THE ENCYCLOPEDIA OF
NORTH AMERICAN
INDIAN WARS,
1607–1890

THE ENCYCLOPEDIA OF NORTH AMERICAN INDIAN WARS 1607–1890

A Political, Social, and Military History

VOLUME I: A–L

Dr. Spencer C. Tucker
Editor

James Arnold and Roberta Wiener
Editors, Documents Volume

Dr. Paul G. Pierpaoli Jr.
Associate Editor

Dr. David Coffey
Dr. Jim Piecuch
Assistant Editors

 ABC-CLIO

Santa Barbara, California   Denver, Colorado   Oxford, England

Library of Congress Cataloging-in-Publication Data

The encyclopedia of North American Indian wars, 1607-1890 : a political, social, and military history / Spencer C. Tucker, editor ; James Arnold and Roberta Wiener, editors, documents volume ; Paul G. Pierpaoli, Jr., associate editor ; David Coffey, Jim Piecuch, assistant editors.
      p. cm.
  Includes bibliographical references and index.
  ISBN 978-1-85109-697-8 (hard back : alk. paper) -- ISBN 978-1-85109-603-9 (ebook)
  1. Indians of North America—Wars—Encyclopedias.   I. Tucker, Spencer, 1937–   II. Arnold, James R.   III. Wiener, Roberta, 1952–
  E81.E984   2011
  970.004'97003—dc23

              2011027913

ISBN: 978-1-85109-697-8
EISBN: 978-1-85109-603-9

15 14 13 12 11   1 2 3 4 5

This book is also available on the World Wide Web as an eBook.
Visit www.abc-clio.com for details.

ABC-CLIO, LLC
130 Cremona Drive, P.O. Box 1911
Santa Barbara, California 93116-1911

This book is printed on acid-free paper ∞
Manufactured in the United States of America

For my girls:
Beverly, Mary Mikel, Paige, and Pam

About the Editors

Spencer C. Tucker, PhD, held the John Biggs Chair of Military History at his alma mater, the Virginia Military Institute in Lexington, for 6 years until his retirement from teaching in 2003. Before that, he was professor of history for 30 years at Texas Christian University, Fort Worth. He has also been a Fulbright Scholar and, as a U.S. Army captain, an intelligence analyst in the Pentagon. Currently the senior fellow of military history at ABC-CLIO, he has written or edited 39 books, including the award-winning *Encyclopedia of the Arab-Israeli Conflict,* the comprehensive *A Global Chronology of Conflict,* and the *Encyclopedia of the Middle East Wars,* all published by ABC-CLIO.

James Arnold is the author of more than 20 military history books and has contributed to numerous others. His published works include *Jeff Davis's Own: Cavalry, Comanches, and the Battle for the Texas Frontier* and *Napoleon Conquers Austria: The 1809 Campaign for Vienna,* which won the International Napoleonic Society's Literary Award in 1995. His two newest titles will be released in 2011: *The Moro War: How America Battles a Muslim Insurgency in the Philippine Jungle, 1902–1913* and *Napoleon's Triumph: The Friedland Campaign, 1807.*

Roberta Wiener is managing editor of the *Journal of Military History.* She coauthored *The American West: Living the Frontier Dream* as well as a number of history books for the school library market and has contributed to several of ABC-CLIO's print and online reference works.

Contents

List of Entries

List of Maps

List of Tables

Preface

Fighting between Native Americans and Europeans represents the most protracted conflict in American history. While most Americans now associate the term "Indian Wars" with the fighting on the Great Plains in the period after the American Civil War, conflict between Native Americans and white settlers in North America began with European colonization in the early 17th century. This struggle can be said to have ended definitively sometime in the first decade or two of the 20th century. Fighting not only occurred between the English-speaking colonists and the Native Americans but also involved immigrants of the other colonial powers, including the Spanish, French, Dutch, and Swedes. There was even fighting between the Russians and Native Americans in the Pacific Northwest and Alaska. Early on, Native Americans helped save European settlements by sharing with the colonists their knowledge of the land and local conditions as well as food supplies, but hopes of peaceful coexistence were soon dashed by the European desire to own the land and to fence it off. The native peoples did not adhere to the concept of private ownership of land.

The Indian Wars introduced the Europeans to a new type of warfare. Europeans were accustomed to standup battles by close formations of men facing one another in the open and trading gunshots at dueling pistol ranges, slashing at one another with pikes, or charging one another with horse cavalry. Conditions in the largely forested North American eastern seaboard in the early 17th century did not lend themselves to this type of fighting. The Native Americans introduced the Europeans to a new type of warfare—the so-called skulking way of war—that emphasized stealth, the bow and arrow, the tomahawk and knife at close quarters, and hit-and-run raids. Although such tactics worked astonishingly well at first, they could not bring the native peoples victory against superior European firepower.

The Indian Wars ended as they only could, in victory for the U.S. Army. A proliferation of tribes and clans with a long record of antagonism between them and competing goals and leaders prevented the native peoples from effectively mobilizing to oppose the growing numbers of white immigrants. Even when they were able to mobilize larger numbers, as in the Great Sioux War of 1876–1877, the Native Americans' lack of logistical services kept them from maintaining a sustained presence in the field. Diseases brought by Europeans such as smallpox, for which the native peoples had no immunity, killed off large numbers of Native Americans. Susceptibility to alien diseases greatly reduced Native American numbers, while the European population steadily increased. The superior military technology of their enemy, including artillery, as well as the coming of the railroads and the government-sanctioned demise of the buffalo all contributed to the inevitable Native American defeat and the movement of many Native American onto government-prescribed reservations.

Although the first major recorded battle between Native Americans and colonists in the New World occurred on the island of Hispaniola in March 1495, in this encyclopedia we treat only warfare in North America proper and after 1776 in the United States. We have included entries on all of the significant Native American tribes, key individuals, battles, wars, weapons, trade, diplomacy (including treaties), and social and cultural topics. We have also included a bibliography and information on rank structure and military awards and decorations. In all, the encyclopedia contains nearly 800 entries. We have tried throughout to be impartial in presenting both sides of a complex and difficult issue.

Although this encyclopedia includes excellent entries on military ranks and the confusing brevet promotion system, an introduction to these subjects may be helpful. In applying military ranks to individuals, we used the officer's rank at the time of a given event. Therefore, George A. Custer, a major general on a provisional basis during the American Civil War, is referred to by his substantive rank, lieutenant colonel, in discussions of his Indian Wars activities. During major conflicts such as the Civil War, the federal government created a separate volunteer organization to meet the emergency rather than expand the regular army. Furthermore, the government allowed regular officers to accept temporary commissions at higher ranks in the volunteers. Thus, Wesley Merritt, a captain in the regular army, came to command a cavalry corps at the close of the Civil War as a major general of U.S. Volunteers. To add to the confusion, the army awarded brevet promotions (largely honorary) for a number of reasons, usually for gallant or meritorious service (but also for 10 years at the same grade). Brevets were awarded in both regular and volunteer organizations, sometimes simultaneously. At the end of the Civil War, then, Ranald Mackenzie held the substantive rank of captain and the volunteer rank of brigadier general, with brevets to brigadier general in the regulars and to major general of volunteers, only to be appointed a colonel when the regular army was reorganized following the war. Although he later earned promotion to brigadier general, most mentions of Mackenzie in this project are as a colonel. Many officers spent the Indian Wars trying to regain their Civil War stars, and more than a few did so. This means that George Crook, for an extreme example, appears as a lieutenant colonel in some entries and as a brigadier general in others. Finally, an officer could be assigned to command at his brevet rank. This usually occurred when the assignment involved the appointment of an officer to a command that included an officer or officers of higher substantive rank or with seniority at the same rank, but brevet ranks also could be employed to add significance to a command or campaign. For this project we have endeavored to sight the brevet rank only when it was in use.

On the encyclopedia I am pleased to again have the assistance of Dr. Jim Piecuch of the Department of History at Kennesaw State University as an assistant editor on a project in this series of encyclopedias covering American wars. Dr. Piecuch contributed substantially as an assistant editor on the earlier set of encyclopedias treating North American colonial warfare. He is a specialist in American colonial history. The other assistant editor is Dr. David Coffey, chair of the Department of History and Philosophy at the University of Tennessee at Martin. He has special expertise in the second half of the 19th century. Dr. Paul G. Pierpaoli Jr. continues in his important role of associate editor. A U.S. history specialist and my right-hand man in the America at War series, he is also a splendid writer and superb editor. Dr. Pierpaoli assigned entries and kept up with them. He also wrote many himself. He and I have also edited all the entries, as have the two assistant editors.

We are indeed fortunate to have the services of distinguished author and historian Robert Utley. Former chief historian of the National Park Service and author of 16 books on the history of the American West, he graciously agreed to write the provocative and informative introductory essay.

As usual, I am grateful for the support of my wife, Dr. Beverly B. Tucker. I take full responsibility for any errors and omissions in the encyclopedia.

SPENCER C. TUCKER

General Maps

EARLY PENETRATION OF NORTH AMERICA BY EUROPEAN NATIONS

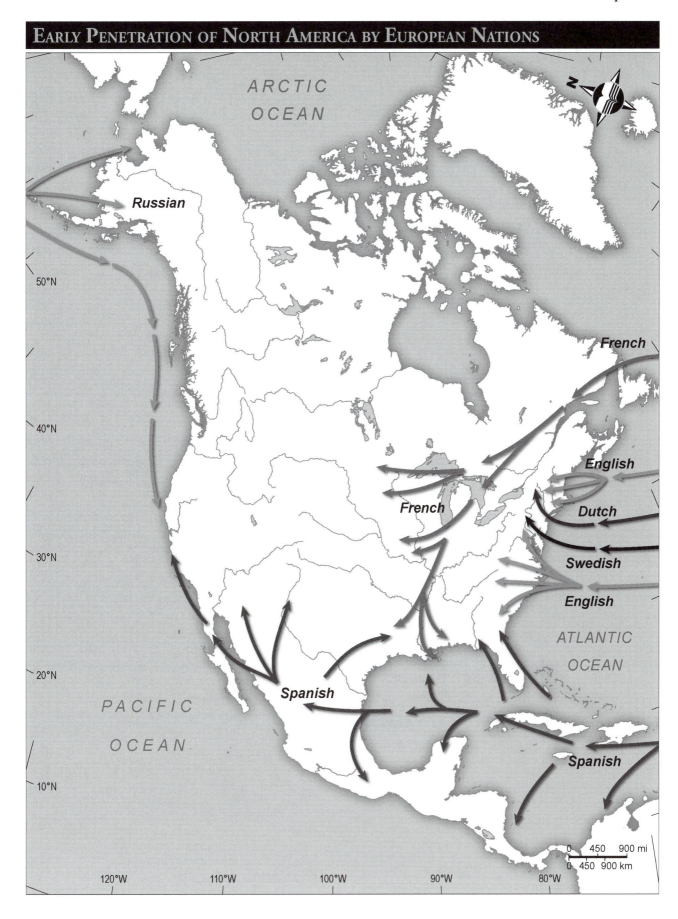

ARCTIC OCEAN

Russian

French

English

Dutch

Swedish

English

French

ATLANTIC OCEAN

Spanish

Spanish

PACIFIC OCEAN

0   450   900 mi
0   450   900 km

INDIAN TRIBES OF NORTH AMERICA

90°W

180°

60°N

150°W

Eskimos   Koyukons

Ingaliks   Tananas

Tanainas

Aleuts

Eskimos

Kutchins

Ahtenas   Hans   Hares

Tlingits

Tutchones

Eskimos

Nahanes
(Kaskas,
Tagish,
Tahltans)

Dogribs

Yellowknifes

Haidas

Sekanis

Chippewyans

CANADA

Eskimos

Tsimshians

Carriers

Beavers

Naskapis

Beothuks

Bella Bellas Bella Coolas
Kwakiutls
Nootkas   Lillooets   Sarcees
Cowichans Stalos Shuswaps
Clallams   Songish

Montagnais

Crees

1   2

Blackfeet

Micmacs
Malecites
Passamaquoddy
Penobscots
Abenakis

Chinooks   4 3   Flatheads   Assiniboines
Tillamooks   Coeur D'Alenes Gros Ventres
Nez Perce
Cayuses
PACIFIC Yuroks Klamaths Bannocks Crows Hidatsas
Wintuns   Shoshonis Arikaras
OCEAN   Pomos Maidus

Ojibwas

Algonquins
Nipissings
Ottawas

Hurons

Menominees
Winnebagos

Massachusetts
Wampanoags
Narragansetts

Fox
Sauks

11 Neutrals

12 14
13 15

Miwoks

Costanos   Yokuts

Chumash

Arapahos
Utes

Cheyennes Poncas
Omahas
Pawnee

Kickapoos
Iowas Miamis
Otos   Illinois
Missouris
Kansas

Delawares
Susquehannocks
Shawnees

Montauks
Manhattans
Powhatans

UNITED

Paiutes

Havasupais
Hualapais

Nahyssans

STATES

ATLANTIC

Halchidhomas Navajos

Yuchis Meherrins
Cherokees

Santees

Mojaves Hopis
Tiwas Cuitoas
Osages

Yavapais   Zunis   Tewas
Yumas Maricopas   Keres   Wichitas
Kohuanas Cocopas Piros Kiowas

Catawbas Cusabos

Sewees

Guales

30°N

Papagos   Comanches Caddoes
Pimas Apaches Kadohadachos
Seris Jumanos Hasinais Natchez Mobiles

5   6

Creeks
7   Hitchitis
8 9   Tunicas

OCEAN

Tacatacuras
Saturiwas

Atakapas Acolapissas
Yaquis   Karankawas

10   Freshwater Indians
Ais

Seminoles Guacatas
Jeagas

Calusas

Coahuiltecs

Gulf of Mexico

Arawaks

MEXICO

Caribs

Totonacs

Tarascans

Mayas

Aztecs

Cuna

1. Columbias
2. Spokanes
3. Pend d'Oreilles
4. Yakimas
5. Napochis
6. Alabamas
7. Tious
8. Choctaws
9. Tohomes
10. Timucuas
11. Pottawatomis
12. Iroquois
13. Mahicans
14. Wappingers
15. Pequots

0   1000   2000 mi
0   1000   2000 km

120°W

90°W

Indian Land Cessions, 1776–1945

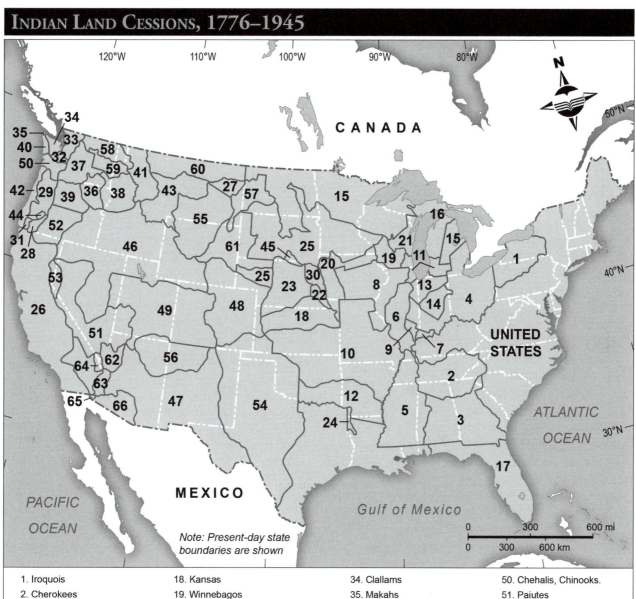

Note: Present-day state boundaries are shown

1. Iroquois
2. Cherokees
3. Creeks
4. Wyandots, Delawares, Chippewas, allied tribes
5. Choctaws, Chickasaws
6. Kaskaskias
7. Delawares
8. Sauks, Fox
9. Piankashaws
10. Osages
11. Ottawas, Chippewas, Potawatomis
12. Quapaws
13. Potawatomis
14. Miamis
15. Chippewas
16. Ottawas, Chippewas
17. Seminoles

18. Kansas
19. Winnebagos
20. Sauks, Fox, Sioux, Omahas, Iowas, Otos, Missouris
21. Menominees
22. Otos, Missouris
23. Pawnees
24. Caddoes
25. Sioux
26. California Indians
27. Sioux, Cheyennes, Arapahos, Crows, Assiniboines, Gros Ventres, Mandans, Arikaras
28. Rogue River Indians
29. Umpquas, Kalapuyas
30. Omahas
31. Chastacostas
32. Nisqually and Suquamish Indians
33. Duwamish and Suquamish Indians

34. Clallams
35. Makahs
36. Walla Wallas, Cayuses, Umatillas
37. Yakimas
38. Nez Perce
39. Confederated Tribes of Middle Oregon
40. Quinaults, Quileutes
41. Flathead Indians
42. Coast Tribes of Oregon
43. Blackfeet, Flathead Indians, Nez Perce
44. Molalas
45. Poncas
46. Shoshonis
47. Apaches
48. Arapahos, Cheyennes
49. Utes

50. Chehalis, Chinooks.
51. Paiutes
52. Klamath Indians
53. Washos
54. Comanches, Kiowas
55. Crows
56. Navajos
57. Arikaras, Gros Ventres, Mandans
58. Methows, Okanagans
59. Coeur d' Alene Indians
60. Gros Ventres, Blackfoots, River Crows
61. Sioux, Northern Cheyennes, Arapahos
62. Hualapais
63. Yumas
64. Mojaves
65. Cocopas
66. Papagos, Pimas, Maricopas

WAR ON THE NORTHERN PLAINS, 1866–1890

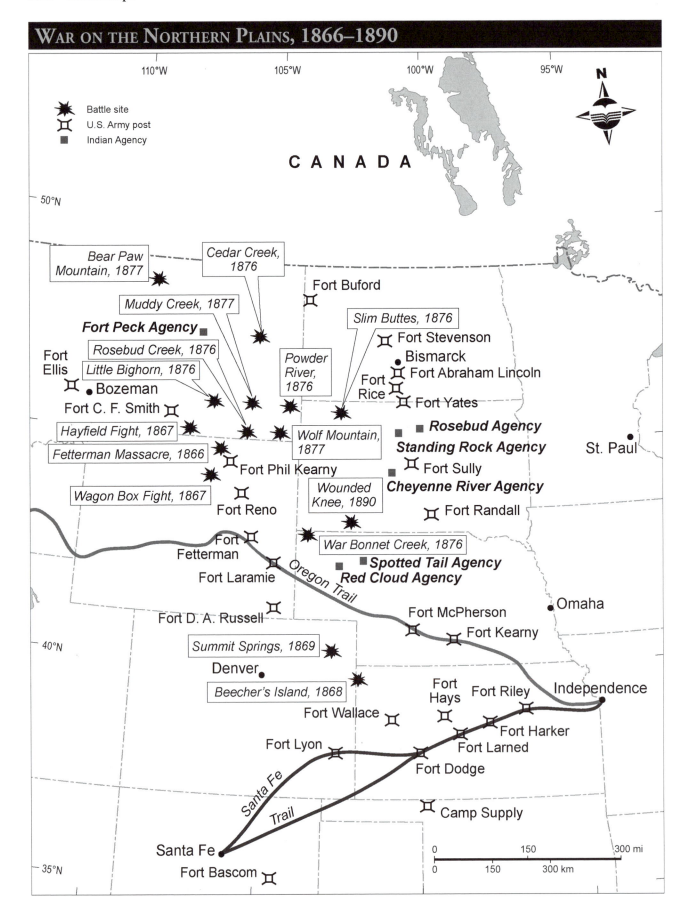

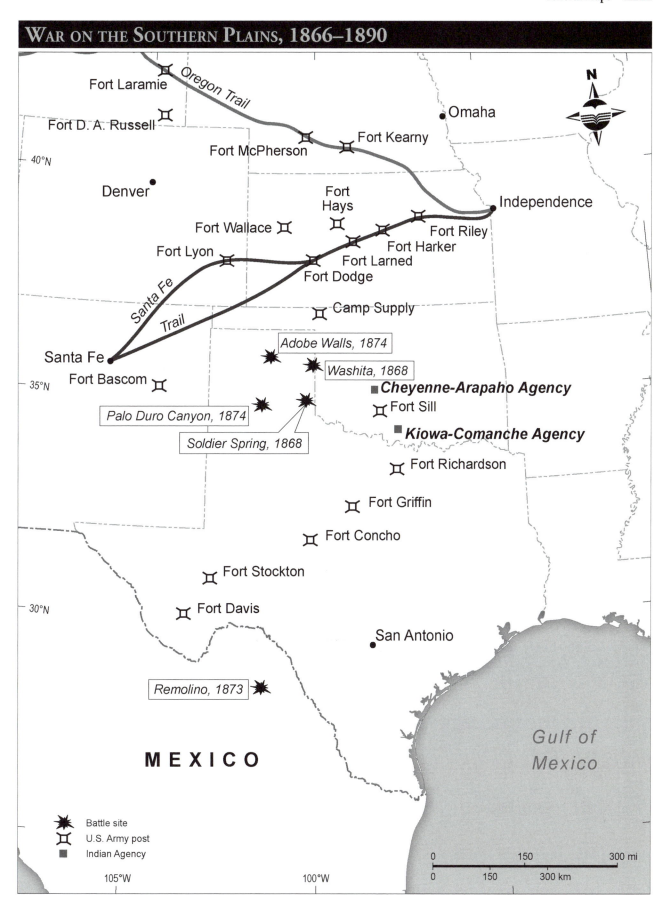

WAR ON THE SOUTHERN PLAINS, 1866–1890

Fort Laramie

Oregon Trail

Fort D. A. Russell

Omaha

Fort McPherson

Fort Kearny

40°N

Denver

Fort
Hays

Independence

Fort Wallace

Fort Riley

Fort Lyon

Fort Harker

Santa Fe

Fort Larned

Fort Dodge

Trail

Camp Supply

Adobe Walls, 1874

Santa Fe

Washita, 1868

Fort Bascom

■ **Cheyenne-Arapaho Agency**

35°N

Fort Sill

Palo Duro Canyon, 1874

■ **Kiowa-Comanche Agency**

Soldier Spring, 1868

Fort Richardson

Fort Griffin

Fort Concho

Fort Stockton

30°N

Fort Davis

San Antonio

Remolino, 1873

MEXICO

Gulf of
Mexico

✴ Battle site

✡ U.S. Army post

■ Indian Agency

| 0 | 150 | 300 mi |

| 0 | 150 | 300 km |

105°W

100°W

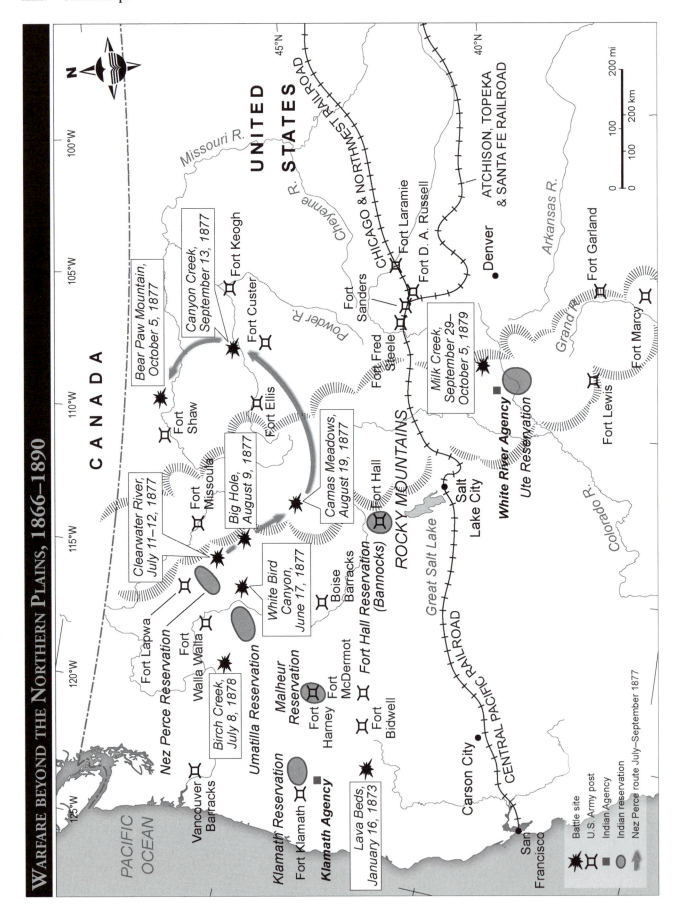

WARFARE BEYOND THE NORTHERN PLAINS, 1866–1890

CANADA

UNITED STATES

PACIFIC OCEAN

Vancouver Barracks

Nez Perce Reservation

Fort Lapwa

Fort Walla Walla

Klamath Reservation

Fort Klamath

Klamath Agency

Umatilla Reservation

Malheur Reservation

Fort Harney

Fort McDermot

Fort Bidwell

Lava Beds, January 16, 1873

Birch Creek, July 8, 1878

White Bird Canyon, June 17, 1877

Boise Barracks

Fort Hall Reservation (Bannocks)

Fort Hall

Camas Meadows, August 19, 1877

Big Hole, August 9, 1877

Clearwater River, July 11–12, 1877

Fort Missoula

Fort Shaw

Fort Ellis

Bear Paw Mountain, October 5, 1877

Canyon Creek, September 13, 1877

Fort Custer

Fort Keogh

Missouri R.

Cheyenne R.

Powder R.

ROCKY MOUNTAINS

Great Salt Lake

Salt Lake City

Carson City

San Francisco

CENTRAL PACIFIC RAILROAD

Fort Fred Steele

Fort Sanders

Fort Laramie

Fort D. A. Russell

CHICAGO & NORTHWEST RAILROAD

Denver

Milk Creek, September 29– October 5, 1879

White River Agency

Ute Reservation

Grand R.

Fort Lewis

Fort Garland

Fort Marcy

Arkansas R.

Colorado R.

ATCHISON, TOPEKA & SANTA FE RAILROAD

125°W 120°W 115°W 110°W 105°W 100°W

45°N 40°N

200 mi

100

100 200 km

Battle site

U.S. Army post

Indian Agency

Indian reservation

Nez Perce route July–September 1877

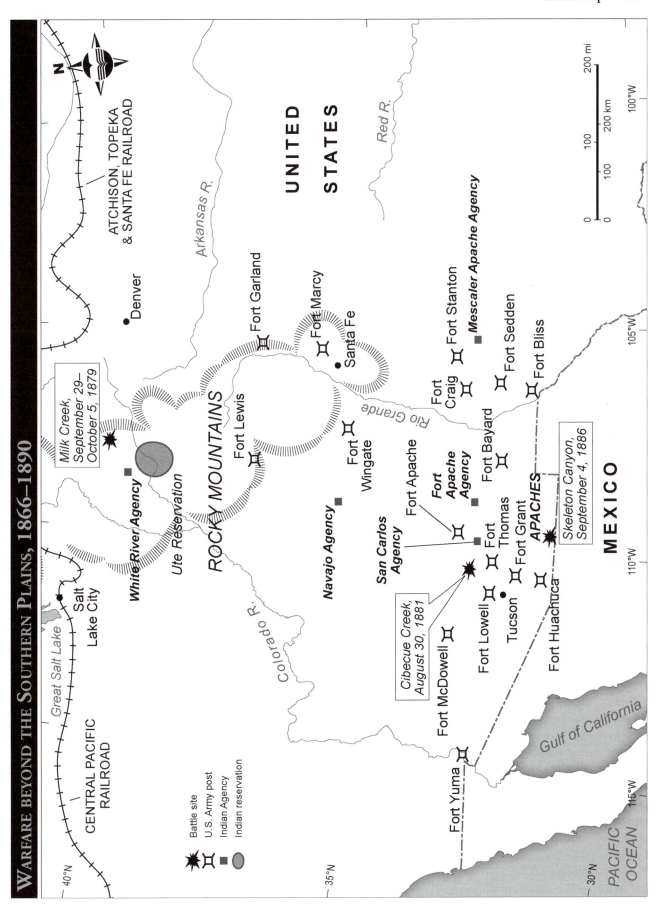

Warfare Beyond the Southern Plains, 1866–1890

N

200 mi

0   100   200 km

0   100   100

ATCHISON, TOPEKA & SANTA FE RAILROAD

UNITED STATES

Arkansas R.

Red R.

Denver

Fort Garland

Fort Marcy

Santa Fe

Fort Stanton

Mescaler Apache Agency

Fort Sedden

Fort Bliss

Milk Creek, September 29–October 5, 1879

White River Agency

ROCKY MOUNTAINS

Fort Lewis

Fort Craig

Fort Bayard

Fort Wingate

Fort Apache

Fort Apache Agency

Skeleton Canyon, September 4, 1886

Ute Reservation

Navajo Agency

San Carlos Agency

Fort Thomas

Fort Grant

APACHES

MEXICO

Rio Grande

Colorado R.

Salt Lake City

Great Salt Lake

CENTRAL PACIFIC RAILROAD

Cibecue Creek, August 30, 1881

Fort McDowell

Fort Lowell

Tucson

Fort Huachuca

Fort Yuma

Gulf of California

PACIFIC OCEAN

Battle site
U.S. Army post
Indian Agency
Indian reservation

40°N

35°N

30°N

115°W

110°W

105°W

100°W

Overview

Four Centuries of Conflict

When Christopher Columbus and some of his followers waded ashore in the Bahamas on October 12, 1492, to establish the first lasting contact between the Old World and the New World, the Europeans were greeted warmly by the island's Taino inhabitants. As the natives and newcomers examined one another, some of the curious Tainos grasped the Europeans' swords, not realizing the sharpness of the blades, and accidentally slashed their hands and fingers. This bloodshed on the very first day of contact, although inadvertent, foreshadowed the 400 years of warfare that would follow this initial encounter, conflicts that would eventually devastate the native population of the Americas and, by the time the last battle was fought in 1890 at Wounded Knee in the United States, see the surviving natives subjugated by the Europeans and their descendants.

Columbus and those Europeans who came after him were not entering empty lands. Although population estimates vary widely, perhaps 8 million–12 million people inhabited the region north of present-day Mexico; some 4 million lived on the islands of the Caribbean; another 18 million or more inhabited Mexico and Central America; and about 10 million–11 million people were subjects of the Inca Empire in South America, between the Andes mountains and the Pacific Ocean. Adding the inhabitants of South America east of the Andes gives the New World an aggregate population of more than 40 million people and possibly as many as 60 million in 1492. The American natives spoke hundreds of languages and dialects, and their cultures varied from small bands of nomadic hunters in Canada to semisedentary agriculturalists in most of North America to the complex, highly organized and stratified empires of the Aztecs in Mexico and the Incas in South America.

Despite later romantic notions of native life imagined by Europeans, the inhabitants of the Americas did not live in peaceable kingdoms, free from conflict. The Tainos in the Caribbean warred sporadically with their Carib neighbors, while the Aztecs in central Mexico had built an empire through conquest, celebrating their victories and honoring their gods with thousands of human sacrifices every year. In western South America, the Incas had conquered a geographically larger if less populous empire, and the inhabitants of North America also battled for resources and to avenge wrongs, albeit on a smaller scale than the wars waged by the great empires in Mexico and South America.

Initial encounters between natives and Europeans were almost invariably cordial. The natives greeted Europeans in accordance with native traditions of hospitality to strangers, enhanced by curiosity about the physically different newcomers and their strange and marvelous weapons, goods, and livestock, which some natives took as signs of great spiritual power. Europeans also preferred to establish good relations, since they needed information from the natives that would enable the Europeans to survive in an unfamiliar environment while learning from the inhabitants what resources and potential riches the new land possessed.

The Spanish Conquest

Despite the peaceful beginnings of the relationship between natives and Europeans, violence soon became commonplace. Columbus and the 1,500 Spanish colonists who accompanied him in 1493 quickly began to exploit the Tainos. Building on the existing Taino tribute system, the Spaniards demanded that Taino caciques (chiefs) turn over a portion of the food and other goods that their people produced to support the newcomers. When caciques began to balk at the Spanish demands, they were killed and their people enslaved. Columbus, as governor of the colony, divided native lands among the colonists and put the inhabitants to work clearing

Christopher Columbus receives ritual gifts from the Cacique Guacanagarís on Hispaniola. Engraving by Theodor de Bry. (Library of Congress)

land, farming, and mining for gold. Natives laboring in this *encomienda* system were treated harshly. Columbus insisted that some of the natives on Hispaniola turn a specified quantity of gold over to the Spaniards every three months, and those who did not meet the quota had their hands cut off. The natives revolted but were quickly suppressed, as their weapons were no match for Spanish soldiers in armor who wielded crossbows and muskets and were supported by artillery, mounted cavalry, and attack dogs.

Those natives who survived the brutal treatment and military onslaught suffered from the new diseases brought by the Europeans. The natives lacked immunity to common European diseases such as measles, mumps, influenza, and, the most devastating of all, smallpox. Epidemics decimated the native population. Hispaniola, home to an estimated 1 million Tainos in 1492, had no native survivors left in 1535 despite the Spaniards' capture and importation of tens of thousands of natives from other islands, the South American mainland, and Florida. To meet their demand for labor, the Spanish began importing African slaves.

After securing control of the Caribbean islands, the Spanish moved to establish themselves on the mainland of North America and South America. In 1519 Hernan Cortes landed on the coast of Mexico. His orders were to establish a trading post, but lured by reports of the wealth of the Aztec Empire, Cortes marched inland. Spanish military technology enabled Cortes to defeat some of the Aztecs' subject peoples, who in turn allied with the Spaniards in the hope of overthrowing their Aztec overlords. Cortes thus estab-

lished a pattern that would be followed by other Europeans: taking advantage of existing native rivalries to gain assistance from one native group against another. Aided by disease, superior weaponry, and his native allies, Cortes completed the conquest of the Aztec Empire in 1521. Francisco Pizarro subjugated the Inca Empire in 1533, although Inca elements held out in Andean strongholds and continued to resist the Spaniards for several years.

Spanish incursions north of Mexico met with less success. The Spaniards subdued the Pueblo peoples and other tribes in the present-day American Southwest but faced frequent revolts. In 1539 Hernando de Soto led 1,000 soldiers into what is now the southeastern United States, marching across a vast expanse of territory and using violence and intimidation to supply his men. De Soto's expedition devastated the native societies of the region before deaths from combat and disease forced the survivors to escape to Mexico.

French-Native Relations

French exploration of North America began in the 16th century, but it was not until 1604 that the French succeeded in establishing a permanent colony in Acadia (Nova Scotia). Four years later a second colony was established at Quebec. Unlike the Spaniards, the French had neither the military might nor the desire to forcibly subdue the natives. Few French colonists were willing to brave the harsh Canadian climate and settle in North America, so the French were always heavily outnumbered by the natives. Furthermore, the main goal of French colonization was to profit from the fur trade, and since traders relied on the natives to trap beaver and other fur-bearing animals, the French could not afford to alienate their native trading partners.

Samuel de Champlain, founder and first governor of Quebec, set the tone for relations between the French and the natives in North America. He scrupulously purchased the land on which his colonists settled and integrated the French within the existing native trade and alliance system. French traders, the coureurs de bois, quickly settled in native communities and married native women, strengthening ties between the two societies. Missionaries, notably the Jesuits, pursued a similar course, learning native languages and then settling among the various nations to carry out their work of conversion. While the Jesuits were not always welcome, they eventually won acceptance, if few converts, in the native communities where they lived and added another link to the relationship between the French and the natives.

Champlain's judicious conduct helped to forge a strong military alliance with the natives. Unlike other Europeans, he insisted that the natives be treated on their own terms; thus he refused to force the natives to submit to French law. Natives who killed French colonists paid an indemnity in goods, a traditional native practice, rather than being punished by French standards with the imposition of the death penalty, a practice not employed by most native societies. On the other hand, when a French colonist killed a native, Champlain compensated the native's family with trade goods but

Depiction of Spaniards under Hernando de Soto torturing Native Americans in present-day Florida. (Library of Congress)

also executed the French offender. This fairness earned Champlain and his successors the respect of the natives, who often turned to French governors to mediate disputes among themselves.

French willingness to accommodate the natives came with a price, however, as Champlain learned in 1609. Huron and Algonquian diplomats called at Quebec that year and asked Champlain for warriors to join in an expedition against their Iroquois enemies to the south. Realizing that his alliance with the natives obligated him to participate, Champlain and one or two French soldiers accompanied the Native force, and French firearms proved crucial in the defeat of a Mohawk war party. The battle helped to cement the French alliance with the Hurons and various Algonquian-speaking tribes of Canada but also drew the French into these nations' long-standing conflict with the Iroquois Confederacy, of which the Mohawks were a member. The resulting warfare would continue until the Grand Paix of 1701 ended French-Iroquois hostilities, which resumed with the outbreak of the French and Indian War five decades later.

The alliance between the French and the natives persisted, with some disruptions, until France was expelled from North America in 1763. Many native nations fought alongside France in the various colonial wars against Great Britain that raged intermittently beginning in 1689. Nevertheless, French relations with some native groups were marked by hostility and violence, notably the French campaign to eliminate the Fox (Mesquakie) tribe during 1712–1737 and the French war against the Natchez people during 1729–1733.

English-Native Relations

Sir Walter Raleigh, the driving force behind English colonization in North America, believed that the Spanish experience provided the English with a textbook example of how not to treat the natives. Raleigh believed that fair treatment would win the goodwill of the natives, resulting in their voluntary submission to the Crown of England and peaceful coexistence. However, by the time the first permanent English colony was established at Jamestown, Virginia, in 1607, Raleigh had lost his influence. In any case, he had failed to take into account the deep cultural divide between the natives and the English. Key aspects of native society, including decentralized leadership based on persuasion and consensus, communitarian property ownership that in regard to land was based on usage

Engraving showing Native Americans and colonists meeting for the first time; from *The True Travels of Captaine John Smith*, published in 1630.
(John Smith, *The True Travels, Adventures, and Observations of Captaine John Smith*, 1630)

rights, and nature-based religious beliefs stood in sharp contrast to the English system of rigid hierarchical government, private property and individual land ownership, and formal religious systems. Such differences, exacerbated by the English desire to take native lands and impose their political, economic, and religious practices on the natives, made conflict virtually inevitable.

In Virginia, responsibility for diplomacy with the tribes of the Powhatan Confederacy fell to John Smith, who adopted a harsh policy. Smith frequently forced the natives to supply the English with food but was careful not to press too hard and provoke open warfare. In 1609 Smith returned to England, and the following year English demands for supplies and land sparked the first of three Anglo-Powhatan wars. Unlike the natives, who sought to minimize casualties and take captives for adoption into their tribes, the

English waged total war, targeting noncombatants as well as crops and other essential supplies. When the final war ended in 1646, the once-powerful Powhatan Confederacy survived only as a remnant on a few small parcels of its original lands, which were in effect the first native reservations.

To the north in New England, relations began peacefully. A smallpox epidemic had nearly annihilated the coastal tribes shortly before the Pilgrims arrived and founded Plymouth Colony in 1620; the surviving natives helped the newcomers survive the first winter and begin farming the following spring. The Puritans who settled Massachusetts Bay in 1630 also established good relations with their native neighbors, but the New England colonies soon came into conflict with the Pequot nation in the Connecticut River Valley. Irritated by the Pequots' stubborn independence and egged on by their Mohegan allies, who were rivals of the Pequots, the colonists began hostilities against the Pequots in the summer of 1636. The Pequot War ended in 1638 with the Pequots virtually annihilated.

The colonists' victory over the Pequots intimidated the other New England tribes, and the colonies met almost no opposition as they expanded during the next four decades. However, the colonists' seemingly endless desire for land and their efforts to impose their law, religion, and customs on the natives led Metacom (King Philip) of the Wampanoags to organize a coalition of tribes to oppose the English. The resulting conflict, known as King Philip's War (1675–1676), saw many New England settlements devastated, but the natives of the region suffered immense losses. No longer able to oppose the English, many of the survivors moved farther away from the colonists.

New York succeeded in avoiding hostilities with the natives by virtue of having inherited the Dutch alliance with the Iroquois upon England's conquest of the Dutch colony of New Netherland in 1664. The Dutch had waged brutal warfare against the Algonquian-speaking tribes of the Hudson River Valley, but after an early conflict with the Mohawks, the Dutch sought peace with the Iroquois, who became New Netherland's partner in the fur trade. After assuming control of the colony, English officials continued the Dutch policy of conciliating the Iroquois, both to profit from the fur trade and to keep the confederation as a buffer between New York and New France.

In the southern colonies, which were settled in the late 17th and early 18th centuries, warfare also erupted between the English and the natives. The causes were similar: the colonists' land hunger, trade abuses, and attempts to enslave the natives. The two most violent conflicts were the Tuscarora War (1711–1713) in North Carolina and the Yamasee War (1715–1717) in South Carolina, both of which ended with the defeat of the natives.

Native-colonial relations were more peaceful in a few colonies. Roger Williams in Rhode Island and William Penn in Pennsylvania, both of whom sought to create religious havens for those fleeing persecution in England or in neighboring colonies, established good relations with the natives, as did James Oglethorpe in Georgia, in another utopian experiment, in the 1730s. These colonies were exceptions, however, and by the mid-18th century both Pennsylvania and Georgia were enmeshed in the seemingly endless conflict between the British colonists and the natives.

Imperial Warfare

In 1689 the European War of the League of Augsburg spilled over into North America as both France and England tried to strike a blow at each other's colonies. While the English colonists strove, with little success, to strike Montreal and other key French posts, the French and their native allies mounted raids on the New England and New York frontiers to keep the English on the defensive. Neither side gained a decisive advantage by the time the conflict, known to the English colonists as King William's War, ended in 1697. Peace brought no change to the situation in North America, although the

Iroquois, angered by the lack of English support, opted for neutrality by signing a peace agreement with New France in 1701.

Another European conflict, the War of the Spanish Succession, broke out shortly afterward. Once again fighting extended to the colonies. Forces from South Carolina, augmented by native allies, invaded Spanish Florida in 1702 but failed to capture St. Augustine. The English and natives then overran Spanish posts to the west before being checked by the French-allied Choctaws. To the north, the French and their native allies resumed their strategy of raiding the English frontier, their most notable success being an attack on Deerfield, Massachusetts, in February 1704. An expedition from New England captured Port Royal, Acadia, in 1710, and France was forced to cede that province to Britain in the 1713 Treaty of Utrecht; the British renamed the colony Nova Scotia.

King George's War (1744–1748), known as the War of the Austrian Succession in Europe, followed a similar pattern. While the British and their colonists targeted key French positions such as the fortress of Louisbourg on Cape Breton Island, which they captured in June 1745, the French and their native allies used raiding to maintain pressure on the borders of the British colonies. The war came to an indecisive conclusion in 1748, with the British returning Louisbourg to France.

The peace of 1748 brought only the briefest respite to North America. Seeking to shore up the links between their possessions in Canada and those along the Mississippi River, the French began constructing forts in the Ohio River Valley. This region was also claimed by the British, and when Virginia sent troops in 1754 in an unsuccessful effort to oust the French, fighting erupted that sparked the French and Indian War (1754–1763).

The British government, hoping for a quick victory, sent troops to seize French Fort Duquesne at the Forks of the Ohio River in 1755. General Edward Braddock, the British commander, squandered an opportunity to gain support from native nations in the Ohio Valley area when he refused to promise that the tribes could keep their land in exchange for assisting the British. Angered, the natives sided with the French and helped to rout Braddock's force in July 1755. The natives followed up the victory by launching devastating raids along the frontier from New England to Virginia over the next two years.

Despite the natives' important contributions to the French war effort, the French military commander, General Louis-Joseph, Marquis de Montcalm, alienated his allies in 1757 after capturing Fort William Henry in New York. Montcalm allowed the British and colonial garrison to withdraw with their possessions, depriving the natives of plunder and captives, their traditional rewards for service with the French. The infuriated natives attacked the British and the colonists as they evacuated the fort and then returned home, where most sat out the remainder of the war. With little native aid and facing a much superior British and colonial force, Montcalm was driven back to the heart of New France in the Saint Lawrence River Valley. In 1759 the Iroquois, recognizing that the tide had turned against the French and hoping to share in the spoils of victory, joined the British. That September Quebec capitulated to the British, and under the terms of the Treaty of Paris, signed in 1763, France ceded Canada to Britain and Louisiana to Spain, ending the French presence in North America.

The British and colonial victory aroused the fears of the natives in the Ohio Valley and Great Lakes region. Having lost the protection of the French, they now stood alone against an expected onslaught of land-hungry colonists. Hoping to forestall this disaster and perhaps entice the French to return, Ottawa war leader Pontiac organized a coalition of tribes and launched a series of assaults on British posts beginning in May 1763. Pontiac's Rebellion failed to drive out the British but forced a change in British policy to the natives' benefit. Officials in London, unwilling to engage in costly wars with the natives and recognizing that their own colonists' insatiable desire for land was the root of the problem, responded with the Proclamation of 1763. The edict forbade colonial settlement west of the Appalachians and strengthened the powers of the British Indian superintendents to regulate trade and the sale of native lands east of the Appalachians. The new policy angered many colonists, who believed that their victory in the French and Indian War entitled them to seize native lands.

Native Americans and the American Revolution

Although never completely effective, the new British policy won the goodwill of the natives. Thus, when the American Revolution began in 1775, the royal government could count on the support of most tribes. Both the British and the Americans debated the benefits of utilizing the natives, but it was the natives themselves who chose to take action. Most realized that an American victory would deprive them of British protection and unleash a horde of intruders onto their territory, and therefore most natives fought on behalf of the Crown. A few tribes, such as the Catawbas in South Carolina and the Oneidas of the Iroquois Confederacy, supported the Americans in hopes of preserving their lands and independence.

In the North, Mohawk leader Joseph Brant led most of the Iroquois in support of the British. Frequently working in company with Loyalist rangers, Brant's native forces won several important victories. Brant's success forced General George Washington to dispatch an expedition under Major General John Sullivan that devastated the Iroquois homeland in 1779. Undeterred, Brant returned to the offensive the following year. The Shawnees and other Ohio Valley nations also operated against Americans on the frontier, but British forces never cooperated effectively with any of the native operations in the North, greatly reducing their overall effectiveness.

The story was similar in the South. Ignoring the advice of British Indian agents, the Cherokees attacked the Virginia and Carolina frontiers in 1776, only to suffer a disastrous defeat after initial successes. The Cherokees' failure dampened the enthusiasm of the other southern tribes, who generally remained on the sidelines until the British occupied Savannah, Georgia, at the end of 1778. Efforts to coordinate Creek attacks with British operations in Georgia failed because of slow communications and the great distances involved. After the British captured Charleston, South Carolina, in May 1780 and occupied that state and Georgia, the southern natives offered their services, only to be rejected by the British commander in the South, Lieutenant General Charles, Earl Cornwallis. By the time Cornwallis asked for native assistance in late 1780, the Creeks and Choctaws were committed to the defense of British West Florida against Spanish attacks. Their efforts failed to prevent the loss of that province in May 1781. Meanwhile, the Americans had driven the British to the environs of Charleston and Savannah, making cooperation with the natives impossible. In the 1783 Treaty of Paris, the British ignored their native allies and ceded the region between the Appalachians and the Mississippi River to the United States.

U.S.-Native Relations

As the natives had expected, American independence was followed by an influx of settlers onto native lands. Sporadic fighting occurred along the entire western frontier but was most serious in the Northwest, where a coalition of tribes led by Miami war chief Little Turtle and Blue Jacket of the Shawnees effectively opposed American expansion. The natives defeated U.S. military expeditions in 1790 and 1791 before they were finally defeated in 1794 and then were forced to make peace the following year.

Shawnee leader Tecumseh refused to accept defeat. While his half brother, the prophet Tenskwatawa, preached a native spiritual

Mohawk Indian chief Joseph Brant (1742–1807) fought with the British during the American Revolutionary War. A highly effective military leader, he also was regarded as a humane warrior. (Chaiba Media)

Political cartoon from 1833 satirizing the policies of President Andrew Jackson (on horseback with Martin Van Buren behind him), including his Indian removal program. (Library of Congress)

revival, Tecumseh began organizing a native confederacy to continue resisting American expansion. While Tecumseh was away on a diplomatic mission in 1811, Major General William Henry Harrison marched against Tenskwatawa's village, Prophetstown, on the Wabash River. Despite Tecumseh's admonition not to give battle, Tenskwatawa attacked Harrison and was defeated in the Battle of Tippecanoe. Harrison's victory undermined Tecumseh's efforts to form a native alliance, and Tecumseh turned to the British in Canada for assistance.

During the War of 1812, Tecumseh's Shawnees and other natives fought well in conjunction with the British until October 1813, when the combined forces were defeated and Tecumseh was killed in the Battle of the Thames in Canada. The Creek War, fought in the South during the War of 1812, was considered part of the larger conflict by Americans, although its origins were separate. Some southern native nations had tried to adopt American culture, which sparked a civil war among the Creeks. Nativist Red Sticks opposed the accommodationist policies of the White Stick Creek faction, and the dispute erupted into civil war in 1813. When Red Stick attacks struck both their White Stick rivals and American settlers, the U.S. government responded with force. In 1814 Major General Andrew Jackson crushed the Red Sticks and forced the Creek Nation to cede much of its territory in the Southeast.

Jackson's experience fighting natives in the Creek War and the First Seminole War (1817–1818) convinced him that natives and white Americans could not peacefully coexist. After his election as president of the United States in 1828, Jackson proposed removing all of the native nations in the East to land west of the Mississippi

River. The Indian Removal Act, passed by Congress in 1830, led many nations to accept removal to Indian Territory (present-day Oklahoma). Many Cherokees refused to leave their homes, however, and were forcibly removed along the so-called Trail of Tears in 1838. Many Seminoles also resisted removal, igniting the Second Seminole War (1835–1842). The survivors won a reservation in their Florida homeland, but tensions with whites led to the Third Seminole War (1855–1858); by its conclusion, most of the surviving Seminoles had been sent to Indian Territory, with only a handful left in Florida.

Indian Wars of the West

The Third Seminole War marked the end of native warfare east of the Mississippi, yet a whole new field of conflict had opened in the West. The triumph of the United States in the Mexican-American War (1846–1848) secured the cession of a vast expanse of territory in the Southwest and in California. Lured by the discovery of gold in California and the ideology of Manifest Destiny (the belief that it was Americans' right to spread their superior culture across the continent even at the expense of Native Americans, Mexicans, and others deemed inferior), thousands of settlers set out for the West. The result was a series of conflicts with the natives of the region, from the Great Plains to the Southwest and the Pacific Northwest.

On the southern Plains, the Kiowas, Comanches, Southern Cheyennes, and other nations signed treaties agreeing to live in peace with the settlers, but white encroachment on native lands led to tensions that quickly resulted in sporadic warfare. By 1864 several Southern Cheyenne bands were at war with the Americans,

The Sand Creek Massacre of November 29, 1864, in which Colorado militia attacked a peaceful Cheyenne village. Painting by Robert Lidneux, 1936. (Courtesy, History Colorado, Decorative and Fine Arts Collection, 20020087)

and U.S. troops slaughtered a peaceful Southern Cheyenne band at Sand Creek, Colorado, in November 1864, provoking further native attacks. The Kiowas and Comanches also began fighting the Americans to protect their lands and way of life. Hostilities culminated in the Red River War of 1874–1875. U.S. forces defeated the natives, who surrendered most of their territory and were confined to reservations.

Farther west, the Navajos attempted to remain at peace but eventually began retaliating against New Mexicans who raided their food supplies and livestock. The U.S. Army, preoccupied with subduing the Mescalero Apaches, did not focus its attention on the Navajos until 1863. Army officers then ordered the Navajos to a reservation. The Navajos refused and were defeated in 1864.

Although the Mescaleros had been defeated, other Apache bands went to war against the United States after Cochise, a prominent Chiricahua leader, was falsely accused in 1861 of kidnapping an American boy. Cochise waged a decade-long guerrilla war against the United States before making peace in 1872. Leadership of Apache resistance was subsequently assumed by Victorio and Geronimo, who continued to fight the Americans, in Geronimo's case until his surrender in 1886.

On the northern Plains, the various Sioux bands and their allies, the Northern Cheyennes and Arapahos, resisted the tide of white settlement for nearly 30 years. Intermittent fighting began in the 1850s, and the first major Sioux war erupted in 1862. The Santee

Sioux had sold much of their land and accepted a reservation in Minnesota, only to be cheated out of their annuity payments by corrupt traders and Indian agents. Frustrated and starving, the Santees led by Little Crow went to war, inflicting heavy losses on civilians and soldiers before being defeated.

Red Cloud of the Lakota Sioux led a more successful resistance during 1866–1868. An influx of settlers and the construction of forts along the Bozeman Trail in Wyoming threatened traditional Sioux hunting grounds. Red Cloud responded by attacking civilians and soldiers along the trail, isolating the forts, and annihilating a unit of cavalry in the December 1866 Fetterman Massacre. In the 1868 Fort Laramie Treaty the U.S. government agreed to abandon the forts and close the Bozeman Trail in exchange for peace, giving the natives a rare victory in their wars to defend their territory.

Red Cloud's triumph was short-lived, however. The discovery of gold in the Black Hills of South Dakota in 1874, territory reserved to the natives by the treaty that ended Red Cloud's War, brought a rush of miners onto Native American land. Federal officials offered to purchase the territory, and when the natives refused to sell, the government appropriated the land. Native resistance culminated in the 1876–1877 Great Sioux War. The most notable action was the near destruction of Lieutenant Colonel George A. Custer's command in the June 1876 Battle of the Little Bighorn. Despite this success, the Sioux and their allies could not withstand the forces brought against them, and by 1877 the Sioux and their allies had surrendered except for Sitting Bull, who had led his followers to Canada.

Another war in 1877 involved the Nez Perce of Oregon. Chief Joseph and other leaders declined to move their bands to a reservation, and in the spring of 1877 the army threatened to remove them by force. Before Joseph could comply, some Nez Perce warriors killed a few white settlers, and when Joseph attempted to negotiate a peaceful resolution, he was attacked by troops and civilian volunteers. The Nez Perce then waged a running battle across Idaho and Montana in an epic bid to remain free. However, they failed to reach Canada and were forced to surrender.

There was little native resistance after 1877, as most tribes had been defeated and confined to reservations. However, in 1890 military authorities feared a revival of Native American warfare as a new nativist religious movement swept across the West. Inspired by Wovoka, a Paiute prophet, who predicted the resurrection of Native American dead and renewal of the earth if his followers performed the Ghost Dance ritual, thousands of Native Americans began performing the dance. As the movement spread eastward it became more militant, especially on the Sioux reservations, and some Native Americans left their reservations to avoid white scrutiny. One proponent of the Ghost Dance movement, Big Foot of the Miniconjou Sioux, was leading his people to the Pine Ridge Reservation in South Dakota to surrender when he was confronted by U.S. troops at Wounded Knee. On December 29 as the soldiers began to disarm the Sioux, shots were fired. More than 150 Sioux and 25 soldiers died in the ensuing battle. Although the last Sioux refugees from the reservations did not surrender until January 1891, the Battle of Wounded Knee is generally accepted as marking the end of the Indian Wars in North America.

JIM PIECUCH

Introduction

When Europeans first landed on the North American continent, they entered a land already populated by people who had lived there for millennia. A people of diverse culture, language, and lifestyle, they clustered in communities, ranged as nomads, or lived semi-nomadically.

"Indians," the Europeans labeled them. The term originated in the erroneous Spanish belief that Columbus had landed on an island in the Indian Ocean. Although historically inaccurate, for the non-Indian world "Indian" prevailed until recent decades. "Native American" now appears to have displaced Indian. It suffers the same inaccuracy as Indian because many non-Indians are also native Americans. Further complicating the issue, the native peoples themselves do not regard themselves as either Indians or Native Americans or any other term that collectivizes them. They look on themselves as Creek, Cherokee, Sioux, Cheyenne, Comanche, Ute, Apache, Nez Perce, or whatever tribal group they belong to. Unless dealing with separate tribes, however, writers must use a collective word. Most modern Indians seem not to object to either label.

European colonists and the Americans who followed confronted the Indians not only in war but in other relationships as well. More often than war, peace or even friendship prevailed. Political, economic, and cultural maneuvering or competition ruled these exchanges. Interaction, whether peaceful or violent, nearly always produced acculturation—changes in values, attitudes, institutions, and material culture. Nor was acculturation confined only to one side. Both changed, often radically—a process that continues to this day.

Even so, the worldview of each remained essentially beyond the understanding of the other. The European invasion condemned the two peoples to physical union, while a great cultural chasm condemned them never really to see or understand each other.

Their two distinct mindsets accommodated only marginally to each other. As historian Calvin Martin has written, "Surely this is the most poignant message of Indian-White relations: 500 years of talking past each other, of mutual incomprehension."

Many Indian wars grew from roots of mutual incomprehension.

Less abstract causes of course added weight: competition for tribal lands, pressures that produced intertribal conflicts over hunting territories, trade with the newcomers, resources, weapons, slaves, and in the West the horses introduced by the Spanish.

In the beginning mutual incomprehension appeared only as European and Indian began to talk to one another. The first Europeans came for reasons other than conquest. Encountering peoples that posed obstacles, they turned to conquest. With superior weapons, they readily conquered.

The Spanish laid the groundwork, in the sixteenth century ravaging the islands of the Carribean and the mainland that became New Spain. In their quest for mineral wealth, they perpetrated slaughter, cruelty, and slavery on man, woman, and child. Their savageries would today defy description had they not been described by the first Spanish priest ordained in the New World, Bartolomé de Las Casas. On the mainland, the Spanish found the riches they sought. But when they ventured northward into the present-day American Southwest and Southeast, they discovered none. Even so, they inflicted the same atrocities described by Las Casas on the native peoples living there.

The English landing in Tidewater Virginia and on the Massachusetts coast early in the seventeenth century brought with them attitudes toward natives similar to those of the Spaniards. Except for the Pilgrims and Puritans seeking religious freedom, they came for the same reasons: the land's resources.

English and Spanish drew strength from a scourge of rapidly spreading European diseases against which the Indians had no immunity. As early as the first part of the seventeenth century, disease had wiped out as much as seventy percent of the Indian population. Disease would continue to take its toll, even to the present day.

Not that the Indians failed to retaliate. Both in Virginia and Massachusetts bloody massacres of the invaders studded the history of conquest. As the colonial powers pushed inland, from east and south, war produced massacres on both sides.

In the seventeenth century the French came with the same objective as the English and Spaniards—exploitation of whatever wealth their part of the continent yielded. They promptly cultivated friendly relations with the tribes they met in present-day Canada and the American Midwest as far south as the Gulf of Mexico. Mutual incomprehension lessened with the passage of time, but it never ended. Occasionally hostilities disturbed relations, as some tribes frustrated France's imperial designs; but more often France's wars with England in Europe spread to America and swept the tribes into alliance with the French, and sometimes the English. These encounters pitted Indian against white and well as Indian against Indian. In this warfare the French held the upper hand. Their forested environment favored the masterful ambush tactics of their Indian allies. In the end, though, the English prevailed.

The French spread through the forests and along the rivers and lakes to live mainly by harvesting fur-bearing animals. Combined with the Indian trade, this rarely brought into play the issue of how the land should be used. The Spaniards sought mineral wealth, the French fur-bearing animals. Neither involved serious competition for land.

But for the English, land and its resources undergird most warfare. Finding no natural treasures, the English turned to agriculture—tobacco, cotton, rice, and on the far frontiers grains—which did require land. Indian subsistence patterns, depending on both wild animals and vegetation, interfered with English agriculture. Ridding the land of its Indian occupants, when they refused to move or sell, often led to war. Competing land uses also invoked mutual incomprehension The Indians worshiped deities residing in the natural world and sought a life dependent on its fruits and in harmony with it. The Christian God mandated that his people subdue and destroy the wilderness and make it blossom with the results of their industry. The Indians' communal use of large areas of land could not be viewed as the basis of true ownership, especially when they used so little of it in the approved Christian fashion. In the white mind, the Indians were simply part of the wilderness, to be subdued either by war or agreements that came to be labeled treaties

For the English, the Indian trade brought profits but also ill-will that played a role in hostilities. Most traders were unscrupulous and constantly cheated the Indians. At the same time, the trade stirred animosities among neighboring tribes, which maneuvered for supremacy in the trading relationship. Together with other causes, trade frequently sparked wars between white and Indian and between Indian and Indian. The European powers took advantage of the long history of intertribal warfare to play off one tribe against another.

Not only wealth motivated the European colonizers, but souls as well: convert the Indians to Christianity. The English cared little for saving souls, but Spanish and French priests and missionaries went among them to spread word of the white man's God. For a people with differing but profound spiritual beliefs, Christianity held little appeal. Here too mutual incomprehension prevailed. Sometimes wars broke out, sometimes the Indians faked conversion, sometimes they embraced Christianity, sometimes they practiced a dual system, above ground and underground. Whether success or failure, the drive to save souls contributed to the colonial Indian wars.

The French and Indian War of 1754-63 and the American Revolution of 1776-81 ended the wars of the colonial era and ushered in the era of relations between white American and American Indian. In the first, like others powered mainly by European antagonisms, the English finally expelled the French from the New World and left their Indian allies still harboring animosity toward the English victors. In the latter, the former English subjects proclaimed themselves independent Americans and fought for five years until the English at last concluded further fighting not worth the cost. The colonies became the United States of America.

Tribal lands brought about the first hostilities between westward-moving Americans and the Indian tenants of the land west of the Appalachian Mountains. As tenaciously as the tribes had defended their land through the colonial period, they fought back as white American emigrants sought to seize their land. At first, to overcome the resistance, the United States relied on militia, which proved ineffective, on occasion disastrously so. Gradually a weak regular army took shape and performed better, inflicting severe defeats on the peoples of the Old Northwest.

As the nineteenth century advanced, however, new attitudes toward Indians began to unfold in white minds. Some people, usually those closest to the frontier, favored outright extermination. Others, usually those along the more urbanized eastern seaboard, viewed the Indians as humans possessed of rights that ought to be respected. A third group drew inspiration from President Thomas Jefferson. He envisioned the United States as a vast continental nation (or several nations of similar bent) stretching from sea to sea. Tribes impeding the westward movement could simply be moved farther west, into the huge unsettled regions beyond the frontier.

Jefferson's unsettled regions of course were scarcely unsettled; on the contrary, Indians inhabited all of them. Even so, "Indian Removal" ultimately became the law of the land. To carry it out, the U.S. Army had to fight some tribes, while others yielded to the threat of war or to heavy-handed diplomacy. By whatever means, Indian Removal cleared most of the lands east of the Mississippi River of Indians. The movement, however, could hardly be considered humane. It spawned intratribal factions and wrought hardship, suffering, death, conflict with tribes already living in destinations, and for all political, economic, and cultural devastation.

The Louisiana Purchase (1803), the Mexican War (1846-48), and settlement with England over the disputed Oregon country (1846) realized the Jeffersonian vision of a continental nation. In the western half of the continent, Americans encountered new tribes of Indians, as well as some that had been evicted by the Indian Removal program. As whites moved west, seeking mineral, agricultural, and other natural bounty, wars moved with them.

Remaining behind were new and differing attitudes toward Indians. Frontiersmen still advocated extermination. But by mid-century a growing body of opinion favored "civilizing" the Indians by transforming them into good American citizens in all but skin color. Inevitably, echoing the colonial quest for souls, civilization could occur only in tandem with Christianity. Civilization programs ultimately dominated public policy and lessened the impulse for war.

Indians of course did not want to be civilized; they had their own civilization. Government, therefore, confronted the challenge of how and where to civilize them. Indian Removal provided no answer because it had aimed only to move tribes out of the way without changing them. The solution, byproduct of the larger purpose of clearing the tribes from lands coveted by white people, lay in reservations. By war or treaty, Indians would be confined to designated lands called reservations, thus getting them out of the path of white travel routes and settlement and establishing a laboratory in which to test theories of Christianization and civilization.

In the years after the American Civil War, increasingly influenced by humanitarian opinion and organized groups in the East, the government attempted a policy of "conquest by kindness"— get the Indians settled on reservations without resorting to war. Treaties between the United States and a tribe or tribes provided the mechanism without resort to war. Frequently, however, only war could force treaties, war that pitted the U.S. Army against the Indians. The history of Indian warfare in the last half of the nineteenth century typically was a record of campaigns to force tribes onto reservations where they had agreed by treaty to settle or war to return them to reservations from which they had fled in disgust. The tools for producing civilization, working imperfectly on some, not at all on others, failed to produce civilization.

Four hundred years of Indian warfare in North America came to an end in 1886 when the Apache Geronimo surrendered to the U.S. Army. Some would post the date at 1890, although the tragedy at Wounded Knee was not the culmination of a war but of a religious movement.

Indian warfare in North America differed radically from warfare elsewhere in the world. It did not consist of the conventional set-piece battles that characterized European wars, featuring maneuvering units, artillery, and standup attacks and withdrawals by infantry and cavalry. Rather American wars more accurately deserve the term guerrilla warfare, featuring ambush, surprise, and sudden attacks on enemy concentrations that involved noncombatants. A surprisingly small number of encounters even warrant the label "battle."

In the Eastern woodlands, both the colonial powers and the early Americans waged an especially brutal form of war. They located Indian villages, drove out the inhabitants, burned the dwellings, and applied the torch to the cornfields and other means of subsistence.

The American West , with its plains, mountains, and deserts, called for different strategies than the woodlands. In the final decades of hostilities, generals introduced a concept that had worked for the Union in the Civil War: "total war." Make war on the entire population, ran the argument, discover a winter village if possible and attack, then hound the fugitives relentlessly until exhaustion, hunger, and insecurity led to surrender. Indians also practiced total war, rarely sparing women and children.

American Indian wars differed from those elsewhere in another way. Unless surprised, Indians declined to fight unless virtually certain of winning. This occurred mainly in the ambush at which they excelled. When their women and children were threatened, even in a direct surprise attack, Indians usually fled and scattered while men provided rear-guard actions.

Traditional Indian weaponry consisted principally of bow and arrow, lance, tomahawk, knife, and a defensive hide shield. Gradually, however, they acquired European firearms, usually in trade and usually inferior to those of their opponents. By the 1860s, trade yielded firearms often superior to those of the military, such as repeating rifles against the army's single-shot weapons. The lack of skilled marksmen lessened this advantage. The principal arms of Europeans and Americans were muskets followed in the nineteenth century by rifles and metallic cartridges. Pistols and later revolvers constituted sidearms. Cavalry sabers proved useless in fighting Indians. Artillery played a minor role.

In the Eastern woodlands, Indians traveled and fought largely on foot—ideal for ambushing formally organized European or American troops moving in conventional formation on roads. In the western plains, mountains, and deserts, nomadic tribes moved and sometimes fought on horseback. (Spaniards brought horses to the New World, allowing pedestrian tribes to become nomads.)

Finally, the Indian wars of America not only pitted Indian against European invader but Indian against Indian. Tribes had been fighting one another for centuries, largely over hunting grounds but by long tradition as well. The advent of Europeans and their successor Americans not only failed to unite the tribes in the common defense but also failed to interrupt the long history of intertribal wars. Alliances formed and ended, but Indian against Indian persisted. Intertribal warfare formed a backdrop for wars with the invaders but also played a part in those wars.

Indian warfare wound its way prominently through four centuries of American history. That the Indians were never conquered but adapted time and again to changing circumstances may be ironic, but they continue to this day as a vibrant element of the American people, nurturing their identity and proud of it.

ROBERT M. UTLEY

Abenakis

Native American group indigenous to northern New England and Quebec and the Maritimes in Canada. The Abenakis ("People of the Dawn") were an Algonquian-speaking people who resided in present-day Maine, New Hampshire, Vermont, and Quebec. Historians often divide the Abenakis into Eastern Abenakis, centered in Maine, and Western Abenakis, centered in Vermont. However, the basis for these distinctions is more linguistic than geographic or political, and they were not in use during the colonial period. The British often called all Abenakis "eastern Indians." The Abenakis were hunter-gatherers, although they supplemented their diet and livelihood with fishing and agriculture, primarily corn. Abenaki tribes were autonomous, and inter-Abenaki wars were not uncommon.

The first recorded Abenaki meeting with Europeans occurred during the French expedition under Giovanni de Verrazano in 1524, but there is evidence that the Abenakis had earlier contact with Europeans. In 1604 Samuel de Champlain met with an Abenaki chief at Norumbega. The Abenakis traded furs with the French, Dutch, and English.

European diseases such as smallpox ravaged the native tribes of New England in the early 17th century. Those diseases made it far easier for Catholic missionaries from New France to make inroads with the Abenakis. Indeed, the Abenakis eventually became allies of the French in part because of the influence of missionaries. Jesuits over the course of the 17th century gained many Abenaki adherents to Catholicism. After early failures at conversion, the Jesuits turned to syncretism and over time to more conventional Catholicism.

The Abenakis and other Algonquian groups were subject to frequent raids by the Iroquois, who were supplied with firearms by the Dutch and later the English. The English colonies of New England and the Iroquois impinged on Abenaki territory, which made the tribe a natural ally of the French. In 1650 with French assistance, a series of Abenaki groups formed a coalition to guard against the Iroquois Confederacy.

In 1663 the Iroquois attacked an Abenaki group known as the Sokokis. In 1669 the Iroquois defeated a multitribal Algonquian force. Growing English settlements replaced the Iroquois as the major threat to the Abenakis, particularly after the English elimination of the Pequots in 1637. The Abenaki position between Quebec and New England, the fact that French immigration was far less robust than that of the English, and the greater facility of French traders and missionaries with the tribe all served to place the Abenakis firmly in the French camp in any conflict.

During King Philip's War (1675–1676), the Abenakis fought against English encroachment and demands to disarm. Because of English attacks, many Abenaki refugees fled to French mission villages in Quebec. Mission villages there such as St. Francis and Bécancour proved to be another link between the Abenakis and the French, and Catholicism became far more prevalent among the Abenakis from this point onward. In 1689 during King William's War (1689–1697), the Abenakis fought with the French against the English in New England, mainly by raids and guerrilla warfare. When the war concluded, the Abenakis continued to fight the English-allied Iroquois until 1701, when the latter made peace with the French. In 1699 the Abenakis signed an agreement to remain neutral in future conflicts between England and France.

During Queen Anne's War (1702–1713) the Abenakis, despite their prior agreement to remain neutral, fought the British. Their most famous raid of the war was against Deerfield, Massachusetts, where the French, Abenakis, and other natives inflicted numerous

An Abenaki sachem intercedes to stop a confrontation between two Abenakis and a British officer, saving the life of the latter. Etching from *Bickerstaff's Boston Almanack*, 1768. (Library of Congress)

casualties, captured some 100 colonists, and burned the town. In 1713 the war ended when the British and the Abenakis signed a treaty. Abenaki tribes lost land at the conclusion of the war, notably in Acadia, which the French ceded to the British. The Abenakis then began a war without French support, although allegedly it had been urged by French Jesuits such as Sebastian Rale. In Dummer's War (1722–1727), the Abenakis faced off with Massachusetts and New Hampshire over British encroachment on Abenaki land. At Pigwacket in 1725 the Abenakis went down to defeat, and a chief, Paugus, was killed. Most of the Eastern Abenakis stopped fighting, but the Western Abenakis led by Grey Lock continued to fight until 1727.

In Maine, the British destroyed the Abenaki settlements of Penobscot and Norridgewock. But the Abenakis, particularly in western Massachusetts, conducted guerrilla raids with some success before coming to terms with the British. At Norridgewock the Jesuit priest Sebastian Rale, a spiritual leader of the Abenakis, was killed and scalped by the British and their native allies.

During King George's War (1744–1748), the Abenakis raided throughout New England and New York. They undertook these efforts both with their French allies and alone. The mission Abenakis, who had fled during the destruction of their lands by the British, were also active in the war effort.

During the French and Indian War (1754–1763) the Abenakis again sided with the French, and in most campaigns Abenaki warriors were present. One Abenaki band, the Penobscot, initiated the massacre of the British at Fort William Henry in August 1757. In retaliation, in October 1759 a British force under the command of Major Robert Rogers razed the Abenaki mission village of St. Francis (in Quebec). With the removal of the French from North America in 1763, the Abenakis had to deal with British demands for land with no European ally to aid them. The French and Indian War had destroyed many villages and increased the stream of Abenakis into the mission villages of Quebec.

In the American Revolutionary War (1775–1783), Abenakis fought with both the British and Americans. Colonel John Allan, the Continental Congress's agent to the eastern Native Americans, convinced some Abenaki groups to join the American cause. Other groups of Abenakis, many of them the mission Indians of Quebec centered at St. Francis, fought alongside the British.

With the American victory in 1783, Abenaki land rights were increasingly endangered. Many states, in violation of federal law, negotiated their own agreements with Abenaki tribes in an attempt to gain as much land as possible. After the Revolution most Abenakis left for Canada, although some remained and assimilated into American life.

In 1805 the British set aside land for the Abenakis within Canada. Abenaki animosity toward the United States over the loss of tribal lands led many warriors, particularly those from villages on the St. Francis River south of Montreal, to fight for the British during the War of 1812. For the most part, the Abenakis conducted raids across the border or harassed American forces when they invaded Canada. Abenaki warriors were present at the Battle of Chateauguay on October 26, 1813, serving under Colonel Charles de Salaberry. That battle ended the American invasion led by Major General Wade Hampton. The war concluded on the terms of status quo ante bellum and thus failed to resolve Abenaki grievances against the United States. During the 20th century, many Abenaki tribes struggled to gain recognition from both state and federal governments.

MICHAEL K. BEAUCHAMP

See also

Deerfield, Massachusetts, Attack on; France; French and Indian War; Great Britain; Iroquois Confederacy; King George's War; King Philip's War; Native Americans and the American Revolutionary War; Native Americans and the War of 1812; Norridgewock, Battle of; Queen Anne's War; Rogers's Raid on St. Francis

References

Calloway, Colin G. *The Western Abenakis of Vermont, 1600–1800: War, Migration, and the Survival of an Indian People.* Norman: University of Oklahoma Press, 1990.

Calloway, Colin G., ed. *Dawnland Encounters: Indians and Europeans in Northern New England.* Hanover, NH: University Press of New England, 1991.

Morrison, Kenneth M. *The Embattled Northeast: The Elusive Ideal of Alliance in Abenaki-Euramerican Relations.* Berkeley: University of California Press, 1984.

Abenaki Wars

Start Date: 1675
End Date: 1678

Conflict between the Abenakis and English settlers, a result of King Philip's War (1675–1676). The Abenaki Wars were not true warfare in the classic sense, as they involved little actual combat; instead, they were marked chiefly by a massive Abenaki population displacement along the northern frontier. Constituent bands of the Algonquian-speaking Abenakis included the Androscoggin, Kennebec, Maliseet, Passamaquoddy, Pennacook, Penobscot, Saco, and Wawenock peoples who lived in the areas of Maine, New Hampshire, and New Brunswick. These bands had formed a loose confederacy by the end of the 16th century. A second group of Abenakis lived in the area now known as Vermont, but this group acted largely independently of the more eastern bands.

The Abenakis generally aligned themselves with the French to the north in Canada rather than with the English to the south in Massachusetts. From their first contact with Europeans, the Abenakis traded with them and had enjoyed good relations with the English in the first half of the 17th century; however, by the 1650s, the Abenakis had gravitated toward the French. Catholic French missionaries, dispatched to Abenaki towns, promised the Abenakis protection against their aggressive Iroquois neighbors. French interest in the fur trade strengthened ties. The English to the south, by contrast, had little interest in commercial ties with the Abenakis. The gradual expansion of the English north toward Abenaki territory also heightened tensions and led to a decline in amicable relations between the English colonists and the Abenakis.

The Abenaki Wars began as an outgrowth of King Philip's War. Refugees from the southern tribes, also Algonquian speakers, fled to the Abenakis in an attempt to avoid the campaigns of the English. Contributing to the already tense situation, Massachusetts settlers living near the Abenakis insisted on the submission of the Native Americans, demanding that the Abenakis relinquish their firearms to demonstrate that they were not in league with the Wampanoags. Without firearms and cut off from trade with the English on which they depended, the Abenakis faced starvation and hardship. The English failed to help matters when they overturned the canoe containing the children and wife of Abenaki chieftain Squando into the Saco River, leaving them to drown. In 1675 several Abenaki bands moved north to the French-established missions, while other bands remained neutral. In general the Abenakis retreated northward rather than engage the English, but English raiding parties continued to push the Abenakis off of their lands.

In 1676 following the end of King Philip's War, the English in Massachusetts saw little need to compromise with the Abenakis. Thus, the Abenakis continued to flee Massachusetts until 1678, when conflict ended with an uneasy agreement to cease hostilities. The treaty, negotiated by Governor Edmund Andros of New York, officially ended the war but did little to address its root causes. Continuing tension over English expansion onto Abenaki lands ensured persistent conflict. Furthermore, Abenaki alignment with the French meant that the French would seek the aid of their native allies against the English whenever war in Europe broke out.

The Abenaki Wars contributed to a sense of crisis in the Massachusetts Bay Colony following King Philip's War. Displaced refugees from the fighting along the Maine border created a sense of impending doom in the towns where they sought refuge. English refugees from the Maine frontier sojourned across Massachusetts, and their stories of Native American brutality convinced many that Satan was at work. The evident union of the heathen Native Americans with the Catholic French offered further proof of satanic agency to New Englanders.

The end of the First Abenaki War failed to secure a lasting settlement, leading to three more distinct wars between the Abenakis and the English. A second war erupted in 1688 and did not end until 1699; although it began and ended separately from King William's War (1689–1697), the French attempted to capitalize on the conflict in order to further their fight against the English. The Third Abenaki War likewise overlapped with Queen Anne's War (1702–1713). The Abenakis seized the opportunity of renewed conflict between France and England in an attempt to settle old scores. For instance, a party of Abenakis accompanied the group of French soldiers and Indians that attacked Deerfield, Massachusetts, in 1704.

Conflict erupted again in the Fourth Abenaki War of 1722–1727 largely because of continued English expansion into Maine. Abenaki auxiliaries accompanied French soldiers into battle as late as the French and Indian War of 1754–1763. The French defeat in that conflict spelled disaster for the Abenakis, who dispersed and were driven from their land.

Peter C. Luebke

See also

Abenakis; Deerfield, Massachusetts, Attack on; French and Indian War; Iroquois; King Philip's War; King William's War; Queen Anne's War; Wampanoags

References

Calloway, Colin G. *The Western Abenakis of Vermont, 1600–1800: War, Migration, and the Survival of an Indian People.* Norman: University of Oklahoma Press, 1990.

Grenier, John. *The Far Reaches of Empire: War in Nova Scotia, 1710–1760.* Norman: University of Oklahoma Press, 2008.

Grenier, John. *The First Way of War: American War Making on the Frontier.* Cambridge: Cambridge University Press, 2005.

Haefeli, Evan, and Kevin Sweeney. *Captors and Captives: The 1704 French and Indian Raid on Deerfield.* Amherst: University of Massachusetts Press, 2003.

Morrison, Kenneth M. *The Embattled Northeast: The Elusive Ideal of Alliance in Abenaki-Euramerican Relations.* Berkeley: University of California Press, 1984.

Norton, Mary Beth. *In the Devil's Snare: The Salem Witchcraft Crisis of 1692.* New York: Knopf, 2002.

Sévigny, P. André. *Les Abénaquis: Habitat et Migrations (17e et 18e siècles).* Montréal: Les Éditions Bellarmin, 1976.

Abihkas

See Creeks

Acoma Pueblo, Battle of
Start Date: January 22, 1599
End Date: January 24, 1599

Fierce battle at Acoma Pueblo in northern New Spain (New Mexico) between Spanish forces and Acoma natives that resulted in the deaths of some 800 Acomas. Located on a mesa 357 feet above the desert floor west of the Rio Grande Valley, Acoma Pueblo (or Sky City) was home to approximately 6,000 Keresan-speaking Acomas at the end of the 16th century. Irrigated fields of corn and beans encircled the steep slopes of the mesa, and residents traveled between village and farmland by using a combination of stairs and hand and toe holes carved into the red rock. Prior to the arrival of the Spanish, Acoma had been inhabited for at least 500 years, making it one of the oldest continuously occupied settlements in North America.

In the early 16th century, the viceroy of New Spain authorized expeditions north of Mexico in hopes of discovering riches rumored to be found among the adobe towns scattered across the landscape. Francisco Vásquez de Coronado, governor of the province of New Galicia in northern Mexico, led the largest of these expeditions from 1540 to 1542. Coronado's captain of artillery, Hernando de Alvarado, visited Acoma with a small force of men on his way back from a foray to Zuni Pueblo in 1540 and noted the pueblo's virtually impregnable position atop the mesa.

Coronado's accounts of his unprofitable expedition dissuaded further ventures into pueblo country for more than half a century. In 1595 Juan de Oñate led an expedition up the Rio Grande Valley to spread the Catholic faith, pacify the natives, and establish a permanent colony in the northern provinces of New Spain. In 1598 after a series of delays, Oñate and 500 men, women, and children entered New Mexico near present-day El Paso, Texas. By late May, Oñate had reached the upper Rio Grande and encountered the first of many pueblos that he formally claimed for Spain. In July 1598 Oñate arrived at the confluence of the Chama River and the Rio Grande and established his headquarters at Ohke Pueblo, which he renamed San Juan and made the capital of the new colony.

Oñate dispersed friars from San Juan to the pueblos and personally led a party of colonists and soldiers on a reconnaissance of the province. On October 27, 1598, Oñate arrived at Acoma, ascended the mesa, and entered the city. Residents of the pueblo disagreed on how best to deal with the Spanish. Ultimately the natives decided to treat Oñate and his party hospitably and gave them (as well as their horses) food and water. Before leaving, the governor informed the inhabitants of Acoma that they were now under Spanish rule.

In December 1598 Oñate's nephew, Juan de Zaldivar, arrived at the base of Acoma Pueblo at the head of a column of 30 soldiers en route to a rendezvous with his uncle. Zaldivar demanded food for his hungry men. The Acomas refused to comply. They did, however, agree to trade cornmeal for tools if the Spaniards could wait until they completed the grinding process. After waiting three days for the promised cornmeal, Zaldivar and 16 of his men ascended the mesa and entered the city. What happened next is not entirely clear. Native accounts blame the ensuing violence on the Spaniards' mistreatment of Acoma women and exploitation of the pueblo's hospitality. Spanish survivors claimed that the Acomas attacked by design. Either way, Zaldivar and his men were quickly overwhelmed. Only 4 of the 16 men were able to flee to the desert floor and safety. Zaldivar was among the dead.

When Oñate received word that his nephew had been killed, the governor dispatched Juan's brother, Vicente de Zaldivar, along with a force of 70 men to punish the pueblo. On January 22, 1599, Spanish soldiers arrived at Acoma and under the cover of darkness managed to scale the steep-sided mesa and haul a cannon to the top. Zaldivar besieged the city for three days. Cannon fire destroyed adobe walls, and soldiers slaughtered villagers fighting to save their homes and families. When the carnage ended, approximately 800 Acoma men, women, and children lay dead; another 580 were taken captive.

Oñate quickly orchestrated a trial, over which he presided, and found the Acomas guilty of treason against Spain. Adolescents were sentenced to 20 years of servitude, and adult men were to have one foot amputated. The mutilation was to be conducted in the plazas of pueblos along the Rio Grande as a lesson to those who might question Spanish authority. The inhabitants of Acoma eventually rebuilt their city, but the bitter memory of the events of January 1599 contributed to the Pueblo Revolt of 1680 and remained fixed in Indian minds for centuries to come.

ALAN C. DOWNS

See also

New Mexico; Oñate, Juan de; Pueblo Revolt; Pueblos

INDIAN REBELLIONS AGAINST THE SPANISH ON THE SOUTHERN PLAINS

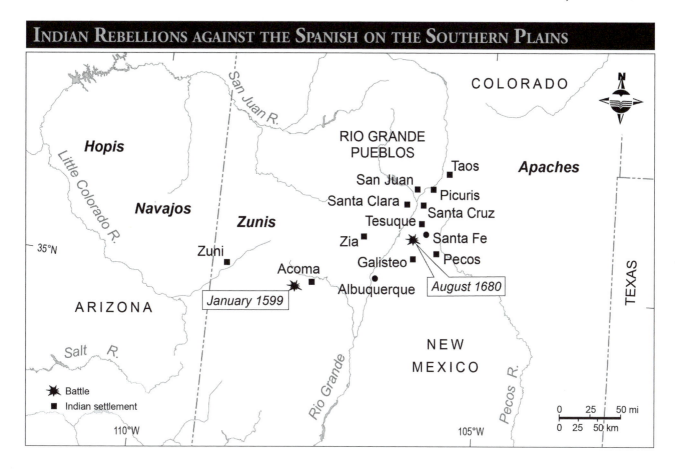

References

Josephy, Alvin M., Jr. *500 Nations: An Illustrated History of North American Indians.* New York: Knopf, 1994.

Simmons, Marc. *The Last Conquistador: Juan de Oñate and the Settling of the Far Southwest.* Norman: University of Oklahoma Press, 1991.

Adobe Walls, First Battle of
Event Date: November 25, 1864

Battle fought between a New Mexico Volunteer Infantry unit and Kiowa and Comanche warriors in the Texas Panhandle on November 25, 1864. The structure that came to be known as Adobe Walls began as a trading post established in 1843 near the Canadian River in what is today Hutchinson County, Texas, by Bent, St. Vrain and Company to trade with the Kiowas and Comanches. Originally built of logs, the outpost was soon converted to adobe and became known as Fort Adobe. The fort was an 80-foot rectangle with 9-foot-high adobe walls and a single entrance. Traders occupied the fort only on an intermittent basis because of persistent Native American attacks. In 1849 as a result of the consistent attacks, the company detonated the interior of the fort, leaving behind just the outer walls.

In the autumn of 1864 Colonel Christopher "Kit" Carson was dispatched from Fort Bascom, New Mexico, to reestablish control of the Santa Fe Trail. Carson commanded a 300-man force of volunteers drawn from California and New Mexico. Traveling along with Carson's detachment were some 70 Ute and Apache allies. The trail had been subject to repeated attacks by the Comanche, Kiowa, and Kiowa Apache tribes in the area. The attacks along the Santa Fe Trail also threatened the lines of communication and supply between New Mexico and the eastern United States during the American Civil War.

On the morning of November 25, 1864, Carson's advanced force, mostly cavalry supported by two howitzers, attacked a Kiowa village of some 150 lodges near the old Fort Adobe, routing the Native Americans. The assault was so successful that Carson's men were inside the fort's walls within two hours. The Kiowas fled, and Carson's men followed until they encountered a much larger force of Kiowa, Comanche, and Kiowa Apache warriors operating out of substantial villages nearby and whose presence had been unknown to Carson's men.

Estimates vary as to the size of the Native American force, but it may have been somewhere between 3,000 and 7,000 warriors. Instead of directly engaging this force, Carson wisely turned back to the ruins of Fort Adobe, which he used for defensive purposes. The ruins of Fort Adobe served as a hospital and a corral in addition to providing a firm base throughout the battle.

Carson was familiar with the fort and the area, having worked there earlier in his life. He and his men repulsed a series of determined attacks led by Kiowa chief Dohasan. The defenders were successful, thanks in large part to the devastating effect of their two 12-pounder howitzers. The outcome of the battle may well have been different had Carson not had access to Fort Adobe and the howitzers.

When the last Native American assault had been blunted, Carson's men burned the nearby Kiowa village and destroyed its winter store of foodstuffs and other supplies. But concern for his trailing infantry and lengthy supply train prompted Carson to withdraw. During the fight, Carson's unit suffered 2 dead and 10 wounded. Native American casualties were much higher, with an estimated 50 to 150 killed or wounded.

The First Battle of Adobe Walls was a tactical victory for Carson in that he inflicted more casualties, held off a significantly larger force, and destroyed a large Kiowa village along with its invaluable stores. But the overall objective of the campaign was not achieved, for the Santa Fe Trail continued to be subject to Native American attacks. Still, the battle was widely perceived as an American victory and greatly enhanced the reputation of Kit Carson.

The Adobe Walls site remained abandoned until 1874, when a series of merchants established stores there to benefit from the trade in buffalo hides. Several hundred buffalo hunters began operating in the area, which would ultimately lead to the Second Battle of Adobe Walls on June 27, 1874, whereupon the fort was abandoned again. In 1978 the site became a Texas state archaeological landmark.

MICHAEL K. BEAUCHAMP AND PAUL G. PIERPAOLI JR.

See also
Adobe Walls, Second Battle of; Apaches; Carson, Christopher Houston; Comanches; Kiowas; Utes

References
Baker, T. Lindsay, and Billy R. Harrison. *Adobe Walls: The History and Archeology of the 1874 Trading Post.* College Station: Texas A&M University Press, 1986.
Dixon, Olive K. *Life of "Billy Dixon": Plainsman, Scout and Pioneer.* Dallas: P. L. Turner, 1914.

Adobe Walls, Second Battle of
Event Date: June 27, 1874

Battle between white buffalo hunters and Native Americans at the Adobe Walls outpost, located in the Texas Panhandle just above the Canadian River and not far from the old trading post established in 1843. By 1874 buffalo hunters ranging across the Great Plains had decimated the herds on which the indigenous tribes of the southern Plains relied for their existence. This brought to prominence a Comanche medicine man named Isatai (Wolf Ass), who claimed the power to make warriors immortal and the ability to cough ammunition from his mouth. Isatai's call for war encouraged enough young men, roughly 300 from the Kiowa, Comanche,

and Cheyenne tribes, under the command of the Comanche Quanah Parker, to launch an attack on the outpost at Adobe Walls.

Although the old post—site of a battle in 1864—had earlier been abandoned, the economic opportunity created by the lucrative buffalo-hunting business encouraged adventurous entrepreneurs to reestablish a trading post near the old Adobe Walls in 1874. As spring turned to summer, word began to spread that Quanah Parker was attacking hunting parties, and many hunters thus began to gather at Adobe Walls for mutual protection.

By late June 1874, 28 hunters and a handful of storekeepers were gathered at the post. Parker planned his attack for the early morning darkness of June 27. As fate would have it, an accident at a local saloon had almost every man at Adobe Walls awake and inside when the attack was launched. As the warriors swept toward the outpost, they killed 2 men sleeping in their wagon outside the enclosure. The men working in the saloon heard the gunfire and immediately fired into the darkness at the attackers. This initial fusillade alerted all who were still asleep, and within a matter of minutes the hunters and traders had occupied all three buildings in the outpost.

The warriors swarmed around the buildings, firing in the windows and attempting to cut firing holes in the roofs, but effective fire from the hunters' large-caliber buffalo rifles pushed back the initial attack. Parker's warriors then withdrew and laid siege to the tiny outpost. During this time, several frontier legends were born. A young Bat Masterson got his first taste of combat and was witness to the legendary marksmanship of one Billy Dixon, who killed a warrior at a reported distance of 1,500 yards.

In addition to the two men killed in the wagon, one man was killed in the initial battle, and another man accidentally shot himself. Seven Cheyennes and 6 Comanches were killed, and more than 20 were wounded, including Quanah Parker. Disillusioned by the false claims of the prophet Isatai, the warriors abandoned the siege after only two days.

After the battle, the occupants of Adobe Walls recognized the folly of establishing an outpost in hostile territory and abandoned the venture. Within weeks, Comanche and Kiowa warriors destroyed the buildings. The Second Battle of Adobe Walls was also the opening fight in what came to known as the Red River War, the final gasp of the once great southern Plains tribes.

PATRICK R. JENNINGS

See also
Adobe Walls, First Battle of; Cheyennes; Comanches; Kiowas; Quanah Parker; Red River War

References
Baker, T. Lindsay, and Billy R. Harrison. *Adobe Walls: The History and Archeology of the 1874 Trading Post.* College Station: Texas A&M University Press, 1986.
Groneman, William. *Battlefields of Texas.* Plano, TX: Republic of Texas Press, 1998.
Nye, Wilber S. *Plains Indian Raiders: The Final Phase of Warfare from the Arkansas to the Red River.* Norman: University of Oklahoma Press, 1968.

Agriculture

While popular imagination sometimes stereotypes North America's native peoples solely as nomadic hunters, many if not most practiced agriculture, or the domestication of plants for human consumption. At least half of the earth's staple vegetable foods, the most important being corn (maize) and potatoes, were first cultivated by Native Americans, who often drew more of their sustenance from agriculture than from hunting and gathering. By the year 800 CE, agriculture was an established way of life for many native peoples in North America.

At first sight, many immigrating Europeans did not recognize Native American agriculture because it did not resemble their own. Native Americans did not domesticate draft animals and only rarely plowed their fields. Sometimes crops were grown in small clearings amid forest. When Europeans first laid eyes on North America, it was much more densely forested than it is today. The parklike appearance of many eastern forests was a result of native peoples' efforts to manage plant and animal life.

Some native peoples used fire to raze fields for farming and to drive game while hunting. These were not fires left to blaze out of control, however. For instance, Navajos who used range fires customarily detailed half of their hunting party to contain and control the fire and to keep it on the surface, where the flames would clear old brush so that new plant life could self-generate instead of destroying the forest canopy.

Agricultural Contributions to the World

Native Americans first cultivated many of the foods that today are taken for granted as everyday nourishment. Peanuts and corn, for example, are both indigenous to the Americas, as are all edible beans except horse beans and soybeans, all squashes (including pumpkins), Jerusalem artichokes, the "Irish" potato, the sweet potato, sunflowers, peppers, pineapples, watermelons, cassava, bananas, strawberries, raspberries, gooseberries, and pecans.

Native American agriculture has influenced eating habits around the world so completely that many people forget the culinary origins of their food. Before the voyages of Christopher Columbus, the Italian food of today (with its tomato-based sauces) was unknown; tomatoes grew only in the New World. The Irish cooked their food without potatoes. Europeans satisfied their desire for sweets without chocolate. Corn was unknown outside the Americas. These crops were produced by experimentation by many Native American cultures over thousands of years. Knowledge of plant life was passed along from generation to generation with other social knowledge, usually by the elder women of a native tribe or nation.

Food Production and Spiritual Life

The production of food is woven into Native American spiritual life. Among the Iroquois and many other native peoples, for example, festivals highlight the key role of the so-called three sisters (corn, squash, and beans). Archaeologists suggest that the food complex of corn, beans, and squash was transferred northward from Mexico as a set of rituals before it became an agricultural system. By practicing the rituals, Native Americans in the corn-growing areas of North America became farmers. Corn requires a 160-day frost-free growing season; the northern limit of corn cultivation also often marks the limit of intensive native agriculture.

Agriculture among Native American peoples enabled higher population densities. The Native Americans in Maine, who did not use widespread agriculture, sustained an average density of about 40 people per 100 square miles, while Native Americans in southern New England, who raised crops (corn being their major staple), averaged 287 people (seven times as many) on the same amount of land.

Native American agriculture often seemed disorderly to European eyes, accustomed as they were to large fields of a single crop. Native fields showed evidence of thought and practice, however. Samuel de Champlain described how Native Americans planted corn on small hills mixed with beans of several types. John Winthrop, describing Native American fields in Massachusetts shortly after the Puritans' arrival, said that their agriculture "load[ed] the Ground with as much as it will beare." Native farming methods (usually the responsibility of women, except when growing tobacco) not only kept weeds at a minimum but also preserved soil moisture.

Many native peoples offered their thanks to the plants as well as to the animals that they consumed out of a belief that the essence of life animating human beings also is present in the entire web of animate and inanimate life and objects. Long before a science of sustained-yield forestry evolved, Native American peoples along the Northwest Coast harvested trees in ways that would ensure their continued growth as part of a belief that trees are sentient beings. Some Native Americans charted farming cycles through complicated relationships with the sun and moon. In addition to domesticating and breeding dozens of food plants, they also harvested the wild bounty of the forests for hundreds of herbs and other plants used to restore and maintain health.

Pueblo Agriculture: Water Is Life

Long before the arrival of Europeans, the ancestors of today's Pueblos were creating a corn-based culture in the Chaco Canyon of present-day New Mexico. The Pueblos of the Rio Grande are cultural and economic inheritors of the Mogollon, Ancestral Puebloan, and Hohokam communities to the west and southwest of the upper Rio Grande Valley. The cultivation of corn was introduced into the area about 3000 BCE. About 2000 BCE, beans and squash were added. Cotton later became a fourth staple crop.

Also about 2,000 years ago, irrigation was introduced to supplement dry farming in the area. The Pueblos used brief, heavy precipitation to advantage by constructing some of their irrigation works at the bases of steep cliffs that collected runoff. The residents of this area constructed roads that often ran for hundreds of miles to provide a way to share food surpluses; if one pueblo had

Depiction of Timucua Indians in Florida at work in agriculture by Theodor de Bry in 1591. The men are preparing the field while the women plant corn and beans. (Library of Congress)

a bad harvest, others would make up the shortfall. The cultivation of corn in Chaco Canyon supported a civilization that constructed the largest multifamily dwellings in North America. Such a high degree of agricultural organization supported a culture that dominated the turquoise trade in the area. Turquoise was important as a liquid asset, a medium of trade. Pueblo centers such as Pueblo Bonito became centers of trade, manufacturing, and ceremony.

The vital role of water and irrigation in Pueblo agriculture is illustrated by the fact that the great classic Pueblo civilizations were destroyed by a drought so severe that not even ingenious water management could cope with it. In the 13th century, residents abandoned most pueblo settlements outside the Rio Grande Valley after 50 years of drought that destroyed their agricultural base.

Following the Spanish colonization of New Mexico, access to water became a crucial cause for conflict. Land without water is worthless in the arid Southwest. Paradoxically, the Pueblos in 1680 used the waters of the Rio Grande to defeat the Spanish, staging their revolt while the river was flooding to keep Spanish reinforcements out.

The irrigation of farmland was the key factor in Pueblo agricultural land use. To plan, construct, and maintain elaborate irrigation systems, cooperation among several villages was crucial. The irrigation systems needed routine maintenance that rendered

clans inefficient, so nonkinship associations were created to cope with the work. This organizational framework had other community functions and revolved primarily around the spiritual life of the Pueblos. The basic rationale for the nonkinship associations was irrigation, however.

The Importance of Corn

Corn, the major food source for several agricultural peoples across the continent, enjoyed a special spiritual significance. Corn and beans (which grow well together because beans, a legume, fix nitrogen in their roots) were often said to maintain a spiritual union. Some peoples, such as the Omahas of the eastern Great Plains, "sang up" their corn through special rituals. Some groups cleaned their storage bins before the harvest so that the corn would be "happy" when it was deposited. The Pawnees grew 10 varieties of corn, including a variety (called holy or wonderful corn) that was used only for religious purposes and was never eaten. The Mandans had a corn priest who officiated at rites during the growing season. Each stage of the corn's growth was associated with particular songs and rituals, and spiritual attention was said to be as important to the corn as proper water, sun, and fertilizer. Among the Zunis, a newborn child was given an ear of corn at birth and endowed with a corn name. An ear of maize was put in the place of death as the heart of the deceased and later used as seed corn to begin the cycle of life anew. To the Navajos, corn was as sacred as human life.

Corn is intertwined with the origin stories of many Native American peoples. The Pueblos say that corn was brought to them by Blue Corn Woman and White Corn Maiden, who emerged to the surface of the earth from a great underground kiva (sacred place). At birth each infant is given the seed from an ear of corn as a fetish to carry for life as a reminder that the Corn Mothers brought life to the Pueblos. The corn fetish has a practical side as well. Should a harvest completely fail for drought or other reasons, the fetishes may become the seed corn for the next crop.

Corn's biological name is *Zea mays,* from which the name "maize" is derived. The first distant relatives of today's foot-long ears of corn were probably grown in central Mexico near Teoti-huacán around 5000 BCE from a wild grass called *teosinte.* Early corn was small, perhaps three to four inches long, with two rows of mismatched kernels. Utilization of corn spread to South America as well as to the Ancestral Puebloan country in present-day Arizona and New Mexico first as a wild grain and then as an agricultural product, gradually increasing in length and quantity of kernels. Corn was firmly established as a staple in the Southwest by the sixth century. By the year 1000, corn had spread over all areas of North and South America that had the requisite growing season and had become a stable crop of many native peoples across the hemisphere. As the use of maize spread north and south from Mexico, native peoples domesticated hundreds of varieties and bred them selectively so that the edible kernels grew in size and numbers.

Corn was introduced in eastern North America about 200 CE and had become a dominant food source across much of the region (from southern Ontario to northern Florida) by about 800. During this time Native American farmers took part in the selective breeding of several strains of corn to increase production as well as hardiness in the face of freezes and drought. By 900 a major advance in breeding, commonly called flint or eastern eight row, secured corn's dominance of agricultural food production throughout the East because it was hardier than earlier strains. The spread of corn as a staple crop did not reach its greatest extent until 100 years before Christopher Columbus's first voyage in 1492.

When colonists arrived in eastern North America, many of the native peoples they met farmed corn in large tracts. John Winthrop, governor of Massachusetts Bay Colony, admired abandoned native cornfields and declared that God had provided the epidemic that killed the people who had tended them as an act of divine providence, clearing the way for the Puritans. Native Americans taught the Puritans which seeds would grow in their territory. Most of the seeds brought by the Puritans from England did not sprout when planted in the area that the colonists called New England.

Corn also enhanced the role of agriculture in many Native American economies. The oral history of the Iroquois, for example, holds that corn had a key role in establishing agriculture as a major economic enterprise. The Iroquois adopted corn as a staple crop and developed large-scale agriculture shortly after 1000. Their ability to produce a surplus of corn played a role in the political influence of the Iroquois Confederacy, which reached through a chain of alliances from their homelands in present-day upstate New York across much of New England and the Mid-Atlantic region.

The adoption by the Iroquois of corn-based agriculture along with cultivation of beans and squash (the three sisters) played an important role in their adoption of a matrilineal social structure and a consensus-based political system.

BRUCE E. JOHANSEN

See also

Corn; Iroquois Confederacy; Mohawks; Navajos; Pawnees; Pueblos; Winthrop, John; Wyandots

References

Ballantine, Betty, and Ian Ballantine. *The Native Americans: An Illustrated History.* Atlanta: Turner Publishing, 1994.

Brandon, William. *American Heritage Book of Indians.* New York: Dell, 1961.

Cronon, William. *Changes in the Land: Indians, Colonists, and the Ecology of New England.* New York: Hill and Wang, 1983.

Deloria, Vine, Jr. *God Is Red.* Golden, CO: Fulcrum, 1992.

Dozier, Edward P. *The Pueblo Indians of North America.* New York: Holt, Rinehart and Winston, 1970.

Grinde, Donald A., Jr., and Bruce E. Johansen. *Ecocide of Native America.* Santa Fe, NM: Clear Light Publishers, 1995.

Hughes, J. Donald. *American Indian Ecology.* El Paso: Texas Western Press, 1993.

Sando, Joe S. *The Pueblo Indians.* San Francisco: Indian Historian Press, 1976.

Agriculture, Subsistence

See Subsistence Agriculture

Akanseas/Akensas

See Quapaws

Alabamas

See Creeks

Albany Conference
Event Date: May 1, 1690

Conference of delegates from the New England colonies and New York at Albany, New York, on May 1, 1690, to develop a common means to defend themselves from the French and their Native

American allies. The meeting was convened following the February 1690 attack on Schenectady, New York. This conference is considered the first intercolonial American congress.

From 1688 to 1697, France and a coalition of European powers, known as the League of Augsburg (after 1689 the Grand Alliance), fought each other in what became known as the War of the League of Augsburg. In 1689 Louis XIV of France invaded the Rhine Palatinate. The Glorious Revolution (1688–1689) in England overthrew King James II, and William, the prince of Orange, became William III of England. Louis supported a counterrevolution in Ireland to keep William from sending troops to the continent, but the rebels lost the Battle of the Boyne in 1690. After eight years of fighting France had captured some forts and territory, but the exhaustion of the belligerents and the defection of Savoy from the Grand Alliance in 1696 led to the Treaty of Ryswick in 1697.

The American counterpart to this conflict, known as King William's War (1689–1697), was the first of the French and Indian wars that would occur over the next 75 years. Fighting first broke out between the English and French on Hudson Bay and between the Iroquois and the French in western New York. Louis de Buade, Comte de Frontenac et de Palluau, the governor-general of New France (Canada) during 1672–1682 and 1689–1698, sent French troops with their Native American allies, especially the Algonquins and Abenakis, to attack English settlements along the frontier with New France and the Iroquois, allied with the British. On February 9, 1690, 200 French soldiers and Native Americans attacked and burned Schenectady, New York, resulting in the deaths of 62 of its inhabitants, including women and children; the destruction of 60 buildings; and 27 survivors taken as prisoners back to New France.

In the wake of these attacks, delegates from the New England colonies and New York met at Albany on May 1, 1690, to form a confederation for their mutual defense and develop a plan for a concerted attack on New France. This was crucial because England had only a few regular soldiers in North America. The delegates at the conference decided on a two-pronged invasion of Canada. On May 11 Sir William Phips, the governor of Massachusetts, seized Port Royal, the capital of French Acadia. In August, Colonel John (Fitz-John) Winthrop led a land force to attack Montreal, while Phips led a naval force to attack Quebec via the Saint Lawrence River. Both expeditions were humiliating financial disasters for the English and were made worse when the French recaptured Port Royal. The Quebec expedition was the only major offensive in North America of this war. For the remainder of the conflict, the English colonists could only defend themselves against French attacks.

The war ended with the inconclusive Treaty of Ryswick, signed on September 30, 1697. The treaty restored the prewar status quo in the colonies and turned the Hudson Bay dispute over to a group of commissioners, who failed to reach an agreement.

ROBERT B. KANE

See also
Abenakis; Algonquins; Iroquois; King William's War; Winthrop, John (Fitz-John)

References
Barr, Daniel P. *Unconquered: The Iroquois League at War in Colonial America.* Westport, CT: Praeger, 2006.
Bolton, Herbert Eugen, and Thomas Maitland Marshall. *The Colonization of North America, 1492–1783.* New York: Macmillan, 1920.
Peckham, Howard Henry. *The Colonial Wars, 1689–1762.* Chicago: University of Chicago Press, 1964.

Albany Congress
Start Date: June 19, 1754
End Date: July 11, 1754

The Albany Congress, also known as the Albany Conference, met from June 19 to July 11, 1754, to repair deteriorating relations between the government of New York and the Iroquois Confederacy. In 1753 Mohawk leader and spokesman Chief Hendrick (Theyanoguin) informed Governor George Clinton that "the Covenant Chain is broken between you and us" and that New York's proximity to New France necessitated good relations to protect the fur trade and maintain frontier defenses. The French had already begun reasserting old claims to the territory from the Great Lakes down the Ohio and Mississippi rivers and asserting new claims to the Wyoming Valley. This was emphasized by the construction of Fort Duquesne at the Forks of the Ohio. The British Board of Trade ordered the northern colonies to convene at Albany to renegotiate Native American alliances and trade agreements and to assess the status of frontier defenses. As the delegates arrived, George Washington's skirmish with the French at Jumonville's Glen in May and his besiegement at Fort Necessity should have added a note of dire urgency to the proceedings.

On the contrary, however, the Albany Congress became a tangle of political intrigue interlaced with the backroom maneuvering of land speculators primarily from New York, Connecticut, and Pennsylvania. They all coveted Wyoming Valley territory and other Iroquois lands and sent agents to negotiate purchases of lands occupied by the Delawares and Susquehannocks, who were generally not privy to the proceedings. Spurious land claims conflicted with fraudulent deals brokered by unscrupulous Indian representatives and white middlemen, and these exacerbated preexisting rivalries centered on territorial claims and acquisitions. New York, which saw itself as the primary theater in any future colonial war with France, demanded that Virginia, Pennsylvania, and New England assist in financing the construction of a string of defensive forts in Iroquoia, demands that were summarily rejected. New England was particularly loath to do anything for the benefit of New York, as Massachusetts intermittently clashed with New York over joint claims to the land in present-day Vermont. Furthermore, New England saw no sense in committing precious funds to an endeavor that would not protect its region and was also concerned about the threat from New France.

The political and economic ambitions of the presiding officer, New York governor James Delancey, who was also New York City's most powerful merchant, were also on display at the Albany Congress. The assembly provided Delancey a platform from which to advance his mercantile interests in the Iroquois fur-trading network as well as the political and financial aspirations of William Johnson, an influential Mohawk Valley trader. Together they cultivated the patronage of Thomas Pownall, a younger brother to the secretary of the Board of Trade, who sent to the Earl of Halifax reports of the Albany Congress that emphasized the positive contributions of Delancey and Johnson. Benjamin Franklin, a Pennsylvania delegate, likewise worked with Pownall to advance an idea that he had for an intercolonial union. However, like the politico-mercantile intrigue that infected the Albany Congress, larger scale political rivalries involving the American and British clients of aristocratic patrons in England precluded substantial progress toward viable colonial defense.

Franklin's Albany Plan of Union, for which the Albany Congress is best known and which Pownall enthusiastically supported, involved an ambitious redefinition of the colonies' status within the British Empire. Cognizant of the uneven British administration of colonial affairs in America and the dangers of American disunion, Franklin proposed to solve these problems with the creation of a Grand Council composed of elected delegates from each colony. The council would administer matters directly involving military defense, Indian affairs, intercolonial relations, and western land policies and would also have the power to tax the colonies for mutual defense. The council would be overseen by a royally appointed president-general who would report to the British secretary of state for the Southern Department and thus streamline imperial administration. Despite some initial interest in the plan, it was soundly rejected by the delegates who knew that their respective assemblies would not share authority with another body and also by the British government, which did not wish to relinquish its growing direct control over the American colonies. Although the Albany Congress was a failure in terms of grand designs, it turned out to be lucrative for a number of men, especially William Johnson, who was appointed superintendent for northern Indian affairs in 1756 and who eventually received a knighthood for his work during the French and Indian War.

JOHN HOWARD SMITH

See also
Covenant Chain; Delawares; French and Indian War; Iroquois Confederacy; Johnson, Sir William; Susquehannocks

References
Anderson, Fred. *Crucible of War: The Seven Years' War and the Fate of the Empire in British North America, 1754–1766.* New York: Vintage Books, 2001.
Jennings, Francis. *Empire of Fortune: Crowns, Colonies, and Tribes in the Seven Years War in America.* New York: Norton, 1988.
Olsen, Alison Gilbert. "The British Government and Colonial Union, 1754." *William and Mary Quarterly,* 3rd Ser., 17(1) (January 1960): 22–34.

Aleut Rebellion
Start Date: 1761
End Date: 1766

Sporadic conflict occurring between Russian fur traders and the Aleut peoples in the Aleutian Islands, situated in present-day southwestern Alaska. In the 17th century, Russian fur traders began making moves toward Siberia and beyond in search of animals that yielded highly valuable pelts including sea otters, which were abundant in Alaska and the Aleutian Islands. By the mid-1700s traders had begun to penetrate the Aleutian Islands in search of pelts. Because many of these traders were not skilled at hunting sea otters, they began to coerce the local Aleut population into doing the hunting for them. This resulted in the shameful exploitation of the Native Americans.

The Russians coerced many Aleutian males into undertaking long hunts that took them far from their families and homes. Sometimes they were gone for six months or more, which severely disrupted tribal and family life. Other times the Russians would hold Aleut women and children hostage, not releasing them until the males returned with an adequate supply of pelts.

In 1761 on the Aleutian island of Umnak, a group of Aleuts attacked Russian fur traders who had attempted to coerce them into hunting sea otters. This began a five-year struggle, albeit a sporadic one, in which Aleuts and Russians engaged in a low-level war against each other. Seeking retaliation for the Aleut attack, the Russians shelled several Aleut villages, killing a number of people. Other Aleuts were captured and enslaved. During the course of the next several years, the Aleuts conducted raids on Russian settlements. The Aleuts also seized at least four Russian ships and killed their crews. The Aleut Rebellion came to an end in 1766.

PAUL G. PIERPAOLI JR.

See also
Russia

References
Chevigny, Hector. *Russian America: The Great Alaskan Venture, 1741–1867.* New York: Viking, 1965.
Starr, S. Frederick, ed. *Russia's American Colony.* Durham, NC: Duke University Press, 1987.

Alexander
See Wamsutta

Algonquins
Native American people who occupied the Ottawa River Valley, the border between the present-day Canadian provinces of Ontario and Quebec. Both Algonquin and Algonkin are acceptable spellings of the tribal name, although in their own language the

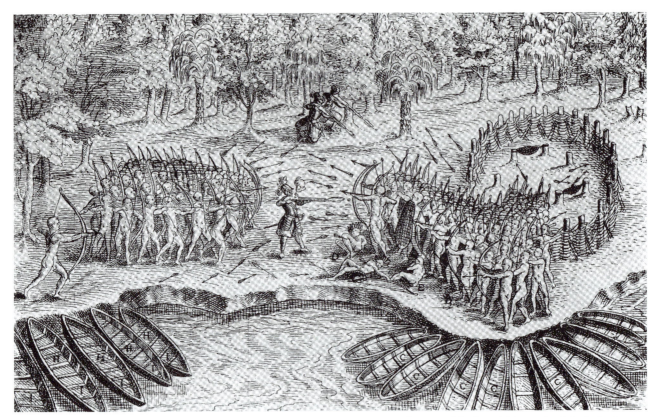

Depiction of the July 30, 1609, battle on the shores of Lake Champlain. The illustration appeared in Samuel de Champlain's 1613 book. In the battle, Champlain killed two chiefs with a single bullet, leading to the defeat of the Iroquois, who nonetheless remained lasting enemies of the French. (Library of Congress)

Algonquins call themselves Anishnabe or Anishinabe, meaning "original person" (the plural is Anishnabek or Anishnabeg). The word "Algonquian" (Algonkian) refers to a group of languages that include those of not only the Algonquins but also the Cheyennes, Arapahos, Crees, Blackfeet, and Ojibwas, among others. Algonquian is in fact the largest North American native language group. The Iroquois, however, referred to the Algonquins as the Adirondacks (literally "they eat trees").

In 1603 when they first encountered the French, the Algonquins probably numbered some 6,000 people. In 1768 the British estimated the Algonquin population at 1,500 people. The Algonquins were a seminomadic people, being too far north for settled agriculture. In contrast to the neighboring Iroquois to the west and the south, who lived primarily by agriculture in large fortified communities, the Algonquins were hunter-gatherers and trappers who lived in villages. Their shelters were of birchbark, known as waginogans or wigwams, and Algonquins traveled by water in birchbark canoes. In winter the villages split into smaller extended family units for hunting. The harsh winter conditions would not allow additional burdens, and the Algonquins were in consequence often known to kill the sick or badly injured among them. Algonquins were patrilineal, with hunting rights passed down from father to son. The Algonquins were known as fierce warriors, and they dominated the Iroquois until those tribes came together in the Iroquois Confederacy.

When Jacques Cartier first arrived in the Saint Lawrence River Valley in 1534, he found only Iroquoian-speaking people living in the area between Stadacona (Quebec) and Hochelaga (Montreal), but following near-continual warfare between the Iroquois and the Algonquins from 1570 and the resultant formation of the Iroquois Confederacy, the Iroquois drove the Algonquins north from the Adirondack Mountains and the upper Hudson River Valley. The Alqonquins in turn displaced or absorbed Iroquoian-speaking native peoples along the Saint Lawrence.

In 1603 Samuel de Champlain made contact with the Algonquins when he established a French trading post along the Saint Lawrence at Tadoussac. He soon learned that the Hurons rather than the Algonquins dominated the upper Saint Lawrence. Anxious to secure both free passage and furs, in 1609 Champlain joined the French to the struggle among the natives of the region by committing himself to aiding the Algonquins, Montagnais, and Hurons in an expedition against the Mohawks of the Iroquois Confederacy. Although by the time of the battle the French contingent numbered only Champlain and two others, their firearms proved the difference in battle, and the Mohawks fled.

This victory brought a formal alliance between the French and the Algonquins and also brought about trade in furs in exchange for the European tools and weapons sought by the Native Americans. By 1610 the Algonquins, led by their chief, Piskaret, dominated the Saint Lawrence Valley. In the process, however, the

French had made an implacable enemy of the Mohawks. In 1614 Champlain participated in an Algonquin-Huron attack on the Oneida and Onondaga nations of the Iroquois Confederacy, cementing Iroquois enmity toward the French. Soon the French were doing most of their fur trading with the Hurons rather than the Algonquins, much to the displeasure of the latter.

Intermittent fighting continued between the Mohawks and the Algonquins and Montagnais. In 1629 the Mohawks attacked the Algonquins and Montagnais near Quebec in what is usually considered the beginning of the so-called Beaver Wars (1641–1701). This fighting was prompted by the desire of the Iroquois to expand northward. From 1629 to 1632 the Mohawks, taking advantage of the temporary defeat of the French by the English, drove the Algonquins and Montagnais from the upper Saint Lawrence Valley. Peace terms allowed the French to return to Quebec in 1632, when they sought to restore their alliances by furnishing firearms to a number of native groups. This effort proved unsuccessful, especially as the Dutch in turn provided the Mohawks with large quantities of the latest firearms. By the end of the 1640s the Mohawks and Oneidas had driven the remaining Algonquins and Montagnais from the upper Saint Lawrence and lower Ottawa River areas. The Iroquois had also defeated the Hurons.

The arrival of a contingent of regular French troops in 1664 allowed the Quebec government to conclude peace with the Iroquois three years later. The French then resumed trading with the western Great Lakes region. The peace also permitted the Algonquins, now greatly reduced in number, to begin returning to the Ottawa Valley.

Although only some Algonquins converted to Catholicism, the nation as a whole was bound to the French cause during the French and Indian War (1754–1763). In August 1760 after British forces had taken Quebec, the Algonquins and other Native American allies of the French made peace with the English, agreeing to remain neutral in any future fighting between the English and the French. This agreement helped to seal the fate of New France.

The Algonquins continued their new loyalty to the British, fighting on their side during the American Revolutionary War (1775–1783) and taking part in Lieutenant Colonel Barry St. Leger's campaign against Patriot forces in the Mohawk Valley in 1777. Following the war when many British Loyalists fled to Canada, the British government settled a number of them on lands in the lower Ottawa Valley purchased from the Algonquins. Despite this the Algonquins also fought on the British side in the War of 1812, helping to defeat U.S. troops in the Battle of Chateauguay in October 1813. The reward to the Algonquins for their loyalty was to be continually pushed off their ancestral lands.

Ultimately purchases by the Canadian government resulted in the establishment of reserves (reservations) for the Algonquins in their former homeland. Today the majority of remaining Algonquins live on nine reserves in the province of Quebec and one reserve in Ontario.

SPENCER C. TUCKER

See also
Beaver Wars; Champlain, Samuel de; Iroquois; Iroquois Confederacy; Mohawks; Wyandots

References
Ceci, Lynn. *The Effect of European Contact and Trade on the Settlement Pattern of Indians in Coastal New York, 1524–1665.* New York: Garland, 1990.
Clement, Daniel, ed. *The Algonquins.* Hull and Quebec: Canadian Museum of Civilization/Musée Canadien des Civilisations, 1996.
Couture, Yvon H. *Les Algonquins.* Quebec: Éditions Hyperborée, 1983.
Greer, Allan, ed. *The Jesuit Relations: Natives and Missionaries in Seventeenth-Century North America.* Boston: Bedford/St. Martin's, 2000.
Strong, John A. *The Algonquian Peoples of Long Island from Earliest Times to 1700.* Interlaken, NY: Empire State Books, 1997.
White, Richard. *The Middle Ground: Indians, Empires, and Republics in the Great Lakes Region, 1650–1815.* New York: Cambridge University Press, 1991.

Allilimya Takanin
See Looking Glass

American Horse
Birth Date: ca. 1840
Death Date: December 16, 1908

Sioux (Lakota) leader who came of age at a crucial time when the Lakotas were poised on the verge of war with the United States. The son of Sitting Bear, chief of the True Oglala band and keeper of the tribe's winter count, American Horse was born around 1840. He gained his skills as a warrior in raids and battles with the Crows, Shoshones, and other Plains tribes. Charles A. Eastman, Dakota author and physician at Pine Ridge Reservation, noted that as a young man American Horse demonstrated abilities as an impersonator and orator. These skills would serve him later as he negotiated with whites and other Lakotas.

American Horse's experience fighting soldiers began in 1866 when Oglala chief Red Cloud opposed the U.S. Army's construction of forts to protect miners along the Bozeman Trail in the Powder River Country of northeastern Wyoming and southeastern Montana. The Powder River area had been previously promised to the Native Americans by treaty. After meeting with Colonel Henry Carrington at Fort Laramie and learning that the army intended to build three forts, Red Cloud began a war designed to force the soldiers to abandon their forts and the trail.

In December 1866 American Horse was among 10 warriors under Oglala leader Crazy Horse who lured Captain William Fetterman and his 80 men into an ambush. Ordered to protect a woodcutting detail, Fetterman instead pursued Crazy Horse's warriors into an ambush. The warriors killed all the soldiers in

Lakota leader American Horse, circa 1900. His willingness to work with U.S. authorities to ensure his people's welfare earned him considerable criticism from his own people. (Library of Congress)

short order. The army eventually closed the three Bozeman Trail forts as part of an agreement to end hostilities with Red Cloud.

The Great Sioux Reservation was created by the Treaty of 1868. American Horse joined his band at Pine Ridge, where he worked to ensure peace with the whites and his people's accommodation to the reservation. He also became active in tribal politics. In September 1877 he joined fellow Oglala leaders in attempting to persuade Crazy Horse to surrender to the army. Crazy Horse was arrested and murdered on September 5, 1877. Two weeks later American Horse joined other Lakota leaders in a mission to Washington, D.C., to oppose the relocation of the Pine Ridge Agency to the Missouri River.

American Horse also worked actively to remove Pine Ridge agent Valentine McGillycuddy. Assigned to Pine Ridge in 1879, McGillycuddy entered into a protracted struggle with Red Cloud. McGillycuddy's attempts to remove the popular leader as head chief met strong opposition. As American Horse pointed out, Red Cloud was elected by the council, and the agent's attempts to undercut him were only causing trouble and ill feelings among the Sioux. American Horse and his allies eventually had McGillycuddy removed in 1886.

American Horse's willingness to work with the U.S. government to ensure his people's welfare opened him to criticism by his own people. In 1889 the Crook Commission came to Pine Ridge to negotiate another land cession. Although American Horse favored signing the agreement and spoke in support of it, he was equally vocal in opposing the government's decision to cut the Native Americans' beef ration in December 1889.

Although American Horse was usually regarded as a friend of the whites, he remained critical of the government's fraudulent and often violent methods of dealing with the Lakotas. As interest in the Ghost Dance movement grew in the autumn of 1889, American Horse feared that the government would send troops to suppress the ceremony. He warned his tribesmen that the Lakotas could not hope to fend off the federal government. Although he worked to prevent conflicts between the Ghost Dancers and the military and remained opposed to the dance, he also strongly criticized the army for killing unarmed women and children.

After the Battle of Wounded Knee in 1890, American Horse joined some of his contemporaries in traveling with the Buffalo Bill Wild West Show. American Horse also worked diligently to help his people adjust to reservation life. He died at Pine Ridge on December 16, 1908.

STEVE POTTS

See also

Buffalo Bill's Wild West Show; Carrington, Henry Beebe; Crazy Horse; Crook, George; Fetterman Massacre; Ghost Dance; Great Sioux Reservation; Lakota Sioux; Pine Ridge Reservation; Powder River Expedition; Red Cloud; Red Cloud's War; Wounded Knee, Battle of

References

Bray, Kingsley M. *Crazy Horse: A Lakota Life.* Norman: University of Oklahoma Press, 2006.
Eastman, Charles A. *Indian Heroes and Great Chieftains.* Lincoln: University of Nebraska Press, 1991.

American Revolutionary War

See Native Americans and the American Revolutionary War

Amherst, Jeffrey
Birth Date: January 29, 1717
Death Date: August 3, 1797

British Army officer, commander in chief of British forces in America (1758–1763), and commander in chief in Britain (1778–1782, 1793–1797). Jeffrey Amherst was born on January 29, 1717, on his family's estate of Brooks Place in Riverhead, Kent, England. Amherst's military career began in 1731 when his powerful neighbor and patron, Lionel Cranfield Sackville, Duke of Dorset, used his influence with Sir John Ligonier to help Amherst obtain a commission in the 1st Foot Guards. Amherst first saw active service during the War of the Austrian Succession (1740–1748) as an aide-de-camp to Ligonier. Amherst secured the rank of lieutenant colonel by 1745. During the early part of the Seven Years' War (1756–1763), he served on the staff of William Augustus, Duke of Cumberland, second surviving son of King George II.

Lieutenant General Jeffrey Amherst commanded British forces in North America during 1758–1763 and brought the French and Indian War to a successful conclusion for Great Britain. Amherst's decision to end the practice of gift-giving to Native Americans led to considerable unrest and Pontiac's Rebellion in 1763. (Library of Congress)

Amherst's career accelerated in 1758 when Prime Minister William Pitt appointed him, with the temporary rank of major general, to command a joint Anglo-American expedition to capture the French fortress of Louisbourg on Cape Breton Island in North America. British and American forces landed on June 8, 1758, and forced the garrison's surrender on July 26. The British owed their success as much to naval superiority as to Amherst's abilities, although he effectively managed both the siege and his sometimes impetuous subordinate James Wolfe.

In 1758 Pitt appointed Amherst to overall command in North America. Amherst marched from Albany and occupied Fort Ticonderoga and Crown Point before poor weather ended the campaign. In the opinion of some Amherst moved too sluggishly, but he recognized the importance of pacing his own advance with that of Wolfe down the Saint Lawrence River. Wolfe prevailed at Quebec, and the following year Amherst commanded a successful offensive against Montreal, forcing the surrender of New France on September 8, 1760. Rarely before had any commander coordinated the convergence of three forces from such widely distant starting points. Amherst received honors for his accomplishment, including promotion to lieutenant general in January 1761.

Although Amherst disliked American provincial troops, he maintained the all-important working relationship with American colonial officials. Americans later named several towns for him including Amherst, Massachusetts, home of the University of Massachusetts and Amherst College.

France's surrender altered the balance of power to the disadvantage of many northern Native American tribes. This situation called for skillful diplomacy, but Amherst was lacking in this area. He sought to halt the British practice of providing gifts to the Native American tribes, which the latter regarded not as simple grants but instead as the reasonable cost of purchasing their political partnership. British officers experienced in Amerindian politics warned Amherst that his policy change would bring war. Even though Amherst's intransigence brought about the ensuing conflict known as Pontiac's Rebellion (1763), he acted forcefully to quell the rebellion. During the conflict the British allegedly employed biological weapons, namely blankets contaminated with smallpox. While Amherst approved of their use, several subordinates likely introduced biological agents on their own initiative. Amherst was subsequently recalled and left for Britain on November 10, 1763.

While Amherst never received the public accolades he hoped for upon his return, he did garner several promotions and offices, was made a peer, and sat in the House of Lords. He was offered command of British forces in America in 1774 and 1777 but declined both times. In 1778 he was promoted to general, became commander in chief in Britain, and organized the defense of Britain against the planned Franco-Spanish invasion of 1779. In 1780 he commanded the forces that suppressed the Gordon Riots. He was recalled as commander in chief in 1795 and was promoted to field marshal that year. Amherst died on August 3, 1797, at Riverhead, Kent. While he never enjoyed consistent success, he was nevertheless one of the foremost British soldiers of the 18th century and contributed significantly to the development of early America.

MARK H. DANLEY

See also
Amherst's Decree; French and Indian War; Pontiac's Rebellion

References
Knollenberg, Bernhard. "General Amherst and Germ Warfare." *Mississippi Valley Historical Review* 41(3) (December 1954): 489–494.

Long, J. C. *Lord Jeffery Amherst: A Soldier of the King.* New York: Macmillan, 1933.

Nester, William R. *"Haughty Conquerers": Amherst and the Great Indian Uprising of 1763.* Westport, CT: Praeger, 2000.

Whitworth, Rex. "Field Marshal Lord Amherst: A Military Enigma." *History Today* 9(2) (February 1959): 132–137.

Amherst's Decree

Decree issued in August 1761 by Major General Sir Jeffrey Amherst, the British Army commander in chief in North America, that strictly regulated trade and exchanges with Native Americans in the North American colonies. A direct cause of Pontiac's Rebellion (1763), Amherst's Decree marked a dramatic shift in Britain's policies toward Native Americans as the French and Indian War (1754–1763) drew to a close.

With French power in North America diminishing in the late 1750s, France's traditional Native American allies sought new arrangements with the British. Amherst attempted to regulate Anglo–Native American relations by enacting a series of rules for such relations in the late summer and autumn of 1761. In August of that year Amherst, simultaneously issuing a proclamation to all colonial governors and sending instructions to northern Indian superintendent Sir William Johnson, announced a four-part policy change mandating that traders were prohibited from journeying to native villages to conduct business, compelling the native peoples to transport their trade goods to British forts; British officials would no longer bestow large gifts upon tribes, which threatened a substantial component of the Native American economy; Native Americans were to be denied access to alcohol; and only very limited amounts of ammunition or gunpowder could be transferred to native peoples. By these means Amherst hoped to not only control Anglo-American contact with Native Americans but also transform them into the British conception of sober hardworking people.

Johnson vociferously protested Amherst's Decree. He argued that such measures would disastrously disrupt native societies and give them a common grievance that might unite them against the British. Amherst turned a deaf ear to his arguments, however, and the policies remained in place. As Johnson feared, the decree indeed prompted a violent response from the aggrieved tribes in the form of Pontiac's Rebellion.

ELIZABETH DUBRULLE

See also

Amherst, Jeffrey; French and Indian War; Johnson, Sir William; Pontiac's Rebellion

References

Anderson, Fred. *Crucible of War: The Seven Years' War and the Fate of the Empire in British North America, 1754–1766.* New York: Vintage Books, 2001.

Jennings, Francis. *Empire of Fortune: Crowns, Colonies, and Tribes in the Seven Years War in America.* New York: Norton, 1988.

Sosin, Jack M. *Whitehall and the Wilderness: The Middle West in British Colonial Policy, 1760–1775.* Lincoln: University of Nebraska Press, 1961.

Amonute

See Pocahontas

Anglo-Powhatan War, First
Start Date: August 9, 1610
End Date: April 5, 1614

The first war between a Native American nation and the English, which began in Virginia in 1610. The main catalyst for war was European encroachment on traditional Powhatan lands and the latter's violent reaction to these usurpations. By the end of the war the issue of land ownership remained unresolved as European settlements covered an ever-increasing area. The only solution for the Native Americans was to retreat to the interior in the face of steady European migration westward.

It took only three years for large-scale violence to erupt between Native Americans and English settlers, who had arrived at Jamestown in 1607. Sporadic violence between the colonists and the Powhatans had taken place from the beginning, but leaders on both sides had tried to exercise restraint. There was of course a clash of cultures, but the concept of land ownership was the chief cause of antagonism. The natives used land communally; private ownership was an entirely foreign concept for them. Europeans, on the other hand, believed strongly in private land ownership and erected fences and walls to demarcate such ownership. As more and more Europeans arrived in Virginia, they also cut down the forests and killed or drove away the game on which the Indians depended for both food and clothing.

Chief Powhatan, leader of the confederacy of tribes that bore his name, naively believed that he could tolerate a colonial trading post at Jamestown, where his people would have access to European trade goods such as metal tools. Powhatan slowly realized that Europeans had come to the New World not to trade but primarily to obtain land that heretofore was within his area of control. Ultimately war became Powhatan's answer to European encroachment.

Although the Europeans possessed firearms, Powhatan's warriors were armed with the bow and arrow, a highly effective weapon in the early 17th century. The Indians also enjoyed the advantage of knowing the land.

In 1610 Powhatan informed the Jamestown settlers that he would tolerate no further exploration of the region. He also warned the English to restrict themselves to Jamestown, the trading post he had desired from the beginning. On July 6, 1610, almost immediately after Powhatan's warning, members of the Nansemond tribe murdered a group of English settlers who were living among them.

That summer Thomas West, Lord de la Warr, the newly arrived governor of Virginia, chose to ignore Powhatan's continuing threats and sent a group of explorers up the James River to search for valuable minerals. At the time the colonists still harbored quixotic visions of becoming rich from discoveries of precious metals such as gold and silver. At the Indian village of Appomattox, the natives convinced the explorers to enter their village to eat and rest. The explorers naively accepted the offer, and all but one were slain.

The settlers sought retribution, and on August 9, 1610, acting on de la Warr's orders, George Percy, who was a member of the powerful Northumberland family and had been appointed a deputy in the colony's government, led 70 men to the Powhattan village of Paspahegh. There the English took captive a wife and children of Chief Wowinchopunch, who ruled the town but was subordinate to Powhatan. The wife was taken into the woods and killed. Once they reached the James River, the English threw the children into the water and shot them as they struggled to escape.

In all some 50 natives were slain. Wowinchopunch vowed revenge for the attack. Percy's men burned some other Indian villages and seized their stocks of corn before returning to Jamestown.

The fighting quickly spread. Native warriors, led by Opechancanough, attacked Jamestown and laid siege to its fort. The settlers raided native villages and burned crops. Over a three-year span both sides continually harassed the other, although no pitched battles occurred. The actual number of fatalities on both sides is unknown.

The war was fought native-style, replete with ambushes, kidnappings, and torture, until 1614. Powhatan's favorite daughter, Pocahontas (Matoaka), had been lured aboard an English ship, captured by Captain Samuel Argall, and held hostage since April 1613. Three months later Powhatan agreed to negotiate an end to the violence and offered the English food in return for his daughter's release. Argall saw the value of his prisoner and made greater demands. Powhatan accordingly offered a considerable ransom for Pocahontas's return. In the meantime English reinforcements arrived, lifting the native siege of Jamestown.

In the end the English arrived at a political solution. John Rolfe had settled in Jamestown in 1610. He introduced tobacco as a cash crop and was among the wealthiest Virginians. Rolfe and Pocahontas married at Jamestown on April 5, 1614. The wedding of Powhatan's daughter to one of the most important men in Virginia sealed the peace agreement, which required Powhatan to return all of the English captives, runaways, tools, and firearms in his people's possession.

THOMAS JOHN BLUMER

See also

Anglo-Powhatan War, Second; Jamestown; Nansemonds; Native American Warfare; Opechancanough; Pocahontas; Powhatan Confederacy

References

Gleach, Frederic W. *Powhatan's World and Colonial Virginia.* Lincoln: University of Nebraska Press, 1997.

Noel-Hume, Ivan. *The Virginia Adventures: Roanoke and Jamestown.* Charlottesville: University of Virginia Press, 1994.

Rountree, Helen C. *Pocahontas's People: The Powhatan Indians of Virginia through Four Centuries.* Norman: University of Oklahoma Press, 1990.

Anglo-Powhatan War, Second
Start Date: March 22, 1622
End Date: 1632

Armed conflict between the Powhatan people and English settlers near Jamestown, Virginia. Also known as the Virginia-Indian War of 1622–1632, the Second Anglo-Powhatan War began on March 22, 1622, with a massive surprise assault by the Powhatans on the English settlers near Jamestown.

The Powhatans' attack stemmed from native fears that the English were becoming too numerous and were taking too much territory. However, hostilities had been simmering between the English and the Powhatans since the end of the First Anglo-Powhatan War (1610–1614). The Powhatans were frustrated by English exploration, demands for food, and the way in which they self-righteously pushed their culture and religion on the natives.

After Chief Powhatan settled that first war without a victory in 1614, his actual power declined. Although Powhatan remained paramount chief until his death in 1618, his younger brother Opechancanough and others hostile to the English dominated Powhatan diplomacy after that time.

For years Opechancanough lulled the colonists into a sense of security with friendly overtures and by ignoring their abuses. The English saw the period between 1613 and 1622 as a golden age in their relations with the Powhatans, trading freely with the natives and frequently welcoming them on their plantations and in their homes. The English thus felt shocked and betrayed when the attack occurred.

While Opechancanough was appeasing the English, he quietly negotiated with the various Powhatan tribes to join in a fight that would eliminate the English threat. More tribes were persuaded to fight after 1617, when tobacco became an extremely profitable crop in Virginia. Between 1617 and 1622 some 3,000 English settlers arrived to take advantage of the tobacco boom. Thus, settlement spread far beyond Jamestown and put unprecedented pressure on the local natives.

Just before the first assault on March 22, 1622, two Powhatans betrayed Opechancanough's plans and warned the English of the coming attack. Nonetheless, the native offensive was indeed costly to the colonists. The Powhatans killed 347 settlers that day, about one-fourth of the entire English population in the colony.

Once the colonists regrouped from the devastating attack, bitter fighting ensued. The English launched raids against Powhatan towns and sniped at any native in range of their firearms. They made treaties with the Powhatans only to break them, such as in 1623 when the English brought poisoned wine to a feast to toast a new peace accord.

Still, nearly another quarter of the English population died in the following year from small-scale native raids, starvation, and dysentery and other diseases. The climax of the war came in a large-scale battle at the town of Pamunkey in 1624 in which the English were victorious. The native threat to the English diminished greatly afterward, and warring parties finally negotiated a peace in 1632.

The Second Anglo-Powhatan War permanently changed English views toward Native Americans. Prior to 1622 many settlers envisioned living harmoniously among the natives, whom they expected to convert to Christianity and English cultural mores. The English, however, had not recognized how these goals were nearly impossible to achieve. Working against them were deep-seated cultural differences and their desire to settle on "unoccupied" native land. As a result of the conflict, the English no longer desired to incorporate Powhatans as English subjects. Most English now wanted to rid the land of natives altogether or at the least to keep them as servants or slaves.

Seventeenth-century engraving by Theodor de Bry depicting the surprise massacre of English residents near Jamestown, Virginia, on March 22, 1622, that began the Second Anglo-Powhatan War (1622–1632). (Library of Congress)

Another result of the war was that King James I came to believe that the Virginia Company of London was mismanaging the colony and endangering the lives of the settlers. In 1624 the king declared Virginia a royal colony, which gave the settlers many new rights that they had not enjoyed under company control.

JENNIFER BRIDGES OAST

See also

Anglo-Powhatan War, First; Anglo-Powhatan War, Third; Jamestown; Opechancanough; Powhatan; Powhatan Confederacy

References

Axtell, James. *After Columbus: Essays in the Ethnohistory of Colonial North America.* New York: Oxford University Press, 1988.

Rountree, Helen C., ed. *Powhatan Foreign Relations, 1500–1722.* Charlottesville: University Press of Virginia, 1993.

Rountree, Helen C., and E. Randolph Turner III. *Before and After Jamestown: Virginia's Powhatans and Their Predecessors.* Gainesville: University Press of Florida, 2002.

Anglo-Powhatan War, Third
Start Date: March 18, 1644
End Date: October 1646

The last major conflict between the English colonists and the Powhatan Confederacy in Virginia. Also known as the Virginia-Indian War of 1644–1646, it broke the power of the Powhatans forever.

Following their defeat in the Second Anglo-Powhatan War (1622–1632), the natives watched the growing number of settlers in Virginia occupy more and more Powhatan land. Eager to profit from the sale of tobacco, a crop that rapidly depleted the soil, the English expanded their settlements from the area along the James River to territory on the York, Rappahannock, and Potomac rivers. At the same time Virginia's settler population grew rapidly, reaching an estimated 8,000 people in 1640.

Opechancanough, the Powhatan leader, had few options. His people, whose population had declined in size, had been pushed to the far western reaches of their land. If the Powhatans chose to abandon their homes and try to reestablish themselves among their native enemies to the west, they might lose their cultural identity and possibly their lives. To allow the English to occupy their remaining territory would leave the Powhatans powerless and render the destruction of their culture certain. War, the only remaining choice, seemed reckless given the odds against the Powhatans and the likelihood that defeat would mean annihilation.

Although Opechancanough was elderly (reportedly nearly 100 years old) and frail, he remained determined. Believing that the turmoil caused by the English Civil War might distract the Virginians and perhaps even bring Catholic Maryland into alliance with the Powhatans, he organized an attack on the Virginia settlements. Opechancanough also had the support of the native tribes along the Rappahannock.

The Powhatans and their allies struck on March 18, 1644. Borne on a litter by some of his men, Opechancanough led attacks on plantations in the heart of the English settlements along the James River. Other native parties attacked settlers on the upper reaches of the York and Rappahannock. The assault took the colonists by surprise, and 400–500 were killed in the initial onslaught. Many others abandoned their farms and took refuge in fortified buildings. Although the Powhatans killed many more settlers than they had in their attack of 1622, the impact of the new attack was less significant given the increase in settler population. While the attack of 1622 killed 25 percent of the English population, that of 1644 brought the deaths of 8.3 percent of the settlers.

As in 1622, the Powhatans hesitated after their initial victories. Regrouping swiftly, the Virginians launched counterattacks against native towns, burning buildings and crops and killing any natives they found. Within six months the settlers had reoccupied all of their abandoned plantations, and the Powhatans and their allies were in retreat. Sporadic fighting continued until the late summer of 1646, when Opechancanough was captured and brought to Jamestown. Shortly afterward he was murdered by one of his guards, who shot him in the back.

Opechancanough's death marked the end of Powhatan resistance. His successor, Necotowance, signed a treaty with Virginia in October 1646 in which the Powhatans ceded most of their remaining land to the English. The natives would henceforth be confined to the small portion of their territory allotted to them by the victors, in effect the first Indian reservations in North America. The Powhatans also agreed to surrender all English prisoners and firearms, to return any runaway servants who might come to them, and to pay an annual tribute of furs to Virginia. Unfortunately, only a few

years passed before the English grew covetous of the land left to the Powhatans in the treaty. Thus, in less than 40 years the powerful Powhatan Confederacy had been destroyed, and English domination of the Tidewater region of Virginia had been secured.

JENNIFER BRIDGES OAST AND JIM PIECUCH

See also

Anglo-Powhatan War, First; Anglo-Powhatan War, Second; Opechancanough; Powhatan Confederacy; Virginia-Indian Treaty of 1646

References

Axtell, James. "The Rise and Fall of the Powhatan Empire." Chapter 10 in *Natives and Newcomers: The Cultural Origins of North America*. New York: Oxford University Press, 2001.

Rountree, Helen C. *Pocahontas's People: The Powhatan Indians of Virginia through Four Centuries*. Norman: University of Oklahoma Press, 1990.

Rountree, Helen C., and E. Randolph Turner III. *Before and After Jamestown: Virginia's Powhatans and Their Predecessors*. Gainesville: University Press of Florida, 2002.

Ani-yun-wiyas

See Cherokees

Apache Pass, Battle of
Start Date: July 15, 1862
End Date: July 16, 1862

Definitive engagement in the war between Chiricahua and Mimbres Apaches led by Cochise and the U.S. Army at Apache Pass, Arizona (New Mexico Territory) during July 15–16, 1862. In 1862 a Confederate presence in New Mexico prompted Union Army colonel Edward R. S. Canby to request reinforcements. Consequently, Brigadier General James Carleton led the 1st California Volunteer Infantry to New Mexico via the Apache Pass, located east of Tucson. Cochise had posted scouts throughout the region and knew that Carleton was en route. Cochise convinced Mangas Coloradas, leader of the Mimbres Apaches, to join him in ambushing the troops at the springs in Apache Pass. The combined forces of Mimbres and Chiricahuas well exceeded 500 warriors.

Cochise stationed his warriors behind boulders, trees, and breastworks. The plan was to kill the soldiers while they rested at camp following an exhausting 19-hour march through arid and hot desert country. On July 15 Captain Thomas Roberts's Company E of the 1st California Infantry, with two howitzers, marched into Apache Pass. As the soldiers entered the pass, some warriors opened fire on the rear of the column, killing one man. The remaining troops quickly returned fire, killing four Apaches. Assuming a defensive formation they then continued their march, as their need for water was critical.

The soldiers reached an abandoned station house built of stone that afforded substantial cover. However, the water was still another 500 yards away. Roberts then deployed men on both sides of the canyon with the goal of reaching the water source. The Apache warriors responded by opening fire on the soldiers, killing one and wounding another. Roberts then ordered his men to fall back and sent some up the hillside in hopes of flanking the dug-in Apaches. This tactic also failed, as Cochise had protected his flanks. Four hours had now elapsed.

Recognizing the almost impregnable position of the Apache warriors, Roberts ordered the howitzers to open fire. For at least two hours his men fired at the hillside where the Apaches hid behind rocks and breastworks. Apache casualties from shards of rock mounted. Cochise watched in dismay as the howitzer fire forced his shell-shocked warriors to retreat out of range, thus allowing the soldiers to reach the water.

As the main column approached the following day, July 16, only scattered firing occurred in the pass. By now Cochise had taken the bulk of his force to his stronghold in the Dragoon Mountains. Estimates of Apache casualties in the battle vary from 10 to more than 40. U.S. losses were reported as 2 dead and 2 wounded. Within a few months the army constructed Fort Bowie at Apache Pass, and the fort became the center of operations against the Chiricahua Apaches. While Cochise continued his war for several more years, he never again directly engaged the army in battle.

GENE MUELLER

See also

Apaches; Apache Wars; Canby, Edward Richard Sprigg; Carleton, James Henry; Cochise

References

Aleshire, Peter. *Cochise: The Life and Times of the Great Apache Chief.* New York: Wiley, 2001.

Roberts, David. *Once They Moved like the Wind: Cochise, Geronimo, and the Apache Wars.* New York: Touchstone, 1993.

Apaches

Generic term used to describe numerous separate Native American groups who traditionally habituated the American Southwest (principally Arizona and New Mexico). The term "Apache" means "enemy" and was a name given to these people by the Zuni tribe of New Mexico. The Apaches referred to themselves as "the people." They spoke a variety of different but related dialects, including Chiricahua, Jicarilla, Mescalero, Mimbreño, White Mountain, and Aravapai.

Because the Apaches were a seminomadic people who were never united as a nation but instead identified themselves by virtue of family or clan relationships and the region in which they ranged, anthropologists and historians have often differed when identifying specific bands, leading to much confusion in the historical record. Perhaps the best approach is to group them into the six geographic regions that comprise Apacheria. First, the Lipan Apaches were the easternmost band and ranged in what is now western Texas from the Edwards Plateau to the Rio Grande. Second, the Jicarilla Apaches ranged in what is now northeastern New Mexico, east of the Rio Grande and north of Sante Fe and Las Vegas to Taos. Third, the Mescalero Apaches ranged in the Sierra Blanca and Sacramento Mountains of south-central New Mexico. Fourth, the Gila Apaches, which included the Mimbres, Warm Springs, and Mogollon bands, ranged in the upper regions of the Gila River along the New Mexico–Arizona border from the Datil Mountains south to Chihuahua. Fifth, the Western Apaches include the Coyotero or White Mountain Apaches, who ranged in the middle Gila River region of eastern Arizona, and the Aravapai, San Carlos, and Tonto bands, who ranged in eastern and central Arizona. Sixth, the Chiracahua Apaches ranged from the Dragoon Mountains of southern Arizona into northern Mexico. Because many of these regions overlapped, it is not surprising that one band often viewed another with suspicion and mistrust and that some bands occasionally warred with other Apache bands, a likely reason why they never unified as a cohesive group or nation.

In general the Apaches drew a clear distinction between raiding, for which they were well known, and warfare. Raiding was undertaken solely for the purpose of stealing goods, principally horses and livestock. Raiding parties, which usually engaged no more than 15 individuals, launched stealth attacks to avoid detection or a larger conflict. In addition to raiding, the Apaches also hunted small and large game, gathered wild foods, and engaged in small-scale agriculture. Corn was a principal crop, as were beans and squash. Most Apaches also engaged in trade among themselves and with other Native American groups as well as nonnatives. Warfare, usually undertaken to avenge a hostile act or to eliminate an imminent threat, was more methodical and was mainly designed to kill as many of the enemy as possible. War chiefs would sometimes raise several hundred warriors to engage in a military attack.

Throughout the 17th and 18th centuries the Apaches resisted Spanish efforts to move into their lands. The Apaches also raided into northern Mexico to acquire horses and take captives, who were incorporated into the tribe. The efforts of Spain (and Mexico after its independence) to suppress the Apaches resulted in lasting enmity. Indeed, hatred of the Mexicans was so strong, in large measure because of the bounties that Mexico paid for Apache scalps, that most Apaches at first welcomed the arrival of American forces during the Mexican-American War (1846–1848). Once it became clear that Americans intended to stay in the Southwest, the Apaches proved to be among the most difficult foes that the United States would face during the Indian Wars of the 19th century.

The Lipans were among the first to suffer the consequences of American expansion, which is ironic because they had befriended the first American immigrants who settled in Texas after Mexico achieved its independence from Spain and had supported them during the Texas Revolution against Mexico (1835–1836). After Texas won independence in 1836, the Lipans soon became allies of the new Republic of Texas, even joining in military actions against

Coyetero Apaches near Camp Apache, Arizona Territory, 1873. Photograph by Timothy O'Sullivan. (Library of Congress)

the Comanches. In 1842 Mexico's Army of the North invaded Texas, recapturing San Antonio and several nearby towns. While the Texans were raising a militia to oppose this invasion, Lipan warriors defended Austin, Houston, and other Texas cities from surprise attack by Mexican forces. In addition, when Alexander Somervell led a daring punitive expedition into Mexico in November 1842, Lipan warriors rode alongside him, prompting Texas president Sam Houston to promise that Texas would always be "kind" to the Lipans.

Unfortunately for the Lipans, after the United States annexed Texas in 1845, the U.S. government subjected the state's Native Americans to its national policies of Indian removal. Throughout the 1850s the U.S. Army increased troop strengths at forts on or near Lipan lands and mounted punitive raids against Lipan encampments. Although the American Civil War (1861–1865) halted attacks against the Lipans for a time, the army reentered Texas in force after the war and in 1872 and 1873 conducted a brutal campaign of annihilation against the Lipans. In raids on both sides of the Rio Grande, U.S. cavalry units attacked Apache encampments, killing Lipans on sight—sometimes women along with the men—and destroying their homes, crops, livestock, and ponies, thus rendering desperate any Lipans who might have escaped the raiders. By 1880 most of the surviving Lipans had scattered, giving up their land and traditional way of life to hide among the Tejano populations (Hispanic Texans), especially around San Antonio, Corpus Christi, and the Rio Grande, while others moved onto the Mescalero Reservation in New Mexico. Today the Lipan Apache tribe is petitioning the State of Texas for official recognition.

The Mescaleros, from the Spanish term for "mescal makers," had traditionally warred with the Comanches and routinely raided the Pueblos. During the early 1850s the Mescaleros also began attacking white settlers in New Mexico and stagecoaches on the San Antonio–El Paso road. In 1854 Brigadier General John Garland, commander of the Department of New Mexico from 1853 to 1857, launched two campaigns into the Sierra Blanca region, but neither succeeded in encountering the Mescaleros. In January 1855, however, Captain Richard S. Ewell and Captain Henry W.

Stanton led a two-pronged invasion of the Capitan Mountains that resulted in the deaths of 15 Mescalero warriors, including war chief Santa Anna, and just 2 American deaths, including Stanton. In addition, Lieutenant Samuel D. Sturgis led 18 dragoons and 6 civilians in a chase of a Mescalero raiding party that had attacked the Eaton Ranch outside Santa Fe. Sturgis and his men pursued the raiders for more than 100 miles before finally cornering them, killing 3 warriors, wounding 4, and recovering all the stolen livestock. Following the 1855 campaign, the Mescaleros pursued peace and promised to refrain from future raids in exchange for annual government subsidies. They also allowed the government to build Fort Stanton near Bonita in New Mexico Territory.

Although the Mescaleros remained at peace for the next six years, the outbreak of the American Civil War and the abandonment of Fort Stanton in 1861 caused the Mescaleros to resume raiding, in part because promised government subsidies were not provided. In August 1862 alone, government authorities reported that the Mescaleros killed 46 whites and captured several others. After Brigadier General James H. Carleton assumed command of the Department of New Mexico in September 1862, he ordered Christopher "Kit" Carson and the 1st New Mexico Cavalry to reactivate Fort Stanton and dispatched four companies of California volunteers under Captain William McClean and Captain Thomas L. Roberts against the Mescaleros. Although approximately 100 Mescalero fled to the Guadalupe Mountains, the majority went to Fort Stanton to seek peace. Carleton forced chiefs Cadete, Chato, and Estrella to agree to removal to the Bosque Redondo Reservation in eastern New Mexico. Facing harsh conditions and forced to share the reservation with the Navajos, the Mescaleros fled Bosque Redondo in December 1863 and returned to the Sierra Blanca. Although a few Mescaleros would join other Apache bands in raids afterward, the majority remained peaceful, and the tribe remains in the Sierra Blanca today.

Like the Mescaleros, the Jicarillas, the Spanish term for "little basket," had alternately traded with and raided against the Pueblos. The Jicarillas also frequently raided both Mexican and white settlers. After a series of Jicarilla attacks threatened to close the Santa Fe Trail in 1854, the U.S. Army launched a series of campaigns to stop the depredations. On March 5, 1854, Lieutenant David Bell and 30 men of the 2nd Dragoon Regiment attacked a Jicarilla camp along the Canadian River approximately 50 miles from Fort Union, killing several warriors, including Chief Lobo Blanco. A few weeks later Chief Chacon retaliated by ambushing Lieutenant John W. Davidson's company of the 1st Dragoons approximately 25 miles south of Taos, killing 22 and wounding 36. Upon receiving news of the ambush, army officials dispatched 200 dragoons and 100 riflemen under Lieutenant Colonel Philip St. George Cooke to Taos, where they were joined by 36 Pueblos and Mexicans under Captain James Quinn. Guided by Carson, Cooke's force pursued Chacon to the Rio Caliente, where on April 8 they surprised Chacon's camp, killing 5 warriors and wounding 8. Seventeen Jicarilla women and children later froze to death in the flight following the battle.

Two months later Carson led Carleton's 100 dragoons and Quinn's Pueblo-Mexican force in a devastating expedition northeast of Taos. On June 4 they surprised a Jicarilla camp at Raton Pass, killing several warriors, destroying 22 lodges, and capturing 38 ponies. The 1854 campaign effectively ended Jicarilla resistance. Chacon settled his tribe at Chama and attempted to farm. The Jicarillas would be moved several times, including a brief tenure on the Mescalero Reservation, before finally receiving their current reservation in northern New Mexico in 1887.

Although the Gila Apache bands had remained fairly peaceful in the early years of American occupation of New Mexico and Arizona, this began to change after the Gadsden Purchase of 1853 opened a southern route to California and Gila Apache raids prompted military action. In March 1856 army officials ordered a two-pronged invasion by dragoons and infantry into the Gila region. Lieutenant Colonel David T. Chandler led a column into the Mogollon Mountains and attacked a Mogollon Apache camp in southwestern New Mexico, killing several Apaches and capturing several hundred head of livestock. Chandler's forces then converged with Lieutenant Colonel John H. Eaton's column along the upper Gila River and marched into Arizona, where they mistakenly attacked Chief Delgadito's peaceful Mimbres band. Although Chandler quickly recognized his mistake and apologized, he was reprimanded by officials in Washington.

In 1857 Garland launched a much larger invasion into the Gila region. Colonel William W. Loring moved from the north with three companies of Mounted Riflemen, two companies of the 3rd Infantry Regiment, and a company of Pueblo warriors, while Lieutenant Colonel Dixon S. Miles advanced from the south with three companies of the 1st Dragoons, two companies of Mounted Riflemen, two companies of the 3rd Infantry Regiment, and one company of the 8th Infantry Regiment. Although the Mogollon and other Gila Apaches evaded Garland's forces, the Western Apaches were not as fortunate. On June 27 a detachment of the American force under Captain Richard S. Ewell attacked a Coyotero Apache camp along the Gila River, killing or wounding 40 warriors and capturing 45 women and children. Mangas Coloradas and later Victorio as well as other Mimbres and Warm Springs Apaches frequently raided with the Chiricahuas and other warring factions.

In the aftermath of the attack on the Coyotero Apaches, the U.S. Army soon confronted the Chiricahua Apaches, who proved to be by far the most difficult Apache band to suppress. Although the Chiricahuas had long engaged in regular raids against Mexicans and other Native American groups, they had cooperated with Brigadier General Stephen W. Kearny when he moved through their territory into California during the Mexican-American War. Throughout the 1850s the Chiricahuas remained at peace with the United States. In October 1860, however, things changed dramatically when a Coyotero raiding party attacked John Ward's ranch in the Sonoita Valley and abducted Ward's six-year-old stepson. Ward incorrectly blamed the raid on Cochise's band of Chiricahuas, who had heretofore had peaceful relations with

Americans. Lieutenant Colonel Pitcairn Morrison, commander of Fort Buchanan, responded in January 1861 by dispatching Lieutenant George N. Bascom and a company of mounted infantry to Cochise's camp at Apache Pass to demand the return of the livestock and Ward's stepson. When Cochise and five others met with Bascom and denied involvement in the raid, fighting broke out after Bascom attempted to seize Cochise. Although Cochise escaped, the other five Chiricahuas, three of whom were related to Cochise, were taken hostage. Cochise then responded by seizing three whites and placing Bascom under siege. After Bascom was reinforced, Cochise executed his captives and fled to Mexico. Bascom retaliated by hanging three of his Chiricahua hostages and three Coyoteros.

The so-called Bascom Affair resulted in 25 years of bitter conflict with the Chiricahuas. In the immediate aftermath, Cochise joined forces with Mimbres chief Mangas Coloradas (identified as a Chiricahua by many scholars) in attacking settlements in eastern Arizona and western New Mexico, including Pinos Altos, where a gold strike in 1860 had brought an influx of 2,000 miners by 1861. The withdrawal of federal troops from the region after the outbreak of the American Civil War further emboldened the Apaches. By the summer of 1862, however, the tide began to turn against them. On July 15 Cochise and Mangas ambushed an army detachment under Captain Thomas L. Roberts in Apache Pass, but Roberts's skillful use of howitzers turned the ambush into a crushing defeat, with the Apaches losing many warriors. After Carleton took command of the Department of New Mexico in September 1862, he made suppression of Cochise and Mangas a top priority. On January 18, 1863, Mangas was captured by Captain E. D. Shirland after being lured into the captain's camp under a flag of truce. Mangas was then killed by Shirland's guards. By the end of the following year, Mangas's band was virtually exterminated.

With the end of the American Civil War, the U.S. Army increased its presence in the Southwest. In addition, gold and silver strikes in New Mexico and Arizona increased the number of white settlers. The resulting tensions led to events such as the Camp Grant Massacre on April 30, 1871, when 148 Tucson settlers attacked an Aravapai and Pinal Apache village at dawn, ruthlessly slaughtering as many as 150 Apaches, mainly women and children, in their sleep and taking 29 children captive. Outrage in the East forced President Ulysses S. Grant to extend his peace policy to the Apaches. Toward this end, Grant instructed Brigadier General Oliver O. Howard to make peace with Cochise. With the assistance of Thomas J. Jeffords, Howard traveled to Cochise's camp in the autumn of 1872 and succeeded in negotiating a peace whereby Cochise would go to the Chiricahua Reservation near Fort Bowie. Similar agreements were made with the Warm Springs, Mimbres, Mogollon, San Carlos, Aravaipa, Pinal, and White Mountain Apaches. Approximately 5,000 Apaches agreed to live in peace on reservations in exchange for government rations.

Although many Apaches genuinely wanted peace and attempted to live on the reservations, just as many found it difficult to adjust to a sedentary lifestyle and had no interest in adopting the white man's culture. Consequently, many Apaches simply used the reservations as a staging point for raids. Officials estimated that 54 raids were carried out between September 1871 and September 1872, resulting in the deaths of 44 people and the loss of 500 head of livestock. In other cases the Apaches revolted in response to the government's broken promises. Membres chief Victorio, who was Cochise's son-in-law, is perhaps the best example of this. Having been promised a reservation at Ojo Caliente, their traditional home by which the band is known, the Warm Springs Apaches were forcibly removed to San Carlos in 1877. Over the next two years Victorio and his band would flee San Carlos twice, leading the army on a fruitless chase across New Mexico and western Texas. Eventually Victorio fled to Mexico, where he was killed by Mexican militia in 1880.

Of all the Apaches who resisted reservation life, Geronimo proved to be the most difficult to apprehend. On October 1, 1881, he fled San Carlos with 74 Chiricahuas and headed to the Sierra Madre in Mexico, where he joined other renegade Apaches under Nana. Over the next five years Geronimo launched repeated raids across the border and even returned briefly to life on the reservation. By 1886, however, the combination of unprecedented cooperation between the U.S. and Mexican forces, Brigadier General George S. Crook's skillful use of Apache scouts, and relentless pressure applied by Crook's replacement, Brigadier General Nelson A. Miles, forced Geronimo to capitulate. After a period of exile in Florida, he and his followers were permanently settled at Fort Sill, Oklahoma. Geronimo died there in 1909. Although 187 of his followers were allowed to relocate to the Mescalero Reservation in 1914, 84 chose to remain at Fort Sill, where slightly more than 600 lived in 2010.

Although Americans have tended to view the Apaches as one of the more bellicose tribes in North America, such a view is clearly one-sided. For the most part the Apaches were no more warlike than any other Native American group. Rather, white encroachment and bad dealings with the U.S. government forced them to resort to violence as a way to preserve their lands and their way of life.

JUSTIN D. MURPHY AND PATRICK R. RYAN

See also

Apache Pass, Battle of; Apache Wars; Bosque Redondo; Carleton, James Henry; Carson, Christopher Houston; Cochise; Comanches; Cooke, Philip St. George; Crook, George; Fort Sill; Geronimo; Grant's Peace Policy; Howard, Oliver Otis; Kearny, Stephen Watts; Mangas Coloradas; Miles, Nelson Appleton; Navajos; Ojo Caliente Reservation, New Mexico; Pueblos; San Carlos Reservation; Santa Fe Trail; Victorio

References

Aleshire, Peter. *Reaping the Whirlwind: The Apache Wars.* New York: Facts on File, 1998.

Schilz, Thomas F. *Lipan Apaches in Texas.* El Paso: Texas Western Press, 1987.

Sturtevant, William C., ed. *Handbook of North American Indians,* Vol. 10, *Southwest.* Washington, DC: Smithsonian Institution, 1983.

Thrapp, Dan L. *The Conquest of Apacheria.* Norman: University of Oklahoma Press, 1967.

Utley, Robert M. *Frontier Regulars: The United States and the American Indian, 1866–1891.* New York: Macmillan, 1973.

Utley, Robert M. *Frontiersmen in Blue: The United States and the Indian, 1848–1865.* Lincoln: University of Nebraska Press, 1967.

Worcester, Donald E. *The Apaches: Eagles of the Southwest.* Norman: University of Oklahoma Press, 1979.

Apache Wars
Start Date: 1861
End Date: 1886

No formal declaration of hostilities signaled the beginning of the bloody Apache Wars in the American West. Instead, two separate incidents, one in 1860 and another in 1861, caused a great deal of anguish on the part of the Mimbres and Chiricahua Apaches and sparked a decades-long resistance that came to be known by that name. The conflict did not end until 1886, when Chiracahua leader Geronimo surrendered to U.S. forces.

In 1860 Mangas Coloradas, a well-respected chief, lived with his Mimbres Apache followers in southern New Mexico. In May of that year prospectors discovered gold in the heart of Mimbres territory, causing an influx of more than 700 miners, which the Mimbres had never expected. In the spirit of friendship, the chief visited a mining camp and was immediately captured, bound, and whipped. A second offense occurred early in 1863 when Mangas became a prisoner of the military at Fort McLane. Two army privates taunted him by pressing hot bayonets to his feet. When he strenuously objected, they killed him. The Apaches considered both of these events worthy of revenge.

At about the same time Cochise, Mangas's son-in-law, was the victim of similar abuse. Cochise ranged with his Chiricahua Apache band across deserts, grasslands, and mountains in the southeastern corner of Arizona. Known by the Americans as a friendly and cooperative Apache, Cochise had an agreement with the U.S. government to supply wood to the Butterfield Stage Station in the Sulphur Springs Valley. In February 1861 he received word that a contingent of soldiers had arrived and camped nearby and that they wanted to speak with him. Trusting the Americans' word, Cochise complied only to be mistakenly accused by young army lieutenant George N. Bascom of kidnapping a rancher's son. Cochise, although wounded in the fracas, escaped, but his companions, five male relatives, were held and subsequently killed. According to Apache custom, the murders demanded reprisal, so Cochise killed frontiersmen, drovers, stagecoach passengers, mail riders, members of the U.S. military, and anyone else who set foot in his territory. By August 1861 much of Arizona that had been settled by nonnatives was deserted. For a time the Apaches were convinced that they had driven the Americans out of the area.

The whites had not disappeared, however, and the Apache Wars continued for 25 years. During those decades the frontier advanced farther and farther west. A tide of miners, merchants, businessmen, charlatans, religious men and women, schoolteachers, the military, mercenaries, scalp hunters, and settlers all risked their lives entering the areas in which Mangas, Cochise, and their followers camped. These people expected protection from the forts that had been established across the Southwest after the Treaty of Guadalupe Hidalgo in 1848 and the Gadsden Purchase in 1853.

Contrary to standard U.S. military practices, the Apaches remained in small bands, each independent of the other and with each warrior completely acclimated to the harsh terrain and arid climate and able to travel 40 miles a day on foot without food or water. Each was supremely confident in his abilities, waiting for orders from no superior, never at a loss to know exactly when to attack or when to retreat, relying solely on guerrilla warfare, traveling at night, and hiding during the day in rocky points and high places. Often using the element of surprise or a planned ambush, Apaches attacked, murdered, plundered, scattered, and then regrouped at predetermined sites, carrying with them the rifles, shotguns, pistols, and ammunition taken from their enemies.

Despite the advantages that a guerrilla force has when protecting its homeland and in addition to the Apaches' extremely competent leadership, one fight in particular, the Battle of Apache Pass (July 15–16, 1862), showed how vulnerable the Native Americans were to superior American firepower. Apache Pass, located in southeastern Arizona, is a narrow defile between the Chiricahua Mountains to the south and the Dos Cabezas range to the north. The area contained a flowing spring, the only reliable water supply for miles around. As Brigadier General James H. Carleton led a regiment of California volunteers eastward from California to fight the Confederates in New Mexico during the American Civil War (1861–1865), he passed through Apache Pass. When the army entered the pass on July 15, Apache warriors were on the cliffs high above the spring and were ready to do battle. Kicking down rocks and boulders and using traditional weapons as well as firearms, they killed 2 soldiers and wounded 2 others. But then the army's howitzers responded. Having experienced nothing similar in the past, the terrified Apaches fled from their positions but not before losing an estimated 10–40 warriors. Cochise's warriors halfheartedly resumed the battle the next day, but the troops again fired their howitzers, and the Apaches scattered once more. Never again did Mangas Coloradas and Cochise fight together. As a consequence of the Battle of Apache Pass, Carleton recommended that a fort be established in the vicinity; it was built and was designated Fort Bowie.

Throughout the Civil War years Carleton and other officers established a number of new forts and camps, while volunteer units campaigned relentlessly against the Apaches and other groups. The Mescalero Apaches were particularly hard hit during this period. The return of the regular army in 1867 followed by some notable success in the field did little to quiet unrest, as various bands of Apaches and Yavapais continued to raid roads, settlements, and

CAMPAIGNS AGAINST THE APACHES, 1880s

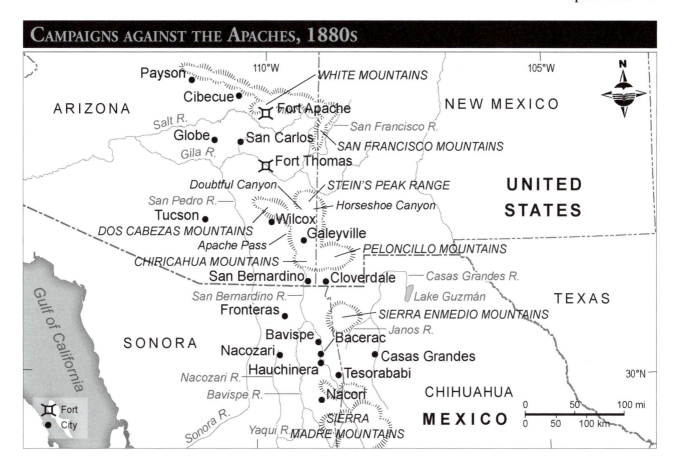

mining camps. Complicating matters for the army was a civilian population with little interest in pursuing peaceful coexistence with the Indians. Depredations perpetrated by settlers, such as the infamous Camp Grant Massacre of 1871 in which perhaps 150 Apaches, mostly women and children, were murdered, made President Ulysses S. Grant's peace policy almost impossible to implement.

In 1872 Brigadier General Oliver O. Howard arrived in Arizona in hopes of establishing a lasting peace with the Apaches. He proved partially successful in that he negotiated a settlement with Cochise that ended the vaunted leader's war making. Howard also helped establish a more workable reservation system. Despite these advances, Apache and Yavapai raiding continued, prompting department commander Lieutenant Colonel George Crook to launch his highly successful Tonto Basin Campaign during the winter of 1872–1873. Crook established a new model for operating against the Apaches, including the extensive use of Indian scouts and pack mule trains in place of cumbersome wagons. The peace overtures of Howard combined with Crook's inspired campaigning brought a semblance of order to the Southwest that lasted to some degree for many years.

Following the death of Cochise in 1874 other leaders emerged, including his son Naiche (Nachez) and the shaman Geronimo, who carried on the Apache Wars. Never a chief, Geronimo's remarkable abilities as a medicine man served the group as it continued to defy U.S. plans to settle the American West. While the white settlements

in Arizona enjoyed relative peace for many years, Apaches used the reservations in Arizona and New Mexico as protected bases from which to raid northern Mexico. The government's decision to consolidate most of Arizona's Apaches on the inhospitable San Carlos Reservation in 1876 contributed to a resumption of major hostilities throughout the region. Several hundred Apaches, including Geronimo's Chiricahuas, raided both sides of the border, which brought a significant military response and a renewed effort to confine the Chiricahuas and their Warm Springs Apache allies from New Mexico on the San Carlos Reservation.

The Warm Springs faction led by the formidable Victorio broke from the reservation. Beginning in 1879 Victorio and his followers staged a bloody rampage on both sides of the porous border in what became known as the Victorio War. For two years this gifted warrior occupied considerable numbers of U.S. and Mexican troops, including most of the 9th and 10th U.S. Cavalry regiments, before he and his band were wiped out by Mexican irregulars in the mountains of northern Mexico in October 1880.

By 1880 most of the West's Native American nations had capitulated and lived on reservations that encompassed only a small portion of their traditional homelands. The remaining areas now opened for settlement. However, a small group of Apaches defied U.S. authority and fought on. Although many Apaches of notable stature participated, Geronimo emerged as the most significant leader in the final stage of the Apache Wars.

Chiricahua Apache prisoners, including Geronimo (first row, third from right), on an embankment in Arizona outside their railroad car in 1886, following Geronimo's surrender on September 4, 1886. (National Archives)

In 1881 prompted by the deplorable conditions at the San Carlos Agency and the killing of a popular shaman in a fight at Cibecue Creek, Apaches left the reservation in large numbers. Some attacked nearby Fort Apache. In September, Geronimo and some 70 Chiricahuas bolted for Mexico, where they joined others including the remnants of Victorio's band. From Mexico the Apaches raided furiously, attracting a heavy but ineffectual military response. In September 1882 General Crook returned to command the Department of Arizona. Crook's arrival roughly coincided with the implementation of a reciprocal crossing agreement between the United States and Mexico that Crook soon exploited, leading a large expedition into Sonora in May 1883. Pressured by U.S. and Mexican troops, the Indians proved willing to negotiate, and Crook met with Geronimo, Nana, Natchez, and others, securing Geronimo's promise to return to the reservation. Geronimo appeared to have reneged until he and 80 followers finally arrived in March 1884.

Geronimo's return to San Carlos proved short-lived, as he led another breakout in May 1885. Bloody raiding across Arizona, New Mexico, and northern Mexico followed, with the predictable military response. Crook sent two columns into Mexico, while hundreds of other troops picketed the border and protected key areas. The campaign proved fruitless, which only encouraged more raids. In late 1885 Crook dispatched two more columns, these largely comprised of Indian scouts. The detachment led by the gifted Captain Emmet Crawford located the fugitive Apaches, but so too did Mexican militia, who attacked the soldiers and scouts, killing Crawford. Again the Apaches reached out, resulting in a famous meeting among Crook, Geronimo, and other Apache leaders in March 1886 at the Cañon de los Embudos.

It appeared that the Apache Wars were over, but Geronimo failed to report as promised. Crook now asked to be relieved and was replaced by Brigadier General Nelson A. Miles, who launched a massive effort to catch Geronimo, including a grueling 2,000-mile march through northern Mexico led by Captain Henry Lawton. But a large military effort never worked against the Apaches. In the meantime, Miles ordered relocation of all Chiricahua and Warm Springs Apaches on the reservation to prisons in Florida. Having failed to catch Geronimo and his small band of followers with upwards of 5,000 regular troops, Miles sent Lieutenant Charles B. Gatewood and 2 Indian Scouts into Mexico to bring in Geronimo. In early September 1886 Gatewood's scouts located the impoverished Indians. Geronimo, upon learning that his people had been moved to a distant land, recognized the futility of continued resistance. He agreed to return with Gatewood to U.S. soil and surrendered to General Miles in Skeleton Canyon, Arizona, on September 4, 1886.

Within days Geronimo and the remaining Chiricahuas, including the loyal scouts so instrumental during the long campaign, were loaded on trains for the trip to prisons in Florida.

H. HENRIETTA STOCKEL AND DAVID COFFEY

See also

Apache Pass, Battle of; Apaches; Carleton, James Henry; Cochise; Crook, George; Gatewood, Charles Bare; Geronimo; Mangas Coloradas; Manuelito; Miles, Nelson Appleton; Victorio

References

Debo, Angie. *Geronimo: The Man, His Time, His Place.* Norman: University of Oklahoma Press, 1976.

Sweeney, Edwin R. *Cochise: Chiricahua Apache Chief.* Norman: University of Oklahoma Press, 1991.

Sweeney, Edwin R. *Mangas Coloradas: Chief of the Chiricahua Apaches.* Norman: University of Oklahoma Press, 1998.

Thrapp, Dan L. *The Conquest of Apacheria.* Norman: University of Oklahoma Press, 1967.

Utley, Robert M. *Frontier Regulars: The United States and the American Indian, 1866–1891.* New York: Macmillan, 1973.

Apalachee Revolt
Event Date: February 1647

Insurrection of the Apalachee people against the Spanish in Florida. In response to a variety of grievances, disputes with Spanish officials, and fears of Spanish colonization, Apalachee warriors revolted against Spanish missionaries in 1647. The Spaniards had developed friendly relations with the Apalachees beginning in 1597. After the initial meeting between the two nations, informal missionary work began throughout Florida, but officially sanctioned missions did not appear in Apalachee territory until the early 1630s.

Unlike other areas where the Spaniards built missions, officials in St. Augustine considered the Apalachee region an excellent location for a future settlement. Thus, the government in St. Augustine kept a closer eye on the activities of its missions there than in other Spanish-administered areas. Franciscan friars entered Apalachee communities and went to work converting the native population.

By 1635 approximately 5,000 of the 34,000 residents of Apalachee had converted to Catholicism.

Despite the Franciscans' success, the missionaries injected significant tensions in Apalachee communities. Compared to Catholic missionary work elsewhere, the Spaniards in Florida rarely entered an area with a heavy hand. By the late 1630s, however, Spanish soldiers descended upon the province, and tensions between the Apalachees and Spaniards increased.

In part the soldiers entered the area to provide protection for the missionaries and act as peacemakers between the Apalachees and their neighbors. Prior to the arrival of the missionaries, the Apalachees had fought nearly constant wars with their neighbors. The Florida government hoped to establish Spanish settlements in Apalachee Province, however, and to many Apalachees the first soldiers brought a glimpse of a future dominated by the demands of the Spanish government.

Spain's desire to settle the area became very clear when the government at St. Augustine appointed an official governor of the province in 1645. The Apalachees were to become something more than just a target for conversion; they were to be colonized. As more Apalachees converted to Catholicism, additional conflicts emerged between the converted and those who rejected the new religion. Catholic friars and converted native peoples began to ban traditional religious practices. Also, any social activities considered offensive to the Catholic faith were forbidden. For the Apalachees who had rejected the new religion, these changes represented a cultural attack. Internal dissent coupled with a growing Spanish presence helped create an environment primed for rebellion.

Factions within the Apalachee community ultimately led to revolt. In February 1647 Apalachee warriors attacked, killing three friars in the initial raid. In addition, the leaders of the revolt captured and killed the deputy governor and his family. After killing the principal leaders at Mission San Luis, the Apalachees moved throughout the region and destroyed seven of the eight Catholic compounds. Most participants in the revolt were non-Catholics, but the warriors also received help from members of the neighboring Chisca community.

When authorities in St. Augustine learned of the revolt, the reaction was swift and strong. Officials sent a large group of Timucuan warriors and several dozen Spanish soldiers to quell the rebellion. The Apalachees, however, stood their ground and fought the Timucuas to a draw. Shortly after the initial response to the revolt, Timucuan, Spanish, and Christian Apalachee forces came together to fight the rebellious faction. Ultimately these combined forces prevailed, capturing and executing the leaders of the revolt.

Unlike other native revolts, this one did not drive the Spaniards from the area. Instead, Christian Apalachees found common cause with the Spaniards, and together each side helped rebuild Apalachee Province and its missions. Catholic missionaries then renewed their efforts with the Apalachee communities until virtually every inhabitant of the province accepted Christianity.

SHANE A. RUNYON

See also
Apalachees

References
Hann, John H. *Apalachee: The Land between the Rivers.* Gainesville: University Press of Florida, 1988.
Hann, John H., and Bonnie G. McEwan. *The Apalachee Indians and Mission San Luis.* Gainesville: University Press of Florida, 1998.

Apalachees

A group of Native Americans who lived in the Florida Panhandle area through the 18th century. Prior to European contact, the Apalachee chiefdom participated in a trade network that spanned much of Florida and extended through present-day Georgia, Alabama, and the Mississippi River Valley. As soon as the first Spaniards crossed Apalachee territory in the early 16th century, however, the Apalachees became associated with the Spaniards and conducted most of their business with Europeans, a relationship that eventually turned deadly.

According to anthropologists, the Apalachees assumed many characteristics of Mississippian cultures. They spoke a language related to the Muskhogean language family, organized their communities along the lines of other Mississippian cultures, and accepted a shared leadership by peace and war rulers. In the early 17th century Catholic missionaries entered Apalachee territory.

Before the first missionaries constructed churches and attempted to convert the natives, the Apalachees interacted with the Spanish government based in St. Augustine, Florida. Initial contact between the two nations helped curb tensions between the Apalachees and their frequent enemy, the Timucuas. Timucuan and Apalachee communities maintained a near-permanent state of war. The arrival of the Spaniards created a power structure that settled many of these disputes.

The Franciscan Order built the first missions in Apalachee Province in the 1630s. Tensions between the newcomers and the Apalachees followed a familiar pattern seen throughout Spanish North America, but when soldiers accompanied missionaries in the late 1630s, hostilities came to a head. Apalachee violence against the Spaniards peaked with the Apalachee Revolt in 1647. Following the violence, Spanish officials took a more active role in the management of Apalachee Province.

Authorities in St. Augustine viewed Apalachee Province as an ideal location for Spanish settlement. After the revolt, St. Augustine instituted a labor requirement known as the *repartimiento*. Under this system, the Apalachees were expected to provide food and labor for the benefit of the Spanish Crown and the protection it provided. In the late 17th century this tribute grew to include mandatory labor on Spanish fortifications such as the Castillo de San Marcos and participation in wars that Spain fought against nearby native communities.

Throughout the remainder of the 17th century, the Apalachees and Spaniards clashed frequently. Although most members of the Apalachee community eventually accepted Catholicism, many refused to bow to other Spanish demands. When the British settled Carolina in 1670, Apalachee and Spanish interests came together for the purposes of mutual defense. Unfortunately, the Spaniards could not defend the Apalachees, and in a series of raids in 1704, James Moore, the governor of Carolina, captured hundreds of Apalachees as slaves. As a result of Moore's attacks and slave raids by other native communities, the remaining Apalachees fled to Pensacola and dispersed under Spanish protection in the early 1700s. A number were taken in by the Creeks and Yamasees, while still others sought refuge in French-controlled Mobile for a time. At the end of the French and Indian War (1754–1763), most remaining Apalachees settled in Rapides Parish, Louisiana, where remnants of the tribe still survive. In 2010 the tribal office in Libuse, Louisiana, administered to about 300 Apalachees.

SHANE A. RUNYON

See also
Apalachee Revolt; Creeks; French and Indian War; Yamasees

References
Hann, John H., and Bonnie G. McEwan. *The Apalachee Indians and Mission San Luis.* Gainesville: University Press of Florida, 1998.
McEwan, Bonnie G., ed. *The Spanish Missions of La Florida.* Gainesville: University Press of Florida, 1993.

Appalachian Mountains

Extending from Newfoundland and Labrador in the far north to Georgia and Alabama to the far south, the Appalachian Mountains stretch for more than 1,500 miles. They form the predominant inland highlands of Maine, New Hampshire, Vermont, New York, Massachusetts, Connecticut, Pennsylvania, West Virginia, Maryland, Kentucky, Virginia, Tennessee, North Carolina, South Carolina, Georgia, and Alabama. Including the associated foothills, the Appalachians are anywhere from 100 to 300 miles in width. Unlike North American mountain ranges in the far West, the average elevation of the Appalachian Mountains, at about 3,000 feet above sea level, is not very lofty. The tallest peak in the chain is Mount Mitchell in North Carolina at 6,684 feet. Most of the Appalachians are heavily forested and comparatively sparsely populated.

The Appalachian Mountains were the first real frontier for Europeans settling on the eastern seaboard of North America and provided the setting for several battles of the French and Indian War (1754–1763). Early European immigrants to North America established settlements in the coastal areas in the early 1600s, but the Piedmont areas (Appalachian foothills) were not settled until decades later. This was at least in part because of Native American resistance. Westward settlement beyond the Piedmont was frequently stymied by the physical obstacles presented by the

Vista of the Blue Ridge Mountains, a physiographic province of the Appalachian Mountains, from Raven's Roost in Virginia. (Alwekelo/Dreamstime.com)

Appalachians, not to mention the harsher climate and poor soil that are found in the highlands.

The Appalachian region was occupied by Native Americans of various tribal affiliations, and until the mid-1700s only a few white trappers were willing to brave the wilds of the mountain chain. Most of the region's Native Americans were agriculturalists who relied on fishing and extensive hunting grounds to supplement their diets. They also moved their villages frequently to prevent them from depleting their natural resources. As Algonquian migration increased during the first six decades of the 17th century, so did Algonquian conflicts with the Iroquois. The Iroquois had monopolized the fur trade with the Dutch and British and used their influence with the British to displace the Algonquian-speaking tribes. As white settlement increased, displaced tribes found fewer unoccupied lands on which to settle. This led to increasing conflict between Native Americans and colonists.

Native American stewardship of these lands largely determined European settlement of the Appalachian Mountains, which began in earnest after 1730 when Robert Dinwiddie, lieutenant governor of Virginia, awarded 1,000 acres each to every family willing to settle west of the Blue Ridge Mountains. Prior to that, settlement of western South Carolina began after the Yamasee War

(1715–1717). Hostilities between the British and the Yamasee, Cherokee, and Catawba tribes were frequent after 1713.

Soon settlers built forts in western Virginia to protect the growing population from Native American attacks. Yet settlement along the Wilderness Road and in the Shenandoah Valley actually decreased during the French and Indian War until after the British capture of Fort Duquesne in 1758. Once the British won the French and Indian War in 1763, London set out to tighten control over the most abundant land in the colonies: the Appalachians and the territory west of the mountains. The British government's first move was to issue the Royal Proclamation of 1763, which restricted white settlement on the lands west of the Appalachians. The Crown hoped to avoid future conflicts with Native Americans by preventing white encroachment on their lands. Settlers, however, openly defied the proclamation and quickly spread into the Appalachian region.

British forts in the highlands could not impede westward movement. Likewise, the small number of soldiers garrisoned at trans-Appalachian forts made enforcing the standing rules of conduct between whites and Native Americans virtually impossible. Native uprisings were common, as were murders and rapes of both whites and Native Americans. While the Proclamation of

1763 set the Appalachian Mountains as the boundary between white settlements and Native American lands, it was essentially worthless in practice. Enforcing the boundary proved impossible, and the colonial governments could not or made little effort to control squatters who illegally claimed Native American lands for themselves. Indeed, the proclamation served only to antagonize British settlers who believed that they had a right to settle in the highlands after their sacrifices in the French and Indian War and caused increased tension between whites and Native Americans.

Prior to the American Revolutionary War (1775–1783), most Native American who did not want to live under colonial laws had been forced west of the Appalachians. After that war, relatively few Native Americans remained within the settled areas of the newly established United States. The Cherokees, who survived European diseases as well as the deprivations of the American Revolutionary War, had allied themselves with the British and upon the colonists' victory ceded 4 million acres of land to the United States.

The Cherokees, who lived mainly in the southern Appalachian region, successfully adapted to the white economy and modeled their villages, government, agriculture, and society after those of the Americans. No matter how well the Cherokees adapted to white ways, however, they were viewed by most whites as savages and were subjected to frequent efforts to remove them farther to the west, which culminated in the U.S. government's Indian removal actions of the 1830s and the infamous Trail of Tears. In New York, the Iroquois's defense of the Mohawk Valley led to constant conflict with whites, which eventually subsided when they were defeated during the War of 1812.

REBECCA TOLLEY-STOKES

See also

Algonquins; Catawbas; Cherokees; French and Indian War; Indian Removal Act; Iroquois; Native Americans and the American Revolutionary War; Native Americans and the War of 1812; Proclamation of 1763; Yamasee War

References

Drake, Richard. *A History of Appalachia.* Lexington: University Press of Kentucky, 2001.

Ward, Matthew C. *Breaking the Backcountry: The Seven Years' War in Virginia and Pennsylvania, 1754–1765.* Pittsburgh, PA: University of Pittsburgh Press, 2003.

Appomattocks

Native Americans residing in eastern Virginia. The Appomattocks belonged to a group of Algonquian-language tribes living in eastern Virginia that the leader Powhatan organized into the Powhatan Confederacy in the late 16th century. They lived in the area at the falls of the James River and adjacent to a James River tributary, the present-day Appomattox River. Captain John Smith noted the presence of their village in a 1612 map summarizing his earlier explorations of the region.

Much of the history of the Appomattocks is bound up with that of the Powhatan Confederacy. Powhatan, their chief, oversaw a confederacy of similarly cultured tribes, each owing their ultimate allegiance to Powhatan but retaining some local governing institutions (such as their own chief, called the *weroance*) and a sense of their ethnic identity. It was the confederacy's great task to confront the colony at Jamestown and the growing English expansion up the James River and beyond. Powhatan employed a number of both conciliatory and hostile methods for checking English encroachment, most notably the legendary rescue of captured English leader John Smith by his daughter Pocahontas. While some members of the Powhatan Confederacy maintained peaceful—or sometimes ambiguous—relations with the English, the English viewed the Appomattocks as generally hostile.

Indian-English relations deteriorated with the death of Powhatan in 1618. Growing English pressure on Indian lands meant an inevitable escalation of hostility. Powhatan's successor, Opechancanough, pursued a much more confrontational policy that became open warfare after a 1622 Indian attack that killed nearly 350 English settlers. As members of the Powhatan Confederacy, the Appomattocks were caught up in the resulting conflict. The years from 1622 to 1624 and 1644 to 1646 were ones of violent warfare that claimed lives and property. In 1646 Opechancanough was captured, ending all hope for a successful campaign against English conquest of native lands in eastern Virginia.

By the mid-1640s the Appomattocks had abandoned some of their traditional lands. The site of the native village of Appomattock came under English rule in 1652. English settlement moved steadily up the James River, displacing the Appomattocks with settlements and thriving tobacco plantations. During this time the Appomattock population declined, and the landholdings of the Appomattocks continued to shrink.

The fate of the Appomattocks indeed may have been sealed with the Treaty of Middle Plantation. Originally signed by area tribes in 1677, the Appomattock *weroance* was not allowed to sign until 1680. The treaty made the signers subjects of the English Crown. Documentary evidence of the Appomattocks after 1680 is scarce until their final mention in the early 18th century. Their last appearance in the historical record is the word "Appomattock" engraved on a bronze badge (probably issued in 1711), which was likely given to Indian tribes as a hunting permit by the colonial government. Their name survives only in the Anglicized version, "Appomattox," which names both the town of Appomattox and the river.

CHARLES ALLAN

See also

Algonquins; Anglo-Powhatan War, First; Anglo-Powhatan War, Second; Anglo-Powhatan War, Third; Opechancanough; Powhatan; Powhatan Confederacy; Smith, John

References

Feest, Christian F. *The Powhatan Tribes.* New York: Chelsea House, 1990.

Gleach, Frederic W. *Powhatan's World and Colonial Virginia.* Lincoln: University of Nebraska Press, 1997.

Rountree, Helen C. *Pocahontas's People: The Powhatan Indians of Virginia through Four Centuries.* Norman: University of Oklahoma Press, 1990.

Rountree, Helen C. *The Powhatan Indians of Virginia: Their Traditional Culture.* Norman: University of Oklahoma Press, 1989.

Arapahos

Native American group also known as the Inuna-Ina, meaning "the people" or "our people." The word "Arapaho" was picked up by traders and fur trappers from the Absaroke (Crow) name "Alappaho," meaning "people with many tattoos." The Arapahos lived on the western plains (in what is now eastern Colorado, Wyoming, and Kansas) when they first encountered white Americans. Unlike neighboring plains tribes, Arapahos speak an Algonquian language, which suggests that they at one time lived east of the Great Lakes.

Fighting at various times with the Lakotas, Cheyennes, Kiowas, Comanches, Pawnees, and Utes, the Arapahos moved south from the Black Hills, taking control of the upper South Platte River area. By 1730, raids on Comanche and Kiowa tribes had provided a supply of horses, which the southern nations had acquired from Spanish settlements in Mexico. The Arapahos were not an agricultural group. Bison, other game, and roots and berries provided most of what the Arapaho people needed. They supplemented these with trade with the agricultural Arikaras, Mandans, and Hidatsas.

Around 1820 the Arapahos began to form their most enduring alliance with the Cheyennes, initially to fight the Lakotas to the north and the Kiowas and Comanches to the south. Both later allied with the Lakota Nation in the final conflicts with the U.S. government, although the Arapahos persistently tried to find peaceful accommodation with the encroaching tide of Americans.

Trade with Americans and Europeans was a part of Arapaho life from the early 19th century. Metal knives, arrow points, cooking pots, and other implements were obtained in return for buffalo robes, as were brass wire and colored beads for decoration. Most of all, as enemy tribes to the east acquired guns and ammunition, tribes farther west, including the Arapahos, sought to purchase them as well. Large numbers of Americans began passing through Arapaho lands in the 1840s en route to California. These migrations were sufficiently intrusive to disrupt the bison herds, beginning a sharp decline in the game on which all Plains tribes relied. By the 1850s bison were so scarce that woven blankets and

Buffalo meat dries at an Arapaho camp near Fort Dodge, Kansas, in 1870. The Arapahos most likely migrated to the western Great Plains from Minnesota, where they came to rely on the buffalo and other game. (National Archives)

other trade clothing became an absolute necessity for many Native Americans.

The Arapahos refrained from attacking passing wagon trains but often sought presents in return for allowing safe passage through their territory. Lines of warriors often rode up to caravans waving American flags and showing papers from military officers attesting to their good character. The United States acknowledged Arapaho and Cheyenne control of the territory between the North Platte and Arkansas rivers in 1851 as part of a general treaty with most of the Plains tribes. However, by 1858 the Pikes Peak Gold Rush brought massive settlement into the area, creating the city of Denver and splitting the Arapahos permanently into northern and southern branches. Northern Arapahos moved into the upper North Platte and Sweetwater River basins, while the Southern Arapahos moved toward the Canadian and Cimarron rivers in western Indian Territory (Oklahoma).

The Arapahos first went to war on a large scale against American soldiers and settlers in 1864. A small number of Southern Arapahos were camped with the Cheyenne band under Black Kettle at Sand Creek, Colorado, when the settlement and its people were nearly wiped out on November 29, 1864, by Colorado militia commanded by Colonel John Chivington. Most of the other Southern Arapahos, led by Little Raven, were camped nearby. While Arapaho elders, women, and children fled to Kiowa territory to the south, most adult men joined Southern Cheyenne bands in the war against the intruders through the following spring.

Between 1865 and 1869, Little Raven tried to keep his people away from continued fighting between the army and the Southern Cheyennes while seeking a reservation on the North Canadian River. The reservation established between the Arkansas and Cimarron rivers in 1867 during the Medicine Lodge Creek Treaty Council was too close to the fighting. Americans in the area, civilian or military, retaliated against any Native American peoples for raids on settlements and wagon trains. In 1869 Little Raven brought his band to Fort Sill (Oklahoma), and President Ulysses S. Grant established a reservation on the Canadian River by executive order.

Northern Arapahos joined the Northern Cheyennes and several Lakota bands in a successful war, led by Oglala chief Red Cloud, over U.S. attempts to build forts along the Bozeman Trail. The United States then agreed to remove military posts from the Black Hills and Powder River basin and guaranteed the land by treaty to the Native American nations in possession. Arapaho warriors participated in the Battle of the Little Bighorn in 1876 that wiped out Lieutenant Colonel George Custer's battalion of the 7th Cavalry. Arapaho scouts provided considerable assistance to the army in its retaliatory campaign against the Lakotas and Cheyennes during 1876–1877.

In the meantime, Northern Arapaho leaders Medicine Man and Black Bear sought to establish friendly relations with the U.S. military, with the goal of obtaining a reservation in Wyoming. The Arapahos' valuable scouting services convinced military officers to arrange for them to settle on a portion of the Shoshone Reservation. Nevertheless, there were frequent clashes with settlers. In addition, a white mob ambushed and killed Black Bear. A Northern Arapaho delegation, led by Black Coal and Sharp Nose, met with President Rutherford B. Hayes in Washington in 1877, leading to permanent settlement on the Shoshone Reservation, in the Great Basin area, in 1878.

CHARLES ROSENBERG

See also

Cheyennes; Chivington, John; Comanches; Lakota Sioux; Little Bighorn, Battle of the; Oglala Sioux; Pawnees; Red Cloud; Sand Creek Massacre; Utes

References

Fowler, Loretta. *Arapaho Politics, 1851–1978: Symbols in Crises of Authority*. Lincoln: University of Nebraska Press, 1982.

Fowler, Loretta. *Indians of North America: The Arapaho*. New York: Chelsea House, 1989.

Kroeber, A. L. *The Arapaho*. Lincoln: University of Nebraska Press, 1983.

Salzmann, Zdenek. *The Arapaho Indian: A Research Guide and Bibliography*. New York: Greenwood, 1988.

Trenholm, Virginia Cole. *The Arapahoes: Our People*. Norman: University of Oklahoma Press, 1970.

Arapahos, Northern

A small Algonquian-speaking Plains tribal group closely aligned with both the Gros Ventres of northern Montana and southern Canada and with the Southern Arapahos. The Northern Arapahos' early history is debated; however, by the late 1700s and very early 1800s, they were located on the Great Plains and had become a horse-dependent nomadic people. Although they retained the creator god of the Algonquian-speaking peoples (Manitou), they had also adopted the Sun Dance common among Plains tribes. Like all Plains groups, the Northern Arapahos relied heavily on buffalo for their food, clothing, and shelter requirements. Indeed, bison were at the center of their economic system and were key to their trade relations with other Native American groups and white traders.

The Arapahos, both Northern and Southern, had a long-standing alliance with the more numerous Cheyennes, another Algonquian-speaking Plains tribe. The two Arapaho groups often camped together and frequently hunted and waged war together. The Northern Arapahos were primarily located in Wyoming and western Nebraska along the Platte River basin. They often visited among their southern cousins in Kansas and eastern Colorado in the Arkansas River basin. The reason for the split between northern and southern groups is conjectural, being attributed to the coming of the white man and the development of the Oregon Trail, which split the buffalo herds, as well as to a desire on the part of the southerners to more widely partake of the horse market of the southern Plains.

As with their Cheyenne and Lakota allies, until the 1830s the Northern Arapahos were almost continuously at war with the Shoshones, Crows, and Pawnees as well as with the Comanches and Kiowas. The Northern Arapahos had initially begun to settle their

Arapaho Powder Face, along with his wife and baby on a buffalo robe, Indian Territory (present-day Oklahoma), 1870. (National Anthropological Archives, Smithsonian Institution, NAA INV 9153700)

References

Seger, John H. *Early Days among the Cheyenne and Arapahoe Indians.* Norman: University of Oklahoma Press, 1934.

Trenholm, Virginia Cole. *The Arapahoes: Our People.* Norman: University of Oklahoma Press, 1970.

Arapahos, Southern

Small Algonquian-speaking Plains tribe closely aligned with both the Gros Ventres of northern Montana and southern Canada and with the Northern Arapahos. The early history of the Southern Arapahos is subject to conjecture; however, by the late 1700s and early 1800s they were already located on the Great Plains and had become a nomadic people who relied heavily upon the horse. Although they retained the creator god of the Algonquian-speaking peoples, Manitou, they had also adopted the Sun Dance that was common among Plains tribes. Like all Plains tribes, the Southern Arapahos relied heavily on buffalo for their food, clothing, and shelter requirements. Indeed, bison were at the center of their economic system and were key to their trade relations with other Native American groups and white traders.

The Arapahos, both Northern and Southern, had a long-standing alliance with the more numerous Cheyennes, another Algonquian-speaking Plains tribe. The two peoples often camped, hunted, and waged war together. The Southern Arapahos were primarily located in western Kansas and eastern Colorado in the Arkansas River basin. They frequently visited among their Northern Arapaho cousins in Wyoming and western Nebraska along the North Platte River basin. The reason that the Arapaho split is subject to debate. Some argue that the split can be attributed to the coming of whites and the development of the Oregon Trail, which divided the buffalo herds, sparking a desire on the part of the southerners to participate actively in the horse market of the southern Plains.

As with their Cheyenne and Lakota allies, the Southern Arapahos were almost continuously at war with the Shoshones, Crows, and Pawnees as well as with the Comanches and Kiowas until the 1830s. The Southern Arapahos had initially begun to settle their differences with the Comanches and Kiowas of the southern Plains but became involved with the Cheyennes in their major confrontation with the Comanches and Kiowas at Wolf Creek in 1838.

The Southern Arapahos were very closely aligned with their Southern Cheyenne neighbors. Like the Southern Cheyennes, the Southern Arapahos were more inclined to make accommodations with the ever-increasing white population. Whether this was due to the temperament of their leaders or a more complete understanding of the numbers and power of the whites is unclear. What is certain is that the Southern Arapahos tried to maintain a more peaceful approach than their northern brethren. This was costly to them on a number of occasions. Their close affiliation with the Southern Cheyennes resulted in many Southern Arapahos

differences with the Comanches and Kiowas of the southern Plains but became involved with the Cheyennes in their major confrontation with the Comanches and Kiowas at Wolf Creek in 1838.

The Northern Arapahos were active participants in the Native American wars of the 1850s and in Red Cloud's War (1866–1868). By most accounts, they were not present at the Battle of the Rosebud (June 17, 1876) but did participate in the Battle of the Little Bighorn (June 25–26, 1876). Subsequent to these engagements, some Arapahos served as scouts, principally for Brigadier General Nelson A. Miles. The Northern Arapahos seem not to have gotten along as well with the Lakotas as did their Cheyenne allies, and this quiet resentment may have been part of the reason for the willingness of some Arapahos to serve as scouts.

According to the terms of the 1868 Fort Laramie Treaty, the Northern Arapahos were to locate on South Dakota's Great Sioux Reservation along with the Lakotas. This, however, did not sit well with the Northern Arapahos because of lingering resentment toward the Lakotas, so the Northern Arapahos asked for their own reservation. Meanwhile they stayed in Wyoming, and most refused to settle in Indian Territory (Oklahoma) with their southern brethren. Not until 1878 did they agree to join the eastern Shoshones' Wind River Reservation located in west-central Wyoming.

JOHN THOMAS BROOM

See also

Cheyennes; Comanches; Crows; Fort Laramie, Treaty of (1851); Fort Laramie, Treaty of (1868); Kiowas; Lakota Sioux; Pawnees; Red Cloud's War; Shoshones camping with Southern Cheyenne chief Black Kettle's band and suffering accordingly in both the Sand Creek Massacre in 1864 and the Washita River Massacre (Battle of the Washita) in 1868. Although some Southern Arapaho warriors fought with the Kiowas and Comanches against whites in the late 1860s and early 1870s, most remained peaceful and resided with their Cheyenne allies on the combined Cheyenne-Arapaho Reservation in Indian Territory (present-day Oklahoma).

The Southern Arapahos still reside with their longtime friends the Southern Cheyennes in Oklahoma, although there are contact and visiting with their Northern Arapaho cousins who reside on the Wind River Reservation in Wyoming.

JOHN THOMAS BROOM

See also

Cheyennes; Comanches; Crows; Kiowas; Lakota Sioux; Pawnees; Red
Cloud's War; Sand Creek Massacre; Shoshones; Washita, Battle of the

References

Seger, John H. *Early Days among the Cheyenne and Arapahoe Indians.*
Norman: University of Oklahoma Press, 1934.
Trenholm, Virginia Cole. *The Arapahoes: Our People.* Norman:
University of Oklahoma Press, 1970.

Arikaras

A Caddoan-speaking native people closely related to the Pawnees. Arikara means "horn," which refers to a traditional hairstyle worn by the tribesmen. As Caddoan-speaking peoples moved gradually northwest from their original homes in the southeastern Plains, the Arikaras became the northernmost of this linguistic group. The Arikaras migrated north from Nebraska into the Dakotas in the 1500s. Their political structure was decentralized, with villages often combining to create informal confederations of named bands.

By the early 1700s French traders observed that the Arikaras resided in 40 villages stretching from the present-day Nebraska–South Dakota border to central South Dakota near present-day Pierre. By the mid-1700s the Arikaras had moved farther up the Missouri River, concentrating near present-day Pierre and Mobridge, South Dakota. As with their Pawnee relatives, the Arikaras built earthen lodges, hunted buffalo, fished, and farmed, growing corn, squash, beans, and sunflowers. After European contact they became active participants in the fur trade. As with most Plains people, buffalo hunting was the central focus of the Arikaras' economic activity. Their villages became popular stops for traders eager to obtain furs and for other Native Americans eager to exchange their furs for European trade goods. The Arikaras became active commercial entrepreneurs and middlemen in this trade. By the late 1700s they had also acquired horses.

In the early 1780s the first of several devastating smallpox epidemics struck the Arikaras, drastically reducing their population. By the time Meriwether Lewis and William Clark ascended the

An Arikara family in 1908. The Arikaras followed an agricultural style of life along the Missouri River. (Library of Congress)

Missouri River in 1804, the remaining Arikaras were concentrated in three villages near the confluence of the Grand and Missouri rivers. Warfare with the neighboring Lakotas, regular outbreaks of disease, rivalries with fur traders, and troubles with the U.S. government (such as the 1823 Arikara War) eventually led the Arikaras to abandon these villages permanently in 1833.

The Arikaras eventually moved north to join the Mandans and Hidatsas. Another smallpox epidemic in 1837 cost the Arikaras nearly half their population. From 1863 to 1886 the Arikaras shared the Like-a-Fishhook Village on the Fort Berthold Reservation with the Mandans and Hidatsas. A treaty in 1871 ceded much of this land to the U.S. government.

Like their neighbors, the Arikaras were encouraged to adopt farming and the dominant American culture. They also served with distinction as army scouts, most notably during the Great Sioux War of 1876–1877. By the late 1880s many Arikaras lived on small individual plots of land clustered around Nishu, North Dakota. Missionaries and government agents made active attempts at converting the Arikaras and transforming them into small farmers. In 1934 the Arikaras, Mandans, and Hidatsas formally adopted the Indian Reorganization Act and became known officially as the Three Affiliated Tribes.

The Arikaras and their neighbors suffered greatly when the Garrison Dam was constructed in 1954. Relocated from their river-bottom homes, the Arikaras now live near White Shield, North Dakota. Most remain small farmers and ranchers.

STEVE POTTS

See also
Arikara Scouts; Arikara War; Pawnees

References
Krause, Richard A. *The Leavenworth Site: Archaeology of an Historic Arikara Community.* University of Kansas Publications in Anthropology 3. Lawrence: University of Kansas Press, 1972.
Meyer, Roy W. *The Village Indians of the Upper Missouri: The Mandans, Hidatsas, and Arikaras.* Lincoln: University of Nebraska Press, 1977.
Rogers, J. Daniel. *Objects of Change: The Archaeology and History of Arikara Contact with Europeans.* Washington, DC: Smithsonian Institution Press, 1990.

Arikara Scouts

Native American scouts belonging to the Arikara tribe who served with the U.S. Army on the northern Plains between 1865 and 1881. In the 19th century, the Arikaras were a sedentary tribe whose main sources of subsistence were corn horticulture and the buffalo hunt. They lived in semipermanent earth lodge villages along the Missouri River. Like many other sedentary tribes, they were often harassed by the more powerful Lakotas (Sioux). In the 1860s the Arikaras began to serve as scouts for the U.S. Army, partly for self-preservation. The first Arikara scout was Bloody Knife, who joined Brigadier General Alfred Sully's campaign against the Sioux in 1865. Bloody Knife later gained fame as Lieutenant Colonel George A. Custer's favorite scout. In 1867 Colonel Philippe Regis de Trobriand, commanding officer at Fort Stevenson, North Dakota, became the first officer to systematically enlist Arikara warriors for scouting services.

Arikara scouts served in several major military campaigns as well as in nonmilitary expeditions. These campaigns included the Northern Pacific Railroad Expedition of 1872, the Yellowstone Expedition of 1873, the Northern Boundary Surveys of 1873–1874, the Black Hills Expedition of 1874, the Little Bighorn Campaign of 1876, and several follow-up campaigns in the Great Sioux War of 1876–1877, including the disarmament of the Sioux at the Standing Rock and Cheyenne River reservations in 1876.

Arikara scouts are perhaps best remembered for their participation in the Battle of the Little Bighorn on June 25, 1876. Some 40 Arikaras served with Custer and Brigadier General Alfred H. Terry. About 16 Arikaras rode into the battle with Major Marcus A. Reno, and 3 perished in the fight: Bloody Knife, Bobtail Bull, and Little Brave (aka Little Soldier or Bear's Trail). Another scout, Goose, was severely wounded. Despite later criticisms from certain military officials and newspaper correspondents, most scouts performed well in the battle and continued to serve loyally afterward. The last Arikara scouts were mustered out after Sioux chief Sitting Bull surrendered at Fort Buford, North Dakota, in 1881.

Following their service, the Arikara veterans applied for military pensions. Because of complications concerning their names (mustering officers had difficulty accurately recording their Native American names) and the loss of discharge papers in Washington, D.C., only a few scouts were able to obtain pensions. To draw the attention of the Pension Office and to set the record straight on their role at the Little Bighorn, the scouts related their story of the campaign to North Dakota historian Orin G. Libby in 1912. The result was the publication in 1920 of *The Arikara Narrative of the Campaign against the Hostile Dakotas, June, 1876,* which has since been reissued under a slightly different title. The book is still one of the most important sources on the Battle of the Little Bighorn.

Presently, the Arikaras share a reservation with the Mandans and Hidatsas on the Fort Berthold Indian Reservation in North Dakota. Many Arikara people trace their ancestry to one or more of the scouts.

MARK VAN DE LOGT

See also
Arikaras; Bloody Knife; Custer, George Armstrong; Great Sioux War; Little Bighorn, Battle of the; Reno, Marcus Albert; Sioux; Sully, Alfred; Terry, Alfred Howe

References
Dunlay, Thomas W. *Wolves for the Blue Soldiers: Indian Scouts and Auxiliaries with the United States Army, 1860–90.* Lincoln: University of Nebraska Press, 1982.
Gray, John S. "Arikara Scouts with Custer." *North Dakota History* 35 (December 1968): 443–478.
Greene, Candace. "Arikara Drawings: New Sources of Visual History." *American Indian Art Magazine* 31(2) (2006): 74–85, 99.
Libby, Orin G. *The Arikara Narrative of Custer's Campaign and the Battle of the Little Bighorn.* Norman: University of Oklahoma Press, 1998.

Arikara War
Event Date: 1823

Brief conflict between the Arikara tribe and the U.S. Army and the first significant military confrontation between the United States and western Native Americans. The Arikara War began in the spring of 1823, a result of increasing tensions between white fur traders and the Arikaras, who lived north of the Grand River in present-day South Dakota.

The troubles began when St. Louis fur entrepreneur William Ashley moved north into Arikara territory in early 1823. His Missouri Fur Company expedition had stopped to trade at two Arikara villages on the west bank of the Missouri River. The villages were popular with passing explorers, including Meriwether Lewis and William Clark. Since the early 1800s the Arikaras had played an active role as commercial middlemen in the fur trade. However, they now feared that competition with Ashley would end their control of the Missouri River trade.

On June 2, 1823, the Arikaras attacked Ashley's camp and killed 14 fur traders there. Ashley's men fled south and marched to Fort Atkinson (Nebraska), arriving on June 18. Upon their arrival they informed the U.S. garrison of the June 2 massacre. Colonel Henry Leavenworth, commander of the 6th Infantry Regiment, and Indian agent Benjamin O'Fallon subsequently decided to mount a military expedition to punish the Arikaras.

Leavenworth left Fort Atkinson on June 22 with 230 men and two guns. They were later joined by Missouri Fur Company head Joshua Pilcher and 60 trappers, along with a howitzer. Later approximately 750 Lakotas, recruited by Pilcher, also joined the expedition to punish their traditional enemy.

On August 9 the Lakotas began their attack on the Arikara villages. The following day Leavenworth shelled the villages. The Lakotas subsequently left the siege to raid Arikara cornfields and gardens, and Leavenworth soon turned to negotiating with the Arikaras.

After several days of fruitless talks, the Arikaras slipped out of their villages on August 14 and fled north to seek refuge with their Mandan and Hidatsa allies. Leavenworth soon headed back to Fort Atkinson, while an angry Pilcher burned the Arikara villages. Leavenworth's leniency toward the Arikaras—he did not press for a complete victory—proved controversial and later spawned a debate between those Americans seeking accommodation with Native Americans and those seeking the complete subjugation or extermination of Native Americans.

The outcome of the brief Arikara War drastically affected the regional fur trade and relations among the Arikaras, fur traders, and the U.S. government. No longer able to count on safe passage along the Missouri River, Ashley sought a new route to the Rocky Mountains. His subsequent course through South Pass into the central Rockies shifted the fur trade and pioneered new paths that later settlers would take.

The Arikaras returned to their burned villages in 1824, rebuilt them, and signed a peace treaty with the U.S. government in 1825. They abandoned their villages in 1833, however, and began a series of migrations, eventually settling among the Mandans and Hidatsas. The Arikaras remain on the Fort Berthold Reservation in North Dakota.

STEVE POTTS

See also

Arikaras; Fur Trade; Lakota Sioux

References

Krause, Richard A. *The Leavenworth Site: Archaeology of an Historic Arikara Community.* University of Kansas Publications in Anthropology 3. Lawrence: University of Kansas Press, 1972.

Nester, William R. *The Arikara War: The First Plains Indian War, 1823.* Missoula, MT: Mountain Press, 2001.

Nichols, Roger. "Backdrop for Disaster: Causes of the Arikara War of 1823." *South Dakota History* 14(2) (1984): 93–113.

"Official Correspondence Pertaining to the Leavenworth Expedition of 1823 into South Dakota for the Conquest of the Ree Indians." *South Dakota Historical Society Collections* 1 (1902): 179–256.

Arikaree Fight

See Beecher Island, Battle of

Arrow

See Bow and Arrow

Artillery

The monopoly generally enjoyed by European settlers to the New World over their Native American adversaries in the use of artillery was representative not only of their enormous advantage in technology and war matériel but also of the superior level of organization and training that they could potentially bring to bear. Early colonial settlements and fortifications equipped with cannon had an advantage in firepower that indigenous attackers could not match during a direct assault. Early in the colonial period, major settlements such as Jamestown, Plymouth, Boston, St. Augustine, and New Amsterdam all boasted artillery pieces in their defenses for use against both indigenous threats and rival colonial powers. Still developing into an efficient military art in the 16th and 17th centuries, artillery was often relegated to a defensive role because of its expense as well as lack of mobility, poor roads, the densely wooded terrain of eastern North America, and the generally fluid nature of frontier warfare.

Artillery pieces of the colonial period ran a gamut of sizes and had evocative names such as falcon, minion, and basilisk, which generally indicated the size of the bore and length in relation to caliber. These names were not, however, necessarily applied consistently across nationalities or even by different founders. Likewise, the weight of the pieces themselves ranged from less than 200 pounds to several thousand pounds, and their shot could vary in weight from less than 1 pound to more than 50 pounds. While the larger pieces had theoretical ranges of up to several thousand yards, effective aimed fire for the small to midsized pieces was typically as little as several hundred yards.

The type of ammunition used depended on the situation. The earliest projectiles were solid, first of stone and then of lead and iron. Solid projectiles (known as shot) were employed for distance and accuracy. Solid shot could be heated in furnaces, and hot shot was used to set fire to wooden structures and ships. By the late 18th century, ammunition included grapeshot, a collection of balls in a sack lashed to a wooden spindle that broke open on firing, and canister, a sheet-metal container of musket shot or scrap metal that broke apart on firing and had the effect of a giant modern shotgun. Grapeshot and canister were particularly effective against personnel at short ranges.

Explosive shell, or bombs, were hollow spheres filled with gunpowder and fused to detonate above or among an enemy. In the late 18th century, Henry Shrapnel, a British officer, invented

The lightweight (362-pound) U.S. Army 1.65-inch Hotchkiss breechloading rifled steel mountain gun. (A.B. Dyer, *Handbook for Light Artillery*, 1908)

spherical case shot, providing an antipersonnel projectile with greater range than canister. Instead of the shell simply fragmenting, it was filled with iron pellets that would continue traveling forward in a cone-shaped pattern.

By the early 18th century, artillery had developed into three basic types: the gun, the mortar, and the howitzer. The gun was relatively long and fired its projectile on an essentially flat trajectory. The mortar fired on a steep trajectory and was useful for lobbing shells behind defensive works and fortifications. Mortars ranged in size from small coehorns, which had a 4.5-inch bore and an overall length of 13 inches, weighed 86 pounds, and could be transported by two men by means of carrying handles on each side of the wooden mount, to large pieces of as great as 13-inch bore. The howitzer was a hybrid capable of firing at a higher trajectory than a gun but with greater range than a mortar of comparable size and was also capable of firing scattershot in an antipersonnel role. Furthermore, the earlier names had given way to designations based specifically on either the weight of the shot or the diameter of the bore (e.g., a 6-pounder gun, an 8-inch mortar, etc.), and European nations began adopting standard systems of calibers and lighter and more mobile field pieces on better carriages.

In its wars with the Native Americans on its frontiers in the late 18th and early 19th centuries, the U.S. Army employed artillery with mixed results. Major General John Sullivan used it effectively in his campaign against the Iroquois and their Loyalist allies in 1779, but the three small pieces with Brigadier General Josiah

Harmar's column never fired a shot in anger during his unsuccessful 1790 expedition against the Miamis and Shawnees. The two companies of artillery with Major General Arthur St. Clair in 1791 failed to prevent his disastrous defeat at the Battle of the Wabash. Despite Major General "Mad" Anthony Wayne's hopes for the small 3-inch howitzers that accompanied him in his 1794 campaign, they did not contribute decisively to his victory in the Battle of Fallen Timbers (August 20, 1794) because of their inability to keep up with the advancing infantry over difficult terrain. The standard field pieces of the time, 3- and 6-pounder guns and 5.5-inch howitzers, were thus considered even more unfit for use on the frontier except in forts.

The development of a standardized system of ordnance in the 1830s and 1840s did provide the U.S. Army with a more suitable artillery piece as the frontier expanded onto the Great Plains and into the far West. Ordnance included the lightweight Model 1841 12-pounder mountain howitzer, which was capable of firing an 8.9-pound projectile 900 yards. Light enough for the tube, carriage, and ammunition to be carried by three mules and with the development of the prairie carriage, the Model 1841 howitzer was able to keep up with the rest of a column in mobile warfare over rugged terrain. The howitzer provided invaluable support on multiple occasions, such as during the Battle of Apache Pass (July 15–16, 1862), the defense of Fort Ridgely (August 20–22, 1862), the First Battle of Adobe Walls (November 25, 1864), at Soldier Spring (1868), and in the Modoc War (1872–1873).

Illustration of an 1883 Gatling gun. This crank-operated weapon was capable of firing 350 rounds per minute from 10 rotating barrels but was prone to fouling and jamming. (A.B. Dyer, *Handbook for Light Artillery*, 1908)

The advent of widespread use of rifling and breech-loading technology both in artillery and in small arms during the American Civil War (1861–1865) brought additional changes to the use of artillery. Rifling, or grooves on the interior of a weapon's bore that cause a projectile to spin, greatly increased both range and accuracy. With new breech-loading rifles, Native American marksmen could conceivably outrange the mountain howitzer. In response to pressure from U.S. Army officers, the War Department ordered the Hotchkiss 1.65-inch breech-loading rifled steel gun. Although firing a comparatively small projectile, it weighed a mere 117 pounds and had an effective range of 4,000 yards. First employed in 1877 against the Nez Perces, its advantages in mobility and range soon made it the dominant artillery piece on the frontier. The Hotchkiss played a significant role in the unfortunate Battle of Wounded Knee (December 29, 1890).

Other field pieces that saw service on the frontier included the Model 1838 24-pounder coehorn mortar, the Model 1857 bronze 12-pounder smoothbore Napoleon, the iron 3-inch Ordnance rifle, and the Gatling gun. The coehorn could fire a 17-pound explosive shell 1,200 yards and was light enough to be manhandled by two to four soldiers on a wooden bed. The Napoleon had an effective range of more than 1,600 yards, but its tube alone weighed 1,230 pounds. The 3-inch Ordnance rifle had slightly greater range at

1,830 yards and weighed a bit less with an 830-pound tube but, as with the Napoleon, lacked the mobility often desired for frontier campaigning. Introduced in the Civil War and classified as artillery, the Gatling gun was an early crank-operated automatic weapon that was capable of firing 350 rounds per minute from a bank of 10 rotating barrels. However, it was prone to fouling and jamming when overheated, and many commanders did not wish to burden their columns with the difficulty of transporting such an unwieldy weapon.

Even when suitable field pieces were available, the 19th-century army lacked any clear doctrine for the employment of artillery in situations other than traditional European-style warfare. The employment of artillery on campaigns against Native Americans was at the discretion of local commanders. Many prominent officers viewed artillery as an unnecessary encumbrance, while others, such as Major General Nelson A. Miles, considered it a necessity. Further complicating the issue were the War Department's economy measures, which ensured that even those artillery companies that were nominally to be provided with horses and mounted for use in the field were often simply detailed and equipped as infantry. When regular artillerymen were unavailable, infantry soldiers and cavalrymen often served field pieces themselves.

JOSEPH R. FRECHETTE

See also
Adobe Walls, First Battle of; Apache Pass, Battle of; Fallen Timbers, Battle of; Gatling Gun; Harmar, Josiah; Miles, Nelson Appleton; Modoc War; Native American Warfare; St. Clair, Arthur; St. Clair's Campaign; Wabash, Battle of the; Wayne, Anthony; Wayne's Campaign; Wounded Knee, Battle of

References
Dastrup, Boyd L. *King of Battle: A Branch History of the U.S. Army's Field Artillery.* Washington, DC: U.S. Army Training and Doctrine Command and U.S. Army Center of Military History, 1993.
Peterson, Harold L. *Round Shot and Rammers.* Harrisburg, PA: Stackpole, 1969.
Utley, Robert M. *Frontier Regulars: The United States and the American Indian, 1866–1891.* New York: Macmillan, 1973.
Utley, Robert M. *Frontiersmen in Blue: The United States and the Indian, 1848–1865.* Lincoln: University of Nebraska Press, 1967.
Yates, Larry. *Field Artillery in Military Operations Other than War: An Overview of the U.S. Experience.* Fort Leavenworth, KS: Combat Studies Institute Press, 2004.

Ash Hollow, Battle of
Start Date: September 2, 1855
End Date: September 3, 1855

Military engagement along the Platte River in present-day Garden County, Nebraska, between U.S. forces commanded by Brevet Brigadier General William S. Harney and Brulé Sioux led by Little Thunder. The Battle of Ash Hollow is also referred to as the Battle of Blue Water Creek. The clash resulted from disputes involving violations of the 1851 Treaty of Fort Laramie. This treaty stipulated where Native Americans could move about unhampered while not impeding the progress of western settlers moving along the so-called California Road, which was part of the Oregon Trail.

This particular encounter was triggered by the so-called Grattan Massacre a year earlier. In August 1854 a Mormon traveling west on the Oregon Trail complained that a Sioux named High Forehead had stolen his cow. In reality the cow, with bleeding hooves, had been abandoned, and High Forehead had slaughtered it for food. When negotiations for compensation failed, the commander at Fort Laramie ordered one of his junior officers, Second Lieutenant John Grattan, to arrest the Native American. Grattan thus led a patrol of 30 men and artillery to capture High Forehead. Grattan's troops encountered the Sioux, who were offended by such a show of force. After an angry exchange the troops fired, killing Chief Conquering Bear. During the ensuing engagement, the Sioux killed Grattan and 29 of his soldiers. The remaining soldier later died of his wounds at Fort Laramie.

Although Grattan was blamed for the skirmish, President Franklin Pierce demanded that the military take action. Pierce ordered General Harney to defeat the Sioux and enforce all stipulations of the Fort Laramie Treaty. Harney set out in August with some 600 men, consisting of elements of the 2nd Dragoons, the 6th and 10th Infantry, and the 4th Artillery.

By September 1 the soldiers came upon the Brulé village along the Platte River in a place called Blue Waters. During the night of September 2, Harney ordered a flanking maneuver led by Lieutenant Colonel Philip St. George Cooke and Captain Henry Heth to establish a blocking position, into which he would drive the Sioux. The next morning Harney advanced with the infantry toward the village. Convinced that he had the Sioux trapped, he entered into negotiations with Chief Little Thunder and demanded that the men responsible for the Grattan Massacre and other outrages be handed over. While the parley was in progress, with Little Thunder rebuffing Harney's demand, some of the Sioux discovered Cooke's men.

Learning that Cooke's men had been spotted, Harney ordered his men to attack the Sioux camp. Some Sioux fled into caves along the river as soldiers fired into the village, killing many women and children in the process. Other warriors fled on horseback in an attempt at escape and were pursued by Heth's men. The encounter lasted several hours, during which Harney's force soundly defeated the Sioux. More than 80 Sioux were killed, and a large number were wounded. Army casualties were 4 killed, 7 wounded, and 1 missing.

In October 1855 Harney negotiated a peace treaty with the Sioux. The Battle of Ash Hollow allowed the U.S. Army to enforce peace without further bloodshed in Sioux territory and protected settlers traveling the Oregon Trail for years to come. Some newspapers hailed the battle as a heroic victory for the U.S. military over the Native Americans. Others called it butchery and an excuse to justify expanding the U.S. Army.

CHARLES FRANCIS HOWLETT

See also
Brulé Sioux; Cooke, Philip St. George; Fort Laramie, Treaty of (1851); Fort Laramie, Treaty of (1868); Grattan Massacre; Harney, William Selby; Oregon Trail

References
Beck, Paul N. *The First Sioux War: The Grattan Fight and Blue Water Creek, 1854–1856.* Lanham, MD: University Press of America, 2004.
Paul, R. Eli. *Blue Water Creek and the First Sioux War, 1854–1856.* Norman: University of Oklahoma Press, 2004.
Robbins, James S. *Last in Their Class: Custer, Pickett and the Goats of West Point.* New York: Encounter Books, 2006.
Werner, Fred H. *With Harney on the Blue Water: Battle of Ash Hollow, 1855.* Greeley, CO: Werner Publications, 1988.

Ashishishe
See Curly

Athapascans

A large group of Native Americans inhabiting vast stretches of territory from far northern Canada and Alaska through southern

Canada who share a common language family, known as Athapascan. Athapascan-speaking peoples ranged from the Arctic Circle, Alaska, the Yukon Territory, the Northwest Territories of Canada, and south into the northern reaches of British Columbia, Alberta, Saskatchewan, and Manitoba. In the American Southwest, the Apaches and Navajos were Athapascan-speaking groups.

The term "Athapascan" includes a large number of individual Native American nations, tribes, and bands. Archaeologists believe that most Athapascans crossed from Siberia to Alaska between 10,000 and 15,000 years ago via the land bridge crossing the Bering Strait. As the Ice Age descended, they moved farther to the south.

For much of their existence, this large group centered their lives around seasonal hunting, fishing, and gathering. Most hunted all types of game, large and small. By the mid-19th century many Athapascans had built permanent villages, which some still inhabit. They often erected summer camps far away from the main villages, however, to facilitate hunting. As they came into increasing contact with Europeans, they adopted certain aspects of European lifestyles.

The Athapascan language family is the second-largest indigenous linguistic family in North America, second only to the Uto-Aztecan family. The term "Athapascan" is derived from Lake Athapasca, located in far northwestern Saskatchewan. The name was apparently coined by Albert Gallatin in his 1836 North American language classification study. Athapascans do not use the term, however, and prefer to be referred to by their tribe, specific language, or location.

PAUL G. PIERPAOLI JR.

See also
Apaches; Navajos

References
Nelson, Richard K. *Hunters of the Northern Forest.* Chicago: University of Chicago Press, 1973.
Savinshinsky, Joel. *The Trail of the Hare.* New York: Gdon and Breach, 1994.

Atkinson, Henry
Birth Date: 1782
Death Date: June 14, 1842

U.S. Army officer. Henry Atkinson was born in Person County, North Carolina, in 1782. He was appointed a captain of infantry by President Thomas Jefferson and commanded a company of the 3rd Infantry Regiment in the Louisiana Territory in 1808. During the War of 1812 Atkinson served as inspector general under major generals Wade Hampton and James Wilkinson on the New York–Canadian border from 1813 to 1814. Atkinson was then promoted to colonel and commanded first the 37th Infantry Regiment in 1814 and then the 6th Infantry Regiment in 1815.

In 1819 Atkinson led the 6th Infantry from Plattsburg, New York, to the Missouri River, where his men constructed Fort Atkinson on the Nebraska side across from present-day Council Bluffs, Iowa. Atkinson also supervised the initial construction of Fort Leavenworth (Kansas). He was concurrently assigned as commander of the Ninth Military District, which encompassed much of the western half of the United States including Illinois, Kentucky, and Tennessee as well as all the territory west of the Mississippi and from Missouri north to the Canadian border.

Between 1819 and 1842 Atkinson commanded this region, although the designation of the command changed from time to time. He was promoted to brigadier general in 1820.

Atkinson led explorations of the Missouri as far upriver as the confluence of the Missouri and the Yellowstone. He also selected the site and supervised the construction of Jefferson Barracks, Missouri. At both Fort Atkinson and Jefferson Barracks, he encouraged the development of post farms both to improve the quality of food for soldiers and to reduce the cost of maintaining the then-remote installations.

General Atkinson took a balanced approach to the problem of white–Native American conflict in the West. He often criticized white settlers and traders for causing problems and tried to ensure that allegations of wrongdoing were investigated prior to engaging in operations to punish Native Americans. He also tried to limit and even prohibit the sale or trade of alcohol to the Native Americans.

Atkinson's most significant military operations occurred in the course of the 1832 Black Hawk War, during which he was both the overall commander and the field commander at the end of the conflict. While he was criticized for the opening operations of the war, he was successful in bringing the war to a conclusion at the Battle of Bad Axe (August 1–2, 1832). There Atkinson defeated the Sauks and Foxes and their allies under the overall leadership of Chief Black Hawk prior to the arrival of reinforcements led by Brigadier General Winfield Scott. Atkinson then directed the relocation of the Sauks and Foxes back across the Mississippi River to a reservation along the Iowa River. He was later involved in the relocation of the Winnebago tribe from its ancestral lands in Wisconsin and Illinois across the Mississippi River to Iowa.

Unlike many of his contemporaries in the army, Atkinson was seldom involved in controversy and served quite competently and professionally until his death at Jefferson Barracks, Missouri, on June 14, 1842.

JOHN THOMAS BROOM

See also
Bad Axe, Battle of; Black Hawk; Black Hawk War; Sauks and Foxes; Scott, Winfield; Winnebagos

References
Hagan, William T. "General Henry Atkinson and the Militia." *Military Affairs* 23(4) (Winter 1959–1960): 194–197.
Nichols, Roger L. *General Henry Atkinson: A Western Military Career.* Norman: University of Oklahoma Press, 1965.

Wesley, Edgar Bruce. "Life at a Frontier Post: Fort Atkinson, 1823–1826." *Journal of the American Military Institute* 3(4) (Winter 1939): 202–209.

Attakullakulla

Birth Date: ca. 1712
Death Date: ca. 1780–1785

Cherokee leader. Born sometime around 1712 on Sevier Island in the French Broad River of Tennessee, Attakullakulla (also known as Little Carpenter) became an important peace chief who shaped diplomatic relations between the Cherokees and the Europeans for more than 50 years. In his youth he was one of seven Cherokees who traveled to London in 1730 to meet England's King George II. A leading peace chief by 1738, Attakullakulla was decidedly pro-British.

Captured by French-allied Ottawa warriors about 1740, Attakullakulla was held captive until 1748. On his return to the Overhill Cherokees around 1750, he became the top lieutenant to his uncle Connecorte (Old Hop), the head chief of Chota and considered the Cherokees' best warrior.

In the 1750s and 1760s, Attakullakulla dominated Cherokee diplomacy. Although he usually favored the British, he was a consummate diplomat, always hoping for a peaceful resolution to problems but looking out for the best interests of the Cherokees. He negotiated with both French and British officials and also curried favor among the Virginians and South Carolinians as he negotiated advantageous trade relations. He championed the cause of increased military protection in the form of European forts, especially Fort Loudoun.

With the outbreak of the French and Indian War (1754–1763), Attakullakulla and other Cherokees fought alongside the British. The Cherokee Nation as a whole, however, remained divided, eventually leading to the Cherokee War (1759–1761). In 1759 Governor William Henry Lyttelton of South Carolina took hostage a Cherokee delegation, including the great war chief Oconostota. Attakullakulla successfully negotiated Oconostota's release, but the remaining hostages were killed. As a result, the Cherokees besieged Fort Loudoun and cut off all supplies to it.

Attakullakulla attempted to negotiate and prevent the escalation of violence. When he was unsuccessful, he warned the British of an impending attack and eventually ransomed Lieutenant John Stuart, helping him escape to Virginia. Stuart and Colonel James Grant negotiated peace with the Cherokees in 1761. Attakullakulla was also part of the larger peace process again in 1763, when the French and Indian War ended.

Attakullakulla remained active in diplomatic affairs through the 1770s. He unsuccessfully argued against the 1776 Cherokee attack on the southern colonies and helped to negotiate the 1777 Treaty of Long Island of Holston (referring to the Holston River) with the Patriots, which ended the war. He lost prominence, however, as a large faction of Cherokees under his son, Dragging Canoe, continued fighting the Americans. Attakullakulla died sometime between 1780 and 1785 at an unknown location.

LISA L. CRUTCHFIELD

See also
Cherokees; Cherokee War; Oconostota

References
Hatley, Tom. *The Dividing Paths: Cherokees and South Carolinians through the Revolutionary Era.* New York: Oxford University Press, 1995.
Oliphant, John. *Peace and War on the Anglo-Cherokee Frontier 1753–63.* Baton Rouge: Louisiana State University Press, 2001.

Auglaize

See Glaize, The

Auglaize, Council on the

See Council on the Auglaize

Augur, Christopher Columbus

Birth Date: July 10, 1821
Death Date: January 16, 1898

U.S. Army officer. Christopher Columbus Augur was born in Kendall, New York, on July 10, 1821, but grew up in Michigan. He graduated from the U.S. Military Academy, West Point, in 1843 and was commissioned a second lieutenant. Augur served in a variety of posts, mostly in the American West, and during the Mexican-American War (1846–1848). From 1855 to 1858 he participated in the Yakima-Rogue War (1855–1858) in the Pacific Northwest. In 1856 as a captain, Augur was principally responsible for constructing Fort Hoskins along the Luckiamute River in Oregon. In 1860 he was appointed commandant of cadets at West Point.

Promoted to major in 1861, in the opening months of the American Civil War (1861–1865) Augur organized defenses in Washington, D.C., before being given command of a brigade, with the rank of brigadier general of Volunteers, in November 1861. He subsequently saw action along the Rappahannock River and at Fredericksburg in April 1862. Given command of a division in Major General Nathaniel Banks's II Corps, Augur performed well in Virginia. During the Battle of Cedar Mountain (August 9, 1862), he was seriously wounded. Cited for gallantry during the battle, he was promoted to major general of Volunteers later in the month. He did not recover from his wounds until November 1862, when he was assigned to New Orleans to serve as Banks's second-in-command specifically upon Banks's request.

Brigadier General Christopher Columbus Augur, who commanded the Department of the Platte, played a key role in bringing about the 1867 Medicine Lodge and 1868 Fort Laramie treaties. (Library of Congress)

Augur's remaining field service during the war occurred in the Mississippi River campaigns, during part of which he commanded a division in the Army of the Gulf. In early 1863 he took command of the District of Baton Rouge, and he played a key role in the successful siege of Port Hudson, Louisiana, from March 4 to July 8, 1863. Augur next commanded XXII Corps and then the Department of Washington, D.C., from October 1863 until early 1866. He was by then well known for his strong managerial skills.

From 1867 to 1871 Augur commanded the Department of the Platte. Promoted to brigadier general in the regular army in 1869, he subsequently commanded the Department of Texas (1871–1875) during that department's most active role in the Indian Wars and then commanded the Department of the Gulf (1875–1878). As commander of the Department of the Platte, he played a key role in formulating the 1867 Medicine Lodge Treaty and the 1868 Treaty of Fort Laramie. After 1878 he held a variety of command posts, mostly in the East, before retiring as a brigadier general in 1885. Augur then resided in Virginia. He died in Washington, D.C., on January 16, 1898.

PAUL G. PIERPAOLI JR.

See also
Fort Laramie, Treaty of (1868); Medicine Lodge Treaty; Yakima-Rogue War

References
Augur, E. P. *The Augur Family*. Middletown, CT: Self-published, 1904.
Eicher, John H., and David J. Eicher. *Civil War High Commands*. Stanford, CA: Stanford University Press, 2001.

Augusta, Congress of
Start Date: November 3, 1763
End Date: November 10, 1763

General congress among the governors of the four southernmost colonies and the leaders of the five major southeastern Native American confederacies in Augusta, Georgia, held during November 3–10, 1763. The royal governors of the four southern British colonies (Francis Fauquier of Virginia, Arthur Dobbs of North Carolina, Thomas Boone of South Carolina, and James Wright of Georgia) joined John Stuart, the British superintendent of Indian affairs for the southern department, to meet with Native American representatives for the Catawbas, Cherokees, Creeks, Chickasaws, and Choctaws. The native delegation totaled more than 900 people. The main goals of the congress were to repair Anglo–Native American relations after the French and Indian War (1754–1763), to settle grievances over the deerskin trade, and to establish a firm boundary between white settlements and Native American hunting grounds. The treaty signed on November 10 mostly unified various prior agreements made separately between the governors and the Native Americans, with one important exception. The Creeks, for the first time since 1733, ceded territory to Georgia in exchange for an enforceable boundary.

Land cessions and a peaceful south were priorities for the British government in 1763. Having exhausted its coffers in defeating France and Spain in North America, Britain soon found itself fighting Pontiac's Rebellion (1763) in the Ohio Valley and Great Lakes region. Recognizing that anti-British sentiment still lingered among southern tribes, the royal government ordered the governors to call a general meeting and prevent a southern expansion of the Native American uprising. Fauquier, Dobbs, and Boone attended out of obligation to the royal government but felt little pressing need to do so, as their colonies had largely settled Native American affairs in separate treaties during the last days of the French and Indian War.

The same was true for many of the Native American delegates. The Catawbas and Cherokees used the congress to raise long-standing complaints of trader abuse and white encroachment, but little new came from the talks. The Chickasaws, staunch British allies and far removed from the irritation of British settlers, made few demands. The Choctaws, at war with the Creeks, believed that the journey was too dangerous and sent only two representatives. Despite the congress's goal of universality, its main significance lay in the particulars of Georgia-Creek relations.

For Georgia's Wright, the congress was crucial. For many of the Creeks, avoiding the congress was equally important. Anglo-Creek relations had been strained by the war with France, fueled by Creek fears that the British wanted to seize all the Creek lands. Word had quickly spread in advance of the congress that the British wanted to purchase Creek lands in Georgia, giving new life to old fears. A month before the congress these tensions increased when Creek warriors killed a number of Georgia traders. Wright, whose young and sparsely populated colony would bear the brunt of an Anglo-Creek war, eagerly sought to ease tensions, convincing the governors to move the congress from Charles Town (present-day Charleston, South Carolina) to Augusta to assuage Creek concerns. Even with this concession, few Upper Creeks (among whom anti-British feeling ran deepest) attended, and none of their most influential leaders went.

The Lower Creeks were ultimately persuaded to attend and to cede lands due to the influence of the respected traders Lachlan McGillivray and George Galphin. At the congress they allowed Georgia's territory to increase dramatically from the original seacoast grants made in 1733, giving Georgia its first true native boundary. The Upper Creeks disagreed with the cession but ultimately ratified it a year later.

For the Creeks, the Augusta Congress was the major turning point in their relations with the British. The Creeks' decades-old policy of neutrality was unsustainable without European rivals competing for their affections, and they now found themselves encircled by a British government constantly demanding land cessions, a process that would continue under the U.S. government until the era of removal beginning in the 1830s.

ROBERT PAULETT

See also

Catawbas; Cherokees; Cherokee War; Chickasaws; Choctaws; Creeks; French and Indian War; Indian Presents; Pontiac's Rebellion; Proclamation of 1763; Stuart, John

References

Cashin, Edward J. *Lachlan McGillivray, Indian Trader: The Shaping of the Southern Colonial Frontier.* Athens: University of Georgia Press, 1992.

Corkran, David H. *The Creek Frontier, 1540–1783.* Norman: University of Oklahoma Press, 1967.

De Vorsey, Louis, Jr. *The Indian Boundary in the Southern Colonies, 1763–1775.* Chapel Hill: University of North Carolina Press, 1966.

Hahn, Stephen C. *The Invention of the Creek Nation, 1670–1763.* Lincoln: University of Nebraska Press, 2004.

B

Bacon's Rebellion
Start Date: June 1676
End Date: January 1677

Violent uprising in Virginia led by Nathaniel Bacon, a member of the rural planter class. At one time identified as the first manifestation of revolutionary sentiment in English North America, Bacon's Rebellion is now seen as more the result of a power struggle between two colonial leaders.

A number of factors contributed to the unrest, chief among them a declining economy brought on by a sharp drop in the price of tobacco, the result of increasing competition from Maryland and the Carolinas. This economic crisis affected small farmers and planters alike, and many Virginia farmers relied almost exclusively on tobacco cultivation. The ongoing Anglo-Dutch wars also wrought considerable havoc, disrupting trade and increasing the price of imported English manufactured goods. A series of natural disasters had also taken a heavy toll. These included hurricanes, dry spells, and hailstorms.

Internal Virginia politics played the key factor in the outbreak of the rebellion. In an effort to expand their landholdings, the colonials increasingly encroached onto native lands in the western part of the colony, leading to armed conflict. The natives found themselves a ready scapegoat for the colony's other problems.

In July 1675, apparently in a dispute over nonpayment of trade items, members of the Doeg tribe raided the plantation belonging to Thomas Mathews near the Potomac River in the Northern Neck area of Virginia. Several Doegs were killed in the raid. Unfortunately, the colonists then mounted a retaliatory strike against the wrong tribe, the Susquehannocks, and this led to a series of native raids along the western frontier.

Hoping to prevent the spread of hostilities, Virginia governor Sir William Berkeley ordered an investigation. This led to a meeting between the colonists and natives and the murder of several chiefs. Throughout the crises Berkeley sought to please both sides, leading to anger on the part of many western colonists, who believed that the government had abandoned them in the face of the native threat.

The leader of the western colonists was the intemperate yet eloquent Nathaniel Bacon, a distant relative of Berkeley and a member of the House of Burgesses since 1675. Bacon opposed Berkeley's conciliatory policies and disregarded a direct government order by seizing some members of the Appomattox tribe for allegedly stealing corn, whereupon Berkeley reprimanded him. In the western part of the colony most likely a majority of the colonists sided with Bacon, believing that Berkeley was taking the natives' side.

Berkeley sought to pursue a middle course, ordering local natives to give up their powder and ammunition while, in March 1676, calling the Long Assembly. This body declared war on hostile natives and took steps to strengthen Virginia's frontier defenses. But this action necessitated a sharp increase in taxes. The assembly also took charge of trading with the natives, insisting that this be done through a government commission, supposedly to see that the natives were not receiving arms and ammunition, but the commission also brought financial gain to close associates of the governor.

Bacon was one of those who had traded with the natives and was adversely affected by this decision. In addition, he was angry because Berkeley had denied him a commission as a militia officer. Bacon then secured his election as the "general" of a local militia unit, promising to pay for its operations against the natives from his own pocket.

In 1676, Nathaniel Bacon led a revolt of colonial Virginia's frontier settlers. Known as Bacon's Rebellion, it was fought against Virginia governor William Berkeley and involved harsh actions against Native Americans. (Library of Congress)

When Bacon and his men drove a number of friendly Pamunkeys from their lands, Berkeley rode to Bacon's headquarters at Henrico with a force of 300 well-armed men to confront him, whereupon Bacon and his 200 men fled into the forest. Berkeley then issued two decrees, the first declaring Bacon a rebel and the second pardoning his men if they would return to their homes. Bacon would lose his seat on the council, to which he had won election that year, but Berkeley promised him a fair trial. Bacon failed to comply with Berkeley's order. Instead Bacon led an attack on the friendly Occaneechee natives along the Roanoke River, the border between Virginia and North Carolina, seizing their stocks of beaver pelts in the process.

With events now seemingly spinning out of control, Berkeley announced that he was ready to forgive Bacon's disobedience and pardon him if he agreed to be sent to England for trial there before King Charles II. The House of Burgesses, however, insisted that Bacon apologize and ask for the governor's forgiveness. At the same time Bacon, supported by the western landowners who approved of his actions toward the natives, won election to the House of Burgesses.

In June 1676 Bacon traveled to Jamestown to take part in the new assembly. He has been mistakenly credited for a number of political reforms enacted by this assembly, including granting freedmen the right to vote and limiting the terms of officeholders. Bacon's only real platform, however, was his opposition to natives.

On his arrival at Jamestown, Bacon was arrested and taken before Berkeley and the council, where he apologized for his actions. Berkeley then pardoned Bacon and allowed him to take his seat. Neither Berkeley nor the council understood the level of support that Bacon enjoyed. That support became clear when in the midst of debate over policies regarding the natives, Bacon stalked out of the meeting and left Jamestown, only to return a few days later with some 500 armed followers, who surrounded the assembly house.

Bacon then confronted Berkeley and demanded that he be placed in charge of all the colony's forces against the natives. Berkeley courageously refused this demand, which was made at gunpoint, and offered to grant Bacon his previous militia commission but not control of the Virginia forces. With some of Bacon's men threatening to shoot members of the House of Burgesses, Berkeley at length gave in and granted Bacon's request that he be made "general" and commander of the Virginia Militia and be allowed to lead it free of government interference in a campaign against the natives.

For the next three months Bacon was in firm control of Jamestown, and on July 30 he issued his "Declaration of the People," claiming that Berkeley was corrupt and had shaped his native policies in order to bring financial reward to himself and his friends. Bacon also issued a decree requiring an oath in which the swearer would have to agree to obey him in any manner that Bacon deemed necessary. Berkeley meanwhile fled to his estate of Green Spring on the Eastern Shore and once again declared Bacon a rebel. Much to his dismay, the governor found that he could attract few armed supporters. Indeed, many Virginians were upset with Berkeley for turning on Bacon in the middle of a campaign against Native Americans.

Bacon used his authority as commander of the militia to lead a force of about 1,000 colonists against the natives, not to the western part of the colony, where the threat actually lay, but against the peaceful Pamunkeys, who had been friendly with the English since 1646. The colonists drove the Pamunkeys into Dragon Swamp, pursuing them during a three-week span and killing or capturing only 10, 7 of them women and children. Bacon then dismissed most of his force and pressed on with some 150 of his most loyal followers. Shortly thereafter they came across a Pamunkey camp, where they killed 53 natives, most of them women and children. Bacon declared the campaign at an end. In none of his fighting against the natives did he do battle with those who were actually hostile.

Bacon emerged from the campaign to learn that Berkeley's followers had infiltrated the ships of the Virginia navy, enabling the governor's return to Jamestown. Bacon then marched on Jamestown, besieging it. On September 16 Berkeley's supporters briefly sallied from Jamestown and attacked Bacon's siege positions, only to be driven back with a dozen casualties. Berkeley departed again with his followers for the Eastern Shore.

Bacon now overreached. On September 19 he ordered Jamestown, the oldest permanent English settlement in the New World, burned to the ground, although he did save most of the valuable state records. This deed led many Virginians to question their support for Bacon, who lost other followers by admitting to his military force both indentured servants and slaves. This decision threatened to overturn the entire social order of the colony.

On October 26, 1676, Bacon died abruptly of "Bloodie Flux," a fever accompanied by virulent dysentery that was probably a direct result of the time spent in the backwoods and swamps. An obscure follower, Joseph Ingram, took over for him, and the rebellion turned from its chief raison d'être of warfare against hostile natives to mere looting and robbery.

Gradually Berkeley's forces grew in strength. They controlled the waters and, aided by the addition of several larger merchant vessels that they intercepted on arrival from England, mounted increasing numbers of raids up the James River and York River against rebel strongholds. Resistance strengthened before the chief rebel stronghold of West Point, whereupon Berkeley authorized Thomas Grantham, captain of the merchantman *Concord,* to negotiate the surrender of the remaining rebels. There Grantham secured the surrender of some 700 freemen, servants, and slaves in January 1677. Bacon's Rebellion was for all intents and purposes at an end.

In the spring of 1677 at Middle Plantation the Virginia government entered into a number of peace treaties with the natives in an effort to repair relations; the Susquehannocks had apparently left western Virginia in mid-1676. Charles II had reacted to news of the rebellion by recalling Berkeley and dispatching a force of 1,000 soldiers, who arrived after the rebellion was over. The first regular English troops to be stationed in Virginia, they were soon withdrawn. Bacon's Rebellion was in no way a precursor of the American Revolutionary War.

JAIME RAMÓN OLIVARES AND SPENCER C. TUCKER

See also

Appomattocks; Berkeley, William; Jamestown; Occaneechees; Pamunkeys; Powhatan Confederacy; Susquehannocks; Virginia-Indian Treaty of 1677/1680

References

Shea, William L. *The Virginia Militia in the Seventeenth Century.* Baton Rouge: Louisiana State University Press, 1983.

Washburn, Wilcomb E. *The Governor and the Rebel: A History of Bacon's Rebellion in Virginia.* Chapel Hill: University of North Carolina Press, 1957.

Webb, Stephen Saunders. *1676: The End of American Independence.* New York: Knopf, 1984.

Wertenbaker, Thomas Jefferson. *Torchbearer of the Revolution: The Story of Bacon's Rebellion and Its Leader.* Princeton, NJ: Princeton University Press, 1940.

Bad Axe, Battle of
Start Date: August 1, 1832
End Date: August 2, 1832

Engagement that took place during August 1–2, 1832, between the Sauks and Foxes under the leadership of Chief Black Hawk and U.S. Army troops and militia from Illinois and the Michigan Territory. The Battle of Bad Axe, sometimes called the Bad Axe Massacre, was fought near present-day Victory, Wisconsin, in the southwestern portion of the state along the Mississippi River. It was the last major battle of the short-lived Black Hawk War (1832).

The Black Hawk War began in the spring of 1832 when Chief Black Hawk and his followers attempted to halt the encroachment of white settlement on what had been their lands. Black Hawk's men were often called the British Band because the chief had made an alliance with Great Britain during the War of 1812 and was still closely linked to the British in Canada.

The British Band numbered nearly 1,500 warriors in the spring of 1832 when it crossed into Illinois and began attacking white American settlements. Black Hawk meanwhile believed that he would receive aid in money, weapons, supplies or even soldiers from the British. Such aid was not forthcoming, however, and the Illinois state and Michigan territorial militias soon arrived on the scene to protect the settlers.

By the summer the militias, now aided by U.S. Army regulars under Brevet Brigadier General Henry Atkinson, were closing in on Black Hawk's band. The two sides fought a small skirmish, resulting in a victory for the Americans. After the battle, Black Hawk and his men retreated toward the Mississippi River.

As they approached the river on August 1, Black Hawk and 500 of his followers, who now included women and children, were faced with two options. They could cross the river or continue along the riverbank until they reached the safety of other Native American tribes in the area, particularly the Winnebagos. Black Hawk favored the latter, but many of his followers began building rafts and started to cross the river. This effort took considerable time, and while a number of Native Americans were able to cross, many others were trapped by the arrival of the steamboat *Warrior,* which had been pressed into service by the U.S. government when the Black Hawk War began. Realizing that the situation was now hopeless, Black Hawk tried to wave a white piece of cloth to surrender, but he was either not seen or his communication was misunderstood or ignored by the Americans on the *Warrior,* who opened fire. Twenty-three Native Americans, including 1 woman, were killed by the time the shooting stopped.

Black Hawk and some of his followers fled north toward Canada, but many stayed behind to fight. The second day of the battle, August 2, turned into a massacre as the soldiers killed everyone who tried to run for cover or cross the river. More than 150 people were killed outright, including women and children. Reportedly the soldiers scalped most of the dead. U.S. forces captured an

The steamer *Warrior* fires at Indians on a raft during the Battle of Bad Axe in the short-lived 1832 Black Hawk War. Illustration from *Das illustrierte Mississippithal* by H. Lewis. Düsseldorf: Arnz & Co, 1857. (Library of Congress)

additional 75 Native Americans. Army casualties amounted to 5 killed and 19 wounded.

Those Native Americans who escaped across the river found only temporary reprieve, for many of them were subsequently killed by Sioux warriors acting with the army. The Sioux brought 68 scalps and 22 prisoners to U.S. Indian agent Joseph M. Street in the weeks after the battle.

The Bad Axe Massacre was the last major action of the Black Hawk War. Chief Black Hawk escaped but eventually surrendered at the end of August. He was held in a prison in St. Louis, Missouri, before being sent to Washington, D.C., in 1833. In the capital he met briefly with President Andrew Jackson before being sent to another prison in Virginia. Black Hawk was eventually released and returned to his tribe.

SETH A. WEITZ

See also

Black Hawk; Black Hawk War; Sauks and Foxes

References

Bowes, John P., and Paul C. Rosier. *Black Hawk and the War of 1832: Removal in the North.* New York: Chelsea House, 2007.

Jung, Patrick J. *The Black Hawk War of 1832.* Norman: University of Oklahoma Press, 2007.

Trask, Kerry A. *Black Hawk: The Battle for the Heart of America.* New York: Holt, 2006.

Baker Massacre

See Marias Massacre

Bannock War
Event Date: 1878

Uprising of the Bannock tribe against white settlers of Oregon and Idaho in 1878. The Bannocks, a subdivision of the Shoshone Nation, had long resented white encroachment on their ancestral lands. This animosity peaked after the Native American defeat during the 1877 Nez Perce War and after the Bannocks failed to receive several deliveries of supplies from Indian agents.

In the spring of 1878 several Bannock bands congregated on the Camas Prairie in southern Idaho to gather camas roots, a major part of their diet. They discovered, however, that white settlers had encroached on the land and decimated the root fields by grazing hogs and cattle there. On May 30 a Bannock shot and killed 2 white herders and wounded another. This incident sharply divided the tribe. Most left for the reservation at Fort Hall, but a group of about 200 warriors under the leadership of Chief Buffalo Horn banded together with the intention of driving out the white settlers by force.

News of the herders' killings reached Boise Barracks. Captain Reuben Bernard of the 1st U.S. Cavalry Regiment and Colonel Orlando Robbins of the territorial militia mobilized forces to meet the Bannock threat. Meanwhile, Buffalo Horn and his warriors set out on a path of destruction toward eastern Oregon. They burned settlements, looted homes, attacked wagon trains, and indiscriminately killed whites. On June 8 a civilian volunteer company from Silver City intercepted Buffalo Horn with a raiding party of 50 warriors near South Mountain and engaged them in a brief skirmish, during which Buffalo Horn was killed. The remaining members of the band withdrew to Stein's Mountain in an effort to recruit support from other tribes. There they secured reinforcements from disaffected Paiute, Umatilla, and Cayuse warriors and also secured new leadership under Malheur Paiute chief Egan.

Robbins and Bernard continued their chase of the hostiles, now led by Egan, catching up with them at Silver Creek on June 22, 1878. Scouting the Native American camp that night, Bernard planned an attack for the following morning. On June 23 he sent Robbins's scouts on a charge through the Native American camp in order to drive them into his dismounted cavalry hidden in an ambush position farther downstream. In the ensuing melee some of the Native Americans escaped, but nearly 100 died. Bernard's forces suffered only 5 killed. Among the casualties was Chief Egan, desperately wounded allegedly at the hands of Robbins himself.

Survivors of the battle, now under the leadership of Chief Otis (Oytes), escaped to John Day River, where they expected to join warriors from other tribes. Brigadier General Oliver O. Howard, commander of the Department of the Columbia, assumed leadership of Bernard's column on June 25. Howard dispatched 12 scouts under Robbins ahead of the main body to locate the remaining hostile Native Americans. On July 8 Howard and Bernard received word from scouts that the hostiles had created a defensive position high on the cliffs above Birch Creek, near Pilot Butte. In spite of the steep ridges, Bernard's troops charged the position, forcing the Native Americans to withdraw again.

Howard then moved north to Fort Walla Walla in an attempt to cut off the retreat. The Native Americans changed course, however, and moved southward to the Umatilla Reservation in an attempt to coerce that tribe's support. Troops of the 21st Infantry Regiment under the command of Captain Evan Miles abandoned their plan to reinforce Howard and instead met this new threat near Cayuse Station. On July 13 nearly 500 hostiles launched a surprise attack on Miles's exhausted troops, but the soldiers quickly regrouped and counterattacked, causing the Native Americans to flee southward. The neutral Umatillas, who were prepared to do battle, observed the fight, waiting to side with the victor. They thus offered their services to the United States against the Bannocks in exchange for amnesty.

On July 16 a band of Umatillas approached the retreating Bannocks under the guise of discussions and assassinated Chief Egan. Native American resistance dwindled away during the remainder of the summer. The remaining hostile bands scattered throughout the countryside, occasionally murdering local whites and destroying their property. Many others returned to the reservation. Troops under Colonel Nelson A. Miles defeated a Bannock band attempting to retreat through the Yellowstone Valley on September 4. Lieutenant Colonel James W. Forsyth with several troops of the 1st Cavalry subdued the last hostile contingent on September 20 along the John Day River. The last 131 Bannocks surrendered to the U.S. Army shortly thereafter. After a brief detention at Fort Keogh, they were moved permanently to the Fort Hall Reservation.

BRADFORD A. WINEMAN

See also

Forsyth, James William; Fort Walla Walla; Howard, Oliver Otis; Miles, Nelson Appleton; Shoshones

References

Brimlow, George Francis. *The Bannock Indian War of 1878.* Caldwell, ID: Caxton Printers, 1938.

Glassley, Ray Hoard. *Pacific Northwest Indian War.* Portland, OR: Binfords and Mort, 1953.

Barbed Wire

From the first domestication of animals, men sought to find effective barriers to contain them. Fences of both wood and stone appeared, but by the second half of the 19th century ranchers in the vast expanse of the North American West employed fences of smooth wire strung between posts. Wire was easily erected, relatively inexpensive, would not rot, and was unaffected by fire. Smooth wire was not terribly effective as a barrier, however, as cattle could push through it. By the 1860s manufacturers experimented with adding sharp points to the wire. In 1868 Michael Kelly invented a wire with points that was used in quantity until 1874, when Joseph Glidden of DeKalb, Illinois, came up with a process whereby barbs were placed at intervals on smooth wire and fixed in place by a twisted second wire. Subsequently hundreds of patents were issued on thousands of varieties of barbed wire based on this principle.

Barbed wire was one of the many factors disrupting the traditional Native American way of life in the West. Heretofore Native Americans had roamed the Great Plains without restrictions and without any sense of private land ownership. In many respects, therefore, barbed wire became a cultural weapon. The buffalo no longer had the same ability to roam freely, and Native Americans no longer had the same freedom to hunt them. Barbed wire thus helped destroy the communal nature of Native American society and contributed to the near extinction of the vast Plains buffalo herds in the last quarter of the 19th century.

Barbed wire also came to have military uses. The British employed it to protect their military encampments during the Boer War (1899–1902), but World War I (1914–1918) saw its most extensive employment. Once the front lines on the Western Front stabilized at the end of 1914, both sides erected wire barriers to break up enemy attacks and to prevent trench raids to secure prisoners. Belts of barbed wire became a ubiquitous feature of no-man's-land and contributed greatly to the heavy casualties of the war. The need to deal with barbed-wire obstacles was one of the motives behind British and French development of the tank. During World War II (1939–1945) barbed wire was a feature of concentration camps and prisoner of war facilities. More lethal razor wire was developed and utilized during the Vietnam War (1965–1973) and other late-20th-century conflicts.

SPENCER C. TUCKER

See also
Buffalo

References

McCallum, Henry D., and Frances T. McCallum. *The Wire That Fenced the West.* Norman: University of Oklahoma Press, 1965.

Razac, Olivier. *Barbed Wire: A Political History.* New York: New Press, 2002.

Simpson, Andy, ed. *Hot Blood and Cold Steel: Life and Death in the Trenches of the First World War.* London: Tom Donovan, 1993.

Barboncito
Birth Date: 1820
Death Date: March 16, 1871

Navajo leader who signed a treaty with the U.S. government in 1868 that eventually resulted in the creation of the Navajo Nation, the largest Native American homeland in the United States. Born in 1820 in Cañon de Chelly (Canyon de Chelly) in present-day Arizona, Barboncito's oratorical skills, strong personality, and pragmatism enabled him to become one of the council chiefs of the Navajo people. His name, which literally means "little beard" in Spanish, referred to what the Navajo people called a mustache. Unlike most Navajo men, Barboncito had an ample mustache.

Following the American invasion of Santa Fe during the early stages of the Mexican-American War (1846–1848), Barboncito, along with several other Navajo chiefs, signed the Doniphan Treaty with the United States. Although both sides agreed to coexist peacefully, conflict quickly erupted when American settlers began seizing Navajo land. Nevertheless, throughout the 1850s Barboncito consistently sought a peaceful resolution to differences between the Navajos and the United States. In 1860, however, Barboncito initiated armed resistance against rapidly increasing American encroachment onto Native American–held lands. In 1864 Colonel Christopher "Kit" Carson forced 8,000 Navajos and many Mescalero Apaches to march more than 300 miles to the Bosque Redondo reservation in New Mexico. While some 200 Navajos died on the so-called Long Walk, more than 2,000 died of hunger and disease at the new reservation.

In 1868 Barboncito led a Navajo delegation to Washington, D.C., to petition President Andrew Johnson to return the Navajos to their

Navajo chief Barboncito signed a treaty with the U.S. government in 1868 that led to the creation of the Navajo Nation, the largest Native American homeland in the United States. (National Anthropological Archives, Smithsonian Institution, OPPS NEG 55766)

native homeland. Barboncito was able to arrange a compromise that ensured peace, and on June 1, 1868, the Navajo chiefs, led by Barboncito, signed a treaty with the United States that resulted in the return of the Navajo people to their traditional homeland. Occupying 26,000 square miles in northeastern Arizona, southeastern Utah, and northwestern New Mexico, the Navajo Nation allowed the Navajos to continue their cultural traditions on a reduced portion of their ancestral lands at a time when most American Indians were being deported to distant reservations, where they were subjected to intensive cultural assimilation programs. Barboncito died peacefully at his home in Cañon de Chelly on March 16, 1871.

MICHAEL R. HALL

See also
Apaches; Bosque Redondo; Canyon de Chelly, Arizona; Carson, Christopher Houston; Navajos

References

McNitt, Frank. *Navajo Wars: Military Campaigns, Slave Raids, and Reprisals.* Albuquerque: University of New Mexico Press, 1990.

Thompson, Gerald. *The Army and the Navajo: The Bosque Redondo Reservation Experiment, 1863–1868.* Tucson: University of Arizona Press, 1976.

Bascom Affair
Start Date: January 27, 1861
End Date: February 18, 1861

Event that triggered the Apache Wars (1861–1866) fought between the United States and the Apaches in the American Southwest. The Bascom Affair began on January 27, 1861, when a group of Coyotero Apaches raided John Ward's ranch along Sonoita Creek in present-day Arizona. The Coyoteros stole 20 head of cattle and abducted Felix, the 12-year-old son of Ward's Mexican mistress, Jesusa Martínez. Ward's ranch, of which he took possession in 1857, was located on land acquired by the United States from Mexico in the 1853 Gadsden Purchase. Whereas many Native Americans initially welcomed the transition from Mexican to American control, the American quest to acquire land during the 1850s quickly led to tensions between whites and Native Americans.

After returning to his ranch and learning of the Apache raid, Ward set off for Fort Buchanan, about 12 miles northeast at the head of the Sonoita Valley, to report the incident to Lieutenant Colonel Pitcairn Morrison, the commander of the fort. The next morning Morrison dispatched Second Lieutenant George N. Bascom and a contingent of troops to investigate the events at Ward's ranch. Bascom, an inexperienced soldier who graduated at the bottom of his class at the U.S. Military Academy and was only recently assigned to Fort Buchanan, mistakenly assumed that the raid had been conducted by the Chokonen band of Chiricahua Apaches led by Cochise.

On January 29, 1861, Morrison ordered Bascom and 54 men mounted on mules to hasten to Apache Pass, about 150 miles to the northeast, and rescue the boy and the stolen cattle. Ward and an interpreter accompanied the expedition. On February 3, 1861, Bascom's command arrived at Siphon Canyon, a short distance from Cochise's camp at Goodwin Canyon. Upon learning of Bascom's presence, Cochise, who had been friendly toward Americans up to this point, and six members of his family went to greet Bascom's party. After inviting Cochise and his family into a tent, Bascom demanded the return of the boy and the cattle. Notwithstanding Cochise's vehement denial that he had knowledge of the raid on Ward's farm, Bascom informed Cochise that he was a hostage. Following a scuffle Cochise was able to escape, but his family remained prisoners of Bascom.

After a series of skirmishes between Americans and Cochise's followers in the area surrounding Apache Pass, Bascom's troops executed Cochise's family on February 18, 1861, in retaliation for the Americans who had been killed by Cochise's men. Bascom returned to Fort Buchanan the next day and was commended by Morrison, despite the fact that the kidnapped boy, who had been adopted by the White Mountain Apaches and later became a U.S. Army scout known as Mickey Free, was not recovered. The moment Cochise learned that his brother and nephews had been executed proved cathartic for the Apaches. Cochise's Chiricahua

Apaches, joined by Mangas Coloradas and his Mimbres, launched the Apache Wars, which lasted with only brief respites until 1886, when Geronimo finally surrendered.

MICHAEL R. HALL

See also
Apaches; Apache Wars; Cochise; Geronimo; Mangas Coloradas; Victorio

References
Aleshire, Peter. *Cochise: The Life and Times of the Great Apache Chief.* New York: Wiley, 2001.
Roberts, David. *Once They Moved like the Wind: Cochise, Geronimo, and the Apache Wars.* New York: Touchstone, 1993.
Sweeney, Edwin R. *Cochise: Chiricahua Apache Chief.* Norman: University of Oklahoma Press, 1991.

Bates Creek, Battle of
See Dull Knife Fight

Bear Paw Mountains, Battle of
Start Date: September 30, 1877
End Date: October 5, 1877

The last battle of the Nez Perce War of 1877. The Battle of Bear Paw Mountains between U.S. forces and the Nez Perce tribe took place from September 30 to October 5, 1877. The Bear Paw Mountains are located 16 miles south of present-day Chinook, Montana, less than 40 miles from the Canadian border. The battle ended a longer conflict that had begun 14 years earlier when the U.S. government sought to reduce reservation boundaries to protect 19,000 Americans who had invaded tribal lands in search of gold and furs.

In an effort to keep the peace, Nez Perce leader Lawyer and other members of the treaty faction had signed a new pact with the United States (the so-called Thief Treaty of 1863) that reduced the reservation by 6 million acres. Old Joseph and White Bird, furious that the terms of an 1855 agreement had been altered, rejected the new treaty provisions. While most of the Nez Perces abided by the new confines, the nontreaty bands refused. Joseph's band continued to occupy the Wallawa Valley in northeastern Oregon. Before his death in 1871, Old Joseph made his son Young Joseph promise that he would never sell tribal lands. Young Joseph's people managed to live in peace among the whites until the rapidly growing settler population brought renewed pressure for their removal. By 1877 Joseph and others appeared ready to comply.

On June 14, 1877, the situation turned violent when Nez Perce warriors attacked a group of local settlers, killing four of them. Brigadier General Oliver O. Howard, in the area to negotiate with Joseph, mobilized the army in response.

On June 17, 1877, the Battle of White Bird Canyon in Idaho Territory formally began the Nez Perce War. Rather than stand and

A scene from the Battle of Bear Paw Mountains, September 30–October 5, 1877, the culminating engagement of the Nez Perce War. Illustration from *Harper's Weekly*, November 17, 1877. (Library of Congress)

fight, Joseph, Looking Glass, and White Bird fled into the mountains with 800 men, women, and children. During the 1,500-mile trek that followed, the Nez Perces outflanked and eluded more than 2,000 U.S. soldiers. During the retreat the Nez Perces fought only defensive battles, a tactic that they quickly perfected as the fleeing band found refuge in canyons and forests and among Yellowstone Park's steaming geysers en route to sanctuary in Canada.

In late September 1877 the Nez Perces camped on the banks of Snake Creek, located just north of the Bear Paw Mountains. Believing that they had outmaneuvered Howard's soldiers, Looking Glass persuaded tribal leaders to permit a rest before making the final push into Canada. This halt proved to be a major error, for it enabled additional army forces under Colonel Nelson A. Miles to catch up.

On September 30, 1877, Miles and 400 men of the 2nd Cavalry, the 7th Cavalry, and the 5th Infantry (mounted) along with 40 Native American scouts attacked the unsuspecting Nez Perce camp. The 7th Cavalry struck the camp, while the 2nd Cavalry captured all of the Indian ponies. Again the Nez Perces proved their discipline under fire, concentrating on the officers and noncommissioned officers. Miles then wisely broke off the attack and settled in for a siege. Both sides had suffered heavy losses during the initial skirmish. Miles lost 2 officers and 21 enlisted men killed and 4 officers and 38 enlisted men wounded. Among the Nez Perces dead was Joseph's brother Ollokot, a Nez Perce leader. During the battle and the siege that followed some 300 Nez Perce men, women, and children managed to elude the soldiers and ultimately reach Canada. Those who remained responded to the assault by digging rifle pits and preparing for a long siege.

By day's end, Miles had encircled the Nez Perce camp. A stalemate then ensued until Brigadier General Oliver O. Howard, who had trailed the Indians from the start, arrived with reinforcements on October 4. Howard, however, left Miles in command.

The Nez Perces now debated the course of action to follow. Joseph favored negotiations, while White Bird and Looking Glass favored an attempt to break out. On October 5 an army sniper killed Looking Glass. Joseph then decided to meet with Howard and Miles. That same day Joseph handed his rifle to Miles and said, "From where the sun now stands I will fight no more forever."

During their trek the Nez Perces had fought 18 armed engagements, winning most of them. Joseph surrendered only 87 men, 184 women, and 147 children. The dispirited Nez Perces, now wards of the government, experienced still more heartache as sickness and death took their toll during a prolonged exile in Kansas and Indian Territory (present-day Oklahoma). Although some Nez Perces returned to a diminished reservation at Lapwai in 1885, Joseph and 150 of his followers were relocated to the Colville Reservation in central Washington.

JON L. BRUDVIG

See also

Howard, Oliver Otis; Joseph, Chief; Miles, Nelson Appleton; Nez Perce War; White Bird Canyon, Battle of

References

Beal, Merril D. *"I Will Fight No More Forever": Chief Joseph and the Nez Perce War*. Seattle: University of Washington Press, 1963.

Greene, Jerome A. *Nez Perce Summer, 1877: The U. S. Army and the Nee-Me-Poo Crisis*. Helena: Montana Historical Society Press, 2000.

Hampton, Bruce. *Children of Grace: The Nez Perce War of 1877*. New York: Holt, 1994.

Miles, Nelson A. *Personal Recollections and Observations of General Nelson A. Miles*. 2 vols. Lincoln: University of Nebraska Press, 1992.

Wooster, Robert. *The Military and United States Indian Policy, 1865–1903*. New Haven, CT: Yale University Press, 1988.

Wooster, Robert. *Nelson A. Miles and the Twilight of the Frontier Army*. Lincoln: University of Nebraska Press, 1993.

Bear River, Battle of
Event Date: January 29, 1863

Massacre at a Shoshone village along the Bear River in southern Idaho on January 29, 1863, by California volunteers led by Colonel

Patrick Edward Connor. Tension between the Shoshones, led by Chief Bear Hunter, and Mormon farmers had mounted after the latter began moving from northern Utah into the Cache Valley of southern Idaho in the spring of 1860. With the outbreak of the American Civil War (1861–1865), however, some 2,500 Union troops departed Utah to fight in the East. Consequently, defense of the Utah Territory fell to volunteer militia forces. Colonel Patrick Edward Connor, a California businessman and a veteran of the Mexican-American War (1846–1848), organized approximately 1,000 California volunteers and marched to Utah in 1862, ostensibly to protect the Overland Mail Route.

Upon Connor's arrival, Utah's territorial government requested that he mount an attack against the Shoshones in the Cache Valley, where young warriors had been attacking Mormon settlements. Although Connor had no love for the Mormons, he despised Native Americans. After he assembled some 300 California volunteers at Salt Lake City's Camp Douglas and vowed that no prisoners would be taken, he and his men, led by famed Mormon scout Orrin Porter Rockwell, marched north to the confluence of Beaver Creek and Bear River, where Chief Bear Hunter and some 450 Shoshones had established their winter camp.

Arriving at the village at approximately 6:00 a.m. on January 29, 1863, Connor and his men found the Shoshones well entrenched behind a 10-foot embankment along Beaver Creek. Nevertheless, Connor ordered his troops to attack across the open plain. After his troops suffered approximately 20 casualties in the initial attack, Connor directed his men to pull back and surround the village to prevent any possibility of the Shoshones escaping. Over the next two hours Connor's men fired indiscriminately into the village, killing men, women, and children. Once the Shoshones ran out of ammunition, Connor's forces moved into the village, turning the battle into a massacre in which they shot every person they could find, raped women, and killed those who were wounded.

Of the 450 Shoshones in the village, approximately 250 were slain, including Chief Bear Hunter, his subchief Lehi, and at least 90 women and children. Before departing for Salt Lake City, Connor's men burned all 75 Shoshone lodges and confiscated 1,000 bushels of flour and 175 ponies. Approximately 150 women and children were left in the desolated village with hardly any food in the dead of winter. Connor carried his 14 dead and 53 wounded troops back to Salt Lake City, where Mormon settlers hailed him and his men for their deliverance.

JUSTIN D. MURPHY

See also

Connor, Patrick Edward; Shoshones

References

Barrett, Carole A. *American Indian History*. Pasadena, CA: Salem Press, 2003.

Madsen, Brigham D. *The Shoshoni Frontier and the Bear River Massacre*. Salt Lake City: University of Utah Press, 1985.

Utley, Robert M. *The Indian Frontier of the American West, 1846–1890*. Albuquerque: University of New Mexico Press, 1984.

Bear Spring, New Mexico

See Ojo Oso, New Mexico

Beaver Wars

Start Date: 1641
End Date: 1701

Series of wars fought by the five nations of the Iroquois Confederacy (the Mohawks, Oneidas, Onondagas, Cayugas, and Senecas) against the French and their Native American allies. Historians have long debated Iroquois motivations in pursuing these conflicts (also known as the Iroquois Wars and the French and Iroquois Wars), which were punctuated by lulls, treaties, and truces. The Iroquois appear to have had two primary goals for their offensives. First, in need of a reliable source of European goods, the Iroquois sought to gain control of the fur-trading routes to their north and west and then move the beaver pelts from the upper Great Lakes to their Dutch (later English) trading partners at Fort Orange (present-day Albany, New York). The second goal was an extension of the traditional practice of the Mourning War. Having been devastated by outbreaks of European diseases in the 1630s, the Iroquois sought captives, some of whom would be adopted by clans to replace their dead. This was a long-standing practice in Iroquois culture.

At odds with New France, the Iroquois desired a reliable supplier of European trade goods and thus developed a trade relationship with the Dutch. Beaver pelts were the primary currency of the trade, but the Iroquois seem to have trapped most of the beavers in their territory by the beginning of the 1640s. Even if there were sufficient beaver pelts in Iroquoia by this time, they were not the thicker (and more valuable) pelts from the upper Great Lakes. Dependent on European weapons, tools, and cloth and needing captives to replace the dead, the Iroquois began the so-called Beaver Wars by launching a series of attacks against other Iroquoian speakers in the early 1640s.

By virtue of their location, the Wyandots (Hurons) served as middlemen in the fur trade, acquiring pelts from tribes such as the Nipissings to their north and the Ottawas to their west in exchange for maize. The Wyandots then traded the pelts to the French for European goods. The Iroquois attacked the Hurons in 1648 and followed up with attacks that devastated Huronia in March 1649. Several aspects of the 1649 attack on the Hurons signaled that the Iroquois were practicing a new form of warfare. The Five Nations attacked during a time of year when warfare was usually suspended because of the difficulty of travel, and they struck in great force (estimated at 1,000 men) rather than in small groups. They were also very far from their homes in Iroquoia. In addition, they unveiled a new tactic: fighting at night.

While the Hurons had the military capacity to respond in the wake of the 1649 attacks, the assault seems to have had an unnerving effect on them. The majority of the Hurons chose to flee in an effort to escape the Iroquois. Most Hurons went to Ganadoe (now Christian) Island in Lake Huron's Georgian Bay, where many of them perished of starvation during 1649–1650. Some went to Quebec, whereas others fled and were dispersed throughout the Great Lakes region and the Ohio Country.

The Iroquois followed up with other attacks in 1650. Many of the Hurons were captured or fled to the western Great Lakes or the Ohio Country. Presumably, the confederation asked the Eries and a confederacy known as the Neutrals to join the Longhouse (the metaphor for the Iroquois League). When they refused, the Iroquois, well equipped with firearms obtained from the Dutch, devastated both nations, carrying off many of their people into captivity.

If the Iroquois goal in these campaigns was to gain control of the Huron fur-trading routes, they failed. Instead, the elimination of the Hurons shifted the epicenter of the trade westward, and Algonquian-speaking peoples, such as the Ottawas, replaced the Hurons as middlemen. The Five Nations, moreover, could not sustain this conflict without resting and rebuilding their stocks of muskets and ammunition. To facilitate this and to keep New France from attacking them, the Iroquois allowed the French to send missionaries among them.

The Iroquois, however, soon found themselves at war again, this time with the Iroquoian-speaking Susquehannocks. Quite numerous, backed by the colonies of Maryland and Delaware, and able to obtain powder and firearms from Swedish traders, the Susquehannocks were a formidable foe. Unable to fight the Susquehannocks and to continue their campaign in the Great Lakes region, the Iroquois made peace with their enemies to the north and west. The Susquehannock threat came to an end but for reasons that had nothing to do with the Iroquois. Attacked by Virginians in the opening phases of Bacon's Rebellion in 1676, the Susquehannocks were dispersed, and many were incorporated into the Seneca tribe.

Freed of the threat to their south, the Iroquois renewed their assault on the peoples of the Ohio Country and the Great Lakes. But over time the ongoing conflict served to weaken the Five Nations. Their enemies acquired European weaponry, while Iroquois losses mounted. The French even invaded Iroquoia and burned a Seneca town. The Mourning War tradition began to change the demographic makeup of Iroquoia, so much so that one Jesuit claimed that there were more adoptees than native-born people among the Iroquois. Moreover, neither the French nor the Iroquois could hope to control the fur trade. The founding of the English Hudson's Bay Company shifted much of the fur trade northward.

In 1701 with the Iroquois weakened and having failed to gain control over the fur trade, the Iroquois leader Decanisora came up with a cunning diplomatic solution to their difficulties. In what came to be known as the Grand Settlement of 1701, the Five Nations began a new policy best described as armed neutrality. In separate treaties, the Iroquois promised the French that they

would remain neutral in future conflicts and assured New York that they would aid that colony, provided it fulfilled certain promises that the Iroquois knew would not be kept. For the next half century the Iroquois would invoke these agreements to ensure a steady flow of gifts. This diplomatic maneuvering would end only toward the end of the French and Indian War (1754–1763), when the then Six Nations joined the English in the conflict.

ROGER M. CARPENTER

See also

Decanisora; French and Indian War; Fur Trade; Indian Presents; Iroquois; Iroquois Confederacy; Iroquois Treaties of 1700 and 1701; Mohawks; Mourning War; Native American Warfare; Oneidas; Onondagas; Ottawas; Senecas; Susquehannocks; Wyandots

References

Carpenter, Roger M. *The Renewed, the Destroyed, and the Remade: The Three Thought Worlds of the Iroquois and the Huron, 1609–1650.* East Lansing: Michigan State University Press, 2004.
Hunt, George T. *The Wars of the Iroquois: A Study in Intertribal Trade Relations.* Madison: University of Wisconsin Press, 1940.

Beecher Island, Battle of
Start Date: September 17, 1868
End Date: September 25, 1868

Military engagement between Major George A. Forsyth's company of 50 scouts and 500–600 Arapaho, Northern Cheyenne, and Oglala Sioux warriors during the 1867–1869 Southern Plains War. The Battle of Beecher Island (also known as the Arikaree Fight) took place during September 17–25, 1868, in northeastern Colorado along the Arikaree River, near present-day Wray, Colorado. There Forsyth's command was able to hold out for more than a week against an overwhelming force before being relieved.

In the summer of 1868, Oglala Sioux and Cheyenne war parties moved east through northwestern Kansas to battle their traditional enemies, the Pawnees. While passing through the Solomon and Saline valleys, the warriors raided several farms, murdering scores of settlers, burning farms and barns, and carrying off one woman into captivity. In response, Major General Philip Sheridan authorized his longtime aide Forsyth, with Lieutenant Henry Ward Beecher as his second-in-command, to raise a company of settlers to pursue the hostiles. Forsyth's command included a number of veterans of both sides of the American Civil War (1861–1865), with several noted frontiersmen as scouts. The unit, dubbed the "Solomon Avengers," was well armed with Spencer repeating carbines and soon set out in unsuccessful pursuit of the hostiles.

On September 10 Forsyth's command left Fort Wallace in western Kansas to intercept a party of raiders. Four days later his men came across a pronounced trail and followed it westward along the Arikaree Fork of the Republican River. On the morning of September 17 the scouts, 50 in number, were attacked by a large party of as many as 600 warriors, led by Northern Cheyenne warrior Roman

Major George Alexander Forsyth's 50-man company defeats some 500–600 Northern Cheyennes, Arapahos, and Oglala Sioux under war chief Roman Nose in the Battle of Beecher Island, Colorado, fought during September 17–25, 1868. The survival of Forsyth's men is one of the most celebrated events of the western Indian Wars. Art by Rufus Fairchild Zogbaum (1849–1925). (Library of Congress)

Nose. Realizing that they would be ridden or shot down if they attempted to escape, the scouts took shelter on a 200-foot-long by 40-foot-wide island in the nearly dry streambed of the Arikaree.

Despite suffering several casualties, including Beecher who was mortally wounded, the men were able to dig shallow entrenchments in the sandy soil and hold off several Native American charges. That night Forsyth, badly outnumbered, still surrounded, and with all of his horses dead, dispatched two scouts—Jack Stilwell and Pierre Trudeau—to cover the 85 miles to Fort Wallace and secure assistance. The men arrived safely on September 22. The remaining scouts on Beecher Island managed to hold off successive attacks, surviving mainly on putrid horse flesh, until September 25, when Captain Louis Carpenter and the buffalo soldiers of Troop H of the 10th Cavalry Regiment arrived with ambulances and supplies. In the battle Forsyth lost 6 killed and 15 wounded. Accounts of Native American losses vary between 9 and more than 30 killed, including Roman Nose, and perhaps as many as 60 or 70 wounded.

The battle helped to convince Sheridan, commander of the Department of the Missouri, that small units of militia were insufficient to maintain peace on the frontier. Nonetheless, the

successful defense of the island by a small group of whites with superior technology against a large Native American force echoed similar events elsewhere in the world and became an American metaphor for the Western conquest of indigenous peoples.

CHRISTOPHER M. REIN

See also

Arapahos; Buffalo Soldiers; Cheyennes, Northern; Forsyth, George Alexander; Oglala Sioux; Pawnees; Roman Nose; Sheridan, Philip Henry

References

Dixon, David. *Hero of Beecher Island: The Life and Military Career of George A. Forsyth.* Lincoln: University of Nebraska Press, 1994.

Grinnell, George Bird. *The Fighting Cheyenne.* 1915; reprint, Norman: University of Oklahoma Press, 1989.

Monnett, John H. *The Battle of Beecher Island and the Indian War of 1867–1869.* Niwot: University Press of Colorado, 1992.

Belknap, William Worth
Birth Date: September 22, 1829
Death Date: October 11, 1890

U.S. Army officer and secretary of war (1869–1876). William Worth Belknap was born on September 22, 1829, in Newburgh, New York. He studied law at Princeton University from 1846 to 1848, practiced law for a time, and served a term in the Iowa legislature from 1857 to 1858.

In December 1861 Belknap secured a commission as major in the 15th Iowa Volunteer Infantry and served with distinction in the American Civil War (1861–1865). Wounded in the Battle of Shiloh (April 6–7, 1862), he was promoted to lieutenant colonel. Distinguishing himself again in the Battle of Corinth (October 3–4), he received promotion to colonel in June 1863. Belknap fought in the Vicksburg Campaign and won promotion to brigadier general of Volunteers. He then served in the Atlanta Campaign as a highly effective brigade commander, leading it in both Major General William T. Sherman's March to the Sea and the subsequent Carolinas Campaign. Belknap was rewarded by advancement to major general of Volunteers in March 1865.

Following the war, Belknap returned to Iowa and became an internal revenue collector. On Sherman's recommendation, President Ulysses S. Grant offered Belknap, a personal friend, the position of secretary of war to fill the vacancy created by the death of John A. Rawlins. Belknap accepted the post on November 3, 1869. His tenure as secretary of war saw the army sharply reduced in size, with low morale because of the lack of personnel to deal with Indian threats in the West. By the end of 1871 the army was down to just 33,000 men and the next year to 31,500 men.

Morale in the army also suffered with the sharp increase in the cost of goods at trading posts, the result of Belknap having given the concessions at the various forts to friends, family members, and politicians, who in many cases then sold the rights to others—often to those who originally held the concessions—who then raised prices to recover their costs. Several army officers brought the high prices to the attention of Belknap, only to have him dismiss their claims. In addition to low morale, desertions increased during Belknap's tenure.

Sherman, now the commanding general of the army, sharply disagreed with Belknap's policies. Following a February 9, 1876, article in the *New York Herald* about bribery involving the trading posts, the Committee on Expenditures in the War Department began an investigation. Caleb Marsh testified that he was then paying Belknap for the trading post concession at Fort Sill (Oklahoma). Belknap denied any wrongdoing, but the U.S. House of Representatives voted unanimously to impeach him.

Belknap resigned on March 2, 1876. This left the Senate in a quandary because private citizens could not be impeached. The Senate nonetheless proceeded with a trial in July 1876 but in a vote on August 1, 1876, failed to convict. Belknap then practiced law, first in Philadelphia and then in Washington, D.C., where he died on October 11, 1890.

DALLACE W. UNGER JR.

See also

Grant, Ulysses Simpson; Indian Ring Scandal; Sherman, William Tecumseh

References

Cooper, Edward S. *William Worth Belknap: An American Disgrace.* Madison, NJ: Fairleigh Dickinson University Press, 2003.

Morris, Roy, Jr. *Fraud of the Century: Rutherford B. Hayes, Samuel Tilden, and the Stolen Election of 1876.* New York: Simon and Schuster, 2003.

Summers, Mark Wahlgren. *The Era of Good Stealings.* New York: Oxford University Press, 1993.

Bent, Charles

Birth Date: November 11, 1799
Death Date: January 19, 1847

American pioneer and merchant who in 1846 served as the first civilian governor of American-controlled New Mexico. Born on November 11, 1799, in Charleston, West Virginia, Charles Bent moved to St. Louis, Missouri, with his family in 1806. Bent joined the Missouri Fur Company in 1822, becoming a partner in 1825. Finding too much competition in the Missouri fur trade, Bent and his brother William led a trading expedition over the Santa Fe Trail in 1828.

Discovering trade in Mexican-controlled New Mexico profitable, the Bent brothers formed the Bent and St. Vrain Company with local fur trader Ceran St. Vrain in 1832. The company subsequently built a series of fortified trading posts along the Santa Fe Trail, the most important of which was a massive adobe brick structure near La Junta, Colorado, called Bent's Fort (or Bent's Old Fort), constructed between 1833 and 1834. Located just across the Arkansas River north of the boundary between Mexico and the United States, Bent's Fort would be an important staging ground

Charles Bent was one of the most prominent businessmen in New Mexico at the outbreak of the Mexican-American War and was that territory's first American governor. His murder by Latinos and Native Americans on January 19, 1847, began the Taos Revolt. (Mercaldo Archives)

for military expeditions into New Mexico during the Mexican-American War (1846–1848).

In 1835 Bent, who had a very low opinion of local Latinos, built his home in Taos, New Mexico. In August 1846 in the very early stages of the Mexican-American War, Brigadier General Stephen Watts Kearny's force of 1,700 American troops captured Santa Fe without resistance. On September 22, 1846, Kearny, before departing for California, appointed Bent the governor of a provisional U.S. government in New Mexico. Bent was determined to govern the territory efficiently, immediately requesting from Washington, D.C., money to create schools, a mail system, and other essential services. Ignoring warnings from locals in Santa Fe that he remain there, Bent decided to return to his home in Taos in early January 1847. Unbeknownst to Bent, a group of disaffected Mexicans was plotting to overthrow the American regime and kill him.

On January 19, 1847, Latino and Native American insurrectionists murdered Bent and several of his friends at the Bent home in Taos, thus igniting the Taos Revolt, a local uprising against American rule. The revolt resulted in the death of 17 other Americans. Sixteen of the leaders of the Taos Revolt were eventually captured, tried, convicted, and hanged in Taos.

MICHAEL R. HALL

See also
Bent, William; Bent's Fort; Kearny, Stephen Watts; New Mexico; Santa Fe Trail; Taos Revolt

References
Crutchfield, James Andrew. *Tragedy at Taos: The Revolt of 1847*. Plano: Republic of Texas Press, 1995.
McNierney, Michael. *Taos 1847: The Revolt in Contemporary Accounts*. Boulder, CO: Johnson Publishing, 1980.

Bent, William
Birth Date: May 23, 1809
Death Date: May 19, 1869

American fur trapper and merchant who managed Bent's Fort (also known as Old Bent's Fort), a privately owned fortified trading post of the Bent and St. Vrain Company, located on the border between the United States and Mexico along the Arkansas River (present-day southeastern Colorado). Born on May 23, 1809, in St. Louis, Missouri, William Bent was the younger brother of Charles Bent. Charles Bent, murdered at the start of the Taos Revolt in 1847, was briefly governor of U.S.-controlled New Mexico. In 1832 the Bent brothers formed the Bent and St. Vrain Company with Ceran St. Vrain and built a series of fortified trading posts along the Santa Fe Trail, the most important being Bent's Fort, a massive adobe brick structure near La Junta, Colorado. Located just across the Arkansas River north of the boundary between Mexico and the United States, Bent's Fort, constructed in 1833, facilitated trade with New Mexico as well as with local Native Americans. In 1835 William Bent married a Cheyenne woman and established friendly relations with Cheyenne chief Black Kettle, which further increased trade with the local Native American population.

During the Mexican-American War (1846–1848), Bent's Fort served as an important staging area for military expeditions into New Mexico. Bent, however, became annoyed by the outbreak of disease caused by the presence of so many American troops at the fort. After the war he offered to sell the fort to the United States, but the Americans refused because the fort's strategic value had been greatly diminished as a result of the Treaty of Guadalupe Hidalgo. Having terminated his business relationship with St. Vrain, on August 21, 1849, a disgruntled Bent burned Fort Bent. Bent, who was horrified by the slaughter of Cheyennes in the 1864 Sand Creek Massacre, died on May 19, 1869, in Westport, Kansas.

Michael R. Hall

See also
Bent, Charles; Bent's Fort; Black Kettle; Cheyennes; New Mexico; Sand Creek Massacre; Santa Fe Trail; Taos Revolt

References
Crutchfield, James Andrew. *Tragedy at Taos: The Revolt of 1847*. Plano: Republic of Texas Press, 1995.
Lavender, David. *Bent's Fort*. Garden City, NY: Doubleday, 1954.

Benteen, Frederick William
Birth Date: August 24, 1834
Death Date: June 22, 1898

U.S. Cavalry officer. A descendant of Dutch immigrants, Frederick William Benteen was born in Petersburg, Virginia, on August 24, 1834. In 1849 he moved with his family to Missouri, where he entered service in the Union Army at the outbreak of the American Civil War (1861–1865), against his pro-Confederate father's wishes. As a first lieutenant in the 10th Missouri Cavalry, Benteen fought in numerous small skirmishes as well as larger engagements, including at Pea Ridge and Vicksburg. Promoted to major in December 1862 and to lieutenant colonel in February 1864, he enjoyed a distinguished record until he was mustered out of service in June 1865.

Benteen briefly served as colonel of the 138th Colored Volunteers (July 1865–January 1866) before accepting a regular army commission as a captain in the 7th U.S. Cavalry in July 1866. While serving with the 7th Cavalry, Benteen continued to build his military reputation. However, during the Washita Campaign in 1868 he developed a toxic relationship with his regimental commander, Lieutenant Colonel George Armstrong Custer. Benteen's controversial public criticism of Custer's conduct during the campaign created tension within the regiment and between the two men that would last until Custer's death.

From 1867 until 1882 Benton commanded H Troop of the 7th Cavalry. During the Battle of the Little Bighorn (June 25–26, 1876), Custer divided his regiment into three battalions, with Benteen given command of H, D, and K troops. Sent on a fruitless scouting mission, Benteen received an urgent but cryptic message from Custer to join him and the rest of the regiment in an attack on a Native American village along the Little Bighorn River. Before Benteen reached the field, Custer's detachment was annihilated. Arriving at the battle site, Benteen rallied the remaining forces of Major Marcus Reno's battalion and orchestrated a stalwart two-day defense against numerous Sioux attacks on a hill four miles south of where Custer had come under attack. While Benteen's performance most likely saved the regiment from total destruction, the army later forced him to defend his actions in a court of inquiry investigating the Little Bighorn defeat. The court exonerated him and Reno of wrongdoing, but many in the army continued to blame Benteen for Custer's demise.

Following the Little Bighorn fiasco, Benteen fought in the campaign against the Nez Perces in 1877. He was promoted to major in 1882, but his behavior became increasingly erratic. While commander of Fort Duchesne, Utah, in 1884, he was arrested and suspended for a year on half-pay for drunken and disorderly conduct. He was granted disability and was allowed to retire in 1888. In 1890 he received a brevet to brigadier general for his service at Little Bighorn and against the Nez Perces. Benteen died in Atlanta, Georgia, on June 22, 1898.

Bradford A. Wineman

See also

Cavalry Regiment, 7th U.S.; Custer, George Armstrong; Great Sioux War; Little Bighorn, Battle of the; Nez Perce War; Reno, Marcus Albert

References

Benteen, Frederick W. *Camp Talk: The Very Private Letters of Frederick W. Benteen of the 7th U.S. Cavalry to His Wife, 1871 to 1888.* Mattituck, NY: J. M. Carroll, 1983.

Laudenhiem, Jules C. *Custer's Thorn: The Life of Frederick W. Benteen.* Westminster, MD: Heritage Books, 2007.

Mills, Charles K. *Harvest of Barren Regrets: The Army Career of Frederick William Benteen, 1834–1898.* Glendale, CA: Arthur H. Clark, 1985.

Bent's Fort

Thriving center of Native American trade located on the north bank of the upper Arkansas River (present-day southeastern Colorado) in the 1830s and 1840s. In 1830 brothers Charles and William Bent and Ceran St. Vrain formed the Bent and St. Vrain Company to trade with the Plains Indians. Three years later the Bents and St. Vrain established Bent's Fort, designed to serve as the hub of their trading activities. The fort quickly became a center for Native American and settler commerce on the Santa Fe Trail, with the partners exchanging various trade goods for buffalo hides. As the Bents' reputation for fair dealing spread among the Cheyennes, Comanches, Utes, Arapahos, Kiowas, and other area tribes, the partners came to dominate Native American trade on the southern Plains. Many tribes, especially the Cheyennes, moved whole villages to the Arkansas River area to be closer to the fort.

In 1835 Colonel Henry Dodge, commander of the 1st Dragoons, organized a peace council at Bent's Fort between the Cheyennes and Arapahos and their enemies. The Bent brothers were such effective peacemakers that in 1846 their fort became headquarters for the Upper Platte and Arkansas Indian Agency. William Bent lived with his Cheyenne wife, Owl Woman, in her nearby village. Bent's Fort quickly declined as a trade center after the Mexican-American War (1846–1848), and the Native Americans gradually left the area. Charles Bent was killed in 1847, and two years later William Bent and Ceran St. Vrain decided to abandon the fort. In 1853 William Bent constructed Bent's New Fort, located some 40 miles downstream on the Arkansas River.

PAUL DAVID NELSON

See also

Arapahos; Cheyennes; Comanches; Dodge, Henry; Kiowas; Native American Trade; Santa Fe Trail; Utes

References

Comer, Douglas C. *Ritual Ground: Bent's Old Fort, World Formation, and the Annexation of the Southwest.* Berkeley: University of California Press, 1996.

Lavender, David. *Bent's Fort.* Garden City, NY: Doubleday, 1954.

Berkeley, William
Birth Date: January 1, 1606
Death Date: July 9, 1677

Governor of the English colony of Virginia (1640–1652 and 1660–1677). Born in Somerset, England, on January 1, 1606, William Berkeley was educated at St. Edmond Hall and Merton College, Oxford. He studied law at the Middle Temple in London before

Illustration of Bent's Fort on the Santa Fe Trail, circa 1845. (Library of Congress)

Sir William Berkeley was governor of Virginia during 1640–1652 and 1660–1677. His generally conciliatory policies toward Native Americans led to Bacon's Rebellion, which, although Berkeley finally put it down, nonetheless ended his tenure as governor. (Maurice du Pont Lee)

embarking on a tour of continental Europe. In 1632 he secured a position in the household of King Charles I. Berkeley took part in the First Bishops' War (1639) and the Second Bishops' War (1640) and was knighted for this service.

Berkeley's parents owned stock in the Virginia Company, and friends and relatives assisted Berkeley in purchasing the post of governor of Virginia from its then-current occupant, Sir Francis Wyatt. Charles I approved, and in 1642 Berkeley arrived at Jamestown, Virginia, to take up his post. He became the longest serving of all English North American colonial governors and of all Virginia governors, colonial or modern.

Berkeley soon established a plantation near Jamestown, where as one of the planter elite he experimented with the production of crops for export other than tobacco. These included flax, rice, and fruits. Berkeley sought to make Jamestown the center of a diverse colonial trade that would increase the wealth of both Virginia and himself. A proponent of free trade and autonomy, Berkeley found himself at odds with the Crown's mercantilist principles, symbolized in the Navigation Acts.

In 1644 Berkeley traveled to England to secure arms for use in fighting the Native Americans during the Third Anglo-Powhatan War (1644–1646). In October 1646 he signed the peace treaty that established reservations for the Native Americans who had been part of Powhatan's Confederation and required them to pay annual tribute to the Virginia government.

With the onset of the English Civil War (1642–1651), the loyalty of many royal governors was severely tested. In 1649 Berkeley declared Virginia loyal to Charles I. As a result, in 1652 Parliament dispatched a military expedition to Virginia. Berkeley surrendered to these forces but not before winning terms that kept Virginia's political institutions largely intact. He then retired to his estate near Jamestown until he was returned to power in January 1660 following the death of Governor Samuel Mathews.

During his second period as governor, Berkeley sought to implement his economic plans for Virginia. Toward that end and to secure funding, he traveled to England in 1661. King Charles II supported the idea of economic diversification but refused additional immediate funding and rejected Berkeley's appeal for free trade.

Berkeley returned to Virginia in late 1662. His plans for economic diversification were largely unsuccessful, and he became increasingly unpopular as a result of taxes imposed to support that effort. Maryland's failure to honor an agreement regulating the production of tobacco also led to a sharp decrease in the price of that commodity, for which many small tobacco farmers blamed Berkeley. War with the Dutch also affected Virginia trade and its overall economy. Finally, Berkeley found himself sharply at odds with many settlers in western Virginia regarding his conciliatory policy toward the Native Americans in the face of mounting Indian raids in the 1670s. This came to a head following a Doeg raid in July 1675. Berkeley misread the situation, and his failure to mount a major punitive operation drew the anger of many westerners. Many of these settlers sought an all-out war against the Native Americans that would allow them to take the Native Americans' land.

All of these grievances found expression in the summer of 1676 in a rebellion against the colonial government. The planter Nathaniel Bacon and his followers seized control of the capital of Jamestown, forcing Berkeley to flee. A reaction to Bacon's excesses enabled forces loyal to Berkeley to regain control following Bacon's death from fever and dysentery in October 1676 and before the arrival of a sizable English military expedition to Virginia to accomplish the same end. Berkeley ordered the leaders of the rebellion hanged.

Berkeley quarreled with new officials sent out by London and resigned his office in May 1677. He returned to England in an effort to clear his name, but before he could accomplish this he died in Twinkenham, England, on July 9, 1677.

JAIME RAMÓN OLIVARES AND SPENCER C. TUCKER

See also
Bacon's Rebellion

References
Washburn, Wilcomb E. *The Governor and the Rebel: A History of Bacon's Rebellion in Virginia.* Chapel Hill: University of North Carolina Press, 1957.
Webb, Stephen Saunders. *1676: The End of American Independence.* New York: Knopf, 1984.

Biduyé

See Victorio

Bierstadt, Albert
Birth Date: January 7, 1830
Death Date: February 18, 1902

German American painter who produced a large body of work in the last half of the 19th century and is best known for his landscapes of the American West. Albert Bierstadt, the sixth child of Henry and Christina Bierstadt, was born on January 7, 1830, in Solingen, Prussia. Two years later the family migrated to New Bedford, Massachusetts. By the time Bierstadt reached adulthood, he had attempted to both teach art and exhibit his own work, apparently without showing any extraordinary propensity for either.

In 1853 Bierstadt sailed for Germany to study art in Düsseldorf. There he showed significant growth, working tirelessly among a community of artists that included fellow German American Émanuel Leutze and American landscape painters Worthington Whittredge and William Stanley Haseltine. Back in New Bedford by late 1857, Bierstadt displayed his work the following spring at the National Academy of Design in New York. With his skills honed

Albert Bierstadt's large panoramic landscapes of the West were wildly popular with the public and with wealthy collectors in the years after the Civil War and helped to shape American perceptions of the rugged country west of the Mississippi River. (Library of Congress)

and his works garnering attention, the ambitious young painter looked for an opportunity to establish his place in the art world.

Bierstadt's subsequent travels into the American frontier proved enormously influential. In the spring of 1859 he joined the expedition of Colonel Frederick W. Lander to survey western lands for a possible rail line through the South Pass of Wyoming. Then four years later Bierstadt made a deeper foray into the West, traveling to California and Oregon and making a lengthy stay in Yosemite Valley. The scenes he witnessed and other scenes gathered from subsequent trips inspired most of his remaining life's works. From his New York City studio on 10th Street, an artists' enclave, he produced landscapes characteristic of the Hudson River School: large-scale majestic interpretations of American nature. They came at a fortuitous time. Americans had recently poured into the far West, leaving those in the East hungry for visual representations of the accounts they read and for diversion from the bloody American Civil War (1861–1865). Bierstadt's art portrayed boundless western lands and celebrated unparalleled natural beauty that suggested tranquility and portended a limitless future for the young nation. He quickly found some of the notoriety and wealth that he craved, with *The Rocky Mountains, Lander's Peak* (1863) selling for the unprecedented price of $25,000 and his renditions of the Rockies, Sierra Nevadas, and Yosemite highly desired. By the end of the 1860s he exhibited his art in Europe, gained an audience with Britain's Queen Victoria, and was made a knight in the Legion of Honor by France's Napoleon III.

Bierstadt's good fortune continued through the next decade, although his work always faced intense scrutiny. Critics complained that he was driven by the desire for fame and financial gain, that his work lacked creativity, and that he shared the fixation of Düsseldorf-trained artists on detail. By the 1880s as public tastes changed toward the impressionistic, even buyers' interest in Bierstadt's work waned, so much so that he declared bankruptcy in 1894 and died in relative obscurity on February 18, 1902, in New York City.

Native Americans commonly appeared in Bierstadt's paintings of western scenes, but he offered little insight into their lives and cultures. They typically were mere props, such as trees and wildlife, on nature's stage. On the rare occasions that they were a primary focus, Bierstadt settled for stereotypes. In *The Landing of Columbus* (1893), for example, indigenous people, situated in the darkness of shadow, bow obsequiously before the newly arrived Europeans, who stand in light. If his art distorted nature, it nevertheless was a view popular among many mid-19th-century Americans.

Mark Thompson

See also
Literature and the American Indian Wars; Rocky Mountains

References
Anderson, Nancy K., and Linda S. Ferber. *Albert Bierstadt: Art & Enterprise.* New York: Hudson Hills, 1990.
Baigwell, Matthew. *Albert Bierstadt.* New York: Watson-Guptill Publications, 1981.

Big Bend, Battle of
Event Date: May 12, 1860

Initial battle of the 1860 Paiute War. The Battle of Big Bend, also known as the First Battle of Pyramid Lake, was fought approximately 35 miles northeast of present-day Reno, Nevada, between Paiute warriors and local white militiamen on May 12, 1860. From the onset of the California Gold Rush in 1849, tensions between whites and the Paiutes had steadily mounted as settlers traversed Paiute territory along the California Trail. By 1860 mining operations within Nevada itself were bringing increased numbers of settlers into the territory, making conflict with the Paiutes virtually unavoidable. Indeed, in the spring of 1860 Paiutes from across the Southwest gathered at Pyramid Lake in a war council. While the council was taking place, news arrived that whites at the Williams Station trading post on the Carson River had kidnapped and raped two Native American girls and that their families had retaliated on May 7 by burning down the station and killing five whites. Although war chief Numaga had counseled peace, he correctly recognized that the Williams Station incident meant war and began preparations for the inevitable white attack to come.

News of the Paiute attack on Williams Station spread rapidly, and soon 105 mounted but poorly armed white volunteers assembled at Virginia City. They were in four detachments: the Genoa Rangers under Captain Thomas F. Condon Jr., the Silver City Guards under Captain Richard G. Watkins, the Carson City Rangers under Major William M. Ormsby, and the Virginia City Hearties under Captain Archie McDonald. Departing Virginia City on the morning of May 9, the volunteers arrived at Williams Station on May 10, buried the dead from the prior attack, and decided to march overland to the Big Bend of the Truckee River, camping near present-day Wadsworth. On the morning of May 12 they continued north up the Truckee River, where shortly after noon they were ambushed by Paiute warriors armed with bows and poison-tipped arrows and some firearms. Well hidden behind rocks and clumps of sage brush, the Paiutes fired their weapons and then quickly dispersed before the whites could respond.

After the initial ambush, Ormsby assumed leadership of the ragtag volunteers, almost all of whom had little or no military experience. Spotting a band of warriors on an elevated plateau overlooking the river bottom, Ormsby led approximately half of his men in an attack up a ravine around 4:00 p.m. The result was a disaster, as the whites were soon surrounded on three sides. Ormsby was killed in the ensuing panic as his men attempted to flee back to the river bottom, where their compatriots, seeing the conflict above going badly, had begun to disperse. The Paiutes pursued the fleeing whites until dark. Subsequent reports put the number of dead whites at 42, with another 30 missing and only 33 making it back to their communities.

The Paiutes claimed to have lost only three warriors wounded and two horses killed, but their victory proved to be short-lived. California responded to news of the disaster at Big Bend by sending a force of some 750 troops into Nevada, where they defeated the Paiutes near Pinnacle Mountain, bringing the Paiute War to a close a short time later.

JUSTIN D. MURPHY

See also
California Gold Rush; Paiutes, Northern

References
Allred, B. W. *Great Western Indian Fights.* Lincoln: University of Nebraska Press, 1966.
Egan, Ferol. *Sand in a Whirlwind: The Paiute Indian War of 1860.* Lincoln: University of Nebraska Press, 2002.

Big Foot
Birth Date: ca. 1826
Death Date: December 29, 1890

Lakota Sioux leader killed during the Battle of Wounded Knee in December 1890. Big Foot (also known as Spotted Elk and Si Tanka) was probably born in 1826 and was the son of Lone Horn, a leader of the Miniconjou band of the Teton Lakotas (Sioux). Big Foot's place of birth is not known for certain, but it was probably western South Dakota or western Nebraska. A leader known for his keen diplomatic skills, Lone Horn arranged numerous agreements between his people and the Crows and Cheyennes, and he apparently passed his negotiating talents to his son, who took over after his father's death.

Big Foot fought with the Miniconjous during the Great Sioux War (1876–1877) and surrendered to U.S. troops in 1877. Placed on the Cheyenne River Reservation, he opposed further land agreements and concessions, but he was also a realist who worked hard not to anger the U.S. government.

During the Ghost Dance movement, Big Foot supported the right of his people to engage in the dance even though it proved highly unpopular with U.S. authorities. Indeed, Big Foot hoped that the dance would restore his tribe's traditional way of life. Although he grew disillusioned with the dance and abandoned it in early December 1890, many of his people continued it.

On December 19, 1890, Big Foot was headed toward his reservation agency to receive annuities when he learned of the death of Sitting Bull. After several days of discussions with his people, Big Foot moved with his band to Pine Ridge, where they camped near Wounded Knee Creek (present-day South Dakota).

Although Lakota leaders at Pine Ridge worked hard to negotiate a peaceful resolution to the standoff between the Ghost Dancers and the U.S. Army, a series of misunderstandings and Major General Nelson A. Miles's uncompromising stance virtually ensured a violent outcome.

On December 29, 1890, troops of Colonel James W. Forsyth's 7th Cavalry Regiment surrounded Big Foot's camp. Directed to disarm the Native Americans, Forsyth called upon Big Foot, then

Big Foot became chief of the Miniconjou band of the Teton (Lakota) Sioux following the death of his father Long Horn. Big Foot, also known as Si Tanka and Spotted Elk, was killed in the Wounded Knee Massacre of December 29, 1890. (National Archives)

almost 65 years old and wracked with pneumonia, to order his people to surrender their guns. When few guns were produced, troops began searching the camp. A single gunshot, probably fired in error, set off a melee in which the troops fired on the Miniconjous and on each other in the ensuing confusion.

By the time the chaos and smoke cleared, Big Foot's band lay shattered. More than 250 of the 400 Native Americans in the camp had been killed, many of them women and children. Among the dead was Big Foot. One of the most enduring images of the massacre at Wounded Knee is the photograph of Big Foot's crumpled body frozen in the snow, still partly wrapped in a blanket. On January 4, 1891, Big Foot and the rest of the Lakota dead were buried in a ditch dug into the frozen ground at Wounded Knee.

STEVE POTTS

See also
Forsyth, James William; Ghost Dance; Miles, Nelson Appleton; Miniconjou Sioux; Pine Ridge Reservation; Sitting Bull; Wounded Knee, Battle of

References
Mooney, James. *The Ghost Dance Religion and the Sioux Outbreak of 1890.* Lincoln: University of Nebraska Press, 1991.
Utley, Robert M. *The Last Days of the Sioux Nation.* 2nd ed. New Haven, CT: Yale University Press, 2004.

Big Hole, Battle of the
Start Date: August 9, 1877
End Date: August 10, 1877

Major engagement of the Nez Perce War of 1877. This pitched battle between U.S. forces and bands of the Nez Perce tribe occurred during August 9–10, 1877, along the north fork of the Big Hole River in present-day Beaverhead County, Montana. Two U.S. Army columns pursued the Nez Perces under Chief Joseph as they moved up the Bitterroot Valley. On August 6 they reached the Big Hole basin in their effort to reach Canada and freedom. There Chief Looking Glass insisted that they stop for a time to rest, believing that they were sufficiently clear of the army column under Brigadier General Oliver O. Howard. Although Joseph and others protested, Looking Glass remained adamant.

Unknown to the Nez Perces, however, a second army column led by Colonel John Gibbon, commander of the District of Montana, had joined the chase. At Missoula, Gibbon assembled a force of 15 officers and 146 enlisted men. Later 45 volunteers also joined. On August 4 Gibbon set out in pursuit of the Nez Perces up the Bitterroot Valley.

Gibbon's scouts located the Nez Perce encampment on August 8 and kept it under observation while the rest of the force caught up, which occurred later that day. Gibbon then deployed his men to be able to launch an attack at sunrise on August 9. Believing themselves to be safe, the Nez Perces had not posted guards and thus were caught by surprise.

The soldiers charged the camp, firing as they advanced. Although they had been taken by surprise, Nez Perce warriors fought back as they and the women and children tried to flee into nearby woods. The fighting in the camp was at times hand to hand.

Within about 20 minutes Gibbon's command had secured the encampment and attempted to burn the tepees, which proved difficult because of heavy dew. While Gibbon's men tried to destroy the camp, the Indians regrouped and opened fire on the soldiers from covered positions surrounding the village. The Nez Perces then counterattacked, forcing Gibbon's men to withdraw to a nearby wooded hill. The soldiers dug in to hold off the warriors as the remainder of the Nez Perces buried their dead and fled. The Nez Perce warriors continued to hold Gibbon's soldiers at bay throughout the remainder of that day and the next. Gibbon brought up a howitzer, but the soldiers were only able to fire a single round before the Nez Perces captured and dismantled it. Neither side was able to gain a decisive advantage, and on the night of August 10 the warriors broke contact and slipped away to join the others. The following day, Howard arrived with his column to take up the pursuit again.

During approximately 36 hours of fighting, Gibbon's force suffered 28 dead: 22 soldiers, 1 civilian guide, and 5 civilian volunteers. Another 39, including Gibbon, were wounded. Indian losses, most of them in the initial assault, were much higher. Between 60 and 90 Nez Perce perished, many of them women and children. The number of wounded is unknown. One consequence of the battle was that Looking Glass, who had insisted that the fugitives stop to rest, lost much of his influence. The remaining Nez Perces moved east into the area of Yellowstone National Park and then turned north toward Canada. In 1992 federal legislation incorporated the Big Hole National Battlefield with the Nez Perce National Historical Park, making it part of a unique system of 38 different sites in five states.

DALLACE W. UNGER JR. AND SPENCER C. TUCKER

See also

Gibbon, John; Howard, Oliver Otis; Joseph, Chief; Looking Glass; Nez Perces; Nez Perce War

References

Greene, Jerome A. *Nez Perce Summer, 1877: The U. S. Army and the Nee-Me-Poo Crisis.* Helena: Montana Historical Society Press, 2000.

Hampton, Bruce. *Children of Grace: The Nez Perce War of 1877.* New York: Holt, 1994.

Johnston, Terry C. *Lay the Mountains Low: The Flight of the Nez Perce from Idaho and the Battle of the Big Hole, August 9–10, 1877.* New York: St. Martin's, 2000.

Billy Bowlegs
Birth Date: 1810
Death Date: 1859

Seminole chief, participant in the Second Seminole War (1835–1842), and a key combatant in the Third Seminole War (1855–1858). Billy Bowlegs, whose Seminole name of Holata Micco, or Halpuda Mikko, means "Alligator Chief" and who was also known as Billy Bolek, was born sometime in 1810 in north-central Florida (near present-day Micanopy). He was descended from a long line of chieftains, and his father was a local chief.

By the early 1830s Bowlegs had risen to some prominence among the Seminoles, and he had become increasingly impatient with U.S. attempts to move the Seminoles out of Florida and confiscate their lands. In 1832 he signed the controversial Treaty of Payne's Landing, which had committed numerous Seminole bands to relocate to the west. However, once the U.S. government order to move was received, Bowlegs refused to comply.

In 1835 the Second Seminole War began. During the course of the seven-year conflict Bowlegs became a most influential leader, especially after Chief Osceola surrendered to American forces and Chief Micanopy died. Indeed, by the end of the war in 1842, Bowlegs and his band of some 200 warriors were among the most

prominent Seminoles remaining in Florida. In 1842 U.S. government officials ordered Bowlegs to Washington, D.C., presumably to impress upon him the power of the federal government.

Upon returning to Florida, Bowlegs lived with his people in relative peace, although increasing numbers of white settlers and surveyors making their way into Florida began to impinge upon Seminole lands. By the early 1850s the pressures created by increased white settlement put the Seminoles on the defensive once more, and raids against whites became increasingly common. In 1855 Colonel William Selby Harney, head of a U.S. Army surveying corps, destroyed Bowlegs's banana crop in southwestern Florida. This action combined with increased white settlement precipitated the Third Seminole War.

Instead of waging pitched set-piece battles, Bowlegs insisted on a guerrilla-style war, to which U.S. forces were initially unable to respond. Using the vast, dense, and largely impenetrable Everglades, Bowlegs's forces easily evaded American troops. In late 1857 the U.S. War Department decided to employ shallow-draft boats to help U.S. soldiers penetrate the Everglades. In November of that year they managed to locate and destroy Bowlegs's camp headquarters.

After several months of negotiations, Bowlegs and his followers agreed to relocate to Indian Territory (Oklahoma) on May 7, 1858. This officially ended the Third Seminole War and all but

Seminole chief Billy Bowlegs was a key figure in the Third Seminole War (1855–1858). (Library of Congress)

ended the Seminole reign in Florida. Afterward there were fewer than 300 Seminoles remaining in the entire peninsula. To coax Bowlegs into accepting the U.S. terms, the U.S. government authorized a payment to him in the amount of $10,000. Each of his followers received $1,000. Bowlegs died in 1859 shortly after arriving in Indian Territory.

PAUL G. PIERPAOLI JR.

See also

Harney, William Selby; Osceola; Payne's Landing, Treaty of; Seminoles; Seminole War, First; Seminole War, Second; Seminole War, Third

References

Covington, James W. *The Billy Bowlegs War, 1855–1858: The Final Stand of the Seminoles against the Whites.* Chuluota, FL: Mickler House, 1982.

Missall, John, and Mary Lou Missall. *The Seminole Wars: America's Longest Indian Conflict.* Gainesville: University Press of Florida, 2004.

Birch Coulee, Battle of
Event Date: September 2, 1862

Engagement between volunteer and militia forces and the Dakota Sioux on September 2, 1862, during the Minnesota Sioux Uprising. The battle occurred in Renville County in south-central Minnesota. The Dakota conflict in Minnesota, which began on August 17, 1862, with the murder of four white settlers, was the first in a series of bloody interactions between the Dakota Sioux and whites in the upper Midwest during the last half of the 19th century.

When Minnesota governor Alexander Ramsey learned of Dakota attacks on settlers and troops from Fort Ridgely, he appointed Colonel Henry Hastings Sibley, a politician and frontier trader, to lead volunteer forces against the Dakotas. Sibley soon left for Fort Snelling before moving on to Fort Ridgely to begin the campaign. Before departing Sibley aided displaced settlers; gathered supplies, guns, and ammunition; and recruited additional troops. He reached Fort Ridgely on August 29.

On August 31 Sibley sent Major Joseph R. Brown and some 150 men to bury the dead settlers, repair the ferry crossing the Minnesota River, and scout the area for Indians. Knowing that the Native Americans took advantage of geography to mount attacks on unwary whites, Sibley warned Brown about camping near gullies and trees where ambushes were likely. Brown divided his burial party into two groups. They came together at the top of a wooded ravine called Birch Coulee about 15 miles from Fort Ridgely. There they set up camp in an area that was not easily defended.

Just before dawn on September 2 sentries at the fort heard rifle fire. Sibley dispatched 240 men toward Birch Coulee. The troops there had met with heavy Native American fire, and the commander of the troops sent a message to the fort requesting reinforcements. Sibley and his forces arrived just before midnight. Early the next morning he advanced, using cannon fire to drive the Indians out of the woods.

What Sibley found was the war's worst disaster: 13 men and 90 horses dead and 47 men wounded. Their ammunition nearly expended and without water for 36 hours, Brown's men were on the verge of collapse. Dakota leader Mankato and his warriors had scored a major victory, having lost only several men in the attack.

When Sibley returned to Fort Ridgely, he sent his resignation to Governor Ramsey. Although criticized by some of his troops and by a local newspaper editor who called him "the state undertaker," Sibley was persuaded to remain in command of the militia unit.

The Battle of Birch Coulee changed the nature of conflict. Sibley had left a note for Little Crow, the Dakota leader, attached to a stake on the battlefield. After three days, two messengers returned to Sibley under a flag of truce. They revealed that Little Crow held many white women and children as captives and considered the mixed-blood Dakotas as captives too. This initial contact led to a continuing exchange of notes between the two men. Sibley also learned of dissension within Native American ranks. Some Dakotas opposed war but feared the anger of their fellow tribesmen. Sibley now had to contend with freeing the white and Native American captives as well as quelling the conflict.

After the debacle at Birch Coulee, Sibley received additional supplies and more trained troops. The U.S. government also assigned Major General John Pope to the army's new Department of the Northwest, where he quickly asked for additional help and reassured Sibley of his support. On September 18 Sibley moved across the Minnesota River and advanced against the Indians. He soon met Little Crow in battle. The Battle of Wood Lake (September 22, 1862) led to Little Crow's retreat and eventual freedom for the white and Native American captives.

STEVE POTTS

See also

Dakota Sioux; Little Crow; Minnesota Sioux Uprising; Pope, John; Sibley, Henry Hastings; Wood Lake, Battle of

References

Folwell, William Watts. *A History of Minnesota,* Vol. 2. Rev. ed. St. Paul: Minnesota Historical Society Press, 1961.

Gilman, Rhoda R. *Henry Hastings Sibley: Divided Heart.* St. Paul: Minnesota Historical Society Press, 2004.

Lass, William E. *Minnesota: A History.* 2nd ed. New York: Norton, 1998.

Birch Creek, Battle of
Event Date: August 15, 1877

Skirmish between the fleeing Nez Perces and white teamsters and traders at Birch Creek (Monteview, Idaho) on August 15, 1877, during the Nez Perce War. After the Battle of Big Hole (August 9–10, 1877), Nez Perce chief Joseph and his warriors crossed the Continental Divide at Bannock Pass into the Lemhi Valley, moving south. On July 15 as a band of Nez Perces traversed the Birch Creek Valley in the southwestern corner of present-day Clark County, Idaho, it came upon a supply train including 8 wagons, 30 mules,

3 teamsters, and 5 others. The train was bound for Salmon City, Idaho, from Corrine, Utah.

A force of approximately 60 well-armed Nez Perce warriors forced the wagon train to stop and demanded that the teamsters feed them, which they did. The Indians then ordered the train to accompany them to their camp, located about two miles upriver. Once everyone had arrived at the camp, the Nez Perces inquired about buying the goods being carried in the wagon train. A sizable quantity of whiskey was among the products being carried, so the teamsters sold the Native Americans a portion of the whiskey.

As the warriors imbibed more and more whiskey, they grew increasingly belligerent toward the whites. Sensing impending danger, one of the freighters, Albert E. Lyons, made his way out of the camp undetected. It is impossible to tell for sure what happened next, but the Nez Perces apparently allowed three Chinese passengers to leave the camp. A conflict subsequently ensued between the inebriated Nez Perces and the remaining teamsters and passengers, resulting in the deaths of four whites. The Nez Perces abandoned their camp shortly afterward. Sometime after that U.S. forces found the battered bodies of the four white men; all had been shot.

Paul G. Pierpaoli Jr.

See also

Big Hole, Battle of the; Joseph, Chief; Nez Perces; Nez Perce War

References

Josephy, Alvin M. *The Nez Perce Indians and the Opening of the Northwest.* New Haven, CT: Yale University Press, 1965.

Nerburn, Kent. *Chief Joseph and the Flight of the Nez Perce: The Untold Story of an American Tragedy.* New York: HarperCollins, 2005.

Utley, Robert M. *The Indian Frontier of the American West, 1846–1890.* Albuquerque: University of New Mexico Press, 1984.

Bison

See Buffalo

Black Elk
Birth Date: ca. 1863
Death Date: August 19, 1950

Oglala Sioux spiritual leader who came of age during the late 19th century as white encroachment reached his homeland. Black Elk was born circa December 1863 probably along the Little Powder River (Wyoming) and was known as a traditional spiritual leader, although he spent much of his later life as a Roman Catholic. Black Elk was only 11 years old in the summer of 1874 when, by his own account (published in *Black Elk Speaks* in 1932), an expedition under Lieutenant Colonel George Armstrong Custer invaded the Paha Sapa (Black Hills), land that was sacred to the Lakotas. The Black Hills previously had been guaranteed to the Lakotas "in perpetuity" in the Fort Laramie Treaty of 1868. Custer's expedition

was a geological mission, not a military one; it was looking for gold and found it. In the expedition's wake several thousand gold seekers began pouring into the Black Hills, ignoring the treaty.

In the words of Black Elk, the Lakota and Cheyenne warriors "painted their faces black" and went to war to regain the Black Hills. The result was the Great Sioux War of 1876–1877 that included the Battle of the Little Bighorn in June 1876, in which Black Elk participated. The young Black Elk tried to take the first scalp, but the soldier under Black Elk's knife proved to have an unusually tough scalp, so Black Elk shot him. The battle provoked momentary joy among the Sioux and Cheyennes, who for decades had watched their hunting ranges infringed upon by what Black Elk characterized as the gnawing flood of the Wasi'chu (literally "takers of the fat").

In 1886 when Black Elk was 23 years of age he joined Buffalo Bill's Wild West Show. After a tour of large cities on the eastern seaboard, the troupe traveled to England. Black Elk later said that he greatly disliked his involvement in the Wild West Show. After the December 1890 Wounded Knee tragedy in which he was wounded, Black Elk watched his people, once the mounted lords of the Plains, become hungry, impoverished prisoners held on 13 government reservations. After his first wife became a Roman Catholic, Black Elk converted to Catholicism in 1903.

Portrait of Oglala Sioux spiritual leader Black Elk, 1885. (Getty Images)

Black Elk's views of Native American life reached large audiences beginning in the early 20th century through the edited books of John Neihardt, the best-known of which is *Black Elk Speaks.* The first three decades of Black Elk's life are chronicled in Neihardt's book *Black Elk Speaks,* first published in 1932; much of the same period was covered in Joseph Epes Brown's *The Sacred Pipe: Black Elk's Account of the Seven Rites of the Oglala Sioux* (1949).

Another book, Michael Steltenkamp's *Black Elk: Holy Man of the Oglala* (1993), describes Black Elk's final years as a Roman Catholic missionary. Steltenkamp, a Jesuit as well as an anthropologist, said he learned of Black Elk's conversion from Lucy Looks Twice, Black Elk's only surviving child, who died in 1978. Steltenkamp wrote that the Catholic Church had sent Black Elk on fundraising trips to cities such as New York City; Boston; Chicago; Washington, D.C.; and Omaha. In 1934 shortly after publication of *Black Elk Speaks,* Black Elk complained that Neihardt had not written enough about his life as a Catholic.

During his later years Black Elk combined Catholic missionary work with occasional showmanship at South Dakota tourist attractions that capitalized on his image as a Lakota holy man. Steltenkamp wrote that Black Elk saw no contradictions in mixing the two interpretations of the "great mystery." Black Elk died on August 19, 1950, at Pine Ridge, South Dakota. He is said to have believed that lights in the sky would accompany his death. The night that Black Elk died, the Pine Ridge area experienced an intense and unusually bright meteor shower.

BRUCE E. JOHANSEN

See also

Buffalo Bill's Wild West Show; Fort Laramie, Treaty of (1851); Fort Laramie, Treaty of (1868); Great Sioux War; Lakota Sioux; Little Bighorn, Battle of the; Wounded Knee, Battle of

References

Black Elk. *The Sacred Pipe.* Edited by Joseph Epes Brown. New York: Penguin, 1973.

Brown, Dee. *Bury My Heart at Wounded Knee.* New York: Holt, Rinehart and Winston, 1970.

Nabokov, Peter. *Native American Testimony.* New York: Viking, 1991.

Neihardt, Hilda. *Black Elk & Flaming Rainbow: Personal Memories of the Lakota Holy Man.* Lincoln: University of Nebraska Press, 1995.

Neihardt, John. *Black Elk Speaks.* Lincoln: University of Nebraska Press, 1932.

Rice, Julian. *Black Elk's Story.* Albuquerque: University of New Mexico Press, 1991.

Blackfoot Confederacy

Native American confederacy made up of three tribes of Algonquian-speaking peoples. The three tribes were the Northern Blackfeet or Siksikas, the Bloods or Kainahs, and the Piegans or Pikunis, each of which had a variable number of bands. The Blackfeet (also known as Blackfoot) were the westernmost Algonquian-speaking nation. The Blackfoot home extended from the North Saskatchewan River in the north to the Missouri River in the south and from the Rocky Mountains in the west to the South Saskatchewan River in the east, being divided about equally between what is now Canada and the United States.

Having migrated in the precontact period to the northern Great Plains, the Blackfoot tribes were unfamiliar with the horse until about 1730, when a Shoshone war party attacked a Piegan Blackfoot party and inflicted heavy losses because the Shoshone were mounted. In this prehorse period, the three Blackfoot tribes harvested buffalo primarily by the drive method, either running the bison over a cliff or running them into an enclosure. The Blackfeet relied heavily on buffalo for their food, clothing, and shelter needs and also engaged in trade using buffalo products as far south as northern Mexico.

Once acquainted with the horse, by the mid-1700s the Blackfeet became inveterate horse raiders, seizing horses from tribes to their south and west. Horses helped the Blackfeet stage raids against enemy tribes, which became a significant component of their economic and military culture. Horses also transformed their hunting patterns, especially after the Blackfeet began using firearms. Their lodges became significantly larger, and they increased their personal possessions. Blackfoot society also became more stratified, with wealth being identified by both the number and quality of an individual's horses.

Around the mid-18th century, the Blackfeet acquired smoothbore muzzle-loading muskets from their neighbors to the east and north, who had obtained the weapons from French and British traders. The French appear to have made contact with the Blackfeet first. By the time the British had established extensive direct contact with the Blackfeet, the Blackfeet had defeated the French in the French and Indian War (1754–1763). The Hudson's Bay Company became the principal trade contact with the Indians. The Blackfeet were not especially interested in hunting beavers, preferring to trade buffalo hides and other large-game animal hides for the increasingly important trade goods of the Europeans. The Blackfeet were considered skilled and shrewd traders and often successfully played American, French, and British traders against each other.

Following a July 1806 skirmish between Americans and the Blackfeet during the Lewis and Clark expedition, there existed a long-term enmity between the Blackfeet and American traders and trappers. This issue was not solved until 1830, when former employees of the Hudson's Bay Company now in the employ of the American Fur Company made contact and peace with the Piegan tribe. Once again the Blackfeet resisted trading in beaver pelts, but the increasing demand for buffalo hides nevertheless resulted in a lucrative trade for them.

Relations between the Americans and the Blackfeet were formalized in an 1855 treaty and with the creation of an Indian agency and reservation for the Blackfeet at Fort Benton, Montana. The American Civil War (1861–1865) disrupted these positive relations, however, and by the late 1860s increasing numbers of white settlers engaged in ranching and prospecting resulted in increasing hostility. In January 1870 a U.S. Army attack on a Piegan band along the Marias River resulted in the deaths of 173 Native Americans, including a large number of women and children. Although the ensuing scandal prevented the transfer of the Indian Bureau from the Interior Department to the War Department, the impact of the massacre along with the effects of repeated outbreaks of smallpox led the Blackfoot tribes to seek peace with the Americans. After 1870 no further outbreaks of violence on the part of the Blackfeet occurred, but gradually they were compelled to cede much of their land to the United States. Today the Blackfoot Reservation is located on the Marias and Cut Bank rivers in north-central Montana.

JOHN THOMAS BROOM

See also
Buffalo; Fort Laramie, Treaty of (1851); Fort Laramie, Treaty of (1868); Lewis and Clark Expedition; Marias Massacre

References
Ewers, John C. *The Blackfeet: Raiders of the Northwestern Plains.* Norman: University of Oklahoma Press, 1958.
Ewers, John C. *Indian Life on the Upper Missouri.* Norman: University of Oklahoma Press, 1968.
Ewers, John C. "Were the Blackfoot Rich in Horses?" *American Anthropologist,* n.s., 45(4), pt. 1 (October–December 1943): 602–610.
Grinnell, George Bird. "Early Blackfoot History." *American Anthropologist* 5(2) (April 1892): 153–164.
Haines, Francis. "The Northward Spread of Horses among the Plains Indians." *American Anthropologist,* n.s., 40(3) (July–September 1938): 429–437.
Nugent, David. "Property Relations, Production Relations, and Inequality: Anthropology, Political Economy, and the Blackfeet." *American Ethnologist* 20(2) (May, 1993): 336–362.
Sundstrom, Linea. "Smallpox Used Them Up: References to Epidemic Disease in Northern Plains Winter Counts, 1714–1920." *Ethnohistory* 44(2) (Spring 1997): 305–343.

Blackfoot Sioux

One of seven subbands of the Teton Sioux. Referred to as the Lakota or Western Sioux, the Tetons inhabited parts of present-day Nebraska, Wyoming, Montana, and the Dakotas during the 1800s. The Blackfoot Sioux refer to themselves as the Sihasapas ("black foot" in Lakota). Close relatives of the Hunkpapa Lakotas, the Sihasapas joined the Sioux migration from their original home in central Minnesota onto the Plains in the mid-1700s. As the Sihasapas moved west, they fought with the Assiniboines, Crows, Mandans, Arikaras, and Hidatsas over hunting territories and trading rights. Lakota strength grew during the 19th century, and the Blackfoot band expanded its territory at the expense of its enemies. By the mid-1800s the Blackfoot Sioux

Blackfoot man and woman wearing striped trade blankets, with their horse and travois. (Library of Congress)

lived along the Missouri River in present-day north-central South Dakota.

The tribe exhibited all of the Plains cultural and economic characteristics, which included widespread use of horses, the primacy of the buffalo hunt, and the use of buffalo for food, clothing, and shelter. They also engaged in raiding and trading.

Although the Blackfoot Sioux were not involved in the Dakota Uprising (1862) in Minnesota, they fell prey to the aftermath of that struggle when Brigadier General Alfred Sully's expeditions during 1863–1865 marched into Dakota Territory to punish the Sioux. Blackfoot warriors were among the Lakotas who were attacked at Whitestone Hill (1863) and Killdeer Mountain (1864). These battles drove many Sihasapas into the ranks of the Sioux who opposed the reservation system.

During the Battle of the Little Bighorn (June 25–26, 1876), 34 Sihasapa lodges, led by Crawler and Kill Eagle, fought alongside their Lakota allies. Indeed, Kill Eagle recorded one of the most vivid accounts of the battle. Most of the Blackfoot Sioux who fought at the Little Bighorn surrendered to U.S. troops in the autumn of 1876 and were returned to the reservation. In 1877 some Sihasapas fled into exile in Canada, where they settled near Wood Mountain in Saskatchewan. Most Blackfoot Sioux returned to the United States in 1881 and were sent to Standing Rock Reservation.

Other Blackfoot Sioux meanwhile had remained on the Standing Rock Reservation. John Grass, a Sihasapa leader, was considered to be a progressive because he encouraged the Blackfoot people to farm and attend mission schools. Grass and Gall (Pizi) opposed further land cessions in the 1880s, but their cooperation with Standing Rock agent James McLaughlin probably won the Lakotas the best deal they could have received.

After the Ghost Dance movement ended in 1890, the Blackfoot Sioux settled in as farmers and ranchers on the Cheyenne River and Standing Rock reservations and began the difficult process of assimilating American cultural practices.

STEVE POTTS

See also

Ghost Dance; Killdeer Mountain, Battle of; Lakota Sioux; Little Bighorn, Battle of the; Minnesota Sioux Uprising; Standing Rock Reservation; Sully, Alfred; Whitestone Hill, Battle of

References

DeMallie, Raymond J., ed. *Handbook of North American Indians: Plains*, Vol. 13, pt. 2. Washington, DC: Smithsonian Institution, 2001.
Gibbon, Guy. *The Sioux: The Dakota and Lakota Nations*. Malden, MA: Blackwell, 2003.

Black Hawk
Birth Date: ca. 1767
Death Date: October 3, 1838

Leader of the Sauks and Foxes and an inveterate foe of American expansion. Black Hawk (Makataimeshekiakiak), a member of the Thunder Clan of the Sauks and Foxes, was born around 1767 and grew up at Saukenuk in northeastern Illinois. He joined his first war party at age 15 and fought in successive wars and raids against neighboring Osages and Cherokees. A chief since 1788, Black Hawk resented American interference in Native American affairs and became stridently pro-British in outlook. This conflicted directly with most tribal elders, who were friendly toward the United States and received gifts and annuities in return.

By 1804 Black Hawk's dislike turned to hatred when Indiana territorial governor William Henry Harrison persuaded several Sauk and Fox chiefs to sell most of their land east of the Mississippi River. Black Hawk refused to sign the treaty and remained at his village of Saukenuk. When the War of 1812 erupted eight years later, his warrior band joined Tecumseh's pantribal pro-British alliance in their struggle against the whites. Pan-Indian unity proved fleeting, however. Despite Black Hawk's best efforts, the Sauk and Fox nation split into the British band under himself and a pro-American faction allied to Chief Keokuk.

Black Hawk fought and helped defeat the Americans in the Battle of Frenchtown in January 1813 and participated in the unsuccessful siege of Fort Meigs that May. When British forces failed to dislodge Major George Croghan from Fort Stephenson in August 1813, however, Black Hawk grew disillusioned and withdrew to his homeland for the winter. He reentered the fray in July 1814 when

Black Hawk was a chief of the Sauk and Fox Indians. Allied with the British during the War of 1812, Black Hawk went to war again in 1832 to halt the encroachment of white settlers on tribal lands. (Peter Newark American Pictures/The Bridgeman Art Library International)

his warriors ambushed and defeated a detachment of the 1st U.S. Infantry Regiment on Campbell's Island in the Mississippi River.

In September, Black Hawk enjoyed similar success when he drove off an expedition under Major Zachary Taylor at Rock River, Illinois. Black Hawk was understandably upset with his British allies when they signed a peace treaty with the Americans and abandoned all their western conquests to the United States. Throughout the spring of 1815 Black Hawk raided several settlements near Fort Howard, Missouri, in protest. The following year he sullenly concluded a peace treaty with the United States, the last Sauk and Fox war chief to do so.

For the next 20 years Black Hawk lived in an uneasy truce with his white neighbors at Saukenuk, but in 1829 the Illinois state government applied pressure on the Native Americans to move. When the old chief refused, in June 1831 Governor John Reynolds called out the militia to evict them by force. Bloodshed was averted, however, when the Sauks and Foxes slipped quietly across the Mississippi River into Iowa and endured an uncomfortable winter there. Black Hawk had meanwhile come under the influence of White Cloud, a Winnebago prophet, who urged action against the whites, and Black Hawk decided to reclaim his ancestral home. On April 5, 1832, the tribe, numbering 1,400 men, women, and children, crossed into Illinois for the stated purpose of occupying Saukenuk. It was hoped that hostilities could be avoided.

Predictably, the Americans reacted by summoning the troops of Brigadier General Henry Atkinson and Colonel Henry Dodge, who immediately marched against the Indians. The Sauks and Foxes, having received no pledge of assistance from the neighboring Winnebago and Potawatomi tribes, decided that the odds were too steep and tried to surrender. When two of their peace envoys were killed by Illinois militia, the Battle of Stillman's Run erupted on May 14, 1832, and Black Hawk was again victorious. Black Hawk and the tribe then reached the Mississippi River and prepared to cross. They were in the act of building rafts when they were attacked by the steamboat *Warrior* on August 1, 1832.

Again the Native Americans tried to signal their surrender but to no avail. After inflicting considerable losses, the *Warrior* withdrew because of lack of fuel just as Atkinson's column arrived. An intense battle ensued in which 150 Native Americans were slain and a like number captured. Several survivors made their way across to the west bank of the Mississippi, where they were immediately attacked by Sioux war parties. Black Hawk was eventually captured and taken east to meet with President Andrew Jackson. After several months of confinement at Fort Monroe, Virginia, Black Hawk was released into the custody of rival chief Keokuk.

Back in Iowa, Black Hawk dictated his memoirs, a stinging indictment against white injustice, to Indian agent Antonine LeClaire. When published in 1833, this book—*Autobiography of Ma-Ka-Tai-Me-She-Kia-Kiak, or Black Hawk, Embracing the Traditions of His Nation, Various Wars in Which He Has Been Engaged, and His Account of the Cause and General History of the Black Hawk War of 1832, His Surrender, and Travels through the United States; Also Life, Death and Burial of the Old Chief, Together with a History of the Black Hawk War*—became a national best seller. Black Hawk died in Keokuk's village on October 3, 1838. The defeat of Black Hawk signaled the collapse of Native American resistance to white expansion east of the Mississippi.

BRUCE E. JOHANSEN

See also

Bad Axe, Battle of; Black Hawk War; Keokuk; Sauks and Foxes; Native Americans and the War of 1812; Stillman's Run, Battle of; Winnebagos

References

Black Hawk. *Black Hawk: An Autobiography.* Edited by Donald Jackson. 1833; reprint, Urbana: University of Illinois Press, 1964.

Jung, Patrick J. *The Black Hawk War of 1832.* Norman: University of Oklahoma Press, 2007.

Trask, Kerry A. *Black Hawk: The Battle for the Heart of America.* New York: Holt, 2006.

Black Hawk War
Event Date: 1832

Conflict fought between factions of the Sauk (Sac) and Fox (Mesquakie) people and the United States. The fighting occurred throughout northern Illinois and southern Wisconsin. As with most Native American wars, the root cause of the conflict was land, particularly disputes that arose from the Treaty of 1804.

The Algonquian-speaking Sauk and Fox tribes had originally lived near the Saint Lawrence River, but with the arrival of European settlers onto their ancestral homelands, the tribes were slowly forced south and west to territory in Illinois and Wisconsin. During the French and Indian War (1754–1763), many had fought with the British and presumed that at the conclusion of the war the British government would protect their land from American encroachment. This, of course, did not occur, and the outcome of the American Revolutionary War (1775–1783) ensured American dominance of the area.

Almost immediately after American independence in 1783, white clamor for the tribes' land grew. The Northwest Ordinance of 1787 even went so far as to devise a scheme for dividing up the lands without Native American consent. Tensions between the tribes and white settlers steadily increased. Repeated attempts by the American government to negotiate a treaty that called for the Sauks and Foxes to vacate the land were rebuffed.

Pressure mounted on the administration of Thomas Jefferson to remove the Sauks and Foxes from their land as white settlement in the region between the Appalachian Mountains and the Mississippi River steadily grew. Increasingly the presence and the intransigence of the Native Americans became intolerable to most Americans. Moreover, conflict between the Sauks and Foxes and the Osage tribe heightened tensions between the Sauks and the United States. The Osages had signed a treaty with the U.S. government that frustrated the Sauks and Foxes, who wished to make war against their long-time enemy. Older members of the tribes, however, sought to alleviate tensions between themselves and the settlers by securing the release of numerous captive warriors and reaching a peace with the American government. They reasoned that such a peace would strengthen the tribes in relation to their Native American rivals and would secure American-made goods.

In 1804 a delegation of Sauk and Fox leaders went to St. Louis to negotiate for the release of captured warriors, make amends for attacks on white settlers, and secure American goods and arms. Coincidentally, William Henry Harrison, governor of the Indiana Territory, was also in St. Louis. The lands occupied by the Sauks and Foxes fell within Harrison's jurisdiction, and he sought to remove the tribes from their land. Not much is known about the treaty negotiations except that at the end of the talks, the Sauk and Fox diplomats had agreed to vacate all lands east of the Mississippi River for a very modest sum of money. They then were supposed to move into present-day Iowa.

Upon the delegates' return, the 1804 treaty was immediately repudiated by a number of the tribal elders and young leaders, who argued that the delegation had not been authorized to cede lands. Most Sauks and Foxes remained on their lands and refused to relocate west of the Mississippi. One of the more vocal opponents of the treaty was Black Hawk, a young chief.

Following the War of 1812 in which the Sauks and Foxes backed the British, the U.S. government began to press the Sauks and Foxes to move across the Mississippi to Iowa. Black Hawk refused to leave. However, a growing faction of the tribe under the leadership of Keokuk, a rival of Black Hawk, came to the conclusion that moving across the river was the best thing for the tribe. In 1829 Keokuk and a significant portion of the tribe moved to Iowa. However, Black Hawk and his followers remained near present-day Rock Island, Illinois, vowing to resist any attempts to move them.

Black Hawk mistakenly believed that the British would aid him in his fight with the Americans. In 1831 he and his followers were forced off their land by Illinois militiamen and into Iowa, where they took up residence with Keokuk's band. However, in 1832 Black Hawk led some 400 warriors and their families back into Illinois, hoping to join the Rock River Winnebago tribe and settle in the region. The Illinois militia and federal troops pursued Black Hawk and his followers across northern Illinois.

The Black Hawk War was short but bloody, and Native American forces scored a stunning victory in the Battle of Stillman's Run on May 14, 1832, routing a contingent of the Illinois militia. However, the war soon turned against Black Hawk, who was soundly defeated at the mouth of the Bad Axe River in southern Wisconsin on August 2, 1832. As many as 150 Native Americans died in this battle, while some 75 were captured, including Black Hawk, who was imprisoned. A subsequent treaty between the Sauks and Foxes and the United States, signed on September 21, 1832, forced the Sauks and Foxes to cede much of their lands in Iowa.

RICK DYSON

See also

Bad Axe, Battle of; Black Hawk; Harrison, William Henry; Keokuk; Osages; Sauks and Foxes; Stillman's Run, Battle of; Winnebagos

References

Black Hawk. *Black Hawk: An Autobiography.* Edited by Donald Jackson. Urbana: University of Illinois Press, 1964.

Jung, Patrick J. *The Black Hawk War of 1832.* Norman: University of Oklahoma Press, 2007.

Trask, Kerry A. *Black Hawk: The Battle for the Heart of America.* New York: Holt, 2006.

Wallace, Anthony F. C. "Prelude to Disaster: The Course of Indian-White Relations Which Led to the Black Hawk War of 1832." *Wisconsin Magazine of History* 65 (1982): 247–288.

Black Hills, South Dakota

The Black Hills, located in western South Dakota and northeastern Wyoming, have a widely varied landscape that includes canyon lands and gulches with large boulders, rocky outcrops and caves, steep ridges, rolling hills, upland prairies, and valleys. The mountain ranges average about 2,950–3,300 feet; the highest point at 7,130 feet is Harney Peak. The area of the Black Hills' core highland is 688 square miles, while the foothills area covers an additional 900 square miles. The Black Hills are the sacred ground and home territory of the Teton Sioux, or Lakotas.

The Lakotas found strong religious significance in the Black Hills because they are the traditional birthplace of the Sioux Nation. The Lakotas are also known to be the caretakers and protectors of the Black Hills, which they call He Sapa. Furthermore, the Lakotas found psychological and physical remedial elements in "the heart of everything that is" because the Black Hills provided the Lakotas with every basic necessity. The region was also the Lakotas' hunting grounds for buffalo, which yielded food, clothing, shelter, and tools.

In the 1868 Treaty of Fort Laramie, the U.S. government set the Black Hills within the Great Sioux Reservation, and whites were not allowed inside the reservation. However, an 1874 expedition led by Lieutenant Colonel George A. Custer to identify a suitable location for a new military post also discovered gold, and a subsequent geological expedition headed by Walter P. Jenny in 1875 confirmed the area's mineral richness. Such discoveries were bound to attract unwanted visitors and invite conflict. The federal government therefore sought to negotiate new treaties to purchase the land from the Lakotas. The Lakotas vigorously opposed opening the hills to white settlers and rejected all attempts at negotiation, but this failed to discourage gold seekers. The government at first attempted to prevent the encroachment of prospectors, which proved impossible, and soon miners flooded the hills.

Soon a gold rush engulfed the Black Hills. Boomtowns such as Deadwood, which boasted some 25,000 residents by 1876, and Lead, home of the Homestake Mine, sprang up seemingly overnight. The Homestake became the greatest and most enduring gold

Floor of Spearfish Canyon in the Black Hills of South Dakota. (Shutterstock)

mine. (Until it closed in 2002, it was the oldest, largest, and deepest mine in the Western Hemisphere. Homestake Mine extended more than 8,000 feet below the town of Lead.) Miners eventually transitioned to mining for hard-rock and ore within the hills.

The Lakotas considered the invasion of gold miners and army troops a violation of the 1868 treaty and consequently threatened war. Indeed, opening of the Lakota land led to the Great Sioux War (1876–1877). Without a suitable new treaty, the federal government demanded that the tribes report to their agencies or be declared hostile. When some bands failed to report, the army was sent to round up the Native Americans. This led to a three-pronged invasion, with the army hoping to trap the Lakotas and their allies. Oglala Sioux leader Crazy Horse, however, stopped Brigadier General George Crook at Rosebud Creek in early June 1876. Shortly afterward on June 25, 1876, Crazy Horse, along with other Lakota leaders and hundreds of Northern Cheyenne warriors, dealt Custer's 7th Cavalry a devastating blow in the Battle

of the Little Bighorn, killing Custer and wiping out his entire battalion. The government was determined to punish the Indians and after a brutal winter campaign forced Crazy Horse and most of the Lakota and Cheyenne leaders to surrender in 1877. As a result, the Lakotas were obliged to cede the Black Hills to the U.S. government for only a fraction of their value.

JUSTIN D. MURPHY AND LORIN M. LOWRIE

See also

Black Hills Gold Rush; Crazy Horse; Crook, George; Custer, George Armstrong; Fort Laramie, Treaty of (1851); Fort Laramie, Treaty of (1868); Great Sioux War; Lakota Sioux; Little Bighorn, Battle of the; Oglala Sioux; Rosebud, Battle of the

References

Froiland, Sven. *Natural History of the Black Hills.* Sioux Falls, SD: Center for Western Studies, 1978.

Lazarus, Edward. *Black Hills/White Justice: The Sioux Nation versus the United States, 1775 to the Present.* New York: HarperCollins, 1991.

Black Hills Gold Rush
Event Date: 1874

Gold rush that began with the July 1874 discovery of deposits in the Black Hills of present-day western South Dakota and eastern Wyoming. Following Red Cloud's War (1866–1868), the United States withdrew the army from the Black Hills. Negotiations between the U.S. government and the Sioux Nation finally resulted in the 1868 Treaty of Fort Laramie, which set aside the Black Hills, sacred to the Sioux, for the "absolute and undisturbed use and occupation" of the Sioux. The treaty, however, was ambiguous regarding the right of the U.S. military to make incursions into the region for surveying and exploration purposes.

In 1872 Secretary of the Interior Columbus Delano, observing that too large an allotment of land had been reserved for the approximately 20,000 Sioux, suggested that mineral deposits and natural resources in the Black Hills merited investigation and exploration. Accordingly, Lieutenant Colonel George Custer was ordered to scout out possible sites for a fort within the area. The Custer expedition, which numbered about 1,000 men, left Fort Abraham Lincoln in the Dakota Territory on July 2, 1874. In mid-July Custer's party found gold deposits near the present-day town of Custer, South Dakota. Custer immediately sent word of the gold to his commanding officer, Brigadier General Alfred H. Terry. By the time Custer's expedition had returned to Fort Abraham Lincoln on August 30, 1874, word of the gold discovery had been leaked to the press, and the gold rush into the Black Hills was under way.

The U.S. military initially attempted to prevent prospectors from moving into the region. This proved almost impossible, and by January 1875 an estimated 15,000 white miners were in the Black Hills. The government then sought to negotiate a revision of the 1868 treaty that would allow for white settlement in the region. When Sioux leaders Red Cloud, Spotted Tail, and Crazy Horse refused to approve these exceptions, President Ulysses S. Grant decided to terminate the treaty in its entirety.

On December 6, 1875, the Sioux were ordered to move onto reservation land designated by the government. Any Sioux failing to follow this directive would be declared hostile. Authority over these hostiles was transferred from the secretary of the interior to the War Department on February 1, 1876. The army was then sent into the Black Hills, resulting in the Great Sioux War (1876–1877) and the ill-fated Battle of the Little Bighorn (June 25–26, 1876), in which Custer and an entire battalion of the 7th Cavalry were killed on the first day of the battle.

This Sioux victory was short-lived, as military reinforcements quickly subdued the Sioux and their Cheyenne allies. Sioux leader Sitting Bull retreated into Canada, while Crazy Horse was murdered in captivity on September 5, 1877. Red Cloud and Spotted Tail were forced to surrender the Black Hills in 1878, and the Pine Ridge and Rosebud agencies were established as the new home for the Sioux Nation.

RON BRILEY

See also

Black Hills, South Dakota; Crazy Horse; Custer, George Armstrong; Fort Laramie, Treaty of (1851); Fort Laramie, Treaty of (1868); Great Sioux Reservation; Great Sioux War; Little Bighorn, Battle of the; Pine Ridge Reservation; Red Cloud; Red Cloud's War; Sioux; Sitting Bull; Terry, Alfred Howe

References

Jackson, Donald. *Custer's Gold: The United States Cavalry Expedition of 1874.* New Haven, CT: Yale University Press, 1966.

Lazarus, Edward. *Black Hills/White Justice: The Sioux Nation versus the United States, 1775 to the Present.* New York: HarperCollins, 1991.

Parker, Watson. *Gold in the Black Hills.* Norman: University of Oklahoma Press, 1966.

Black Hills War

See Great Sioux War

Black Hoof
Birth Date: ca. 1740
Death Date: 1831

Shawnee leader. The life of Shawnee leader Black Hoof (Catecahassa) in many ways paralleled the life of his tribe. He often said that he was not sure where he was born, but most historians agree that it was in the area of present-day Ohio, probably around 1740. By the time Black Hoof was a young man, he was living with the rest of his tribe in the Ohio Country.

Black Hoof was well known among the Ohio tribes as an excellent orator and warrior. While little is known about his early life, he claimed to have participated in the 1755 Battle of the Monongahela (Braddock's Campaign) during the French and Indian War (1754–1763). He also claimed that he joined in every major battle against the Americans over a span of 40 years.

Black Hoof entered the historical record in 1795 when he placed his mark on the Treaty of Greenville. The defeat that the Native Americans had suffered at the 1794 Battle of Fallen Timbers changed Black Hoof greatly. He came to the conclusion that war against the Americans was unwinnable. If the tribes were to survive, he opined, then they must become year-round farmers.

Black Hoof retired to the village of Wapakoneta in present-day Shelby County, Ohio. There he encouraged the Shawnees to live in peace with the Americans and adopt their ways. In 1808 he went to Philadelphia, where he asked the Society of Friends (Quakers) to help his people. Quakers subsequently traveled to Wapakoneta, where they taught the Shawnees how to raise livestock, build barns and fences, and operate flour and sawmills.

Black Hoof was an outspoken critic of Tecumseh and Tenskwatawa (the Prophet) and was able to keep most of the Ohio Shawnees loyal to the Americans during the War of 1812. Black Hoof signed the second Treaty of Greenville in 1814, the Treaty of Spring Wells in 1816, and the Treaty at the Foot of the Rapids in 1818, by which the Shawnees gave up most of their remaining lands in northwestern Ohio. Black Hoof received a 10-mile-square grant around the council house at Wapakoneta as part of the last treaty.

As with so many chiefs who had been loyal to the United States, Black Hoof was stunned when the government forced his tribe west following passage of the Indian Removal Act in 1830. Black Hoof died in Wapakoneta, Ohio, in 1831, shortly after the Shawnees living in Wapakoneta had surrendered their land to the Americans.

MARY STOCKWELL

See also

Braddock's Campaign; Fallen Timbers, Battle of; Greenville, Treaty of; Indian Removal Act; Little Turtle's War; Shawnees; Tecumseh

References

Clark, Jerry E. *The Shawnee.* Lexington: University Press of Kentucky, 2007.

Johnston, John. *Recollections of Sixty Years.* Whitefish, MT: Kessinger, 2010.

Black Kettle
Birth Date: ca. 1803
Death Date: November 27, 1868

Southern Cheyenne leader. Black Kettle (Mo-to-vato, Mo-ke-ta-va-ta) was born around 1803, possibly near the Black Hills of present-day South Dakota. As a youth he distinguished himself in warfare against the Utes, Pawnees, and Comanches, emerging as a leader of the Southern Cheyennes by 1861. That year he joined several Cheyenne and Arapaho leaders in signing the Treaty of Fort Wise. In this agreement the tribes gave up most of their land claims in exchange for a reservation south of the Arkansas River.

Black Kettle's assent to the treaty was consistent with his efforts to coexist with the growing number of American settlers rather than resist them, a policy that earned him a reputation as a peace chief. He constantly sought accommodation despite suffering repeated abuses at the hands of the Americans.

In 1864 Colonel John M. Chivington of the Colorado Volunteers responded to sporadic Native American attacks on settlers by launching a campaign against area tribes. Black Kettle and 400 followers encountered some of Chivington's troops in May on the Smoky Hill River. When a Cheyenne leader approached to explain that his people were peaceful, the soldiers opened fire and killed 28 Native Americans before Black Kettle ordered the Cheyennes to cease resistance. The incident triggered reprisals by other Native American groups, and soon war engulfed the Colorado region.

Still hoping for peace, Black Kettle opened negotiations with Major Edward Wynkoop. In mid-September 1864 Black Kettle accompanied Wynkoop to Denver for talks with Chivington, who

Black Kettle, chief of the Southern Cheyennes, sought peace with whites but was killed along with many of his people in an attack by Lieutenant Colonel George A. Custer's 7th Cavalry on his peaceful camp on the Washita River in western Oklahoma on November 27, 1868. (Courtesy of the Oklahoma Historical Society, 6737A)

ordered Black Kettle to take his people to Fort Lyon, where they would be safe. Black Kettle complied. Upon reaching the fort he was ordered by Major Scott Anthony to camp at Sand Creek, 40 miles away.

Early on the morning of November 29, 1864, Chivington and his troops attacked the camp. Black Kettle held a pole with an American flag and shouted reassurance to his people but to no avail. Approximately 200 people died in what became known as the Sand Creek Massacre. Black Kettle managed to escape.

The Sand Creek Massacre led many Cheyennes to renew their campaign against the Americans. However, Black Kettle angered Cheyenne militants by leading his remaining supporters south of the Arkansas River to avoid the fighting. He persisted in his efforts to secure peace, signing the Little Arkansas Treaty in 1865 and the Medicine Lodge Treaty two years later. The latter required the southern Plains nations to give up their remaining land and settle in Indian Territory (Oklahoma).

Most Native Americans were slow to comply with the treaty. In the autumn of 1868 Major General Philip Sheridan ordered all peaceful Native Americans to report to Fort Cobb in Indian Territory. Black Kettle did so, but Colonel William B. Hazen told him that he had no authority to protect Black Kettle's people, who would have to surrender to Sheridan. Black Kettle returned to the Cheyenne camp on the Washita River, where Lieutenant Colonel George A. Custer's 7th Cavalry attacked them on November 27, 1868. Black Kettle, true to his principles, did not resist and was killed while trying to flee.

JIM PIECUCH

See also

Cheyennes; Cheyennes, Southern; Chivington, John; Custer, George Armstrong; Medicine Lodge Treaty; Sand Creek Massacre; Washita, Battle of the

References

Brown, Dee. *Bury My Heart at Wounded Knee.* New York: Holt, Rinehart and Winston, 1970.

Hoig, Stan. *The Peace Chiefs of the Cheyennes.* Norman: University of Oklahoma Press, 1980.

Utley, Robert M. *The Indian Frontier of the American West, 1846–1890.* Albuquerque: University of New Mexico Press, 1984.

Black Point, Attacks on
Event Dates: October 12, 1676, May 14–16, 1677, and June 29, 1677

Series of three skirmishes between Native Americans and English colonists during King Philip's War (1675–1676). Black Point, the site of a small English settlement and stronghold, was located in present-day Scarborough County, Maine, just south of Portland. The initial attack on Black Point came on October 12, 1676, when Mugg Hegon, the Androscoggin sachem (chief), led 50–100 native warriors against the English there.

The native attack was an extension of King Philip's War that had been raging for months between Massachusetts settlers to the south and the Wampanoags. By 1676, the violence had spilled north into Maine; several English settlements and farms had already been targets of native raids. Mugg did not attack immediately. Instead, he called for the post to surrender. He also offered to let the English leave with their possessions. While the fort's English commander, Captain Henry Jocelyn, was talking with Mugg, most of the English settlers fled Black Point by boat. Jocelyn, who had heretofore enjoyed cordial relations with Mugg, had no choice but to surrender, as the garrison was much reduced. Mugg kept his word and permitted Jocelyn and the remaining settlers to leave with their possessions. Without a shot being fired, Mugg and his men had forced the English to abandon Black Point.

Mugg had no use for the fort at Black Point and abandoned it by November 1676, believing that he had ousted the settlers

for good. Nevertheless, the English reestablished the garrison at Black Point early the following year. Captain Bartholomew Tippen was the garrison's new commander. With the English garrison reconstituted and settlers beginning to return, Mugg once again attacked Black Point. This time the English were prepared and did not flee.

The battle began on May 14, 1677, and ended on May 16. Tippen and his men held back the large contingent of warriors, losing just three men in the three-day fight. Native losses were greater, and Tippen allegedly shot and killed Mugg on May 16. Mugg's death was a severe blow to the natives, who quickly withdrew before day's end.

This English victory was fleeting, however. Just six weeks later on June 29, 1677, a force of 40 raw colonial recruits, led by Captain Benjamin Swett and Lieutenant James Richardson, along with 200 allied native warriors arrived at Black Point by ship. Their goal was to neutralize hostile natives in the area and end any threat to Black Point. A group of men from the garrison joined them as they disembarked. The English then spotted enemy warriors fleeing and gave chase. As it turned out, the flight served as bait for an ambush, into which the English quickly fell. The ambush cost the English 40 dead, including both commanders, and their native allies lost 20 warriors.

The attacks at Black Point were only three episodes in the ongoing hostilities between English settlers and Native Americans in Maine that continued into the 18th century.

DALLACE W. UNGER JR.

See also

King Philip's War; Metacom; Wampanoags

References

Lincoln, Charles H., ed. *Narratives of the Indian Wars, 1675–1699.* New York: Barnes and Noble, 1959.

Mather, Increase, and Cotton Mather. *The History of King Philip's War by Rev. Increase Mather; Also, A History of the Same War by the Rev. Cotton Mather.* Edited by Samuel Gardner Drake. 1862; reprint, Bowie, MD: Heritage Books, 1990.

Schultz, Eric B., and Michael J. Tougias. *King Philip's War: The History and Legacy of America's Forgotten Conflict.* Woodstock, VT: Countryman, 1999.

Black Robes

French Jesuit missionaries who operated in New France beginning in 1625 with the arrival of Jean de Brébeuf and innovated conversion methods among the Native Americans inhabiting the region. Nicknamed "Black Robes" by the Native Americans for their distinctive black cassocks, they were unique in the Americas for their conversion methods, determining that it was necessary for a missionary to live amid the natives as one of them. In so doing, the Black Robes were well equipped to translate Christianity into verbal and cultural terms that the natives could understand.

The Black Robes prepared themselves by living among France's peasantry, but nothing could have readied them for the privations and ordeals of life among the Algonquins and other native nations. The natives considered the Frenchmen to be ugly and stupid, their robes effeminate and ungainly for travel in the wilderness, and their ignorance of basic survival skills a liability to a party on the move. The Algonquins especially ridiculed the inability of the Black Robes to speak the native language fluently.

The best that a new arrival could do was stand aside and observe, learning as much as he could until he developed the strength and stamina to paddle a canoe nonstop for several hours, carry it in a portage, sleep on the frozen ground in tight quarters, stomach the native cuisine, learn the elaborate customs, and—most important—master the language such that he could be deemed a "man of sense" and an asset to that particular community. Only the rare missionary could gain the respect of the natives. Indeed most washed out, usually quite early and most often because of an inability to learn the language.

However, years of experience allowed successful missionaries to prepare guides for those who followed, which along with their annual reports, published in Paris from 1632 to 1673 and known as *The Jesuit Relations,* constitute a sympathetic study of native societies in the early colonial period. Once the Black Robes earned esteem, the natives found much to admire in the priests: their indifference to wealth; their ability to withstand carnal desires (though puzzling), which meant that they would not accost young girls or married women; and their courage and ability to endure discomfort ranging from ridicule from their companions to bodily torture from their enemies.

Being bound by their rule never to carry a weapon or shed blood was considered a great liability, however, as the Indians could never understand a people who would not take up a hatchet in self-defense. But the priests' ability to endure all manner of hardship nevertheless garnered much respect.

The mastery of protocol meant that priests could become important leaders in native communities, and the rare priest who climbed to such a height found conversion a relatively easy business. However, each priest had to win his own victories, which did not enhance the general reputation of the missionaries or the French as a whole. The sum total was disappointing progress, which accounts for the gradual abandonment of such nuanced conversion approaches after 1672, although Jesuit missionaries continued their work well into the 18th century.

JOHN HOWARD SMITH

See also
Algonquins; Missionaries; Wyandots

References
Axtell, James. *The Invasion Within: The Contest of Cultures in Colonial North America.* New York: Oxford University Press, 1985.

Greer, Allan, ed. *The Jesuit Relations: Natives and Missionaries in Seventeenth-Century North America.* Boston: Bedford/St. Martin's, 2000.

Black Swamp

The Black Swamp (also called the Great Black Swamp), which once extended over 12 counties in present-day northwestern Ohio and northeastern Indiana, played an important role in the 1794 Battle of Fallen Timbers. Geologists believe that this region was created by the passing of the glaciers at the end of the Ice Age. As the earth warmed and the glaciers melted, they left behind an ancient lake called the Glacial Maumee Lake. The southwestern corner of this lake became the Black Swamp as the earth grew even warmer and the shores of the ancient lake receded to the outlines of present-day Lake Erie. Today the Maumee, Auglaize, and Portage rivers are the major waterways in the region. Other rivers that once ran through the swamp included the Sandusky, Ottawa, Tiffin, and Blanchard.

Parts of the Black Swamp were flat and inundated by water most of the year. Here ash, elm, cottonwood, and sycamore trees grew so tall that they blocked out the sun. In other places that were slightly more elevated and less prone to flooding, beech, maple, linden, and tulip trees thrived. Oak and hickory stood on the highest sandy ground that was well drained. Still other parts of the Black Swamp were marshes or prairies where grasses and wild flowers grew so thick that they were virtually impenetrable.

Mosquitoes in the Black Swamp often infected people with malaria. The humidity in summer could be unbearable, while the swampy ground in rainy seasons made it impossible for people or animals to cross through it. Still, the Ottawas made the Black Swamp their home in the late 18th and early 19th centuries. The bottomland along the rivers was excellent for farming, while the shallow rivers provided for superb fishing.

Because it was so difficult to pass through, the Black Swamp was used for defensive purposes by Native Americans. Little Turtle, the Miami leader of Ohio's confederated tribes in the 1790s, was certain that the swamp would act as a barrier to protect the tribes from an American attack. He was surprised when Brigadier General "Mad" Anthony Wayne marched his army through the Black Swamp in the summer of 1794 and defeated the confederated tribes at the Battle of Fallen Timbers. But even Wayne did not think that the region was valuable, and he surrendered it to the Ohio tribes in the Treaty of Greenville (1795).

Settlers who poured into Ohio after the end of the War of 1812 generally avoided the Black Swamp. But by the 1830s and 1840s when the best land in the state had already been settled, the Black Swamp suddenly seemed valuable. Many German immigrants entered the region once the Miami and Erie Canal was completed, and they realized that there was excellent soil beneath the tangled trees and thick prairie grass. By the 1850s a concerted effort was under way to drain the Black Swamp. By 1890 most of the Black Swamp had been drained and settled. Today, some of the most productive farmland in the world can be found along the rivers of the Black Swamp. Vestiges of the swamp can still be found in marshy wildlife preserves along the shore of Lake Erie.

MARY STOCKWELL

See also

Fallen Timbers, Battle of; Greenville, Treaty of; Little Turtle; Little Turtle's War; Miamis; Ottawas; Wayne, Anthony; Wayne's Campaign

References

Good, Howard. *Black Swamp Farm.* Columbus: Ohio State University Press, 1997.

Kaatz, Martin Richard. "The Black Swamp: A Study in Historical Geography." *Annals of the Association of American Geographers* 45(1): 1–35.

Mollenkopf, Jim. *The Great Black Swamp: Historical Tales of 19th Century Northwest Ohio.* Toledo, OH: Lake of the Cat Publishing, 1999.

Blockhouses

Often crude but effective fortifications used frequently on the American frontier during the 17th, 18th, and 19th centuries. While many fortifications used in North America, especially during the colonial period, employed the principles of European military engineering, blockhouses were commonsense expedients to the problem of frontier defense. Consequently, although blockhouses were occasionally used by regular military forces, they were more typically constructed by militiamen or provincials because of their simple design and the relative ease with which they could be erected.

A typical blockhouse was a two-story square or rectangular building with a sloping roof. Blockhouses were usually constructed of logs or thick planks to protect the defenders from enemy musket fire. In the far West, especially in the Southwest, some blockhouses were constructed of adobe. Frequently the second floor was constructed to overhang the first so that defenders could fire down on an enemy pressed against the lower wall. Loopholes in the walls allowed the defenders to engage the enemy while remaining hidden from view and protected from fire. Occasionally blockhouses mounted light artillery pieces and incorporated such additional defensive measures as earthworks or a palisade.

A frontier community might build a blockhouse to serve as a place of refuge and defense in the event of a Native American attack, much like a garrison house. For example, in the 17th

Types of Fortifications Used during the Early American Indian Wars

Name	Description
Abatis	Obstruction made of trees placed in front of a field fortification
Blockhouse	One- or two-story structure used by militias and usually made of logs
Breastworks	Temporary chest-high defensive structures made of earth or timber
Fort	Permanent structure used for protection or defense
Garrison House	Private dwellings used for local defense
Presidio	Permanent Spanish fort, often made of adobe and used for defense against Indians
Redoubt	Unsophisticated temporary fully enclosed field fortification, often made of earth

century Sir William Johnson, founder of Johnstown, New York, constructed two blockhouses adjacent to his home at Johnson Hall in the Mohawk Valley.

Blockhouses could also serve as stand-alone fortifications, much like European-style redoubts. In this capacity, a blockhouse might be used to defend an avenue of approach or a key piece of terrain, such as a river ford or portage. Blockhouses might also be constructed at intervals along an army's line of supply. Fort Ingoldsby, a blockhouse, was constructed in 1709 near Stillwater, New York, in support of Colonel Francis Nicholson's planned invasion of Canada along Lake Champlain. Supplies for his army at Wood Creek moved north from Albany in several stages based on the navigability of the Hudson River. At Stillwater, the small garrison of Fort Ingoldsby oversaw and protected the transfer of supplies from wagons to boats for the continued move northward.

Finally, blockhouses might serve as component parts of larger fortifications. In some instances these structures were placed at the corners of curtain walls in lieu of angled bastions. In this case the deficiencies of blockhouses became apparent, as they did not allow for interlocking fields of fire or all-around protection, a key advantage of angled-bastion fortifications. At other times, well-built blockhouses could serve as strong points within a larger fortification.

Thomas A. Rider II

See also

Forts, Camps, Cantonments, and Outposts; Johnson, Sir William

References

Barry, William E. *The Blockhouse and Stockade Fort.* Kennebunk, ME: Enterprise Press, 1915.

McCully, Bruce T. "Catastrophe in the Wilderness: New Light on the Canada Expedition of 1709." *William and Mary Quarterly,* 3rd ser., 11 (1954): 441–456.

Roberts, Robert B. *New York's Forts in the Revolution.* Cranbury, NJ: Associated University Presses, 1980.

Bloody Brook Massacre
Event Date: September 19, 1675

Native American ambush of colonial militiamen and a supply column near Deerfield, Massachusetts, on September 19, 1675. In mid-September 1675 as fighting along Massachusetts's western frontier worsened during King Philip's War (1675–1676), colonial officials decided to abandon a number of outlying towns and consolidate their defenses. Deerfield, Massachusetts, was one of the towns abandoned, but its grain warehouses and barns were full of drying corn, food that would be greatly needed that winter. In mid-September 1675 Captain Thomas Lathrop was ordered to protect the wagon caravan carrying the corn from Deerfield south to Springfield. Lathrop and his Essex County militia company of some 60–70 men loaded the carts during the night of September 18.

The next morning, September 19, Lathrop and his company, as well as local teamsters in charge of the carts, set off. Captain

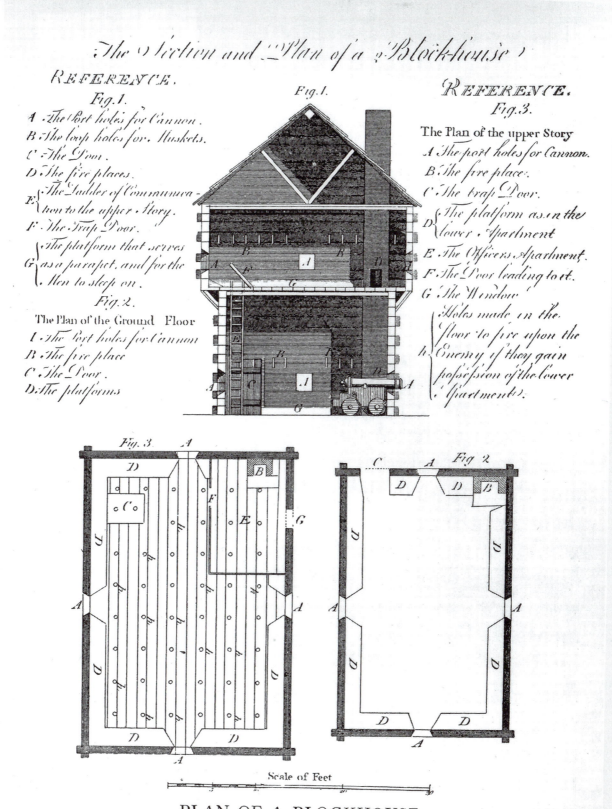

The Section and Plan of a Block-house

REFERENCE.
Fig. 1.
A . The Port holes for Cannon .
B . The loop holes for. Muskets .
C . The Door .
D . The fire places .
E { The Ladder of Communica- tion to the upper. Story .
F . The Trap Door .
G { The platform that serves as a parapet, and for the Men to sleep on .

Fig. 2.
The Plan of the Ground Floor
A . The Port holes for Cannon
B . The fire place
C . The Door .
D . The platforms

REFERENCE.
Fig. 3.
The Plan of the upper Story
A . The port holes for Cannon .
B . The fire place .
C . The trap Door .
D { The platform as in the lower. Apartment
E . The Officers Apartment .
F . The Door leading to it .
G . The Window
{ Holes made in the floor to fire upon the
h { Enemy if they gain possession of the lower Apartments .

Fig. 1.

Fig. 3.

Fig. 2.

Scale of Feet

PLAN OF A BLOCKHOUSE
Lent by William D. Patterson, Wiscasset

Section and plan of a colonial-era blockhouse. (Library of Congress)

Samuel Mosley's militia company scouted the area ahead of the wagon train. Lathrop reportedly was confident that no Indian party would attack such a large military force. He believed that Native American war parties struck only defenseless garrison houses and isolated farms. Accordingly, Lathrop had not positioned flankers or a vanguard. The wagon train traveled south along the forest path. When it reached Muddy Brook, about five miles south of Deerfield, Lathrop and his men found themselves quickly surrounded by hundreds of Wampanoags, Pocumtucks, Nipmucks, and other Native Americans.

The Indians attacked with deadly speed and efficiency, and from that point Muddy Brook was known as Bloody Brook. In his history of the war, Increase Mather claimed that Lathrop's men were so confident and carefree that they had placed their muskets in the carts in order to eat wild grapes along the stream bank, rendering the men defenseless. The ambush was over in just a few minutes. At least 60 colonials were slain, including Captain Lathrop and 15 of the Deerfield men. Hearing the frantic calls of Lathrop's bugler, who had escaped the carnage, Captain Mosley and his company hurried to the scene, rushing the Indians and scattering the scalp hunters. As Mosley's scouting unit and the few survivors from the ambush struggled back to Deerfield that evening, they were taunted by Indians in the distance, who held aloft as trophies clothing stripped from the colonial dead. The next day Mosley and his men returned to Bloody Brook to bury the English dead, including Lathrop.

When news of the ambush traveled east, the entire colony, and especially Essex County, went into mourning. Reverend William Hubbard called it "that most fatal day, the saddest day that ever befel New England," and "the Ruine of a choice Company of young men, the very Flower of Essex."

The Bloody Brook Massacre is only one example of the style of wilderness warfare known as the skulking way of war. Native Americans had long practiced the tactic of ambush, and their adoption of European firearms only made it more deadly. While colonial militias throughout the colonies were at first overwhelmingly the victims of ambush and other types of irregular warfare, some militia commanders adopted Indian tactics with much success.

KYLE F. ZELNER

See also

Deerfield, Massachusetts, Attack on; King Philip's War; Narragansetts; Nipmucks; Skulking Way of War; Wampanoags

References

Hubbard, William. *The History of the Indian Wars in New England, from the First Settlement to the Termination of the War with King Philip in 1677*. Edited by Samuel Gardner Drake. 1864; Facsimile reprint, Bowie, MD: Heritage Books, 1990.

Malone, Patrick M. *The Skulking Way of War: Technology and Tactics among the New England Indians*. Lanham, MD: Madison Books, 2000.

Mather, Increase, and Cotton Mather. *The History of King Philip's War by Rev. Increase Mather; Also, A History of the Same War by the Rev. Cotton Mather*. Edited by Samuel Gardner Drake. 1862; reprint, Bowie, MD: Heritage Books, 1990.

Melvoin, Richard I. *New England Outpost: War and Society in Colonial Deerfield*. New York: Norton, 1989.

Zelner, Kyle. "Essex County's Two Militias: The Social Composition of Offensive and Defensive Units during King Philip's War, 1675–1676." *New England Quarterly* 72(4) (1999): 577–593.

Bloody Knife
Birth Date: ca. 1840
Death Date: June 25, 1876

Native American scout of mixed Arikara and Hunkpapa Sioux ancestry. Bloody Knife (Tamena Way Way or Nes I Ri Pat in Arikara) was perhaps the most famous Native American scout to serve the U.S. Army. Lieutenant Colonel George Armstrong Custer once called Bloody Knife his favorite scout. Bloody Knife's life is surrounded by myth, however, and it is difficult to separate the legend from the actual man. Details of Bloody Knife's early life are sketchy. He was probably born around 1840, but his place of birth is not known. His mother was an Arikara, and his father was a Hunkpapa Sioux, but Bloody Knife grew up among his father's people. According to legend, during his childhood Bloody Knife and future Hunkpapa war leader Gall developed an intense hatred for each other. When his parents separated in 1856, Bloody Knife moved with his mother back to his Arikara relatives near Fort Clark in present-day North Dakota. Life there was dangerous.

Sioux war parties frequently attacked Arikaras who ventured out from the village. Even though he was part Hunkpapa, Bloody Knife was not safe from such attacks. Once he was ambushed by Gall's Hunkpapas, stripped of his clothes, and beaten severely with coup sticks. In 1862 another Sioux war party killed two of his brothers in an ambush.

After working as a hunter and messenger for the American Fur Company for several years, Bloody Knife joined Brigadier General Alfred Sully's Sioux expedition as a scout in 1865. Later that year Bloody Knife led a group of soldiers to a Hunkpapa village to arrest Gall. On this occasion the soldiers bayoneted Gall but prevented Bloody Knife from killing him. Gall eventually recovered from his wounds and reportedly took revenge years later during the Battle of the Little Bighorn.

Bloody Knife later served as a scout at Fort Stevenson, Fort Buford, Fort Rice, and Fort Lincoln. He took part in the first Yellowstone Expedition in 1872. The following year he met Custer at Fort Rice. Custer was impressed with Bloody Knife's skills as a scout, and the two men soon developed a friendship. In 1873 Bloody Knife joined Custer on the second Yellowstone Expedition, during which the troops fought several battles with the Sioux. In 1874 Bloody Knife served in the Black Hills Expedition and was awarded an additional $150 for his "invaluable assistance."

In 1876 Custer appointed Bloody Knife head scout during the expedition that led to the fateful Battle of the Little Bighorn (June

Bloody Knife, a Sioux serving with the U.S. 7th Cavalry, was Lieutenant Colonel George A. Custer's chief scout. Here, Bloody Knife is pictured scouting for Custer during the Yellowstone Expedition of 1873. Bloody Knife was shot and killed in the Battle of the Little Bighorn on June 25, 1876. He had reportedly warned Custer against the attack. (National Archives)

25–26, 1876). Bloody Knife reportedly cautioned Custer against an attack but nevertheless rode into battle with Major Marcus A. Reno's battalion. Bloody Knife was killed while standing next to Reno, which allegedly traumatized Reno. Bloody Knife's remains were later mutilated by the Sioux.

In 1879 Bloody Knife's widow, Young Owl Woman (also known as She Owl), applied for and eventually received her husband's outstanding pay. After the Battle of the Little Bighorn, the surviving Arikara scouts composed a song in Bloody Knife's honor.

MARK VAN DE LOGT

See also

Arikaras; Arikara Scouts; Custer, George Armstrong; Gall; Great Sioux War; Hunkpapa Sioux; Little Bighorn, Battle of the; Reno, Marcus Albert; Sioux; Sully, Alfred

References

Custer, Elizabeth B. *Boots and Saddles: Life in Dakota with General Custer.* Norman: University of Oklahoma Press, 1961.

Dunlay, Thomas W. *Wolves for the Blue Soldiers: Indian Scouts and Auxiliaries with the United States Army, 1860–90.* Lincoln: University of Nebraska Press, 1982.

Gray, John S. "Arikara Scouts with Custer." *North Dakota History* 35 (December 1968): 443–478.

Gray, John S. "Bloody Knife, Ree Scout for Custer." *Chicago Westerners Brand Book* 17(12) (February 1961): 89–96.

Greene, Candace. "Arikara Drawings: New Sources of Visual History." *American Indian Art Magazine* 31(2) (2006): 74–85, 99.

Grinnell, George B. "Bloody Knife." In *Handbook of American Indians North of Mexico,* edited by Frederick W. Hodge, 155. Washington, DC: U.S. Government Printing Office, 1906.

Grinnell, George B. "Bloody Knife, the Ree." *Forest and Stream* 74(10) (March 5, 1910): 370–371.

Innis, Ben. *Bloody Knife: Custer's Favorite Scout.* Bismarck, ND: Smoky Water, 1994.

Libby, Orin G. *The Arikara Narrative of Custer's Campaign and the Battle of the Little Bighorn.* Norman: University of Oklahoma Press, 1998.

Blue Jacket
Birth Date: ca. 1743
Death Date: ca. 1810

Shawnee war chief who played a prominent role in resisting British and then American western encroachment into the Old Northwest. Weyapiersenwah, better known as Blue Jacket, was born probably in 1743 in what is now south-central Ohio. Details of Blue Jacket's early life are so obscure that a persistent myth that he was actually a white Shawnee captive named Marmaduke Van Swearingen gained credence after the 1870s. This myth is now annually celebrated in an outdoor play performed each year in Xenia, Ohio. Blue Jacket's most recent biographer, John Sugden, has conclusively shown, however, that Van Swearingen and Blue Jacket were two different individuals.

Blue Jacket first came to prominence in Lord Dunmore's War (1774), which pitted the Virginia colony against the Shawnee and Mingo tribes. Shawnee displeasure at the Iroquois' sale of their land to Virginians at Fort Stanwix in 1768 burst into open warfare when American frontiersmen brutally murdered the pregnant sister of Mingo chief Logan. This murder was one of a number of brutal slayings along the Ohio River in 1774. Shawnee and Mingo forces attempted to stem the tide of settlers into their Kentucky hunting grounds, only to be defeated at Point Pleasant (in present-day West Virginia) on October 10, 1774.

The Shawnees were initially neutral during the early years of the American Revolutionary War (1775–1783), but the murder of Chief Cornstalk in October 1777 led many Shawnees to fight with the British, and Blue Jacket rose to great prominence during the ensuing years. By 1778, however, his town on Deer Creek (35 miles south of Columbus in present-day Ohio) near the Scioto River was abandoned, and Blue Jacket moved to present-day Bellefontaine, Ohio. The British defeat in the American Revolution removed a valuable ally in the defense of Shawnee lands. Regardless, the Shawnees and many other northwestern nations continued to fight against the newly independent United States. Following the destruction of his Ohio settlement by frontiersmen under Brigadier General Benjamin Logan in 1786, Blue Jacket negotiated a peace treaty at Limestone, Kentucky, in 1787 and moved into the region of the Miami River in northwestern Ohio.

In 1788 Blue Jacket raided Kentucky and together with the Miami chief Little Turtle (Michikinakoua) led confederated Indian forces in the defeat of an American military force under Brigadier General Josiah Harmar in October 1790. This was followed by a convincing defeat of another American army under Major General Arthur St. Clair, governor of the Northwest Territory, at the Wabash River on November 4, 1791. These battles were all part of Little Turtle's War (1785–1795). In June 1794 Blue Jacket took command of the Ohio Indian forces but was decisively defeated by Brigadier General "Mad" Anthony Wayne at Fallen Timbers, Ohio, on August 20, 1794. While many Shawnees, including Tecumseh, refused to admit defeat, Blue Jacket signed the Treaty of Greenville on August 3, 1795, which ceded most of present-day Ohio to the United States and ended Little Turtle's War.

Following his defeat, Blue Jacket lived near Fort Wayne and later Detroit. In July 1805 he signed the Treaty of Fort Industry, which ceded the rest of northwestern Ohio to the United States. In his later life Blue Jacket witnessed the rise of Tecumseh and the new Pan-Indian movement that continued to resist American westward expansion prior to the War of 1812, and there is evidence to suggest that for a time Blue Jacket was a follower of Tecumseh's half brother Tenskwatawa (the Prophet). Blue Jacket, one of the most prominent Shawnee leaders of his time, probably died in 1810 in northern Indiana or southern Michigan. Two of his surviving sons, George Blue Jacket and Jim Blue Jacket, continued his path of resistance, following Tecumseh into his ill-fated alliance with the British during the War of 1812.

RORY T. CORNISH

See also

Fallen Timbers, Battle of; Greenville, Treaty of; Harmar, Josiah; Little Turtle; Little Turtle's War; Logan, Benjamin; Mingos; Native Americans and the American Revolutionary War; Old Northwest Territory; Shawnees; St. Clair, Arthur; Tecumseh; Tenskwatawa; Wayne, Anthony; Wayne's Campaign

References

Colloway, Colin. "Beyond the Vortex of Violence: Indian-White Relations in the Ohio Country, 1783–1815." *Northwest Ohio Quarterly* 64 (1992): 16–26.
Colloway, Colin. "We Have Always Been the Frontier: The American Revolution in Shawnee Country." *American Indian Quarterly* 16 (1992): 39–52.
Sugden, John. *Blue Jacket: Warrior of the Shawnees*. Lincoln: University of Nebraska Press, 2000.

Blue Licks, Kentucky, Action at
Event Date: October 19, 1782

Military engagement on October 19, 1782, in which Kentucky frontiersmen were ambushed by pro-British Native American warriors at Blue Licks, Kentucky, during the American Revolutionary War (1775–1783). In August 1782 Loyalist captain William Caldwell,

Simon Girty, and Alexander McKee crossed the Ohio River with 300 warriors and on August 15 besieged Bryan's Station near Lexington, Kentucky. Unable to compel its surrender, they withdrew on August 18 toward the Ohio River, making no attempt to disguise their march. At Bryan's Station more than 200 militiamen, commanded by John Todd, Stephen Trigg, Daniel Boone, and others, quickly assembled. Refusing to heed Boone's advice to await reinforcements, 182 mounted men under Colonel Todd set out on August 18 to pursue their adversaries. Meanwhile, Caldwell and his party had arrived at the lower Blue Licks, crossed the Licking River, and arrayed themselves in ambush position.

On August 19 the Kentuckians reached the Blue Licks and observed Native Americans on the north side of the Licking River. Boone, suspecting that the warriors were deliberately exposing themselves to lure an assault, pleaded with Todd to await reinforcements coming forward under Benjamin Logan. Apparently at this point Major Hugh McGary accused Boone of cowardice, and Boone bristled that he was ready to fight, disadvantage or not. Others sided with McGary. Todd, despite Boone's further pleas that he wait, decided to advance. Once across the Licking River, the Kentuckians moved forward in three columns for about a mile, with Boone commanding the left, Todd commanding the center, and Trigg commanding the right. A scouting party that included McGary and 27 others led the way. Suddenly the Americans were fired upon by Caldwell's concealed warriors. All but three of the scouts were killed; McGary was one of the few who survived.

Within seconds, Trigg's men on the right were fighting for their survival. They held their ground for about five minutes, but their flanks were enfiladed, their commander was killed, and they were practically annihilated. Shortly thereafter the center under Todd also disintegrated. Todd and his men fled in disarray, leaving only the left flank under Boone still engaged. At McGary's urging, Boone was soon in headlong retreat, pursued by the Native Americans toward the Licking River. In the melee Boone's son, Israel, was mortally wounded, but Boone was compelled to abandon Israel and flee for his life.

Later that day reinforcements under Logan met the retreating survivors and prepared to repel any pursuing warriors, but none followed. On August 24 Logan and his men reclaimed the battlefield and the American dead, including Israel Boone. Seventy-seven Americans were killed, 12 were wounded, and 8 were captured; most of the captives were burned alive. Seven Native Americans were killed, and 10 were wounded; the rest escaped across the Ohio River.

PAUL DAVID NELSON

See also

Boone, Daniel; Girty, Simon; Native Americans and the American Revolutionary War

References

Adams, Michael C. C. "An Appraisal of the Blue Licks Battle." *Filson History Quarterly* 75 (2001): 181–203.

Cotterill, Robert S. "Battle of Upper Blue Licks (1782)." *Historical Quarterly* 2 (1927): 29–33.

Wilson, Samuel M. *The Battle of the Blue Licks, August 19, 1782.* Lexington, KY: n.p., 1927.

Blue Water Creek, Battle of

See Ash Hollow, Battle of

Boomtown

Term used to refer to a town or city that experiences exponential population and economic growth over a short span of time; sometimes a boomtown could later experience a commensurate loss of population and economic activity in a short period of time. Boomtowns were largely associated with the western mining and cattle frontiers. For example, cattle ranching benefited greatly from the successful conclusion of the Texas Revolution in 1836, the annexation of Texas to the United States in 1845, and the Mexican-American War (1846–1848). This added millions of acres of open grasslands to the Union and opened the way in the years following the American Civil War (1861–1865) for large cattle trails northward across Indian Territory (Oklahoma) to the railheads in Kansas. These cattle towns along the route experienced a boom-and-bust cycle in which, as the railroad linked them to markets in the east, they grew at rapid rates and then later declined as rail routes moved closer to the source.

Annual cattle drives, which reached their peak from 1866 to 1880, brought big money into these towns. The drives followed four major trails from Texas northward: the Sedalia and Baxter Springs trails to Arkansas and Missouri; the Chisholm Trail to Ellsworth, Kansas; the Western Trail to Dodge City, Kansas; and the Goodnight-Loving Trail to Pueblo and Denver, Colorado. There were few stops along the way. Cowboys slept on the prairie and ate from chuck wagons while watching the herds. When they reached the railheads, the men were paid. A mix of money and alcohol, coming with a break from a long period of boredom, produced plenty of gunfights and brawling. The business opportunities, however, generated interest by settlers, and as more permanent residents appeared, they demanded a certain amount of "civilization," passing ordinances that protected farmers' lands from cattle grazing. Lawmen such as James Butler, Wild Bill Hickok, Wyatt Earp, and Bat Masterson were employed to establish order among the rowdy cowhands. As permanent settlers built schools, banks, and businesses and established cultural amenities, they desired the wild cowboys in their towns even less. Of course, towns then paid the price in a declining economy that had profited from the lucrative, if seasonal, influx of transients.

Eventually it was the extension of the railroad farther west, and not local ordinances, that consigned the recent boomtown to its

Stereograph of men and a wagon posed in front of the "Colorado Curiosities" shop, perhaps a taxidermist, on 16th Street in Denver, Colorado, circa 1875. Painted on the wagon cover is "Home from the Black Hills, Busted." (Library of Congress)

bust cycle. As the railheads stretched throughout Texas and the West, the need for cattle drives evaporated, and so did much of the prosperity that came with them. Towns such as Abilene, Ellsworth, Wichita, and Dodge City, Kansas, all experienced rapid growth and, to varying degrees, rapid decline.

The same was true for mining towns established in the Arizona, Colorado, Dakota, Montana, New Mexico, and Nevada territories and California. Rich mines at Bisbee and Tombstone in Arizona, Bodie and Calico in California, and Goldfield in Nevada all thrived with prospectors and merchants, only to turn into ghost towns when the ore veins dried up. Towns such as Deadwood and Lead in the Black Hills of the Dakota Territory sprang up within areas set aside for Indian use by treaty. Mining towns across the West helped to create animosity and spawn conflict with the Indians. As with the cow towns of Kansas, the mining towns could be lawless and ultimately dangerous places.

The expansion of the railroad and even a small population growth increased tensions with Native Americans and led to calls by farmers and townspeople for government protection. Further incursions onto Native American lands brought a series of wars with virtually all of the Plains tribes from 1866 to 1890, culminating with the U.S. Army forcing most of the tribes onto designated reservations. Meanwhile, the boomtowns became little more than local supply sources for farmers or points of historic interest about the Wild West. A few, such as Wichita, managed to remain regional economic centers.

LARRY SCHWEIKART

See also
Cattle Industry; Railroads

References
Atherton, Lewis. *The Cattle Kings.* Bloomington: Indiana University Press, 1961.

Dykstra, Robert. *The Cattle Towns.* New York: Atheneum, 1970.

Fitzgerald, Daniel. *Ghost Towns of Kansas: A Traveler's Guide.* Lawrence: University Press of Kansas, 1988.

Jordan, Terry G. *North American Cattle Ranching Frontiers: Origins, Diffusion, and Differentiation.* Albuquerque: University of New Mexico Press, 1993.

Schweikart, Larry, and Bradley J. Birzer. *The American West.* New York: Wiley, 2003.

Boone, Daniel
Birth Date: October 22, 1734
Death Date: September 26, 1820

Famed pioneer, politician, and militiaman. Daniel Boone was born on October 22, 1734, in Berks County, Pennsylvania. In 1750 he moved with his family from the Pennsylvania frontier to the North Carolina backcountry, settling along the Yadkin River. Boone likely had no formal education, but his brother Samuel's wife taught him to read and write. By his early teens, Boone had already developed skills as a hunter and trapper and soon became a highly regarded backwoodsman and an excellent shot. In the process, he quickly came to love both the solitude of the wilderness and the challenge of the hunt.

In 1755 as a member of the North Carolina Militia, Boone became a teamster in British major general Edward Braddock's army that marched against the French at Fort Duquesne in western Pennsylvania. Boone fled with the other teamsters when the British forces were attacked and decisively defeated. Back in North Carolina the following year, Boone sought to make a living as a blacksmith and teamster, but increasing debts persuaded him to leave North Carolina. When his wife refused to move to Florida in 1765, Boone looked west. He had heard many glowing reports about the Kentucky country. After an initial sojourn, Boone set out in 1769 on a two-year exploring and trapping expedition beyond the Cumberland Gap. Taken with the fertility of the Bluegrass Country along the Kentucky River, he led an abortive attempt to settle the area in 1773. The group of about 50 settlers returned to North Carolina after a force of Delawares, Cherokees, and Shawnees captured and killed 2 in their party, including Boone's son James.

In 1775 Boone finally succeeded in relocating to Kentucky. Acting as an agent for a North Carolina land speculator, Boone marked out the Wilderness Road, helped negotiate the purchase of Kentucky land from the Cherokees, and settled his family in Boonesborough. Once the American Revolutionary War (1775–1783) began, the British encouraged the trans-Appalachian tribes, who were already concerned with white encroachment, to resist the new settlers. In July 1776 a war party of Shawnees and Cherokees captured Boone's daughter Jemima and two other girls. Boone led a small party of men who rescued the girls three days later, an exploit that James Fenimore Cooper drew upon for his highly successful 1826 novel, *Last of the Mohicans.*

Boone and 16 other men were captured by Shawnees in 1778. The Shawnees adopted into the tribe several of the captives including Boone, whom they renamed Sheltowee, or Big Turtle. Boone ingratiated himself with the Shawnees by persuading them that in the spring of 1779 he would help negotiate the surrender of the remaining Boonesborough settlers. Four months into his captivity, however, Boone learned of a Shawnee plan to attack Boonesborough and escaped. He traveled 160 miles in only four days to reach his settlement. Even though Boonesborough had only 60 able-bodied men, the settlers were prepared and resisted a 10-day siege. Some of the settlers were unhappy with Boone's relationship with the Shawnees and charged him with treason in this episode, but a court-martial conducted by the Kentucky Militia vindicated him.

Boone remained in the Kentucky country until 1799. To support his large family he tried surveying, running a tavern and a store, and speculating in land. He filed dozens of claims for thousands of acres, but the claims were so poorly drawn up that he eventually lost virtually all the land in litigation with other

Daniel Boone was a highly regarded backwoodsman who established a route through the Appalachians and helped establish Kentucky's first white settlement. His battles with the region's Native Americans were the stuff of legend. (Library of Congress)

claimants. Whenever circumstances and time permitted, Boone returned to trapping and hunting. While he had a well-deserved reputation as a pioneer loner, he also often stepped forward as a community leader. He served as a deputy surveyor, coroner, and county sheriff. He also won election to several terms in the Virginia state assembly and served as a militia officer. In the latter capacity Boone participated in numerous conflicts with Native Americans, including the action at Blue Licks in 1782 that claimed his son Israel. But as his beloved Kentucky increased in population and as he grew ever more frustrated with his lost land claims, Boone decided to accept an offer from the Spanish government to move to Missouri in 1799.

Besides granting him several thousand acres, the Spanish named Boone a syndic, or chief magistrate. His responsibilities included recommending applicants for land grants and supervising the surveys of the land. He settled in the Femme Osage district about 60 miles from St. Louis. Unfortunately for Boone, after the United States purchased the Louisiana Territory in 1803, all Spanish land claims were subject to review, and his were not confirmed. Boone appealed to Congress, which in 1814 awarded him 850 acres. In his last years, even though well past 70 years old, Boone continued to hunt, trap, and explore. He grudgingly granted interviews to numerous inquisitive visitors eager to meet the famed pioneer. Boone died in the home of his son, Nathan, in St. Charles County, Missouri, on September 26, 1820.

LARRY GRAGG

See also

Blue Licks, Kentucky, Action at; Boonesborough, Kentucky; Cherokees; Cooper, James Fenimore; Cornstalk; Delawares; French and Indian War; Native Americans and the American Revolutionary War; Shawnees

References

Faragher, John Mack. *Daniel Boone: The Life and Legend of an American Pioneer.* New York: Holt, 1992.

Lofaro, Michael A. *The Life and Adventures of Daniel Boone.* Lexington: University Press of Kentucky, 1986.

Boonesborough, Kentucky

Site of an early American settlement in Kentucky that was important as a sanctuary against Shawnee and British attacks during the American Revolutionary War (1775–1783). Boonesborough, located in central Kentucky, was founded in 1775 by the organizers of the Transylvania Company. In the spring of 1775 Richard Henderson, Daniel Boone, and other land-hungry speculators organized this company to establish a colony on a large tract of land encompassing northern, central, and western Kentucky.

The company purchased the land from the Cherokee tribe in March 1775 over the opposition of the Virginia government, which then controlled the area, and began organizing two pioneer parties to move in and found a settlement. One party would be led by Boone, who had earlier explored the land and already had a settlement site in mind. He would blaze a trail that Henderson would follow shortly thereafter.

On March 10, 1775, Boone's pioneers set out on their westward trek. Along the way three were killed, and many others fled back to their homes. Henderson's party, following on March 20, also lost most of its members to faintheartedness.

The remaining pioneers reached the proposed site of Boonesborough in early April 1775. Boone's contingent was the first to arrive. They built a camp on the bank of the Kentucky River and surveyed a large number of two-acre parcels of land. Henderson arrived a few days later, surveyed more lots, and distributed them by lottery. He then began construction of a fort, but it was not to be completed until 1778, when Native Americans threatened to evict the settlers. Henderson's settlers were reluctant to assist in providing for their own defense, and they also suffered from hunger because of the failure to preserve meat. Many returned east before the year was out.

Henderson also organized a government for the Transylvania Colony and on May 8, 1775, made Boonesborough its capital, in honor of Daniel Boone. But the Virginia legislature, which nominally controlled the area, refused to recognize the colony's legitimacy, and by 1778 the colony was largely defunct. Henderson thereupon lost all interest in Boonesborough and Kentucky and returned to Virginia.

During the Revolutionary War, Boonesborough was both a way station for settlers and a refuge from Native American attacks. The local Native Americans were a constant menace, conducting raids, kidnapping settlers, and killing the unwary. In September 1778 Native Americans led by Black Fish, a Shawnee chief, and his British supporters unsuccessfully besieged the fort at Boonesborough for 10 days. A year later Virginia granted Boonesborough a town charter, and the place became a center for tobacco storage and inspection in the 1780s. Also, a ferry was established at Boonesborough to cross the Kentucky River.

Even when the Native American threat waned in the 1790s the town did not flourish, and it gradually disappeared during the 19th century. Today it is merely an unincorporated part of Madison County that is the site of a state park, where a reconstructed fort and a museum document its role in pioneer history.

PAUL DAVID NELSON

See also

Boone, Daniel; Cherokees; Native Americans and the American Revolutionary War; Shawnees

References

Harrison, Lowell H., and James C. Klotter. *A New History of Kentucky.* Lexington: University Press of Kentucky, 1997.

Lofaro, Michael A. *Daniel Boone: An American Life.* Lexington: University Press of Kentucky, 2003.

Ranck, George Washington. *Boonesborough: Its Founding, Pioneer Struggles, Indian Experiences, Transylvania Days, and Revolutionary Annals.* Louisville: J. P. Morton, 1901.

Bosque Redondo

Site of a U.S. military post, Fort Sumner, and an infamous Indian reservation in east-central New Mexico from 1863 to 1868. Established on October 31, 1862, by order of Brigadier General James H. Carleton, Bosque Redondo was located on 40 square miles of land on the Pecos River.

In 1862 Carleton, responding to escalating violence involving the Navajos, the Mescalero Apaches, and New Mexican settlers, developed a plan to remove the Native Americans from their lands. The U.S. government intended to use the reservation as a place to assimilate both tribes into American culture and help them become self-sufficient. Colonel Christopher "Kit" Carson, who defeated the Mescalero Apaches in 1862, eventually moved 500 of them to Bosque Redondo. In 1864 the Navajos, having been essentially starved into submission by Carson's efforts, were forced into a perilous 300-mile march, known as the Long Walk, to Bosque Redondo. As many as several thousand Navajos died during this relocation, although approximately 9,000 arrived at the reservation.

The Bosque Redondo site was chosen for this mass relocation, despite the fact that it lacked abundant firewood, had only salty drinking water, and was located on a disease-prone marshy floodplain. Carleton intended for the Indians to become self-sufficient farmers, but the harsh environment led to many crop failures. To make matters worse, government rations were often inadequate. Food and firewood shortages, beginning in the winter of 1864, increased tensions. Dysentery was a frequent problem, caused by the poor water supply, and other diseases, such as malaria and measles, ran rampant.

Most of the Mescalero Apaches escaped the reservation on November 3, 1865. The government eventually established a much more suitable reservation for the Mescaleros in the mountains of southern New Mexico. In 1868 the U.S. government finally recognized the continued suffering of the Navajos and the financial burdens of the reservation. The Navajos and the U.S. government signed a treaty on June 1, 1868, allowing the Navajos to return to their traditional lands. The treaty also offered the Navajos financial and livestock resources for their rehabilitation. The Bosque Redondo reservation became synonymous with misery and death and stood as another ugly example of failed Indian management. Its closing in 1868 and the closing of the adjoining Fort Sumner a year later were welcomed by Indians and the government alike.

DEREK N. BOETCHER

See also
Apaches; Carleton, James Henry; Carson, Christopher Houston; Fort Sumner; Navajo Removal; Navajos; Navajo War

References
Bailey, Lynn R. *Bosque Redondo: An American Concentration Camp.* Pasadena, CA: Socio-Technical Books, 1970.
Thompson, Gerald. *The Army and the Navajo: The Bosque Redondo Reservation Experiment, 1863–1868.* Tucson: University of Arizona Press, 1976.

Bouquet, Henry
Birth Date: ca. 1719
Death Date: August 25, 1765

British Army officer. Born in Rolle, Switzerland, most likely in 1719, Henry Bouquet was the son of a hotel proprietor. Bouquet entered foreign military service at a young age, first with the United Provinces of the Netherlands and then with Sardinia. He returned to Dutch pay after the War of the Austrian Succession (1740–1748), eventually attaining the rank of captain commandant of the Swiss Guards.

In the Netherlands in 1755, Bouquet met another countryman, James Prevost, who persuaded him to travel to the New World as a field officer in a proposed foreign Protestant colonial regiment to be raised in Pennsylvania by the British government. Granted authority in 1756 by the British government to hold a military commission, Bouquet became lieutenant colonel of the 1st Battalion of the 60th (Royal American) Regiment of Foot. He remained in British North America with the regiment for the remainder of his life.

Bouquet's association with the western frontier began soon after his arrival in the Mid-Atlantic colonies. Although transferred south to Charles Town (Charleston), South Carolina, with five of his companies to bolster defenses there through 1757, he returned to Pennsylvania as a principal commander in British brigadier general John Forbes's 1758 expedition against Fort Duquesne. This successful advance was marred by a defeat at the Battle of Grant's Hill (September 14, 1758) in which the Royal Americans suffered 42 casualties. Nevertheless the advance continued, with the French abandoning their base at the Forks of the Ohio in November. The site was then occupied by British troops, who constructed a massive structure that they named Fort Pitt. Bouquet spent much of his time as a commander of advanced posts, for his battalion provided most of the troops to these remote installations. Logistics, American Indian diplomacy, and garrison duties absorbed his attention until the outbreak of Pontiac's Rebellion in the early summer of 1763.

Bouquet played a pivotal role in quashing this insurrection. While leading a relief column to the aid of the besieged Fort Pitt, he was ambushed by Shawnee and Delaware warriors at Bushy Run on August 5, 1763. As in earlier irregular actions fought throughout the French and Indian War (1754–1763), the initiative lay with the attackers, who chose their ground carefully. Withdrawing to a defensive position at Edge Hill, however, Bouquet tricked the Indians into staging a reckless assault across open ground the following day. Native resolve crumbled in the face of a daring British bayonet counterattack and heavy cross fire. The Native Americans then abandoned both the field and the siege of Fort Pitt. This victory was followed up a year later with a measured advance by British forces into the upper Muskingum Valley. The 1764 campaign, designed and led by Bouquet, was a complete success, which forced Ohioan natives to sue for peace.

Bouquet did not live long enough to enjoy the fruits of victory. Naturalized by parliamentary statute on June 2, 1762, he was promoted to brigadier general three years later and given command of British troops in the Southern Department. He died at Pensacola, West Florida, on August 25, 1765, the day after arriving to take up his new post.

ALEXANDER V. CAMPBELL

See also
Bushy Run, Battle of; Delawares; French and Indian War; Pontiac's Rebellion; Shawnees

References
Hutton, Sir Edward. *Colonel Henry Bouquet: A Biographical Sketch.* Winchester, UK: Warren and Son, 1911.
Steele, Ian K. *Warpaths: Invasions of North America.* New York: Oxford University Press, 1994.
Waddell, Louis W., and Bruce D. Bomberger. *The French and Indian War in Pennsylvania, 1753–1763: Fortification and Struggle during the War for Empire.* Harrisburg: Pennsylvania Historical and Museum Commission, 1996.

Bow and Arrow

The primary weapon of Native American warriors and hunters used throughout North and South America until the early 1800s, when firearms became the preferred weapon. The material employed in making bows varied from region to region. Wood from the Osage orange (bois d'arc) tree was widely recognized as the best bow-making material. However, Osage orange grew only in the valleys of the Red and Arkansas rivers in southern Oklahoma and northern Texas, so native bow makers had to use the best materials at hand. Eastern Woodlands warriors fashioned their bows from hardwoods such as ash, oak, hickory, and maple. These tribes frequently used the self-bow, which was at least four feet long and fashioned out of a single piece of wood.

Occasionally bows were fitted with a smaller reverse bow attached to the front in an attempt to generate more resistance and thus impart more force to the launched arrow. Plains warriors often chose horn or antler as their materials of choice for making composite bows. Used in both war and hunting, Native American bows were often offset by native defensive capabilities. In the Northeast, for example, Iroquois and Wyandot (Huron) warriors wore armor made of bark and reeds that could deflect an arrow. But this did not mean that Europeans could dismiss native bowmen as ineffective. During his incursion into the American Southeast, Spaniard Hernando de Soto and his men discovered that although their plate armor could deflect Apalachee arrows, the latter could penetrate chain mail, and even if they did strike plate armor, the arrows, made of cane, splintered, causing painful injuries when they shattered.

New England colonists soon discovered that Native American arrows were driven with such force as to actually penetrate through a human body. There is little technical data regarding Native American bows from the colonial period. Cabeza de Vaca noted that the arrows of Apalachee warriors in Florida penetrated full-grown poplar trees to a depth of six inches. Europeans in the

Native American from Florida holding bow and arrow. Painting by John White. (Library of Congress)

colonial period also soon discovered that their firearms were frequently no match for well-armed tribes with bows and arrows. Indeed, because of the cumbersome and slow-loading firearms of the day, Native American warriors could shoot multiple arrows with great accuracy in the same time that it took a colonist to load and fire just a single round.

Prior to European contact, native warriors tipped their arrows with bone, horn, obsidian, flint, and, in some cases, copper from the upper Great Lakes region. When more durable European-manufactured products became available, the native people eagerly adopted them. The Iroquois, for instance, cut up copper pots and transformed them into arrowheads. Recognizing a potential market, Europeans soon began offering ready-made iron arrowheads as a trade item.

While native warriors recognized the power of firearms—and were perhaps fascinated by them as novelties—these did not immediately replace the bow and arrow. The early matchlock weapons were heavy and clumsy and required yards of specially treated cord, known as match, in order to operate. However, with the advent of flintlock weapons, native demand for firearms increased. Once native warriors became dependent on firearms beginning in the mid-1700s, they lost their skills at making and using the bow and arrow. This left them at the mercy of colonial governments, which could in time of conflict simply cut off their supplies of shot and gunpowder. By the early 1800s most tribes in North America had adopted firearms as their preferred weapons, and the bow and arrow was relegated largely to ceremonial uses.

ROGER M. CARPENTER

See also
Apalachees; Firearms Trade; Iroquois; Wyandots

References
Given, Brian J. *A Most Pernicious Thing: Gun Trading and Native Warfare in the Early Contact Period.* Ottawa, Ontario: Carleton University Press, 1994.
Mason, Otis T. *North American Bows, Arrows, and Quivers.* Washington, DC: Smithsonian Institution Press, 1893.

Mitch Boyer, born to a Sioux mother and a French Canadian fur trapper in 1837, served as a scout, guide, and interpreter for the army. This photograph, from circa 1875, shows him with a velvet cloth around his shoulders decorated with sequins and fringe, a polka-dot kerchief, and a fur hat with two stuffed woodpeckers. (Denver Public Library, Western History Collection, Charles A. Nast, X-31214)

Boyer, Mitch
Birth Date: 1837
Death Date: June 25, 1876

Scout, guide, and interpreter who facilitated the exploration of the American West and also accompanied Lieutenant Colonel George Armstrong Custer's 7th Cavalry during the Battle of Little Bighorn (June 25–26, 1876). Born sometime in 1837 in the Dakotas to a Sioux mother and John Baptiste Boyer, a French Canadian hunter and fur trapper, Mitch Boyer was baptized at Fort Pierre (present-day South Dakota) in 1840 with his three sisters, who were triplets. His given name, Michel (Michael), was frequently shortened to Mich by his family. English speakers who heard his name pronounced wrote it as "Mitch." Some 20th-century scholars have mistakenly assumed that "Mitch" was a nickname derived from "Minton" or "Milton."

In 1848 the Boyer family moved westward to Wyoming, settling near Fort Laramie. By the time Boyer reached adulthood he was able to speak English, French, Sioux, and Crow. He was also an accomplished frontiersman, excelling in survival skills.

Possessing the features of a Native American and dressing as an American, Boyer was adept in his interactions between American and Indian cultures. As such, he earned the respect of both Native Americans and whites for his skills as a scout, a guide, and an interpreter. After his father was killed by a group of Native Americans in 1863, Boyer consistently aided the U.S. Cavalry in its efforts to pacify the American West. In 1868 he served as an official interpreter at Fort Kearny (Nebraska). Boyer worked for the 2nd Cavalry as a guide for the military escort for the Northern Pacific Railroad survey team in the Dakotas and Montana from 1870 to 1872. From 1872 to 1876 he worked for the army at the Crow Indian Agency in Montana. Killed in the Battle of Little Bighorn on June 25, 1876, Boyer was subsequently buried in a mass grave with the slain troops of the 7th Cavalry.

MICHAEL R. HALL

See also
Crows; Custer, George Armstrong; Little Bighorn, Battle of the; Sioux

References
Brown, Dee Alexander. *Showdown at Little Big Horn.* Lincoln: University of Nebraska Press, 2004.
Gray, John S. *Custer's Last Campaign: Mitch Boyer and the Little Bighorn Reconstructed.* Lincoln: University of Nebraska Press, 1991.

Bozeman, John
Birth Date: ca. 1835
Death Date: April 20, 1867

Western pioneer responsible for blazing the Bozeman Trail to Montana. John Bozeman was born in Pickens County, Georgia, sometime in 1835; little is known about his early years. In 1849 Bozeman's father left his family to seek his fortune in the California Gold Rush. Bozeman never saw his father again. When Bozeman left Georgia in 1861 to try his own hand at mining, first in Colorado and then in Montana in 1862, he too left behind a family.

Bozeman, who remained in Montana after his gold claims failed to pan out, hoped to discover a more direct route to the goldfields of southwestern Montana. He believed that a new trail would enable him and others to garner quick wealth by making it easier to transport the ore from the ground back to the eastern financial centers. He also hoped to facilitate supplying the miners' camps in the region.

In 1863 Bozeman and John Jacobs, a fellow miner and pioneer, began their quest in Virginia City in the Montana Territory. They worked their way eastward through the Rocky Mountains in Montana, onto the plains, and south into Wyoming, where they connected with the Oregon Trail just west of Fort Laramie in southeastern Wyoming. Bozeman's explorations did indeed lead to a quicker route to Montana. Unfortunately, the trail bisected the hunting grounds of the Sioux in the Powder River basin, leading to years of conflict between the whites and Native Americans, including Red Cloud's War (1866–1868), which compelled the army to remove its three forts from the region. Prior to the opening of the Bozeman Trail, travel to Montana had been difficult and arduous, accomplished either overland from Colorado or up the Missouri River via steamboat from St. Louis to one of several Montana towns.

Bozeman led the first group of settlers over the trail in 1864 from Missouri to Montana. He and the immigrants arrived in what became known as the Gallatin Valley, where they found fertile soil and an excellent site for a town. There they founded the town of Bozeman, Montana, that same year. Bozeman remained in the vicinity of the town for the rest of his life. He tried farming but found it not to his liking. Instead, Bozeman became an adventurer sojourning in the hinterlands and returning to town to regale the residents with stories of his travels. On April 20, 1867, Bozeman was murdered by unknown assailants while on a trip along the Yellowstone River. For many years his death was attributed to members of the Blackfoot tribe. However, more recently that theory has come under suspicion, and some historians attribute his death to his white traveling companion, Tom Cover.

RICK DYSON

See also

Blackfoot Sioux; Bozeman Trail; California Gold Rush; Fort Laramie; Red Cloud's War; Rocky Mountains; Sioux

References

Burlingame, Merrill. "John M. Bozeman, Montana Trailmaker." *Mississippi Valley Historical Review* 27(4) (1941): 541–568.
Doyle, Susan Badger. "Journeys to the Land of Gold: Emigrants on the Bozeman Trail." *Montana: The Magazine of Western History* 41(4) (1991): 54–67.

Smith, Sherry. "The Bozeman Trail: To Death and Glory." *Annals of Wyoming* 55(1) (1983): 32–50.

Bozeman Trail

Overland route in the American West first scouted by pioneer and land speculator John M. Bozeman in 1863. The Bozeman Trail linked the Oregon Trail to the gold-mining areas of Montana, turning north from the main trail approximately 80 miles past Fort Laramie and following the eastern edge of the Bighorn Mountain range through treaty-granted Indian lands and then curving west at the north end of the range and ending in Virginia City in southwestern Montana.

The fact that the trail traversed Indian territory became a significant concern. Migrant and freight traffic on the trail certainly irritated the region's Native Americans. However, it was the U.S. Army's post–American Civil War (1861–1865) establishment of forts (Forts Phil Kearny, C. F. Smith, and Reno) and garrisons under the leadership of Colonel Henry B. Carrington in 1866 that provoked the strongest reaction from the Sioux, led by Chief Red Cloud. The Sioux would be supported by several allied groups, including the Arapahos and Cheyennes.

The resulting conflict, Red Cloud's War (1866–1868), led to the deaths of 81 army personnel in the Fetterman Massacre near Fort Phil Kearny on December 21, 1866; the Hayfield Fight near Fort C. F. Smith on August 1, 1867; and the Wagon Box Fight near Fort Phil Kearny on August 2, 1867.

The U.S. Army was not able to suppress Indian resistance, and the Peace Commission of 1867 finally produced the Treaty of Fort Laramie in 1868. Under its terms, the army agreed to abandon the Bozeman Trail and the defensive forts along it by August 1868. The Indian tribes thus regained formal control of the region.

The Bozeman Trail was used by more than 3,500 settlers and for limited freight activity but, because of the security threat from the Indian tribes, primarily served as a military road. The Bozeman Trail's chief legacy was Red Cloud's War. In the 1880s after the end of the Indian Wars, the route was again used by settlers moving into Montana.

JEROME V. MARTIN

See also

Bozeman, John; Carrington, Henry Beebe; Fetterman Massacre; Fort Laramie; Fort Laramie, Treaty of (1868); Fort Phil Kearny; Hayfield Fight; Oregon Trail; Red Cloud; Red Cloud's War; Wagon Box Fight

References

Johnson, Dorothy M. *The Bloody Bozeman: The Perilous Trail to Montana's Gold.* New York: McGraw-Hill, 1971.
Larson, Robert W. *Red Cloud: Warrior-Statesman of the Lakota Sioux.* Norman: University of Oklahoma Press, 1997.
Lass, William E. *From the Missouri to the Great Salt Lake: An Account of Overland Freighting.* Lincoln: Nebraska State Historical Society, 1972.
Utley, Robert M. *Frontier Regulars: The United States and the American Indian, 1866–1891.* New York: Macmillan, 1973.

Wagon Roads and Railroads

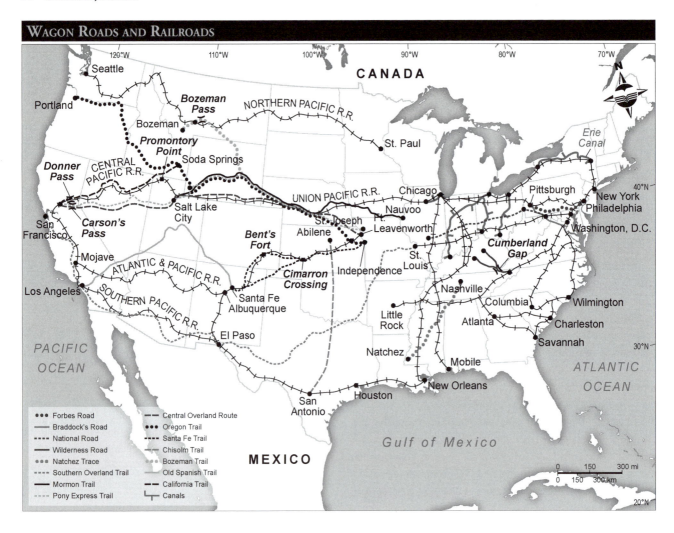

Braddock, Edward

Birth Date: December 1694
Death Date: July 13, 1755

British major general in the French and Indian War (1754–1763) who led the disastrous 1755 campaign against Fort Duquesne. Edward Braddock was born in London in December 1694 and was the son of Major General Edward Braddock (1664–1725), a lifelong officer in the Coldstream Guards, one of the finest British regiments. In 1710 Braddock's father purchased a commission for him in the Coldstream Guards.

The younger Braddock's subsequent military career was marked primarily by routine duty. He became a lieutenant in the regiment's grenadier company in 1716 but saw no action in the Jacobite Uprising of 1715. He also experienced little combat during the War of the Austrian Succession (1740–1748) or the Jacobite Rising of 1745.

Braddock became first major of the regiment in 1744 and led a routine reconnaissance to Ostend in Flanders the same year. In 1747, now a lieutenant colonel, he served under the Prince of

Orange in Holland during the siege of Bergen-op-Zoom. In 1753 Braddock sold his commission in the Coldstream Guards for £5,000 and purchased the colonelcy of the 14th Regiment of Foot. Shortly thereafter he became governor of Gibraltar, where his regiment was posted.

The imperial confrontation that became the French and Indian War provided Braddock with his greatest military opportunity. Following the surrender of Virginia Militia lieutenant colonel George Washington at Fort Necessity in July 1754, Britain decided on a strong response to include attacks against France's Ohio forts, Nova Scotia, Fort Niagara, and French posts along the Lake George–Lake Champlain corridor, including Crown Point. This plan called for a commander in chief with sweeping authority to supervise all military operations there and direct civilian colonial authorities to provide logistical support. Although Braddock had no prior experience directing a major military campaign and had seen little action in his 45-year army career, he was tapped for the position in the autumn of 1754 and became a major general as a result. He arrived in Virginia in February 1755.

Major General Edward Braddock assumed command of British forces in North America in 1755, only to have his column defeated and himself killed by French and Indian forces near Fort Duquesne that July. (Corbis)

Braddock personally assumed command of the expedition against Fort Duquesne, which he launched from Alexandria. He quickly developed a reputation as a stern, impatient officer who was unwilling to heed the advice of colonial military men experienced in wilderness fighting. His roughshod treatment of civil authorities and provincial assemblies greatly contributed to the logistical difficulties that marked his effort against Fort Duquesne. He conducted what was essentially a European-style campaign, which ended in the destruction of his force by the French and their Native American allies several miles from his objective on July 9, 1755. Braddock was mortally wounded in the debacle and died on July 13. To disguise his place of death, he was buried by retreating British forces along the road that bears his name near present-day Uniontown, Pennsylvania.

JOHN R. MAASS

See also

Braddock's Campaign; French and Indian War; Washington, George

References

Kopperman, Paul E. *Braddock at the Monongahela*. Pittsburgh: University of Pittsburgh Press, 1977.

McCardell, Lee. *Ill-Starred General, Braddock of the Coldstream Guards*. Pittsburgh: University of Pittsburgh Press, 1958.

Braddock's Campaign
Start Date: March 1755
End Date: July 1755

Failed British offensive against French Fort Duquesne in 1755 during the French and Indian War (1754–1763). When news of the French victory over the Virginia militia at Fort Necessity arrived in London in September 1754, the British cabinet debated a new course of action against the French. The Earl of Albemarle, governor of Virginia in absentia and a career soldier, recommended that "officers, and good ones," be sent to North America. The king's principal minister, the Duke of Newcastle, concurred but believed that a regiment of Highlanders might help still more. The Duke of Cumberland, the king's son and captain general of Britain's armed forces, went further, proposing two Irish regiments (the 44th and 48th) and a commander in chief for the forces in America.

By November, Cumberland's plan had been adopted, and Major General Edward Braddock was named commander in chief for North America. Before his departure from England on January 13, 1755, Braddock received orders to attack Fort Duquesne, Niagara, Crown Point, and Fort Beauséjour. Once in America, however, it was left to his discretion whether to attack them in succession or simultaneously.

On his arrival at Williamsburg, Virginia, in March, Braddock found that colonial officials had been quite busy over the winter. Particularly notable was Massachusetts governor William Shirley's effort, which raised an extra 2,000 troops for the Beauséjour operation. Both Shirley and British Indian agent William Johnson proposed that the main British attack be directed against Niagara, but Braddock stuck to his orders to focus on Fort Duquesne. Nevertheless, Braddock exercised his discretion in allowing Shirley and Johnson to attack Niagara and Crown Point, respectively, while Braddock took his own force of 2,200 men to Fort Duquesne. The remainder of colonial forces, under the command of Nova Scotia governor Charles Lawrence and Colonel Robert Monckton, attacked Fort Beauséjour.

As with Shirley and Johnson's campaign in New York and Virginia lieutenant colonel George Washington's ill-fated operations against Fort Duquesne the previous summer, Braddock envisioned a road-building project through the wilderness punctuated by a European-style siege. At first he proposed to take a large contingent with supplies for a major siege, but he soon split his force into roughly equal parts: one to transport the immense train of baggage and artillery, and the other, a flying column, to scout ahead and prepare for the siege.

Alert to the dangers of wilderness warfare, Braddock regularly employed more than a third of his force for screens and patrols. In June and July the army advanced steadily and thwarted the attempts of French commander Claude Pierre Pécaudy de Contrecoeur to disrupt its progress. Despite native raids on the colonial frontier, Braddock continued forward, increasing the panic at Fort Duquesne.

On July 8 as Braddock forded the Monongahela River, only 10 miles away Contrecoeur prepared a last desperate attempt by sending about half of Fort Duquesne's garrison against Braddock. With 36 officers, 72 colonial regulars (*troupes de la marine*), 146 Canadian militiamen, and 637 American Indian allies under his command, Captain Daniel Liénard de Beaujeu was supposed to attack Braddock's column east of the Monongahela, but his force was dispatched too late. Ultimately the two forces met just west of the river shortly after noon on July 9.

As he continued his march on Fort Duquesne, Braddock sent forward a vanguard of about 300 men followed by an independent company and 250 workers. The main body of 500 men followed with the artillery, and another 100 men covered the rear. Unlike past marches, however, Braddock missed a key terrain feature on the morning of July 9, a hill to his right and front from which scouts would have been able to detect Beaujeu's approach and prepare an adequate defense.

Braddock's screening forces were unusually small and close to the main body that morning, and the main body was split along the road, with only two ranks to either side of the artillery train. This deployment may have reflected Braddock's confidence in his progress, but it left his force more vulnerable to surprise.

When the French and Native Americans attacked, Braddock's men fought bravely but paid the price for their commander's errors. The opening volleys went well for the British, killing Beaujeu. But the vanguard, flanked by Beaujeu's native allies, fell back on the main body, which Braddock had ordered to advance. The units became intermingled, and Braddock's regulars, strung out on either side of the baggage train, struggled to form a line of battle. Having fallen victim to an ambush, Braddock was unable to use the light infantry tactics that had served him throughout his march.

To make matters worse for Braddock and his men, their battlefield was a Native American hunting ground that concealed hunters and exposed prey. Braddock's men, still trying to form ranks, soon became targets for Indian marksmen; the officers on horseback were the most vulnerable of all. Although the British and some colonials fought bravely for more than three hours, they were unable to form units larger than a platoon, and most of their fire proved ineffective.

Unaccustomed to the war whoops and military tactics of the natives, the regulars attempted to form companies, fire in volleys, and look for the visual cues of the European battlefield. Panic in the British ranks caused several incidents of friendly fire, increasing the confusion. Braddock's force also became an increasingly dense mass as the terror of battle drove men closer together. In reality, they only proved to be an easier target.

Discipline finally and irretrievably crumbled when Braddock was shot from his horse. The workers, the rear guard, and most of the provincial troops had already fled, leaving no one available to cover the withdrawal. The constant pressure from Canadians and Indians turned the retreat into a rout and entirely reversed the previous month of British progress. Braddock's force had lost two-thirds of its numbers and most of its supplies and equipment. French and native losses totaled fewer than 40. The progress made on Braddock's road once promised a steady flow of supplies from Virginia and Maryland to Fort Duquesne; that same road now rendered the British colonies more vulnerable than ever.

The French victory on the Monongahela released forces from their defense of Fort Duquesne and rendered abortive Shirley's proposed expedition to Niagara. Although Shirley took over command of colonial forces from the deceased Braddock, Shirley's relations with Johnson steadily deteriorated as they squabbled over supplies at Albany. Johnson later allied with the faction led by Lieutenant Governor James DeLancey of New York and Thomas Pownall of New Jersey to intrigue against Shirley, undermining his authority by the spring of 1756. Major General John Campbell, Earl of Loudoun, then replaced Shirley as commander in chief. Campbell made several important logistical and administrative reforms but proved militarily ineffective. Only when Major General Jeffrey Amherst took over British military operations in 1758 did British forces return to the offensive against Fort Duquesne—this time successfully—under Brigadier General John Forbes.

MATT SCHUMANN

See also
Amherst, Jeffrey; Braddock, Edward; French and Indian War; Johnson, Sir William

References
Anderson, Fred. *Crucible of War: The Seven Years' War and the Fate of the Empire in British North America, 1754–1766.* New York: Vintage Books, 2001.

Frégault, Guy. *Canada: The War of the Conquest.* Translated by Margaret M. Cameron. London: Oxford University Press, 1969.

Pargellis, Stanley. "Braddock's Defeat." *American Historical Review* 41(2) (January 1936): 253–269.

Brant, Joseph
Birth Date: ca. 1742
Death Date: November 24, 1807

Mohawk leader. Joseph Brant was born Thayendanega around 1742 at an Iroquois settlement in present-day Ohio and was related by marriage to British northern Indian superintendent Sir William Johnson. Johnson took an interest in young Brant and groomed him as one of his protégés, arranging for him to be educated with a small group of native youths at Eleazar Wheelock's Indian Charity School.

As a young man Brant twice visited England and made a favorable impression on London society, counting the Prince of Wales among his friends. Brant was also admired for his membership in the Masons and for having translated the Bible (and later the

Mohawk Joseph Brant (Thayendanega) fought on the British side during the American Revolutionary War and proved to be a highly effective and humane miliary leader. (Library of Congress)

Book of Common Prayer) into Mohawk. His last visit to England coincided with the outbreak of the American Revolutionary War (1775–1783). In July 1776 Brant arrived in New York and made his way back to Mohawk country.

Brant offered his services to the British Crown and led Mohawk warriors in several campaigns, participating in the battles at Oswego and Fort Stanwix in 1777. He also led Mohawk warriors—in the first battle in which Iroquois fought Iroquois—at Oriskany that same year. Late the next year he led a raid on Cherry Valley, New York.

Along with his effectiveness as a leader, Brant acquired a reputation as a humane warrior. At Cherry Valley, he was said to have protested to the British commander over the killing of noncombatants. Others argued that this reputation was unjustified, pointing out that Brant could be as harsh as any other Native American warrior with his prisoners, expecting them to keep pace with a retreating war party.

As with other Native American allies of the British, Brant was angered by the terms of the Peace of Paris, the treaty that ended the American Revolutionary War. Particularly galling was the transfer of native lands to the Americans. Brant argued that the Americans had beaten the British, not the Iroquois. However, he believed that the Iroquois position was untenable in the new

United States. After a large Continental Army expedition in 1779 known as the Sullivan Campaign for its commander, Major General John Sullivan, that was aimed at breaking forever the power of the Iroquois Confederacy, which had sided with the British, and had devastated Iroquoia, Brant used his influence to secure reserves for the Mohawks along the Grand River in Ontario and convinced many of his people to move there.

In the early 1790s a native confederacy under the Miami chief Little Turtle defeated American military expeditions led by Josiah Harmar and Arthur St. Clair in the Ohio Country. Brant and other Iroquois leaders recommended that Little Turtle, Blue Jacket, and other leaders negotiate a peace with the Americans that would leave their gains in place. Brant died on November 24, 1807, at Burlington, Ontario.

ROGER M. CARPENTER

See also

Blue Jacket; Iroquois; Iroquois Confederacy; Johnson, Sir William; Little Turtle; Mohawks

References

Graymont, Barbara. *The Iroquois in the American Revolution.* Syracuse, NY: Syracuse University Press, 1972.
Kelsay, Isabel Thompson. *Joseph Brant, 1743–1807: Man of Two Worlds.* Syracuse, NY: Syracuse University Press, 1984.

Brims of Coweta
Birth Date: Unknown
Death Date: ca. 1730–1733

Creek *mico* ("headman") and leader of Coweta, the Lower Creeks' most prominent settlement. In the late 17th century the Creeks were strategically located among the French in Louisiana, the Spanish in Florida, and the English in South Carolina. The nation was comprised of many different towns with individual leaders and encompassed two general areas: the Upper Towns and Lower Towns. The headman of the premier Lower Town, Coweta, was able to bring his people together and direct their diplomacy for several decades. That headman was known as Brims, or Emperor Brims, because of his influence and stature among the Creeks. Nothing is known of the circumstances of Brims's birth or his early years.

After Carolina's founding in 1670, the English slowly made inroads to the interior native tribes. By the 1680s Indian agent Henry Woodward had established contact with the Creeks. Anxious to counterbalance Spanish power in the region, Brims created a strong alliance with Woodward and subsequently opened an important economic connection with the English through trade. In August 1705 both the Upper and Lower Creeks cemented the relationship with a formal alliance.

Quickly, however, trade abuses against the Native Americans became so rampant that many of the southeastern natives revolted, leading to the Yamasee War (1715–1717). Brims and the Creeks joined the revolt, which initially favored the natives and almost wiped out South Carolina. But the English eventually regained the upper hand, largely because of native allies such as the Cherokees. The English ultimately dispersed the Yamasees, selling many of them into slavery, and concluded peace negotiations with the Creeks in November 1717.

In the years after the Yamasee War, Brims became most known for his policy of neutrality and manipulative diplomacy. He sought bargaining power for the Creeks, hoping for leverage against the three European nations. He therefore determined to fight none and court all in an effort to keep the Creeks powerful.

To that end, in 1717 Brims allowed the French to build Fort Toulouse, gave permission to the Spanish to build a fort in Coweta, received the English, and allowed his niece, Mary Musgrove, to marry an Englishman to solidify the alliance. Clearly Brims planned to keep the Creeks in the good graces of all three European nations, enabling him to play one against the other. He directed this policy until his death sometime between 1730 and 1733. Yet even after his death, his successors continued the policy. This allowed the Creeks to remain power brokers in the region throughout the 18th century.

LISA L. CRUTCHFIELD

See also
Creeks; Musgrove, Mary; Yamasees; Yamasee War

References
Corkran, David H. *The Creek Frontier, 1540–1783*. Norman: University of Oklahoma Press, 1967.
Hahn, Stephen C. *The Invention of the Creek Nation, 1670–1763*. Lincoln: University of Nebraska Press, 2004.

Britain
See Great Britain

Brodhead Expedition
Start Date: August 11, 1779
End Date: September 14, 1779

Expedition led by Colonel Daniel Brodhead against Native Americans in the Allegheny Valley from August 11 to September 14, 1779, in support of the Patriot invasion of the Iroquois country. Throughout the American Revolutionary War (1775–1783), American settlements on the frontiers of Pennsylvania and New York were the targets of attacks by Loyalists and Native Americans. On February 27, 1779, Congress directed Continental Army commander General George Washington to launch punitive attacks against frontier Native Americans and the British post of Fort Niagara.

Brodhead, commander at Fort Pitt, was to first strike north, his force of more than 600 men destroying Native American villages and crops along the way. He was then supposed to march to Genesee, where he would rendezvous with Major General John Sullivan and assist in an attack on Fort Niagara.

Departing Fort Pitt, Brodhead proceeded into country that was almost impassable due to rough terrain and thick forests. In the midst of these harsh surroundings, on August 15 his advance party of 25 men, under Lieutenant John Harding, surprised a Seneca war party. When the Senecas prepared themselves for action, brandishing their tomahawks, Harding and his party attacked with fury. Soon the warriors broke and ran, some plunging into the river and others escaping through the thick underbrush. Five Senecas were killed; there were no losses among Harding's men. By this time Brodhead as a precaution had deployed his entire force for battle, but this skirmish was the only resistance that he met during the entire campaign.

That same day Brodhead's expedition reached Buchan, Pennsylvania, where the men left all their baggage under guard. Proceeding to the Seneca settlements about 20 miles farther, the Americans burned eight abandoned towns and threw the warriors' military gear into the Allegheny River. Over the next three days Brodhead's troops cut down 600 acres of corn, piled it in heaps, and burned it. Proceeding on toward Genesee, Brodhead came within 50 miles of his destination but decided to turn back because he was unfamiliar with the territory and had no guides to lead him. On his return march, his soldiers burned the old Native American towns of Conauwago and Mahusquachinkocken. They arrived back at Fort Pitt on September 14 laden with plunder and proudly displaying the scalps they had taken from their enemies. In the course of 33 days, Brodhead had marched almost 400 miles without the loss of a single man, perhaps a record for a Revolutionary War campaign. Brodhead received the thanks of Congress and congratulations from Washington.

Although Brodhead's expedition produced no smashing military triumph, the Americans considered it a success. His projection of American power into seemingly impenetrable country had shown the Native Americans that none of their towns were secure. More importantly, Brodhead found awaiting him at Fort Pitt a delegation of Wyandot warriors who sued for peace because their dream of an Iroquois alliance was permanently shattered by his and Sullivan's successes.

PAUL DAVID NELSON

See also
Iroquois; Native Americans and the American Revolutionary War; Senecas

References
Brady, William J. "Brodhead's Trail up the Allegheny, 1779." *Western Pennsylvania Historical Magazine* 37 (1954): 19–31.
Buck, Solon, and Elizabeth Hawthorn Buck. *The Planting of Civilization in Western Pennsylvania*. Pittsburgh: University of Pittsburgh Press, 1939.

Brookfield, Siege of

Start Date: August 2, 1675
End Date: August 5, 1675

Native American assault on a central Massachusetts town (also known as Quabaug) by the Nipmuck tribe during August 2–5, 1675, in the early months of King Philip's War (1675–1676). The siege demonstrated that additional aboriginal groups besides the Wampanoags, led by King Philip (Metacom), would become adversaries of New England colonists in the conflict. Prior to August 1675, hostilities had involved only the Wampanoags and English colonists and militiamen in the western portions of Plymouth Colony and the eastern area of Narragansett Bay. In addition, attacking warriors attempted to employ a number of siege techniques, demonstrating a Native American facility for technical innovation.

On August 2, 1675, a party of English colonists with some Native American guides left Brookfield to meet with local sachems (chiefs). When the latter failed to arrive at the appointed time and place, the English party went in search of them and in so doing fell into an ambush prepared by Nipmuck warriors. The survivors of this attack retreated to Brookfield and, with residents of the town, defended themselves during the ensuing siege in the settlement's garrison house from that evening to the early morning of August 5. The Nipmucks abandoned their assault upon the arrival of colonial militiamen, who were notified by a colonist who had crept out of Brookfield in the midst of the siege.

The primary eyewitness account of the siege, written by militia captain Thomas Wheeler, notes that attacking warriors "used several Strategems" to fire the garrison house. During the first day the Nipmucks used fire arrows, placed and set alight combustible materials such as flax and hay at the side of the house, and "shot a Ball of wild Fire" at the building. The English defenders checked all these attempts to burn the garrison house, but by the following night warriors had constructed three devices to burn the structure.

Engraving of Nipmuck Indians attacking a building at Brookfield, Massachusetts, during their siege of that town in August 1675 early in King Philip's War. (Library of Congress)

One was a cart filled with flammable matter and fitted with planks to protect from the colonists' gunfire those Nipmucks pushing the vehicle. The other two devices were made of two sets of poles lashed together and set on small wheels, the front ends of the poles joined by an axle set within a barrel.

Rain helped foil the use of these siege devices on the evening of August 4. That same night reinforcements in the form of 46 Englishmen and five natives under Major Simon Willard and Captain John Parker arrived at Brookfield. Warriors constructing the siege engines failed to hear shots fired by scouts warning them of the soldiers' approach, allowing Willard and his men to reach the garrison house. The Native Americans subsequently engaged the reinforced English force in a firefight but then abandoned the siege on the early morning of August 5.

MATTHEW S. MUEHLBAUER

See also
King Philip's War; Metacom; Nipmucks; Wampanoags

References
Bodge, George Madison. *Soldiers in King Philip's War*. 3rd ed. Baltimore: Genealogical Publishing, 1967.
Leach, Douglas Edward. *Flintlock and Tomahawk: New England in King Philip's War*. East Orleans, MA: Parnassus Imprints, 1992.
Wheeler, Thomas. "A Thankefull Remembrance of Gods Mercy to Several Persons at Quabaug or Brookfield. . . ." In *So Dreadfull a Judgement: Puritan Responses to King Philip's War, 1676–1677*, edited by Richard Slotkin and James K. Folsom, 234–257. Middletown, CT: Wesleyan University Press, 1978.

Brown, Thomas
Birth Date: 1750
Death Date: August 3, 1825

Loyalist partisan and British Indian agent. Thomas Brown was born in Whitby, England, in 1750. He immigrated to Georgia in 1774, settling north of Augusta. An ardent Loyalist, Brown quickly came into conflict with Georgia's revolutionary movement. On August 2, 1775, a rebel mob attacked Brown, partially scalped him, and applied burning wood to his feet. As soon as he recovered he escaped to South Carolina, where he aligned himself with leading backcountry Loyalists. After South Carolina revolutionaries suppressed the Loyalists, in January 1776 Brown escaped to East Florida.

Brown urged aggressive action against the rebels, a plan that coincided with the ideas of East Florida's governor, Patrick Tonyn. In June 1776 Tonyn appointed Brown lieutenant colonel in the East Florida Rangers, a regiment of Loyalist refugees. Brown augmented his force by spending several months soliciting help from Britain's Creek and Seminole allies.

On February 17, 1777, Brown attacked Fort McIntosh in Georgia with 50 warriors and 20 rangers, forcing the garrison to surrender the next day. The Americans retaliated by invading East Florida but were thwarted by resistance from Brown's force of rangers and

Native Americans. Brown then resumed his raids against Georgia, and on March 13, 1778, Brown's force captured Fort Barrington on the Altamaha River. The rangers and Native Americans helped turn back another attempted American invasion of Florida in July.

After the death of southern Indian superintendent John Stuart in February 1779, the British government appointed Brown superintendent of the Creeks and Cherokees. Brown's rangers occupied Augusta after British forces captured Charleston in May 1780. There Brown conferred with Creek and Cherokee leaders, who asked for his aid in driving out settlers who had occupied their lands west of the Appalachians in violation of the British government's Proclamation of 1763. Brown favored the plan and asked Lieutenant General Charles Cornwallis, British commander in the South, for permission to attack the overmountain settlements. Cornwallis, who harbored a low opinion of Native Americans, refused, and the overmountain settlers were left free to destroy Major Patrick Ferguson's Loyalist militia at King's Mountain, South Carolina, on October 7.

Meanwhile, American partisans attacked Augusta on September 14, 1780. Brown's rangers and several hundred warriors held out for five days, when they were relieved by British troops from South Carolina. The following year the Americans again besieged Augusta, forcing Brown, his rangers, and some Native Americans to surrender on June 5, 1781. Brown was paroled to Savannah and was later exchanged.

With the Americans in control of the backcountry, Brown found it nearly impossible to communicate with his native allies. Some groups of Creeks, Cherokees, and Choctaws managed to reach Savannah, but they were too few to do more than annoy the Americans. When the British evacuated Savannah in July 1782, Brown urged tribal leaders to align themselves with the Spanish.

Brown then went to East Florida but left because Britain had ceded the province to Spain in the final peace settlement. He eventually obtained a land grant on the island of St. Vincent, where he operated a sugar plantation until his death on August 3, 1825.

JIM PIECUCH

See also
Cherokees; Choctaws; Creeks; Native Americans and the American Revolutionary War; Seminoles; Stuart, John

References
Cashin, Edward J. *The King's Ranger: Thomas Brown and the American Revolution on the Southern Frontier*. New York: Fordham University Press, 1999.
Piecuch, Jim. *Three Peoples, One King: Loyalists, Indians, and Slaves in the Revolutionary South, 1775–1782*. Columbia: University of South Carolina Press, 2008.

Brulé Sioux

One of the seven major bands of the Lakota Sioux tribe, also known as the Sicangus. This band of the Lakotas (the westernmost tribe of the Sioux) first became known to white Europeans while the

Brulé warriors. The Brulé are one of the seven major bands of the Teton (Lakota) Sioux. Photo taken by Edward S. Curtis, circa 1907. (Library of Congress)

Brulé Sioux still lived a woodlands lifestyle along the Mississippi River in Minnesota. Their name is derived from the French, who may have been the first Europeans to make contact with them. The Brulé Sioux were initially known as the Teton Sioux prior to their move west toward the Missouri River and farther west into western Dakota and northwestern Nebraska, which occurred probably by the late 1770s.

During their period in Minnesota, the Brulés were semi-sedentary, relying on grains and local hunting and fishing with occasional forays onto the prairies and plains in search of buffalo, which at that point was not an important part of their diet or lifestyle. However, a combination of increasing pressure from the Ojibwa (Chippewa) tribe and white encroachment on their lands as well as the pull of the horse-centered Plains culture drew the Brulés farther and farther west and onto the Plains proper. By the late 1700s they and the other Lakota bands were pressing the Cheyennes and Crows off their lands in the vicinity of the Black Hills.

Once on the Plains, the Brulés along with their Lakota cousins came to epitomize Plains culture, with large horse herds, conical buffalo-hide lodges, seasonal migrations to follow the buffalo herds, and the Sun Dance as the center of their spiritual life. By the early 19th century the buffalo had become the central part of the Brulés' way of life. From the buffalo came most of their food, clothing, and shelter. The Brulés also traded buffalo hides with other Native Americans and white traders.

The Brulés eventually ranged across western South Dakota, western Nebraska, western Kansas, and eastern Colorado, but the early heartland of their territory was the White River country

of western South Dakota. They later moved farther south to the Platte River basin. Initially hostile to the Cheyennes, the Brulés later allied with them in their wars against other Native American groups, such as the Crows, Arikaras, and Pawnees, as well as against American settlers.

The opening of the Oregon Trail in the early 1840s resulted in increasing pressures on the Brulés as large numbers of both westward-bound whites and settlers moving onto the Great Plains began to the crowd the Brulés out. This also shifted and in time destroyed the buffalo herds on which the Brulés depended. Serious troubles between the Brulé band and whites began in the mid-1850s as a result of the 1854 Grattan Massacre and the army expedition that followed. This conflict would continue off and on until 1868.

The most famous of the Brulé chiefs was Spotted Tail, who was renowned as both a warrior and a leader. By 1855 he was already influential among the Brulés. The overrunning of Little Thunder's village in the autumn of 1855 by Brigadier General William S. Harney's forces had a tremendous impact on Spotted Tail's life. He was wounded there and, after surrendering to Harney, spent four months at Fort Leavenworth, Kansas. When Spotted Tail returned to the Brulés, he was a changed man.

The impact of the 1855 conflict had a profound effect on many of the Lakotas, not least of all the Brulés. For Spotted Tail, the number of whites and their wealth seemed nearly incomprehensible. He now understood that the fate of the Brulés was no longer in their own hands but instead was in the hands of the whites. Spotted Tail led the southern bands of the Brulés onto reservation land following the 1868 treaty that concluded Red Cloud's War

(1866–1868). Some of the northern bands of the Brulés, however, remained allied with their Oglala Sioux cousins and continued to fight against the increasing encroachment of white settlers. They participated in the Battle of the Rosebud (June 17, 1876) and the Battle of the Little Bighorn (June 25–26, 1876).

The Brulés now reside primarily on the Rosebud Reservation in southwestern South Dakota.

JOHN THOMAS BROOM

See also

Buffalo; Cheyennes; Grattan Massacre; Harney, William Selby; Lakota Sioux; Little Bighorn, Battle of the; Oregon Trail; Red Cloud's War; Rosebud, Battle of the; Spotted Tail

References

Dyke, Paul. *Brule: The Sioux People of the Rosebud.* Flagstaff, AZ: Northland, 1971.

Goldfrank, Esther S. "Historic Change and Social Character: A Study of the Teton Dakota." *American Anthropologist,* n.s., 45(1) (January–March 1943): 67–83.

Hyde, George E. *Spotted Tail's Folk: A History of the Brulé Sioux.* The Civilization of the American Indian Series 57. Norman: University of Oklahoma Press, 1961.

Price, Catherine. "Lakotas and Euroamericans: Contrasted Concepts of 'Chieftainship' and Decision-Making Authority." *Ethnohistory* 41(3) (Summer 1994): 447–463.

Buffalo

A bovine mammal, the natural habitat of which was the Great Plains of North America. To the Native Americans of the resource-poor Great Plains, the vast herds of buffalo (also known as bison) were the very foundation of life. Buffalo skins were used for shelter and clothing. Meat provided food, bones could be fashioned into tools and weapons, and tendons were stretched to form the strings of the bow and arrow. Dried buffalo dung served as fuel. Indeed, the constant search for the buffalo determined that the Plains Indians would be migratory hunters.

Beginning with the 1851 Fort Laramie Conference and Treaty, the U.S. government pursued a policy of concentrating the Plains Indians on reservations. Following the American Civil War (1861–1865), the government became more aggressive in enforcing this policy as conflict increased between Native Americans and the growing number of white settlers. The Native Americans were not predisposed to accept the artificial boundaries of the reservation largely because the buffalo ignored such boundaries. Indians thus had no compunction about leaving the reservation to pursue the buffalo, even when this put them in direct conflict with the U.S. Army. Native Americans and white settlers also fought over the prime traditional buffalo hunting grounds, such as the Black Hills in the Dakota Territory or along the Bozeman Trail in Wyoming. Moreover, to the Indians these lands were important cultural locations because they played a central role in tribal origins. Loss of this land thus had a devastating impact.

Buffalo Population Decline

Date	Estimated Population
Precolonial era	60,000,000
1800	40,000,000
1850	20,000,000
1865	15,000,000
1870	14,000,000
1875	1,000,000
1880	395,000
1885	20,000
1890	1,091
1895	Fewer than 1,000
1902	1,940
1983	50,000
2004	350,000
2010	365,000

Generals William T. Sherman and Philip Sheridan had defeated the Confederacy by destroying the South's resource base. After 1865 they turned the same techniques against the Native Americans of the Great Plains. Sherman and Sheridan reasoned that there were only two ways to compel the Indians to adhere to the reservation policy and end conflict with white settlers. One way was the outright extinction of the Indians. The second way, and seemingly the more humane option, was to remove the temptation that lured Native Americans off the reservation. This meant slaughtering the massive buffalo herds. Although the U.S. Army did not directly participate in this planned extinction of the buffalo, it did protect the thousands of white buffalo hunters on the Plains.

Indeed, buffalo hunters swarmed the Plains, killing animals by the thousands. As the railroads cut deeper into the Plains, they left no refuge for the buffalo. Buffalo skins, meat, and bones supplied the food, clothing, shoe, fertilizer, and other industries in the East. From 1865 to 1875, the buffalo herd north of the Union Pacific Railroad was driven to near extinction. Between 1875 and 1885, the herd south of that line suffered the same fate. By 1890, there were perhaps only several hundred wild buffalo remaining.

Congress passed several bills to halt the wholesale slaughter of the buffalo, but General Sherman persuaded President Ulysses S. Grant to veto the legislation. The Texas state legislature also debated granting protection to the buffalo, but a personal appearance by General Sheridan convinced the legislature otherwise. By 1890, destruction of the buffalo had broken the Native Americans' resistance. Without the buffalo, the Plains Indians became anchored to the reservation and reliant on the U.S. government for food, shelter, and basic supplies.

GREGORY J. DEHLER

See also

Black Hills, South Dakota; Bozeman Trail; Fort Laramie, Treaty of (1851); Fort Laramie, Treaty of (1868); Grant, Ulysses Simpson; Railroads; Sheridan, Philip Henry; Sherman, William Tecumseh

References

Danz, Harold. *Of Bison and Men.* Boulder: University of Colorado Press, 1997.

Isenberg, Andrew C. *The Destruction of the Bison: An Environmental History, 1750–1920.* New York: Cambridge University Press, 2000.

Roe, Frank Gilbert. *The North American Buffalo: A Critical Study of the Species in Its Wild State.* Rev. ed. Toronto: University of Toronto Press, 1970.

Buffalo Bill

See Cody, William Frederick

Buffalo Bill's Wild West Show

Large-scale western-themed live performances produced by legendary frontiersman William "Buffalo Bill" Cody beginning in 1883. Buffalo Bill's Wild West Show entertained audiences in America and Europe for 30 years and helped create a lasting image of the American West, some of which was admittedly inaccurate or overly romanticized. The action-packed shows thrilled audiences with steers, broncos, buffalo, bears, cowboys, and Indians.

After initial success in an 1872 stage show in Chicago called *Scouts of the Prairie,* in 1873 Cody organized his own troupe of actors, and for the next decade the cast performed a spectacle known as *Scouts of the Plains.*

In 1883 Cody initiated Buffalo Bill's Wild West Show in Omaha, Nebraska. In the tradition of such popular spectacles as Barnum and Bailey's Circus, Cody made Buffalo Bill's Wild West Show a traveling production. The outdoor event was designed to entertain as well as educate the audience. The cast, which included as many as 1,200 performers, included real cowboys and Native Americans. Although most Americans and Europeans initially used the term "cowboy" as an insult and viewed cowboys as uncivilized ruffians, Buffalo Bill's portrayal of the virtuous and hardworking cowboy changed their opinion.

In 1887 Buffalo Bill's Wild West Show traveled to the United Kingdom for Queen Victoria's Golden Jubilee. The show's success there helped to improve Anglo-American relations. In 1889 Cody toured Europe. His image as both a civilized man and a frontiersman helped to persuade many Europeans that Americans were not barbarians.

Although Cody initially gained fame as an Indian fighter and a U.S. Army scout during the Indian Wars, he treated Native Americans in his show with respect. Sitting Bull was a frequent

William Cody, known as Buffalo Bill, drew large crowds during the late 1800s and early 1900s to his often exaggerated shows depicting scenarios from the history of the West. (Library of Congress)

participant in the show during the 1880s. The show provided Native Americans with an opportunity to showcase their culture at a time when it was threatened by Americanization and U.S. attempts at cultural assimilation. Cody, who frequently referred to Native Americans as Americans, argued that rather than being bloodthirsty savages, they were merely trying to preserve their cultural heritage. Thus, although the show portrayed Native American attacks on wagon trains and stage coaches, it also highlighted reenactments of Native American attempts to resist Americanization, such as the Ghost Dance.

The show began with a massive parade of Native Americans, U.S. cavalrymen, Cossacks, Gauchos, and other recognizable horsemen. The authentic costumes of the horsemen added to the spectacle. In addition to reenactments of historical events in the West, the show featured feats of skill such as shooting, bronco riding, and roping. One of the most famous performers was Annie Oakley, who engaged in shooting exhibitions with her husband Frank Butler. Committed to women's rights, Cody paid female performers the same as male performers. In the show, women frequently outrode and outgunned the male performers. One of the most popular celebrities in the show was Martha Jane Cannary Burke, popularly known as Calamity Jane. Buffalo Bill's Wild West Show frequently ended with a reenactment of Custer's Last Stand—the Battle of the Little Bighorn (June 25–25, 1876)—with Cody playing Lieutenant Colonel George A. Custer.

In 1912 after a series of poor economic investments, Cody borrowed $20,000 from fellow entertainer Harry Tammen to finance his shows. In 1913 when Cody arrived in Denver, Colorado, the show was seized by law enforcement officials and sold at auction because of unpaid debts to Tammen. For the next two years Cody was forced to work in Tammen's Sells-Floto Circus to pay off his debt. In 1915 after paying his debt, Cody performed with Pawnee Bill's Far East Show. Unable to retire because of heavy personal indebtedness, Cody performed until he died in 1917.

Ironically, despite the popular acclaim for Cody's engaging portrayal of the West and Native American culture, the American West was dramatically transformed during the 30 years that the show toured the United States and Europe. Buffalo herds had been virtually eliminated; white settlers, prospectors, and speculators dominated the Great Plains; and the Native Americans, in the aftermath of the Indian Wars, were confined to reservations. By 1900 the West portrayed in Buffalo Bill's Wild West Show no longer existed. Be that as it may, there can be little doubt that Buffalo Bill Cody and his Wild West Show had a profound influence on perceptions—the myths and realities—of the American West in the last third of the 19th century. Indeed, the show still resonates to the present, and characters such as Annie Oakley and Calamity Jane are still part of the American lexicon.

MICHAEL R. HALL

See also
Buffalo; Cody, William Frederick; Custer, George Armstrong; Ghost Dance; Little Bighorn, Battle of the; Sitting Bull

References
Carter, Robert A. *Buffalo Bill Cody: The Man behind the Legend.* Hoboken, NJ: Wiley, 2000.
Kasson, Joy S. *Buffalo Bill's Wild West: Celebrity, Memory, and Popular History.* New York: Hill and Wang, 2000.
Warren, Louis S. *Buffalo Bill's America: William Cody and the Wild West Show.* New York: Knopf, 2005.

Buffalo Hump
Birth Date: ca. 1800
Death Date: 1870

Principal Comanche war chief of the Peneteka band and leader of the 1840 Linnville Raid. Born around 1800, Buffalo Hump grew to prominence as a warrior during the 1830s, leading raids into Mexico and fighting against the Cheyennes and Arapahos. His most famous raid came in 1840 in retaliation for the Council House Fight in San Antonio, where Comanche leaders and their families had gone to negotiate with Texas colonels Hugh M. McLeod and William G. Cooke. When McLeod and Cooke demanded that the Comanches return all white captives, a fight broke out in which 35 Comanches were killed and another 27 were captured.

Upon receiving news of this treachery, the Comanches tortured and killed 13 of their white captives, and Buffalo Hump organized the largest raiding party in Comanche history, estimated at 500–600 warriors. Moving down the Guadalupe Valley, Buffalo Hump's force proceeded to the Gulf Coast, attacking farmsteads on the outskirts of Victoria on August 6 and burning the town of Linnville to the ground on August 8. The Comanches killed at least 23 settlers and seized more than 1,500 horses.

In the aftermath of the Linnville Raid, Texas militia pursued Buffalo Hump's force, which had split up as it headed back north, and defeated Buffalo Hump in the Battle of Plum Creek near present-day Lockhart. Buffalo Hump lost more than 50 warriors in the battle. The Texans continued their pursuit and attacked a Comanche camp some 300 miles northwest of Austin, killing as many as 100 Comanches, capturing 34 women and children, and recovering approximately 500 horses.

Buffalo Hump's raid had a significant impact on Texas politics, as Texans had paid a high price for President Mirabeau B. Lamar's war policy against Native Americans. Voters returned Sam Houston to the presidency in December 1841. Hoping to secure peace with the Comanches, Houston agreed to meet with Buffalo Hump and other Comanche chiefs at Council Springs in 1842. Although Buffalo Hump rejected Houston's attempt to keep the Comanches north of the San Saba River, Houston did succeed in getting Buffalo Hump to agree to end hostilities.

While Buffalo Hump continued to lead raids into Mexico, he recognized that the increasing number of white settlers in Texas was shifting the balance of power away from the Comanches. In

1847 he joined other Comanche chiefs in accepting a treaty that allowed German colonists to settle between the Llano and Colorado rivers. After a cholera outbreak that decimated the Comanches in 1849, Buffalo Hump signed a new treaty in December 1850 by which Judge John H. Rollins, who had become Texas's Indian agent in 1849, succeeded in convincing Buffalo Hump and the Comanches to agree to remain above the Llano River, a boundary limit that Buffalo Hump had previously steadfastly rejected.

Although Buffalo Hump was among the Comanche leaders who agreed in 1856 to settle on a reservation along the Brazos River, he initially resisted efforts to take up farming and led hunting parties north of the Red River in pursuit of buffalo herds. In 1858 he and a large number of Comanches, including members of other bands, left the reservation and moved to the Wichita Mountains. U.S. cavalry under Major Earl Van Dorn attacked his camp in October 1858, killing approximately 80 Comanches. Although Buffalo Hump managed to escape and fled north to the Arkansas River, Van Dorn pursued him and struck his camp near old Fort Atkinson some 15 miles south of the Arkansas on May 13, 1859. Following this defeat, Buffalo Hump agreed to settle on the Kiowa-Comanche Reservation near Fort Cobb in Indian Territory (Oklahoma) and even attempted to take up farming to set an example for his tribe. Buffalo Hump was among Comanche, Kiowa, Cheyenne, and Arapaho chiefs who met with U.S. officials at the Little Arkansas on October 14, 1865, and agreed to the Little Arkansas Treaty, which ceded all territory north of the Arkansas River, and accepted the reservation in Indian Territory. Buffalo Hump died near Fort Cobb sometime in 1870.

JUSTIN D. MURPHY

See also

Comanches; Penateka Comanches

References

Brice, Donaly E. *The Great Comanche Raid: Boldest Indian Attack of the Texas Republic.* Austin, TX: Eakin, 1987.

Hoig, Stan. *Tribal Wars of the Southern Plains.* Norman: University of Oklahoma Press, 1993.

Richardson, Rupert Norval. *The Comanche Barrier to South Plains Settlement.* Austin, TX: Eakin, 1996.

Buffalo Soldiers

Term used to refer to African American troops who served on the western frontier from 1866 to 1917. The policy mandating racial segregation in the American military survived until the early 1950s. The name "buffalo soldiers" was given to these troops by the Cheyennes, who asserted that the black soldiers fought as fiercely and courageously as a wounded buffalo. The appellation was proudly adopted by all African American troops on the frontier. Buffalo soldiers served in four regiments of the U.S. Army: the 9th and 10th Cavalry regiments as well as the 24th and 25th Infantry regiments. These units were born out of regiments of

African American soldiers of the U.S. Army's 25th Infantry Regiment, some wearing buffalo robes. Fort Keogh, Montana, 1890. (Library of Congress)

the United States Colored Troops (USCT) that had served in the Union Army during the American Civil War (1861–1865). During their existence the buffalo soldiers fought in every major war with Native Americans on the western frontier, often bearing the brunt of the fighting. The buffalo soldiers also fought at the 1898 Battle of San Juan Hill in the Spanish-American War, assisted in fighting Filipino insurgents in the Philippines during 1899–1902, and formed the core of troops who pursued Mexican revolutionary Pancho Villa during the 1916–1917 Punitive Expedition.

At the conclusion of the Civil War, a significant number of African American troops wished to remain in the U.S. Army. In reward for their wartime service, Congress responded by authorizing six black regiments (two cavalry, four infantry) that were later consolidated into four regiments. The pay was steady at $13 a month; soldiers were also provided with room, board, clothing, a pension, and a modicum of protection from the worst abuses of discrimination suffered in Jim Crow America. The buffalo soldiers were greatly admired by the African American community. In addition to serving as occupation forces in the Reconstruction-era South, these troops were also sent to forts throughout the American West. The buffalo soldiers were charged with protecting white settlers against warring Native American tribes as well as preventing whites from encroaching upon tribal lands. The buffalo soldiers ably assisted in subduing the Cheyenne, Kiowa, Comanche, Apache, Sioux, and Arapaho tribes.

Army life on the frontier was hard, with soldiers living in isolated forts, riding and marching for days on end, and fighting Native Americans warriors who attacked out of nowhere. Life for the buffalo soldiers could be even harder, as they faced hostility and ostracism from their white comrades in arms and many times from their white officers. Often the very people whom the buffalo soldiers were ordered to protect despised them, and in many towns they entered they were barred from eating in the saloons, sleeping in the hotels, and shopping in the stores.

Nonetheless, the buffalo soldiers served with distinction, drawing praise from their white officers and respect from their Native American adversaries. The black regiments were known for low desertion and high reenlistment rates and for continuity of leadership. Twenty buffalo soldiers were awarded the Medal of Honor, the highest honor in the American military. Without doubt, the men as a whole served capably and honorably.

RICK DYSON

See also

Geronimo; Grierson, Benjamin Henry; Hatch, Edward; Infantry Regiment, 24th U.S.; Infantry Regiment, 25th U.S.

References

Carlson, Paul H. *The Buffalo Soldier Tragedy of 1877.* College Station: Texas A&M University Press, 2003.
Christian, Garna L. *Black Soldiers in Jim Crow Texas, 1899–1917.* College Station: Texas A&M University Press, 1995.
Fowler, Arlen L. *The Black Infantry in the West, 1869–1891.* Norman: University of Oklahoma Press, 1996.
Leckie, William H., and Shirley A. Leckie. *The Buffalo Soldiers: A Narrative of the Black Cavalry in the West.* Norman: University of Oklahoma Press, 2003.
Taylor, Quintard. "Comrades of Color: Buffalo Soldiers in the West 1866–1917." Special issue, *Colorado Heritage* (Spring 1996): 3–27.

Buffalo War

See Red River War

Bureau of Indian Affairs

One of the largest divisions of the U.S. Department of the Interior and charged with representing Native American interests. The Bureau of Indian Affairs (BIA) predates the creation of the Department of the Interior, established in 1849, by almost 25 years. Established as the Office of Indian Affairs in 1824 under the tutelage of Thomas L. McKenney, one of the 19th century's most noteworthy Indian reformers, the BIA is the oldest bureau in the federal government.

The BIA has functioned somewhat like a city, state, or federal government for Native Americans, providing various services from education to law enforcement. The main mission of the BIA is to protect Native Americans, their land, and their resources, but in recent years the BIA has begun to relinquish its responsibility over program administration to Native American nations. Since 1972 Native Americans have greatly influenced hiring and promotions within the BIA.

From the earliest times of European settlement in the New World, whites had to contend with those who inhabited the land first. With the establishment of the United States, the new government came to perceive Native Americans not only as enemies but also as wards of the state. The framers of the Articles of Confederation and later of the U.S. Constitution of 1787 foresaw the need for a governmental program to deal with Native Americans. Initially the secretary of war (beginning with Henry Knox in 1786) was in charge of Indian-related affairs. Then in 1806 the Office of the Superintendent of Indian Trade was created. In 1824 Secretary of War John C. Calhoun established the BIA in the Department of War, with McKenney as the first head. Calhoun did so without congressional approval, however. Congress finally gave the office statutory authority in 1832, and with it the chief was titled "Commissioner of Indian Affairs."

The BIA was officially established by Congress in 1834 but remained a part of the War Department until 1849, when responsibility for the BIA shifted to the Interior Department. That shift resulted in a nearly century-long struggle between civilian officials and the military over who should control Indian affairs. From 1849 until 1977 the BIA fell under the control of an official within the Interior Department who often had little interest in Indian affairs. In 1977 the position of assistant secretary of Indian affairs

U.S. Government Indian Service Field Units, 1802–1903

Year	Superintendencies	Territorial Governors	Agencies	Subagencies
1802	4	3	6	—
1818	4	4	15	10
1834	4	3	18	27
1843	5	2	10	14
1853	9	4	25	3
1863	13	5	55	1
1873	4	—	77	1
1883	—	—	65	—
1893	—	—	58	4
1903	—	—	64	—

was created within the department, finally giving Native American issues an equal voice within the department.

Over the years there has been much criticism of the BIA for ineptitude, graft, and fraud. The BIA oversaw the relocation of many tribes to reservations, with often tragic results for the Native Americans. Often BIA officials charged with doling out aid to Native Americans engaged in thievery and chicanery, which only further antagonized the Native Americans. By the early 1860s the BIA was rife with corruption. In 1869, Ely Parker the BIA's first Native American commissioner of Indian affairs, engaged in Herculean efforts to clean up the BIA, but his tenure met with only limited success because of bureaucratic inertia and political scheming. The Indian Ring Scandal investigations of the late 19th century led to the resignation of Commissioner Ezra A. Hayt, but the investigations did little to curb the excesses of agents in the field.

The Society of American Indians, an early 20th-century Pan-Indian rights group, harshly denounced the BIA and demanded its abolition, but these recommendations were ignored. In 1987 the *Arizona Republic* newspaper reinforced such criticism, stating that in spite of the money spent to improve the lives of Native Americans, "Washington has succeeded primarily in building the most intractable and convoluted bureaucracy in the federal government." At times the BIA has been accused of being the worst-managed agency in the U.S. government.

In the 1960s President Lyndon Johnson's War on Poverty program enabled tribal leaders to solicit grants from federal agencies and administer programs themselves. This broke the agency's monopoly on funding, allowing tribes to develop relationships with a wide network of federal agencies. The new policy of self-determination in the 1970s reversed older tribal termination policies and ushered in a broader appreciation of Indian culture and tribal governments. Congress also enacted a series of laws, including the Indian Self-Determination Act, the Indian Child Welfare Act, and the Health Care Improvement Act, that were designed to improve life on reservations without eliminating tribal government. In 1975 Congress appointed the American Policy Review Commission, composed mostly of Native Americans, to investigate the BIA.

Headed by Ernest L. Stevens, a Wisconsin Oneida, 11 task forces investigated tribal conditions and recommended in its final report that the BIA needed to endorse, without any limitations, tribal sovereignty. In 1977 Congress elevated the position of commissioner of Indian affairs to assistant secretary of the interior, which gave the head of the BIA a full voice in policy decisions.

Today according to *The United States Government Manual, 2008/2009,* the principal objectives of the BIA are "to encourage and assist Indian and Alaska Native people to manage their own affairs under the trust relationship to the Federal Government; to facilitate, with maximum involvement of Indian and Alaska Native people, full development of their human and natural resource potential; to mobilize all public and private aids to the advancement of Indian and Alaska Native people for use by them; and to promote self-determination by utilizing the skill and capabilities of Indian and Alaska Native people in the direction and management of programs for their benefit." Since 1996, however, the BIA has been embroiled in a lawsuit alleging that it has not fulfilled its obligation of properly managing lands held in a trust for the benefit of Native Americans. The plaintiffs of *Elouise Pepion Cobell, et al. v. Gale A. Norton, Secretary of the Interior, et al.* have claimed that neither the sale of millions of acres of land nor profits from any possible sales can be accounted for. A recent ruling in *Cobell v. Norton* ordered that the management and accounting of the trust be evaluated. The case is ongoing.

The BIA, which in 2010 employed about 12,000 people (95 percent of whom are Native Americans), has area offices in several cities, including Aberdeen, South Dakota; Albuquerque, New Mexico; Anadarko and Muskogee, Oklahoma; Billings, Montana; Juneau, Alaska; Minneapolis, Minnesota; Phoenix, Arizona; Portland, Oregon; and Sacramento, California. The BIA provides services to approximately 1.5 million people in 562 federally recognized Native American tribes in the continental United States and Alaska and administers 55.7 million acres of tribal, federal, and individually owned land.

PAUL G. PIERPAOLI JR.

See also

Calhoun, James Silas; Indian Ring Scandal; Parker, Ely Samuel; Reservations

References

Jackson, Curtis. *A History of the Bureau of Indian Affairs and Its Activities among Indians.* San Jose, CA: R & E Publishing, 1977.

Prucha, Francis Paul. *American Indian Policy in the Formative Years: Indian Trade and Intercourse Acts, 1790–1834.* Cambridge: Harvard University Press, 1962.

Prucha, Francis Paul. *The Great Father: The United States Government and the American Indians.* 2 vols. Lincoln: University of Nebraska Press, 1984.

Taylor, Theodore W. *The Bureau of Indian Affairs.* Boulder, CO: Westview, 1984.

The United States Government Manual, 2008/2009. Washington, DC: U.S. Government Printing Office, 2009.

Viola, Herman J. *Thomas L. McKenney: Architect of America's Early Indian Policy, 1816–1830.* Chicago: Sage Books, 1974.

Burnt Corn Creek, Battle of
Event Date: July 27, 1813

The first battle of the Creek War (1813–1814) waged on July 27, 1813, at Burnt Corn Creek in southern Alabama. The Battle of Burnt Corn Creek can also be considered an ancillary part of the War of 1812. The battle was fought between U.S. militia forces and warriors of the Red Stick faction of Creeks returning from Pensacola, Florida, with guns and ammunition secured from the Spanish and British.

In mid-July 1813 a group of Red Sticks (so-named because they painted their war clubs red), led by Peter McQueen, Josiah Francis, and High Headed Jim, went to Pensacola to obtain weapons from Forbes and Company, the British trading firm there. They also sought weapons and ammunition from the Spanish governor. Both McQueen and Francis were pro-British at a time in which Britain and the United States were engaged in the War of 1812. At first Forbes and Company was reluctant to provide the weapons, but eventually company officials gave in. The Spanish governor and merchants at Pensacola provided additional weapons and military supplies to the Red Sticks.

News of the Red Stick departure from Pensacola northwestward toward their homeland soon reached American settlers in southern Alabama. In short order, a group of Alabama militiamen under the command of Colonel James Caller and Captain Dixon Bailey moved to intercept the war party. The militia, which was stationed at Fort Mims, consisted of whites and mixed-blood Native Americans (many of them of Creek ancestry) loyal to the United States.

The militia located the Red Sticks, now led by McQueen, at Burnt Corn Creek about 90 miles north of Pensacola, and on July 27, 1813, Caller launched a surprise attack against them. The militiamen routed the Red Sticks in a battle lasting several hours.

Caller, however, made a serious mistake by not pursuing the Red Stick survivors. Instead, he and his men began rummaging through the equipment and supplies that they had captured. While they were thus preoccupied, the Red Sticks rallied and regrouped. The Red Sticks then counterattacked and drove the militia from the battlefield, recapturing much of their lost equipment and supplies. Having suffered casualties, the militia was not able to regroup for another attack. The Americans sustained losses in the battle of 2 killed and 15 wounded. Creek losses are unknown.

The Battle of Burnt Corn Creek marked the beginning of the Creek War, which pitted the United States and its Creek (White Sticks) and Cherokee allies against the hostile Creek Red Sticks. The Red Sticks believed that the attack at Burnt Corn Creek had been unprovoked and called for revenge against American settlers and their Creek allies. This led to the massacre at Fort Mims on August 30, 1813, where as many as 500 whites died.

DALLACE W. UNGER JR.

See also
Creeks; Creek War; Fort Mims, Battle of; Native Americans and the War of 1812; Red Sticks

References
Axelrod, Alan. *America's Wars.* New York: Wiley, 2002.
Remini, Robert Vincenti. *Andrew Jackson and His Indian Wars.* New York: Penguin, 2001.
Vandervort, Bruce. *Indian Wars of Mexico, Canada and the United States, 1812–1900.* New York: Routledge, 2006.
Wright, J. Leitch, Jr. *Creeks and Seminoles: The Destruction and Regeneration of the Muscogulge People.* Lincoln: University of Nebraska Press, 1986.

Bushy Run, Battle of
Start Date: August 5, 1763
End Date: August 6, 1763

Clash between British and colonial troops, under the command of Colonel Henry Bouquet, and warriors of the Shawnee, Delaware, Mingo, and other Native American groups from the Ohio River and Great Lakes region 25 miles from Fort Pitt (later Pittsburgh, Pennsylvania). The Battle of Bushy Run, which took place during August 5–6, 1763, on the Pennsylvania frontier occurred during Pontiac's Rebellion (1763) and was arguably the most intensely fought field action of the conflict. Following this engagement, warriors abandoned attacks on and near Fort Pitt.

During the summer of 1763, Native American warriors attacked settlements and isolated garrisons on the Pennsylvania frontier. Fort Pitt (Fort Duquesne before 1758), the largest and most important garrison in the region, was the target of sporadic attacks beginning in June and came under constant fire beginning on July 28, 1763. However, advancing warriors broke off these attacks on August 2 when they received word of an approaching relief column led by Colonel Bouquet. Three days later at about noon, warriors ambushed the column's advance guard a mile from Bushy Run.

Bouquet sent two light infantry companies to support his vanguard. The assailants fell back before his soldiers' charges but shifted to attack the British force's flanks until they threatened Bouquet's baggage train. Bouquet took up a position at the top of nearby Edge Hill, which his forces improved by building temporary defensive works with flour bags.

Native American warriors renewed their assaults on August 6. Still surrounded, Bouquet devised a ruse to take advantage of his foes' boldness. He moved two companies off his perimeter and had nearby units change position as if the first two companies were retreating. Subsequently many warriors rushed through the gap; however, when they were within the British lines, the first two units charged out from a location previously hidden from view and routed the surprised warriors. The latter received fire from other units on the perimeter as they fled and were then pursued

Dowd, Gregory Evans. *War under Heaven: Pontiac, the Indian Nations, and the British Empire.* Baltimore: Johns Hopkins University Press, 2002.

Nester, William R. *"Haughty Conquerers": Amherst and the Great Indian Uprising of 1763.* Westport, CT: Praeger, 2000.

Chief Pontiac of the Ottawa tribe, leader of a federation of Native Americans against the colonists, meets with a delegation of British and Pennsylvania officers, among them Colonel Henry Bouquet, and prepares to sign a peace treaty following the Battle of Bushy Run during August 5–6, 1763. Original engraving by Charles Grignion (1717–1810). (Library of Congress)

by the charging British troops. The Native Americans who had not fallen into but witnessed the effectiveness of Bouquet's trap also abandoned the fight.

Although victorious, Bouquet's force sustained heavy casualties. Of about 400 men in the engagement, some 50 were killed and another 60 wounded. Moreover, Bouquet had to abandon and destroy the flour bags intended for Fort Pitt in order to use the pack horses to carry his wounded men.

MATTHEW S. MUEHLBAUER

See also

Bouquet, Henry; Delawares; French and Indian War; Mingos; Pontiac's Rebellion; Shawnees

References

Anderson, Fred. *Crucible of War: The Seven Years' War and the Fate of the Empire in British North America, 1754–1766.* New York: Vintage Books, 2001.

Bouquet, Henry. *The Papers of Colonel Henry Bouquet.* Ser. 21634. Edited by Sylvester K. Stevens and Donald H. Kent. Harrisburg: Pennsylvania Historical and Museum Commission, 1940.

Bouquet, Henry. *The Papers of Colonel Henry Bouquet.* Ser. 21649, pt. 2. Edited by Sylvester K. Stevens and Donald H. Kent. Harrisburg: Pennsylvania Historical and Museum Commission, 1942.

Butler, John
Birth Date: 1728
Death Date: May 12, 1796

Pioneer, wealthy New York landowner, and Loyalist during the American Revolutionary War (1775–1783) who led the irregular unit known as Butler's Rangers during 1774–1784. John Butler was born in 1728 in New London, Connecticut. Soon thereafter his family moved to the western frontier in New York's Mohawk Valley, settling near present-day Fonda, New York. His father began purchasing tracts of land in the area, and the family was quite comfortable financially. During the French and Indian War (1754–1763) Butler saw action as a captain and commanded numerous Native American warriors who had allied with the British during the conflict. He participated in the Battle of Fort Ticonderoga, the Battle of Niagara, and the Battle of Montreal, among other battles.

After the war Butler concentrated on augmenting his family's already-impressive landholdings in New York. By the eve of the American Revolutionary War, Butler had amassed some 26,000 acres of land. He served for a time as a local judge and was a lieutenant colonel in the Tryon County Militia. In the early 1770s Superintendent of Northern Indian Affairs Sir William Johnson appointed Butler as one of his chief deputies. Meanwhile, Butler won a seat in the New York colonial assembly. He managed to cultivate good relations with most of the Native Americans in his area.

When war began between the Patriots and the British in April 1775, Butler promptly joined the Loyalist cause, becoming a colonel in the British Army. In May of that same year he left New York for Canada, where he participated in the defense of Montreal and was charged with developing alliances with the Native Americans. In the spring of 1777 Butler was given permission to recruit an irregular armed force of Loyalists who would fight alongside some of the Iroquois allied with the British against the Patriots.

Butler's force, dubbed Butler's Rangers, took part in the Saratoga Campaign (June–October 1777) with no small measure of success. Indeed, the rangers played a significant role in the Battle of Oriskany on August 6, 1777. In the late spring of 1778 Butler and his force began preparations for a campaign into Pennsylvania. In June 1778 Butler, along with some 20 rangers and an undetermined number of Iroquois warriors, arrived in Pennsylvania's Wyoming Valley (near present-day Wilkes-Barre) determined to harass the local Patriot population and defeat armed forces in the region. Butler's campaign resulted in the crushing defeat of a

Patriot force under Lieutenant Colonel Zebulon Butler (his cousin) at Forty Fort and the torching of nearly 1,000 homes in the area. Unfortunately, the fighting at Forty Fort quickly got out of control, as Butler's Native American allies killed scores of Patriots, bringing American losses there to more than 340. The debacle came to be known as the Wyoming Valley Massacre and is also known as the Battle of Wyoming.

Similar depredations followed, and by 1779 Butler was both universally feared and despised by most Americans. The November 1778 Cherry Valley Massacre in New York, in which 14 soldiers and 30 civilians died at the hands of Butler's Rangers and their Native American allies, only deepened that animosity.

Butler's force ranged from Niagara all the way to eastern Illinois. In 1779 Continental Army major general John Sullivan and Brigadier General James Clinton launched a punitive expedition against Butler and the Iroquois in western New York. Butler and his allies were defeated temporarily, and Butler was compelled to withdraw to his makeshift headquarters at Fort Niagara. Although Butler had been chastened by the Sullivan-Clinton Expedition, he nevertheless continued to wage a guerrilla-style war in New York's Mohawk and Schoharie valleys for the remainder of the war. His hit-and-run raids, made even more deadly by Native American participation, proved the bane of locals in the area until the unit was finally disbanded in 1784.

Forced to give up his lands in New York, in 1784 Butler began farming in the Niagara region, where he soon established himself as a successful landowner. He subsequently became involved in politics in Upper Canada (present-day Ontario) and once again served as a local militia leader. On May 12, 1796, Butler died at Niagara (present-day Niagara Falls), Canada.

PAUL G. PIERPAOLI JR.

See also

Brant, Joseph; French and Indian War; Iroquois; Iroquois Confederacy; Native Americans and the American Revolutionary War; Oriskany, Battle of; Sullivan-Clinton Expedition against the Iroquois; Wyoming, Battle of

References

Cook, Frederick. *Journals of the Military Expedition of Major General John Sullivan against the Six Nations of Indians in 1779.* 1887; reprint, Freeport, NY: Books for Libraries Press, 1972.

Mann, Barbara Alice. *George Washington's War on Native America, 1779–1782.* Westport, CT: Praeger, 2005.

Butterfield Overland Mail Route

Stagecoach route used to convey U.S. mail and passengers from the East Coast to California that was in operation from 1857 to 1861. The Butterfield Overland Mail Route linked two eastern termini—Tipton, Missouri, and Memphis, Tennessee—with San Francisco. The two routes converged at Fort Smith, Arkansas, and then headed west through Indian Territory (present-day Oklahoma), Texas, New Mexico, and Arizona and finally to San Francisco. The Butterfield Route was approximately 2,800 miles long and was almost 600 miles longer than east-west routes farther

A Butterfield coach leaves Atchison, Kansas, in 1866. The Butterfield Overland Mail Route ran from St. Louis to San Francisco via El Paso, Tucson, and Los Angeles during 1857–1861 and was often subject to Indian attack. (Corbis)

to the north, but it was essentially snow-free, making winter travel much faster and easier than on routes farther to the north. Stagecoaches left each terminus point semiweekly in both directions. Four-horse coaches or spring wagons were employed during the journey, which provided for both passenger and mail service.

The route was named for John Warren Butterfield, a stage and freight line operator who helped found Wells Fargo and American Express. Concerned that it was taking far too long to move mail from east to west, the U.S. government contracted with Butterfield in 1857 to carry letters and small parcels to California on the stipulation that the entire journey would average 25 days or less. Butterfield was paid $600,000 to fulfill the contract, an astronomical sum at the time and the largest government contract to date. The contract went into force in September 1858.

The route was subdivided into eight segments (from west to east): San Francisco to Los Angeles (460 miles); Los Angeles to Fort Yuma (280 miles); Fort Yuma to Tucson (280 miles); Tucson to El Paso (360 miles); El Paso to Fort Chadbourne, Texas (460 miles); Fort Chadbourne to Colbert's Ferry, Oklahoma (280 miles); Colbert's Ferry to Fort Smith, Arkansas (190 miles); and Fort Smith to Tipton (320 miles). Average total time traveled was 596.3 hours. At its peak of operations in 1860, the Butterfield Route employed 800 workers and used 250 stagecoaches. At the time approximately 1,800 horses and mules were used, and the company staffed 130 relay stations and redoubts along the way to serve passengers, riders, and horses.

The route was fraught with perils both natural and man-made. In the summer this southern route, which traversed deserts that had virtually no easily accessed water supplies and had temperatures between 100 and 115 degrees, proved brutal to both stage drivers and the animals that pulled the stagecoaches. Much of the route went through sparsely populated areas where medical services were few and far between. Stage drivers were ever mindful that the Butterfield Route traversed lands inhabited by sometimes hostile Native Americans, so there was a constant threat of attack, especially on the far western portions.

The coming of the American Civil War (1861–1865) and the advent of the Pony Express in 1860, however, dealt a severe blow to the Butterfield Overland Mail Route. The U.S. government now sought faster mail service for the West, which the Pony Express and then railroads were able to provide. In March 1861 the U.S. Congress officially discontinued the Butterfield service, and on June 30 the service ceased operations. Newer routes farther to the north were utilized, and the Pony Express offered mail delivery in a fraction of the time, as its riders ran nonstop in a relay system. From 1861 to 1862 the Butterfield Route was used by the Confederate States of America but on a limited scale. Wells Fargo continued to use the route to bring miners and supplies to the Southwest, but completion of the transcontinental railroad in 1869 rendered the route obsolete. Three Civil War skirmishes, all in Arizona, were fought at or close to Butterfield Mail outposts: the Battle of Stanwix Station, the Battle of Picacho Pass (Peak), and the Battle of Apache Pass.

Paul G. Pierpaoli Jr.

See also

Overland Trail; Pony Express; Railroads; Santa Fe Trail; Wells Fargo

References

Conkling, Roscoe P., and Margaret B. Conkling. *The Butterfield Overland Mail, 1857–1869.* 3 vols. Glendale, CA: Clark, 1947.

Ormsby, Waterman L. *The Butterfield Overland Mail.* 1942; reprint, San Marino, CA: Huntington Library, 1955.

Williams, J. W. "The Butterfield Overland Mail Road across Texas." *Southwestern Historical Quarterly* 61 (July 1957): 22–41.

C

Caddos

Native American nation of scattered autonomous villages and complexes. The Caddo people resided in the entire lower Red River area, which included much of present-day Oklahoma, Texas, Louisiana, and Arkansas. The Caddos are believed to have numbered some 8,000 people at the time of first European contact.

The word "Caddo" is a French abbreviation of *Kadohadacho*, derived from the term *kaadi,* meaning "chief." The term identifies both the Caddo Nation and the language spoken by the Wichitas, Kichais, Pawnees, and Arikaras. Spanish references to the Caddos as Tejas or Teches, meaning "friend," became the basis for the name of the state of Texas.

The Caddos were composed of several dozen loosely organized tribes and confederacies, the most important of which were the Hasinais, Natchitoches, Caddos proper (Kadohadachos or Cadodachos), Adais, Eyishes, and Tulas. Mentioned in 17th-century records, the Caddos were recognized as having controlled their lands prior to Spaniard Hernando de Soto's excursion. Members of his expedition had entered Caddo territory at Chaguate on the Ouachita River near present-day Malvern and Arkadelphia, Arkansas, in June 1541. By 1686, the Caddos had allied with their old rivals, the Wichitas, and were in conflict with the Choctaws, the Chickasaws, the Osages, and the Tonkawas.

Known as the Earth House People for their earthen temples and mounds, the Caddos were also recognized for having well-established communities and ceremonial centers in small and larger townships. They were basically an agricultural people and had farmsteads along the larger rivers. They did not build fortifications. Their dwellings were circular and both grass-thatched and earth-covered. Around the walls were couches that served as seats during the day and beds at night. The Caddos made bows and arrows and hunted deer and buffalo, among other animals. They also fished.

In the summer many Caddos went naked, and in the winter they draped themselves in animal skins. They produced pottery and traded salt, conch shells, copper, cotton, and turquoise, which they secured from the Southwest. After European contact, the Caddos became great horsemen and hunters as their homeland shifted westward.

The French established early their control over all the Caddo tribes, except for the Adais near whom the Spanish had located. In 1714 the French founded a trading post at present-day Natchitoches, Louisiana, and by 1730 there were several hundred Natchitoches dwellings near the post. The Caddos hoped to remain neutral, trading with both colonial powers, but this proved impossible. In fighting between France and Spain, the Adais particularly suffered, their villages being divided between the two colonial powers.

In the Treaty of Fontainebleau in 1762, France compensated Spain for losses incurred while fighting on the French side in the Seven Years' War (1756–1763) by giving it the Louisiana Territory. This transaction was not completed until 1769 but produced great anger among the Caddos, who did not believe that the French had the right to cede their land. The Spanish succeeded in winning Caddo loyalty, however, through the fur trade and presents. Caddo chief Tinihiouien meanwhile negotiated several treaties ceding land to the Spanish.

When the United States took control of the Louisiana Territory in 1803, a number of Caddos were compelled to move west into Spanish-controlled Texas. After the successful Texas Revolution of 1836 the Texas government did not adequately protect the tribe from white aggression, so by the early 1840s the tribe had relocated again to the Brazos River Valley. Eventually the Caddos

Caddo chief Long Hat's family compound near Binger, Indian Territory (Oklahoma), photograph circa 1870 by William Soule. (National Anthropological Archives, Smithsonian Institution, NAA INV 01623401)

settled in Indian Territory (Oklahoma) on a reserve along the Washita River. In the American Civil War (1861–1865) the Caddos sided with the Union, and numerous Caddos served as scouts for the U.S. Army.

RAESCHELLE POTTER-DEIMEL AND SPENCER C. TUCKER

See also

Arikaras; Chickasaws; Choctaws; Indian Territory; Osages; Pawnees; Soto, Hernando de

References

Hudson, Charles. *Knights of Spain, Warriors of the Sun: Hernando de Soto and the South's Ancient Chiefdoms.* Athens: University of Georgia Press, 1997.

Swanton, John R. *The Indians of the Southeastern United States.* Washington, DC: Smithsonian Institution Press, 1946.

Vega, Garcilaso de la. *The Florida of the Inca.* Translated by John and Jeannette Varner. Austin: University of Texas Press, 1996.

Caesar
Birth Date: Unknown
Death Date: Unknown

A Cherokee chief of the early 18th century who was at different times a warrior, a slave trader, and a slave. The precise time and place of

Caesar's birth and death, his real name, and how he acquired the name Caesar are unrecorded. He evidently had been supplying South Carolina with Native American slaves and capturing runaways when he himself was captured and sold to John Stephens, a Savannah planter, in 1713. At the prompting of Flint, another Cherokee chief, Caesar soon escaped from captivity. The Cherokees offered to pay restitution to Stephens, since their own tradition recognized the enslavement of war captives as a legal right.

In 1714 Caesar and Flint were approached by Eleazar Wigan and Alexander Long, two South Carolina traders who claimed to have grievances against the Yuchis. (The Yuchis are believed to be the people identified in the 17th century as the Westos.) The traders persuaded Caesar and Flint to lead a Cherokee attack against the Yuchi village of Chestowee (Tsistuyi) on the Hiwassee River (present-day Polk County, Tennessee), even though Chestowee was on friendly terms with the colony.

The traders would take the captives, who would be sold into slavery, and in return the Cherokees would have their debts canceled and receive ammunition, powder, and trade goods. Governor Charles Craven received advance word of the attack but was unable to stop it. Caught by surprise but unwilling to become slaves, many of the Yuchis killed each other, leaving only one woman and five children to be taken captive. The incident created a scandal and led to a trial, perhaps the first in the colony in which

Cherokees testified. The Cherokees claimed that they were told the governor had authorized the operation. Wigan and Long had their trading licenses revoked.

In 1715 the colonial government offered Wigan £500 to persuade the Cherokees to join South Carolina in the Yamasee War (1715–1717). He brought Caesar from Echota, on the upper Chattahoochee River, to Charles Town (present-day Charleston, South Carolina) with a delegation of 120 natives. There Caesar appeared to commit the Cherokees to a joint war effort, but he had no real authority to do so, and the warriors failed to appear as promised. Charitey Hagey (known as the Conjuror), a chief from another Cherokee village, took a neutralist position and offered to mediate between South Carolina and the Creeks, an ally of the Yamasees. The colonial authorities, suffering from the war, were intrigued by this offer, but the prospect threatened to undermine Caesar's authority and usefulness as the leader of the pro-British war faction. Yet another faction, little known to the colonists, sought an alliance with the Creeks against South Carolina.

Caesar was apparently instrumental in orchestrating the massacre of a large Creek delegation visiting the Cherokees on January 26, 1716. The brutal act ended the possibility of an accommodation with the Creeks and forced the Cherokees into the war on the side of South Carolina. With the forging of the Cherokee alliance, the Native American coalition fighting South Carolina soon began to unravel.

SCOTT C. MONJE

See also
Cherokees; Westos; Yamasee War

References
Gallay, Alan. *The Indian Slave Trade: The Rise of the English Empire in the American South, 1670–1717*. New Haven, CT: Yale University Press, 2002.
McDowell, William L., Jr., ed. *Journals of the Commissioners of the Indian Trade, September 20, 1710–August 29, 1718*. Columbia: South Carolina Archives Department, 1955.
Reid, John Phillip. *A Better Kind of Hatchet: Law, Trade, and Diplomacy in the Cherokee Nation during the Early Years of Contact*. University Park: Pennsylvania State University Press, 1976.

Cahokia-Fox Raid
Event Date: June 1, 1752

An attack by Fox warriors and their native allies on a Cahokia village on the banks of the Mississippi River in present-day Illinois on June 1, 1752. The inhabitants of the Cahokia village included members of the Michigamea Nation and numbered roughly 400 people, including men, women, and children. The raid was a devastating blow to the Cahokia tribe, driving them further into a state of dependence on the French and weakening their tribal identity.

Allies of the French, the Cahokias had broken a French-sponsored treaty between themselves and their native rivals to the north by trespassing onto non-Cahokia lands for a hunting excursion in 1751. During the trip the Cahokia party captured and mistreated

some members of the Fox (Mesquakie) tribe. The Foxes retaliated the following year with a raiding party of 400–500 warriors from the Fox and other northern tribes. The party filled 60 canoes, which stole past French forts on the Mississippi toward their objective.

Taking advantage of the absence of some members of the Cahokia tribe at the Corpus Christi feast held at nearby French Fort de Chartres, the Fox raiding party attacked. Despite the close proximity of the fort, no help from it was forthcoming. The Foxes easily took the village, destroying a great part of it and taking hostages. The attackers scalped the dead and abused corpses, both those killed during the raid and those already buried in the village graveyard. The Cahokia hostages remained in bondage for some years, with at least a few returning to the tribe after French diplomatic efforts to secure their release.

The raid effectively began the Cahokias' downward spiral toward eventual extinction and removed them from their ancestral area. Unable to recover, reduced to a state of dependency on the fading power of France, and stricken by demographic decline, many of the remaining Cahokias merged with their culturally close cousins, the Peorias. The Peoria tribe eventually settled in Oklahoma.

Although there is no historical proof, many observers have suggested French duplicity in the raid. The French often portrayed themselves as the protectors of their native allies against hostile threats, but it was the French who benefited most from this arrangement. The British pressed hard against French possessions in the region, and the French could not afford to have the Cahokia tribe defect to the British side. It would have been to the French advantage to create a situation in which the Cahokias could not collude with France's native enemies or with the British, who had hitherto been associated with native foes of the Cahokias. The existence of this strategy can only be inferred by the French modus operandi in other native areas, the suspicious passage of the Fox raiding party past French forts, and suggestive remarks made by French officials in the region.

CHARLES ALLAN

See also
Mesquakies

References
Hauser, Raymond E. "The Fox Raid of 1752: Defensive Warfare and the Decline of the Illinois Indian Tribe." *Illinois Historical Journal* 86(4) (1993): 210–224.
Temple, Wayne C. *Indian Villages of the Illinois Country*, Vol. 2, pt. 2. Springfield: Illinois State Museum Scientific Papers, 1966.

Calhoun, James Silas
Birth Date: 1802
Death Date: July 2, 1852

Whig politician, soldier, and first governor of New Mexico Territory (1851–1852). James Silas Calhoun was born in 1802 in Columbus, Georgia. From 1838 to 1839 he served as mayor of

Columbus; he also served in the Georgia state legislature from 1838 to 1840 and again in 1845. From 1841 to 1842 he served as the U.S. consul in Havana, Cuba. During the Mexican-American War of 1846–1848, Calhoun initially held a volunteer commission as a captain; by war's end he had been promoted to colonel. During the conflict he served under Major General Zachary Taylor, and the two men became friends and political allies.

In 1849 Taylor, now president of the United States, named Calhoun superintendent of Indian affairs for New Mexico, part of the territory newly won from Mexico. Taylor apparently had an ulterior motive in the appointment, hoping that Calhoun would help pave the way for New Mexican statehood, which Taylor greatly favored. Taylor's untimely death in July 1850, however, combined with the Compromise of 1850 ensured that New Mexican statehood would be postponed and that the region would remain a territory.

Calhoun made it clear that he did not want to be territorial governor and that he preferred to remain as superintendent of Indian affairs for New Mexico. Nevertheless, President Millard Fillmore named Calhoun territorial governor, and he was inaugurated on March 3, 1851. He also continued to act as superintendent of Indian affairs.

Calhoun was almost immediately overwhelmed by the problems he faced as governor. In 1851 he wrote to a colleague that "everybody and everything in this country appears at cross purposes." Calhoun lamented that civilian and military officials in New Mexico were engaged in a virtual war, that the U.S. military refused to accord the governor the right to dispatch Indian agents to certain regions, that U.S. citizens were being uncooperative, and that even Christian missionaries were at loggerheads. Amid this chaos Calhoun was expected to administer a territory that had almost no money under a political system in which the governor had little actual authority.

The problems that Calhoun faced as the first governor of New Mexico Territory were emblematic of the larger problems that the United States faced in governing the newly won territories in the American Southwest. The lack of financial resources, the bickering between civilian and military authorities, and the general lack of organization lent an air of chaos to the entire region. Amid the maelstrom were dozens of Native American tribes, many of which suffered because of such disorganization and widespread unrest. Not surprisingly, some tribes engaged in warfare among themselves and against American and Mexican citizens. In the early spring of 1852 Calhoun's health began to rapidly deteriorate, no doubt precipitated by the stresses of his job.

In early May 1852 Calhoun, probably suffering from scurvy and jaundice, decided to leave Santa Fe for his hometown in Georgia. Before departing he told associates that he hoped to make it back to Georgia before he died. Reportedly he took a coffin with him for the trip in case he died en route. Calhoun died near Independence, Missouri, on July 2, 1852, never making it to Georgia. Little had been accomplished in New Mexico during Calhoun's

abbreviated tenure, and that territory remained in chaos for several years thereafter.

PAUL G. PIERPAOLI JR.

See also

New Mexico; Taylor, Zachary

References

Keleher, William A. *Turmoil in New Mexico.* Facsimile of 1952 ed. Santa Fe, NM: Sunstone, 2008.

Lamar, Howard R. *The Far Southwest, 1846–1912: A Territorial History.* Albuquerque: University of New Mexico Press, 2000.

Calhoun, John Caldwell
Birth Date: March 18, 1782
Death Date: March 31, 1850

Political leader, secretary of war (1817–1825), vice president (1825–1832), and secretary of state (1844–1845). One of the most dominant political figures in the United States during the first half of the 19th century, John Caldwell Calhoun was born on March 18, 1782, in what became Abbeville, South Carolina. He graduated from Yale College in 1804 and studied law in Connecticut. He returned to South Carolina in 1807 and was admitted to the bar. Although a gifted lawyer, he disliked the profession and decided that he could best serve his state and country as a planter and in public service. Calhoun was elected to the South Carolina legislature in 1808 as a Democratic-Republican. In 1810 he won election to the U.S. House of Representatives for the first of three terms, serving until November 1817. Calhoun quickly established himself as one of the War Hawks, calling for an aggressive stance toward Great Britain during the Napoleonic Wars. During the War of 1812 he did his best to raise funds to prosecute the war, weed out unfit officers and cabinet members, and strengthen the unity of the nation.

Following the war, Calhoun became known as a nationalist. He called for federal support of internal improvements such as canals and roads. He also drafted a bill to create the Second Bank of the United States and supported a protective tariff.

From 1817 to 1825 Calhoun served as secretary of war in President James Monroe's cabinet, proving to be one of the most effective secretaries of war in the nation's history. Calhoun established military posts in the West, which would prove essential for westward expansion and the prosecution of the Indian Wars. He also created the first general staff and established the position of commanding general of the army. Calhoun also developed the expansible army concept, or what would be known as skeletonizing today. The concept called for an officer-heavy force that could be rapidly expanded by volunteers in time of war. Congress rejected the plan because of its expense, however. Calhoun wanted to court-martial Andrew Jackson for his invasion of Spanish Florida in 1818, but the president countermanded him. In 1821 the regular army was set at seven regiments of infantry and four of artillery. The cavalry

South Carolinian John C. Calhoun, while primarily known for his defense of slavery and states' rights, was also a highly effective secretary of war during 1817–1825. Calhoun established many military posts in the West that proved essential for subsequent westward expansion. (Library of Congress)

was done away with entirely, although the Corps of Engineers was retained.

In 1824 Calhoun was the presidential candidate selected by the Republican congressional caucus. In the past this choice was the party's certain nominee. By 1824, however, local party organizations were exerting their power, and Calhoun could not overcome Jackson, Henry Clay, and John Quincy Adams. Calhoun was nominated for vice president and was inaugurated in 1825 along with President-elect John Quincy Adams. Calhoun joined a pro-Jackson faction, worked for Jackson's election in 1828, and was again elected vice president, but Calhoun soon became alienated from the president. Calhoun's earlier attempt to censure Jackson over Florida was also a sensitive issue.

In 1832 Calhoun resigned the office of vice president and was elected senator from South Carolina. He held the office for the rest of his life, with a short interval as secretary of state under John Tyler from 1844 to 1845. As senator, Calhoun helped negotiate the Compromise Tariff of 1833 that ended the Nullification Crisis. He became best known as a champion of slavery and states' rights. While serving as secretary of state, Calhoun argued forcefully for the annexation of Texas, seeing Texas as additional slave territory and believing that it could be a buffer between the United States and British interests in Mexico. Conversely, Calhoun opposed the Mexican-American War (1846–1848). He feared that the United

States would add vast new territories from Mexico that would bring the question of slavery's spread to the fore and expand the scope and powers of the federal government. He opposed the admission of Oregon and California as free states in 1848 and 1849 because that move would upset the regional balance in Congress.

Toward the end of his life, Calhoun warned against the dissolution of the Union if the federal government did not protect slavery. At an 1850 meeting of representatives of the slave states in Nashville, Tennessee, Calhoun gave a fiery speech on March 4 against any compromise. He died on March 31, 1850, in Washington, D.C., before the Compromise of 1850 was reached. Calhoun had warned darkly—and presciently—that the Union would be dissolved within 12 years if slavery was not guaranteed.

TIM J. WATTS

See also
Jackson, Andrew

References
Bartlett, Irving H. *John C. Calhoun: A Biography*. New York: Norton, 1993.
Lander, E. M. *Reluctant Imperialists: Calhoun, the South Carolinians, and the Mexican War*. Baton Rouge: Louisiana State University Press, 1980.

California Gold Rush
Start Date: 1848
End Date: 1855

Large influx of prospectors who flocked to California beginning in 1848 after the discovery of significant gold deposits there. Ten days prior to the February 2, 1848, signing of the Treaty of Guadalupe Hidalgo, which formally ended the Mexican-American War (1846–1848), James W. Marshall discovered gold in California. Although this had no influence on the negotiations for or ratification of the treaty, it did have a major impact on California and the United States.

With the end of hostilities in California in January 1847, Americans and Europeans in northern California turned to speculation, mostly in land. Approximately 1,000 white immigrants had arrived in the region during 1846. With the expectation that immigration over the next few years would be at least as large, speculators anticipated an increase in the demand for land. One such speculator was John Sutter, already the owner of 48,827 acres at the junction of the Sacramento and American rivers known as New Helvetia, including Sutter's Fort. Besides laying out a town near the fort, he decided that he could make money by harvesting trees and selling lumber to the buyers of his lots and anyone else who needed lumber during the expected building boom. What he needed for this, of course, was a sawmill.

Because Sutter had a number of enterprises absorbing most of his time, he decided that a partner could do most of the work on the project, to be paid with a portion of the proceeds. His partner in the sawmill enterprise was James W. Marshall. Finding a suitable spot on the American River, Marshall began construction of the sawmill with a crew of Mormons. By January 1848 they had most of the building completed and had dug several thousand yards of dirt for the dam and channel above the mill to power it. Running out of time, Marshall decided to let the water cut the channel below the mill when the men were not working on the mill itself. Shutting the water source each morning, Marshall would walk the lower channel to inspect how well the channel was being cut. On the morning of January 24, 1848, he saw shiny yellow specks in a pool of water. Finding a couple of nuggets, he returned to camp and tested the material. Convinced that he had gold, he took the samples and went to see Sutter a few days later. Sutter and Marshall agreed to keep the discovery quiet, although Marshall allowed the workers to look for gold in their off-hours.

When Sam Brannan, a Mormon and the editor of the *California Star* newspaper, visited the site in March, he reported the discovery, but there was no immediate excitement. In May, however, he returned with enough evidence to stir the population. The California Gold Rush was on.

The impact of the gold rush on California, especially on northern California, was dramatic. Although many sailors had jumped ship in California before, now ship captains could not find anyone to hire at all. Day laborers left for the gold mines as well. Not long after the day laborers had gone to seek their riches, shop owners and almost everyone else departed in the rush to become rich.

In the early days, a placer miner panned for gold using a pick, a shovel, a pan, and water to separate the alluvial deposits from the gold. Soon sluice boxes were built to run the water through and into which the loose material would be dropped. A sluice box uses a series of short obstructions to catch the heaviest pieces that drop to the bottom, while the water washes the lighter material away. Later during the gold rush, miners dug deep holes and tunnels, especially when a vein of gold ore was discovered. By 1853 hydraulic mining was the main method employed in the extraction process. Hydraulic mining involved forcing water through a large nozzle, like a fire hose nozzle, under high pressure. With this constant stream of water, miners washed away the hillsides to get to the gold. Quite obviously such techniques wrought terrible environmental damage, including severe soil erosion and flooding.

By August 1848 news of the gold discovery had reached the East Coast, and on December 5, 1848, President James K. Polk officially announced the discovery of gold in California. At a time in which the typical day laborer made just $2 a day, the average individual was taking in $50 per day working in the gold mines. With predictable and great speed, gold fever swept the United States. Some men abandoned their homes and families and started up the Oregon Trail with only what they could carry. Many of the people who headed for California during the gold rush never returned home or even asked for their families to join them. By 1855 hundreds of thousands of people had migrated to California, the largest

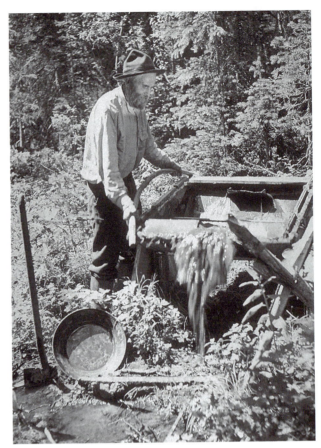

Sluicing and panning operations for gold in California, late 19th century. (Getty Images)

migration of its kind in U.S. history. The huge influx of people brought many problems, which the new California government was not able to handle. Prices for all kinds of goods skyrocketed, and a lawless element appeared. Indeed, the vigilante movement helped bring forth cries for official law and order. The value of the gold found during the California Gold Rush well exceeded the cost of the Mexican-American War for the United States. The gold rush ended around 1855.

The California Gold Rush proved catastrophic for the region's Native Americans. Prospectors and miners who flooded the state destroyed fish dams built by Native Americans, fouled salmon streams, and drove away wild game. While some Native Americans joined in the gold frenzy, others fell prey to racism. Hoping to mobilize the Native Americans to work in the mines and on the ranches springing up in the area, California decreed that Native Americans not working for ranchers or who did not possess government papers would be subject to arrest and trial. By the beginning of 1849, some 4,000 Native Americans were involved in gold prospecting. Soon the number of whites in California exploded, so that by the early 1850s they outnumbered Native Americans by a ratio of 2 to 1; Native Americans had outnumbered whites by almost 10 to 1 in the late 1840s.

Native Americans were devastated by white violence and encroachment, disease, starvation, and unscrupulous speculators. Between 1848 and 1860, about 12 percent of the entire Native American population in California (about 4,675 people) died at the hands of the U.S. military or local and state militias. Some, such as the Modocs, fought back but to little lasting effect.

As for Sutter, the discovery of gold on his land was the beginning of the end. His workers ran off, immigrants squatted on his lands, and gold seekers took his equipment and killed his livestock. In 1849 Sutter helped frame the California State Constitution, but the new government refused to recognize his land grant, and Sutter died, nearly impoverished, on June 18, 1880.

RICK GRISET

See also

Modocs; Modoc War

References

Brands, H. W. *Age of Gold.* New York: Doubleday Division, Random House, 2002.

De Voto, Bernard. *The Year of Decision: 1846.* Boston: Little, Brown, 1943.

Hammond, George P., ed. *The Larkin Papers.* 11 vols. Berkeley: University of California Press, 1959.

Rohrbough, Malcolm J. *Days of Gold: The California Gold Rush and the American Nation.* Berkeley: University of California Press, 1997.

Camas Meadows, Battle of
Event Date: August 20, 1877

Skirmish between U.S. Army troops and the Nez Perces led by Chief Joseph during the Nez Perce War of 1877. The engagement occurred at present-day Kilgore, Idaho, in the eastern part of the state. At the time of the battle, U.S. forces under Brigadier General Oliver O. Howard had been in pursuit of the Nez Perces, who were attempting to flee Idaho and seek refuge in Canada. With Colonel John Gibbon's force still recovering from the Battle of the Big Hole (August 9–10, 1877) just days earlier, Howard was now on his own, hoping to overtake and capture the fleeing Nez Perces before they could reach the border. Several of his cavalry units, which were running ahead of his regular infantry, were reportedly only a day behind the Nez Perces. These units were Companies B, I, and K of the 1st Cavalry Regiment, Company L of the 2nd Cavalry Regiment, and 53 mounted volunteers from Montana. Howard joined the advance cavalry units later.

On the evening of August 19 the U.S. force made camp at a site that the Nez Perces had used the previous night, near the confluence of East Camas and Spring creeks. In the early morning hours before dawn, approximately 200 Nez Perce warriors rode back to their abandoned camp with the intention of stealing horses and pack mules. Before daylight the warriors had managed to take approximately 150 mules. When they next began to approach the horses,

which were heavily guarded, firing commenced, and the Nez Perces began a fighting withdrawal. A small contingent of cavalrymen gave chase and recaptured a few mules. However, the troops were forced back by the Nez Perces, who greatly outnumbered them. Upon General Howard's arrival, the warriors broke contact and continued their flight. The engagement lasted about three hours.

The Americans suffered 2 fatalities and 11 wounded. No losses were reported for the Nez Perces. Although a small skirmish in relative terms, the Battle of Camas Meadows was noteworthy because the loss of Howard's pack mules meant that he had little maneuverability. The Nez Perces were thus able to continue their flight for Canada, and Howard's opportunity to overtake them had been lost.

PAUL G. PIERPAOLI JR.

See also

Big Hole, Battle of the; Gibbon, John; Howard, Oliver Otis; Joseph, Chief; Nez Perces; Nez Perce War

References

Josephy, Alvin M. *The Nez Perce Indians and the Opening of the Northwest.* New Haven, CT: Yale University Press, 1965.

Nerburn, Kent. *Chief Joseph and the Flight of the Nez Perce: The Untold Story of an American Tragedy.* New York: HarperCollins, 2005.

Utley, Robert M. *The Indian Frontier of the American West, 1846–1890.* Albuquerque: University of New Mexico Press, 1984.

Camels

During the 19th century, the U.S. Army experimented with the possibility of using camels for military transport in areas with problematic terrain and a lack of roads, such as the desert Southwest. The initial idea of using camels for military transport was suggested by Second Lieutenant George H. Crosman in 1836 during the Second Seminole War (1835–1842) in Florida. Crosman argued that camels were superior to horses and mules as pack animals because of their strength, endurance, tolerance for high heat, and limited need for water. Camels could easily carry more than 800 pounds of cargo, travel 40 miles per day, and survive without water for a week. In addition, camels' feet were well-suited to grassy and sandy plains as well as rocky terrain and did not require shoeing.

Although the U.S. government ignored his recommendation, the U.S. Army revived the possibility of using camels for military transport after the United States acquired the American Southwest following the Mexican-American War (1846–1848). Given the rough terrain of the Southwest, some military analysts believed that camels might be the best way to supply the U.S. Army in the area during the Indian Wars.

In 1853 Crosman, who had by then been promoted to major, befriended Major Henry C. Wayne, a quartermaster, who introduced Crosman to President Franklin Pierce's secretary of war, Jefferson Davis. Concerned about the pacification and economic

Members of the U.S. Camel Corps in the Southwest, 1857. Although the Camel Corps experiment was largely a failure, the corps did play a key role in surveying and mapping the region. (Getty Images)

development of the American Southwest, Davis, an advocate of building transcontinental railroads, saw the potential value in creating a U.S. Army Camel Corps. After a period of intense lobbying, Davis was able to convince the U.S. Congress to authorize funds to experiment with the possibility of launching a Camel Corps. On March 3, 1855, Congress authorized $30,000 for the initiative. In June 1855 Davis sent Wayne in USS *Supply* to North Africa to obtain camels for the venture. In Egypt, Wayne discovered that Bactrian camels (two-humped camels indigenous to Asia) were best suited to carrying supplies, while Arabian camels (one-humped camels indigenous to the Middle East) were best suited to carrying passengers.

Wayne purchased 33 Bactrian and Arabian camels in Egypt and recruited five Egyptians to care for the animals and teach the Americans how to train them. On April 29, 1856, the *Supply* arrived in Indianola, Texas, with its cargo of camels. Davis promptly sent the ship back to Egypt to purchase 40 more camels. In the meantime, the recently arrived camels were transported to Camp Verde near San Antonio, Texas, for training.

In June 1857 President James Buchanan placed the camels under the command of Edward Fitzgerald Beale, a noted frontiersman and explorer, who was charged with surveying and building a 1,000-mile-long wagon road across Arizona between Fort Defiance and the Colorado River. Initially Beale opposed the

camel experiment. Assisted by two Middle Eastern camel trainers, Georges Caralambo (Greek George) and Hadji Ali (Hi Jolly), Beale was pleasantly surprised at the durability of the camels in the American Southwest. In 1858 Beale used them to survey and build a wagon road between Fort Smith, Arkansas, and Fort Defiance. During the 1860s and 1870s Beale's wagon trail along the 35th Parallel was a popular route to California.

Despite this success, many military officials were unconvinced of the viability of investing in a Camel Corps. In 1858 Buchanan's secretary of war, John B. Floyd, urged Congress to purchase 1,000 camels, but Congress refused to act on his recommendation. During the American Civil War (1861–1865) the camels were all but forgotten by military officials. The remaining camels owned by the U.S. Army were sold to circuses, zoos, and private citizens, including Beale, following the Civil War. Some camels were released into the wild to roam the American Southwest.

MICHAEL R. HALL

See also

Davis, Jefferson; Seminole War, Second

References

Faulk, Odie B. *The U. S. Camel Corps: An Army Experiment.* New York: Oxford University Press, 1976.

Thompson, Gerald. *Edward F. Beale and the American West.* Albuquerque: University of New Mexico Press, 1983.

Cameron, Alexander
Birth Date: ca. 1719
Death Date: December 27, 1781

British commissary to the Cherokees (1762–1779) and superintendent of the Choctaws and Chickasaws (1779–1780). Alexander Cameron was born in Scotland, perhaps in 1719 or 1720; little is known about his youth. In 1738 Cameron went to the British colonies as a private in James Oglethorpe's 42nd Regiment of Foot. Commissioned an ensign in South Carolina in 1761, Cameron served at Fort Prince George.

In 1762 John Stuart, newly appointed British superintendent of Indian affairs for the South, appointed Cameron commissary to the Cherokees. Known as "Scotchie" to the Cherokees, his role was to promote peace. Cameron succeeded in gaining the trust of the Cherokees and securing an important British ally.

Cameron's role as peace facilitator, created to diminish the threat of Native American attack on British settlements, required his immersion in Cherokee culture. Accordingly, Cameron took a Cherokee wife, fathered three children with her, and became increasingly sympathetic to the Cherokees. When land encroachment by the colonists threatened the peace, Cameron endeared himself to the Cherokees by enforcing a British edict that allowed them to drive intruding colonists from their land.

When the American Revolutionary War (1775–1783) began, both sides sought Native American alliances. After Cameron refused the Patriots' request for assistance, members of the new American government attempted to undermine his influence among the Cherokees. In 1776 Cameron received orders to prepare the Cherokees for action against the rebels. However, he tried to restrain them from opening hostilities until the British were ready to act. Unwilling to wait because they saw war as a chance to evict settlers from their land, the Cherokees rejected Cameron's advice and attacked settlements in Georgia and the Carolinas in late June 1776. Cameron then led bands of Loyalists and Cherokees against American settlers. These attacks made Cameron hated by both sides, as it was virtually impossible to distinguish between rebels and Loyalists. During the autumn and winter the Cherokees were unable to withstand the American counterattacks and were forced to surrender vast tracts of land as the price of peace.

The peace negotiations fractured the Cherokee Nation. Dragging Canoe refused to participate and with his followers, known as the Chickamauga Cherokees, continued fighting. Following the destruction of many Chickamauga villages and attempts by Cherokee leaders to turn him over to the rebels, Cameron and some of the Chickamaugas moved south toward Pensacola, Florida. By 1778 Cameron was leading Chickamauga attacks against Georgia.

Upon Stuart's death in March 1779, Cameron was appointed superintendent of the Choctaws and Chickasaws. He maintained his relations with the Chickamaugas, who resumed attacks on the Americans that summer but failed to achieve much success.

In 1780 Cameron mobilized the Choctaws to help defend Pensacola from an expected Spanish attack. The British commander at Pensacola, Major General John Campbell, called for Choctaw aid each time an attack appeared imminent and then dismissed the warriors when the threat did not materialize. Cameron warned Campbell that repeated false alarms would make the Choctaws reluctant to turn out in the future, while Campbell accused Cameron and the Choctaws of insufficient cooperation. The dispute may have been a factor in Cameron's decision to resign his post in October 1780. Cameron retired to Savannah, Georgia, where he died on December 27, 1781.

JASON LUTZ AND JIM PIECUCH

See also
Cherokees; Chickamaugas; Chickasaws; Choctaws; Native Americans and the American Revolutionary War; Stuart, John

References
Nichols, John L. "Alexander Cameron, British Agent among the Cherokee, 1764–1781." *South Carolina Historical Magazine* 97(2) (April 2006): 94–114.
Piecuch, Jim. *Three Peoples, One King: Loyalists, Indians, and Slaves in the Revolutionary South, 1775–1782.* Columbia: University of South Carolina Press, 2008.

Camp Grant Massacre
Event Date: April 30, 1871

Massacre that occurred on April 30, 1871, that was perpetrated by a confederacy of Anglo-Americans, Mexican Americans, and Tohono O'odham warriors that murdered more than 100 western Apaches, mostly unarmed children and women, who had surrendered to the U.S. Army at Camp Grant, just north of Tucson, Arizona. Another 30 or so children were taken captive.

Following the finalization of the Gadsden Purchase in 1853, American settlers began to enter the San Pedro Valley, the fertile land to the east of present-day Tucson. However, western Apache groups such as the Aravaipa and Pinal bands had control of the valley, as they had since at least the late 1700s. To protect pioneers and subdue Native Americans who refused to submit to U.S. authority, the government established military posts in the region to strike directly into Apache communities. On May 8, 1860, the United States erected Fort Aravaypa at the confluence of the San Pedro River and the Aravaipa Creek. In 1865 the fort was renamed Camp Grant in honor of Ulysses S. Grant.

On February 28, 1871, Lieutenant Royal E. Whitman, then in charge of Camp Grant, reported that a small group of elderly Apache women had come to the post looking for several stolen children and hoping to make a lasting peace with the government. Whitman encouraged the Apaches to come in, and soon dozens of Aravaipa and Pinal Apaches were encamped at the fort and receiving rations of corn, flour, beans, coffee, and meat. By late March more than 400 Apaches had arrived, settling peacefully at a traditional site called *gashdla'á cho o'aa* ("Big Sycamore Stands There"), five miles from Camp Grant up the Aravaipa Creek.

Despite the amiable settlement at Camp Grant, the Chiricahua Apaches continued raiding. While the Apaches at Camp Grant almost certainly did not commit these depredations, residents in Tucson assumed that they did. After the government refused pleas for protection, William Oury conspired with another prominent Tucson citizen, Jesus Maria Elías, to seek revenge on the Apaches near Camp Grant. The men recruited dozens of local residents and scores of Tohono O'odham warriors. On the afternoon of April 28, 1871, the group met in secrecy and was provided weapons and provisions by the adjutant general of Arizona, Samuel Hughes.

After nearly continuous travel, they arrived at Big Sycamore Stands There in the early morning hours of April 30; they attacked immediately, catching the Apaches off guard. The attack was over in half an hour. The murders were brutal: children were hacked apart, and girls were raped. The soldiers at Camp Grant did not hear the screams and gunshots because of the distance from the Apache settlement. When the attackers left, more than 100 Apaches were dead, nearly all women and children, and some 30 children were taken as captives. A half dozen of the children lived for a while with highly regarded Tucsonans, such as Leopoldo Carrillo and Francisco Romero, but were reluctantly returned to Apache relatives in 1872. The rest of the children were sold into slavery in Sonora, Mexico, for $100 each.

The vigilante group returned to a jubilant Tucson, while the reaction on the East Coast and even among military personnel was horror and disbelief. When local authorities did not press charges, President Ulysses S. Grant threatened to impose martial law to prosecute those responsible. On October 23, 1871, a grand jury handed down 111 indictments, 108 for murder and 3 for misdemeanors, with Sidney R. DeLong as the lead defendant. A weeklong trial was held in December 1871. The jury deliberated for 19 minutes before announcing a verdict of not guilty on all counts.

After the massacre, the Apaches at Camp Grant dispersed throughout southern Arizona. They returned to the post in the spring of 1872 for peace talks and agreed to settle on the San Carlos River to the north. Although this pact did not relinquish Apache territory, Anglo-American and Mexican American pioneers soon spread into the San Pedro Valley and made it their home. When the Apaches later tried to return and settle in the San Pedro Valley during the 1880s, they were run off their traditional lands.

CHIP COLWELL-CHANTHAPHONH

See also

Apaches

Reference

Colwell-Chanthaphonh, Chip. "Western Apache Oral Histories and Traditions of the Camp Grant Massacre." *American Indian Quarterly* 27(3–4) (2003): 639–666.

Camps

See Forts, Camps, Cantonments, and Outposts

Canada

Whether a colony of France or of Great Britain or an autonomous member of the British empire, Canada played a significant role in various Indian wars beginning in the 1600s and enduring until the closing of the frontier in the 1890s. For almost 300 years Canada served as a supplier of munitions, a base of operations, an ally, and a place of refuge for numerous Native American tribes. Canada's role in the numerous Native American wars can be divided into three periods: the French era (ca. 1608–1763), the British era (1763–1867), and nationhood (1867–present).

During the Indian wars of the French era, the colony of Canada, known then as New France, served multiple roles. During four imperial wars—the War of the League of Augsburg (1689–1697), also known as King William's War; the War of the Spanish Succession (1702–1713), also known as Queen Anne's War; the War of the Austrian Succession (1744–1748), also known as King George's War; and the Seven Years' War (1756–1753), also known as the French and Indian War (1754–1763)—Indian tribes in Canada allied with the French to attack the English settlers to the south. In these conflicts Canada served as both a supplier of weapons and a refuge for Native Americans. For example, the Abenaki settlement at Odenak, Quebec, was settled specifically as a refuge. Beyond the imperial conflicts, Native Americans were regularly supplied with munitions, ostensibly for hunting, but many of these weapons were used against American frontier settlements. The Micmacs and Abenakis, among others with support from the French, strongly resisted English settlement along the frontier until the collapse of French control on the Atlantic coast in 1761. Other examples include King Philip's War (1675–1676), when defeated Native Americans moved closer to Canada and aligned themselves with the French for protection.

The British era initially witnessed a relative lull in terms of Canada's involvement in Native American wars. However, with the outbreak of the American Revolutionary War (1775–1783), Canada once more became a significant factor in native warfare. During the Revolutionary War, Fort Niagara in Canada served as a refuge for Native American warriors and Loyalist civilians alike. At the end of the conflict many Iroquois moved to Canada, eventually settling along the Grand River. Similar to the French early on, the British made use of tribal hostility toward American settlements during 1783–1814 to further their own interests. Officially British Indian agents encouraged their former allies to make peace with Americans while at the same time distributing arms for hunting. Tecumseh and the Indian confederation opposing American settler expansion westward, for instance, made use of Britain's desire to remain on friendly terms with the Native Americans to meet in safety and seek supplies in Canada.

Political cartoon from *Frank Leslie's Illustrated Newspaper*, September 24, 1881. A woman labeled "Canada" addresses a troubled Uncle Sam, saying: "Well, Uncle Sam, I have no trouble with my Indian. Treat him no longer as a pauper or a pensioner, but give him good land and implements, and tell him he has got to earn his own being or starve. And stick to your word! That's my plan." (Library of Congress)

During the War of 1812, British and Indian troops fought together against American forces in nearly all of the battles. Native support was essential in the capture of Fort Mackinaw and Fort Detroit as well as in the defeat of invading U.S. troops at Queenston Heights. Native warriors, with supplies from Canada, also engaged Americans along the frontier independently.

From 1815 until the 1860s, American Indian agents regularly suspected Britain of arming and encouraging Native American attacks, although the British officially discouraged such actions. Nevertheless, in 1838 during the heightened tensions between Britain and the United States and with cross-border raids originating from American soil, British Indian agent George Ironside Jr. suggested that Native American and British troops capture Mackinaw and Detroit before attacking the American frontier. This initiative was politely rejected. Also in the 1830s, various Pottawatomi, Ojibwa, and Ottawa people fled to Canada to avoid removal.

During the national era (1867–present), Canada served mainly as a place of refuge for Native Americans fleeing conflict in the United States. Sitting Bull and his Sioux followers fled to Canada in 1876 during the Great Sioux War, as did other Sioux people after the Battle of Wounded Knee (1890). Chief Joseph of the Nez Perces, however, failed to reach safety in Canada in 1877. Canadians after 1867 encouraged Native Americans to return home but refused to force refugees such as Sitting Bull and his followers to leave. As the Indian Wars came to an end, Canada ceased to be seen as a supplier of munitions and a place of refuge.

Karl S. Hele

See also
Abenakis; French and Indian War; Iroquois; Joseph, Chief; King George's War; King William's War; Micmacs; Native Americans and the American Revolutionary War; Native Americans and the War of 1812; Ojibwas; Ottawas; Pottawatomis; Queen Anne's War; Tecumseh; Thames, Battle of the; Sitting Bull

References
Allen, Robert S. *The British Indian Department and the Frontier in North America, 1755–1830.* Ottawa: Information Canada, 1975.

Allen, Robert S. *His Majesty's Indian Allies: British Indian Policy in the Defense of Canada, 1774–1815.* Toronto: Dundurn, 1992.

Benn, Carl. *The Iroquois in the War of 1812.* Toronto: University of Toronto Press, 1988.

Borneman, Walter R. *The French and Indian War: Deciding the Fate of North America.* New York: HarperCollins, 2006.

Leckie, Robert. *"A Few Acres of Snow": The Saga of the French and Indian Wars.* New York: Wiley, 1999.

Sugden, John. *Tecumseh: A Life.* New York: Holt, 1997.

Vandervort, Bruce. *Indian Wars of Mexico, Canada and the United States, 1812–1900.* New York: Routledge, 2006.

Canby, Edward Richard Sprigg
Birth Date: November 9, 1817
Death Date: April 11, 1873

U.S. Army officer. Edward Richard Sprigg Canby was born on November 9, 1817, at Platt's Landing, Kentucky. As a boy he moved with his family to neighboring Indiana. Canby graduated from the U.S. Military Academy, West Point, in 1835. Commissioned a second lieutenant, he saw action in the Second Seminole War (1835–1842) in Florida and then fought in the Mexican-American War (1846–1848), earning promotion to first lieutenant in 1846. He was twice brevetted (major and lieutenant colonel) for gallantry in the latter conflict.

In 1855 after numerous staff assignments, Canby was promoted directly to major in the 10th Infantry Regiment. In November 1860 he launched an offensive against the Navajos in New Mexico that is known as Canby's Campaign. Commanding under his brevet rank of lieutenant colonel, he led elements of the 10th Infantry Regiment from Fort Garland, New Mexico, to Fort Defiance, where he was to link up with the 5th and 7th Infantry regiments and 2nd Dragoon Regiment. The fighting endured through December but was inconclusive. In January 1861 Canby launched another offensive. This time he was more successful, and by April he had negotiated treaties with 54 Navajo leaders, guaranteeing food, clothing, and protection in return for a sustained peace.

In April 1861 when the American Civil War (1861–1865) began, Canby was still at Fort Defiance. Within weeks of the start of the conflict he was named commander of the Department of New Mexico, having been appointed colonel of the new 19th Infantry Regiment. The beginning of the war made it impossible for the U.S. government to fulfill its obligations, and the Navajos renewed

Brigadier General Edward R. S. Canby took command of the Department of the Columbia in 1870. On April 11, 1873, Canby and a civilian were murdered while attempting to negotiate a peace settlement with the Modoc Indians. The popular Canby thus became the only general to lose his life in the American Indian Wars. (Library of Congress)

troops who helped capture Confederate forts in highly effective cooperation with Union naval forces under Rear Admiral David G. Farragut during the Battle of Mobile Bay on August 5, 1864.

Canby then commanded the land forces attempting to take Mobile, which finally fell on April 12, 1865. On May 26, 1865, more than a month after General Robert E. Lee's surrender at Appomattox Court House, Canby had the distinction of accepting the surrender of the last major Confederate commands, those of Lieutenant General Richard Taylor and General Edmund Kirby Smith. During the army reorganization in 1866, Canby was confirmed in the regular rank of brigadier general. He then held a variety of posts—including the department encompassing the District of Columbia, Maryland, Delaware, and parts of Virginia and then North Carolina and South Carolina—before taking command of the Department of the Columbia in 1870. There he oversaw numerous campaigns against and peace initiatives with the Native Americans. In Siskiyou, California, on April 11, 1873, Canby and a civilian negotiator were treacherously murdered, and another civilian was badly wounded during peace talks with hostile Modocs. Canby thus became the only full-rank general officer to be killed during the Indian Wars after the American Civil War.

PAUL G. PIERPAOLI JR. AND DAVID COFFEY

See also

Canby's Campaign; Seminole War, Second; Navajos

References

Cottrell, Steve. *Civil War in Texas and New Mexico Territory.* Greta, LA: Pelican, 1998.
Larson, Carole. *Forgotten Frontier: The Story of Southeastern New Mexico.* Albuquerque: University of New Mexico Press, 1993.

their attacks. Now concerned chiefly with the Confederate threat, Canby could do little to respond to the renewed Navajo raids.

When Confederate troops invaded the territory in early 1862, Canby oversaw the Union counteroffensive, but his federal troops were defeated on February 21, 1862, at Val Verde, New Mexico. A month later at the Battle of Glorieta Pass (March 26–28, 1862), sometimes referred to as the Gettysburg of the West, Canby's force, now reinforced by a contingent of Colorado volunteers, suffered a tactical battlefield defeat.

The battle turned into a strategic victory, however, when Colorado volunteers under Major John M. Chivington captured the Confederate supply train at Johnson's Ranch. This forced a Confederate withdrawal to Santa Fe. Supply shortages, above all of food, then caused the Confederates to quit New Mexico.

Appointed brigadier general of volunteers, Canby went east, serving for almost two years as adjutant general in Washington, D.C. In July 1863 he commanded the Union troops who put down the New York City draft riots. On May 7, 1864, Canby was advanced to major general of volunteers and took command of the Military Division of West Mississippi. In that post he commanded Union

Canby's Campaign
Start Date: 1860
End Date: 1861

Abortive U.S. military campaign against the Navajos in New Mexico Territory during 1860–1861. After the United States established its authority in New Mexico following the Mexican-American War (1846–1848), conflict with the Navajos escalated throughout the 1850s as whites, supported by the U.S. Army, began seizing Navajo grazing lands. Indeed, territorial governor Abraham Rencher (1857–1861) placed primary blame for the growing conflict on Colonel Benjamin L. Bonneville, who in 1858 had forced a harsh treaty on the Navajos, taking away most of their land in New Mexico proper, and on local white militia who attacked the Navajos without authorization. Given these conditions, Rencher warned officials in Washington that the Navajos would have little recourse but to turn to banditry, making a full-scale war inevitable.

Just as Rencher predicted, hard-pressed Navajo warriors began attacking supply trains in western New Mexico, leading to a vicious cycle of reprisals by the army and white settlers and counterreprisals by the Navajos. Angered that whites had burned his home and killed some 50 of his sheep, Manuelito led some 1,000 Navajo warriors in an attack on April 30, 1860, that nearly overran Fort Defiance, the chief army post in New Mexico Territory, located near present-day Window Rock, Arizona. Rencher now had no choice but to seek army assistance, and federal officials ordered Major Edward R. S. Canby, under his brevet rank of lieutenant colonel, to lead elements of the 10th Infantry Regiment stationed at Fort Garland, New Mexico, to Fort Defiance, where they would be joined by the companies of the 5th and 7th Infantry regiments and the 2nd Dragoon Regiment.

Canby's Campaign began in November 1860 when he departed Fort Defiance with 600 soldiers accompanied by Ute scouts and a small contingent of New Mexico volunteers under Captain Blas Lucero. Canby divided his force into three detachments, leading one himself and placing the other two under Major Henry Hopkins Sibley and Captain Lafayette McLaws. During the next month Canby's men killed some 35–40 Navajos, seized more than 1,000 Navajo horses, and killed several thousand Navajo sheep.

Lack of water and forage caused by the severe drought of 1860 forced Canby to return to Fort Defiance in December without securing a peace treaty. Nevertheless, he launched a second campaign from Fort Defiance in January 1861, focusing primarily on the destruction of Navajo crops and livestock. By April, Canby had succeeded in negotiating a series of treaties with 54 Navajo chiefs, guaranteeing food, clothing, and the army's protection in return for peace.

Unfortunately, the outbreak in April 1861 of the American Civil War (1861–1865) prevented the federal government from fulfilling its promises to the Navajos. Canby, appointed colonel of the new 19th Infantry Regiment, took command of the Department of New Mexico, but his chief concern was to defend New Mexico from Confederate attack. Consequently, the Navajos took advantage of the situation by renewing attacks on white settlements, for which they were subsequently forced to pay a heavy price during the Long Walk to Bosque Redondo in 1864.

Justin D. Murphy

See also

Bosque Redondo; Canby, Edward Richard Sprigg; Manuelito; Navajo Removal; Navajos; Sibley, Henry Hastings; Utes

References

Keleher, William A. *Turmoil in New Mexico.* Facsimile of 1952 ed. Santa Fe, NM: Sunstone, 2008.

Larson, Carole. *Forgotten Frontier: The Story of Southeastern New Mexico.* Albuquerque: University of New Mexico Press, 1993.

Utley, Robert M. *Frontiersmen in Blue: The United States and the Indian, 1848–1865.* Lincoln: University of Nebraska Press, 1967.

Cannibalism

The ritual consumption of human flesh. Although cannibalism is frequently associated with starvation as a means to sustain life, during the North American Indian Wars ritual cannibalism served as a frequent if not necessarily widespread practice, particularly during the colonial period. Cannibalism by North American indigenous peoples is a controversial subject. While reports of ritual cannibalism (anthropophagy) abound throughout the historical record, some modern studies call into question the veracity of these reports and note the lack of reliable eyewitness accounts.

For centuries ritual cannibalism was uncritically accepted either as an indicator of native ferocity and savagery (and therefore justification for missionization and exterminative practices on the part of colonizers) or as one aspect of native peoples' deeply ceremonial practice of warfare. Undoubtedly the early history of North America depends on written sources that largely represent the colonizers' point of view. Therefore, any discussion of cannibalism must consider the Eurocentric bias inherent in the sources from which the information is drawn. From Christopher Columbus's first writings in America onward, cannibalism appears to have been an act that Europeans expected to find among the newly encountered indigenous peoples. While use of the word "anthropophagous" to refer to the consumption of human flesh dates to antiquity, the word "cannibal" has its origins during the invasion of the Americas. The term evolved from Carib (Canib), the name applied by the Arawaks to their neighbors and subsequently used by Europeans. (The defiant Caribs were thus depicted as ferocious cannibals, perhaps to justify their extermination.) This idea spread, appearing in works from Columbus to Shakespeare, such that by the early 18th century the terms "cannibal" and "anthropophagus" were synonyms. The term "cannibal" came to denote any person or group who ate human flesh.

The extent of cannibalism in the Americas was likely exaggerated by European colonizers who expected to find it practiced in the uncivilized wilderness. Numerous books that were widely read in medieval and early modern Europe, including those by Augustine, Pliny, John Mandeville, and Marco Polo, created a vast catalog of grotesque qualities, placing cannibals alongside dog-headed men and amazons, labels ready to be applied to America's exotic indigenous "others." And certainly, applying the cannibal label to a troublesome native group could justify that peoples' enslavement or extermination. However, reports of ritual cannibalism are too numerous to suggest that it did not occur on some level.

Vivid after-action reports by European and later American soldiers include frequent mentions of Indian allies partaking of the flesh of slain enemies. This practice in some form appears to have been common among dozens of tribes, including the Iroquois and Hurons, and extended into the 19th century.

The flesh of slain warriors was consumed in order to incorporate the warrior's spirit or to honor his bravery. But the practice could apparently also demonstrate dishonor or disdain. Cannibalism might form part of an elaborate torture ritual as well.

In Huron tradition, ritual cannibalism occurred in cases of extreme grief, when a captive (usually male) would be executed and small amounts of the person eaten in order to both honor the captive and to engage in collective healing on the part of the captors. Evidence suggests that cannibalism likely occurred in ritual settings to varying degrees across the Americas. However, the point that these occurrences may have been exaggerated in the European and American literature to emphasize Native American savagery, and therefore to justify colonization, cannot be ignored.

DANIEL MORLEY JOHNSON

See also
Iroquois; Wyandots

References

Arens, William. *The Man-Eating Myth*. New York: Oxford University Press, 1979.

Barker, Francis, et al., eds. *Cannibalism and the Colonial World*. Cambridge: Cambridge University Press, 1998.

Churchill, Ward. "*Man Corn*" [Review]. *North American Archaeologist* 21(3) (2000): 268–288.

Hulme, Peter. *Colonial Encounters: Europe and the Native Caribbean, 1492–1797*. London: Methuen, 1986.

Sanday, Peggy Reeves. *Divine Hunger: Cannibalism as a Cultural System*. Cambridge: Cambridge University Press, 1986.

Sioui, Georges E. *Huron Wendat: The Heritage of the Circle*. Lansing: Michigan State University Press, 2000.

Canonchet
Birth Date: Unknown
Death Date: April 2, 1676

Sachem (chief) of the Narragansett tribe who became the principal military leader of the Native American alliance during King Philip's War (1675–1676). Nothing is known of the birth or early life of Canonchet (Nanunteeno). At the time the Narragansetts were the most powerful tribe in New England, able to muster more than 2,000 warriors. Despite declaring that his people would take no active part in the conflict, in 1675 Canonchet took in refugees from tribes at war with New England colonists. Alarmed by this seemingly hostile action, the colonists declared war and launched a winter offensive against the Narragansetts in Rhode Island.

The colonial force located a weakened entry way into Canonchet's stronghold, leading to a decisive English victory that left 600 Narragansetts dead in the Great Swamp Fight of December 19, 1675. Canonchet and most of his men escaped, however, to join the forces led by Metacom (King Philip). Canonchet proved to be the best military leader in the native alliance, ambushing and nearly annihilating a small English column commanded by Captain Michael Pierce in March 1676 and then capturing and burning the towns of Rehoboth and Providence.

Canonchet realized the importance of food to the Native Americans, so in April 1676 he led a handful of warriors on a dangerous mission to acquire seed corn. He was intercepted by a combined force of colonists and Mohegan warriors. Taken prisoner, Canonchet was brought to trial, convicted, and beheaded in Stonington, Connecticut, on April 2, 1676. His death was a fatal blow to the fortunes of Metacom's rebellion and the entire Narragansett tribe.

Only 500 Narragansetts escaped death or enslavement out of a pre-war population of about 5,000.

ANDREW C. LANNEN

See also
Great Swamp Fight; King Philip's War; Metacom; Narragansetts

References

Adams, James Truslow. *The Founding of New England*. New York: Atlantic Monthly Press, 1921.

Bourne, Russell. *The Red King's Rebellion: Racial Politics in New England, 1675–1678*. Oxford: Oxford University Press, 1990.

Canochet's Fort
See Great Swamp Fortress

Canoes

Watercraft. Early canoes, known as dugout canoes or dugouts, were hollowed out from logs with primitive tools and by fire and are the earliest types of watercraft identified by archaeologists.

The watercraft most identified as a canoe, however, is the lightweight shallow-draft boat made of birchbark or other waterproof material stretched over a wood frame. The basic design of the former type has remained unchanged for thousands of years. It is long and narrow with a rounded bottom and sides. The boat is tapered at both front and back with raised points at either end. The canoe was originally designed and used by the Native Americans, but it was rapidly adopted by the English, French, and other Europeans in the New World.

The canoe's design makes it ideal for waterborne transportation along rivers and lakes. The canoe is lightweight but holds considerable cargo. Unlike most European designs, the canoe is propelled by individuals facing forward so the occupant can easily see the direction of travel. The person (or people) responsible for moving the canoe sits or kneels facing forward and uses a front-to-back stroke to pull a single two-handed paddle through the water. If there is only one person, he or she might alternate paddling sides to maintain course or to perform what became known as the J stroke. Named for the path of the paddle in the water, this stroke pulls the bow back on course at the end of the rearward motion.

The canoe design is adaptable from small one- and two-person sizes that were about 10 to 12 feet in length to versions as long as 24 feet that could carry 10 or 12 people or several thousand pounds of cargo.

Canoes were also easy to build. They were generally made by building a birch or pine frame, held together with pine or other roots and sealed with hot pine tar. The covering was of birch, cedar, or elm bark, all of which were smooth, flexible, and durable. The lightweight design made it easy to remove canoes from the water and carry them overland (portage), making canoes ideal for the small trading and warring parties that crisscrossed the frontier. The

Menominee Indians spear salmon by torchlight from birchbark canoes on the Fox River in Wisconsin. (Native Stock Pictures)

end result was a craft perfectly suited for traveling long distances in shallow lakes and rivers. In areas in which there were few or no roads, canoes were often the only viable means of transportation.

JOSEPH ADAMCZYK

See also

Native American Warfare

References

Adney, Edwin Tappan, and Howard Irving Chapelle. *The Bark Canoes and Skin Boats of North America*. Washington, DC: Smithsonian Institution Press, 1993.

Poling, Jim, Sr. *The Canoe: An Illustrated History*. Woodstock, VT: Countryman, 2001.

Cantonments

See Forts, Camps, Cantonments, and Outposts

Canyon Creek, Battle of
Event Date: September 13, 1877

Engagement during the 1877 Nez Perce War that occurred along Canyon Creek, not far from present-day Yellowstone National Park in eastern Idaho. In early 1877 the U.S. government ordered

the Nez Perces in the Wallowa Valley (present-day northeastern Oregon), where several hundred lived peacefully in defiance of an earlier treaty, to relocate to the Lapwai Reservation in Idaho. Although Nez Perce chief Joseph attempted to negotiate a compromise, Brigadier General Oliver O. Howard issued an ultimatum backed by the threat of military action and forced removal, which Joseph reluctantly accepted. While the tribe was preparing to move to Idaho in June 1877, however, young warriors within the tribe began raiding white settlements along the Salmon River.

Realizing that the U.S. Army would retaliate for the raids, Joseph attempted to lead his people to Canada in hopes of finding sanctuary there. With Howard in hot pursuit, the Nez Perces, with no more than 300 warriors, fought engagements against the much larger American forces in White Bird Canyon and on the Clearwater River, eluding the Americans in the Bitterroot Mountains. Checked in the Battle of the Big Hole (August 9–10, 1877), the Nez Perces were forced southeastward into the vicinity of Yellowstone National Park, where they eluded Colonel Samuel Sturgis and the 7th Cavalry Regiment by fleeing northward up Clark's Fork of the Yellowstone River, attacking white settlements as they went.

By September 10 Sturgis had converged with Howard near the mouth of Clark's Fork and on the following day renewed his pursuit of the Nez Perces, who were then moving toward Canyon Creek, which cuts through the sheer cliffs on the north bank of the Yellowstone. From there they hoped to escape to the prairie beyond. When Nez Perce warriors attacked a stagecoach at the mouth of Canyon Creek on September 11, survivors alerted Sturgis to the Native Americans' location. Arriving at Canyon Creek on September 13, Sturgis ordered his men to dismount, which in retrospect was a tactical error. They then began a fruitless long-range firing contest that served only to alert the Nez Perces to their location. As most of the tribe escaped up Canyon Creek, well-placed Nez Perce marksmen held off the cavalry trying to advance on foot and turned back a halfhearted cavalry charge. By the end of the day Sturgis had suffered casualties of 3 dead and 11 wounded, while only a few Nez Perces suffered minor wounds.

Although the Battle of Canyon Creek was yet another humiliating defeat for the U.S. Army, it bought the Nez Perces only three more weeks of freedom. On September 30 Colonel Nelson B. Miles and 400 soldiers surrounded the Nez Perce camp at Bear Paw Mountain, forcing them to surrender six days later only some 40 miles south of the Canadian border.

JUSTIN D. MURPHY

See also

Bear Paw Mountains, Battle of; Cavalry Regiment, 7th U.S.; Clearwater River, Battle of; Howard, Oliver Otis; Joseph, Chief; Nez Perces; Nez Perce War; White Bird Canyon, Battle of

References

Beal, Merril D. *"I Will Fight No More Forever": Chief Joseph and the Nez Perce War.* Seattle: University of Washington Press, 1963.

Brown, Mark H. *The Flight of the Nez Perce.* Lincoln: University of Nebraska Press, 1967.

West, Elliott. *The Last Indian War: The Nez Perce Story.* New York: Oxford University Press, 2009.

Canyon de Chelly was a natural stronghold protecting the Navajos from Spanish and American incursions. The stronghold lasted for many decades, until Colonel Christopher ("Kit") Carson destroyed much of the Navajo livestock and crops and forced the Indians to evacuate the area in January 1864. (Photos.com)

Canyon de Chelly, Arizona

A traditional stronghold of the Navajos during their various confrontations with Spain, Mexico, and the United States until Colonel Christopher "Kit" Carson finally forced the tribe to evacuate the area in January 1864. Located in northeastern Arizona at an elevation ranging from 5,000 to 6,000 feet, Canyon de Chelly consists of four main gorges, including Canyon del Muerto, and many branching ravines. The vertical red sandstone walls of Canyon de Chelly rise from a height of 30 feet at the canyon mouth to nearly 1,000 feet in the canyon depths, making access to the canyon floor extremely difficult. Small Navajo settlements were scattered through the canyon.

Following their occupation of Canyon de Chelly in about 1700, the Navajos conducted raids against Spanish and Pueblo settlements along the Rio Grande Valley, many of which originated in Canyon de Chelly. Reprisals by Spanish, Mexican, and eventually U.S. forces followed. Early armed clashes in the canyon included Spanish Lieutenant Antonio Norbona's 1805 expedition into Canyon del Muerto, during which numerous Navajo women and children were killed at Massacre Cave, and skirmishes in 1849 with U.S. Army troops led by Lieutenant Colonel John M. Washington in Canyon del Muerto.

During the American Civil War (1861–1865), Navajo attacks originating from the Canyon de Chelly area intensified against American settlers as army units were redeployed to the East. In June 1863 Brigadier General James H. Carleton ordered Carson to initiate a campaign to punish the Navajos. This rapidly developed into a scorched-earth operation that sought to relocate the entire Navajo population to Fort Sumner (Bosque Redondo) in New Mexico.

In January 1864 Carson led a 16-day operation to depopulate Canyon de Chelly. Advancing along the canyon's frozen streambed, sometimes through two feet of snow, Carson's forces encountered ineffectual resistance from a starving Native American population. As Carson's troops advanced, they systematically destroyed Navajo homes and peach orchards. Navajo losses included 23 killed and 34 captured and the surrender of 200 others. The survivors subsequently participated in the infamous Long Walk to Fort Sumner, described by some as a death march, where 9,022 Navajos were interned as of March 1865. It is believed that as many as several thousand Navajos died en route. Following the conclusion of a peace treaty with the Navajos on June 1, 1868, they were permitted to return to their ancestral homes, and Canyon de Chelly became part of the large Navajo Reservation.

GLENN E. HELM

See also

Carleton, James Henry; Carson, Christopher Houston; Fort Sumner; Navajo Removal; Navajos; Pueblos

References

Bailey, Lynn R. *The Long Walk: A History of the Navajo Wars, 1848–68.* Los Angeles: Westernlore, 1964.

Ortiz, Alfonso, ed. *Handbook of North American Indians,* Vol. 10. Washington, DC: Smithsonian Institution, 1983.

Spicer, Edward H. *Cycles of Conquest: The Impact of Spain, Mexico, and the United States on the Indians of the Southwest, 1533–1960.* Tucson: University of Arizona Press, 1962.

Underhill, Ruth M. *The Navajos.* Norman: University of Oklahoma Press, 1956.

Captain Jack

See Kintpuash

Captain O'Beel

See Cornplanter

Captivity Narratives

One of the most popular literature genres in the colonial period and beyond. Captivity narratives are the often sensationalized accounts of white colonists who were kidnapped by Native Americans, lived with them for a period of time, and then were freed. Part morality tale, part religious and national propaganda, and part gory thriller, captivity narratives were essentially propagandistic in nature and intent whether they reinforced prejudice against Native Americans or against the French in Canada. Nevertheless, the popular appeal of captivity narratives lay in their more titillating, voyeuristic aspects.

The earliest published account of European captivity by Native Americans was that of Álvar Núñez Cabeza de Vaca in 1542, but the popular genre was innovated by Increase Mather and Mary Rowlandson of New England in the publication *The Sovereignty and Goodness of God* (1682). In 1681 Mather suggested that he and his colleagues collect stories of "special providences" concerning New England to be evaluated, sorted, and eventually anthologized. This effort became *Wonders of the Invisible World* (1693), but he thought Rowlandson's story too compelling to await later publication. Rowlandson had been taken captive during Metacom's raid on the central Massachusetts town of Lancaster in February 1676 and ransomed after three months. Thus her harrowing experience seemed to him a perfect allegory for a second-generation New England that—in the opinion of clerical elites—had slipped from its religious moorings. Rowlandson may also have felt a need to write a faithful rendition of her ordeal to quell rumors that she had been sexually abused by her captors. With Mather most likely serving as her editor, she produced *The Sovereignty and Goodness of God.*

Rowlandson's narrative became the standard blueprint on which all future captivity narratives were built. A devout pure woman is ruthlessly captured by "savages," forced to endure all manner of physical and emotional torments for a length of time, and then is finally redeemed to rejoin English society. Although usually exaggerated in the narratives, there is some truth to the methods that indigenous peoples typically used to subdue white hostages during their captivity, consisting mainly of forcing them to travel long distances on foot and to subsist on meager rations of whatever could be foraged on the trail. It was a physically exhausting ordeal to people unaccustomed to it, and Rowlandson frequently complained of her aches and pains as she reluctantly accommodated herself to life in Native American society. She eventually learned to accept the "filthy trash" that the Native Americans ate, and along the way she gradually won the respect and honor of her captors, meeting with Metacom himself and being temporarily adopted into his household. This she took as evidence of her racial superiority, when in fact King Philip (Metacom) was merely protecting and humoring his valuable investment. After a total of 20 "removes" that took her throughout western Massachusetts and present-day Vermont, she was redeemed by her husband Joseph in May 1676.

In this regard, captivity narratives can be studied as another form of archetypal story involving a hero's transformation through symbolic death and rebirth. The hero or heroine is somehow separated from the comfortable and familiar and is compelled to undertake an extended journey that is multilayered, in that the journey is literal, psychological, and metaphorical. According to Joseph Campbell's interpretation of the monomyth, the hero's journey consists of three distinct stages: separation, transformation, and

Popular Narratives of European Captivity by Native Americans

Captive	Title of Narrative	Publication Date
Álvar Núñez Cabeza de Vaca	*The Narrative of Cabeza De Vaca*	1542
Mary Rowlandson	*The Sovereignty and Goodness of God*	1682
John Williams	*The Redeemed Captive, Returning to Zion*	1707
Elizabeth Hanson	*God's Mercy Surmounting Man's Cruelty Exemplified in the Captivity . . . of Elizabeth Hanson*	1728
Charles Saunders	*The Horrid Cruelty of the Indians*	1763
Mary Jemison	*The Life of Mary Jemison: The White Woman of the Genesee*	1824

Poster advertising a book about the kidnapping of two white women by Native Americans in the early 19th century. This genre of literature, known as the captivity narrative, was often sensationalistic and exploited white fears of Native Americans. (Library of Congress)

enlightened return. Native American captivity narratives that followed Rowlandson's extremely popular book generally kept to the same monomythic progression that she described, however much the details varied. Although this suggests that Native American abduction practices and initiation and adoption rites shared similar dynamics and that white captives' reactions tended to be roughly similar, the formulaic nature of the narratives that gained in popularity in 18th-century British America indicates a high degree of borrowing that belies their essentially propagandistic nature.

The second best-selling captivity narrative was John Williams's memoir *The Redeemed Captive, Returning to Zion,* published in 1707. Williams, a minister of the Congregational Church in the western Massachusetts town of Deerfield, was captured with a number of his family members and parishioners in the French and native raid on the town in 1704 during Queen Anne's War. The white captives were marched north through winter snow to Montreal and the surrounding Kahnawake Mohawk villages over the course of nearly two months from March through April 1704. Following the by now conventional model for captivity narratives, Williams recounts the rigors and cruelties of the forced march through the New York wilderness, the fear of starvation and sudden death, and the horror at the witnessing of burdensome children and the wounded being killed or abandoned to die, including his wife Eunice. However, whereas Rowlandson devotes some space in her narrative to a denigration of the Christianized praying Indians, whom she suspected as traitors and spies to their white civilizers, Williams's narrative is most concerned with describing the attempts by the French Jesuit missionaries to convert him and his fellow captive parishioners to Catholicism. Williams's *Redeemed Captive* inaugurated the subgenre of anti-Catholic captivity narrative, which remained wildly popular until the American Revolutionary War (1775–1783).

Indeed, this became the basic threefold purpose of captivity narratives: to reinforce prejudice against the native peoples, particularly those allied with the French; to stoke the fires of anti-Catholic bigotry; and to invigorate Francophobic British nationalism and imperialism. Captivity narratives were most popular in New England, where anti-Catholic prejudice was regularly expressed at Pope's Day celebrations every November 5 (Guy Fawkes Day in England). Production and sales of captivity narratives consequently rose with the outbreak of King William's War (1675–1676), Queen Anne's War (1702–1713), King George's War (1744–1748), and the French and Indian War (1754–1763). The latter conflict was the most catastrophic of the four, involving as it did colonial militia forces under British Army command. This war took on distinctly religious and even apocalyptic tones, as New England clergymen often described it as the first skirmishes in the foretold War of Armageddon.

Although not as numerous or quite as popular as they were in the 17th and 18th centuries, captivity narratives continued to attract sizable audiences in the 19th century. Perhaps one of the most successful involved the captivity of Mary Jemison by the Shawnees. Her story, published in 1824 as *The Life of Mary Jemison: The White Woman of the Genesee,* tells the saga of a white woman who thoroughly adapted to Native American ways, twice married Iroquois men, and raised her children immersed in the Shawnee culture. Indeed, Jemison became a noted leader among the Shawnees. The book has been published in many editions over the years.

JOHN HOWARD SMITH

See also

Captivity of Europeans by Indians; Iroquois; Jemison, Mary; King Philip's War; Metacom; Rowlandson, Mary White; Shawnees

References

Axtell, James. "The White Indians of Colonial America." *William and Mary Quarterly,* 3rd ser., 32(1) (January 1975): 55–88.

Demos, John. *The Unredeemed Captive: A Family Story From Early America.* New York: Knopf, 1994.

Derounian-Stodola, Kathryn Zabelle, and James A. Levernier. *The Indian Captivity Narrative, 1500–1900.* New York: Twayne, 1993.

Fitzpatrick, Tara. "The Figure of Captivity: The Cultural Work of the Puritan Captivity Narrative." *American Literary History* 3(1) (Spring 1991): 1–26.

Pearce, Roy Harvey. "The Significances of the Captivity Narrative." *American Literature* 19(1) (1947): 1–20.

Captivity of Europeans by Indians

Native Americans took Europeans captive to demonstrate personal courage, replace lost family or tribe members, and for ransom. Most natives valued captives over scalps and certainly over territory as a mark of prowess in combat. Captivity was most prevalent in the colonial era but continued to occur, although with less frequency, in the 19th century. During that century, the captivity narratives that emerged from such occurrences tended to be more sensationalized; some appeared as outright fictionalized accounts.

Native American war parties would go to some length to return with captives but would often execute prisoners and take their scalps as opposed to releasing them if return was impractical. Thus, adult women and adolescents of both genders stood a better chance of surviving the trek back to native territory than adult men, often seen as dangerous, or young children or infants, who slowed the march.

Upon reaching the captors' settlement, some captives were offered the opportunity to assimilate into the native social structure, replacing a lost member by taking on the member's role and status, sometimes without regard to age or gender. European captives sometimes married natives, and children were adopted into Native American families.

Other captives became ritual sacrifices, either in vengeance or as a mark of respect. Some warrior peoples believed that torture gave a captive the opportunity to demonstrate courage. This honor was lost on most captives, who did not meet the warriors' expectations of stoicism or clever insults. Those who did show courage

Depiction of the surrender of Native Americans during Pontiac's Rebellion in November 1764. The Indians are relinquishing their British captives to Colonel Henry Bouquet. The war itself did not end until 1766, when Pontiac agreed to the Treaty of Oswego. (Library of Congress)

might earn a reprieve or at least respect for their religious teachings, as did several missionaries. Other captives were eaten, either in accordance with custom or to show defiance of European values.

Native Americans who had converted to Catholicism or were in need of trade goods could ransom British prisoners to the French in Canada, where the captives were exchanged through negotiations between Europeans. The French were anxious to avoid the opprobrium that came with their native allies executing prisoners. The capture and ransoming of captives became a central part of the economy of many tribes located between the colonial empires.

Those captives who survived removal and were offered a place in native society, especially children, often assimilated and resisted repatriation. Adult women who had converted from Protestantism to Catholicism and/or taken Native American husbands also often declined to return, fearful of the contempt that their former neighbors might show them. By rejecting their birth culture, these so-called European transplants posed serious spiritual and cultural problems for colonists.

GRANT WELLER

See also

Black Robes; Captivity Narratives; Captivity of Indians by Europeans; Jemison, Mary; Mourning War; Native American Warfare; Rowlandson, Mary White; Scalping

References

Axtell, James. "The White Indians of Colonial America." *William and Mary Quarterly,* 3rd ser., 32(1) (January 1975): 55–88.

Colley, Linda. *Captives: The Story of Britain's Pursuit of Empire and How Its Soldiers and Civilians Were Held Captive by the Dream of Global Supremacy, 1600–1850.* New York: Pantheon, 2002.

Doyle, Robert. *A Prisoner's Duty: Great Escapes in U.S. Military History.* Annapolis, MD: Naval Institute Press, 1997.

Doyle, Robert. *Voices from Captivity: Interpreting the American POW Narrative.* Lawrence: University Press of Kansas, 1994.

Steele, Ian K. *Betrayals: Fort William Henry & the "Massacre."* Oxford: Oxford University Press, 1990.

Captivity of Indians by Europeans

Just as Native Americans took Europeans captive since first contact in the 16th century, so too did Europeans capture Native Americans. Europeans valued native captives both for their labor and as potential converts to Christianity and European culture. Native Americans' resistance generally proved effective on both counts.

Colonists at war with native societies tended to kill as many men as possible to eliminate future military threats, leaving a skewed proportion of women and children as captives. Captives were valued mainly for their labor as domestic or field servants or slaves, these concepts being flexible in many cases. Over time many colonists became disillusioned with native labor. Europeans had developed a distorted picture of the gendered division of labor in Native American societies, believing that their women would welcome the opportunity to serve white families rather than their assumably lazy or abusive husbands. Instead, the unfamiliar tasks and negative racial and cultural attitudes set up barriers to effective use of native labor, and native servants or slaves dropped in value compared to European indentured servants or imported African slaves.

Another factor contributing to the reduced value placed on Native American captives was their tendency to escape. Even in cases where the captive's original family and society were inaccessible because of removal of the captive or destruction of the society, escapees could often find native communities closely matching their language and traditions in which the custom of adoption allowed them to assume a better social position than that of a servant or slave in colonial society. In some cases natives still living in their own communities encouraged or assisted escaping captives.

Many efforts were made to convert Native American captives to Christianity and convince them to adopt colonial or European cultural values. Although feelings of cultural superiority ran both ways, European attitudes were tinged with a racism that prevented a native from fully assimilating into white society. This failure to assimilate caused much anxiety among Europeans, but they never discovered a solution to the problem.

Other native captives had value not as laborers or converts but instead as hostages or subjects for exchange. Europeans sometimes took native notables hostage for the good behavior of their people or to convince natives suspected of criminal or warlike behavior to submit to white jurisprudence. These efforts did not often work, as nonnatives failed to understand the more consensual view of leadership held by most indigenous peoples or the complex relationships among different tribes and nations.

GRANT WELLER

See also

Caesar; Captivity Narratives; Captivity of Europeans by Indians; Captivity of Indians by Indians; Native American Warfare

References

Axtell, James. *The Invasion Within: The Contest of Cultures in Colonial North America.* New York: Oxford University Press, 1985.

Fickes, Michael. "'They Could Not Endure That Yoke': The Captivity of Pequot Women and Children after the War of 1637." *New England Quarterly* 73(1) (March 2000): 58–81.

Sainsbury, John. "Indian Labor in Early Rhode Island." *New England Quarterly* 48(3) (September 1975): 378–393.

Captivity of Indians by Indians

Native American warfare was often an affair of vengeance. For many tribes the goal was to take scalps on a scalp-for-scalp basis. If a war party went out to avenge the death of a family member, it did not matter if the scalp of an old woman or a child was brought home in triumph. Custom required that the one originally killed had to be avenged so that her or his spirit might rest.

Natives also sought to replace deceased tribal members by capturing people from rival tribes and adopting them (known as a mourning war). Raiding parties took captives and transported them to the raiders' home nation. Once safely delivered to the village, the prisoners' fate was determined by tribal leaders and in many cases the relatives of slain natives. In many tribes the latter decided whether they would adopt a particular captive to replace a lost family member or instead demand the prisoner's execution. Captured women and children were usually adopted and gradually assumed the identity, language, and customs of their captors. Occasionally men were adopted, and in some cases tribal leaders assigned captives, regardless of age or gender, to labor as slaves.

Most male captives were shown little consideration. On arrival in the capturing nation, if they were not selected for adoption or enslavement they were used for murderous sport. Ritual torture was often the rule; the Iroquois were particularly notorious in this regard. The goal of the one being tortured was to remain stoic to the end.

On August 30, 1763, for example, King Haigler of the Catawbas was assassinated by a Shawnee war party that had entered the nation for that purpose. Although they were pursued by the infuriated Catawbas, the killers escaped. Five years later on May 1, 1768, a group of Shawnees was taken captive by the Catawbas. One man was certainly identified as one of those who had murdered King Haigler.

Realizing his fate, the captured man refused to walk and was tomahawked on the spot. The other six Shawnees were not so fortunate. On May 24, 1768, they were delivered to the Catawba towns and executed Catawba style. First they were beaten unconscious with switches and then revived with cold water. This process was followed repeatedly. During this time of torture a Catawba woman known as Betty took a liking to one of the victims. She requested that his life be spared, but her plea was denied. Rather than see him continue to suffer, Betty took a tomahawk and killed the captive herself. When the Catawbas grew tired of this sport, the remaining five were given to young boys, who used them for target practice with their bows and arrows. The men finally died in this gruesome fashion.

Native Americans also occasionally practiced vengeance on the dead. At one time, for example, the Catawbas dug up the bodies of Senecas and scalped the corpses.

THOMAS JOHN BLUMER AND JIM PIECUCH

See also

Captivity Narratives; Captivity of Europeans by Indians; Captivity of Indians by Europeans; Catawbas; Haigler; Iroquois; Iroquois Confederacy; Mohawks; Mourning War; Oneidas; Onondagas; Scalping; Senecas; Tuscarora War

References

Brown, Douglas S. *The Catawba Indians: The People of the River.* Columbia: University of South Carolina Press, 1966.

Haefeli, Evan, and Kevin Sweeney. *Captives among the Indians: First Hand Narratives of Indian War Customs, Tortures and Habits of Life in Colonial Times.* New York: Outing, 1916.

Russell, Carl P. *Guns on the Early Frontier: A History of Firearms from Colonial Times through the Years of the Western Fur Trade.* Berkeley and Los Angeles: University of California Press, 1957.

Carbines

Short-barreled shoulder-fired personal weapons used extensively by mounted troops. The carbine is similar to the rifle in design but is shorter in length. The carbine was the primary weapon used by cavalry troops during the Indian Wars. Until the 19th century, carbines, like muskets, were muzzle loaders. In the second half of the 19th century breech-loading carbines were introduced. Breech-loading carbines could be opened at the breech block, allowing the firing chamber to be loaded directly. This carbine was also a favored firearm of Native American warriors. The carbine provided both a good combination of ease of use on horseback and a reasonable range of fire. Carbines of this period were approximately 40 inches in overall length, including a rifled barrel of about 24 inches long.

Carbines varied extensively but can be characterized by the differences in their firing mechanisms and type of ammunition. Both single-shot and repeating carbines were common. The single-shot carbine required that each shot be loaded and fired separately. Repeaters allowed several cartridges to be loaded at one time and fired in sequence before reloading.

American single-shot carbines of the 19th century. Carbines were essentially shorter, lighter versions of rifles. They fired the same ammunition, although often at a lower velocity. The carbine was intended for cavalry use. (Dover Publications)

The percussion cap system was common in the early and mid-19th century. This system consisted of two parts. A cartridge, usually made of paper or specially treated linen and containing powder and bullet, was loaded into the firing chamber. The chamber was then closed. When the trigger was pulled, an external firing ignition system, usually a percussion cap containing fulminate of mercury, was struck by the hammer. The hot gases thus generated were channeled into the chamber, firing the cartridge. This system meant that most of the carbines were single-shot weapons; however, several repeating carbines of varying success were developed.

The development of self-contained cartridges allowed for effective repeating mechanisms to be designed. Rigid metal cartridges contained the powder, bullet, and igniter in one case. This along with the toughness of the metal cartridge made possible the design of magazines able to hold several cartridges. Both tube- and box-type magazines were developed. The firing systems were designed so that the fired round could be extracted and the next round loaded into the chamber, the breech sealed, and the hammer cocked all in one mechanical operation. The rate of fire could thus be greatly increased. By the mid-19th century, several designs of repeating carbines were in production. The most popular design was the Winchester carbine that had several models in production.

The breech-loading carbine, using self-contained cartridges of either single or repeating shot, was ideal for the mounted soldier. The short length, when compared to a rifle, and the ability to quickly load while on horseback greatly increased the efficiency of fire for mounted troops. By the end of the Indian Wars, all U.S. mounted troops were armed with carbines.

Several models and manufacturers were utilized by the army. The most common carbine of the U.S. Cavalry was the single-shot breech-loading Springfield Armory carbine of the Sharps design. Some 700,000 of the 1873 Model .45-70 were produced in both rifle and carbine versions (the infantry model had a 32.63-inch barrel, while the cavalry version had a 22-inch barrel). The Springfield carbine, the standard cavalry weapon in most of the Indian campaigns after the American Civil War (1861–1865), had a muzzle velocity of 1,100 feet per second. A trained cavalryman could fire up to about 20 aimed shots per minute. The U.S. War Department believed that the reliability of this carbine and the large supply of weapons and parts overcame the disadvantage of its slower firing rate, when compared to repeaters. The carbine was also the preferred weapon of Native American warriors; however, they were forced to use any type of firearm they could procure, so there was little standardization.

LAWRENCE E. SWESEY

See also
Pistols; Rifles

References
Bilby, Joseph G. *A Revolution in Arms: A History of the First Repeating Rifles.* Yardley, PA: Westholme Publishing, 2006.
Myatt, Frank. *Firearms: An Illustrated History of the Development of the World's Military Firearms during the 19th Century.* New York: Crescent Books, 1979.

Carleton, James Henry
Birth Date: December 27, 1814
Death Date: January 17, 1873

U.S. Army officer. James Henry Carleton was born in Lubec, Maine, on December 27, 1814, the son of a ship captain. In his youth Carleton yearned to be an author, actually carrying on a written correspondence with Charles Dickens about his literary aspirations. Although this ambition went largely unrealized, Carleton kept voluminous journals and military writings for the remainder of his life. In 1838 he received a commission as a lieutenant in the Maine Militia. On October 18, 1839, he was appointed a second lieutenant in the U.S. Army 1st Dragoons and was assigned to Fort Gibson in Indian Territory (Oklahoma), where he became involved in a number of expeditions.

Promoted to first lieutenant in 1845, Carleton served under Brigadier General Stephen W. Kearny on the Rocky Mountain Expedition to the South Pass in 1846. During the Mexican-American War (1846–1848), Carleton served on the staff of Major General John Wool, earning promotion to captain in 1847, and saw action at the Battle of Buena Vista, for which Carleton was brevetted to major for gallantry. During the 1850s he saw extensive duty in the Southwest.

Following the outbreak of the American Civil War (1861–1865), Carleton, a major in the newly formed 6th U.S. Cavalry Regiment, was ordered to raise a relief force and proceed to New Mexico to stymie any attempts by Confederates to take control of the region. In August 1861 while organizing his forces, he entered the volunteer organization as colonel of the 1st California Infantry. He then commanded the so-called California Column on its epic march to the Rio Grande. In charge of 2,350 men, Carleton marched his troops from Wilmington, California, to El Paso, Texas, in what was one of the longest infantry marches in U.S. history. In the process Carlton retook Tucson, which had been occupied by Confederate forces. His arrival at El Paso ended the Confederate threat to the New Mexico Territory.

In April 1862 Carlton was promoted to brigadier general and assigned command of the Department of New Mexico, which he kept under martial law. Persistent problems with Native American tribes in the region led to a relentless campaign to force them onto reservations. Carleton's orders were to kill all Native American

Brigadier General James H. Carleton commanded U.S. forces in New Mexico during the Civil War. He waged relentless campaigns against the Mescalero Apaches and the Navajos to force them onto reservations. (Library of Congress)

warriors and capture the women and children. His principal field commander was Colonel Christopher "Kit" Carson of the 1st New Mexico Cavalry. With the help of Carson and other subordinates, the Mescalero Apaches were subdued and relocated to a reservation. Carleton then ordered his army to destroy all crops in Navajo territory and starve the Native Americans there into submission. Prior to the end of the Civil War in 1865, Carleton was brevetted major general of volunteers. He was also brevetted to the same rank in the U.S. Army. His volunteer regiments remained in action in the West against restless tribes until relieved by regulars at the end of 1866.

Carleton returned to the regular army after the war as a lieutenant colonel in the 4th Cavalry, serving in Texas. He wrote numerous articles on military subjects as well as a book on the Battle of Buena Vista, published in 1848. Still on active duty, Carleton died from pneumonia in San Antonio on January 17, 1873.

Charles Francis Howlett

See also
Apaches; Carson, Christopher Houston; Navajo Removal; Sibley, Henry Hastings; Wool, John Ellis

References
Hunt, Aurora. *Major General James H. Carleton, 1814–1873: Western Frontier Dragoon.* Glendale, CA: Clark Publishers, 1958.

Hutton, Paul Andrew, ed. *Soldiers West: Biographies from the Military Frontier.* Lincoln: University of Nebraska Press, 1987.

Thompson, Gerald. *The Army and the Navajo: The Bosque Redondo Reservation Experiment, 1863–1868.* Tucson: University of Arizona Press, 1976.

Carleton's Campaign

Start Date: 1863
End Date: 1864

Campaign against the Mescalero Apaches and Navajos between 1863 and 1864 that culminated in the forced removal of the Navajos, known as the Long Walk, to the Bosque Redondo Reservation in eastern New Mexico. Although Brevet Lieutenant Colonel Edward R. S. Canby had established peace with the Navajo in early 1861, the outbreak of the American Civil War (1861–1865) that year prevented the United States from fulfilling its promises to provide food, clothing, and protection to the tribe. More important, Canby, who had been appointed brigadier general of volunteers and given command of the Department of New Mexico, was soon preoccupied with defending New Mexico against a Confederate invasion mounted by Brigadier General Henry Hopkins Sibley in 1862. Consequently, the Navajos took advantage of the situation by raiding white settlements and disrupting mail service to California. Unfortunately for the Navajos, once the Confederate invasion was defeated, the full brunt of federal power was directed against them.

Brigadier General James H. Carleton, who succeeded Canby as commander of the Department of New Mexico on September 18, 1862, was determined to crush Native American resistance in New Mexico. Having under his command the 1st New Mexico Cavalry led by Colonel Christopher "Kit" Carson, the 1st California Cavalry, the 5th U.S. Infantry, the 1st New Mexico Infantry, and the 1st and 5th California Infantry, Carleton moved against the Mescalero Apaches in the spring of 1863 and then turned his attention to the Navajos, ordering Navajo chiefs Barboncito and Delgadito to relocate to the new reservation established for the Mescalero Apaches at Bosque Redondo near Fort Sumner along the Pecos River in eastern New Mexico.

When the Navajos refused to submit to this order, Carleton ordered Carson to lead the 1st New Mexico Cavalry to Fort Wingate (near present-day Grants, New Mexico) and Fort Defiance (near present-day Window Rock, Arizona), which was renamed Fort Canby, in preparation for a campaign against the Navajos. Beginning in June 1863 Carson's men, joined by Ute and Zuni warriors, began attacking Navajo farms and seizing Navajo livestock. During the next six months Carson kept steady pressure on the Navajos, killing a reported 78 warriors and destroying crops, orchards, and dwellings. By January 1864 the majority of the Navajos had been forced into their traditional stronghold of Canyon de Chelly, which Carson and his men entered on January 12, 1864.

By mid-March the Navajos were on the verge of starvation, and approximately 6,000 assembled at Fort Wingate and Fort Canby to surrender. Approximately 2,400 Navajos were then marched to Bosque Redondo, with at least 200 dying en route. By the end of 1864 almost 8,000 Navajos had surrendered and relocated to Bosque Redondo.

Although Carleton's Campaign had brutally and effectively crushed the Navajos, his attempt to "civilize" the Navajos at Bosque Redondo proved an abject failure. There was not enough land to support the Navajos and their livestock, and the attempt to force them to live alongside their traditional enemy, the Mescalero Apaches, resulted in continual turmoil. Indeed, the Mescalero Apaches fled the reservation in late 1865, and Carleton was relieved of his command in the autumn of 1866. Even hard-nosed Lieutenant General William Tecumseh Sherman, who met with Navajo leaders at Fort Sumner in 1868, recognized the futility of the Bosque Redondo experiment and agreed to a new treaty with the Navajos on June 1, 1868, that allowed them to return to their traditional homeland.

JUSTIN D. MURPHY

See also

Apaches; Barboncito; Bosque Redondo; Canby, Edward Richard Sprigg; Canyon de Chelly, Arizona; Carleton, James Henry; Carson, Christopher Houston; Delgadito; Navajo Removal; Navajos; Sherman, William Tecumseh

References

Dutton, Bertha Pauline. *American Indians of the Southwest.* Albuquerque: University of New Mexico, 1994.

Keleher, William A. *Turmoil in New Mexico.* Facsimile of 1952 ed. Santa Fe, NM: Sunstone, 2008.

Utley, Robert M. *Frontiersmen in Blue: The United States and the Indian, 1848–1865.* Lincoln: University of Nebraska Press, 1967.

Utley, Robert M., and Wilcomb E. Washburn. *Indian Wars.* New York: American Heritage Press, 2002.

Carr, Eugene Asa

Birth Date: March 20, 1830
Death Date: December 2, 1910

U.S. Army officer. Eugene Asa Carr was born in Erie County, New York, on March 20, 1830. He was appointed to the U.S. Military Academy, West Point, in September 1846; graduated in 1850; and was then commissioned a second lieutenant in the Regiment of Mounted Riflemen. During the next decade Carr served primarily in the American West. On October 10, 1854, he was badly wounded by an arrow in a skirmish with Apache warriors near Limpia, Texas. Returning to duty, Carr was promoted to first lieutenant in the 1st Cavalry in 1855 and to captain in 1858.

At the beginning of the American Civil War (1861–1865), Carr was stationed at Fort Washita in Indian Territory (Oklahoma). Within weeks he was assigned to Brigadier General Nathaniel Lyon's

Brigadier General Eugene A. Carr (1830–1910) is generally regarded as one of the more effective army officers in the West during the post–Civil War period. (Library of Congress)

command in Missouri, where he saw action at the Battle of Wilson's Creek (August 10, 1861). On August 16 Carr entered the volunteer establishment as colonel of the 3rd Illinois Cavalry. In the succeeding months he helped push Confederate forces out of Missouri.

During the Battle of Pea Ridge (March 7–8, 1862), Carr was wounded three times but refused to leave the field of battle; he was later (in 1893) awarded the Medal of Honor for his actions there. On March 7, 1862, Carr was made a brigadier general of volunteers. During the Vicksburg Campaign (April 1–July 4, 1863) he commanded a division and helped to secure the city for the Union. He then went to Arkansas but saw only sporadic action. During the Siege of Mobile (March 25–April 12, 1865) he commanded a division under Major General Edward R. S. Canby.

Following the end of the Civil War, Carr assumed the regular army rank of major and was later assigned to the 5th Cavalry Regiment on the frontier. His first major action came against the Cheyennes on July 11, 1869, at the Battle of Summit Springs in Colorado. The Cheyenne Dog Soldiers, as the elite warriors were called, were routed in the engagement. Carr's second objective, the rescue of two white female captives, met with mixed results because one of the women was killed before she could be rescued. Carr's actions nonetheless helped to solidify his reputation as a successful Indian fighter.

By the time of the Great Sioux War (1876–1877), Carr was a lieutenant colonel of the 5th Cavalry Regiment. As such, he participated in the hunt for those responsible for defeating Lieutenant Colonel George A. Custer, but the subsequent failure of Carr's superiors, brigadier generals Alfred Terry and George Crook, to catch Custer's killers left Carr frustrated.

On April 29, 1879, Carr was promoted to colonel and given command of the 6th Cavalry Regiment. The 6th Cavalry faced Carr's old nemesis, the Apaches, in Arizona and New Mexico. Carr led expeditions against the Apaches in 1880, including the effort to catch the notorious Apache leader Victorio. By August 1881, more trouble unfolded. A new militant Native American prophet had emerged, preaching a message that troubled local white settlers. Carr moved to take the prophet into custody on August 30 at a village on Cibecue Creek. The prophet's supporters resisted, aided by a company of White Mountain Apache army scouts who unexpectedly turned on the soldiers. One U.S. officer and eight soldiers died in the melee.

Subsequent newspaper stories greatly exaggerated the events at Cibecue Creek, claiming that Carr's entire command was wiped out. Matters worsened when the Apache war leader Geronimo arrived and convinced others to join him. Many blamed Carr for the events at Cebicue Creek, and he demanded a court of inquiry to clear his name. The court found that he had made minor misjudgments but in general exonerated him. Still, Carr was haunted by the Cibecue Creek episode for the remainder of his life, and he refought the battle in print with his critics on many occasions.

Carr's last Native American campaign came in late 1890 as part of the effort to round up Sioux who had left the reservation to follow the Ghost Dance religion. Carr arrived at Wounded Knee, South Dakota, after the December 29 battle had ended. During the campaign Carr's image was immortalized by the great Western artist Frederic Remington in a work titled *General Carr Receiving a Report*.

Carr was promoted to brigadier general on July 21, 1892. He wanted to continue in the U.S. Army but was retired on February 15, 1893, after 43 years of service. Although hampered somewhat by a touchy ego and a combative nature, Carr became one of the more effective frontier commanders, a determined and relentless campaigner. He died on December 2, 1910, in Washington, D.C.

ALAN K. LAMM

See also

Apaches; Custer, George Armstrong; Dog Soldiers; Geronimo; Ghost Dance; Great Sioux War; Little Bighorn, Battle of the; Remington, Frederic; Summit Springs, Battle of; Victorio; Wounded Knee, Battle of; Wovoka

References

King, Charles. *Campaigning with Crook*. 1880; reprint, Norman: University of Oklahoma Press, 1967.

King, James T. *War Eagle: A Life of General Eugene A. Carr*. Lincoln: University of Nebraska Press, 1963.

Utley, Robert M. *Frontier Regulars: The United States and the American Indian, 1866–1891*. New York: Macmillan, 1973.

Warner, Ezra J. *Generals in Blue: Lives of the Union Commanders*. 1964; reprint, Baton Rouge: Louisiana State University Press, 2006.

Carrington, Henry Beebe
Birth Date: March 2, 1824
Death Date: October 26, 1912

Attorney, U.S. Army officer, educator, and author. Henry Beebe (sometimes spelled Beebee) Carrington was born in Wallingford, Connecticut, on March 2, 1824. After graduating from Yale University in 1845 he taught natural science and Greek at the Irving Institute in Tarrytown, New York, and attended Yale Law School in 1847. While at Yale he became known for his staunch advocacy of abolition. In 1848 Carrington moved to Columbus, Ohio, where he took up the practice of law. Between 1848 and 1861 he became involved with numerous Free Soil and Republican Party politicians.

In 1857 Carrington began serving as an adjutant general of Ohio and was instrumental in reorganizing the state militia. By the time the American Civil War (1861–1865) began, Carrington's troops were well enough organized that several regiments were immediately dispatched to western Virginia. In May 1861 he received a direct appointment to colonel in the U.S. Army and thereafter served principally in administrative assignments. He was promoted to brigadier general of volunteers in November 1862. In Ohio and Indiana, Carrington drew criticism for his summary trials of civilians suspected of pro-Confederate Copperhead activities. He then spent the remainder of the war in Tennessee, where he supervised trials of accused guerrillas.

When the war ended Carrington remained in the army as colonel of the 18th Infantry Regiment, and in late 1865 he was appointed commander of the Mountain District, Department of the Missouri, with the rank of colonel. In 1866 he moved his regimental headquarters to Colorado and was assigned the task of defending the Bozeman Trail against Native American raids. He personally supervised the construction of Fort Phil Kearny (in present-day Wyoming), from which he would administer his command. In the interim Carrington reacted hesitantly during several Native American skirmishes, leading some of his subordinates to question his abilities.

On December 6, 1866, a large contingent of warriors led by Red Cloud attacked a woodcutting detail just outside the walls of Fort Phil Kearny. When Carrington learned of the attack he dispatched a relief force, but the unit was badly mauled, and 2 men were killed. Carrington thus forbade any of his men to pursue Native American attackers. On December 21 Red Cloud mounted another attack on a U.S. wood train, and this time Captain William Fetterman demanded that Carrington allow him to lead the relief effort. Carrington agreed but gave Fetterman strict orders not to pursue the warriors beyond the immediate confines of the area. Once Fetterman arrived on the scene the warriors fled, but against orders he pursued the warriors (who numbered about 2,000). Within 20 minutes Fetterman and his entire force of 80 men had been killed. It was the largest loss in any U.S. battle with Native Americans in the West to that point in time.

Because of his past reluctance to engage Native Americans in combat and his unpopularity among his subordinates, rumors quickly surfaced that Carrington had recklessly sent his men into combat against an enemy that greatly outnumbered them. Commanding general of the army General Ulysses S. Grant sought to court-martial Carrington, but the Fetterman Massacre, as it came to be called, instead was resolved by a court of inquiry. Carrington was cleared of any wrongdoing, and it was determined that the cause of the tragedy had been Fetterman's refusal to obey orders. Nevertheless Carrington's military career was effectively over, and he resigned his commission in 1870.

Thereafter Carrington enjoyed a successful career as a college professor in Indiana, a prolific writer, and the negotiator of several treaties between the U.S. government and Native Americans, including one with the Flathead tribe in Montana. He wrote 11 books, including the very popular *Battles of the American Revolution* (1876). Carrington died on October 26, 1912, in Boston, Massachusetts.

PAUL G. PIERPAOLI JR.

See also
Fetterman, William Judd; Fetterman Massacre; Fort Phil Kearny; Red Cloud

References
Brown, Dee. *The Fetterman Massacre.* Lincoln: University of Nebraska Press, 1984.
Brown, Dee. *Fort Phil Kearny: An American Saga.* New York: Putnam, 1962.
Johnston, Terry C. *Sioux Dawn: The Fetterman Massacre, 1866.* New York: St. Martin's, 1991.

Carson, Christopher Houston
Birth Date: December 24, 1809
Death Date: May 23, 1868

Fur trapper, mountaineer, military officer, and renowned Indian fighter. Christopher Houston "Kit" Carson was born in Madison County, Kentucky, on December 24, 1809. Before he was 2 years old his family moved to Missouri, where he spent most of his youth. At age 14 Carson was apprenticed to a saddle maker but later ran away and joined a wagon train headed west to Santa Fe, New Mexico. Carson soon found himself in the occupation of fur trapper and mountaineer. This provided the foundation for almost everything else he did for the rest of his life. He traveled all over the West as far as California hunting, trapping, and ranching. He often lived with various Native American tribes. In the process he took at least two Native American wives and learned at least four Native American languages.

Although Carson deservedly gained a reputation as one who had fought Native Americans, he also became known as someone who could work with them and served as an Indian agent for the Ute tribe from 1854 to 1861. With the outbreak of the American

Christopher ("Kit") Carson was renowned as a frontiersman and U.S. Army scout, but he also led harsh army campaigns against several Indian tribes. Of these, his campaign against the Navajos is the most controversial. (Library of Congress)

Civil War (1861–1865), Carson resigned that post and joined the Union forces as a lieutenant colonel in the New Mexico volunteers but was quickly promoted to colonel. Union troops turned back an invading Confederate force at Glorieta Pass (March 26–28, 1862), but the disruption and lack of soldiers elsewhere in New Mexico led to attacks against settlers by Native American tribes, including the Mescalero Apaches, Comanches, Kiowas, and Navajos.

In mid-1862 Brigadier General James H. Carleton became commander of the Department of New Mexico. Carson was his principal field commander. Carleton believed that there could be no peace between whites and Native Americans unless the Native Americans were removed to remote locations away from white settlements. Although Carson did not relish fighting Native Americans and tried to resign his post, claiming that he had joined the army to fight Confederates, he finally agreed to stay on. He then led military campaigns against several different tribes. But it would be his campaign against the Navajos that would prove most controversial.

In December 1862 Carleton informed a group of Navajo leaders that he intended to relocate the tribe several hundred miles from their current homeland to the Bosque Redondo reservation on the Pecos River in eastern New Mexico. He gave the Navajos until July 20, 1863, to surrender and comply with the order or face war. When the Navajos did not surrender, war became certain.

Beginning in late July 1863, Carson led five separate missions through Navajo country, conducting a total-war campaign that would be imitated by Union generals against the Confederacy in the East. During the Navajo War, Carson used his contacts with the Utes to bring them into the fighting against the Navajos. He reported that during one single mission he and his men confiscated or destroyed more than 2 million pounds of grain. This relentless army pursuit and the seizure or destruction of foodstuffs, homes, and even clothes had a pronounced effect on the Navajos' ability and willingness to continue fighting.

Also devastating to the Navajos were the continued attacks by the Utes and other traditional enemies. The combination of Native American and U.S. attacks, especially Carson's invasion of the Navajo stronghold in Canyon de Chelly, proved overwhelming, and soon small bands of Navajos began turning themselves in. By the end of January 1864, between 6,000 and 8,000 Navajos (one-half to two-thirds of the tribe) had come forward to be removed to Bosque Redondo.

Charges at the time that Carson had ordered Navajos shot down without first offering them the chance to surrender now appear inaccurate. Accounts indicate that at different times he released Navajos so they could coax others into turning themselves in. There were, of course, some treacherous acts such as soldiers killing innocent Navajos who had surrendered, but Carson roundly decried these, realizing that they worked against the overall goal of rounding up the Navajos. Recent scholarship also discounts as exaggerations accounts of thousands of Navajos starving to death because of devastation wrought by Carson's forces.

In late November 1864, with the Mescalero Apache and Navajo tribes either at Bosque Redondo or on their way there, Carleton sent Carson and several hundred soldiers in search of the Kiowas, leading to the inconclusive First Battle of Adobe Walls (November 25, 1864), during which Carson was fortunate enough to be able to retreat from a much larger Native American force. Nevertheless, Carson's forces did inflict considerable casualties during the fight, mainly with howitzers.

Carson was neither an avowed friend nor enemy of Native Americans. At times he fought them, and at other times he befriended them, a behavior and attitude not uncommon to many whites of the time. Carson was awarded a brevet to brigadier general of volunteers in 1865. He then moved to Colorado to command Fort Garland before leaving the post in 1866 because of poor health. Carson died near Fort Lyons, Colorado, on May 23, 1868.

DAVID SLOAN

See also

Adobe Walls, First Battle of; Apaches; Bosque Redondo; Carleton, James Henry; Comanches; Kiowas; Navajos; Navajo War; New Mexico; Utes

References

Carter, Harvey Lewis. *Dear Old Kit: The Historical Christopher Carson.* Norman: University of Oklahoma Press, 1968.

Gordon-McCutchan, R. C., ed. *Kit Carson: Indian Fighter or Indian Killer?* Niwot: University Press of Colorado, 1996.

Trafzer, Clifford E. *The Kit Carson Campaign: The Last Great Navajo War.* Norman: University of Oklahoma Press, 1990.

Casco, Treaty of

Treaty signed on April 12, 1678, between the magistrates of Massachusetts and the Penobscots of Maine at Fort Loyal on Casco Bay, ending three years of armed hostilities between the two groups. In 1675 New England was wracked by Native American warfare. What was initially a conflict between Metacom (King Philip) and Plymouth Colony became a regional confrontation involving all of New England. Following King Philip's War (1675–1676) the broader hostilities and tensions continued, and the skirmishes led to numerous deaths on both sides.

As the violence escalated, the Penobscots became the first tribe to sue for peace. Peace articles were drawn up in Boston on November 6, 1676, and a local chieftain, Madockawando, officially ratified them. Despite the initial treaty, New England colonists soon renewed the conflict.

Following two additional years of fighting in which the Penobscots destroyed all English settlements in northern Maine, both sides agreed to the Treaty of Casco on April 12, 1678. Under its terms, the Penobscots allowed the English to regain their farms in return for paying rent to the natives. Thus the Treaty of Casco safeguarded Penobscot land rights. The peace was kept until the outbreak of King William's War in 1689.

JAIME RAMÓN OLIVARES

See also

Dummer's Treaty; King Philip's War; King William's War; Metacom

References

Day, Gordon M. *In Search of New England's Native Past: Selected Essays by Gordon M. Day.* Edited by Michael K. Foster and William Cowan. Amherst: University of Massachusetts Press, 1998.

Leach, Douglas Edward. *Flintlock and Tomahawk: New England in King Philip's War.* East Orleans, MA: Parnassus Imprints, 1992.

Catawbas

Native American tribe located primarily in the western Carolinas, near the border of present-day North and South Carolina, about 20 miles south of Charlotte, North Carolina. The Catawba Reservation, whose headquarters is near Rock Hill, South Carolina, is near the center of what once was a very large territory, extending from south-central Virginia through North Carolina and including much of South Carolina. Today the Catawba Nation consists of some 2,000 people on a tract of land only slightly larger than 15 square miles on the North Carolina–South Carolina border. At their peak the Catawbas controlled some 55,000 square miles.

Since before the arrival of the Spanish, the Catawbas were held in great awe by neighboring chiefdoms. The Catawbas were particularly known as warriors of great skill. This respect continued through the colonial period. It is significant that they knew better than to fight Hernando de Soto in the 16th century, for they understood the Europeans' superior military power. Instead they dealt with the potential threat diplomatically, a concept that worked rather well. The Catawbas' political approach was always marked by practicality. The Catawbas could not, however, escape the ravages of disease brought by European contact. Their population base dwindled from many thousands before the arrival of the Spanish to several hundred at the end of the colonial period. Indeed, the Catawbas were decimated by smallpox epidemics in 1718, 1738, and 1759.

The Catawbas first appeared on the colonial battlefield beside British settlers during the Tuscarora War (1711–1713). The Catawbas were crucial to the defeat of the Tuscarora tribe of North Carolina. Through this war the Catawbas managed to make long-lasting enemies of the Iroquois as the Tuscarora fled north. Those Tuscaroras not lucky enough to escape North Carolina were sold into slavery. The problem for the Catawbas was made more acute when the Tuscaroras joined the Iroquois Confederacy as the sixth member nation in 1722. During the Yamasee War (1715–1717), the Catawbas changed sides and fought briefly with their fellow natives against the British. The Catawbas quickly saw the folly of this alliance, however, and made peace with the British. This marked the last time that the Catawbas would fight against British settlers. Indeed, the Catawbas became loyal allies of the Carolinas, enjoyed cordial relations with colonial governments, and engaged in a robust trade with the Europeans.

In spite of their dwindling numbers, the Catawbas continued to serve the Carolinas. They also did much to disguise their growing demographic weakness. This was largely accomplished by sending incorrect population figures to colonial authorities. The Catawbas also made some temporary population gains by incorporating smaller Catawban-related tribes. The Carolinas in turn used the Catawbas as a buffer between the settlements and the Cherokee Nation to the west. During the French and Indian War (1754–1763), the Catawbas sent warriors to fight alongside the British.

The Catawbas suffered from Iroquois war parties throughout the period and lost more population to an escalating war of vengeance. This consisted of a constant parade of Iroquois war parties seeking Catawban scalps and captives from the early 18th century until well after the Treaty of Albany (1759). The situation had become so bad in the mid-1750s that New York and South Carolina negotiated a peace between the Catawbas and the Iroquois Confederacy in 1759.

Wars of vengeance with other tribes did not cease, however. In 1763 a Shawnee war party assassinated the famed Catawba chief King Haigler. When South Carolina joined the independence effort against Great Britain, there was no debate among the Catawbas. They gave their all to the colonists' effort. As the years progressed, the Catawbas gradually adapted to European warfare tactics and weaponry. During the Tuscarora War (1711–1713) and the Yamasee War (1715–1717), the Catawba went into battle with the bow and arrow and the war club. By the time of the French and Indian War, the Catawbas were using firearms almost exclusively, although they sometimes struggled to obtain powder and flints.

The few remaining Catawbas signed a treaty with the state of South Carolina in 1840, ceding their land claims there and agreeing to relocate to North Carolina. They were not welcomed in North Carolina, however, so many joined the Cherokees and Pamunkeys. By the mid-1850s many of the Catawbas who had joined the Cherokees returned to South Carolina. Others went west. The Catawbas in South Carolina eventually negotiated a deal with state officials in which they secured a reservation of 603 acres in the northwestern part of the state and an annuity from the state. The reservation lands were not well suited for agriculture, however. As a result, in the last half of the 19th century many Catawbas were forced into sharecropping. In the early 20th century many took jobs in the area's booming textile mills. The tribe was able to purchase more land and extend its reservation in the 1950s.

THOMAS JOHN BLUMER

See also

Cherokees; Haigler; Iroquois; Iroquois Confederacy; Native Americans and the American Revolutionary War; Shawnees; Tuscaroras; Tuscarora War; Yamasees; Yamasee War

References

Brown, Douglas S. *The Catawba Indians: The People of the River.* Columbia: University of South Carolina Press, 1966.
Hudson, Charles M. *The Catawba Nation.* Athens: University of Georgia Press, 1970.
Merrell, James H. *The Indians' New World: Catawbas and Their Neighbors from European Contact through the Era of Removal.* Chapel Hill: University of North Carolina Press, 1989.

Catecahassa

See Black Hoof

Catlin, George
Birth Date: July 26, 1796
Death Date: December 23, 1872

Noted American painter and collector who specialized in portraying Native Americans of the West. George Catlin was born on July 26, 1796, at Wilkes-Barre, Pennsylvania, and was a self-taught artist who painted in the American Romantic tradition. Growing up in the Susquehanna Valley, Catlin collected Native American curiosities and formed a short-lived friendship with an Oneida family who camped on the family farm. He briefly embarked on a legal career before turning to art.

Artist George Catlin (1796–1872) created paintings that captured the Native American way of life on the prairies in the 19th century. (Hayward Cirker, ed., *Dictionary of American Portraits*, 1967)

Catlin is best known for his paintings and sketches of Native Americans of the Great Plains and for his artifact collection. Along with his artwork, Catlin published books about Plains Indian life as well as his experiences while living among the Native Americans and traveling in Europe. Catlin also promoted justice for the Native Americans. Like others in the 1830s and 1840s, he advocated that a large reservation be established for the remnants of the "Indian race." Catlin's work and Indian Gallery, displayed in Europe for more than 30 years, helped establish the Plains Indian as the "typical" North American Indian in popular imagination.

Catlin's initial artistic endeavors were miniatures of locals and some oil-on-canvas paintings of notables, such as Sam Houston. In 1827 Catlin expanded his repertoire by painting Niagara Falls as well as the Erie Canal and the Welland Canal. It was during his efforts to establish his artistic career that Catlin met in Philadelphia a delegation of western chiefs who were heading to Washington for treaty negotiations. This meeting gave Catlin the impetus to travel to the West to paint the last remaining tribes there.

In 1830 Catlin arrived in St. Louis, where he became a protégé of Brigadier General William Clark. From 1831 to 1836 Catlin visited and painted various Plains nations, including the Pawnees, Blackfeet, Crows, Osages, Comanches, Kiowas, and Ojibwas. In 1837 Catlin opened his Indian Gallery in New York City.

He subsequently offered to sell his collection of approximately 500 paintings and thousands of artifacts to the U.S. government, which declined his offer. In 1839 he transported the collection to England. On February 1, 1840, he opened the gallery at the Egyptian Hall in Piccadilly. The gallery drew thousands, including commoners and royalty.

As interest in the display gradually waned, Catlin utilized showmanship to keep the crowds coming. Initially employing English cockneys to play Native Americans, he hired a group of Canadian Ojibwas and later a group of Iowas to re-create aspects of their culture for entertainment and education. Realizing that England was tiring of the exhibition, Catlin moved the entire gallery, including the Iowas, to Paris, amid great fanfare. Tragedy soon resulted. Catlin's wife, son, and four of the Iowas died in France of disease, probably smallpox. Catlin hired Ojibwa performers, eight of whom became ill with smallpox; two of the performers died shortly after reaching Belgium. The others were hospitalized in Brussels at Catlin's expense. These misfortunes forced Catlin to mortgage his collection, which was sold to cover debts.

During the 1850s Catlin set out to paint the Indians of Central and South America as well those along the West Coast of the United States. He eventually completed 600 new paintings. In 1871 he returned to New York to display his work. Unable to secure funds, he accepted free housing at the Smithsonian Institution, where he lived in poverty until his death in Jersey City, New Jersey, on December 23, 1872. Significant collections of Catlin's work are now located at the Smithsonian Institution and the American Museum of Natural History.

KARL S. HELE

See also

Blackfoot Confederacy; Clark, William; Comanches; Crows; Kiowas; Ojibwas; Oneidas; Osages; Pawnees

References

Dippie, Brian W. *Catlin and His Contemporaries: The Politics of Patronage*. Lincoln: University of Nebraska Press, 1990.

Ewers, John C., ed. *George Catlin's "Indian Gallery": Views of the American West*. Richmond: Virginia Museum of Fine Arts, 1992.

Flavin, Francis. "The Adventurer-Artists of the Nineteenth Century and the Image of the American Indian." *Indiana Magazine of History* 98(1) (2002): 1–29.

Cattle Industry

The cattle industry, which began with the first Spanish settlers in the Southwest and the Jamestown colony (Virginia) in the early 1600s, spread steadily to Texas and the Great Plains. By the mid-1800s large cattle ranches had been established in Texas and then, later in New Mexico, Wyoming, and Montana. Cattle were rounded up, branded, and herded to market on long cattle drives. From the railheads in Missouri and Kansas, the animals were shipped to stockyards and slaughterhouses in Chicago, where they were processed. The meat was then sent to the East Coast. The cattle industry entered a new era by the late 1800s with the introduction of barbed wire, large self-contained ranches, refrigerated rail cars, and federal regulation of land and food.

Cattle, first imported to Jamestown in 1611, became common in the colonies with the arrival of Swedes and Danes in the mid-1600s. Although most herds in colonial America numbered fewer than 20 animals, some herds were as large as 200 animals. As U.S. boundaries expanded, the cattle frontier did as well, moving into the Mississippi River region in the 1820s. Meanwhile, the grazing of cattle in the Northeast, dominated as it was by small farms, pushed cattle ranchers farther west. On the other end of the continent, Spaniards brought cattle into California, Arizona, and New Mexico by the 1600s. When the United States defeated Mexico in the Mexican-American War (1846–1848), a lack of currency among occupation forces led to cattle being a means of exchange, while in California, cattle hides routinely served as currency. The war also brought an increase in business for cattle ranchers, who sold beef to the army.

Although Scandinavian- and English-bred cattle did not fare well on the dry Plains, new breeds such as the longhorn survived well. Cattle ranching on a large scale originated sometime before the American Civil War (1861–1865), mostly on the Texas grasslands. Herds were driven eastward to New Orleans to be shipped to the cities of the East. These cattle drives provided the basis for the legendary northward drives that occurred after the Civil War. Texas land stretching from San Antonio to Laredo provided some of the best cattle-raising territory.

Allowing cattle to roam on vast ranges, however, invited rustling and theft and the reintroduction of the old Spanish practice of branding, whereby a hot iron was applied to the hindquarters of a cow. Branding itself constituted a cultural phenomenon on the Plains that involved cowboys cutting a single animal out of the herd (a process that required a highly trained horse and a skilled rider), roping it, tying it down, and applying the unique brand.

By 1848 Texas required all brands to be registered with county clerks, and a new game of branding by ranchers and altering brands by rustlers ensued. Brands became increasingly complex and hard to alter. Once barbed wire came into widespread use in the 1870s, branding became less important.

Not surprisingly, the growth of the cattle industry meant more tension between whites and Native Americans as settlers and ranchers sought grazing lands on Native American territory.

Beginning in the 1860s, long cattle drives northward to railheads ensued. The spring roundup gathered together all of an owner's cattle, which were strung out over the grasslands, and headed them to train routes in Kansas along any of several famous cattle trails, including the Chisholm, the Goodnight-Loving, and the Western trails. These cattle drives required full-time ranch employees and temporary hired cowboys to push the herd through bad weather, Native American attacks, and attempts by rustlers to pick off stragglers.

The drives were sometimes dangerous and often alternately boring and difficult; they required cowboys to exercise great skill, as their profit depended on getting every head to market. The 700-mile-long Goodnight-Loving Trail, which ran west of Fort Worth through New Mexico and then northward to Colorado, was characteristic of the main cattle trails. In a single year, as many as 260,000 cattle could be herded north to the rail links. Similar trails in the North, such as the Oregon and Northern trails, brought cattle from Oregon and Montana. These cattle were transported to Chicago slaughterhouses developed by Gustavus Swift and Philip Armour or to Omaha's Cudahy Brothers stockyards; Chicago's famous Consolidated Union Stock Yards opened in 1865. From those points, the sides of beef would be packed in refrigerated railroad cars and shipped eastward.

By the 1870s as many as 300,000 cattle grazed on the Great Plains at any given time, and it is thought that in Wyoming alone 70,000 cattle were on the ranges in 1870. But the significance of Chicago as a location for the slaughterhouses also led to Illinois becoming a leading beef producer. Cattle drives peaked in the late 1870s, when as many as half a million cattle a year were herded north. After that, the introduction of barbed wire and the extension of the railroads through Texas and across the Plains ended the legendary drives and brought the cattle industry into a new era of fenced ranges and federal regulations.

LARRY SCHWEIKART

See also

Oregon Trail; Railroads

References

Birzer, Bradley J., and Larry Schweikart. *The American West.* New York: Wiley, 2003.

Dale, E. Everett. *The Range Cattle Industry.* Norman: University of Oklahoma Press, 1930.

McCoy, Joseph G. *Historical Sketches of the Cattle Trade of the West and Southwest.* Lincoln: University of Nebraska Press, 1985.

Pelzer, Louis. *The Cattlemen's Frontier.* Glendale, CA: Arthur H. Clarke, 1936.

Skaggs, Jimmy M. *The Cattle Trailing Industry: Between Supply and Demand.* Lawrence: University of Kansas Press, 1973.

Cavalry, Native American

The term "cavalry" traditionally refers to soldiers or warriors who fight mounted on horseback, although the term is not usually applied to irregular mounted units such as the Native Americans. When the Spanish introduced horses into North America in the late 1500s, the western tribes quickly incorporated them into their way of life. From the American Southwest, horses spread northward and eastward in the 16th and 17th centuries and had a tremendous impact on native societies in the West and Southwest. Horses also induced certain tribes, such as the Sioux, Cheyennes, and Comanches, to migrate to the Plains and adopt a nomadic or seminomadic lifestyle based on hunting the vast

herds of bison. Prior to the arrival of the horse, the Plains were largely devoid of tribes.

Horses revolutionized western Indian warfare by turning warriors from foot soldiers into cavalrymen. Surprise attacks by small but highly mobile mounted war parties replaced pitched battles fought by large native armies. Body armor disappeared, and shield sizes decreased. Instead of clubs, the mounted warrior depended almost exclusively on the bow and arrow until the introduction of firearms. Since American Indians did not use saddles, the lessened weight gave their horses an advantage in speed and distance over the saddled horses of European and later U.S. cavalry. In addition, American Indians had an advantage in knowing where water sources could be found on the Plains. Consequently, American Indian war parties could generally outrun their pursuers. Ultimately, destruction of the buffalo herds, superior American firepower and numbers, and intertribal rivalries enabled the United States to defeat Native Americans in the Indian Wars.

Among the first tribes to take full advantage of the military opportunities afforded by horses was the Apaches. Horses made the Apaches the supreme military power on the southern Plains until their expansion was checked by the Pawnees, Osages, Kiowas, Comanches, and other tribes. Because of the great economic and strategic importance of horses, horse raids became the most common type of intertribal warfare. Horses known for their great

Pawnee scouts in 1869. The Pawnee scouts provided invaluable service to U.S. Army cavalry units in campaigns against the Sioux and Cheyennes during the 1860s and 1870s. (Library of Congress)

speed and stamina (so-called war or buffalo horses) were particularly sought after by Native American war parties. Capturing such horses, which were always kept close to their owners' lodges at night, required great skill and daring.

American Indians perfected mounted warfare. At an early age, Native American boys learned to ride without stirrups or saddles, to shield their bodies by hanging down the side of the horse while handling the bow and arrow or firing rifles from underneath its head, and to lift up heavy objects, such as fallen comrades, at high speed. By the time boys reached adulthood, they were expert horsemen. While highly trained, Native American cavalrymen were not as well organized as their U.S. Army counterparts, and combats tended to be of an individual nature.

By contrast, U.S. cavalrymen typically did not fight on horseback but instead used horses only to get close to the enemy and then dismounted for battle. The idea of employing Native Americans as cavalry troops for the U.S. Army did not take hold until the American Civil War (1861–1865). During this conflict, Cherokee-born Brigadier General Stand Watie commanded two Confederate Indian cavalry regiments and achieved several successes in battles in Indian Territory (Oklahoma).

After the Civil War, the U.S. Army began to experiment with Native American cavalry. The Army Reorganization Act of 1866 authorized the army to enlist up to 1,000 Indian scouts. Most of them were organized as cavalrymen and attached to regular army units as guides, but a few all-Indian units were also organized. Perhaps the best known of these was the Pawnee Battalion commanded by Frank North that was intermittently active between 1864 and 1877. Other Indian units (usually not larger than company size) included the Apache scouts in the Southwest and the Arikara and Crow scouts who served with Lieutenant Colonel George Armstrong Custer at the 1876 Battle of the Little Bighorn. However, most western tribes furnished scouts for the army at some point.

Native Americans signed up as scouts with the army for a variety of reasons: to escape the confines of the reservation, to earn income, to fight traditional enemies, to earn war honors, to capture horses, or to improve their bargaining position when dealing with the U.S. government. When serving against people of their own nationality, scouts sometimes hoped to persuade their opponents to surrender and avoid bloodshed. Apache scouts, for example, persuaded Apache war leader Geronimo to surrender in 1886.

Compared to white soldiers, Indian scouts performed remarkably well. Lieutenant John G. Bourke, who served alongside Indian scouts in a number of military campaigns, called them "the finest light cavalry in the world." Sixteen Indian scouts were awarded the Medal of Honor.

Although the Indian Wars ended in 1890, the U.S. Army continued to experiment with Native American troops. In 1891 the army initiated a program that created Native American companies attached to regiments stationed in the West. Among these units were Lieutenant Edward Casey's company of Cheyenne soldiers of the 8th Cavalry Regiment and Captain Hugh L. Scott's all–Native American company of the 7th Cavalry Regiment. Unfortunately, racial prejudice among the upper echelon of the army brought an end to this experiment. In 1897 the last of the Indian units was disbanded.

In 1916, however, following Mexican bandit Pancho Villa's attack on Columbus, New Mexico, the U.S. Army authorized the formation of a small unit of Apache scouts that took part in Brigadier General John J. Pershing's Punitive Expedition into Mexico.

Although the success of Pershing's Apache scouts revived the idea in some quarters of forming new all-Indian units, the War Department rejected such proposals. By now, Native Americans had been successfully integrated into the army. During World War I (1914–1918), American Indians served alongside whites not only in the cavalry but also in all branches of the military.

MARK VAN DE LOGT

See also

Cavalry, U.S. Army; Custer, George Armstrong; Geronimo; Horses; Pawnees; Scouts, Native American; Watie, Stand

References

Dunlay, Thomas W. *Wolves for the Blue Soldiers: Indian Scouts and Auxiliaries with the United States Army, 1860–90.* Lincoln: University of Nebraska Press, 1982.

Ellis, Richard N. "Copper-Skinned Soldiers: The Apache Scouts." *Great Plains Journal* 5 (Spring 1966): 51–65.

Hauptman, Laurence M. *Between Two Fires: American Indians in the Civil War.* New York City: Free Press, 1995.

Roe, Frank G. *The Indian and the Horse.* Norman: University of Oklahoma Press, 1979.

Smits, David D. "'Fighting Fire with Fire': The Frontier Army's Use of Indian Scouts and Allies in the Trans-Mississippi Campaigns, 1860–1890." *American Indian Culture and Research Journal* 22(1) (1998): 73–116.

Cavalry, U.S. Army

During the Indian Wars, cavalry units of the U.S. Army served as the primary combat force against western Native American tribes. Practicing the traditional missions of reconnaissance, security, and mounted assault, cavalry units had a mixed record of battlefield success against various tribes.

In the conflicts with the Indians that followed the American Revolutionary War (1775–1783), many of the tribes of the Southeast and the Old Northwest Territory were defeated by regular infantry units. Most fighting took place in wooded areas and challenging terrain that were unsuited for cavalry actions. However, by the 1840s the conflict between the U.S. government and Native Americans shifted to the West. The California Gold Rush that began in 1848, new land acquired via the 1848 Treaty of Guadalupe Hidalgo that ended the Mexican-American War (1846–1848), and a belief in Manifest Destiny encouraged thousands of white Americans to move west. Within this context, the U.S. government was pressured to provide protection for its citizens and establish sovereignty over territories claimed by native tribes.

A series of western forts that delineated the frontier stretched from the Rio Grande in the South to the Red River in the North. In theory these posts served as lines of communication, protected western travelers, and enabled cavalry patrols to keep the Native Americans peaceful and confined to their reservations. This combination of mounted patrolling and fort construction, however, enjoyed limited success because of the vast expanses in the West.

Because mounted troops were more expensive to maintain than infantry, Congress had historically been reluctant to fund a large mounted force. Although the 1st and 2nd Dragoons were established in 1833 and 1836, respectively, and a regiment of Mounted Riflemen was established in 1846, these were used more as mounted infantry than as European-style cavalry. It was not until 1855 that the 1st and 2nd Cavalry regiments were established through the efforts of U.S. secretary of war Jefferson Davis. The 2nd Cavalry in particular gained distinction as a training ground for officers during the American Civil War (1861–1865), including in its ranks Albert Sidney Johnston, Robert E. Lee, John Bell Hood, and George H. Thomas. With the beginning of the Civil War, all mounted forces were redesignated cavalry, with the 1st and 2nd Dragoons becoming the 1st and 2nd Cavalry and the Mounted Riflemen becoming the 3rd Cavalry.

Although Congress initially set the number of cavalry regiments at 6 in the immediate aftermath of the war, in 1866 Congress voted to increase the number of regiments to 10 in order to meet the needs of Reconstruction in the South and conflict with Native Americans on the frontier. Each cavalry regiment was comprised of 12 troops (officially listed as companies prior to 1883). The 9th and 10th regiments were composed of African American enlisted men (buffalo soldiers) commanded mostly by white officers. Despite subsequent reductions in the total overall strength of the U.S. Army, the basic structure of the cavalry remained the same during the American Indian Wars of the post–Civil War era. Indeed, after George Armstrong Custer's defeat at Little Bighorn in 1876, Congress authorized an increase of 2,500 men in the army's strength in order to bolster the numbers of each cavalry troop to 100 enlisted men. In reality the actual strength of a troop was much lower, averaging just 58 men (46 privates) in 1881. Cavalry squadrons (officially listed as battalions prior to 1889) consisted of 2 or more troops and fluctuated in strength according to the needs of a campaign. With such a skeleton force stretched across frontier outposts, cavalrymen rarely assembled together as entire regiments. Consequently, the first loyalty among cavalrymen was to their fellow troopers.

The average cavalryman found army service to be routine and monotonous. The food was usually poor, the pay was low, and desertion rates were extremely high (less so in the black 9th and 10th regiments). With reenlistment rates very low, cavalry ranks were often filled with inexperienced men. Cavalrymen were usually armed with a single-shot carbine and a pistol in preference

U.S. Army Troops Assigned to Indian Duty, 1862–1865

Region	Number of Troops
Central Plains	2,500–3,500
Northern Plains	4,500–5,000
Southwest	2,500–4,000
Pacific Coast, Inland Empire, and the Great Basin	5,000–6,000

to the traditional saber, which was rarely carried in the field, and cavalry doctrine dictated that soldiers fight dismounted with a combination of controlled fire against attacking warriors. The drawn-saber and bugle-sounded charges of Hollywood almost never occurred. Frequently, sabers were boxed and stored in the supply room.

Campaigning required extensive supply trains that carried rations and extra ammunition and pulled small howitzers or sometimes Gatling guns. Even the food for the cavalry's grainfed horses had to be hauled. This long logistical tail hindered the army's mobility against Native Americans and frustrated soldiers, who soon learned that warriors refused to fight according to cavalry doctrine.

As conflicts between white settlers and Native Americans escalated, the primary mission of the cavalry was to enforce the numerous treaties signed between the government and the western tribes. When the Native Americans violated these treaties by leaving the reservation or raiding white settlements and travelers, cavalry units were dispatched to punish the guilty and force the others back onto reservations. In reality, finding villages or interdicting small bands of well-mounted warriors who fought using sudden raids and delaying tactics against ponderous army columns proved to be virtually impossible.

However, by the late 1860s army planners developed a new strategy of winter campaigning. Conditioned to camping for long months along waterways, the Native Americans stockpiled food and supplies to endure the extremely cold winter conditions of the Great Plains. Army leaders sought to take advantage of these stationary targets and were able to attack villages and destroy the Native Americans' food, shelter, clothing, and pony herds. Army leaders also sought to exploit traditional animosities between various tribes and employed Native Americans as scouts.

As the Indian Wars continued, the same scenario repeated itself in relations between the government and the tribes. Peace commissioners would renegotiate treaties and force the Native Americans onto smaller marginal tracts of land that white settlers did not want. When it became evident that the promised annuities, education, and other social services were not going to be provided, many Native Americans left the reservations and tried to continue their traditional way of life. This often precipitated armed struggle with American forces.

When gold was discovered in the Black Hills in 1874, the government tried to force the Sioux to cede that territory to the United States, although the territory had been reserved to the tribe by the

1868 Treaty of Fort Laramie. In an attempt to force the Sioux to surrender the land, the most well-known cavalryman of the time, Lieutenant Colonel George Armstrong Custer, led one of three offensive columns against the Sioux during the Great Sioux War (1876–1877). On June 25, 1876, Custer divided his regiment and with his battalion attacked a Native American encampment along the Little Bighorn River. In the ensuing action, he and his battalion of some 225 men were surrounded and killed. However, aside from the dramatic defeat of Custer, most of the fighting between U.S. Army cavalry units and Native American warriors consisted of brief small-unit engagements. Even full-scale wars typically lasted less than one year.

By 1886 the Indian Wars were practically over, and much of the U.S. Cavalry's attention was focused on defeating the Apache chief Geronimo. His small band of warriors used the southern boundary between Mexico and the United States to frustrate both governments, which sought to stop the Apaches' raiding. Eventually 6th Cavalry lieutenant Charles Gatewood and his Indian scouts located and forced Geronimo to surrender in September 1886.

By 1889 the Native Americans' traditional way of life had all but ended. Native Americans were confined on reservations and suffering from high incidences of disease, alcoholism, malnutrition, and depression. The Ghost Dance phenomenon that spread across the West promised the Native Americans salvation and a return to their ancestral lands. Concerned government authorities wanted to outlaw the dance and arrest tribal leaders who supported it. After Sitting Bull was killed on December 18, 1890, a band of Miniconjou Sioux under Chief Big Foot left the reservation, but the 7th Cavalry found and surrounded them. On December 29, 1890, the last battle of the Indian Wars occurred at Wounded Knee (South Dakota) during which an accidental rifle discharge resulted in the deaths of at least 150 Native Americans and 25 U.S. soldiers.

During the Indian Wars, regular cavalry units participated in more than 1,000 engagements and suffered more than 2,000 total battle casualties. Although defeats such as Custer's were rare, highly mobile Native American warriors proved to be capable adversaries.

DONALD L. WALKER JR. AND JUSTIN D. MURPHY

See also
Buffalo Soldiers; California Gold Rush; Cavalry, Native American; Cavalry Regiment, 4th U.S.; Cavalry Regiment, 5th U.S.; Cavalry Regiment, 6th U.S.; Cavalry Regiment, 7th U.S.; Cavalry Regiment, 8th U.S.; Cavalry Regiment, 9th U.S.; Cavalry Regiment, 10th U.S.; Custer, George Armstrong; Dragoon Regiments, 1st and 2nd; Fort Laramie, Treaty of (1868); Geronimo; Geronimo Campaign; Ghost Dance; Little Bighorn, Battle of the; Manifest Destiny; Sitting Bull; Wounded Knee, Battle of

References
Utley, Robert M. *Frontier Regulars: The United States and the American Indian, 1866–1891.* New York: Macmillan, 1973.
Utley, Robert M. *Frontiersmen in Blue: The United States and the Indian, 1848–1865.* Lincoln: University of Nebraska Press, 1967.
Utley, Robert M., and Wilcomb E. Washburn. *Indian Wars.* New York: American Heritage Press, 2002.

Cavalry Regiment, 3rd Colorado

Colorado volunteer cavalry regiment best remembered for its participation in the notorious Sand Creek Massacre of November 29, 1864. This wanton killing of peaceful Arapahos and Cheyennes was one of the most brutal in the history of the American West and helped spark some 20 years of war between Native Americans and whites in the region.

During the American Civil War (1861–1865), many of the Union garrisons were withdrawn from the western posts. Protection of settlements, trails, and mining operations became the responsibility of locally raised regiments of volunteers. The situation in Colorado was no different. During the 1850s and 1860s, gold strikes drew thousands of whites to the Colorado Territory. They forced the Cheyennes and Arapahos off their traditional lands and onto reservations, compelling the Native Americans to strike back where they could, attacking stagecoaches, wagon trains, and small groups of whites. Attacks occurred within 20 miles of Denver. Some historians estimate that during the summer of 1864, as many as 400 whites were killed in such raids.

To help protect supply lines, Governor John Evans called for a regiment of volunteers to serve for 100 days. This regiment, the 3rd Colorado Cavalry, was raised under the authority of the U.S. War Department. The men, however, were largely untrained, and many were among the worst of Denver's citizens. The regiment's commanding officer, named in October 1864, was Colonel George Shoup, who had previously served as a lieutenant in the 1st Colorado Cavalry. The regiment was not fully equipped until November because blizzards in October and early November shut down the supply routes into Denver.

At the time Colonel John Chivington, known for his hostility to Native Americans, was the federal district commander in Colorado. Chivington was determined to use the 3rd Colorado Cavalry to attack any Native Americans he could locate. Chivington ordered 2 companies stationed on the Platte River Trail to keep that supply route open. He then took the other 10 companies to Fort Lyon, located on the Arkansas River. Chivington was unable to find any Native Americans except those under Chief Black Kettle. Camped along Sand Creek 40 miles north of Fort Lyon, Black Kettle believed that he had made an agreement with U.S. authorities and that his group was under the protection of the federal government.

Chivington nevertheless decided to attack Black Kettle's camp before the regiment's enlistments expired. With about 700 men and four guns, Chivington led his men on a forced night march to Sand Creek. On the morning of November 29 they attacked Black Kettle's camp. When Black Kettle saw the soldiers, he raised a white flag and a U.S. flag given to him by Abraham Lincoln.

Chivington disregarded these flags and pressed the attack. After killing as many Native Americans as they could, the soldiers returned to the camp and mutilated the dead. At least 200 Native Americans, mostly women and children, died. Chivington was never held accountable for his actions. The 3rd Colorado Cavalry was mustered out of service on December 31, 1864, and was never reactivated.

Tim J. Watts

See also
Arapahos; Black Kettle; Cheyennes; Chivington, John; Sand Creek Massacre

References
Dunn, William R. *"I Stand by Sand Creek": A Defense of Colonel John M. Chivington and the Third Colorado Cavalry.* Fort Collins, CO: Old Army, 1985.
Scott, Robert. *Blood at Sand Creek: The Massacre Revisited.* Caldwell, ID: Claxton, 1994.

Cavalry Regiment, 4th U.S.

U.S. Army cavalry regiment that traces its lineage to the 1st Cavalry, formed in March 1855 at Jefferson Barracks near St. Louis, Missouri. Organized into 10 companies, each consisting of 50 privates plus officers and noncommissioned officers, the regiment averaged about 400 men present for duty at a given time. Posted to the West, the regiment initially operated in the Kansas and Indian (Oklahoma) territories from forts such as Cobb, Riley, Kearny, and Leavenworth.

Led by Colonel Edwin V. "Bull" Sumner, the then 1st Cavalry actively campaigned to suppress the Comanche and Cheyenne tribes in the late 1850s. Simultaneously the regiment struggled to maintain order in so-called Bleeding Kansas (1854–1856) as slavery and antislavery proponents clashed over the territory's statehood.

Following the secession of Texas from the Union in March 1861, the regiment evacuated its forts in Indian Territory and, eluding Texas troops in pursuit, concentrated at Fort Leavenworth, Kansas, at the end of the month. The U.S. War Department reorganized the army's cavalry regiments in August 1861, and the 1st Cavalry became the 4th Cavalry. The 4th Cavalry served throughout the American Civil War (1861–1865), primarily in the western theater of operations.

When the war ended in 1865, the War Department ordered the 4th Cavalry to Texas, where it reestablished federal authority from San Antonio south to the Rio Grande. In 1871 29-year-old Colonel Ranald Slidell Mackenzie assumed command. Easily the most dashing commander in the regiment's history, Mackenzie turned the 4th Cavalry into one of the finest mounted units in the army and, on commanding general William Tecumseh Sherman's orders, moved it to Fort Richardson, northwest of Fort Worth, in late January 1871. For the next several years Mackenzie's troops campaigned across western Texas and New Mexico, along the Rio Grande, and across the border into Mexico. The 4th Cavalry played a significant role in the Red River War (1874–1875), especially in the decisive Battle of Palo Duro Canyon. The regiment then moved to the northern Plains in the aftermath of the Battle of the Little

Bighorn and played a major role in suppressing the Cheyennes, defeating Dull Knife and destroying his village in November 1877. After a brief return to the Rio Grande that featured another cross-border incursion, Mackenzie and the 4th Cavalry moved to Colorado to assist in putting down the Ute uprising. The regiment then moved to Arizona, where it participated in the long Geronimo Campaign. Colonel W. B. Royall succeeded Mackenzie in 1882.

In 1883 the regimental headquarters, along with Troops B, D, and I, moved to Fort Huachuca in the Arizona Territory, while the remainder occupied scattered posts in other parts of the territory. Following Apache warrior Geronimo's raids into the Southwest, Captain Henry W. Lawton's B Troop led the pursuit to Mexico in May 1885. Following Geronimo's surrender in August 1886, Lawton personally escorted his captive to Florida.

With the Indian threat over, the 4th Cavalry relocated to Fort Walla Walla, Washington. The regiment later fought in the Philippine-American War (1899–1902) during the first year of that conflict and as the 4th Mechanized Cavalry Group in 1943 during World War II (1939–1945). Squadrons of the 4th Mechanized Cavalry Group served with different divisions during the Vietnam War (1955–1975), during Operation Desert Storm (1991), and during Operation Iraqi Freedom (2003–2010).

Stephen A. Bourque and David Coffey

See also
Comanches; Dull Knife; Geronimo; Geronimo Campaign; Great Sioux War; Kickapoos; Lawton, Henry Ware; Mackenzie, Ranald Slidell; Mackenzie's Mexico Raid; Red River War

References
Sawicki, James A. *Cavalry Regiments of the U.S. Army.* Dumfries, VA: Wyvern Publications, 1985.
Stubbs, Mary Lee, and Stanley Russell Conner. *Armor-Cavalry, Part I: Regular Army and Army Reserve.* Washington, DC.: U.S. Army Center of Military History, 1969.
Utley, Robert M. *Frontier Regulars: The United States and the American Indian, 1866–1891.* New York: Macmillan, 1973.
Utley, Robert M. *Frontiersmen in Blue: The United States and the Indian, 1848–1865.* Lincoln: University of Nebraska Press, 1967.

Cavalry Regiment, 5th U.S.

One of the finest mounted regiments in the U.S. Army. The 5th U.S. Cavalry Regiment grew out of the 2nd U.S. Cavalry Regiment, organized on May 28, 1855, in Louisville, Kentucky. It was redesignated the 5th U.S. Cavalry Regiment during the general army reorganization in 1861. In 1855 Secretary of War Jefferson Davis had handpicked the officers of the newly formed 2nd Cavalry. Among the military luminaries associated with the 2nd Cavalry were a number of future leaders during the American Civil War (1861–1865), including Robert E. Lee, Albert Sidney Johnston, and John Bell Hood. During the regiment's early service on the frontier, it participated in some 40 engagements with various Native American tribes throughout the American Southwest. Occasionally units of the regiment pursued Mexican raiders back across the Rio Grande.

With the beginning of the Civil War in 1861, the regiment was recalled from frontier service and redesignated the 5th U.S. Cavalry. The 5th Cavalry had the distinction of being present at the first major engagement of the Civil War, the First Battle of Bull Run (July 21, 1861) and the last major engagement at Appomattox Court House (April 9, 1865). In between, the 5th Cavalry took part in more than 125 battles and engagements.

During the immediate post–Civil War period, the 5th Cavalry performed occupation duty in small detachments throughout the South. In the autumn of 1868 the regiment received orders to deploy to Nebraska and Kansas to assist in policing the frontier, where it served under the capable leadership of Major Eugene Carr.

As part of Major General Philip Sheridan's campaign of 1868–1869, the regiment fought in the culminating battle at Summit Springs, Colorado. Five companies of the regiment, guided by the scout William "Buffalo Bill" Cody, pursued a band of Cheyenne Dog Soldiers led by Chief Tall Bull that had raided settlements in Colorado and Kansas. On July 11, 1869, the troops surprised the Cheyenne warriors at Summit Springs, killing 50 warriors during the brief fight and capturing another 117, including Tall Bull, with only 1 soldier wounded.

Following the disastrous defeat of the 7th Cavalry during the Battle of the Little Bighorn (June 25–26, 1876), the 5th Cavalry helped defeat the Sioux and Cheyennes. The regiment, under the command of decorated Civil War veteran Colonel Wesley Merritt, formed part of Brigadier General George Crook's force. En route to reinforce Crook, Merritt's command fought a minor skirmish with a band of Cheyennes near Hat Creek, Nebraska, now known as War Bonnet Creek, on July 17, 1876. The regiment joined Crook on August 3, 1876, and was present during September 9–10, 1876, at Slim Buttes, Montana, the first significant clash with Native Americans since the Battle of the Little Bighorn.

One of the last major engagements for the 5th Cavalry during the Indian Wars came during the Ute War on September 29, 1879, along Milk Creek in Colorado. A force of 300–400 Ute warriors had trapped elements of the 4th Infantry and the 5th Cavalry, under the command of Major Thomas Thornburgh, along the creek. Thornburgh's band held out for eight days until Merritt arrived with the remainder of the regiment to lift the siege. For this action, 11 5th Cavalry troops received the Medal of Honor.

At the conclusion of the Indian Wars, the 5th Cavalry Regiment returned to constabulary duties on the frontier. The regiment next saw action during the Spanish-American War (1898).

M. R. Pierce

See also

Carr, Eugene Asa; Cheyennes; Cody, William Frederick; Crook, George; Dog Soldiers; Little Bighorn, Battle of the; Merritt, Wesley; Milk Creek, Battle of; Sheridan, Philip Henry; Slim Buttes, Battle of; Summit Springs, Battle of; Tall Bull; Utes; Ute War

References

Ferris, Robert, ed. *Soldier and Brave: Historic Places Associated with Indian Affairs and Indian Wars in the Trans-Mississippi West.* Washington DC: United States Department of the Interior, 1971.

Sawicki, James A. *Cavalry Regiments of the U.S. Army.* Dumfries, VA: Wyvern Publications, 1985.

Utley, Robert M. *The Indian Frontier of the American West, 1846–1890.* Albuquerque: University of New Mexico Press, 1984.

Yenne, Bill, *Indian Wars: The Campaign for the American West.* Yardley, PA: Westholme Publishing, 2006.

Cavalry Regiment, 6th U.S.

One of the most productive and well-regarded mounted units of the Indian Wars. The 6th U.S. Cavalry Regiment began as the 3rd Cavalry Regiment by presidential proclamation in May 1861 at the start of the American Civil War (1861–1865) and was redesignated the 6th Cavalry in August 1861. Recruits came primarily from Pennsylvania, Ohio, and parts of New York. The regiment first saw action in the Civil War during the Peninsula Campaign of March–August 1862 as part of the Army of the Potomac. During the 1863 Battle of Chancellorsville, the regiment participated in a major raid behind Confederate lines led by Major General George Stoneman. The 6th Regiment ended the Civil War as part of the Union force that defeated the Confederate forces of the Army of Northern Virginia in the Battle of Sayler's Creek on April 6, 1865.

Following the war, the regiment was sent west. Detachments of the 6th Cavalry were stationed at small forts throughout the Department of Texas from 1865 to 1871. The 6th Regiment became increasingly involved in peacekeeping between the Texans and the Kiowa and Comanche tribes. By 1871 after increasing numbers of clashes with local tribes, the regiment's primary mission became pacification of the Native Americans.

In July 1874 the 6th Cavalry formed part of a five-pronged pincer movement converging in the Texas Panhandle to subdue the Kiowas and Comanches. During this campaign, known as the Red River War (1874–1875), Civil War veteran Colonel Nelson A. Miles commanded the eight companies of the 6th Cavalry.

One memorable fight occurred during September 12–14, 1874, at Buffalo Wallow in the Texas Panhandle. Miles, short on supplies, sent out a 6-man patrol to locate his missing supply column. En route 125 warriors surrounded the patrol, which was commanded by Sergeant Zachariah Woodall. The troops held out for a day and a half before a relief column arrived; all members of the patrol subsequently received the Medal of Honor. Shortly thereafter the regiment transferred to Arizona, where it would spend the next decade guarding or pursuing renegade Apaches such as Victorio and Geronimo. In 1879 Colonel Eugene A. Carr took command of the regiment, and under Carr the 6th Cavalry became one of the most effective units in the army.

A member of the 6th Cavalry Regiment poses on horseback at Fort Niobrara, Nebraska, circa 1886. (Denver Public Library, Western History Collection, NS-83)

In September 1880 the 6th Cavalry formed part of a joint force of American and Mexican cavalry dispatched to capture Apache chief Victorio. After a long and arduous pursuit through northern Mexico, the Mexican cavalry cornered and killed the Apache chief. In 1881 during the opening stages of what became known as the Geronimo Campaign, elements of the 6th Cavalry were caught in a desperate situation when Carr's Apache scouts mutinied at Cibecue Creek. After the trouble at Cibecue, the 6th Cavalry returned to its base at Fort Apache, where it had to fight off a rare Indian attack on a military post. In July 1882 Captain Adna Chaffee's company of the 6th Cavalry defeated a band of White Mountain Apaches in the Battle of Big Dry Wash. Chaffee's troop also accompanied Brigadier General George Crook into Mexico in May 1883, while Lieutenant Charles Gatewood of the 6th Cavalry led a detachment of Indian scouts on an expedition that netted Geronimo's surrender. When Geronimo and others fled the reservation again in 1885, the 6th Cavalry once more joined the pursuit, and Gatewood secured Geronimo's final surrender in 1886.

One of the final engagements for the 6th Cavalry in the Indian Wars occurred on January 1, 1891, as one of the events related to the Battle of Wounded Knee when two companies of the regiment defeated an undetermined number of Lakota Sioux near the mouth of Little Salt Grass Creek along the White River.

At the conclusion of the Indian Wars, the 6th Cavalry returned to frontier constabulary duties. The 6th Cavalry next saw action in the Spanish-American War (1898) when it served alongside the Rough Riders in the Battle of San Juan Hill.

M. R. PIERCE AND DAVID COFFEY

See also

Apaches; Carr, Eugene Asa; Chaffee, Adna Romanza, Sr.; Cibecue Creek, Incident at; Comanches; Gatewood, Charles Bare; Geronimo; Kiowas; Miles, Nelson Appleton; Red River War; Sioux; Victorio; Wounded Knee, Battle of

References

Ferris, Robert, ed. *Soldier and Brave: Historic Places Associated with Indian Affairs and Indian Wars in the Trans-Mississippi West.* Washington DC: United States Department of the Interior, 1971.

Sawicki, James A. *Cavalry Regiments of the U.S. Army.* Dumfries, VA: Wyvern Publications, 1985.

Utley, Robert M. *The Indian Frontier of the American West, 1846–1890.* Albuquerque: University of New Mexico Press, 1984.

Yenne, Bill. *Indian Wars: The Campaign for the American West.* Yardley, PA: Westholme Publishing, 2006.

Cavalry Regiment, 7th U.S.

U.S. cavalry unit involved in two of the most infamous events of the Indian Wars—the Battle of the Washita (November 27, 1868) and the Battle of Wounded Knee (December 29, 1890)—and perhaps the most identifiable defeat suffered by the U.S. Army, the Battle of the Little Bighorn (June 25–26, 1876). Constituted on July 28, 1866, the 7th U.S. Cavalry Regiment was formally organized at Fort Riley, Kansas, on September 21, 1866. Although Colonel A. J. Smith originally headed the regiment, for most of its first 10 years actual command fell to Lieutenant Colonel George A. Custer, a hero of the American Civil War (1861–1865). The 7th Cavalry was organized as a regiment containing 12 companies, with 4 companies per battalion (renamed squadrons in 1883).

Cavalry troops were armed with .45-caliber revolvers and single-shot Springfield carbines. The 7th Cavalry was unusual in that it also had a band. The outfit was nicknamed "Garryowen" after it adopted the Irish quick-step tune of the same name as the official song of the regiment. This same tune was later adopted by the 1st Cavalry Division in 1981.

The 7th Cavalry was posted to Fort Riley from 1866 to 1871 and participated in three notable campaigns during that period, mostly against the Southern Cheyennes, including the November 1868 strike into Indian Territory (Oklahoma) that featured the Battle of the Washita River, which is sometimes referred to as the Washita Massacre. Attacking the village of Cheyenne chief Black Kettle at dawn on a freezing morning, Custer's troops devastated the village, indiscriminately killing dozens of women and children.

But the campaign was considered a success and restored Custer to prominence.

From 1871 to 1873 the regiment was assigned to Reconstruction duty in the South and was divided among several posts performing various constabulary duties. The regiment was charged primarily with enforcing federal tax laws and suppressing Ku Klux Klan activities in Alabama, Georgia, Kentucky, North Carolina, and South Carolina.

In 1873 the 7th Cavalry was moved to Fort Abraham Lincoln (near present-day Bismarck) in the Dakota Territory. The next year the unit carried out a reconnaissance of the Black Hills and made its discovery of gold public. The ensuing gold rush precipitated the Great Sioux War (1876–1877) with the Lakota tribe and its allies. As the spearhead of a massive punitive campaign, the 7th Cavalry suffered a spectacular defeat at the hands of the Lakotas and Northern Cheyennes at the Battle of the Little Bighorn. During the fight, Custer was killed along with 241 soldiers. Surviving troops under Major Marcus Reno and Captain Frederick Benteen were eventually rescued, but the regiment was crippled for months to come. Two dozen soldiers from the unit earned the Medal of Honor for their actions during the battle. The next year the 7th Cavalry participated in the Nez Perce War, serving under Colonel Nelson Miles in the Battle of Bear Paw Mountain (September 30–October 5, 1877). That fight led to the surrender of most of Chief Joseph's Nez Perce warriors.

The 7th Cavalry completed its controversial participation in the Indian Wars with the tragic Battle of Wounded Knee on December 29, 1890. Sent to the Pine Ridge Reservation to quell a potential uprising related to the Ghost Dance movement and escort a band of Lakotas back to their agency, the regiment under Colonel James Forsyth instead accidentally precipitated a slaughter when efforts to disarm the Indians went terribly wrong. At least 150 Lakotas perished in the melee, and another 50 were wounded. The 7th Cavalry lost 25 men killed and 39 wounded.

After the Indian Wars, the 7th Cavalry continued to serve with distinction in the Mexican Expedition (1916–1917), World War II

An illustration of a Sioux attack on a company of the 7th Cavalry Regiment on June 24, 1867. (Library of Congress)

(1939–1945), the Korean War (1950–1953), and the Vietnam War (1965–1973) and, more recently, in the Middle East.

ANDREW BYERS AND DAVID COFFEY

See also

Bear Paw Mountains, Battle of; Benteen, Frederick William; Custer, George Armstrong; Great Sioux War; Joseph, Chief; Little Bighorn, Battle of the; Miles, Nelson Appleton; Nez Perces; Nez Perce War; Reno, Marcus Albert; Washita, Battle of the; Wounded Knee, Battle of

References

Utley, Robert M., and Wilcomb E. Washburn. *Indian Wars.* New York: American Heritage Press, 2002.

Yenne, Bill. *Indian Wars: The Campaign for the American West.* Yardley, PA: Westholme Publishing, 2006.

Cavalry Regiment, 8th U.S.

In response to the growing problems in policing the frontier, the U.S. Congress authorized the formation of additional cavalry regiments after the American Civil War (1861–1865). The 8th U.S. Cavalry Regiment was thus organized on September 21, 1866, at Angel Island, California. Colonel J. Irvin Gregg, a proven cavalry officer and Civil War veteran, commanded the new regiment.

Once assembled and trained, the 8th Cavalry Regiment deployed to the Arizona Territory and immediately waged campaigns against the Yavapai and Hualapai tribes. During the period April 10–18, 1867, two companies of the 8th Cavalry based at Fort Whipple near Prescott, Arizona, killed 53 Yavapais in four separate engagements, losing just 1 trooper. Throughout the summer of 1867 and into the winter of 1868, the 8th Cavalry continuously faced the Yavapais and Hualapais. Dozens of Native Americans died in these engagements, with minimal losses to the 8th Cavalry.

As hostilities with the Yavapais and Hualapais subsided, a new enemy appeared, the Apaches. The Apaches' tactics of small guerrilla raids posed a different threat to U.S. forces, and there were few large-scale engagements. Most battles were in fact skirmishes between handfuls of troops and warriors. However small these engagements, they nonetheless netted a significant number of Medals of Honor for members of the 8th Cavalry. Between April 1868 and November 1869, 41 troopers of the regiment received the coveted award.

By 1871, an uneasy truce existed between the settlers and the Apaches. However, by the end of that year, with the truce broken, the 8th Cavalry returned to the field. It took two more years of hard campaigning under Brigadier General George Crook to broker another truce.

I Troop of the 8th U.S. Cavalry Regiment at Fort Meade, South Dakota, in 1889. Photo by John Grabill. (Library of Congress)

In 1874 the 8th Cavalry returned to action, this time against the Kiowas and Comanches. This struggle came to be known as the Red River War (1874–1875), during which elements of the 8th Cavalry, commanded by Major William Price, formed the western element of a five-pronged assault converging in the Texas Panhandle along the Red River. The campaign began in late August. In early September elements of the regiment linked up with Colonel Nelson Miles's beleaguered force on the Llano Estacado (Staked Plains), straddling the Texas–New Mexico border. After departing on September 12, a combined force of Kiowas and Comanches ambushed the column containing members of the 8th Cavalry along with Miles's men. The surrounded troops fought off the warriors for several hours before the attackers withdrew. The Red River War ended with the surrender of Comanche chief Quanah Parker on June 2, 1875.

With the end of the Red River War, the 8th Cavalry returned to constabulary duties throughout the Southwest. In May 1888 with an influx of settlers into the Department of Dakota, the regiment relocated to parts of South Dakota and Montana. This deployment required the regiment to march 2,600 miles to its new posts, the longest march by a cavalry regiment in the history of the U.S. Army. At the conclusion of the Indian Wars, the 8th Cavalry returned to constabulary duties on the frontier. The regiment next saw action in 1898 during the Spanish-American War.

M. R. Pierce

See also

Apaches; Comanches; Crook, George; Hualapais; Kiowas; Miles, Nelson
    Appleton; Quanah Parker; Red River War; Yavapais

References

Ferris, Robert, ed. *Soldier and Brave: Historic Places Associated with Indian Affairs and Indian Wars in the Trans-Mississippi West.* Washington DC: United States Department of the Interior, 1971.
Sawicki, James A. *Cavalry Regiments of the U.S. Army.* Dumfries, VA: Wyvern Publications, 1985.
Utley, Robert M. *The Indian Frontier of the American West, 1846–1890.* Albuquerque: University of New Mexico Press, 1984.
Yenne, Bill. *Indian Wars: The Campaign for the American West.* Yardley, PA: Westholme Publishing, 2006.

Cavalry Regiment, 9th U.S.

African American cavalry regiment commanded by white officers, with other African American units known as the buffalo soldiers. In August 1866 commander of the Military Division of the Gulf, Major General Philip Sheridan, obtained authorization from the War Department to raise an African American cavalry regiment. On September 21, 1866, at Greenville, Louisiana, the 9th U.S. Cavalry Regiment was created under the command of Colonel Edward Hatch, who had risen to brevet major general during the American Civil War (1861–1865). Following training, in June 1867 the regiment transferred to Texas to begin peacekeeping duties in the Southwest.

On September 14, 1868, the 9th Cavalry fought a major battle against a band of Apaches that had attacked a wagon train. During the ensuing fight, known as the Battle of Horsehead Hill, 9th Cavalry troops suffered only minor casualties while killing more than two dozen Apaches. These losses temporarily crippled this band of Native Americans.

Between 1869 and 1874 nearly all of western Texas was a war zone, pitting the U.S. Army against the Kiowa and Comanche tribes. The 9th Cavalry, constantly in the thick of battle, fought several significant engagements with the Native Americans. Two of the more notable battles occurred in September and October 1869. On September 16, 1869, four companies of the 9th Cavalry came across a Native American encampment of 200 lodges. During the ensuing assault, there were more than 20 Native American casualties to just 3 wounded troops. A month later, on October 28, a band of more than 500 Kiowa and Comanche warriors ambushed some 200 troops along the Brazos River. Badly outnumbered, the troops nevertheless repulsed several attacks while sustaining only minor casualties themselves.

In 1874 the regiment returned to constabulary duties until 1877, when the charismatic Apache chief Victorio led nearly 300 members of his tribe off its reservation. For the next three years

A photograph of an unidentified African American soldier of the 9th Cavalry Regiment in 1870. Note the marksman badge, sharpshooter medal, and kepi with crossed sabres. (Getty Images)

the 9th Cavalry, along with much of the rest of the U.S. Army in the Southwest, attempted to subdue Victorio and his followers. The conflict that resulted began on September 4, 1877, when Victorio raided an army post near Ojo Caliente, New Mexico, leaving 5 soldiers and 3 civilians dead. Victorio then led the cavalry on a fruitless chase through the harsh terrain of the Southwest. On numerous occasions the 9th Cavalry, along with other army units, had isolated Victorio and his band. Yet the elusive chief always managed to escape. Victorio was also causing problems for the Mexican government, and in the autumn of 1880 a joint force of U.S. and Mexican cavalry sought to put an end to Victorio. On October 16, 1880, Mexican militia finally cornered and killed Victorio in the state of Chihuahua.

At the conclusion of the Indian Wars, the 9th Cavalry returned to constabulary duties on the frontier. During its campaigns on the frontier, 11 9th Cavalry troops earned Medals of Honor for gallantry, more than any other African American regiment. The regiment next saw action during the Spanish-American War in 1898 alongside Theodore Roosevelt's Rough Riders.

M. R. PIERCE

See also

Apaches; Buffalo Soldiers; Comanches; Hatch, Edward; Kiowas; Sheridan, Philip Henry; Victorio

References

Ferris, Robert, ed. *Soldier and Brave: Historic Places Associated with Indian Affairs and Indian Wars in the Trans-Mississippi West.* Washington DC: United States Department of the Interior, 1971.

Leckie, William H., and Shirley A. Leckie. *The Buffalo Soldiers: A Narrative of the Black Cavalry in the West.* Norman: University of Oklahoma Press, 2003.

Sawicki, James A. *Cavalry Regiments of the U.S. Army.* Dumfries, VA: Wyvern Publications, 1985.

Utley, Robert M. *The Indian Frontier of the American West, 1846–1890.* Albuquerque: University of New Mexico Press, 1984.

Yenne, Bill. *Indian Wars: The Campaign for the American West.* Yardley, PA: Westholme Publishing, 2006.

Cavalry Regiment, 10th U.S.

African American cavalry regiment commanded by white officers. Troops in this and other African American units in the West were known as buffalo soldiers. The 10th U.S. Cavalry was organized on September 21, 1866, at Fort Leavenworth, Kansas, under the command of Colonel Benjamin H. Grierson, a celebrated veteran of the American Civil War (1861–1865). Because of the high enlistment standards established by Grierson, it took more than a year to fully man the regiment. Transferring to Fort Riley, Kansas, in August 1867, the regiment spent the next eight years in Kansas and the Indian Territory (present-day Oklahoma). As part of Major General Philip Sheridan's winter campaign of 1868, the 10th Cavalry fought numerous battles against Cheyenne,

Comanche, and Kiowa warriors. The regiment saw action in the 1874 Red River War, when it contributed to the five-pronged pincer action to trap the Native Americans along the Red River in the Texas Panhandle.

In 1875 the 10th Cavalry, now headquartered at Fort Concho in western Texas, began patrolling mail routes and guarding the Texas-Mexico border. Troops of the regiment scouted thousands of miles of the harsh desolate territory, opening hundreds of miles of roads and stringing some 200 miles of telegraph line. While the 10th Cavalry's efforts eased white expansion into the Southwest, this expansion inevitably increased friction between settlers and Native Americans. These events culminated in 1877 when U.S. and Mexican forces launched a concerted effort to pursue and capture the Apache war chief Victorio.

Shortly after leading 300 of his followers off their reservation, Victorio began hostilities with a raid on an army post on September 4, 1877, that left 5 soldiers and 3 civilians dead. Over the next three years, the 10th Cavalry was heavily involved in the long and arduous campaign to apprehend Victorio. On three separate occasions Grierson set traps for Victorio, but each time the chief eluded capture. Eventually a combined effort by the United States and Mexico defeated Victorio, with Mexican irregulars cornering and killing Victorio on October 16, 1880.

Following the death of Victorio, a new chief, Geronimo, led the recalcitrant Apaches, and the 10th Cavalry was in action again. Geronimo proved as evasive as Victorio. Indeed, six long years passed before Geronimo surrendered on September 4, 1886, at Fort Bowie, Arizona. However, Geronimo's capture did not end the conflict with the Apaches.

Four years later elements of the 10th Cavalry fought an engagement on the Salt River in the Arizona Territory. On March 7, 1890, after a 250-mile pursuit, K Company of the 10th Cavalry along with a detachment from the 4th Cavalry nabbed a renegade band of Apaches who had killed a Mormon freighter. During the action, Sergeant William McBryar's coolness and bravery under fire earned him the Medal of Honor.

From 1891 to 1898, the 10th Cavalry served at various posts throughout Montana and the Dakotas as part of the Department of Dakota. The 10th Cavalry's next action came during the Spanish-American War (1898) alongside Theodore Roosevelt's Rough Riders at San Juan Hill.

M. R. PIERCE

See also

Apaches; Buffalo Soldiers; Cavalry Regiment, 9th U.S.; Cheyennes; Comanches; Geronimo; Grierson, Benjamin Henry; Kiowas; Red River War; Sheridan, Philip Henry; Victorio

References

Ferris, Robert, ed. *Soldier and Brave: Historic Places Associated with Indian Affairs and Indian Wars in the Trans-Mississippi West.* Washington DC: United States Department of the Interior, 1971.

Leckie, William H., and Shirley A. Leckie. *The Buffalo Soldiers: A Narrative of the Black Cavalry in the West.* Norman: University of Oklahoma Press, 2003.

Drawing by Frederic Remington of the Buffalo Soldiers of the 10th Cavalry Regiment, 1886. (Library of Congress)

Sawicki, James A. *Cavalry Regiments of the U.S. Army.* Dumfries, VA: Wyvern Publications, 1985.

Utley, Robert M. *The Indian Frontier of the American West, 1846–1890.* Albuquerque: University of New Mexico Press, 1984.

Cayugas

Tribe of Native Americans who traditionally occupied the Northeast Culture Area and were a part of the Iroquoian language group. The Cayugas were one of the five original tribes of the Iroquois Confederacy. In pre-European society, Cayuga hunting territory was largely located in present-day New York state and Ontario, particularly in the Finger Lakes District (Cayuga Lake still bears their name).

Traditionally the Senecas were located to the west of the homelands of the Cayugas and the Onondagas. In 1660 after disease had decimated the Cayugas, their population was reported to have been only 1,500. As a member of the Iroquois Confederacy, the Cayuga tribe played a fundamental part in colonial warfare in North America.

There is some speculation about the precise definition of the word "Cayuga," but it has been reported to mean "where the boats were taken out," "where the locusts were taken out," or "mucky land," all of which refer to the lands that the tribe traditionally occupied. Their name in the Iroquois Confederacy council, however, alludes to them as "those of the great pipe."

The Cayugas operated on a system of matrilineal descent, with the matron of each clan appointing a spokesman (or chief) for the clan. Accordingly, Cayuga women were politically powerful and influential. Generally, Cayuga males spent much time away from their tribe hunting, fishing, trading, and fighting. The women remained in the village and provided sustenance by raising crops for the remaining tribe members. Corn was their main staple, but squash, pumpkins, and beans were also grown. Cayuga villages usually consisted of 20 to 50 longhouses that sheltered 15 to 30 people each.

Although the Cayugas were small in number and territory, they had great clout in the Iroquois Confederacy. They sent 10 chiefs (or sachems) to the council of 50 chiefs and were a fierce fighting force within the confederacy. From 1667 to 1684 they were constantly engaged in the Beaver Wars (1641–1701) with neighboring tribes and became involved in European conflicts as well. The Cayugas were officially neutral during the French and Indian War (1754–1763) but generally fought with the French. During the American Revolutionary War (1775–1783) the Cayugas sided with the British and lost all their traditional homelands in the aftermath. After the American Revolution, many Cayugas moved onto reserve land in Ontario that the British set aside for the Six Nations of the Iroquois Confederacy. This had been one of the results of the 1784 Treaty of Fort Stanwix, which had expressly established Iroquois territorial boundaries.

By 1807 the Cayugas had temporarily abandoned their New York land claims, and most lived among the Senecas on their reservation. Others went to the Ohio Country to live among Iroquois groups there. During the War of 1812, the Cayugas living in Ohio, along with their Iroquoian allies, fought on the American side against the British. In the aftermath of the 1830 Indian Removal Act, the remaining Cayugas in Ohio and elsewhere were relocated to Indian Territory (Oklahoma). Today the language of the Cayugas is still spoken, and many Cayugas continue to live in Ontario on reserve land. As a tribe the Cayugas have never given up their land claims in New York, and they have a strong case because their treaties were negotiated by state officials rather than by federal representatives after the American Revolution. The Cayuga land claims are still being negotiated by courts in the United States.

TAKAIA LARSEN

See also

Beaver Wars; Indian Removal Act; Iroquois; Iroquois Confederacy; Iroquois Treaties of 1700 and 1701; Longhouse; Senecas

References

Fenton, William N. *The Great Law and the Longhouse: A Political History of the Iroquois Confederacy.* Norman: University of Oklahoma Press, 1998.

Richter, Daniel K. *The Ordeal of the Longhouse: The People of the Iroquois League in the Era of European Colonization.* Chapel Hill: University of North Carolina Press, 1992.

Speck, Frank G. *Midwinter Rites of the Cayuga Long House.* Lincoln: University of Nebraska Press, 1995.

Wait, Mary Van Sickle, and Will Heidt Jr. *The Story of the Cayugas.* Ithaca, NY: De Witt Historical Society of Tompkins County, 1966.

Centennial Campaign

See Great Sioux War

Chacato Troubles

Start Date: 1674
End Date: 1676

Native American rebellion against Spanish missionaries. During 1674–1680 the Spanish established two missions, San Carlos de Chacatos and San Nicolas de Tolentino, under the auspices of

fathers Rodrigo de la Barreda and Miguel de Valverde in present-day Jackson County, Florida. The missions were part of an effort to convert the Chacato (Chatot) tribe to Christianity. The Chacatos are believed to have been related to the Choctaws.

In 1674 a few months after the establishment of the missions, the Chisca (Yuchi) tribe, which lived nearby, began to incite a rebellion among the Chacatos against the missionaries. A force of Spanish soldiers under the command of Captain Juan Fernandez de Florencia, deputy governor of Apalachee Province, was sent to quell the uprising. Florencia was successful in ending the disturbance, and the mission work continued peacefully.

However, when the Spanish soldiers withdrew in late 1674, the Chacatos once again revolted and completely destroyed the missions of San Carlos and San Nicolas. The missionaries, urgently seeking help, fled to the mission of Santa Cruz de Sabacola. As a result of the second uprising, Florencia returned to the Chacatos' tribal lands in 1676 with a large force of Spanish soldiers and mission natives from Apalachee Province. Convinced that the Chiscas were again responsible for the Chacatos' latest rebellion, Florencia crossed the Choctawhatchee River and attacked a Chisca village, killing hundreds of people. After the removal of the Chiscas, the Chacatos were relocated eastward to the vicinity of present-day Sneads, where in 1680 a new mission known as Señor San Carlos de Chacatos was established among them.

In 1696, however, this new mission became the focus of hostilities between the Spanish and the Native Americans to the north in what are now Alabama and Georgia. Several of the Chacatos were killed, and others were carried away as captives. The few survivors fled to the region of San Luis (Tallahassee), then to the French settlements near Mobile, and later to Texas and Oklahoma. As a result, the Chacatos disappeared as a people in the early 1700s.

KATJA WUESTENBECKER

See also

Apalachees; Choctaws; Spain

References

McEwan, Bonnie G., ed. *The Spanish Missions of La Florida.* Gainesville: University Press of Florida, 1993.

Milanich, Jerald T. *Laboring in the Fields of the Lord: Spanish Missions and Southeastern Indians.* Washington, DC: Smithsonian Institution Press, 1999.

Chaffee, Adna Romanza, Sr.

Birth Date: April 14, 1842
Death Date: November 1, 1914

U.S. Army officer. Born on April 14, 1842, in Orwell, Ohio, Adna Romanza Chaffee Sr. served in the army from 1861 to 1906. During this time he took part in the American Civil War (1861–1865), the Indian Wars, the Spanish-American War (1898), and the 1900 Boxer Rebellion. At the outset of the Civil War, he enlisted in the Union Army. On July 22, 1861, he was assigned to the 6th Cavalry

Adna Romanza Chaffee's 45-year army career included three decades of exemplary service on the Great Plains and in the Southwest. Chaffee was chief of staff of the army during 1904–1906 as a lieutenant general. (Library of Congress)

Regiment as a private, and he would remain with the same regiment for more than a quarter century. He won promotion to sergeant for his performance in the 1862 Peninsula Campaign. He fought in the bloody Battle of Antietam (September 17, 1862) and in May 1863 was commissioned a second lieutenant. Wounded at the Battle of Gettysburg (July 1–3, 1863), he narrowly escaped capture. In February 1865 Chaffee was commissioned a first lieutenant, and because of his valor at the Battle of Dinwiddie Court House on March 31, 1865, he was brevetted captain.

Chaffee remained in the army following the war. Promoted to captain in 1867, he was posted to Fort Griffin in north-central Texas in 1868. In March 1868 he won a brevet to major following an engagement against the Comanches at Paint Creek, Texas. For three decades he fought in a series of Indian conflicts on the Great Plains and in the Southwest against Cheyennes, Comanches, Kiowas, and Apaches, including the Red River War (1874–1875) and Geronimo Campaign (1881–1886). Chaffee also proved an able and humane Indian agent. He amassed one of the more impressive service records in the frontier army, but the fact that he remained a captain for more than 20 years offers a graphic example of the impossibly slow pace of promotion in the post–Civil War army.

In 1888 Chaffee was finally promoted to major and transferred to the 9th Cavalry Regiment. In 1894 he was assigned to Fort Leavenworth, where he taught military tactics for two years. Chaffee was transferred to the 3rd Cavalry Regiment in 1897 and promoted to lieutenant colonel.

Following the outbreak of war with Spain in April 1898, Chaffee was promoted to brigadier general of U.S. Volunteers and assumed command of a brigade of volunteers in May. Following his important role in the U.S. victory in the Battle of El Caney on July 1, 1898, he was promoted to major general of volunteers. In May 1899 he was promoted to colonel in the regular army and assigned to the 8th Cavalry Regiment. From the conclusion of the Spanish-American War to May 1900, Chaffee served as chief of staff to Major General Leonard Wood, U.S. military governor of Cuba.

In July 1900 Chaffee was assigned to command the U.S. China Relief Expedition, a force of 2,500 men charged with relieving the foreign legations at Beijing during the Boxer Rebellion. Promoted to major general in the regular army in 1901, from July to October 1902 Chaffee served as military governor of the Philippines during the latter part of the Philippine-American War (1899–1902). Returning to the United States, he commanded the Department of the East from October 1902 to October 1903. Promoted to lieutenant general in January 1904, he then served as army chief of staff during 1904–1906. In that position he implemented significant organizational reforms. Chaffee retired from active duty in February 1906 and died of typhoid on November 1, 1914, in Los Angeles, California.

MICHAEL R. HALL

See also

Apaches; Cavalry Regiment, 6th U.S.; Cheyennes; Comanches; Kiowas

References

Barr, Ronald J. *The Progressive Army: US Army Command and Administration, 1870–1914.* New York: St. Martin's, 1998.

Carter, William H. *The Life of Lieutenant General Chaffee.* Chicago: University of Chicago Press, 1917.

Champlain, Samuel de
Birth Date: July 3, 1567
Death Date: December 25, 1635

French explorer, writer, cartographer, colonizer, governor of New France, and founder of Quebec. Born in Brouage, southeast of Rochefort, France, on July 3, 1567, Samuel de Champlain was the son of a ship's captain. Champlain was briefly educated by parish priests and spent several years working aboard his father's ship. He then became a billeting officer for the French Army (1594–1598) and served on chartered French ships carrying cargo to and from the West Indies from 1599 to 1601.

Champlain's time in the West Indies fueled his curiosity about the New World, and upon his return to France he was appointed a royal geographer. In 1603 he journeyed to Canada with noted explorer Francis Grave Sieur du Pont Pontgravé, who established a trading post at Tadoussac. Champlain then traveled up the Saint Lawrence River to the Lachine Rapids before returning to Tadoussac and embarking with Pontgravé for France.

Champlain returned to Canada in 1604 in an expedition headed by Pierre Du Gua de Monts to Acadia and helped found St. Croix in 1604 and Port Royal in 1605. Having learned from the established explorers of his day, Champlain mapped New England as far south as Martha's Vineyard (Massachusetts). He returned to France in 1607.

In 1608 Champlain returned to North America with 32 colonists to found a fur-trading outpost at Quebec. There he built upon the work of Jacques Cartier and allied himself with the local Huron (Wyandot) and Algonquin tribes. Champlain twice assisted the Hurons in defeating their rivals, the Iroquois, during 1609–1610, leading to 150 years of hostility between the Iroquois and the French.

In 1612 Champlain was appointed commandant of New France. He regularly traveled to France (making 21 Atlantic crossings between 1603 and 1633) and promoted trade, exploration, missionary work, and military alliances with the Native Americans. Champlain carried the first Recollet and Jesuit missionaries to New France in 1615 and 1625, respectively, and pushed for agricultural colonization to diminish dependence on the fur trade. He hoped that increased self-sufficiency would render New France better able to compete with English colonies to the south.

Champlain also conducted a series of explorations that made clear the vast extent and military importance of many of North America's most important waterways. He made the first ascent by a European of the water route between the Saint Lawrence River and the Hudson River, and in 1609 he discovered the lake that bears his name. Champlain made the first European traverse of the Ottawa River to the head of Lake Huron and then to Lake Ontario in 1613, and in 1615 he finally reached Georgian Bay. Champlain kept meticulous maps and journals of each expedition and then published his findings in a series of books. These detailed accounts dramatically increased French (as well as English) interest in Canada.

English forces captured Quebec from Champlain after a year-long siege in 1629. When the city was ceded back to France in the Treaty of St. Germain-en-Laye in March 1632, Champlain returned despite the fact that he was already 65 years old. Appointed governor of New France by King Louis XIII in 1633, Champlain inaugurated a period of expansion, founding settlements at Beauport and at Trois Rivières in 1634. He also reestablished Jesuit missionaries among the Hurons.

Champlain died in Quebec on December 25, 1635. He is buried there in the Church of Notre-Dame de la Recouvrance and is remembered as the founder of French Canada. There is a large statue of Champlain in the Old City.

LANCE JANDA

See also

Algonquins; France; Iroquois; Trois-Rivières; Wyandots

References

Litalian, Raymonde, and Denis Vaugeois, eds. *Champlain: The Birth of French America.* Translated by Kathe Roth. Montreal: McGill-Queen's University Press, 2005.

Morison, Samuel Eliot. *Samuel de Champlain: Father of New France.* New York: Little, Brown, 1972.

Cheroenhakas

See Nottoways

Cherokee Alphabet

An 86-character syllabary that captures the 86 syllables of the spoken Cherokee language. Sequoyah, a Cherokee also known by the English name of George Gist, invented the Cherokee alphabet sometime between 1815 and 1821. The written syllabary that he developed enabled the Cherokees to become a literate culture that possessed the ability to disseminate oral tradition and tribal history as well as to conduct business, communicate written laws, and inform tribal members of events not only between widely separated tribal groups in an age of limited transportation but also to subsequent generations. This written culture allowed the Cherokees to promote tribal unity and harmony while also adapting to cultural and political challenges brought about by increased contact with European settlers.

Sequoyah, a trader, silversmith, and sometime blacksmith, was born in Tennessee around 1760 and fought alongside the Americans in the War of 1812. His invention assigned a unique symbol for each of the 86 syllables that he identified within his native language. This system was easy to teach and to learn, and the written language spread rapidly after 1821. As early as 1808, the Cherokees had developed a legal code that was now easily communicated in their native language using the syllabary. By 1827 the Cherokees were publishing a newspaper, the *Cherokee Phoenix,* that they were able to disseminate among the geographically disparate villages in their homelands of Tennessee, North Carolina, and Georgia and to tribal members known as the Old Settlers who had previously removed to present-day Arkansas. One of the early uses of the alphabet was to translate the Bible into written Cherokee. An 1828 treaty between the Old Settlers and the U.S. government officially recognized Sequoyah's accomplishment with the promise of a $500 payment. Sequoyah lived in Indian Territory until about 1842, when he traveled to Mexico to visit a remote band of Cherokees. Companions reported his death to tribal officials in 1845, although it is believed that he died some two years earlier.

The invention of the syllabary gave the Cherokees the ability to organize tribal affairs, communicate over long distances, record

Cherokee Alphabet

Sounds represented by vowels.

a as _a_ in _father_ or short as _a_ in _rival_
e as _a_ in _hate_ or short as _e_ in _met_
i as _i_ in _pique_ or short as _i_ in _pit_

o as _aw_ in _law_ or short as _o_ in _not_
u as _oo_ in _fool_ or short as _u_ in _pull_
v as _u_ in _but_, nasalized.

Consonant Sounds.

g nearly as in English, but approaching to k. d nearly as in English, but approaching to t. h, k, l, m, n, q, s, t, w, y, as in English.
Syllables beginning with g, except ꮟ have sometimes the power of k, ꭲ, ꮝ, ꮗ, are sometimes sounded to, tu, tv; and syllables written with tl,
except ꮑ, sometimes vary to dl.

A sample of the characters of Sequoyah's Cherokee alphabet. (Corbis) their history and culture, and develop strong educational and religious traditions. These resulted in a more informed society and the enhancement of political discourse within the Cherokee Nation.

DEBORAH KIDWELL

See also

Cherokees; Sequoyah

References

Conley, John R. *The Cherokee Nation: A History.* Albuquerque: University of New Mexico Press, 2005.

Foreman, Grant. *Sequoyah.* Norman: University of Oklahoma Press, 1938.

Pierce, Earl Boyd, and Rennard Strickland. *The Cherokee People.* Phoenix: Indian Tribal Series, 1973.

Woodward, Grace Steele. *The Cherokees.* Norman: University of Oklahoma Press, 1982.

Cherokees

One of the so-called Five Civilized Tribes and the largest single Native American group in the American Southeast upon first European contact. The name "Cherokee" is probably from the Creek *tciloki,* meaning "people who speak differently." Their self-designation was Ani-yun-wiya, meaning "Real People." Along with the Creeks, Choctaws, Chickasaws, and Seminoles, the Cherokees were designated the Five Civilized Tribes by the Americans because by the early 19th century many members of these tribes dressed, farmed, and governed themselves much like white Americans. The Cherokees were formerly known as Kituhwas. Cherokee is an Iroquoian language and had three dialects, which were mutually intelligible with difficulty.

The tribe's chief deity was the sun, which may have had a feminine identity. The people conceived of the cosmos as being divided into three parts: an upper world, this world, and a lower world. Each contained numerous spiritual beings that resided in specific places. The four cardinal directions were replete with social and spiritual significance. Tribal mythology, symbols, and beliefs were complex, and there were also various associated taboos, customs, and social and personal rules.

The various Cherokee villages formed a loose confederacy. There were two chiefs per village: a red (or war) chief and a white chief (Most Beloved Man or Woman) who was associated with civil, economic, religious, and juridical functions. Chiefs could be male or female, and there was little or no hereditary component. There was also a village council in which women sat, although usually only as observers. The Cherokee were not a cohesive political entity until the late 18th century at the earliest.

Towns were located along rivers and streams. They contained a central ceremonial place and in the early historic period were often surrounded by palisades. People built rectangular summer houses of pole frames and wattle with walls of cane matting and clay plaster and gabled bark or thatch roofs. The houses, about 60 or 70 feet by 15 feet, were often divided into three parts: a kitchen, a dining area, and bedrooms. Some were two stories high, with the upper walls open for ventilation. There was probably one door.

The Cherokee were primarily farmers. Women grew corn (three kinds), beans, squash, sunflowers, and tobacco, the latter used ceremonially. Wild foods included roots, crab apples, persimmons, plums, cherries, grapes, hickory nuts, walnuts, chestnuts, and berries. Men hunted various animals, including deer, bears, raccoons, rabbits, squirrels, turkeys, and rattlesnakes. The men also fished occasionally; they also collected maple sap in earthen pots and boiled it into syrup.

Cherokee pipes were widely admired and easily exported. The people also traded maple sugar and syrup. They imported shell wampum that was used as currency. Their plaited cane baskets, pottery, and masks carved of wood and gourds were of especially fine quality.

In addition to the red (war) chief in each village, there was also a War Woman, who accompanied war parties. She fed the men, gave advice, and determined the fate of prisoners. Women also distinguished themselves in combat and often tortured prisoners of war. The people often painted themselves as well as their canoes and paddles for war. The party carried an ark or medicine chest to war and left a war club engraved with its exploits in enemy territory.

The Cherokees probably originated in the upper Ohio Valley, the Great Lakes region, or someplace else in the present-day northeastern United States. They may also have been related to the Mound Builders. The town of Echota, located on the Little Tennessee River, may have been the ancient capital of the Cherokee Nation.

The Cherokees encountered Hernando de Soto around 1540, probably not long after they arrived in their historic homeland. Spanish attacks against the Native Americans commenced shortly thereafter, although new diseases probably weakened the people even before Spanish soldiers began killing them. There were also contacts with the French and especially the English in the early 17th century. Traders brought guns around 1700, along with debilitating alcohol.

The Cherokees fought a series of wars with the Tuscaroras, Shawnees, Catawbas, Creeks, and Chickasaws early in the 18th century. In 1760 the Cherokees, led by Chief Oconostota, fought the British as a protest against unfair trade practices and violence practiced against them as a group. The Cherokees raided settlements and captured a British fort but were defeated after two years of fighting by the British scorched-earth policy. The peace treaty cost the Cherokees much of their eastern land, and in fact they never fully recovered their prominence after that time.

Significant depopulation resulted from several epidemics in the mid-18th century. Cherokee support for Britain during the American Revolutionary War (1775–1783) brought retaliatory attacks by southern state militias. Finally, some Cherokees who lived near Chattanooga relocated in 1794 to Arkansas and Texas

Photograph of a Cherokee family living in a log cabin on the Qualla Indian Reservation in North Carolina. The woman is grinding corn with a log pestle and mortar. (Native Stock Pictures)

and in 1831 to Indian Territory (Oklahoma). These people eventually became known as the Western Cherokees.

After the American Revolutionary War, the Cherokees adopted British-style farming, cattle ranching, business relations, and government, becoming relatively cohesive and prosperous. They also owned slaves and sided with the United States in the Creek War (1813–1814). The tribe enjoyed a cultural renaissance between about 1800 and 1830, although they were under constant pressure for land cession and were plagued by internal political factionalism.

The Cherokee Nation was founded in 1827 with Western democratic institutions and a written constitution (which specifically disenfranchised African Americans and women). By then the Cherokees were intermarrying regularly with nonnatives and were receiving increased missionary activity, especially in education. Sequoyah (also known as George Gist) is credited with devising a Cherokee syllabary and thus providing his people with a written language. During the late 1820s the Cherokee people began publishing a newspaper, the *Cherokee Phoenix.*

The discovery of gold in Cherokee territory led in part to the 1830 Indian Removal Act, requiring the Cherokees (among other tribes) to relocate west of the Mississippi River. Gold also brought squatters and prospectors onto Cherokee land. The tribe sought federal assistance from the U.S. Supreme Court. In *Cherokee Nation v. Georgia* (1831), Chief Justice John Marshall ruled that the court had no jurisdiction in the case but that the Cherokees had an "unquestionable right" to their lands. In a separate case, *Worcester v. Georgia* (1832), the Marshall court ruled that the Cherokee Nation was a "distinct political community" in which Georgia law did not apply. President Andrew Jackson refused to enforce the Court's rulings or support the Cherokees in their fight against illegal encroachment.

When a small minority of Cherokees signed the Treaty of New Echota, ceding the tribe's last remaining eastern lands, local nonnatives immediately began appropriating their land and plundering their homes and possessions. Native Americans were forced into internment camps where many died, although more than 1,000 escaped to the mountains of North Carolina, where they became the progenitors of what came to be called the Eastern Cherokees.

The removal, known as the Trail of Tears, began in 1838. The Cherokees were forced to walk some 1,000 miles through severe weather without adequate food and clothing. About 4,000 Cherokees, almost a quarter of the total, died during the removal, and more died once the people reached Indian Territory (Oklahoma), where they joined—and largely absorbed—the group already there. Following their arrival in Indian Territory, the Cherokees quickly adopted another constitution and reestablished their institutions and facilities, including newspapers and schools. Under Chief John Ross, most Cherokees supported slavery and also supported the Confederate cause in the Civil War.

The huge "permanent" Indian Territory was often reduced in size, however. When the northern region was removed to create the states of Kansas and Nebraska, Native Americans living there were again forcibly resettled. One result of the Dawes Severalty Act (1887) was the "sale" (the virtual appropriation) of roughly 2 million acres of Native American land in Oklahoma. Although the Cherokees and other tribes resisted allotment, Congress forced them to acquiesce in 1898. Their land was individually allotted in 1902 at about the same time that their Native American governments were officially terminated.

Ten years after the Cherokee removal, the U.S. Congress ceased efforts to round up the Eastern Cherokees. The Cherokees received North Carolina state citizenship in 1866 and incorporated as the eastern band of Cherokees in 1889. In the early 20th century, many Eastern Cherokees were engaged in subsistence farming and in the local timber industry. Having resisted allotment, the tribe took steps to ensure that it would always own its land.

In the 1930s the United Keetoowah Band (UKB), a group of full-bloods opposed to assimilation, formally separated from the Oklahoma Cherokees. (The name "Keetoowah" derives from an ancient town in western North Carolina.) The group originated in the antiallotment battles at the end of the 19th century. In the early 20th century the UKB reconstructed several traditional political structures, such as the seven clans and white towns, as well as some ancient cultural practices that did not survive the move west. They received federal recognition in 1946.

BARRY M. PRITZKER

See also

Creek War; Dawes Severalty Act; Indian Removal Act; Sequoyah; Trail of Tears

References

Dowd, Gregory Evans. *A Spirited Resistance: The North American Indian Struggle for Unity, 1745–1815*. Baltimore: Johns Hopkins University Press, 1992.

Ehle, John. *Trail of Tears: The Rise and Fall of the Cherokee Nation*. New York: Doubleday, 1988.

Thornton, Russell. *The Cherokees: A Population History*. Lincoln: University of Nebraska Press, 1990.

———————————

Cherokees, Campaigns against
Event Dates: 1760–1761, 1773–1774, 1776–1777, 1779–1780, and 1782

Series of punitive campaigns by British colonial and later American militias against the Cherokee Nation. The Cherokee Nation, a formidable power before the American Revolutionary War (1775–1783), strongly supported the British during that conflict in an effort to stop the encroachment of European settlers upon their lands. The Cherokees had endured conflict with white settlers during 1760–1761, but the coming of the Revolution saw these conflicts increase dramatically, with a series of debilitating campaigns taking place in 1773–1774, 1776–1777, 1779–1780, and 1782. The Cherokees emerged from the Revolutionary War a weakened people, unable to resist continued pressure from white settlers that eventually drove them from their ancestral region.

The Cherokee Nation sprawled over the mountain country from North and South Carolina and northern Georgia to the future state of Tennessee. The Lower Towns clustered in upcountry South Carolina east of the Appalachian Mountains. The Middle Towns occupied the fertile valley of Cowee along the northward-flowing Little Tennessee River and the southern-flowing tributaries of the Savannah River. The Overhill Settlements lay to the west of the mountains.

Colonial South Carolinians regarded the rivers flowing south and east out of the Cherokee country as a potential avenue of invasion by the French and their Native American allies. To prevent this, in 1756 Governor James Glen persuaded the Overhill chiefs to allow him to build Fort Loudoun on the Little Tennessee River.

During the French and Indian War (1754–1763) the Cherokees aided the British but went to war against their erstwhile allies after Virginians slaughtered a Cherokee party returning home from service with the British. The Cherokees attacked Fort Loudoun and massacred most of the garrison. That episode launched three decades of sporadic warfare between the Cherokees and white settlers. In 1760 and 1761 British expeditions devastated the Lower and Middle Towns but could not penetrate the Overhill Settlements.

This intermittent warfare interfered with the Cherokees' usual hunting patterns, and they became heavily indebted to their suppliers. Their traders, in turn, owed money to the merchants in England and Scotland. An arrangement was made whereby the Cherokees exchanged land in northern Georgia for the royal government's assumption of Cherokee debts.

The Treaty of Augusta (1773) confirmed this cession. However, the land in question was also claimed by the Creek Nation, and warriors from the Lower Creek towns raided frontier settlements in Georgia during the winter of 1773–1774. Governor James Wright disappointed settlers by declining to demand further land cessions as a condition of peace. The perception that the royal government favored the interests of Indian traders over those of the settlers had much to do with the growth of the Revolutionary movement in the Georgia and Carolina backcountry.

Although the British Proclamation of 1763 prohibited colonial settlement west of the Appalachian Mountains, pioneers moved into the Watauga and Holston valleys in the Cherokee Overhill country. Speculators met with Cherokee chiefs in March 1775 and claimed that the tribe had ceded a huge territory amounting to the future state of Kentucky and much of Tennessee. Dragging Canoe, son of the Cherokee leader Attakullakulla, showed his disgust with the proceedings by leaving the conference in a fury and later led a secessionist movement westward to the Chickamauga River. John Stuart, the British Indian superintendent, declared the transaction illegal, and the chiefs claimed that they had been duped. Nevertheless, the interlopers remained on the Watauga and Holston rivers.

The Revolutionary movement in the South gathered strength in 1775, fueled partly by a false rumor that Stuart intended to launch an Indian war against the frontier settlements. By the late summer of 1775, Loyalists and Patriots engaged in armed conflict in the South Carolina backcountry. Dragging Canoe and other Cherokee militants believed that the war provided them an opportunity to drive out encroaching whites and avenge past wrongs. Over the protests of Stuart and the Cherokee peace faction headed by Attakullakulla, the militants attacked the southern frontier on June 28, 1776.

Continental Major General Charles Lee ordered a three-pronged retaliatory attack against the Cherokees by the militias of Georgia, the Carolinas, and Virginia. In August 1776 South Carolina general Andrew Williamson led 1,000 South Carolinians, later reinforced by Georgians, in the destruction of the Lower Towns. In September, Williamson's troops joined Brigadier General Griffith Rutherford's North Carolinians in a devastating expedition against the Middle Towns. Finally, in October, Virginians under Colonel William Christian approached the Overhill Settlements along the western side of the mountains and destroyed many of those towns.

A delegation of older chiefs signed a peace treaty with Georgia and South Carolina at DeWitt's Corner, South Carolina, and with North Carolina and Virginia at Long Island on the Holston River in 1777. The agreements required the Cherokees to cede vast tracts of land. Dragging Canoe and many of the younger warriors, however, continued hostilities. In April 1779, Virginia governor Patrick Henry organized a punitive invasion of the Chickamauga country. Although it seemed that Cherokee resistance was finally crushed, the reoccupation of Georgia and South Carolina by the British Army between 1778 and 1780 and the resumption of British supplies of ammunition caused isolated bands of Cherokees to resume their struggle against the frontier settlements. Cherokees fought alongside Thomas Brown's King's Rangers at Augusta, Georgia, in September 1780 in a four-day battle to repulse Lieutenant Colonel Elijah Clarke's Patriot raiders, and Cherokee warriors harassed Clarke's retreating Georgians as they made their way back to the mountains.

As he moved into the South Carolina backcountry, British lieutenant general Charles Cornwallis initially disdained the use of Native Americans in warfare. After the Loyalists' defeat at Kings Mountain in October 1780, however, Cornwallis ordered Brown, Stuart's successor as superintendent of the Creeks and Cherokees, to launch attacks on the Watauga and Holston settlements. The raids caused the inhabitants under John Sevier and Arthur Campbell to retaliate against Native American villages, destroying 1,000 houses and burning 50,000 bushels of corn. Even as the British prepared to evacuate Georgia in 1782, Brown ordered his deputy, Thomas Waters, to recruit Cherokees for new raids in the Georgia and South Carolina backcountry. Clarke chased Waters and his Native American allies to Florida, and South Carolina's Andrew Pickens led another attack on the Cherokee Middle Towns.

The final withdrawal of the British from South Carolina and Georgia in 1782 forced the Cherokees to conclude peace at the cost of the surrender of large tracts of land in both South Carolina and North Carolina. Having learned the bitter lesson of the futility of warfare against white settlers, the Cherokee Nation tried another tactic to hold on to its land. Over the next 50 years, the Cherokees adopted several basic features of European American civilization, including farming and writing. Even these alterations, however, could not stop the inexorable invasion of aggressive American settlers, and in the 1830s the Cherokees were forced to abandon the Southeast entirely and embark on the Trail of Tears to Oklahoma.

EDWARD J. CASHIN

See also

Cherokees; French and Indian War; Native Americans and the American Revolutionary War; Trail of Tears

References

Hatley, Tom. *The Dividing Paths: Cherokees and South Carolinians through the Revolutionary Era.* New York: Oxford University Press, 1995.

O'Donnell, James H., III. *The Cherokees of North Carolina in the American Revolution.* Raleigh: North Carolina Department of Cultural Resources, Division of Archives and History, 1976.

O'Donnell, James H., III. *Southern Indians in the American Revolution.* Knoxville: University of Tennessee Press, 1973.

Cherokee War

Start Date: October 5, 1759
End Date: November 19, 1761

A protracted and devastating frontier conflict that weakened the Cherokee Nation but did not break its traditional alliance with Great Britain. Throughout the 17th and 18th centuries, the Cherokees, an Iroquoian-speaking assemblage of tribes, were the largest ethnic bloc along the southern Appalachian highlands, an area encompassing parts of present-day West Virginia, Virginia, Kentucky, Tennessee, Georgia, and the Carolinas.

The tribe itself, numbering as many as 21,000 people in 1735, was a regional power to be reckoned with. Early on the Cherokees had established friendly trade relations with English colonial settlements in Virginia and the Carolinas and fought alongside them and against their traditional Creek and Yamasee rivals in 1716. The English saw the Cherokees as a potential ally against the French-influenced Shawnees and Creeks, situated respectively to the north and south. In 1730 several leading Cherokee chiefs arrived in London for a formal appearance at the court of King George II. There a formal treaty of alliance was sealed with several individuals, the most prominent being Oconostota, who held the title "Great Warrior," and Attakullakulla, a peace chief.

The next 25 years proved both peaceful and prosperous, but the onset of the French and Indian War (1754–1763) plus a rising tide of white encroachment on Cherokee territory led to increasing friction between the erstwhile allies. The British, for their part, sought to protect the Cherokees from French attacks and influence by constructing Fort Prince George near Keowee (South Carolina) in 1753 and Fort Loudoun near Chota (Tennessee) in 1756. Whatever military benefits these posts conferred was basically negated by the growing perception and resentment among Cherokees that their territorial rights were being infringed upon.

By 1758 many elements within the tribe waxed openly hostile toward the British, and a single provocation could transform simmering resentment into frontier violence. When the French and Indian War began in 1754, the Cherokees dutifully dispatched war bands to assist Brigadier General John Forbes in his campaign against Fort Duquesne. But on the return home, these same warriors were attacked and killed by Virginia militiamen who claimed that the warriors had stolen their horses. The tribesmen were understandably enraged when their slain warriors were then scalped by the militiamen, who subsequently collected bounties on the scalps. These acts triggered a spate of retaliatory raids against British settlements across the southern frontier, resulted in the deaths of at least 20 whites, and prompted the former consorts to take up arms against each other.

On October 5, 1759, Governor William Henry Lyttelton of South Carolina officially declared war against the Cherokees and prepared to lead an armed expedition of 1,300 men against them in the field. Word of this spurred several Cherokee chiefs, including Oconostota, to visit Charles Town (present-day Charleston, South Carolina) in an attempt to forestall hostilities. The chiefs were nevertheless taken prisoner by Lyttelton and were marched under guard to Fort Prince George. There the governor met with Attakullakulla and demanded that 24 warriors known to have murdered settlers be turned over for punishment. The peace chief agreed to comply on December 26, 1759, and arranged the release of Oconostota. However, the remaining 24 chiefs and tribal leaders were to be retained as hostages.

A short truce ensued between the antagonists until February 16, 1760, when Oconostota lured the commander of Fort Prince George into the open for a parley and had him killed. The enraged British garrison then slaughtered all the hostages in retaliation, ending any chance for a peaceful negotiated settlement.

For many weeks into the war, Cherokee bands raided and terrorized frontier settlements with impunity, forcing Lieutenant Governor William Bull, Lyttelton's successor, to appeal to Major General Jeffrey Amherst, supreme British commander, for assistance. Amherst responded by dispatching several British regiments under Lieutenant Colonel Archibald Montgomery, who arrived at Charles Town on April 1, 1760. Once augmented by supplies and militia, Montgomery marched 1,600 soldiers and militiamen to the relief of Fort Prince George. From there the force embarked on a punitive expedition against the Cherokee Lower Towns.

The British first moved against the nearby village of Keowee, which they devastated on June 1, 1760. They then proceeded against a larger settlement at Echoe (in North Carolina). Here the Cherokees established an effective ambush, which was sprung on June 27, 1760. Montgomery suffered 20 killed and 70 wounded before driving off his antagonists, after which he withdrew to Charles Town.

Considering the disparity in numbers and equipment, this was a considerable Cherokee victory and inspired the Overhill bands of the tribe to continue fighting. Here Oconostota's warriors managed to blockade Fort Loudoun and starve it into surrender. Captain Paul Demere, the commander, had been promised free passage back to British territory, but on August 8, 1760, angry Cherokees attacked his column, killing Demere and 32 others and taking the remainder hostage. This proved to be the largest humiliation for British troops during the entire war.

The loss of Fort Loudoun prompted Amherst to detail 2,500 British and Scottish troops under Lieutenant Colonel James Grant to Charles Town as reinforcements in the spring of 1761. Grant took the offensive on March 20 by marching to Fort Prince George, where he conferred with Attakullakulla. The colonel brushed off the chief's peace offer as being impossible to accept following the Fort Loudoun massacre and then set about chastising the Cherokees further.

The British marched in force toward the Middle Towns, and on June 10, 1761, only two miles from where Montgomery's force had been ambushed, the Cherokees launched another devastating attack. Grant managed to repel the warriors, driving them from the field, but at a cost of 10 killed and 50 wounded. The victorious British then spent an entire month systematically devastating native villages, crops, and fields, forcing upwards of 5,000 Cherokees to flee into the wilderness. The natives proved unable to sustain this swath of destruction, and many chiefs, unable to secure assistance from neighboring tribes, believed that they had no recourse but to sue for peace.

Attakullakulla, Oconostota, and other tribal leaders subsequently conferred with Grant at Fort Prince George that autumn and formalized a peace treaty on September 23, 1761. The treaty stipulated that the tribe would renounce and summarily cease all contacts with the French and recognize the sovereignty of British courts over wanted fugitives hiding on native land. In addition, the terms of the treaty pushed the South Carolina border 26 miles past the village of Keowee. The British demanded that the Cherokees hand over several chiefs for execution. But Attakullakulla, having ventured to Charles Town to confer with the lieutenant governor, had this demand rescinded. A separate arrangement signed with Virginia on November 19, 1761, finally brought the Cherokee War to an end.

Afterward the Cherokees and the British normalized relations to the extent that lingering anger and resentment on both sides allowed. The natives in particular had sustained considerable loss of life, displacement of entire communities, and the surrender of valuable hunting grounds. In their weakened condition, the Cherokees were unable to stem the rising tide of colonial encroachment along the frontier, despite the best attempts of British authorities to contain it east of the Appalachians. But whatever reservations they may have entertained against their former allies, the tribe trusted the emerging American nation even less. In 1776, perhaps thinking that they had no choice, the Cherokees went to war as an ally of Great Britain and suffered commensurately for it.

JOHN C. FREDRIKSEN

See also

Attakullakulla; Cherokees; French and Indian War; Oconostota

References

Bryant, James A. "Between the River and the Flood: The Cherokee Nation and the Battle for European Supremacy in North America." Master's thesis, College of William and Mary, 1999.

Fabel, Robin F. A. *Colonial Challenges: Britons, Native Americans, and Caribs, 1759–1775.* Gainesville: University Press of Florida, 2000.

Nelson, Paul D. *General James Grant: Scottish Soldier and Royal Governor of East Florida.* Gainesville: University Press of Florida, 1993.

Oliphant, John. *Peace and War on the Anglo-Cherokee Frontier 1753–63.* Baton Rouge: Louisiana State University Press, 2001.

Cheyenne-Arapaho War

Start Date: 1864
End Date: 1867

Military conflict involving the U.S. military and the Southern Cheyennes and Arapahos from 1864 to 1867. The Cheyenne-Arapaho War is sometimes called the Colorado War because most of the conflict occurred there.

The Colorado Gold Rush had accelerated the American conquest of the central Plains, marginalizing and driving to poverty the Cheyennes and Arapahos who for decades had controlled the area. Cutting tribal lands to pieces, large numbers of white prospectors, traders, and others flocked to the Denver area and began to take control of the river valleys and fertile grasslands, pivotal grazing areas for buffalo and the tribes' horse herds. As the competition for subsistence, pastures, commerce, and living space in the central Plains intensified, the power of the Cheyennes and Arapahos declined. The Cheyennes and Arapahos had sustained alliances for generations while carving themselves room as middlemen in the lucrative Plains commerce, but in the 1860s both were divided in their policies for dealing with the white settlers. Some sought to retain or regain power through war, while others preferred a potentially more secure life isolated from whites.

Influenced by a desire for statehood and personal ambitions, Colorado officials—foremost among them Governor John Evans and local military commander and Methodist minister John M. Chivington—provoked the war. Seemingly uncooperative

Cheyennes and Arapahos stood in the way of settling the lands of eastern Colorado and western Kansas. Colorado officials believed that Native Americans should either be removed to reservations or destroyed. One goal was to consolidate them on the Upper Arkansas Reservation, created by the Fort Wise Treaty of 1861. However, only a fraction of Cheyennes and Arapahos recognized the agreement, which made the two tribes relinquish most of their territory.

In the spring of 1864 whites believed that a large-scale Native American revolt was at hand, and thus the settlers created a war where none had existed. They even raised a specific unit, the volunteer 3rd Colorado Cavalry Regiment, to respond to tribal offenses, real and imagined.

A year of violence began in April 1864 when troops exchanged fire with Cheyennes suspected of stealing horses. In mid-May a group of Cheyennes on their way to hunt buffalo was attacked by soldiers. Twenty-eight Cheyennes died. As scattered raids occurred during the summer, Coloradoans increasingly desired more aggressive actions. However, many Native Americans wanted negotiations and peace. After coming to terms with Colorado officials, some Cheyennes under Black Kettle and Arapahos under Little Raven and Left Hand settled near Fort Lyon, believing that they were under government protection. On the morning of November 29, 1864, a portion of them faced a shocking attack by Colorado volunteers. The resulting Sand Creek Massacre saw Chivington and his militia attack Black Kettle's sleeping village. Men, women, and children perished in the brutal killings of approximately 200 people.

Not surprisingly, outraged Cheyennes, Arapahos, and some Sioux retaliated against white settlements and travelers during the winter of 1865. They twice sacked the town of Julesburg and attacked ranches, wagon trains, and stage stations. They also ripped up miles of telegraph wire, cutting off Denver from the East. At least 30 soldiers, freighters, travelers, and settlers died in the assaults. By then, military subjugation had gained wide acceptability, including in Washington, D.C.

In the summer of 1865 the U.S. Army launched its biggest offensive yet against the Plains tribes. But the central Plains were largely empty of hostiles. Many of the Cheyennes and the Arapahos had moved north to join their kinsmen and the Sioux in areas that were still relatively free from large-scale white intrusions. Large army columns faced massive logistical difficulties when operating far from their bases in the Plains. Lack of knowledge concerning the terrain, weather, distances, and the enemy, in addition to voluminous desertion, plagued the troops. The military takeover of the Plains proved impossible, as the army was beaten not by the enemy but by its own carelessness and inabilities. Peace again became an option.

After the Sand Creek Massacre, Black Kettle's Cheyennes moved south of the Arkansas River to avoid fighting. They signed the Little Arkansas Treaty in October 1865 that created another illusion of peace, terminated their rights to the hunting grounds of western Kansas, and made them live south of the Arkansas River. Still, a majority of the Native Americans saw the vast central Plains as their birthright. The summer of 1867 witnessed another futile army campaign, which insulted the Native Americans even more. In the autumn of 1867 the Medicine Lodge Treaty, which many Cheyennes and Arapahos signed, called for a permanent relocation and created a combined Cheyenne-Arapaho reservation on Creek and Seminole lands in Indian Territory (Oklahoma). That treaty brought an end to the Cheyenne-Arapaho War, at least in theory.

Sporadic fighting between some Southern Cheyennes and Arapahos and the settlers continued, however. Army campaigns during 1868–1869 drove most of them to their newly assigned reservations. Battles at the Washita River in western Indian Territory in 1868 and at Summit Springs in 1869, in addition to the Red River War of 1874–1875, are among the best-known episodes of these last conflicts between the central Plains tribes and the Americans.

JANNE LAHTI

See also

Arapahos; Black Kettle; Cheyennes; Chivington, John; Medicine Lodge Treaty; Red River War; Sand Creek Massacre; Sioux; Summit Springs, Battle of; Washita, Battle of the

References

Utley, Robert M. *Frontier Regulars: The United States and the American Indian, 1866–1891.* New York: Macmillan, 1973.
Utley, Robert M. *The Indian Frontier of the American West, 1846–1890.* Albuquerque: University of New Mexico Press, 1984.
West, Elliott. *The Contested Plains: Indians, Goldseekers, and the Rush to Colorado.* Lawrence: University Press of Kansas, 1998.

Cheyenne Campaign
Start Date: May 1857
End Date: September 1857

U.S. military campaign against Cheyennes during the spring and summer of 1857. Although the Cheyennes had agreed in the 1851 Fort Laramie Treaty to refrain from attacking white settlers traveling across Kansas and Nebraska along the trails to Oregon and California and to remain at peace with other tribes, chiefs found it virtually impossible to enforce treaty restrictions on younger warriors. Indeed, Cheyenne raids against their traditional enemies, the Pawnees, not only violated the treaty but also made incidents with settlers crossing the Plains inevitable.

Although U.S. Army colonel William S. Harney, commander at Fort Kearny, had warned Cheyenne chiefs in early 1856 that he would attack them ruthlessly if they continued to raid against the Pawnees, the conflict between proslavery and antislavery forces in Kansas prevented him from launching a campaign. Nevertheless, numerous incidents escalated tensions during 1856. In June, Captain Henry W. Wharton attempted to arrest 3 Cheyenne warriors at Fort Kearny because a white settler had been killed not far from the fort. In August, Wharton dispatched elements of the

1st Cavalry under Captain George H. Stewart against the Cheyennes after they attacked a stage coach. In an attack on a Cheyenne camp along the Platte River, Stewart's troops killed 10 Cheyennes, wounded 10 more, and seized camp provisions. When the Cheyennes retaliated by attacking white settlers crossing the Plains, Secretary of War Jefferson Davis authorized a campaign against them in the spring of 1857.

In May 1857 the campaign commenced from Fort Leavenworth with three columns under the overall command of Colonel Edwin Vose Sumner, a veteran of the Mexican-American War (1846–1848) who had assumed command of the new 1st Cavalry Regiment in 1855. Sumner's column of two companies from the 1st Cavalry and two companies from the 2nd Dragoons was to advance up the Platte along the Overland Trail to Fort Laramie and then swing south. Major John Sedgwick's column of four companies from the 1st Cavalry was to advance up the Arkansas along the Sante Fe Trail to the foothills of the Rockies (near present-day Pueblo, Colorado) and then swing north to converge with Sumner. Lieutenant Colonel Joseph E. Johnston headed a third column of four companies from the 1st Cavalry and two companies from the 6th Infantry Regiment charged with surveying the southern boundary of Kansas and providing support to Sumner if possible.

Each column was supported by two howitzers. During their advance neither Sumner nor Sedgwick encountered hostiles, and the two companies of the 2nd Dragoon Regiment were detached from Sumner's column and transferred to Utah, where Harney had been sent to suppress the Mormons. Upon arriving at Fort Laramie, three companies of the 6th Infantry were attached to Sumner's column, which then moved south to meet Sedgwick. Johnston meanwhile completed the survey of Kansas's southern border without incident but was too far away to play a role in the campaign against the Cheyennes.

After converging with Sedgwick's column near present-day Greeley, Colorado, in mid-July, Sumner led the combined force eastward in search of the Cheyennes. On July 29 scouts located a large force of Cheyennes along the Solomon River. Approximately 300 Cheyenne warriors, who had been told by their medicine man that they could not be harmed by the American guns because they had bathed in a "holy lake," formed a line from the banks of the Solomon to nearby bluffs and prepared to meet the American forces in a pitched battle. To their surprise, Sumner ordered his cavalry, approximately 300 strong, to draw their sabers and charge instead of opening fire and waiting to bring up his infantry or howitzers. The ferocity of the charge and the realization that the medicine man's magic protected them against guns, not sabers, caused the Cheyennes to flee in panic. Sumner's cavalry followed in hot pursuit for seven miles. Casualties were relatively light on both sides, with nine Cheyenne warriors killed and two cavalrymen killed and another eight wounded, including Lieutenant J. E. B. Stuart.

After spending two days building an earthen embankment on the Solomon, where Sumner left his infantry behind to take care of the wounded, he pursued the trail left by the Cheyennes, eventually finding their hastily abandoned village and burning their lodges. Sumner then proceeded to Bent's Fort on the Arkansas River, where he confiscated the allotment of firearms and ammunition that the Indian agent was supposed to distribute to the Cheyennes and Arapahos. Although Sumner planned to continue the campaign, in early September he received orders to send most of his men to Utah to join Harney. Consequently, the Cheyenne Campaign of 1857 ended rather abruptly. In the weeks that followed, the Cheyennes launched a series of raids along the Platte, leading general in chief of the army Brevet Lieutenant General Winfield Scott to criticize Sumner's effectiveness. In reality, the Cheyenne Campaign had produced an important psychological victory over the Cheyennes. For the next seven years the Cheyennes remained relatively peaceful despite an onrush of miners and settlers into Colorado.

JUSTIN D. MURPHY

See also

Cheyennes; Davis, Jefferson; Fort Laramie; Fort Laramie, Treaty of (1851); Harney, William Selby; Overland Trail; Pawnees; Santa Fe Trail

References

Bonvillain, Nancy. *The Cheyennes: People of the Plains.* Brookfield, CT: Millbrook, 1996.

Utley, Robert M. *Frontiersmen in Blue: The United States and the Indian, 1848–1865.* Lincoln: University of Nebraska Press, 1967.

Cheyennes

Great Plains tribe located during the 1800s between the Yellowstone River to the north and the Arkansas River to the south, encompassing a large region from the Black Hills in South Dakota to southeastern Colorado. The Cheyennes, an Algonquian-speaking nation, were first encountered by Europeans as woodland Indians in Minnesota west of the headwaters of the Mississippi River. The Cheyennes were reported by the French explorer Louis Hennepin about 1680. The name "Cheyenne" was from the Sioux term meaning "foreign speakers." The Cheyennes were essentially sedentary during this period, harvesting wild rice and planting maize, beans, and squash. They also hunted for deer and ventured onto the prairies for bison. There is evidence that they produced some pottery during this period, a skill they later abandoned.

During the first half of the 18th century, the Cheyennes and the Sioux were pushed by the Ojibwas out of the extensive woodland lakes region of Minnesota to the prairies of southern and western Minnesota and the eastern Dakotas. By 1766 the Cheyennes, now living a nomadic lifestyle, were located by Jonathon Carver along the Minnesota River Valley. They had temporarily replaced farming with bison hunting and food gathering.

Continuing their westward migration, the Cheyennes again adopted a sedentary lifestyle in the late 18th century while still hunting bison on a seasonal basis. They had now settled in a number of walled villages along the present boundary between North and South Dakota. While the younger men left on the available horses to hunt bison, the older men, most women, and the children would remain behind. Several villages were destroyed in the late 1700s by Ojibwa war parties. A small tribe, the Cheyennes were forced out before other migrating groups of Native Americans moving west and were drawn to the Great Plains because of the horse and the bison.

Because of the Ojibwa threat and the lure of the bison- and horse-rich Great Plains, the Cheyennes abandoned agriculture once more and advanced farther onto the Plains. By the end of the 1700s they were west of the Missouri River and possessed enough horses to become fully nomadic. The transition into a nomadic lifestyle on the Great Plains was facilitated when a Cheyenne holy man named Sweet Medicine returned from the Black Hills with a sacred bundle of four arrows, two to give luck in hunting and two for war.

The Cheyennes split into two groups—Northern and Southern—comprised of several smaller bands. The Northern division remained close to the Lakotas in Wyoming, Nebraska, Montana, and South Dakota. The Southern division moved farther south into Colorado and Kansas, where they began to push the Kiowas out. The Cheyennes were often willing to wage a more intense form of warfare than their neighbors. Once the tribe had decided on war, they were willing to engage in decisive action. By the mid-1830s, skirmishing between the Kiowas and the Cheyennes had become quite intense.

In 1838 the Cheyenne (now partnered with the Arapahos) declared war on the Kiowas. At the 1838 Battle of Wolf Creek, the two met in a set-piece battle. The Cheyennes approached a large Kiowa village and attacked. Although the Battle of Wolf Creek was a draw, both sides realized that the level of casualties involved in further fighting would be devastating. The Kiowas made peace overtures, and in 1840 a peace was concluded between the Cheyennes and Kiowas. They agreed that the Cheyennes would remain north of the Arkansas River, while the Kiowas would remain south of it.

Movement along the Oregon Trail led to tension with whites but little direct conflict until the 1850s, when the discovery of gold in the Colorado Rockies led to a large migration of whites across prime Cheyenne hunting grounds. In 1857 the army conducted a brief but fruitful campaign against Cheyennes on the southern Plains, which forestalled wider conflict for a number of years. A third band of Cheyennes, the Dog Soldiers, had now developed. The Dog Soldiers were originally a warrior society, many of whose members had intermarried with Lakota women, and were more aggressive than the other Cheyennes. By 1864, small-scale raids on whites by the Dog Soldiers had increased, and open war broke out between the Cheyennes and the settlers. Some Cheyenne elders desired peace. One in particular, Chief Black Kettle, sought accommodation with the whites. Assured that if he encamped near Fort Lyon along Sand Creek he and his band would be safe, Black Kettle went so far as to raise a white flag and an American flag over his encampment.

Cheyenne chiefs White Antelope, Alights-on-a-Cloud, and Little Chief, circa 1851–1852. (Getty Images)

However, the 3rd Colorado Cavalry Regiment and other militia units under Colonel John Chivington, a Methodist minister and a politician, attacked the camp at sunrise on November 29, 1864. The attack, known as the Sand Creek Massacre, ended with 100–200 Cheyennes killed. Among the dead were a number of Arapahos as well. Two-thirds of the casualties were women and children. Although the attack was condemned by the U.S. Army, the Cheyennes and their allies—the Lakotas, Arapahos, Kiowas, and Comanches—were incensed by the massacre.

Black Kettle fled to Indian Territory (Oklahoma), keeping his band together and his young men from taking revenge. He was surprised again, however, in his winter camp along the Washita River. The 7th U.S. Cavalry under Lieutenant Colonel George Custer, on the trail of a band of hostiles made up of Kiowas, Comanches and Cheyennes, lost track of its target. Instead, Custer attacked Black Kettle's camp on the morning of November 27, 1868, killing the unlucky chief and dozens of Cheyenne men, women, and children.

In retribution, Cheyennes isolated the town of Denver and other white settlements in Colorado, launching attacks on farmers, ranchers, stage coaches, and travelers. Before long such attacks were occurring throughout Wyoming, Colorado, western Kansas,

and Nebraska. Continuing throughout 1865 and into 1866, the conflict merged with Red Cloud's War (1866–1868) in the Powder River Country of Wyoming and Montana.

During the war, the Cheyennes fought around Fort Phil Kearny, which precipitated the December 21, 1866, Fetterman Massacre. Many Cheyennes were also at the Beecher's Island fight between September 17 and 24, 1868. Here Major George Forsyth and 51 volunteer scouts were surrounded and unhorsed on a small island in the Arickaree Fork of the Republican River. Although the losses were light on both sides, Cheyenne war leader Roman Nose was killed on the afternoon of the first day as he led a charge on the scouts.

The Southern Cheyennes aligned with the Kiowas and Comanches as they attempted to slow settlement on the southern Plains and the massive slaughter of the bison herd. They participated with the Kiowas and Comanches in the Second Battle of Adobe Walls (June 27, 1874) and during the subsequent Red River War (1874–1875), after which they remained largely peaceful and settled on their reservation in Indian Territory.

The Northern Cheyennes generally rode with their Lakota allies and participated in actions throughout the late 1860s and mid-1870s. Chief Dull Knife's band fought at the Battle of the Little Bighorn (June 25–26, 1876) against Custer's 7th Cavalry. The last major action of the Cheyennes was the defeat of Dull Knife's band in winter camp by Colonel Ranald Mackenzie's 4th Cavalry on November 26, 1876. Led by Pawnee scouts, Mackenzie destroyed Dull Knife's village, forcing the chief's surrender.

The Northern Cheyennes were then moved south to Indian Territory. In 1878, homesick for their northern Plains, 300 Cheyenne warriors, women, and children under chiefs Little Wolf and Dull Knife broke away from the Fort Reno area in Oklahoma and evaded patrols. Dull Knife's band was eventually caught and imprisoned at Fort Robinson until it moved onto the reservation in Montana at Fort Keogh, where they were joined by Northern Cheyennes who had been at Pine Ridge with the Lakotas and some Southern Cheyennes from Oklahoma.

JOHN THOMAS BROOM

See also

Adobe Walls, Second Battle of; Arapahos; Black Kettle; Cheyenne Campaign; Cheyennes, Northern; Cheyennes, Southern; Chivington, John; Comanches; Custer, George Armstrong; Dull Knife; Fetterman Massacre; Kiowas; Lakota Sioux; Little Bighorn, Battle of the; Little Wolf; Mackenzie, Ranald Slidell; Ojibwas; Oregon Trail; Red Cloud's War; Sand Creek Massacre

References

Brown, Dee. *Action at Beecher Island.* New York: Modern Press Editions, 1967.

Carlson, Paul H. *The Plains Indians.* College Station: Texas A&M University Press, 1998.

Chalfant, William Y. *Cheyennes and Horse Soldiers: The 1857 Expedition and the Battle of Solomon's Fork.* Norman: University of Oklahoma Press, 1989.

Goodrich, Thomas. *Scalp Dance: Indian Warfare on the High Plains, 1865–1879.* Mechanicsburg, PA: Stackpole, 1997.

Grinnell, George Bird. *The Cheyenne Indians,* Vols. 1 and 2. Lincoln: University of Nebraska Press, 1972.

Hedren, Paul L., ed. *The Great Sioux War, 1876–77.* Helena: Montana Historical Society Press, 1991.

Hoig, Stan. *Tribal Wars of the Southern Plains.* Norman: University of Oklahoma Press, 1993.

Moore, John H. *The Cheyenne.* Malden, MA: Blackwell, 1996.

Cheyennes, Northern

An Algonquian-speaking Plains nation located during the 1800s between the Yellowstone River in the north and the Arkansas River in the south. In the mid-1830s the Cheyennes split into two divisions—Northern and Southern—each of which was comprised of several smaller bands. The Northern Cheyennes remained close to the Lakotas in Wyoming, Nebraska, Montana, and South Dakota. Despite the split, however, the Northern Cheyennes remained closely aligned with the Southern Cheyennes. As with most Plains tribes, the Northern Cheyennes were seminomadic, relying principally on the buffalo for their food, clothing, and shelter needs and

for trade with other Native Americans and, later, with Americans. The buffalo remained at the center of the Cheyenne economic and social systems until the tribe's forced relocation to reservation lands in the late 1870s.

The Cheyennes were generally prone to wage a more intense form of warfare than their neighbors. Once they had decided to go to war, the Cheyennes were willing to engage in decisive action. By the mid-1830s, skirmishing between the Kiowas and the Cheyennes had become intense and frequent. In the summer of 1838, the Cheyennes, along with the Arapahos, went to war against the Kiowas and Comanches. At the Battle of Wolf Creek in 1838, the two met in a seldom-seen set-piece battle. The Cheyennes approached a large Kiowa village and attacked. Although the Battle of Wolf Creek was a draw, both sides realized that if the war continued, the level of casualties would be devastating. The Kiowas made peace overtures, and in 1840 a peace was concluded between the Cheyennes and the Kiowas. The Cheyennes agreed to remain north of the Arkansas River, while the Kiowas would remain south of it.

In the 1851 Fort Laramie Treaty, the Cheyennes formally agreed that their land would encompass the area roughly between the North Platte River and the Arkansas River. The treaty also officially recognized the division of the Cheyennes into northern and southern branches.

Movement along the Oregon Trail led to tension between the Northern Cheyennes and whites, but little conflict ensued until the mid-1850s, when the discovery of gold in the Colorado mountains led to mass movement of whites across prime Cheyenne hunting grounds. Ignoring the 1851 Fort Laramie Treaty, the Cheyennes isolated Denver and other white settlements in Colorado and attacked farmers, ranchers, stage coaches, and travelers throughout Wyoming, Colorado, western Kansas, and Nebraska. Continuing throughout 1865 and into 1866, the conflict merged with Red Cloud's War (1866–1868) in the Powder River Country of Wyoming and Montana.

The Cheyennes fought around Fort Phil Kearny and were participants in the Fetterman Massacre (December 21, 1866) in which 80 U.S. soldiers were killed. Many Cheyennes were also at the Battle of Beecher Island (September 1868). During the fighting the losses were relatively light on both sides, but Northern Cheyenne war leader Roman Nose was among those killed while leading a charge on U.S. scouts.

The Northern Cheyennes rode with their Lakota allies during actions against the U.S. Army throughout the late 1860s and 1870s, including the Battle of the Rosebud (June 17, 1876) against Brigadier General George Crook's force. Dull Knife's band fought at the Battle of the Little Bighorn (June 25–26, 1876) against Lieutenant Colonel George Custer's 7th Cavalry. The last major action of the Cheyennes was the defeat of Dull Knife's band in winter camp by Colonel Ranald Mackenzie's 4th Cavalry on November 26, 1876.

The Northern Cheyennes were subsequently relocated south to Indian Territory (Oklahoma). In 1878, homesick for their northern

Plains, 300 Northern Cheyenne warriors, women, and children led by chiefs Little Wolf and Dull Knife broke away from the Fort Reno area in Oklahoma, evaded patrols, and headed northwest. Dull Knife's band was imprisoned at Fort Robinson, Nebraska, until it was allowed to move onto the Tongue River Reservation in eastern Montana, where it was joined by Northern Cheyennes who had been at Pine Ridge, South Dakota, along with the Lakotas and some Southern Cheyennes from Oklahoma.

JOHN THOMAS BROOM AND PAUL G. PIERPAOLI JR.

See also

Arapahos; Beecher Island, Battle of; Cheyennes, Southern; Comanches; Dull Knife; Fetterman Massacre; Fort Laramie, Treaty of (1851); Fort Laramie, Treaty of (1868); Kiowas; Little Bighorn, Battle of the; Little Wolf; Red Cloud's War; Roman Nose; Rosebud, Battle of the

References

Brown, Dee. *Action at Beecher Island.* New York: Modern Press Editions, 1967.

Carlson, Paul H. *The Plains Indians.* College Station: Texas A&M University Press, 1998.

Chalfant, William Y. *Cheyennes and Horse Soldiers: The 1857 Expedition and the Battle of Solomon's Fork.* Norman: University of Oklahoma Press, 1989.

Goodrich, Thomas. *Scalp Dance: Indian Warfare on the High Plains, 1865–1879.* Mechanicsburg, PA: Stackpole, 1997.

Grinnell, George Bird. *The Cheyenne Indians,* Vols. 1 and 2. Lincoln: University of Nebraska Press, 1972.

Hoig, Stan. *Tribal Wars of the Southern Plains.* Norman: University of Oklahoma Press, 1993.

Cheyennes, Southern

An Algonquian-speaking Plains nation. The Cheyennes and the Sioux had been gradually pushed by the Ojibwas to the south and west out of the extensive woodland and lakes region of eastern Minnesota and to the prairies of southern and western Minnesota and eastern South Dakota. By 1766 they were located along the Minnesota River, living a nomadic lifestyle. They had replaced farming with buffalo hunting and food gathering for a time. They relied heavily on buffalo for their food, clothing, and shelter needs and for trade with other Native Americans and, later, with white settlers and traders. Buffalo remained at the center of their economic and social systems until their forced relocation to reservation lands by the late 1860s. A relatively small tribe, the Cheyennes split into two primary divisions—Northern and Southern—sometime after 1832.

By about the mid-1830s the Southern Cheyennes had moved south into eastern Colorado and western Kansas, where they began to encounter the Kiowas. Soon thereafter, skirmishing between the Kiowas and the Cheyennes became intense. The

Southern Cheyenne chief Stump Horn and his family with their horse-drawn travois in 1890. Photograph by Christian Barthelmess. (National Archives)

Cheyennes were willing to wage a more intense form of warfare than their neighbors. Once the tribe had decided on war, they sought to engage in decisive action. In 1837 fighting broke out, pitting the Southern Cheyennes and Southern Arapahos against the Comanches. In 1838 the Cheyennes decided on war against the Kiowas and Comanches. At the Battle of Wolf Creek, the two groups met in a seldom-seen set-piece battle. The Cheyennes approached a large Kiowa village and attacked. Although the Battle of Wolf Creek was a draw, both sides realized that the level of casualties from continuing such warfare would be devastating. The Kiowas made peace overtures, and in 1840 peace was concluded, with the Cheyennes agreeing to remain north of the Arkansas River.

In the Fort Laramie Treaty of 1851, the Cheyennes agreed that their land would encompass the area roughly between the North Platte River and the Arkansas River. The treaty also officially recognized the division of the Cheyennes into northern and southern branches.

Increased settler traffic and white settlement on Cheyenne hunting grounds led to small-scale raids on whites by the vaunted Cheyenne Dog Soldiers. Although the Southern Cheyennes had sought to avoid conflict with whites more so than did their northern cousins, open war broke out between the Cheyenne and the settlers in 1864. A number of Southern Cheyenne leaders had long desired peace, and one, Chief Black Kettle, sought accommodation with the whites. Assured that if he camped near Fort Lyon along Sand Creek in Colorado he and his band would be protected by U.S. forces, Black Kettle went so far as to raise an American flag and a white flag over his encampment.

On November 29, 1864, the 3rd Regiment of Colorado Cavalry under Colonel John Chivington, a Methodist minister and a politician, attacked Black Kettle's camp at sunrise. The attack turned into a massacre, with at least 130 Cheyennes and Arapahos killed, many of them women and children. Both the U.S. government and the U.S. Army condemned the attack.

Black Kettle subsequently fled to Indian Territory (Oklahoma), keeping his band together and his young warriors peaceful. In November 1868 he was again surprised in his winter camp along the Washita River. Lieutenant Colonel George A. Custer's 7th Cavalry Regiment had lost the trail of a band of hostile Kiowas, Comanches, and Cheyennes and instead attacked Black Kettle's camp on the morning of the November 27, 1868. Black Kettle was among those killed.

The Southern Cheyennes aligned with the Kiowas and Comanches as they attempted to slow settlement on the southern Plains and oppose the massive slaughter of the buffalo herds. In addition, the Southern Cheyennes participated with the Kiowas and Comanches in the Second Battle of Adobe Walls (June 27, 1874) and the Red River War (1874–1875), the last major action on the southern Plains, after which they remained peaceful and resided on their reservation in Indian Territory, along with the Arapahos.

JOHN THOMAS BROOM

See also

Adobe Walls, Second Battle of; Arapahos; Black Kettle; Cheyennes, Northern; Chivington, John; Comanches; Custer, George Armstrong; Dog Soldiers; Fort Laramie, Treaty of (1851); Fort Laramie, Treaty of (1868); Kiowas; Red River War; Sand Creek Massacre; Washita, Battle of the

References

Carlson, Paul H. *The Plains Indians.* College Station: Texas A&M University Press, 1998.

Chalfant, William Y. *Cheyennes and Horse Soldiers: The 1857 Expedition and the Battle of Solomon's Fork.* Norman: University of Oklahoma Press, 1989.

Goodrich, Thomas. *Scalp Dance: Indian Warfare on the High Plains, 1865–1879.* Mechanicsburg, PA: Stackpole, 1997.

Grinnell, George Bird. *The Cheyenne Indians,* Vols. 1 and 2. Lincoln: University of Nebraska Press, 1972.

Hedren, Paul L., ed. *The Great Sioux War, 1876–77.* Helena: Montana Historical Society Press, 1991.

Moore, John H. *The Cheyenne.* Malden, MA: Blackwell, 1996.

Chichimecos

See Westos

Chickahominys

Native American tribe that lived between the Chickahominy River and the James River in eastern Virginia. Chickahominy territory extended into present-day New Kent County, Virginia. Essentially the name "Chickahominy" means "coarse-pounded corn people" and may possess a connection to the word "rockahominy," a coarse cornmeal often consumed by Native Americans and later European colonists during hunting. The Chickahominys were Algonquian speakers and occasionally allied with the Powhatan Confederacy, best known for its chief Powhatan and his early contacts with the English colonists. As with the Powhatans and other eastern tribes, the Chickahominys subsisted by hunting, fishing, trapping, and raising crops, corn in particular.

At the time of the English landings in Virginia in 1607, the Chickahominy tribe was already present in the region. Although the Powhatans vastly outnumbered the Chickahominys, the former were never able to gain complete suzerainty over the latter. By the same token, the Chickahominys did send men to fight alongside the Powhatans as a part of their alliance.

The alliance arrangement between the two tribes greeted the English on their arrival in Jamestown in 1607. Shortly thereafter, several Chickahominy warriors captured Captain John Smith as he explored the Chickahominy River. In accordance with their relationship to the Powhatan Confederacy, they turned the English captain over to Chief Powhatan. This set in motion the sequence of events that eventually led to Smith's alleged rescue from execution by Powhatan's daughter Pocahontas.

Around 1615 after the First Anglo-Powhatan War (1610–1614), the Chickahominys negotiated a treaty with the English colonists, represented by Sir Thomas Dale. The Chickahominys made this peace with the colonists to preserve some of their autonomy in relation to both the Powhatan Confederacy and the growing English presence. One facet of the agreement included a promise to supply the English with military assistance when called upon. Still, when forced to choose sides in the Second Anglo-Powhatan War (1622–1632), the Chickahominys chose to remain loyal to the Powhatans.

As English settlements expanded and native attempts to stop or slow the growth of these settlements met with continued failure, the Chickahominys were reduced in numbers. They made a shaky peace with the English in 1632 that held until the outbreak of the Third Anglo-Powhatan War (1644–1646). That conflict saw the tribe lose much of its native territory to the colonists. The Chickahominys joined other groups in a forced relocation to the region known as the Pamunkey Neck. Later, in 1718, they were removed from this area as well. This resulted in a gradual migration to Chickahominy Ridge (in present-day Charles City County, Virginia), where a number of Chickahominys still reside.

The governing style of the Chickahominys was at variance with their native neighbors. As opposed to rule by a chief or any other single dominant figure, the Chickahominys were ruled by a council of elders. Although many contemporaries commented on the different organization of the Chickahominy government, none left any real explanation as to how and why it was organized as it was.

In the early 20th century the tribe established its own school, and in 1972 the tribe purchased additional land, some of which was used as a tribal buffer zone. The State of Virginia formally recognized the Chickahominys in 1983. Today about 750 Chickahominys live within a five-mile radius of the tribal center, and perhaps several hundred more live in other areas of the United States. Despite their travails and dislocations, the Chickahominys have maintained their tribal and cultural identities.

James R. McIntyre

See also

Anglo-Powhatan War, First; Anglo-Powhatan War, Second; Anglo-Powhatan War, Third; Jamestown; Pocahontas; Powhatan; Powhatan Confederacy; Smith, John

References

Gleach, Frederic W. *Powhatan's World and Colonial Virginia.* Lincoln: University of Nebraska Press, 1997.

Rountree, Helen C. *Pocahontas's People: The Powhatan Indians of Virginia through Four Centuries.* Norman: University of Oklahoma Press, 1990.

Chickamaugas

A group of Cherokees that separated from the Overhill Cherokees to continue fighting the Patriots during the American Revolutionary War (1775–1783) after the majority of Cherokees had sued for peace. The Chickamaugas were not a tribe; rather, they were an amalgamation of Indians from several tribes who first banded together to fight white settlers and then Patriots in the late 1700s. Their territory was mainly eastern Tennessee.

As soon as the Cherokee Chickamaugas separated from the other Cherokees, a small number of British Loyalists, Upper Creeks, and Shawnees joined the relocated Cherokee Chickamaugas in southeastern Tennessee. These new allies aided the Cherokee Chickamaugas in their fight against the Americans and helped them create an alliance network that spread from the Ohio River down to Florida and west to the Mississippi River. The Cherokee Chickamaugas continued to fight the Americans until 1795.

At the beginning of the American Revolutionary War, the Cherokees lived in three distinct collections of communities known as the Overhill Towns, the Middle Towns, and the Lower Towns. The Overhill Towns occupied eastern Tennessee, the Middle Towns were situated in the mountains of North Carolina, and the Lower Towns were located in South Carolina. Angered by the seizure of lands by American frontiersmen and encouraged by their British Loyalist allies as well as Shawnees from the Ohio River Valley, the Cherokees launched attacks on American frontier settlements across the South in June 1776. Because they began these attacks before their allies were ready to assist, however, the Cherokees were soon defeated by the Americans. Troops from Virginia defeated the Overhill Towns at the same time that forces from North Carolina devastated the Middle Towns and South Carolinians and Georgians laid waste to the Lower Towns.

As a consequence of this defeat, the Cherokees had to cede additional land to the victors in the Treaty of De Witt's Corner (May 20, 1777) and the Treaty of Long Island of Holston (July 2, 1777). These treaties precipitated the creation of the Chickamauga Cherokees, a separatist movement that continued to resist the Americans and the implementation of the two treaties until 1795.

The Chickamaugas were a collection of primarily Overhill Cherokees, Upper Creeks, some Shawnees, and British Loyalists. The Cherokee Chickamaugas dominated and were led by Tsiyu Ganisini, commonly known as Dragging Canoe. Dragging Canoe led the relocation of this faction of Cherokees down the Tennessee River to the vicinity of Chickamauga Creek, a tributary of the Tennessee River located just north of the future town of Chattanooga, Tennessee. As soon as they had relocated, the Cherokee Chickamaugas began a military campaign against the American frontier that lasted until 1795. The Chickamaugas kept up their campaign with British aid from Detroit and later Spanish governmental and British trader support from Florida and also sustained Native American alliances with northern and southern tribes. The most important of these were with the Upper Creeks, the Choctaws, the Chickasaws, and the Shawnees.

Even though it was the Chickamaugas who carried on the war with the Americans, all the Cherokee towns suffered the consequences. During 1780 Patriot and Indian fighter John Sevier destroyed many of the Overhill communities as well as many of the

Chickamauga settlements. Sevier later burned 15 Middle Towns in 1781. These strikes against the Cherokees caused many more Cherokees to join the Chickamaugas in the early and middle years of the 1780s. However, American forces wore down this native resistance over time.

Eventually the U.S. government organized the Southwest Territory in 1790, which later produced the states of Kentucky and Tennessee. The new territorial government used federal funds to end Chickasaw and Choctaw contributions to the Chickamauga movement by promising food, farm supplies, and other needed items to these two nations. The government of the Southwest Territory also armed its 15,000 males over the age of 21 and began to organize and prepare to use them against the Chickamaugas. Then, through diplomacy, the U.S. government shut down the Chickamauga supply lines from the British in Detroit and Florida. Finally, the Shawnees and their northern allies were defeated by American forces at the Battle of Fallen Timbers (August 20, 1794). They too could no longer support the Chickamaugas. Furthermore, many Chicamauga Cherokees and those Cherokees not aligned with the Chickamaugas argued for an end to hostilities to spare them from further invasions by American forces. Thus, the Chickamaugas faced large numbers of American frontiersmen on all sides, a growing peace party in their midst, and increasing pressure from other Cherokees to end hostilities.

The futility of the Chickamauga position now became apparent, and the Chickamaugas negotiated an end to hostilities with the Americans in 1795. Afterward most of the Cherokee Chickamaugas rejoined their Cherokee brethren in the southern Appalachians, but many fled to Spanish territory across the Mississippi River for protection. Those still living in southern Appalachia were removed to Indian Territory (Oklahoma) in 1839, along with their Cherokee brethren, as a result of the Indian Removal Act of 1830. This precipitated what came to be called the Trail of Tears.

DIXIE RAY HAGGARD

See also

Cherokees; Chickasaws; Choctaws; Creeks; Fallen Timbers, Battle of; Great Britain; Indian Removal Act; Native Americans and the American Revolutionary War; Shawnees; Spain; Trail of Tears

References

Calloway, Colin G. *The American Revolution in Indian Country: Crisis and Diversity in Native American Communities.* Cambridge: Cambridge University Press, 1995.

Dowd, Gregory Evans. *A Spirited Resistance: The North American Indian Struggle for Unity, 1745–1815.* Baltimore: Johns Hopkins University Press, 1992.

Downes, Randolph C. "Cherokee-American Relations in the Upper Tennessee Valley, 1776–1791." *East Tennessee Historical Society's Publications* 8 (1936): 35–53.

Hatley, Tom. *The Dividing Paths: Cherokees and South Carolinians through the Revolutionary Era.* New York: Oxford University Press, 1995.

O'Donnell, James H., III. *The Cherokees of North Carolina in the . American Revolution.* Raleigh: North Carolina Department of Cultural Resources, Division of Archives and History, 1976.

Chickasaws

One of the so-called Five Civilized Tribes of the Southeast (in addition to the Cherokees, the Choctaws, the Creeks and the Seminoles). Sharing the Western Muskogean language family with the Choctaws, the Chickasaws settled primarily in present-day northern Mississippi. Based on their shifting fortunes in war and diplomacy, the Chickasaws also claimed territory extending into present-day Alabama, Kentucky, South Carolina, Georgia, and Tennessee. Consequently they battled a wide assortment of tribes, including the Choctaws, the Cherokees, the Caddos, the Shawnees, and the Illinois. Chickasaw military operations extended north beyond the Ohio River and as far south as the Gulf of Mexico.

The Chickasaws constructed permanent communities in Mississippi and Alabama that featured palisades for defense and space reserved for such public events as councils and athletic competitions. The primary unit of social organization for the Chickasaws was the house group, which was based on matrilineally related women residing with their husbands, children, and unmarried brothers. House groups functioned as part of larger clans, each of which took the name of an animal with which it identified based on spiritual visions.

The Chickasaw economy was a mixed one in which women tended crops and the men hunted, fished, and trapped. Trade with other tribes and the Europeans was also part of the Chickasaws' economic activities. Because the Chickasaws lived in towns, their population was concentrated. There were likely six to eight Chickasaw towns at the time of first European contact.

Placing a higher premium on mobility than did the Choctaws, the Chickasaws heavily relied on horses for hunting, devoting relatively less energy to agriculture. As such, they helped pioneer equestrian warfare in the Southeast. Male prisoners taken in battle were usually executed, which left captured women and children as the primary sources of slaves. Nonetheless, the Chickasaws adopted a fair number of war captives to augment their population. By the middle of the 18th century, trade with the British had brought African slaves into Chickasaw communities.

Warfare served a variety of purposes for the Chickasaws. All males who fought in battle attained adulthood and prestige among their peers. Clans used raids to avenge homicides within their communities, as their law allowed for killing the culprit or, in his absence, a male relative. In the event of a female victim, retaliation on a woman from the offending clan was acceptable. Separating military from civil leadership, larger campaigns were conducted by experienced war leaders who could only persuade fellow tribesmen to join them in combat.

Prior to battle, warriors fasted for three days in a hot house, consuming only herbal tea. Abstinence from sexual activity was also mandated. Several nights of ritualistic dancing culminated in a speech by a retired warrior, ceremonial smoking, and the striking of a red war pole. Each member of the expedition struck the pole while wearing full war paint and regalia.

Chickasaw stick ball players; painting by George Catlin (1796–1872), who specialized in paintings of Native Americans. (Native Stock Pictures)

In fighting colonial forces, the Chickasaws sought to employ tactics of ambush and surprise to avoid the conventional battle that favored European firepower. When both sides were ready to negotiate, the Chickasaws hosted enemy emissaries with elaborate entertainment. They passed a white calumet pipe among those assembled while the Eagle Dance was performed (with a heavy use of red and white colors to symbolize the duality of war and peace).

The ill-fated Spanish expedition led by Hernando de Soto initiated first European contact with the Chickasaws in 1540. Chickasaw-Spanish relations developed amicably at first, and the Spanish remained for about five months. But then de Soto demanded that 200 Chickasaw men serve as porters for travels that would ultimately take him to the Mississippi River. The Chickasaws refused to cooperate and assaulted the Spanish camp under cover of darkness. With the loss of roughly 40 men and nearly all of his equipment, de Soto was fortunate that the Chickasaws chose not to follow up on their initial attack.

During the colonial period, the Chickasaws were aggressively courted by the British, French, and Spanish as each colonial power vied for security and commerce in the region. The eclipse of Spanish influence in North America rendered this a two-way competition by the late 1600s. Although the French made progress in developing a friendly faction, the Chickasaws increasingly gravitated toward the British. This affiliation produced a flourishing trade of horses, guns, textiles, and metals for slaves and pelts.

As the Chickasaws' partnership with the British solidified, the French gradually discarded diplomacy in favor of brutal attacks. During the 18th century the French employed the Choctaws and other native allies to carry these out. Indeed, the French went so far as to hire Iroquois mercenaries from New York, but they never achieved a decisive victory. In fact, the defeat of two French armies at the hands of the Chickasaws helped to destabilize the standing of New France with its Algonquian allies. These periodic conflicts consumed precious French resources and lasted until France lost its hold on the North American mainland in 1763.

The Chickasaws briefly battled the British during Pontiac's Rebellion (1763). They also contested the Cherokees to the northeast. The Chickasaws backed the British during the American Revolutionary War (1775–1783) and did so in large part over fears of the relentless westward expansion of colonists.

During the war, a promising development emerged in the form of a proposed confederacy of the Chickasaws, Cherokees, Choctaws, and Creeks. They were all to attack the western frontier in conjunction with British forces. This ambitious campaign was forestalled when George Rogers Clark led an intrepid collection of American and French backwoodsmen to recapture a British outpost at Fort Sackville in Vincennes (present-day Indiana). In the process they seized supplies destined for Britain's Native American allies. Realizing that the proposed operation was now a dead letter, the grand council for Pan-Indian action never convened. The aborted plan proved to be a fateful episode for the Chickasaws.

The Treaty of Paris (1783) and the removal of their British ally was a great blow to the Chickasaws. In what was at best a delaying tactic, they attempted to play the Spanish and Americans against each other for commerce along the Mississippi River. The tribe refused to join in Tecumseh's alliance against the Americans in 1811 and instead fought with Major General Andrew Jackson against the Red Stick Creeks during the War of 1812. The Chickasaws helped Jackson defeat the Creeks at the Battle of Horseshoe Bend (March 27, 1814). During the 1820s many Chickasaws moved west.

By 1830 the Chickasaw Nation, a mere shadow of its former self in size, power, and cultural homogeneity, ceded its remaining territory in Mississippi. As feared, the Chickasaw peoples had been decimated by white encroachment, sporadic warfare, and diseases brought to the continent by Europeans. They soon proceeded along the infamous Trail of Tears to Indian Territory (Oklahoma) in the 1830s. During the American Civil War (1861–1865) the Chickasaws allied with the Confederacy, although their fealty was more symbolic than military. As one of the Five Civilized Tribes, they were exempted from the 1887 Dawes Severalty Act, but in 1889 the Curtis Act stripped the Chickasaws of their right to self-governance in preparation for Oklahoma statehood.

JEFFREY D. BASS

See also

Chickasaw Wars; Choctaw-Chickasaw War; Choctaws; Creeks; Creek War; Dawes Severalty Act; Horseshoe Bend, Battle of; Pontiac's Rebellion; Red Sticks; Tecumseh; Trail of Tears

References

Dowd, Gregory Evans. *A Spirited Resistance: The North American Indian Struggle for Unity, 1745–1815.* Baltimore: Johns Hopkins University Press, 1992.

White, Richard. *The Middle Ground: Indians, Empires, and Republics in the Great Lakes Region, 1650–1815.* New York: Cambridge University Press, 1991.

Chickasaw Wars
Start Date: March 1736
End Date: April 1740

Major military campaigns in the American Southeast that reflected both the Anglo-French struggle for continental supremacy and the long-standing Choctaw-Chickasaw rivalry. Although the French committed more forces to these conflicts than in previous native encounters, they remained in search of a decisive victory over the Chickasaws that would deprive the British of a vital commercial and military partner. In the end, the Chickasaw Wars contributed to the steady decline of New France in terms of strategic assets and its standing among native tribes.

The Chickasaw Wars followed on the heels of the Natchez War (1729–1733) that had pitted the French and the Choctaws against the Natchez and the Chickasaws, with the British assisting the latter coalition. By 1733, hostilities had subsided out of a recognition by most of the involved parties that regrouping was essential. Still chafing under French authority, the Choctaws mounted an independent assault on the Chickasaws in 1734. Roughly 600 warriors tricked the Chickasaws into leaving their forts and entering into an ambush. This bold strike convinced the Chickasaws to lobby harder for peace and to accede to a standing French demand to eliminate the Natchezes, who had sought refuge within their territory. In 1734 it briefly appeared as though a lasting peace could be achieved because the Choctaws and the Chickasaws were exhausted and the French were stretched dangerously thin in maintaining their security commitments in North America.

In April 1735, however, a contingent of French soldiers transporting 1,700 pounds of gunpowder happened upon a larger force of Natchezes and Chickasaws on a mission to rescue their captured women from the Illinois. The alarmed French quickly opened fire, which led to the defeat of both the soldiers and any hope for peace in the region. Although a delegation of Chickasaw chiefs employed diplomacy to return the French prisoners taken in the engagement, French resolve had hardened. The governor of Louisiana, Jean-Baptiste Le Moyne de Bienville, was finally prepared to launch a major French invasion of Chickasaw lands, a task previously relegated to the Choctaws. The French constructed Fort Tombeché (Alabama) along the Tombigbee River as a staging point for the assault.

By March 1736 Bienville had assembled about 460 French soldiers in addition to 100 Swiss mercenaries and 45 African slaves. He could soon expect a sizable Choctaw war party to arrive. But the French operation was plagued by poor coordination of forces. In February, Pierre d'Artaguette had departed from the Illinois country with 145 French troops and a contingent of 326 natives, including Iroquois, Miamis, Arkansas, and Illinois warriors. By moving into Chickasaw territory ahead of the now-delayed Bienville, the force tipped its hand that a major incursion was afoot. There is evidence that the French allies in d'Artaguette's force had grown disenchanted and deliberately discarded bread to reveal their presence.

Running low on supplies, d'Artaguette opted in March to attack the Chickasaw village of Ogoula Tchetoka. The assault was thwarted, however, when 400 Natchez and Chickasaw warriors arrived to outflank the invaders. D'Artaguette's native allies deserted him, and he suffered serious injuries during what degenerated into a pell-mell retreat. Only a remnant of the original French force escaped as the Chickasaws made away with a considerable cache of gunpowder. French prisoners, including d'Artaguette and a Jesuit priest, were tossed into a fire; the Chickasaws viewed such treatment as an appropriate form of revenge and a means of purification. The captives might well have been spared, but word of Bienville's advance ruined any chance for negotiation.

Unaware of this horrendous turn of events, Bienville began his assault along the Tombigbee River in May 1736. About 600

Choctaws joined him, including the devious Chief Red Shoes, who periodically shifted his favor between the French and the British. Bienville wished to locate the Natchezes and quarreled with Choctaw chiefs who preferred to concentrate on the Chickasaws.

Choctaw guides misled the French and forced a battle against several Chickasaw villages in the vicinity of present-day Tupelo, Mississippi. At this site the Chickasaws enjoyed the strongest defensive position in their entire nation as they retreated inside a collection of sturdy forts atop steep ridges. Bienville's initial attack was composed entirely of Europeans and gained little while absorbing heavy casualties. Bienville had his troops march in ranks with their officers prominently displayed in a classic example of losing a battle in the New World with tactics typical of the Old World. The attackers wore heavy woolen bags to protect them from musket fire but suffered from shots aimed at their vulnerable legs. When the Europeans threw grenades, the defenders often retrieved them quickly enough to employ against the assault. Dumbfounded over the ineptitude of the French, the Choctaws joined the melee but to no avail.

Having presided over the worst defeat ever inflicted on the French by Native Americans, Bienville began a retreat with his demoralized force that proceeded only four miles. He pleaded successfully with Choctaw chiefs for them to remain with him. On returning to New Orleans, Bienville liberally placed blame for the fiasco with the Choctaws, his own troops, and the British. Authorities in Paris expected him to resume the offensive.

Allowing for time to marshal his forces, Bienville's second invasion did not begin until July 1739. In the meantime, the Choctaws had grown more effective in raiding Chickasaw territory and consequently were more frustrated with French timidity. Learning from the French to concentrate on the destruction of crops and horses, the Choctaws had weakened Chickasaw morale to the point where there was strong momentum for peace. Sensing the weariness of their hosts, the Natchezes grew increasingly uncomfortable residing among the Chickasaws. Anxious to support their clients, British agents helped to broker a settlement between the Chickasaws and the Choctaws in 1738 using the mysterious Red Shoe. But a rival Choctaw faction commenced hostilities and plunged the region into full-scale war yet again.

At Fort Assumption near present-day Memphis, Tennessee, the French had amassed enough gunpowder, artillery, and grenades to launch their greatest assault against the Chickasaws. Bienville now commanded approximately 1,000 Frenchmen, 500 northern native allies, and 1,000 Choctaws. But poor weather, illness, and desertion took its toll on this force before it ever saw battle. By February 1740 Bienville had lost too many horses and oxen to transport his cannon. He informed his already skeptical native allies that the French could not attack. This disclosure was particularly infuriating to the Choctaws, whom the French had restrained from launching a major assault of their own despite recent success in raiding the Chickasaws.

Bienville agreed to provide about 200 French troops to accompany 337 natives for a reduced operation. Red Shoes dispatched warriors to alert the Chickasaws to the impending onslaught, but distrust among the Chickasaws rendered this initiative useless.

Pierre Joseph de Celeron commanded the French expedition that moved against Ogoula Tchetoka. Discovering a Chickasaw fort, the French endeavored to erect a fort of their own. Disgusted with what they perceived as the lack of an offensive spirit, the Choctaws abandoned the operation. Only frantic entreaties kept the northern natives on board. Negotiations produced a peace settlement whereby the northern warriors retired and the Chickasaws promised to deliver the Natchezes.

The Choctaws remained free to battle the Chickasaws with French logistical support, and the Chickasaws allowed French commerce to resume along the Mississippi. By April 1740, Bienville left for New Orleans having achieved only mixed results. The French had finally completed their quest for revenge against the Natchezes for a revolt initiated in 1729 with the wholesale slaughter of colonists. But unable to produce decisive victories over the Chickasaws or compete with British traders for native commerce, the ongoing revelation of French weakness compromised its military, diplomatic, and economic operations throughout North America.

The peace of 1740 proved fragile in implementation. Northern warriors continued to harass the depleted Chickasaws, who were for the most part attempting to make good on their promise concerning the Natchezes. Bienville continued exhorting the Choctaws to raid Chickasaw territory but was soon replaced as governor. Considerable strife lay ahead in the quest for supremacy among Europeans and natives in the Southeast.

Jeffrey D. Bass

See also

Chickasaws; Choctaw-Chickasaw War; Choctaws; Ogoula Tchetoka, Battle of; Natchez Revolt; Natchez War; Red Shoe

References

Atkinson, James R. *Splendid Land, Splendid People: The Chickasaw Indians to Removal.* Tuscaloosa: University of Alabama Press, 2004.

Axtell, James. *The Indians' New South: Cultural Change in the Colonial Southeast.* Baton Rouge: Louisiana State University Press, 1997.

Chillicothe, Ohio, Battles on the Little Miami River
Event Dates: August 8, 1780 and November 1, 1782

Two attacks led by Colonel George Rogers Clark and a force of Virginia and Kentucky militia against the Shawnees in the Ohio River Valley. The first battle took place on August 8, 1780, and was followed two years later by another attack on November 1, 1782. Clark carefully planned these engagements and received the support of the Virginia government, which sought the removal of the Shawnees from what they considered sovereign U.S. territory.

At the time the Shawnees were wedged between the white settlers of Virginia and Kentucky to the south and east and the hostile

Mingo tribe to the north, who were allied with the British during the American Revolutionary War (1775–1783). The Shawnees had unsuccessfully fought steady white encroachment, mainly from Virginia, for years prior to 1780. The tribe was divided into five divisions: the Chillicothes, Thawekilas, Maquachakes, Piquas, and Kispokis. The tribe was also divided among a war faction anxious to ally with the British, a band that favored neutrality, and a contingent sympathetic to the colonists. In 1777 a group of Shawnee warriors had joined the Mingos, at the urging of British Governor Henry Hamilton at Detroit, and began attacking frontier settlements.

That same year Chief Cornstalk, leader of the Maquachakes, who had long pleaded for peace with the colonists, was killed by American militia, driving more Shawnees to side with the British. Two years later John Bowman raided the town of Chillicothe with a group of Kentucky frontiersmen. The invaders were repelled, but the Shawnee leader, Chief Black Fish, was killed. The Native Americans, weakened by a brutal winter and a mass migration of their tribe farther west, looked to the British for help when Clark's force invaded in the summer of 1780.

In August 1780 when Clark's regiment of nearly 1,000 men neared, the Shawnees burned the town of Chillicothe and fell back 12 miles to the town of Piqua on the Miami River (also known as the Mad River). The conflict was decided when Clark ordered his artillery to fire on the village council house, where many Shawnees had taken refuge. Militia casualties numbered 14 killed and 13 wounded. Shawnee losses were almost triple that, but Clark's raiders inflicted the most damage after the battle. For two days the marauders burned cornfields and plundered Shawnee graves. An estimated 500 acres of corn were destroyed. Evidence of the devastation from Clark's raid was substantiated by a white captive, Mary Erskine, who attested that the tribe subsisted on meat all the next winter. Many fled to Detroit for aid.

The first battle of the Miami River was a minor skirmish that did succeed in further weakening the Shawnees in the Ohio Valley. Ironically, Clark's cousin, Joseph Rogers, was killed by the white invaders during the engagement. The cousin had been presumed dead in 1776 when a supply train carrying gun powder from Fort Pitt to Kentucky was ambushed. He had in fact been captured by the Shawnees. Rogers, dressed in Native American garb, was shot and killed while running toward the militia lines.

The Shawnees did not remain idle after Clark's first raid and continued their hostility toward white settlers on the frontier. Clark mounted another incursion into the area after Kentucky militiamen were ambushed and routed at the Battle of Blue Licks on August 19, 1782. He set off on November 1, 1782, with close to 1,000 men including Daniel Boone, whose son was killed at Blue Licks. Clark advanced against the same area he had attacked two years before. The raid was not as hotly contested as the previous one, as most of the Shawnee warriors were away hunting. Clark burned five villages and again destroyed crops. The countryside was ravaged, and Clark's men razed a British supply station

known as Loramie's Store. The Shawnees suffered 10 dead, 7 prisoners, and 2 whites recaptured, while the raiders suffered 1 killed and 1 wounded.

The 1782 invasion was the last major offensive mounted in the Old Northwest Territory during the American Revolution. These two minor engagements temporarily dissuaded other tribes in the area from attacking white settlements, however.

WILLIAM WHYTE

See also

Blue Licks, Kentucky, Action at; Boone, Daniel; Clark, George Rogers; Cornstalk; Mingos; Native Americans and the American Revolutionary War; Old Northwest Territory; Shawnees

References

Bodley, Temple. *George Rodgers Clark: His Life and Public Services.* Boston: Houghton Mifflin, 1926.

Bodley, Temple. "The National Significance of George Rodgers Clark." *Mississippi Valley Historical Review* 11(2) (September 1924): 165–189.

Calloway, Colin G. *The American Revolution in Indian Country: Crisis and Diversity in Native American Communities.* Cambridge: Cambridge University Press, 1995.

Calloway, Colin G. "'We Have Always Been the Frontier': The American Revolution in Shawnee Country." *American Indian Quarterly* 16(1) (1992): 39–52.

Chippewas
See Ojibwas

Chivington, John
Birth Date: February 21, 1821
Death Date: October 4, 1894

Ordained Methodist minister, volunteer officer, and perpetrator of the 1864 Sand Creek Massacre. John Chivington was born on February 21, 1821, in Lebanon, Ohio, where he worked on the family farm and in the lumber business. He received little formal education. Chivington converted to Methodism in October 1842 and decided to study for the ministry. In 1844 he was ordained as a Methodist minister. He served Methodist congregations in Illinois and then Missouri, where in 1856 his vocal opposition to slavery nearly provoked a violent encounter with some members of his church. As a result, Chivington was reassigned to Nebraska and in 1860 became presiding elder of the Rocky Mountain Conference in the Colorado Territory.

When the American Civil War (1861–1865) broke out, Chivington helped organize the 1st Regiment of Colorado Volunteers for the Union. Declining an offer to serve as the unit's chaplain, he resigned from the ministry and took a commission as major in the regiment. In March 1862 he led the unit on a grueling 13-day

Portrait of colonel and Methodist minister John M. Chivington, who led an attack on Cheyenne chief Black Kettle's peaceful village on November 29, 1864. Known as the Sand Creek Massacre, it brought the deaths of some 200 Indian men, women, and children. (Denver Public Library, Western History Collection, Z-128)

400-mile march to New Mexico to join Union forces opposing Confederate brigadier general Henry Sibley's invasion of that territory. Chivington fought in the battles at Apache Canyon and Glorieta Pass during March 26–28, 1862, participating in the decisive march around the Confederate lines that destroyed Sibley's wagon train and forced the Confederates to retreat east to Texas.

Returning to Colorado, Chivington was promoted to colonel and was appointed military commander of the Colorado Territory. In 1863 he was unable to protect Colorado from a series of Cheyenne attacks that threw the territory into turmoil until cold weather ended the raiding. When a small group of Cheyennes renewed their harassment in the spring of 1864, Chivington and Governor John Evans formed a new limited-enlistment volunteer regiment, the 3rd Colorado Cavalry, and Chivington led the unit in search of the attacking parties. Chivington's efforts accomplished little, and by the late summer of 1864 he was publicly urging the slaughter of the Cheyennes as the only means to end the raids.

Failing to find the hostile Cheyennes, on the early morning of November 29, 1864, Chivington and his troops instead attacked a peaceful party of 600 Cheyennes and Arapahos of Black Kettle's

village camped at Sand Creek in eastern Colorado. Only 35 warriors were in the camp, and two-thirds of the Native Americans were women and children. Chivington's force easily overwhelmed the defenseless camp, killing at least 130 Native Americans, although some estimates put the death toll at more than 200. Less than a dozen of Chivington's men were killed, most of them by friendly fire. When the slaughter ended, the soldiers scalped and mutilated the Native American corpses, displaying body parts as trophies.

Public outrage at the Sand Creek Massacre caused Congress to launch an investigation. Chivington insisted that he thought the Native Americans were hostile, but many of his officers testified that he knew otherwise. Chivington avoided a court-martial by resigning his commission in 1865. He then moved to Nebraska and California before returning to Ohio, where the stain of Sand Creek thwarted his candidacy for the state legislature in 1883. After his political defeat Chivington moved to Denver, where he died on October 4, 1894.

JIM PIECUCH

See also
Arapahos; Black Kettle; Cavalry Regiment, 3rd Colorado; Cheyennes; Sand Creek Massacre; Sibley, Henry Hastings

References
Craig, Reginald S. *The Fighting Parson: The Biography of Colonel John M. Chivington*. Los Angeles: Westernlore, 1959.
Scott, Robert. *Blood at Sand Creek: The Massacre Revisited*. Caldwell, ID: Claxton, 1994.

Choctaw-Chickasaw War
Event Date: 1752

Unsuccessful French-Choctaw campaign against the Chickasaws and the last in a series of nearly uninterrupted conflicts over the previous two decades between two longtime native rivals spurred on by European intrigues. The Choctaw-Chickasaw War of 1752 served as a futile last gasp in the French attempt to eradicate the Chickasaws as British allies in the American Southeast.

By the 1740s the French-allied Choctaws had lost three successive wars to the Chickasaws. These setbacks severely damaged French credibility, but the Chickasaws had lost as much as three-fourths of their population in the process. In 1742 Pierre de Rigaud de Vaudreuil, as newly appointed governor of Louisiana, inherited the onerous task of maintaining French interests in the region. The exhausted Chickasaws initiated peace overtures with the French in 1743, but Vaudreuil demanded cessation of all trade with Britain and the consent of the Choctaws as preconditions.

Vaudreuil hoped to stall negotiations while awaiting reinforcements with which to subdue the Chickasaws. But French priorities lay elsewhere, and the reinforcements never arrived. With diplomacy stymied, both the Choctaws and the Chickasaws resorted to periodic raids while pressing their respective European allies for more trade as an inducement to continue fighting.

The French paid Choctaw warriors for Chickasaw scalps, and Chickasaw prisoners were made available for enslavement. Vaudreuil's alleged commitment to peace appears even weaker in light of instructions he received from Paris in 1751 to encourage internecine warfare among the Choctaws, his own allies. The governor had no moral qualms in executing this policy, but he worried that the Choctaws would recognize his strategy as a means of rendering them more dependent on the French. As the Choctaws bickered over which European power to favor, a civil war ensued during 1746–1750, with the French faction emerging victorious.

In the meantime, British naval exploits during King George's War (1744–1748) reduced French supplies to the point where the Choctaws felt little incentive to attack their neighbors at the behest of New France. As Chickasaw raids had now intensified, in 1752 the French finally convinced the unenthusiastic Choctaws to act. Scholars disagree on the number of French troops involved in the Choctaw-Chickasaw War, with estimates ranging from 700 to as few as a handful.

The Choctaw-dominated invasion force moved along the Tombigbee River (located in present-day western Alabama) in September 1752, just as the French and the Choctaws had done during an earlier war in 1736. The Chickasaws, however, refused to engage their enemies in a conventional battle that would likely have favored the invaders. The result was a hit-and-run guerrilla-style war, with most of the Chickasaws remaining in their well-fortified towns. As such, the French and the Choctaws settled for razing deserted villages and depriving the Chickasaws of crops and livestock. The 1752 war concluded without any alteration in the regional balance of power. France's eviction from the North American mainland in the Treaty of Paris (1763) ultimately ensured Chickasaw dominance over the Choctaws.

JEFFREY D. BASS

See also

Chickasaws; Choctaw Civil War; Choctaws; King George's War

References

Atkinson, James R. *Splendid Land, Splendid People: The Chickasaw Indians to Removal*. Tuscaloosa: University of Alabama Press, 2004.

White, Richard. *The Middle Ground: Indians, Empires, and Republics in the Great Lakes Region, 1650–1815*. New York: Cambridge University Press, 1991.

Choctaw Civil War

Start Date: 1746
End Date: 1750

Intertribal conflict among the Choctaws precipitated by the ongoing Anglo-French rivalry. The Choctaw Civil War ensued when Choctaw war chief Red Shoe, a longtime ally of France, switched allegiance to Britain. The civil war can also be seen as one more conflict, along with King George's War (1744–1748), in the colonial competition involving France, Britain, and Spain in North America that devastated the indigenous peoples.

Although the French had been in North America a few years longer than the British, the French and the British had only arrived in southeastern North America in the early 1700s. Spain had older, albeit more contested, ties with powerful southeastern tribes such as the Choctaws and the Chickasaws. The arrival of the French along the Gulf Coast (Choctaw territory) and the British in inland Chickasaw territory led to logical trade alliances between the French and Choctaws and between the British and the Chickasaws. French colonists who had trouble inland with the Natchezes and the Yazoos turned to their Choctaw allies for help. The resultant destruction of the Natchez tribe and the establishment of New Orleans in 1718 further advanced the French-Choctaw alliance. Because New Orleans then functioned essentially as a port of illicit trade and piracy, it also served to bring the French and the Choctaws into conflict with the British-Chickasaw alliance and Spain.

Neither France nor Britain wanted the age-old Choctaw-Chickasaw rivalry to end. Nevertheless, in 1741 the Choctaw chief Red Shoes tried to negotiate a treaty between the two tribes, perhaps realizing that their real enemy was the ever-growing number of European colonists. Both British and French representatives worked feverishly to thwart the treaty, and French governor Pierre de Vaudreuil was successful in doing so by 1744. However, bad blood eventually emerged between Vaudreuil and Red Shoe that would have serious future consequences.

In 1744 the Franco-British rivalry erupted into King George's War. During the conflict, the British fleet blockaded New World shipping. The blockade had little effect on French colonists, who by this time were largely self-sufficient. However, it did have a major impact on France's ability to supply European goods to its native allies. As a result, some Choctaw chiefs, headed by Red Shoe, asked the British to open trade especially for guns, which were vital to Choctaw survival.

As with most Native American groups, the Choctaw Nation was a complex political unit in which each part had some autonomy in certain domestic and foreign affairs. The Choctaws consisted of about eight tribes and many clans numbering perhaps 40,000 people in all by the mid-18th century. Some groups remained loyal to the French, other groups sided with British traders, and still other groups remained neutral.

From 1746 to 1748 Red Shoe remained in control with British support. But discontent was rising within the Choctaw Nation. Governor Vaudreuil ultimately conspired with Red Shoe's Choctaw rivals to murder Red Shoe in June 1748. A full-blown Choctaw civil war then ensued.

During the second phase of the war, from 1748 to 1750, the brother of Red Shoe carried on the intertribal conflict with British support. Ultimately the French faction dominated and won the war outright by September 1750. In the end British support for the Choctaws who had allied with them was minimal, as the British stood to win either way. The British certainly did not want to incur the wrath of their longtime allies, the Chickasaws, by support-ing the Choctaws. Yet the British hoped to reduce French–Native American power in the region. The Choctaw Civil War served both purposes, making the British the clear winners. The British went on to defeat a weakened French–Native American alliance in the French and Indian War (1754–1763). In a sense, the civil war was a precursor to the much larger Franco-British conflict. The Choctaw Civil War and disease combined to decimate the formerly power-ful southeastern tribe. Usually able to field around 3,000 warriors and up to 600 in a single battle well into the 1700s, the Choctaws emerged from the civil war with fewer than a third that number.

CHRISTOPHER HOWELL

See also

Chickasaws; Choctaw-Chickasaw War; Choctaws; King George's War; Red Shoe

References

Daunton, Martin, and Rick Haltern, eds. *Empire and Others: British Encounters with Indigenous Peoples, 1600–1850.* Philadelphia: University of Pennsylvania Press, 1999.

Gayarre, Charles. *History of Louisiana.* 3 vols. 1909; reprint, Ann Arbor: University of Michigan Press, 2005.

Nester, William R. *The Great Frontier War: Britain, France, and the Imperial Struggle for North America, 1607–1755.* Westport, CT: Praeger, 2000.

Peyser, Joseph. *Letters from New France (Chickasaw Wars).* Norman: University of Oklahoma Press, 1983.

Woods, Patricia Dillon. *French-Indian Relations on the Southern Frontier, 1699–1762.* Ann Arbor: University of Michigan Research Press, 1980.

Choctaws

Native American group whose territory included east-central Mississippi as well as parts of Alabama. The Choctaws were one of the so-called Five Civilized Tribes of the American Southeast (along with the Chickasaws, the Creeks, the Seminoles, and the Cherokees). The Choctaw Nation traditionally resisted developing dependency on Europeans, whereas the English, French, and Span-ish vied for resources and influence among indigenous peoples.

The Choctaws had developed a multiethnic confederacy in present-day east-central Mississippi by the late 17th century. Reputedly the one-time brethren of the Chickasaws, the Choctaws became renowned farmers and fierce warriors. Because of their agricultural prowess, they enjoyed a diverse economy that also included hunting, fishing, gathering, and trapping.

Choctaw competitiveness manifested itself in a rough version of stickball known as *toli,* or "little brother of war." These contests trained men for battle and sometimes settled political disputes. Opposing towns sometimes invoked witchcraft in an effort to influence the outcome.

Four social ranks differentiated Choctaw males. The grand chiefs, village chiefs, and war chiefs occupied the highest rung. Under them were the *hatak holitopa,* or "beloved men." The

tashka ("warriors") held the third level. At the bottom were the *hatak imatahali* ("youth" or "supporting men") who had not seen combat or had slain only women and children. The political organization and social structure of the Choctaws centered on the *iksa* ("clan"), with their matrilineal kinship networks. Traditional political power hierarchies tended to be weak, however.

The size and central location of the Choctaw Nation rendered it strategically vital for imperial ambitions in the region. The French secured the first sustained European contact with the Choctaws through a trading post, which prompted the English to befriend the adjacent Chickasaws and Quapaws with the promise of weap-ons in exchange for Choctaw slaves. By 1699 the Choctaws had lost nearly 2,000 people to English-inspired slave raids and military assaults. In 1702 the Choctaws allied with the French to gain fire-arms. However, a lack of immunity to European diseases reduced the Choctaw population by roughly 5,000 within 15 years.

In 1711 the British along with the Chickasaws and the Creeks launched a major campaign that inflicted on the Choctaw losses to death and slavery in excess of 400. But after 1715 when the British had faced a rebellion of their own among Native Americans, an effort was begun to entice the Choctaws to abandon the French.

Because indigenous slaves were perishing rapidly in South Carolina, the British favored commerce with the Choctaws while increasing the importation of African slaves. The French coun-tered with an increasingly large volume of gifts to selected Choc-taw chiefs. But a lack of effective hierarchy in Choctaw society rendered these expenditures ineffective in securing strong influ-ence. Indeed, Choctaw chiefs routinely redistributed European goods to their people. They thus perceived French gifts in terms of their own cultural interpretation as an affirmation of friendship. But French authorities grew to resent what they deemed an arro-gant expectation of tribute.

Financial strains on New France in the early 18th century reduced its generosity as officials resorted to bypassing civil chiefs in favor of direct scalp bounties to warriors. The British had their own difficulties thanks to a bloody uprising known as the Yamasee War (1715–1717). The Choctaw alliance with the French was solidified in the aftermath of the Natchez Revolt (1729) in which French settlers along the Mississippi River were slaughtered and enslaved.

The Choctaws played an important role in exacting retribution on the Natchezes in the conflicts of the early 1730s. Because some of the Natchezes had fled to the Chickasaws, the French aimed to eradicate the Natchezes and compel the Chickasaws to renounce their alliance with the British. The French then constructed a fort in Choctaw territory along the Tombigbee River and initiated two unsuccessful wars with the Chickasaws.

By the mid-18th century an intense effort by the French and Brit-ish to curry favor among the Choctaws had plunged the nation into civil war. French officials showered the war chief Red Shoe (Shu-lush Homa) with gifts and medals to help him supplant civil chiefs and turn him into a pliable client. But the ambitious leader created

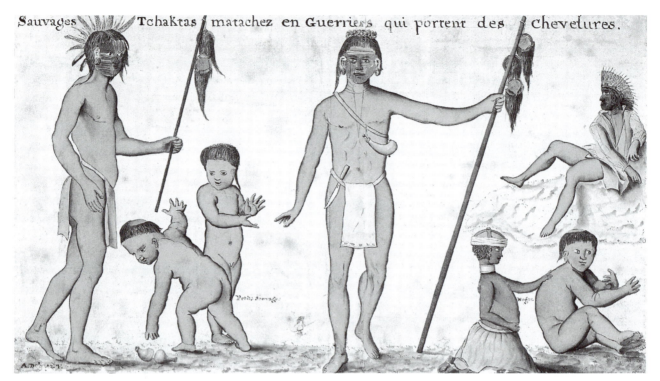

Sauvages Tchaktas matachez en Guerriers qui portent des chevelures.

An 18th-century sketch of Choctaw warriors and children. One of the so-called Five Civilized Tribes, the Choctaws were an ethnically mixed people who lived in present-day Mississippi and part of Alabama. Although Choctaw assistance was critical to the victories of Major General Andrew Jackson in the Creek War (1813–1814), the Choctaws lost the remainder of their land and were removed to the West beginning in 1831. (Corbis)

an independent power base from which to play the French and the British against each other (as well as against Choctaw factions) during the 1730s with a series of intricate diplomatic maneuvers.

When Red Shoe parleyed with the British and the Chickasaws in 1745, the French arranged for the murder of several delegates. Red Shoe retaliated by ordering the slaying of a French officer and two traders the following year. The Choctaw system of justice did not prescribe death for the perpetrators despite the fact that the French had executed two of their own in 1738 for the murder of a Choctaw couple. The Choctaws attempted to placate the French by killing more of the Chickasaws and the British, but internal divisions deepened.

Meanwhile, the British hoped to compel more trade with the Choctaws. But the Choctaws required only a small range of goods, generally clothing, textiles, metal tools, and blankets. The British consequently promoted rum and the credit necessary to purchase it as a means to create commercial dependency. Numerous Choctaw hunters soon languished in debt as they desperately sought the animal pelts necessary to settle accounts. Feeling betrayed over a partnership with few dividends, the French hired an assassin who murdered Red Shoe in 1747. A civil war ensued, as no other leader could maintain his delicate equilibrium of power and diplomacy. The conflict was slowed by a smallpox epidemic, but the pro-French faction ultimately triumphed.

Following the Treaty of Paris in 1763, the French eviction from the North American mainland left the Choctaws vulnerable

to attacks from their neighbors. For more than a decade the British periodically agitated the Creeks into attacks. But the Choctaws subsequently used the threat posed by Spanish Florida to gain commercial and diplomatic advantages with the British. Choctaw warriors joined British forces arrayed against the Spanish during the American Revolutionary War (1775–1783), but meager pay and supplies led many of the fighters to depart before battle. Many Choctaws assisted the British in the unsuccessful defense of Pensacola against a Franco-Spanish assault in 1781 but left when the town surrendered in May.

During the Creek War (1813–1814) and the War of 1812 the Choctaws, after having rebuffed Shawnee leader Tecumseh's invitation to join his confederacy, sided with the Americans, serving as messengers and scouts. The Choctaws participated in the Battle of Econochaca (December 23, 1813), also known as the Battle of Holy Ground; the Battle of Horseshoe Bend (March 27, 1814); and the Battle of New Orleans (January 8, 1815). After the Indian Removal Act of 1830 was passed, the Choctaws were forcibly removed from their ancestral lands by the U.S. government to Indian Territory (Oklahoma).

JEFFREY D. BASS

See also

Chickasaws; Chickasaw Wars; Choctaw-Chickasaw War; Choctaw Civil War; Creek-Choctaw Wars; Creeks; Natchez Revolt; Natchez War; Native Americans and the War of 1812; Red Shoe; Slavery among Native Americans; Tecumseh

References

Carson, James Taylor. *Searching for the Bright Path: The Mississippi Choctaws from Prehistory to Removal.* Lincoln: University of Nebraska Press, 1999.

Galloway, Patricia. "Choctaw Factionalism and Civil War, 1746–1750." *Journal of Mississippi History* 44 (1982): 289–327.

Galloway, Patricia. *Choctaw Genesis, 1500–1700.* Lincoln: University of Nebraska Press, 1995.

Church, Benjamin
Birth Date: 1639
Death Date: January 17, 1717

New England soldier and frontiersman and the first of the so-called border captains who figure so prominently in the history and mythology of the colonial wars against Native Americans. Benjamin Church was born in 1639 at Duxbury in Plymouth Colony, the son of a carpenter and veteran of the Pequot War (1636–1638). To the dismay of the more conventional English soldiers in Plymouth and Massachusetts Bay colonies and the Puritan divines, particularly Increase Mather, Church counseled adopting Native American ways of fighting (the so-called skulking way of war). He also urged the use of Native American allies to defeat Metacom (King Philip) and his warriors in King Philip's War (1675–1676).

Church practiced what he preached. He taught colonials under his command to move silently through the forests and swamps, to "scatter" as the Native Americans did if attacked, and to "never fire at an Indian if you can reach him with a hatchet."

Ranging through Massachusetts and Rhode Island, Church's mixed band of Native Americans and handpicked Plymouth soldiers burned enemy villages and crops and took many native prisoners. Finally, on August 12, 1676, Church and his rangers tracked the Native American leader Metacom to his camp near Mount Hope, Rhode Island, and killed him when he tried to escape. The dead chief's head was cut off and taken to Plymouth, where it remained atop a pole for some 25 years as a trophy of English victory. For his exploits, the Plymouth authorities awarded Church the sum of 30 shillings.

Church frequently fell out with colonial leaders over treatment of native foes during the war. On more than one occasion, Native Americans he had convinced to surrender or who had been captured were sold into slavery, to his great fury. This was the fate of Metacom's wife and son, taken by Church and his rangers 10 days before they killed the Native American leader.

When King William's War (1689–1697) began, Church was commissioned a major and led Plymouth forces in the fight against the French and their Native American allies in Maine, then part of Massachusetts. His troops participated in the Battle of Brackett's Woods, which helped lift the siege of Fort Loyal. Church led three more expeditions into Maine and what is today New Brunswick,

New England frontiersman Benjamin Church (1639–1717) was an accomplished military leader who adopted Native American methods of warfare. (Library of Congress)

Canada, in 1690, 1692, and 1696. These were in retaliation for French and Native American raids against the northern borders of New England.

In March 1704 Church, although by now a rotund 65-year-old, was granted a commission as colonel of Massachusetts troops and was ordered to raid into Acadia. The raids were in revenge for French and native destruction of the town of Deerfield, Massachusetts, the month before. Fortified by a promise of £100 for each Native American scalp and moving from place to place by whaleboat and taking to snowshoes when necessary, Church's 550 New England volunteers attacked native villages, seized and burned the towns of Les Mines (Grand Pré) and Chignecto, and threatened the French base at Port Royal.

The Acadia raid was Church's last campaign. He retired to his farm at Little Compton, Rhode Island, where he and his son Thomas composed the two volumes of his memoirs of King Philip's War and the struggles against the French and Native Americans, the primary material for which was a diary Church had kept over the years. The volumes are noteworthy for the author's insistence on the importance of human agency—his own, primarily—in the victories of the colonists over their enemies. Other contemporary historians of the wars, such as William Hubbard and Cotton Mather, had seen the triumphs as evidence of God's will. Publication of his memoirs made Church a model for other border captains, such as Robert Rogers, to follow. Church died on January 17, 1717, near his home at Little Compton, Rhode Island.

BRUCE VANDERVORT

See also

Deerfield, Massachusetts, Attack on; King Philip's War; King William's War; Metacom; Skulking Way of War

References

Church, Benjamin, and Thomas Church. *Entertaining Passages Relating to Philip's War, Which Began in the Month of June 1675*. Boston: B. Green, 1716.

Church, Benjamin, and Thomas Church. *The History of King Philip's War, Commonly Called the Great Indian War, of 1675 and 1676; Also of the French and Indian Wars at the Eastward, in 1689, 1690, 1692, 1696, and 1704*. Exeter, NH: J. & B. Williams, 1829.

Leach, Douglas Edward. *Arms for Empire: A Military History of the British Colonies in North America, 1607–1763*. New York: Macmillan, 1973.

Slotkin, Richard. *Regeneration through Violence: The Mythology of the American Frontier, 1600–1860*. Middletown, CT: Wesleyan University Press, 1973.

Church of Jesus Christ of Latter-day Saints

See Mormonism

Cibecue Creek, Incident at
Event Date: August 30, 1881

Skirmish between elements of the U.S. 6th Cavalry and the Apaches on August 30, 1881, near Cibecue Creek, Arizona. Following the successes of Brigadier General George Crook's campaigns in Apacheria, the White Mountain Apaches had been peaceful for several years. Nevertheless, an aging White Mountain medicine man named Nochaydelklinne told of visions of an Apache resurgence and the disappearance of the white man, all of which would occur when the corn turned green. As the old medicine man's words reached more and more restless Apaches living on the San Carlos Reservation in Arizona, Indian agent J. C. Tiffany appealed for army assistance. On August 29, 1881, Colonel Eugene A. Carr led a large detachment of the 6th Cavalry from Fort Apache to investigate.

Carr and his command of some 80 soldiers and 23 White Mountain Apache scouts marched to the medicine man's village at Cibecue Creek and demanded that he come with the soldiers to Fort Apache or be killed. Although Nochaydelklinne initially declined, the White Mountain scouts encouraged him to go along for the sake of peace. After a short march Carr selected a campsite for the night, perhaps deciding to talk with the hundreds of Apaches who had thus far peacefully followed the soldiers as they traversed the reservation. The Apache scouts grew more agitated by the growing numbers of hostile Apaches and by the apparent disrespect toward Nochaydelklinne, who was guarded by 10 soldiers and a sergeant.

Witnesses later noted that without warning or provocation, a Scout, Sergeant Dead Shot, gave a war whoop and shot a nearby soldier. The white sergeant guarding the medicine man immediately drew his revolver and shot Nochaydelklinne in the head, at which time several other Apache scouts and the White Mountain people following the detachment opened fire on the cavalry. Amazingly the medicine man was still moving, so two Apaches, a young man and a woman, attempted a rescue but were killed by the soldiers. Realizing that Nochaydelklinne was the focus of the battle, the sergeant killed the old man with an ax. By now several of the Apache scouts had been subdued, while others ran away. The Apaches followed the soldiers and drove off Carr's pack mules and extra horses. Recognizing the difficulty of his situation, Carr ordered his men to create a breastwork of ration boxes, cans, and rocks. From this hastily constructed position they faced approximately 600 Apaches.

Throughout the late afternoon and early evening the Apaches made no concerted attempt to assault the cavalry position, so Carr had his dead rolled up in tent canvas and, to the sound of taps, buried where they fell. Later that night Carr pulled out under cover of darkness and marched to Fort Apache, a distance of 45 miles. Although the Apaches followed closely, they did not attack the column. The 6th Cavalry lost one officer and six enlisted men killed in the fighting at Cibecue Creek. According to those Apaches interviewed by General Crook after the incident and following campaign, the shooting began when Carr's cook, frightened by the scouts' wailing, opened fire on the crowd.

PATRICK R. JENNINGS

See also

Apaches; Apache Wars; Carr, Eugene Asa; Crook, George

References

Cozzens, Peter, ed. *Eyewitnesses to the Indian Wars, 1865–1890*. 5 vols. Mechanicsburg, PA: Stackpole, 2001–2006.

Thrapp, Dan L. *The Conquest of Apacheria*. Norman: University of Oklahoma Press, 1967.

Wellman, Paul I. *Death in the Desert: The Fifty Years' War for the Great Southwest*. Lincoln: University of Nebraska Press, 1987.

Civil War

See Native Americans and the Civil War

Clark, George Rogers
Birth Date: November 19, 1752
Death Date: February 13, 1818

Frontiersman and soldier. Born in Albemarle County, Virginia, on November 19, 1752, George Rogers Clark studied surveying and read history and geography as a youth. In 1772 he traveled by flatboat down the Ohio River, establishing a homestead at the mouth of the Kanawha River. In 1774 Clark served as a captain in the Virginia Militia in Lord Dunmore's War but saw no fighting. A year later he set out for Kentucky on a surveying trip for the Ohio Company.

Establishing himself among the few settlers in the region of present-day Kentucky, Clark worked to promote orderly government. On the beginning of the American Revolutionary War (1775–1783), he and his neighbors declared for the Patriot cause. By 1776 they were under attack by Native Americans from north of the Ohio River who had been encouraged by British lieutenant governor Henry Hamilton at Detroit.

In the summer of 1776 Clark traveled to Williamsburg, Virginia, where he petitioned Governor Patrick Henry for assistance in defending Kentucky. In response, the government created Kentucky Country in December and gave Clark 500 pounds of gunpowder. After his return home in March 1777, he was appointed major of militia, with orders to defend Kentucky. Fending off Native American attacks during the summer and autumn, Clark became convinced that Americans should wrest the Northwest Territory from British control. In October he again returned to Virginia and persuaded the governor to accept his idea. Clark was promoted to lieutenant colonel in the Virginia State Line, and in the spring of 1778 he organized an army of 175 men near Louisville.

On June 28 Clark marched across the Illinois Country toward Kaskaskia. He arrived at the town on the evening of July 4,

Although he was a surveyor by profession, George Rogers Clark (1752–1818) spent most of his adult life on the frontier fighting both Native Americans and the British. (Library of Congress)

surprising the garrison and forcing its capitulation. With the assistance of friendly inhabitants, he quickly sent detachments to Vincennes and Cahokia, and he convinced local Native Americans to join him. Hamilton, alarmed at Clark's success, marched on October 7 with a force of 500 British regulars, Canadian militia, and Native Americans to retake the Illinois posts. He forced the tiny American garrison at Vincennes to surrender on December 17, 1778, and then suspended operations for the winter.

On January 29, 1779, Clark, who was then at Kaskaskia, learned of Hamilton's success and decided to retake Vincennes immediately. Clark set out on February 5 with 170 men, and after a march of almost 200 miles through freezing marshy plains, he arrived at Vincennes on February 23, forcing Hamilton to surrender two days later.

During the course of the next three years, Clark operated mostly from Fort Nelson at the Falls of the Ohio, trying to capture Fort Detroit while fending off British attempts to regain control of the Illinois Country. Although he never mobilized the resources to seize Detroit, he was successful in keeping control of his conquests. In the summer of 1780 he thwarted four British attacks west of the Appalachians. Clark retaliated by successfully attacking the Shawnees on the Little Miami River. In 1781 while he was in Virginia seeking more military assistance, he was involved in a skirmish with British regulars. Commanding 250 men, he ambushed a part of Brigadier General Benedict Arnold's invading force at Hood's Ferry in early 1781, killing 17 and wounding 13. Back in Kentucky and promoted to brigadier general, Clark led an expedition against the Shawnees at Chillicothe on November 4, 1782.

Following the Revolutionary War, Clark served for a number of years on the Federal Board of Commissioners. In 1786 he was one of three commissioners who concluded the Treaty of Fort McIntosh with the Native Americans north of the Ohio River. The ineffectiveness of the treaty soon became clear, and Clark led an expedition in the autumn of 1786 and early 1787 against the Wabash tribe, during which he confiscated goods from Spanish merchants in Vincennes. When his men mutinied he had to call off the attack, and his reputation suffered. The master intriguer, James Wilkinson, taking advantage of the situation to remove a perceived rival to his own preferment, successfully campaigned to destroy Clark's credibility. For the remainder of his life Clark was out of favor with the governments of both the United States and Virginia and was constantly harassed by creditors. Although he claimed unpaid obligations of $20,000 for his services during the Revolutionary War, he collected nothing.

In an attempt to restore his fortunes, Clark tried to secure permission from Spanish authorities to found a colony in Spanish Louisiana. Having no success, he set out to found a colony near Natchez without Spain's consent but was stymied when President George Washington issued a proclamation banning the scheme. In 1793 Clark accepted a French commission as a major general to lead an American filibustering campaign against Spanish territory. When the U.S. government insisted that he cease and desist, he refused and lived for a time in St. Louis. In 1803 he settled at Clarksville in the Northwest Territory (Indiana) and drank to excess. After suffering a stroke in 1809, he moved to his sister's home near Louisville, Kentucky. Belatedly, in 1812, the Virginia General Assembly, in recognition of his services in the Revolution, voted to award him a sword and half-pay of $400 per year. Clark died on February 13, 1818, in Louisville.

PAUL DAVID NELSON

See also

Blue Licks, Kentucky, Action at; Chillicothe, Ohio, Battles on the Little Miami River; Clark's Ohio Campaign, First; Clark's Ohio Campaign, Second; Piqua, Battle of; Shawnees

References

Harrison, Lowell Hayes. *George Rogers Clark and the War in the West.* Lexington: University Press of Kentucky, 1976.
Palmer, Frederick. *Clark of the Ohio: A Life of George Rogers Clark.* Whitefish, MT: Kessinger, 2004.

Clark, William
Birth Date: August 1, 1770
Death Date: September 1, 1838

Frontiersman, explorer, and soldier who along with Meriwether Lewis commanded the Corps of Discovery from 1803 to 1806; governor of the Missouri Territory; and the first U.S. superintendent of Indian affairs. Known among the Native Americans of the American West as "Red Head," William Clark was born on August 1, 1770, in Caroline County, Virginia. He was the younger brother of frontiersman and American Revolutionary War hero George Rogers Clark.

Clark's upbringing combined Virginia plantation society with the Ohio River frontier of Kentucky. Clark received a commission as an ensign in the U.S. Army in 1788 and as a captain of the Virginia Militia in 1790. He met Meriwether Lewis in 1794 when they both served during Little Turtle's War (1786–1795). In 1796 Clark resigned from the military to manage his family's Kentucky plantation.

In 1803 Lewis invited Clark to share command of the expedition to explore the Louisiana Purchase, which became known as the Lewis and Clark expedition. Clark was a good judge of character and played an important role in selecting men to staff the expedition. He served as the expedition's cartographer and artist, skillfully making maps and sketching plants, animals, objects, and Native Americans. By dead reckoning, Clark estimated that the distance the expedition had traveled from the mouth of the Missouri River to the Pacific Ocean was 4,142 miles, and he was off by only about 40 miles. Although he lacked Lewis's scientific training, Clark was practical and resourceful. He was a strong leader whose experience as a frontiersman made him effective in his dealings with Native Americans encountered along the way.

With the party's limited medical supplies, Clark provided medical care to the Nez Perces in exchange for horses and food, which the party badly needed to make the eastward crossing of the Rocky Mountains. On the return trip, Lewis and Clark separated after crossing the Bitterroot Mountains. Clark led his party over Bozeman Pass and explored the Yellowstone Valley to the Missouri River, where he reunited with Lewis. Together they returned to St. Louis in September 1806.

Following the expedition, Clark resigned his commission in the army. President Thomas Jefferson appointed him brigadier general of the militia of the Louisiana Territory and Indian agent for the West. Clark soon settled in St. Louis. In the early 19th century St. Louis was the hub of activity in the West, and it was from there that Clark carried out his governmental duties.

In 1808 Clark ordered the construction of Fort Osage (near present-day Kansas City), which became a center for western Indian affairs. President James Madison appointed Clark governor of the newly created Missouri Territory in 1813. Clark, however, lost the election for governor after Missouri entered the Union as a state in 1821.

In 1822 Clark became U.S. superintendent of Indian affairs, the first person to hold the newly created post. In 1824 he became surveyor general for the states of Illinois, Missouri, and Arkansas, with the responsibility of arranging for the rectangular survey of public lands in those states in preparation for opening them to

Virginia militia officer William Clark led, with Meriwether Lewis, the expedition to explore the 1803 Louisiana Purchase. He was subsequently a highly effective Indian agent and governor of the Missouri Territory. (Library of Congress)

settlement. Native American affairs occupied much of Clark's time during his years in St. Louis. In 1825 he negotiated the Treaty of Prairie du Chien, which established boundaries of lands claimed by the Sauk, Fox, Sioux, Iowa, and other tribes in the Old Northwest. The treaty allowed the U.S. government to make treaties with individual tribes for land cessions. Clark died in St. Louis on September 1, 1838.

Doug Dodd

See also
Lewis, Meriwether; Lewis and Clark Expedition; Nez Perces; Old Northwest Territory; Prairie du Chien, Treaty of

References
Ambrose, Stephen E. *Undaunted Courage: Meriwether Lewis, Thomas Jefferson, and the Opening of the American West.* New York: Simon and Schuster, 2003.
Cutwright, Paul Russell. *Lewis and Clark: Pioneering Naturalists.* Lincoln: Bison/University of Nebraska Press, 2003.
Ronda, James P. *Lewis and Clark among the Indians.* 2nd ed. Lincoln: University of Nebraska Press, 2002.

Clark's Garrison, Battle of
Event Date: March 12, 1676

Key engagement in the Native American uprising in New England known as King Philip's War (1675–1676). The Battle of Clark's Garrison, which occurred on March 12, 1676, in Plymouth Colony, helped reshape colonial military tactics and the treatment of combat in the New England legal system. Indeed, after the attack English settlers concluded that only the heavy use of indigenous forces, hit-and-run operations, and vicious treatment of enemy captives would subdue the rebellion and prevent similar occurrences.

During the height of King Philip's War, numerous surprise attacks on lightly defended colonial outposts terrorized New Englanders. Such was the fate of a garrison house owned by William Clark that was located several miles south of Plymouth. The eldest son of a wealthy Boston importer, Clark appears to have been targeted because local natives knew of his military supplies through an ongoing commercial relationship. The home was fortified to serve as a common defensive position in the event of hostilities, but archaeologists have not found any evidence of palisades. When warriors attacked the garrison, settlers offered little resistance because most males were attending a Sabbath meeting. One of Clark's sons, Thomas, was left for dead with a tomahawk wound. He later recovered to spend the rest of his life with a silver plate attached to his head.

Accounts of colonial fatalities ranged as high as 11 and included Clark's wife, Sarah. Casualty figures may have been inflated by the powerful and imposing minister Increase Mather, who used the war as a sign of divine retribution for the failure of Puritans to maintain their special covenant with God. Because the victims had not respected the Sabbath, Mather characterized the Clark's

Garrison tragedy as a lesson to those who succumb to materialism. He was contributing to a growing sense of declension that gripped New England and preoccupied Puritans who already believed that nothing happened by chance.

The number of native attackers remains unclear, as Mather's records do not match those of the Plymouth General Court. In September 1676 colonial troops produced a collection of surrendered natives to Plymouth magistrates with confessions that three of them had participated in the attack on noncombatants at Clark's home. A purported testimonial from a native woman augmented the case, and the accused were put to death without regard to their status as prisoners of war. In effect the Plymouth General Court regarded this attack as a crime against humanity as civil authorities swiftly discarded military distinctions in their rulings.

With the conflict dissipating after the death of the charismatic Metacom (King Philip) in August 1676, New England courts increasingly used their power as a form of vengeance to conclude what had become a war of attrition. Soon New England Native American tribes would no longer enjoy their status as sovereign nations, as treason ranked among the charges leveled against them.

Jeffrey D. Bass

See also
King Philip's War; Metacom

References
Drake, James D. *King Philip's War: Civil War in New England, 1675–1676.* Amherst: University of Massachusetts Press, 1999.
Lepore, Jill. *The Name of War: King Philip's War and the Origins of American Identity.* New York: Knopf, 1998.

Clark's Ohio Campaign, First
Start Date: November 1, 1782
End Date: November 17, 1782

Military campaign directed against the Shawnees conducted during the American Revolutionary War (1775–1783) in the Ohio River Valley. The campaign is named for its commander, Virginia Militia brigadier general George Rogers Clark. Although there was a sharp reduction in combat operations following the British defeat at Yorktown in October 1781, to the west small-scale massacres and revenge killings that had begun in 1777 continued to exact a toll on settlers and natives alike. The central issue was land ownership. A number of settlers had moved onto lands west of the line delineated by the Proclamation of 1763 and supposedly off-limits to their settlement. This was especially true following the beginning of the Revolutionary War, when many settlers chose to disregard the British prohibitions in the region. Encouraged by the British, however, the Native Americans zealously defended their territorial rights.

On June 4, 1782, Colonel William Crawford led a raid into the Ohio River Valley near Sandusky. Then in August some 50 British rangers and 300 Native Americans raided into Kentucky and on August 19 near the Licking River in present-day Robertson County ambushed and routed 182 Kentucky militiamen. Clark, although he had not been present at the battle, was much criticized for the outcome, and he undertook command of a retaliatory operation.

Clark assembled some 1,050 men, the largest number he had ever commanded. Among those participating was Daniel Boone. On November 1, 1782, the men crossed the Ohio River into Shawnee territory at present-day Cincinnati. Clark's men burned five Shawnee villages, including Old Chillicothe, along the Little Miami River. The Americans also destroyed Loramie's Store, a British trading post.

The Shawnees generally fell back before Clark's army, but a skirmish, known as the Battle of Piqua, did occur between the Native Americans and the militiamen on November 4 near what is now Springfield, Ohio. The expedition, which ended on November 17, did little to ease tensions between the Native Americans and settlers, which became one of the causes for the War of 1812.

JAMES R. MCINTYRE AND SPENCER C. TUCKER

See also

Blue Licks, Kentucky, Action at; Boone, Daniel; Clark, George Rogers; Old Northwest Territory; Proclamation of 1763

References

Harrison, Lowell Hayes. *George Rogers Clark and the War in the West.* Lexington: University Press of Kentucky, 1976.

Nester, William R. *The Frontier War for American Independence.* Mechanicsburg, PA: Stackpole, 2004.

Clark's Ohio Campaign, Second
Start Date: September 1786
End Date: October 1786

Unsuccessful foray against hostile Native American towns on the Wabash River in the Old Northwest Territory (present-day Indiana). In the 1780s, tensions ran high between the tribes north of the Ohio River and white settlers impinging upon their territory. In response, on April 18, 1785, Congress appointed Brigadier General George Rogers Clark, Richard Butler, and Oliver Wolcott as special commissioners to negotiate with the Native Americans in the Northwest.

In November 1785 chiefs of the Wyandot and Delaware tribes met with the commissioners at Fort Finney, near present-day Cincinnati. They were joined by the Shawnees in January 1786. On February 1 the tribes agreed to the Treaty of Fort Finney, which

Destruction of a Wabash River Indian village. Brigadier General George Rogers Clark reluctantly accepted command of an expedition to punish Indian raiders living along the upper Wabash in 1786. (North Wind Picture Archives)

recognized American sovereignty north of the Ohio River. In return the Native Americans were guaranteed territory between the Big Miami and Wabash rivers. Soon thereafter, however, the Shawnees repudiated the treaty because white settlers continued to impinge upon their lands. In early July the Native Americans organized the Wabash Confederacy, vowing to drive the settlers from the region, and immediately commenced attacks on Kentucky settlements.

When Congress responded weakly to these assaults, Governor Patrick Henry of Virginia authorized the Kentucky Militia to raid Native American towns on the Wabash. Thereupon the militia officers requested that Clark take command of an expedition. The general accepted but only reluctantly because he was uncertain that the Kentucky Militia could be ordered outside Virginia, which at the time controlled Kentucky. He decided to tell the soldiers nothing and hope for the best.

By mid-September 1786 Clark had collected 1,200 militiamen at Clarksville (Indiana) in preparation to attack Native Americans on the upper Wabash. Half the militia had not reported, however. Colonel Benjamin Logan finally collected 790 of the recalcitrants and in early October led them on a successful raid at the head of the Great Miami River against the Shawnees, who had been weakened because their warriors had joined the Wabash Indians to confront Clark's force. As Clark marched northward on September 17, his authority began to erode as word spread among the men that he had no sanction to lead them beyond the borders of Kentucky. Finally discipline broke down almost completely, and Clark was compelled to march to Vincennes to collect supplies rather than drive directly into Native American territory. At Vincennes, Clark found only sufficient provisions to sustain his army for a few days' marching.

Nevertheless, Clark continued northward on October 3. Three days later when he was only two days away from the Wabash villages and had every hope of a victory, half of his men mutinied. He pleaded, without success, for the mutineers to follow him. Instead they decamped southward. The loyal half of his force was now too small to continue operations. Clark thus returned to Vincennes and in mid-October established there a garrison of 150 men in hopes of intimidating the Shawnee and Wabash tribes. Despite his own military setback, he played upon Logan's triumph against the Shawnees to persuade the Native Americans to agree to an armistice until a peace council could be held at Vincennes in 1787.

PAUL DAVID NELSON

See also
Delawares; Logan, Benjamin; Old Northwest Territory; Shawnees

References
Bakeless, John. *Background to Glory: The Life of George Rogers Clark.* Philadelphia: Lippincott, 1957.
Harrison, Lowell Hayes. *George Rogers Clark and the War in the West.* Lexington: University Press of Kentucky, 1976.
Helderman, L. C. "The Northwest Expedition of George Rogers Clark, 1786–1787." *Mississippi Valley Historical Review* 25 (1938): 317–334.

Clearwater River, Battle of
Start Date: July 11, 1877
End Date: July 12, 1877

Engagement between Nez Perce Native Americans under Chief Joseph and the U.S. Army under Brigadier General Oliver Otis Howard. The confrontation at the Clearwater River occurred in Idaho County, Idaho, and was part of the larger Nez Perce War. General Howard's troops had begun pursuing the Nez Perces following the defeat of U.S. soldiers at the Battle of White Bird Canyon (June 17, 1877). Howard, who became the first and only commissioner of the Bureau of Refugees, Freedmen, and Abandoned Lands after the American Civil War (1861–1865), had assumed command of the Department of the Columbia in the Pacific Northwest. He promptly dispatched a small contingent of troops to capture Chief Looking Glass, who had joined forces with Chief Joseph.

Learning that Looking Glass had combined with Joseph, Howard's objective was then to pursue the joint Nez Perce force, round it up, and escort the Nez Perces to a reservation. Howard's force consisted of four companies of the 1st Cavalry Regiment, six companies of the 21st Infantry Regiment, and five companies of artillerymen from the 4th Artillery Regiment. There were some 500 men in all.

On July 11, 1877, Howard's soldiers surprised the Nez Perces, numbering about 300 warriors, encamped on the Clearwater River. Howard's men charged into Chief Joseph's force, which had surrounded a civilian village at the bottom of the ravine. Chief Toohoolhoolzote, however, managed to hold his men together despite a withering attack until four other groups of Nez Perces could come to their rescue and surround the attacking soldiers. Howard's men were then pushed back from the canyon onto open grasslands. The fighting lasted for several hours until the army brought up howitzers and opened artillery fire. Still, some of Joseph's warriors managed to capture a few of the howitzers, only to have Lieutenant Charles F. Humphrey of the 4th Artillery lead a charge on the Native American position and regain control of them. For his act of bravery, Humphrey was later awarded the Medal of Honor.

The battle continued into the night and the next day. Howard had placed his troops in a difficult situation, however. He now began looking for a breakout maneuver despite the protection that his artillery was providing. The battle ended when troops from Fort Klamath approached the Nez Perce rear. Scrambling to avoid capture, Joseph and his warriors escaped across the Clearwater River.

During the engagement, Howard lost 17 men killed along with 27 wounded. Chief Joseph suffered 4 killed and 6 wounded. Instead of immediately pursuing Joseph and the fleeing Nez Perces, Howard waited until the next day to move, thus giving the Nez Perces a considerable head start across Idaho and into Montana. Howard ordered Major Edwin Mason of the 21st Infantry Regiment with elements of five cavalry companies to lead the chase, while

Howard led the remainder of his forces through the mountains. Even though Howard's command had sustained the greater number of casualties, the battle was touted as a victory for the army because Chief Joseph and his Nez Perces had been forced from Idaho into Montana.

CHARLES FRANCIS HOWLETT

See also

Howard, Oliver Otis; Joseph, Chief; Looking Glass; Nez Perces; Nez Perce War; White Bird Canyon, Battle of

References

Carpenter, John A. *Sword and Olive Branch: Oliver Otis Howard.* Pittsburgh: University of Pittsburgh Press, 1964.

Dillon, Richard H. *North American Indian Wars.* New York: Facts on File, 1983.

Greene, Jerome A. *Nez Perce Summer, 1877: The U. S. Army and the Nee-Me-Poo Crisis.* Helena: Montana Historical Society Press, 2000.

Sweeney, Jerry K., and Kevin B. Byrn, eds. *A Handbook of Military History.* Lincoln: University of Nebraska Press, 2006.

Clinch, Duncan Lamont
Birth Date: April 6, 1787
Death Date: November 27, 1849

U.S. Army officer and veteran of the First Seminole War (1817–1818) and the Second Seminole War (1835–1842). Duncan Lamont Clinch was born in Edgecombe County, North Carolina, on April 6, 1787. Orphaned at a young age, he entered the U.S. Army in 1808 as a first lieutenant in the 3rd Infantry Regiment, an appointment that he secured with the assistance of U.S. congressman Thomas Blount.

Clinch saw sporadic action during the War of 1812 and was stationed in Louisiana and then Plattsburg, New York. He was promoted to captain in December 1810 and to lieutenant colonel in August 1814. In 1819 he was promoted to colonel and given command of the 8th Infantry Regiment.

At the beginning of the First Seminole War in July 1816, Clinch was ordered to the Florida Gulf Coast, where he was to lay siege to and attack an old British-built fort on the Apalachicola River known as Negro Fort, so-named because runaway slaves were often harbored there by the Seminoles and Choctaws. Clinch worked in tandem with a river-borne force of gunboats, which opened fire on the fort on July 27, igniting its powder magazine. The ensuing explosion and fire killed most of the fort's inhabitants. As many as 300 men, women, and children lost their lives. While some criticized Clinch for the incident, most did not hold him responsible, believing that the explosion had been unintentional, an unfortunate result of a wartime operation. Nevertheless news of the assault enraged the Seminoles, who stepped up their assaults against American forces. By 1817 the First Seminole War was under way and would endure until 1818.

In April 1829 Clinch was brevetted brigadier general. During the Second Seminole War he again commanded forces against the recalcitrant Seminoles. He saw only one major action, the Battle of Withlacoochee, on December 30, 1835. The day prior he led about 700 men from Fort Drane to a large Seminole encampment along the Withlacoochee River. His purpose was to attack and disperse the Native American congregation. The Seminoles, however, were well prepared and withstood Clinch's assault on December 30. He was compelled to withdraw to Fort Drane, having suffered only minimal losses.

In April 1836 Clinch tendered his resignation to President Andrew Jackson, who implored Clinch to reconsider. Saddled with eight children and a plantation to manage in Georgia, however, Clinch resigned on September 21, 1836. Upon retirement he oversaw Refuge Plantation, which he had inherited from his first wife's father, on the Satilla River in southeastern Georgia.

A Whig, Clinch briefly became involved in politics and served in the U.S. House of Representatives from February 1844 until March 1845. He died in Macon, Georgia, on November 27, 1849.

PAUL G. PIERPAOLI JR.

See also

Jackson, Andrew; Seminoles; Seminole War, First; Seminole War, Second

References

Missall, John, and Mary Lou Missall. *The Seminole Wars: America's Longest Indian Conflict.* Gainesville: University Press of Florida, 2004.

Patrick, Rembert Wallace. *Aristocrat in Uniform, General Duncan L. Clinch.* Gainesville: University of Florida Press, 1963.

Cochise
Birth Date: ca. 1810
Death Date: June 8, 1874

Chiricahua Apache leader. Born circa 1810 probably in present-day southeastern Arizona, Cochise spent much of his youth fighting Mexicans who routinely trespassed on Chiricahua lands. He also launched devastating raids into the Mexican provinces of Chihuahua and Sonora, often in concert with Mangas Coloradas, leader of the Mimbres Apaches. Cochise's keen intelligence and finely honed military skills led to his emergence as leader of the Chiricahuas by 1856.

Although he continued to battle the Mexicans after the United States acquired his Arizona homeland from Mexico in 1848, a result of the Mexican-American War (1846–1848) and the 1848 Treaty of Guadalupe Hidalgo, Cochise remained at peace with the Americans. The Chiricahuas took no hostile action against the stagecoach stations built in their territory along the road from the Rio Grande to Tucson, nor did they harass travelers.

The situation changed in February 1861, however, when U.S. Army lieutenant George Bascom summoned Cochise to a

A master of hit-and-run tactics, Chiricahua Apache leader Cochise was one of the most feared Native American warriors in the Southwest during the 1860s and early 1870s. (Bettmann/Corbis)

conference at Apache Pass, located in far southeastern Arizona in present-day Cochise County. Bascom falsely accused Cochise of stealing cattle and kidnapping a boy. Cochise explained that the raid that Bascom described had been carried out by Coyotero Apaches and offered to negotiate for the boy's release, but Bascom did not believe Cochise and attempted to arrest him. Cochise escaped by cutting through the wall of the tent where the meeting took place. However, Bascom seized five of Cochise's relatives who had accompanied him to the meeting.

In an effort to free the hostages and secure bargaining power, Cochise captured three whites. Bascom refused to exchange Cochise's relatives for these prisoners, insisting that Cochise must also return the boy and the cattle. The Chiricahua leader responded by surrounding the troops at Apache Pass and launching a series of raids against travelers and other soldiers in the area. Seeing that Bascom would not yield, Cochise executed his prisoners. Bascom retaliated by hanging the Chiricahua hostages. Cochise responded with further raids.

Soon afterward the U.S. government withdrew most of its troops from the Southwest for service in the American Civil War

(1861–1865). Cochise and Mangas Coloradas took prompt advantage by intensifying their attacks on settlers and travelers and besieging the mining camp at Pinos Altos, forcing most of the prospectors to flee. They met no resistance from the small Confederate detachment that had occupied Tucson.

In the summer of 1862 a unit of California Volunteers under Brigadier General James Carleton marched into Arizona and drove out the Confederates. Cochise and Mangas Coloradas ambushed Carleton's force at Apache Pass on July 15. After their initial assault was repulsed, the troops fought their way through to Apache Springs. Apache sharpshooters tried to deny the soldiers access to the water but were driven off by artillery fire.

From his nearly inaccessible stronghold in the Dragoon Mountains of Arizona, Cochise continued to wage a guerrilla war against both soldiers and civilians, although his 300 Chiricahua fighting men were vastly outnumbered. His determination to continue resistance increased after U.S. troops captured Mangas Coloradas under a flag of truce and then murdered the Mimbres leader in January 1863.

By late 1869 Cochise had grown tired of fighting and sent word through intermediaries to American officials that he was willing to make peace. The U.S. government was similarly inclined, and its emissaries proposed that the Chiricahuas and Mimbres share a reservation in New Mexico. Cochise approved, but his people preferred to remain in the Arizona mountains. He also distrusted both the government and the settlers, and therefore in the early spring of 1871 he declined an invitation to visit Washington, D.C. In April 1871 Cochise's worries were confirmed when about 150 Avaraipa and Pinal Apaches, who had accepted a reservation at Camp Grant, were attacked and massacred by white Arizona settlers.

President Ulysses S. Grant denounced the massacre and ordered the army and the Bureau of Indian Affairs to make peace with the Apaches. Cochise had been raiding in Mexico and upon his return found that Brigadier General George Crook had troops searching southern Arizona for the Chiricahuas. Cochise then led his people to New Mexico, where he contacted Brigadier General Gordon Granger. The two met at Cañada Alamosa in March 1872 and discussed peace terms, but the Chiricahuas returned to the Dragoon Mountains upon learning that the government had ordered that all Apaches were to be sent to Fort Tularosa.

On October 1, 1872, Brigadier General Oliver O. Howard, who had taken charge of the effort to negotiate with Cochise, reached the Chiricahua camp with the assistance of Cochise's friend Thomas Jeffords. After 10 days of discussions Cochise agreed to end the fighting and accept a reservation in the mountains of southeastern Arizona.

Cochise had suffered from a stomach ailment since at least 1872 and was in declining health. He died on June 8, 1874, at his camp in the Dragoon Mountains.

JIM PIECUCH

See also

Apache Pass, Battle of; Apaches; Apache Wars; Camp Grant Massacre; Carleton, James Henry; Crook, George; Grant, Ulysses Simpson; Howard, Oliver Otis; Mangas Coloradas

References

Brown, Dee. *Bury My Heart at Wounded Knee.* New York: Holt, Rinehart and Winston, 1970.

Sweeney, Edwin R. *Cochise: Chiricahua Apache Chief.* Norman: University of Oklahoma Press, 1991.

Utley, Robert M. *The Indian Frontier of the American West, 1846–1890.* Albuquerque: University of New Mexico Press, 1984.

See also

Bacon's Rebellion; Jamestown; Pamunkeys; Powhatan Confederacy; Virginia-Indian Treaty of 1677/1680

References

McCartney, Martha W. "Cockacoeske, Queen of Pamunkey: Diplomat and Suzeraine." In *Powhatan's Mantle: Indians in the Colonial Southeast,* edited by Peter H. Wood, Gregory A. Waselkov, and M. Thomas Hatley, 173–195. Lincoln: University of Nebraska Press, 1989.

Washburn, Wilcomb E. *The Governor and the Rebel: A History of Bacon's Rebellion in Virginia.* Chapel Hill: University of North Carolina Press, 1957.

Cockacoeske

Birth Date: ca. 1640
Death Date: 1686

Pamunkey leader who remained loyal to Virginia's colonial leaders during English conflicts with native peoples. Cockacoeske became the Pamunkeys' *weronsqua* (female leader) in 1656 after her husband, Totopotomy, the tribe's leader, died in battle fighting neighboring natives hostile to the colonial government.

In 1676 Cockacoeske appeared at the Virginia General Assembly with an interpreter and her son, John West. When assembly members asked Cockacoeske to supply warriors to help defeat Nathaniel Bacon's rebellion (1676–1677), she remained quiet and then yelled her husband's name when pressured to commit forces. She then stated that the Pamunkeys had in the past sacrificed for government causes without compensation. When officials continued to request troops, she finally agreed to provide 12 warriors.

When Bacon's forces raided Pamunkey villages, Cockacoeske told her people to flee and not fight. Rebels captured and killed several natives. Terrified when she saw the carnage and destruction wrought by the raids, Cockacoeske hid in nearby woods for days. On February 20, 1677, she asked that the General Assembly recover seized Pamunkey property and land and compensate her people. Assembly members countered that she had to prove that the items belonged to the Pamunkeys. Cockacoeske pressed her demands directly with King Charles II's commissioners. In due course they instructed the General Assembly to assist her because they realized full well that the government needed her as an ally.

During negotiations for the 1677 Virginia-Indian Treaty (also known as the Treaty of Middle Plantation), Cockacoeske secured terms favorable to expand her power. The treaty stated that she was the leader of the Pamunkeys and several nearby tribes. Cockacoeske aspired to create a confederacy similar to that created by Powhatan. The uncooperative tribes did not pay the tributes she demanded, however, insisting that they had not agreed to such stipulations. Cockacoeske complained to colonial officials but did not achieve her ambitions before her death in 1686.

ELIZABETH D. SCHAFER

Cody, William Frederick

Birth Date: February 26, 1846
Death Date: January 10, 1917

American frontiersman, U.S. Army civilian scout, and celebrated entertainer. William Frederick ("Buffalo Bill") Cody was born on February 26, 1846, in Scott County, Iowa. In 1853 the Cody family moved to Kansas. In 1858 after his father's death, Cody obtained employment with a wagon train to help support his family. At the outbreak of the American Civil War (1861–1865), Cody sought to enlist in the Union Army but was refused because of his age. He enlisted in the 7th Kansas Cavalry in 1863 and served as a scout for the duration of the war.

In 1867 the Kansas Pacific Railroad hired Cody to hunt buffalo to feed the railroad workers. While working for the railroad Cody, who killed more than 4,000 buffalos, earned a reputation as an expert shot. The railroad workers, impressed by Cody's skills, honored him with the nickname "Buffalo Bill." From 1868 to 1872 Cody served as a civilian scout for the U.S. Army during the Indian Wars. In 1872 the U.S. government awarded Cody the Medal of Honor for gallantry in action while serving as a scout for the 3rd Cavalry Regiment. The medal was revoked in February 1917 just after Cody's death because he was a civilian and thus was ineligible for the award under guidelines set in 1917. The medal was restored to Cody in 1989.

To generate a positive image of the U.S. Army in the West, army officials often organized elaborate hunting adventures for foreign and domestic dignitaries. Cody led a number of these expeditions, protected by the U.S. military. The hunting expeditions were eagerly followed by newspaper readers around the world.

In 1872 novelist Ned Buntline convinced Cody to play himself in the stage production of Buntline's novel *Scouts of the Prairie.* Smitten with the theater, Cody formed his own troupe of frontier actors in 1873. Because the majority of the actors were frontiersmen, the dramatic productions were fairly credible. In 1876 after the outbreak of the Great Sioux War (1876–1877), Cody was once again employed by the U.S. Army as a civilian scout. To avenge the death of Lieutenant Colonel George Armstrong Custer and his men at the Battle of the Little Bighorn (June 25–26, 1876), Cody

Coeur d'Alenes

Native American tribe of the Pacific Northwest who spoke a Salishan language of the interior, as opposed to those groups who spoke a coastal version of the Salishan language. The name "Coeur d'Alene" was derived from the French for "awl heart," or "sharp-hearted," reportedly a reference made by a trader alluding to the shrewd trading skills of these Native Americans. Their self-designation was Skitswish, perhaps meaning "foundling."

In the 18th century the Coeur d'Alenes lived along the Spokane River upstream from Spokane Falls and on Lake Coeur d'Alene. The region of more than 4 million acres was fertile and well watered. In the early 19th century, the tribe lived in central Idaho, eastern Washington state, and western Montana. The mountains in this area helped to protect their horses against raiders from the Plains tribes. The Coeur d'Alenes sporadically fought with the Spokane tribe in the 1790s until both groups achieved an enduring peace by the early 1800s. Today's Coeur d'Alene Reservation is located in Benewah and Kootenai counties in Idaho.

Like all Salish peoples, the Coeur d'Alenes probably originated in British Columbia. They migrated to the Plateau during the prehistoric period, keeping some Pacific coast attributes even after they adopted Plateau culture. They acquired the horse around 1760, at which time they gave up their semisedentary lives to hunt buffalo, Plains style. Thus, the buffalo became a key aspect of their culture and economic system, providing items for trade as well as food, clothing, and shelter. The tribe also engaged in seasonal small-scale agriculture to supplement its diet.

The Coeur d'Alenes' traditional antipathy toward outsiders made it difficult for trappers to penetrate their territory. A Jesuit mission was established in 1842, however, foreshadowing the significant role the Jesuits were to play in the later history of the Coeur d'Alenes. The Jesuits successfully influenced the tribe to give up buffalo hunting and begin farming as a primary occupation.

In the meantime, intermittent warfare with other Native American tribes and Europeans, in addition to disease, had decreased the Coeur d'Alene population by about 85 percent by 1850. In 1858 the Coeur d'Alenes fought the ill-fated Coeur d'Alene War (with the help of tribes such as the Northern Paiutes, the Palouses, and the Spokanes). Although the immediate cause of this conflict had been white treaty violations and encroachments on tribal territory, it can be seen as an extension of the wider Yakima-Rogue War (1855–1858) and the general Plateau Native American resistance struggle during that time.

The roughly 600,000-acre Coeur d'Alene Reservation was created in 1873, at which time the Native Americans ceded almost 2.4 million acres to the federal government. However, pressure from miners soon forced the tribe to cede almost 185,000 more acres in the late 1880s. Most of the rest of the Coeur d'Alenes' land was lost to the allotment process in the early 20th century. In 1894, 32 Spokane families joined the reservation. Most Coeur d'Alene people became Catholics, farmers, and stockbreeders. In 1958 the tribe

William "Buffalo Bill" Cody was a scout, Pony Express rider, showman, and legend of the American frontier. His Wild West Show drew huge crowds in the late 19th and early 20th centuries. (Library of Congress)

shot to death and then scalped Yellow Hair, a Cheyenne warrior, during the Battle of Warbonnet Creek (July 17, 1876) in the Nebraska Territory.

In 1883 Cody formed the Buffalo Bill Wild West Show. For the next 30 years the Wild West Show entertained audiences all over America and Europe. Members of the show's cast included Sitting Bull, Annie Oakley, Wild Bill Hickok, and Calamity Jane. Cody invested his earnings in economic development projects throughout the West. In 1896 he helped establish Cody, Wyoming. He was also an early supporter of Native American rights and women's suffrage. Cody was incredibly popular and well respected, and U.S. presidents frequently consulted with him about matters pertaining to the West. Beginning in 1912 Cody's finances sharply deteriorated. He went heavily in debt, a situation that he was never able to rectify completely. Because of his indebtedness, Cody performed until his death on January 10, 1917, in Denver, Colorado.

MICHAEL R. HALL

See also

Buffalo; Buffalo Bill's Wild West Show; Custer, George Armstrong; Great Sioux War; Little Bighorn, Battle of the; Sitting Bull

References

Carter, Robert A. *Buffalo Bill Cody: The Man behind the Legend.* Hoboken, NJ: Wiley, 2000.

Warren, Louis S. *Buffalo Bill's America: William Cody and the Wild West Show.* New York: Knopf, 2005.

was awarded more than $4.3 million in land claims settlements. There are now about 2,000 people identified as Coeur d'Alenes.

BARRY M. PRITZKER

See also

Buffalo; Coeur d'Alene War; Paiutes, Northern; Palouses; Reservations; Spokanes; Yakima-Rogue War

References

Peltier, Jerome. *A Brief History of the Coeur d'Alene Indians, 1806–1909.* Fairfield, WA: Ye Galleon, 1981.

Teit, James, and Franx Boaz. *Coeur d'Alene, Flathead, and Okanogan Indians.* Fairfield, WA: Ye Galleon, 1985.

Coeur d'Alene War
Event Date: 1858

Conflict between the U.S. Army and Native Americans in the interior Pacific Northwest (present-day Washington and Idaho) from May to September 1858. The war began when Indian tribes of the Pacific Northwest—the Coeur d'Alenes, Palouses, and Spokanes—united to resist U.S. domination.

In May 1858 Brevet Lieutenant Colonel Edward J. Steptoe departed Fort Walla Walla with 158 men to investigate accounts that some Palouse warriors had murdered miners to the north of the fort. On May 16 a force of some 1,000 Indians surrounded Steptoe's men, and his attempts to parley failed. The next morning he tried to retreat to the fort as Palouse, Coeur d'Alene, and Spokane warriors harassed his formation from all sides. Steptoe then led his men to a hill, where they repulsed a full-scale Native American attack with their two howitzers, using up almost all of their ammunition. To avoid being massacred, the soldiers left the hill that night, abandoning their howitzers and their dead, and made it to Walla Walla five days later. This engagement prompted what would be called the Coeur d'Alene War.

Brevet Brigadier General Newman S. Clarke, commanding the Department of the Pacific, ordered a two-pronged response to this assault. Colonel George Wright was to proceed north from Fort Walla Walla, following the path taken by Steptoe, and Major Robert S. Garnett was sent from Fort Simcoe to pursue the Palouses involved in the murder of the miners. Garnett soon hunted down most of the killers, several of whom were executed. This prompted the remaining fugitives to flee to the Spokane tribe for protection.

Colonel Wright meanwhile set out to subdue the hostile Native Americans. Wright left the Snake River on August 27, 1858, with about 600 men and a pack train of 400 mules. A Jesuit priest from the Coeur d'Alene mission informed him that the Indians had been emboldened by their recent victory and sought war. On September 1 Wright engaged the main body of these Native Americans at the Battle of Four Lakes, near present-day Spokane, Washington. After easily taking the Native Americans' position on a central hill, he attempted to drive them from the forest and away from ravines near the lakes. With artillery and rifle fire that outranged that of

the Indians, he was ultimately able to bring them into the open. Four dragoon units, led by Captain (Brevet Major) William Grier, then smashed into the Native Americans, forcing them to flee. Not a single U.S. soldier was killed or injured, while 20–60 Native Americans died during the fight.

Wright again caught up with a Native American force on September 5. In the Battle of Spokane Plain, the Indians set a grass fire, concealing themselves behind a wall of smoke, yet they were again outgunned by the army howitzers and long-range rifles. Eventually this fire drove them into the open, where Grier's dragoons dealt the decisive blow with a saber charge.

The Battle of Four Lakes and the Battle of Spokane Plain marked the end of Native American opposition in the Northwest. By late September the hostile Spokanes, Palouses, and Coeur d'Alenes had all surrendered to Wright. Fifteen Native Americans—those accused of inciting the attack on Steptoe's force—were executed.

CAMERON B. STRANG

See also

Coeur d'Alenes; Fort Simcoe; Fort Walla Walla; Four Lakes, Battle of; Palouses; Spokanes; Steptoe, Edward Jenner; Wright, George

References

Burns, Robert Ignatius, S.J. *The Jesuits and the Indian Wars of the Northwest.* New Haven, CT: Yale University Press, 1966.

Utley, Robert M. *Frontiersmen in Blue: The United States and the Indian, 1848–1865.* Lincoln: University of Nebraska Press, 1967.

Coffee, John
Birth Date: June 22, 1772
Death Date: July 7, 1833

Tennessee Militia officer. Born on June 22, 1772, in Prince Edward County, Virginia, John Coffee soon moved with his family to North Carolina, where his father became a successful planter. Following his father's death, in 1798 Coffee migrated to Davidson County, Tennessee. There he engaged in the burgeoning river trade with various partners including Andrew Jackson, who became a lifelong friend. After marrying in 1809, Coffee abandoned his mercantile ventures and relocated to a plantation in Rutherford County, Tennessee, where he pursued a lucrative career in land speculation. His subsequent election as clerk of the Rutherford County Court helped solidify his political contacts.

The declaration of war against Great Britain in June 1812 propelled Coffee into the military spotlight. When the call came to Tennessee in late 1812 for an expedition to the Gulf Coast, it fell to Coffee to raise and lead a volunteer cavalry regiment, of which he was elected colonel. Arriving in mid-February 1813, the Tennessee army, led by Andrew Jackson (then major general of the Tennessee Militia), loitered in the vicinity of Natchez, Mississippi, for a month until being informed by the federal government that

Tennessee militia brigadier general John Coffee (1772–1833) served under Major General Andrew Jackson during the Creek War of 1813–1814 and fought in the Battle of New Orleans in January 1815. (Hulton Archive/Getty Images)

its services were no longer required. An angry Jackson, with Coffee at his side, marched the troops back to Tennessee.

When the Red Stick faction of the Creek tribe attacked the settlement at Fort Mims along the Tombigbee River in the Mississippi Territory in late August 1813, the fight that the Tennesseans had sought finally presented itself. The Tennessee legislature called for 3,500 troops to commence a campaign against the Creeks to eliminate the Native American "menace" once and for all. Coffee, promoted from colonel to brigadier general, commanded a unit of some 1,200 dragoons in the force led by Jackson.

The Red Stick Creeks, always outmanned and outgunned, put up a desperate but ineffective resistance, as the Tennesseans forced their way into the Creek Nation, killing as many warriors as they could along the way. Coffee and his mounted men soundly defeated the Red Sticks at Tallushatchee on November 3, 1813, and, with Jackson, won another victory at Talladega on November 9, 1813. At Emuckfaw Creek on January 22, 1814, the Tennesseans were besieged by Creek forces, but a counterattack led by Coffee routed the Red Sticks. Wounded during the engagement, Coffee had to be carried on a litter during the withdrawal of Jackson's troops to their post at Fort Strother. En route the Red Sticks struck the rear guard of the Tennessee army at Enitachopco Creek on January 24, 1814. The initial panic of the Tennesseans was staved off by Jackson's artillery, and Coffee is said to have demanded that he be taken off his litter and put on a horse to ride into the thick of battle.

By March 1814, Jackson had amassed an army of 5,000 to administer the final blow against the Red Sticks. This occurred on March 27, 1814, at a curve in the Tallapoosa River known as Horseshoe Bend, where Jackson's forces slaughtered nearly 900 Red Stick warriors, the largest single defeat of Native Americans by whites in North American history. Coffee commanded the mounted men and allied Indians in this climactic battle of the Creek War.

In the autumn of 1814 the theater of action shifted to Pensacola, where on November 7, 1814, Jackson initiated an unauthorized attack against the Spanish, who were harboring British troops and refugee Indians. Coffee then joined Jackson at New Orleans in mid-December 1814 and participated in all of the engagements against the British, including the Battle of New Orleans (January 8, 1815). During the campaign Coffee's men occupied the extreme left of Jackson's defensive line.

At the conclusion of the war, Coffee returned to his lucrative land speculation career. For the next several years he orchestrated appointments for himself to head surveys of public lands in Alabama. In 1819 he moved his family to Florence, Alabama, where he exercised nearly complete control over the public lands. By the time of his death on July 7, 1833, in Florence, Coffee had became one of the most influential planters of the Tennessee Valley.

Tom Kanon

See also

Creek War; Emuckfaw Creek, Battle of; Enitachopco Creek, Battle of; Fort Mims, Battle of; Horseshoe Bend, Battle of; Jackson, Andrew; Tallushatchee, Battle of

References

Chappell, Gordon T. "The Life and Activities of General John Coffee." *Tennessee Historical Quarterly* 1 (June 1942): 125–146.

Owsley, Frank L., Jr. *Struggle for the Gulf Borderlands. The Creek War and the Battle of New Orleans, 1812–1815.* Gainesville: University Presses of Florida, 1981.

_____

Colorado War

See Cheyenne-Arapaho War

_____

Colorow
Birth Date: ca. 1808
Death Date: 1855

Ute leader known for his intrepid fighting skills and diplomatic prowess. Colorow Ignacio Ouray Walkara (usually called Walker by whites), of the Timpanogo band of Utes, was born probably in 1808 near the Spanish Fork River in present-day Utah. In his youth he became well respected as a warrior and for his expert horsemanship and marksmanship. Reputedly more than six feet tall, Colorow projected a commanding presence. Over the years he learned both Spanish and English as well as several other Native American languages, making him practically indispensable as a negotiator and diplomat.

Colorow soon assumed a leadership role among the Utes and assembled a band of warriors that included Utes, Shoshones, and Paiutes. During the early 1840s Colorow led numerous raids into New Mexico and southern California, in the process making off with more than 3,000 horses. He traded frequently with both white pioneers and Mexicans, usually trading horses for whiskey and other spirits.

In 1847 Brigham Young sent a group of Mormons west to Utah. Initially Colorow and the Utes welcomed the arrival of the Mormons and cooperated with the pioneers quite closely, teaching them about the geography and climate of the region and instructing them in how to cultivate crops. During the first winter of the Mormons' stay, a severe measles epidemic broke out. The Mormons shared with the Utes their limited supply of medicine designed to ease the symptoms of the illness. In turn when the Mormons' food supply ran low toward the end of winter, Colorow ordered that some of the Ute food supply be shared with them. By 1850 Colorow had negotiated a trade arrangement with the Mormons and had been baptized into the Mormon Church.

By the early 1850s increased pressures on the Utes by U.S. Army forces, white speculators, pioneers, and traders caused relations with the Mormons to sour. The Mormons also did not approve of Ute raiding, occasional trading of Native American slaves, and the frequent trade of distilled spirits, which was strictly forbidden by them. Also, as white traders began to move into the region in larger numbers, Colorow blamed the Mormons for the intrusions.

In 1853 Colorow precipitated a brief war, known as Walker's War, after a confrontation between a Ute group and white settlers resulted in the deaths of several Utes. Colorow then took to hit-and-run raids on Mormon settlements in southern and central Utah. To avoid violence, Young advised Mormons in the area to temporarily leave outlying farms and ranches and take refuge in centralized, well-fortified areas. In the spring of 1854 Walker's War concluded when Colorow and Young personally negotiated an end to the bloodshed. In all, perhaps as many as 15 whites died during the brief war; it is believed that an equal number of Native Americans died. While the agreement ended the war, none of the problems that had provoked the hostilities was solved. It is thought that Colorow was rebaptized in July 1854, along with some 120 of his followers, before his death at Meadow Creek, Utah, in 1855.

PAUL G. PIERPAOLI JR.

See also
Paiutes, Northern; Shoshones; Utes

References
Bailey, Paul D. *Walkara: Hawk of the Mountains.* Los Angeles: Westernlore, 1954.
May, Dean L. *Utah: A People's History.* Salt Lake City: Bonneville Books, 1987.

Colt, Samuel
Birth Date: July 19, 1814
Death Date: January 10, 1862

Inventor and industrialist. Samuel Colt was born in Hartford, Connecticut, on July 19, 1814. Indentured to a farm in Glastonbury at age 11, he attended school there and became fascinated by the *Compendium of Knowledge,* a scientific encyclopedia. This led to his decision to become an inventor and produce a firearm that could shoot multiple times without reloading.

In 1829 Colt began working in his father's textile mill in Ware, Massachusetts, providing Colt access to tools and skilled workers. He built a galvanic cell and used it to explode a charge in Lake Ware. In 1832 Colt's father sent him to sea with the plan that he would become a sailor. On his first voyage Colt built a model revolver, said to have been inspired by the movement of the ship's wheel and the clutch mechanism that held it.

Returning home that same year Colt again worked for his father, who financed the manufacture of his first two pistols. Both were failures because they had been poorly made of inferior materials. That same year, 1832, Colt applied for a patent on his revolver. He then traveled and made a modest living performing nitrous oxide (laughing gas) demonstrations. In 1835 he traveled to Britain and there secured a patent for his revolver. Returning to the United States, he there secured a patent for his "revolving gun" in 1836.

That same year Colt formed the Patent Army Manufacturing Company in Paterson, New Jersey. Its first product was a small five-shot .28-caliber revolver, but its most famous early design was the 1838 Colt Holster Model Paterson Revolver No. 5. Better known as the Texas Paterson, it was a .36-caliber gun with five cylinders and came in 4- to 12-inch barrel lengths. This was the first revolving cylinder pistol in general use. Each chamber was separately loaded from the muzzle end and had its own nipple for the copper percussion cap. The drum chamber moved each time the hammer was cocked. The Mexican-American War (1846–1848) brought an order for 1,000 of Colt's revolvers, establishing his business. The California gold rush and western expansion greatly assisted the business, and his patent gave him a virtual monopoly.

Colt revolvers were adopted by both the army and navy and saw wide service in the Mexican-American War (1846–1848), the American Civil War (1861–1865), and fighting with Native Americans in the West.

Colt did not claim to have invented the revolver, which is attributed to Elisha Collier of Boston, but did greatly improve and popularize it. His was the first truly practical revolver and repeating firearm. Colt greatly accelerated the employment of interchangeable parts in manufactured goods. He also experimented with underwater mines, and tensions with Great Britain led Congress to appropriate funds for his project at the end of 1841. The next year Colt destroyed a small ship with a mine in a demonstration for

See also
Colt Revolver; Rifles; Telegraph

References
Grant, Ellsworth S. *The Colt Legacy.* Providence, RI: Mowbray, 1982.
Hosley, William. *Colt: The Making of an American Legend.* Amherst: University of Massachusetts Press, 1996.
Kelner, William L. "On Samuel Colt and the Patent Arms Manufacturing Company, New Jersey." Unpublished master's thesis, Fairleigh Dickinson University, 1969.
Kinard, Jeff S. *Pistols: An Illustrated History of Their Impact.* Santa Barbara, CA: ABC-CLIO, 2003.
Myatt, F. *Illustrated Encyclopedia of Pistols and Revolvers.* London: Salamander Books, 1980.
Taylorson, A. *The Revolver.* 3 vols. London: Arms and Armour, 1966–1970.

American inventor and industrialist Samuel Colt perfected a revolving-cylinder pistol in the 1830s. His Colt revolver was widely utilized during the Indian Wars in the West. (Hayward Cirker, ed., *Dictionary of American Portraits,* 1967)

President John Tyler. Colt also developed an underwater telegraph cable to capitalize on Samuel Morse's invention of the telegraph. In 1855 Colt completed construction of a new plant at Hartford, Connecticut, at the time the largest arms manufacturing facility in the world. He was apparently a model employer, building factory housing for his workers and mandating a 10-hour workday and a 1-hour lunch break. He also established a club for his employees where they could relax and read newspapers.

On the outbreak of the Civil War, in May 1861 Colt accepted a volunteer commission as colonel of the 1st Regiment Colts Revolving Rifles of Connecticut, which was armed with his revolving rifle. The unit never was established, however, and Colt was discharged the next month. Colt died in Hartford on January 10, 1862. At the time of his death his estate was estimated at $15 million.

Colt's resolute wife Elizabeth carried on the firm after his death. Probably the most famous early revolver in U.S. history was the Colt .45 Model 1873 "Peacemaker." Designed for the U.S. Army and still in production, it was widely used in the American West in fighting against the American Indians. The cavalry version had a 7.5-inch barrel and was officially known as the Single Action Army Revolver, Model 1873 Six-shot Caliber .45 Colt.

SPENCER C. TUCKER

Colt Revolver

The standard U.S. military sidearm employed during the later American Indian Wars. Designed by William Mason and Charles B. Richards of the Colt Patent Firearms Company of Hartford, Connecticut, the caliber .45 Model 1873 Colt Single Action Army (SAA) revolver was easily the most famous revolver ever manufactured. With its classic lines, beautiful balance, and hard-hitting nearly half-inch .45-caliber Colt cartridge, it won instant popularity when first issued. Replacing earlier percussion weapons, the six-chambered Model 1873 served as the U.S. regulation sidearm from 1873 to 1892, when it was redesignated as a substitute standard. The government declared it obsolete in 1909.

The Model 1873 was Colt's first cartridge revolver manufactured with a solid frame, a structurally much sounder design than the company's earlier two-piece frame designs. The revolver was fitted with a swing-down loading gate hinged to the right side of the frame behind the cylinder and a spring-loaded spent-casing extractor on the lower right of the barrel. Originally designating the pistol as the Model P in 1873, Colt produced 357,859 Model 1873s in various calibers before ceasing production in 1941. Of these, the federal government purchased some 37,000 revolvers chambered for the center-fire .45-caliber Colt cartridge.

The revolvers issued to the cavalry were fitted with 7.5-inch barrels, with artillery models being manufactured with 5.5-inch barrels. Standard military examples were fitted with walnut grips and finished with blued barrels, grip straps, and triggers with case-hardened frames and hammers. The revolver was originally issued with a black leather full-flap holster of American Civil War (1861–1865) vintage that completely enclosed the weapon. In 1874 the U.S. Army adopted a half-flap model embossed with the "U.S." insignia that partially exposed the butt of the grip. Although a popular weapon, the Model 1873 did exhibit serious deficiencies. Its internal mechanism was relatively fragile for a military sidearm and was prone to breakage, a possibly fatal drawback in combat.

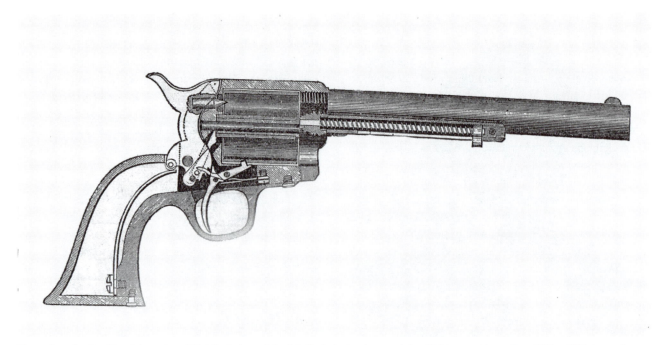

Illustration of a .45 caliber Colt revolver. Officially designated the Colt Single Action Army and the official army sidearm from 1873 to 1892, it was also known as "the Peacemaker" and the weapon that "won the West." (A.B. Dyer, *Handbook for Light Artillery*. New York: John Wiley & Sons, 1908)

The Model 1873 was also somewhat obsolescent when compared to other double-action contemporary designs, most notably those produced by Smith and Wesson and by British firms such as Adams and Webley. As a single-action revolver the Colt required the user to cock the hammer before each shot, whereas double-action revolvers could be fired conventionally or by simply squeezing the trigger to both cock and drop the hammer for rapid fire. In addition, the Colt required the individual removal of spent cartridge cases by manually rotating the cylinder to align the chambers with the ejection rod, a process eliminated by Smith and Wesson's top-break designs that merely required tilting the hinged cylinder and barrel assembly forward to automatically eject all of the spent casings with one motion.

Despite such flaws, the Model 1873 served the army well in the West and to a limited extent in the Philippines during the Spanish-American War (1898) and the Philippine-American War (1899–1902), in Mexico during the U.S. interventions there (1914 and 1916–1917), and during World War I (1914–1918). It was known as the "Peacemaker" and the "Frontier Six-Shooter," and its aficionados included such western personalities as William F. "Buffalo Bill" Cody, Bat Masterson, and the Earp brothers as well as President Theodore Roosevelt and General George S. Patton, who owned a brace of ivory-gripped Colts.

JEFF KINARD

See also

Cody, William Frederick; Rifles

References

Flayderman, Norm. *Flayderman's Guide to Antique American Firearms.* Iola, WA: Krause Publications, 1998.

Kinard, Jeff S. *Pistols: An Illustrated History of Their Impact.* Santa Barbara, CA: ABC-CLIO, 2003.

Comanche Campaign
Start Date: 1867
End Date: 1875

Series of skirmishes and small battles between the U.S. Army and white settlers on one side and the Comanches, along with their Kiowa, Arapaho, and Southern Cheyenne allies, on the other. The hostilities took place mainly in Kansas, Colorado, New Mexico, and parts of Texas. After decades of incessant raids on white settlements by the Comanches throughout the southern Plains and northern Mexico, the U.S. government called for a meeting of the Comanches and other southern Plains tribes at Medicine Lodge Creek, 60 miles south of Fort Larned (Kansas), in October 1867. The Comanches believed that the resulting treaty would not be enforceable and was unlikely to resolve the differences between the tribes and white settlers but signed it anyway. Some Comanches accepted a reservation in southwestern Indian Territory (Oklahoma), which they would share with several Kiowa bands. Others refused to go to the reservation. The annuities promised by the U.S. government failed to materialize, so the Comanches and their allies continued their raids against the whites.

Throughout the late 1860s the raids intensified, as the Comanche were now hard-pressed to provide for themselves because the buffalo herds upon which they relied were being reduced at an alarming rate; the bison would be hunted nearly to extinction by the late 1870s. By 1871 U.S. Army commander General William T. Sherman and Lieutenant General Philip Sheridan, commander of the Military Division of the Missouri, had instituted a scorched-earth policy toward the Comanches. This meant that their winter camps, supplies, and animals were to be destroyed and that non-combatants were to be killed. Although this strategy was difficult to carry out over the vast Comanche territory, the Comanches would nevertheless feel the full impact of the policy, which did not end until their final surrender in 1875.

The first major U.S. military strike began in the autumn of 1871 with Colonel Ranald Mackenzie's 4th Cavalry marching through western Texas's Blanco Canyon onto the Staked Plains, where Tonkawa scouts found the Comanche war chief Quanah Parker leading a large Kwahadi Comanche band. The troops pushed the Kwahadis deep into the region until cold weather halted their drive.

In the spring of 1872 Mackenzie changed his strategy, instituting a border patrol system anchored by newly established forts. With 300 soldiers and Tonkawa scouts, he tracked Comanche Rancherias, charted war and hunting trails, and mapped the sites of Comancheros (New Mexican Hispanic traders). Avoiding direct confrontation, he wore down the Comanches by disrupting their seasonal cycle of activities, including trade.

In September 1872 the 4th Cavalry attacked a Kwahadi-Kotsoteka camp of 262 lodges on the North Fork of the Red River. In a brutal engagement the soldiers killed 24 warriors, captured more than 100 women and children, seized horses and mules, and burned lodges, robes, and food. Pursuing Comanche parties managed to recapture most of the animals in night raids, but the fight left the Comanches destitute.

In 1874 the Comanches followed a mystic Kwahadi medicine man, Isatai, who promised a restoration of Comanche power. He claimed that he could raise the dead, stop bullets in midflight, and regurgitate all the cartridges that the Comanches would need. By mid-June 1874 some 700 warriors and their families had gathered on Elk Creek to follow Isatai. At dawn on June 27, 1874, Isatai and Quanah Parker led an attack on a well-armed group of buffalo hunters at Adobe Walls, a small trading post in the Texas Panhandle. The assault, known as the Second Battle of Adobe Walls, failed, thanks largely to the high-powered rifles of the post's defenders and demoralization among the attackers. Isatai's horse was killed by a stray shot, and his support quickly evaporated.

The U.S. government now ordered all Comanches and Kiowas to return to their agency by August 3, 1874, at Fort Sill. The deadline passed with no answer, and the Native Americans remained in place. In what became known as the Red River War, generals Sherman and Sheridan now sent five columns, 1,400 soldiers in all, from every direction to converge upon Comanche and Kiowa sanctuaries in the canyons along the Caprock and plains of the Texas Panhandle. The advancing troops meaningfully engaged the

Comanches only once, but their looming presence prevented fleeing Comanche bands from searching for the few remaining bison and making preparations for the winter.

On September 28, 1874, Mackenzie's 4th Cavalry attacked a serpentine village of several hundred Comanches, Kiowas, and Southern Cheyennes in Palo Duro Canyon. Scattered across the canyon floor, the tribes failed to organize a united defense. Instead they fled onto the open plains, leaving their possessions behind. Mackenzie ordered the camp and all of its supplies destroyed. Soldiers captured some 1,500 Indian ponies, most of which Mackenzie ordered killed. This defeat ended all hopes of a Comanche victory. Half-starved and worn out from incessant skirmishing, the Native Americans returned to their reservations for good by the summer of 1875, with Quanah Parker and his band being the last to submit.

JOHN THOMAS BROOM

See also

Adobe Walls, Second Battle of; Arapahos; Cheyennes; Cheyennes, Southern; Comanches; Kiowas; Kotsoteka Comanches; Kwahadi Comanches; Mackenzie, Ranald Slidell; Medicine Lodge Treaty; Palo Duro Canyon, Battle of; Quanah Parker; Sheridan, Philip Henry; Sherman, William Tecumseh

References

Ferhenbach, T. R. *Comanches: The History of a People*. New York, Anchor Books, 2003.

Hoig, Stan. *Tribal Wars of the Southern Plains*. Norman: University of Oklahoma Press, 1993.

LaVere, David. *Contrary Neighbors: Southern Plains and Removed Indians in Indian Territory*. Norman: University of Oklahoma Press, 2000.

Powers, William K. *Indians of the Southern Plains*. New York: Capricorn Books, 1972.

Wallace, Ernest, and E. Adamson Hoebel. *The Comanches: Lords of the South Plains*. 1952; reprint, Norman: University of Oklahoma Press, 1986.

Comancheros

New Mexican traders of Hispanic origin based in central and northern Mexico who traded with Native American peoples in eastern New Mexico and western Texas, most predominantly with the Comanche people (hence the name Comanchero). In the late 1860s and early 1870s the U.S. Army worked to end the exchange of goods and livestock between the Comanches and the Comancheros. Originally called Viageros ("travelers"), these frontiersmen traded liquor, munitions, food, and manufactured goods for stolen cattle and horses or buffalo hides.

By the 1860s a pattern had developed whereby the Comanches would rustle cattle herds in Texas and trade them to the Comancheros, who in turn sold them in New Mexico. One contemporary estimated that between 1860 and 1867, the Comanches had stolen about 300,000 cattle and 100,000 horses from Texas.

A. B. Norton, U.S. superintendent of Indian affairs in New Mexico, accused the Comancheros of inciting these Indian raids to facilitate their trade, and he therefore revoked all trading licenses in 1867. Yet the trading ban could not be enforced, so Colonel George Washington Getty, the new district commander, placed guarded picket posts along all known trade routes. From their base at Fort Bascom, the soldiers were able to confiscate several fraudulent trading licenses along with the cattle and goods being trafficked, significantly decreasing the Comanchero trade during 1868–1869.

In 1870, however, the force stationed at Fort Bascom was reduced to only a few men, emboldening the Comancheros and permitting a robust revival of their illegal trade. In 1871 Colonel John Irwin Gregg reinforced the fort and ordered Major D. R. Clendenin to patrol the frontier between Fort Bascom and Fort Sumner. In May of that same year one of these patrols came across a band of 21 Comancheros who briefly employed bows and muskets to fight off the 11 cavalrymen until the Comancheros were finally overpowered. The patrol took 700 cattle from them, and although their orders were to kill all confiscated livestock, the soldiers ran out of ammunition after dispatching only 250.

In 1872 a small force from the 4th Cavalry Regiment overtook a party of 15 Comancheros, killing 2 and capturing 1 before the rest could make their escape. The captive, Polonio Ortiz, told his army interrogators who his fellow traders were, which trails they used, and who bought their cattle. Based on this information, both Colonel Gregg and Colonel Ranald S. Mackenzie led large forces into the backcountry in an effort to suppress the trade. Although neither of their expeditions encountered the traders, they did explore much unknown land as well as intimidate New Mexicans, making them hesitant to buy stolen cattle. This fear was also fed by the raids of John Hittson, a Texan who led a large contingent of civilians into New Mexico to collect cattle that they claimed had been stolen from Texas.

With the market for stolen cattle disappearing, the Comanchero trade began to dwindle. During a patrol of the trading routes in 1873, the cavalry rode more than 1,000 miles without seeing a single trader. The final blow to the Comanchero trade was dealt when the U.S. Army defeated the Comanches, Cheyennes, Arapahos, and Kiowas in the Red River War (1874–1875). The Comancheros, who had traded with the Comanches since the 18th century, now had to seek another livelihood.

CAMERON B. STRANG

See also

Adobe Walls, Second Battle of; Arapahos; Cheyennes; Comanches; Fort Bascom; Fort Sumner; Gregg, John Irvin; Kiowas; Mackenzie, Ranald Slidell

References

Kavanagh, Thomas W. *Comanche Political History: An Ethnohistorical Perspective, 1706–1875.* Lincoln: University of Nebraska Press, 1996.

Kenner, Charles S. *A History of New Mexican–Plains Indian Relations.* Norman: University of Oklahoma Press, 1969.

Comanches

A Native American group of the southern Great Plains. The Comanches were an offshoot of the Shoshones of the Upper Platte River area of Wyoming. Between 1650 and 1700 or so the Comanches became an autonomous group, although they were never really a unified tribe. Rather, they were subdivided into as many as 12 independent groups. Their language was of the Uto-Aztekan family, and they were linguistically and in many ways culturally identical to the Shoshones, whose wider range had been in the Great Basin and Rocky Mountain area. The first European contact with the Comanches occurred in New Mexico in 1705, when the Spaniards first encountered them. The Spaniards named them "Comanche," from the Ute name "Komantcia," which translates loosely as "enemy." The Comanches' name for themselves was "Nermernuh," which means "the people."

After the split with the Shoshones, the Comanches migrated east and south for a time toward eastern Wyoming and Colorado, western Nebraska, and Kansas before settling on the southern Plains. From the 1700s their principal range became northwestern Texas, western Oklahoma, eastern Colorado, eastern New Mexico, and southern Kansas. The area in time became known as the Comancheria. However, the area in which they conducted raids was much larger, stretching from eastern Kansas and Nebraska deep into Mexico and from the Gulf Coast of Texas to Santa Fe, New Mexico. It is believed that at their peak the Comanches numbered about 20,000 people.

The Comanches' migration from the Rocky Mountains to the southern Plains was influenced by several factors. The abundance of bison lured them onto the Plains, while the growing power of tribes to their north, such as the Kiowas and later the Cheyennes and Lakotas, pushed them farther south, where the allure of Spanish horse herds became a major factor. The Comanches had obtained horses early. By the time of their first encounter with the Spanish, the Comanches already had substantial herds. Indeed,

Population History of Indians in Texas, 1690–1890

Tribe	1690 Population	1890 Population	Reduction
Akokisa	500	Extinct	100%
Arapahos	*3,000	5,630	+88%
Biduis	500	Extinct	100%
Caddos	8,500	536	94%
Cheyennes	*3,500+	5,630	+61%
Coahuiltecans	7,500	Extinct	100%
Comanches	7,000	1,598	77%
Karankawans	2,800	Extinct	100%
Kichais	500	66	87%
Kiowa Apaches	*300+	326	+9%
Kiowas	*2,000	1,140	43%
Lipan Apaches	500	60	88%
Mescalero Apaches	700	473	32%
Tonkawans	1,600	56	97%
Wichita	3,200	358	89%

*Population as of 1780

Illustration of a Comanche village by George Catlin, 1844. (Hulton-Deutsch Collection/Corbis)

their culture was dominated by the horse, the bison, and raiding. In the early years, most Comanches were hunter-gatherers; however, as they migrated farther south, hunting became the central part of their cultural and economic activities.

The various Comanche bands did not have a unitary leader, or chief. Instead, each group chose a small group of leaders and advisers who carried out the governing functions of the whole band, including warfare. Thus, most Comanche clans had a war chief, a peace chief, and a small group of elders who handled other concerns, including the settling of disputes and the assignment of particular tasks.

The Comanches were divided into a shifting number of bands, the principal ones being the Honey-eaters (Penatekas), who were located at the southern and eastern side of their range in Texas; the Yap-eaters (Yapparikas), located along the northern side of the range; and the Antelopes (Quahadi, Kwahadi), located in the western area of the range, principally on the Staked Plains. The Wanderers (Nokonis), who ranged along the headwaters of the Brazos River in Texas, and the Buffalo-eaters (Kotsotekas), of the Canadian River Valley, were other prominent bands. Band membership was partially by family association and partially by choice. Members were free to shift from band to band.

The Comanches were bellicose and aggressive, driving various Apache tribes off the southern Plains and then raiding into the regions of the Lipan Apaches in Texas and the various Apache groups of eastern New Mexico. The Comanches warred on an almost constant basis with the Utes and engaged in raids deep into Mexico until their free roaming days drew to a close in the 1870s. In addition, the Comanches warred against tribes to their east in Texas and Oklahoma and against Prairie tribes such as the Osages and Pawnees. Throughout the early 1800s, the Comanche presence on the southern Plains stopped Spanish and later Mexican expansion from New Mexico and Texas and halted French penetration of the area. Texan and American expansion, while not halted, was slowed as the fortunes of the Comanches and the Americans ebbed and flowed. During the American Civil War (1861–1865), the Comanches forcefully drove back the Texas frontier by as much as 100 miles in some areas.

Despite their warlike ways, the Comanches could also make peace with long-standing enemies. In the 1790s the Comanches made peace with their northern enemies: the Kiowas and the associated Kiowa Apaches. Later in 1840 the Comanches and Kiowas made peace with the Cheyennes and Arapahos. These peace arrangements held fairly firm and served to protect the Comanches from attacks from the northern end of their range. After the 1790s and again after the 1840 peace arrangements with the Kiowas and the Cheyennes, the Comanches were often joined on their long-distance raids by young warriors from these tribes.

In 1786 the Comanches made peace with the New Mexicans under Don Juan Bautista de Anza, and their raids on Spanish and (later) Mexican settlements in New Mexico stopped. This treaty, signed in Taos, was the result of successful military campaigns on the part of de Anza, his insistence on the entirety of the Comanche people agreeing to the treaty, and the arrangement for traders from New Mexico known as Comancheros to provide trade goods previously denied to the Comanches, specifically guns and ammunition. Despite the agreement with de Anza in New Mexico, the Comanches continued their raiding into northern Mexico and Texas.

The initial purpose of warfare for the Comanches was to maintain their hold on Comancheria, their bison-hunting grounds. Additionally, they raided for horses, captives, and material goods. The Comanches raided other tribes, the Mexicans, Texans, American settlers, and even the U.S. Army for horses. Indeed, the Comanches accumulated some of the largest horse herds of any Plains people. When making peace with the Cheyennes and Arapahos, the Comanches greatly impressed their northern neighbors with the number of horses given as gifts.

The Comanches angered and frightened settlers with their habit of taking captives. The captives served several purposes. Young captives were often brought up within Comanche families as adopted children to increase tribal numbers. Some were kept as slaves to perform menial tasks around the band's camps, while others managed and guarded the horse herds. Women were sometimes taken as secondary wives but more often simply to be raped and mutilated in an almost casual way on the trip back to Comancheria. In addition, the Comanches learned quickly that captured white children and women would be ransomed by the white New Mexicans and other settlers with whom they traded.

Usually, however, fancy cloth, trinkets, cooking utensils, and arms and ammunition were the primary objective of Comanche raiding. In 1840 a Comanche raiding party under Buffalo Hump raided as far east as Linnville, Texas, at Lavaca Bay on the Gulf Coast. On reaching Linnville, the Comanches captured so much booty that it slowed down their escape, and they were caught by a hastily raised group of Texas Rangers and civilian volunteers. The resulting action fought at Plum Creek on August 12, 1840, resulted in at least 80 dead Comanche warriors.

The Comanches had adopted firearms but preferred bows and arrows, lances, and clubs in their warfare. In addition to the tangible results of raiding, the Comanches held the warrior in high esteem. While some tribes allowed as many as four warriors to count coup, the Comanches recognized only the first two warriors to strike an enemy as coup counters, meaning that only they received primary credit for the raid or attack. As such, raiding and hunting were the paths to manhood for young Comanche men. The Comanches rarely engaged in large-scale warfare, preferring instead a raid-and-ambush strategy. On the few occasions in which the Comanches did engage in large attacks they suffered heavy casualties, the most notable being after their one experiment with large-scale fighting at the Second Battle of Adobe Walls (June 27, 1874) in the Texas Panhandle.

As the 19th century progressed, increasing white settlement, the extermination of the southern bison herd, and the expansion of the railroads spelled the end of the Comancheria. The Medicine Lodge Treaty, which most Comanche bands signed, sought to concentrate the Comanches and Kiowas on a reservation in western Indian Territory (Oklahoma), which would be overseen by a new military post, Fort Sill. Most Comanches had no faith in the treaty, nor did most intend to recognize its stipulations. In fact, the treaty led to a brief but intense Comanche attempt to beat back white civilization. The reign of the Comanches on the southern Plains came to an end in June 1875 when the last of the major Comanche bands, under Quanah Parker, surrendered to Colonel Ranald S. Mackenzie and moved to the reservation at Fort Sill.

JOHN THOMAS BROOM

See also
Adobe Walls, Second Battle of; Apaches; Arapahos; Buffalo; Cheyennes; Fort Sill; Kiowas; Kotsoteka Comanches; Kwahadi Comanches; Mackenzie, Ranald Slidell; Nakoni Comanches; Quanah Parker; Shoshones; Utes

References
Ferhenbach, T. R. *Comanches: The History of a People.* New York: Anchor Books, 2003.
Hoig, Stan. *Tribal Wars of the Southern Plains.* Norman: University of Oklahoma Press, 1993.
LaVere, David. *Contrary Neighbors: Southern Plains and Removed Indians in Indian Territory.* Norman: University of Oklahoma Press, 2000.
Wallace, Ernest, and E. Adamson Hoebel. *The Comanches: Lords of the South Plains.* 1952; reprint, Norman: University of Oklahoma Press, 1986.

Commissioner of Indian Affairs, Office of
See Office of Commissioner of Indian Affairs

Connor, Patrick Edward
Birth Date: March 17, 1820
Death Date: December 17, 1891

U.S. Army officer. Patrick Edward Connor was born in County Kerry, Ireland, on March 17, 1820. In 1828 he arrived in the United States, and in 1839 he enlisted in the U.S. Army. He saw action during the Second Seminole War (1835–1842) before his enlistment expired, and in 1845 he became a naturalized U.S. citizen. After relocating to Texas, he joined an independent company of Texas volunteers and saw action in the Mexican-American War

As a colonel, Patrick E. Connor led the fight against the Shoshone Indians in the West during the Civil War. (Library of Congress)

(1846–1848), rising to the rank of captain. He resigned his commission in 1847 to pursue various business interests.

Connor eventually followed the gold rush to California, where he came to command a California Militia unit known as the Stockton Blues. When the American Civil War (1861–1865) began, Connor recruited men to enlarge the unit, which ultimately became the 3rd California Volunteer Infantry Regiment, and he became its colonel. He was subsequently ordered to Utah Territory, where he was to protect overland trails and control the Mormons, who appeared on the edge of rebellion.

Connor was dissatisfied with his assignment and sought action on the battlefields of the East. He personally entreated his friend, Major General Henry W. Halleck, to authorize the transfer of his regiment to the East. Halleck demurred and suggested that Connor scout the area around present-day Salt Lake City. Over Mormon objections, Connor established Fort Douglas.

Meanwhile, Connor dealt with problems arising from tensions between white miners and settlers and the Shoshones near the Idaho-Utah border. On January 29, 1863, after marching his men more than 140 miles through bitter weather and a frozen countryside, Connor's force attacked a Shoshone camp near the Bear River. The engagement saw the deaths of between 200 and 400 Native Americans, many of them women and children. Connor also confiscated large caches of weapons and captured a large

store of Shoshone wheat. In February 1863 Connor was promoted to brigadier general of volunteers and given command of the District of Utah. He made Fort Douglas his headquarters.

Shortly after the Civil War ended in April 1865, Connor was brevetted major general of volunteers. In July 1865 Major General Grenville M. Dodge sent Connor and a force to the Powder River, where he was to conduct punitive raids against the Arapahos, Cheyennes, and Sioux, who had been raiding the Bozeman Trail. The operation lasted until early September and saw little sustained military action except for the Battle of the Tongue River (August 29), a victory for Connor's forces. The expedition temporarily brought a halt to the Bozeman Trail raids but did not break Native American resistance, especially among the Sioux.

In 1866 Connor mustered out of the volunteer army. Thereafter he settled in Salt Lake City, established a newspaper there, and became involved in a mining venture. He also helped recruit men—many of them Confederate Civil War veterans—for the state militia and was often involved in their training. Connor founded the town of Stockton, Utah, naming it in honor of his old California Militia unit. He died in Salt Lake City on December 17, 1891.

PAUL G. PIERPAOLI JR.

See also

Arapahos; Bear River, Battle of; Bozeman Trail; Cheyennes; Dodge, Grenville Mellen; Powder River Expedition; Shoshones; Sioux

References

Madsen, Brigham D. *Glory Hunter: A Biography of Patrick Edward Connor.* Salt Lake City: University of Utah Press, 1990.

Utley, Robert M. *Frontiersmen in Blue: The United States and the Indian, 1848–1865.* Lincoln: University of Nebraska Press, 1967.

Connor's Powder River Expedition
Start Date: August 11, 1865
End Date: September 24, 1865

Inconclusive campaign led by Brigadier General Patrick E. Connor against northern Native American tribes along the Powder River in 1865. With the outbreak of the American Civil War (1861–1865), Native American tribes in the western United States took advantage of the war to reassert control over their ancestral lands. This was especially true on the northern Plains. The end result was widespread attacks on isolated frontier forts and white settlements. In many cases citizen militias took matters into their own hands, helping to spark the Sand Creek Massacre in 1864 during which Colonel John Chivington led Colorado militia in a vicious assault against Cheyenne chief Black Kettle's peaceful village. That action resulted in some 150 Native American deaths, more than half of whom were women and children. In retaliation, the Sioux, Cheyennes, and Arapahos launched raids along the Platte River and against Fort Laramie.

With the Civil War drawing to a close, however, the U.S. Army was in a position to shift resources and manpower to the West and felt compelled to act swiftly because many soldiers' terms of service were soon to expire. Consequently, Major General Grenville Dodge, commander of the Department of Missouri and the Department of Kansas at Fort Leavenworth, ordered Brigadier General Patrick E. Connor, who two years earlier had led a successful attack against the Shoshones in the Battle of Bear River (sometimes described as a massacre), to lead a three-pronged punitive expedition to the Powder River.

Connor's force numbered approximately 2,400 men and was comprised primarily of volunteers from California, Kansas, and Nebraska. Colonel Nelson Cole's column proceeded up the Loup Fork of the Platte River to the forks of the Little Powder and Big Powder rivers and then to the Tongue River, where they were to be met by Lieutenant Colonel Samuel Walker's column, which marched north from Fort Laramie and then swung west of the Black Hills. Meanwhile, Connor led the third column from the north bend of the North Platte River to the Powder River, arriving on August 11 and building a stockade, named Fort Connor, before advancing to the Tongue River.

Arriving at the Tongue River on the morning of August 29, Connor attacked Chief Black Bear's camp of approximately 500 Arapahos. Catching the natives by surprise, Connor's forces used howitzers to devastating effect, killing approximately 60 Arapahos, including Black Bear's son. Following the victory, Connor waited in vain for the arrival of the columns of Cole and Walker, both of which had gotten lost. By the time Connor's scouts located them on September 19, Cole's and Walker's men were on the verge of starvation, primarily because Connor had brought the bulk of supplies with his column.

While Connor debated on a course of action, a courier arrived on September 24 with orders relieving him of his command. The expedition then straggled back to Fort Laramie. The limited success of the expedition, its high cost, and outrage with Connor's order that all Native American males over age 15 should be summarily shot contributed to the decision to pursue a peace policy with the Plains tribes.

JUSTIN D. MURPHY

See also

Arapahos; Bear River, Battle of; Black Kettle; Connor, Patrick Edward; Chivington, John; Dodge, Grenville Mellen; Fort Laramie; Native Americans and the Civil War; Sand Creek Massacre

References

Brady, Cyrus Townsend. *The Sioux Indian Wars: From the Powder River to the Little Big Horn.* New York: Barnes and Noble, 1992.

McDermott, John D. *Circle of Fire: The Indian War of 1865.* Mechanicsburg, PA: Stackpole, 2003.

U.S. Army Military History Institute, and Bruce Reber. *The United States Army and the Indian Wars in the Trans Mississippi West, 1860–1898.* Carlisle Barracks, PA: U.S. Army Military History Institute, 1978.

Conquistadors

Term used in reference to the Portuguese and Spanish soldiers, explorers, and adventurers who brought much of the Americas under the control of the kingdoms of Spain and Portugal from the late 15th century through the 17th century. Meaning literally "the conqueror," the term "conquistador" referenced the kinship that the Spanish explorers felt with those who had accomplished the *reconquista* ("reconquest") of Spain from Muslim Moorish control in 1492. Many conquistadors were initially poor, as tradition prohibited Spanish noblemen from engaging in manual work. Some were escaping the religious prosecution of the Spanish Inquisition. Areas in the New World that came under Spanish and Portuguese control included Mexico, most of South and Central America, parts of the Caribbean, and much of the present-day United States.

The Spanish and Portuguese fought for control over these new colonies. This rivalry was finally settled under papal arbitration in the Treaty of Tordesillas of 1494. This treaty divided the territory conquered outside of Europe between the Spanish Crown and the Portuguese along a north-south meridian running 1,100 miles west of the Cape Verde Islands off the west coast of Africa. The territory to the east would belong to Portugal, and the land to the west would belong to Spain. In 1506 Pope Julius II officially sanctioned this division. This opened the way for Spanish exploration and colonization in the New World except for Brazil, most of which fell under Portuguese dominion.

The Spanish conquest of the Americas began in 1492 with the arrival of Christopher Columbus, an Italian by birth. The Caribbean regions were conquered first, but these did not provide sufficient treasure to make the conquerors rich. Juan Ponce de León secured the island of Puerto Rico, while Diego Velázquez took Cuba. Hernán Cortés became the first significantly successful conquistador. He overpowered the Aztecs during 1520–1521 and brought Mexico under Spanish rule. Francisco Pizarro was responsible for conquering the Incas in South America. In 1520 Ferdinand Magellan's discovery of the straits at the tip of South America led the Spanish conquistadors to the Pacific and Asia. Miguel López de Legazpi, who arrived in the Philippines in 1565, opened the way for the Spanish conquest in the Pacific. In North America, conquistadors Hernando de Soto and Francisco Coronado had extensive and devastating contact with native populations.

The conquistadors brought with them European diseases such as smallpox, influenza, measles, and typhus, which were disastrous to the Native American populations who had no immunity to them. European diseases in many cases wiped out between 30 percent and 90 percent of the native populations. In respect to the Aztecs and the Incas, the diseases badly weakened their populations, which had significantly outnumbered the Spanish, and aided the Spanish conquistadors in their effort to colonize the Americas.

The legends of immeasurable wealth located in golden cities (such as El Dorado) enticed many Spanish adventurers to leave

Seventeenth-century painting of the conquest of Tenochtitlán (present-day Mexico City) by Hernán Cortés in 1521. (Library of Congress)

for the Americas. Oftentimes they came back empty-handed; however, those who did manage to bring precious metals back to Spain propagated the impression of seemingly endless sources of gold and silver in the New World. Over time the Spanish monarchs, relying too heavily on these imports and engaging the country in extensive foreign wars, overstretched the Crown's budget to the point of bankruptcy. This undermined the Spanish and European economies and led to rampant inflation in Spain.

Native American populations suffered greatly at the hands of the conquistadors. Wanton killings, enslavement, rape, torture, and other abuses perpetuated the stereotype of Spanish cruelty that came to be known as the Black Legend. This term referred to the infamous Spanish Inquisition and later to the behavior of the Spanish conquistadors in the colonies. Early Protestant historians, describing the period of Spanish colonization, often depicted the Spanish conquistadors as being fanatical, cruel, intolerant, and greedy, in the process perpetuating the Black Legend.

Accounts of the mistreatment of the natives by the conquistadors contributed to the passage of the Spanish colonial laws, known as the New Laws, in 1542. They were designed to protect the rights of Native Americans and to prevent the exploitation of indigenous peoples by the conquistadors. The enslavement of the natives in the New World colonies came under further scrutiny in the Valladolid Debate of 1550–1551. This debate sought to

determine whether Native Americans had souls, as white Europeans were believed to possess. Bartolomé de Las Casas, a Dominican friar, argued that the full humanity of the natives was evident because they indeed did possess souls. The Jesuit priest Juan Gines de Sepulveda, however, maintained that the indigenous peoples in the New World did not have souls and therefore could be enslaved. King Charles I of Spain (r. 1516–1556; Holy Roman Emperor Charles V during 1519–1558), when confronted with this debate, ordered an end to the aggression against the natives and also ordered a jury of eminent scholars to hold a hearing on the subject. The jury ruled in favor of treating the natives as human beings, who were presumed to have immortal souls. This ruling did little to change Spanish colonial policy, however, as most conquistadors ignored or circumvented the royal edicts, which were virtually unenforceable at such a distance from Spain.

Before attacking native populations, the conquistadors would often read to them a document known as the Requirement. The document provided an overview of world history, with the focus on Christianity as propagated by the Catholic Church, and demanded that the indigenous peoples accept the king of Spain as their supreme ruler on behalf of the pope and allow missionaries to introduce them to the Christian Gospel. This document came into being after the Catholic Church in Spain had asserted that the wars against Native American peoples were unjust and immoral.

In contrast to the Moors, who were Muslims and rejected Christ as the Messiah, the indigenous people in the colonies had never come into contact with Christianity. For the conquistadors, the Requirement served as a loophole to put the native populations in a position in which they would reject Christianity and could therefore be attacked without facing the wrath of the Catholic Church or the king.

Often by force, the Native Americans were gradually converted to Christianity. In so doing, the conquistadors purged most native cultural practices. Oftentimes, however, the natives would blend their traditional customs and beliefs with Catholic traditions. In contrast to religion, the Spanish language was not normally imposed on the conquered populations. After the heavy damage sustained by Spain during the Peninsular War (1808–1814) and decades of imperial overstretch, Spain was unable to maintain its colonies. This led to a wave of independence movements in its New World colonies during the first part of the 19th century.

ANNA RULSKA

See also

Missionaries; Ponce de León, Juan; Slavery among Native Americans; Spain

References

Hakim, Joy. *The First Americans.* New York: Oxford University Press, 1993.

Jones, Mary Ellen. *Christopher Columbus and His Legacy: Opposing Viewpoints.* San Diego: Greenhaven, 1992.

Wood, Michael. *Conquistadors.* Berkeley: University of California Press, 2000.

Cooke, Philip St. George
Birth Date: June 13, 1809
Death Date: March 20, 1895

U.S. Army officer. Philip St. George Cooke was born on June 13, 1809, in Leesburg, Virginia, and graduated from the U.S. Military Academy, West Point, in 1827. Commissioned a second lieutenant of infantry, he was promoted to first lieutenant and transferred to the 1st Dragoons in 1833. Cooke served in the Black Hawk War of 1832 and was promoted to captain in 1835. During the Mexican-American War (1846–1848) he marched to New Mexico with Colonel Stephen Watts Kearny and then cut a separate route to California, where Cooke earned promotion to major and a brevet to lieutenant colonel. Promoted to lieutenant colonel and assigned to the 2nd Dragoons, he fought against the Apaches in New Mexico in 1854 and the Sioux in Nebraska in 1855 before participating in the Mormon Campaign in 1857. He became colonel in 1858. In 1861 Cooke published a book titled *Cavalry Tactics,* which helped him to become known by many as the "Father of American Cavalry."

In April 1861 the American Civil War (1861–1865) erupted and divided Cooke's family as well as the nation. His son, John R. Cooke, became a Confederate general; two of his daughters also sided with the South. One of those daughters was married to Confederate cavalry general J. E. B. Stuart. Another daughter was married to Union brigadier general Jacob Sharpe.

Cooke was promoted to brigadier general in the regular army in November 1861 and was placed in command of cavalry forces in Washington, D.C. He participated in the March–August 1862 Peninsula Campaign and saw action in command of a cavalry division in the Siege of Yorktown (April 5–May 3, 1862), the Battle of Williamsburg (May 5, 1862), and the Seven Days' Campaign (June 25–July 1, 1862).

Cooke's wartime leadership produced controversy. Early on he was criticized for not pursuing aggressively enough his Confederate opponent and son-in-law, J. E. B. Stuart. Then Cooke was humiliated when Stuart circled the entire Union Army in June 1862. Many speculated that the reason Cooke was not forceful was that he feared the humiliation of losing a battle to Stuart. As a result of his actions at Gaines's Mill (June 27) in the Seven Days' Campaign, Cooke was attacked for advancing without orders and launching an ill-fated cavalry charge that attempted to save some cannon in danger of being captured but only resulted in heavy casualties among his men. Critics claimed that Cooke was too wedded to the idea of a saber charge to realize that such tactics were suicidal against entrenched infantry. Cooke also saw action in the Battle of White Oak Swamp on June 30, 1862. On July 5 Cooke asked to be relieved of command, pending an investigation of his actions at Gaines's Mill.

Cooke never again served in the field during the Civil War and instead was limited to administrative duties. Until August 1863 he served on the courts-martial staff, after which he commanded the District of Baton Rouge, Louisiana, until May 1864. From May 1864 to April 1865 he had charge of the Union's recruiting effort. Cooke was brevetted major general on March 13, 1865.

Following the Civil War, Cooke remained in the army and commanded the new Department of the Platte, which included Iowa, Nebraska, Utah, and part of the Dakota and Montana territories. Cooke's headquarters was in Omaha, Nebraska. His department saw a heavy flow of white immigrants, who preferred using the Great Platte River Road and the new Bozeman Trail.

In his final days in uniform, Cooke, ever the cavalry traditionalist, resisted efforts to eliminate the saber, even though it was not practical for fighting Native Americans in the West. Like many of his fellow army officers, he was often more sympathetic toward the Native Americans than he was toward the white settlers and even learned to speak several different Native American languages. Furthermore, like many officers, he believed that it was whites who had corrupted the Native Americans with their introduction of alcohol and gambling.

Cooke retired from active duty on October 29, 1873, after more than 50 years in the military. He spent his retirement years writing about his experiences. He died in Detroit, Michigan, on March 20, 1895.

ALAN K. LAMM

See also
Apaches; Black Hawk War; Bozeman Trail; Great Platte River Road; Sioux

References
Cooke, Philip St. George. *Cavalry Tactics.* Washington, DC: U.S. Government Printing Office, 1861.
Cooke, Philip St. George. *The Conquest of New Mexico and California.* New York: Putnam, 1878.
Cooke, Philip St. George. *Scenes and Adventures in the Army: Or, Romance of Military Life.* Philadelphia: Lindsay and Blakiston, 1857.
Longacre, Edward G. *Lincoln's Cavalryman: A History of the Mounted Forces of the Army of the Potomac.* Mechanicsburg, PA: Stackpole, 2000.
Young, Otis E. *The West of Philip St. George Cooke.* Glendale, CA: Arthur H. Clark, 1955.

Cooper, James Fenimore
Birth Date: September 15, 1789
Death Date: September 14, 1851

American novelist who treated the colonial experience in many of his novels and glorified Native Americans. Born on September 15, 1789, in Burlington, New Jersey, James Fenimore Cooper moved with his family in 1790 to Cooperstown, then a small village in upstate New York on the edge of the frontier. Not a good student, he was often in trouble. He studied at Yale during 1803–1805 but was expelled for blowing up another student's door. Cooper's father arranged for him to go to sea, preparatory to entering the U.S. Navy. The experience gave Cooper a love of the sea as a place of freedom and adventure. Appointed a midshipman in January 1808, he was assigned to the U.S. Navy brig *Wasp.* When his father died in 1809, Cooper inherited $50,000 and resigned his commission in May 1811. By 1820 he had gone through his inheritance and faced financial ruin. In desperation, he turned to writing as a career.

Cooper's first novels were published anonymously. His first, *Precaution,* appeared in 1820 and was a failure. His second, *The Spy* (1821), was a patriotic historical treatment of the American Revolutionary War (1775–1783). It was one of the first novels written by an American with an American setting and characters. *The Spy* was hugely popular. His next novel, *The Pioneers* (1823), was autobiographical and dealt with the founding of Cooperstown. A prevalent theme in the novel was the conflict between taming the wilderness and preserving it. In this novel Cooper introduced his most memorable character, Natty Bumpo, an aged hunter who became the symbol of the American frontiersman. The character was based on Daniel Boone and other scouts and explorers. Natty Bumpo appeared in four other Cooper novels, including *The Last of the Mohicans* (1826), Cooper's most famous work. Known as the Leatherstocking Tales, the five novels are *The Pioneers* (1823), *The Last of the Mohicans* (1826), *The Prairie* (1827), *The Pathfinder* (1840), and *The Deerslayer* (1841).

Cooper's works were widely read by both Americans and Europeans. His descriptions of the frontier and its effect on the American character were highly influential. His depiction of American expansion as inevitable and correct conformed with the Manifest Destiny philosophy accepted by many Americans of his day.

During the 1830s Cooper's popularity declined, and his elitist approach alienated many. Cooper disliked the "tyranny" of popular democracy and favored a republic controlled by the elite. His later writings were often suffused with polemics against the vulgar crowd. He also became known for his many libel suits against publishers critical of his ideas and writings.

Cooper supported the Mexican-American War (1846–1848), seeing it as part of the mission of the United States to spread liberty around the world. He wrote one novel set during the war, *Jack Tier; Or the Florida Reefs* (1848). One of the most important themes of the novel was that of a benevolent U.S. government rescuing Mexico from ambitious and dishonest rulers. Among his 52 books is the first scholarly study of the early U.S. Navy, *History of the Navy of the United States of America* (1839).

The first American to support himself completely by writing novels, Cooper, despite his quirks, helped to create a unique American genre of literature, capturing the influences of nature

James Fenimore Cooper was the first writer to capture the popular imagination with myths rooted in America's own history and the first to support himself with his own writings. His novels embodied the ideals—courage, integrity, and love of the wilderness—of a nation destined to expand and prosper. Among his 52 books is the first scholarly study of the early U.S. Navy. (National Archives)

and the frontier experience in his stories. Although he believed that it was the duty of the United States to expand across the continent, Cooper also decried the destruction of the wilderness and the Native Americans, whom he viewed as noble. Cooper died at Cooperstown on September 14, 1851.

TIM J. WATTS

See also
Boone, Daniel; Literature and the American Indian Wars; Mahicans

References
Dekker, George, and John P. McWilliams, eds. *James Fenimore Cooper: The Critical Heritage.* London: Routledge and Kegan Paul, 1973.
McWilliams, John. *Political Justice in a Republic: James Fenimore Cooper's America.* Berkeley: University of California Press, 1972.

Coosaponakeesa
See Musgrove, Mary

Córdova, Francisco Hernández de
Birth Date: Unknown
Death Date: 1517

Spanish explorer and slave trader. The date and place of birth for Francisco Hernández de Córdova (also spelled Francisco Fernández de Córdoba) are unknown, and his early years remain an enigma. Córdova was the first Spaniard to explore Mexico's Yucatan Peninsula. On February 8, 1517, Córdova and 110 men left Cuba in three ships bought on credit from the governor of Cuba, Diego Velásquez. Although the initial goal of the expedition was to procure slaves on the small islands off the coast of Honduras, storms drove Córdova off course. His expedition landed on an unknown coastline in March 1517. Córdova inquired of the native peoples where he was. They replied (in their own language) "Tectetan," which meant "I do not understand you." Henceforth, the Spaniards called the region "Yucatan."

Although a few shipwrecked Spanish sailors had found refuge on the Yucatan Peninsula prior to Córdova's arrival, Córdova was the first European to explore the region. He initially landed on the northeastern end of the peninsula and continued northwest. Almost immediately he realized that the natives he encountered on the peninsula, the Mayas, had a civilization far more advanced than any of the other native civilizations that the Spaniards had encountered in the Caribbean. In his report to Velásquez, Córdova noted that the Mayas constructed buildings made of limestone, had sophisticated agricultural techniques, and wore fine cotton clothing and gold jewelry. The Mayan people, however, greeted Córdova's expedition with great hostility. During the course of their journey, more than half of the expeditionary force was killed, and the remainder of the soldiers, including Córdova, were wounded.

Following several months of exploration, Córdova returned to Cuba and presented his report to the governor. Córdova died there shortly after his arrival later in 1517 of wounds he had received at the hands of the Mayas. Velásquez was absolutely convinced of the importance of Córdova's discovery, however. Indeed, Córdova's expedition opened the door for Juan de Grijalva's expedition to the Yucatan Peninsula in 1518 and, most important, Hernán Cortés's lucrative foray into Mexico in 1519.

MICHAEL R. HALL

See also
Spain

References
Díaz del Castillo, Bernal. *The Discovery and Conquest of Mexico.* Cambridge, MA: Da Capo, 2004.
Lockwood, C. C. *The Yucatan Peninsula.* Baton Rouge: Louisiana State University Press, 1989.

Corn

Cereal grain first domesticated by Native Americans in northern Central America perhaps 7,000 years ago. Corn (maize) was unique to the Americas but spread to other parts of the world after Europeans took it back with them to the Old World beginning in the late 15th century. There are dozens of varieties of corn, which can be cultivated almost anywhere in the world where there are sufficient rainfall or irrigation and an adequate growing season. Corn grows on long, straight stalks and develops into the characteristic ear of corn that contains the actual corn kernels. The kernels are well protected by a fibrous husk that must be removed to access the corn itself.

Corn is one of the world's basic staple crops, and because it can be stored for long periods, dried, and ground, it has been a food staple for many centuries. Corn can be grown in climates ranging from tropical to arid to nearly arctic. Corn can also be used for animal feed. Native Americans wasted almost nothing of their corn yields, using almost all parts of the plant for a variety of purposes. They also used it to produce corn liquor.

The first corn plants were probably cultivated by Native Americans in central Mexico. It is believed that corn was first grown in caves near Teotihuacàn and was taken from a wild grass known as teosinte. Early varieties of corn were much smaller than today's varieties, with ears perhaps only three to four inches long. Before long, corn cultivation spread throughout Central and South America and to the north into present-day Arizona and New Mexico. Over the years Native American breeding resulted in larger corn stalks and ears. Some 1,500 years ago corn was a staple crop as far north as the American Southwest; by 800 CE it had become a staple in areas that ranged from southern Ontario, Canada, to Florida. Native Americans in the more temperate areas of North America continually bred and cross-bred corn varieties to increase yield and to make them less susceptible to frost and drought. By 900 flint, or

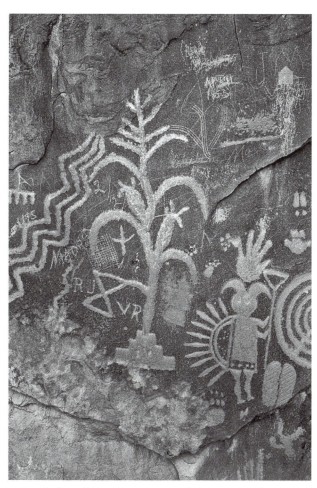

A petroglyph panel from circa 1500–1700, depicting corn and a Navajo deity, located in Largo Canyon in northwestern New Mexico. This area is known as the birthplace of Navajo culture. (iStockPhoto.com)

European colonists first landed on the shores of eastern North America, they were awestruck by perfectly planned and well-cultivated tracts of corn. These tracts were quite large and usually far exceeded the size of the typical European farm of that era. Native Americans initially helped the early colonists choose the proper seeds to sow, as the seeds they had brought with them were ill-suited for the New England climate and soil.

Native Americans continued to rely on corn and corn cultivation long after the arrival and settlement of Europeans in the New World. Because of the versatility and ease of cultivation of corn, Europeans also made corn a staple, using it for both human and animal consumption. Today corn is the most-cultivated crop in the world, with more than 1 billion metric tons produced every year. The United States is by far the world's largest corn producer, growing on average about 323 million metric tons per year.

Paul G. Pierpaoli Jr.

See also

Agriculture; Corn Liquor; Subsistence Agriculture

References

Ballantine, Betty, and Ian Ballantine. *The Native Americans: An Illustrated History*. Atlanta: Turner Publishing, 1994.

Cronon, William. *Changes in the Land: Indians, Colonists, and the Ecology of New England*. New York: Hill and Wang, 1983.

Hughes, J. Donald. *American Indian Ecology*. El Paso: Texas Western Press, 1993.

Josephy, Alvin. *America in 1492: The World of the Indian Peoples before the Arrival of Columbus*. New York: Knopf, 1992.

eastern eight-row corn, had ensured the centrality of corn in Native American agriculture because it was hardier than earlier varieties.

Native Americans knew, however, that corn cultivation tended to deplete the soil, so they often planted it with beans, which return nutrients such as nitrogen to the soil. Before long corn, beans, and squash became the three staple crops grown by virtually all Native Americans to some extent, prompting scholars to refer to them as the "three sisters." Corn was more than just a basic food item and modicum of exchange. Its centrality to Native American cultures meant that it often became a sacred item. Corn was often part of Native American rituals, and the Pawnees, who grew at least 10 different varieties of corn, included a variety that they called "wonderful" or "holy" corn, which was used strictly for religious purposes and was never consumed for food. The Navajos considered corn as sacred as human life itself.

In the East, corn cultivation, and specifically the ability to cultivate a surplus of the crop, helped to build and maintain the powerful Iroquois Confederacy, which at its zenith ranged from upstate New York to much of New England and south to the Mid-Atlantic. The Iroquois were masterful cultivators of the three sisters, which kept their well-organized agricultural pursuits in balance. When

Corn Liquor

Intoxicating beverage, usually of low quality. Corn liquor, or more accurately corn whiskey, was used by many merchants as a trading item in the American West. During the first two decades of the 19th century, corn liquor became an important element of the fur trade with the Native Americans. The liquor was usually distilled locally and brought directly to Native American tribes.

The primary goal of using alcohol to trade for furs and other goods with the Native Americans was to bind certain tribes as well as their chiefs to a single trader or his company. Initially corn liquor was used only by independent fur traders to compete against the two major fur-trading companies of that time, the Hudson's Bay Company and the American Fur Company.

By the 1820s independent fur traders were becoming more and more successful in the Indian trade, with the heavy inclusion of alcohol as a trade commodity. Afraid of the new rivals, both major fur-trading companies also began to trade alcohol with the Native Americans, each blaming the other company for starting the alcohol trade.

The resultant heavy use of alcohol by Native Americans brought destruction and suffering to many different tribes. Indeed, no other originally European-produced commodity created the same serious difficulties among Native Americans as did alcohol. The reasons for the heavy use of alcohol may have been the consequences of suffering a series of destabilizing events before the liquor trade began: epidemic diseases, violent removals from ancestral lands, and the diminution of native cultures. Increasing quantities of available alcohol only exacerbated these long-standing problems.

ALEXANDER EMMERICH

See also

Corn; Fur Trade; Hudson's Bay Company; Native American Trade

References

Lealand, Joy. *Firewater Myths: North American Indian Drinking and Alcohol Addiction.* New Brunswick, NJ: Rutgers Center for Alcohol Studies, 1976.

Mancall, Peter C. *Deadly Medicine: Indians and Alcohol in Early America.* Ithaca, NY: Cornell University Press, 1995.

Unrau, William E. *White Man's Wicked Water: The Alcohol Trade and Prohibition in Indian Country, 1802–1892.* Lawrence: University Press of Kansas, 1996.

Cornplanter

Birth Date: ca. 1740
Death Date: February 18, 1836

Prominent Seneca chief. Cornplanter, also known as Kaiiontwa'ko ("By What One Plants"), John O'Bail, and Captain O'Beel, was born

Portrait of Seneca chief Cornplanter (Kaiiontwa'ko) by 19th-century American painter Charles Bird King, from *The Indian Tribes of North America.* (Thomas L. McKenney and James Hall, *The Indian Tribes of North America*, 1836–1844)

to a Seneca woman and a Dutch trader around 1740 at Canawagus in present-day New York. Cornplanter's native relatives included his half-brother Handsome Lake, an Iroquois Confederacy chief, and his nephew Governor Blacksnake.

Initially Cornplanter argued adamantly for Native American neutrality during the American Revolutionary War (1775–1783). He made his position clear during a meeting of the Iroquois Confederacy, stating that "war is war, death is death, a fight is a hard business." Accused of cowardice, Cornplanter eventually decided to enter the war on the side of the British. He served as second-in-command under Mohawk chief Joseph Brant during several engagements, including the Battle of Wyoming Valley (Wyoming Valley Massacre) of 1778 and the Cherry Valley Campaign (Cherry Valley Massacre) of 1780. Alarmed by Cornplanter's victories, the Continental Congress sent Major General John Sullivan to remove the Iroquois threat. After defeating British and Iroquois forces at Newtown, Sullivan systematically destroyed many Iroquois settlements throughout upstate New York.

After the devastation of the Sullivan Expedition and the end of the Revolutionary War, Cornplanter devoted his life to promoting peace between whites and Native Americans. He worked to keep the Senecas neutral during subsequent conflicts. Cornplanter played an important role in the treaty negotiations at Fort Stanwix (1784) and Fort Harmar (1789), although he did not actually sign either document. He also participated in negotiations in 1794, 1797, and 1802 that ceded large portions of native-held land. Although well intentioned, Cornplanter received heavy criticism from the Senecas as a result of the concessions he made. In appreciation of his efforts, the U.S. government awarded Cornplanter and his heirs a grant of land on the western bank of the Allegheny River in Pennsylvania. Cornplanter died on this land on February 18, 1836. His heirs, however, were robbed of their inheritance in 1964 when the Kinzua Dam at Warren, Pennsylvania, permanently flooded the area.

PAUL G. PIERPAOLI JR.

See also

Brant, Joseph; Fort Harmar, Treaty of; Iroquois Confederacy; Native Americans and the American Revolutionary War; Senecas; Sullivan-Clinton Expedition against the Iroquois; Wyoming, Battle of

References

Abler, Thomas S. *Cornplanter: Chief Warrior of the Allegheny Senecas.* Syracuse, NY: Syracuse University Press, 2007.

Graymont, Barbara. *The Iroquois in the American Revolution.* Syracuse, NY: Syracuse University Press, 1972.

Cornstalk

Birth Date: ca. 1720
Death Date: November 10, 1777

Shawnee leader who lobbied for good relations with British colonists. Cornstalk was born in Pennsylvania around 1720. Like many other warriors who were unhappy with the British Crown after

1763, Cornstalk led raids against Virginia's frontier settlements during Pontiac's Rebellion (1763). Following the Native American defeat at Bushy Run (1763), however, Cornstalk recognized the folly of armed resistance. He spent the rest of his life working to forge a peaceful accommodation with the westward-moving British colonists.

Cornstalk's diplomatic measures were tested in 1774 when Governor Lord Dunmore of Virginia dispatched soldiers to the Ohio Valley following a series of frontier murders and revenge raids. By October 1774 some 1,100 soldiers had invaded Shawnee territory. Although Cornstalk counseled peace, the Shawnees voted to attack the invaders. Cornstalk subsequently led Shawnee, Mingo, Delaware, Wyandot, and Ottawa warriors against the unsuspecting Virginia camp at Point Pleasant on October 10, 1774. Following a humiliating defeat, Cornstalk led a Shawnee delegation to Camp Charlotte and accepted Lord Dunmore's peace terms.

Cornstalk honored the treaty provisions and encouraged other Native Americans to embrace peaceful neutrality during the American Revolutionary War (1775–1783). In 1777 the Shawnee leader visited Fort Randolph to inform the Americans that the Shawnees, including his own band, would ally with the British. Cornstalk, along with Red Hawk, a young Delaware chief, and his son Ellinipisco, were then detained. When a young soldier was killed and scalped while hunting for deer, an angry mob of John Hall's Rockbridge volunteers murdered Cornstalk and his two companions on November 10, 1777.

JON L. BRUDVIG

See also
Bushy Run, Battle of; Lord Dunmore's War; Pontiac's Rebellion; Shawnees

References
Holton, Woody. "The Ohio Indians and the Coming of the American Revolution in Virginia." *Journal of Southern History* 60 (August 1994): 453–478.
Lambert, Harold. "Cornstalk: King of the Rhododendron Country." *West Virginia History* 19 (1957–1958): 194–203.
Sugden, John. *Blue Jacket: Warrior of the Shawnees.* Lincoln: University of Nebraska Press, 2000.

Coronado, Francisco Vásquez de
Birth Date: 1510
Death Date: September 22, 1554

Spanish explorer and provincial governor. Francisco Vázquez de Coronado was born in Salamanca, Spain, in 1510 of noble parentage. In 1535 he moved to Mexico in the company of Viceroy Antonio de Mendoza to seek fame and fortune. Coronado served in various political offices and ultimately rose to become the governor of the province of Nueva Galicia in western Mexico.

The Spaniards had long heard tales of cities of gold located in the northern interior of the continent, and legend had it that the famed Seven Cities of Cibola existed in the uncharted wilds of North America. Allegedly these cities held riches that surpassed even those of the Aztec and Incan empires. Two alleged eyewitness accounts held particular influence over the Spaniards' lust for riches. One account was that of Álvar Núñez Cabez de Vaca, who traveled throughout Texas and told of seeing precious metals in the mountains of northwestern Mexico. However, the most tempting account of riches came from Friar Marcos de Niza, who discovered "seven cities of gold," the smallest being larger and richer than Mexico City.

On hearing these stories, Mendoza appointed Coronado commander of an expedition charged with finding the Seven Cities of Cibola. The expedition, consisting of 300 Spanish soldiers and a large contingent of Native American allies, left Culiacan on April 22, 1540. The caravan moved north, reaching the Zuni village of Hawikuh, supposedly one of the Seven Cities, in present-day Arizona. The Spanish laid siege to the village and captured it on July 7, 1540. However, the settlement was not a city of gold but rather a small native community. The other alleged cities turned out to be simple villages as well.

Undeterred, Coronado led his men east on an arduous trek through present-day New Mexico, Texas, and Oklahoma and into Kansas in search of the golden city of Quivera. Coronado found nothing more than a settlement of seminomadic Native Americans. Failure though it was, Coronado's expedition extended Spanish influence into much of today's southwestern United States. Coronado was also the first Spaniard to make contact with many unknown Native American tribes, establishing a pattern of hostility and distrust for centuries to come.

In July 1542 Coronado returned to Mexico City, where he faced an inquiry for the mistreatment of natives he encountered. Found guilty several years later, he was removed from office. Coronado died on September 22, 1554, in Mexico City.

RICK DYSON

See also
Pueblos; Spain

References
Bolton, Hebert Eugene. *Coronado: Knight of Pueblos and Plains.* Albuquerque: University of New Mexico Press, 1990.
Flint, Richard. *Great Cruelties Have Been Reported: The 1544 Investigation of the Coronado Expedition.* Dallas: Southern Methodist University Press, 2002.
Hammond, George Peter, and Agapito Rey, eds. *Narratives of the Coronado Expedition, 1540–1542.* New York: AMS Press, 1977.
Lecompte, Janet. "Coronado and Conquest." *New Mexico Historical Review* 64(3) (1989): 279–304.

Corps of Discovery
See Lewis and Clark Expedition

Council on the Auglaize
Event Date: September 30, 1792

Pan-Indian conclave convened at the mouth of the Auglaize (Glaize) River in northwestern Ohio on September 30, 1792, that was designed to deal with continued settler advances into the Old Northwest Territory and to reaffirm Native American support for the British. As many as 30 tribes were represented, including the Shawnees, Wyandots, Delawares, Miamis, Ottawas, Ojibwas, Pottawatomis, Cherokees, and Creeks and the Seven Nations of Canada. In all more than 1,000 chiefs, warriors, and their families converged at the Auglaize in what was then the largest such meeting ever held. British and American representatives were also present.

Most of the major decisions were made during the first week of October. It is not entirely clear when the council ended, although it is unlikely that it went beyond the end of October. Indeed, continued delays compelled many attendees to leave early.

After they had defeated the Americans at the November 4, 1791, Battle of the Wabash, Ohio tribes such as the Miamis and Shawnees were convinced that they now held the upper hand in the battle against the westward advance of the United States. Indeed, they were more determined than ever to maintain the Ohio River as the boundary between their territory and that of the United States. They received support from tribes such as the Wyandots and Delawares, which had previously been unwilling to join the confederation against the United States. The major tribes living in the Ohio Country subsequently agreed to meet in a grand council, including tribes from all over the East, to determine future strategy and their response to President George Washington's request for peace negotiations. The tribes had not held a similar council since 1788.

Washington was hopeful that he could convince the Native Americans to sign a peace treaty and thus avoid another military disaster in the western region. He had already sent five emissaries to meet with Ohio tribes in 1792. The first two had been captured by the British, and the second two had been killed. Brigadier General Rufus Putnam, the fifth emissary, was able to win approval for a peace treaty that was later ignored by all parties. The latest emissary was Captain Hendrick Aupaumut from the Indian reservation at Stockbridge, Massachusetts. He went to the Council on the Auglaize in an effort to convince the tribes to make peace with the United States.

The tribes refused to discuss peace with Aupaumut, however, and instead asserted that the Ohio River must be recognized as the border between Native American territory and the United States. They also asserted that they wanted no compensation from the government with the exception of the Shawnees, who sought to be paid for the loss of Kentucky following Lord Dunmore's War of 1774. The tribes demanded that the government send honest agents, not "proud land jobbers," to negotiate a peace treaty. They also told Aupaumut that an Iroquois warrior would take these demands back to Israel Chapin, the government agent of the Iroquois, who would relay the information to Washington's administration. In the end, the council dispersed with a renewed commitment to fighting westward expansion across the Ohio River, renewed tribal fealty to the British, and a vow not to negotiate with Americans who did not deal in good faith. The council did nothing to end Little Turtle's War (1786–1795).

President Washington responded by sending Timothy Pickering, Beverly Randolph, and Benjamin Lincoln to negotiate with the tribes at Detroit in July 1793. Secretary of War Henry Knox had authorized the American negotiators to recognize Native American title to the western country and to return all territory north of the Ohio River to them with the exception of Ohio Company lands and the Symmes Purchase. Forts Harmar and Washington would also be abandoned, and the tribes would receive annuities totaling $50,000 as a lump sum and $10,000 yearly. The tribal representatives rejected these offers and again demanded that the Ohio River be recognized as the boundary of their country. In turn, Knox ordered Brigadier General Anthony Wayne to confront the confederated tribes, which eventually led to the August 20, 1794, Battle of Fallen Timbers. That engagement handed the Native Americans a resounding defeat and effectively broke their power in the Old Northwest Territory.

Mary Stockwell and Paul G. Pierpaoli Jr.

See also
Fallen Timbers, Battle of; Glaize, The; Little Turtle's War; Old Northwest Territory; Wabash, Battle of the; Washington, George

References
Hurt, R. Douglas. *The Ohio Frontier: Crucible of the Old Northwest, 1720–1830.* Bloomington: Indiana University Press, 1996.

Willig, Timothy D. *Restoring the Chain of Friendship: British Policy and the Indians of the Great Lakes, 1783–1815.* Lincoln: University of Nebraska Press, 2008.

Counting Coup

Cultural tradition of Native Americans who lived on the Great Plains that was particularly prevalent among the Sioux and Cheyenne peoples. The challenge and practice of counting coup allowed young men to demonstrate to their peers and to tribal leaders that they were brave, honorable, and heroic. This prerequisite for admission to warrior societies involved public displays of valor that did not inflict bodily harm or cause the death of the opponent. The primary objective of this ritual was to touch, tap, or lightly strike an enemy with a coup stick or to steal a horse or other valuables in plain view of the enemy.

Coup, a French term for a blow or sudden attack, was rehearsed and executed with regularity and in the presence of eyewitnesses. Warriors launched their attacks in plain sight—sneak attacks or ambushes did not qualify—and feathers were awarded as tribal acknowledgment of the coup. In Plains culture, an impressive

Buffalo-hide shield of a Shoshone warrior in a full-length feather headdress on horseback counting coup with an enemy Crow brave who has a rifle. (Native Stock Pictures)

headdress was a symbol of honor and distinction. Young boys were gradually assimilated into warrior groups through past stories of heroic coups, especially by tribal leaders.

The exact origins of this rite of passage are deeply buried in the traditions of warrior societies. However, it is well known that Plains tribes favored martial practices that were not fatal encounters. The demands of a hunting society required a constant supply of healthy men to ensure that basic needs were met. In the era prior to white contact, it was virtually unknown for Plains peoples to engage in conflicts that produced a large number of deaths. The arrival of the U.S. Army on the Plains disrupted the practice of counting coup because the goal of the U.S. military was to inflict numerous casualties through constant and ruthless pursuit.

JAMES F. CARROLL

See also

Cheyennes; Dog Soldiers; Sioux

References

Denig, Edward Thompson. *Five Indian Tribes of the Upper Missouri.* Norman: University of Oklahoma Press, 1976.

McGinnis, Anthony. *Counting Coup and Cutting Horses: Intertribal Warfare on the Northern Plains, 1738–1889.* Evergreen, CO: Cordillera, 1990.

Covenant Chain

A system of treaties, alliances, and councils between the five nations of the Iroquois Confederacy (the Senecas, the Cayugas, the Onondagas, the Oneidas, and the Mohawks) and the English North American colonies. After 1720, the confederation expanded to include six nations with the addition of the Tuscaroras.

The first recorded agreement of the Covenant Chain was that negotiated with New York governor Edmund Andros in 1677. A visible emblem of the chain appeared in 1692, with a treaty recorded on the Guswenta, a four-foot-long two-row wampum belt. One row symbolized the Iroquois and the other row the settlers, representing an arrangement that was equal as brothers rather than dominant and subordinate, as father to son. A three-link silver chain was made to make the metaphor tangible.

In place between the late 17th century and the 1760s, the Covenant Chain dealt with issues of settlement, trade, and the episodic violence between the colonials and the Iroquois Confederacy. The Iroquois spoke for the tribes they had subordinated in battle, creating a greater illusion of unity in Native American councils than actually existed, given that the Iroquois government included not only the 50 hereditary chiefs of the Five Nations but also a multitude of village leaders. The treaties that comprised the chain were renewed regularly. Generally, the renewals entailed the polishing of the wampum belt's silver chain and the providing of aid to the Iroquois Confederacy.

Because most of the negotiations occurred in New York's Mohawk Valley, that colony served as the principal colonial negotiator. Over time Massachusetts, Connecticut, Rhode Island, and Maryland joined the chain as well. In 1720 the Tuscaroras, scattered from their home in North Carolina after the Tuscarora War (1711–1713), also joined the Covenant Chain.

In June 1753 the Mohawks announced that colonial seizure of Iroquois lands had broken the chain. In July 1754 leaders from seven colonies, fearful of French efforts to assert control over the Ohio Valley, met with Iroquois leaders at Albany to restore the chain. The meeting dealt principally with land disputes between Native Americans and the British and the growing tensions with France. The Albany Congress also introduced the Iroquois condolence ceremony, which remained part of the native negotiating process for years to come. The Iroquois Confederacy remained neutral during the early years of the French and Indian War (1754–1763).

In 1760 the Seven Nations (or Seven Fires) of Canada decided to abandon the French side in the war. They promptly joined the Covenant Chain after a meeting with British major general Jeffrey Amherst and Indian superintendent Sir William Johnson. In the autumn of 1768 a meeting at New York's Fort Stanwix polished the tarnished chain and set the boundaries for hunting grounds as promised in the Proclamation of 1763. During the American Revolutionary War (1775–1783), four of the six Iroquois nations fought alongside the British. Clearly, however, after 1763 the tenor of the Covenant Chain had changed. The withdrawal of the French from North America had more to do with this than any other single development.

JOHN H. BARNHILL

See also

Albany Congress; Decanisora; French and Indian War; Iroquois; Iroquois Confederacy; Johnson, Sir William; Mohawks; Proclamation of 1763; Tuscarora War

References

Jennings, Francis. *The Ambiguous Iroquois Empire: The Covenant Chain Confederation of Indian Tribes with English Colonies from Its Beginnings to the Lancaster Treaty of 1744.* New York: Norton, 1984.

Nobles, Gregory H. *American Frontiers: Cultural Encounters and Continental Conquest.* New York: Hill and Wang, 1997.

Richter, Daniel K., and James H. Merrell, eds. *Beyond the Covenant Chain: The Iroquois and Their Neighbors in Indian North America, 1600–1800.* Syracuse, NY: Syracuse University Press, 1987.

Cowetas

See Creeks

Crawford, Emmet
Birth Date: September 6, 1844
Death Date: January 18, 1886

U.S. Army officer. Emmet Crawford was born in Philadelphia, Pennsylvania, on September 6, 1844; little else is known about his youth. In May 1861 after lying about his age, he enlisted in the U.S. Volunteers as a private in the 71st Pennsylvania Infantry. During the American Civil War (1861–1865) he saw action in the Battle of Antietam (September 17, 1862) and also in the Battle of Fredericksburg (December 13, 1862), during which he was wounded. He later accepted a commission as a first lieutenant in the 13th U.S. Colored Infantry and received brevets to captain and major.

Crawford joined the regular army after the war. Commissioned a second lieutenant, he served in the African American 37th and 39th (later the 25th) Infantry regiments and in 1870 became a first lieutenant in the 3rd Cavalry. Posted to Arizona late in 1870, he was transferred in 1872 to Fort Robinson, Nebraska. As commander of Company G, Crawford served under Brigadier General George Crook during the 1876 Powder River Expedition and in the Battle of the Rosebud (June 17, 1876). During that campaign Crawford assisted in driving away the Sioux from a ridge overlooking Crook's camp on June 9, 1876. Crawford's men rode up the

ridge, dismounted, and chased the Sioux across two other ridges. On June 17 Crawford helped drive back Sioux warriors who were attempting to attack the soldiers from the rear. He also participated in the Battle of Slim Buttes (September 9–10, 1876) during which he led a charge against a Sioux village.

Promoted to captain in 1879, Crawford again joined General Crook, this time in Arizona. There Crawford was military commandant at the San Carlos Reservation and played a role in the campaign to compel Geronimo to surrender. Capable and respected by his Indian charges, Crawford, along with Lieutenant Charles Gatewood, organized, trained, and led several companies of Apache scouts, who became Crook's primary weapon in the pursuit of Geronimo. Crawford then led two expeditions into the Mexican Sierra Madres, the second of which resulted in his death. On January 11, 1886, he was shot and mortally wounded during an attack by a troop of Mexican irregulars while attempting to negotiate with Geronimo. Crawford died during the return trip from Mexico near the village of Nacori on January 18, 1886.

GENE MUELLER

See also

Apaches; Apache Wars; Crook, George; Gatewood, Charles Bare; Geronimo; Rosebud, Battle of the; Scouts, Native American; Slim Buttes, Battle of

References

Greene, Jerome A., ed. *Battles and Skirmishes of the Great Sioux War, 1876–1877: The Military View.* Norman: University of Oklahoma Press, 1993.

Schmitt, Martin F., ed. *General George Crook: His Autobiography.* Norman: University of Oklahoma Press, 1986.

Crazy Horse
Birth Date: ca. 1840
Death Date: September 5, 1877

Lakota Sioux war chief and one of the most widely known leaders of the centuries-long Native American resistance to white expansion across North America. Paradoxically, he has also remained one of the most mysterious figures in American history. Most sources accept that Crazy Horse was born sometime in 1840, although cases have been made for alternative dates ranging from 1841 to 1845. His father, who survived him and became one of the major sources of information about him, had also been called Crazy Horse, but when his son reached maturity and wished to take that name, his father took the name Worm. The tribal affiliation of Crazy Horse's mother is also somewhat ambiguous: most sources identify her as a Brulé Sioux, but some contend that she was a Miniconjou Sioux.

As a young warrior, Crazy Horse earned a reputation for being both skilled and fearless in battles against the Lakotas' tribal enemies: the Arikaras, Blackfeet, Crows, Pawnees, and Shoshones. But relatively few of his exploits against these enemies survived in Lakota oral tradition after the wars with the U.S. military had greatly reduced the population and the cohesion of the tribe.

After the Lakotas allied themselves with the Cheyennes, Crazy Horse distinguished himself in his first battles against the U.S. military, at Red Buttes and Platte River Bridge Station. But Crazy Horse first came fully to the attention of the U.S. military and of the American public during Red Cloud's War (1866–1868). In violation of existing treaties, the U.S. Army had constructed forts along the Bozeman Trail, which provided an eastern route to gold-rich Virginia City, Montana. On December 21, 1866, Crazy Horse led a small contingent of warriors who lured cavalry and infantry units away from Fort Phil Kearny and into a trap. Outnumbered more than 10 to 1, the 80 soldiers were quickly wiped out in what became known as the Fetterman Massacre. The commander of the doomed infantry unit, Captain William Fetterman, had boasted that he could subdue the whole Sioux Nation with the exact number of soldiers who perished with him in what was, to that point, the worst defeat suffered by the army during the wars with the Plains Indians.

On August 2, 1867, Crazy Horse attempted to repeat the success that he had achieved against Fetterman's force. The Lakotas surprised a woodcutting party sent out from Fort Phil Kearny. In what became known as the Wagon Box Fight, the soldiers surprised and eventually drove off the Lakotas with the much-enhanced firepower provided by their recently issued breech-loading rifles.

Ten years later during what became known as the Great Sioux War (1876–1877), Crazy Horse led about 1,500 Lakota and Cheyenne warriors against Brigadier General George Crook's roughly equal force of cavalry, infantry, and Native American allies in the Battle of the Rosebud (June 17, 1876). Although neither side committed fully enough to the battle to sustain sizable losses, Crook's advance into Sioux territory was temporarily checked, delaying his rendezvous with the 7th Cavalry under Lieutenant Colonel George A. Custer.

All Native American sources agree that Crazy Horse had a decisive role in the annihilation of Custer's battalion at the Battle of the Little Bighorn (June 25–26, 1876), but nothing is known about Crazy Horse's specific actions during the engagement. Nonetheless, his notoriety following the massacre of Custer and his troops made Crazy Horse a prime target of the forces sent to subdue the Sioux and the Cheyennes.

Likewise, after Crazy Horse's surrender in May 1877, any rumors of further insurrection among the Lakotas increased the suspicion surrounding him. Not surprisingly, he was eventually killed at Camp Robinson on September 5, 1877, when such rumors led to an order for his arrest. Although there were numerous eyewitnesses, the details of how he was fatally stabbed have remained ambiguous, leading to a continuing series of theories about why he was killed and at whose orders. Even those who accept that he was bayoneted by an impetuous soldier cannot agree on the identity of that soldier or whether he was acting out of heightened anxiety or deep-seated animus.

Although Crazy Horse is being honored with a mountaintop sculpture rivaling the nearby Mount Rushmore, there is only one surviving photograph of the Lakota war chief. And, fittingly, much doubt has been cast on whether or not the figure in the photograph is actually Crazy Horse.

MARTIN KICH

See also

Brulé Sioux; Cheyennes; Cheyennes, Northern; Crook, George; Fetterman Massacre; Little Bighorn, Battle of the; Miniconjou Sioux; Oglala Sioux; Red Cloud's War; Rosebud, Battle of the; Sioux; Wagon Box Fight

References

Ambrose, Stephen E. *Crazy Horse and Custer: The Parallel Lives of Two American Warriors.* New York: Anchor Books, 1996.

Blevins, Winfred. *Stone Song: A Novel of the Life of Crazy Horse.* New York: Forge, 1995.

Matthiesen, Peter. *In the Spirit of Crazy Horse.* New York: Viking, 1991.

McMurtry, Larry. *Crazy Horse.* New York: Lipper/Viking, 1999.

Sandoz, Mari. *Crazy Horse: The Strange Man of the Oglalas.* 3rd ed. Lincoln: University of Nebraska Press, 2008.

Creek-Cherokee Wars
Event Dates: 1716–1727 and 1740–1754

The Creek Nation and the Cherokee Nation fought several wars in the North American Southeast. These conflicts sprang from disputes over hunting grounds, frustrations over Carolina settlers' designs on their lands, and alliances forged with other native tribes. The fighting occurred in two phases: one from 1716 to 1727 and the other from 1740 to 1754. The Creeks and Cherokees were two of the most populous Native American nations in the Southeast, and any conflict involving them was bound to impact settlers in the Carolinas and Georgia.

Hostilities between the Creeks and Cherokees began in 1716 during the Yamasee War (1715–1717). The fighting started when the Cherokees assassinated Creek diplomats sent to the Lower Cherokee towns to secure support for an assault on South Carolina. During the war, Cherokee warriors, assisted by Carolina settlers, repeatedly raided Upper Creek towns. The settlers, made aware of the precariousness of their southern frontier during the Yamasee War, aided the Cherokees in the expectation that intertribal warfare would weaken both nations and prevent them from attacking British settlements. The situation was further complicated by warfare between the Creeks and the pro-French Choctaws.

Attempts of officials in Charles Town (present-day Charleston, South Carolina) to influence the Creek-Cherokee War to British advantage were not successful. As the fighting on the frontier escalated, South Carolinians increasingly feared for their safety. In 1725 the British sent Tobias Fitch, agent to the Creeks, to secure an end to the war. Despite this and other British efforts, the Creeks and Cherokees continued the fight.

In March 1726 several hundred Cherokee and Chickasaw warriors moved against the Creeks. Operating under the British flag in the false belief that they enjoyed the support of the Crown, the warriors destroyed most of the Creek village of Cussita. The attack terrified many of the British settlers, who feared that it would bring closer ties between the Spanish and the Creeks. After a small force of about 40 Creek warriors attacked and defeated some 500 Cherokee and Chickasaw warriors, officials in Charles Town renewed their push for peace. By January 1727 these officials had negotiated an end to the fighting.

Fighting between the Creeks and Cherokees resumed in 1740 shortly after onset of the Anglo-Spanish War (1739–1744), also known as the War of Jenkins' Ear, between Britain and Spain. The Creeks remained largely neutral during the fighting in America, whereas many Cherokees allied themselves with the British. Hostilities began when Creeks attacked a Cherokee war party that had entered Creek country. The Cherokee warriors, who were on their way to attack the Choctaws and their French allies, believed that an ongoing war between the Creeks and Choctaws would allow them to march safely through Creek territory. In this the Cherokees miscalculated.

Fighting between the Creeks and the Cherokees continued for several years until the onset of King George's War (1744–1748) between Britain and France. British officials then sought to secure Indian allies and end the Creek-Cherokee dispute. In 1745 despite a recently negotiated truce with the Creeks, the Cherokees allowed the Senecas to use their territory as a staging ground for attacks on the Creeks. When Cherokee warriors joined the fighting, Creek-Cherokee hostilities resumed. In late 1748 Governor James Glen of South Carolina tried to arrange another truce. The French, correctly assuming that peace between the two Native American nations would benefit the British, sought to disrupt the peace talks by arranging for Creek headman Acorn Whistler to lead an attack on the Cherokees. Despite this action, the Creeks and Cherokees came to an agreement. They settled on boundaries for their hunting grounds, and the Cherokees agreed to stop allowing northern natives passage through their lands to attack the Creeks. Glen guaranteed the agreement, promising to punish transgressors.

The treaty did not hold. Although the Upper Creeks and Cherokees refrained from warfare, in 1750 several Lower Creek towns waged war on their Cherokee neighbors. This fighting was prompted primarily by frustrations caused by what the Lower Creeks saw as Cherokee control of valuable hunting grounds and continued Cherokee assistance to the northern native parties in attacks on the Creeks.

Malatchi, Creek headman of the important Coweta village, led a campaign that sought to seize control of hunting grounds from the Cherokees. In April 1750 Malatchi and 500 Lower Creek warriors attacked and razed the Lower Cherokee towns of Echoi and Estatoe. The Creeks continued on the offensive, and when South Carolina restricted trade with the Cherokees for a series of frontier depredations in 1751, the Creeks escalated their campaign

to acquire Cherokee lands. This effort was largely successful. All but three of the Lower Cherokee towns were destroyed, and many Cherokees were made refugees. As a result of the fighting, the Creeks secured much of the disputed hunting ground between the Little River and the Broad River north of present-day Savannah, Georgia.

In 1752 Acorn Whistler and other Creeks assassinated Cherokee diplomats while they were in Charles Town. Governor Glen demanded justice, and under great pressure from British officials the Creeks finally executed Acorn Whistler. In May 1753 Creek officials traveled to Charles Town to negotiate another peace treaty with the Cherokees. Small skirmishes plagued the region during the following year, but in April 1754 at Coweta the Creeks and Cherokees negotiated a formal end to the war and secured a peace settlement.

ANDREW K. FRANK

See also

Cherokees; Chickasaws; Choctaws; Creek-Choctaw Wars; Creeks; Iroquois; King George's War; Senecas; Yamasee War

References

Alden, John Richard. *John Stuart and the Southern Colonial Frontier.* Ann Arbor: University of Michigan Press, 1944.

Corkran, David. *The Cherokee Frontier: Conflict and Survival, 1740–1762.* Norman: University of Oklahoma Press, 1962.

Hahn, Stephen C. *The Invention of the Creek Nation, 1670–1763.* Lincoln: University of Nebraska Press, 2004.

Oatis, Steven J. *A Colonial Complex: South Carolina's Frontiers in the Era of the Yamasee War, 1680–1730.* Lincoln: University of Nebraska Press, 2004.

Creek-Choctaw Wars
Start Date: 1702
End Date: October 1776

Series of pitched conflicts and low-level skirmishes between the Creek Nation and the Choctaw Nation. Warfare constantly plagued relations between the Creeks and the Choctaws during the colonial period. Although the incidents are not always technically defined as wars, slave raids and disputes over hunting grounds periodically caused military conflicts between the two southeastern nations. According to some anthropologists, these disputes predated the region's settlement by the Spanish and the British. However, they became more pronounced and frequent in the colonial period.

The Creeks and the Choctaws both emerged as distinct communities during the late 17th century as disease and warfare destroyed the pre-Columbian chiefdoms in the American Southeast. Both nations spoke variants of the Muskogee language, employed similar horticultural practices, used comparable gender norms, and had similar cosmologies. These similarities did not, however, prevent the tensions that were fostered by their proximity to one another. The Creeks primarily lived along the rivers in what became Georgia, northern Florida, and Alabama. The Choctaws lived to the west in what became Louisiana, Alabama, and Mississippi.

At the start of the 18th century, the Creeks initiated the first Creek-Choctaw war. Encouraged by English officials and armed with English muskets, bands of Creek warriors repeatedly marched on several Choctaw towns in an attempt to capture slaves. These slaves were valuable commodities in South Carolina, and this lure would shape the behavior of the Creeks for more than a decade. The British alliance with the Creeks, who obtained a reputation for their martial prowess, led the Spanish and French to forge their own alliances with various southeastern tribes. The Choctaws found allies in traders and officials from French Louisiana.

Soon the fighting between the Creeks and the Choctaws became immersed in the Franco-British rivalry. In the early years the Creeks were the aggressors in most of the campaigns. This was especially true during Queen Anne's War (1702–1713), when approximately 1,000 Creek warriors attacked the Choctaws and their French allies in 1711. The Creeks launched similar, albeit smaller, slaving campaigns in the following years.

After demand for Native American slaves declined in South Carolina following the Yamasee War (1715–1717), warfare between the Creeks and the Choctaws remained constant in the southern interior. Although tensions did not explode into large-scale warfare, disputes over trade and hunting parties caused ongoing troubles between the nations. Repeated efforts by British officials to resolve the territorial disputes failed. In the most notable attempt, in 1759 British southern Indian superintendent Edmond Atkin traveled to the Creek village of Tuckebatchee to delineate the boundary between the nations. The Creeks denied the existence of a boundary between the nations, and the fighting over hunting grounds continued.

Following the French and Indian War (1754–1763), the nature of Creek-Choctaw warfare changed once again. With France's withdrawal from the American Southeast, Great Britain became the major force in the region. Hoping to create a profitable and peaceful new order, Great Britain organized a regional congress in 1763 to be held at Augusta, Georgia. When the Choctaws indicated their desire to participate, some Creek warriors threatened to kill any Choctaws who traveled through Creek country in order to attend. The Creeks, fearful that their long-term enemy would obtain guns and other supplies from the British, had hoped that France's demise would lead to the deterioration of the Choctaws' position.

Most Choctaws heeded the warning, but Red Shoe, a lesser-known chief, traveled through Chickasaw territory in order to avoid the Creeks and still reach Augusta. After he met with the British, he traveled by boat to Mobile in West Florida. The Creeks, outraged at the emerging diplomatic and economic relationship between the Choctaws and the British, tried to prevent the alliance from being sealed. In 1763 the Creeks attacked the Choctaws and reinitiated the Creek-Choctaw Wars. The Creeks had hoped to

force the British into choosing sides rather than making peace with both nations. Rather than siding with their longtime Creek allies as many Creek headmen had anticipated, the British chose to supply both the Creeks and the Choctaws. With ample and uninterrupted supplies, the Creek-Choctaw Wars became a bloody campaign that preoccupied the warriors of both nations. The desire by British officials to keep the two nations as allies and to focus Creek attention on the Choctaws rather than the expanding colony in Georgia led to the continuation of this policy until 1776. During this time several leading headmen were killed, the harvest of deerskins fell precipitously, the debts of Creek hunters skyrocketed, and few diplomatic solutions were found.

The Creek-Choctaw Wars finally came to a close in 1776, as the American Revolutionary War (1775–1783) led the British to demand a peace rather than continue fueling the dispute. That October, British Indian superintendent John Stuart met with headmen from the Creek and Choctaw nations in Pensacola and negotiated an end to the war.

ANDREW K. FRANK

See also
Augusta, Congress of; Choctaws; Creeks; French and Indian War; Queen Anne's War; Red Shoe; Stuart, John; Yamasee War

References
Alden, John Richard. *John Stuart and the Southern Colonial Frontier.* Ann Arbor: University of Michigan Press, 1944.
Corkran, David. *The Cherokee Frontier: Conflict and Survival, 1740–1762.* Norman: University of Oklahoma Press, 1962.
Hahn, Stephen C. *The Invention of the Creek Nation, 1670–1763.* Lincoln: University of Nebraska Press, 2004.
Oatis, Steven J. *A Colonial Complex: South Carolina's Frontiers in the Era of the Yamasee War, 1680–1730.* Lincoln: University of Nebraska Press, 2004.
Wright, J. Leitch, Jr. *Creeks and Seminoles: The Destruction and Regeneration of the Muscogulge People.* Lincoln: University of Nebraska Press, 1986.

Creeks

Multiethnic Native American group, also known as the Muskogees, who in the colonial and early national period lived in the southeastern portion of North America in what is now Florida, Georgia, and Alabama. The location of the Creeks in British Georgia and South Carolina, French Louisiana, and Spanish Florida allowed them to play the colonial powers against one another and protect their own interests throughout the colonial period. The Creeks tended to pursue a policy of neutrality when it came to the wars that consumed their European neighbors and also vigorously protected their interests against their Choctaw and Cherokee neighbors.

Organized in the 17th century after the disease-induced collapse of the southeastern chiefdoms that once dominated the region, the Creeks obtained their name from the English, who

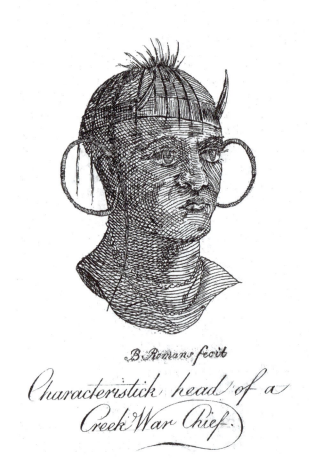

B. Romans fecit

Characteristick head of a Creek War Chief.

A Creek war chief with typical hooped earrings and skullcap, 1775. (Getty Images)

noted that their villages were always built near inland waters. The Spanish similarly called them Tallapoosa Indians, after one of the rivers along which they primarily lived. At its height, the Creek Confederacy included approximately 60 villages.

Comprised of a diversity of ethnic and linguistic groups, the Creeks remained decentralized throughout the colonial period. Nevertheless, Muskogee became the dominant language of the confederacy. A series of rituals, such as the Green Corn Ceremony, and a system of matrilineal clans unified them as a people. The Creeks were an agricultural society, with women farming corn, beans, and squash. Men hunted in order to augment their diet and provide skins for the marketplace.

An amorphous polity known as the Creek Confederacy slowly emerged, but at best the Creeks were an alliance of loosely affiliated villages. Rather than a centralized nation, Creeks primarily associated themselves with their village. During the colonial period they typically referred to themselves as Cowetas, Abihkas, Hichitis, and Alabamas rather than as Creeks. Unbeknownst to colonial officials, many of the most prominent leaders represented only a minority interest or a single village. For example, Tomochichi, one of Georgia governor James Oglethorpe's closest allies, represented the

Yamacraws, one of several conquered groups among the Creeks. The Creek spokesperson Brims, frequently called "Emperor Brims," was similarly misunderstood. Rather than a national leader in the early 17th century, Brims was simply the *mico* ("head chief") of Coweta, one of the most powerful Creek villages.

Power in Creek society was primarily organized around villages and matrilineal clans, and authority was extended to individuals who could convince rather than coerce others into agreement. As a result Creek power was extremely localized and fluid, and Creek villages were largely autonomous entities. The confederacy served as an organizing principle for trade and war and did not act as a centralized nation. Marriages, trade, and clan ties connected the villages, but individual villages were free to choose with whom to ally themselves or make war against. As a result, Creek villages often divided against one another during the colonial wars. In addition, most villages often tried to remain neutral in the colonial wars even as neighboring Creek villages went to war.

The emergence of the deerskin trade and the presence of Spanish and British neighbors shaped the diplomatic history of the Creeks. Connections and resistance to slave raiders also helped define the position of the Creeks in the region. During the Yamasee War (1715–1717), the Creeks primarily allied themselves with the French in order to counter trade abuses by the British. The Cherokees took this opportunity to secure an alliance with the British. As a result, the devastating Creek-Cherokee Wars (1716–1754) ensued.

After the Yamasee War, many Creek leaders decided that neutrality was the best policy. Most towns created trading alliances with the British. The Creeks allowed traders to reside in their village and often marry the daughters of influential leaders. At the same time, Upper Creek villages in the west encouraged the French to build Fort Toulouse (Alabama) to bring supplies and trade goods into the region. Similarly, several Creek villages negotiated alliances with the Spanish in Florida.

Despite the hopes of many European diplomats, trade connections and pledges of peace did not necessarily lead to allies during wartime. Although some Creek warriors accompanied Governor Oglethorpe in his invasion of Florida in 1743, most Creeks refrained from participating. During King George's War (1744–1748), most Creek villages remained neutral even as some villages felt pulled by British or French relationships.

Creek neutrality in terms of their European neighbors did not result in a colonial peace, however. Instead, the Creeks fought several wars with their Cherokee and Choctaw neighbors during the colonial period.

The Creeks fought two wars with the Cherokees. The first took place during the Yamasee War, and the other occurred in the 1740s and early 1750s. These wars resulted from conflicts over hunting grounds and as attempts to conquer each other's territory. The Creeks also fought a series of bloody wars with the Choctaws, known as the Creek-Choctaw Wars (1702–1776). The conflicts began as reciprocal slave raids and as extensions of the French-English rivalry in the region. These slave raids were often encouraged by European neighbors. In 1711, for example, the British armed more than 1,000 Creek warriors as they marched on their French-Choctaw enemy.

Hostilities between the Creeks and Choctaws were the most severe after the French and Indian War (1754–1763). When the British called for a congress at Augusta, Georgia, to establish the postwar order, the Creeks sought to exclude their longtime Choctaw enemies. The British provided guns and ammunition to both sides in the ensuing war, and the Creeks and Choctaws remained at arms until the American Revolutionary War (1775–1783), during which some—but not all—Creeks sided with the British. Thereafter the Creeks had to contend with the new state of Georgia and the U.S. government, neither of which had much regard for former treaties or Creek land rights.

In the early 19th century, continued white encroachment onto Creek lands threatened to boil over into open warfare. By 1810 most Creeks were divided on how to deal with white encroachment. The so-called Red Sticks, the more militant faction, favored war, while the White Sticks sought peace. The War of 1812 provided the perfect context for the Red Sticks, influenced by Shawnee chief Tecumseh's concept of unified Native American resistance, to go on the offensive. In January 1813 a contingent of Red Sticks took part in a battle with U.S. forces at the Raisin River in which the Americans were badly mauled. That August, Red Eagle (William Weatherford) commanded some 1,000 Red Stick warriors in an attack on Fort Mims, resulting in the deaths of hundreds of white settlers. By now the Creek War (1813–1814) was in full swing, and Major General Andrew Jackson was charged with defeating the Red Stick Creeks and their allies. Sporadic warfare ensued until the Battle of Horseshoe Bend (March 27, 1814) in which the Native Americans were convincingly defeated.

Jackson imposed upon the Creeks—both those who were pro-American and those who had waged war—the punitive Treaty of Fort Jackson (also known as the Treaty of Horseshoe Bend), signed on August 9, 1814. The agreement compelled the Creeks to surrender some 23 million acres of their land to the U.S. government, which would then be opened to white settlers. In 1836 as part of the 1830 Indian Removal Act, the Creeks—along with the Choctaws, Chickasaws, Cherokees, and Seminoles—were relocated by force to Indian Territory (Oklahoma). The resulting Trail of Tears was catastrophic to the Creeks, who lost 3,500 people (out of a total of 15,000) during the forced march and relocation. Today most surviving Creeks continue to reside in Oklahoma, but a small number remain in Georgia, Alabama, and Florida.

ANDREW K. FRANK

See also
Augusta, Congress of; Brims of Coweta; Creek-Cherokee Wars; Creek-Choctaw Wars; Creek War; Fort Jackson, Treaty of; Fort Mims, Battle of; French and Indian War; Horseshoe Bend, Battle of; Indian Removal Act; Jackson, Andrew; King George's War; Raisin River Massacre; Red Sticks; Tecumseh; Tomochichi; Trail of Tears; Yamasee War

References
Alden, John Richard. *John Stuart and the Southern Colonial Frontier.* Ann Arbor: University of Michigan Press, 1944.
Braund, Kathryn E. Holland. *Deerskins & Duffels: The Creek Indian Trade with Anglo-America, 1685–1815.* Lincoln: University of Nebraska Press, 1993.
Hahn, Stephen C. *The Invention of the Creek Nation, 1670–1763.* Lincoln: University of Nebraska Press, 2004.
Wright, J. Leitch, Jr. *Creeks and Seminoles: The Destruction and Regeneration of the Muscogulge People.* Lincoln: University of Nebraska Press, 1986.

Creek War
Start Date: 1813
End Date: 1814

Civil war between the Lower Creeks (mainly White Sticks) and the Red Stick Creeks (largely Upper Creeks). The United States eventually became involved in the conflict on the side of the White Sticks. The Creek intratribal disagreement over the nation's relationship to the United States and other issues caused a major division within the Creek Nation. The United States became involved in the war with the Battle of Burnt Corn Creek on July 17, 1813, and the massacre at Fort Mims on August 30. The Creek War is usually seen as a part of the War of 1812.

Creek reactions to American encroachment onto their lands, along with the U.S. government's efforts to "civilize" the Creeks, broke the nation into two factions. Located in present-day northern and central Alabama and southern Georgia, Creek territory was prime land for growing cotton, a highly prized crop. The faction that opposed the U.S. efforts, not to mention its land policies, was the Red Sticks, so-named because they painted their war clubs red. The Red Sticks, influenced in part by the Shawnee leader Tecumseh, favored joining Tecumseh's Pan-Indian alliance to resist white expansion and urged the rejection of white goods and culture in favor of a return to traditional native ways. By 1813 the Red Sticks were receiving support from the British, who were at war with the United States; some of the aid was funneled through Spanish Florida.

The White Sticks, in contrast to the militants, believed that the best course for the Creeks to follow was to work with the United States, even if to do so meant ceding additional land and adopting American cultural practices.

Open fighting between the two sides broke out in 1813 when a Red Stick war party was ambushed by White Sticks. The White Sticks captured the Red Stick leader and executed him. The United States entered the war on July 27, 1813, with the Battle of Burnt Corn Creek. An Alabama Militia unit intercepted a group of Red Sticks returning from Pensacola, Florida, where they had received weapons and ammunition from the British and Spanish. The militia unit, commanded by Colonel James Caller, found the Red Sticks encamped near Burnt Corn Creek about 90 miles north of

An officer attempts to protect a woman during the Red Stick Creek attack on Fort Mims, Alabama, on August 30, 1813. The Red Stick victory here left 250–500 men, women, and children dead and brought greater U.S. involvement in the Creek War. (Library of Congress)

Pensacola and surprised them on July 27. Winning an initial easy victory, the militia did not pursue the Red Sticks, who then rallied and counterattacked, routing the militia and recapturing their supplies. The militia suffered 2 dead and 15 wounded. Creek losses in the encounter are unknown.

On August 30, 1813, the Red Sticks launched a retaliatory strike on Fort Mims, where the Alabama Militia was stationed. The fort, to which a number of civilians and White Stick refugees had fled, was about 25 miles southwest of the Burnt Corn Creek battlefield. The odds should have been in favor of the fort's defenders, but the commander of the post, Major Daniel Beasley, had failed to heed warnings that a Red Stick war party was nearby and took no precautions to secure the fort. The Red Sticks gathered information about the fort and identified its weaknesses. On the day of the attack, one of the fort's gates was left open. The Red Sticks launched a surprise attack, quickly overran the fort, and killed almost all of the inhabitants, including women and children. As many as 500 people died, while only 36 escaped.

The U.S. response to the Fort Mims massacre was swift and strong. The government dispatched forces under Major General Andrew Jackson to the area. Jackson commanded 5,000 Tennessee militia and several hundred Cherokee and White Stick allies.

On November 3, 1813, a detachment from Jackson's force ambushed a group of Red Sticks at Tallushatchee, Alabama. The Red Sticks suffered 186 killed, including women and children, while U.S. loses were 5 killed and 41 wounded. Later in the month, the White Sticks asked Jackson to attack the Red Sticks who were laying siege to the White Stick village at Talladega. Moving quickly, Jackson launched his attack on November 9, 1813. Jackson estimated Red Stick strength at some 1,080 warriors. Despite the large number of Red Sticks, Jackson won a victory. At the end of the battle, the Americans counted 290 dead Red Sticks for U.S. losses of 15 killed and 85 wounded.

Jackson spent the remainder of the year hunting down the Red Sticks, training his men, and seeking to hold his force together. The enlistment period for many of the volunteers was coming to an end, and a large number wished to return home. Jackson was also beginning to experience supply problems. At the beginning of 1814, however, he received replacement volunteers and 600 U.S. regulars of the 39th Infantry Regiment.

CREEK WAR, 1813–1814

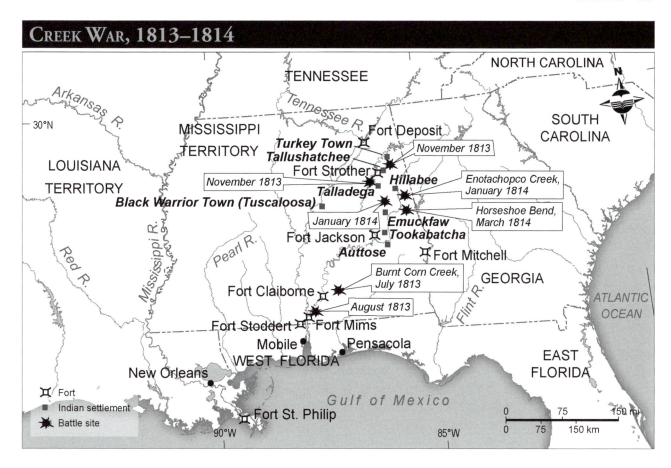

In March 1814 Jackson moved his force against the Red Stick encampment at Horseshoe Bend along the Tallapoosa River in Alabama, where the Red Sticks had built a fortified encampment. Jackson advanced toward the camp with 2,000 infantry, 700 cavalry and mounted riflemen, and 600 Native American allies (500 Cherokees and 100 White Stick Creeks). There were about 1,000 warriors and 300 women and children at the Red Stick camp.

The Battle of Horseshoe Bend occurred on March 27, 1814. Jackson's men arrived in front of the encampment to find it protected by a barricade of logs and earth at least eight feet in height with firing ports. Jackson sent his Native American allies and most of his cavalry around the camp on the other side of the river to prevent the Red Sticks from escaping or being reinforced. This force eventually helped support the main attack by crossing the river and moving against the encampment from the rear.

The attack on the barricade proved to be difficult, but Jackson's troops were eventually able to breach it. This action and the attack from the rear led the Red Stick defenders to attempt to flee. They had little success. Red Stick losses in the battle were 557 killed and 400 warriors captured. Most of the women and children were captured and turned over to Jackson's Native American allies. Jackson lost 32 killed and 99 wounded among his own troops, Cherokee losses were 18 killed and 36 wounded, and the allied White Sticks lost 5 dead and 11 wounded. Although it would be several months

before the Creek War officially ended, the Battle of Horseshoe Bend broke the back of Red Stick resistance.

Georgia Militia forces under the command of Brigadier General John Floyd also undertook action against the Red Sticks, albeit in a somewhat haphazard and ineffective manner. The end of November 1813 saw Georgia forces attack the Red Stick village of Auttose. The assault was a success in that the Red Sticks were scattered from their village stronghold and lost as many as 200 dead. Floyd's forces suffered 11 dead and 54 wounded. But on January 29, 1814, the Red Sticks attacked Floyd's position at Calibee Creek (in eastern Alabama) and inflicted heavy casualties. As many as 22 of his men died, and another 140 were wounded. The Red Sticks lost 37 warriors. While Floyd's men successfully held off the Red Sticks, the general saw the attack as a defeat and withdrew. The Georgians would not launch any subsequent attacks during the remainder of the war. The Mississippi Militia under Brigadier General Thomas Flournoy never actively engaged the Red Sticks but did destroy a number of Red Stick villages and outposts.

In August 1814 Jackson called all Creek leaders to a meeting at Fort Jackson (near Watumpka, Alabama) to negotiate a treaty ending the war. The only Creek leaders who attended, however, were the White Stick leaders, who were shocked to learn the terms of the treaty. It demanded 23 million acres of Creek land (about half of all their territory) and 4 million acres from the Cherokees. This land was to come not just from the defeated Red Sticks but also from the Native Americans allied with the United States during the war.

White Stick complaints had no effect on Jackson, who blamed the White Sticks as much as the Red Sticks for the war. Indeed, Jackson told the White Sticks that they should have prevented the conflict and that because they had not, they were equally responsible for it. Knowing that their only alternative to signing the treaty was to go to war against the United States, White Stick and Cherokee chiefs signed the Treaty of Fort Jackson (Horseshoe Bend) on August 9, 1814.

DALLACE W. UNGER JR. AND PAUL G. PIERPAOLI JR.

See also

Burnt Corn Creek, Battle of; Cherokees; Creeks; Fort Jackson, Treaty of; Fort Mims, Battle of; Horseshoe Bend, Battle of; Jackson, Andrew; Native Americans and the War of 1812; Shawnees; Tallushatchee, Battle of; Tecumseh

References

Ethridge, Robbie. *Creek Country: The Creek Indians and Their World.* Chapel Hill: University of North Carolina Press, 2003.

Remini, Robert Vincenti. *Andrew Jackson and His Indian Wars.* New York: Penguin, 2001.

Wright, J. Leitch, Jr. *Creeks and Seminoles: The Destruction and Regeneration of the Muscogulge People.* Lincoln: University of Nebraska Press, 1986.

Croatans

An Algonquian Native American tribe of the eastern tidewater of North Carolina; the term "Croatan" also identifies the eastern coastal area or present-day North Carolina. During efforts to establish the first English settlement in the New World on Roanoke Island from 1585 to 1587, the neighboring Croatans (Croatoans) maintained friendly relations with the English longer than any other tribe. After Queen Elizabeth I granted him a patent for colonization in 1584, Sir Walter Raleigh sponsored a New World expedition commanded by Philip Amandas and Arthur Barlowe. Following favorable exchanges with Algonquian natives on North Carolina's Outer Banks, the explorers returned to England with Native American leaders Wanchese and Manteo, the latter a Croatan.

Little is known about the Croatans, although it can be surmised that they were similar to neighboring tribes in eastern North Carolina in that they led a seminomadic existence that depended on hunting, gathering, and small-scale agriculture. Because of their proximity to the coast, they also likely engaged in fishing. Their language was of Algonquian extraction.

In 1585 Raleigh sponsored a colonizing expedition of more than 100 men. Commanded by Sir Richard Grenville, the expedition included Wanchese, Manteo, and Sir Ralph Lane, who would become the first governor of Virginia, an area that at the time included present-day eastern North Carolina as well as Virginia

to the north. The colonists established a fort on Roanoke Island, and Lane explored inland searching for the gold and silver that the natives had described. Misunderstandings with neighboring tribes escalated, however, possibly driven by drought conditions. The interactions between Native Americans and Europeans followed a classic pattern. Initially peaceful trade transactions were soon marred by cultural misunderstandings and then violence.

On July 11, 1585, Grenville and his men began an exploration of the mainland, entering several native towns along the way. When it was discovered the following day that a silver cup was missing, Grenville focused on the village of Aquascogoc. When Native Americans there denied taking it, his men burned their village and cornfields. Such accumulated acts of force by the English led to a 1586 native uprising, and the mounting conflicts were too much for the limited English garrison to subdue. Leaving just 15 men behind, Lane and the others returned to England in June 1586 when Sir Francis Drake's supply ships arrived. The following year, 117 men, women, and children arrived at Roanoke Island to establish a colony but found the English post abandoned.

Hostilities continued with surrounding tribes despite attempts by the Croatans to maintain peaceful relations with the settlers. Tensions escalated when English soldiers misidentified and attacked friendly Croatan men, women, and children on August 9, 1587, in retaliation for a previous attack by the Roanoke tribe. Following the incident, Manteo and the Croatans seemingly maintained friendly relations while other tribes did not. When the situation worsened, colonists persuaded their governor, John White, to return to England for supplies and support.

Because of England's war with Spain and the attack of the Spanish Armada in 1588, three years passed before White successfully mounted a rescue mission. Upon his return in August 1590 he found no evidence of surviving colonists. However, the word "Croatoan" was carved into a tree trunk. Some historians suggest that colonists fled to the Croatans because of threats from other Native Americans or possibly the Spanish. White was forced to abandon his search and returned to England before he could explore further. Speculation continues whether or not the Roanoke Island colonists intermingled with the Croatans, later called the Hatteras Indians.

LISA HEUVEL

See also

Spain

References

Axtell, James. *The Indians' New South: Cultural Change in the Colonial Southeast.* Baton Rouge: Louisiana State University Press, 1997.

Horn, James. *A Land as God Made It: Jamestown and the Birth of America.* New York: Basic Books, 2005.

Kupperman, Karen Ordahl. *Roanoke: The Abandoned Colony.* Lanham, MD: Rowman and Littlefield, 1984.

Shields, E. Thomason, and Charles R. Ewen, eds. *Searching for the Roanoke Colonies: An Interdisciplinary Collection.* Raleigh: Office of North Carolina Department of Cultural Resources, 2003.

Crockett, David
Birth Date: August 17, 1786
Death Date: March 6, 1836

Soldier, frontiersman, politician, and one of the best-known frontier folk heroes of the 19th century. David (Davy) Crockett was born into a poor frontier family on August 17, 1786, in Greene County in eastern Tennessee. He only rarely attended school and was hired out by his father in 1798 to help on a cattle drive to Virginia. Crockett ran away when his employer tried to keep him against his will. Crockett made his way back to Tennessee but soon was off again on his own.

Crockett married in August 1806 and moved to middle Tennessee in 1811. He moved his family to his first home outside the mountains in Franklin County, near the border with the Mississippi Territory. Crockett proved to be a poor farmer, but he was an excellent hunter. In 1813 he joined the Tennessee Militia units headed to Alabama following the massacre at Fort Mims during the Creek War (1813–1814). He participated in the militia's campaign under Major General Andrew Jackson against the Red Stick faction of the Creeks. Crockett apparently served primarily as a scout and guard for the horse herds. After his first enlistment expired, he returned home. In the late summer of 1814, Crockett enlisted again and spent the autumn of 1814 at Pensacola.

After the war, Crockett was elected a lieutenant in the 32nd Militia Regiment of Franklin County. His wife died that summer, and Crockett married a widow with two children the following year. In 1817 they moved to Lawrence County, Tennessee. Crockett soon established himself there and was appointed justice of the peace. He apparently used stories about his exploits in the war against the Creeks to enhance his reputation. He was elected colonel of the 57th Militia Regiment in 1818, and in 1821 he was elected to the state legislature.

Although Crockett lacked formal schooling, he was not as illiterate as the public image that he had created. He established himself as a supporter of settlers' rights on public lands. He won reelection in 1823 but was defeated in 1825.

In 1827 Crockett was elected to the U.S. House of Representatives. He campaigned as an honest country boy who was an outstanding hunter and a straight shooter in every sense of the term. He soon became a noted member of the House, thanks to his backwoods persona. Strangers called him Davy, a name appropriate to that image.

Crockett's support for settlers' rights, for the Bank of the United States, and against Native American removal brought him into conflict with President Andrew Jackson. The anti-Jackson faction, later to become the Whig Party, took interest in Crockett as a potential national candidate. He was reelected to the House in 1829 but was defeated in 1831. With the Whigs' support, Crockett won reelection in 1833.

David ("Davy") Crockett was a frontiersman, soldier, and politician who became a mythic hero for his role in the defense of the Alamo during the Texas War of Independence of 1835–1836. (Nathaniel W. Stephenson, *Texas and the Mexican War*, 1921)

In 1833 a book of frontier stories titled *Sketches and Eccentricities of Colonel David Crockett of West Tennessee* made its appearance. Supposedly written by Crockett, it was in fact ghostwritten by an anonymous Whig and was enormously popular. The book made Crockett into a folk hero among eastern readers. Although Crockett probably supplied many of the stories, he was apparently embarrassed by the extent to which the truth was bent. He then wrote, with help, his own autobiography, titled *A Narrative of the Life of David Crockett of the State of Tennessee.* Published in 1834, the book could be viewed as a campaign biography for a future run for the presidency. Crockett spent a month traveling through the Northeast to promote the book and to make himself known to voters. In his autobiography, he again portrayed himself as a simple frontiersman, honest and straightforward, who stood up for the ordinary man rather than as a politician.

His opposition to Jackson ultimately led to Crockett's political demise, and Crockett was defeated in the election of August 1835. On November 1, 1835, he and a small party left for Texas to seek their fortunes. In early February 1836 he arrived in San Antonio, where he joined the garrison of the Alamo. He died there on March 6, 1836, during the Battle of the Alamo, when Mexican forces under General Antonio López de Santa Anna attacked the fort. Crockett's frontiersman reputation long survived him, and he remains part of American legend to this day.

TIM J. WATTS

See also

Creeks; Creek War; Fort Mims, Battle of; Jackson, Andrew; Native Americans and the War of 1812; Red Sticks

References

Hollman, Robert E. *Davy Crockett*. Dallas, TX: Durban House Publishing, 2005.

Remini, Robert Vincenti. *Andrew Jackson and His Indian Wars*. New York: Penguin, 2001.

Croghan, George
Birth Date: ca. 1720
Death Date: August 31, 1782

Trader, land speculator, and diplomat. Born around 1720 in Dublin, Ireland, George Croghan received what is believed to have been only a rudimentary education. In 1741 he immigrated to Pennsylvania. Once there, he embarked on a career that included roles as a frontier diplomat, a Native American trader, and a speculator.

When he first arrived in North America, Croghan traded with natives in an area ranging from western Pennsylvania as far west as the Ohio River Valley. However, this trade was cut short by the beginning of the French and Indian War (1754–1763). During the conflict Croghan served as a local militia commander and helped survey the route for what became the path of British major general Edward Braddock's campaign to reach the Monongahela River. According to one biographer, Croghan even assisted in carrying the mortally wounded general from the field during the 1755 battle.

After Braddock's defeat, Croghan turned from his business interests as a trader to become a full-time diplomat. In 1756 he began a term of service under Sir William Johnson as deputy superintendent of Indian affairs for the Northern District. Croghan continued in this post until 1772. During his tenure he took part in several notable conferences, including the Easton Conference of 1758 and the Fort Stanwix Conference. Likewise, he helped put an end to Pontiac's Rebellion (1763) by convincing a number of the western tribes to negotiate at a conference at Detroit.

Throughout his life in the colonies Croghan also speculated in land in the frontier territories. By 1773 he had accumulated vast tracts in both western Pennsylvania and western New York. After that, however, he was forced to sell off much of this property in order to meet various obligations. His contemporaries often viewed Croghan with distrust in financial matters, and this hurt him when it came to redeeming the expenses of his various diplomatic efforts, since these always included gift giving. Croghan died on August 31, 1782, in Passyunk, Pennsylvania, now a part of the city of Philadelphia.

JAMES R. MCINTYRE

See also

Braddock's Campaign; Easton Conference and Treaty; French and Indian War; Indian Presents; Johnson, Sir William; Pontiac's Rebellion

References

Anderson, Fred. *Crucible of War: The Seven Years' War and the Fate of the Empire in British North America, 1754–1766*. New York: Vintage Books, 2001.

Volwiler, Albert T. *George Croghan and the Westward Movement, 1741–1782*. 1926; reprint, New York: AMS Press, 1971.

Wainwright, Nicholas B. *George Croghan, Wilderness Diplomat*. Chapel Hill: University of North Carolina Press, 1959.

Crook, George
Birth Date: September 8, 1828
Death Date: March 21, 1890

U.S. Army officer. George Crook was born near Dayton, Ohio, on September 8, 1828. He graduated from the U.S. Military Academy, West Point, in 1852 and was commissioned a second lieutenant in the 4th Infantry. His first assignment was in the Pacific Northwest. He was promoted to first lieutenant in 1856 and to captain in 1861 following the outbreak of the American Civil War (1861–1865). In September 1861 Crook entered the volunteer establishment as colonel of the 36th Ohio Infantry and participated in actions in western Virginia. On May 23, 1862, he was wounded at Lewisburg, Virginia; he was promoted to brigadier general of volunteers on September 7, 1862. Crook commanded a brigade in the Kanawha Division in the Battle of South Mountain (September 14, 1862) and in the ensuing Battle of Antietam (September 17, 1862). In the early months of 1863 he played a prominent role in operations in eastern Tennessee before assuming command of the 2nd Cavalry Division in the Army of the Cumberland in July 1863.

Given command of the Kanawha District in February 1864, Crook led a series of operations to disrupt Confederate communications between eastern Tennessee and Lynchburg, Virginia. During Major General Philip Sheridan's Shenandoah Valley Campaign (August 7, 1864–March 2, 1865), Crook commanded the Department of Western Virginia and the Army of Western Virginia (VIII Corps) and played a conspicuous role in the succession of Union victories during that campaign. In October 1864 Crook was promoted to major general and continued to command the Department of Western Virginia from his headquarters in Cumberland, Maryland. On February 21, 1865, Crook and Brigadier General Benjamin Kelley were taken prisoner by Confederate partisans in a daring raid. Exchanged on March 20, Crook subsequently led a cavalry division in the Army of the Potomac as it drove toward Appomattox. Crook was brevetted major general in the regular army on March 27, 1865.

After the Civil War, Crook reverted to lieutenant colonel in the regular army and assumed command of the 23rd Infantry Regiment. He spent the next few years fighting the Paiutes in the

George Crook (1828–1890), who ended his military career as a major general, is widely regarded as one of the most capable army leaders against hostile Native Americans in the West and developed many of the techniques employed with success by the army there. (Library of Congress)

Idaho Territory. In 1871 in a rather controversial move, Crook was assigned to command the Department of Arizona while still a lieutenant colonel. There he met Captain John G. Bourke, an outstanding officer who would later immortalize Crook in such books as *On the Border with Crook* and *With General Crook in the Indian Wars.*

In Arizona, Crook developed three key methods that helped him to become, in the view of many, the nation's premier Indian fighter. First, he employed Native Americans not only as scouts but also to provide insight into the possible courses of action of his foes. Second, he discarded his wagons and used only mule trains, giving him greater flexibility and speed. Third, he followed his adversaries wherever they went, even into northern Mexico, until he could bring them to battle. After the notable success of his 1872–1873 campaign, in another controversial move he was promoted directly to brigadier general. Crook's approach paid off, and by early 1875 the hostile Apaches had been temporarily subdued. Crook then worked to improve the lot of the Apache people and show them that the benefits of peace outweighed those of war.

In March 1875 Crook was named commander of the Department of the Platte, headquartered in Omaha, Nebraska. He participated in the Great Sioux War (1876–1877) and commanded one of three converging columns during the army's spring offensive. In the Battle of the Rosebud (June 17, 1876), Crook's men engaged Native Americans under Chief Crazy Horse in a spirited

stand-up fight unusual for Native Americans and were forced to fall back and regroup, rendering Crook unable to support the other columns or to communicate news of his setback. Following the devastating defeat of Lieutenant Colonel George A. Custer's 7th Cavalry at the Little Bighorn, Crook largely directed the army's response, including Colonel Ranald S. Mackenzie's destruction of Cheyenne chief Dull Knife's village.

In 1882 Crook returned to Arizona, where he once again employed his innovative approaches, including a heavy reliance on Indian scouts and small expeditions, but his efforts to deal with the Apaches encountered strong opposition from civilian agents and his old roommate, now rival, Lieutenant General Philip Sheridan. Crook's opponents were strengthened when Geronimo led a group of Chiricahuas off the San Carlos Agency on May 17, 1885. Crook's forces wore Geronimo down, and the Apache leader finally agreed to surrender. Sheridan rejected Crook's terms, however, and demanded Geronimo's unconditional surrender. Geronimo and some of his men again fled U.S. control, and Sheridan blamed Crook and his Apache scouts. Crook was replaced by Brigadier General Nelson A. Miles.

Crook spent the last years of his life attempting to win the return of Apaches from imprisonment in Florida to Arizona and battling with Miles and Sheridan in print. President Grover Cleveland promoted Crook to major general in April 1888 and assigned him to command the Division of the Missouri. Crook died in Chicago on March 21, 1890, while still on active duty.

ALAN K. LAMM

See also

Apaches; Cheyennes; Crawford, Emmet; Crazy Horse; Custer, George Armstrong; Dull Knife; Gatewood, Charles Bare; Geronimo; Great Sioux War; Little Bighorn, Battle of the; Mackenzie, Ranald Slidell; Miles, Nelson Appleton; Paiutes, Northern; Rosebud, Battle of the; Scouts, Native American; Sheridan, Philip Henry; Sioux

References

Aleshire, Peter. *The Fox and the Whirlwind: General George Crook and Geronimo, A Paired Biography.* New York: Wiley, 2000.
Crook, George. *General George Crook: His Autobiography.* Edited by Martin F. Schmidt. Norman: University of Oklahoma Press, 1960.
Hutton, Paul Andrew. *Phil Sheridan and His Army.* Lincoln: University of Nebraska Press, 1985.
Hutton, Paul Andrew, ed. *Soldiers West: Biographies from the Military Frontier.* Lincoln: University of Nebraska Press, 1987.

Crows

A northern Plains tribe whose traditional territory was located in the Yellowstone River Valley. The Crows, who now reside on a reservation outside of Billings, Montana, are part of the Siouan language group. The name they apply to themselves is Absaroka, which is derived from a bird of the Great Plains. The Crows are most closely related to the Hidatsa tribe of the upper Missouri River Valley. It is Crow lore that they split from the Hidatsas but

Painting of Crow Indians by Karl Bodmer, circa 1832. (Library of Congress)

remained friendly with them thereafter. Anthropologists disagree as to the date of the split, but it was definitely prior to contact with whites and most likely pre-Columbian. The Hidatsas were sedentary farmers relying primarily on maize for their diet, supplemented with some gathering efforts and hunting of the ubiquitous bison of the Plains.

It is believed that the Crows and the Hidatsas split after a disagreement over the division of spoils from a hunt. The Crows evolved into a seminomadic tribe and would travel every summer to visit and trade with their Hidatsa cousins along the Missouri River. The Crows would bring meat, furs, buffalo hides, and sometimes horses to exchange for grain, trade goods, and guns. It was on one of these summer trading migrations that the Crows encountered the Lewis and Clark expedition in 1805. By that time the Crows had become typical northern Plains Indians. They had substantial horse herds, primarily hunted bison, lived in tepees, and engaged in the Sun Dance ritual. Crow society was both matrilineal and matriarchal, and it was not uncommon to find women at the top of a Crow governing hierarchy.

The Crows, as was common among the Plains tribes, divided themselves into bands that came together as a nation only periodically. The Crows were divided into three principal bands: the River Crows, who lived primarily along the Yellowstone River;

the Mountain Crows, who lived higher up along the tributaries of the Yellowstone River; and the Kicked-in-the-Bellies, who spent part of their time with the Mountain Crows, especially during the summer months, but moved away from them in the autumn and winter.

The Crows possessed war clubs, as did other Plains tribes, and warfare was central to the Crow lifestyle. Indeed, success in the hunt and in war was the sign of manhood and also the means to both respectability and wealth among the Crows. The principal mode of warfare was the raid on another tribe's village for horses, to count coup (thus displaying courage), and to take captives. Skirmishes between tribes as they hunted buffalo were also common. Large-scale set-piece battles with large bodies of warriors were quite uncommon, and casualties were assiduously avoided. Despite this, the numbers of the slain could, over time, become quite large.

The Crows were first noted by Europeans in about 1715 or 1716 by fur traders of the Hudson's Bay Company. Some 18th-century accounts refer to the Crows as "Rocky Mountain Indians." At the time, the Crows hunted from the Black Hills west along the present-day Wyoming-Montana state line to the Yellowstone Basin. This territory included some of the richest of the northern Plains hunting grounds, especially the Powder River Country. The

Crows shared this area with various other tribes, including for a time the Comanches and the Kiowas before they migrated south to the Arkansas River basin and the Red River basin of Texas. To the north and west lay the hunting grounds of the Blackfeet, the Shoshones, and the Utes, with whom the Crows often engaged in warfare. To the east and south the Crows engaged in intermittent warfare with the Pawnees along the Platte River in present-day Nebraska.

The Crows' most notable enemies, however, were the Lakotas and the other members of the Lakota alliance, principally the Cheyennes. Probably around 1780, the Lakotas drove the Crows from the Black Hills and continued to push them farther west. By the 1850s the Lakota were contesting the Powder River Country with the Crows.

Although the Crows initially resented white intrusion onto their hunting grounds, they were far more concerned with the active aggression of the Lakotas. Even though the Lakotas invited the Crows to join with them during the Powder River War of 1866–1867, the Crows declined, still seeing the Lakotas as the larger threat. The Crows never engaged in serious conflict with the whites and often saw themselves as allied with the whites against the Lakotas. The Crows, however, often provided scouts to U.S. Army columns, including Lieutenant Colonel George Custer's Little Bighorn expedition in 1876. Evidently, both the Crow and Arikara scouts tried to warn Custer of the danger involved due to the unprecedented size of the horse herds they observed. Custer chose to attack anyway. The Crows, in spite of their awareness of the size of the Lakota alliance, rode with the column. In an ironic twist of history, the Little Bighorn battlefield is located on the present-day Crow Reservation in Montana.

The Crows continued to provide scouts to the U.S. Army even after the Custer disaster and continued to engage the Lakotas unilaterally. With the end of large-scale campaigning, the Crows settled down on a large reservation covering much of southern Montana within their old home range. They were eventually relocated on a much smaller reservation in south-central Montana but still within the heart of their home territory. The Crows gradually adopted ranching, retained mineral rights to their lands, and were reasonably successful in adapting to the new conditions, maintaining a strong identity and strong tribal sense on their own terms.

JOHN THOMAS BROOM

See also

Arikaras; Blackfoot Sioux; Buffalo; Cheyennes; Custer, George Armstrong; Lakota Sioux; Little Bighorn, Battle of the; Powder River Expedition; Shoshones; Utes

References

Carlson, Paul H. *The Plains Indians*. College Station: Texas A&M University Press, 1998.

Dunlay, Thomas W. *Wolves for the Blue Soldiers: Indian Scouts and Auxiliaries with the United States Army, 1860–90*. Lincoln: University of Nebraska Press, 1982.

Goodrich, Thomas. *Scalp Dance: Indian Warfare on the High Plains, 1865–1879*. Mechanicsburg, PA: Stackpole, 1997.

Hoxie, Frederick E. *Parading through History: The Making of the Crow Nation in America, 1805–1935*. New York: Cambridge University Press, 1997.

Lowie, Robert H. *The Crow Indians*. Lincoln: University of Nebraska Press, 1983.

Curly
Birth Date: ca. 1859
Death Date: May 21, 1923

Crow scout who served Lieutenant Colonel George Armstrong Custer during the Great Sioux War (1876–1877) and a key figure in the mythology surrounding the Battle of the Little Bighorn (June 25–26, 1876). Born in the Montana Territory in approximately 1859, Curly (also known as Ashishishe), fought the Sioux before

Curly, a Crow scout for Lieutenant Colonel George Armstrong Custer at the Battle of the Little Bighorn in 1876. (National Archives)

contracting with the U.S. Army under Colonel John Gibbon in April 1876. Establishing himself as a valuable scout, Curly was one of several Crow scouts with Custer's 7th U.S. Cavalry Regiment dispatched to locate the Sioux on June 22, 1876. Curly and his fellow scouts guided Custer's men and discovered the large Sioux encampment on the Little Bighorn River.

When the 7th Cavalry prepared to attack the Sioux on June 25, 1876, Custer dismissed Curly and the other scouts, declaring that they had done their duty. Viewing the ensuing battle from a distance and concluding that the soldiers had lost, Curly left to find Gibbon. On June 27 Curly appeared near the confluence of the Bighorn and Little Bighorn rivers, recounting what he saw to crew members of the steamboat *Far West,* which then carried the news eastward. Regarded by many as the lone survivor of the battle, his ambiguous stories helped shape the myth of Custer's Last Stand. For instance, Curly, along with Sitting Bull, reported that Custer was among the last soldiers to die in a "last stand," something that has never been proven definitively. After the Battle of the Little Bighorn, Curly lived on the nearby Crow Reservation, serving with the Crow police and recounting his story to interviewers. He died there on May 21, 1923.

ADAM R. HODGE

See also

Custer, George Armstrong; Gibbon, John; Great Sioux War; Little Bighorn, Battle of the; Scouts, Native American; Sioux; Sitting Bull

References

Connell, Evan S. *Son of the Morning Star: Custer and the Little Bighorn.* New York: North Point Press, 1984.

Fox, Richard Allan. *Archaeology, History, and Custer's Last Battle: The Little Big Horn Reexamined.* Norman: University of Oklahoma Press, 1993.

Curtis, Samuel Ryan
Birth Date: February 3, 1805
Death Date: December 26, 1866

U.S. Army general. Samuel Ryan Curtis was born on February 3, 1805, in Clinton County, New York, but moved to Ohio with his family as a youth. He graduated from the U.S. Military Academy, West Point, in 1831 and was assigned to the 7th U.S. Infantry Regiment. Curtis resigned his commission the following year, returned to Ohio, studied law, and was admitted to the bar in Zanesville. From 1837 to 1839 he worked as a civil engineer on a project along the Muskingum River. Subsequently he worked in the same capacity for the National Road.

When the Mexican-American War (1846–1848) began, Curtis, who held a commission in the Ohio Militia, became first the state's adjutant general and then colonel of the 3rd Ohio Volunteer Regiment. The regiment did not see combat, but Curtis served as military governor of several occupied Mexican towns.

Back in civilian life after the war, Curtis moved to Iowa and continued to practice law. In 1856 he became mayor of Keokuk and subsequently served in the U.S. House of Representatives from 1857 until his resignation in 1861. A member of the Republican Party, Curtis leaned toward abolitionism and was an early supporter of Abraham Lincoln. However, in early 1861 Curtis served on the peace commission in Washington, seeking yet another sectional compromise.

When the American Civil War (1861–1865) began, Curtis once again offered his services and was elected colonel of the 2nd Iowa Volunteer Regiment. He was prompt in marching his regiment to occupy the town of Hannibal, Missouri, at the request of Brigadier General Nathaniel Lyon, who commanded Union field forces in Missouri at that time, and the favorable attention of that movement earned Curtis promotion to brigadier general. In December 1861, Major General Henry W. Halleck, commanding the Department of Missouri, assigned Curtis to command the Army of the Southwest. In February 1862 Curtis succeeded in pushing Confederate forces out of the southwestern corner of Missouri. Curtis's army saw much action in the early spring of 1862 in northwestern Arkansas. On March 7–8, 1862, at the Battle of Pea Ridge, Curtis successfully thwarted a Confederate offensive; it was the most important victory gained west of the Mississippi. Curtis received promotion to major general, effective March 21.

In September, Curtis was made commander of the Department of Missouri but in that role tended to come into conflict with the governor of Missouri, who was offended by Curtis's antislavery views. To mollify the governor, Lincoln relieved Curtis of his command on May 12, 1863.

The following January, however, Lincoln assigned Curtis to command of the Department of Kansas. Such western commands in the Civil War were seen as convenient places to shelve inconvenient officers, but in 1864 Curtis gathered the forces available to him and on October 23 met and defeated Confederate forces under Brigadier General Sterling Price at Westport (near Kansas City). Curtis's final Civil War assignment was to the Department of the Northwest. In this post he oversaw but did not actively participate in engagements with Native Americans in Minnesota and the Dakota Territory, chiefly against the Sioux. These conflicts had been spillovers from the Minnesota Sioux Uprising of 1862.

After the Civil War, Curtis served very briefly as an Indian peace commissioner and as a consultant to the Union Pacific Railroad. He died in Council Bluffs, Iowa, on December 26, 1866.

STEVEN E. WOODWORTH

See also

Minnesota Sioux Uprising; Sioux

References

DeBlack, Thomas A. *With Fire and Sword: Arkansas, 1861–1874.* Fayetteville: University of Arkansas Press, 2003.

Eicher, John H., and David J. Eicher. *Civil War High Commands.* Stanford, CA: Stanford University Press, 2001.

Custer, George Armstrong
Birth Date: December 5, 1839
Death Date: June 25, 1876

U.S. Army officer and one of the youngest generals in the American Civil War (1861–1865) who went on to an infamous career on the frontier in the Indian Wars. George Armstrong Custer was born on December 5, 1839, in New Rumley, Ohio, although he spent part of his childhood with his half sister in Monroe, Michigan. Custer often accompanied his father to local militia drills and by the age of 4 could go through the manual of arms perfectly. At age 16 he was admitted to the U.S. Military Academy at West Point, performing just well enough to graduate last in his class in 1861.

Despite his mediocre record as a student, Custer excelled during the Civil War. Shortly after graduating from West Point, he was assigned to a regiment on its way to the First Battle of Bull Run (July 21, 1861). His daring reconnaissance patrols and valor brought him to the attention of Union Army commander Major General George B. McClellan. As a captain and a staff officer for McClellan and Major General Alfred Pleasonton, Custer demonstrated his potential to such an extent that he was promoted to brigadier general on June 29, 1863, and given command of the 2nd Brigade of the 3rd Cavalry Division at the age of 23.

With his flamboyant uniform—which he designed personally—and his long flowing reddish hair, Custer immediately became a national hero. From the Battle of Gettysburg (July 1–3, 1863) through the end of the war, he was renowned for his fearless and often decisive cavalry charges and earned the respect of his men and superiors. In October 1864 he took charge of the entire 3rd Cavalry Division and became a close confidant of Major General Philip Sheridan during the Shenandoah Valley Campaign (August 7, 1864–March 2, 1865). Custer also intrepidly led his force in the Third Battle of Winchester (September 19, 1864) and in the Battle of Fisher's Hill (September 22, 1864) and the Battle of Five Forks (April 1, 1865), among many other battles. By the end of the war he had been promoted to major general and was considered one of the most brilliant cavalry officers in the Union Army.

Following the war, Custer returned to the regular army with the permanent rank of lieutenant colonel and was assigned to the 7th Cavalry Regiment. Because his commanding officer was frequently absent, the 7th Cavalry was, for all intents and purposes, Custer's regiment. He quickly made a name for himself on the Plains. Dressed in fringed buckskin instead of a traditional uniform, he was the embodiment of the dashing Indian fighter. His best-selling book *My Life on the Plains* (1874) and several popular magazine articles helped to reinforce his reputation as a military genius. Yet the Custer myth did not always square with reality.

Indeed, Custer's first experience fighting the Native Americans in 1867 ended in humiliating failure during a campaign against the Cheyennes. Not only did he fail to defeat any Native Americans, but he was court-martialed and sentenced to a year's suspension from rank and pay for being absent without leave (AWOL). He

Lieutenant Colonel George Armstrong Custer. A brigadier general in the Civil War, the flamboyant Custer became infamous in the Indian Wars. His 7th Cavalry Regiment was largely obliterated in the Battle of the Little Bighorn on June 25, 1876, in what became known as Custer's Last Stand. (Library of Congress)

rebounded from this personal setback in 1868 when he surprised Chief Black Kettle's Cheyenne village in a brutal and strategically questionable attack at the Battle of the Washita (November 27, 1868). This victory helped to burnish Custer's public reputation.

In 1874 Custer and the 7th Cavalry escorted a large exploratory expedition that, among other things, located gold in the Black Hills of the Dakota Territory, and the U.S. government subsequently attempted to buy the Black Hills from the Sioux. When this effort failed, the government essentially appropriated the land and attempted to confine the Sioux and Northern Cheyennes to significantly reduced reservations. But in the spring of 1876 thousands of Sioux and Cheyennes left the reservation for hunting grounds in the Powder River and Yellowstone River valleys, which gave American officials the necessary justification to send in the military to resolve the situation. The result was the Great Sioux War of 1876–1877. The 7th Cavalry spearheaded Brigadier General Alfred Terry's column, part of a large three-pronged campaign to subdue the wayward Indians.

On June 25, 1876, Custer's scouts located a massive village on the Little Bighorn River in southwestern Montana. Perceiving an opportunity, Custer divided his 7th Cavalry into three battalions and without waiting for the commands of Terry and Colonel John Gibbon to arrive rashly attacked the village of Sioux leaders Sitting

Bull and Crazy Horse. Sending a battalion under Major Marcus Reno to strike the village directly, Custer led his battalion of some 225 men in an effort to outflank the Sioux. Reno's force was quickly repulsed with heavy loses but managed to retreat to a ridge where survivors were joined by the third battalion, that of Captain Frederick Benteen, and held out until the Indians withdrew.

Custer soon found himself outnumbered 10 to 1 and surrounded. In one of the most famous and controversial battles in American history, the Sioux slaughtered "Long Hair"—the name the Sioux had given Custer—and all of his men, including Custer's younger brother Tom. Custer's Last Stand, as the battle is also known, stunned Americans and attached to Custer an immortality that he probably did not deserve but that fit with his reputation and public persona. The shocking development galvanized the army, which mobilized resources from across the West for a punitive campaign that brought an end to Sioux and Cheyenne dominance.

ANDY JOHNS

See also

Benteen, Frederick William; Cheyennes; Crazy Horse; Gibbon, John; Great Sioux War; Little Bighorn, Battle of the; Reno, Marcus Albert; Sioux; Sitting Bull; Terry, Alfred Howe; Washita, Battle of the

References

Ambrose, Stephen E. *Crazy Horse and Custer: The Parallel Lives of Two American Warriors.* New York: Anchor Books, 1996.
Monaghan, Jay. *Custer: The Life of General George Armstrong Custer.* Lincoln: University of Nebraska Press, 1971.
Wert, Jeffrey D. *Custer: The Controversial Life of George Armstrong Custer.* New York: Simon and Schuster, 1996.

Custer, Thomas Ward
Birth Date: March 15, 1845
Death Date: June 25, 1876

U.S. Army officer, younger brother of George A. Custer, and rare two-time winner of the Medal of Honor. Thomas Ward Custer was born near New Rumley, Ohio, on March 15, 1845. When the American Civil War (1861–1865) began, Thomas Custer was only 16 years old but lied about his age and enlisted as a private in the 21st Ohio Infantry Regiment. He saw extensive action in the western theater before his enlistment expired in 1864. Thanks in large part to his brother, then a brigadier general of volunteers, the younger Custer received a direct commission as a second lieutenant in the 6th Michigan Cavalry in late 1864 and was assigned a staff position with his brother in Virginia.

Custer soon developed a reputation for reckless bravery, which was only enhanced at the Battle of Five Forks (April 1, 1865) when he had five horses shot from under him. Two days later at the Battle of Namozine Church he captured a Confederate battle flag and was awarded his first Medal of Honor. Three days after that, on April 6, at the Battle of Sayler's Creek he captured another

Confederate battle flag and won a second Medal of Honor. His brother later said that Tom should have been the general and he the lieutenant.

Custer was brevetted through major of volunteers and later through lieutenant colonel in the regular army. After mustering out of the volunteers, in 1866 he joined the regular army as a second lieutenant in the 1st Infantry but was soon promoted to first lieutenant and transferred to his brother's unit, the 7th U.S. Cavalry Regiment. On November 28, 1868, Thomas Custer participated in the Battle of the Washita, which proved a devastating blow to the Cheyennes. During the fight he was wounded in his right hand by a bullet.

In June 1873 Custer was part of an expedition that explored the Yellowstone region. While there he was with his brother as part of a detachment that was ambushed by a band of Sioux on August 4. A week later Custer commanded Company B in the Battle of the Yellowstone and successfully avoided the same kind of trap that had killed 80 soldiers in the 1866 Fetterman Massacre.

In 1874 Custer was sent to the Standing Rock Agency, a reservation in the Dakota Territory. His mission was to arrest the Sioux warrior Rain in the Face, who had boasted of killing four white men. During the arrest Custer slapped Rain in the Face. The warrior later escaped custody, vowing to cut Custer's heart out. That same year Custer was part of the Black Hills expedition dispatched to explore that region. Gold was soon discovered, which led to a great many white prospectors moving into the area. The Black Hills, however, were protected by treaty and were considered sacred by the Sioux, who vowed to keep the whites out. This conflict set the stage for the Great Sioux War (1876–1877) and the final events of Custer's life.

On December 2, 1875, Custer was promoted to captain and later that month took command of Company C; soon he had the opportunity to lead his company into battle. Responding to Sioux and Cheyenne attacks on trespassing white settlers and mass defections from the reservations, the federal government sent in the army in what became known as the Great Sioux War. On May 17, 1876, the 7th Cavalry left Fort Abraham Lincoln to join the campaign against the Sioux. Custer was at his brother George's side when both died at the Battle of the Little Bighorn on June 25, 1876. Tom's younger brother, Boston, died that day too, as did his favorite nephew, 18-year-old Henry Armstrong Reed, and his brother-in-law, Lieutenant James Calhoun. Tom Custer's body was scalped and mutilated and could only be identified by a tattoo bearing the initials "TWC" on his arm. He was hastily buried beside his brother George on the battlefield; later Tom's body was removed and reburied at Fort Leavenworth, Kansas.

ALAN K. LAMM

See also

Black Hills, South Dakota; Cavalry Regiment, 7th U.S.; Cheyennes; Custer, George Armstrong; Fetterman Massacre; Great Sioux War; Little Bighorn, Battle of the; Sioux; Washita, Battle of the

References

Day, Carl F. *Tom Custer: Ride to Glory.* Spokane, WA: Arthur H. Clark, 2002.

Custer, Elizabeth. *"A Beau Sabreur" in Uncle Sam's Medal of Honor: Some of the Noble Deeds for Which the Medal Has Been Awarded; Described by Those Who Have Won It.* Edited by Theodore F. Rodenbaugh. New York: n.p., 1886.

Custer, Elizabeth. *Boots and Saddles, or Life in the Dakotas with General Custer.* 1885; reprint, Norman: University of Oklahoma Press, 1977.

Custer, Elizabeth. *Tenting on the Plains.* 1893; reprint, Norman: University of Oklahoma Press, 1971.

Custer's Last Stand

See Little Bighorn, Battle of the

Custer's Last Stand in Art

The annihilation of Lieutenant Colonel George Armstrong Custer's cavalry unit at the Battle of the Little Bighorn (June 25–26, 1876) has perhaps captured the American imagination more than any other military event in U.S. history. The battle's combination of pathos, tragedy, bravado, and carelessness has served as a cautionary model for future warriors and military commanders alike.

The year 1876 was to be a year of celebration for the U.S. centennial, which made Custer's Last Stand even more noteworthy to artists and journalists alike.

Centennial America craved information about the demise of the 7th Cavalry, and artists did their best not to disappoint. First there was John Mulvany's *Custer's Last Rally,* completed in 1881 and praised and touted by no less than writer Walt Whitman, who was said not to be able to contain his emotions when observing the painting. Mulvany, an Irishman, dedicated two years to research, visiting the battlefield, interviewing Native Americans and soldiers, and striving for historical perfection. The massive canvas measured 11 by 20 feet and was taken on tour to Boston, New York, and Pittsburgh. Mulvany, never completely satisfied, later removed the saber from Custer's hand, replacing it with a revolver. The artist also shortened Custer's hair after learning that Custer had done so before the march. The painting was acquired by the H. J. Heinz Company in 1898 and displayed in its Pittsburgh auditorium and was also shown in Atlantic City and in various European cities before being sold several more times.

Artist Frederic Remington was not pleased by Mulvany's success, as he saw subject matter of the American West as his exclusive area. Remington thus created a small piece that he gave to Custer's widow and then did a larger painting completed in 1895 showing a small group of cavalrymen standing alone and titled *The Last Stand,* which is now in the Amon Carter Museum in Fort

Artist Charles M. Russell's 1903 painting depicts the defeat of Lieutenant Colonel George Armstrong Custer's 7th Cavalry Regiment in the Battle of the Little Bighorn on June 25, 1876. (Library of Congress)

Worth, Texas. Charles Russell, a contemporary, did variations in two works, one called *Custer's Last Stand* (1895) and another, *The Custer Fight* (1903), reproduced in *Scribner's Magazine*.

In 1884 Cassily Adams painted his own rendition of the event, called *Custer's Last Fight,* drawing from descriptions left by Native Americans who fought there and from pictures of cavalrymen, their armaments, and uniforms and a long-haired Custer. Adams, who studied at the Boston Academy of Arts and at the Cincinnati Art School, spent a year painting the 9.5-foot by 16.5-foot painting, which was first displayed by the St. Louis Arts Club. The painting became an immediate sensation and was sold and moved numerous times until 1945, when it was lost in a fire at Fort Bliss, Texas. When the original was lost, Otto Becker created a smaller lithograph version of the Adams work and was also charged with painting a Custer work from sketches left by Adams. Adams's work was cut up to create details for the lithographic rendition, commissioned by Anheuser-Busch. The pieces were put back together and hang in the St. Louis offices of the company. This work has been reprinted in the hundreds of thousands and is still available. It is probably the Custer work that has had the greatest audience. This painting, finished in 1895, shows a heroic Custer with shorter hair and standing nobly with a revolver in each hand.

There have been perhaps 200 serious attempts at creating Custer in art forms. Indeed, one of the participants in the battle, Red Horse, had created some 42 drawings on manila paper depicting events, with stick figures representing the combatants. These are in the collection of the Smithsonian Institution. Another notable painting called *Custer's Last Stand* was created in 1899 by E. S. Paxson. An imposing work at 5 by 9 feet, Paxson's painting has some 200 figures, many drawn from photographs of the personalities and from descriptions by Native Americans and soldiers who were close to the battle scene. Some have called it the best representation of the battle. It was displayed at the 1893 Chicago World's Fair and now hangs in Science Hall at Montana State University in Missoula, Montana.

Notable modern studies have been created by Eric von Schmidt, whose father, Harold von Schmidt, an illustrator for popular magazines, had done his own *Custer's Last Stand* for *Esquire* in 1950. His son produced an acclaimed study titled *Here Fell Custer,* which was selected by the National Park Service as the official painting of the disaster. It is displayed in the wayside exhibit at Last Stand Hill at the Little Bighorn Battlefield Monument.

A curious art exhibit was produced by Thom Ross, who created an art installation project of 120 to 200 full-sized figures inspired by the figures in the Becker lithograph cut out of plywood and placed in various positions. This was in celebration of the 125th anniversary of the battle. Martin Pate has painted various segments of the battle, which were chosen by the National Park Service for roadside exhibits at the battlefield site. Pate has also done a painting titled *In the Arms of Immortality.* There were other works too, such as a *Custer's Last Fight* painted by W. H. Leigh in 1939 and privately held at the Frank Phillips Ranch in Bartlesville, Oklahoma.

A popular depiction of Custer's Last Stand was in the cyclorama production that was shown successfully in Boston in 1889. This painting replaced that of the Battle of Gettysburg, which moved to Gettysburg. A number of artists worked on the massive canvas under direction of E. Pierpont, who had visited the battlefield and examined available paintings. What happened to the cyclorama is unknown.

JACK J. CARDOSO

See also

Custer, George Armstrong; Little Bighorn, Battle of the

References

Donnelle, A. J., ed. *Cyclorama of the Battle of the Little Bighorn.* New York: Promontory, 1966.

Donovan, James. *A Terrible Glory: Custer and the Little Bighorn.* New York: Little, Brown, 2007.

Russell, Don. *Custer's Last; Or, the Battle of the Little Big Horn in Picturesque Perspective, Being a Pictorial Representation of the Late and Unfortunate Incident in Montana as Portrayed by Custer's Friends and Foes, Admirers, and Iconoclasts of His Day and After.* Fort Worth, TX: Amon Carter Museum of Western Art, 1968.

Viola, Herman. *Little Bighorn Remembered: The Untold Indian Story of Custer's Last Stand.* New York: Times Books, 1999.

D

Dade's Massacre
Event Date: December 28, 1835

Ambush of 108 U.S. troops by Seminole warriors on December 28, 1835, in central Florida near present-day Bushnell at the beginning of the Second Seminole War (1835–1842). On December 23, 1835, U.S. Army major Francis L. Dade of the 4th Infantry Regiment departed Fort Brooke (at present-day Tampa) with 107 men to march 100 miles to Fort King (present-day Ocala) in order to resupply and reinforce its garrison.

The months preceding Dade's march witnessed increasing disharmony between the Seminoles and whites. According to the Treaty of Payne's Landing, which was signed on March 28, 1833, and ratified by the U.S. Senate in April 1834, the Seminoles had three years to move from Florida to lands west of the Mississippi River. The United States, represented by Seminole agent Wiley Thompson, understood the removal period to end in 1835, while many Seminole chiefs simply did not recognize the treaty as either valid or binding. When President Andrew Jackson authorized the U.S. Army to forcibly remove the Seminoles, relations rapidly deteriorated.

Under the leadership of Halpatter Tustenuggee (Alligator), Micanopy, and Ote Emathla (Jumper), the Seminoles began a wave of violence whose primary objectives were to kill Agent Thompson and severely cripple the American military. The southern fork of this two-pronged offensive was an effort to ambush Dade's men as they moved northward on the road from Fort Brooke to Fort King. Dade had arrived at Fort Brooke on December 21 and had volunteered to take command of the column from Captain Washington Gardiner, whose wife was then quite ill.

The men in Dade's column, artillerymen trained to fight as infantry, were escorted by a guide, a slave named Louis Pacheco.

They departed Fort Brooke on December 23. The terrain between the two forts contained dense vegetation, and there was only the one road and limited trails. Dade's column moved at a very slow pace and was under the observation of Seminole scouts from the moment it departed Fort Brooke. On the sixth day, December 28, apparently not expecting contact with Seminole warriors and bracing for an unusually cold and damp morning by wearing their overcoats over their cartridge boxes, Dade's soldiers continued north in two columns. Some 180 Seminole warriors meanwhile moved into position on the west side of the road, directly opposite a pond to the east. Because Dade had failed to post flankers on either side of the column, the Seminoles waited undetected.

The Seminoles' initial volley cut down nearly half of the soldiers, including Dade. The survivors began to seek cover behind trees and got their only artillery piece, a 6-pounder, into action. The cannon delayed the Seminoles for nearly 45 minutes, during which time the soldiers hastily constructed a triangular breastwork of felled trees nearly 200 yards south of the initial area of contact.

Nevertheless, all of the men in Dade's command except 3 were dead by 4:00 p.m. The warriors later killed 1 of the survivors as he attempted to reach Fort Brooke, while another reached the safety of the fort only to die of his wounds. The total number of U.S. troops to die was thus 107. The survivor, Private Ransome Clarke, arrived at Fort Brooke several days after the fight. Clarke, Louis Pacheco (who had betrayed Dade and his men by joining the Seminoles during the battle), and Alligator provided the only eyewitness accounts of the action. Seminole losses were reportedly 3 killed and 5 wounded.

JEFFERY P. LUCAS

Dade's Massacre on December 28, 1835, touched off the Second Seminole War (1835–1842). On this date, a Seminole war party attacked a column of 108 men in central Florida commanded by Major Francis L. Dade, killing all but 3 of them. Seminole losses were reportedly only 3 dead and 5 wounded. (Corbis)

See also

Indian Removal Act; Payne's Landing, Treaty of; Seminoles; Seminole War, Second

References

Laumer, Frank. *Dade's Last Command.* Gainesville: University of Florida Press, 1995.

Laumer, Frank. *Massacre.* Gainesville: University of Florida Press, 1968.

Mahon, John K. *History of the Second Seminole War, 1835–1842.* Rev. ed. Gainesville: University Press of Florida, 1991.

Dakota-Ojibwa Conflict

See Ojibwa-Dakota Conflict

Dakota Sioux

Native American tribal group that consisted of seven bands located in Minnesota and the Dakota Territory and roughly divided into two subgroups, the Eastern or Santee Dakota Sioux, consisting of the Mdewakanton, Sisseton, Wahpeton, and Wahpekute bands inhabiting the eastern and central regions; the Western or Yankton Dakota Sioux, consisting of the Yankton and Yanktonais bands occupying the western region; and the Tetons, residing on the westernmost fringe of the Dakota Sioux territory. As with most Native Americans of this region, the Dakota Sioux were seminomadic hunters and gatherers.

The first recorded historical mention of the Sioux people was by the Jesuits in the 1640s. There is some suggestion that they resided near the confluence of the Mississippi and Minnesota rivers for several generations. Their own traditions have them originating in the Northeast and then moving southwest. This movement westward was primarily because of nearly constant fighting with the Chippewas, who had firearms supplied by the French, while the Sioux were forced to rely almost entirely on bows and arrows.

During the American Revolutionary War (1775–1783) and the War of 1812, most of the Dakotas adhered to the English. Peace was established between the Dakotas and the United States in a treaty of July 1815, and in August 1825 boundary lines were set between the Dakotas and the United States and the Dakotas and the various tribes in the Northwest.

Prior to the Indian Wars of the middle and late 19th century, the U.S. government concluded three treaties with the Dakota Sioux: the Treaty of 1837, the Treaty of Traverse des Sioux (1857), and the Treaty of Mendota (also 1857). Through these treaties the Dakota Sioux agreed to cede land to the United States in most of eastern and central Minnesota, move to the Redwood Agency and the Yellow Medicine Agency reservations in western Minnesota, cease warring with the Ojibwa tribe to their north, and adopt a semisedentary agricultural lifestyle. The Dakota Sioux agreed to these conditions in exchange for annuities, rations, and services to be performed or delivered by the government through the Indian agencies. In 1862 approximately 6,000 Native Americans were located at the Redwood Agency Reservation, the more developed facility, whereas 4,000 were located at the Yellow Medicine Agency Reservation.

Most of the eastern subdivision of the Dakota Sioux lived on or around one of the reservations together with sizable populations of Franco-Dakotas, Anglo-Dakotas, and white government employees and their families. By 1860 only a quarter of the Native Americans had adopted agriculture, leaving many of them dependent on the rations provided by the government as wild game was depleted. The outbreak of the American Civil War (1861–1865) delayed annuity payments and shipments of rations to the Indians, while corrupt traders and agency officials diverted annuity funds to pay individual debts, sold goods distributed under the treaty at high prices in the agency store, and issued rations preferentially to those who had adopted agriculture. These developments contributed to increased debt and privation among the Indians.

A poor harvest in 1861 followed by a harsh winter in 1861–1862 left the Dakota Sioux of all lifestyles destitute by the summer of 1862. Tensions among the Indians, traders, and government

Dakota Sioux perform a traditional Dog Dance, 1868. Painting by Seth Eastman (1808–1875). (Getty Images)

employees came to a head on August 17, 1862, when four Dakota Sioux killed several whites while stealing food and then appealed to the hunters' lodge among the largest band, the Mdewakantons, on the Redwood Agency for support.

With many able-bodied white men serving in the Union Army in the East and posts garrisoned by uneasy and inexperienced militia, the hunters among the Dakota Sioux saw an opportunity to end their forced acculturation to white ways. On August 18, 1862, they won the support of Chief Little Crow of the Mdewakantons and attacked the Redwood Agency, killing two dozen whites. Thereafter the resultant war, known as the Dakota War or the Minnesota Sioux Uprising, became both widespread and racial in nature, spreading far beyond the agency area but failing to involve other tribes of the northern Plains. The most notable engagements occurred at Fort Ridgeley, New Ulm, and Wood Lake, where desperate battles raged and Indians massacred civilians between August 19 and 23, 1862. More than 400 whites were killed in the first days of the war, and another 100 more were slain during the next six weeks. Still hundreds of others were taken prisoner, sharing in the suffering of the Sioux. Indian casualties were also significant.

Hostilities ended on September 26, 1862, when many warriors surrendered. More than 300 Native Americans were convicted of capital offenses; however, after President Abraham Lincoln ordered a review of trial transcripts that uncovered numerous errors, all but 39 capital convictions were overturned. Thirty-eight Indians (1 was granted a reprieve) were hanged en masse at Mankato, Minnesota, on December 26, 1862. The other convicted warriors and survivors were moved to Davenport, Iowa.

Brigadier General Henry H. Sibley led an expedition to pursue approximately 500 Indians who had escaped to the Dakota Territory in June and July 1863. By then the Dakota Sioux were weary of war and retreated deeper into Dakota Territory, Nebraska, and Canada, fighting only rearguard actions and thus ending sustained Sioux resistance. Eventually the Dakota Sioux returned to Minnesota and their reservations. Today the Lower Sioux Indian Reservation has a population of 335.

MARCEL A. DEROSIER

See also

Little Crow; Minnesota Sioux Uprising; Ojibwas; Sibley, Henry Hastings

References

Anderson, Gary Clayton. *Little Crow: Spokesman for the Sioux.* St. Paul: Minnesota Historical Society Press, 1986.

Anderson, Gary Clayton, and Alan R. Woolworth, eds. *Through Dakota Eyes: Narrative Accounts of the Minnesota Indian War of 1862.* St. Paul: Minnesota Historical Society Press, 1988.

Clodfelter, Michael. *The Dakota War: The United States Army versus the Sioux, 1862–1865.* Jefferson, NC: McFarland, 1998.

Deloria, Vine, Jr. *Singing for a Spirit: A Portrait of the Dakota Sioux.* Santa Fe, NM: Clear Light Publishers, 2000.

Davis, Jefferson

Birth Date: ca. June 3, 1808
Death Date: December 6, 1889

U.S. Army officer, politician, secretary of war (1853–1857), and president of the Confederate States of America (1861–1865). Jefferson Davis was born in Christian County, Kentucky, possibly on June 3, 1808, although the exact date and year of his birth are not known for certain. He attended Transylvania University in Lexington, Kentucky. In 1824 he entered the U.S. Military Academy at West Point, graduating in 1828. Commissioned a second lieutenant in the 1st U.S. Infantry Regiment, Davis was assigned to the northwestern frontier. In 1832 he served very briefly in the Black Hawk War, as he had been away in Mississippi for much of that conflict. He subsequently courted and won the hand of Sarah Knox Taylor, daughter of his commanding officer, Colonel Zachary Taylor. As Taylor opposed their marriage, Davis resigned his commission in 1835, married Sarah Taylor, and moved to Brierfield, a plantation on the banks of the Mississippi River north

West Point–trained Jefferson Davis, future president of the Confederate States of America, distinguished himself as the colonel of a volunteer regiment from Mississippi in the Battle of Buena Vista (February 22–23, 1847) during the Mexican-American War and as U.S. secretary of war (1853–1857). (Bettmann/Corbis)

of Natchez, Mississippi, which Davis's older brother Joseph had given him.

Following his wife's death shortly after their marriage, Davis secluded himself for several years before returning to public life. In 1844 he campaigned for James K. Polk in the latter's successful presidential bid, and the following year Davis ran successfully for a seat in the U.S. House of Representatives.

With the beginning of the Mexico-American War (1846–1848), Davis resigned his seat in Congress to accept the colonelcy of the 1st Mississippi Rifle Regiment. He soon found himself under the command of his once-reluctant father-in-law, now a major general. Taylor welcomed Davis into his military family. Upon arriving on the Rio Grande, Davis immediately set about training and organizing his unit. As a former regular officer, he drilled his men diligently and often, and his political connections enabled him to arm them with percussion cap rifles. Although the unit was arguably one of the best-trained volunteer regiments in Taylor's command, many suspected that Davis's special relationship with Taylor affected the major general's decision to include the 1st Mississippi Rifles in his march into northern Mexico as summer drew to a close.

At the Battle of Monterrey (September 21, 1846) Davis performed exceptionally well, staging a daring and successful assault on Fort Teneria. In the Battle of Buena Vista (February 23, 1847) Davis's men again played a pivotal role when they helped blunt a charge by Mexican lancers. But his command sustained high casualties including Davis, who was struck in the ankle by a musket ball. Although badly wounded, he refused to leave the battlefield, remaining mounted the rest of the day. Taylor gave Davis much of the credit for the American victory and offered to secure Davis's appointment as brigadier general. When it came, Davis and his regiment were back in Mississippi. The now-popular war hero, who was recovering from his wound, declined an army career in favor of an appointment to Mississippi's vacant seat in the U.S. Senate in 1847. Davis was elected to a full term the next year.

Davis served in the Senate until September 1851. In 1853 President Franklin Pierce appointed him secretary of war. In that office Davis lent strong support to the army's ongoing modernization program, including adoption of the new Springfield rifled musket. He also agitated for the building of a transcontinental railroad along a southern route. This was a major factor in inciting Native Americans in the Southwest to revolt against white encroachment on their ancestral lands. Davis also expanded the number of western forts to increase the army's ability to protect settlers from Native American attacks. As one of the most influential members of Pierce's cabinet, Davis took a leading role in securing the president's approval for the 1854 Kansas-Nebraska Act, which reopened the sectional turmoil that led to the American Civil War (1861–1865). Upon leaving his post, in 1857 he returned to the U.S. Senate, where he again became a leading voice for the South.

In response to the 1860 elections, seven states in the Deep South, including Mississippi, seceded from the Union. Davis strongly approved, despite his earlier statements against secession, and resigned his U.S. Senate seat. In February 1861 the Montgomery Convention named Davis president of the Confederate States of America. Davis performed fairly well as president, although critics claimed that his prior military experience caused him to interfere in army operations instead of leaving decisions to his generals. Even his supporters admitted that he made some very poor strategic and personnel decisions that hastened the South's defeat. At the war's end in 1865 Davis fled Richmond, but Union cavalry apprehended him in Georgia. He was imprisoned for two years.

Following his release, Davis served as president of an insurance company. In 1877 he moved to the Beauvoir estate near Biloxi, Mississippi, as a guest of its owner. He inherited it in 1879. There he wrote his two-volume memoir *The Rise and Fall of the Confederate Government.* Davis died in New Orleans on December 6, 1889.

Ethan Rafuse

See also
Black Hawk War; Railroads

References
Cooper, William J., Jr. *Jefferson Davis, American.* New York: Knopf, 2000.
Davis, William C. *Jefferson Davis: The Man and His Hour.* New York: HarperCollins, 1991.
Monroe, Haskell M., James T. McIntosh, Lynda Lasswell Crist, and Mary Seaton Dix, eds. *The Papers of Jefferson Davis.* 12 vols. Baton Rouge: Louisiana State University Press, 1974–2008.

Dawes Severalty Act

Legislation passed by the U.S. Congress on February 8, 1887, sometimes known simply as the Dawes Act, designed to redistribute land to Native Americans. The Dawes Severalty Act was named for its chief sponsor and author, Senator Henry L. Dawes, a Republican from Massachusetts. Congress amended the act in 1891 and again in 1906 via the Burke Act. The Dawes Act remained the law until 1934, when it was repealed.

The Dawes Act allowed the president of the United States, with tribal approval, to subdivide Indian reservations into individual homesteads consisting of 160-acre plots. The federal government would hold the deeds for these lands in trust for 25 years. Most of the lands were located in Oklahoma. Reservation land in excess of that allocated to Native American individuals would be sold by the U.S. government to white settlers.

By the mid-1880s, eastern reformers influenced by Christian humanitarianism and the disturbing account of federal Indian policy depicted in Helen Hunt Jackson's *Century of Dishonor* (1881) began to advocate individual land allotment as a practical policy to provide Native Americans with an economically self-sufficient lifestyle. Reformers tended to see Native American adherence to hunting, which pulled them off the reservation and put them in direct conflict with white settlers and the U.S. Army, as the main reason for violence.

The rapid extermination of the buffalo in the 1870s forced the Native Americans to stray even farther from the reservations while, at the same time, making them more dependent upon federal assistance for basic sustenance. By encouraging an agrarian-based and settled lifestyle, reformers hoped to eliminate both dependence and violence. In 1884 an allotment plan was applied to the Omaha Reservation. Senator Henry Dawes used the Omaha example as a model for the bill that would ultimately bear his name.

Almost immediately, rampant corruption among the federal Indian agents and the white settlers' ever-increasing demand for land dashed the high hopes of the reformers. An 1891 amendment allowed Native Americans to lease their lands to white settlers if they chose. Many Native Americans chose this option and either became wage earners on other people's lands or simply adhered to the nomadic camp lifestyle that was so familiar to them. As reservations were opened for allotment between 1891 and 1900, one of the key factors determining which reservation to allot was white interest in the land. In the Great Plains, where land was highly prized, all of the reservations were allotted under the terms of the Dawes Act. In the Southwest, however, where there was little white demand for land, none of the reservations were opened per the Dawes Act.

The Dawes Act had a profoundly negative impact on Native Americans. In breaking up the reservations and placing the Native Americans on inadequate agricultural lands, the Dawes Act only plunged Native Americans into greater poverty. Indeed, evidence suggests that fewer Native Americans farmed the land after the Dawes Act than before it. Under the excuse that the Native Americans could feed themselves, the federal government provided little assistance. The loss of common areas meant that hunting and grazing of livestock were not options for Native Americans. Not surprisingly, the legislation interfered with tribal self-governance and seriously disrupted Native American cultural observances.

Between 1903 and 1907 a series of laws removed many protections that existed for the Native Americans under the Dawes Act, such as eliminating the 25-year trustee period, which was partly accomplished by the 1906 Burke Act. By 1934 it had become evident that the Dawes Plan had failed. Of the 136.3 million acres under Native American control when Congress passed the Dawes Act in 1887, only 34.2 million remained in their hands in 1934. The act clearly benefited white settlers more than the Native Americans. In 1934 the Dawes Act was repealed as part of the Indian Reorganization Act.

Gregory J. Dehler

See also
Grant's Peace Policy; Indian Reorganization Act; Indian Territory; Reservations

References
Carlson, Leonard A. *Indians, Bureaucrats and Land: The Dawes Act and the Decline of Indian Farming.* Westport, CT: Greenwood, 1981.

Fowler, Loretta. *The Columbia Guide to American Indians of the Great Plains.* New York: Columbia University Press, 2003.

McDonnell, Janet L. *The Dispossession of the American Indian, 1887–1934.* Bloomington: Indiana University Press, 1991.

Decanisora
Birth Date: Unknown
Death Date: 1720s

Onondaga diplomat and orator. Decanisora, known as Teganissorens to the French, represented the Iroquois Confederacy in negotiations with New France and New York in the late 17th and early 18th centuries. His precise birth and death dates are unknown. In a time of declining Iroquois strength, he used diplomacy to divide New France from its Native American allies and to balance the French and English against each other. The first recorded mention of Decanisora was in 1682. In that year he offered assurances of peace to the French in Montreal, hoping to immobilize them, while Iroquois war parties attacked the Illinois and the Miamis, who were allies of the French.

By 1693 the Iroquois had suffered heavy losses in the Beaver Wars (1641–1701) as well as in King William's War (1689–1697). The Iroquois thus began sounding out the French for peace. In 1694 Decanisora approached the English and voiced frustration with English efforts to prevent negotiations with the French; the English were unable to prevent French attacks, much less oust the French from Canada as promised. He informed the English that the Iroquois would be compelled to seek unilateral peace unless additional military supplies were forthcoming. The English immediately complied. Now in a stronger position, Decanisora insisted to the French that peace talks must include the English and that the negotiations must be held in Albany, New York. He knew, however, that neither the French nor the English were prepared to negotiate with each other. Meanwhile, other Iroquois delegations informed the western tribes that the French were abandoning them and negotiating a separate peace with the Iroquois, which soon resulted in a separate peace between the Iroquois and the western tribes.

War between the Iroquois and the French soon resumed, but now the Iroquois were better supplied, and the French were shorn of allies. It is not clear, however, to what extent this outcome was planned and to what extent it was the result of ongoing politics between pro-English and pro-French factions in the Iroquois Council.

In 1697 the French and English concluded peace. This transformed the geopolitical situation for the Iroquois, but the New York authorities apparently neglected to inform them of such. The Iroquois learned of the treaty from the governor of New France late in 1699. Decanisora expressed particular irritation because the English continued to press the Iroquois to fight. At the same time, the Iroquois were once again under attack from French-allied tribes to the west. Rumors spread among the Iroquois that the two European powers were conspiring to attack them.

At this point the Iroquois shifted to a true neutralist position while still attempting to balance the French and English against one other. In 1701 Decanisora led a delegation that agreed to a peace treaty with New France and, at French insistence, with its Native American allies. One provision in the treaty called on the Iroquois to remain neutral during any future Anglo-French conflict. The Iroquois also renewed their alliance, the so-called Covenant Chain, with the English, but held the English at arm's length, denying them permission to build a fort on Onondaga territory for another quarter century. The Iroquois maintained their neutrality in Anglo-French wars for the next half century.

Decanisora was courted by both English and French governors, who recognized him as being highly influential within the Iroquois Confederacy. In 1721 the Onondaga Council replaced him as chief orator, possibly because of his memory loss. His wife, a Christian Mohawk accused of witchcraft, was murdered in 1700 by an Onondaga, possibly a member of a rival faction. Details of Decanisora's death are unknown.

Scott C. Monje

See also
Beaver Wars; Covenant Chain; Iroquois; Iroquois Confederacy; Iroquois Treaties of 1700 and 1701; King William's War

References
Eccles, W. J. "Teganissorens (Decanesora)." In *Dictionary of Canadian Biography,* Vol. 2, 619–623. Toronto: University of Toronto Press, 1969.

Fenton, William N. *The Great Law and the Longhouse: A Political History of the Iroquois Confederacy.* Norman: University of Oklahoma Press, 1998.

Jennings, Francis. *The Ambiguous Iroquois Empire: The Covenant Chain Confederation of Indian Tribes with English Colonies from Its Beginnings to the Lancaster Treaty of 1744.* New York: Norton, 1984.

Deerfield, Massachusetts, Attack on
Event Date: February 29, 1704

Raid on and near destruction of the English settlement of Deerfield, Massachusetts, on February 29, 1704, by a combined force of Native Americans and French, resulting in the deaths of 41 English colonists and the capture of 112 more. As the northwesternmost town in Massachusetts, Deerfield had been a frequent target of Native American assaults during King Philip's War (1675–1676) and King William's War (1689–1697). To the English, Deerfield was merely a small exposed settlement in the middle Connecticut River Valley. However, to various Native American groups, the town symbolized English intrusion onto their lands as well as a source for potential captives for ransom or adoption.

With the outbreak of Queen Anne's War (1702–1713), the town was once again at direct risk for assault. In May 1703 New York's

Native Americans transport colonists captured during the Deerfield Massacre on February 29, 1704. The raid, led by combined French and indigenous forces, nearly destroyed the English settlement and brought the deaths of 41 English colonists and the capture of 112 others. (Library of Congress)

governor received word of a French and Native American raiding party gathering at Fort Chambly and intent on attacking Deerfield. Similar warnings would come four more times during 1703 and into early 1704. In October 1703 two Deerfield men were captured while working in the nearby fields. In response to this raid and repeated alarms, Deerfield's inhabitants temporarily crowded into the stockade that surrounded several houses in the center of the town. Massachusetts also sent 20 militiamen from neighboring towns to stiffen the town's defenses. But because nothing else happened, the people of Deerfield began to let down their guard.

A raiding party was indeed aiming at Deerfield, however. In the winter of 1703–1704 French lieutenant Jean Baptise Hertel de Rouville led a force composed of 48 French and Canadians and between 200 and 250 Pennacooks, Abenakis, Hurons, Kahnawake Mohawks, and Iroquois of the Mountain toward Deerfield.

Just before daybreak on February 29, 1704, de Rouville's forces struck. Some of the raiders climbed a snowdrift that had accumulated at the base of the stockade and opened the north gate. The remainder of the attackers then streamed in. The various Native American parties spread throughout the town, bent on acquiring captives for ransom and adoption. Many families in the northern part of town were surprised and quickly captured, but the

uncoordinated nature of the attack allowed some English settlers to mount a defense or to hide. The settlers in Benoni Stebbins's house managed to hold out for more than two hours. Alerted by sounds of the fight and a few Deerfielders who managed to flee, militiamen from nearby Northampton, Hadley, and Hatfield came to Deerfield's relief. This makeshift force managed to drive de Rouville's raiders from the village. However, as the English militiamen chased the French and Native Americans through the town's North Field, they fell into an ambush and were forced back after losing nine men.

Although de Rouville's expedition suffered 10 dead (3 French and 7 Native Americans) and 22 French and an unknown number of Native Americans wounded, his force had devastated Deerfield. The town was left in shambles, with 17 houses and barns completely destroyed. Human losses were even greater. Forty-one inhabitants died in Deerfield, uncounted others were wounded, and 112 were carried off as captives, including the town's minister, John Williams. Two young men escaped soon after, but 21 captives did not survive the march to French and Native American communities to the north. At least 62 Deerfield captives eventually returned to New England, many of them resettling in their former Deerfield hometown. However, others chose to remain among their captors. Eight young girls, including Eunice Williams, daughter of the town's minister, married natives and remained among the Kahnawake Mohawks or the Iroquois of the Mountain (although 1 of the girls subsequently returned to New England). Ten women and 6 men married French colonists, while 2 captives married each other, and all were integrated into Canadian society.

The Deerfield raid was a great success for the French. By spreading fear among the English and putting them on the defensive, de Rouville had helped protect France's underpopulated colonies.

DAVID M. CORLETT

See also
Abenakis; Captivity of Europeans by Indians; Iroquois; King Philip's War; King William's War; Mohawks; Pennacooks; Queen Anne's War; Wyandots

References
Demos, John. *The Unredeemed Captive: A Family Story from Early America.* New York: Knopf, 1994.

Haefeli, Evan, and Kevin Sweeney. *Captors and Captives: The 1704 French and Indian Raid on Deerfield.* Amherst: University of Massachusetts Press, 2003.

Williams, John. *The Redeemed Captive, Returning to Zion.* Boston: B. Green, 1797.

Degataga
See Watie, Stand

Delaware Prophet
See Neolin

Delawares

Native American group of the Algonquian linguistic family located, at the time of first European contact, in present-day Delaware, New Jersey, southeastern New York, and southeastern Pennsylvania. The Delawares (Lenni Lenapes) were one of the most influential groups of native peoples during the colonial period. Their history is inextricably tied with that of British and French colonization in North America. Lenni Lenape, which translates as "original people," is the term that the Delawares used to describe themselves. In recognition of this claim, other Algonquian peoples of the Northeast often referred to the Lenni Lenapes as "grandfathers." The English christened them "Delawares," as they lived mainly along the Delaware River.

From the early 17th century to the beginning of the American Revolutionary War (1775–1783), the Delawares engaged in trade, diplomacy, and warfare with the Swedes, Dutch, British, French,

and finally the nascent American nation. By the 1680s, however, the Delawares had entered into a lengthy peace with the English colony of Pennsylvania. Unfortunately, the long peace with the Quaker colony gave way in the 18th century to events that would see the Delawares much reduced in numbers, influence, and territory.

Myth holds that the Delawares migrated across an ocean to the west, crossed the continent, and settled on the eastern seaboard. The story of the migration of the Delawares has been recorded in a pictographic account, of debatable authenticity, known as the *Wallum Ollum.* In any case, the Delawares soon settled into a seasonal round of life in which they planted maize, beans, and squash in the spring; fished and clammed along the coast in the summer; and hunted in the autumn.

The Delawares had their first recorded contact with Europeans in 1609. In that year, according to a native story recorded by Moravian missionary John Heckewelder in the early 19th century, they encountered the explorer Henry Hudson. Uncertain if Hudson's ship was an island or a large canoe, reportedly a few Delawares in a canoe approached cautiously. Hudson welcomed them aboard and showered them with gifts. During a subsequent visit from the Dutch, the Delawares learned more about the character of Europeans. Amused that the natives used ax heads as pendants and stockings as tobacco pouches, the Dutch demonstrated the proper use of these items. When the Dutch asked for a piece of land that could be enclosed by an ox hide, the Delawares agreed and then watched in dismay as the hide was cut into a single long, continuous strip that encircled a much larger area than the intact pelt. The Delawares now knew that they would have to exercise caution in their dealings with the newcomers.

The Delawares probably had contacts with the Swedish colony in what is now southern Pennsylvania and New Jersey. As the Swedes had difficulty telling one group of native peoples from another, it is impossible to verify this with certainty.

The most notable contacts between the Delawares and the Europeans began with the founding of Pennsylvania in the 1680s. Although William Penn, like other Englishmen, did not view natives as equals, he did believe that they should be dealt with fairly. Penn duly purchased lands from the Delawares and maintained peaceful relations with them. Indeed, Penn's dealings with the Delawares were so amicable that other Native Americans moved from other English colonies to Pennsylvania.

The era of peaceful dealings with Pennsylvania came to an end, however, when Penn's heirs assumed control of the colony in the early 18th century. Relations became strained as the colony expanded and then came to a head with the fraudulent land deal known as the Walking Purchase (1737). In short, Penn's heirs produced a document that they claimed Penn and the Delawares had signed years earlier. The questionable agreement had purportedly granted a tract of land to the colony equivalent to what a man could traverse in a day and a half. The colony fixed the walk so as to acquire considerably more land, and the Delawares protested and refused to move. Realizing that they could not force the

Engraving of a Delaware Indian man, woman, and child living in New Sweden and holding axes and bow and arrows. (Getty Images)

Delawares out of the colony on their own, Pennsylvania called on the Iroquois Confederacy to evict them.

Some Delawares indeed complied with the order of the Onondaga spokesman Cannestego that they relocate to western Pennsylvania. A few, however, remained in the eastern part of the colony and New Jersey. But the majority went west, beyond the Allegheny and Monongahela rivers and into the Ohio Country, far beyond the effective reach of the Iroquois and beyond easy reach of British traders.

In the 1740s British traders began to establish trading relations and posts in the Ohio Country, allowing the Delawares to trade with them and obtain superior-quality British goods. The French, who also claimed the Ohio Country, evicted the British traders. By pressing their claims, the Delawares helped precipitate the French and Indian War (1754–1763). The French promised the Delawares that they could regain their old lands. Convinced that the French would win the war, western Delawares joined them and launched attacks on British settlements in western Pennsylvania and Virginia. Delaware warriors also participated in the 1755 Battle of the Monongahela that resulted in the defeat of a sizable British force under Major General Edward Braddock, who was attempting to take Fort Duquesne from the French. As the war went on, however, the French had difficulty supplying their native allies with weapons and trade goods. Thus, the Delawares and other natives sat out the later stages of the conflict.

Among the Delawares in the Ohio Country, a prophet named Neolin came to prominence when he began preaching a movement that called for the Delawares and other natives to forsake items of European manufacture and to return to the ways of their ancestors. It was too late for natives to do this, as they were by then too dependent on European goods. Nevertheless, Neolin's message was co-opted by the Ottawa-Annisgheg chief Pontiac, who fomented a rebellion against the British in 1763.

The Delawares remained split after Pontiac's Rebellion (1763). With the beginning of the American Revolutionary War, many Delawares sided with the British. However, a few sided with the Americans, becoming the first group of natives to sign a treaty of alliance with the fledgling new nation in 1778.

As white encroachment proceeded apace, some Delawares moved west into Missouri and Texas, where they adopted a Plains lifestyle based upon buffalo. Among the defeated tribes at the 1794 Battle of Fallen Timbers, still other Delawares also moved west, into Indiana and Kansas. There they warred with the Pawnees. During the 1860s this Delaware band was relocated to Indian Territory (Oklahoma). By this time the Delawares were scattered about Canada and the United States, from Massachusetts to Kansas.

ROGER M. CARPENTER

See also
Algonquins; Braddock's Campaign; Fallen Timbers, Battle of; French and Indian War; Iroquois Confederacy; Neolin; Pawnees; Pontiac; Pontiac's Rebellion; Walking Purchase

References
Kraft, Herbert C. *The Lenape: Archaeology, History, and Ethnography.* Newark: New Jersey Historical Society, 1986.

Richter, Daniel K., and James H. Merrell, eds. *Beyond the Covenant Chain: The Iroquois and Their Neighbors in Indian North America, 1600–1800.* Syracuse, NY: Syracuse University Press, 1987.

Weslager, C. A. *The Delaware Indians: A History.* New Brunswick, NJ: Rutgers University Press, 1972.

Delgadito
Birth Date: ca. 1830
Death Date: 1870

Navajo political and religious leader. Born near Nazlini (Arizona) around 1830, Delgadito was among the first renowned Navajo silversmiths, emerging as a tribal leader in the Canyon de Chelly region of present-day Arizona. After initially adopting an accommodating position toward white encroachment, by the early 1860s Delgadito, his brother Barboncito, and the formidable Manuelito, among others, grew increasingly defiant. Still, Delgadito joined other Navajo leaders in an 1861 meeting with U.S. Army colonel E. R. S. Candy, during which the Native Americans vowed to promote peaceful relations.

In 1862 with the American Civil War (1861–1865) raging in the East, Brigadier General James Carleton assumed command of the

New Mexico Territory and soon moved against the tribes, essentially demanding in meetings with Delgadito and others that all peaceful Navajos be relocated to a reservation on the Pecos River in eastern New Mexico or face military action. The Navajos, even those notoriously inclined toward peace, resisted, and in 1863 Carleton delivered on his promise, unleashing hundreds of troops under Colonel Christopher "Kit" Carson in a scorched-earth campaign against the Navajos. Delgadito, hoping to broker peace and avoid the devastation that loomed, agreed to lead some 500 of his people away from their beloved homeland, thus becoming the first important Navajo to take up residence at the wretched Bosque Redondo reservation.

Although the journey to Bosque Redondo proved perilous (many Navajos died en route) and the stay there even more so, Delgadito managed to endure long enough to sign the 1868 treaty that allowed his people to return to their now significantly downsized homeland. He died near Chinle (Arizona) in 1870.

DAVID COFFEY

See also

Barboncito; Bosque Redondo; Canby, Edward Richard Sprigg; Canyon de Chelly, Arizona; Carleton, James Henry; Carson, Christopher Houston; Manuelito; Navajo Removal; Navajos; Navajo War

References

Brown, Dee. *Bury My Heart at Wounded Knee.* New York: Holt, Rinehart and Winston, 1970.

Dunlay, Thomas W. *Kit Carson and the Indians.* Lincoln: University of Nebraska Press, 2000.

Iverson, Peter. *Diné: A History of the Navajos.* Albuquerque: University of New Mexico Press, 2002.

Demographics, Historical

Historical demography entails the study of fertility and mortality patterns along with changes in historic populations. Several themes dominate the discussion of Native American historical demography. These include the demographic collapse of many populations over several centuries following 1492, the establishment of sustained contact between the Old World and the New World, and the survival and recovery of some Native American populations. A number of factors contributed to demographic collapse, including war, slavery, and the introduction of highly contagious diseases such as smallpox and measles to which the Native Americans had no immunity.

Smallpox created such chaos in the Inca Empire that Francisco Pizarro was able to seize an empire as large and populous as Spain and Italy combined with a force of only 168 men. According to demographer Henry Dobyns, by the time imported diseases were done with Native Americans, 95 percent of them had died. This was the worst demographic collapse in recorded human history.

Dobyns has estimated that the population of Mexico declined from between 30 million and 37.5 million people in 1520 to 1.5 million in 1650, a holocaust of a severity unknown in the Old World. Even if the argument is made that Dobyns's figures are too high, cutting them almost in half, to 20 million in 1520, would still produce a mortality rate in 130 years of 92.5 percent.

A second theme in Native American historical demography is cultural and biological mixing. This is called *mestizaje* in Spanish and *mestissage* in French and entailed not only biological mixing with peoples from Europe and Africa but also sociocultural mixing.

Today a general consensus exists that the Americas sustained large populations when Europeans first established continuous contact after 1492 and that the native populations experienced drastic declines in numbers after 1492. Instead of engaging in a numbers game, trying to make educated guesstimates of contact population sizes, this entry explores the dynamics of population decline. There is one fundamental assumption made in the model of virgin soil epidemics that native populations in the Americas were more susceptible to epidemics of highly contagious crowd diseases such as smallpox introduced after 1492. This may be an overly simplistic assumption that does not take into consideration other factors related to mortality during epidemics and patterns of morbidity and mortality. An examination of contemporary European demographic patterns calls into question the assumption of high susceptibility and the buildup of immunities to disease. A host of maladies routinely killed as many as 10–20 percent of children in Europe, and the individuals lucky enough to survive built up some immunity from their exposure as well as from antibodies acquired from their mothers. However, surviving childhood disease did not mean that adults could not become ill from the same diseases a second time.

Until the acceptance by doctors of the germ theory in the late 19th century, there were few effective treatments for the maladies introduced into the New World from the Old World. Medical knowledge had a basis in the ancient Greek humoral theory, which posited that disease was caused by an imbalance in the four basic elements: earth, air, water, and fire. According to the humoral theory, a fever is caused by an excess of fire, and the proper treatment is to reduce the fire. This gave rise to bloodletting as a common treatment, which, of course, only weakened the patient by depleting the immunological system. The other prevailing theory for the cause of disease was miasma, which held that clouds of noxious gas floating in the air caused disease. The gas originated from rotting vegetation, rotting corpses, and garbage, among other things. Practical responses to the belief in miasma included the clearing of garbage and the drainage of standing water, which could be beneficial. Garbage, for example, attracted rats that could carry fleas. Mosquitoes breed in standing water and carry a variety of diseases, including yellow fever and malaria. Doctors also made use of what most accurately could be called folk remedies. A 1797 document distributed throughout Spanish California suggested, among other things, cleaning the eyes of smallpox victims with water made from rose petals. This treatment first appeared in a 15th-century Spanish medical text.

American Indian Demographic Change by Region

Region	Notable Tribes	Date of Initial Estimate	Number of Tribes at Initial Estimate	Number of Tribes in 1907	Population at Initial Estimate	Population in 1907
Northern Atlantic Region	Abenakis, Iroquois, Delawares	1600	24	10	55,600	21,900
Southern Atlantic Region	Cherokees, Powhatans, Tuscaroras	1600	35	15	52,200	2,170
Gulf Coast Region	Creeks, Miamis, Seminoles	1650	39	12	114,400	62,700
Central Region	Illinois, Shawnees, Yuchis	1650	12	10	75,300	46,130
Southwest Region	Kiowas, Navajos, Pueblos	1680	25	19	72,000	53,830
Southern Plains Region	Apaches, Comanches, Kickapoos	1690	12	7	41,000	2,860
California Region	Chumash, Miwoks, Shastas	1780	45	36	260,000	18,800
Northern Plains Region	Dakota Sioux, Missouris, Sauks	1780	20	19	100,800	50,480
Northwest Region	Chinooks, Modocs, Suquamish	1780	95	83	88,800	15,430
Central Mountains Region	Arapahos, Cheyennes, Sashonis	1845	6	6	19,300	11,540

Smallpox was one of the great killers of Native Americans, and two treatments reached the Americas in the 18th century. The first was called inoculation by variation and entailed injecting a healthy person with pus from a ripe pustule from a smallpox victim. The expectation was that the individual inoculated would develop a milder infection, and evidence from the period suggests that mortality rates were lower among those inoculated when compared to people naturally infected. At the same time, there was considerable resistance to the use of inoculation when introduced in the 18th century, primarily because of the fear that inoculation would help spread the contagion. Doctors in Mexico first used inoculation by variation during a smallpox outbreak in Mexico City in 1779, and Dominican missionaries successfully inoculated native residents of several missions in Baja California in 1781.

The second smallpox prophylaxis introduced in the 18th century was the cowpox vaccine, first described in the late 1790s by English doctor Edward Jenner. Jenner was a country doctor, and he noted that milkmaids did not contract smallpox, which was still a problem in England. Milkmaids inhaled dry cowpox pustules and became infected with cowpox, which is related to smallpox but is not fatal to humans. The milkmaids developed antibodies that protected them from smallpox. In 1803 the Spanish government sent a medical team to the Americas to disseminate the cowpox vaccine. The team transported the vaccine on the arms of infected children and maintained the chain of infection from child to child.

Extensive trade networks existed in the Americas prior to the arrival of Europeans, and diseases may have been conducted along them. For example, archaeologists have encountered evidence of trade, including copper bells produced in central Mexico and bird plumes in sites in northern Mexico such as Casas Grandes in Chihuahua and in the native communities of New Mexico. Conversely, turquoise from New Mexico has been discovered in pre-Hispanic sites in central Mexico.

When Europeans arrived in different parts of North America and came into contact with native populations, disease spread to the natives as a result of these contacts. Contagion, carried in the bodies of traders or other travelers, spread from one native community to another. Early accounts of European exploration and colonization report the spread of epidemics in advance of Europeans.

The assumption cannot be made that disease spread uniformly among native populations or that rates of morbidity and mortality were uniform from population to population. A number of factors limited the rates of morbidity and mortality. Maladies such as smallpox and measles spread through contact between people sneezing or in other ways of exchanging body fluids. Contagion spreads in dense populations but not as easily among dispersed populations, particularly among small bands of hunter-gatherers that migrated in search of food within a clearly defined but often extensive territory. In the 16th and early 17th centuries, for example, Spaniards explored and conquered the populations living in western Mexico in Sinaloa and Sonora and up into what today is the southwestern United States, including Arizona and New Mexico. The first Spanish descriptions of the region described sophisticated tribal states based on compact nucleated communities. In some areas such as northern Sonora and southern Arizona, this settlement pattern gave way to a more dispersed *rancheria* settlement pattern characterized by homesteads dispersed over a large area, usually in a river floodplain. Scholars speculate that the more dispersed settlement pattern was an adaptation resulting from the spread of lethal epidemics in the 16th and 17th centuries.

Several other factors influenced the impact of epidemics on native populations. The frequency of epidemics is important, and it is possible to construct tentative epidemic chronologies in some regions of European settlement. For an epidemic to spread among and between populations, there must be enough susceptible individuals not previously exposed to the contagion to maintain the chain of infection. Moreover, pathogens such as smallpox are inefficient in the sense that either they kill the host or the host survives. The pathogen then dies out, and the epidemic ends until the next outbreak, which will occur when once again there are enough susceptible hosts to maintain the chain of infection. Generally a given pathogen finds enough susceptible hosts about once a generation, after a population has recovered and grown following the previous epidemics. However, if a series of epidemics spread through a population with a greater frequency, the possibility of recovery following the outbreak is diminished.

Useful parallels can be drawn between demographic trends among the native populations in the Americas and contemporary European populations. Two aspects of demographic patterns in Europe are relevant to a discussion of Native American population trends. The first is the culling of the population by lethal epidemics, such as the Black Death in the 14th century that killed perhaps a third of Europe's population, and its subsequent outbreaks. The epidemics slowed or temporarily stopped population growth, but after the epidemic episodes the population recovered. Early modern Europe was a patriarchal society, and the father generally controlled the lives of his children until such time as he decided to let them marry. Moreover, in rural communities, a son generally could not start a family until he had his own land and could establish economic independence. Mortality crises (mortality at three times the normal rate) often caused a redistribution of wealth and enabled sons to marry at a younger age. European populations rebounded or recovered following epidemics as a result of increased birthrates. Discussions of epidemics in the Americas in the 16th and 17th centuries focus on reports of horrific mortality, but rarely do they examine whether the native populations rebounded or recovered following the epidemics.

The second parallel consists of patterns of mortality in nonepidemic years in European populations when maladies such as smallpox and measles became established as endemic maladies that killed as many as 10–20 percent of the children every year. Contagion spread and reached epidemic proportions when a large pool of susceptible people had been born since the previous epidemic outbreak. To understand the recovery of larger native populations, it is necessary to document the patterns of mortality among native populations in nonepidemic years, when maladies such as smallpox became chronic childhood diseases. Furthermore, it is essential to examine birthrates and the age and gender structure of a population to show whether sufficient numbers of women of childbearing age survived epidemics to reproduce.

At the same time, other factors also contributed to native population losses, although all causes for depopulation were interrelated and should not be discussed in isolation. These include war; famine resulting from food shortages and crop losses due to drought, excessive rainfall, frost, locust infestation, and other causes; enslavement; and migration. People died in war, but in the early modern period more casualties resulted from the spread of disease and famine than from actual battlefield losses. Armies on campaign in contemporary Europe lived in filthy conditions and bred disease. The armies then spread disease when they moved from place to place. The same occurred in the Americas. Moreover, armies lived off the land and took food supplies that civilian populations needed to survive. Additionally, armies deliberately destroyed crops to weaken the enemy. This occurred, for example, during the Sullivan-Clinton Campaign against the Iroquois during the American Revolutionary War (1775–1783). In the summer of 1779, Continental Army troops under Major General John Sullivan and Brigadier General James Clinton attacked Native Americans who had sided with the British in the war. The troops systematically destroyed growing crops, and many Iroquois died from starvation during the ensuing winter.

Famine also contributed to mortality, and epidemics frequently occurred in conjunction with it. Some scholars believe that food shortages led to the weakening of the immunological system, which then resulted in epidemic outbreaks. However, recent studies have suggested that the relationship between famine and epidemics can be traced to the movement of large numbers of people in search of food who spread disease as they moved from place to place. Studies of historical famines have identified one common phenomenon: the movement of people from the countryside into towns and cities and the discovery of abandoned bodies of famine and disease victims. Priests recorded in burial registers the discovery of the dead on the steps of churches or near cemeteries.

Migration, forced or voluntary, contributed to mortality and population losses as well. The Trail of Tears (the forced relocation of thousands of Cherokees in the late 1830s) is a good example of how migration contributed to population losses. Causes for mortality during the forced relocation to Indian Territory (Oklahoma) included accidents, food shortages, and the less than ideal hygienic conditions on the trail. But again the movement of peoples also contributed to the spread of epidemics. The enslavement of Native American peoples was common and also contributed to population losses. Slavery removed adults from the population, and the enslavement of women of childbearing age had the greatest consequence. Moreover, the forced movement of people also contributed to the spread of disease.

Did the native populations acquire immunities to smallpox and the other maladies brought to the Americas after 1492? No convincing evidence exists to support this assumption. New insights on this subject come from recent research on historic epidemics in Spanish America that are documented in detail in burial registers and censuses that recorded the number of deaths or in some instances the actual numbers of victims of contagion during an outbreak. Burial registers exist for Spanish Americans from the 17th century, but records are more complete for the 18th century, some two centuries after the Spanish arrived in the Americas. As suggested, the frequency of epidemic outbreaks and the initial size of a population are critical factors in determining epidemic mortality and the short- and long-term consequences of epidemics.

Biological mixing and sociocultural passing, known as miscegenation, also contributed to demographic change following the arrival in the Americas of peoples from the Old World. Recent studies of *mestizaje* and the creation of race and caste categories in Spanish America provide insights that can also be applied to other parts of the Americas. One recent study compared the race and caste categories on the colonial north Mexican frontier with those in a rural zone in Bolivia dominated by haciendas and corporate indigenous communities. The Spanish caste system created categories that ostensibly delineated degrees of mixture based on the documentation of bloodlines and skin color but also on the application of sociocultural and economic criteria that shifted over time. Under the caste system, the Spanish collapsed all Native American ethnic groups into a single fiscal category of "Indian," based on an obligation to pay tribute and provide labor services.

The stereotypical sociocultural and economic criteria used to define Indian status shifted over time and were idiosyncratic. In the Cochabamba region of Bolivia, for example, the Spanish government and later the Bolivian government categorized Indians as residents of corporate native communities legally recognized by the Crown. At the same time, residents of those communities could move to the Spanish towns, adopt a European style of dress, learn a little Spanish, and pass as people categorized as being of mixed European and native ancestry. They also passed from the ranks of tribute payers.

During the 19th century following Bolivian independence, the economy of the Cochabamba region shifted, and in the 1870s the government passed legislation that abolished the corporate native communities and attempted to force the community residents to take private title to their lands. There was also a growth in the number of smallholders identified by government officials as not being natives, since the definition of Indian status was linked to residence in corporate native communities with communal land tenure. As this sociocultural and economic shift occurred, the population defined as being Indian came to be people of mixed ancestry. This change did not include a distinction based on language, because even today Quechua is still the dominant language spoken in the countryside.

A similar creation of a caste system did not occur on the northern Mexican frontier, primarily because rigid distinctions between native and nonnative peoples were not as important. Sacramental registers and censuses did not record or did not consistently record race and caste terms. At the same time the Spanish engaged in the practice of creating new "ethnicities" in an attempt to make order out of the many native polities and communities that existed in northern Mexico and in what today is the American Southwest. One example is the creation of the ethnic group "Apaches" to identify different bands of Native American peoples spread across Arizona, New Mexico, Texas, and neighboring regions. A second example is the creation of an ethnic group called "Nijoras," natives who in reality were slaves brought into Sonora by the Spaniards from the Colorado River area ostensibly as war captives who had been ransomed.

Many native communities, bands, and polities disappeared in the centuries following the arrival of the Europeans, whereas other groups survived, recovered, and experienced population growth after about 1900. A variety of factors help explain survival and later population growth. Two key factors were improvement in health care and the development of medicines to combat disease in the late 19th century and the 20th century, including the mass inoculation of nonnative populations in the Americas that brought pathogens such as smallpox under control. The control of smallpox in the cities in the Americas meant that there were fewer epidemic outbreaks that could spread to the native populations. Moreover, in the United States and Canada the creation of reservations managed—and mismanaged—by bureaucracies such as the Bureau of Indian Affairs led to public health measures for native populations. At the same time, the relocation of native groups to reservations with the sociocultural changes that the bureaucrats attempted to impose created new problems, such as sociocultural disintegration, poverty and marginalization, alcoholism and fetal alcohol syndrome, and high rates of suicide.

Some Native American groups survived by incorporating new members to replace those killed in recurring epidemics. This was the practice among the Iroquois, for example. The Iroquois engaged in wars with neighboring groups and incorporated captives into their communities. The introduction of the horse revolutionized the society and culture of Native American peoples who previously had lived on the fringes of the Great Plains. The horse made it possible to live full-time on the Great Plains and follow the huge buffalo herds; living in a more dispersed and shifting settlement pattern buffered somewhat the spread of epidemics. Larger native populations suffered declines resulting from disease and the other factors already discussed, but the degree of decline did not reach a threshold at which the drop in the number of women of childbearing age precluded recovery.

In the 20th century native populations grew in the Americas, as did the number of those who desired to be considered natives. As occurred in the United States in 1970 and 1980, changes in the definitions of census categories could greatly expand the number of people categorized as "American Indian." The 1990 census reported that 1.8 million people classified themselves as Native American, more than three times as many as the 523,600 reported 30 years earlier. The 1890 U.S. census had reported 228,000 American Indians. The trend continued in the 2000 census, in which more than 4.1 million people said they were at least partially Native American, an increase of more than 100 percent in 10 years and 13 times the official figure of about 300,000 a century earlier. Part of the increase was due to an excess of births over deaths among Native Americans. The census figures must be qualified, however, because they rely on self-identification.

ROBERT H. JACKSON

See also
Apaches; Iroquois; Medicine, Military; Medicine, Native American

References
Cook, Nobel David. *Born to Die: Disease and New World Conquest, 1492–1650.* Cambridge: Cambridge University Press, 1998.
Cook, Sherburne, and Woodrow Borah. *Essays in Population History.* 3 vols. Berkeley: University of California Press, 1971–1979.
Denevan, William. *The Native Population of the Americas in 1492.* Madison: University of Wisconsin Press, 1976.
Dobyns, Henry. *Their Numbers Become Thinned: Native American Population Dynamics in Eastern North America.* Knoxville: University of Tennessee Press, 1983.

Driver, Harold E. *Indians of North America*. 2nd ed. Chicago: University of Chicago Press, 1969.

Jackson, Robert H. *Race, Caste, and Status: Indians in Colonial Spanish America*. Albuquerque: University of New Mexico Press, 1999.

Shoemaker, Nancy. *American Indian Population Recovery in the Twentieth Century*. Albuquerque: University of New Mexico Press, 2000.

Stannard, David. *American Holocaust: The Conquest of the New World*. Oxford and New York: Oxford University Press, 1992.

White, Richard. *The Middle Ground: Indians, Empires, and Republics in the Great Lakes Region, 1650–1815*. New York: Cambridge University Press, 1991.

Demoiselle, La

See Old Briton

Department of the Interior

See Bureau of Indian Affairs

Devil's Hole Road, Battle of
Event Date: September 14, 1763

Ambush by Native Americans of a British supply convoy during Pontiac's Rebellion (1763). The British routinely sent supply convoys to Detroit overland from Fort Niagara to Lake Erie. This portage passed through Seneca territory. On September 14, 1763, a combined force of 300 Seneca, Ottawa, and Ojibwa warriors set an ambush for a British convoy on its way to Detroit. The natives chose a location near a ravine close to the whirlpool known as Devil's Hole in the Niagara River Gorge.

The British convoy consisted of 25 wagons accompanied by only 31 soldiers. The Native American ambush took the convoy by surprise and killed all but 2 of the soldiers. The musket fire alerted two companies of the British 80th Regiment nearby. These men then rushed to rescue their comrades but instead ran into a second ambush. During this engagement approximately half of the soldiers from the 80th Regiment became casualties.

Some 80 British soldiers were killed during the two ambushes. These actions effectively closed the portage between Fort Niagara and Lake Erie and prevented the British from resupplying Detroit. The British garrison at Fort Niagara spent the next several weeks trying to reopen the portage, but the Senecas continued to attack the convoys even when they were well guarded. This combined with deteriorating weather conditions halted all attempts to resupply Detroit. The garrison undoubtedly would have been starved into surrender but was saved by Pontiac's truce.

DALLACE W. UNGER JR.

See also

Native American Warfare; Ojibwas; Ottawas; Pontiac's Rebellion; Senecas

References

Anderson, Fred. *Crucible of War: The Seven Years' War and the Fate of the Empire in British North America, 1754–1766*. New York: Vintage Books, 2001.

Brumwell, Stephen. *Redcoats: The British Soldier and War in the Americas, 1755–1763*. Cambridge: Cambridge University Press, 2002.

Steele, Ian K. *Warpaths: Invasions of North America*. New York: Oxford University Press, 1994.

Deyohninhohakarawenh

See Theyanoguin

Digger Indians

A pejorative term first applied by white Americans to the desert Native American tribes of the Great Basin region, such as the Paiutes and Maidus. The term "digger Indians" has been used to identify Native Americans of the central Plateau region to include Utah, Arizona, Nevada, Idaho, and Oregon as well as California. Eventually this became a term preferred by many whites to describe all of California's Native American population. Labeling these Native Americans as "diggers" helped create a mind-set among Americans that such tribes were subhuman. This in turn made it easier to pursue a brutal policy of extermination that devastated California Indians in the years following the California Gold Rush, which began in 1848.

While the union of Spaniards and Indians created the mestizo or mixed-race peoples of Mexico and while the Spaniards had built a system of 21 missions in California to proselytize Native Americans, there had been less interest in assimilation of Native Americans during the Americans' inexorable march westward. Indeed, Americans encountered Indian tribes eking out subsistence in the desert approaches to California and interpreted their lack of institutional sophistication as an indication of social and spiritual inferiority. Many of these Native Americans had experienced decades of demographic decline because of exposure to diseases such as smallpox. Pioneering Americans, accustomed to encountering vigorous Plains tribes such as the Sioux and Cheyennes, invariably portrayed these Native Americans as inferior and frequently described them as being animal-like.

European settlers had never been particularly impressed with the Native Americans of California, although their numbers were large (compared to the rest of what is now the United States) and their cultures were diverse and long-standing. This stereotyping of California's native peoples was exacerbated by American encounters with desert Indians who scratched out a living in the harsh environs of the Great Basin region in Utah, Nevada, and California.

Often living on grubs, roots, rats, and other sparse fare, the Native Americans of the Great Basin were remarkably knowledgeable at surviving some of the harshest environmental conditions on the planet. Their lifestyles were nevertheless described in the most scornful terms by encroaching Americans, who designated them "diggers" as a way of describing their perceived lack of sophistication. Encroaching on their tribal hunting grounds and resource base, outsiders often attacked impoverished Native Americans for real and perceived crimes, including the theft of cattle. Indian children were often taken from their families and sold to ranchers as virtual slave labor in the 1850s in California.

Labeling the Native Americans as "diggers" somehow seemed to legitimize the seizure of their lands before, during, and after the California Gold Rush. Newspaper accounts through the 1870s described the killing of Native Americans as "good hauls of diggers." By 1900 the Native American population of California had declined to approximately 10,000 people, a monumental demographic reduction from an estimated 300,000 Native Americans there in 1750. Several notorious massacres occurred in California in the 1850s and 1860s, and the State of California was actually reimbursed by the federal government for bounties paid at the rate of $5 dollars per head and 50 cents per scalp.

The horrific mistreatment of the so-called digger Indians helped revive a nascent Indian reform movement. Following the gold rush period, many social reformers attempted to help the survivors by establishing reservations for the remaining tribal groups and boarding schools for their youth. Ironically, Californians celebrated the discovery in 1911 of the Stone Age man Ishi, whose Yahi tribe had been effectively wiped out in the campaign against the diggers.

RANDAL BEEMAN

See also

California Gold Rush; Paiutes, Northern

References

Cooke, Sherburne. *The Population of the California Indians, 1769–1970.* Berkeley: University of California Press, 1976.

Heizer, Robert F. *The Destruction of the California Indian.* Lincoln, NE: Bison Books, 1993.

Hurtado, Albert L. *Indian Survival on the California Frontier.* New Haven, CT: Yale University Press, 1988.

Dime Novels

Inexpensive pocket-sized formulaic melodramatic novels ranging from 25,000 to 30,000 words and sold from about 1860 to 1895. Dime novels were the dominant form of popular fiction and were an inseparable part of the day-to-day life of most young men in the last half of the 19th century. The dime novel often tended toward very patriotic and nationalistic tales of adventure and chaste romance while conveying a puritanical sense of morality, rugged individualism, and a clearly defined portrait of the American

Cover of *The Lost Trail,* a dime novel published by Beadle and Company, 1864. (Library of Congress)

frontier, where the Indian was portrayed as either a bloodthirsty redskin or a noble savage.

The dime novel format evolved from the story paper, an eight-page tabloid-sized weekly that serialized novels and included other materials to appeal to the entire family. Revolutions in publishing technology and the centralization of the publishing industry, the availability of cheap paper, and improvements in distribution were among the factors that led Irwin P. Beadle and his brother Erastus to develop the concept of a series of short pocket-sized novels bound in cheap groundwood, or pulp paper, and published every fortnight. In 1860 the publishing firm of Beadle & Adams issued the first in its series of Beadle's Dime Novels, *Malaeska, the Indian Wife of the White Hunter.* The book was written by a respected author, Ann S. Stephens. Soon the Yellow Beadles, as they were called, gained an enormous following. The exciting adventures of such characters as Buffalo Bill Cody and Wild Bill Hickok in books that were cheap and small enough to tuck into a pocket or hide in a textbook made them requisite reading for most young men of the day.

Beadle's novels offered the working classes of the East an affordable and portable form of escapism. In the dimers, as they were sometimes called, readers were shown a wild West filled with romance, adventure, and the opportunity to make something of one's life. The dime novels began less than 50 years after the nation's last war with Britain and reflected this with an intense nationalism and a strident patriotism. In the early Westerns especially they painted a clear picture of a frontier infested with Indians, inviting the reader to join in the push of Manifest Destiny.

The advent of the American Civil War (1861–1865) meant a further increase in the market for Beadle's dime novels. Soldiers desired the books because they fit easily into pockets and were exciting reading. Beadle's novels were delivered to the troops in bales by trains, and many reports exist of dead soldiers being buried with their Beadle in their pocket. Nearly 5 million Beadles sold during the war years even though they were unavailable in the Confederacy.

The success of Beadles led to the development of many competing publishing houses, most notably Street & Smith and George Munro. These publishers and the Beadles added many new genres to the dime novel format. As the western frontier was settled, detective stories set in Chicago moved to the forefront. Changes in postal rates and production techniques led most publishers to shift from the dime format to the magazine format in the 1920s, marking the beginning of the end of the dimers.

Dime novels were most often written under pen names, but many well-known writers of the day, including Horatio Alger Jr., Ned Buntline, Bret Harte, and Louisa May Alcott, slummed and wrote a dimer or two.

B. KEITH MURPHY

See also

Literature and the American Indian Wars; Manifest Destiny

References

Burns, Terry. *Trails of the Dime Novel.* Laurel, MD: Echelon, 2004.

Denning, Michael. *Mechanic Accents: Dime Novels and Working Class Culture in America.* London: Verso, 1998.

Dodge, Grenville Mellen
Birth Date: April 12, 1831
Death Date: January 3, 1916

U.S. Army officer, congressman, railroad builder, and land developer. Born in Danvers, Massachusetts, on April 12, 1831, Grenville Mellen Dodge was educated at Dunham Academy in New Hampshire and then Norwich University in Vermont, from which he graduated with a degree in civil engineering in 1851. He moved to Iowa that same year and was an engineer and a surveyor for railroads, including the Union Pacific. He also became a partner in the Baldwin & Dodge Banking Firm.

Dodge organized the Council Bluffs Guards and was commissioned a colonel in the 4th Iowa Infantry Regiment in July 1861 after the start of the American Civil War (1861–1865). Shortly

Major General Grenville M. Dodge commanded the Department of the Missouri during the Civil War. After the war, as chief engineer of the Union Pacific Railroad, he played a key role in construction of the Transcontinental Railroad. (Library of Congress)

thereafter he received command of the 1st Brigade, 4th Division, Army of the Southwest. Dodge fought in Arkansas in the Battle of Pea Ridge (March 7–8, 1862), also known as the Battle of Elkhorn Tavern, during which he had three horses shot from under him and was wounded in the side. Promoted to brigadier general of volunteers for his role in that battle, he took command of the District of the Mississippi, earning the attention of Major General Ulysses S. Grant for his espionage networks and rebuilding of the Mobile & Ohio and other western railroads.

Promoted to major general of volunteers in June 1864, Dodge commanded XVI Corps during Major General William T. Sherman's Atlanta Campaign. Dodge led his corps in the Battle of Ezra Church (July 28, 1864). Wounded in the head by a Confederate sharpshooter on August 19, 1864, during the siege of Atlanta, he returned to active duty that December as commander of the Department of the Missouri, a post he held until the end of the war. The department was subsequently expanded to include the departments of Kansas, Nebraska, and Utah.

Dodge's soldiers were kept busy against the Native Americans, for in the summer of 1865 the Cheyennes, Arapahos, and

Sioux raided the Bozeman Trail and other overland mail and travel routes. Dodge then ordered a punitive operation against the hostiles. This operation became known as the Powder River Expedition and was also known as the Connor Expedition for its commander Brigadier General Patrick E. Connor. The only major engagement of the campaign, the Battle of the Tongue River (August 29, 1865), resulted in an army victory against the Arapahos. Fighting in the Powder River area, however, eventually led to Red Cloud's War (1866–1868).

Resigning his army commission in May 1866, Dodge returned to the railroad business as chief engineer of the Union Pacific Railroad. In this position he became a key figure in the construction of the transcontinental railroad. He also won election to the U.S. House of Representatives as a Republican from Iowa and served in the House form 1867 to 1869. He spent much of his time away from the capital, however, engaged in railroad construction, but while in Washington he lobbied forcefully for the railroads and internal improvements in the West. Employed by financier Jay Gould in 1873, Dodge supervised the laying of some 9,000 miles of railroad track. Later he also supervised the laying of railroad track in Cuba. Involved in a number of different businesses, he became immensely wealthy with a fortune estimated at some $25 million.

A staunch Republican and personal friend and confidant of both President William McKinley and Secretary of War Russell A. Alger, Dodge believed that war with Spain would bring economic instability. He therefore encouraged McKinley to secure a peaceful solution to the growing tension with Spain over Cuba. On the declaration of war, Dodge was offered command of I Corps, but he declined in order to continue his business pursuits. Throughout the war, however, he remained in close touch with McKinley and Alger.

Following the war Dodge reluctantly agreed to chair a commission created by McKinley to investigate the notorious Embalmed Beef Scandal and the practices of the War Department during the war. The commission, officially called the Commission to Investigate the War Department, came to be known simply as the Dodge Commission.

Dodge retired to Council Bluffs, Iowa, in 1907. He wrote several books of recollections of the Civil War and construction of the transcontinental railroad. He died at Council Bluffs on January 3, 1916.

Spencer C. Tucker

See also

Bozeman Trail; Powder River Expedition; Red Cloud's War

References

Alger, Russell A. *The Spanish-American War.* New York: Harper and Brothers, 1901.

DeMontravel, Peter R. *A Hero to His Fighting Men: Nelson A. Miles, 1839–1925.* Kent, OH: Kent State University Press, 1998.

Dodge, Grenville M. *The Battle of Atlanta and Other Campaigns, Addresses, Etc.* Council Bluffs, IA: Monarch Publishing, 1911.

Dodge, Grenville M. *How We Built the Union Pacific Railway.* Council Bluffs, IA: Monarch Publishing, 1908.

Hirshon, Stanley P. *Grenville M. Dodge: Soldier, Politician, Railroad Pioneer.* Bloomington: Indiana University Press, 1967.

Leech, Margaret. *In the Days of McKinley.* New York: Harper and Brothers, 1959.

Dodge, Henry

Birth Date: October 12, 1782
Death Date: June 19, 1867

U.S. Army officer and politician. Henry Dodge was born in Vincennes, Indiana, on October 12, 1782. He received his education on the hardscrabble Missouri frontier, learning to understand the intricacies of Native American society, culture, and warfare. During the War of 1812 he was elected captain of a mounted rifle company. He soon established himself as an adept Indian fighter, ultimately rising to the rank of lieutenant colonel in command of a Missouri mounted rifle battalion. He saw service during the relief of the Boone's Lick, Missouri, settlement in the summer of 1814, earning him an appointment later in the year to major general in the Missouri Militia. Following a Native American raid

Army officer Henry Dodge distinguished himself in combat against Native Americans during the War of 1812 and again in the Black Hawk War of 1832. He subsequently commanded the 1st U.S. Dragoons, a mounted infantry unit specifically designed for frontier service. (North Wind Picture Archives)

on the settlement, Dodge sheltered some 500 Miami tribesmen, undoubtedly saving their lives in the process.

Following the war Dodge moved to Wisconsin, where he found work mining minerals. When troubles with Native Americans there flared, he raised a company of mounted rifles in August 1827 in support of Brigadier General Henry Atkinson's army. The mere presence of these troops dissuaded Native American aggression and averted a conflict. The Black Hawk War of 1832 found Dodge a colonel commanding Michigan Militia troops. His effective leadership here gained him an appointment endorsed by President Andrew Jackson to command a regiment of mounted rangers in June 1832. On July 21, 1832, Dodge fought Chief Black Hawk to a draw at Wisconsin Heights, and Dodge played an important role in the final defeat of Black Hawk in the Battle of Bad Axe (August 1–2, 1832).

In 1833 as a reward for his services during the Black Hawk War, Dodge was selected to command the 1st U.S. Dragoons, a mounted unit purposefully designed for frontier service. This unique unit was the first standing regular army cavalry regiment authorized since the War of 1812. The dragoons were to ride into battle, thus providing speed and mobility, and then fight dismounted without the reduction in firepower faced by traditional cavalry. This combination of speed and firepower was believed to be an answer to the long-standing shortcomings of traditional formations operating against Native Americans on the frontier.

For the next two years Dodge and his dragoons traveled throughout the western territories, ranging from the southern Indian Territory (Oklahoma) to eastern Kansas and as far west as the Rocky Mountains. By demonstrating the power of the American military to the Native Americans, Dodge's travels helped to forestall hostilities and generally quieted the region.

In June 1836 Dodge returned to civilian life, where he held appointments as governor of the Wisconsin Territory from 1836 to 1841 and again from 1845 to 1848. The sprawling territory ultimately became the states of Wisconsin, Iowa, and Minnesota. During his tenure in office, Dodge arranged a treaty with the Menominee tribe on January 18, 1838, that secured 4 million acres for Michigan and Wisconsin.

Dodge served as a territorial delegate to Congress from 1841 to 1845 and, upon Wisconsin's attainment of statehood in 1848, as U.S. senator from that state from 1848 to 1857. He was also courted for the 1844 Democratic presidential nomination but declined. Dodge died in Burlington, Iowa, on June 19, 1867.

ROBERT J. DALESSANDRO

See also

Atkinson, Henry; Bad Axe, Battle of; Black Hawk; Black Hawk War; Dragoon Regiments, 1st and 2nd; Native Americans and the War of 1812

References

Clark, James I. *Henry Dodge, Frontiersman: First Governor of Wisconsin Territory*. Madison: State Historical Society of Wisconsin, 1957.

Meudt, Edna. *Promised Land: The Life and Times of Henry Dodge, First Territorial Governor of Wisconsin*. Fennimore, WI: Westburg Associates Publishers, 1977.

Dog Soldiers

One of the six Cheyenne warrior bands, perhaps the most warlike of all the Plains tribes, also known as Dog Men (the Cheyenne phrase is Hotamétaneo'o). The Dog Soldiers were critical to Cheyenne governance and led the Cheyenne resistance to American westward expansion from the 1830s until they were defeated in the Battle of Summit Springs in northeastern Colorado on July 11, 1869. Even after that, however, Dog Soldiers were involved in other Cheyenne struggles against U.S. troops.

The Dog Soldiers were held in reverence by other Cheyennes because of their bravery and prowess in battle and were known for their sashes, called dog ropes, made of tanned skins and decorated with porcupine quills and human hair that the four designated bravest Dog Soldiers would wear into battle. The dog rope hung over the right shoulder and down to the ground, where it would be staked to the ground with a sacred arrow or metal pin during battle. This symbol of resolve meant that the Dog Soldier was left to defend his piece of ground to the death, if necessary, in order to cover the possible retreat of the rest of the band.

The Dog Soldiers policed Cheyenne encampments during war and peace and also were in charge of tribal buffalo hunts and the distribution of meat after the hunt. Dog Soldier policing was especially important during wartime, as it kept individual warriors from seeking personal glory and thus allowed large bands to approach their enemies unawares. For example, Dog Soldier policing enabled some 3,000 Cheyennes to remain undetected until they began their assault on Camp Dodge in 1865.

The Dog Soldiers came together in the late 1830s under the leadership of Porcupine Bear, who was deemed an outlaw after he murdered his cousin. Porcupine Bear and his followers were alienated from the tribe, which led to their independence because they were then only governed by what became the war leaders of the Dog Soldier Clan. Soon the Dog Soldiers grew to become more than half the military arm of the Cheyennes.

The Dog Soldiers staunchly opposed white expansion and refused to sign treaties with the U.S. government or to be limited to reservations. Instead, they fought to retain their freedom, even when the Council of Forty-Four (a civil council of chiefs) had voted for peace. This aggressive posture made the Cheyennes the target of American military aggression that culminated in the massacre of Black Kettle's tribe at Sand Creek, Colorado, in November 1864.

The Dog Soldiers led a coalition of Cheyenne, Arapaho, and Lakota warriors to avenge the Sand Creek Massacre in 1865. Under the leadership of Roman Nose, the Dog Soldiers devastated nearly 400 miles of white settlements from Kansas through Colorado and laid siege to Denver. The U.S. government threatened the Cheyennes with extermination unless the raiding stopped. Until 1877 the Dog Soldiers led the Cheyennes in continual conflict against American expansion and played key roles in many critical engagements with U.S. forces, including the Battle of the Little Bighorn (June 25–26, 1876) in which the Dog Soldiers along with Arapaho and Lakota Sioux warriors almost destroyed the 7th Cavalry. In response to Little Bighorn, the U.S. Army, working with Pawnee and Shoshone mercenaries, pursued the Dog Soldiers and eventually subdued them.

B. Keith Murphy

See also

Black Kettle; Cheyennes; Little Bighorn, Battle of the; Roman Nose; Sand Creek Massacre; Summit Springs, Battle of

References

Afton, Jean, David Fritjof Halaas, and Andrew E. Masich. *Cheyenne Dog Soldiers: A Ledgerbook History of Coups and Combat.* Niwot: University Press of Colorado, 1997.

Broome, Jeff. *Dog Soldier Justice: The Ordeal of Susanna Alderdice in the Kansas Indian War.* Lincoln, KS: Lincoln County Historical Society, 2003.

Do-ne-ho-ga-wa

See Parker, Ely Samuel

Dover, New Hampshire, Attack on

Start Date: June 27, 1689
End Date: June 28, 1689

Native American attack on the English settlement of Dover, New Hampshire, during June 27–28, 1689. Relations between New Hampshire colonists and their Native American neighbors had been generally satisfactory in the 17th century. Indeed, peace had been maintained until the final stages of King Philip's War (1675–1676).

In the autumn of 1676 many New Hampshire natives had accepted Major Richard Waldron's invitation to a meeting at his home in Dover. Waldron had been conducting considerable trade with the Native Americans, all the while earning a reputation as an unsavory and unscrupulous businessman. The natives were accompanied by several tribal leaders who had fought alongside Metacom (King Philip). A detachment of Massachusetts soldiers, who had stopped in Dover on their way to Maine to subdue some of Metacom's supporters there, quickly recognized Metacom's entourage. At Waldron's suggestion, the natives agreed to participate in a mock battle with the colonists, during the course of which the Massachusetts troops captured most of the native

warriors. Metacom's supporters were kept as prisoners, and the New Hampshire warriors were released.

The natives considered Waldron's role in the affair a serious breach of trust, and they retaliated with attacks on New Hampshire settlements. Hostilities ended with the signing of a peace treaty in 1678, but the Native Americans remained distrustful of the colonists. Indeed, their belief that Waldron was cheating them in the fur trade by using false weights further strained relations, especially since they had to sell land to pay their debts to the traders. Furthermore, the Native Americans suspected the New England governments of trying to incite the Mohawks to attack them.

Despite these strains, Pennacook sachem (chief) Passaconaway and his successor Wonalancet urged a policy of accommodation, and the smaller tribes followed their lead. By 1685, however, Kancamagus had succeeded his aged uncle Wonalancet as sachem of the Pennacooks. Unlike his predecessors, Kancamagus refused to tolerate further abuses from the colonists. He therefore urged the Ossipees and other tribes to unite with the Pennacooks to strike back at the English.

Kancamagus finally made his attack on the night of June 27, 1689, targeting the settlement at Dover (or Cocheco, as the natives knew it), home of the despised Waldron. Although friendly natives warned colonial officials of the impending attack, a message dispatched to Dover did not arrive in time. That evening several Native American women arrived at the town and announced that others were on their way to trade. The women secured lodging in four of the town's five palisaded garrison houses. After the colonists were asleep, the women opened the doors and gates of three houses, enabling the warriors, who had gathered outside, to enter. At the fourth garrison, a young man awoke and managed to bar the door.

Kancamagus's men killed Waldron, his trading partner Richard Otis, and several other occupants of Waldron's and Otis's garrisons. Altogether, 23 colonists were slain, and 29 others were carried off as prisoners. Because the natives apparently held no animosity toward most of the colonists, they allowed many of their captives to escape. The raiding party burned a total of six houses and a mill before withdrawing on the early morning of June 28.

A party of colonists pursued the raiders but failed to catch them. During the next several years, however, troops from New Hampshire and Massachusetts hunted down the Pennacooks and their allies until the surviving natives finally took refuge with the French in Canada.

Jim Piecuch

See also

King Philip's War; Mohawks; Pennacooks

References

Belknap, Jeremy. *The History of New Hampshire.* 3 vols. New York: Arno, 1972.

Stackpole, Everett S. *History of New Hampshire,* Vol. 1. New York: American Historical Society, 1916.

Dragoon Regiments, 1st and 2nd

U.S. Army regiment first organized in 1833 and then in 1836 reorganized and expanded into two dragoon regiments (later the 1st and 2nd Cavalry). In the U.S. system, the dragoons were basically medium cavalry, expected to use horses for mobility and speed but usually to fight dismounted, although they were certainly capable of mounted fighting. With the westward expansion of the United States, it became evident that mounted troops were required to cover the vast stretches of territory and compete with Native American warriors. Thus, despite a traditional fiscal aversion to regular mounted troops, in 1833 the U.S. Regiment of Dragoons was formed at Jefferson Barracks, Missouri, and included many veterans of the battalion of Mounted Rangers authorized by Congress a year earlier. The regiment, commanded by a colonel, originally Henry Dodge, and comprised of a headquarters and 10 companies, totaled 34 officers and 714 enlisted men.

In 1836 Congress authorized a second dragoon regiment, commanded initially by Colonel David Twiggs. The two regiments were now designated the 1st U.S. Dragoons and the 2nd U.S. Dragoons. No sooner was it established than much of the 2nd Dragoons was employed, both mounted and dismounted, in Florida in the Second Seminole War (1835–1842). Following that war, the 2nd Dragoons was reorganized as the Regiment of Riflemen but was remounted as dragoons the following year, rejoining its fellow regiment in the West.

Dragoon weapons included a heavy saber, a carbine, and pistols. The original Henry carbine gave way to the musketoon, replaced in 1858 by the Sharp's rifled carbine. Single-shot muzzle-loading "horse pistols" (the holsters were mounted on the horse) had been replaced by 1849 by Samuel Colt's cap-and-ball six-shooter and by the early 1850s by Colt's revolvers. Although sabers continued to be issued, they were of little use in fighting Native Americans and were often not carried in the field.

Until the Mexican-American War (1846–1848) began, the 1st Dragoon Regiment was employed in scouting Native American warriors along the 1,000 miles of western frontier and from Missouri to the Rocky Mountains. There were numerous expeditions associated with the Cherokee, Iowa, Kansas, Pawnee, Pottawatomi, Osage, Otoe, Sauk, and Sioux nations. Particularly notable were the 1834 Pawnee Expedition and the 1845 expedition to the South Pass of the Rocky Mountains. During these years, however, there was little fighting, and most disturbances were settled with a show of force, notably with the Osages in 1837 and 1838 and the Cherokees in 1839 and 1840. Dragoons were also engaged in exploration and in building roads and bridges.

The Mexican-American War found most of the 1st Dragoons in Colonel (later Brigadier General) Stephen Watts Kearny's Army of the West engaged in seizing New Mexico, Arizona, and then California. Two companies that remained in New Mexico participated in Brigadier General Sterling Price's retaliatory attacks at Pueblo de Taos against Mexicans and then Native Americans who had revolted and killed the American governor there. Four of its companies served in Major General Winfield Scott's advance from Vera Cruz to Mexico City. The 2nd Dragoons fought with Brigadier General Zachary Taylor's army and then with Scott's army.

Following the Mexican-American War, both regiments as well as the Regiment of Mounted Riflemen, constituted in 1846, protected and policed the trails and settlements of California, Utah, and Oregon. The massive westward expansion triggered by the 1848 discovery of gold in California resulted in confrontations between Native Americans and the white invaders of their lands. The 1st Dragoons were heavily engaged with the Apaches, while the 2nd Dragoons faced the Cherokees. Companies of both regiments, however, were employed throughout the country's expanded area.

Two new cavalry regiments were formed in 1855, and in 1861 the five mounted regiments were redesignated as cavalry, with the 1st and 2nd Dragoons becoming the 1st and 2nd Cavalry, the Mounted Rifles becoming the 3rd Cavalry, and the 1st and 2nd Cavalry becoming the 4th and 5th Cavalry. These units fought in the American Civil War (1861–1865) and the later Indian Wars. Modern U.S. Army troops still serve in these regiments.

Philip L. Bolté

See also

Apaches; California Gold Rush; Carbines; Cavalry Regiment, 4th U.S.; Cavalry Regiment, 5th U.S.; Cherokees; Colt Revolver; Kearny, Stephen Watts; Mexico; Mounted Riflemen, Regiment of; Scott, Winfield; Seminole War, Second; Taylor, Zachary

References

Adams, George Rollie. *General William S. Harney: Prince of Dragoons.* Lincoln: University of Nebraska Press, 2001.

Johnson, Swafford. *History of the U.S. Cavalry.* New York: Smithmark Publishers, 1994.

Wellman, Paul I. *Death in the Desert: The Fifty Years' War for the Great Southwest.* Lincoln: University of Nebraska Press, 1987.

Duck River Massacre
Event Date: May 16, 1812

Native American raid on a white settler's home. On May 16, 1812, a party of five Creek warriors decided to raid a remote Tennessee settlement near the mouth of the Duck River in Humphreys County. The band of Native Americans, led by Little Warrior of the Creek war faction (Red Sticks), attacked the house of Jesse Manley, where the families of Manley and John Crawley, both absent at the time, had taken shelter. The assault resulted in the deaths of seven of the inhabitants, including five children, Mrs. Manley, and a young man in the village who had been asked to look after the two families. Martha Crawley, wife of John Crawley, was taken captive by the Creeks and forced to march back to the Creek Nation as a hostage.

The incident at Duck River created a wave of fear and fury throughout the western frontier. The initial response by Tennessee Militia units failed to locate Crawley or her captors. One incensed Tennessean was Andrew Jackson, then brigadier general of the Tennessee Militia, who urged the governor of the state to authorize a military expedition into Creek territory for the purposes of rescuing Crawley and, more importantly, to exact retribution against the Creeks.

Meanwhile, reports filtered back to Tennessee of the fate of Crawley. Rumors printed in the newspapers stated that she had been severely whipped and exhibited naked in Creek villages. Unbeknownst to Tennesseans, however, Crawley had escaped her abductors sometime in late June 1812. Her rescue was facilitated through the intervention of a blacksmith named Tandy Walker at St. Stephens on the Tombigbee River.

Before news of her rescue reached the Tennesseans, however, the United States had declared war against Great Britain. Because it was assumed that most Indian depredations on the frontier were provoked by British intrigue, the Crawley affair took on wider ramifications. Prowar advocates used the incident along with Indian-hating rhetoric to inflame the nation against western Native Americans hostile to white encroachment. In Tennessee, the Duck River Massacre gave impetus to the desire of many whites for an invasion of the Creek Nation, particularly after the massacre at Fort Mims in the Mississippi Territory on August 30, 1813.

As for Crawley, she gave a deposition upon her return to her settlement providing details of her captivity, none of which matched the sensationalism depicted in the press. Still, the indiscriminate murders on the Duck River and the capture of a white woman provided a justification for punitive action against the Creeks, resulting in the Creek War (1813–1814). Indeed, the concluding treaty of the conflict—the Treaty of Fort Jackson—in August 1814 mentioned the incident as a reason for the United States going to war against the Creeks.

Tom Kanon

See also

Creeks; Creek War; Fort Mims, Battle of; Jackson, Andrew; Native Americans and the War of 1812

References

Kanon, Tom. "The Kidnapping of Martha Crawley and Settler-Indian Relations Prior to the War of 1812." *Tennessee Historical Quarterly* 64 (2005): 3–23.

Owsley, Frank Lawrence, Jr. *Struggle for the Gulf Borderlands: The Creek War and the Battle of New Orleans, 1812–1815.* Gainesville: University Presses of Florida, 1981.

Dudley, Joseph
Birth Date: September 23, 1647
Death Date: April 2, 1720

British colonial official, military officer, and governor of Massachusetts (1702–1715) during Queen Anne's War (1702–1713). Joseph Dudley, the son of Massachusetts governor Thomas Dudley

and Catherine Hackburn, was born in Roxbury, Massachusetts, on September 23, 1647. The younger Dudley graduated from Harvard College in 1665, represented Roxbury in the Massachusetts General Court (1673–1676), and served with provincial forces in King Philip's War (1675–1676). Afterward he held various provincial offices until 1685, when King James II appointed him president of the council created to govern Massachusetts and New Hampshire. In 1686 Sir Edmund Andros succeeded Dudley as council president, although Dudley continued to serve as a councilor.

The New Englanders ousted Andros in 1689 amid the turmoil associated with the Glorious Revolution, and Dudley spent 10 months in prison for his support of Andros. On his release Dudley went to England, rehabilitated his political career, returned to North America, and served briefly as chief justice of New York. He was appointed governor of Massachusetts in April 1702.

As governor, Dudley almost immediately had to face the crisis brought on by the outbreak of Queen Anne's War. French and Native American raiding parties from Canada and Acadia attacked the province's western frontier as well as settlements in what is now Maine. The most devastating raid was made against Deerfield on February 29, 1704. Dudley responded by sending provincial militia to strike the French at Minas and Beaubassin in Acadia during the following summer. The success of this expedition helped to secure the frontier, and in 1706 Dudley secured the

As governor of Massachusetts (1702–1715) during Queen Anne's War, Joseph Dudley came under great criticism for his failure to prevent fierce French-supported raids by the Abenakis against frontier settlements. (Library of Congress)

release of the remaining Deerfield captives. However, he failed in two efforts to capture Port Royal in Acadia, from which French privateers harassed colonial shipping. The town finally fell to a combined British and colonial assault in October 1710.

Dudley's political patrons lost power when Queen Anne died in 1714, resulting in Samuel Shute replacing him as governor in 1715. Dudley died in Roxbury, Massachusetts, on April 2, 1720.

JIM PIECUCH

See also

Deerfield, Massachusetts, Attack on; King Philip's War; Queen Anne's War

References

Johnson, Richard R. *Adjustment to Empire: The New England Colonies, 1675–1715.* New Brunswick, NJ: Rutgers University Press, 1981.

Kimball, Everett. *The Public Life of Joseph Dudley: A Study of the Colonial Policy of the Stuarts in New England, 1660–1715.* Harvard Historical Studies, Vol. 15. New York: Longmans, Green, 1911.

Dull Knife
Birth Date: ca. 1810
Death Date: 1883

Northern Cheyenne chief who fought with the Lakota Sioux at the Battle of the Little Bighorn (June 25–26, 1876). Morning Star, better known as Dull Knife, the name given him by the Sioux, was born around 1810 along Rosebud Creek in present-day Montana. Dull Knife's Northern Cheyennes were allies of the Lakota Sioux in the Great Sioux War (1876–1877). At the Battle of Little Bighorn, Dull Knife's Cheyenne warriors were initially rebuffed by Lieutenant Colonel George Armstrong Custer's force. However, once Major Marcus A. Reno's battalion retreated, the Cheyennes joined the Lakota Sioux in annihilating Custer's battalion. Following the Battle of the Little Bighorn, the U.S. Army mobilized a huge field force to track down Dull Knife, his band, and the other perpetrators of Custer's demise. Colonel Ranald S. Mackenzie's cavalry troops finally defeated the Cheyennes along Bates Creek near the Red Fork of the Powder River, destroying Dull Knife's village and valuable stores. This victory, dubbed the Dull Knife Fight (November 25, 1876), led to the surrender in 1877 of Dull Knife and most of the Northern Cheyennes, who were removed to the Darlington Reservation in Indian Territory (Oklahoma). In September 1878, however, Dull Knife led his Cheyennes north to their traditional territory in Montana. Pursued, they eventually surrendered and were confined at Fort Robinson, Nebraska. During a desperate attempt to escape, most of Dull Knife's band was killed on January 9, 1879. Dull Knife did manage to get away, but he surrendered at the Pine Ridge Agency with fewer than 50 of his band. He died in the Rosebud Valley sometime in 1883, a year before the establishment of the Cheyenne Reservation at Tongue Creek.

JASON N. PALMER

Northern Cheyenne chief Morning Star, better known as Dull Knife. In 1878, he led several hundred of his people in an epic march north from a reservation in Oklahoma toward their homeland in Montana. (National Archives)

See also

Cheyennes, Northern; Custer, George Armstrong; Dull Knife Fight; Dull Knife Outbreak; Great Sioux War; Lakota Sioux; Little Bighorn, Battle of the; Mackenzie, Ranald Slidell; Reno, Marcus Albert

References

Greene, Jerome A., ed. *Lakota and Cheyenne: Indian Views of the Great Sioux War, 1876–1877.* Norman: University of Oklahoma Press, 1994.

Werner, Fred H. *The Dull Knife Battle: "Doomsday for the Northern Cheyennes."* Greeley, CO: Werner Publications, 1981.

Dull Knife Fight
Event Date: November 25, 1876

Battle fought on November 25, 1876, between U.S. Army forces under Colonel Ranald S. Mackenzie and Northern Cheyenne warriors under Chief Dull Knife (also known as Morning Star). The Dull Knife Fight (also known as the Battle of Bates Creek)

marked the last significant engagement of the Great Sioux War (1876–1877). Allies of the Lakota Sioux in the Great Sioux War, Dull Knife's band of Cheyennes had helped annihilate much of Lieutenant Colonel George Armstrong Custer's command in the Battle of the Little Bighorn (June 25–26, 1876). During the autumn and winter following Custer's Last Stand, Brigadier General George Crook sent columns of cavalry and infantry in pursuit of the Cheyennes and Lakota Sioux, which precipitated the Dull Knife Fight.

Crook departed Fort Fetterman, located 11 miles northwest of present-day Douglas, Wyoming, on November 14, 1876, with nearly 1,500 cavalry and infantry of the 2nd, 3rd, 4th, and 5th Cavalry regiments and the 4th, 9th, 14th, and 25th Infantry regiments. Some 400 Pawnee, Shoshone, and Arapaho scouts and some 300 civilian teamsters responsible for 168 wagons also accompanied the army. Crook's Native American scouts reconnoitered the Cheyenne camp near the North Fork of the Powder River along Bates Creek west of present-day Kaycee, Wyoming, on November 22. Crook then ordered Colonel Mackenzie to take about 1,100 cavalrymen of the 2nd, 3rd, 4th, and 5th U.S. Cavalry regiments and drive off the Cheyennes, wreck the village, destroy their winter food supply, and capture their ponies.

Mackenzie's troops made a difficult night march on November 24 and attacked at dawn the next morning, November 25. The Cheyennes had been celebrating a victory over a band of Shoshone warriors, and surprise was complete. In frigid weather Mackenzie's troops burst upon the village, driving 400 Cheyenne warriors and their families from their lodges. The Cheyennes fled west down the valley, leaving behind their lodges, ponies, and most of their belongings. Several Cheyenne warriors took up a position in a draw near a butte in the middle of the valley. At this spot hand-to-hand fighting caused most of the casualties on both sides of the engagement. Colonel Mackenzie sent Lieutenant John A. McKinney and A Troop, 4th Cavalry, to counterattack a party of Cheyennes intent on recapturing their pony herd. Ambushed from a high-walled ravine, McKinney fell, hit by six bullets. H Troop, 5th Cavalry, commanded by Captain John M. Hamilton, helped rescue A Troop from its precarious situation.

Most of the Cheyennes escaped up the valley, leaving a small group of warriors on the high bluffs to cover their withdrawal. Dull Knife's and Little Wolf's bands suffered 40 killed and an estimated equal number of wounded in the engagement. Mackenzie's troops lost Lieutenant McKinney and suffered 6 enlisted men killed and 26 men wounded.

Unable to pry the Cheyenne rear guard from its outcrop, the troops returned to the Cheyenne village and began its destruction. The cavalrymen demolished and burned approximately 200 lodges, captured and took away nearly 600 ponies, and destroyed the winter stores of several tons of buffalo meat. Temperatures that night dropped to about 30 degrees below zero. Without shelter and with little more than the clothes on their backs, the Cheyennes

faced brutal conditions in their effort to reach Crazy Horse's band of Lakota Sioux. Dull Knife and Little Wolf finally surrendered what remained of their bands, along with Crazy Horse and other Lakota Sioux, to the U.S. Army at the Red Cloud Agency on May 5, 1877, effectively ending the Great Sioux War.

JASON N. PALMER

See also

Cheyennes, Northern; Crook, George; Custer, George Armstrong; Dull Knife; Great Sioux War; Little Bighorn, Battle of the; Little Wolf; Mackenzie, Ranald Slidell

References

Greene, Jerome A., ed. *Lakota and Cheyenne: Indian Views of the Great Sioux War, 1876–1877.* Norman: University of Oklahoma Press, 1994.

Werner, Fred H. *The Dull Knife Battle: "Doomsday for the Northern Cheyennes."* Greeley, CO: Werner Publications, 1981.

Dull Knife Outbreak
Start Date: September 1878
End Date: March 1879

Cheyenne trek led by Dull Knife that began in August 1878 from Indian Territory (present-day Oklahoma) to the Bighorn Mountains in Wyoming near the headwaters of the Powder River. The harrowing march of Dull Knife and his Cheyenne compatriots from U.S. Army captivity toward their homeland in present-day Wyoming, known as the Dull Knife Outbreak, added a sad chapter to the tragic closing stages of the Great Sioux War.

Northern Cheyenne leaders Dull Knife (Morning Star was his Cheyenne name, but he is better known by the name of Dull Knife, given to him by the Lakota Sioux) and Little Wolf were among the Cheyennes who had allied with the Lakota Sioux and defeated Lieutenant Colonel George Armstrong Custer and his 7th Cavalry Regiment in the Battle of the Little Bighorn. Dull Knife, Little Wolf, and their followers were pursued by the army and surrendered in May 1877. They were then relocated to Indian Territory (Oklahoma).

It was soon clear that the promises of adequate resources on the reservation were untrue. Game was nearly nonexistent, promised government rations failed to arrive on time and in sufficient quantity, and many Cheyennes either starved to death or perished of fever, probably malaria. In August 1878 with half of the Cheyennes who had been sent to Indian Territory now dead, Dull Knife and Little Wolf pleaded with Indian agent John Miles to let the survivors return to their ancestral homes in the Powder River basin of Wyoming and Montana. Miles refused.

Dull Knife and Little Wolf now took matters into their own hands. On September 9 they led some 350 Cheyennes from the reservation and began a march on foot to their homelands. There were perhaps only 70 warriors among them. Pursuing cavalry and

Arapaho scouts caught up with them on the Little Medicine Lodge River, but the Cheyennes refused to surrender. Three soldiers and an Arapaho scout were killed, and the Northern Cheyennes continued their trek, repelling attacks, capturing arms, and taking food from settlements that they encountered.

After crossing the Arkansas and South Platte rivers, the Indians split into two groups at White Clay Creek, Nebraska. Little Wolf led 115 Cheyennes to the Sand Hills, while Dull Knife planned to lead the remainder to the Red Cloud Agency, where they would surrender.

Dull Knife's band arrived at the Red Cloud Agency in Nebraska only to find it abandoned. They then trekked to Fort Robinson, where they surrendered on October 23. Dull Knife and his band were there for two months when they were informed that they would have to return to Indian Territory, but they refused.

Denied food, water, and heat until they relented, several days later on the night of January 9, 1879, the Cheyennes killed 2 guards in an escape attempt. Some 50 of the fleeing Cheyennes were shot down by soldiers as they ran from the fort, and other Cheyennes were discovered nearby in the course of the next days and ordered to surrender. Many chose to fight to the death. Fewer than 100 were herded back to Fort Robinson. Dull Knife and his wife and son, traveling at night on foot, managed to make it to the Pine Ridge Agency 18 days later. They and their few remaining followers were eventually allowed to stay there until they received a reservation of their own, which occurred a year after Dull Knife's death in 1883.

Meanwhile, Little Wolf and the remaining Cheyennes had proceeded to the Nebraska Sand Hills, where they were able to survive that winter. Along the Little Missouri River in Montana, Little Wolf surrendered his band to Lieutenant William P. Clark of the 2nd Cavalry Regiment on March 27, 1879. The Cheyennes were escorted to Fort Keogh, where Little Wolf and many of his followers signed on to help U.S. troops fight the Sioux.

BRUCE E. JOHANSEN

See also
Cheyennes; Dull Knife; Great Sioux War; Little Bighorn, Battle of the; Little Wolf; Pine Ridge Reservation; Powder River Expedition

References
Little Eagle, Avis. "Remains of Dull Knife's Band Make Final Journey Home." *Indian Country Today,* October 14, 1993.
Sandoz, Mari. *Cheyenne Autumn.* 1953; reprint, Lincoln: University of Nebraska Press, 1992.
Wiltsey, Norman B. *Brave Warriors.* Caldwell, ID: Caxton, 1963.

Dummer's Treaty

Peace treaty formally ending hostilities in Dummer's War (1722–1727). The treaty was signed by Massachusetts officials and local Native Americans and was named for Massachusetts's acting governor, William Dummer. Armed conflict began in 1722 with Native American (mainly Abenaki) raids on British settlements in Maine (then part of Massachusetts Bay Colony). In 1723 the British struck back, beginning in Casco Bay. As in many other areas of North America, relations between British colonists and Native Americans had steadily deteriorated as a result of increasing land encroachments by white settlers.

In 1723 a group of Penobscots murdered five white settlers, including a militia captain. When news of the massacre reached Boston, the colonial government decided to retaliate. In 1724 in a series of raids, the local militia destroyed numerous indigenous villages. The natives responded in equally violent fashion. In late 1724 after suffering heavy losses, the two sides agreed to begin discussions for a peace treaty.

Although active negotiations began in 1725, Dummer's Treaty was not signed until 1727, as Governor Dummer sought an agreement mainly on his terms, which greatly complicated the negotiating process. It was probably the most important treaty between the Native Americans of Maine and the Maritime Provinces with the colony of Massachusetts. The chief representative for the Native Americans was Chief Sauguaaram (also known as Loron). The treaty ended all hostilities but also affirmed the existence of the Abenakis' original land titles. The Native Americans also received promise of a Catholic missionary priest as well as fishing, hunting, and land-use rights in perpetuity. Dummer's Treaty became a model for subsequent treaties between the British and Native Americans.

JAIME RAMÓN OLIVARES

See also
Abenakis; Dummer's War

References
Delanie, Phillip, ed. *A Companion to American Indian History.* Malden, MA: Blackwell, 2004.
Ghere, David L. "Mistranslation and Misinformation: Diplomacy on the Maine Frontier, 1725–1755." *American Indian Culture and Research Journal* 8 (1984): 3–26.

Dummer's War
Start Date: July 25, 1722
End Date: 1727

War between British colonists and various Native American groups, primarily the Abenakis, in New England. The 1713 Treaty of Utrecht, ending the War of Spanish Succession—known in America as Queen Anne's War (1702–1713), which ended with the Treaty of Portsmouth (1713)—had put a halt to most violence in northern New England; however, the roots of further conflict continued to grow from 1713 to 1722. No longer threatened by native attacks, New England settlers and traders once again expanded into the northern and eastern frontiers of the region, intruding on Abenaki lands and disrupting their lives. Religion furthered the

Death of Father Sébastien Râle of the Society of Jesus. Killed by the English and Mohawks at Norridgewock, August 23, 1724. The event took place during Dummer's War (1722–1727). The illustration serves as the frontispiece of the *Indian Good Book*. (Maine Historical Society)

divide between natives and the English as Jesuit priests such as Sébastien Râle at Norridgewock continued to proselytize among the Abenakis. Largely dependent on British trade goods, the natives restrained their anger until Massachusetts attempted to arrest Râle in the winter of 1722 and plunder his church.

The Abenakis responded to British encroachments with open insolence and property destruction, causing many British families to flee exposed areas. Hoping to coerce the natives into a settlement, the Massachusetts legislature halted all trade with the Abenakis in September 1721. The next summer the Abenakis raided the lower settlements of the Kennebec River near Brunswick, where they burned homes and took more than 60 captives (most of whom they later released) but avoided indiscriminate bloodshed. On July 25, 1722, Governor Samuel Shute of Massachusetts denounced the eastern natives as rebels, essentially declaring war. Shute soon left for England, leaving the conduct of the war to Lieutenant Governor William Dummer, who served as acting governor and for whom the conflict was named.

Native American raiding parties struck across northern New England, engulfing Maine, New Hampshire, and western Massachusetts in war once more. New England went on the offensive in 1723, burning the Penobscot village of Panawanske (Old Town) in February. Convinced that Râle was inciting the natives to violence, New England leaders were determined to stamp out his influence for good. After unsuccessful winter expeditions in 1723 and 1724, captains Johnson Harmon and Jeremiah Moulton led forces up the Kennebec River in August 1724. Undetected, the New England forces attacked Norridgewock, killing Râle and several Abenaki

leaders and burning the village. The Abenakis were less aggressive following this defeat.

In addition to organized expeditions, British colonial governments encouraged private actions against hostile natives by offering an extraordinarily high bounty of £100 for each scalp of male Abenakis over 12 years of age. Private citizens organized and equipped armed companies, essentially business ventures, to range against the natives in hopes of gathering scalps and sharing the profits. Captain John Lovewell led one such company toward Pigwacket, where on May 8, 1725, his party was mauled by native warriors. The company lost nearly a third of its men, including Lovewell.

Peace negotiations eventually followed, but Dummer wanted peace on his terms and had difficulty obtaining agreement among the various Abenaki bands. Androscoggins, Kennebecs, and Canadian mission Native Americans continued sporadic raids on eastern frontier settlements into 1726. A formal peace was declared with Dummer's Treaty in 1727.

Fighting continued, however, in western New England in 1727, where the war was known as Grey Lock's War. Grey Lock, a Western Abenaki leader and possible refugee from King Philip's War (1675–1676), led numerous raids against British settlements in the Connecticut River Valley. He ignored repeated efforts by New York, the Iroquois, and the Penobscots to end the war. However, once the Eastern Abenakis had come to terms with the British, Grey Lock ended his war but without signing a peace agreement.

Peace was followed by another spurt of British expansion as the Massachusetts government approved the creation of a series of new townships across northern New England to establish a buffer against northern and eastern natives, satisfy the land demands of veterans of King Philip's War and King William's War, and strengthen its claims to the region.

Following Dummer's War, the Massachusetts government took greater control of the Indian trade, establishing three truck houses in frontier regions as the only sanctioned locations for trade with the natives. Also as a result of aggressive British actions against Abenaki villages, the Abenakis dispersed north and eastward in small groups, many moving to Canada.

DAVID M. CORLETT

See also

Abenakis; Dummer's Treaty; Indian Presents; King William's War; Lovewell, John; Norridgewock, Battle of; Queen Anne's War

References

Leach, Douglas Edward. *Arms for Empire: A Military History of the British Colonies in North America, 1607–1763.* New York: Macmillan, 1973.

Morrison, Kenneth M. *The Embattled Northeast: The Elusive Ideal of Alliance in Abenaki-Euramerican Relations.* Berkeley: University of California Press, 1984.

Steele, Ian K. *Warpaths: Invasions of North America.* New York: Oxford University Press, 1994.

Dunmore, Fourth Earl of

See Murray, John, Fourth Earl of Dunmore

Dunmore's War

See Lord Dunmore's War

Duston, Hannah
Birth Date: December 1657
Death Date: 1730

Settler of Haverhill, Massachusetts, captured by Native Americans during King William's War (1689–1697) and celebrated for killing nine of her captors. Born in Haverhill, Massachusetts, in December 1657, Hannah Emerson married Thomas Duston (his name appears in various sources as Dustin, Dustan, and Durstan), a farmer from Dover, New Hampshire, in 1677. The couple had eight children. The family resided in Haverhill.

When Haverhill was raided by natives on March 15, 1697, Duston had just given birth to her eighth surviving child. Thomas Duston and their other children were away from the house when the attack began and found shelter in a nearby garrison. However, Hannah and her nurse, Mary Neff, were quickly captured, and the infant was killed.

The natives marched their captives to a small island settlement near the confluence of the Contoocook and Merrimack rivers, just upriver from present-day Concord, New Hampshire. Duston, Neff,

and Samuel Lennardson, a young English boy captured at Worcester eight months previously, were held by an extended native family of two men, three women, and seven children.

Informed of the long march to Canada and the gauntlet they would face at its conclusion, the 3 captives contrived to escape. Lennardson convinced a warrior to explain how to kill and scalp a person. On the night of March 30, 1697, as the natives slept, Duston and Lennardson killed and scalped 10 of their captors and returned to Haverhill. On April 21 Duston and her husband presented the scalps to the Massachusetts General Court, petitioning for the appropriate scalp bounty. Thomas Duston received £25 on behalf of his wife. Neff and Lennardson received half that amount, although Duston reportedly killed 9 of the 10 natives herself.

Duston's deeds were celebrated throughout New England, most notably by Cotton Mather in his *Magnalia Christi Americana,* and she thus became a frontier legend. Duston survived her husband and died sometime in 1730.

DAVID M. CORLETT

See also

Captivity Narratives; Captivity of Europeans by Indians; King William's War; Scalp Bounty

References

Mather, Cotton. *Magnalia Christi Americana; Or, the Ecclesiastical History of New-England from Its First Planting in the Year 1620, unto the Year of Our Lord, 1698; In Seven Books.* London: n.p., 1702.

Ulrich, Laurel Thatcher. *Good Wives: Image and Reality in the Lives of Women in Northern New England, 1650–1750.* New York: Knopf, 1982.

Dutch-Indian Wars
Event Dates: 1639–1645, 1655, 1659–1660, and 1663–1664

A series of conflicts between European settlers in New Netherland and neighboring Algonquian-speaking tribes. Tensions flared into four periods of open warfare: Kieft's War (1639–1645), the Peach War (1655), the First Esopus War (1659–1660), and the Second Esopus War (1663–1664).

Residents of New Netherland carried on a profitable fur trade with the Iroquoian Mohawk people of the upper Hudson River Valley but increasingly viewed the Algonquian people—the Hackensacks, Raritans, and Wecquaesgeeks, among others—of the lower Hudson as an obstacle to the colony's expansion. Director General Willem Kieft had purchased several large tracts of land around New Amsterdam from the Algonquian tribes. Dutch settlers quickly moved onto the tracts and established farms. The European practice of fencing fields and letting livestock roam clashed, however, with the natives' open-field agriculture. When European hogs and cattle damaged native crops, the Native Americans retaliated by killing and eating the livestock.

Kieft aggravated the growing native hostility by ordering the tribes to pay a tribute to the colonial government. Indeed, Kieft sent a boat to collect the tribute from the riverside native villages. At one village in early 1640 the crew began loading furs without permission and sparked an armed skirmish.

Shortly thereafter Kieft received word of Raritans killing hogs belonging to a Dutch planter on Staten Island, although in fact Dutch seamen were the culprits. On July 16, 1640, Kieft sent a punitive expedition of some 70 soldiers and sailors against a band of Raritans near Staten Island with orders to demand satisfaction and, if that was not forthcoming, to destroy the Raritans' corn crop and take prisoners. During the expedition, Dutch commander Cornelis Van Tienhoven walked away rather than restrain his men, and the troops immediately began to kill Raritans.

Kieft mistakenly believed that his attack would subdue the Raritans, but it only enraged them. Although conflicting reports obscure whether a particular incident triggered Kieft's War, a picture emerges of a cycle of murder and revenge, some of it fueled by alcohol, the colonists' main stock in trade. On September 1, 1641, the Raritans retaliated for the July 1640 expedition, killing four Dutch men and burning several houses on Staten Island. Kieft then called for the other tribes to turn on the Raritans. Enough of them did so that the Raritans sued for peace by the end of the year.

In the meantime, in August 1641 a Wecquaesgeek man had robbed and murdered a Dutch craftsman, claiming that he was avenging the long-ago murder of his uncle by Dutch traders. Kieft demanded, without result, that the killer be turned over to him for punishment. The end of hostilities with the Raritans freed Kieft to seek redress from the Wecquaesgeeks. He mounted an expedition against them in March 1642, but the soldiers failed to find the native encampment.

Frightened by how near they had come to being attacked, the Wecquaesgeeks sued for peace. They promised to turn over the fugitive but never did. In the summer of 1642 the son of a Hackensack sachem, while drunk, shot and killed a Dutch man at work on a Staten Island farm and then fled the area. Again Kieft demanded custody of the fugitive but to no avail.

In February 1643 Kieft decided that the time had come to mount an attack so brutal that it would end all native resistance. He chose two targets: an encampment at Pavonia, where several hundred Tappan and Wecquaesgeek people had taken refuge after an attack by the Mohawks, and an encampment of Hackensacks on Manhattan Island. On the night of February 25, 1643, Kieft ordered his militia to massacre the refugees. Eighty Dutch soldiers torched the Pavonia encampment as their victims slept and killed some 80 defenseless men, women, and children. Some 50 volunteers attacked the refugees on Manhattan, killing another 40 of them.

Kieft's massacre ignited a general Indian uprising against colonial settlements—both Dutch and English—throughout New Netherland. Eleven tribes mounted attacks on the colony's farms and settlements, and the colonists fled to the New Amsterdam fortifications. Many Dutch families desperately sought passage back to the Netherlands. In late April 1643 the tribes accepted the terms

of a peace treaty. However, Kieft insulted the sachems by giving them only the bare minimum of the expected gifts.

The young men of the tribes agitated for a return to war, and violent incidents proliferated. In August 1643 the Wappinger tribe began attacking trading ships on the Hudson. The violence quickly escalated, and within a month 1,500 warriors from seven tribes had attacked and occupied much of Manhattan.

Kieft then hired John Underhill, the New England officer who had taken part in the 1637 massacre of the Pequots, to lead a militia force of some 40 English volunteers. Underhill's troops joined with Dutch militia and swept through the countryside, killing more than 100 Native Americans and mutilating several prisoners. A third of the war's native casualties occurred on one night in February 1644. In an action similar to that of the Pequot massacre, Underhill led a 130-man force in the slaughter of more than 500 Wecquaesgeeks and Wappingers in present-day Westchester County, New York, setting fire to their village and killing them as they fled.

Some of the Algonquian tribes sued for peace in April 1645, and by August all parties had signed a treaty. Kieft's War ended with more than 1,500 Algonquians killed and the countryside virtually emptied of Dutch settlers. The thinning of both populations reduced the opportunities for conflict. However, colonists complained bitterly about Kieft's incompetence, some calling him too bellicose and others saying that he failed to prosecute the war with sufficient vigor. Their complaints spurred the West India Company to replace him with Petrus Stuyvesant, who arrived in May 1647. European immigration surged, and once again natives and colonists struggled for control of the land. Isolated killings occurred, but unlike his predecessor, Stuyvesant showed restraint.

The so-called Peach War began in 1655 with the murder of a native woman as she picked peaches from a colonist's trees. Nearly 2,000 Mahican, Esopus, and Hackensack people had come down the river to invade an enemy people, the Canarsies of Long Island. Camped on Manhattan, they foraged for food, and a hot-tempered Dutch landowner shot the woman in his orchard. To avenge her death, on September 15 hundreds of warriors invaded Manhattan Island, Staten Island, and Long Island. During a three-day rampage they burned farms and orchards and captured nearly 100 women and children. The attack took place while Stuyvesant was absent in Delaware subjugating the Swedes. On Stuyvesant's hurried return, colonial forces retaliated against native villages and farms, although peace negotiations began in October. While the combatants did not bring the war to a formal conclusion, hostilities ceased, and the Native Americans began ransoming their prisoners. The episode caused the deaths of some 50 colonists and 60 Native Americans, the loss of some 500 cattle, and the destruction of 28 farms.

Stuyvesant began instructing his colonists to live together in defensible villages rather than on their scattered farms. The settlers, however, preferred to live independently and thus remained isolated and vulnerable to attack. They also gave the natives brandy

Illustration showing New Netherland governor Willem Kieft and his men massacring Mohawk Indians during the Dutch-Indian Wars of 1639–1664. The fighting in this period was triggered by the often brutal treatment of the Indians by the Dutch. (North Wind Picture Archives)

in exchange for furs. Young men of the Esopus tribe, fueled by the brandy, harassed colonists around the village of Esopus, a Dutch settlement between New Amsterdam and Fort Orange (Albany). Stuyvesant visited Esopus in 1657 and sternly admonished both settlers and natives to refrain from liquor trafficking. He insisted on the fortification of Esopus and stayed long enough to see it accomplished. The situation returned to a semblance of tranquility, but resentment simmered on both sides.

On September 20, 1659, a colonist gave 8 Native Americans brandy in payment for harvesting his corn. They proceeded to have a loud party just outside of Esopus. Several settlers then attacked them after they had fallen asleep and killed 1 of them. The next day some 500 Native Americans avenged the murder

by destroying the settlers' crops, killing livestock, and burning barns. The Esopus and Wappinger peoples attacked colonists' farms and villages along the Hudson River and laid siege to Esopus for 23 days. Stuyvesant raised an army of some 300 men and came to its aid on October 10, but the natives had already abandoned the siege.

After a quiet winter, Stuyvesant and his force again sailed north in March 1660 to finish the war. After a series of skirmishes and the killing of the eldest Esopus chief, the combatants signed a treaty in July 1660.

Still resentful that Stuyvesant had deported 11 captives to slavery in the West Indies during the previous war, the Esopuses began a new series of attacks on June 7, 1663. They massacred the inhabitants of Wiltwyck (formerly Esopus), including women and children, leaving more than 20 dead and taking nearly 50 prisoners. Calling for volunteers among the panic-stricken populace, Stuyvesant was able to assemble only 150 men, 80 of whom were mercenaries. Their capable leader, Martin Cregier, received a description of the terrain from a woman who had escaped from her captors. On September 3 Cregier led a successful expedition from Wiltwyck, killed some 30 of the Native Americans, and recovered a number of prisoners.

The remnants of the Esopuses continued to harass the settlers until a second expedition in October destroyed what was left of the Esopus crops. The surviving Esopuses took refuge with the Wappingers. Although the two tribes planned a joint attack, they lacked the resources to carry it out. Instead, they sued for peace near the end of 1663. Distracted by the growing English threat, Stuyvesant accepted their offer. A treaty concluded on May 16, 1664, divested the Esopus people of all their land near Wiltwyck.

ROBERTA WIENER

See also
Kieft, Willem; Kieft's War; Stuyvesant, Petrus

References
De Forest, John William. *History of the Indians of Connecticut from the Earliest Known Period to 1850*. Hamden, CT: Archon Books, 1964.

Jameson, J. Franklin, ed. *Narratives of New Netherland, 1609–1664*. New York: Scribner, 1909.

Kammen, Michael. *Colonial New York: A History*. New York: Scribner, 1975.

Rink, Oliver A. *Holland on the Hudson: An Economic and Social History of Dutch New York*. Ithaca, NY: Cornell University Press, 1986.

Taylor, Alan. *American Colonies: The Settling of North America*. New York: Viking/Penguin, 2001.

Van der Zee, Henri, and Barbara Van der Zee. *A Sweet and Alien Land: The Story of Dutch New York*. New York: Viking, 1978.

Dutch-Mohawk Treaty

Treaty of alliance made in 1643 between the Mohawks and the Dutch colonists of New Netherland. Both the Mohawks and Dutch settlers in New Netherland came under increasing pressure in the early 1640s from their Native American neighbors and other European colonial powers. France was expanding its settlements in Canada, and the French, together with their Algonquian and Huron allies, posed a significant military threat to the Mohawks. But the more immediate danger came from the French-allied natives' challenge to Mohawk dominance of the regional fur trade.

Dutch claims to the territory along the Connecticut River were jeopardized by the growing number of New Englanders settling in the area. At the same time, tensions with New Netherland's neighbors had led to a series of conflicts called Kieft's War (1639–1645), named after the colony's governor, Willem Kieft.

In these circumstances the Dutch and the Mohawks recognized the benefits of an alliance. Building on earlier treaties of friendship entered into between the Dutch traders at Fort Orange (Albany) and the Mohawks, Kieft began negotiations to formalize the relationship between the Mohawks and the colonial government. The actual treaty has not been found, although references to it elsewhere give some information regarding its terms.

The treaty was apparently an economic agreement as well as a political alliance. The Dutch affirmed the Mohawks' position as intermediaries in the fur trade with New Netherland and provided firearms with which the Mohawks could oppose the efforts of the pro-French tribes to gain a larger share of the trade and direct it to New France. The Mohawks agreed in turn to serve as intermediaries for the Dutch in the colonists' disputes with other natives in the area and later played a crucial role in bringing the Esopus tribe to negotiate with the Dutch during the Esopus Wars (1659–1660 and 1663–1664).

The Dutch-Mohawk Treaty remained in effect to the benefit of both parties until the English capture of New Netherland in 1664. The English then followed in the footsteps of the Dutch and formed their own alliance with the Mohawks.

JIM PIECUCH

See also
Kieft, Willem; Kieft's War; Mohawks

References
Jennings, Francis. *The Ambiguous Iroquois Empire: The Covenant Chain Confederation of Indian Tribes with English Colonies from Its Beginnings to the Lancaster Treaty of 1744*. New York: Norton, 1984.

Trelease, Allen W. *Indian Affairs in Colonial New York: The Seventeenth Century*. Ithaca, NY: Cornell University Press, 1960.

E

Easton Conference and Treaty
Start Date: October 11, 1758
End Date: October 26, 1758

Meeting of various Native American groups, Pennsylvania representatives, and British royal officials held at Easton, Pennsylvania, from October 11 to 26, 1758, sometimes referred to as the Easton Congress. The Easton Conference was the largest meeting of its kind in the colony's history. The congress and resulting treaty came about at the height of the French and Indian War (1754–1763) and must be viewed within the context of that conflict. The 1758 meeting was actually the culmination of a series of conferences held at the same location beginning in 1756. The negotiations involved a variety of groups, often with competing interests.

For the British, the key issue at the time was their desire to ensure the support of the Iroquois and Ohio-area tribes or at least to guarantee their neutrality in the war against the French. The outcome of the negotiations at Easton held special importance for Brigadier General John Forbes, whose campaign against the French at Fort Duquesne hung in the balance. George Croghan was the chief representative of the British government. In addition, several groups represented various Pennsylvania interests at the conference. On the Native American side, the Iroquois Confederacy, the Delawares, the Shawnees, and others were represented. Altogether there were some 500 Native American representatives from 13 nations present at Easton.

The various indigenous groups sought a redress of grievances stemming from previous land agreements, most notably the Walking Purchase. Likewise, there existed internal divisions among the natives as the Iroquois sought to reimpose their hegemony over various tribes they considered dependent, such as the Delawares.

The Delaware chief Teedyuscung, who played a significant role in the two previous Easton conferences, thus had his prestige undercut by the representatives of the Iroquois Confederacy.

The atmosphere at the conference was tense and confused from the start, with Teedyuscung frequently drunk and then ignored by the other tribal leaders in their private councils. The meeting ended on October 26 with the promise by British officials to look into the various native claims of mistreatment in land dealings. Furthermore, the British promised to keep land beyond the Appalachian Mountains free from white settlement. This pronouncement was key in that it allowed the Iroquois to use their considerable influence with the Ohio tribes to keep them neutral.

The British pledge cleared the way for Forbes to advance on Fort Duquesne and force the French to abandon that post. On the Native American side, the Iroquois succeeded in reasserting their hegemony at the cost of Teedyuscung's reputation. Likewise, they believed that they had achieved a clear guarantee of protection from the British Crown for the lands beyond the Appalachians.

JAMES R. MCINTYRE

See also
Croghan, George; Delawares; French and Indian War; Iroquois; Iroquois Confederacy; Shawnees; Teedyuscung; Walking Purchase

References
Anderson, Fred. *Crucible of War: The Seven Years' War and the Fate of the Empire in British North America, 1754–1766.* New York: Vintage Books, 2001.

Chidsey, A. D. *A Frontier Village: Pre-Revolutionary Easton.* Easton, PA: Northumberland County Historical and Genealogical Society, 1940.

Wainright, Nicholas. *George Croghan, Wilderness Diplomat.* Chapel Hill: University of North Carolina Press, 1959.

Econochaca, Battle of
Event Date: December 23, 1813

Battle fought as part of the Creek War (1813–1814) at the Creek stronghold of Econochaca in present-day Lowndes County, Alabama, on December 23, 1813, between American forces and Creek warriors. The Battle of Econochaca is also known as the Battle of Holy Ground. Brigadier General Ferdinand L. Claiborne of the Mississippi Territorial Militia commanded the American army of some 1,200 men, composed of militia from the Mississippi Territory, the U.S. Army 3rd Infantry Regiment, and Choctaw allies. The Creek force, the total number of which is unknown, was led by William Weatherford, also known as Red Eagle. The Holy Ground had become a refuge for fugitive Creeks displaced from their homes because of the war and was thus a high-priority target for American forces.

Econochaca, protected by fallen timber and stakes driven firmly into the ground, was situated on a small wooded plateau, with ravines and swamp on three sides and the Alabama River on the other. Claiborne's army advanced on the village in three columns. The initial attack by Major Joseph Carson's column about noon was immediately followed up by Colonel Gilbert Russell's 3rd Regiment. A small mounted force, led by Major Henry Cassels, was ordered to take a position on the far side of the settlement to cut off any retreating Creeks. Cassels, however, did not get into position quickly enough after the attack began, and consequently most of the Creeks escaped. About 33 on the Creek side died in the brief engagement, including 12 African Americans fighting as allies of the Creeks. American casualties amounted to 1 man killed and 20 wounded. The Americans were unsuccessful in their pursuit of the fleeing Creeks.

The Americans then looted Econochaca, which contained about 200 houses and a large supply of provisions. One significant find was correspondence between the Spanish governor at Pensacola, Gonzalez Manrique, and the chiefs of the Creek Nation, indicating a link between the two. Following the capture of the Holy Ground, the Americans destroyed another Creek village farther up the Alabama River, but the expedition ended in January 1814 when most of Claiborne's troops were discharged at the expiration of their enlistments.

Despite the Creeks' escape from Econochaca, the battle's real importance lay in the fact that it proved false predictions made by Creek prophets who had pronounced the site as consecrated and surrounded by a magic barrier that would strike dead any white man who tried to pass through it. This victory by the Americans had a severe negative effect on Creek morale for the remainder of the war.

Tom Kanon

See also
Choctaws; Creeks; Creek War; Native Americans and the War of 1812; Weatherford, William

References
Claiborne, J. F. H. *Mississippi, as Province, Territory and State, with Biographical Notices of Eminent Citizens.* 1880; reprint, Baton Rouge: Louisiana State University Press, 1964.
Halbert, H. S., and T. H. Ball. *The Creek War of 1813 and 1814.* University: University of Alabama Press, 1969.
Owsley, Frank L., Jr. *Struggle for the Gulf Borderlands. The Creek War and the Battle of New Orleans, 1812–1815.* Gainesville: University Presses of Florida, 1981.

Ecuyer, Simeon
Birth Date: Unknown
Death Date: Unknown

Swiss-born soldier in the Royal American Regiment and commander of Fort Pitt during 1761–1763 who was best known for employing a crude form of germ warfare against the Delawares during Pontiac's Rebellion (1763). No reliable birth information is available for Simeon Ecuyer, and his early years are shrouded in obscurity.

Ecuyer entered the historical record near the end of the French and Indian War (1754–1763). Beginning in 1761 Ecuyer, a captain, took command of Fort Pitt (present-day Pittsburgh, Pennsylvania). The fort had withstood repeated attacks and siege attempts before the British finally forced the French to abandon the post in 1758. As soon as the French and Indian War ended in 1763, another conflict flared, this one between the British and Native American tribes in the Ohio Valley and Great Lakes region.

The renewed warfare was instigated by Ottawa chief Pontiac. He and other native leaders believed that they had just cause for rebellion, including new policies instituted by the British commander in chief in North America, Major General Jeffrey Amherst, that included an end to the French practices of gift giving, a staple of Native American diplomacy. In the spring of 1763 in what became known as Pontiac's Rebellion or Pontiac's War, area natives advanced on Fort Pitt, burning homes as they advanced. The attacks forced dozens of frightened colonists into the confines of the fort. Realizing that this post was now terribly overcrowded, the warriors laid siege to it, allowing no one to enter or exit. In May or June 1763 Captain Ecuyer informed Colonel Henry Bouquet that he feared an outbreak of disease because of conditions. Indeed, right after the letter was sent smallpox broke out within the fort. Ecuyer quarantined those affected and stubbornly refused to capitulate to the besiegers.

On June 24, 1763, according to the journal of the trader William Trent, two native chiefs entered Fort Pitt to convince Ecuyer to give up the fight. He refused, but he did present them with two blankets and a handkerchief. All three articles had come from the smallpox victims.

Historians are still in disagreement over who actually hatched the plan to infect the natives with contaminated articles. But Trent's journal leaves little doubt that it was Ecuyer who carried out the deed. In a July 1763 letter, Amherst had mentioned that the natives should be infected with smallpox, though it is unlikely that he had heard about Ecuyer's action. Whether he had mentioned this previously to Ecuyer cannot be determined, but it is obvious that Amherst would have approved of it in any case. In a matter of several months, a smallpox epidemic swept through the native populations of the Ohio River Valley. Whether it was a result—direct or indirect—of Ecuyer's deed at Fort Pitt cannot be definitively established.

In July 1763 a group of Shawnee and Delaware warriors assaulted Fort Pitt. Sometime during the fight and the ensuing siege, Ecuyer was wounded. The garrison nevertheless fended off the attackers until Bouquet arrived with some 400 reinforcements. Bouquet took command of Fort Pitt in August 1763. Little is known of Ecuyer's remaining years, and the circumstances of his death remain obscure.

PAUL G. PIERPAOLI JR.

See also

Bouquet, Henry; Delawares; French and Indian War; Pontiac's Rebellion; Shawnees

References

Darlington, Mary C., ed. *Fort Pitt and Letters from the Frontier.* Pittsburgh: J. R. Weldin, 1892.

McConnell, Michael N. *A Country Between: The Upper Ohio and Its Peoples, 1724–1774.* Lincoln: University of Nebraska Press, 1992.

Peckham, Howard H. *Pontiac and the Indian Uprising.* Princeton, NJ: Princeton University Press, 1947.

Edged Weapons

During the Indian Wars, particularly those of the colonial era and the early national period, edged weapons appeared in great variety and design. Traditionally, edged weapons provided a relatively inexpensive means of conducting combat. The most common types of edged weapons in North America were swords, pikes, knives, hatchets, and bayonets.

In the Spanish Empire, the common *espadon* (two-handed sword) of medieval Europe eventually gave way to the lighter and more flexible rapier. The rapier possessed distinctive *quillons* (protective metal rings about the handle) and a long thin double-edged blade. Elsewhere, rancheros and soldiers alike carried less fanciful *espadas anchas* (common swords). Although the Spanish government formally adopted a cavalry, light infantry, and dragoon sword in the 18th century, the conservative nature of Spain's bureaucracy and the need for economy required the heavy reuse and refurbishment of old swords. Most Spanish colonial swords proved ruggedly simple in design and were worn either in the belt or over the shoulder.

In Europe, the British Army relied essentially on two types of slightly curved single-edged swords that saw widespread use in America and were unofficially known as the Model 1742 and the Model 1751. However, the English were not known for their cutlery; as a consequence, many army and navy officers frequently purchased their swords from abroad. At the time Solingen, Toledo, Valencia, and Milan produced some of the finest blades in Europe. Furthermore, neither the British Army nor the Royal Navy standardized their sword designs until after the American Revolutionary War (1775–1783). Consequently, the actual design and acquisition of swords often fell on individual regimental commanders and ship captains. Despite the popularity of the weapon, the French and Indian War (1754–1763) proved the relative uselessness of the sword. Although edged weapons remained the weapon of choice among cavalry, elsewhere such pieces were fast becoming strictly ceremonial because of the growing lethality of artillery and muskets.

As with the British, the French also realized the sword's impracticality during the French and Indian War. After 1764 French infantry no longer employed swords as combat weapons, although the cavalry did retain them, as did noncommissioned officers, musicians, and grenadiers. The French did not standardize their sword design until 1767.

Colonial American swords revealed tremendous variety in both style and design. American militiamen not only used swords made in Europe and by local smiths but also made use of family heirlooms and captured pieces. In the end, no truly innovative sword designs or patterns emerged in America. As a rule, American-made swords tended to be of poorer quality than their European counterparts. However, beginning in the 18th century, the immigration of German swordsmiths—with their patterns, molds, and tools—slowly but steadily increased the viability of the craft in the British colonies.

On both sides of the Atlantic, other types of swords also existed. For example, hunting swords and small swords remained popular among the civilian population, whereas fanciful and often bejeweled town or walking swords continued to be used within diplomatic and court circles.

Another broad class of swords, the cutlass (also known as a hanger) was a short single-edged weapon. In the military, swords generally fell into one of two categories: foot (as a backup weapon for infantry) and mounted (as a primary weapon for cavalry). Generally, officers' swords possessed such fineries as engraving, silver inlay, and handles made of bone or ivory.

Another popular edged weapon was the pike. A weapon ancient in design, it consisted of an iron or brass blade attached to the end of a long thin wooden pole. The pike went by various names, including bill, gisarme, lance, partisan, poleaxe, spontoon, halberd, and even half-pike. Although similar in design, each name suggested a slight variation in pattern. For example, a full pike measured 14–16 feet in length, whereas a half-pike came to 6–8 feet; a fauchard was a pike with spikes protruding from the dull side of the blade, and a halberd flaunted a head

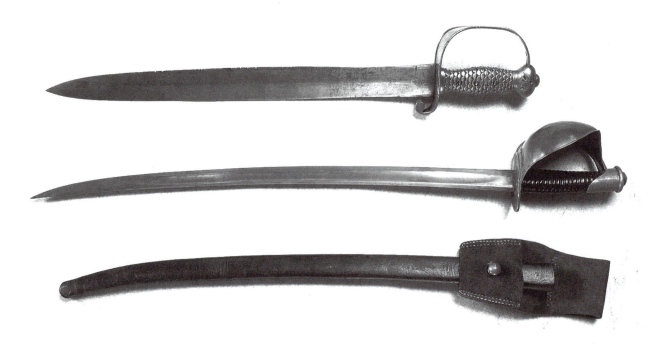

Short sword, hanger sword, and navy cutlass with scabbard. (Tria Giovan/Corbis)

with a long spear point and a crescent-shaped blade. Originally introduced to the Americas by the Spanish, the pike normally served as a weapon against cavalry to protect infantry made temporarily vulnerable when reloading their muskets. Although pikes proved effective against cavalry, they too became obsolete with the emergence of improved firearms and artillery. Also, the sheer length of pikes (up to 22 feet) rendered them impractical in North America's heavily wooded terrain. Consequently, by the end of the 17th century Europeans and Americans alike abandoned the use of pikes as formal weapons. They were, however, retained as ceremonial pieces employed by officers and court officials.

The most commonly used polearm, however, was the hatchet. In the colonial period, the hatchet resembled the European half-ax or American felling ax. Simple in design, hatchets entailed the same fundamental construction: a short wood or iron handle with a forged iron head. The blade edge normally flared out slightly so that it was approximately twice the width of the base of the blade. Easily repaired by camp blacksmiths, hatchets were generally preferred over bayonets because of their ruggedness and utility. The hatchet consisted of a handle (or helve) that fit into the eye of the head. The blunt end of the hatchet head was the poll, and the sharp-edged end was referred to as the bit. One curious innovation—the pipe tomahawk—appeared in the early 1700s. It incorporated a smoking pipe into the body of the handle; a cast brass version appeared around 1750. Another (but less common) innovation was the so-called spontoon hatchet, an unwieldy weapon that used the head design of a traditional long polearm. Other designs included a hammer poll (which was

just as the name suggests) and the less common (and decidedly unwieldy) spiked poll, which featured a picklike extension opposite the blade. Militia laws long required soldiers to carry both a sword and a hatchet, but by the time of the American Revolutionary War, most colonies had resorted to the hatchet alone because of the latter's versatility and low cost. Eventually both the French and British made the hatchet a standard piece of soldiers' equipment.

As with the hatchet, the knife dates to antiquity (in fact, the word "knife" descends from the Anglo-Saxon *cnif*). The value of the knife traditionally lay in its simple design, ease of manufacture, and practical use as both a weapon and a tool for the soldier. People employed a wide variety of knives in the colonial period. For example, soldiers used a rifle knife—with a short blade of about three to four inches in length—during combat to trim the excess cloth from musket-ball patches.

Daggers were more fanciful and a bit less common. Such weapons were normally finely made double-edged knives with blades approximately six inches long and a small hand guard. They usually possessed such adornments as silver hilts and ivory grips. Generally, daggers were carried by officers.

The most common blade of all, however, was the formidable-looking hunting knife. Also known as the fighting or scalping knife, this particular weapon brandished a cutting edge up to 12 inches in length. Handles on knives tended to be made of either antler, cow horn, or wood. As with many edged weapons, however, knives lost their primacy as combat weapons with the advent of advanced muskets and artillery. A notable exception was the Bowie knife, a large fixed-blade knife with a blade length of 6 to 24 inches that was popularized by Colonel James "Jim" Bowie in the early 19th century.

The bayonet also came into prominence during the colonial period. The exact origins of the weapon remain unclear. The Old French word for arrow was *bayon,* and in the 17th century the term "bayonet" referred to a dagger; another theory holds that the weapon was developed in the French town of Bayonne. In any case, the bayonet—a blade approximately 16 inches long attached to the muzzle of a musket—emerged in France as early as the 1640s.

Bayonets allowed a soldier protection against enemy cavalry during the dangerous lull required to reload a musket. In short, the bayonet crudely merged the pike with the musket. The original prototype of the bayonet, the plug, consisted of a blade attached to a tapered wooden handle, the latter part fitting snugly into the muzzle of the musket. Unfortunately, plug bayonets usually proved a nuisance to soldiers. The plug's handle could break off inside the musket barrel and could also be rendered useless because of the buildup of hard gunpowder residue inside the muzzle. Moreover, the plug bayonet also required the soldier to completely remove the entire blade each time to fire and reload.

A solution to such problems, the so-called socket bayonet, emerged in Sweden in the 1680s. By attaching the bayonet to the exterior surface of the muzzle using a hollow metal cylinder, a soldier could load and fire a musket while the bayonet was attached. By the early 18th century, the socket bayonet became standard throughout European and American armies. It would remain essentially unchanged for the next 150 years and would be employed by the U.S. Army throughout virtually all of the Indian Wars.

FRANK HARPER

See also
Artillery; Muskets; Rifles

References
Peterson, Harold L. *Arms and Armor in Colonial America, 1526–1783.* Harrisburg, PA: Stackpole, 1956.
Wilbur, C. Keith. *Picture Book of the Continental Soldier.* Harrisburg, PA: Stackpole, 1969.
Wilkinson-Latham, Robert. *Swords in Color: Including Other Edged Weapons.* New York: Arco, 1978.

8th U.S. Cavalry Regiment
See Cavalry Regiment, 8th U.S.

El Popé
See Popé

Emistisiguo
Birth Date: ca. 1718
Death Date: 1782

Prominent chief of the Upper Creeks from approximately 1763 until his death in 1782. Born in what is now western Georgia about 1718, Emistisiguo rose to a prominent leadership position in the Creek Confederacy. He participated in the war against the neighboring Choctaws from 1763 to 1776 and took the leading diplomatic role in the Creeks' territorial dispute with Georgia in 1773 and 1774.

After the Creeks ceded a large amount of land to that colony in 1773, several disgruntled warriors launched attacks against colonists in these ceded lands at the beginning of 1774. The Georgians retaliated, and officials halted all trade with the Creeks. These actions threatened to spark all-out war. To resolve the dispute, in October Emistisiguo traveled to Savannah, where, with representatives of the Lower Creeks, the native leaders reached agreement with Governor Sir James Wright and British Indian superintendent John Stuart to halt their attacks in exchange for a resumption of trade.

At the start of the American Revolutionary War (1775–1783), Stuart understood that Britain could rely on the support of the Creeks, Cherokees, Choctaws, and Chickasaws, all of whom considered the westward expansion of the colonies a significant threat. These tribes believed that if the British prevailed in the war, they would protect native land rights from further encroachment. However, divisions prevailed among the Creeks, as many leaders hesitated to join the war against the colonists without assurances of British support. Emistisiguo disagreed and led his followers against the rebels, often cooperating closely with Lieutenant Colonel Thomas Brown's Loyalist Florida Rangers.

Other Creeks, influenced by American agent George Galphin, attempted to kill Emistisiguo and some British agents in 1777 but failed. Stuart eventually secured the allegiance of these dissidents, but Emistisiguo, undaunted, continued to harass the Americans on the frontier.

After British forces had been confined to Savannah in 1782, Emistisiguo led several hundred Creeks in an attempt to reach the town. Finding his way blocked by American troops under Brigadier General Anthony Wayne, Emistisiguo launched a surprise night attack on the American camp near Gibbons's Plantation. Wayne's troops repulsed the Native Americans after a fierce struggle in which Emistisiguo was killed.

JAIME RAMÓN OLIVARES AND JIM PIECUCH

See also
Augusta, Congress of; Creeks; Native Americans and the American Revolutionary War

References
Cashin, Edward J. *The King's Ranger: Thomas Brown and the American Revolution on the Southern Frontier.* New York: Fordham University Press, 1999.

Cochran, David H. *The Creek Frontier, 1549–1783.* Norman: University of Oklahoma Press, 1967.

Wright, J. Leitch, Jr. *Creeks and Seminoles: The Destruction and Regeneration of the Muscogulge People.* Lincoln: University of Nebraska Press, 1986.

Emuckfaw Creek, Battle of
Event Date: January 22, 1814

Military engagement between Tennessee militia and White Stick Creeks and Cherokee allies on one side and Red Stick Creeks on the other. The battle took place on January 22, 1814, at Emuckfaw, a Red Stick settlement located in southeastern Alabama. Although they forced the Americans to retreat at Emuckfaw, the Red Sticks lost their best opportunity for a quick victory over the United States and its Native American allies during the Creek War (1813–1814).

The Creek War, which coincided with the War of 1812, began as a civil war between two rival Creek factions: the Red Stick Creeks, encouraged by Tecumseh, who supported the British and wanted to end American expansion in Alabama and southern Georgia, and the White Stick Creeks, who favored a conciliatory policy toward the United States. The Red Sticks, whose name was derived from the red-colored war clubs used by their warriors and the magical red sticks used by Creek shamans, championed traditional Creek

values and, beginning in 1813, actively sought to expel white settlers from Alabama and southern Georgia.

Following the slaughter of 250 white and mixed Creek settlers by Red Stick warriors near Mobile, Alabama, in August 1813, the United States initiated military activities to crush the British-supplied Red Stick uprising. Tennessee militia under Major General Andrew Jackson therefore spent most of the War of 1812 fighting Native Americans rather than British troops.

On January 17, 1814, Jackson and his men departed from Fort Struther in northern Alabama to confront the Red Sticks at the village of Emuckfaw. More than 90 percent of Jackson's 1,000 men, however, were inexperienced recruits lacking discipline who had just arrived at Fort Struther on January 14. In addition, the troops were forced to march through difficult terrain in territory occupied by hostile forces. On January 21, 1814, Jackson's troops encamped along Emuckfaw Creek, about 12 miles from the village of Emuckfaw. Jackson immediately sent out scouts, who discovered an encampment of about 500 Red Sticks located approximately three miles away.

At dawn on January 22, 1814, the Red Sticks attacked Jackson's encampment but were repelled. Taking the initiative, Jackson sent a force of 200 Americans and 200 Native American allies led by Brigadier General John R. Coffee to attack the Red Stick encampment. Finding the Red Stick encampment too well defended, Coffee ordered his troops to return to Jackson's camp. The Red Sticks, however, immediately counterattacked Jackson's encampment. In the ensuing battle 54 of Jackson's men were killed and a number

The Battle of Emuckfaw Creek, January 22, 1814, during the Creek War. (Getty Images)

were wounded, while the Red Sticks suffered only 24 fatalities. Realizing his precarious situation and unwilling to suffer a defeat, Jackson ordered a withdrawal to Fort Struther.

On January 23, 1814, Jackson's troops encamped on the Enitachopco Creek, about 30 miles north of Emuckfaw, on their way back to Fort Struther. Although Jackson's troops passed the night without incident, they were again attacked by Red Stick warriors on the morning of January 24, 1814, as they attempted to cross Enitachopco Creek. Jackson's men were able to repel the attack. Nevertheless, Jackson realized the difficulty of fighting the Red Stick Creeks in hostile territory without sufficient reinforcements and continued the retreat to Fort Struther. Regardless, the Red Creeks had lost their best chance for a decisive victory against Jackson's forces, who resumed the offensive in mid-March 1814, leading to Jackson's defeat of the Red Sticks in the Battle of Horseshoe Bend on March 27, 1814, and precipitating the surrender of the Red Sticks five months later.

MICHAEL R. HALL

See also

Creeks; Creek War; Horseshoe Bend, Battle of; Jackson, Andrew; Native Americans and the War of 1812; Red Sticks; Tecumseh

References

Debo, Angie. *Road to Disappearance: A History of the Creek Indians.* Norman: University of Oklahoma Press, 1979.

O'Brien, Sean Michael. *In Bitterness and in Tears: Andrew Jackson's Destruction of the Creeks and Seminoles.* Guilford, CT: Lyons, 2005.

Encomienda

A feudalistic arrangement that involved land allotments—but not grants—as well as a tributary system of labor for Spanish conquistadors. The word *encomienda* comes from the Spanish word *encomendar,* meaning "to entrust." Spanish conquistadors employed the *encomienda* system throughout the Spanish Empire in return for services to the Crown. The *encomendero,* or holder of the *encomienda,* received a revocable grant from the Crown that included the labor of native peoples occupying the land. The *encomendero* did not actually possess native lands, although his absolute power made him the de facto local ruler.

First used in Spain against the Moors and then established by the Castilian Crown for the empire in May 1493, the *encomienda* was designed to spread Catholicism and Spanish civilization to the natives as well as to protect them against outside attack. For such services, natives were bound to provide labor to the *encomendero.* By the Law of Burgos, any *encomendero* with 50 people or more under his care was required to instruct one young male who could teach the others the tenets of Catholicism and other "civilizing" lessons. The Crown also encouraged intermarriage as a means of civilizing the natives.

The *encomienda* was not inheritable, and the natives theoretically retained ownership of their lands as well as independence from *encomendero* legal or political control. In practice, however, they were often subjected to significant and arbitrary exploitation at the hands of the *encomienda* holder. Far from official oversight and control, the conquistadors indulged their voracious appetites for wealth. Unwilling to perform manual labor themselves, ambitious *encomenderos* acquired lands and established a plantation-style economy based on unpaid labor performed by the natives.

The *encomenderos* eventually became a landed gentry living off the backs of indigenous peoples, many of whom became virtual slaves. Empowered to set the amounts of tribute (tax) that could be collected from the natives, *encomenderos* used that power to exact huge concessions from them. Very soon abuses of the system in the Caribbean contributed to major population losses. The Caribbean *encomienda* was all but defunct within a generation.

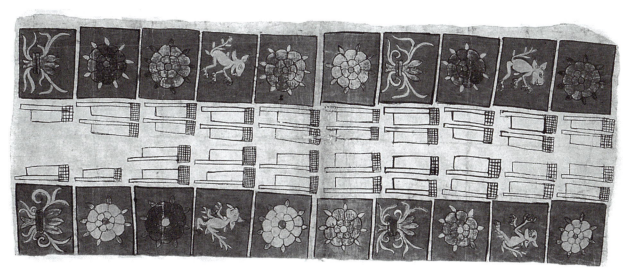

Leaf from the *Huejotzingo Codex* depicts the variety and quantity of woven cloth given in tribute by the people of the Puebla region of Mexico to the Spanish administration, 1531. (Library of Congress)

The New Laws of 1542 and the establishment of the Council of the Indies set limits on the amount of tribute and established local government in the form of the Audienca. However, the *encomenderos* quickly took control of local governments, and the *encomienda* continued, although it ultimately evolved into the *repartimiento*, finally becoming debt peonage.

JOHN H. BARNHILL

See also
Spain

References
Bannon, John F., ed. *Indian Labor in the Spanish Indies.* Boston: D. C. Heath, 1966.
Himmerich y Valencia, Robert. *The Encomenderos of New Spain.* Austin: University of Texas Press, 1991.
Simpson, Lesley Byrd. *The Encomienda in New Spain.* Berkeley and Los Angeles: University of California Press, 1950.

Endicott, John
Birth Date: ca. 1588
Death Date: March 15, 1665

Governor of Massachusetts (1628–1630, 1644–1645, 1649–1650, 1652–1654, 1655–1665) and colonial military leader best known for his exploits during the Pequot War (1636–1638). John Endicott (also spelled Endecott) was born in Devon, England, about 1588. It is believed that he had some military service before joining the New England Company and leading a group of colonists to Salem, Massachusetts, in 1628.

Endicott served as governor of Massachusetts Bay Colony until the arrival of John Winthrop in 1630. A staunch Puritan, Endicott is often associated with his harsh persecution of religious dissenters, such as the tearing down of Thomas Morton's maypole and the hanging of Quakers.

In 1636 Endicott led a group of 90 colonial volunteers on a preemptive strike against the natives of Block Island and the Pequots. This action precipitated the Pequot War. Outraged by the assault, the Pequots retaliated against the English at Fort Saybrook. The war culminated in the 1637 Mystic Fort Fight, which killed 700 Pequots and virtually extinguished that tribe.

Considered an upstanding citizen of Salem and Massachusetts Bay, Endicott held several high offices, including the governorship, for multiple terms. After the death of John Winthrop in 1649, Endicott served as either governor or deputy governor of the colony until his death on March 15, 1665, at Boston.

SARAH E. MILLER

See also
Endicott Expedition; Mystic Fort Fight; Pequots; Pequot War

References
Cave, Alfred A. *The Pequot War.* Amherst: University of Massachusetts Press, 1996.

Portrait of John Endicott (1588–1665), colonial magistrate, soldier, and governor of the Massachusetts Bay Colony. Endicott is best known for leading the preemptive attack that began the Pequot War (1636–1638). (Library of Congress)

Mayo, Lawrence Shaw. *John Endecott: A Biography.* Cambridge: Harvard University Press, 1936.

Endicott Expedition
Event Date: August 1636

Military expedition mounted by Massachusetts Bay Colony against Native Americans on Block Island (now part of Rhode Island) that precipitated the Pequot War (1636–1638). In July 1636 a ship captained by John Gallop came on John Oldham's pinnace near Block Island. Seeing a number of Block Island natives on board, Gallop investigated. A fight ensued in which Gallop and his men killed 10 or 11 of the natives before discovering Oldham's body below deck.

The Block Islanders paid tribute to the Narragansetts, and Massachusetts then sent a delegation to the Narragansetts to investigate Oldham's murder and whether that tribe was hostile to the English. The investigators returned with a report that the leading Narragansett sachems (chiefs) were loyal and willing to punish those responsible. Nonetheless, Governor Henry Vane of Massachusetts ordered John Endicott (also spelled Endecott) to lead a force of volunteers from the colony against Block Island.

Vane's instructions to Endicott were to take possession of the island, killing all the native adult males there and capturing the women and children (who would then be sold as slaves). Immediately thereafter Endicott was to sail to Pequot territory and there demand the surrender of those natives responsible for the 1634 murder of colonist John Stone. The Pequots were to pay damages in wampum and turn over several Pequot children as hostages to ensure the tribe's future good behavior.

Endicott's force of some 90 men set sail in five ships on August 24. Endicott had the assistance of captains John Underwood, Nathaniel Turner, and William Jenningston and an Ensign Davenport as well as two native guides. High waves and wind at Block Island prevented their ships from landing, and the men had to disembark offshore and wade in, whereupon they promptly came under native attack. Musket fire soon compelled the natives to retreat.

During a two-day period Endicott and his men attempted to do battle with the natives, who had sought refuge in the swamps on the island. The colonists burned two abandoned villages and set fire to much of the island, including its cornfields. After having killed perhaps as many as a dozen natives and being unable to locate the remainder, Endicott ordered his men to return to their ships to fulfill the second part of his orders.

Endicott first sailed to Fort Saybrook at the mouth of the Connecticut River on Long Island Sound. His men remained there for four days because of bad weather. The commander of the fort, Lieutenant Lion Gardiner, was a strong critic of the expedition. Fearing native retribution on Saybrook, he questioned why Massachusetts leaders would be mounting a military expedition to avenge the murder of a Virginian and warned Endicott of the likely repercussions.

When Endicott's ships finally sailed up the Pequot River (now known as the Thames River), the Pequots inquired as to the reason for the English presence. Endicott remained on his ship and did not answer. The next day the Pequots sent an emissary to meet with Endicott, who then revealed the purpose of his expeditionary force, saying that he had come to avenge the killing of Virginian John Stone. The envoy replied that the sachem Sassacus and others had killed Stone in retaliation for the murder of the sachem Tatobem. The Dutch had captured and killed the grand sachem, and the Pequots had taken revenge on Stone, not recognizing that he was English. In their defense, the Pequots believed that it had been an honest misunderstanding and that the murder had been justified. They therefore refused to surrender those involved in the attack.

The envoy departed and asked the English to wait for a response. Fearing a trick, the English went ashore, ready to do battle. The Pequots asked for time, claiming that their principal sachems were away. Endicott took this as a ruse by which the Pequots would gain time to prepare for battle, and he ordered an attack.

Here, as on Block Island, the Pequots refused to fight; they simply fled. Endicott repeated the tactics of Block Island, destroying the Pequot settlements and crops. Endicott's force then returned to Massachusetts Bay, having failed to accomplish any of the mission's objectives.

As Gardiner predicted, Endicott's actions led to war. Despite defense of the action by new governor John Winthrop (1637–1640) as necessary to avenge the deaths of two Englishmen, colonial settlements and trading posts on the Connecticut River soon came under attack by angry Pequots. This fighting soon expanded into the destructive Pequot War.

SARAH E. MILLER AND SPENCER C. TUCKER

See also

Endicott, John; Narragansetts; Pequots; Pequot War; Sassacus; Winthrop, John

References

Cave, Alfred A. *The Pequot War.* Amherst: University of Massachusetts Press, 1996.

Mayo, Lawrence Shaw. *John Endecott: A Biography.* Cambridge: Harvard University Press, 1936.

Sylvester, Herbert Milton. *Indian Wars of New England,* Vol. 1. Cleveland, OH: Arthur H. Clark, 1910.

Vaughan, Alden T. "Pequots and Puritans: The Causes of the War of 1637." *William and Mary Quarterly,* 3rd ser., 21(2) (April 1964): 256–269.

Enitachopco Creek, Battle of
Event Date: January 24, 1814

Engagement between Major General Andrew Jackson's Tennessee militia and their White Stick Creek and Cherokee allies on one side and Red Stick Creeks on the other. The battle occurred at Enitachopco Creek on January 24, 1814, during the American retreat from the January 22 Battle of Emuckfaw Creek. Enitachopco Creek is located in southeastern Alabama some 30 miles north of Emuckfaw, a Red Stick encampment. Red Stick Creeks attacked American troops and their White Stick Creek and Cherokee allies as they attempted to cross Enitachopco Creek. Although the Red Sticks inflicted significant casualties on Jackson's force, which continued its hasty retreat, the Red Sticks lost a second opportunity to gain a decisive victory during the Creek War (1813–1814).

The Creek War, which coincided with the War of 1812, began as a civil war between two factions of the Creek Confederacy: the Red Sticks, encouraged by Tecumseh, who received arms from the British and wanted to end American expansion in Alabama and southern Georgia, and the White Stick Creeks, who favored a conciliatory policy toward the United States.

Beginning in 1813, the Red Sticks actively sought to expel white settlers from Alabama and southern Georgia. Following the slaughter of 250 white and mixed Creek settlers by Red Stick warriors near Mobile, Alabama, in August 1813, the United States initiated military activities to crush the Red Stick uprising. Tennessee militia under Jackson therefore spent most of the War of 1812 fighting Native Americans rather than British troops.

On January 17, 1814, Jackson and his troops departed from Fort Struther in northern Alabama to attack the Red Sticks at the village of Emuckfaw. More than 90 percent of Jackson's 1,000 men, however, were inexperienced recruits lacking discipline who had just arrived at Fort Struther on January 14. On January 21, 1814, Jackson's troops encamped along Emuckfaw Creek, about 12 miles away from the village of Emuckfaw. At dawn on January 22, 1814, Red Stick warriors attacked Jackson's encampment but were repelled. Taking the initiative, Jackson sent a force of 200 Americans and 200 Native American allies under Brigadier General John R. Coffee to attack the Red Stick encampment. Finding the Red Stick encampment too well defended, Coffee ordered his troops to return to Jackson's camp. The Red Sticks, however, immediately counterattacked Jackson's encampment. In the ensuing Battle of Emuckfaw Creek, 54 of Jackson's men were killed and several more were wounded, while the Red Sticks only suffered 24 fatalities. Realizing his precarious situation and unwilling to risk a defeat, Jackson ordered a retreat to Fort Struther.

On January 23, 1814, Jackson's troops encamped on the Enitachopco Creek, about 30 miles north of Emuckfaw, on their way back to Fort Struther. Although Jackson's troops passed the night without incident, they were attacked by Red Stick warriors on the morning of January 24, 1814, as they attempted to cross Enitachopco Creek. Surprisingly, Jackson's troops, who were in a state of panic, were able to repel the attack, in which they sustained 24 fatalities. Nevertheless, Jackson fully realized the difficulty of fighting the Red Sticks in hostile territory without sufficient reinforcements, and he continued the retreat to Fort Struther. Regardless, the Red Sticks had lost yet another opportunity for a decisive victory against Jackson's forces, who resumed the offensive in mid-March 1814. This ultimately led to Jackson's defeat of the Red Sticks at the Battle of Horseshoe Bend on March 27, 1814, culminating in the surrender of the Red Sticks in August 1814.

MICHAEL R. HALL

See also

Creeks; Creek War; Emuckfaw Creek, Battle of; Horseshoe Bend, Battle of; Jackson, Andrew; Native Americans and the War of 1812; Tecumseh

References

Debo, Angie. *Road to Disappearance: A History of the Creek Indians.* Norman: University of Oklahoma Press, 1979.

O'Brien, Sean Michael. *In Bitterness and in Tears: Andrew Jackson's Destruction of the Creeks and Seminoles.* Guilford, CT: Lyons, 2005.

Eries

See Westos

Esopuses

Native American group that occupied the Hudson River Valley and the Delaware River Valley as the Dutch and English began to colonize the region in the early 17th century. The Esopus people were a classic colonial tribe in the sense that they organized during the colonial period in response to changing colonial power relations among native tribes and between natives and Europeans. Indications point to Delaware (Lenni Lenape) ancestral roots. The Esopus tribe, along with the Dutch, controlled much of the vital Hudson River trade from the Great Lakes to the Atlantic in the early 1600s. As with most native groups of the region, the Esopuses relied on agriculture, hunting, fishing, and trapping as the basis of their economy. As the colonial period progressed, fur trapping became especially important for trade with the Europeans.

In the pre-Columbian period, Algonquian legends suggest that the Lenape, the Nanticoke, the Powhatan, and the Shawnee peoples all came from an Algonquian-speaking Lenape homeland, probably associated with mound-building cultures. The Lenapes (or "true ancestor people") slowly migrated and were transformed into the Delaware peoples who occupied much of present-day New York by 1600. The northern Lenapes occupied the region from the headwaters of the Delaware River to the Catskills and the western shore of the Hudson River. By the mid-17th century, these Munsee-speaking peoples, or "people of the stoney country," were known as the Esopuses, who were subdivided into four principal tribal groups: Catskills, Memekotings, Waranawonkongs, and Warasinks.

As the Dutch settled the Hudson Valley from 1610 to 1664, they established a relationship with the Esopus people that was alternatively cooperative and antagonistic. By 1660 the Dutch numbered 10,000 people; the Esopuses numbered perhaps 15,000. The Esopus people, as with many other native groups, were not really a tribe or even a nation. Rather, they were a set of linguistically and territorially related clans and bands that defined relationships of power with one another and with Europeans on that level. The so-called Wolf and Turkey clans were the most prominent. They also had the most dealings with the Dutch.

With the French in Canada, the English in New England, and the Dutch and the Swedes along the Hudson and Delaware rivers, power relationships in the 1600s changed radically for the Esopuses. Conflicts with the Dutch, the Mohawks, and the Senecas left the Esopuses with little population and even less land. Indeed, the Esopus Wars (1659–1660 and 1663–1664) with the Dutch decimated the tribe. A smallpox epidemic in the mid-17th century further weakened the tribe and forced the Esopuses into refugee status with the Iroquois after 1664. The Esopuses became wards of the Iroquois, supplying some manpower and foodstuffs in return for protection. The English takeover of Dutch New Netherland in 1664 cemented the fate of the Esopuses by cutting off further trade through the Dutch. Eventually the surviving Esopus people, who had lost all of their landholdings to the Dutch and the English, migrated west and south to settle in central Pennsylvania, where other Delaware tribes already resided. Others may have made their way as far west as Wisconsin, and today a small number of Native Americans in Shawano County, Wisconsin, and Ontario, Canada, claim to be Esopus descendants.

CHRISTOPHER HOWELL

See also

Delawares; Dutch-Indian Wars; Esopus Wars; Iroquois; Iroquois Confederacy

References

Brink, Andrew. *Invading Paradise: Esopus Settlers at War with the Natives, 1659, 1663.* New York: Random House, 2003.

Dolan, Edward. *The American Indian Wars.* Brookfield, CT: Millbrook, 2003.

Goodfriend, Joyce. *Revisiting New Netherland: Perspectives on Early Dutch America.* Boston: Brill Academic, 2005.

Jacobs, Jaap. *New Netherland: A Dutch Colony in Seventeenth-Century America.* Boston: Brill Academic, 2004.

Mabie, Roger. *Indian Tribes of Hudson's River: 1700–1850.* Utica, NY: North Country Books, 1992.

Merwick, Donna. *The Shame and the Sorrow: Dutch-Amerindian Encounters in New Netherland.* Philadelphia: University of Pennsylvania Press, 2006.

Esopus Wars

Start Date: 1659
End Date: 1664

Armed conflict between the Dutch and their native allies and the Esopus Nation, centered in the Hudson River Valley. The Esopus Wars were part of a long history of conflict between European settlers and natives in the northeastern region of North America. Between 1614 and 1640, some 2,000 Dutch colonists settled on Esopus (Waranawonk) lands along the Hudson, from Long Island to Kingston, New Netherland (present-day Kingston, New York). They did so under the auspices of the Dutch West India Company. By 1640 a series of Dutch–Native American conflicts had developed, stemming from land issues and revenge killings. The last of these conflicts were the Esopus Wars. Ironically, those wars ended with the Dutch destruction of much of the Esopus tribe by 1664, the same year in which the English invaded New Amsterdam and put an end to Dutch colonization in North America. After 1664 the Iroquois Confederacy replaced the Esopus people as the major native power in the Hudson River Valley.

In the early 1600s, French, English, and Dutch colonists flowed into a region that was already experiencing complicated political affairs between indigenous tribes. The river valleys were key strategic transport corridors for both trade and maintaining maritime power. In New Netherland, the Hudson River, with its mouth at Long Island, was a vital corridor for both Native Americans and Europeans. The natives wanted to be involved in trade to receive goods such as firearms and liquor, whereas the Europeans desired native lands along the Hudson River and those lands' resources, such as beaver pelts. A classic colonial confrontation soon ensued, with both natives and colonists using the other to reconfigure power relationships in the valley.

At the time of the first Dutch settlement in 1614, the Susquehannocks controlled the east bank of the Hudson, the Esopus people controlled the west bank, and the Mohawks controlled the upper reaches around the Catskill Mountains. The Dutch then established Fort Orange (Albany, New York) on the Hudson River in 1614, Fort Good Hope (Hartford, Connecticut) on the Connecticut River in 1624, and Fort Amsterdam (New York City) on Manhattan Island in 1626. Although claimed by England, which was often preoccupied by war with France and Spain, the region was actually controlled by Native Americans. The Esopuses and other natives tolerated the Dutch presence because the Europeans offered an additional outlet for trade, especially for guns that were vital to native diplomatic negotiations and warfare. With the French in Canada, the English in New England, and the Dutch in New Netherland, the Hudson River became the strategic center of trade, with New Amsterdam the key port.

Dutch expansion upriver, the devastation wrought by Old World diseases, and increasing conflict between native tribes all took their toll on indigenous peoples along the Hudson River. News of the 1636–1638 Pequot War in New England and the virtual extermination of the once-powerful Pequot Nation also heightened tensions and increased the flow of native refugees into the region. This powder keg ignited over a series of revenge killings that led to Kieft's War (1639–1645) with the Raritans around Long Island. This was followed by wars involving the Iroquois (1642–1655), the Anglo-Dutch wars (1652–1654, 1664–1667) centered on New Amsterdam, the capture of New Sweden by the Dutch in 1655, and a final conflict with the Raritans known as the Peach War (1655–1657). Both the Dutch and the Esopus tribe found themselves increasingly drawn into these conflicts on opposing sides. Eventually they confronted each other over control of the Hudson River.

During 1652–1655 the Dutch settlement of Kingston, New Netherland, established the Dutch at both ends of the valley. By 1660 the Dutch population was at 10,000. Centered on a small settlement known today as Esopus, Dutch–Native American land conflicts developed into full-scale war all along the river. The Mohawks entered on the side of the Dutch and turned the tide against the Esopus tribe. The Mahicans then intervened as peacekeepers and ended the First Esopus War in 1660. But because the natives were mobile seasonally, the European-style treaty proved inadequate because Mohawk, Mahican, and Dutch interests were advanced at the expense of the Esopuses.

Mahicans settled on Esopus lands to act as a buffer against future conflict. Eventually the Esopuses left the lands to the Mohawks. Many Esopus refugees fled to Mahican buffer lands only to find that they could not reacquire their homelands when the conflict ended. The return of captives also worked against the

Esopuses, as many rejoined the tribe from captivity with diseases that spread rapidly.

The Esopuses fared even worse in the Second Esopus War (1663–1664). They and the Susquehannocks had dominated the Hudson Valley up to the Dutch arrival. Now both groups found their gunpowder and weapon supplies severely limited. Also, their access to European trade goods had almost been cut off. This was largely the result of Dutch success in halting Swedish and English shipments in 1655 by capturing New Sweden and a peace treaty with England that ended the First Anglo-Dutch War (1652–1654). By 1663 the trade guns still available to the Esopus warriors were at best old and unreliable and at worst deadly to the user. Mohawks, supplied by the English and granted access by the Dutch, now poured into Esopus territory. Most Esopus people fled as refugees to Mahican lands in the Catskills, never to return to their former home.

In 1664 a British fleet captured New Amsterdam, and the role of the Dutch and the Esopuses as major powers in the Hudson River Valley ended. The British and the Iroquois now replaced them. The Esopus tribe sold the last of its lands in 1677 to newly arrived French Huguenots and moved west with the permission of their Iroquois landlords to Pennsylvania's Wyoming Valley.

CHRISTOPHER HOWELL

See also

Dutch-Indian Wars; Esopuses; Native American Trade

References

Brink, Andrew. *Invading Paradise: Esopus Settlers at War with the Natives, 1659, 1663.* New York: Random House, 2003.

Dolan, Edward. *The American Indian Wars.* Brookfield, CT: Millbrook, 2003.

Goodfriend, Joyce. *Revisiting New Netherland: Perspectives on Early Dutch America.* Boston: Brill Academic, 2005.

Jacobs, Jaap. *New Netherland: A Dutch Colony in Seventeenth-Century America.* Boston: Brill Academic, 2004.

Mabie, Roger. *Indian Tribes of Hudson's River: 1700–1850.* Utica, NY: North Country Books, 1992.

Merwick, Donna. *The Shame and the Sorrow: Dutch-Amerindian Encounters in New Netherland.* Philadelphia: University of Pennsylvania Press, 2006.

Evans, John
Birth Date: March 9, 1814
Death Date: July 2, 1897

Physician, educator, railroad financier, politician, and governor of Colorado Territory from 1862 to 1865. John Evans was born in Waynesville, Ohio, on March 9, 1814. In 1838 he graduated with a medical degree from Clermont Academy and subsequently moved to Attica, Indiana, where he practiced medicine. He also founded the Indiana Central State Hospital in Indianapolis. He began investing in the burgeoning railroad industry and became quite wealthy as a result. In the meantime he moved to Chicago,

where his money and contacts made him a formidable political force. He taught at Chicago's prestigious Rush Medical College, founded the Illinois Medical Society, and studied the 1848–1849 cholera epidemic in Chicago, which prompted the U.S. Congress to mandate quarantine laws during future epidemics. In 1851 Evans cofounded Northwestern University. The suburb in which it is located, Evanston, was named in his honor.

By 1852 Evans had been elected to the Chicago City Council and had established the Illinois Republican Party. In this capacity he became a close associate and political ally of Abraham Lincoln. Evans continued to teach and remained an influential figure in Illinois Republican politics. After Lincoln became president in 1861, he offered Evans the governorship of Washington Territory, but Evans turned it down, not wanting to relocate to a distant and sparsely populated locale. The following year he accepted Lincoln's offer to become governor of Colorado Territory.

Evans immediately set about to establish rail and telegraph lines throughout the territory; the former would eventually become part of a transcontinental railway. He is credited with making Denver a major western metropolis, and he founded the Denver Seminary, which is now Denver University. Although economic development and eventual statehood preoccupied much of Evans's time

Governor of the Colorado Territory John Evans was widely blamed for having given Colonel John M. Chivington free rein, leading to the Sand Creek Massacre of 1864. Condemnation of this event brought Evans's resignation as territorial governor in 1865. (North Wind Picture Archives)

as governor, he was also forced to deal with hostile Native Americans, especially the Arapahos and Cheyennes. Indeed, by 1864 Native Americans had all but closed down Colorado's overland trails and were harassing newly arriving white settlers.

That same year Evans appointed Colonel John Chivington to lead the Colorado Volunteers, a force of 800 cavalrymen whose task it would be to subdue the Native Americans and reassure nervous white settlers. While Evans had empowered Chivington to use force if necessary to curb Native American attacks, he had also empowered Major Edward Wynkoop, commander of Fort Lyon, to engage the Southern Cheyennes in peace talks, which produced an uneasy cease-fire by September 1864.

While Evans was away in Washington, D.C., Chivington and his men attacked a peaceful band of Cheyennes and Arapahos at Sand Creek in east-central Colorado, shattering the fragile peace. Evans had apparently instructed Chivington not to honor the earlier peace. The November 29, 1864, Sand Creek Massacre, as it came to be called, resulted in the killing of 88 unarmed women and children and 60 men. Upon his return Evans commended Chivington for his work, but there were already rumors circulating that the incident at Sand Creek had been an unprovoked massacre and not the result of a Native American attack. Soon the rumors spurred an official investigation in Washington. President Andrew Johnson, angered that Evans at best had made light of the massacre and at worst had tried to cover it up, requested Evans's resignation on July 18, 1865. Evans complied, but he remained a popular figure in Colorado. Chivington was never censured for his part in the massacre.

With his political career over, Evans once again became a key proponent of railroad development. Thanks largely to his efforts, a Union Pacific rail line, linking Denver with Cheyenne, Wyoming, was opened in June 1870, providing a major economic boon for Denver. Until his death in Denver on July 2, 1897, Evans remained active in the railroad industry and was principally responsible for founding five railroad companies within Colorado.

PAUL G. PIERPAOLI JR.

See also
Black Kettle; Chivington, John; Sand Creek Massacre

References

Hoig, Stan. *The Sand Creek Massacre*. Norman: University of Oklahoma Press, 1961.

Hughes, J. Donald. *American Indians in Colorado*. Boulder, CO: Pruett Publishing, 1977.

Josephy, Alvin M., Jr. *The Civil War in the American West*. New York: Knopf, 1991.

Everglades

Geographic location of significant U.S. operations against the Seminole peoples during the Second Seminole War (1835–1842). The Everglades are a vast subtropical wetlands and swamp located in southern Florida in what are now parts of Broward, Miami-Dade, Palm Beach, Collier, and Monroe counties and are fed by a series of slow-moving rivers and creeks. One of the main sources of the Everglades wetlands is Lake Okeechobee. The Everglades run south from Lake Okeechobee to the Florida Bay and from the Big Cypress Swamp to the west (in the 19th century) to the Atlantic coast to the east. The Everglades encompassed as many as 4.5 million acres before modern development and explosive growth resulted in the loss of more than half that area. The Everglades region was difficult to penetrate because of its shallow slow-moving waters and hot humid climate. Natural predators such as alligators, which are abundant throughout the marshlands and swamps, as well as snakes and insects carrying diseases such as yellow fever and malaria also made the Everglades a forbidding place. While these characteristics made the Everglades seem impenetrable to the white man, the Seminoles used the region as their base of operations in conflicts with Florida settlers.

During the Second Seminole War (1835–1842), the United States used amphibious tactics to bring the fight to the Seminoles, who were using the difficult terrain and topography of the Everglades as a safe haven. The attacks into the Everglades, which consisted of a mixture of sailors, marines, and soldiers traveling by canoe or flat-bottom boat, set a precedent for cooperation between the commands of the U.S. Army and the U.S. Navy. The flotilla of small craft used to navigate the rivers and swamps of southern Florida, known as the Mosquito Fleet, was the first U.S. force designed specifically for riverine warfare.

U.S. Navy lieutenant Levin M. Powell spearheaded the effort to infiltrate the Everglades and thus initiated army-navy cooperation and designed specialized boats for conducting shallow-river warfare. From 1836 to 1838 he led a series of missions to track down Indian settlements in an effort to kill Seminole leaders and destroy their crops and other supplies. On January 10, 1838, Powell's force of 55 sailors and 25 soldiers was defeated while attempting to destroy a settlement, and 4 of his men were killed. Powell returned to the Everglades the following year as part of a force led by Colonel James Bankhead that forced a contingent of Seminoles to flee their village. This was the first successful attack against the Seminoles in the Everglades. The approach that Powell introduced for fighting in Florida, using a mixed force with a variety of small craft, worked because it used irregular tactics against an enemy that also relied on guerrilla warfare.

In December 1840 U.S. Army colonel William S. Harney employed Powell's strategy and an African American guide named John to surprise and destroy the camp of Seminole war chief Chakaika. The raid was a rout, and Chakaika and several of his warriors were killed. Some were also captured.

From December 31, 1840, to January 19, 1841, U.S. Navy lieutenant John T. McLaughlin and his black and Seminole guides led a flotilla of canoes from east to west across the Everglades. Although they failed to do any direct damage to their enemy, they wreaked havoc on the Seminoles' stores of food and powder and kept the Native Americans constantly on the retreat. McLaughlin and his men became the first whites to cross the entire width of Florida's Everglades, and in so doing they charted much unexplored territory.

Although the army and navy continued to conduct amphibious missions in the Everglades until the war's end in 1842, there were few direct engagements with the Seminoles. U.S. forces did, however, wage a version of total war in an effort to undermine the Seminoles' ability to fight and force them to capitulate. This goal and the coordination of the army and navy to conduct amphibious strikes anticipated military tactics that would prove definitive in future wars.

CAMERON B. STRANG

See also

Harney, William Selby; Native American Warfare; Seminoles; Seminole War, Second

References

Buker, George E. *Swamp Sailors: Riverine Warfare in the Everglades, 1835–1842.* Gainesville: University of Florida Press, 1975.

Mahon, John K. *History of the Second Seminole War, 1835–1842.* Rev. ed. Gainesville: University Press of Florida, 1991.

F

Fallen Timbers, Battle of
Event Date: August 20, 1794

Significant engagement fought just south of present-day Toledo, Ohio, between U.S. troops and Native Americans that secured control of much of Ohio from the Native Americans. In the 1783 Treaty of Paris that ended the American Revolutionary War (1775–1783), the British government acknowledged U.S. claims west of the Appalachians and made no effort to protect Native American lands in the Ohio Valley. Incursions by American settlers there led to serious problems because the Native American leaders refused to acknowledge U.S. authority north of the Ohio River. Although between 1784 and 1789 the U.S. government persuaded some chiefs to relinquish lands in southern and eastern Ohio, most Native Americans refused to acknowledge the validity of these treaties.

Encouraged by the British, leaders of the Miami and Shawnee tribes insisted that the Americans fall back to the Ohio River. When the settlers refused, the Miamis attacked them, prompting Northwest Territory governor Arthur St. Clair to send U.S. troops and militia against the Native Americans along the Maumee River. Brigadier General Josiah Harmar led an expedition in October 1790, the first for the post-Revolution U.S. Army. Setting out with 1,300 men, including 320 regulars and Pennsylvania and Kentucky militiamen, Harmar divided his poorly trained force into three separate columns. Near present-day Fort Wayne, Indiana, the Miamis and Shawnees, led by Miami chief Little Turtle, defeated Harmar in detail, the troops sustaining 300 casualties.

In the autumn of 1791 St. Clair, commissioned a major general, led a second expedition of the entire 600-man regular army and 1,500 militia. On November 3 the men camped along the upper Wabash River at present-day Fort Recovery, Ohio. The next morning Little Turtle and his warriors caught them by surprise and administered the worst defeat ever by Native Americans on the British or Americans, inflicting some 800 casualties. Native American losses were reported as 21 killed and 40 wounded.

President George Washington did not attempt to conceal these twin disasters from the American people, and in December 1792 Congress voted to establish a 5,000-man Legion of the United States, commanded by a major general and consisting of four sublegions led by brigadier generals. Washington appointed retired general Anthony "Mad Anthony" Wayne to command the legion.

Wayne set up a training camp 25 miles from Pittsburgh, Pennsylvania, at a site he named Legionville and put the men through rigorous training. In May 1793 he moved the legion to Fort Washington (Cincinnati) and then a few miles north to a new camp, Hobson's Choice. In early October, Wayne moved north with 2,000 regulars to Fort Jefferson, the end of his defensive line. When Kentucky mounted militia arrived, Wayne moved a few miles farther north and set up a new camp, naming it Fort Greeneville (now Greenville, Ohio) in honor of his American Revolutionary War commander, Major General Nathanael Greene.

In December 1793 Wayne sent a detachment to the site of St. Clair's defeat on the Wabash. On Christmas Day 1793 the Americans occupied the battlefield and constructed Fort Recovery on high ground overlooking the Wabash. Aided by friendly Native Americans, the soldiers recovered most of St. Clair's cannon, which the Native Americans had buried nearby. These were incorporated into Fort Recovery, which was manned by an infantry company and a detachment of artillerists.

Wayne's campaign timetable was delayed because of unreliable civilian contractors, Native American attacks on his supply trains,

Major General Anthony Wayne's Legion of the United States defeats Native Americans at the Battle of Fallen Timbers on August 20, 1794. The battle restored U.S. military prestige and broke forever Native American power in the eastern region of the Northwest Territory. (Library of Congress)

the removal of some of his men elsewhere, and a cease-fire that led him to believe that peace might be in the offing. But Little Turtle, Shawnee war chief Blue Jacket, and other chiefs rejected peace negotiations, in part because of a speech by British governor-general in Canada Sir Guy Carleton, who predicted war between Britain and the United States and pledged British support for the Native Americans. In February 1794 Carleton ordered construction of Fort Miami on the Maumee River to mount cannon larger than those that Wayne might be able to bring against it, further delaying Wayne's advance.

On June 29, 1794, Little Turtle struck first at Fort Recovery, Wayne's staging point for the invasion. A supply train had just arrived there and was bivouacked outside the walls when 2,000 warriors attacked. Although a number of soldiers were killed, the Native Americans were beaten back with heavy casualties and two days later withdrew. Never again were the Native Americans able to assemble that many warriors. The repulse also prompted some of the smaller tribes to quit the coalition and led to the eclipse of Little Turtle, who was replaced as principal war leader by the less effective Blue Jacket.

Wayne now had 2,000 men. In mid-July some 1,600 Kentucky militia under Brigadier General Charles Scott began to arrive. Wayne also could count on 100 Native Americans, mostly Choctaws and Chickasaws, from Tennessee. On July 28 Wayne departed

Fort Greeneville for Fort Recovery. Washington warned that a third straight defeat "would be inexpressibly ruinous to the reputation of the government."

The Native Americans were concentrated at Miami Town, the objective of previous offensives, and the rapids of the Maumee River around Fort Miami. A 100-mile-long road through the Maumee River Valley connected the two. Wayne intended to build a fortification at midpoint on the road, allowing him to strike in either direction and forcing the Native Americans to defend both possible objectives. By August 3 he had established this position, Fort Adams, and had also built a second fortified position, Fort Defiance, at the confluence of the Auglaize and Maumee rivers. Wayne then sent the chiefs a final peace offer. Little Turtle urged its acceptance, pointing out the strength of the force opposing them and expressing doubts about British support. Blue Jacket and British agents wanted war, which a majority of the chiefs approved.

Having learned of a Native American concentration near Fort Miami, Wayne decided to move there first. After a difficult crossing of the Maumee River, on August 15 Wayne's men were still 10 miles from the British fort. Sensing an impending fight, Wayne detached unnecessary elements from his column to construct a possible fall-back position, Fort Deposit, manned by Captain Zebulon Pike and 200 men.

On August 20 Wayne again put his column in motion, anticipating battle that day with either the Native Americans or the British. Indeed, more than 1,000 warriors and some 60 Canadian militiamen were lying in wait for the Americans, hoping to ambush them from the natural defenses of a forest before its trees had been uprooted by a tornado; the forest had been transformed into a chaos of twisted branches and broken tree trunks.

Blue Jacket had expected Wayne to arrive on August 19, not anticipating the daylong delay. In preparation for battle, the Native Americans began a strict fast on August 18 and then continued it the next day. When the Americans did not arrive, many of the Native Americans, hungry and exhausted, departed for Fort Miami.

Wayne marched his men so as to be ready to meet an attack from any quarter. His infantry were in two wings: Brigadier General James Wilkinson commanded the right, and Colonel John Hamtramck commanded the left. A mounted brigade of Kentuckians protected the left flank, while legion horsemen covered the right. Additional Kentucky horsemen protected the rear and served as a reserve. Well to the front, Major William Price led a battalion to trigger the Native American attack and allow Wayne time to deploy the main body.

When the Native Americans did open fire, Price's men fell back into Wilkinson's line. Wayne rallied his men and sent them to defeat the ambush with an infantry frontal attack driven home with the bayonet. At the same time, the horsemen closed on the flanks. The Native Americans were routed, fleeing the battle toward Fort Miami. The killing went on to the very gates of the fort while the British looked on. Wayne's losses in the battle were 33 men killed and 100 wounded (11 of them mortally), while Native American losses were in the hundreds.

Although Wayne disregarded Fort Miami, he destroyed Native American communities and British storehouses in its vicinity. The soldiers then marched to Miami Town. They occupied it without opposition on September 17 and razed it. They then built a fort on the site of Harmar's 1790 defeat, naming it Fort Wayne.

The Battle of Fallen Timbers broke forever the power of the Native Americans in the eastern region of the Northwest. The battle also led the British to evacuate their garrisons below the Great Lakes and did much to restore U.S. military prestige. Wayne is justifiably known as the father of the U.S. Army.

On August 3, 1795, chiefs representing 12 tribes signed the Treaty of Greenville, Wayne having revealed to them that the British had agreed to withdraw their forts and recognize the boundary set in the 1783 Treaty of Paris. The Treaty of Greenville set a definite boundary in the Northwest Territory, forcing the Native Americans to give up once and for all most of the present state of Ohio and part of Indiana. Increased settler movement into the Ohio Country and ensuing Native American resentment and turn to the British helped set the stage for the War of 1812 in the Old Northwest.

SPENCER C. TUCKER

See also

Blue Jacket; Delawares; Greenville, Treaty of; Little Turtle; Little Turtle's War; Miamis; Mingos; Ojibwas; Ottawas; Pottawatomis; Shawnees; Tecumseh; Wayne, Anthony; Wyandots

References

Millett, Allan R. "Caesar and the Conquest of the Northwest Territory: The Wayne Campaign, 1792–95." *Timeline: A Publication of the Ohio Historical Society* 14 (1997): 2–21.

Nelson, Paul David. *Anthony Wayne: Soldier of the Early Republic.* Bloomington: Indiana University Press, 1985.

Nelson, Paul D. "Anthony Wayne's Indian War in the Old Northwest, 1792–1795." *Northwest Ohio Quarterly* 56 (1984): 115–140.

Palmer, Dave R. *1794: America, Its Army, and the Birth of the Nation.* Novato, CA: Presidio, 1994.

Sword, Wiley. *President Washington's Indian War: The Struggle for the Old Northwest, 1790–1795.* Norman: University of Oklahoma Press, 1985.

Tebbel, John W. *The Battle of Fallen Timbers, August 20, 1794.* New York: Franklin Watts, 1972.

Falls Fight
Event Date: May 19, 1676

Massacre of Native Americans by New Englanders during King Philip's War (1675–1676). The Falls Fight assault, which took place on May 19, 1676, helped cripple native resistance and allowed for a venting of colonial frustrations over the guerrilla tactics used against their communities. Settlers learned from engagements such as this to fight counterinsurgencies by relying on native allies, stealth, and the merciless treatment of captives.

Although most natives of southern New England had answered the call of the Wampanoag sachem Metacom (King Philip) to attack English settlements, the momentum in the conflict began to shift in favor of the colonists by the spring of 1676. Intelligence arrived at Hatfield, Massachusetts, regarding an encampment of Pocumtucks 20 miles away near the falls of the Connecticut River at a site known as Peskeompskut. An assortment of warriors, women, children, and the elderly had gathered at this popular fishing spot to resupply.

Captain William Turner commanded a small garrison at Hatfield, and he recruited men and boys from surrounding towns to mount an assault on Peskeompskut. A Baptist imprisoned several times in Puritan New England for his religious beliefs, Turner owed his billet to the widespread damage suffered in Massachusetts that overrode concerns over spiritual compatibility. Weakened by illness during his latest incarceration, he led a force of roughly 150 men. They thoroughly lacked discipline, experience, and expertise. Little more than a rabble, Turner's force reached Peskeompskut at dawn on May 19 intent on allowing no quarter to a foe whose assaults had threatened every New England colony.

The prearranged signal for the surprise attack against the unguarded native position entailed firing directly into the wigwams. The ensuing bloodbath left several hundred natives dead, including women and children. Not a single prisoner was taken. Turner's men rejoiced at suffering only one fatality.

The engagement, however, was far from over. The sounds of battle had roused other natives along the Connecticut River, who prepared an ambush. Negligent in planning for his retreat, Turner divided his forces, only to face a withering onslaught. Thirty-nine colonists, including Turner, died in the ensuing melee. Although technically the campaign was a triumph for the colonists, the high casualty rate of the ambush rendered the earlier victory less important. As word spread of the slaughter, there was no public outcry to reassess the conduct of the war. Attitudes were now hardening among New Englanders as the conflict grew dangerously close to genocide. Indeed, wracked with guilt and uncertainty over the maintenance of what they believed was their unique covenant with God, Puritans embraced a spirit of vengeance that manifested itself on the battlefields and in the courtrooms of their land during and after King Philip's War.

The Falls Fight was notable as the first clear-cut English victory in the war (more specifically, in the western theater). The battle also decimated a still-powerful native force, which adversely affected morale among the native combatants, and also served to propel the bulk of Metacom's forces out of the Connecticut River Valley and toward the south and east, into Rhode Island and the eastern reaches of Massachusetts and Connecticut.

Finally, the Falls Fight can be seen as a sort of unintended pincer movement against Metacom's forces. The chief had to make the decision whether to retreat west or east. He chose the east because he feared conflict with tribes to his west, in particular the Mohawks. But the eastern region would prove to be no more hospitable, as it was the center of colonial power. In effect, Metacom's forces were stuck between threats on either side. It would thus only be a matter of time before they would meet the brunt of colonial strength, which would bring about the downfall of Metacom.

JEFFREY D. BASS

See also
King Philip's War; Metacom; Wampanoags

References
Drake, James D. *King Philip's War: Civil War in New England, 1675–1676.* Amherst: University of Massachusetts Press, 1999.
Lepore, Jill. *The Name of War: King Philip's War and the Origins of American Identity.* New York: Knopf, 1998.

Falmouth, Battle of
Start Date: May 16, 1690
End Date: May 20, 1690

Battle in which French and allied Native American forces captured Fort Loyal and Falmouth (now Portland, Maine, then part of Massachusetts) as part of a three-pronged attack against English settlements during King William's War (1689–1697). In early 1690 three raiding parties comprised of Native Americans and Frenchmen departed Canada to attack New England's northern and eastern frontiers. One party of 60 Abenakis and 50 French troops under René Robineau, Sieur de Portneuf, targeted Falmouth and Fort Loyal on the shores of Casco Bay, Maine. By the time Portneuf reached Falmouth in May, his party had grown to 400 or 500 men, having been strengthened by local Abenakis and a French raiding party that had struck Salmon Falls in March.

Falmouth was protected by four garrison houses and Fort Loyal, a picketed stockade on the bluff along the bay that mounted a few light cannon to command water and land approaches to the town. A large portion of the garrison had departed on a scouting expedition on May 10, however, leaving Captain Sylvanus Davis and perhaps 100 men in the garrison.

Portneuf intended to surprise the garrison, but his eager Native American allies gave away their presence by ambushing a solitary settler early on May 16. Davis then dispatched a scouting party of 30 men to investigate the shots, but they too fell into an ambush, and only a handful escaped back to the fort. Falmouth's soldiers and settlers defended the four garrison houses until nightfall and then withdrew into Fort Loyal.

On the morning of May 17 the Abenakis and Frenchmen plundered and burned the deserted village and then turned on Fort Loyal. For three days Portneuf's forces maintained a withering volley of fire on the English fort, wounding many of Davis's men. At the same time French soldiers crept toward the fort, eventually placing incendiaries against the palisade's base.

Badly outnumbered and threatened with a fiery end, Davis negotiated a surrender with Portneuf on May 20. The French granted quarter to the garrison and promised safe passage to the nearest English town. When the English gave up the fort, however, the French declared them traitors and rebels for supporting the claims of William of Orange against their rightful king, James II. Bargains with rebels being void, the Frenchmen and Abenakis killed or wounded numerous English soldiers and inhabitants and took as prisoners more than 70 men, women, and children, most of whom remained in Abenaki hands.

Combined with attacks on Schenectady, New York, and Salmon Falls, New Hampshire, the destruction of Falmouth caused considerable panic along the New England and New York borders. The New England frontier contracted as soldiers and settlers west of Wells, Maine, abandoned posts and homes. The Abenakis were encouraged by their successes and French participation, and they continued their attacks on English settlements even after Portneuf and his French soldiers returned to Quebec.

DAVID M. CORLETT

See also
Abenakis; France; King William's War

References
Leach, Douglas Edward. *Arms for Empire: A Military History of the British Colonies in North America, 1607–1763.* New York: Macmillan, 1973.
Williamson, William D. *The History of the State of Maine: From Its First Discovery, A.D. 1602, to the Separation, A.D. 1820, Inclusive.* 2 vols. Hallowell, ME: Glazier, Masters, 1832.

Fetterman, William Judd
Birth Date: 1833
Death Date: December 21, 1866

U.S. Army officer. William Judd Fetterman was born in 1833, probably in New London, Connecticut. Little is known of his early life. In May 1861 after the start of the American Civil War (1861–1865), he was commissioned a lieutenant in the 18th Infantry Regiment in Delaware. Fetterman commanded a company of the 18th Infantry in the siege of Corinth, Mississippi, in March 1862. At the Battle of Stones River (December 31, 1862) in Tennessee, he was cited for gallantry. Brevetted major, Fetterman throughout 1864 commanded a battalion in Major General William T. Sherman's drive on Atlanta. Fetterman saw action at Resaca, Kennesaw Mountain, and Peachtree Creek and then took part in the siege of Atlanta. He was brevetted lieutenant colonel in December 1864.

After the war, Fetterman remained in the army as a captain and in November 1866 was posted to Fort Phil Kearny in Wyoming guarding the Bozeman Trail. He was contemptuous of the fighting ability of the Cheyenne and Sioux warriors and boasted that he could ride through the entire Sioux Nation with a force of only 80 men. He also criticized the actions of the post commander, Colonel Henry Carrington, which Fetterman claimed were not sufficiently aggressive to ward off threats from the Native Americans. He went so far as to accuse Carrington of timidity and even cowardice.

Captain William Judd Fetterman disobeyed orders and led 80 soldiers to their deaths near Fort Kearny in Wyoming Territory on December 21, 1866, in an Indian ambush known as the Fetterman Massacre. (Hayward Cirker, ed., *Dictionary of American Portraits*, 1967)

On December 6, 1866, a war party of Sioux, Arapaho, and Cheyenne warriors led by the Oglala Sioux Red Cloud attacked an unescorted wood train not far from Fort Phil Kearny. Carrington's retaliatory force ran into an imposing assemblage of Indians and was driven back into the fort, suffering two dead and five wounded. As a result, Carrington forbade any pursuit in the future.

On December 21 Red Cloud mounted another decoy strike on the wood train, and Fetterman demanded to be allowed to lead the relief force. Carrington ordered him to relieve the wood train but gave him strict instructions not to pursue the Indians beyond Lodge Trail Ridge. Fetterman selected 79 men, a mix of infantry and cavalry. His total force was thus the exact number with which he claimed he could ride through the entire Sioux Nation.

Fetterman then set out with his men. The warriors broke off the assault on the woodcutting detail and fled. Fetterman pursued, violating his orders by passing Lodge Ridge Trail. His men were then cut off by a vastly superior Native American force. In some 20 minutes, an estimated 2,000 warriors had wiped out the entire force, including Fetterman. The Fetterman Massacre, as it would come to be called, was the greatest U.S. military loss in any Native American battle in the West to that point. Carrington was initially blamed for the disaster but was exonerated when it became clear, largely thanks to Carrington's version of events, that Fetterman had disobeyed orders.

RALPH MARTIN BAKER

See also
Arapahos; Cheyennes; Red Cloud; Sioux

References
Brown, Dee. *The Fetterman Massacre.* Lincoln: University of Nebraska Press, 1984.
Johnston, Terry C. *Sioux Dawn: The Fetterman Massacre, 1866.* New York: St. Martin's, 1991.

Fetterman Massacre
Event Date: December 21, 1866

Massacre of 80 U.S. soldiers by Sioux, Cheyenne, and Arapaho warriors on December 21, 1866, near Fort Phil Kearny in Wyoming. The Fetterman Massacre took place within the context of Red Cloud's War (1866–1868). The U.S. Army had constructed a series of forts along the Bozeman Trail, with Fort Phil Kearny as the major installation. The post was designed and commanded by Colonel Henry Carrington of the 18th Infantry Regiment. Fort Phil Kearny was strategically located but was several miles away from the nearest stand of timber, required as a fuel source in the winter. Each day a small detachment of soldiers was sent about an hour distant to obtain wood, and on most days the men were attacked by Native Americans.

In November 1866, 33-year-old Captain William Fetterman arrived at Fort Phil Kearny. Fetterman's wartime experiences during the American Civil War (1861–1865) led him to look with contempt upon Native Americans who fought using hit-and-run tactics. He also believed that Colonel Carrington was too timid and that more aggressive action was needed against the area's hostile tribes. Indeed, Fetterman often bragged that with just 80 soldiers, he could defeat the entire Sioux Nation.

By early December 1866, the Oglala Sioux chief Red Cloud and the Northern Cheyenne chief Roman Nose had gathered several thousand warriors (mainly Sioux, Cheyennes, and Arapahos) a mere 50 miles from the fort. When another army wood train ventured out on December 6, a large party of warriors attacked it and then nearly defeated a relief party that Carrington sent out. Carrington now forbade any more retaliatory operations. On December 19 another wood train was attacked and was rescued by a detachment under Captain James Powell that drove the attackers off, but Powell, as ordered, refused to pursue the warriors and fall into their trap. The next day a heavily armed detachment accomplished its mission without incident. Carrington planned one last wood train for the season before taking a break for winter.

That last wood train headed out on December 21 and came under attack. This time, according to the most widely accepted account, Captain Fetterman insisted that he be permitted to lead the rescue party. Carrington relented but ordered Fetterman not to pursue the warriors beyond Lodge Trail Ridge. In an ironic twist of fate, Fetterman's relief party had exactly 80 men, including

Massacres during the American Indian Wars

Name	Date	Location	Committed By	Committed Against
Bloody Brook Massacre	September 19, 1675	Near Deerfield, Massachusetts	Group of Wampanoag, Pocumtuck, and Nipmuck warriors	Colonial militiamen and supply column
Camp Grant Massacre	April 30, 1871	Camp Grant, north of Tucson, Arizona	Confederacy of Anglo-Americans, Mexican Americans, and Tohono O'odham warriors	Surrendered Apaches, mainly women and children
Dade's Massacre	December 28, 1835	Central Florida	Seminole warriors	U.S. troops
Duck River Massacre	May 16, 1812	Tennessee	Creek warriors	White settler's home
Fetterman Massacre	December 21, 1866	Near Fort Phil Kearny, Wyoming	Sioux, Cheyenne, and Arapaho warriors	U.S. troops
Gnadenhutten Massacre	March 8, 1782	East-central Ohio	U.S. militiamen	Moravian-Delaware Indians, mainly women and children
Good Friday Massacre	March 22, 1622	Virginia	Powhatan warriors	English settlers
Grattan Massacre	August 19, 1854	Near Fort Laramie, Nebraska Territory	Brulé Sioux	U.S. troops
Hillabee Massacre	November 18, 1813	Present-day Cherokee County, Alabama	U.S. troops	Creek warriors
Indian Creek Massacre	May 20, 1832	North-central Illinois	Pottawatomi warriors	White settler's home
Marias Massacre	January 23, 1870	Wyoming	U.S. troops	Blackfoot Sioux, mainly women and children
Meeker Massacre	September 29, 1879	Northwestern Colorado	Ute warriors	Personnel of the White River Indian Agency
Oatman Family Massacre	February 18, 1851	Western Arizona	Yavapai warriors	Royce Oatman family
Pickawillany Massacre	June 21, 1752	Western Ohio	French militiamen and Ottawa, Pottawatomi, and Ojibwa warriors	British fur-trading post and Miami Indian village
Sand Creek Massacre	November 29, 1864	Southeastern Colorado	Colorado volunteers	Southern Cheyennes and Arapahos
Spirit Lake Massacre	March 8–9, 1857	Northern Iowa	Santee Sioux warriors	White settlers
Whitman Massacre	November 29, 1847	Waiilaptu, Oregon Territory	Cayuse warriors	White missionaries
Wounded Knee Massacre	December 29, 1890	Wounded Knee, South Dakota	U.S. troops	Lakota Sioux

Fetterman, the precise number that he claimed he would need to defeat the Sioux Nation.

When Fetterman arrived on the scene with his mixed command of infantry and cavalry, the warriors broke off their attack and began to retreat. One warrior, an Oglala named Crazy Horse, stopped to check his horse to entice the pursuing soldiers to move faster. Others followed Crazy Horse's lead and taunted the soldiers with insults and obscene gestures.

Ignoring his orders, Fetterman pursued the Native American party beyond Lodge Trail Ridge until he and his men suddenly found themselves confronted by some 2,000 warriors. Within 20 minutes, Fetterman's force had been annihilated.

When a relief force arrived, what they found stunned them: 80 dead soldiers had been stripped, and their bodies had been mutilated. The sight of the grotesquely mutilated dead sent the remaining men at Fort Phil Kearny into an understandable panic. The fort's women and children were placed in the powder magazine with orders to blow it up should the fort fall.

The Native Americans did not attack the fort but instead moved on. Initially, Fetterman was proclaimed a hero. Only later did people begin to view his rash actions differently. He had clearly disregarded Carrington's order not to pursue the warriors too aggressively.

Months later an agreement was reached with Red Cloud to close the trail if the Native Americans would permit a railroad line to be built across their lands to the south. As agreed, on July 31, 1868, the last U.S. troops abandoned Fort Phil Kearny, and the Sioux promptly burned the fort to the ground. The Fetterman Massacre was the heaviest U.S. military loss in any battle with Native Americans in the West to that date.

ALAN K. LAMM

See also

Arapahos; Carrington, Henry Beebe; Cheyennes; Crazy Horse; Fetterman, William Judd; Fort Phil Kearny; Red Cloud; Red Cloud's War; Roman Nose; Sioux

References

Brown, Dee. *The Fetterman Massacre.* Lincoln: University of Nebraska Press, 1984.

Johnston, Terry C. *Sioux Dawn: The Fetterman Massacre, 1866.* New York: St. Martin's, 1991.

Monnett, John H. *Where a Hundred Soldiers Were Killed: The Struggle for the Powder River Country in 1866.* Albuquerque: University of New Mexico Press, 2008.

5th U.S. Cavalry Regiment

See Cavalry Regiment, 5th U.S.

Film and the American Indian Wars

The Indian Wars are so central to the story of the American frontier that they form a core segment of the Western genre. Their cinematic depictions underwent dramatic change over the decades, usually, though not always, as a result of the impact of new academic interpretations on popular culture. Sometimes movies were also at the forefront of these changes and for better or worse proved far more influential than any amount of scholarship.

As with all historical topics, there are advantages and disadvantages to the Hollywood treatment. On one hand, the visual element has a reality all its own; no written description could more effectively invoke the paradoxical combination of natural beauty and desolation characteristic of the American frontier than the breathtaking panoramas of Monument Valley in John Ford's *She Wore a Yellow Ribbon* (1949). Likewise, a great performance and subtle script can often provide insight into the personality of a historical figure or character type. Good historical movies can also stimulate our curiosity.

On the other hand, Hollywood tends to add romantic plot lines to improve box office demographics, exaggerate characters or situations for dramatic effect, and downplay the complexities of human beings and institutions in preference for a simple good guys versus bad guys narrative. And like all film genres, these movies have their own set of ubiquitous clichés: the wild cavalry charge on an Indian village; the off-screen massacre of an isolated detachment, homestead, or stagecoach; or the principal Indian character delivering a moving soliloquy in which he describes the plight of his people.

A small handful of classics managed to transcend the medium's limitations. The finest examples were the first two films in John Ford's cavalry trilogy: *Fort Apache* (1948) and *She Wore a Yellow Ribbon.* The third and lesser film was *Rio Grande* (1950). Although these films are fictional and are often dismissed as

overly romanticized, careful viewing reveals them to be surprisingly rich in historical insight.

After *Dances with Wolves* (1989), most films about the Indian Wars chose to ostensibly tell historical rather than fictional stories. Unfortunately, however, these movies often substituted a kind of alleged authenticity of artifacts for interpretive or even factual accuracy. Examples include *Buffalo Soldiers* (1997) and Steven Spielberg's TV miniseries *Into the West* (2005). Many of these films also suffered from a surplus of heavy-handed moralizing and were as historically misleading as anything in the B-Westerns of yesteryear.

There were exceptions, however, such as *Son of the Morning Star* (1991) and Walter Hill's *Geronimo: An American Legend* (1993). Hill's film featured a surprisingly complex screenplay from acclaimed writer John Milius that managed to get much of the details right about Genonimo's guerrilla war in the mid-1880s. Though far from perfect, in their better moments these films managed to evoke what James McPherson called the "larger truth." Their chief failings were dramatic, and for all their historical merit, as movies they simply could not achieve the standard set by Ford.

Perhaps the best way to understand the change in popular views of the Indian Wars is to explore Hollywood's interpretation of the life and death of George Armstrong Custer (1839–1876). More movies have been made about "Yellow Hair's" exploits—real,

John Wayne, an actor known especially for his roles in movies about the American West is shown here in a still from John Ford's film *Fort Apache.* (RKO Radio Pictures/Photofest)

exaggerated, or wholly invented—than all other frontier military figures combined. A discussion of Custer's place in the mythology of the American West belongs elsewhere, but it is worth noting that much of that mythology was established, if not invented, by the movies. Indeed, Custer's epic demise at the hands of Lakota, Cheyenne, and Arapaho warriors in the Battle of the Little Bighorn (June 25–26, 1876), also known as Custer's Last Stand, was the subject of some of the very first movies. And before that it was the frequent climax of the traveling Wild West shows of the late 19th century that did so much to define popular interpretations of the frontier experience.

Until the 1960s, Custer was invariably portrayed as a heroic victim of either the Indians, corrupt government officials, misguided reservation policy, betrayal by his own subordinates, or some combination thereof. The best example was probably *They Died with Their Boots On* (1939), starring Errol Flynn. Here Custer, a victim of scheming and corrupt politicians, was the last to die at Little Bighorn, overrun by an Indian charge after defiantly breaking his saber in half. (Custer actually forbade his troops from carrying sabers prior to an attack lest their clanging alert the enemy.) His heroic sacrifice leads the government to return the Indians' land. The inaccuracies in this version of events are obvious. As one historian put it, "they died with their facts wrong."

By the 1960s, the patron saint of western expansion was beginning to lose his halo. In *Custer of the West* (1967), Robert Shaw's Custer was still brave and even romantic, but some of the darker complexities also appeared for the first time, including his ruthless command style, his feud with the Ulysses S. Grant administration over the Belknap Scandal, and his disputes with subordinates that contributed to his death. Although a few of the events depicted in the film were loosely based on actual history, overall it was mostly just wrong. Surprisingly, one element of continuity with *They Died with Their Boots On* was the portrayal of Custer as sympathetic to the Indians.

Revisionism in all its glory informed the next and arguably the most durable celluloid Custer of all: Richard Mulligan's version in the 1969 epic *Little Big Man*. Here Custer was a megalomaniacal villain, a Custer for the times, personifying all that the so-called New Left feared and loathed about the American propensity for war. Clearly the unpopular Vietnam War had crept its way into this movie. Although such a cartoonish depiction said far more about the 1960s than the 1870s, Mulligan's insane Custer unfortunately was embraced by a generation of historically unsophisticated Americans familiar with slogans such as "Custer Died for Your Sins" as biographical reality.

The next two efforts were both made-for-TV movies. The 1977 Hallmark special *The Court-Martial of George Armstrong Custer* was an attempt to get back to the historical Custer, although the setting was a hypothetical post–Little Bighorn trial in which a surviving Custer was charged with negligence for losing his command. This allowed for plenty of speculation—including about Custer's sexual relationship with wife Elizabeth—but also facilitated the inclusion of many pertinent historical details. Although the film did not include a verdict, it echoed a familiar cinematic theme in strongly implying that Custer was a victim of his political enemies.

The 1991 made-for-TV miniseries based on the book by Evan Connell, *Son of the Morning Star,* represented a far more ambitious attempt to explore the historical Custer. His military career, especially on the frontier, was covered fairly accurately, as were some of the lesser-known aspects of his personal life, such as his relationship with his siblings. Aside from its excellent re-creation of the Battle of the Little Bighorn, however, dramatically the series never managed to transcend its awkward plot structure and lackluster acting, especially Gary Cole's bland Custer. Henry Fonda's fictional Colonel Owen Thursday in *Fort Apache* continued to offer the most enduring and sophisticated celluloid insight into the historical Custer.

If any long-term cinematic trend could be regarded as mostly positive, it was the way in which native peoples were depicted. Until the 1960s, considerable and often insulting historical liberties were commonplace. Actors portraying Indians were usually not real Native Americans at all, they often spoke stereotypical Hollywood gibberish, and, at least in the B-Westerns of the early decades, were seldom little more than human savages. From the 1960s on, however, Indian peoples went from being mere ciphers or targets to protagonists as the movies began to tell the story from their point of view, as in *Little Big Man* (Cheyenne), *I Will Fight No More Forever* (1975, Nez Perce), and, of course, *Dances with Wolves* (Lakota). Not surprisingly, new stereotypes emerged to replace the old, and even as these tribes were portrayed with greater sympathy and accuracy, the Pawnees often took their place as the "bad Indians," as exemplified by *Little Big Man* and *Dances with Wolves.*

Contrary to popular perception, however, the sympathetic portrayal of Indians was not new with *Little Big Man.* As noted above, in *They Died with Their Boots On* the Sioux were driven into hostility by corrupt government officials and land-hungry whites. Similar grievances appeared in many other films, including *Fort Apache* and Chuck Connors's vehicle, *Geronimo* (1962). In each case the Indians' decision to resort to war was presented as a legitimate reaction to white injustice.

Just as Hollywood's portrayal of Indian people reflected changes in scholarship and political culture, so too did its interpretation of the frontier army. Partly a result of the turmoil of the 1960s and partly perhaps a reflection of the cinematic need for dramatic balance, as the Indian rose in esteem, the white soldier declined. The notable exceptions were the African American buffalo soldiers, who were the favorably depicted subject of two films spanning this period of interpretive change: John Ford's *Sergeant Rutledge* (1960) and the TNT movie *Buffalo Soldiers* (1997).

Otherwise, the "blue coats" mutated from the good-natured immigrant heroes of *She Wore a Yellow Ribbon* into agents of militarism or even genocide. In *Little Big Man,* the 7th Cavalry carries out a My-Lai Massacre–like slaughter of Cheyennes at the Battle of the Washita (November 1868). *Soldier Blue* (1970) substituted the

Sand Creek Massacre (November 1864) for Vietnam but kept the increasingly familiar stereotype of psychotic soldiers slaughtering innocent women and children. Later came the insane soldiers of *Dances with Wolves* who inexplicably blow their brains out or sadistically take potshots at wildlife.

Once more, however, this interpretive shift was anticipated by John Ford. *Fort Apache*'s Colonel Thursday was clearly at least partially based on historical figures such as Custer and William Fetterman (1833–1866) who, like Thursday, was lured with his command into a fatal ambush near Fort Phil Kearny in December 1866. In *The Searchers* (1956), which focused on the issue of anti-Indian racism, the army occasionally appeared in the background as a morally ambiguous force, and *Cheyenne Autumn* (1964) presented cinema's first full-blown psychopathic frontier army officer, Karl Malden's uncomplicatedly evil Oskar Wessels.

More recently, productions such as *Ulzana's Raid* (1972), *Son of the Morning Star* (1991), and *Geronimo: An American Legend* (1993) offered a more nuanced view of both Indian and soldier. The latter film in particular represented in some respects a return to the visual and interpretive sensibilities of *Fort Apache*, complete with historical versions of Colonel Thursday (General Nelson A. Miles, 1839–1925) and Captain York (Lieutenant Charles Gatewood, 1853–1896). It remains to be seen, however, if any film about the Indian Wars will ever be able to combine the beauty and power of the fictional work of John Ford with real historical events.

RAYMOND W. LEONARD

See also

Apaches; Buffalo Soldiers; Cheyennes; Cody, William Frederick; Custer, George Armstrong; Dakota Sioux; Fetterman Massacre; Geronimo; Little Bighorn, Battle of the; Sand Creek Massacre

References

Carnes, Mark C., ed. *Past Imperfect: History According to the Movies.* New York: Henry Holt, 1995.

Connell, Evan S. *Son of the Morning Star: Custer and the Little Bighorn.* New York: North Point Press, 1984.

Cowie, Peter. *John Ford and the American West.* New York: Harry N. Abrams, 2004.

Cozzens, Peter, ed. *Eyewitnesses to the Indian Wars, 1865–1890.* 5 vols. Mechanicsburg, PA: Stackpole, 2001–2006.

Eyman, Scott. *Print the Legend: The Life and Times of John Ford.* Baltimore: Johns Hopkins University Press, 2001.

Jones, Douglas C. *The Court-Martial of George Armstrong Custer.* New York: Scribner's, 1976.

Langellier, John Phillip. *Custer: The Man, the Myth, the Movies.* Mechanicsburg, PA: Stackpole, 2000.

Utley, Robert M. *Frontier Regulars: The United States and the American Indian, 1866–1891.* New York: Macmillan, 1973.

Firearms Trade

Firearms played an important, perhaps vital, role in the European settlement of North America. Conflicts between settlers and Native Americans were waged with firearms, and European superiority in these weapons gave them an advantage that the Native Americans could never overcome. Naturally, firearms were prized possessions and became one of the most important trade items for the various cultures involved, both in the colonial era and beyond.

The earliest recorded use of firearms in warfare in what today constitutes the United States and Canada was at the Battle of Lake Champlain in 1609. Samuel de Champlain's intervention against the Iroquois to help his Huron and Algonquin allies created a conflict between the French and the Iroquois that continued for 150 years. The incident taught the Iroquois that they needed firearms to defend their territory against the newcomers. Fortunately for them, the Dutch soon opened trading posts with the natives in New Amsterdam (later New York).

Beginning in 1624, Native Americans were able to obtain firearms in exchange for highly prized beaver pelts. By 1630 the Iroquois had driven the Algonquins from their territory. To protect their native allies and to obtain furs, the French began to arm natives allied with them. The English also supplied weapons to natives in their spheres of influence. An average exchange rate of the 18th century was 1 pelt for 1 pound of shot or 3 flints, 4 pelts for 1 pound of powder, 10 pelts for 1 pistol, and 20 pelts for 1 trade gun.

As the demand for furs continued, the number of firearms manufactured for trade to the Native Americans soared. Most European countries followed a policy of mercantilism with their colonies. According to this theory, only the parent country would produce manufactured goods, and the colonies would supply raw materials. Manufacturing was actively discouraged in the colonies. As a result, the vast majority of the firearms produced during the colonial period came from Europe.

Gradually a specific type of weapon, the trade musket, was developed for trade with Native Americans. The trade musket was the most commonly exchanged weapon during the 17th and 18th centuries in North America. European gun makers during this time created weapons for trade that shared certain characteristics, no matter which country produced them. Trade muskets were all smoothbore weapons. Native Americans wanted a firearm that could be used for hunting or warfare. The trade musket could fire either small shot or a ball. The musket's bore was much smaller than that of European weapons. Eventually the 24-bore was accepted as standard. This meant that a pound of lead would produce 24 balls for a trade musket. In contrast, the English Brown Bess musket was a 12-bore, meaning that only half as many balls could be produced from the same amount of lead. The smaller ball also meant that trade muskets required smaller amounts of gunpowder, an important consideration for Native Americans, who could only secure lead and powder from the colonists. In addition, the smaller-bore weapons meant that more ammunition could be carried for less weight than that for the weapons generally carried by the colonists.

Trade muskets also had shorter barrels than those of their European counterparts. In dense forests, shorter barrels were handier and less likely to catch in brush. A 30-inch barrel was most popular, although other lengths were common. The accompanying loss in accuracy with a shorter barrel was acceptable because most targets were relatively close. The trade musket normally was about four feet long overall, compared to a long rifle that might be up to six feet in length. The trade musket was also plain, without decorations. Many natives preferred to decorate their own weapons with brass tacks, feathers, or paint. Trade weapons were designed to be rugged and stand up to frontier conditions. Trigger guards were also larger than normal to allow firing while wearing mittens.

Gun makers did all they could to reduce the cost of the trade muskets. This fact and the lack of decorations led many to believe that trade muskets were inferior to European weapons. Stories circulated about trade muskets bursting or breaking, and although some such stories were obviously true, the Native Americans who used the muskets were not fools and soon accumulated sufficient experience to recognize an inferior weapon. Keeping trade muskets in working order became such an important issue that most treaties in the 18th century required colonial governments to make gunsmiths available at trading posts to repair Native American weapons.

Beginning in the early 1800s, the standard so-called Indian trade gun became more accurate and had a longer range. The Lewis and Clark expedition reported that the Native Americans they encountered in the Pacific Northwest already possessed such weapons; such was the extent of the firearms trade by the early 19th century. Not until the mid-19th century did Native Americans come to possess carbines and rifles in significant quantities. A good number of these were acquired during raids on white settlements and wagon trains, although most were acquired through trade. Native Americans soon discovered, however, that these firearms were difficult to repair and that ammunition for them was equally difficult to obtain. Principally because of this, the bow and arrow and the lance remained an integral part of the Native American arsenal until the last third of the 19th century. The lightweight and easily repaired Winchester repeating rifle, introduced in 1873, quickly made its way into Native American hands, and the bow and the lance finally became obsolete as weapons of war. The advent of the Winchester rifle, however, only served to increase Native American reliance on white suppliers. By the time that adoption of the rifle had become widespread, the Indian Wars were nearly over.

TIM J. WATTS

See also
Bow and Arrow; Fur Trade; Lance; Muskets; Native American Trade; Rifles

References
Brown, M. L. *Firearms in Colonial America: The Impact on History and Technology, 1492–1792.* Washington, DC: Smithsonian Institution Press, 1980.
Peterson, Harold L. *Arms and Armor in Colonial America, 1526–1783.* Harrisburg, PA: Stackpole, 1956.
Russell, Carl P. *Guns on the Early Frontier: A History of Firearms from Colonial Times through the Years of the Western Fur Trade.* Berkeley and Los Angeles: University of California Press, 1957.

1st and 2nd Dragoon Regiments
See Dragoon Regiments, 1st and 2nd

Flacco the Elder
Birth Date: Unknown
Death Date: Unknown

Lipan Apache chief who frequently allied with Texan Americans. Flacco the Elder and his son Flacco the Younger, who was born ca. 1818, often acted as scouts and guides for Texas settlers against the Mexicans and the Comanches. Flacco the Younger participated in several Texas expeditions into Mexico, including the Somervell Expedition of 1842. Leaving that expedition early with a group of horses that he had managed to round up in Mexico, he was killed under peculiar circumstances near San Antonio in December 1842. Some believed that he had been the victim of Mexican bandits; others suspected that he was killed by a rival Native American tribe, perhaps the Comanches or Cherokees. Flacco the Elder, however, believed that his son had been murdered by two white Texans who had been part of the Somervell Expedition and who had coveted his horses.

President Sam Houston, fearing an outbreak of retaliatory violence on the part of the aggrieved Lipans, insisted that Flacco the Younger's murder had been perpetrated by the Mexicans. Nevertheless, Houston presented gifts to Flacco the Elder and his family and vowed to uncover the circumstances surrounding Flacco the Younger's murder. Houston even sent the grieving chief a poem in honor of his fallen son. In early 1843 the disconsolate Flacco led a band of as many as 400 warriors into northern Mexico, where he joined forces with a contingent of Mescalero Apaches. From there the Apaches conducted raids against Mexican villages and Texan settlements as well. It is not known if Flacco actively encouraged the raids into Texas. Flacco dropped out of the historical record after 1843, and the remaining years of his life and the circumstances of his death are unknown. Some historians have suggested that Flacco the Younger's unsolved murder led to the nearly constant warfare between Texans and the Lipan Apaches during the 1840s and 1850s.

PAUL G. PIERPAOLI JR.

See also
Apaches; Cherokees; Comanches; Houston, Samuel

References
Schilz, Thomas F. *Lipan Apaches in Texas.* El Paso: Texas Western Press, 1987.

Williams, Amelia W., and Eugene C. Barker, eds. *The Writings of Sam Houston, 1813–1863.* 8 vols. 1938–1943; reprint, Austin and New York: Pemberton, 1970.

Flipper, Henry Ossian
Birth Date: March 21, 1856
Death Date: May 3, 1940

First African American graduate from the U.S. Military Academy, West Point. Henry Ossian Flipper was born into slavery in Thomasville, Georgia, on March 21, 1856. He was the eldest of five sons of two slave parents. Growing up in Georgia, he attended schools operated by the American Missionary Association in Atlanta. In 1873 he accepted an appointment to the U.S. Military Academy, where he suffered ostracism from his fellow cadets because of his race. Flipper overcame the prejudice and in June 1877 became the first African American to graduate from West Point. He was commissioned a second lieutenant and was assigned to Company A of the 10th Cavalry.

Flipper served at various posts on the frontier, carrying out assorted missions including scouting, patrolling, and combating local belligerent Native Americans. During his time at Fort Davis in Texas, he led his company in several small skirmishes and expeditions against the Apache war chief Victorio in 1880. While a capable field commander, Flipper excelled particularly in engineering projects at these outposts, working as a surveyor and construction planner. At Fort Sill, Oklahoma, he and his troops drained all of the mosquito-ridden ponds on the installation, which improved the health of the garrison. Flipper's Ditch, which he designed to remove the contaminated water, remains and is now a national historic landmark. Flipper also successfully applied his West Point engineering education in various other projects such as stringing telegraph lines, constructing roads, and erecting post buildings.

While at Fort Davis, Flipper also performed auxiliary duties such as serving as acting assistant quartermaster, post quartermaster, and acting commissary of subsistence, which made him responsible for the installation's supplies and facilities. Once he took on these positions, he left himself exposed to plots by racist white officers to force him out of the army. In 1881 he discovered post funds missing from his quarters and attempted to conceal the loss until he could find or replace the money. Post commander Colonel William R. Shafter of the 1st Infantry accused Flipper of embezzling the money and of conduct unbecoming of an officer and a gentleman. Shafter relieved him of his duties. A court-martial exonerated Flipper of embezzlement but convicted him on the latter charge, resulting in his dismissal from the army on June 30, 1882.

Flipper went on to a successful career as an engineer in Mexico, South America, and Arizona, working on several lucrative surveying, railroad, and mining projects over the next 30 years. Ironically, the same federal government that stripped him of his army career hired Flipper as an engineering and cultural adviser for the

Henry O. Flipper was, in 1877, the first African American to graduate from the U.S. Military Academy at West Point. His military career was cut short because of racism. (Hulton Archive/Getty Images)

Justice Department, the Department of the Interior, and the Senate Committee on Foreign Relations. However, Flipper continued to battle with the government over his conviction, asserting his innocence. He spent the rest of his life lobbying for vindication from his court-martial, including an unsuccessful attempt to have Congress reinstate his commission so that he might participate in the Spanish-American War in 1898.

To bolster his cause Flipper published two books, one an account of his military academy experiences and the other about his ordeal with the army, the second published posthumously. He retired from his engineering career in 1931 and died in Atlanta, Georgia, on May 3, 1940. President Bill Clinton officially pardoned Flipper on February 19, 1999.

BRADFORD A. WINEMAN

See also
Cavalry Regiment, 10th U.S.

References
Dinges, Bruce J. "The Court-Martial of Lieutenant Henry O. Flipper." *American West* 9 (January 1972): 12–17.
Flipper, Henry Ossian. *The Colored Cadet at West Point.* New York: Arno and New York Times, 1969.
Harris, Theodore D., ed. *Black Frontiersman: The Memoirs of Henry O. Flipper, First Black Graduate of West Point.* Fort Worth: Texas Christian University Press, 1997.

Forsyth, George Alexander
Birth Date: November 7, 1837
Death Date: September 12, 1915

U.S. Army officer. George Alexander "Sandy" Forsyth was born on November 7, 1837, in Muncy, Pennsylvania. He attended the Canandaigua Academy in New York, studied law at the Chicago Law Institute, and later apprenticed under attorney Isaac N. Arnold, a noted Illinois Republican and friend to President Abraham Lincoln. With the outbreak of the American Civil War (1861–1865), Forsyth immediately enlisted in the Chicago Dragoons, serving as a private. In September 1861 he secured a commission as a first lieutenant in the 8th Illinois Volunteer Cavalry. He participated in the 1862 Peninsula Campaign in Virginia and the Battle of Chancellorsville in 1863 and then distinguished himself at the Battle of Brandy Station later that year, where he was seriously wounded. Forsyth forged a close relationship with Major General Philip Sheridan during the 1864–1865 Shenandoah Valley Campaign as a staff officer to the general. Mustered out of volunteer service as a major in March 1865, Forsyth was brevetted brigadier general of volunteers for his exemplary service.

Forsyth entered the regular army after the war, and in 1866 he was assigned to frontier duty in the West. Appointed a major in the 9th U.S. Cavalry, in September 1868 he led an independent scout force of 50 men chiefly against the Cheyennes in the regions of Colorado, Kansas, and Nebraska. On September 16 Forsyth and his men set up camp along the Arikaree River, a tributary of the Republican River near present-day Wray, Colorado. The following day a war party of some 1,000 Cheyenne, Sioux, and Arapaho warriors, led by Chief Roman Nose, attacked the bivouacked scouts.

Forsyth quickly organized a credible defense on a small sandy island in the Arikaree River where he and his men held off repeated Native American assaults. In the process Forsyth was wounded three times. The scouts managed to maintain their position for nine days before finally being relieved by a company of African American soldiers from the 10th U.S. Cavalry based at Fort Wallace, Kansas. In the so-called Battle of Beecher's Island, Forsyth lost five men killed including his second-in-command. During the nine-day siege, the U.S. soldiers were forced to eat their own horses because they had no food. Although the action was inconclusive, Forsyth's tenacious defense earned him a brevet to brigadier general and ensured his place in the annals of American frontier history.

Upon Sheridan's promotion to lieutenant general and selection for command of the Division of Missouri, which oversaw military activities throughout the West, Forsyth served as his military secretary from 1869 to 1873. In this post Forsyth was involved in various duties, which included restoring order after Chicago's Great Fire of 1871; organizing a buffalo hunt for Russia's Grand Duke Alexis, the third son of Czar Alexander II; working to ease tensions with the Mormons; and heading a military mission to Japan, China, India, and Europe.

Forsyth continued to serve in a variety of command and staff positions, including lieutenant colonel of the 4th Cavalry during the Apache Wars of the 1880s. In July 1888 in a much-publicized case, he faced a court-martial for submitting fraudulent claims to the U.S. government. Although Forsyth was convicted of the charges, President Grover Cleveland granted some degree of clemency. Nevertheless, the conviction effectively ended Forsyth's military career.

Forsyth was medically retired on March 25, 1890, as a result of "mental and moral derangements of the mind." He published his memoirs that same year and in 1904 was advanced to the rank of colonel on the Retired List. Forsyth died in Rockport, Massachusetts, on September 12, 1915.

ROBERT J. DALESSANDRO AND PAUL G. PIERPAOLI JR.

See also
Apache Wars; Arapahos; Beecher Island, Battle of; Cheyennes; Cavalry Regiment, 4th U.S.; Cavalry Regiment, 9th U.S.; Cavalry Regiment, 10th U.S.; Roman Nose; Sheridan, Philip Henry; Sioux

References
Dixon, David. *Hero of Beecher Island: The Life and Military Career of George A. Forsyth.* Lincoln: University of Nebraska Press, 1994.
Forsyth, George A. *The Story of a Soldier.* New York: D. Appleton, 1900.

Forsyth, James William
Birth Date: August 8, 1835
Death Date: October 24, 1906

U.S. Army officer and longtime staff officer for General Philip H. Sheridan. James William Forsyth was born at Maumee, Ohio, on August 8, 1835. He graduated from the U.S. Military Academy, West Point, in 1856. Commissioned a second lieutenant in the 9th Infantry Regiment, he served for the next five years in the Pacific Northwest. Promoted to first lieutenant in March 1861 and to captain in October 1861, he spent most of the American Civil War (1861–1865) in important staff assignments, first with Major General George McClellan and the Army of the Potomac and later as chief of staff for Major General Philip Sheridan, with whom Forsyth remained closely associated until Sheridan's death in 1888. Forsyth was brevetted through the rank of brigadier general of U.S. Volunteers and in the regular service and, following the close of the Civil War, was elevated to the permanent rank of brigadier general of volunteers before mustering out in January 1866.

In the postwar army reorganization, Forsyth was appointed a major in the new 10th Cavalry Regiment, one of the African American units recently authorized by Congress, but he rarely served with the unit. Instead he held numerous staff assignments, mostly with Sheridan, in the Department of the Gulf and the Department of the Missouri. In 1869 when Sheridan became commander of the massive Division of the Missouri, Forsyth

During his military career, which spanned from the Civil War to the end of the Indian Wars, Major George Alexander ("Sandy") Forsyth participated in more than 70 engagements and was wounded four times. (Library of Congress)

stayed on as aide-de-camp and later as military secretary, serving until 1878. During that period Forsyth joined Sheridan when he represented the United States as an observer of the Franco-Prussian War in 1870 and toured much of Europe. Their return in 1871 coincided with a dramatic escalation of the Indian Wars, and Sheridan's division included the most active area. Somehow Forsyth found time to conduct an exploration of the Yellowstone River and its tributaries in 1875.

After more than 15 years in staff positions, in 1878 Forsyth joined the 1st Cavalry Regiment with a promotion to lieutenant colonel and was active in suppressing the Bannock-Paiute uprising in the Northwest that year. In 1886 he assumed command of the 7th Cavalry, the regiment ravaged a decade before at the Battle of the Little Bighorn (June 25–26, 1876). For three years he devoted himself to developing the Cavalry and Light Artillery School at Fort Riley in Kansas.

On December 29, 1890, Forsyth earned unintentional infamy when the 7th Cavalry ignited a tragic and unplanned battle while trying to disarm several hundred Lakota Sioux men, women, and children under Big Foot. The confrontation at Wounded Knee on the Pine Ridge Agency left more than 150 Native Americans, including dozens of women and children, dead (although some estimates are much higher). Twenty-five troops died, and 39 others were wounded. The regiment lost additional troops in an ambush pursuing another band the following day. Outraged

division commander Major General Nelson Miles blamed Forsyth for the disaster and relieved him from duty, only to be overruled by the secretary of war.

Forsyth went on to earn promotion to brigadier general in 1894 with command of the Department of California until his promotion to major general and retirement in 1897. He died in Columbus, Ohio, on October 24, 1906.

DAVID COFFEY

See also

Cavalry Regiment, 7th U.S.; Cavalry Regiment, 10th U.S.; Ghost Dance; Little Bighorn, Battle of the; Miles, Nelson Appleton; Sheridan, Philip Henry; Wounded Knee, Battle of

References

Morris, Roy, Jr. *Sheridan: The Life and Wars of General Phil Sheridan.* New York: Crown, 1992.

Utley, Robert M. *Frontier Regulars: The United States and the American Indian, 1866–1891.* New York: Macmillan, 1973.

Wooster, Robert. *Nelson A. Miles and the Twilight of the Frontier Army.* Lincoln: University of Nebraska Press, 1993.

Fort Apache

U.S. Army post located on the south bank (east side) of the White Mountain River in eastern Arizona. In May 1870 Major John Green, commanding officer of Camp Goodwin, selected this area as a temporary campsite because Camp Goodwin had become indefensible due to malaria outbreaks and Apache attacks. The new fort was first named Camp Ord in honor of Brigadier General Edward O. C. Ord, commander of the territory. In August 1870 it was named Camp Mogollon, and in September 1870 it was again renamed, as Camp Thomas, in honor of Major General George H. Thomas, the "Rock of Chickamauga." In February 1871 it was finally designated Camp Apache as a sign of friendship with the nearby tribe, the White Mountain Apache Reservation having been established by a presidential executive order. That same year Lieutenant Colonel George Crook was named commander of the Department of Arizona and stationed himself at Camp Apache for a period of time during his Apache campaign of 1872–1873. In April 1879 the military post became Fort Apache. The fort played a conspicuous role in the campaigns against renegade Apaches, including Geronimo, from 1881 to 1886. In August 1881 Colonel Eiugene Carr, two troops of his 6th Cavalry, and two dozen White Mountain Apache scouts, operating out of Fort Apache, engaged in a deadly confrontation at Cibicue Creek, during which the scouts mutinied. Shortly thereafter enraged Apaches attacked the fort, one of few such attacks ever recorded on an army post in the West. The battle at Cibicue and the subsequent attack on Fort Apache ignited a conflict that lasted until Geronimo's surrender in 1886.

Displaced Apaches from various subtribes, including the Chiricahuas and the Yavapais, were placed on the nearby San Carlos Reservation. Conditions on the reservation grew worse

Camp Apache (later Fort Apache) in Arizona Territory, 1871. (Library of Congress)

during the later years of the 19th century because of starvation and overcrowding. In addition, the U.S. government continually reduced the land area of the Apaches based on discoveries of copper, silver, and coal and to provide more farmland and timber for white settlers. The White Mountain Apaches eventually gave up fighting the military in their area, and they pleaded with whites to let them remain in their country. In return, the White Mountain Apaches promised to stop fighting and pledged their help in tracking down the hostile Chiricahuas. White Mountain scouts served throughout the campaigns of the 1880s. The Fort Apache or White Mountain Reservation was established as a separate entity in 1891.

The fort itself encompassed 288 acres, while the Fort Apache Reservation lands covered 1.6 million acres. The reservation lands spread over parts of present-day Navajo, Apache, and Gila counties. Eventually in 1924 Fort Apache was abandoned by the army and was turned over to the Bureau of Indian Affairs to be used as a school. The fort's headquarters building is now the post office for the town of Fort Apache.

JUSTIN D. MURPHY, LORIN M. LOWRIE, AND DAVID COFFEY

See also
Apaches; Crook, George; Geronimo; Yavapais

References
Aleshire, Peter. *Cochise: The Life and Times of the Great Apache Chief.* New York: Wiley, 2001.
Crook, George. *General George Crook: His Autobiography.* Edited by Martin F. Schmidt. Norman: University of Oklahoma Press, 1960.
Fort Apache Indian Reservation: Community Profile. Arizona Department of Commerce, 2008.

Fort Armstrong, Treaty of

Treaty signed on September 21, 1832, at the conclusion of the Black Hawk War between the U.S. government and the Sauk and Fox tribes. The Treaty of Fort Armstrong, negotiated and signed at Rock Island, Illinois, stipulated conditions for an amicable settlement to bring about peace and friendship between the U.S. government and Native Americans. The treaty also provided for a considerable cession of Native American lands to the United States, essentially all Sauk lands east of the Mississippi River and all jointly held Sauk and Fox lands in eastern Iowa. Major General Winfield Scott of the U.S. Army and Illinois governor John Reynolds had empowered their commissioners to enter into talks and themselves signed the treaty, which had been negotiated during September 15–21.

Under the agreement the United States demanded—and received—all lands that the two tribes had title to or had claimed prior to the outbreak of the war except for reservation lands, which were to be set aside for the tribe's explicit habitation. The reservation encompassed 400 square miles of territory on either side of the Iowa River and included Sauk chief Keokuk's principal village, which was some 12 miles from the Mississippi River. In exchange for the huge land cession of well more than 6 million acres, the U.S. government pledged to remunerate the tribes with an annual payment of $20,000 for 30 years, beginning in 1832.

The government further promised to provide the Native Americans with a blacksmith and gunsmith shop for 30 years, including adequate supplies of steel and iron, and an annual shipment (for 30 years) of 40 kegs of tobacco and 40 barrels of salt. The U.S. government also promised to repatriate all prisoners taken during the hostilities but would continue to hold as hostages Black Hawk, his sons, and several other war chiefs as guarantors of good behavior and good faith. To encourage the Sauk and Fox leaders to sign the treaty swiftly, the government offered 35 beef cattle and 12 bushels of salt to be delivered upon signing and a like amount again in April 1833, along with 6,000 bushels of corn.

The Treaty of Fort Armstrong marked the permanent subjugation of the Native American tribes in northern Illinois, southern Wisconsin, and eastern Iowa and facilitated the rapid settlement of these areas by whites looking for arable land upon which to raise crops. The treaty also virtually guaranteed an end to Native American attacks in the region that had culminated in the Black Hawk War, a conflict that had claimed as many as 70 military and civilian lives and perhaps 500 or more Native American lives.

PAUL G. PIERPAOLI JR.

See also

Black Hawk; Black Hawk War; Keokuk; Sauks and Foxes; Scott, Winfield

References

Hurt, R. Douglas. *Nathan Boone and the American Frontier.* Columbia: University of Missouri Press, 1998.
Jung, Patrick J. *The Black Hawk War of 1832.* Norman: University of Oklahoma Press, 2007.

Fort Bascom

U.S. Army post established in 1863 on the south bank of the Canadian River in present-day New Mexico not far from the Texas–New Mexico border. Fort Bascom was one of several forts created by Brigadier General James Henry Carleton that were to control and contain the Kiowas, Comanches, and other tribes in the Staked Plains of the Texas Panhandle (Red River and Canadian River areas). The post was also planned to protect the Santa Fe Trail. Finally, Carleton had hoped to curtail the actions of the Comancheros, American and Mexican renegades who engaged in illegal and illicit trade with the Native Americans.

By all accounts, Fort Bascom was an unimpressive post that was not well constructed and was never fully outfitted or completed. There are no remains left of the fort, the site of which is now located on privately owned land. It is believed that the fort consisted of officers' quarters made of sandstone and several smaller adobe-style structures, which likely served as enlisted men's barracks and storage facilities. When the fort was abandoned in 1870, it had been only partly completed.

Despite its modest appearance and function, Fort Bascom served as a base for several army campaigns against Native Americans. In November 1864 Christopher "Kit" Carson campaigned against the Kiowas and Comanches from Fort Bascom, which culminated in the First Battle of Adobe Walls (November 25) in Texas. Carleton had authorized the punitive mission after several Native American raids on the Santa Fe Trail. During 1868–1869 the fort was again used as a base of operations against Native Americans, this time led by Major General Philip Sheridan. In

1870 the army abandoned Fort Bascom and moved its garrison to Fort Union, New Mexico.

Although deactivated as a permanent post, Fort Bascom continued to see use as a temporary base. Troops from Fort Union took station at or near Fort Bascom during the spring and summer months of 1871, 1872, and 1873 when they were trying to interdict the Comanchero trade and keep tabs on the Comanches and Kiowas on the Staked Plains. In 1874 Fort Bascom served as the final staging area for Major William R. Price's 8th Cavalry battalion in preparation for its participation in the Red River War (1874–1875).

PAUL G. PIERPAOLI JR. AND DAVID COFFEY

See also

Adobe Walls, First Battle of; Carleton, James Henry; Carson, Christopher Houston; Comancheros; Comanches; Kiowas; Red River War; Sheridan, Philip Henry

References

Baker, T. Lindsay, and Billy R. Harrison. *Adobe Walls: The History and Archeology of the 1874 Trading Post.* College Station: Texas A&M University Press, 1986.
Field, Ron. *Forts of the American Frontier, 1820–1891: The Southern Plains and Southwest.* New York: Osprey, 2006.

Fort Greenville, Treaty of

See Greenville, Treaty of

Fort Harmar, Treaty of

Treaty signed between the U.S. government and the Six Nations (Iroquois Confederacy), the Delaware, and the Wyandot tribes at Fort Harmar, on the Muskingum River (near present-day Marietta, Ohio), on January 9, 1789. The treaty's purpose was to renew and confirm the Treaty of Fort Stanwix (October 21, 1784) and the Treaty of Fort McIntosh (January 21, 1785), which had delineated the boundary between U.S. and Native American lands.

The issues at hand were the westward expansion of American settlers across the frontier into Native American territory and the inability of the territorial governors to curb that flow. Moreover, there was concern that the violence between settlers and Native Americans would make the legitimate sale of land in the area known as the Western Reserve impossible, the proceeds of which were intended to pay the federal government's debt. Secretary of War Henry Knox advised the governor of the Northwest Territory, Arthur St. Clair, that the government should take a strong stand with both settlers and Native Americans in order to enforce legitimacy and create an environment of justice and moderation. St. Clair, taking his direction from Knox's clearly articulated belief that peace had its foundations in treaties, sought to bring the chiefs of the Native American tribes to the negotiating table.

Fort Harmar, site of a treaty in 1789 between the U.S. government and the Six Nations, Delawares, and Wyandots. It confirmed earlier treaties but did not last because several tribes refused to sign and many settlers would not abide by its terms. (Getty Images)

St. Clair was successful in bringing representatives from the Delaware, Wyandot, Sac, Ojibwa, Ottawa, and Pottawatomi tribes to Fort Harmar in December 1788. In less than one month, all of the representatives signed a treaty that confirmed the boundaries previously established by the Treaty of Fort McIntosh. The U.S. government agreed to pay the assembled representatives with goods valued at $6,000. The treaty's 15 articles not only clearly delineated geographic boundaries but also promised to increase trade, allow hunting privileges, and punish illegal settlers. Squatters, by the provisions of the treaty, were to be considered outside of the protection of the United States and subject to punishment by the Native American nation upon whose land the settler encroached. Furthermore, both sides at the negotiations were so concerned about the detrimental effects of horse theft that the crime received its own article (Article VI). For this crime, however, the United States was the only adjudicating authority.

Unfortunately, two of the most powerful tribes in the region, the Shawnees and the Miamis, did not send representatives and consequently were not bound by the agreement. Moreover, many settlers flagrantly violated the treaty. The U.S. government could neither control nor coerce frontier settlers, and the treaty quickly proved to be a dead letter. Less than two years after signing the treaty, the U.S. government resolved that the only way to gain control of the region was through punitive military action against the Native Americans. The Northwest Territory was hotly contested over the next four years until the decisive American victory at the Battle of Fallen Timbers (August 20, 1794). That triumph resulted in the 1795 Treaty of Fort Greenville in which the Native Americans ceded most of the Ohio Country to the United States.

JEFFERY P. LUCAS

See also

Fallen Timbers, Battle of; Greenville, Treaty of; Harmar, Josiah; Land Cessions, Northwest Ordinance; Old Northwest Territory; St. Clair, Arthur; Western Reserve

References

Cayton, Andrew R. L. *The Frontier Republic: Ideology and Politics in the Ohio Country, 1780–1825.* Kent, OH: Kent State University Press, 1986.
Hurt, R. Douglas. *The Ohio Frontier: Crucible of the Old Northwest, 1720–1830.* Bloomington: Indiana University Press, 1996.
Kappler, Charles J., comp. and ed. *Indian Affairs: Laws and Treaties,* Vol. 2. Washington, DC: U.S. Government Printing Office, 1904.

Fort Jackson, Treaty of

Treaty between the United States and the Creek Nation that officially ended the 1813–1814 Creek (Red Stick) War. The treaty was negotiated and signed on August 9, 1814, at the newly constructed U.S. outpost of Fort Jackson along the Coosa and Tallapoosa rivers near Wetumpka, Alabama.

Following his great victory over the Red Stick Creeks in the Battle of Horseshoe Bend on March 27, 1814, Major General Andrew Jackson was determined to impose a punitive peace treaty. Jackson's goals were twofold: to end Native American attacks on whites in the lower South and to secure millions of acres of land in Alabama and Georgia for white settlement and farming.

Following several weeks of negotiations, the Treaty of Fort Jackson of August 9, 1814, to which Jackson was himself a signatory, resulted in the transfer to the United States without compensation of approximately 23 million acres of Creek lands, chiefly in central Alabama and southern Georgia. The treaty also granted the U.S. government the right to establish roads, trading posts, and military installations on remaining Creek lands. The treaty was a final blow to Native American power throughout the East except for Florida. Many Creeks who had backed the United States during the Creek War were embittered by their treatment, which for all practical purposes dealt with all the Creeks—hostile or friendly—in a similar manner. Some Creeks went to Florida, where they joined the Seminoles. Creek leader Osceola, for example, refused to abide by the terms of the treaty and relocated to southern Florida. Many Creeks followed him. Eventually a number of these expatriates fought against U.S. forces in the Seminole wars.

PAUL G. PIERPAOLI JR.

See also

Creek War; Horseshoe Bend, Battle of; Jackson, Andrew; Osceola; Red Sticks

References

Hartley, William, and Ellen Hartley. *Osceola: The Unconquered Indian.* New York: Hawthorne Books, 1973.

Kappler, Charles J., ed. *Indian Treaties, 1778–1883.* New York: Interland, 1972.

Owsley, Frank L., Jr. *Struggle for the Gulf Borderlands. The Creek War and the Battle of New Orleans, 1812–1815.* Gainesville: University Presses of Florida, 1981.

Fort Laramie

Important U.S. military post in the West. Located in present-day eastern Wyoming at the junction of the Laramie and North Platte rivers, Fort Laramie served as a supply depot for immigrants traveling along the Oregon, Mormon, and California trails during the 1840s and 1850s and as a staging area for military operations by

Interior of Fort Laramie, by Alfred Jacob Miller, an American painter known for his scenes of the Rocky Mountain region, circa 1837. (Francis G. Mayer/Corbis)

the U.S. Army against Red Cloud and his followers in the 1860s. The fort also served as a way station for the Pony Express during 1860–1861 and as the site of treaty negotiations between the U.S. government and Native American tribes of the Great Plains in 1851 and again in 1868.

Originally built with wooden palisades in 1834 under the guidance of William Sublette and Robert Campbell as a focal point for the burgeoning trade in buffalo robes along the Platte River during the 1830s, Fort William on the Laramie, the name of the original structure, was replaced by a more permanent adobe structure in 1841 called Fort John after John B. Sarpy, an officer in the American Fur Company that had purchased the trading post in 1835.

With the steady increase in overland migration to Oregon, Utah, and the Pacific after 1843, employees at Fort Laramie, as it was popularly known, found themselves dealing less with the fur trade and more with supplying immigrants with provisions, repairing equipment, and servicing livestock as well as providing ferrying services across the Laramie River. News of the discovery of gold in California in 1848 brought even more westward travelers, spurring the government to propose the construction of a chain of military posts adjacent to the trails to protect immigrants. Owing to its strategic location along the migration corridor, Fort Laramie proved ideal for such a mission.

On June 26, 1849, the U.S. Army purchased the adobe trading post from the American Fur Company for $4,000 and proceeded to construct quarters for officers and enlisted men, two stables, and a bakery, all surrounding a large parade ground. By August 12, 1849, Companies A, E, and G of the 6th U.S. Infantry Regiment and Company C of the Mounted Rifles (179 officers and men in all) comprised the fort's first garrison.

In 1851 Fort Laramie was the site of a treaty council between agents of the U.S. government and representatives of major Native American nations of the northern Plains. Signed on September 17, the treaty guaranteed the safety of immigrants along the Oregon Trail in exchange for annuity payments to the tribes whose traditional boundaries the trail crossed. Peace was short-lived, however, as the Grattan Massacre in 1854 ushered in 25 years of sporadic conflict during which the Fort Laramie garrison served as a key component in military expeditions against hostile Native Americans in the Powder River Country, particularly during operations against Red Cloud from 1866 to 1868.

In 1868 Fort Laramie once again served as the locus for treaty negotiations, this time ending hostilities with Red Cloud and creating the Great Sioux Reservation. The discovery of gold in the Black Hills in 1874 soon led to white encroachment onto the reservation, reigniting warfare on the Plains. Troops from Fort Laramie and others supplied from that post participated in the ensuing campaigns against the Sioux and Cheyennes in 1876, including the Battle of the Rosebud on June 17.

As fighting on the Plains subsided and railroads spread across the Plains, Fort Laramie's military mission waned. Troops from the post policed segments of the Cheyenne-Deadwood Stage Road and occasionally offered assistance to nearby civilian authorities in maintaining law and order. Government expenditures for construction and repairs on Fort Laramie ceased in 1886, even though its garrison remained for three more years. The post was finally abandoned in March 1890.

ALAN C. DOWNS

See also

Cheyennes; Fort Laramie, Treaty of (1851); Fort Laramie, Treaty of (1868); Grattan Massacre; Great Sioux War; Oregon Trail; Red Cloud; Red Cloud's War; Rosebud, Battle of the; Sioux

References

Hendron, Paul L. *Fort Laramie and the Great Sioux War.* Norman: University of Oklahoma Press, 1998.
Mattes, Merrill J. *Fort Laramie Park History, 1834–1977.* Washington, DC: U.S. Department of the Interior, 1980.

Fort Laramie, Treaty of (1851)

Treaty signed by Native American tribes of the northern Great Plains and the U.S. government on September 17, 1851. The goals of the treaty were twofold: to formalize relations between the tribes of the northern Plains and the U.S. government and to protect settlers and wagon trains from Native American attacks. Beginning in the 1840s settlers and prospectors migrated to the West in ever-increasing numbers, making their safety a considerable concern for U.S. and territorial officials. At the same time, white encroachment on traditional Native American lands provoked animosity among many Plains tribes.

The Treaty of Fort Laramie involved most Native American groups living south of the Missouri River, east of the Rocky Mountains, and north of the Arkansas River. Specifically, these included the Sioux (Lakota, Dakota, and Nakota), Arapaho, Cheyenne, Assiniboine, Crow, Arikara, and Mandan tribes. Signatories for the federal government included D. D. Mitchell, superintendent of Indian Affairs, and Indian agent Thomas Fitzpatrick.

The document was divided into eight sections. They included the following provisions: first, the tribes involved were to pursue peace among themselves; second, the tribes were to allow the U.S. government to build roads and military outposts within their respective territories; third, the Native Americans were to provide restitution for any damages or crimes involving U.S. citizens; fourth, the tribes involved were to acknowledge the boundaries of their territory and that of the United States and were to select chiefs or leaders with whom the federal government would conduct business exclusively. In return the United States pledged to protect Native Americans from U.S. citizens and pledged to provide certain financial annuities. Failure to abide by any of the treaty's covenants would result in the withholding of such payments.

Originally the annuities were to be in force for 50 years; however, the U.S. Senate, which ratified the agreement on May 24, 1852, reduced that to 10 years with an optional 5 years beyond that, to be determined by the president of the United States. The change caused some difficulty among the tribes, especially the Crows, who were the last to agree to the change.

Because of overly complicated legal terminology and the paucity of good translators and interpreters, many terms in the treaty were not adequately explained to the Native American leaders who helped negotiate it. Because the proceedings had been dominated by the Lakota Sioux, their land boundaries were perhaps the most generous of the tribes present. The Black Hills were thus given to the Lakotas even though much of the area had traditionally been Northern Cheyenne territory. Not surprisingly, this created much friction over who should control the area.

The U.S. government subsequently drew the boundaries of the various tribes' territories, meaning that Washington reserved the right to negotiate with individual nations. This brought about the cession of millions of acres of land to the United States, which was soon opened for white settlement. The 1851 Treaty of Fort Laramie helped settle Oregon and California with large numbers of whites soon thereafter. In the end the treaty was not successful because the intertribal peace pact was eventually shattered by provisions within the treaty itself and because the provisions led to increased tension and misunderstandings between whites and Native Americans.

PAUL G. PIERPAOLI JR.

See also

Arapahos; Arikaras; Cheyennes; Cheyennes, Northern; Crows; Fort Laramie, Treaty of (1868); Sioux

References

Berthrong, Donald. *The Southern Cheyennes*. Norman: University of Oklahoma Press, 1963.

Kappler, Charles J., ed. *Indian Treaties, 1778–1883*. New York: Interland, 1972.

Fort Laramie, Treaty of (1868)

The second of two important mid-19th-century treaties signed by Native American nations of the Great Plains and the U.S. government. The Treaty of Fort Laramie, signed on April 29, 1868, effectively ended Red Cloud's War (1866–1868).

The terms of the treaty guaranteed ownership of the Black Hills to the Lakota Sioux, the removal of military forts along the Bozeman Trail in the Powder River Country, and the establishment—on Lakota land—of the Great Sioux Reservation, a reserve of land covering 26 million acres that ran from the northern boundary of the state of Nebraska to the 46th Parallel, was bordered on the east by the Missouri River and ran westward to the 104th degree of longitude. Moreover, the treaty closed the Powder River Country and the Bozeman Trail to military and settler incursions. The treaty, however, also prophetically designated this same country as "unceded Indian Territory" and therefore left the Lakotas in only temporary ownership of the land outside the official reservation. Additionally, the treaty articles specified the intention of the U.S. government to pursue its stated long-term goals of forced assimilation with agriculture, education, and the division of land held in common.

The treaty document itself is lengthy and relies heavily on dense legal language that often contradicts its own provisions.

Red Cloud himself would later claim that the only provisions of the treaty that he was able to understand were the continued tenure of the Lakotas on their own land and the expulsion of the U.S. military from the Powder River Country.

The Fort Laramie Treaty of 1868 was signed by 25 chiefs and headmen of the Brulés, the Oglalas, the Miniconjous, the Hunkpapas, the Blackfeet, the Pabaskas (Cut Heads), the Itazipacolas (Sans Arcs), and the Oohenupas (Two Kettles), and Santee bands of the Lakota Nation; by the Yanktonais of the Nakota Nation; by the Mdewakantons and Wahpekutes of the Dakota (Santee) Nation; by members of the Inunaina (Arapaho) Nation; and by members of a U.S. treaty commission. The treaty document and a yearlong process of negotiating for signatures were the result of a successful war waged against the United States by the Lakotas, led by Red Cloud. Red Cloud's War (also known as the Bozeman War) was fought in the Wyoming and Montana territories for control over the important hunting grounds of the Powder River Country in north-central Wyoming. The Fort Laramie Treaty was ratified by the U.S. Congress on February 16, 1869.

For the Lakotas and their Native American allies as well as for white settlers and the U.S. government, the Fort Laramie Treaty was important to the history of the late 19th century. Discovery of gold in the sacred Black Hills by Lieutenant Colonel George A. Custer's governmentally sanctioned expedition resulted in the Black Hills Gold Rush, a violation of the treaty's terms that only increased the pressure on Lakota land already under attack by settlement, by the decimation of the great buffalo herds, by the demands of the Northern Pacific Railroad, and by unstable and changing governmental and military policy.

In September 1875 President Ulysses S. Grant sent a special commission to Lakota territory to negotiate for the sale of "unceded Indian Territory" of the 1868 Fort Laramie Treaty and the Black Hills themselves. The Lakotas refused to sell. In November 1875 the Bureau of Indian Affairs ordered all Lakotas who were in the "unceded" hunting lands to come onto the reservation and submit to agency control by January 31, 1876. The government launched a military campaign against the Lakotas who were unwilling or unable to comply with the order. The campaign, which began in the spring of 1876 and lasted into the spring of 1877, was often known as the Great Sioux War and included the Battle of the Little Bighorn (June 25–26, 1876). The Sioux and their allies fought to maintain the ownership of the land that they believed the Fort Laramie Treaty of 1868 had guaranteed them.

As it was in the 19th century, the Fort Laramie Treaty of 1868 remained an important document in the struggle over native rights and land claims in the 20th century. Two important events in the history of the Indian Movement during the 1960s and 1970s were predicated on the language and history surrounding the 1868 Fort Laramie Treaty: the occupation of Alcatraz in 1964 and again in 1969 and the occupation of Wounded Knee in 1973.

In the 21st century, the Fort Laramie Treaty of 1868 continues to be an important aspect of the long-standing Black Hills Land

Indian Peace Commission members meet with Sioux Nation leaders at Fort Laramie, Wyoming, in 1868. The resulting Fort Laramie Treaty ended Red Cloud's War. The treaty guaranteed the Lakota ownership of the Black Hills, but the U.S. government seized the land after gold was discovered there. (National Archives)

Claim wherein the Lakota Nation continues to press the U.S. government for the return of the Black Hills that were guaranteed to them by the 1868 treaty. The U.S. Supreme Court itself ruled in 1980 that the sacred land was indeed unlawfully seized by the government and ruled that the monies that were never paid to the Lakotas, along with interest accrued over time (more than $100 million), be given to them. The Lakotas refused the payment and continue to argue for the return of their land.

KATHLEEN KANE

See also

Black Hills, South Dakota; Black Hills Gold Rush; Great Sioux War; Red Cloud; Red Cloud's War; Sioux

References

Cook-Lynn, Elizabeth, et al., eds. *Black Hills Land Claim.* Special issue of *Wicazo Sa Review* 4(1) (Spring 1988): 1–59.

Deloria, Vine, Jr. *Behind the Trail of Broken Treaties: An Indian Declaration of Independence.* 3rd ed. Austin: University of Texas Press, 1990.

Gonzalez, Mario. "The Black Hills: The Sacred Land of the Lakota and Tsistisistas." *Cultural Survival Quarterly* 19 (1996): 63–69.

Prucha, Francis Paul. *American Indian Treaties: The History of a Political Anomaly.* Berkeley: University of California Press, 1994.

Fort Leavenworth

The oldest U.S. fort west of the Mississippi River. Loocated in the northeastern portion of present-day Kansas along the Missouri River, during the 1840s and 1850s Fort Leavenworth served as the beginning point for traders and immigrants heading to Santa Fe, Oregon, and California. During the Mexican-American War (1846–1848), the fort was an important training and staging area for U.S. troops. Indeed, the forces that secured California in 1846 originated at Fort Leavenworth.

Before 1821 Mexico was a closed economy, unable to trade with the United States. After Mexico gained its independence from Spain that year, U.S. traders quickly opened a trading route to Santa Fe known as the Santa Fe Trail. Each year more and more Americans and their herds of pack mules would cross the Arkansas River into Mexican territory and return with Mexican goods. The smaller groups, however, came under increasing attacks by Native Americans, angered by the trespassing on their lands.

To protect the trade on the Santa Fe Trail, Missouri senator Thomas Hart Benton proposed that an army post be constructed to offer protection to traders. After rejecting a site on the Arkansas River, Congress approved funds for a fort on the Missouri River. In April 1827 Colonel Henry Leavenworth and four companies from the 3rd Infantry Regiment left St. Louis and traveled up the Missouri. Leavenworth rejected the original site for one on higher ground on the west bank of the Missouri. Temporary accommodations for the 188 men were soon built, and the post was named Cantonment Leavenworth on September 19, 1827. Leavenworth himself soon returned to St. Louis, but his name remained. On February 8, 1832, the cantonment was renamed Fort Leavenworth.

Leavenworth provided an important base for trading and exploration expeditions heading west. Steamboats carrying supplies and passengers were able to sail up the Missouri to the fort. Overland trails originating at or near Fort Leavenworth included both the Santa Fe Trail and the Oregon Trail. Thousands of immigrants passed through the area between 1841 and 1858 heading for Oregon and California, and soldiers from the fort provided escorts for travelers and kept the local peace between Native Americans and increasing numbers of white settlers.

When the Mexican-American War (1846–1848) began, Fort Leavenworth was a natural staging area for forces heading west and south. The fort also provided sufficient training grounds for the thousands of volunteers who fought in the war. Congress authorized President James K. Polk to call 50,000 volunteers into federal service, and these men were divided into three armies, with one being organized at Fort Leavenworth. This force became the Army of the West, under the command of Colonel Stephen W. Kearny. Kearny had approximately 1,700 soldiers, consisting of 300 regulars from the 1st Dragoons Regiment and 860 Missouri Mounted Volunteers. After training and equipping his army at Fort Leavenworth, Kearny departed on June 26, 1846. He was accompanied by a train of more than 100 wagons, 500 pack mules, and a large herd of cattle. The Army of the West traveled down the Santa Fe Trail, capturing Santa Fe without a fight, and then proceeded to California, where Kearny quickly secured Los Angeles. Kearny's army returned to the fort on August 22, 1847. The fort also served as a staging area for Santa Fe–bound expeditions led by colonels Alexander W. Doniphan and Sterling Price.

Following the war, Fort Leavenworth remained an important outpost and a gateway to the West. When war with the Mormons threatened in 1857, an army under Albert Sidney Johnston massed at the fort before leaving for Utah. Later, federal troops at Fort Leavenworth secured Kansas for the Union at the start of the American Civil War (1861–1865). The post served as headquarters for the busy Department of the Missouri, which had oversight of a number of important Indian campaigns. In 1874 the military prison opened at the fort. Beginning in the 1880s, Fort Leavenworth housed a series of professional schools for army officers. Today, Fort Leavenworth is the site of the U.S. Army's Command and General Staff College.

Tim J. Watts

See also

Forts, Camps, Cantonments, and Outposts; Kearny, Stephen Watts

References

Hughes, J. Patrick. *Fort Leavenworth: Gateway to the West.* Topeka: Kansas State Historical Society, 2000.

Partin, John W., ed. *A Brief History of Fort Leavenworth, 1827–1983.* Fort Leavenworth, KS: Combat Studies Institute, U.S. Army Command and General Staff College, 1983.

Walton, George H. *Sentinel of the Plains: Fort Leavenworth and the American West.* Englewood Cliffs, NJ: Prentice Hall, 1973.

Fort Mims, Battle of
Event Date: August 30, 1813

Key engagement of the Creek War (1813–1814) between American militia, settlers, and Creek refugees and Red Stick Creeks that occurred on August 30, 1813. Fort Mims was located approximately 50 miles north of Mobile, Alabama. The Creek War was being waged in the southeastern United States simultaneously with the War of 1812, and the horrific details of the demise of the defenders of Fort Mims increased the pressure for U.S. military action against the Creeks in conjunction with operations against the British.

In the Southeast, increasing American encroachment on Creek lands had been accompanied by a significant effort to assimilate the Creeks into American society and resulted in a large proportion of mixed-blood residents in parts of Georgia and Alabama. Inspired by Tecumseh's denunciation of the "civilizing" influences and policies of the U.S. government, Upper Creek nativists (referred to as the Red Sticks for their red-colored war clubs) destroyed a number of assimilated Lower Creek (White Stick) villages during 1812 and 1813. These Red Stick attacks spread panic throughout the region and forced many refugees to seek shelter in nearby U.S. blockhouses and fortified homesteads. The U.S. government attempted to maintain a credible defensive posture during the Creek War (1813–1814). However, on July 27, 1813, near Burnt Corn Creek, Alabama, an American militia unit ambushed a Red Stick force returning from Pensacola, Florida, after its members had purchased Spanish ammunition there. Upon learning that the American militia responsible for the attack at Burnt Corn Creek had come from Fort Mims (one of the region's fortified homesteads near Tensaw Lake), Red Stick leaders Peter McQueen, William Weatherford (Chief Red Eagle), and Paddy Welsh targeted the fort for retaliation.

The small and poorly defended Fort Mims proved no match for the Red Stick assault on August 30, 1813. Nearly 500 refugees had crammed into almost 17 buildings within the 1.25-acre enclosure of Samuel Mims's farm. The fort's commander, Major Daniel Beasley, had no prior military experience and failed to bolster his defenses as ordered by Brigadier General Ferdinand Claiborne, militia commander of the Mississippi Territory. Furthermore, Claiborne had reassigned half of Beasley's garrison to other nearby forts, leaving the settlement weakly defended. Meanwhile, between 800 and 1,000 Red Stick warriors gathered undetected in the woods approximately 400 yards from the fort. Beasley repeatedly ignored intelligence warnings of an impending attack. As the drummer sounded the call to the noon meal, the Red Sticks rushed toward

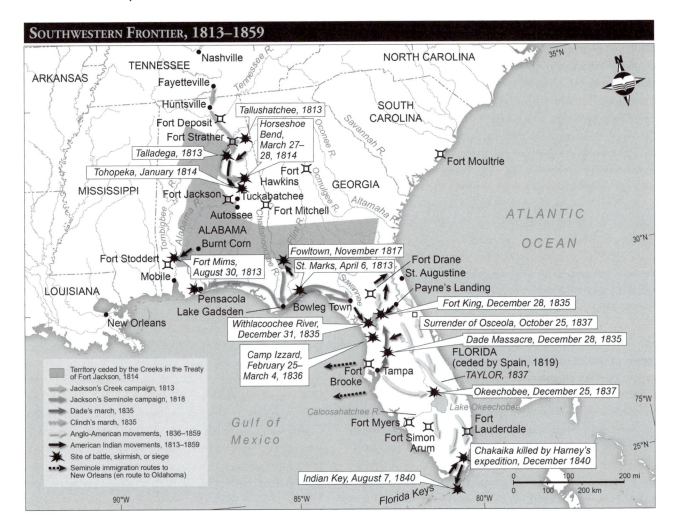

SOUTHWESTERN FRONTIER, 1813–1859

the fort, surprising and overwhelming the inattentive guards before the gate could be closed. Then the Red Sticks' initial momentum stalled. The fort's defenders fled to secondary defensive positions within a corner of the palisade and held out for more than four hours, pouring fire into the attackers before being burned out of their buildings. All but a few were killed trying to escape the flames.

The final toll shocked both sides. Reports indicate that the Red Sticks incurred almost 400 casualties, or 50 percent of their force. The Fort Mims defenders and residents also suffered immensely according to the approximately 15 survivors and witnesses to the battle's aftermath. Red Sticks reportedly killed, scalped, and mutilated between 250 and 500 whites, including women and children. More than 100 slaves were taken by the Creeks and used as human shields at the subsequent Battle of Horseshoe Bend (March 27, 1814). Americans, especially along the southern frontier, were incensed about the Fort Mims attack and clamored for revenge.

The U.S. government called upon the state militias to avenge Fort Mims and subdue the Red Sticks. Tennessee's militia, led by Major General Andrew Jackson, soon shattered Creek resistance, culminating in the 1814 Treaty of Fort Jackson that added nearly 23 million acres to Alabama and Georgia from what had once been

Creek lands. With the Red Stick threat eliminated, the Americans could now focus on the British campaign for New Orleans.

DEREK W. FRISBY

See also

Burnt Corn Creek, Battle of; Creeks; Creek War; Fort Jackson, Treaty of; Jackson, Andrew; McQueen, Peter; Red Sticks; Tecumseh

References

Davis, Karl. "'Remember Fort Mims': Reinterpreting the Origins of the Creek War." *Journal of the Early Republic* 22 (2002): 612–636.
Waselkov, Gregory, A. *A Conquering Spirit: Fort Mims and the Redstick War of 1813–1814.* Tuscaloosa: University of Alabama Press, 2006.

Fort Phil Kearny

Located in Wyoming Territory east of the Bighorn Mountains and on a plateau between Big and Little Piney creeks, Fort Phil Kearny was one of three military outposts along the Bozeman Trail linking Fort Laramie with Virginia City and the newly discovered gold mines in Montana. Built in 1866 by the 18th U.S. Infantry Regiment under the command of Colonel Henry B. Carrington, the

17-acre log stockade fort was the largest of the three posts in the region. Along with those at Fort C. F. Smith to the north and Fort Reno to the south, the garrison at Fort Phil Kearny, which at its peak strength numbered about 550 soldiers and civilians, was charged with protecting travelers along the trail and maintaining peace in the Powder River Country.

Owing to mounting tensions among the Lakotas, Northern Cheyennes, and Arapahos who saw the Bozeman Trail as an intrusion into their traditional hunting grounds, the garrison at Fort Phil Kearny saw almost continual conflict throughout its brief two-year existence. Initially targeting livestock, isolated traders, woodcutting parties, and foragers, Lakota warriors led by Red Cloud and Crazy Horse changed their tactics and attempted to lure military parties away from the protection of the fort and into well-designed ambushes. The most devastating of these engagements occurred on December 21, 1866, when Captain William J. Fetterman and a detachment of 80 men were killed after being lured into the nearby Lodge Trail Ridge and out of visual contact with the fort. Carrington was relieved of command five days later and was replaced by Lieutenant Colonel Henry Wessells.

One positive outcome of the Fetterman Massacre was the recognition by the U.S. Army of the need to replace the muzzle-loading rifles issued to its frontier regulars through 1866 with a new rapid-fire weapon, the Springfield Breech-Loading Rifle Musket, Model 1866. Arriving at Fort Phil Kearny in the early summer of 1867, the new Trapdoor Springfields, as they were commonly called, proved decisive in the next major engagement involving the post's garrison. On August 2, 1867, Captain James Powell and 31 soldiers armed with this new weapon held off several hundred Lakota and Northern Cheyenne warriors as they attempted to attack a woodcutting party near the fort. The so-called Wagon Box Fight lasted five hours until a relief force from the post arrived and drove the warriors away.

The almost constant state of hostilities in the vicinity of the Bozeman Trail in 1867 combined with the completion of the Union Pacific Railroad to the point where travelers no longer needed to use the trail to reach Montana resulted in the rapid decline of civilian traffic along that route. Its usefulness was limited to military supply trains bound for the three forts. Mounting expenses for maintenance of outposts that no longer served their purpose prompted the government to agree to close the Bozeman Trail and abandon the forts in the 1868 Treaty of Fort Laramie. The army withdrew from Fort Phil Kearny in August 1868, and the vacated buildings were soon burned to the ground by Cheyenne warriors.

ALAN C. DOWNS

See also

Arapahos; Bozeman Trail; Carrington, Henry Beebe; Cheyennes; Cheyennes, Northern; Crazy Horse; Fetterman, William Judd; Fetterman Massacre; Lakota Sioux; Red Cloud; Sioux; Wagon Box Fight

References

Larson, Robert W. *Red Cloud: Warrior-Statesman of the Lakota Sioux.* Norman: University of Oklahoma Press, 1997.

Utley, Robert M. *Frontier Regulars: The United States and the American Indian, 1866–1891.* New York: Macmillan, 1973.

Fort Riley

U.S. military post situated at the confluence of the Smoky Hill and Republican rivers in north-central Kansas that was important in both the Indian Wars and the American Civil War (1861–1865). Construction of Fort Riley began in the spring of 1853. The fort was named in honor of brevet Brigadier General Bennett C. Riley, a career U.S. Army officer who led the first military expedition down the Santa Fe Trail in 1829 and who distinguished himself during the Mexican-American War (1846–1848). Fort Riley was one of a series of posts—including Leavenworth (1827), Scott (1843), and Atkinson (1850)—established by the U.S. government to protect travelers, commerce, and settlers during the years of westward expansion. The fort followed the layout of most western posts, and its buildings and fortification were constructed chiefly of limestone.

Fort Riley's initial mission of protecting the frontier settlements from Indian attacks was revised somewhat after the Kansas-Nebraska Bill became law on May 30, 1854. With the opening of two new territories for settlement, the garrison at Fort Riley was ordered to maintain peace and order between proslavery and antislavery settlers during the period of conflict known as Bleeding Kansas. On September 14, 1856, Colonel Philip St. George Cooke and the 2nd Dragoons defused a potentially deadly situation at nearby Lawrence, Kansas, when his troops turned away a threatening Missouri militia of 3,000 men led by U.S. senator David Atchison. Just days earlier, Cooke had led 600 men to the territorial capital of Lecompton to prevent a free-state uprising encouraged by the abolitionist John Brown.

The primary mission of troops stationed at Fort Riley, however, was providing for territorial frontier defense. During the 1850s, post commanders attempted to convince the Sioux, Cheyennes, Kiowas, and other area Native American tribes to allow whites to travel along the Smoky Hill and Platte River trails. Soldiers from Fort Riley regularly escorted mail trains and patrolled trade and travel routes. In May 1857 Fort Riley troops joined Colonel Edwin V. Sumner's campaign against the Cheyennes on the North Fork of the Solomon River. The Cheyennes had been raiding various settlements. Encountering 300 Cheyenne warriors, his men killed 9 and destroyed the winter supply of dried buffalo meat and other goods as the Native Americans fled their abandoned camp.

During the Civil War, Fort Riley was populated with volunteer regiments and remained a staging point to protect westward trails and settlements. The volunteer soldiers held a harsher view toward Plains Indians than did the regulars who preceded them in the Kansas Territory, however. This was evident in March 1863 when a detachment fought a band of Pawnees and soon killed 10 of them.

In 1866 the need to protect crews building the Union Pacific Railroad increased Fort Riley's importance. On September 26, 1866, Lieutenant Colonel George A. Custer's 7th Cavalry was garrisoned at the post.

On March 27, 1867, Major General Winfield Scott Hancock led some 1,400 troops on an expedition down the Santa Fe Trail to harass and capture the Native Americans. Custer's regiment from

Fort Riley, Kansas. Photograph by Alexander Gardner, 1867. (Library of Congress)

Fort Riley was charged with pursuing the Cheyennes. Failing to capture many of the Cheyennes, Custer took leave of his troops and returned to Fort Riley with his men still in the field. He was subsequently court-martialed at Fort Leavenworth and suspended from rank and command for one year, along with forfeiture of pay. The 7th Cavalry would not return to Fort Riley for nearly two decades.

The last clash between soldiers from the post and Native Americans occurred at Wounded Knee, South Dakota, in December 1890 while U.S. troops disarmed and escorted a band of Dakota Sioux back to the Pine Ridge Agency. The engagement at Wounded Knee resulted in at least 150 Native Americans killed.

In 1892 the School of Cavalry and Light Artillery began operations at the post, succeeded by the Mounted Service School in 1907 and the establishment of the permanent Cavalry School after World War I (1914–1918). Presently Fort Riley is home to the 1st Infantry Division.

CHARLES FRANCIS HOWLETT

See also

Cavalry Regiment, 7th U.S.; Cheyennes; Cooke, Philip St. George; Custer, George Armstrong; Dakota Sioux; Kiowas; Pawnees; Santa Fe Trail; Sherman, William Tecumseh; Sioux; Wounded Knee, Battle of

References

Castel, Albert. *A Frontier State at War: Kansas, 1861–1865*. Lawrence: Kansas Heritage Press, 1992.
Goodrich, Thomas. *War to the Knife: Bleeding Kansas, 1854–1861*. Mechanicsburg, PA: Stackpole, 1998.
McKale, William, and William D. Young. *Fort Riley: Citadel of the Frontier West*. Topeka: Kansas State Historical Society, 2000.

Fort Robinson

Major army post that figured prominently in the final stages of the Indian Wars on the northern Plains. In 1874 unrest at the Red Cloud Agency, including the killing of Lieutenant Levi Robinson, prompted the army to establish a military camp near the reservation. Camp Robinson, located near present-day Crawford in northwestern Nebraska and named in honor of the slain officer, quickly became one of the most important posts on the northern Plains, thanks to its proximity to the Black Hills and the Great Sioux Reservation in the Dakota Territory.

An 1874 expedition into the Black Hills confirmed the presence of gold on this sacred Sioux land, and soon a flood of prospectors streamed into the hills, inflaming an already volatile situation. Troops from Camp Robinson and other posts tried to hold back the white encroachment with little success.

In 1876 following the devastating defeat of Lieutenant Colonel George A. Custer in the Battle of the Little Bighorn (June 25–26, 1876), Colonel Ranald S. Mackenzie and his crack 4th Cavalry Regiment took station at Camp Robinson. After disarming the Indians at the Red Cloud Agency, Mackenzie's command took the field and in November destroyed Chief Dull Knife's Cheyenne village, inducing the eventual surrender of Dull Knife and most of his followers. In May 1877 the great Oglala chief Crazy Horse surrendered at Camp Robinson. But Crazy Horse's erratic and threatening behavior while at the Red Cloud Agency unnerved reservation Indians and agents alike. In September, Department of the Platte commander Brigadier General George Crook ordered Crazy Horse's arrest. Crazy Horse refused to submit, and in a melee with soldiers and Indian police he was mortally wounded.

In 1878 Camp Robinson was redesignated Fort Robinson. The Red Cloud Agency was closed, and the inhabitants were relocated to the new Pine Ridge Reservation not far to the north in Dakota Territory. But Camp Robinson retained oversight responsibility for the new reservation. Also in 1878, Northern Cheyennes under Dull Knife and Little Wolf who had been removed to Indian

Territory following their surrender slipped from the Cheyenne and Arapaho Agency in a desperate bid to return to their homeland.

After a harrowing journey during which they had eluded army troops and hostile civilians, Dull Knife and Little Wolf split. Dull Knife and his followers surrendered near Fort Robinson, where they were confined. Harsh measures imposed to induce the Cheyennes to return willingly to Indian Territory led to tragedy in January 1879 when the desperate and hungry Cheyennes bolted from their confinement into the freezing night. Many were cut down at the fort, and dozens of others, including women and children, were gunned down by their pursuers. Thanks to the sympathy that the tragedy invited, Dull Knife and the other survivors were then allowed to reside at Pine Ridge. In 1890 buffalo soldiers from the 9th Cavalry, stationed at Fort Robinson, arrived to help subdue the Ghost Dance movement on the Pine Ridge Reservation but were not engaged in the sad events at Wounded Knee.

After the Indian Wars, the expanded fort enjoyed a productive role in the army. The fort became a giant quartermaster and remount depot during World War I (1914–1918) and served as a German prisoner of war camp during World War II (1939–1945). The army finally abandoned Fort Robinson in 1948.

DAVID COFFEY

See also

Cavalry Regiment, 4th U.S.; Crazy Horse; Crook, George; Dull Knife; Forts, Camps, Cantonments, and Outposts; Great Sioux War; Mackenzie, Ranald Slidell; Red Cloud

References

Prucha, Francis Paul. *A Guide to the Military Posts of the United States, 1789–1895.* Madison: State Historical Society of Wisconsin, 1964.

Utley, Robert M. *Frontier Regulars: The United States and the American Indian, 1866–1891.* New York: Macmillan, 1973.

Forts, Camps, Cantonments, and Outposts

Forts, camps, cantonments, barracks, and outposts served a variety of purposes and became prominent features of the American Indian Wars. The term "fort" implies a large walled defensive structure, but rarely, especially during the 19th century, did forts meet these specifications. Indeed, few forts matched the images of formidable stockades depicted in the movies and on television. Most posts more resembled small villages. The strategic function of forts during the Indian Wars was to project power and influence into a given region; to provide protection for settlers, railroad crews, and miners; to watch over reservations; and to protect peaceful Indians.

On a tactical level, forts contained garrisons of widely varying size and provided bases from which to patrol or campaign. The practical function of most forts, then, was to house troops, but some forts served as marshaling points, logistical centers, supply depots, and administrative headquarters. Some forts functioned in each of these capacities and toward the end of the 19th century operated professional schools for officers. As the United States

expanded and developed and the fight against Native Americans fell increasingly to the government, defense (i.e., the protection against attack) in fact proved an increasingly unimportant function of frontier installations. Native American attacks against military posts grew more and more uncommon, allowing the army to largely abandon defensive works on the frontier.

The different descriptive terms applied to military posts were based to a great extent on the projected function and life expectancy of a given establishment. The term "fort" implied permanence, whereas the terms "camp" and "cantonment" indicated a temporary status. Camps or cantonments might be erected where a long-term military presence was not expected, to meet a particular contingency (Camp Cooper, Texas), or as precursors for more permanent installations (Cantonment Burgwin, New Mexico). In truth, though, the term "fort" was routinely applied to permanent and semipermanent installations as well as to temporary establishments and even outposts, a term rarely found in official use. Also, there were a number of temporary posts established during the War of 1812, the Seminole Wars (1817–1818, 1835–1842, and 1855–1858), and the Mexican-American War (1846–1848) that were termed forts but were obviously not intended to be permanent establishments.

A post's construction often spoke to its true definition, regardless of its designation. The severe fiscal restraints that dictated the U.S. government's approach to military matters mandated that forts and camps be built of locally available materials and by the soldiers themselves although there were exceptions, such as posts erected in the South prior to the American Civil War (1861–1865) where slave labor could be accessed. Some forts therefore boasted impressive stone structures with officers' quarters that rivaled fine civilian homes. Others were little more than a sad array of wood and mud huts. In almost every case the layout was similar, with barracks, officers' quarters, offices, and hospitals arranged along each side of a rectangular parade ground that featured a large flagpole in the center. Warehouses, corrals, and other structures rose behind the primary housing and administrative buildings. Larger posts covered several hundred acres, and the general layout allowed for ready expansion, which frequently occurred. By the mid-19th century, the U.S. Army had developed a more or less set approach to the establishment of military posts, but local conditions and the projected function of a fort largely determined its physical characteristics and size.

During the colonial period, the rival imperial powers more concerned about European competition established numerous forts, many of them quite formidable, in strategically important areas such as the Great Lakes region, the Ohio Valley, and along coastlines. Frontier defense against Native Americans fell to the settlers, who erected forts that were usually small wooden stockades and blockhouses into which the settlers could move during threats. Traders, who coveted Indian markets, also built forts to project their business interests into Indian lands. But official military posts related to Native American warfare, offensive or defensive in nature, were almost nonexistent until after the American

Revolutionary War (1775–1783), when the new U.S. government slowly assumed responsibility for frontier defense.

Philosophical debates over the role of the military in the new republic delayed the establishment of a standing army and assertion of authority into volatile regions until the mid-1780s, when the tiny new army began to reoccupy old forts in the Ohio Valley and establish small new posts to protect settlers moving into the region. (The British continued to garrison some forts in the Great Lakes region until the mid-1790s.) As white settlement into the Ohio Country exploded, the Native Americans resisted, beginning more than a century of constant warfare between the federal government and the Native Americans. Fort Washington, an impressive stockade and blockhouse complex constructed in 1789 near present-day Cincinnati, Ohio, became the staging base for the successful campaigns of the 1790s that drove the Native Americans from the Ohio Country. By the end of the decade the army had established new posts in the Old Southwest and in the Mississippi Valley as well.

The Louisiana Purchase of 1803 brought vast new lands under U.S. dominion; the army occupied former Spanish forts and established new ones in the Trans-Mississippi, near St. Louis and present-day Chicago, and soon up the Mississippi and Missouri rivers. During the War of 1812, American troops manning forts in the Old Northwest suffered devastating losses to the British and their Native American allies, including the surrender of Fort Detroit, but the conclusion of that war came with a new commitment to frontier defense and a much more comprehensive projection of power in the Old Northwest and along the Mississippi and its tributaries, which eventually produced the great bastion at the confluence of the Mississippi and Minnesota rivers, Fort Snelling, among numerous other posts. To the south, where settlers as well as eastern tribes were moving across the Mississippi in large numbers, the army built Fort Smith on the Arkansas River and Fort Towson just above the Red River, the boundary between the United States and Texas, then the northern province of a newly independent Mexico. To anchor the middle of an emerging western line of forts, the army established Jefferson Barracks in 1826 near St. Louis. Although well behind the frontier line when originally activated, Jefferson Barracks grew in size and stature over the next 25 years, serving as a major operational and organizational center especially for mounted units destined for western service. Fort Leavenworth, established in 1827 in present-day Kansas, became another multipurpose installation of considerable importance.

Indian relocation, the Black Hawk War (1832), and the Second Seminole War (1835–1842) dominated the 1830s and led to the construction of a number of temporary posts. In Florida, the army made use of extant coastal fortifications but still found it necessary to construct dozens of forts. By the end of the decade, with most Native Americans now residing west of the Mississippi, the government focused on maintaining order, which meant managing a long frontier, protecting peaceful tribes, and keeping a close watch on white migration westward. This led to the

Fort Snelling, Minnesota, at the confluence of the Mississippi and Minnesota rivers, seven miles north of St. Paul; *Frank Leslie's Illustrated Newspaper*, September 20, 1862. (Library of Congress)

development of a military road, completed in 1845, that stretched from Fort Snelling in the North to Fort Towson in the South, but the Mexican-American War (1846–1848) and unchecked westward expansion soon rendered the road militarily obsolete. In December 1845 Texas entered the Union, bringing not only a crisis with Mexico but a whole new challenge in the form of the Comanches and Kiowas and other mobile warrior tribes. The settlement of Oregon's status, which gave the United States full control of the Pacific Northwest to the 49th Parallel, opened the way for mass migrations across the Great Plains that aroused the Sioux, Cheyennes, and Arapahos. Finally, the conclusion of the Mexican-American War and the Mexican Cession added another 1 million square miles of land to the United States. All of these developments demanded military attention, meaning more forts and more men. Yet the aggregate strength of the regular army at the close of 1848 was less than 11,000, and most of the freshly acquired land had never seen a fort.

To confront the new realities, officers and officials debated the best approach. Many favored saturation, that is, the establishment of forts and camps throughout the West, particularly in likely trouble spots, with troops dispersed among the posts. This approach meant that many forts would be manned by only a company or two, while camps and outposts could expect even smaller troop complements. Others, including Brigadier General Stephen Watts Kearny, advocated the concentration of military assets into a few large forts from which the army could respond as the need arose. Both approaches had merit, but the saturation model initially won out, although the debate continued until the 1880s when, with the Indian Wars waning, the army finally adopted concentration. Saturation proved daunting for an army that never mustered more than 17,000 men in the pre–Civil War years and now had responsibilities in California, the mountainous West, the desert Southwest, and Texas.

Texas alone required a line of forts along the Rio Grande, another along its western frontier, and still another to protect the vital road that ran from San Antonio to California. The great trails—the Santa Fe, the Oregon, and the Bozeman—demanded protection as well, as did the mining centers in Montana and Arizona. The pre–Civil War era produced a number of important new forts including Fort Laramie, a converted trading post on the Oregon Trail; Fort Bliss and Fort Clark along the Mexican border; and Fort Union, an important command center in New Mexico. The saturation approach bore fruit, but the coming of the Civil War in 1861 disrupted the progress except in Minnesota and the Dakota Country, where the Sioux Uprising demanded new posts, most of which proved short-lived, and in the Southwest, where major campaigning resulted in the creation of a dozen new forts.

The post–Civil War years saw the most aggressive employment of forts, a mix of new permanent facilities and temporary posts, as the army pursued its saturation policy with ever-advancing lines of forts in a relentless push to finally subjugate the Native Americans. The authorized size of the regular army grew as well, averaging more than 25,000 soldiers during the 1870s and 1880s, with the vast majority assigned to the frontier. Thus, more posts were required simply to house troops. But the War Department and Congress placed restrictions on the construction of permanent forts and on funds for the construction of any new post, which contributed to the number of small one- or two-company forts and camps that sprang up.

In addition to placing garrisons near known or potential trouble spots, the army established posts such as Fort Sill (Indian Territory), Fort Apache (Arizona), and Fort Robinson (Nebraska) near volatile reservations. The army continued to rely on and develop large administrative and logistical complexes such as Fort Sam Houston, established at San Antonio in the 1870s, that were far removed from the action. Forts played a decisive role in the major campaigns of the 1870s and 1880s, serving as staging areas, supply depots, and rallying points. By 1880 the army operated more than 100 posts in the western United States.

Also by 1880, with the Plains tribes largely subjugated and with railroads crisscrossing the West, Commanding General William T. Sherman and the War Department embraced concentration, cutting the number of active posts over the next decade from 111 to 62. By 1890 many storied forts had outlived their usefulness. Others, however, continued in service, receiving upgrades and new missions. Many posts built in the last third of the 19th century remained vital well into the 20th century. A few of the great frontier posts—Fort Huachuca, Fort Bliss, Fort Riley, Fort Sill, and Fort Leavenworth—remain in service today.

DAVID COFFEY

See also

Black Hawk War; Great Sioux War; Kearny, Stephen Watts; Little Turtle's War; Military Divisions, Departments, and Districts; Old Northwest Territory; Red River War; Seminole War, Second; Sherman, William Tecumseh

References

Prucha, Francis Paul. *A Guide to the Military Posts of the United States, 1789–1895*. Madison: State Historical Society of Wisconsin, 1964.

Prucha, Francis Paul. *The Sword of the Republic: The United States Army on the Frontier, 1783–1846*. New York: Macmillan, 1969.

United States Army. *American Military History*. Washington, DC: United States Army Center of Military History, 1989.

Utley, Robert M. *Frontier Regulars: The United States and the American Indian, 1866–1891*. New York: Macmillan, 1973.

Utley, Robert M. *Frontiersmen in Blue: The United States and the Indian, 1848–1865*. Lincoln: University of Nebraska Press, 1967.

Fort Sill

Military installation located on Medicine Bluff Creek near the eastern base of the Wichita Mountains near present-day Lawton in southwestern Oklahoma. Fort Sill was established on January 7, 1869, during the U.S. Army's 1868–1869 winter campaign,

Photograph of Fort Sill, Indian Territory (Oklahoma), 1889. (Library of Congress)

which is remembered primarily for Lieutenant Colonel George Armstrong Custer's destruction of Cheyenne chief Black Kettle's peaceful village along the Washita River. Colonel Benjamin Grierson and his African American 10th Cavalry troops had camped at the site the prior summer and called it Camp Washita. When Major General Philip Sheridan arrived at Camp Washita in January 1869, he recognized the value of the location and ordered Grierson to erect more permanent structures. Sheridan himself staked out the ground plan. The post was to replace Fort Cobb as the Comanche and Kiowa agency headquarters and serve as the chief base of operations against hostile tribes in the region. On July 2, 1869, Sheridan named the site Fort Sill in memory of his West Point classmate Brigadier General Joshua W. Sill, who had been killed during the American Civil War (1861–1865).

Fort Sill's construction is a testament to the skills and ingenuity of the 10th Cavalry's buffalo soldiers, who hewed logs and quarried stone from nearby sites to build the fort's early structures, many of which still stand, at virtually no cost to the government. One of the most unique structures was a stone corral located approximately one quarter of a mile from the main buildings. Its 8-foot-high stone walls enclosed an area of 20,000 square feet. Rifle loopholes in the walls provided effective defensive fire in the event of an attack, and a deep well provided a reliable and protected water source. Other features of the post included a pentagonal redoubt on the southwest corner of the plateau and two 40-foot-diameter redoubts on the southeast and northeast

corners of the parade grade. A stone blockhouse was erected on Signal Mountain six miles west of the post and served as the chief observation post, using flags, signal lamps, and heliographs to keep the garrison informed about Native American movements.

Fort Sill played a leading role in the campaigns that brought a close to the Indian Wars on the southern Plains. In the spring of 1871 U.S. Army commander General William Tecumseh Sherman arrived at Fort Sill a few days after Kiowas had attacked a wagon train during the Salt Creek Prairie (Warren Wagon Train) Massacre. When he found Satanta, Big Tree, and Satank at the fort to receive their annuities, Sherman ordered that they be arrested and conveyed to Texas for trial. Although a Texas jury convicted and sentenced Satanta to death, the federal government subsequently pressured Texas authorities to parole him in an effort to secure peace with the tribe. Brought back to Fort Sill in September 1873, Satanta pledged to remain at peace. Meanwhile, Comanches under Chief Quanah Parker increased their raids against isolated white settlements and buffalo hunters in Texas. Fort Sill served as one of the principal staging points for the last campaign on the southern Plains, the Red River War (1874–1875). Defeated and on the verge of starvation, the Comanches surrendered, with Quanah Parker bringing in the last band of free Comanches to Fort Sill on June 2, 1875.

Although some consideration was given to closing Fort Sill after the end of the Indian Wars, in the early 20th century it gained a new lease on life as a field artillery training center. Since 1919 Fort Sill has been the home of the U.S. Army's Field Artillery School. In addition, Fort Sill now serves as the home of the U.S. Air Defense Artillery School and numerous other military agencies and units.

JUSTIN D. MURPHY

See also

Black Kettle; Cheyennes; Comanches; Custer, George Armstrong; Grierson, Benjamin Henry; Kiowas; Quanah Parker; Satanta; Sheridan, Philip Henry; Sherman, William Tecumseh; Washita, Battle of the

References

Griswold, Gillett. "Old Fort Sill: The First Seven Years." *Chronicles of Oklahoma* 36(1) (1958): 2–14.
Utley, Robert M. *Frontier Regulars: The United States and the American Indian, 1866–1891.* New York: Macmillan, 1973.

Fort Simcoe

U.S. Army post built in 1859 in what is now south-central Washington state. Fort Simcoe was located in the foothills of the Cascade Mountains along the banks of Toppenish Creek about seven miles west of present-day White Swan, Washington. The principal purpose of the fort was to control the region's Native American tribes and to prevent discord between them and newly arriving white settlers. The area had long been used by Native Americans as a trade and meeting center and was also located near several well-traveled trails.

The installation was designed by the architect Louis Scholl, who also designed Fort Dalles (Oregon). One of Scholl's trademarks was to employ architectural styles prevalent in the East, which explains the neo-Gothic commander's residence, constructed of white clapboards. Major Robert Selden Garnett, who later went on to become a general in the American Civil War (1861–1865), was the fort's first and only commander.

At each corner of the post stood a blockhouse, which was designed to be a stand-alone fortification. Within the installation stood barracks made of logs, three officers' quarters, and numerous outbuildings. Fort Simcoe also had a large parade ground within the confines delineated by the four corner blockhouses. The fort was not surrounded by a contiguous wall or ramparts.

In 1859 after the fort's garrison had been transferred to Fort Colville, the site was used as the headquarters of the Yakima Indian Agency, and several of the buildings were used as schools for Yakima children. The fort was finally abandoned in 1923. In the 1950s the State of Washington leased the site of Fort Simcoe from the Yakima Nation, and it became a state park in 1956. A number of the original buildings remain, including the neo-Gothic commander's residence.

PAUL G. PIERPAOLI JR.

See also

Forts, Camps, Cantonments, and Outposts

References

Frazer, Robert W. *Forts of the West.* Norman: University of Oklahoma, 1965.

Heister, Dean G. *Bugles in the Valley: Garnett's Fort Simcoe.* 1977; reprint, Portland: Oregon Historical Society Press, 2000.

Fort Stanwix, Treaty of

Treaty signed at Fort Stanwix, near Rome, New York, on October 22, 1784, that brought an end to warfare between the United States and the Iroquois Confederacy following the American Revolutionary War (1775–1783), during which most of the Iroquois had served as allies of the British. Included among the signatories were representatives of the Mohawks, Oneidas, Onondagas, Cayugas, Senecas, and Tuscaroras. Signing on behalf of the United States were Oliver Wolcott, Richard Butler, and Arthur Zee, commissioners plenipotentiary for the United States.

The United States offered peace to the Iroquois and pledged to provide protection for them upon several conditions. First, six hostages were to be immediately delivered to the commissioners and would remain in possession of the United States until all prisoners, white and black, taken by the Iroquois during the war were freed. Second, the Oneida and Tuscarora lands upon which Americans were then settled were to remain in their possession. Third, the western boundary of Iroquois lands was to be fixed, and all land claims west of that boundary were to be abandoned by the Six Nations. Fourth, the United States was to provide the Iroquois with certain goods, to be determined at a later date, in recompense and to show good faith.

Although the treaty ended hostilities between the United States and the Iroquois, it failed to distinguish between those tribes who had supported the Americans, such as the Oneidas, who forfeited most of their territory, and those Iroquois who had aided the British. Many of the latter did not participate in the negotiations, choosing instead to relocate to Canada.

BARRY M. PRITZKER

See also

Iroquois; Iroquois Confederacy; Native Americans and the American Revolutionary War

References

Richter, Daniel K. *The Ordeal of the Longhouse: The People of the Iroquois League in the Era of European Colonization.* Chapel Hill: University of North Carolina Press, 1992.
Snow, Dean R. *The Iroquois.* Malden, MA: Blackwell, 1994.

Fort Strother

U.S. fort built under the supervision of Tennessee Militia major general Andrew Jackson, located near Ten Islands on the Coosa River in St. Clair County, Alabama, about 50 miles south of Fort Deposit. Completed in October 1813, Fort Strother served as Jackson's base of operations during his campaign against the Creeks during the War of 1812. A square enclosure measuring 100 yards

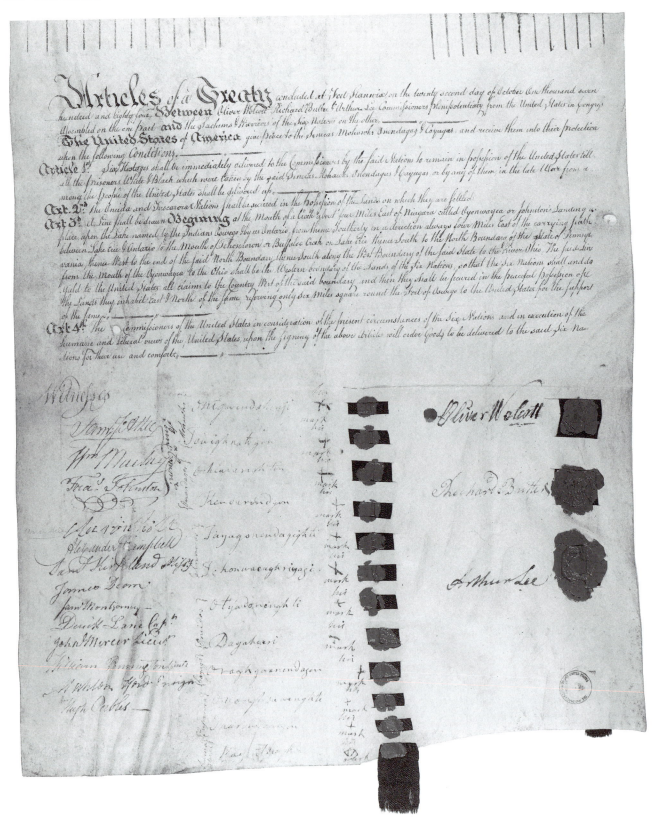

Treaty with the Six Nations concluded at Fort Stanwix, 1784, a cession of land, including a small section of western New York, by the Six (Iroquois) Nations. (National Archives)

by 100 yards, the installation contained eight huts, a supply building, a hospital, and room sufficient for 25 tents. All told, the fort could accommodate about 1,000 men, most of them in tents.

From this base Jackson intended to merge forces with Tennessee Volunteers major general John Cocke's command. Prior to the arrival of Cocke's army, Jackson dispatched Brigadier General John Coffee to disperse hostile Red Stick Creek warriors at Tallushatchee on November 4, 1813. Coffee's detachment killed 186 Creeks there as well as numerous women and children. He returned to Fort Strother with 86 women and children as prisoners, including a 10-month-old orphan boy named Lyncoya whom Jackson sent to his wife Rachel to be raised as their own child.

Fearing an assault on the fort, Jackson rushed to engage the Creeks at Talladega on the morning of November 9, 1813. This victory also marked the first time that he had commanded troops in battle. Jackson then returned to the fort, which was now without provisions, leading to grumbling from his men and several officers. Their pleas to return to the settlements for provisions forced Jackson to compromise by sending a detachment to Fort Deposit.

While at Fort Strother, Jackson constantly wrangled with his soldiers over provisions and their willingness to continue to prosecute the war against the Creeks. This greatly inhibited Jackson's ability to wage an offensive campaign. Worse yet, in mid-December 1813 an entire brigade threatened to mutiny. They acquiesced only when Jackson defiantly threatened to have the protesters shot. By the end of the year, however, Jackson's force was so diminished that the prospect of further operations appeared dubious. In fact, at that point Tennessee's governor recommended that Jackson abandon Fort Strother and terminate the campaign.

In spite of these difficulties, Jackson was determined to push farther into the Creek interior, and in mid to late January 1814 he fought two indecisive battles against the Creeks near the mouth of the Emuckfaw and Enitachopko creeks before returning to Fort Strother. The fort also served as the base of operations for Jackson's March 27, 1814, attack at Tohopeka, also known as Horseshoe Bend. His decisive victory there effectually ended Red Stick Creek resistance and led to the signing of the August 9, 1814, Treaty of Fort Jackson in which the Creeks ceded 23 million acres to the United States.

ROBERT GREG BROOKING

See also

Coffee, John; Creek War; Crockett, David; Emuckfaw Creek, Battle of; Enitachopco Creek, Battle of; Horseshoe Bend, Battle of; Jackson, Andrew; Red Sticks

References

Buchanan, John. *Jackson's Way: Andrew Jackson and the People of the Western Waters.* New York: Wiley, 2001.

Hickey, Donald R. *The War of 1812: A Forgotten Conflict.* Urbana: University of Illinois Press, 1989.

Langguth, A. J. *Union 1812: The Americans Who Fought the Second War of Independence.* New York: Simon and Schuster, 2006.

Remini, Robert Vincenti. *Andrew Jackson and the Course of American Empire, 1767–1821.* New York: Harper and Row, 1977.

Fort Sumner

Military installation established by the U.S. government on October 31, 1862, in an effort to halt the violence between white settlers and the U.S. military on the one side and the Mescalero Apaches and Navajos on the other. Fort Sumner was located on the Pecos River approximately 160 miles southeast of Albuquerque in the east-central part of New Mexico. In 1860 James L. Collins, superintendent of Indian affairs in New Mexico, suggested the creation of a reservation to confine the Native American groups in the area. The plan included the construction of additional forts and reductions in the amount of land allocated to area tribes for hunting and farming. Fort Sumner and its adjoining reservation, built on a 40-square-mile plot of land near Bosque Redondo, was named for late American Civil War (1861–1865) hero Major General Edwin Vose Sumner. Some questioned the feasibility of its location because of the lack of freshwater and the limited amount of wood for fuel and for heating in winter. The purpose of the fort was twofold: to serve as a military base in fighting the local Native American tribes and to guard a reservation for the Navajos and Mescalero Apaches. It was the first reservation to be created west of Indian Territory (present-day Oklahoma).

As the buildings of the installation took shape, ranchers, traders, and stockmen settled in the area surrounding the fort. Many of the Apaches had already been forcibly placed into the encampment at Bosque Redondo, but the Navajos, fighting hundreds of miles distant in their Arizona homelands, would not surrender. To achieve this end, U.S. Army troops destroyed Navajo crops, houses, and livestock, but the Native Americans retreated to Canyon de Chelly. The military, under the orders of Colonel Christopher "Kit" Carson, finally trapped and captured the Navajos in 1863 and organized what would be later called the Long Walk, their forcible removal to confinement at Bosque Redondo. Many Native Americans died during the trek, and among those who made it to Bosque Redondo, still more perished.

The plan for the reservation was poorly designed and executed. From the intermixing of the Mescalero Apaches and Navajos (traditional foes) to the concept of training them as sedentary farmers, the scheme was doomed to failure. Also, farming materials arriving at the reservation were ill-suited to the conditions there, and supplies were insufficient to sustain the inhabitants until the crops matured. Graft and corruption were widespread, with many supplies intended for the Native Americans being sold by unscrupulous whites in positions of authority.

The reservation's inhabitants slowly starved, and many became ill. The supply of wood quickly ran out, and groundwater became too contaminated for drinking. The Apaches at Bosque Redondo were able to escape in November 1865, but the Navajos were forced to endure until June 1, 1868, when the federal government, acknowledging its mistakes, released them from their confinement. That year the Navajos were permitted to return to their ancestral lands in the Four Corners region. Fort Sumner was then officially closed, and the buildings were sold to Lucien B. Maxwell,

Fort Sumner, New Mexico; photograph taken in the 1860s. (Library of Congress)

a well-to-do landowner, in 1870. He died in 1875 and was buried there. The fort's infamous legacy continued when the outlaw Billy the Kid (William H. Bonney) was killed by Pat Garrett in one of the old fort's structures in July 1881.

PAMELA LEE GRAY

See also
Bosque Redondo; Canyon de Chelly, Arizona; Navajos

References
Bailey, Lynn R. *Bosque Redondo: The Navajo Internment at Fort Sumner, New Mexico, 1863–68.* Los Angeles: Western Lore Publications, 1998.
Frazer, Robert W. *Forts of the West.* Norman: University of Oklahoma, 1965.

Fort Walla Walla

A series of trading and military outposts located in southeastern Washington state in and around present-day Walla Walla. The first outpost, also named Fort Nez Perce, was constructed in 1818 along the Columbia River. The outpost, built by the North West Company, a fur-trading venture in the Pacific Northwest, was essentially a fortified trading post designed to serve the growing fur-trapping industry. Supervising the design and construction of the outpost were the fur traders Donald MacKenzie and Alexander Ross, who chose a site along the east bank of the Columbia River

about half a mile north of the mouth of the Walla Walla River and several miles south of the Snake River. This was a strategic site for the fur trade and waterborne commerce and offered a modicum of protection against Native American attack.

Fort Walla Walla featured a double palisade, a unique characteristic of area forts. The inner wall, made of hewn timber, was approximately 12 feet high; the outer wall, made of wooden planks, was about 20 feet high and 6 inches thick. Within the walls were storage facilities and dwellings for traders and their families.

From Fort Walla Walla, MacKenzie set forth on a major expedition along the Snake River in September 1818. Returning to the post in the summer of 1819, he reported major success in his trapping expedition, which attracted others to the area. In 1821 the North West Company merged with the Hudson's Bay Company, and the fort's defenses were strengthened. Fort Walla Walla was used continuously until 1841, when a fire destroyed it. Later that same year it was rebuilt, this time out of adobe-like bricks, which were more durable and less prone to fire than timber. Nevertheless, in 1855 during the Yakima-Rogue War, the outpost burned a second time, destroying much of the structure. Fort Walla Walla was reconstructed a second time, now encompassing some 600 acres, but was abandoned in 1857 when the declining fur trade compelled the Hudson's Bay Company to pull out of the region.

In 1858 the U.S. Army occupied and further fortified the old Fort Walla Walla. The original adobe structures were eventually boarded over and painted white. The army post included officers' quarters, barracks, a large parade ground, stables, a granary, a blacksmith shop, storage and ammunition sheds, and a sawmill. After the end of the American Civil War in 1865, Congress sought to close the fort, but renewed tensions between whites and Native Americans—especially the Modocs—convinced lawmakers to keep it open. Fort Walla Walla remained in service until it was deactivated in 1899. In 1911 the U.S. government officially abandoned it, and the site eventually became home to a museum, a veterans' cemetery, and a Veterans Administration hospital complex. Some buildings dating to the post-1859 period are still standing and have been restored to their 19th-century condition.

PAUL G. PIERPAOLI JR.

See also

Fur Trade; Hudson's Bay Company; Modocs; Modoc War; Nez Perces; Yakima-Rogue War

References

Beckham, Stephen Dow, ed. *Oregon Indians: Voices from Two Centuries.* Corvallis: Oregon State University Press, 2006.

Gibson, Elizabeth. *Walla Walla.* Mount Pleasant, SC: Arcadia, 2004.

Schuster, Helen H. *The Yakimas.* Bloomington: Indiana University Press, 1982.

Fort Washington

One of the first permanent forts established by the United States. Named in honor of President George Washington and regarded as the most important U.S. military outpost during the Indian Wars in the Old Northwest in the early 1790s, Fort Washington was constructed to protect early white settlements in the Symmes Purchase in the Miami Valley in present-day southwestern Ohio. U.S. Army brigadier general Josiah Harmar ordered construction of Fort Washington. The fort was located in the Northwest Territory across the Ohio River from the mouth of the Licking River and adjacent to present-day Cincinnati, Ohio.

The fort was built in 1789 by some 140 men from Fort Harmar under the command of Major John Doughty. The square stockade–style fort was situated on 15 acres of land. Fort Washington had log walls some two stories high with blockhouses on each corner and occupied an area about 180 feet on a side.

Both Harmar in 1790 and Major General Arthur St. Clair in 1791 used the post to launch their disastrous expeditions into Native American territory. The fort was less important to but nonetheless was utilized by Major General Anthony Wayne and his Legion of the United States during their operations of 1793–1794 that culminated in the victory over the Native Americans in the Battle of Fallen Timbers on August 20, 1794. Thereafter Fort Washington fell into disuse. It was abandoned by the army in 1803, replaced by the Newport arsenal and barracks

Fort Washington (Cincinnati), on the Ohio River, was the key U.S. military outpost in the Old Northwest Territory during the late 18th century. (Library of Congress)

located across the Ohio River at Covington, Kentucky, completed around 1807.

SPENCER C. TUCKER

See also

Fallen Timbers, Battle of; Harmar, Josiah; St. Clair, Arthur; Wayne, Anthony

References

Barr, Daniel P., ed. *The Boundaries between Us: Natives and Newcomers along the Frontiers of the Old Northwest Territory, 1750–1850*. Kent, OH: Kent State University Press, 2006.

Bond, Beverly W., Jr. *The Foundations of Ohio*. Columbus, OH: Ohio States Archeological and Historical Society, 1941.

Knopf, Richard C., et al. "The Re-Discovery of Fort Washington." *Bulletin of the Historical and Philosophical Society of Ohio* 11 (1953): 1–12.

Williams, Gary S. *The Forts of Ohio: A Guide to Military Stockades*. Caldwell, OH: Buckeye Book Press, 2003.

Four Lakes, Battle of
Event Date: September 1, 1858

Decisive engagement between the U.S. Army and elements of the Plateau Indians (Yakima, Palouse, Spokane, and Coeur d'Alene tribes) in eastern Washington Territory just southwest of the present-day city of Spokane. The Battle of Four Lakes (also known as the Battle of Spokane Plain) essentially ended the Coeur d'Alene War, the second phase of the on-again, off-again conflict known as the Yakima-Rogue War. The Yakima-Rogue War had its origins in plans by Isaac I. Stevens, the territorial governor, to purchase and clear Native American lands in the Oregon and Washington territories so that a transcontinental railroad could be built linking Puget Sound with the Mississippi River. His efforts began in 1854. Governor Stevens was generally successful in negotiating with tribes west of the Cascade Mountains, but he ran into great difficulty with tribes east of the mountains. At the same time, increased white settlement in the area and increasing encroachment on Native American lands also led to tensions and hostilities.

When Yakima chief Kamiakin learned of Stevens's plans, he organized a unified response among the Plateau tribes, all of which vowed not to give in to U.S. demands. That unanimity crumbled, however, during negotiations, and the Yakimas alone lost 30,000 square miles of their territory in exchange for a small reservation in the Yakima Valley. Many Plateau tribes were outraged, and in September 1855 a U.S. subagent to the Yakimas was murdered, which prompted the Yakima-Rogue War. The fighting lasted only until November 1855, as many of the hostile warriors eluded capture by U.S. forces, fled, and scattered.

The uneasy peace was shattered in July 1858 when open warfare between Plateau tribes and U.S. forces broke out once again. This time the commander of the Department of the Pacific, Brevet Brigadier General Newman S. Clarke, decided to take quick and decisive action to quell the violence. In late July he ordered Colonel George Wright of the 9th Infantry to leave Fort Walla Walla and confront the allied Native Americans on the Spokane Plain. Wright began the expedition with 700 men, who were well armed with the latest long-range rifles.

Along the way Wright's force was harassed by several hit-and-run Native American attacks, which did little to deter the mission. On September 1 the confederated Native American force, numbering as many as 5,000 warriors, massed and attacked the U.S. column. Unaccustomed to fighting against those with long-range rifles, Native American forces were decimated. In wave after wave of suicidal frontal attacks, the warriors were systematically cut down. By day's end the remaining warriors were retreating. Wright did not lose a single man in the fight. Native American losses are unknown, but they are believed to have been very heavy. Wright gave chase, and after a period of four days he had forced the tribes to sue for peace, ending the Yakima-Rogue War for good and compelling the tribes to confine themselves to their respective reservations. Casualty totals for the Battle of Four Lakes have been disputed, as some have posited that the number of warriors present that day was much less than 5,000, indeed perhaps as few as 500, which would have made the fight a far more even affair.

PAUL G. PIERPAOLI JR.

See also

Coeur d'Alenes; Coeur d'Alene War; Fort Walla Walla; Kamiakin; Palouses; Spokanes; Stevens, Isaac Ingalls; Wright, George; Yakima-Rogue War

References

Doty, James, ed. *Journal of Operations of Governor Isaac Ingalls Stevens of Washington Territory in 1855*. Fairfield, WA: Ye Galleon, 1978.

Grassley, Ray. *Indian Wars of the Pacific Northwest*. Portland, OR: Binfords and Mort, 1972.

Miller, Christopher. *Prophetic Worlds: Indians and Whites on the Columbia Plateau*. Seattle: University of Washington Press, 2003.

4th U.S. Cavalry Regiment

See Cavalry Regiment, 4th U.S.

Foxes

See Mesquakies; Sauks and Foxes

Fox Fort, Siege of
Start Date: August 4, 1730
End Date: September 9, 1730

Defensive fortification built by the Fox tribe (Mesquakie, Outagami) in eastern Illinois that was besieged by a large Native

American and French coalition during August and September 1730. According to contemporary French drawings, Fox Fort covered a little more than an acre of land. The fort featured a loose palisade except on the southern side, where the riverbank formed a natural barrier. Trenches were dug along the palisade, and a screen of branches allowed the fort's defenders to shoot between the palisade poles while protected from the view of their enemies. Within the fort were subterranean shelters consisting of burrows four feet deep and covered with reed mats and soil. A series of shallow ditches connected the shelters to one another and to the river. Trees provided shade from the summer sun. The exact location of the fort has long been disputed, but it is believed to have been near the headwaters of the Sangamon River.

In 1729 toward the end of the war between the Foxes and the French and native allies, a group of belligerent young Fox warriors, members of the warrior society known as Kiyagamohag, killed a pair of Kickapoo and Mascouten hunters over a minor grievance. As a consequence, both the Kickapoos and the Macoutens, long-term allies of the Foxes, turned against them and sided with the French. Other past friends such as the Winnebagos, seeing the Fox cause as increasingly hopeless, joined the coalition against them. Fox leaders tried unsuccessfully to persuade their allies to remain at their side but in the end found themselves completely isolated among the Native Americans in the region.

Seeing no other solution to their dilemma, the entire Fox Nation undertook to relocate to the territory of the Senecas (a tribe of the Iroquois Confederacy) in western New York with whom the Foxes had long cooperated in the fur trade. In order to avoid their adversaries in the upper Great Lakes region, the Foxes proceeded to the south, abandoning the familiar woodlands of Wisconsin for the open grasslands of the Illinois Grand Prairie. Their progress was slow because they had with them many elderly people and young children.

Near the Illinois River, the Cahokias (a tribe of the Illinois Confederacy) spotted the Foxes and reported their presence to the Lakes Indians. Some Cahokias trailed the Foxes as they continued their trek. Then on August 4, 1730, the Foxes decided to make a stand in a grove of trees by a small river. The Cahokias harassed them there until the arrival of Kickapoo, Mascouten, and Pottawatomi war parties. Unable to escape any farther, the Fox constructed Fox Fort around the grove.

As the month of August passed, the siege was reinforced by more Illinois, Sauk, Miami, Wea, and Piankashaw war parties and by French soldiers and Creole traders from Fort Chartres, Fort St. Joseph, and Fort Ouiatanon. During the siege the attackers constructed a siege tower, guard posts, and a trench. The Foxes had hoped that the Sauks, the Weas, and the Piankashaws, closely related tribes, would come to their assistance. When those tribes joined the siege instead, the Foxes initiated negotiations, both openly with their enemies as a whole and quietly with the groups related to them. The Foxes released those Illinois whom they had taken captive and asked to be allowed to continue to Seneca territory, but to no avail. They also offered to surrender and to be divided among the Sauks, the Weas, and the Piankashaws, who would teach them to make peace with the French. One French commander was receptive to this proposal, but two others dismissed it as a ruse and an attempt to corrupt the other natives. Quietly the Fox persuaded the Sauks and the Weas to take most of the Fox children out of the fort. The Sauks and the Weas also shared with them some of their surplus food and ammunition. These side deals, when discovered, spurred the Illinois and the French to maintain sporadic gunfire on the fort so as to discourage any further secret meetings.

By early September the Foxes were boiling clothing and moccasins for food. On the other side, more reinforcements arrived—Hurons, Pottawatomis, and Miamis under a French commander—with orders from the governor-general of New France forbidding any negotiated solutions. Then on September 8 after weeks of heat and humidity and near starvation, the remaining Foxes escaped in the dark of night under the cover of a fierce and sudden thunderstorm and made their way southwest across the prairie.

Exhausted, malnourished, and still accompanied by their elderly and some of their children, the Foxes were not difficult to overtake. On September 9 about 12 miles from Fox Fort, they confronted a force of nearly 1,200 attackers and were quickly vanquished. Estimates of the Fox dead include 200–300 warriors and 300–600 women and children. About 50 warriors escaped, some of whom were later captured, tortured, and burned to death.

Scott C. Monje

See also
Fox Wars; France; Sauks and Foxes

References

Edmunds, R. David, and Joseph L. Peyser. *The Fox Wars: The Mesquakie Challenge to New France.* Norman: University of Oklahoma Press, 1993.

Peyser, Joseph L. "The 1730 Fox Fort: A Recently Discovered Map Throws New Light on Its Siege and Location." *Journal of the Illinois State Historical Society* 73 (Autumn 1980): 201–213.

Peyser, Joseph L. "The 1730 Siege of the Fox: Two Maps by Canadian Participants Provide Additional Information on the Fort and Its Location." *Illinois Historical Journal* 80 (Autumn 1987): 147–154.

Fox Wars
Start Date: 1712
End Date: 1737

A series of armed conflicts between the Foxes (also known as the Mesquakies or Outagamis) and New France and its Native American allies between 1712 and 1737. The Fox Wars officially began when the French, the Pottawatomis, the Odawas, the Ojibwas, and the Wyandots destroyed a Fox fort and settlement at Detroit in 1712. The conflict ended when a delegation of Great Lakes tribes traveled to Quebec in 1737 to request that the governor of New

The Siege of Fox Fort (August 4–September 9, 1730) during the Fox Wars, which pitted the French and their native allies against the Foxes. (Library of Congress)

France have mercy on his defeated foe. The Fox Wars became a genocidal conflict as the French sought essentially to exterminate the Fox Nation. By 1737 the Foxes numbered fewer than 1,000 people, whereas at the start of the conflict their population was more than 5,000.

The causes of the Fox Wars, although largely attributed to the arrogance and bellicose nature of the Foxes, had their beginnings in the Beaver Wars (1641–1701) and the reemergence of the fur trade in the Great Lakes. In the 17th century, the Foxes were driven from Michigan lands by the Iroquois, the Hurons, and the Ojibwas. By the 18th century the Foxes had resettled in Wisconsin and engaged in conflict with the Dakota Sioux. In the late 1600s French traders had entered the Wisconsin region, where they initially traded with the Foxes and continued to expand westward. Eventually the French added the Dakota Sioux as customers of European goods, particularly weaponry. The Foxes responded to French trade with their Dakota enemies by harassing and killing French traders, especially those known to be carrying muskets. These actions led the Foxes to seek allies outside the French sphere of influence, and by 1701 they had concluded an alliance with the Iroquois Confederacy. Initially declining fort commander Antoine Laumet de La Mothe de Cadillac's 1701 invitation to establish a village at Detroit, the inhabitants of several Fox villages nevertheless

had decided to relocate to the Detroit region by 1710. This move not only brought the anti-French Foxes closer to the Iroquois and the British but also placed the Foxes among natives who were pro-French and former enemies.

The immediate catalyst of the Fox Wars was an attack by the Ojibwas and Pottawatomis on a group of Mascoutens, who were allied with the Foxes. In the raid 200 Mascoutens died, and the survivors fled to a nearby Fox village. In retaliation, Fox and Mascouten warriors attacked the French and their allies alike, eventually laying siege to Fort Pontchartrain de Detroit. The fort's commander, François de La Forest, under siege and fearful of reprisals from France's native allies for failing to aid them, committed supplies and troops to the battle. Following several days of siege, the Foxes attempted to flee during a thunderstorm.

More than 1,000 Foxes and Mascoutens were killed, and fewer than 100 others managed to escape. Those captured were either executed or sold into slavery. As soon as news of the defeat reached the Foxes and the Mascoutens in Wisconsin, they made the area unsafe for French traders and their allies between 1712 and 1716. This conflict in the Great Lakes forced the French to construct Fort Michilimackinac in 1715 across the Mackinac straits from Fort Buade, which had been neglected since the French had officially abandoned the interior in 1698 due to an overstock of furs.

In 1716, 400 French soldiers, including a battery of artillery, and 1,000 native allies advanced into Wisconsin to attack the Foxes. After a brief siege of one of their villages, the Foxes agreed to keep the peace. This development reopened trade in the Wisconsin region. However, Fox accusations that the Illinois and other French allies continued to raid Fox villages and attack hunting parties, combined with a refusal by the Illinois to return captives, appear to have been the underlying factors of the continued warfare between these two groups. Because the Illinois Country had been placed under the authority of French Louisiana, Quebec governor Charles de la Boische, Marquis de Beauharnois, refused to intervene despite pleas from the Jesuits and the Louisiana governors, Pierre Dugué de Boisbriand (governor during 1724–1726) and Étienne de Périer (governor during 1726–1733). With increasing pressure from Louisiana, Jesuits, and Canadian merchants, Governor Beauharnois dispatched 1,500 men against the Foxes in 1728, an expedition that failed to locate any Fox villages.

In the 1720s the Foxes reaffirmed their alliance with the Iroquois and built new alliances with the Chickasaws and the Abenakis. Kiala, a Fox war chief, recognized the need for a united stance against European colonies. Indeed, his efforts not only challenged the French alliance system but also threatened to cut Louisiana off from New France. Importantly, the French also sought to stop the anti-French Abenakis, led by Nescambiouit, from joining the Foxes in the interior. Such a move by the Abenakis would have strengthened the Foxes while removing a buffer between New England and New France. Hence, Beauharnois saw the destruction of the Foxes as imperative.

In 1730 the Foxes experienced a second disastrous defeat, reminiscent of Detroit in 1712, when they left their villages in the Illinois-Wisconsin region in an attempt to join the Senecas in New York. Trapped during their flight across the Illinois prairie, the Foxes fortified a grove of trees (Fox Fort) and after a siege attempted to sneak away during an intense summer storm. Detected by their attackers and slowed by their families, as many as 1,000 men, women, and children were killed, and dozens were taken captive.

The Foxes sued for peace in 1733, and a delegation of four leaders, including Kiala, arrived in Montreal in 1734 to finalize their surrender. The French arrested the peace delegates, sending one to France to serve in the galleys. Kiala was sold into slavery, and the remainder were scattered among the missions and towns of Quebec. As the French intensified their campaign to exterminate the Foxes, other Great Lakes tribes began to fear the outcome if they allowed the Foxes to be destroyed. During 1734–1735 French native allies released Fox prisoners and began to refuse assistance to the French in what had now become a genocidal conflict. When a group of Great Lakes nations accompanied by the Foxes arrived in Quebec to seek peace in 1737, Governor Beauharnois agreed. His decision was partly motivated by conflicts in the Mississippi region such as the Natchez War (1729–1733) and the Chickasaw Wars (1731–1745), which drew French attention, troops, and supplies.

Furthermore, growing tensions with the British colonies due to their efforts to lure away French Indian allies and increase their presence in the interior, as well as increasing tensions in Europe, contributed to the acceptance of peace in the Great Lakes region.

The Fox Wars are noteworthy not only as an example of attempted genocide by the French but also because the conflict reshaped French policies in the *pays d'en haut* ("upcountry"). First, the Fox Wars made it clear that the French presence in the interior depended on the cooperation and sufferance of the natives. The conflict amply illustrated that despite French efforts to enforce a Pax Gallica, the French were entirely reliant on native cooperation. Second, the wars showed the tribes of the Great Lakes that the French could be dangerous and, most importantly, that the existence of a benign middle ground was tenuous at best. Third, the wars illustrated that canoe routes from Lake Michigan to the Mississippi were not secure. This fact forced the French to rely on the Ohio River system as vital to the maintenance of their American empire and on northerly rivers for westward expansion and trade. Thus, the expansion of the French presence in the Ohio River Valley greatly contributed to the series of conflicts with the British that ended with the conquest of New France in 1760. Finally, the wars showed the French that their alliance system in the Great Lakes was neither stable nor absolute, and the conclusion of the Fox Wars did not end warfare in the Wisconsin-Illinois region. The Illinois continued to suffer raids by the Foxes and others into the 1750s.

KARL S. HELE

See also

Abenakis; Beaver Wars; Chickasaws; Fox Fort, Siege of; France; Native American Warfare; Iroquois; Iroquois Confederacy; Sauks and Foxes

References

Demers, E. A. S. "Native-American Slavery and Territoriality in the Colonial Upper Great Lakes Region." *Michigan Historical Review* 28(2) (2002): 163–172.

Dickason, Olive Patricia. *Canada's First Nations: A History of Founding Peoples from Earliest Times.* 3rd ed. Toronto: Oxford University Press, 2002.

Edmunds, R. David, and Joseph L. Peyser. *The Fox Wars: The Mesquakie Challenge to New France.* Norman: University of Oklahoma Press, 1993.

McNab, David, Bruce W. Hodgins, and Dale S. Standen. "'Black with Canoes': Aboriginal Resistance and the Canoe; Diplomacy, Trade, and Warfare in the Meeting Grounds of Northeastern North America, 1600–1821." In *Technology, Disease, and Colonial Conquests, Sixteenth to Eighteenth Centuries: Essays Reappraising the Guns and Germs Theories,* edited by George Raudzens, 237–292. Boston: Brill Academic, 2001.

Skinner, Claiborne, Jr. "'They Would Not Suffer the French to Live among Them': The Fox Wars, the Emergency of 1747, and the Origins of the Seven Years' War, 1671–1752." In *Entering the 90s: The North American Experience,* edited by Thomas E. Schirer, 27–39. Sault Ste. Marie, MI: Lake Superior State University Press, 1991.

Stelle, Lenville J. "History, Archaeology, and the 1730 Siege of the Fox." *Journal of the Steward Anthropological Society* 18(1–2) (1989): 187–212.

Warren, William W. *History of the Ojibway People.* St. Paul: Minnesota Historical Society Press, 1984.

France

French interests in North American date to 1534, when adventurer Jacques Cartier explored the Saint Lawrence River. New France's existence officially ended in 1763 with the conclusion of the French and Indian War (1754–1763), but French influence can be said to have actually ended with the Louisiana Purchase by the United States in 1803.

Following the initial exploration, during the remainder of the 1500s the French tried several times to establish settlements in North America, including one on the southeastern coast. These failed. In Canada, however, French traders began to establish a fairly elaborate fur trade, which frequently included the area's Native Americans. In 1604 a permanent trading post was established in Port Royal, Acadia (Nova Scotia), which became New France's first successful settlement. Four years later the French established a trade center at Quebec.

For several decades thereafter the pace of French settlement was painfully slow, owing to harsh winter weather, disease, and difficult agricultural conditions. The French Crown attempted to speed up the colonization of New France, but as late as 1660 the census showed just 3,200 French inhabitants. At its height in 1712, New France encompassed an area from Newfoundland to the Rocky Mountains and from Hudson Bay to the Gulf of Mexico. As colonization proceeded, the French established important commercial and cultural ties with many Native American tribes, and Catholic missionaries began ministering to them.

By the early 1700s New France began to thrive, and the 1720 census showed a French population of about 25,000. Beginning in the 1740s, however, conflict with the British and their Native American allies began to tax France's North American colony. The French and Indian War saw New France flounder amid nearly constant warfare. In 1763, upon their defeat, the French turned over control of New France to the British.

The French presence in North America during the colonial period influenced a wide range of Native American military and trade activities. France's colonial officials and military officers, for example, frequently employed Native American warriors as scouts and raiders in operations against other European forces in conflicts such as the French and Indian War. The French use of Native American auxiliaries, although it was essential to success in frontier warfare, represented only one aspect of French–Native American relations, however. The French also allied with certain tribes in strictly intertribal conflicts for religious or economic reasons, as in the case of the Hurons against the Iroquois in the 17th century to retain a modicum of control over the fur trade. While these intertribal conflicts inevitably influenced European colonization, in this context colonial warfare will chiefly be examined by looking at tensions between European powers struggling to establish control over North America. These wars included King William's War (1689–1697), Queen Anne's War (1702–1713), King George's War (1744–1748), and the French and Indian War.

The French approach to fighting with Native American allies against European rivals reflected the nature of France's commercial empire in North America. Motivated by economic and religious goals rather than settlement, the French pursued a form of colonization that was drastically different from that of their British adversary. In stark contrast to the steady encroachment of English settlement on Native American lands, a process in which the colonists exhibited a marked indifference to their relations with the native tribes, the French immersed themselves in Native American society. The low-intensity nature of their colonization dictated that French settlers adopt a posture of cooperation rather than confrontation. This willingness to accommodate Native American culture carried over into the French approach to colonial warfare.

Following a brief experiment with the deployment of one regiment of regulars (or *troupes de terre*) in North America in the mid-17th century, the French adopted a colonial military system that relied heavily on the colonists themselves. To be sure, they frequently employed *troupes de la marine,* recruited in France, in the colonies. These regular European soldiers, however, usually served under leaders born in French Canada. The native-born colonial leaders possessed an expertise in frontier warfare that gave French soldiers a decisive advantage when facing their European rivals. France also depended to a considerable extent on the Canadian Militia, a force well schooled in frontier warfare. The familiarity between French settlers and Native Americans, developed in peacetime, also greatly facilitated operations in times of war.

Anglo-French rivalry did not intensify in North America until the end of the 17th century. Coinciding with the European War of the League of Augsburg, New France initiated King William's War in North America in 1689. To encourage participation by the Native Americans, the French promised them plunder to be gained in raids against English troops and villages. Combined Canadian and Native American forces thereafter conducted a series of small expeditions throughout England's vulnerable northern colonies, including New York, Massachusetts, and New Hampshire. The French treatment of Native Americans during this conflict proved complex.

While the employment of Native American warriors in raids against English villages appeared fairly straightforward, New France's continued conflict with the Iroquois complicated matters. To convince their Algonquian allies to remain in the war against the Five Nations, the French had to emphasize the potential threat that the Iroquois might renew an offensive against these western tribes while discrediting the notion that peace might open beneficial trade with the English. This mutual dependency, in which France required Algonquian allies to successfully gain control over the fur trade while the western tribes needed French assistance in holding off the Iroquois, reflected the nature of an empire of commerce rather than military domination. The relationship established with Algonquians during the war with the Iroquois became invaluable in later efforts against the British. The location of French forts, for example, near Algonquian population centers, coupled with a system of trade in which traders conducted commerce under a permit granted by the government, created an intricate network of communications through which officials could rapidly respond to changes in Native American politics.

Although King William's War ended somewhat indecisively, France and England, along with their colonies, renewed hostilities only five years later. This conflict, known as Queen Anne's War in the colonies, played out in a fashion similar to that of the previous war. Combined Canadian and Native American forces once again launched raids against vulnerable English settlements on the frontier. While embroiled in the East, however, the government of New France lost track of affairs to the west. There relations among Algonquian tribes collapsed into bitter internecine warfare. Trade issues introduced further cracks in the habitual French-Indian alliance. *Fermiers,* or French fur trading companies, began to base the price they paid for furs on supply and demand in Europe by the beginning of the 18th century. Native Americans, with little concept of the world market, grew angry at this seemingly inexplicable variation in price, which was worsened by a reduction in value caused by the glut of fur available on the market.

Consequently, New France's Native American allies began to turn to English traders offering higher prices and better-quality goods in return. Indeed, the 1713 Treaty of Utrecht, which formally concluded the War of the Spanish Succession, as it was known in Europe, guaranteed both the French and the British equal access to trade with the Native Americans. Flush with success, British colonists now set about wresting control of the western trade away from the French, thereby threatening the alliance that had proved so beneficial to France in peace and war.

Three decades of relative peace between Britain and France ensued. The fractures in French–Native American relations that had opened during Queen Anne's War, however, only widened with the advent of King George's War beginning in 1744. Unlike the two previous European colonial conflicts, during this war the French actively sought alliances with the Algonquian tribes against the British. Although they enjoyed initial success, Native American resistance to French diplomacy culminated in open rebellion by 1747. This schism, to be sure, had less to do with French treatment of Native Americans during the conflict and more with fiscal reforms instituted by France prior to the war.

To reduce the expenses of operating in the frontier, the French had simultaneously curtailed the extent of gift giving to Native Americans while adopting a policy of leasing forts to be run by civilians. The lessees of the forts subsequently raised the price of goods to cover the costs incurred by the lease. Additionally, a British wartime blockade limited the amount of French imports into Canada, placing further stress on an already fragile situation.

Native Americans, frustrated by the high prices and dwindling sources of supply, began to heed British warnings that the French could no longer support their needs. Sporadic attacks against French traders and some efforts to secure support from British colonies marred a once-strong alliance. Abandoning accommodation, the French turned to force to dictate their alliance with the Native Americans. Following Queen Anne's War, they demanded that the Algonquian tribes surrender those warriors involved in any killings of French settlers. The language employed by colonial officials also increasingly called for obedience from the Native Americans rather than for alliance.

The signs of this new dynamic in French–Native American relations could be seen quite clearly in the conduct of the French and Indian War. To be sure, this change in the French approach from accommodation to force evolved slowly over time. The most effective military leaders continued to view the Native Americans as allies rather than subordinates. Nevertheless, the relationship between the French and their Amerindian allies had clearly changed. The challenges inherent in waging war with allies separated by vast cultural differences and with whom command relationships remained imprecisely defined are easily detected.

Confusion following the surrender of Fort William Henry in 1757, for example, highlighted some of the difficulties that such operations entailed. Without considering their Native American allies, the French, under General Louis-Joseph, Marquis de Montcalm, offered terms of surrender to the besieged British in keeping with the highest traditions of European military professionalism. The defeated garrison would be allowed to keep its individual weapons and regimental colors and would be guaranteed safe passage to Fort Edward. In addition, the French demanded that these soldiers be paroled for a period of 18 months, during which time they could not serve in a military capacity, and that the British leave behind in the fort all cannon, military stores, and ammunition. Finally, Montcalm expected that all French prisoners in British captivity would be released at Fort Edward. These provisions proved a slap in the face to the Native Americans who had served faithfully alongside their French allies.

The French terms denied Native Americans the booty and prisoners that they customarily relied upon. Angered by this affront, the Native Americans launched aggressive efforts to plunder the British prisoners of their personal possessions, actions that culminated in the violence that came to be known as the Fort William Henry Massacre (August 1757). During the ensuing clash, the Native Americans killed more than 180 British and colonial soldiers and took an additional 300 to 500 as captives. A further testament to the challenges of communication between European and Native American allies, French intercession on behalf of the British compelled the Native Americans to kill many of their recently acquired captives, as they chose to take a scalp rather than suffer the loss of their prize altogether. The Fort William Henry debacle marked a significant turning point in French–Native American relations for the remainder of the war.

The French-allied Native Americans lost considerable faith in their European ally and concluded that their assistance was no longer needed. French recruiting efforts among Native Americans would never again produce the results that had been achieved in the summer of 1756. Furthermore, unbeknownst to either ally, the British at Fort William Henry suffered from smallpox. Thus, as the Native Americans returned to their villages with British possessions, scalps, and prisoners, they spread an epidemic that decimated their populations.

The summer of 1763 offered a poignant conclusion to centuries of French alliance with Native American tribes during North America's colonial wars. Although a preliminary treaty between Britain and France had been signed in Paris in November 1762 marking the end of the conflict known as the Seven Years' War in Europe and the French and Indian War in the colonies, the agreement remained a rumor throughout the frontier. The peace stipulated, among other provisions, that France yield some of its North American possessions to Britain and the remainder to Spain. By this point the British occupied numerous frontier forts in the Old Northwest, including the principal posts of Michilimackinac, Detroit, Niagara, and Pitt. Yet French settlers and the Native Americans with whom they frequently allied found this agreement difficult to conceive, poised as they were on the periphery of empire. Thus, in early May 1763, Pontiac, an Ottawa chief, tapping into Native American sentiment that called for the rejection of European and, more specifically, British culture, organized a loose coalition of Native American warriors in an effort to force a British withdrawal to the Appalachian Mountains.

The offensive, known as Pontiac's Rebellion, enjoyed considerable initial success, capturing most of the British posts in the Northwest within the first two months of fighting. Throughout this conflict the British leadership, including Major General Jeffrey Amherst, commander in chief of the army in America, and Sir William Johnson, superintendent of Indian affairs for the northern district, remained convinced that only the French could have orchestrated such an effective campaign. To be sure, the Native Americans hoped that their defeat of the British would compel the French to return to North America in force. Pontiac, however, much to his chagrin, would receive little support from those French officials still in North America. Embroiled in the siege of Fort Detroit, he received word from a delegation sent to the French garrison in the Illinois Country that no supplies of gunpowder and ammunition would be forthcoming. Although the French would never again play an influential role in the North American frontier, the Native American desire for their return in 1763 underscored the importance of their alliance to the Native Americans.

JAMES K. PERRIN JR.

See also

Algonquins; Amherst, Jeffrey; French and Indian War; Iroquois; Iroquois Confederacy; Johnson, Sir William; King George's War; King William's War; Pontiac's Rebellion; Queen Anne's War

References

Anderson, Fred. *Crucible of War: The Seven Years' War and the Fate of the Empire in British North America, 1754–1766.* New York: Vintage Books, 2001.

Starkey, Armstrong. *European and Native American Warfare, 1675–1815.* Norman: University of Oklahoma Press, 1998.

Steele, Ian K. *Warpaths: Invasions of North America.* New York: Oxford University Press, 1994.

White, Richard. *The Middle Ground: Indians, Empires, and Republics in the Great Lakes Region, 1650–1815.* New York: Cambridge University Press, 1991.

Free, Mickey
Birth Date: 1848
Death Date: 1915

U.S. Army scout and interpreter who assisted the U.S. Army in the Apache Wars (1861–1886). Born in 1848 in Santa Cruz, Sonora, Mexico, to Jesusa Martínez and (possibly) Santiago Tellez, a Mestizo of Irish descent, Mickey Free, whose birth name was Felix, moved to the Sonoita Creek Valley, Arizona, with his mother in 1858 after the death of his father. His mother became the mistress of a local rancher named John Ward, and the family lived on Ward's ranch until January 27, 1861, when a group of White Mountain Apaches raided the ranch and stole 20 head of cattle and captured the young boy.

Ward reported the incident to the commander of nearby Fort Buchanan, who placed Second Lieutenant George N. Bascom in charge of obtaining the boy's release. Bascom, an inexperienced soldier who had graduated at the bottom of his class at the U.S. Military Academy, mistakenly assumed that the raid had been conducted by the Chokonens, a band of Chiricahua Apaches led by Cochise. After a series of skirmishes in the area surrounding Apache Pass, all of which failed to locate the kidnapped boy, Bascom's troops executed Cochise's family. The Bascom Affair triggered the Apache Wars, fought between the United States and the Apaches.

Meanwhile, Felix lived with the White Mountain Apaches, learned their culture, and became trilingual (Spanish, English, and Apache). On December 2, 1872, he enlisted in the U.S. Army as a translator. By this time the one-eyed, light-complected, reddish-haired young man had changed his name to Mickey Free, based on a character in *Charles O'Malley: The Irish Dragoon* (1841), a novel by Irish author Charles Lever. Free served as translator for Brigadier General George Crook during the 1883 Sierra Madre Expedition. Free died sometime in 1915 on the Apache Reservation located near Flagstaff, Arizona.

MICHAEL R. HALL

See also

Apaches; Apache Wars; Bascom Affair; Cochise; Crook, George

References

Radbourne, Allan. *Mickey Free: Apache Captive, Interpreter, and Indian Scout.* Tucson: Arizona Historical Society, 2005.

Roberts, David. *Once They Moved like the Wind: Cochise, Geronimo, and the Apache Wars.* New York: Touchstone, 1993.

Frémont, John Charles
Birth Date: January 21, 1813
Death Date: July 13, 1890

U.S. Army officer, politician, and explorer who played an important role in promoting settlement of the American West. John Charles Frémont was born John Charles Fremon in Savannah, Georgia, on January 21, 1813, the illegitimate son of a Virginia socialite and an impecunious French refugee. In 1837 with the rank of second lieutenant, Frémont entered the U.S. Army's Corps of Topographical Engineers as a protégé of Secretary of War Joel Poinsett. The following year Frémont became an enthusiastic supporter of Missouri senator Thomas Hart Benton and Benton's vision for the westward expansion of the United States. Benton was not only one of the most powerful men in the Senate but was also a close friend and political ally of Andrew Jackson, who, although no longer president, still loomed large on the political landscape of the era. It was therefore particularly reckless of Frémont to provoke Benton's fury by eloping with the senator's daughter, Jessie. Once the

U.S. Army officer John C. Frémont became known as "the Pathfinder of the West" as the result of several important exploring expeditions in the 1830s and 1840s. (George S. Bryan, *The Mentor, Pioneers of the Great West*, vol. 8, no. 1. New York: The Mentor Association, Inc., Feburary 16, 1920)

deed was done, however, Frémont and his new bride succeeded in assuaging the unhappy father and winning him back as a patron for Frémont's army career.

As a member of the topographical engineers, Frémont participated in and later led exploratory expeditions into the western territories of the United States and sometimes Canada and Mexico. In the late 1830s these explorations led him into what later became Iowa, and in the early 1840s he led more dramatic explorations along the Oregon Trail and into the Sierra Nevada. Guided by renowned mountain man Christopher "Kit" Carson, Frémont made a number of geographic discoveries in the West and won the nickname "the Pathfinder." His explorations, which included considerable hardship and danger, and the publicity surrounding them helped to encourage American migration to the West, much to Benton's satisfaction.

When the Mexican-American War (1846–1848) began, Frémont was leading another exploratory expedition in the western mountains. That May after a band of Modocs attacked his party, Frémont attacked a Klamath fishing settlement in Oregon, resulting in a virtual massacre of the Native Americans there. Frémont himself was nearly killed in the engagement. Some weeks later, without authorization, he led his band into California just prior to the official outbreak of hostilities and, with the aid of recent American settlers in the region, successfully established the independent Bear Flag Republic, which soon became part of the United States. By that time, however, Frémont had become embroiled in a dispute with his U.S. Army superior in California, Brigadier General Stephen W. Kearny. Court-martialed and convicted of insubordination, Frémont was pardoned by President James K. Polk but resigned his commission.

As a civilian, in 1848 Frémont led another western expedition, but without Carson and other key guides he lost his way in the snows of the mountains. Several members of the party died, and Frémont and the others narrowly escaped. Landing on his feet again, Frémont became a U.S. senator from California, serving from 1850 to 1851. Meanwhile, gold discovered on his land in California made him rich.

In 1856 Frémont became the first presidential candidate of the newly organized Republican Party. He made a respectable showing in the general election, although he failed to carry his own state of California and lost the electoral vote to Democratic candidate James Buchanan.

During the American Civil War (1861–1865), Frémont served the Union as a major general, first in Missouri, where he embarrassed the Lincoln administration by issuing a harsh and premature proclamation of martial law and emancipation (which the president revoked), and later in what was soon to become West Virginia. There too Frémont proved to be a dismal failure. In the spring of 1862 he blundered militarily and helped to make possible the spectacular success of Confederate major general Thomas J. "Stonewall" Jackson during the Shenandoah Valley Campaign.

After the war President Rutherford B. Hayes appointed Frémont governor of the Arizona Territory, where he served from 1878 to 1881. Frémont died in New York City on July 13, 1890.

ETHAN RAFUSE

See also

Carson, Christopher Houston; Kearny, Stephen Watts; Modocs

References

Chaffin, Tom. *Pathfinder: John Charles Frémont and the Course of American Empire.* New York: Hill and Wang, 2002.

Roberts, David. *A Newer World: Kit Carson, John C. Frémont, and the Claiming of the American West.* New York: Touchstone, 2001.

French and Indian War

Start Date: 1754
End Date: 1763

The last and largest North American conflict between Britain and France and their respective Native American allies. The French and Indian War (1754–1763) began on May 28, 1754. It involved battles on at least three distinct fronts and served as the catalyst for a wider conflict that came to be known in Europe as the Seven Years' War that began there on August 28, 1756, and ended on February 15, 1763. The war saw fighting on land and sea in North America and Europe as well as in India, West Africa, and the Caribbean. The fighting in North America not only confirmed British hegemony on the eastern half of that continent but also affected the war in Europe and set forces in motion that would later influence the American drive for independence. Native Americans played an important role in the conflict.

During the long struggle alliances sometimes shifted, and Native Americans warred against each other as well as against their particular European adversary. The French often claimed the Delawares (Lenni Lenapes), Ottawas, Algonquins, Wyandots, Abenakis, Senecas, Mohawks, and Onondagas as allies. The British, at various points, claimed independent Iroquois bands as allies (although the Iroquois Confederacy declared neutrality) as well as select bands of the Mohawks and Cherokees. The alliance with the Cherokees, however, was short-lived. By 1759, the Cherokees were engaged in their own war with the British.

On August 28, 1753, Robert d'Arcy, Earl of Holdernesse, British secretary of state for the Southern Department (which included North America), sent a circular order to the British North American colonial governors. In it he authorized them to demand a French withdrawal from several disputed territories and, failing that, to force the French out using colonial militia.

Acting on this order, Virginia lieutenant governor Robert Dinwiddie dispatched Major George Washington, who was 21 years old, to Fort Le Boeuf, the nearest known French outpost, in what is now northwestern Pennsylvania. On December 16, 1753, Washington arrived with 11 men and was graciously received by Fort Le Boeuf's commandant, Jacques Legardeur de St. Pierre. St. Pierre patiently received Dinwiddie's demand to withdraw but went only so far as to forward the summons to his superiors in Quebec. This set in motion the second clause of Holdernesse's circular order.

On April 15, 1754, the French presence in western Pennsylvania turned from construction to conquest. A force of 500 men under French captain Claude Pierre Pécaudy, Seigneur de Contrecoeur, forced the surrender of 40 English workmen under Ensign Edward Ward and transformed their Ohio Company trading post into the nucleus of Fort Duquesne at the Forks of the Ohio River. Meanwhile, Washington returned to the frontier with 150 Virginia militiamen and some native allies. On May 28 a detachment of 47 men from this force surprised a party of 35 French and native allies from Fort Duquesne, firing the first shots of the war. Among the 10 French dead was their commander, Ensign Joseph Coulon de Villiers de Jumonville, who received a hatchet blow to the head delivered by Tanaghrisson, the leader of Washington's native allies.

While ministers in Britain and France sought to negotiate their differences in North America, the colonists further heightened tensions. Before the news of Fort Duquesne and Ensign Jumonville's death could reach Europe, French captain Louis Coulon de Villiers, Jumonville's brother, led a force of 600 Canadians and 100 native allies against his brother's supposed murderer. Washington's 500-man militia fought from Fort Necessity, where they were compelled to surrender after a 10-hour fight.

For 1755 both governments planned a proxy war in North America, reinforcing colonial militia with regular European troops. The ministers in London planned one campaign for 1755, but colonial officials requested four smaller ones. The first, during June 2–16, witnessed Nova Scotia lieutenant governor Charles Lawrence and Colonel Robert Monckton leading 250 British regulars and 2,000 colonials to Fort Beauséjour and Fort Gaspéreau on the isthmus connecting Nova Scotia to the Canadian mainland. There the British force defeated 150 French regulars and a few hundred unsteady Acadians. On September 8, 1755, Major General William Johnson's operation against Crown Point achieved a defensive victory at Lake George, capturing the French commander, Marechal de Camp Jean Armand, Baron de Dieskau. Major General William Shirley's campaign to Niagara, however, ended at Oswego when supplies ran short and 2,000 colonial militia fell ill. Meanwhile, on July 9 British major general Edward Braddock's expedition to Fort Duquesne ended in the loss of more than 900 out of his 2,200 troops in the Battle of the Monongahela.

By year's end, ministers in London and Versailles planned new campaigns, expanding operations from North America into the Atlantic and from the Atlantic to the shores of Europe, where nothing short of a diplomatic revolution had occurred. Maria Theresa, the Habsburg empress of Austria, sought to recapture Silesia, which Prussia had invaded and taken in the War of the Austrian Succession (1740–1748), known as King George's War in America. She arranged an alliance with archenemy France, while Britain also switched sides, allying with Prussia. The basic rivalries of

France versus Britain and Austria versus Prussia were maintained, however. Russia also agreed to enter the war against Prussia. King Frederick II of Prussia, aware of the forces massing against him, did not wait to be attacked. Frederick mobilized his own army and on August 28, 1756, began what would become known as the Seven Years' War with an invasion of Saxony en route to the Austrian kingdom of Bohemia.

There was little in the way of large-scale campaigning in North America during 1756 and 1757. The British commander in chief in North America, John Campbell, Fourth Earl of Loudoun, reorganized British forces, which increased by the end of 1757 to 17 regular regiments and more than 10,000 colonial militiamen. Meanwhile, Maréchal de Camp Louis-Joseph, Marquis de Montcalm, commanded some 7,200 French regulars and as many as 17,000 Canadian militiamen. Whereas Loudoun remained quiescent, aborting two projected British operations against Louisbourg, Montcalm won several important victories and attracted large numbers of native allies to the French cause.

Accompanied by 250 native allies, 1,300 French regulars and 1,500 Canadian militiamen raided Oswego late in 1756, leaving the British without their trading and logistical base on Lake Ontario. Abandoned by their Oneida allies, the British garrison of 1,135 men was surprised in their poorly constructed works on the afternoon of August 11 and were compelled to conclude an ignominious surrender.

By 1757 the British attempted to gather their own intelligence and employed Captain Robert Rogers and his 100-man company of green-clad American troops, known as Rogers' Rangers. Discovered and routed in their attempt to reconnoiter Fort Carillon (Ticonderoga) in January 1757, the rangers left Fort William Henry as vulnerable to surprise as Oswego had been in 1756, and the prestige of French victories attracted increasing numbers of native allies. In mid-March a raid on Fort William Henry by Captain François Pierre Rigaud and 1,500 natives, French, and Canadians exposed British weaknesses and destroyed supplies, but Major William Eyre's capable defense saved the fort from immediate capture.

Fort William Henry was in no better shape on August 3 when Montcalm arrived there with some 6,000 French regulars and Canadian militia and 2,000 native allies. British lieutenant colonel George Monro had brought reinforcements to Fort William Henry in the spring and received additional reinforcements later, giving him a total garrison strength of 2,300 British regulars and American colonials. This force held out bravely for a week before surrendering.

On August 9, 1757, Monro negotiated a European-style surrender. Granted the full honors of war, the British garrison was assured safe conduct with all of its effects down the 14-mile road to Fort Edward. Unfortunately for the members of the British garrison, Montcalm had not consulted with his native allies. The natives, seeking plunder and scalps, engaged in what the British and colonial press called a massacre, inflaming public opinion throughout the Anglophone world. Moreover, by trying to restrain his native allies, Montcalm damaged French credibility and gave British Indian commissioner William Johnson an unprecedented opportunity to swing native opinion to Britain's side.

British ships and troops also conducted successful amphibious operations in North America and the Caribbean. The first, against Louisbourg, included Major General Jeffrey Amherst and Colonel (later Brigadier General) James Wolfe. Whereas Lord Loudoun had failed in 1756 and 1757, the expedition in 1758 succeeded brilliantly, taking the fort on July 26.

Wolfe continued with Vice Admiral Charles Saunders up the Saint Lawrence River in 1759. They then waged a lengthy amphibious campaign against the capital of New France, Quebec. In perhaps the most important land battle in the history of North America, the British were victorious in the Battle of the Plains of Abraham outside Quebec on September 13.

The British also enjoyed success in the North American interior. With the American Indian threat largely removed by the Treaty of Easton of August 5, 1757, British colonial forces, backed by regular troops, began a large and virtually continuous three-year offensive. Montcalm blunted the English advance at Ticonderoga on July 8, 1758, and French forces under Chevalier Gaston de Lévis almost retook Quebec following the Battle of Sainte Foy on April 28, 1760, but British operations continued to register slow, cautious progress.

British North American forces under the overall command of Major General James Abercromby in 1758, and Amherst from 1759, had great advantages in numbers and organization and in the quality and creativity of their officers. It was not only Wolfe and Amherst who stood out but also enterprising officers such as Brigadier General John Forbes, whose attack on Fort Duquesne on September 14, 1758, drove the French from western Pennsylvania; Lieutenant Colonel John Bradstreet, whose attack on Fort Frontenac during August 25–27, 1758, threatened the French Canadian war economy; and Indian commissioner Major General William Johnson, who convinced the Iroquois to join the struggle as a British ally in 1759 and whose siege of Niagara during July 6–26, 1759, cleared French influence from New York and the western Great Lakes region and secured British authority over the Ohio Country.

With the fall of Louisbourg and Frontenac and then of Niagara and Quebec, French trade with Canada collapsed. French maritime businesses fell on hard times. With the cancellation of payment on Canadian bills of exchange, merchants trading with Canada were compelled to declare bankruptcy. The Ministry of Marine declared bankruptcy as well in November 1759, and financial problems spread throughout the French government soon thereafter. As French territories in Canada and the Caribbean fell, French subsidies to European allies, notably Austria, dwindled, and French military efforts around the globe weakened substantially after 1760. Meanwhile, the British were able to make regular subsidy payments to Frederick and keep Prussia in the war, although just barely.

The British were successful at sea and in operations in the Caribbean and in India. The last French operation by sea was an assault on Newfoundland in 1762. Though successful, it involved only five ships and 800 men. British colonists in Massachusetts organized a relief expedition of more than 1,500 men under Colonel William Amherst and soon recovered the island. The French campaign in Newfoundland did not truly envision the conquest of that island as an end in its own right; rather, like the British invasion of Belle Isle with 8,000 men on June 7, 1761, it was an attempt to affect the two states' respective bargaining positions at a future peace negotiation.

The first attempt to start peace talks was the Hague Declaration, presented by British and Prussian envoys in the Dutch Republic to their Austrian, French, and Russian counterparts in October 1759. These negotiations failed but led to efforts at a peace congress in Augsburg (Breda) in 1760 and 1761. Britain and France also attempted to negotiate a separate peace in 1761 with envoys Hans Stanley and Sieur de Bussy. Negotiations broke down, however, mostly under Austrian and Spanish pressure and because of concerns over fishing rights near Newfoundland and the return of conquests in Germany. Despite their failure, the talks were restarted through the Sardinian envoys Viry and Solar in 1762 and ended in success near the end of the year.

The negotiations in 1762 were more complex than those of 1761 for several reasons. Changes in the leadership in Spain, in Britain, and finally in Russia altered the international playing field. Spain had slowly edged toward the French camp after the accession of King Carlos III in 1759, and the two states concluded the Third Family Compact on August 15, 1761. With the accession of King George III on October 25, 1760, Britain moved quickly from the hawkish stance of William Pitt the Elder to the more dovish agenda of John Stuart, Third Earl of Bute, and John Russell, Fourth Duke of Bedford.

Finally, with Prussia on the verge of extinction in October 1761, there occurred the so-called Miracle of the House of Brandenburg. On January 5, 1762, Czarina Elizabeth of Russia died. Elizabeth, who hated Frederick and was determined to end his rule, was followed by Czar Peter III, an ardent admirer of the Prussian king. At the czar's command, the Russian Army switched sides and helped the Prussians to achieve victory over the Austrians in battle that July at Burkersdorf. Although Grand Duchess Catherine of Anhalt-Zerbst soon succeeded Peter in a palace coup to become Czarina Catherine II, the die had been cast: Russia declared neutrality, and Frederick and Prussia survived.

When Russia left the conflict, Sweden also declared neutrality, although Spain declared war against Britain on January 4, 1762. In effect Europe experienced a second diplomatic revolution, so that Prussia had an advantage over Austria, and France and Spain had what appeared, at first, to be an upper hand against Britain. Although exhausted financially and militarily, Prussia gained several victories in 1762 and forced Austria to accept the definitive loss of Silesia. British and allied forces meanwhile invaded Havana in Cuba and Manila in the Philippines while repelling a Spanish invasion of Portugal.

Finally convinced of the futility of further conflict, France and Spain expanded on the Viry-Solar talks and found in George III and his envoy, Bedford, remarkable partners for peace. At the prodding of their respective allies, Austria and Prussia made peace at Hubertusburg on February 15, 1763, reaffirming the prewar status quo of 1756 and providing for the definitive secession of Silesia by Austria to Prussia.

Britain, France, and Spain meanwhile concluded the Treaty of Paris on February 10. This agreement formalized a substantial exchange of territories, greatly in Britain's favor. In North America the agreement involved the cession of all of New France to British control except for Louisiana and the small fishing islands of Saint-Pierre and Miquelon, which France ceded to Spain. Britain also acquired Florida from Spain.

By taking large amounts of territory from France yet leaving important naval stations under French control, Britain left open the opportunity for ministers at Versailles to plot their revenge, which occurred during the American Revolutionary War (1775–1783). Meanwhile, Britain had to contend with the difficulties and contradictions inherent in administering its new lands, including the toleration of Catholicism in New France, which was anathema to the Puritan colonists of New England.

Some prominent British officials sought tighter political control over the American colonies, provoking a series of increasingly hostile reactions among the colonists. By 1775, American discontent erupted into full-scale revolt against the mother country, presenting the French with the opportunity for revenge.

MATT SCHUMANN

See also

Amherst, Jeffrey; Braddock's Campaign; Johnson, Sir William; Rogers, Robert; Tanaghrisson; Washington, George

References

Anderson, Fred. *Crucible of War: The Seven Years' War and the Fate of the Empire in British North America, 1754–1766.* New York: Vintage Books, 2001.

Fowler, William, Jr. *Empires at War: The French and Indian War and the Struggle for North America, 1754–1763.* New York: Walker, 2004.

Jennings, Francis. *Empire of Fortune: Crowns, Colonies, and Tribes in the Seven Years War in America.* New York: Norton, 1988.

French and Iroquois Wars

See Beaver Wars

Fur Trade

The North American fur trade comprised an important episode in the continent's history and had far-reaching consequences for the course of European and American westward expansion. Fur traders were the advance guard of European and American society and were typically the first Europeans to encounter Native Americans.

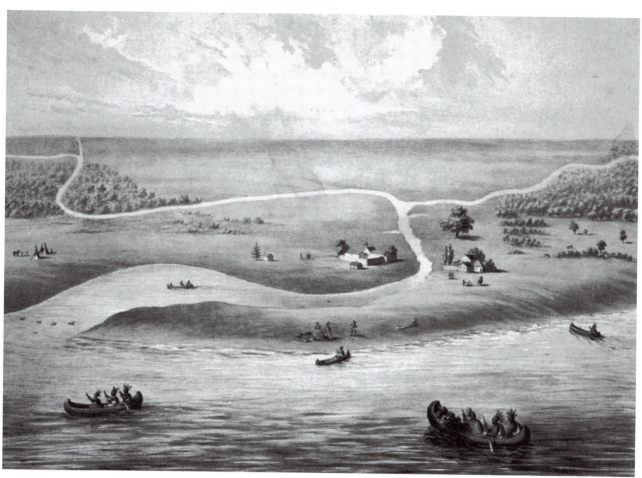

Native Americans engaged in fur trading at a post at the settlement of Chicago, circa 1820. The fur trade was an economic mainstay of Chicago in the early 19th century. (Library of Congress)

The concept of trapping animals and selling their fur to distant consumers also introduced a market economy to the Native Americans' world. In the process, however, the trade hunted many animals to extinction. Moreover, the fur trade was truly an international venture that included not only Native Americans but also the British, French, Russians, Spanish, Dutch, and Americans.

Before Europeans arrived in North America, Native Americans traded furs among themselves. The trade, however, occurred on the local level and served relatively small populations. Also, because many Native American groups had migratory habits, Native Americans did not accumulate more furs than could immediately be put to use or traded for other goods.

When Europeans arrived on the North Atlantic coast in the 16th century, they encouraged Native Americans to assist them in conducting a fur trade on a much larger scale. Presented with abundant and seemingly inexhaustible supplies of fur-bearing animals, Europeans desired sable, mink, otter, ermine, and especially beaver to use in the finest coats, clothes, and hats, establishing a trade to both Europe and parts of Asia. For their part, Native Americans sought iron tools and other items that only Europeans could provide.

Native Americans usually obtained the pelts for French, British, and Dutch traders because the Native Americans knew the land and had experience hunting. As the profits from the trade increased and animal pelts began to grow scarce, competition over trading territory among Native American groups intensified and led to a number of Iroquois wars in the mid-17th century. The Iroquois and their English and Dutch trading partners virtually annihilated the Hurons, who had served as the region's largest fur brokers. This initial phase of the fur trade frequently pitted Native Americans against each other as various groups struggled to achieve or maintain dominance in a particular region.

Meanwhile, another rivalry developed between the European powers to protect their profitable trading empires. Although the French had established a stronghold in Montreal early in the 17th century, the English challenged French dominance in the northern and western fur trade by chartering the Hudson's Bay Company in 1670. The French responded by putting more traders in the field. By 1680, 800 French traders worked in the backcountry and had established strong economic bonds with several Native American groups. The French aggressively continued to establish trading posts throughout the Great Lakes region until the end of the

Average Price of a North American Beaver Pelt in Britain, 1713–1763

Year	Price (shillings)
1713	5.03
1718	5.22
1723	7.84
1728	8.13
1733	8.07
1738	8.32
1743	8.27
1748	8.44
1753	10.87
1758	12.49
1763	16.34

French and Indian War (1754–1763), which ended in their defeat at the hands of the British.

After the French had been swept from the North American continent, the Hudson's Bay Company faced competition from the North West Company, a combination of former French companies and British, Scottish, and New England merchants. The Hudson's Bay Company and the Nor'westers, as the traders and trappers of the North West Company were called, moved aggressively throughout the interior of North America.

In the Ohio Valley and the region around the Great Lakes, the fur trade created a unique society. As in the colonial Northeast, Native Americans played a significant role in the interior fur trade, serving as guides when Europeans pushed into new regions and working as trappers. Native Americans were also an eager market for European goods, contributing to the trade's profitability, as Europeans not only made money trading with the Native American groups but also reaped significant rewards when the furs were sold in Europe. Each group, then, needed the other.

Native Americans often paid a high price for their involvement in the trade, however. European and American traders and trappers introduced alcohol and diseases to Native Americans, with devastating consequences. Epidemics of measles, mumps, influenza, and especially smallpox decimated tribal populations. The resultant decline in Native American populations further opened the door for white settlement, making the fur traders vanguards of European and, later, American empire.

This capitalistic relationship also forged more personal ties between Europeans and Native Americans. European traders frequently married Native American women. In fact, historians now estimate that as many as 40 percent of trappers may have married Native Americans. These unions generally benefited both parties, as European men desired companionship, and Native American women often gained power among their own people and usually a level of material comfort. European traders also used their marriages to gain access to traditional Native American lands and knowledge as well as gain hardworking partners for the arduous labor of the fur

trade. The children resulting from these marriages were known as Métis, who paradoxically fit in both European and Native American societies but who were sometimes ostracized from both.

As trappers moved west, they pushed into the land of the Louisiana Purchase and the Mexican-controlled Rocky Mountain region. Here such famous trappers as Jedediah Smith and Jim Bridger captured the imagination of the American public as they spent years in the mountains trapping beavers and other fur-bearing animals.

The Rocky Mountain trapping system differed substantially from the fur-trapping practices of the Hudson's Bay Company and other colonial traders. Rather than establishing a trading post and having Native American or British trappers periodically go to the post to exchange hides for goods, an American merchant named William Ashley created the annual rendezvous system in 1825. Every year Ashley sent a supply train to a spot in the Rocky Mountains where American trappers, Native Americans, and Mexicans came to trade. The only social event of the year for these trappers, the rendezvous assumed something of a carnival-like atmosphere with a variety of entertainments as well as storytelling, drinking, and dancing. The rendezvous became an important part of the culture of the Rocky Mountain fur trade.

The most successful of the traders was an American named John Jacob Astor. A German by birth, Astor had immigrated to America in the 1780s and shortly thereafter opened his own fur-trading firm in New York City, naming it the American Fur Company. From there he financed an army of trappers who spread out over the North American interior. By 1820 he had nearly established a monopoly on the American fur trade, the profits from which he famously reinvested in Manhattan real estate. He foresaw the decline of the fur trade in the mid-1830s and sold his interest in the business.

By that time fur-bearing animal populations were seriously suffering, hovering on the brink of extinction in many areas of North America. By 1838 the situation was so poor in Mexico, which ruled much of the Rocky Mountain region at the time, that the country declared a moratorium on trapping the animals to allow the populations a chance to recover. This marked the end of the trade in the interior, and by 1840 the Rocky Mountain trapping system had significantly declined. The fur trade in central North America was replaced by a thriving industry in buffalo hides, which would ensure the almost complete extinction of buffaloes by the end of the 19th century.

As some trappers explored the interior of the continent, others extended the trade along the Pacific coast. Since the 1740s, the Russian-American Company had been taking sea otter pelts, which they dubbed "soft gold," in Alaska. Between 1743 and 1800, 100 separate business ventures, all sponsored by the Russian-American Company, obtained pelts worth more than 8 million silver rubles. The Spanish Empire also engaged in some fur-trading activities along the Pacific coast.

The trade along the Pacific coast vastly accelerated at the close of the 18th century after Great Britain's Captain James Cook anchored in Nootka Sound on Vancouver Island in 1778. While on the island Cook obtained sea otter pelts from the Native Americans, and when his ships reached China the crew found that the otter pelts were worth a fortune. When news of this exchange spread, American and British merchants flocked to the Pacific Northwest to join in the trade, quickly out-harvesting Russian and Spanish traders. In fact, they were so successful that the sea otter population had dwindled to dangerously low levels by about 1815. The trade thus faltered, as too few sea otters remained to sustain a profitable business.

In 1811, however, the Pacific Fur Company, a subsidiary of Astor's American Fur Company, established a fur-trading post at Astoria, Oregon, to counter British dominance in the region, which served as the basis for later settlements of American trappers. Undeterred, the Hudson's Bay Company then pursued a policy to make the rich Columbia River region a so-called fur desert. This strategy, pursued by Peter Skene Ogden beginning in about 1834, involved hunting fur-bearing animals to near extinction, making it unprofitable for American fur traders to trap in the region and slowing American migration. The British remained the dominant force in the Northwest until the mid-1840s.

By midcentury the fur trade was exhausted in most of the United States. Only in Alaska did it continue to flourish. Throughout the 20th century furs have remained popular in the fashion world, although hunting for fur has been prohibited in the United States.

ADAM SOWARDS

See also

Beaver Wars; French and Indian War; Hudson's Bay Company; Iroquois; Wyandots

References

Cronon, William. *Changes in the Land: Indians, Colonists, and the Ecology of New England.* New York: Hill and Wang, 1983.

White, Richard. *The Middle Ground: Indians, Empires, and Republics in the Great Lakes Region, 1650–1815.* New York: Cambridge University Press, 1991.

Wishart, David. *The Fur Trade of the American West, 1807–1840: A Geographic Synthesis.* Lincoln: University of Nebraska Press, 1979.

G

Gaines, Edmund Pendleton

Birth Date: March 20, 1777
Death Date: June 6, 1849

U.S. Army officer. Born in Culpepper County, Virginia, on March 20, 1777, Edmund Pendleton Gaines moved with his family to the frontier of North Carolina and Tennessee, where at age 18 he served as a lieutenant of a volunteer company fighting Native Americans. In 1797 he joined the U.S. Army as an ensign and was quickly promoted to lieutenant. Assigned to the Old Southwest, Gaines surveyed the Natchez Trace from 1801 to 1804; served as military collector in Mobile, Alabama; and commanded Fort Stoddert.

Promoted to captain in 1807, Gaines led the troops who apprehended Aaron Burr following the failed Burr Conspiracy, and Gaines testified at Burr's trial. After an extended leave in which Gaines studied and began practicing law in the Mississippi Territory, he returned to active service as a major upon the outbreak of the War of 1812. He was advanced to colonel the following year. Gaines established his military reputation while covering the American retreat after the Battle of Chrysler's Farm on November 11, 1813, after which he was promoted to brigadier general. His defense of Fort Erie during August–September 1814, during which he was wounded, earned him a brevet to major general.

After recovering from his wound, Gaines returned to duty under Major General Andrew Jackson's Southern Command. Dispatched to southwestern Georgia in 1817 to protect settlers against the Seminoles, Gaines constructed Fort Scott on the Flint River and helped precipitate the First Seminole War (1817–1818) when he sent troops to attack Negro Fort, a former British outpost at Prospect Bluff on the Apalachicola River that runaway slaves had

refortified. On July 27, 1816, American gunboats opened fire, striking the fort's powder magazine with heated shot and causing an explosion that killed 270 runaways. After the Seminoles launched retaliatory raids and Chief Neamathla of Fowltown rejected Gaines's demands that those responsible be turned over, Gaines ordered Major David Twiggs to attack Fowltown on November 12. Following the First Seminole War, Gaines was named commander of the new Western Department in 1821 and took the field during Black Hawk's War in 1832 without seeing significant action.

Upon the outbreak of the Second Seminole War (1835–1842) in 1835, Gaines led some 1,100 men to the vicinity of Tampa, Florida, where he was besieged by Seminoles, wounded, and ended up quarreling with Major General Winfield Scott, comparing him to Benedict Arnold. After Gaines's failed Tampa campaign he returned to Louisiana, where he led a force across the Sabine River and held Nacogdoches during the Texas Revolution of 1836.

The ongoing conflict between Gaines and Scott worked more to the detriment of Gaines than to Scott, even though an official court of inquiry in 1837 criticized both commanders. When the War Department rejected Gaines's recommendations for using floating batteries and railroads to improve western defenses, Gaines believed that he had been foiled by Scott. Consequently, in 1840 Gaines bypassed the War Department and sent his recommendations directly to Congress. This may have played a role in his court-martial in late 1846 for raising Louisiana volunteers for Brigadier General Zachary Taylor without the express approval of the War Department. Gaines was acquitted on the grounds that his actions were excusable because Taylor was his subordinate and had been authorized to raise volunteers. Nevertheless, Gaines remained bitter toward Scott, and Taylor and Scott had their own personality clashes during the Mexican-American War (1846–1848). Gaines died in New Orleans on June 6, 1849, without having seen action in the Mexican-American War.

JUSTIN D. MURPHY

See also

Black Hawk War; Jackson, Andrew; Scott, Winfield; Seminole War, First; Seminole War, Second

References

Mahon, John K. *History of the Second Seminole War, 1835–1842.* Rev. ed. Gainesville: University Press of Florida, 1991.

Prucha, Francis Paul. *The Sword of the Republic: The United States Army on the Frontier, 1783–1846.* New York: Macmillan, 1969.

Silver, James W. *Edmund Pendleton Gaines: Frontier General.* Baton Rouge: Louisiana State University Press, 1949.

Gall

Birth Date: ca. 1840
Death Date: December 5, 1894

Hunkpapa Lakota (Sioux) war leader. Gall, also called Pizi, was born around 1840 near the Moreau River in present-day South Dakota. When Gall was young his father died, and the boy was raised by his mother and other relatives. At some point the Hunkpapa leader Sitting Bull adopted Gall as a younger brother. During Red Cloud's War (1866–1868) Gall participated in Sioux attacks against U.S. troops guarding the Bozeman Trail, including the annihilation of a detachment commanded by Captain William J. Fetterman on December 21, 1866. Gall keenly observed the tactics of Crazy Horse and other Sioux leaders and became adept at guerrilla warfare. In addition, Gall was dissatisfied with the terms of the Fort Laramie Treaty that ended the war in 1868.

Impressed by Gall's military abilities and his determination to defend the Sioux culture and lands, Sitting Bull appointed him war leader of the Hunkpapas. Gall led Hunkpapa warriors in the Great Sioux War (1876–1877) and distinguished himself in the Battle of the Little Bighorn (June 25–26, 1876). When Major Marcus Reno's detachment charged into the Hunkpapa camp, the soldiers killed Gall's two wives and three of his children. Infuriated by their deaths, Gall organized the Hunkpapa warriors and led a counterattack that drove Reno's troops from the camp. Gall's force then joined other Sioux under Crazy Horse in the attack that massacred Lieutenant Colonel George Armstrong Custer's battalion.

After the battle, the Hunkpapas attempted to escape pursuing troops. Gall and his warriors skirmished with Brigadier General George Crook's force and ambushed an army wagon train near Fort Keogh, but the Hunkpapas could not shake off their pursuers. In 1877 Sitting Bull led the Hunkpapas into Canada, where he hoped they could live in peace. However, the Sioux struggled to survive there, and in January 1881 Gall and 300 others returned to the United States, going to the Poplar Agency in Montana, where they surrendered to federal officials. Shortly afterward the band was moved to the Standing Rock Reservation in present-day North and South Dakota.

Convinced that accommodation with the whites was the best method to secure Sioux survival, Gall advised his followers to adopt white farming methods and send their children to white-run schools. He abandoned Native American religious practices and joined the Episcopal Church. Agent James McLaughlin later befriended Gall and treated him as the Hunkpapas' leader rather than dealing with Sitting Bull, who had returned to the United States in July 1881.

In 1888 when federal officials proposed a plan to divide the Sioux Reservation into six smaller reservations and take 9 million acres for white settlement, Sitting Bull urged Gall to oppose the measure. Gall was not swayed and signed the treaty on August 3, 1889. That same year he was appointed a judge in the Court of Indian Offenses. In 1890 he worked to prevent his followers from joining the Ghost Dance religious movement that swept through Native American communities. Gall's policies earned him the admiration of most whites, although many Sioux considered him a traitor to his people. He died at Oak Creek, South Dakota, on December 5, 1894.

JIM PIECUCH

A highly effective warrior, Hunkpapa Sioux leader Gall came into prominence at the Battle of the Little Bighorn on June 25, 1876, when he led a counterattack that drove Major Marcus Reno's troopers from the Hunkpapa camp. (National Archives)

See also

Crazy Horse; Crook, George; Dakota Sioux; Fetterman Massacre; Fort Laramie, Treaty of (1851); Fort Laramie, Treaty of (1868); Ghost Dance; Great Sioux War; Hunkpapa Sioux; Little Bighorn, Battle of the; Red Cloud's War; Sitting Bull; Standing Rock Reservation

References

Brown, Dee. *Bury My Heart at Wounded Knee.* New York: Holt, Rinehart and Winston, 1970.

Larson, Robert W. *Gall: Lakota War Chief.* Norman: University of Oklahoma Press, 2007.

Galvanized Yankees and Rebels

The terms "Galvanized Yankees" and "Galvanized Rebels" (or "Galvanized Confederates") were used to describe prisoners of war who were offered their freedom in return for military duty against their former comrades. Very few captured Northerners, perhaps just a few hundred, joined the Confederacy as Galvanized Rebels. Most who did so surrendered to Union troops at the first opportunity so that they could get back home. By far the largest use of ex-prisoners occurred in the North, where more than 6,000 Confederate prisoners availed themselves of the opportunity to leave prison camps to fight for the Union as Galvanized Yankees. They were ultimately organized into six regiments. The first recruitment of prisoners took place in the spring of 1862, when more than 200 incarcerated Confederates at Camp Douglas near Chicago joined Union units; most of these men were foreign-born Germans and Irish. The best known of these men was Henry Morton Stanley, a British citizen who was captured at the Battle of Shiloh (April 6–7, 1862) and then enlisted in an Illinois artillery battery. Stanley later became famous as a newspaper reporter and an African explorer.

The federal government initially resisted such attempts to recruit rebel prisoners. In early 1864 Major General Benjamin F. Butler, in command of the Department of Virginia and North Carolina, received permission to recruit a regiment of ex-Confederates. Organized as the 1st United States Volunteers, this unit first saw active duty in the Norfolk area. Lieutenant General Ulysses S. Grant, however, ordered the regiment to the western frontier rather than have these men fight against their former comrades. Grant saw the need for more soldiers on the Great Plains, which had been denuded of troops earlier in the war, in order to protect settlers, rail lines, and mail routes from Native American attacks.

Thus, between October 1864 and April 1865 five more regiments of Galvanized Yankees were recruited and sent west. The 1st U.S. Volunteers served in Minnesota and the Dakota Territory, the 2nd Regiment served in Arkansas and Kansas, the 3rd Regiment served in Nebraska and the Colorado Territory, the 4th Regiment served in the Department of the Northwest, and the 5th and 6th regiments served in the Nebraska, Colorado, and Utah territories. One company of the 5th Regiment escorted a wagon train into New Mexico. The regiments were mustered out of service between November 1865 and November 1866.

These ex-prisoner units were led by Union officers, who often commented on the high quality of their men. The soldiers comprising these units had differing reasons for joining, primarily wanting to get away from military prison camps. Some saw the chance to desert at the first opportunity and go home (although the desertion rate in these six regiments was remarkably similar to that of the average Union regiment). These men fought hostile Native Americans in numerous skirmishes along the western frontier. Hundreds of these troops died of disease or from the harsh Great Plains weather. When these units were disbanded, a number of men decided to remain out west and start new careers. After the war, the Grand Army of the Republic ignored these so-called white-washed Rebs, while their former comrades in the South wanted nothing at all to do with them.

RICHARD A. SAUERS

See also

Native Americans and the Civil War

References

Brown, D. Alexander. "Galvanized Yankees." *Civil War Times Illustrated* 4(10) (February 1966): 12–21.

Brown, D. Alexander. *The Galvanized Yankees.* Urbana: University of Illinois Press, 1963.

Ganienkehs

See Mohawks

Gatewood, Charles Bare
Birth Date: April 6, 1853
Death Date: May 20, 1896

U.S. Army officer and leader of Indian scouts during the Apache Campaign of the 1880s who played an instrumental role in securing Chiricahua Apache leader Geronimo's surrender in 1886. Born at Woodstock, Virginia, on April 6, 1853, Charles Bare Gatewood graduated from the U.S. Military Academy, West Point, in 1877. Commissioned a second lieutenant in the 6th Cavalry Regiment, he was posted to the Southwest, mostly working out of Camp (later Fort) Apache. He participated in the Victorio Campaign of 1879–1880, but he also devoted himself to understanding Native American culture and language, becoming something of an expert in and admirer of Native American ways in the process. Promoted to first lieutenant, Gatewood had already established himself as a capable leader of Apache scouts when Brigadier General George Crook assumed command of the Department of Arizona in 1882. Crook placed officers with the best grasp of the Apaches in charge of the various reservations and gave Gatewood charge of the difficult White Mountain Agency at Fort Apache, which he administered with notable success.

As the Apaches grew increasingly restive on the reservation, raiding across the Southwest and south into Mexico, Crook mounted a series of partially successful campaigns in which Gatewood and his Scouts figured prominently, but Gatewood's integrity and his sense of justice, driven by a growing sympathy for the Apaches, brought him into conflict with Crook. The escape of Geronimo following his much-celebrated surrender to Crook in March 1886 prompted Crook's removal and caused many to question his methods, including the broad use of Indian scouts.

When a large and grueling campaign into Mexico directed by Crook's replacement, Brigadier General Nelson A. Miles, failed to capture Geronimo, Miles turned reluctantly to Gatewood and his Indian scouts. Gatewood was the only officer available whom Geronimo knew and trusted. Gatewood located Geronimo and convinced him to surrender to General Miles in September 1886. Miles, apparently concerned that Gatewood might garner too much credit for bringing in the dreaded warrior, isolated the lieutenant, resulting in another troubled relationship with a superior.

Repeatedly overlooked for much-deserved promotion to captain, Gatewood was subsequently sent to the Dakota Territory but was not engaged in the final campaign against the Sioux that culminated in the tragedy at Wounded Knee in December 1890. The following year the 6th Cavalry was rushed to Wyoming in response to the so-called Johnson County Range War. In May 1892 Gatewood was badly wounded in the bombing of a building at Fort McKinney by one faction in that conflict. He never fully recovered from his injuries, and his health soon rendered him unfit for field duty. Gatewood died of abdominal cancer at Fort Monroe, Virginia, on May 20, 1896, still a first lieutenant after almost 20 years of service.

DAVID COFFEY

See also

Apaches; Apache Wars; Cavalry Regiment, 6th U.S.; Crook, George; Fort Apache; Geronimo; Mexico; Miles, Nelson Appleton; Scouts, Native American; Sioux; Victorio; Wounded Knee, Battle of

References

Gatewood, Charles B. *Lt. Charles Gatewood and His Apache War Memoir.* Edited by Louis Kraft. Lincoln: University of Nebraska Press, 2005.

Kraft, Louis. *Gatewood and Geronimo.* Albuquerque: University of New Mexico Press, 2000.

Utley, Robert M. *Frontier Regulars: The United States and the American Indian, 1866–1891.* New York: Macmillan, 1973.

Gatling, Richard
Birth Date: September 12, 1818
Death Date: February 26, 1903

Inventor and manufacturer best known for his invention of the Gatling gun, the precursor to the modern machine gun. Richard

Gatling was born on September 12, 1818, in Hertford County, North Carolina, the son of a wealthy planter. While attending local public schools, Gatling helped his father, who had invented several farm machines. Finishing school at age 19, Gatling spent a brief period of time as a schoolteacher, after which he owned and operated a country store for several years.

By age 20 Gatling was devoting most of his time to work on his inventions. He soon turned his attention to agricultural machines and invented and patented a rice-planting machine. In 1844 Gatling began to manufacture his machine in St. Louis, Missouri, while keeping a job as a dry goods clerk. His rice-planting machine was later adapted with great success to the planting of wheat.

The move to St. Louis proved a wise business choice, and by 1845 Gatling was dedicated full-time to the manufacturing and marketing of his machines. During the winter of 1845–1846 he underwent an experience that had a curious impact on his education. While traveling by river steamer en route to Pittsburgh, Pennsylvania, Gatling fell ill with smallpox. Because the steamer was trapped in ice for several weeks, he had to remain in his cabin without medical assistance at the risk of his own life. Determined never to let that happen again, he enrolled at the Indiana Medical College and later the Ohio Medical College in Cincinnati, from which he obtained his doctor of medicine degree in 1850. Although

Richard Jordan Gatling (1818–1903), inventor of the Gatling gun. (Library of Congress)

he never practiced medicine, he was nevertheless able to take care of himself and others in emergency situations.

Gatling's agricultural machine business continued to expand, first to Indianapolis and then to Springfield, Illinois. He also invented and marketed other machines that met with various degrees of success. With the impending American Civil War (1861–1865), Gatling began to turn his attention toward military equipment. He invented a marine steam ram and a rapid-fire gun, which became known as the Gatling gun.

Patented in 1862, the Gatling gun was a hand-cranked weapon with six barrels that revolved around a central shaft. The .58-caliber shells dropped from a hopper mounted on top of the gun. By 1876 the gun had a theoretical firing rate of some 1,200 rounds per minute, but 400 was a more realistic figure for combat.

The early models experienced a number of problems that prevented the device from receiving serious military attention. Gatling's request for a field test was refused, and a fire that destroyed the company that produced the early models of the gun further complicated his efforts to have his invention accepted by the military.

In 1862 a new company was able to produce 12 copies of the Gatling gun that improved upon the earlier models. The U.S. Navy employed a few of Gatling's guns in 1862, and U.S. Army major general Benjamin Butler purchased 12 of them. Gatling, who made the plans for his gun available to foreign governments, continued to meet with strong resistance from the War Department, however. He was finally able to demonstrate an improved model in 1865, manufactured by the Cooper Fire Arms Manufacturing Company of Frankfort, Pennsylvania.

Tested under the direction of Brigadier General Alexander B. Dyer, the gun performed well, and after a few modifications the army agreed to adopt the weapon the following year. The gun underwent further enhancements, with the U.S. Navy adopting the improved 1868 model. The Gatling gun saw service with the army in the Indian Wars in the West. Various models of the gun were adopted and used throughout the world, namely among the French, Russian, and British armies.

In the mid-1880s Gatling sold his patents and manufacturing rights to Samuel Colt's company. The U.S. Army used a later version of the gun during the Spanish-American War (1898), but the gun was reaching the end of its useful life. The army declared it obsolete in 1911.

In 1886 Gatling began working on a cannon by using a new metal alloy. The gun, for which the U.S. Congress had appropriated $40,000, exploded during tests. Gatling was convinced that the gun's breech had been sabotaged at the factory. Disappointed, he turned once more to agricultural machines. He set up a new firm in St. Louis to produce motorized plows. Gatling died on February 26, 1903, while on a visit in New York City.

José Valente

See also
Gatling Gun

References
Johnson, F. Roy, and E. Frank Stephenson Jr. *The Gatling Gun and Flying Machine of Richard and Henry Gatling*. Murfreesboro, TN: Johnson Publishing, 1979.
Wahl, Paul, and Donald R. Toppel. *The Gatling Gun*. New York: Arco, 1965.

Gatling Gun

Famous mechanical-fire gun introduced in 1862 during the American Civil War (1861–1865) by Richard Jordan Gatling. Well aware of problems from the buildup of heat, Gatling designed his gun with six rotating barrels around a central axis, each barrel fired in turn and each with its own bolt and firing pin. In a firing rate of 300 rounds per minute, each barrel would thus be utilized only 50 times.

The Gatling gun employed a hopper for the ammunition. The first model also employed steel cylinders with a percussion cap at the end, a round, and paper cartridges with the charge. The production model did away with the percussion cap in favor of a rimfire cartridge. Turning the crank rotated the barrels, dropped in the rounds, and fired each barrel in turn. By 1876 the Gatling gun had a theoretical rate of fire of 1,200 rounds per minute, although 400 per minute was a more realistic figure for combat conditions.

The U.S. Army's chief of ordnance, Colonel John W. Ripley, who was well known for his opposition to innovative weaponry, blocked adoption of the Gatling gun, and despite Gatling's appeals to President Abraham Lincoln, the army never adopted the gun. Its only use in the Civil War came when Major General Benjamin Butler purchased six of them at his own expense and employed them effectively in the Siege of Petersburg near the end of the war.

In 1864 Gatling redesigned the gun so that each barrel had its own chamber. This helped prevent the leakage of gas. Gatling also adopted center-fire cartridges. These and other refinements produced a rate of fire of about 300 rounds per minute. Finally, in 1866 the U.S. Army purchased 100 Gatling guns, equally divided between 6-barrel models of 1-inch caliber and 10-barrel models of .50-inch caliber. Gatling worked out a licensing agreement with Colt Arms to produce the gun.

The Gatling gun provided effective service in the Indian Wars in the American West and in the Spanish-American War of 1898. The gun remained the standard mechanical rapid-fire weapon until the introduction of the Maxim Gun, the first true machine gun.

Most U.S. Army garrisons in the American West maintained Gatling guns mounted on horse-drawn carriages. Gatlings often accompanied large expeditions into the field and were useful in defending fixed positions such as forts or camps and in supporting assaults. Gatling guns were not decisive in determining the outcome of any wars between Native Americans and the army but were critical at the tactical level in a number of engagements. Lieutenant James W. Pope employed several Gatlings with great effect during a fight with Native Americans in western Texas on August 30, 1874. That same year, Major William Redwood Price utilized some of the guns from the 8th Cavalry during the Red River War against the Cheyennes, Comanches, Kiowas, and Arapahos that stretched from Indian Territory (Oklahoma) into Texas and New Mexico. Gatlings also played a notable role in both the Nez Perce War of 1877 and the Bannock-Shoshone War of 1878, where mountainous terrain often gave Native Americans an advantage and the firepower of Gatlings was critical in supporting attacks.

The most famous incident involving Gatling guns during the period came amid the Great Sioux War (Black Hills War) of 1876–1877. Brigadier General Alfred H. Terry and Colonel John Gibbon included Gatling guns with their columns in a campaign best known for the defeat of George Armstrong Custer at the Battle of the Little Bighorn (June 25–26, 1876). Custer famously declined to take a detachment of Gatling guns into action for fear that they would slow him down, a decision that probably made sense but that historians have understandably questioned ever since.

Gatling guns were also employed effectively by U.S. forces during the Spanish-American War (1898) but were rendered obsolete by true machine guns during World War I (1914–1918). The design was reborn after World War II (1939–1945), however, when electrically fired variants were developed for aircraft and a wide array of ground and naval antiaircraft and antimissile systems.

LANCE JANDA AND SPENCER C. TUCKER

See also

Custer, George Armstrong; Great Sioux War; Little Bighorn, Battle of the; Nez Perce War

References

Berk, Joseph. *Gatling Gun: 19th Century Machine Gun to 21st Century Vulcan.* New York: Paladin, 1991.

Hughes, James B. *The Gatling Gun Notebook: A Collection of Data and Illustrations.* Woonsocket, RI: Andrew Mowbray, 2001.

Wahl, Paul, and Donald R. Toppel. *The Gatling Gun.* New York: Arco, 1965.

Gayanashagowa

See Great Law of Peace of the Longhouse People

Geronimo

Birth Date: June 16, 1829
Death Date: February 26, 1909

Chiricahua Apache war leader and medicine man. Geronimo, named Goyahkla at birth, was born on June 16, 1829, on the upper Gila River near the present-day Arizona–New Mexico border. He was given the name "Geromino" by the Mexicans; Geronimo is Spanish for Jerome, and Saint Jerome is the Catholic saint of lost causes. Legend has it that Mexican soldiers invoked Saint Jerome's name when they fought against Geronimo's raiding parties, and the name eventually stuck. Geronimo was born into the Bedonkohe band, which was closely associated with the Chiricahuas. As a youth Geronimo honed his skills as a hunter and marksman and, most importantly, learned survival skills that would serve him well throughout his storied career.

In 1850 at age 21, Geronimo embarked on an expedition with the Mimbres Apache war leader Mangas Coloradas to Janos, Mexico, where they engaged in raids against several Mexican settlements. The Bedonkohes frequently allied themselves with the more numerous Mimbres band. During Geronimo's absence, a group of Mexicans attacked his family's encampment; Geronimo's mother, wife, and three young children were all slain. The tragedy remained with Geronimo the rest of his life and instilled in him a deep hatred of Mexicans.

After the 1850 expedition, Geronimo continued to develop warrior and raiding skills under Mangas Coloradas. Geronimo engaged in a number of raids against both Mexicans and Americans and is thought to have been a participant in the Battle of Apache Pass in July 1862. He began associating with other notable Apache leaders such as Victorio, Juh, and Cochise and lived among the followers of Cochise. In 1871 during a particularly bloody battle in Arizona against U.S. military forces, Geronimo may have been responsible for the death of Lieutenant Howard B. Cushing. In the meantime, Geronimo continued to raid settlements on both sides of the U.S.-Mexican border and earned infamy in the press in both America and Mexico.

Geronimo eventually allied himself with Victorio and in 1877 took up residence with his followers at the Ojo Caliente Reservation in New Mexico. Shortly after Geronimo's arrival, the reservation agent had him arrested and placed in irons. This began a long series of intrepid breakouts and arrests. Whether Geronimo broke out of imprisonment or was released is somewhat unclear, but by 1878 he was back in Mexico and allied with the Nednhi Apache war chief Juh. Geronimo participated in numerous raids conducted by Juh and his followers. Juh's band subsequently took up residence at the San Carlos Reservation in southern Arizona, where Juh and Geronimo were forbidden to leave by U.S. authorities. Nevertheless, in 1881 Geronimo escaped along with Juh and led their followers into Mexico's Sierra Madre, where they settled for about a year. In 1882 Geronimo and Juh led a daring raid on the San Carlos Reservation, ostensibly to win the release of Chief Loco, but perhaps as many as several hundred Native Americans located there decided to follow Geronimo and Juh.

In 1884 after Geronimo had again returned to San Carlos, he voluntarily surrendered to American authorities; however, less than two years later he eluded officials and was again on the run. Geronimo remained at large until March 1886, when he agreed to surrender to Brigadier General George Crook at Cañon de los Embudos, just south of the U.S.-Mexican border. However, Geronimo and his followers halted temporarily in southeastern Arizona, where an unscrupulous liquor salesman from

Chiricahua Apache leader Geronimo, a pivotal figure during the final phase of the Indian Wars of the late 19th century. In 1886, Geronimo was the last major recalcitrant Indian leader to surrender. (National Archives)

Tombstone clandestinely entered the encampment and proceeded to provide enough liquor to inebriate Geronimo and his followers. The salesman then convinced Geronimo that if he and his followers did not leave the area at once, they would likely be killed by U.S. forces.

Geronimo and his people fled the area and were on the run for at least six months. Meanwhile, Geronimo continued to conduct raids. U.S. forces pursued Geronimo and the Apaches tenaciously, however, and by the late summer of 1886 the Native Americans were exhausted, sick, and hungry. Thus, in early September 1886 Geronimo sent word that he would surrender. He met personally with Brigadier General Nelson A. Miles in Skeleton Canyon, Arizona, to discuss the terms. On September 4 the Apaches formally surrendered. Geronimo and some of his followers remained at Fort Bowie until September 8, at which time they were placed on a train bound for Florida.

Eventually Geronimo and other Apache leaders were detained at Fort Marion in St. Augustine. Their families, however, were sent to Fort Pickens near Pensacola, some 300 miles away. This violated the terms of the surrender, which guaranteed that families would not be split up. By May 1888 the Apaches were reunited in Mount Vernon, Alabama. Geronimo embraced his new life, cooperating with U.S. officials and missionaries, converting to Christianity, and even becoming a local justice of the peace. In 1892 the Apaches were relocated again, this time to Indian Territory (Oklahoma). Geronimo died at the age of 79 at Fort Sill, Oklahoma, on February 26, 1909.

PAUL G. PIERPAOLI JR.

See also

Apache Pass, Battle of; Apaches; Apache Wars; Cochise; Crook, George; Fort Sill; Mangas Coloradas; Miles, Nelson Appleton; Ojo Caliente Reservation, New Mexico; San Carlos Reservation; Victorio

References

Debo, Angie. *Geronimo: The Man, His Time, His Place.* Norman: University of Oklahoma Press, 1976.

Skinner, Woodward B. *The Apache Rock Crumbles: The Captivity of Geronimo's People.* Pensacola: Skinner Publications, 1987.

Stockel, H. Henrietta. *Survival of the Spirit: Chiricahua Apaches in Captivity.* Reno: University of Nevada Press, 1993.

Geronimo Campaign
Start Date: 1881
End Date: 1886

Prolonged U.S. Army campaign to capture Apache warrior Geronimo and his band of followers that lasted from 1881 to 1886. Although not a chief, Geronimo had emerged as the leader of disenchanted Chiricahua and Warm Springs Apache warriors at the San Carlos Reservation, where the U.S. government had concentrated numerous Apache bands. Dissension among the bands combined with increased white settlement in Arizona, where the American population doubled from 40,000 to 80,000 between 1880 and 1882, dramatically increased tensions.

Amid this atmosphere Nakaidoklini, a White Mountain Apache shaman, began preaching that a special dance would bring dead Apaches back to life and cause the whites to disappear. When the U.S. Army suppressed the movement on the White Mountain Apache Reservation, many White Mountain Apaches fled to the Chiricahua camps at San Carlos. Fearing an attack, Geronimo, along with Apache leaders Juh, Nachez, and Chato, fled San Carlos on October 1, 1881, with 74 Chiricahuas and headed to the Sierra Madre in Mexico, where they joined Apaches under Nana.

After resting their forces in the Sierra Madre, in April 1882 Geronimo, Juh, Nachez, and Chato crossed the border into the United States determined to add more Apache warriors to their forces. Slipping around forces that District of New Mexico commander Colonel Ranald S. Mackenzie had stationed along the border, on April 19 Geronimo's warriors attacked the Camp Goodwin subagency and freed Warm Springs leader Loco and several hundred other Apaches. They then made their way up the Gila River before heading to the Peloncillo Range along the Arizona–New Mexico border. They left behind 30–50 whites dead.

On April 23 Lieutenant Colonel George A. Forsyth's patrol, consisting of five troops from the 4th Cavalry Regiment and one scout troop, attacked the Apaches in Horseshoe Canyon, losing five dead and seven wounded and failing to prevent Geronimo's forces from escaping into northern Mexico. Captain Tullius C. Tupper now picked up Geronimo's trail and pursued him into Mexico with two troops of the 6th Cavalry.

On April 28 Tupper caught up with the Apaches but was unable to dislodge them from their well-defended positions and was forced to withdraw. Unfortunately for the Apaches, on April 29 they were ambushed by 250 Mexican infantry troops under Colonel Lorenzo Garcia. Although the Apaches killed 22 Mexican soldiers and wounded 16, they lost 78 people, mostly women and children, before escaping into the Sierra Madre. Meanwhile, Forsyth had tended to his wounded and joined forces with Tupper. On April 30, however, the combined American force was met by Garcia, who ordered them out of Mexico.

The growing unrest among the Apaches convinced General William Tecumseh Sherman, commanding general of the U.S. Army who was actually touring Arizona at the time of Geronimo's raid on the Camp Goodwin subagency, to replace Colonel Orlando B. Willcox with Brigadier General George S. Crook as commander of the Department of Arizona. Upon assuming command at Whipple Barracks on September 4, 1882, Crook set out to establish military control over the reservations by improving conditions and placing trusted officers on each reservation to avoid unnecessary confrontations. He then turned his attention to Geronimo's forces in the Sierra Madre. This task was made easier by improved cooperation with Mexico, which in July 1882 had agreed to a treaty that allowed both Mexican and American troops to cross the border when in pursuit of Apaches. Crook augmented his forces with trusted Apache scouts and replaced supply wagons with pack mules in order to keep his forces provisioned when operating in rugged terrain. These measures would prove to be highly effective in the ensuing campaign.

After Apaches under Chato launched a raid into Arizona and New Mexico in late March 1883 that left at least 11 whites dead, Crook began stockpiling supplies and concentrating forces at Willcox, Arizona, and met with MacKenzie in Albuquerque and Mexican officials in Chihuahua and Sonora to coordinate the campaign. By May 1, 1883, Crook had posted portions of the 3rd and 6th Cavalry at key border crossings and crossed into Mexico with a column of 193 scouts, including 1 of Chato's raiders who had earlier been apprehended, under Captain Emmet Crawford and Lieutenant Charles B. Gatewood; 45 troops of the 6th Cavalry under Captain Adna Chaffee; and a pack train of 350 mules. On May 15 Crawford's scouts attacked a camp led by Chato and Benito, killing 9 warriors and destroying 30 lodges before the Apaches escaped. When a captured Apache girl revealed to Crook that most of the Native Americans would be willing to surrender, he sent her as an emissary to the Apache leaders. Over the next two days Chiricahua and Warm Spring Apaches, including Geronimo, Chato, Benito,

Nachez, Nana, and Loco, came to Crook's camp to discuss terms of surrender.

After a week of negotiations the Apaches agreed to surrender, although Geronimo asked for time to gather his scattered followers. Running low on provisions, Crook was forced to assent to Geronimo's terms and departed Mexico on June 10 with 52 Apache warriors and 273 women and children. Although Crook was somewhat concerned about whether the Apache leaders would honor their promise to surrender and indeed received some ridicule when they were slow to arrive at San Carlos, by mid-March 1884 Nachez, Chato, Mangas, and Geronimo had led their bands to San Carlos. Only a few renegade Apaches remained in the Sierra Madre, and these were not enough to present a major threat. Crook's strategy had proven highly effective. His use of pack mules not only ensured that his troops could remain in the field for a longer amount of time but also enabled them to enter the rugged Sierra Madre, where even few Mexicans had dared to venture. More important, his use of Apache scouts had enabled him to find the Apache camps and also demoralized the Apaches by having their own people assisting the enemy.

Winning the campaign and securing the peace, however, proved to be difficult. Power struggles between the U.S. Army and the Indian agents on the reservations undermined Crook's efforts to maintain positive relations, although he did succeed in winning over Chato. On May 17, 1885, 42 Apache warriors and 92 women and children under Geronimo, Nachez, Chihuahua, Nana, and Mangas fled San Carlos. Geronimo and his followers escaped directly to Mexico, while Chihuahua and his followers raided southeastern Arizona and southwestern New Mexico for three weeks, eluding 20 cavalry troops and 100 scouts before crossing into Mexico.

Crook responded in the same way that he had organized the 1883 campaign, concentrating approximately 3,000 soldiers along the border and sending scouting expeditions into Mexico, but this time he enjoyed less success. Although Crook's scouting expeditions attacked Apache camps on June 23, July 28, August 7, and September 22, in each engagement the Apaches quickly dispersed with minimal losses. In late September, 20 Apache warriors successfully crossed the border into southeastern Arizona and stole a number of horses. This was followed in November by a raid in which Chihuahua's brother, Josanie, led a dozen warriors into Arizona and New Mexico in an area that covered some 1,200 miles. The warriors successfully evaded all army units sent after them, and the raid resulted in the deaths of 38 people and the capture of 250 head of livestock.

Meanwhile, on November 29 Lieutenant General Philip Sheridan arrived at Fort Bowie to confer with Crook and demand more vigorous action. Crook dispatched two columns into Mexico. Crawford commanded two companies composed almost exclusively of White Mountain and Chiricahua scouts led by lieutenants Marion P. Maus and William E. Shipp. Captain Wirt Davis commanded a company of Apache scouts and one cavalry troop. Davis and Crawford moved deep into Mexico, where on January

9, 1886, Crawford succeeded in locating the main Apache camp on the Aros River, approximately 200 miles south of the border. Although the Apaches had fled, Crawford sent an Apache woman as an emissary to the Apache leaders, including Geronimo, who agreed to meet with Crawford at the captured Apache camp on January 11. Before the meeting could take place, however, a force of 150 Mexican militia attacked the camp, not realizing that they were attacking Crawford and Apache scouts rather than Geronimo and his band. After Crawford was killed in the unfortunate engagement, Maus ordered the column to withdraw. Nevertheless, on January 13 Geronimo, Nachez, Chihuahua, and Nana met with Maus and promised to surrender to Crook within two months. Nine Apaches, including Geronimo's wife and Nana, were offered as hostages to demonstrate good faith.

Geronimo and the other Apache leaders met with Crook on March 25 and 27 at Cañon de los Embudos, where they agreed to surrender on the condition that they would not be removed from the Southwest for more than two years. On March 28, however, Geronimo and Nachez, who had obtained mescal from a traveling trader and drank to excess, escaped along with 20 men and 13 women from the escort column that was leading them to Fort Bowie. Meanwhile, Sheridan informed Crook that the agreed-upon terms of surrender were unacceptable.

Once informed of Geronimo's flight, Sheridan demanded a more conventional military strategy of relying on regular troops rather than Apache scouts. On April 1 Crook requested that he be relieved of his command. Sheridan happily complied and promptly appointed Brigadier General Nelson A. Miles commander of the Department of Arizona.

After assuming command at Fort Bowie on April 12, 1886, Miles stationed mobile forces along the border and placed heliograph stations on 27 mountains and high points to keep troops informed about enemy movements. When Apache raiding parties crossed the border on April 27, they were vigorously pursued but not captured. On May 5 Miles dispatched Captain Henry W. Lawton into Mexico with an expeditionary force consisting of 35 troops from the 4th Cavalry, 20 infantrymen from the 8th Regiment, 20 Apache scouts, and 100 pack mules and 30 drivers.

During the course of the next four months Lawton pursued the Apaches across northern Mexico, marching some 2,000 miles, but was unable to force an engagement. Meanwhile, Miles rounded up the Warm Springs and Chiricahua Apaches from the reservations and removed them by train to Florida. In addition, he sent Gatewood and two Apache scouts to join Lawton in Mexico and attempt to negotiate with Geronimo. When Gatewood met with Geronimo on August 24 and informed him that the Chiricahuas were being shipped to Florida, Geronimo agreed to surrender to Miles personally. On September 4, 1886, Miles accepted Geronimo's surrender at Skeleton Canyon on the promise that the lives of the Apaches would be spared and that they would be allowed to rejoin their families in Florida. Although President Grover Cleveland had wanted and even ordered that they be turned over to

civil officials for trial in Arizona, he eventually, albeit reluctantly, accepted the terms that Miles had negotiated.

Geronimo's surrender brought an end to the Indian Wars in the Southwest but did not bring an end to controversy. Despite Miles's promises, Geronimo and his warriors were initially not reunited with their families at Fort Pickens but instead were held at Fort Marion. The Indian Rights Association, which included Crook, successfully pressured the government into reuniting the warriors with their families in 1887. In 1894 the Chiricahuas were transferred to Fort Sill in Indian Territory (Oklahoma). Four years after Geronimo's death at Fort Sill in 1909, 187 Chiricahuas were allowed to join the Mescalero Reservation in New Mexico, but the remainder stayed at Fort Sill.

JUSTIN D. MURPHY

See also

Apaches; Chaffee, Adna Romanza, Sr.; Crawford, Emmet; Crook, George; Fort Sill; Gatewood, Charles Bare; Geronimo; Lawton, Henry Ware; Mackenzie, Ranald Slidell; Miles, Nelson Appleton; San Carlos Reservation; Scouts, Native American; Sheridan, Philip Henry; Willcox, Orlando Bolivar

References

Aleshire, Peter. *The Fox and the Whirlwind: General George Crook and Geronimo, A Paired Biography.* New York: Wiley, 2000.

Utley, Robert M. *Frontier Regulars: The United States and the American Indian, 1866–1891.* New York: Macmillan, 1973.

Worcester, Donald E. *The Apaches: Eagles of the Southwest.* Norman: University of Oklahoma Press, 1979.

Ghost Dance

Pan-Indian religious beliefs and ceremonies that began among various Numic-speaking peoples. The Ghost Dance emerged as a Pan-Indian faith in two movements: 1869–1870 and 1889–1890. Both movements began among the Northern Paiutes of the Walker River Reservation in western Nevada and promised the reunification of the living and the dead on a renewed earth, the return of game animals, and, according to some accounts, the elimination of nonnatives or nonbelievers. Both movements found adherents far beyond the Numu homeland; there were, however, important differences between the two movements. The latter was more widespread and exhibited much greater Christian syncretism. "Ghost Dance" is a non-Indian term; each Native American group has its own specific name for the ceremony.

The Ghost Dance religion exhibited similarities to Pan-Indian religions stretching back to the 18th century. During the French and Indian War (1754–1763), the Delaware prophet Neolin preached that Native American peoples must wean themselves of dependence on the Europeans to clear a path to heaven. His teachings provided the spiritual underpinning of Pontiac's Rebellion (1763). A half century later the Shawnee prophet Tenskwatawa announced a similar prophecy, which played a key role in his brother Tecumseh's attempt to create a Pan-Indian political and

Depiction of a Ghost Dance ceremony. The Ghost Dance movement promised a reunification of the living and the dead on a renewed Earth. Misinterpretation of the movement led to the tragic Battle of Wounded Knee in 1890. Illustration from James Mooney's 1896 report on the Ghost Dance. (James Mooney, *The Ghost Dance Religion*. In the *Fourteenth Annual Report of the American Bureau of Ethnography*, 1896)

military alliance. On the Columbia Plateau, the Prophet Dances and the Dreamer Religion of the Wanapum prophet Smohalla also proposed a millennial vision of a Pan-Indian future.

The first Pan-Indian Ghost Dance movement emerged in the vicinity of the Walker River Reservation around 1869. The 1870 Ghost Dance has remained far more obscure than the religious movement that followed two decades later. The 1870 Ghost Dance prophet was Wodziwob (Gray Hair or Gray Head), a Paiute who lived at Walker River. Announcing his initial prophecies at communal gatherings, Wodziwob told his followers that Native American people could radically transform the present through supernatural means by practicing the prescribed ceremonies. He prophesied a return of the old ways, with all Native Americans—living and dead—reunited on a renewed earth.

The ceremonial base of both Ghost Dance movements was the Great Basin Round Dance, a rite that served a number of important ritual purposes during communal gatherings such as rabbit drives and fish runs. Men, women, and children all participated. The dances occurred five nights in succession, and the cycle could be repeated up to 20 times a year.

The 1870 Ghost Dance spread north and west to the Washoes, Pyramid Lake Paiutes, Surprise Valley Paiutes, Modocs, Klamaths, Shastas, Karoks, Maidus, and Patwins. In California, the dances inspired revivals of preexisting religions (the Kuksu or God Impersonating cult) or were transformed into new belief systems (the Bole-Maru and Dream religions). The 1870 Ghost Dance spread at least as far east as the Rocky Mountains, where the Shoshones, Bannocks, and Utes all practiced the religion continuously throughout the last three decades of the 19th century.

The second Ghost Dance movement also began on the Walker River Reservation. The prophet Wovoka experienced his first vision on New Year's Day in 1889. He reported traveling to heaven and meeting God. He was instructed to return to earth and tell the people to lead good and loving lives and follow a ritual that, if faithfully obeyed, would reunite them with their deceased loved ones and friends in a world without "death or sickness or old age." The first dances took place at Walker River shortly thereafter, and word of the prophecy spread rapidly to reservations across the West. Native American peoples from across the Great Basin attended the second series of dances later that spring, and by the end of 1889 a delegation had arrived from the Lakotas and other Plains peoples.

Broad similarities notwithstanding, several aspects of Wovoka's doctrine marked important departures from the earlier movement. First, the 1890 Ghost Dance was as redemptive as it was transformative. Wovoka did prophesy a radical transformation of the existing order—a renewal of the earth and the reunification of all Native American peoples—but he also preached a gospel of peace, love, and accommodation that, by eliminating many of the causes of internal discord, served to strengthen tribal communities. Caspar Edson, an Arapaho who visited Wovoka in August 1891, was the only Native American person to record a written version of the doctrine: the famed Messiah Letter. Wovoka told his followers to live at peace with the nonnative immigrants. On the other hand, his words also could be interpreted to suggest that nonnatives, or even Native American nonbelievers, would not survive the coming cataclysm. Second, Wovoka's doctrine exhibited far greater Christian influence than the earlier movement. By several accounts, Wovoka claimed that he was Jesus and even reportedly showed the stigmata of crucifixion to a number of Native American seekers, including the Cheyenne holy man Porcupine.

In most accounts, the Ghost Dance of 1890 has been inextricably linked to the tragic events that took place on the Lakota reservations. The popularity and perceived militancy of the religion among the Lakotas (many Lakota dancers wore Ghost Shirts, which were reputed to be bulletproof) panicked white settlers and elicited an overwhelming military response. Following Sitting Bull's assassination at the Standing Rock Agency in December 1890, the Miniconjou (Minneconjou) Sioux leader Bigfoot led his band south toward a hoped-for refuge at the Pine Ridge Agency in present-day South Dakota. Instead, they were intercepted by the U.S. 7th Cavalry. On December 29, 1890, along the banks of Wounded Knee Creek, Bigfoot and more than 150 of his people died as the soldiers' attempt to take them into custody degenerated into a slaughter.

Contrary to popular understanding, the Ghost Dance religion was not a short-lived phenomenon. In many cases, it inspired cultural revitalization among Native Americans. The Lakotas continued to practice the religion for at least two years after the tragedy at Wounded Knee. In 1902 the Lakota apostle Kicking Bear once again visited the prophet Wovoka and later introduced the religion to the Fort Peck Reservation in Montana. The Ghost Dance religion also facilitated the revitalization of Pawnee culture in the 1890s and in the early 20th century, while the Kiowas practiced a modified version of the dance from 1894 to 1916. Moreover, the Ghost Dance continues to be practiced today among the Paiutes, Shoshones, Bannocks, and Utes, with whom it was a customary religious practice long before the movements of 1870 and 1890.

GREGORY E. SMOAK

See also

Neolin; Paiutes, Northern; Sitting Bull; Tecumseh; Wounded Knee, Battle of; Wovoka

References

Hittman, Michael. *Wovoka and the Ghost Dance.* Expanded ed. Edited by Don Lynch. Lincoln: University of Nebraska Press, 1997.

Mooney, James. *The Ghost Dance Religion and the Sioux Outbreak of 1890.* Lincoln: University of Nebraska Press, 1991.

Gibbon, John

Birth Date: April 20, 1827
Death Date: February 6, 1896

U.S. Army officer. John Gibbon was born on April 20, 1827, in Philadelphia, Pennsylvania. He later moved to Charlotte, North Carolina. Gibbon secured an appointment to the U.S. Military Academy, West Point, and was commissioned in the army upon graduation in 1847 and was posted to the artillery.

Gibbon fought in the Mexican-American War (1846–1848) as well as in the Third Seminole War (1855–1858) in Florida. Promoted to first lieutenant in 1850, on September 25, 1854, he was appointed an instructor of artillery at West Point. In 1859 he was promoted to captain and published *The Artillerist's Manual*, which was used by the army for many years.

When the American Civil War (1861–1865) began, three of Gibbon's brothers signed up to fight for the Confederacy, but he

Colonel John Gibbon led U.S. Army forces against the Nez Perce in the hard-fought Battle of the Big Hole River in southwestern Montana during August 9–10, 1877. (Library of Congress)

remained with the Union. Beginning in October 1861 he served as chief of artillery for Brigadier General Irvin McDowell. On May 2, 1862, Gibbon was commissioned a brigadier general of volunteers and was assigned to command a brigade in the Army of the Potomac. Gibbon's "Iron Brigade" became one of the best units in the Union Army.

Gibbon then went on to divisional command in Major General John F. Reynolds's I Corps and was wounded in the Battle of Fredericksburg (December 13, 1862) and then became commander of the 2nd Division of Major General Winfield S. Hancock's II Corps. Gibbon was wounded again during the Battle of Gettysburg (July 1–3, 1863) in which he temporarily exercised corps command.

Upon his recovery, for a short time Gibbon commanded the draft depots in Philadelphia and Cleveland before returning to the 2nd Division to fight during the entirety of Lieutenant General Ulysses S. Grant's Overland Campaign and Siege of Petersburg (June 15, 1864–April 3, 1865). On June 7, 1864, Gibbon was promoted to major general of volunteers. By January 1865 he was commanding XXIV Corps in the Army of the James. He was one of the officers assigned to receive the Confederate surrender at Appomattox. Gibbon achieved great success during the Civil War despite the fact that he had no political connections, so important for gaining rank and honors during that era.

After the Civil War, Gibbon accepted a commission as a colonel in the regular army and was eventually assigned to command the 7th U.S. Infantry Regiment, a unit that he helped shape into one of the premier infantry regiments of the late 19th century. Sent to the West, Gibbon was stationed in Nebraska, the Dakota Territory, the Montana Territory, and the Wyoming Territory. During the Great Sioux War (Black Hills War) of 1876–1877, Gibbon led one of the three converging columns assigned to find and engage the enemy. Gibbon's column arrived too late to save Lieutenant Colonel George Custer's battalion in the Battle of the Little Bighorn (June 25–26, 1876) but did rescue the remainder of the 7th Cavalry and bury the soldiers killed in the battle.

Gibbon's other most noteworthy frontier fight was against the Nez Perces led by Chief Joseph in the Battle of the Big Hole (August 9–10, 1877) in Montana. Gibbon's orders were to force the Nez Perces back to Idaho. He surprised the Nez Perces, inflicting significant casualties, but was then driven back. Gibbon's effort nevertheless had a devastating impact on Joseph's people, who ultimately forced to surrender before they could make their escape into Canada.

Gibbon was promoted to brigadier general in 1885 and took command of the Department of the Columbia in the Pacific Northwest during threatened anti-Chinese riots in Seattle. He retired from the U.S. Army on April 20, 1891. Gibbon devoted much time to writing several dozen articles for various magazines, primarily on his battles with the Native Americans. In 1885 he completed a book on his Civil War experiences titled *Personal Recollections of the Civil War*, which was published posthumously in 1928. He spent the last years of his life in Baltimore, Maryland, where he worked with veterans' groups and Civil War reunions. Gibbon died there on February 6, 1896.

ALAN K. LAMM

See also

Big Hole, Battle of the; Great Sioux War; Joseph, Chief; Little Bighorn, Battle of the; Nez Perces; Nez Perce War; Seminole War, Third

References

Gibbon, John. *Adventures on the Western Frontier.* Edited by Alan and Maureen Gaff. Bloomington: Indiana University Press, 1994.

Gibbon, John. *The Artillerist's Manual.* 1859; reprint, Westport, CT: Greenwood, 1971.

Gibbon, John. *Personal Recollections of the Civil War.* 1928; reprint: Dayton, OH: Morningside, 1977.

Nolan, Alan T. *The Iron Brigade: A Military History.* Bloomington: University of Indiana Press, 1961.

Girty, Simon

Birth Date: ca. 1742
Death Date: February 18, 1818

Loyalist partisan, interpreter, trader, and frontiersman, regarded by many white settlers on the western frontier as a savage and a terrorist. Simon Girty was born in Chambers Mill, Pennsylvania, probably in 1742. When Girty was 10 years old, he and three of his brothers saw their home burned by Lancaster County magistrates. Their father died a violent death a few years later, and their mother married John Turner. In August 1756 the family was captured at the surrender of Fort Granville during the French and Indian War (1754–1763). They were moved to an Indian town, where they saw Turner tortured and burned at the stake in retribution for the Delaware warriors lost in the siege of the fort. Their captors then divided the family among several tribes. The Senecas claimed Girty and returned to their home in western New York, where he quickly learned the language and mastered the tribe's customs. He soon became a full member of the tribe, which gave him the opportunity to learn the other five dialects of the Iroquois Confederacy.

By 1763, treaties had freed the family members, and they regrouped at Pittsburgh, Pennsylvania, where the sons worked as laborers, hunters, and traders and supported their mother. Girty found work as an interpreter for traders moving among the Native American towns of the Ohio and Kentucky countries. Girty's talents as a speaker and his honesty in personal dealings, outgoing nature, and woodland skills made him highly respected and trusted by the Native Americans.

The Pennsylvania Quaker merchants who controlled Fort Pitt saw area tribes as trading partners. During the spring of 1768, however, Fort Pitt was seized by Virginians who, along with their royal governor, John Murray, Lord Dunmore, were interested in expanding their landholdings into the Ohio Valley. They wished to eliminate the Native Americans, whom they viewed as savages and a menace to civilized development. It was not long before a group of Native Americans, including the family of Chief Logan of the Mingos, was ambushed and slain. Logan, who had aided white travelers including Girty, Simon Kenton, and George Rogers Clark in the Ohio Country, took revenge for the atrocities. Chief Cornstalk of the Shawnees also went to war with his large following.

In 1774 Lord Dunmore, anxious to rid his frontier of Native American raiding parties, led one half of his militia army to Fort Pitt, where he hired Girty and Kenton as scouts to maintain communication with the other half of the army. On October 10 Cornstalk took advantage of the split forces and attacked the southern group at Point Pleasant in present-day West Virginia. After the battle, the chiefs and subchiefs of the Shawnees, Wyandots, and Mingos were ready for peace terms, but Logan refused to come to council. Dunmore sent Girty to bring Logan to the meeting. Logan again refused to attend, but Girty returned with Logan's words memorized, as his Seneca family had taught him. These words were recorded by John Gibson and read to Dunmore.

After Dunmore's War, the Pennsylvanians regained control of Fort Pitt and issued a warrant for Girty's arrest because he had taken the oath of loyalty to King George III and was viewed as an agent of Dunmore. Apparently, however, the warrant was never enforced because of Girty's skill as an interpreter and a negotiator.

Upon Cornstalk's murder by Virginia militiamen in 1777, the Native Americans went to war again to stop the flood of settlers into their lands. Having been armed by Henry Hamilton, the lieutenant governor of Canada, the raiding parties became bolder. Girty was then hired by American brigadier general Edward Hand as a scout but resigned after Hand's February 1778 attack on an undefended Native American town in which women and children were murdered. About a month later, Girty departed Pittsburgh with Alexander McKee and Matthew Elliott to join the British at Detroit, taking time to visit his Native American friends along the way. In Detroit, Hamilton hired Girty as an interpreter and agent.

Many frontiersmen hated the Native Americans, misunderstood their ritual warfare, and believed that the Native Americans were incapable of fighting without white leadership. The British kept many agents and rangers in the field to assist their Native American allies, but in most cases the warriors were led by their own chiefs. Girty accompanied some raiding parties as an observer and interpreter, but he was credited with almost every attack throughout the Ohio River Valley. Many of the events that led to his image as a bloodthirsty savage may well have been carried out by his brother James.

After visiting Wyandot villages, Girty settled into his first British assignment with the Mingos along the Scioto River, north of present-day Columbus, Ohio. As a British agent and interpreter, one of his duties was to expel unauthorized whites from the area. This brought him into contact with Moravian missionaries, whom he threatened but never harmed while removing them. Girty's work in eastern Ohio was instrumental in keeping the Delawares neutral during this period.

In the winter of 1778–1779, Girty was east of Fort Laurens (near present-day Canton, Ohio) with a group of warriors who ambushed an American carrying important military plans. These fell into Girty's hands, contributing to the delay of a planned American attack on Detroit.

Girty fought in a fairly large engagement in October 1779. Colonel David Rogers was leading 70 men returning from New Orleans, where they had purchased arms. Girty, along with his brother George, Matthew Elliot, and a mixed party of 50 Shawnee, Wyandot, and Delaware warriors, were about three miles south of the Little Miami River near present-day Dayton, Kentucky. After passing the Licking River on the trip north, Rogers brought his keelboats ashore on the Kentucky side of the Ohio River. It is unclear which group saw the other first, but each underestimated the strength of the other. With Girty relaying directions and taking part in the hand-to-hand combat, the battle turned to his group's favor. In the end Rogers and 41 of his men died, and 5 were captured. This event greatly magnified Girty's prestige with the Ohio tribes, while Pennsylvania and Virginia offered a large cash reward for him.

In 1780 Girty accompanied Colonel Henry Bird, who was leading a raiding force of 150 Loyalists and between 500 and 1,000 Native Americans. Bird invaded Kentucky with a plan to clear it of all supporters of the Virginia government. His campaign was quite successful, but he was nevertheless forced to return to Detroit without having destroyed Kentucky's local government.

Girty now served full-time with the Shawnee tribe and reportedly participated in many battles. The American atrocity against the praying Indians at Gnadenhutten in the Ohio Country in March 1782 outraged Native Americans along the frontier. Girty led reinforcements from Piqua to Upper Sandusky in June against Colonel William Crawford's expedition. Many Americans, including Crawford, were captured. Girty was present as they tortured and burned to death Crawford, whom Girty apparently refused to aid.

In August 1782 Girty evidently joined the British in their attack on Bryant's Station (present-day Lexington, Kentucky). The attackers then withdrew up a buffalo trace, and the Kentuckians followed the raiders to the Blue Licks, where they suffered a major defeat in which Daniel Boone lost his son. This was the last battle of the war for Girty, who returned to Detroit to enjoy his pension from the Crown.

During Little Turtle's War (1785–1795), also known as the Northwest Indian War, Girty reportedly took part in the defeat of Brigadier General Josiah Harmar's force in 1790 and in the Battle of Fallen Timbers in 1794. After that Girty had little involvement in armed conflict, although he did continue to urge tribes to resist white encroachment. He died in Amherstburg, Ontario, on February 18, 1818.

RICHARD CARL REIS

See also
Blue Licks, Kentucky, Action at; Boone, Daniel; Cornstalk; Fallen Timbers, Battle of; French and Indian War; Little Turtle's War; Lord

Dunmore's War; Native Americans and the American Revolutionary War; Old Northwest Territory; Senecas

References
Eckert, Allan W. *The Frontiersman.* Boston: Little, Brown, 1967.
Frederic, Harold. *The Damnation of Simon Girty.* Havelock, NC: Print Shop, 1991.
Truman, Timothy. *Wilderness: The True Story of Simon Girty, Renegade.* Lancaster, PA: 4 Winds, 1990.

Glaize, The

A group of mainly Native American settlements located at the mouth of the Auglaize River where it meets the Maumee River in northwestern Ohio. The Glaize (or Auglaize, sometimes Grand Glaize) consisted of seven towns—three Shawnee, two Delaware, one Miami, and one British—with a combined population of some 2,000 inhabitants. Beginning in 1792, the Glaize became the center of Native American resistance to U.S. expansion across the Old Northwest Territory. In 1794 Major General "Mad" Anthony Wayne destroyed the villages and fields at the Glaize.

Located approximately equidistant from the American Fort Washington and the British Fort Detroit, the Glaize community was ideally suited for its role as the key Indian confederacy town. In 1792 a council took place at the Glaize that drew more than 1,000 warriors and their families in addition to those already settled in the region. Representatives from the Ojibwas, the Ottawas, Iroquois, the Seven Nations of Canada, the Stockbridges, the Mahicans, the Shawnees, and the Delawares gathered there. Delays led to many of the delegates leaving early, but this circumstance did not affect the importance of this or subsequent meetings at the Glaize. This 1792 meeting affirmed anti-American actions and continued alliances with the British but also called into question Britain's ability and willingness to support the confederacy. The British did manage to convince the delegates of British reliability, however.

Prior to the late 18th century, the area known as the Glaize served as a prime hunting and fishing site but did not appear to be permanently settled. The nucleus for the settlement came in 1789 with the first year-round village of Shawnees established under the leadership of Captain Johnny. The movement of six more villages to the area was sparked by American expeditions launched from Cincinnati and Vincennes in 1790 and 1791, respectively. After Brigadier General Josiah Harmar's expedition burned the principal villages near present-day Fort Wayne, Indiana, in 1791, the Native Americans began moving to safer locales. Thus, by 1792 the Glaize had become a major settlement and center of political activity.

The importance of the Glaize and its inhabitants cannot be underestimated. The Shawnee villages were headed by Blue Jacket, the Great Snake, and Captain Johnny. Close to these villages were small settlements of Nanticokes and Chickamauga Cherokees. Within these three villages were Shawnees, Delawares, and Mingos. The Delaware village was headed by the war leader Buckongahelas and the civil leader Big Cat. A small community of Conoys

(originally from the Potomac Bay) also resided near this town. The Miami town was led by Little Turtle, who was seen as the leading warrior of the Northwest Indian Confederacy. Also living at the Miami town was William Wells, an adopted American captive who became a noted warrior and intermediary with the Miamis, and the mixed-blood Miami J. B. Richardville.

The British settlement consisted of traders' houses and warehouses and Indian department buildings and included some French and English families. The important individuals who acted both as traders and representatives of Britain in this settlement were George Ironside, Billy Caldwell, John Kinzie, Alexander McKee, Matthew Elliot, and James and Simon Girty. Each of these men and their children would play important roles in the War of 1812 and the post–Treaty of Ghent era. Finally, a Mohawk woman known as Coocoochee who lived away from the villages served as the entire community's spiritual leader, host, and intermediary between the villages and people at the Glaize. The marriage of Coocoochee's daughter to George Ironside gave the British great influence within the community.

In 1794 after spending months preparing his troops, General Wayne defeated the confederacy at the Battle of Fallen Timbers on August 20. His troops subsequently burned the abandoned villages at the Glaize. This victory forced the Native Americans to sign the Treaty of Greenville in 1795 and led to the reorganization of the Indian confederacy under the leadership of Tecumseh.

KARL S. HELE

See also
Blue Jacket; Council on the Auglaize; Delawares; Fallen Timbers, Battle of; Greenville, Treaty of; Harmar, Josiah; Little Turtle; Little Turtle's War; Miamis; Ojibwas; Old Northwest Territory; Tecumseh; Shawnees; Wayne, Anthony

References
Calloway, Colin G. "'We Have Always Been the Frontier': The American Revolution in Shawnee Country." *American Indian Quarterly* 16(1) (1992): 39–52.
Gaff, Donald H. "Three Men from Three Rivers: Navigating between Native and American Identity in the Old Northwest Territory." In *The Boundaries between Us: Native and Newcomers along the Frontier of the Old Northwest Territory, 1750–1850,* edited by Daniel P. Barr, 143–160. Kent, OH: Kent State University Press, 2006.
Hurt, R. Douglas. *The Ohio Frontier: Crucible of the Old Northwest, 1720–1830.* Bloomington: Indiana University Press, 1996.
Tanner, Helen Hornbeck. "The Glaize in 1792: A Composite Indian Community." *Ethnohistory* 25(1) (1978): 15–39.
Willig, Timothy D. *Restoring the Chain of Friendship: British Policy and the Indians of the Great Lakes, 1783–1815.* Lincoln: University of Nebraska Press, 2008.

Gnadenhutten Massacre
Event Date: March 8, 1782

Massacre of 96 Moravian Delaware Indians, mainly women and children, on March 8, 1782, by American militia troops under the command of Colonel David Williamson near present-day Gnadenhutten in east-central Ohio. The Native Americans who were murdered were all Christians. Following the massacre, the militiamen burned the Moravian Indian mission settlement, including the bodies of those killed. These actions took place during the last full year of the American Revolutionary War (1775–1783).

Moravian missions to the Delawares living in the Ohio Country had begun in 1773. These settlements were never very popular with the Native Americans or the European frontier settlers. Indeed, Ohio Indians accused their Moravian counterparts of witchcraft and of assisting the American settlers during the American Revolution. British officers meanwhile believed that the Moravian Indians and their ministers, such as David Zeisberger and John Heckewelder, were acting as American spies. American military officers sought the support of the Moravian Indians, welcomed them as spies, and attempted to prevent them from being attacked by frontier settlers. The frontier settlers, however, believed that the Moravian Indians were either harboring enemies or were enemies themselves, but American militia units had been restrained from attacking the Moravians in retaliation for Indian raids, and John Heckewelder had even claimed that the Iroquois and the British had plotted in early 1781 to murder the Moravians.

In 1781 to prevent information from reaching the Americans at Fort Pitt, the Wyandots forced the Moravian Indians to relocate near Sandusky, Ohio, and Detroit. Adding to Moravian Indian problems was the alliance of the majority of Delawares with the British that same year. Experiencing starvation conditions in Sandusky, approximately 150 Moravian Indians returned to their settlements at Salem and Gnadenhutten to gather abandoned crops and food stores during the winter of 1782. Sometime earlier the Americans had released several captured Moravian Delawares and informed them that they would not be attacked should they return to harvest their crops in eastern Ohio. While at their villages, the Moravians encountered a retreating raiding party of Shawnees and Wyandots. Based on previous promises, past support of the Americans, and pacifism, the Moravians continued to harvest their crops.

Meanwhile, in response to the raid some 200–300 frontiersmen, organized into a militia, were approaching the Moravian Delawares. When these men encountered the Moravians, the militia initially reassured them that they were to be relocated away from the warring parties. Once the Moravians were gathered at Gnadenhutten, however, Colonel David Williamson and his men accused the Moravians of being spies, harboring enemy Native Americans, and participating in the raids on white settlements. The evidence used to support these accusations was found in the Moravians' homes: axes, pewter basins, spoons, teakettles, pots, cups, saucers, and brands for horses. However, all were European artifacts that the Moravians had adopted at the urging of their missionaries. To the frontiersmen, these artifacts were markers of white civilization and when found in a Native American community pointed to theft.

The Moravian Delawares pled their innocence to no avail. When informed that they were to be executed, the Moravians spent the night praying. On the morning of March 8, 1782, the Moravians were killed with a cooper's mallet. The corpses were then scalped before the entire village was set ablaze. In all, the militiamen murdered 96 men, women, and children, all unarmed pacifists. The surviving Moravians, those few who fled or had not returned to harvest their crops, were escorted back to Detroit.

The Gnadenhutten Massacre helped spur a nativist movement among the Native Americans of the region, and surviving Moravians found it difficult to continue with their adopted religion. The massacre also triggered a series of retaliatory killings by Native Americans. Eventually some of the surviving Moravian Indians settled on the Thames River near present-day London, Ontario. In 1788 Congress granted land in southwestern Ohio to the Moravians in compensation for the massacre. This land was occupied by only a few people until 1823, when it was sold.

KARL S. HELE

See also
Delawares; Iroquois; Moravian Church; Moravian Indian Missions on the Muskingum River; Native Americans and the American Revolutionary War; Shawnees; Wyandots

References
Abel, Mary Bilderback. "Massacre at Gnadenhutten: Recreated Village Marks the Site Where Pennsylvania Backwoodsmen Murdered Ninety-six Christian Indians in 1782." *American History Illustrated* 16(8) (1981): 28–31.
Dowd, Gregory Evans. *A Spirited Resistance: The North American Indian Struggle for Unity, 1745–1815.* Baltimore: Johns Hopkins University Press, 1992.
Sadosky, Leonard. "Rethinking the Gnadenhutten Massacre: The Contest for Power in the Public World of the Revolutionary Pennsylvania Frontier." In *The Sixty Years' War for the Great Lakes, 1754–1814,* edited by David Curtis Skaggs and Larry L. Nelson, 187–214. East Lansing: Michigan State University Press, 2001.

Good Friday Massacre
Event Date: March 22, 1622

Powhatan attack that killed nearly a third of the English settlers in Virginia on March 22, 1622, and precipitated the Second Anglo-Powhatan War (1622–1632). In 1614 after seven years of struggling to keep the colony at Jamestown alive, the English colonists achieved a brief peace when John Rolfe married Pocahontas, Chief Powhatan's daughter. However, she died from disease in England in March 1617, and Powhatan died the following year. The Powhatan chiefdom passed to Powhatan's brother, Opechancanough, who held much contempt for the English colonists.

Opechancanough recognized that the Jamestown colonists threatened his people's way of life. Indeed, by the early 1620s the colonists were no longer struggling to replace their dead;

they were expanding their settlements outward up the rivers and planting tobacco for profit. For a while Opechancanough kept his resentment to himself. To lull the English into a false sense of security and to encourage their vulnerability, he feigned interest in converting to Christianity and invited the colonists to occupy lands that had not been settled by Native Americans. Opechancanough's deception worked. The colonists stopped military drilling, abandoned their construction of fortifications, and expanded across the Virginia countryside, away from the original Jamestown settlement.

Opechancanough continued the deception until the murder of an old Powhatan chief gave him the pretext needed to strike the English settlements. Purposely choosing Good Friday because he knew that the colonists would be preoccupied by the occasion, he launched his attack on March 22, 1622, and in the process killed 347 men, women, and children (nearly a third of the colonists). The survivors fled to Jamestown and a few other well-fortified settlements while the Powhatans destroyed surrounding crops and livestock. After the massacre, an additional 500 white settlers died because of starvation. By the end of 1622, only 180 English people were alive in Virginia.

Despite this terrible setback, the Virginians quickly rallied and developed a counterstrategy, which set in motion the Second Anglo-Powhatan War. The colonists waited until the corn harvest to counterattack their Powhatan neighbors and destroy their food supply. This guaranteed that they would suffer a winter and spring of exposure and starvation. In May 1623 when the Native Americans had reached the height of their suffering, the English pretended that they were ready to negotiate a peace settlement. As the conference concluded, the colonists invited the 250 Powhatan delegates to share in a toast that they had poisoned. The debilitated delegates were then easily killed.

Opechancanough had not attended this conference and continued to resist the English. On April 18, 1644, he launched a second offensive that killed more than 400 colonists, setting off the Third Anglo-Powhatan War (1644–1646). However, this attack did not inflict as much damage on the colonists as the Good Friday Massacre had because the colonial population had risen to almost 10,000. In 1646 the English finally captured Opechancanough, and while he was being taken to Jamestown, an angry soldier shot and killed him.

JOSHUA ADAM CAMPER

See also

Anglo-Powhatan War, Second; Anglo-Powhatan War, Third; Jamestown; Opechancanough; Powhatan; Powhatan Confederacy

References

Doughty, Robert, and Ira Gruber. *American Military History and the Evolution of Western Warfare.* Lexington, MA: D. C. Heath, 1996.

McDougall, Walter. *Freedom Just around the Corner.* New York: HarperCollins, 2004.

Taylor, Alan. *American Colonies: The Settling of North America.* New York: Viking/Penguin, 2001.

Goshute War

Start Date: March 1863
End Date: October 1863

Conflict fought from March to October 1863 within the wider Shoshone (Shoshoni) War of January–October 1863. The Goshute (Goshiute) War consisted of a series of small yet brutal attacks and reprisals between the Goshute tribe and both local militias and California Volunteers in the desert regions southwest of the Great Salt Lake in Utah.

The war was a culmination of several developments in the Great Basin. Beginning in 1847, Mormon settlers began moving into the Goshute homeland, a largely desolate area extending from Tooele Valley, Utah, to the Deep Creek Mountains in eastern Nevada. As governor of the Utah Territory and superintendent of Indian affairs after 1850, Brigham Young encouraged further Mormon settlement, which resulted in the establishment of towns in the areas most utilized by the Goshutes for water, grazing lands, and game. The Goshutes grew increasingly frustrated and desperate in the competition for resources, prompting warriors to steal cattle and livestock from white farmers and ranchers, who retaliated with militia attacks to retrieve stolen stock. Meanwhile, the Mormon-led Walker's War (1853) drove the neighboring Utes into the Tooele Valley, where both tribes formed political and military associations.

Relations worsened between whites and Goshutes with the opening of a private mail route (1854), an overland stage route (1858), and the Pony Express (1860). The stage route established 22 stations along a line running through Fairfield, Simpson Springs, Fish Springs, and Deep Creek, putting further pressure on water and timber supplies.

Warriors attacked settlers, express riders, stages, and migrant trains and miners traveling along the California Trail and the Oregon Trail, which during 1860–1861 led to a series of skirmishes with federal troops stationed at Camp Floyd. Once the army left the region at the start of the American Civil War (1861–1865), the Mormons assumed responsibility for security. A tenuous peace ensued, and settlers and the mail company provided the Goshutes with some assistance.

Delayed subsidies and the threat of widespread starvation by the summer of 1862 saw the Goshutes resume attacks on mail routes and carry out raids for horses, cattle, and provisions. Colonel Patrick Edward Connor soon arrived in the Great Salt Lake region in command of the California Volunteers (3rd California Infantry) to guard the overland mail route from Carson City to Fort Bridger.

A proponent of swift and harsh punishment for Native Americans committing depredations against white settlers, Connor ordered an attack on a Northern Shoshone winter camp at Bear River on January 29, 1863, killing at least 224 people. Turning his attention to the transcontinental stage and mail route traversing Goshute lands, Connor assigned soldiers to coaches and stations. His ruthlessness at Bear River incensed the Goshutes, who made a series of vicious raids including one at Deep Creek Station on March 22, 1863, in which a stage driver and a passenger were killed. That was soon followed by an attack on Eight-Mile Station, where 2 more whites were killed and scalped.

These incidents precipitated a string of violent exchanges and marked the beginning of the Goshute War. By late spring, the stage company had reportedly lost 17 stations, 150 horses, and 16 men. In response, Connor sent Captain Samuel P. Smith to search for and kill any Goshutes he could find in the vicinity of the stations. Favoring hit-and-run attacks rather than pitched battles, Goshute tactics convinced the military that surprise assaults on Goshute encampments could be a more effective strategy.

In early May, Smith's force discovered a mixed group of Native Americans, including some Goshutes, and killed 53 of them. Reprisals followed in June when the Goshutes killed and mutilated 2 stage workers at Point of the Mountain near Salt Lake City. In the same place only two days later, Goshute warriors struck another coach, killing 2 people. Within days of the second incident, Smith had attacked and killed 10 Native Americans at Government Springs and on August 1 led a surprise attack on a Goshute camp north of Schell Creek Station, killing 12 Native Americans, including the wife and child of Chief Peah-namp. The chief avenged these deaths by killing the station keeper and 4 soldiers at Canyon Station and burning it to the ground, rousing Connor to seek cannon and field guns to put an end to Goshute hostility. Facing a superior force in terms of size and weaponry, Goshute chief Tabby saved his people from certain annihilation by convincing his warriors to surrender. According to government records, Goshute casualties numbered about 100 over the course of the year.

The Peace Treaty of Tooele Valley, signed on October 12, 1863, formally ended the Goshute War. Represented by Chief Tabby, Adaseim, Tintsa-pa-gin, and Harry-nup, the Goshutes ensured the safe passage of whites through their homeland and accepted the presence of settlers, miners, stations, military posts, and the operation of the telegraph, stage, and railroad lines. The government, represented by Superintendent of Indian Affairs James Duane Doty and now-Brigadier General Patrick Connor, pledged an annuity of $1,000 per year for 20 years as compensation as well as $1,000 at the treaty signing. The war thus greatly reduced the Goshutes as a military threat, enabled continued settlement of Utah, and helped secure the transcontinental communications and transportation route.

MICHAEL F. DOVE

See also
Bear River, Battle of; Connor, Patrick Edward; Pony Express; Shoshones; Shoshone War

References
Defa, Dennis R. "The Goshute Indians of Utah." In *A History of Utah's American Indians,* edited by Forrest S. Cuch, 73–122. Salt Lake City: Utah State University Press, 2000.
Malouf, Carling. "The Goshute Indians." In *Shoshone Indians,* edited by David Agee Horr, 25–172. New York: Garland, 1974.

Governor Kieft's War
See Kieft's War

Grand Glaize
See Glaize, The

Grant, Ulysses Simpson
Birth Date: April 27, 1822
Death Date: July 23, 1885

U.S. general and president of the United States (1869–1877). Born in Point Pleasant, Ohio, on April 27, 1822, Hiram Ulysses Grant grew up on his father's farm. Securing appointment to the U.S. Military Academy at West Point, Grant discovered that his name had been changed to Ulysses Simpson (his mother's maiden name) Grant, which he kept. He graduated in 1843.

Grant served with distinction in the Mexican-American War (1846–1848), seeing action under Major General Zachary Taylor in northern Mexico in the Battle of Palo Alto, the Battle of Resaca de la Palma, and the Battle of Monterrey. Transferred to Major General Winfield Scott's command in March 1847, Grant fought in the Battle of Cerro Gordo, the Battle of Churubusco, and the Battle Molino del Rey. After the latter battle he was brevetted first lieutenant for gallantry. Promoted to first lieutenant in September 1847, Grant received a second brevet, to captain, following the Battle of Chapultepec.

After the war Grant was on duty in California, where he was promoted to captain in August 1853. Bored and upset at being separated from his wife, he drank heavily and was forced to resign from the army in July 1854, reportedly to avoid a court-martial. He returned to his family in Missouri but was unsuccessful as a farmer and in selling real estate. His father gave him a position as a clerk in the family leather store in Galena, Illinois.

When the American Civil War (1861–1865) began in April 1861, Grant secured a colonelcy of volunteers and command of the 21st Illinois Regiment in June. Promoted to brigadier general of volunteers, he received command of the Southwest Missouri Military District that August. He distinguished himself in the early fighting in Kentucky and in Missouri.

In the subsequent Union river campaigns, Grant worked well with his naval counterpart, Flag Officer Andrew Hull Foote. Now known as "Unconditional Surrender Grant" for the Union victories at Fort Henry and Fort Donelson, he received promotion to major general of volunteers in February 1862.

Grant was preparing to attack Corinth, Mississippi, when he was surprised by Confederates under General Albert Sidney Johnston at Pittsburg Landing (Shiloh) on April 6, 1862. In the ensuing

As president of the United States during 1869–1877, Ulysses S. Grant endeavored to institute a more humane policy toward Native Americans that would integrate them into American society. (Library of Congress)

battle Grant rallied his men and managed to hold; the next day he won the victory.

Pressed to relieve Grant over Shiloh, President Abraham Lincoln demurred. Demoted by a jealous General Henry Halleck, Grant served as second-in-command in Halleck's snail's pace advance on Corinth. Given command of the Army of the Tennessee that October, Grant set his sights on capturing the Confederate stronghold of Vicksburg on the Mississippi River. Disregarding Halleck's instructions to await reinforcements, Grant cut loose from his base at Grand Gulf and moved north, taking Jackson on May 14, 1863. After initial assaults failed, he finally laid siege to Vicksburg, taking the city on July 4, 1863, in one of the most significant Union victories of the war.

Promoted to major general in the regular army and given command of the Military Division of the Mississippi on October 4, 1863, Grant directed the relief of Chattanooga, Tennessee, and then, reinforced, broke the Confederate siege of Chattanooga during October 25–28 and drove the Confederates from both Lookout Mountain and Missionary Ridge during November 24–25.

Named commanding general of the Armies of the United States with the revived rank of lieutenant general in April 1864, Grant opened a multipronged offensive against the Confederates with the main effort coming in Virginia against Confederate general Robert E. Lee's Army of Northern Virginia in the so-called Overland Campaign, beginning in May 1864. A series of bloody rebuffs

followed, but Grant kept pressing the attack. Following bloody engagements in the Wilderness (May 4–7), at Spotsylvania Court House (May 8–17), and Cold Harbor (June 3), Grant attempted to get behind Lee at Petersburg but failed. From August 1864 to March 1865 Grant then laid siege to Petersburg in the longest such operation of the war. His victory at Five Forks (March 29–31, 1865) sealed the fate of Richmond and Petersburg. Lee was forced to surrender at Appomattox Court House on April 9, 1865. Grant's generous terms helped the healing process and set the tone for the other surrenders to follow.

Following the war Grant continued as commanding general of the army and was advanced to full general by act of Congress in January 1866. He has been regarded as a controversial figure for his supposed failure as president. Elected in November 1868 as a Republican to the first of his two terms in office (1869–1877), he was personally honest, but his administration was wracked by scandal. Grant remained popular, however.

In 1869 in an attempt to end violence in the West between Native Americans and whites and to assimilate tribes into U.S. society, Grant enunciated what came to be called Grant's Peace Policy. This marked a departure from previous administrations vis-à-vis Native Americans. Having spent time in the West as an army officer, Grant believed that he comprehended the problems facing Native Americans better than his predecessors and thus sought to address them directly. He was in fact quite sympathetic to their cause and hoped to protect them from further encroachment by white settlers. Grant hoped that Native Americans might be educated, converted to Christianity, and taught how to become self-sufficient farmers. He also hoped to reinforce the existing reservation policy and guarantee those lands for Native American use and habitation.

Part of Grant's policy insisted that Native Americans be relocated to reservations, which was not a departure from previous policies. What Grant sought to do, however, was to end the repeated encroachments on Native American lands that had occurred in the past. The reservations were to be administered by the Bureau of Indian Affairs (BIA), which was to be free of the previous graft and corruption that had been endemic among U.S. Indian agents in the past. In a powerfully symbolic move, Grant ordered the BIA transferred from the War Department to the Department of the Interior to stress that the government did not seek conflict with Native Americans. He also appointed numerous reformers to important BIA posts in an attempt to break with the past.

In the end, however, Grant's policy did not work as intended, chiefly because the government never allocated enough money to carry out its directives. Furthermore, much of the land set aside for Native Americans was ill-suited for agriculture, which flew in the face of Grant's desire to turn Native Americans into reasonably prosperous farmers.

Becoming bankrupt after leaving the presidency when a brokerage firm failed, Grant developed throat cancer but struggled to complete his memoirs in order to provide for his family financially. He completed the task only two days before his death at Mount McGregor, New York, on July 23, 1885. His *Memoirs* (1885) proved a great literary success and reveal the depth of his intelligence and character.

SPENCER C. TUCKER

See also

Bureau of Indian Affairs; Grant's Peace Policy; Parker, Ely Samuel

References

Bunting, Josiah, III. *Ulysses S. Grant.* New York: Henry Holt/Times Books, 2004.

Grant, Ulysses S. *The Personal Memoirs of Ulysses S. Grant.* Introduction by Brooks D. Simpson. Lincoln: University of Nebraska Press, 1996.

McFeely, William S. *Grant: A Biography.* New York: Norton, 1981.

Perret, Geoffrey. *Ulysses S. Grant: Soldier and President.* New York: Random House, 1997.

Grant's Peace Policy

President Ulysses S. Grant's initiative, first enunciated in 1869, to bring about peace in the West and to help Native Americans assimilate to American society was a departure from the policies toward Native Americans of previous and future presidential administrations. Grant had been posted in the West prior to the American Civil War (1861–1865) and was intimately familiar with the Native American problems in that region.

Upon Grant's inauguration to the presidency in March 1869, the principal source of trouble between whites and Native Americans was white settlers' encroachment on Native American lands. For years the settlers had set up homesteads, extracted minerals, grazed cattle, and hunted or habitually passed through Native American lands in violation of numerous treaties signed by the U.S. government and Native American tribes. These encroachments led to a never-ending series of conflicts between Native Americans and white settlers and the U.S. Army.

Native American policy was at a crossroads at the beginning of Grant's first term in office. It was clear that a large number of Americans and U.S. politicians did not care what happened to the Native Americans and only wished to use the Native Americans' land as they pleased. Some extremist Americans actually favored the extermination of the Native Americans. Others wished to assimilate the Native Americans into American society.

Grant was an advocate for Native Americans, and he sought both to safeguard their future and to prevent bloodshed between them and white Americans. He instituted his peace policy in 1869 soon after taking office. The primary thrust of the policy was to assist the Native Americans to assimilate into American society by educating them, converting them to Christianity, and training them to become self-sufficient farmers. Grant hoped to prevent conflict by guaranteeing the Native Americans land upon which whites would be forbidden, reinforcing the reservation system as a way to protect Native Americans. This was certainly not a new

concept, but the activities sponsored on the reservations and those who administered them were new.

Tribes that refused to move to a reservation were to be coerced by the army; if tribes still refused to move, they would be subject to the use of armed force. The reservation system set aside federal lands for Native Americans that would be governed by federal officials. The reservations would be run by the Bureau of Indian Affairs (BIA) with assistance by Indian agents from various religious orders, philanthropic organizations, and the army. It was hoped that these organizations and their workers would be less susceptible to the graft and corruption that had been endemic to government Indian agents for many decades. Heretofore Indian agents had been political patronage appointees, who for the most part were more interested in lining their own pockets than in assisting the tribes under their supervision. Indeed, one of Grant's first actions was to fire all Indian agents and replace them with individuals from churches and religious organizations and orders. Twelve Christian denominations took part in Grant's plan and administered 73 agencies.

In addition, Grant transferred the BIA from the Department of War to the Department of the Interior, a powerful gesture by

Cartoon ridiculing President Ulysses S. Grant's Indian peace policy, showing Indians receiving torn blankets, an empty rifle case, and spoiled beef. Created by Joseph Keppler for *Frank Leslie's Illustrated Newspaper*, September 18, 1875. (Library of Congress)

which he hoped to de-emphasize armed conflict with the Native Americans. One of Grant's most daring moves was to appoint genuine reformers to important positions so that these individuals might implement and enforce the new policy. Jacob D. Cox, a noted advocate of civil service reform, was appointed secretary of the interior, while Grant appointed Ely S. Parker commissioner of Indian affairs. Parker, a member of the Seneca Iroquois tribe, was the epitome of what Grant and the reformers hoped to accomplish with their policy of assimilation. Parker was educated in white church-run schools and went on to become a self-educated engineer as well as a lawyer. Indeed, Parker was a valued member of Grant's staff during and after the Civil War and became a close friend of the president.

Unfortunately, Grant's peace policy was not a success. One of the primary reasons for this was the failure of the federal government to provide adequate financial support to the Indian agencies. Agents' salaries were abysmally low, forcing many to abandon their posts or to turn to graft to supplement their meager salaries. Furthermore, monies provided to the agents to supply the reservations were often too small to provide quality provisions. The land provided for the reservations was poor and often unsuitable to sustain sufficient grazing and farming to support a tribe's needs. This flew in the face of the government's goal of turning Native Americans into successful farmers. Additionally, many Native Americans did not wish to assimilate into white society. Those Native Americans who desired to retain their own cultural identity were disappointed by the poor provisions provided as well as the quality of the land they received. Although there were some success stories, the well-meaning peace policy can only be viewed as a noble failure. In fact, it proved to be a catalyst for destructive conflicts, including the Great Sioux War on the northern Plains and the Nez Perce War in the northwest. Grant's peace policy virtually disappeared after he left office in 1877. His successor, President Rutherford B. Hayes, began phasing the policy out.

RICK DYSON

See also
Bureau of Indian Affairs; Grant, Ulysses Simpson; Great Sioux War; Indian Agents; Nez Perce War; Parker, Ely Samuel; Reservations

References
Armstrong, William H. *Warrior in Two Camps: Ely S. Parker, Union General and Seneca Chief.* Syracuse, NY: Syracuse University Press, 1978.
Bender, Norman J. *New Hope for the Indians: The Grant Peace Policy and the Navajos in the 1870s.* Albuquerque: University of New Mexico Press, 1989.
Bolt, Christine. *American Indian Policy and American Reform.* London: Unwin Hyman, 1987.
Keller, Robert H. *American Protestantism and United States Indian Policy, 1869–82.* Lincoln: University of Nebraska Press, 1983.
Prucha, Francis Ford. *American Indian Policy in Crisis: Christian Reformers and the Indian, 1865–1900.* Norman: University of Oklahoma Press, 1976.

Grattan Massacre
Event Date: August 19, 1854

The massacre of 31 U.S. soldiers by Brulé Sioux warriors east of Fort Laramie in the Nebraska Territory (present-day Wyoming) on August 19, 1854. In mid-August, a large group of Sioux and Cheyennes had gathered outside Fort Laramie to collect their annuity goods. Among them was a Native American named High Forehead, who by luck had stumbled upon a lone cow. The cow, lame with bleeding hooves, had been abandoned by a Mormon migrating west. High Forehead slaughtered the cow for food. The cow's original owner, now at Fort Laramie and learning what had transpired, demanded to be paid for the cow. Sioux chief Bear That Scatters (also known as Conquering Bear) offered the Mormon settler $10 in compensation. The Mormon rejected the offer and demanded $25. When the money was not forthcoming, the Mormon took his complaint to Fort Laramie's commander, Second Lieutenant J. L. Grattan. A recent graduate of the U.S. Military Academy at West Point, the brash young Grattan had gone west to make a name for himself.

Determined to bring the alleged thief to justice, Grattan led a detachment of 30 soldiers with two artillery pieces from Fort Laramie to confront the Sioux on August 19. Reportedly, many of his soldiers were intoxicated. Grattan issued an ultimatum to Bear That Scatters, demanding that the Sioux pay the $25 demanded by the Mormon or surrender High Forehead for punishment. Bear That Scatters protested the ultimatum and attempted to negotiate a compromise. His attempts were futile, however, as the interpreter was inebriated and Grattan was unwilling to listen. As tensions increased, a number of Sioux warriors who had gathered behind their chief began to heckle and shout at the soldiers. Grattan now panicked and ordered his men to open fire. Bear That Scatters fell mortally wounded, the only Sioux to be killed.

Enraged, the Sioux descended upon the soldiers, killing Grattan and all 30 of his men. They next turned on Fort Laramie itself, now defended by only 10 soldiers. A trader, James Bordeau, and several tribal chiefs were able to dissuade the Sioux from attacking the fort but not before they pillaged the government's warehouses. The Sioux then withdrew northward.

Meanwhile, the War Department ordered Brigadier General William S. Harney and 700 men from Fort Leavenworth in a punitive expedition. The Sioux continued to exact revenge for the death of Bear That Scatters, killing 3 members of a mail wagon crew west of Horse Creek and attacking a trading post west of Fort Laramie. But on September 3, 1855, Harney attacked the Sioux camp at Ash Hollow (Bluewater Creek) in present-day Garden County, Nebraska. In the Battle of Ash Hollow, some 100 Sioux, including women and children, perished.

ROBERT W. MALICK

See also
Ash Hollow, Battle of; Brulé Sioux; Fort Laramie; Harney, William Selby

References

Becher, Ronald. *Massacre along the Medicine Road: A Social History of the Indian War of 1864 in Nebraska Territory.* Caldwell, ID: Caxton, 1999.

Marshall, S. L. A. *Crimsoned Prairie: The Wars between the United States and the Plains Indians during the Winning of the West.* New York: Scribner, 1972.

Greasy Grass Creek, Battle of

See Little Bighorn, Battle of the

Great Black Swamp

See Black Swamp

Great Britain

The English government's decision to leave its colonial ventures largely in private hands meant that no coherent policy toward the natives of North America was developed until well into the 18th century. Instead, companies and proprietors operating under royal charters formulated their own policies based on local interests, and even after the Crown assumed control of most of the North American colonies, each colony continued to pursue its own diplomacy with the Native Americans, often in conflict with the aims of neighboring British colonies.

The first successful English colonial project in North America was undertaken by the London (Virginia) Company, which received its charter in 1606 and colonized Virginia at Jamestown the following year. By 1610 the settlers' expansion onto the lands of the Powhatan Confederacy sparked the First Anglo-Powhatan War (1610–1614). A brief interlude of peace was followed by the bloodier Second Anglo-Powhatan War (1622–1632). Major fighting concluded in 1624, although sporadic clashes continued until 1632. The second war led to the Crown taking control of the Virginia colony in 1624; however, the new royal government made no effort to slow the colonists' push onto Powhatan territory, resulting in a Third Anglo-Powhatan War (1644–1646). This conflict destroyed Powhatan power and ushered in several decades of peace in Virginia. The English government played no direct role either in making the policies that led to these wars, in negotiating the peace treaties, or in the fighting. Thus, the colonists were left to defend themselves.

The situation was similar in New England, where the Pilgrims founded Plymouth Colony in 1620 and Puritans settled the Massachusetts Bay Colony a decade later. Early relations with Native Americans in both colonies were peaceful, owing largely to smallpox epidemics that had decimated the New England tribes. As in Virginia, colonial expansion eventually led to hostilities with the Native Americans, fueled in part by the insistence of Massachusetts Bay's governor, John Winthrop, that the Native Americans could not claim title to any land unless they utilized it in the English manner.

Roger Williams, another Massachusetts leader, strongly disagreed with Winthrop. Massachusetts officials, angered by Williams's views, banished him from the colony in 1635, and the following year he established the colony of Rhode Island. Williams purchased land from the local Narragansett people and established good relations with them.

Puritan settlers moving into the Connecticut River Valley encountered the Pequots, the most powerful Native American group in the region. The colonists considered the Pequots a threat, a belief fueled by the assertions of the Mohegans, a rival tribe allied with the colonists. Following the killing of English traders in 1636, the New England colonies went to war against the Pequots. Williams convinced the Narragansetts to assist the English. The Pequot War (1636–1638) nearly annihilated the Pequots and served as a powerful warning to the New England tribes not to resist the English.

Continuing colonial expansion, however, convinced many Native Americans that resistance was essential if they were to maintain their lands and their way of life. In 1675 an alliance of New England nations led by Metacom (called King Philip by the English) of the Wampanoags launched a massive assault against the New England colonies. The conflict, known as King Philip's War (1675–1676), devastated much of the frontier before the fighting ended. The New England colonies mounted a joint effort against Metacom, and the colonists' victory broke the power of the New England Native Americans. Despite the success and severity of the initial Native American attacks, the English government took no part in the conflict.

Similar violence occurred in the Carolinas as those colonies expanded in the early 18th century. North Carolinians' seizure of Native American lands, enslavement of Native American peoples, and defrauding of Native Americans in trade caused the Iroquoian-speaking Tuscarora Nation and several smaller allied tribes of Algonquian speakers to launch a violent attack on settlers on September 11, 1711. The devastating assault and North Carolina's difficulties in mounting an effective response led the colony's officials to appeal to their neighbors for aid. Virginia provided assistance by obtaining pledges of neutrality from several Virginia tribes in exchange for trade benefits and promises to respect Native American land boundaries, while a Virginian emissary secured the neutrality of about half of the Tuscarora towns. South Carolina provided volunteers for military service, including hundreds of the colony's Catawba and Yamasee allies.

The colonists and their Native American allies destroyed the important Tuscarora town of Nehucke in March 1713, killing hundreds of Native Americans and bringing the Tuscarora War (1711–1713) to an end. Harassed by colonists and enemy tribes, many of the surviving Tuscaroras began moving north in the 1720s, joining the Iroquois in present-day New York as the sixth nation of the Iroquois Confederacy.

The southern colonies continued the policy of cooperation against Native American enemies upon the outbreak of the Yamasee War (1715–1717) in South Carolina on April 15, 1715. Despite their nominal status as an ally of South Carolina and the contributions they had made to the defeat of the Tuscaroras, the Yamasees suffered numerous abuses at the hands of the South Carolinians. Yamasee land was occupied without the tribe's consent, colonial traders defrauded the Yamasees to bring them into debt, and then seized Yamasee women and children and sold them into slavery to collect the amounts that they claimed the Yamasees owed them. Unable to obtain redress through diplomatic means, the Yamasees resorted to war.

Despite initial successes and securing assistance from the Creek Confederacy, the Yamasees were soon forced on the defensive as South Carolina forces, augmented by militia from North Carolina and Virginia, carried the war into Yamasee territory. The Creeks appealed to the Cherokees for assistance, but the Cherokees killed the Creek delegates and joined the colonists. The Creeks signed a peace treaty with the colonists in November 1717 and relocated away from colonial settlements. The surviving Yamasees took refuge in Spanish Florida. In all three of the major Native American wars from 1675 to 1717, the colonists had been able to collaborate and emerge victorious without assistance from England.

In contrast to the conflict that plagued other colonies, Pennsylvania enjoyed good relations with the Native Americans during this period. William Penn, the colony's proprietor, insisted that the Native Americans be treated well. He frequently met with Native American leaders, purchased land at fair prices, and did his best to ensure equitable trade. Penn's successful diplomacy, like that of Roger Williams in Rhode Island, demonstrated the extent to which policies toward the Native Americans differed from one colony to another in the absence of any guidance from London.

New York's policy toward its tribal neighbors was dictated largely by the policy that the English inherited from the Dutch when they conquered the New Netherland colony in 1664 and by the power of the Iroquois Confederacy. In a series of wars, the Dutch had decimated or driven off most of the Algonquian-speaking peoples in the vicinity of New Netherland but had sought accommodation with the Iroquois, who in addition to providing the Dutch with furs possessed the power to annihilate the colony. Upon taking control of New Netherland and renaming it New York, English officials in the colony continued to pursue good relations with the Iroquois.

The English failure to establish a coherent imperial policy toward the Native Americans differed drastically from the practices of the French in New France. Beginning with the founding of Quebec in 1608, colonial governor Samuel de Champlain and his successors had nurtured strong trade and political relations with the Native Americans along the Saint Lawrence River and in the Great Lakes region. The alliances forged with the Native Americans had one drawback: they entangled the French in a long-standing war between the Hurons and their Algonquian allies on the one side and their traditional enemy, the Iroquois, on the other side. However, the French succeeded in imposing neutrality on the Iroquois at the start of the 18th century, and the French alliances with the Native Americans would prove essential to the security of New France in the series of conflicts with England that began in 1689. Conversely, the often hostile relationship between the English colonists and the Native Americans would leave England's colonies vulnerable to attack from the French and their Native American allies.

In 1688 the War of the League of Augsburg began in Europe, pitting England and most of the continent against France. The following year the conflict spread to North America, where Iroquois raids into Canada had already reignited the Franco-Iroquois conflict.

Although the North American conflict, known there as King William's War (1689–1697), was an extension of the European war, the English government made little effort to support its colonies or to end its neglect of relations with the Native Americans. The English colonies therefore failed to develop a cohesive policy. While New England leaders mounted a significant military effort in hopes of defeating the French and their Native American allies, officials in New York adopted a more passive policy, preferring to encourage the Iroquois to bear the brunt of the fighting. Joint French–Native American raids struck English frontier settlements in New York, New Hampshire, and northern Massachusetts (present-day Maine) and also harassed the Iroquois, keeping the English largely on the defensive. The English colonists received little aid from their parent country beyond some token naval forces, but eventually the New England militia managed to secure the Maine frontier. The war ended in 1697 with no gains in North America for either side.

Four years later the English colonies lost their most important Native American ally in the northern region. Fighting between the Iroquois and their French and Native American enemies had continued after King William's War ended, and by 1701 the French had gained the upper hand. The Iroquois signed a treaty with New France that year pledging to remain neutral in future wars. While individuals and small groups of Iroquois would occasionally violate the agreement and take part in later conflicts, the treaty effectively removed the Iroquois as a threat to New France while depriving the English colonies of a valuable defensive buffer.

Only one year after the French-Iroquois Treaty, the War of the Spanish Succession (1702–1713) broke out in Europe. Again the conflict extended to North America, where the English colonists termed it Queen Anne's War. Although the English committed more forces to North America than they had in King William's War, officials in London followed their previous practice of leaving Native American affairs in the hands of the colonists.

William Penn (1644–1718) signs a treaty with the Indians on behalf of Great Britain. The British government worked to secure Indian support, first against the French and, after the American Revolution, against the United States. (Library of Congress)

South Carolina recruited Native American allies to strike the Spanish in Florida and achieved considerable success despite failing to capture St. Augustine. A subsequent effort to attack French settlements along the Gulf of Mexico was blocked by the French-allied Choctaws. An attempt in 1707 by a combined force of South Carolina militia and Native American allies to capture Spanish Pensacola also failed.

With the Iroquois adhering to their neutrality, the northern colonies had no significant Native American assistance and suffered from a series of devastating French and Native American raids. New York's leaders, realizing their vulnerability, concluded a separate peace with their Native American neighbors, leaving New England to face the brunt of the assaults. In 1703 French forces supported by strong Native American contingents destroyed the towns of Saco and Wells in Maine and then the following year overran Deerfield, Massachusetts. That colony retaliated with attacks in Maine against the French-allied Abenakis in 1705.

The conflict in New England subsided until 1708 while New France and Massachusetts unsuccessfully tried to negotiate a peace agreement. At the same time, colonial representatives in London pleaded for assistance from British forces. Assistance arrived in 1710 but was directed against the French rather than their Native American allies. A combined British and colonial force captured Port Royal in Acadia that October; however, an attempt to take Quebec in 1711 failed when several transport ships struck rocks in the Saint Lawrence River. More than 900 soldiers and sailors died, and the British commander canceled the operation. The war ended in 1713 with a peace treaty that gave Britain control of Acadia, which was renamed Nova Scotia.

No effort was made by the British government in the decades following the war to frame a consistent colonial policy of any sort, including in regard to Native Americans. Instead, British officials preferred to practice salutary neglect, leaving well enough alone in the colonies. In 1732 King George II did grant James Oglethorpe and a group of trustees a charter to establish the colony of Georgia as a defensive buffer between South Carolina and Spanish Florida. Oglethorpe sought good relations with the colony's Native American inhabitants, a policy that preserved peace and established a prosperous trade in deerskins.

Oglethorpe's policy paid further dividends following the start of the Anglo-Spanish War (1739–1744), also known as the War of Jenkins' Ear. Under Oglethorpe's leadership, a force of Georgia and South Carolina militia along with Native American allies mounted an offensive against St. Augustine in 1740. The Spanish, however, withstood the attack.

In 1744 the conflict broadened when the War of the Austrian Succession (1744–1748), known in the colonies as King George's War, began in Europe. With France now allied with Spain, the British northern colonies again faced the threat of Native American attack. A combined British and New England force captured the French fortress of Louisbourg on Cape Breton Island in June 1745. New England leaders had hoped that this victory would end the Native American threat to their frontiers but were sorely disappointed as French-allied Native Americans staged several attacks that summer against forts and settlements in New Hampshire, Massachusetts, and present-day Maine and Vermont.

The summer raids were followed by an autumn assault on Saratoga by French troops and Native American allies, including some Iroquois. Further attacks on the northern frontier in the spring and summer of 1746 kept the British colonists on the defensive. British officials at last recognized the importance of the Iroquois and urged colonial leaders to secure the confederacy's aid. After two inconclusive conferences, at a July 1748 meeting in Albany, New York, Iroquois leaders told the colonists that they were prepared to assist them. The Iroquois, however, contributed little support, and the colonial frontier continued to suffer from French and Native American raids until the war's end in October 1748. Under the terms of the peace agreement, Britain returned Louisbourg to France.

The British Board of Trade and Plantations, which was responsible for advising the government on colonial matters, decided shortly after the war that the policy of salutary neglect should be ended and that London should assume a larger role in managing colonial affairs. Lord Halifax, the board's president, recommended that the government tighten control over colonial trade and improve the empire's defensive posture in North America. Only the latter plan was partially put into effect, with the establishment of a settlement at Halifax, Nova Scotia, in 1749 as a check on the French at Louisbourg. Despite instructions from Lord Halifax to reach an accommodation with the Micmacs who inhabited Nova Scotia, the new royal governor, Edward Cornwallis, paid little attention to Indian relations. Angered by the British presence, the Micmacs promptly began a war with the Halifax colonists that lasted until the end of the French and Indian War (1754–1763).

With each North American colony still pursuing its own interests, a group of Virginians embarked on a course that would provoke yet another war. In 1749 a group of politically well-connected Virginia land speculators formed the Ohio Company. With the approval of King George II, they procured a grant of 200,000 acres in the Ohio River Valley, territory already claimed by the French. The company sent traders to the area to lure local Native Americans away from their trade connections with the French, and in 1752 the Shawnees, Delawares, Wyandots, and Iroquois signed the Treaty of Logstown, accepting Virginia's claim to the land east of the Ohio River.

The Ohio Company's activities alarmed the French. Determined to oust the British and restore their network of Native American alliances, French troops and Ottawas, Ojibwas, and Pottawatomis allies attacked the Miami village of Pickawillany and its British trading post. The victorious French expelled the traders, and the Miamis switched their allegiance back to the French. Virginia lieutenant governor Robert Dinwiddie responded in 1753 by dispatching George Washington to the region with a demand that the French evacuate their forts. Washington was rebuffed, and the next year Dinwiddie ordered Washington and a militia detachment back to the Ohio Valley to assert Virginia's claim to the territory.

Washington found his force too weak to drive the French from Fort Duquesne at the Forks of the Ohio (present-day Pittsburgh, Pennsylvania) and constructed a fort some distance away. There he was forced to surrender by French troops and their Native American allies in July 1754.

Dinwiddie pressed the British government for assistance. His pleas echoed those of Massachusetts governor William Shirley, who was eager to end the French and Native American threat to the New England frontier. The British government decided to dispatch troops to North America, hoping to win a quick victory over the French and gain territory without provoking a wider European war.

While the British made their preparations, the Board of Trade instructed the northern colonists to meet with the Iroquois and other Native American groups in an effort to mend relations and, if possible, secure Iroquois aid for the coming campaign. Colonial delegates and Iroquois representatives convened at Albany, New York, in June 1754, but achieved nothing. The Iroquois participants, disgusted at the wrangling between the colonial delegates, refused to commit to aiding the colonies.

The failure of the colonists to gain Iroquois support at the Albany Congress was compounded the next year when British major general Edward Braddock arrived with two regular regiments with the assignment to take Fort Duquesne. Representatives of several Ohio Valley Native American nations conferred with Braddock, hoping to secure his pledge that they would retain their lands in exchange for military assistance. Braddock rudely informed the Native American leaders that they would keep none of their territory. Most of the Native Americans promptly joined the French, and the French and Native American force nearly annihilated Braddock's command near Fort Duquesne in July 1755.

The French and Native Americans followed up their victory with devastating raids on the colonial frontier from New England to Virginia. Native American aid enabled the French to maintain the upper hand in the conflict, known in America as the French and Indian War, until 1757. In August of that year after capturing Fort William Henry in New York, the French commander, the Marquis de Montcalm, enraged his Native American allies by allowing the fort's garrison to leave with its possessions. This violated alliance protocol; French leaders had previously allowed the Native Americans to take plunder and captives as compensation for their assistance. The Native Americans responded by attacking the garrison as it left the fort. Montcalm angrily denounced the Native Americans for their behavior, and most of them returned home. Although the Abenakis and a few other northeastern nations continued to aid the French, the loss of most of their Native American allies seriously impaired the French ability to defend Canada. The tide of war shifted in Britain's favor, culminating in the capture of Quebec in 1759.

Seeking to improve Native American relations in order to bolster their position, the British government appointed two superintendents of Indian affairs in 1756. Sir William Johnson, a trader with a Mohawk wife and close ties to the Iroquois, took charge of relations with the Native American nations north of the Ohio River and helped to engineer Iroquois intervention on the British side in 1759. Edmond Atkin, a South Carolinian and a vocal critic of Britain's lack of a consistent policy toward the Native Americans, became superintendent of the nations south of the Ohio.

The British recruited warriors from their Cherokee ally to participate in the 1758 expedition that forced the French to abandon Fort Duquesne. However, some of the Cherokees were killed by Virginians while returning home. The Cherokees responded by attacking the South Carolina frontier in 1759 and were only subdued two years later with the help of a large British force in the first significant campaign undertaken solely against Native Americans by regular troops.

The 1763 Treaty of Paris that ended the French and Indian War ousted France from North America. Realizing that they were now at the mercy of the British and colonists and angered by the tough policies of British commander in chief in North America General Jeffrey Amherst, the northern tribes rallied around Ottawa war leader Pontiac. Pontiac hoped that his Pan-Indian alliance could inflict a severe defeat on the British and permit the Native Americans' traditional ally, France, to return to the continent. The resulting conflict, Pontiac's Rebellion, began in May 1763. After some initial successes the Native Americans were checked, and the individual nations made peace with the British.

Pontiac's Rebellion convinced British officials that a new Native American policy was essential to prevent further warfare on the frontier that had already proved costly in both lives and money. Therefore, instead of imposing harsh terms on the tribes, the British government issued the Proclamation of 1763, which forbade colonial settlement west of the Appalachian Mountains and empowered the Indian superintendents, Johnson and John Stuart, who had replaced Atkin in 1761, to regulate trade and otherwise protect the Native Americans from the colonists' abuses. The proclamation was extremely unpopular among the colonists and was never completely effective. However, it and the subsequent efforts of the Indian superintendents succeeded in winning the goodwill of the Native Americans.

The good relations between the Native Americans and the British enabled the royal government to count on considerable Native American assistance when the American Revolutionary War

A Tory and a Patriot wrestle for a pine tree banner, representing land ownership, while a Native American watches in horror. (Library of Congress)

(1775–1783) began. Nearly all of the major nations supported the British, as they recognized that an American victory would result in an influx of settlers onto their lands.

Cooperation between British and Native American forces proved difficult to achieve, however. Officials in London left strategic and tactical details in the hands of local military commanders and the Indian superintendents. In the North, Mohawk leader Joseph Brant brought most of the Iroquois Confederacy into action on the British side and worked effectively with Loyalist guerrillas in frontier warfare, but the main British forces rarely coordinated their efforts with those of their Native American allies. In the area of present-day Kentucky, the Shawnees also waged a frontier war with little British support.

In the South, Stuart urged the Native Americans to wait for British military assistance before acting, but the Cherokees, eager to avenge their sufferings at the hands of the colonists, ignored Stuart and attacked the frontier in the summer of 1776. A counterattack by militia from the four southernmost states wreaked havoc on Cherokee towns and crops and forced the nation to sue for peace. Although some Cherokees continued to fight the Americans, many stayed aloof from the conflict thereafter, and their defeat caused other southern nations to hesitate in assisting the British. When royal forces did invade Georgia in 1778, coordination with the Creeks could not be achieved due to slow communications and distance.

After the British seized Charleston in 1780 and occupied South Carolina and Georgia, the Cherokees and Creeks offered aid, but it was rejected by the British commander in the South, General Charles Cornwallis. When Cornwallis did call for Native American assistance in late 1780, the Creeks and Choctaws were committed to the defense of Pensacola in West Florida. That city fell to the Spanish in May 1781, and by that time the British were largely confined to the southern coast, and direct communication with their Native American allies had been severed. In the 1783 Treaty of Paris that recognized American independence, British officials ceded all of the territory between the Appalachians and the Mississippi River to the United States without regard for their erstwhile Native American allies.

Faced with the outrage of Joseph Brant, Blue Jacket of the Shawnees, and other Native American leaders, the British government tried to change its position. Officials asserted that the cession of their land claims west of the Appalachians did not effect or extinguish Native American land titles. The governor of Canada, Sir Frederick Haldimand, believed that Native American help would be necessary to defend Canada from an American attack and took steps to mollify the Native Americans, including granting them land in Canada and paying compensation for territory lost to the United States. He also helped to convince leaders in London to retain several forts on American soil that were to be evacuated under the terms of the Treaty of Paris. British officials justified retention of the posts as surety for Congress keeping its promise to compensate the Loyalists for property that the states had seized. Congress claimed that despite its treaty commitment, it had no authority to force the states to make restitution.

From the northwestern forts, British officers and traders engaged in trade with the neighboring Native American nations and dispensed gifts that included arms and ammunition along with encouragement to resist American encroachment. Thus supplied, a Native American alliance led by Blue Jacket and Little Turtle of the Miamis defeated an American expedition in 1790 and a year later inflicted a crushing defeat on a second expedition led by Brigadier General Arthur St. Clair. Encouraged by the Native Americans' success, John Graves Simcoe, lieutenant governor of Upper Canada, pressed his superiors in Quebec and London to provide further support to the Native Americans. Simcoe and others hoped that the Native Americans would force the United States to grant them an independent territory in the Northwest that would be an ally and a defensive buffer for Canada.

Lord Dorchester (Guy Carleton), the new governor of Canada, embraced and went beyond Simcoe's views. Certain that a new Anglo-American war was imminent, beginning in early 1794 Dorchester rallied Native American support, claimed that American actions had invalidated the Treaty of Paris, and ordered Simcoe to move troops from Detroit closer to the Native Americans. Simcoe led 150 men to the Maumee River in Ohio and constructed Fort Miami.

Dorchester's statements were soon disavowed by his superiors in London, and when Major General Anthony Wayne's expedition approached in August 1794, the Native Americans fought without British support and were defeated at Fallen Timbers. The retreating Native Americans sought refuge in Fort Miami, but the commander, Major William Campbell, who had been supplying them, refused to open the fort's gates for fear of starting a war with the United States. The Native Americans made their escape without British aid, but many believed that the British had betrayed them. Later in 1794 the British and U.S. governments signed Jay's Treaty, which was ratified the following year and called for the British to evacuate their posts on American territory, ending direct British support for the Native Americans.

The last significant British involvement in Native American affairs occurred during the War of 1812. Shawnee leader Tecumseh had been working to forge a new Pan-Indian alliance, but his plans had suffered a setback when his brother Tenskwatawa was defeated by American forces at the Battle of Tippecanoe in 1811. When the United States and Britain went to war a year later, Tecumseh allied with the British and was allegedly commissioned a brigadier general in the British Army. His forces fought alongside the British in operations in the Northwest and achieved considerable success. However, in the autumn of 1813 British major general Henry Procter, with whom Tecumseh and his men were cooperating, decided to withdraw into Canada after the American naval victory at the Battle of Lake Erie threatened his supply line. American forces pursued and defeated the Anglo–Native American force at the Battle of the Thames on October 5. Tecumseh was killed, and the American victory signified the end of Native American resistance in the Northwest and effectively ended the British–Native American alliance. When the war ended in 1814, the British provided some of their Native American allies with land in Canada, although most chose to remain in the United States.

JIM PIECUCH

See also

Albany Congress; Anglo-Powhatan War, First; Anglo-Powhatan War, Second; Anglo-Powhatan War, Third; Cherokee War; Fallen Timbers, Battle of; French and Indian War; Iroquois; Johnson, Sir William; King George's War; King Philip's War; King William's War; Native Americans and the American Revolutionary War; Native Americans and the War of 1812; Pequot War; Pontiac's Rebellion; Proclamation of 1763; Queen Anne's War; Stuart, John; Tuscarora War

References

Anderson, Fred. *Crucible of War: The Seven Years' War and the Fate of the Empire in British North America, 1754–1766.* New York: Vintage Books, 2001.

Axtell, James. *Natives and Newcomers: The Cultural Origins of North America.* New York: Oxford University Press, 2001.

Dowd, Gregory Evans. *War under Heaven: Pontiac, the Indian Nations, and the British Empire.* Baltimore: Johns Hopkins University Press, 2002.

Leach, Douglas Edward. *Arms for Empire: A Military History of the British Colonies in North America, 1607–1763.* New York: Macmillan, 1973.

Leach, Douglas Edward. *The Northern Colonial Frontier, 1607–1763.* New York: Holt, Rinehart and Winston, 1966.

Lepore, Jill. *The Name of War: King Philip's War and the Origins of American Identity.* New York: Knopf, 1998.

Piecuch, Jim. *Three Peoples, One King: Loyalists, Indians, and Slaves in the Revolutionary South, 1775–1782.* Columbia: University of South Carolina Press, 2008.

Richter, Daniel K. *The Ordeal of the Longhouse: The People of the Iroquois League in the Era of European Colonization.* Chapel Hill: University of North Carolina Press, 1992.

Robinson, W. Stitt. *The Southern Colonial Frontier, 1607–1763.* Albuquerque: University of New Mexico Press, 1979.

Sosin, Jack M. *Whitehall and the Wilderness: The Middle West in British Colonial Policy, 1760–1775.* Lincoln: University of Nebraska Press, 1961.

Great Law of Peace of the Longhouse People

The oral constitution of the Five Nations (later Six Nations) Confederation, also known as the Iroquois Confederacy or the Haudenosaunee. The Great Law of Peace was also known as the Great Law and the Great Peace. Original member nations were the Senecas, Cayugas, Onondagas, Oneidas, and Mohawks. In 1722 the Tuscaroras became recognized as the sixth member nation of the Iroquois Confederacy. Scholars originally believed that the Great Law of Peace of the Longhouse People (Gayanashagowa) was created in the 1500s as a response to the presence of Europeans on the Atlantic seacoast. More recent studies concerning the founding of the Great Law, however, indicate that it was begun around the end of the 11th century. These studies are in accord with Iroquois beliefs that the Great Peace existed long before the 16th century.

The Great Law of Peace of the Longhouse People was developed by Deganawidah (the Peacemaker) and promulgated by his spokesman Hiawatha in response to the almost continuous warfare among the eventual constituent nations. It was Deganawidah who taught Hiawatha the key ceremonies of the Great Peace, specifically those ceremonies that released grief, commonly referred to as condolence rituals. These rituals were then taken by Hiawatha to the warring nations. The greatest obstacle to the Great Law of Peace was the great warrior-chief Tadadaho of the Onondagas. However, it is believed that Hiawatha and representatives of the other four nations spoke the words of condolence with Tadadaho, curing his body and mind. After this Hiawatha and Tadadaho traveled throughout the lands of the Iroquois, effectively establishing the Great Peace.

In response to Tadadaho's efforts, members of the Onondaga Nation were known as the fire keepers, hosts, and moderators when the Great Council convened. The Great Council consisted of up to 50 chiefs (sachems) representing each of the six nations. The sachems were divided into two moieties—elder and younger—with the Mohawks, Onondagas, and Senecas making up one and the Oneidas, Cayugas, and Tuscaroras making up the other, respectively. To contact or enter the Great Peace, representatives of other nations had to enter metaphorically with the permission of the guardians of either the eastern door (Mohawks) or the western door (Senecas). The council generally met once a year, but more often in times of crisis, to discuss matters of importance to all the nations.

The Great Law of Peace, while not creating true harmony, did create political and legal outlets for the resolution of problems between the constituent tribes. Other nations could join the compact, as did the Tuscaroras in the 1720s.

While often unable to live up to the ideals of the Great Law of Peace, the Iroquois nevertheless struggled to follow its principles. The strength of the Great Peace ensured that the Iroquois Confederacy was able to more or less successfully deal with the strains of European contact until its collapse in the late 1770s during the American Revolutionary War (1775–1783). This meant that the nations were able politically and militarily to dominate many of their neighbors (for example, the dispersal of the Hurons by 1649–1650). Such activities led the Five Nations to become one of the most feared Native American groups by Europeans during the height of the Iroquois Confederacy's power in the 17th and early 18th centuries. The confederacy's power was weakened, however, when it agreed to remain neutral in European conflicts beginning in 1701. Nevertheless, the power of the Great Law of Peace led all the colonial powers in North America to court the Iroquois Confederacy between 1600 and 1814.

KARL S. HELE

See also

Cayugas; Iroquois Confederacy; Longhouse; Mohawks; Native Americans and the American Revolutionary War; Oneidas; Onondagas; Senecas; Tuscaroras

References

Brandão, José António. *Your Fyre Shall Burn No More: Iroquois Policy toward New France and Its Native Allies to 1701.* Lincoln: University of Nebraska Press, 1997.

Fenton, William N. *The Great Law and the Longhouse: A Political History of the Iroquois Confederacy.* Norman: University of Oklahoma Press, 1998.

Parker, A. C. *The Constitution of the Five Nations of The Iroquois Book of the Great Law.* New York: University of the State of New York, 1916.

Richter, Daniel K. *The Ordeal of the Longhouse: The People of the Iroquois League in the Era of European Colonization.* Chapel Hill: University of North Carolina Press, 1992.

Snow, Dean R. *The Iroquois.* Malden, MA: Blackwell, 1994.

Great Platte River Road

Major east-west wagon trail traversing the state of Nebraska and most of Kansas that eventually linked Fort Leavenworth, Kansas, with Fort Laramie, Wyoming. Most of the Great Platte River Road served as a convergence point for the Oregon, Mormon, and California trails. The road was also used by the Pony Express. The Great Platte River Road was constructed during the late 1820s and

1830s and was used principally from about 1841 to 1866. Explorer of the West Robert Stuart has been given credit for being the first American to recognize the importance of the route as early as the 1810s. Many scholars have referred to it as the "superhighway" of its time because it incorporated so many important routes linking east and west. Thousands of migrants seeking a better life in the American West traveled the Great Platte River Road.

Between 1841 and 1866 or so an estimated 250,000 or more people per year traversed the road. Winding its way through often inhospitable prairie lands, the Great Platte River Road presented its travelers with many challenges. Raging blizzards, subzero cold, and scant grazing grounds made winter traveling perilous at best. In the summer, scorching heat, dust, and virtually no shade made the trek an arduous one. Spring rains and snowmelt could easily turn the road into an impassable quagmire. And at any time of the year, Native American raids were a concern.

Over the years, numerous towns and way stations developed along the road to serve travelers. U.S. Army outposts were also constructed to protect the route from Native American attack. Among them was Fort Heath, located near Sutherland's Bluff (O'Fallon).

By the early 1860s railroad travel had begun to diminish the importance of the trail, and by the late 1860s after the transcontinental railroad had linked America's East and West coasts, traffic dropped markedly. In later years much of the road was incorporated into railway routes, and in the 20th century Interstate 80 closely followed the contours of the original route.

PAUL G. PIERPAOLI JR.

See also

Oregon Trail; Pony Express

References

Mattes, Merrill J. *The Great Platte River Road: The Covered Wagon Mainline via Fort Kearny to Fort Laramie.* Nebraska State Historical Society Publications, Vol. 25. Lincoln: Nebraska State Historical Society, 1969.

Olson, James C. *History of Nebraska.* Lincoln: University of Nebraska Press, 1966.

Great Sioux Reservation

Primary reservation for the various Sioux bands from 1868 to 1889. Established in 1868 as part of the Fort Laramie Treaty of 1868, the Great Sioux Reservation set aside land encompassing the present-day state of South Dakota west of the Missouri River, including the sacred Black Hills, for the seven bands of the Lakota Nation, with hunting rights in the nonceded Indian territory bordering the reservation. The treaty, a direct result of Oglala chief Red Cloud's offensive against military outposts on the Bozeman Trail from 1866 to 1868, prohibited unauthorized white settlement in the Black Hills, established agencies on the reservation for the disbursement of federal money and commodities, and stipulated

that no further treaty could cede reservation land without the approval of three-fourths of the adult male population.

The discovery of gold in the Black Hills in 1874 nevertheless led to encroachment onto the reservation by non–Native Americans. Lakota tribal leaders met with President Ulysses S. Grant in Washington, D.C., during the summer of 1875 in an unsuccessful effort to persuade the U.S. government to honor its treaty and remove the trespassers. A subsequent government directive ignoring the treaty's provision for Lakota hunting rights beyond the western boundaries of the Great Sioux Reservation and requiring all tribes to be on the reservation by January 31, 1876, served only to heighten tensions and instigate the so-called Great Sioux War (Black Hills War) of 1876–1877. Successive Native American victories at the Battle of the Rosebud (June 17, 1876) and the Battle of Little Bighorn (June 25–26, 1876) were short-lived, however, and by 1877 the Lakotas and their allies were back on the reservation.

The last decades of the 19th century witnessed the systematic dissection of the Great Sioux Reservation. The passage of the Dawes Severalty Act in 1887 combined with impending statehood status for North Dakota and South Dakota paved the way for the dismantling of the reservation in 1889 into five separate smaller reservations: Pine Ridge, Rosebud, Lower Brulé, Cheyenne River, and Standing Rock. The remaining half of the territory that was once encompassed by the Great Sioux Reservation was subsequently made available for sale to white ranchers and homesteaders.

ALAN C. DOWNS

See also

Black Hills, South Dakota; Dawes Severalty Act; Fort Laramie, Treaty of (1868); Great Sioux War; Lakota Sioux; Little Bighorn, Battle of the; Red Cloud; Rosebud, Battle of the

References

Hendron, Paul L. *Fort Laramie and the Great Sioux War.* Norman: University of Oklahoma Press, 1998.

Utley, Robert M. *Frontier Regulars: The United States and the American Indian, 1866–1891.* New York: Macmillan, 1973.

Great Sioux War

Start Date: 1876
End Date: 1877

Conflict waged in Montana, Wyoming, and the Dakotas during 1876–1877 that pitted the U.S. Army against Lakota Sioux and their allies. Best known as the Great Sioux War or the Black Hills War, it is also known as the Centennial Campaign or Sitting Bull's War. The most famous engagement of the war was the Battle of the Little Bighorn (June 25–26, 1876), also known as Custer's Last Stand.

The underlying causes of the Great Sioux War were ongoing white encroachment into the Black Hills region; Lakota and Cheyenne raids against the Crows, who were U.S. allies; and Lakota resistance to railroad and settler expansion in the Dakota Territory

GREAT SIOUX WAR, 1876

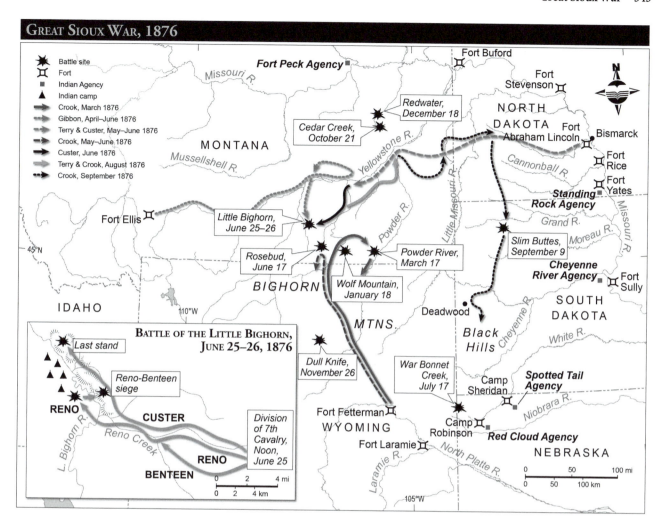

Legend:
- ✹ Battle site
- ⊞ Fort
- ■ Indian Agency
- ▲ Indian camp
- → Crook, March 1876
- → Gibbon, April–June 1876
- → Terry & Custer, May–June 1876
- → Crook, May–June 1876
- → Custer, June 1876
- → Terry & Crook, August 1876
- → Crook, September 1876

Map labels: Fort Peck Agency; Fort Buford; Fort Stevenson; Fort Abraham Lincoln; Bismarck; Fort Rice; Fort Yates; NORTH DAKOTA; Standing Rock Agency; Missouri R.; Redwater, December 18; Cedar Creek, October 21; Yellowstone R.; Cannonball R.; Grand R.; Slim Buttes, September 9; Moreau R.; Cheyenne River Agency; Fort Sully; MONTANA; Mussellshell R.; Fort Ellis; Little Bighorn, June 25–26; Powder R.; Little Missouri R.; Rosebud, June 17; Powder River, March 17; Wolf Mountain, January 18; BIGHORN MTNS.; Deadwood; Black Hills; Cheyenne R.; SOUTH DAKOTA; White R.; IDAHO; Dull Knife, November 26; War Bonnet Creek, July 17; Camp Sheridan; Spotted Tail Agency; Niobrara R.; Fort Fetterman; WYOMING; Camp Robinson; Red Cloud Agency; NEBRASKA; Fort Laramie; Laramie R.; North Platte R.

Inset: BATTLE OF THE LITTLE BIGHORN, JUNE 25–26, 1876 — Last stand; Reno-Benteen siege; RENO; CUSTER; L. Bighorn R.; Reno Creek; RENO; BENTEEN; Division of 7th Cavalry, Noon, June 25; 0 2 4 mi; 0 2 4 km.

and Montana. The most important catalyst, however, was resistance by the Lakotas to a U.S. government order to move onto their assigned reservations in the Dakota Territory. Led by Oglala chief Crazy Horse and the Hunkpapa medicine man Sitting Bull, various bands of the Lakota Nation steadfastly resisted the government order to relocate. Instead, they remained in the Powder River and Yellowstone River country of Wyoming and Montana, where they were joined by hundreds of other Native Americans from reservations.

The army campaign was to begin in early 1876 with three columns moving from the south, the northwest, and the northeast into the Powder River and Yellowstone River country in winter strikes on the Lakota and Cheyenne encampments. This plan miscarried, however, because of the severity of the winter weather. Brigadier General George Crook's Bighorn expedition finally got under way in February, but after the army's success in a fight along the Powder River on March 17, the Lakotas counterattacked Crook's subordinate, and Crook lost the ponies he had captured. He then withdrew to refit his command. Colonel John Gibbon's column did not depart from Fort Ellis in Montana Territory until March 30 and only scouted along the northern bank of

the Yellowstone River. Brigadier General Alfred H. Terry did not depart Fort Abraham Lincoln until May 17, so the notion of winter offensives had by then completely fallen through.

By mid-June 1876 the summertime movement of tribes on reservations to their hunting territories was already under way. Bands led by Sitting Bull and Crazy Horse were now augmented by hundreds of young aggressive warriors. Crook resumed his northward movement into Montana Territory from what is today Sheridan, Wyoming. On June 17, 1876, his troops were attacked by a force of more than 1,000 warriors. In a daylong fight along Rosebud Creek the attackers were repulsed, and the Native Americans sustained heavy casualties. Crook was taken aback by the willingness of the Native Americans to stand and fight and once again pulled back to reorganize his force. However, he was unable to directly communicate news of his setback to the other converging columns, which proceeded unawares.

In the meantime, Gibbon continued to scout the Yellowstone but made no significant contact with the hostile tribes. He eventually linked up with Terry's force, which included the 7th U.S. Cavalry Regiment under Lieutenant Colonel George A. Custer, in mid-June along the Yellowstone River. Terry, Gibbon, and Custer together planned a combined assault on a Native American encampment in the Little Bighorn Valley. Custer would move south along the Rosebud with the fast-moving 7th Cavalry and turn west toward the Little Bighorn to prevent the hostile warriors from escaping south. Gibbon would take his slower-moving infantry down the Little Bighorn, trapping the Native Americans between them.

On June 25 Custer began his westward swing, becoming aware of a large Native American encampment in the Little Bighorn Valley. In the afternoon, after splitting the 7th Cavalry into three battalions, he commenced an attack on the camp, which was the combined encampment of Sitting Bull's and Crazy Horse's warriors reinforced with hundreds of others, without waiting for Gibbon and Terry. Major Marcus Reno's battalion was repulsed and retreated to a hill while under constant attack. Custer's battalion moved north along the river to encircle the village, but this proved impossible because the village was too large. His battalion was surrounded and annihilated in an engagement that lasted a mere 30 minutes. Custer had, however, already summoned Captain Frederick Benteen's battalion forward. Benteen encountered Reno's troops and joined with them instead of continuing to the north. Reno's and Benteen's commands were immobilized because of the loss of horses until June 27, when Gibbon's column arrived. By then the Native Americans had scattered, and Reno's, Benteen's, and Gibbon's men had the grim task of burying the 268 soldiers and civilian scouts who had died at the Battle of the Little Bighorn.

Marches and countermarches engaged U.S. soldiers throughout the summer and early autumn. The only bright spot for the army was an engagement on Warbonnet Creek on July 17 in which Colonel Wesley Merritt and his 5th U.S. Cavalry Regiment intercepted several hundred Cheyennes who were trying to escape the Red Cloud Agency on the Platte River to join their cousins in the hunting territory.

Troops were rushed to the area from across the West, and by late summer some 40 percent of the U.S. Army was involved in the campaign, including all of the army's top Indian fighting officers. By September many of the Native Americans were hungry and tired, having had no time to hunt and being perpetually on the move. On September 9 at Slim Buttes in northwestern South Dakota, Crook managed to destroy a large camp of Miniconjou Lakota under the leadership of American Horse.

Campaigning lasted throughout the autumn and winter of 1876–1877. The army established several semipermanent camps in the heart of unceded Native American hunting grounds, which served as bases from which to harass the still-resistant tribes. Colonel Nelson A. Miles and the 5th U.S. Infantry Regiment attacked several Native American villages, most successfully at Cedar Creek, Montana, on October 21, 1876.

Under Crook's overall command, Colonel Ranald S. Mackenzie and his 4th Cavalry also hit Native American camps, destroying Cheyenne chief Dull Knife's camp during November 25–26. Sitting Bull and his band fled to Canada in January 1877 because of the relentless pressure from Miles, and Crazy Horse surrendered

Two soldiers on either side of Sioux captured after the Battle of Slim Buttes in Wyoming, September 9–10, 1876. Note the 7th Cavalry guidon in front of the tipi, apparently captured by the Sioux during the Battle of Little Bighorn the previous June. (Getty Images)

on May 6, 1877, at Camp Robinson, Nebraska, ending the Great Sioux War.

JOHN THOMAS BROOM

See also

Benteen, Frederick William; Crazy Horse; Crook, George; Custer, George Armstrong; Dull Knife; Gibbon, John; Lakota Sioux; Little Bighorn, Battle of the; Mackenzie, Ranald Slidell; Merritt, Wesley; Miles, Nelson Appleton; Reno, Marcus Albert; Rosebud, Battle of the; Sitting Bull; Slim Buttes, Battle of; Terry, Alfred Howe

References

Carlson, Paul H. *The Plains Indians.* College Station: Texas A&M University Press, 1998.

Gibbon, Guy. *The Sioux: The Dakota and Lakota Nations.* Malden, MA: Blackwell, 2003.

Goodrich, Thomas. *Scalp Dance: Indian Warfare on the High Plains, 1865–1879.* Mechanicsburg, PA: Stackpole, 1997.

Gray, John S. *Centennial Campaign: the Sioux War of 1876.* Norman: Oklahoma University Press, 1988.

Hassrick, Royal B. *The Sioux: The Life and Customs of a Warrior Nation.* Norman: University of Oklahoma Press, 1964.

Hedren, Paul L., ed. *The Great Sioux War, 1876–77.* Helena: Montana Historical Society Press, 1991.

Great Swamp Fight
Event Date: December 19, 1675

Major battle of King Philip's War (1675–1676) that led the heretofore neutral Narragansett tribe to join King Philip (Metacom, Metacomet), leader of the Wampanoags, in his war against the English colonists. In the autumn of 1675, Metacom's forces attacked and destroyed numerous colonial towns in southern New England. In short order his forces grew in both confidence and numbers.

The large and powerful Narragansett tribe, situated in Rhode Island, was officially neutral. However, colonial leaders believed that some Narragansett warriors were secretly joining Metacom's raiding parties and that the tribe itself was harboring wounded warriors. Determined to put an end to such assistance, the commissioners of the New England Confederation (Massachusetts Bay, Connecticut, and Plymouth) recalled most militia units from the western frontier. They also recruited new units, assembling the largest colonial force that America had seen to that point.

The United Colonies placed the troops, drawn from all three colonies, under the overall command of Plymouth governor Josiah Winslow, with Major Samuel Appleton in charge of the Massachusetts men, Major William Bradford commanding the Plymouth contingent, and Major Robert Trent in charge of the Connecticut men. On December 9, 1675, Winslow's entire force, which numbered more than 1,000 colonists and 150 allied Mohegans, marched from Massachusetts Bay toward the Rhode Island stronghold of the Narragansetts.

That year the Narragansetts had decided to winter in a large fortification on the edges of the Great Swamp. The natives felt safe in their nearly completed fortification, especially since they knew that the English disliked fighting in the thick woods and swampy land that surrounded the stronghold.

On December 13, 1675, the majority of the colonial army gathered at Wickford, Rhode Island, on the fringes of the Great Swamp. From there they spent several days attacking nearby native enclaves. The winter weather had made traversing the land easier for the militiamen, for it had stripped the leaves from the underbrush and had frozen the otherwise swampy ground.

In one of these attacks the colonists captured a warrior named Indian Peter, who promised to lead them to the Narragansett fort. After the delayed arrival of troops from Connecticut, Winslow decided that the time had come for the main attack. By then his men were running low on food, and the winter conditions were already taking a toll.

On December 18 the colonial forces, led by Indian Peter, moved into the swamp. They sighted their objective the next afternoon. The fort was constructed of wooden palisades with a mass of brush and timber around the base of the wall and small blockhouses at each corner. A sizable village of huts lay within the walls. At the time of the colonial attack, there were some 1,000 natives in the fort.

Without time to properly plan an attack, the vanguard of the colonial army rushed the fort. With incredible luck they happened on a gap in the wall, although it was protected by a nearby blockhouse. Two companies rushed the opening and broke through, only to lose their captains and be forced back. As other troops rushed forward, they were able to break into the village and force the Narragansetts to fall back. The fight inside became a series of individual battles among the native dwellings.

Winslow, worried about the fierce fighting, gave the order to burn the fort to force the natives into the open. Winslow's aide, Captain Benjamin Church, tried to dissuade him, arguing that the colonials might use the fort for shelter after the battle was won. However, the militiamen began to burn the huts with men, women, and children still inside. It was a scene reminiscent of the English attack on Mystic Fort during the Pequot War (1636–1638).

Soon all the fort was afire. While some warriors escaped into the woods, many more Native Americans—mostly women, children, and the elderly—died in the fire. Contemporary estimates of Narragansett dead ranged from 600 to as many as 1,000. The colonials lost 20 killed and some 200 wounded, about 20 percent of their force. The allied Mohegans suffered 51 dead and 82 wounded.

The colonials took quick stock and then prepared to move back to their base at Wickford. The weather was turning worse, and now that the fort and its dwellings had been destroyed, there was no place to shelter the men, especially the wounded. The colonials quickly fashioned stretchers and began the overnight march to Wickford. The retreat was difficult, especially for the wounded, and conditions sharply deteriorated with the arrival of a winter storm. The colonials also feared a Narragansett counterattack.

By the time the colonials had reached Wickford early the next morning, a number of the wounded had died. Within a month the toll of the dead had risen to 80. Losses were especially high among the officers. Half of the 14 company commanders perished. While the campaign was considered a success, this came at a heavy price.

In the weeks that followed, Winslow's men tried to pursue the Narragansetts who had escaped the fort, but the colonists were undersupplied and unfamiliar with the terrain. Unable to continue their winter campaign, the colonists struggled home by early February in what became known as the Hungry March during which they were reduced to eating a number of their horses in order to survive.

In retrospect, it is questionable whether the campaign was actually successful. Before the attack the Narragansetts were officially neutral. While the colonials had dealt the Narragansetts a terrible blow, the tribe's survivors, determined to exact revenge, now made common cause with Metacom, creating yet another enemy for the United Colonies.

KYLE F. ZELNER

See also

Church, Benjamin; King Philip's War; Metacom; Mystic Fort Fight; Narragansetts; Wampanoags

References

Bodge, George Madison. *Soldiers in King Philip's War.* 3rd ed. Baltimore: Genealogical Publishing, 1967.

Chet, Guy. *Conquering the American Wilderness: The Triumph of European Warfare in the Colonial Northeast.* Amherst: University of Massachusetts Press, 2003.

Leach, Douglas Edward. *Flintlock and Tomahawk: New England in King Philip's War.* East Orleans, MA: Parnassus Imprints, 1992.

Malone, Patrick M. *The Skulking Way of War: Technology and Tactics among the New England Indians.* Lanham, MD: Madison Books, 2000.

Great Swamp Fortress

Redoubt constructed by the Narragansett Indians in the late 17th century in the so-called Great Swamp, located near present-day South Kingstown, Rhode Island. The Great Swamp served as the winter encampment for the Narragansett tribe and was located very close to the Atlantic Ocean. The Great Swamp Fortress (also known as Canochet's Fort, after the military leader who probably created the stronghold) was built well into the swamp itself to make access to it more difficult. By the same token, however, egress out of the fort was also made more difficult. The fort was constructed of earthen berms reinforced by high palisades made out of felled trees and tree limbs.

The Great Swamp Fortress was surrounded by a moat that was fordable only when a log or other device was placed across it. The Narragansetts had erected the fort to be nearer to navigable waters during the cold winter months, but it was increasingly used as a refuge of sorts from the steadily increasing encroachments of English settlers. The redoubt became infamous when settlers savagely attacked it in 1675 during King Philip's War (1675–1676).

The colonists' campaign against the Narragansetts, who had hitherto remained neutral during King Philip's War, was meant as punishment for their failure to turn over Native Americans living among them who were allied with Metacom. The Narragansetts had signed two treaties promising to give up the colonists' enemies by October 28, 1675, and the colonists began preparing for war soon after this deadline had passed. Perhaps the more substantial motive for the attack was the fact that the United Colonies of Plymouth, Massachusetts Bay, and Connecticut feared that the Narragansetts, a militarily powerful group with an estimated 2,000 warriors, would ally with Metacom's forces and greatly weaken the colonial position.

In mid-November the colonies raised an army led by Josiah Winslow, governor of Plymouth, consisting of 1,000 colonists and 150 Mohegans. Its aim was to engage and destroy the Narragansett tribe. Soon after beginning their campaign, the settlers captured a Narragansett named Peter, who guided them to the Great Swamp Fortress. Luckily for the colonials, the usually impassable swamp was frozen over, making possible a direct assault on the fortress.

Winslow's men concentrated their attack, which occurred on December 19, 1675, against a weak point in the fort. Regardless, the Narragansetts repelled the first attack and inflicted heavy losses on the English forces and their Mohegan allies. The second assault, however, succeeded in breeching the Great Swamp Fortress, and close fighting ensued among the densely arranged Indian lodgings. In the midst of the melee the colonists set fire to the fort and the food stores within it. The women and children in the confines of the walls had no chance to escape and were either killed by the colonists or perished in the flames. The battle, known as the Great Swamp Fight, was the bloodiest day of King Philip's War.

CAMERON B. STRANG

See also

Great Swamp Fight; King Philip's War; Metacom; Mohegans; Narragansetts

References

Drake, James D. *King Philip's War: Civil War in New England, 1675–1676.* Amherst: University of Massachusetts Press, 1999.

Schultz, Eric B., and Michael J. Tougias. *King Philip's War: The History and Legacy of America's Forgotten Conflict.* Woodstock, VT: Countryman, 1999.

Greenville, Treaty of

Major treaty between the United States and tribes of the Old Northwest. The signing of the Treaty of Greenville on August 3, 1795, marked the end of British power in the Old Northwest Territory; revealed the strength of the new federal government; formally ended Little Turtle's War (1790–1794), also known as the Northwest Indian War; and dashed any hopes for a Native American confederation to oppose further American settlement in the region. The treaty was signed near Waterville, Ohio, after negotiations between Major General Anthony ("Mad Anthony") Wayne, commander of the Legion of the United States, and several regional tribes, namely the Delawares, Shawnees, Ottawas, Ojibwas, Miamis, Kickapoos, and Pottawatomis. The treaty was intended to set the boundaries between Native American and American lands. Ideally, the treaty could have ended tensions between Native Americans and white Americans but ultimately failed to do so because the Americans did not honor it.

Earlier treaties had structured the American land once owned by Great Britain by opening up the Ohio River Valley to white settlers, who continued to settle on Native American lands. Jay's Treaty of 1794 had formalized the border between the United States and British-controlled Canada, and Great Britain had agreed to surrender its border forts to the United States. To the Native Americans, however, those forts were symbols of British protection, and they thus rejected American rule.

Many regional tribes joined a confederacy to fight American settlement, but others made separate treaties with Americans and ceded large portions of land without authority to do so. The change in power and the increasing loss of land caused resentment among many Native Americans, however. They took out their resentments on white settlers, who then retaliated in kind. The tribes continued to demand that the Ohio River mark the boundary between American and Native American lands, yet white settlers continued to flood into the area.

The failure of negotiations initiated after the Native Americans defeated an American military expedition in 1791 led to another American attempt to subjugate the Native Americans, which culminated with the Battle of Fallen Timbers (August 20, 1794) just south of present-day Toledo, Ohio. There Wayne's Legion of the United States soundly defeated the confederated tribes under Shawnee chief Blue Jacket. The Native Americans then fled to the British-held Fort Miami, where they had been promised protection. They expected the British to help them fight the Americans,

A painting by Howard Chandler Christy depicting the signing of the Treaty of Greenville at present-day Greenville, Ohio, on August 3, 1795. The treaty followed Major General Anthony Wayne's victory in the Battle of Fallen Timbers and led to the cession of extensive Indian lands in the Old Northwest. (Getty Images)

but the British demurred. In November 1794 the Americans negotiated Jay's Treaty, which forced the British to evacuate their posts inside U.S. boundaries.

Several tribal leaders and General Wayne subsequently met to negotiate a new treaty. After eight months of talks, they signed the Treaty of Greenville on August 3, 1795. In it the tribes ceded most of the Ohio River Valley, part of Indiana, 16 sites on Michigan waterways, Mackinac Island, and land around Niagara, Detroit, and Michilimackinac. They also gave up all land south and east of the boundary beginning at the mouth of the Cuyahoga River and then extending southward to Fort Laurens, westward to Fort Laramie and Fort Recovery, and southward to the Ohio River. The Ojibwas, the Ottawas, and the Pottawatomis also ceded Bois Blanc Island, hoping to demonstrate their goodwill toward the Americans. For their part, the Native Americans received cash payments and a promise of annual payments in the future.

BILLIE FORD

See also

Blue Jacket; Fallen Timbers, Battle of; Little Turtle's War; Old Northwest Territory; Wayne, Anthony

References

Hinderaker, Eric. *Elusive Empires: Constructing Colonialism in the Ohio Valley, 1673–1800.* New York: Cambridge University Press, 1997.
Prucha, Francis Paul. *American Indian Treaties: The History of a Political Anomaly.* Berkeley: University of California Press, 1994.

Gregg, John Irvin
Birth Date: July 26, 1826
Death Date: January 6, 1892

U.S. Army officer and commander of the 8th Cavalry Regiment (1866–1879). John Irvin Gregg was born at Bellefonte, Pennsylvania, on July 26, 1826. After working in the family business, he volunteered for service in the Mexican-American War (1846–1848) and in 1847 was commissioned a first lieutenant in the 11th Infantry Regiment. He earned promotion to captain within the year. At the war's conclusion, he mustered out of the service and returned to private life.

When the American Civil War (1861–1865) began, Gregg reentered the army as a captain in the newly formed 3rd Cavalry Regiment (which soon thereafter became the 6th Cavalry Regiment), joining his distant cousin David McMurtrie Gregg. The tall and imposing Irvin Gregg saw extensive action in 1862, fighting with his regulars during the Peninsula Campaign, in the Seven Days' Campaign, the Second Battle of Bull Run, and the Antietam Campaign before moving to the volunteer forces as colonel of the 16th Pennsylvania Cavalry in November 1862. In the Cavalry Corps, Army of the Potomac, he distinguished himself as a brigade commander at Brandy Station, Aldie, and Upperville in June 1863 and at Gettysburg in July. Gregg also saw heavy action in the campaigns of 1864, especially at Yellow Tavern, in the federal raid on Richmond, and at Trevilian Station. Already wounded several times, he was again wounded and captured during the frenetic Appomattox Campaign in April 1865 but was released three days later upon the surrender of Confederate general Robert E. Lee.

Brevetted through major general of U.S. Volunteers and brigadier general in the regular army, Gregg mustered out of the volunteers in August 1865. The following year during a reorganization of the regular army he received an appointment as colonel of the 8th Cavalry Regiment, which curiously pushed him ahead of several of his Civil War superiors such as George Crook, Wesley Merritt, and George A. Custer.

Posted to the Arizona Territory during the volatile postwar period, Gregg commanded the Prescott District out of Fort Whipple, directing numerous expeditions against the Mojaves. He ran afoul of his department commander, Brigadier General Irvin McDowell, when in the spring of 1867 Gregg declared that all Native Americans in his district found off the reservation were hostile, invalidating passes issued by Indian agents. Forced to reverse his position, he instituted a policy that settlers found far too accommodating to the Native Americans. Nor could Gregg please his regiment, which, forced to endure harsh conditions and rigorous campaigning, posted an alarmingly high desertion rate. Gregg narrowly escaped death when a detachment he joined in the field was ambushed by Walapais near Music Mountain in northwestern Arizona. Nevertheless, his persistent campaigning against the Walapais and Yavapais paid off as the army slowly brought order to that region.

Gregg commanded at Fort Union in the New Mexico Territory from 1870 to 1872 and later led a surveying and mapping expedition in the Texas Panhandle. His final years as colonel of the 8th Cavalry were largely uneventful, and he retired on April 2, 1879. Gregg died in Washington, D.C., on January 6, 1892.

DAVID COFFEY

See also

Cavalry Regiment, 8th U.S.; Crook, George; Custer, George Armstrong; Merritt, Wesley; Mojaves; Yavapais

References

Coffey, David. *Sheridan's Lieutenants: Phil Sheridan, His Generals, and the Final Year of the Civil War.* Lanham, MD: Rowman and Littlefield, 2005.

Thrapp, Dan L. *The Conquest of Apacheria.* Norman: University of Oklahoma Press, 1967.

Grierson, Benjamin Henry
Birth Date: July 8, 1826
Death Date: August 31, 1911

U.S. Army officer and commander of the African American 10th Cavalry Regiment. Born on July 8, 1826, in Pittsburgh, Pennsylvania, Benjamin Henry Grierson moved to Ohio and then Illinois with his family. His first career was as a musician and music teacher, including work as a bugler for a militia company. He gave this up in 1854 and tried his hand at business. He also became active in politics, at first with the Know-Nothing Party and then with the new Republican Party, because of his opposition to slavery. Meanwhile, his business venture failed in 1859.

With the beginning of the American Civil War (1861–1865), Grierson enlisted as a private but was commissioned a major of the 6th Illinois Cavalry in October 1861. Promoted to colonel in April 1862, he commanded the regiment in numerous engagements in northern Mississippi and western Tennessee before receiving command of a brigade in December. Grierson gained fame when he led his brigade of 1,700 men almost 900 miles during April 17–May 2, 1863, to divert attention from Major General Ulysses S. Grant's campaign against Vicksburg. This highly successful raid won Grierson promotion to brigadier general of volunteers on June 3, 1863. Grierson fought in the Battle of Brice's Crossroads (June 10, 1864) in Mississippi, withdrawing only after his men ran out of ammunition. He then led raids into Mississippi and against Mobile, Alabama, ending the war as a brevet major general.

Following the Civil War, Grierson elected to stay in the army and accepted appointment as a colonel of the 10th Cavalry, one of two regular army cavalry regiments established for African American soldiers but officered by whites. Unlike some white commanders of black troops, Grierson was sympathetic toward his men and placed great trust in them. After commanding Fort Riley and Fort Gibson in the late 1860s, Grierson selected the site for Fort Sill in Indian Territory (near present-day Lawton, Oklahoma), and from 1869 to 1872 he supervised its construction. He then served as its first commander. Known for his efforts to achieve a fair and lasting peace with Native Americans, he angered a number of whites on the Texas frontier by his advocacy of a peace policy with the Kiowas and Comanches. In May 1871 Grierson arrested chiefs Satanta, Satank, and Big Tree, who had led what was known as the

Colonel Benjamin H. Grierson commanded the 10th U.S. Cavalry Regiment in the West after the Civil War. The 10th was one of two regular army cavalry regiments established for African American soldiers but officered by whites. (Library of Congress)

Warren Wagon Train Raid in northern Texas. During 1873–1874 Grierson was superintendent of the Mounted Recruiting Service at St. Louis, Missouri.

Grierson commanded Fort Concho, Texas, from 1875 to 1878. As commander of the District of the Pecos during 1878–1880, he explored and mapped the Trans-Pecos area and supervised the construction of wagon roads and telegraph lines that opened western Texas to white settlement. During the summer of 1880 Grierson led troops that drove Victorio into Mexico, where Victorio was killed by Mexican militia, ending the Native American threat to western Texas. In 1882 Grierson shifted his headquarters to Fort Davis, which he expanded, and he also invested in land nearby.

Grierson commanded the Department of Texas during September–October 1883. Transferred to Arizona in the spring of 1885, he had charge first of Whipple Barracks and then of Fort Grant. He commanded the District of New Mexico from 1886 to 1888, when he dealt sympathetically with problems on the Jicarilla Apache and Navajo reservations. In 1888 Grierson assumed command of the Department of Arizona. Promoted to brigadier general on April 5, 1890, he retired on July 8. Grierson died on August 31, 1911, in Omena, Michigan.

DANIEL E. SPECTOR AND SPENCER C. TUCKER

See also

Cavalry Regiment, 9th U.S.; Cavalry Regiment, 10th U.S.; Fort Sill; Hatch, Edward; Lone Wolf; Navajos; Victorio; Warren Wagon Train Raid

References

Leckie, William H., and Shirley A. Leckie. *The Buffalo Soldiers: A Narrative of the Black Cavalry in the West.* Norman: University of Oklahoma Press, 2003.

Leckie, William H., and Shirley A. Leckie. *Unlikely Warriors: General Benjamin H. Grierson and His Family.* Norman: University of Oklahoma Press, 1984.

Schubert, Frank N. *Black Valor: Buffalo Soldiers and the Medal of Honor, 1870–1898.* Wilmington, DE: Scholarly Resources, 1997.

Grouard, Frank
Birth Date: September 20, 1805
Death Date: August 15, 1905

Native American scout. Frank Grouard was born on September 20, 1805, of mixed heritage. He claimed that his birthplace was the Society Islands (French Polynesia in the South Pacific), but that is subject to debate. His father, Benjamin Grouard, was allegedly an American of the Mormon faith, and his mother was of Polynesian descent. As a small child, Frank Grouard moved with his family first to Utah and then to southern California. Probably in 1854 his mother returned to the Society Islands, leaving her husband and son behind. The following year he was adopted by a Mormon missionary family and moved with them to Utah. In 1865 at the age of 15, Grouard ran away from home and found work in Montana as a stage driver and express rider. By the late 1860s he had found steady work as a mail carrier.

While on a mail run in 1869 along the Milk River in Montana, Grouard was ambushed and captured by a band of Crow warriors. They stole his possessions and left him in a wooded area, where a group of Hunkpapa Sioux later spotted him and took him in. Sioux leader Sitting Bull later adopted Grouard as a brother. Grouard's dark, slightly exotic features likely convinced the Hunkpapas that Grouard was part Native American. Grouard fully embraced the Sioux way of life, eventually marrying a Sioux woman and learning the Sioux language. Around 1876, however, he decided to leave the Sioux enclave where Sitting Bull and Crazy Horse held forth and went to Nebraska. There Grouard became an emissary at the Red Cloud Agency, where his facility in both English and Sioux proved highly valuable.

Later that year Brigadier General George Crook made Grouard his chief scout. This was ironic because Crook's major goal was the defeat of the Sioux. When Sitting Bull learned that his erstwhile adopted brother was now working for the U.S. Army, he vowed to kill him in battle. Grouard helped Crook locate Crazy Horse's camp near Montana's Powder River in mid-March 1876. By now the Great Sioux War (Black Hills War) of 1876–1877 was in full swing, and Grouard saw action at the Battle of the Rosebud (June 17, 1876).

Grouard was also present during the Battle of Slim Buttes (September 8–9, 1876) and participated in the Yellowstone expeditions. He remained a scout for many years, seeing action during the Ghost Dance rebellion and at the Battle of Wounded Knee on December 29, 1890. By the early 1890s Grouard had become a genuine folk hero of the West. Eventually he moved east to St. Louis, where he died on August 15, 1905. Sitting Bull never had the opportunity to exact his revenge on Grouard, whom he considered an ungrateful turncoat, and bitterly denounced Grouard until his own death in December 1890.

PAUL G. PIERPAOLI JR.

See also

Crazy Horse; Crook, George; Crows; Ghost Dance; Great Sioux War; Hunkpapa Sioux; Little Bighorn, Battle of the; Rosebud, Battle of the; Sioux; Sitting Bull; Slim Buttes, Battle of; Wounded Knee, Battle of

References

Cozzens, Peter, ed. *Eyewitnesses to the Indian Wars, 1865–1890.* 5 vols. Mechanicsburg, PA: Stackpole, 2001–2006.

De Barthe, Joe. *The Life and Adventures of Frank Grouard.* Norman: University of Oklahoma Press, 1958.

Utley, Robert M. *The Last Days of the Sioux Nation.* 2nd ed. New Haven, CT: Yale University Press, 2004.

Guipago

See Lone Wolf

Gun Merchant of Okchai

Birth Date: Unknown
Death Date: Late 1770s

Leader of the Abihka (proper name Enotonachee) town of Okchai who acted as one of the headmen (*mico*) in the Upper Creek Confederacy around 1746–1775. Prior to the mid-1740s, Lower Creek headmen from the Cowetas had taken the lead in Anglo-Creek diplomacy, but a British-Coweta dispute over Mary Musgrove's land claims cooled the relationship. As a result, Upper Creek influence grew. The Gun Merchant of Okchai benefited from this shift in British attention and would remain a major figure in Anglo-Creek relations until well after 1763.

Gun Merchant continued the Cowetas' policy of neutrality toward European powers. During the French and Indian War (1754–1763) he refused to make war on either French or British settlements. This was a difficult position to maintain, however, as Gun Merchant's brother-in-law, the Mortar of the Okchai, continually courted the French in an effort to draw the Creeks into an anti-British alliance during both the French and Indian War and Pontiac's Rebellion (1763).

In addition to maintaining Creek neutrality, Gun Merchant made equity in the deerskin trade a top priority. He made peace with the Cherokees in 1749 and learned from them that Cherokee deerskins fetched better prices from British traders. Thus, he pressed the British for more favorable prices, and in 1756 he went so far as to promise Creek territory for a British fort if trade prices were adjusted. His people rebuffed the fort plan, costing Gun Merchant some prestige, but he nonetheless used his influence in an effort to preserve Creek neutrality during the American Revolutionary War (1775–1783) until he died, sometime in the late 1770s.

ROBERT PAULETT

See also

Brims of Coweta; Cherokees; Creek-Cherokee Wars; Creeks; French and Indian War; Indian Presents; Mortar of the Okchai; Musgrove, Mary

References

Braund, Kathryn E. Holland. *Deerskins & Duffels: The Creek Indian Trade with Anglo-America, 1685–1815.* Lincoln: University of Nebraska Press, 1993.

Corkran, David H. *The Creek Frontier, 1540–1783.* Norman: University of Oklahoma Press, 1967.

Hahn, Stephen C. *The Invention of the Creek Nation, 1670–1763.* Lincoln: University of Nebraska Press, 2004.

H

Haigler

Birth Date: ca. 1700
Death Date: August 30, 1763

Leader of the Catawba Nation (1750–1763). Born about 1700, most likely at the ancient Catawba ceremonial center at Pine Tree Hill (present-day Camden, South Carolina), King Haigler reportedly spoke some English in private but refused to speak English in conference, relying instead on interpreters. As a child he may have been one of the dozen or so hostage students at Fort Christanna. The government of Virginia decided that some Native American children would be "civilized," yet they were held as hostages to ensure compliant behavior by their parents. Haigler's knowledge of English may have come from this experience.

Haigler became king in the autumn of 1750. His predecessor, King Young Warrior, and most of his headmen were murdered by a group of Iroquois as they traveled to Charles Town (present-day Charleston). Haigler, out hunting, was the only headman left to the Catawbas and became king by this accident of history.

Haigler's first task as king was to end the genocidal war between the Catawbas and the Iroquois. The situation had indeed become so dire that the Catawba men were afraid to venture from their village to go hunting. To accomplish the desired results, King Haigler traveled by ship from Charles Town to New York. From New York he traveled up the Hudson River to Albany, then a frontier post. He was accompanied by six of his headmen and Governor James Glen of South Carolina. At Albany, Haigler successfully negotiated a peace treaty with the Iroquois.

In 1757 King Haigler became involved in the French and Indian War (1754–1763). Supporting the English against the French, he led a band of his men to Fort Duquesne. Back home in 1760, he negotiated the Treaty of Pine Tree Hill. In this now-lost document, King Haigler reserved for his people only 2 million acres of the estimated original 50,000 square miles of Catawba land, ceding the remainder to the colonists. He also agreed to abandon the Catawba ceremonial center of Pine Tree Hill and relocate the nation to Kings Bottoms in Lancaster County, South Carolina. Nonetheless, North Carolina authorities were not pleased with the apparent generosity of South Carolina in allowing such a large Native American reservation. The border between the two Carolinas had not yet been delineated, and some of the reservation land was claimed by North Carolina (and is indeed part of present-day North Carolina).

On August 30, 1763, King Haigler was attacked and killed by a Shawnee war party. Several months later some of the Catawbas, ruled by a regent, traveled to Augusta, Georgia. The Catawbas agreed to a further reduction of their land base to 144,000 acres centered at their sacred ground at Kings Bottoms between Lancaster and York counties in South Carolina. Catawba claims to this same 144,000-acre reservation became a thorn in South Carolina's side for 230 years. The land issue created by Haigler finally ended with a settlement in 1993.

A wealth of material has been preserved on King Haigler, mostly in papers in South Carolina. Thinking far ahead of his time, at one point he begged the colonial governments to prohibit the sale of liquor to his people. On another occasion he made an eloquent speech on the worth of women. Today, King Haigler is memorialized by Catawba potters who continue to make pipes in his honor, although no true portraits of him survive. If the pipes are attached as lugs to a large jar, the vessel is known as a King Haigler pot.

THOMAS JOHN BLUMER

See also

Catawbas; French and Indian War; Iroquois; Pine Tree Hill, Treaty of; Shawnees

References

Brown, Douglas S. *The Catawba Indians: The People of the River.* Columbia: University of South Carolina Press, 1966.

McDowell, William L., ed. *Documents Relating to Indian Affairs, 1754–1765.* The Colonial Records of South Carolina, Series 2, The Indian Books, Department of Archives and History. Columbia: University of South Carolina Press, 1970.

Halpuda Mikko

See Billy Bowlegs

Hancock, Winfield Scott
Birth Date: February 14, 1824
Death Date: February 9, 1886

U.S. Army officer. Winfield Scott Hancock was born on February 14, 1824, in Montgomery Square, Pennsylvania. He was educated in local schools before obtaining an appointment to the U.S. Military Academy at West Point. Upon graduation in 1844, Hancock was commissioned a second lieutenant in the infantry. He served at various posts in the West, on recruiting duty, and in the fighting around Mexico City in September 1847 during the Mexican-American War (1846–1848).

Returning to the United States in 1848, Hancock was again assigned to western posts. In 1856 he was sent to Florida as quartermaster of Fort Myers during the Third Seminole War (1855–1858); he then served in Kansas, Utah, and California. When the American Civil War (1861–1865) began, he was a captain serving as chief quartermaster of southern California.

In September 1861 Hancock was commissioned a brigadier general of Volunteers and was assigned to the Union Army of the Potomac. He saw action throughout 1862, earning command of a division that autumn. Promoted to major general of Volunteers, he assumed command of II Corps after the Battle of Chancellorsville (May 1–4, 1863).

During the Battle of Gettysburg (July 1–3, 1863), Hancock played a crucial role in the Union victory, placing II Corps in a strong defensive position on July 1 and helping to stymie General Robert E. Lee's attempt to turn the left flank on July 2. Hancock also led his troops in the repulse of Pickett's Charge on July 3, receiving a severe wound from which he never completely recovered. After a six-month convalescence, he returned to action in 1864, fighting in all of the major battles in Virginia until November, when he took command of the Veteran Volunteer Corps being formed in Washington, D.C. In the meantime he garnered promotion to brigadier general in the regular army.

Winfield Scott Hancock distinguished himself as a major general of volunteers in the Civil War. After the war, he remained in the army and commanded the Department of the Missouri. (Library of Congress)

After the end of the war, Hancock remained in the military and was promoted to major general in the regular army in 1866. At the specific request of General William T. Sherman, in August 1866 Hancock received command of the Military Department of the Missouri. In March 1867 Hancock led an expedition of 1,400 men across the southern Plains to intimidate the Native Americans in the region. The troops marched across Kansas without opposition. Several meetings with Cheyenne leaders in mid-April 1867 frustrated Hancock, as the Native Americans attended reluctantly but declared their desire for peace. He narrowly escaped death at one conference when Cheyenne leader Roman Nose was dissuaded by another chief from killing him. When the Cheyennes refused to cooperate, Hancock concluded that they wanted war and on April 19 burned an abandoned camp at Pawnee Fork, sparking retaliatory attacks on nearby settlers.

Four months later Hancock briefly took charge of reconstruction efforts in Texas and Louisiana, during which he precipitated a donnybrook with Republicans because he refused to use military power in the stead of civil courts. He then assumed command of the Division of the Atlantic in March 1868. A year later he was assigned to the Department of Dakota, where he supervised various operations against the Sioux and Blackfoot but did not directly participate. Hancock took steps in 1872 to prevent whites from traveling to the Black Hills, which had been reserved for the Sioux. In November 1869 he resumed command of the Division of the Atlantic.

Hancock was the Democratic candidate for president in 1880 but lost a close election to James Garfield. While still on active duty at his home at Governor's Island, New York, Hancock died on February 9, 1886.

JIM PIECUCH

See also

Blackfoot Confederacy; Black Hills, South Dakota; Cheyennes; Roman Nose; Sherman, William Tecumseh; Sioux

References

Brown, Dee. *Bury My Heart at Wounded Knee.* New York: Holt, Rinehart and Winston, 1970.

Jordan, David M. *Winfield Scott Hancock: A Soldier's Life.* Bloomington: Indiana University Press, 1988.

Handsome Lake
Birth Date: ca. 1735
Death Date: August 10, 1815

Prominent Seneca prophet and religious leader. Handsome Lake was born sometime around 1735 near present-day Avon along the Genessee River in upstate New York. Little is known of his early years, but gradually he became a respected Seneca leader. Cornplanter was his half brother. Handsome Lake watched with increasing chagrin as Iroquois traditional cultural values steadily eroded, especially after the conclusion of the French and Indian War (1754–1763). He also grew discouraged over repeated land cessions to the Americans in the aftermath of the American Revolutionary War (1775–1783).

In the late 1790s Handsome Lake suffered from a serious illness, thought to have been precipitated by heavy alcohol consumption. In 1799, however, he had the first of several visions that not only transformed his own life but also created a new religious movement among the Senecas and other Iroquois tribes. Known as the Good Word, or the Longhouse Religion, Handsome Lake's religion principally entailed a new moral code, some of which was akin to certain Christian denominational doctrines. Handsome Lake preached against the evils of drunkenness, promiscuity, witchcraft, gambling, and fighting. He suggested that if the Iroquois did not subscribe to this moral code, their world would be destroyed by a mass conflagration. Handsome Lake believed that following the precepts of his Good Word would help his people maintain their cultural and social identity and help in resisting white encroachments on their lands.

Handsome Lake became prominent among many Iroquois because of his religious vision, and as the 19th century progressed, more and more Iroquois adopted the Longhouse Religion; some Iroquois continue to practice it today. At the start of the War of 1812 Handsome Lake urged Iroquois neutrality in the conflict, but

Cornplanter and Red Jacket concluded a defensive pact with the Americans. After that Handsome Lake remained aloof from political decisions but continued to maintain an influential role in the religious and cultural realms. He died on August 10, 1815, at the Iroquois' Onondaga Reservation in New York state.

PAUL G. PIERPAOLI JR.

See also

Cornplanter; Iroquois Confederacy; Red Jacket; Senecas

References

Barr, Daniel P. *Unconquered: The Iroquois League at War in Colonial America.* Westport, CT: Praeger, 2006.

Wallace, Anthony F. C. "Origins of the Longhouse Religion." In *Handbook of North American Indians,* edited by William C. Sturtevant, 445–448. Washington, DC: Smithsonian Institution, 1978.

Harmar, Josiah
Birth Date: November 10, 1753
Death Date: August 20, 1813

Continental Army officer during the American Revolutionary War (1775–1783) who later commanded the U.S. Army on the frontier and was defeated by a Pan-Indian contingent in 1790. Josiah Harmar was born in Philadelphia on November 10, 1753.

U.S. Army commander Brigadier General Josiah Harmar, a competent regimental officer during the American Revolutionary War, failed to understand the nuances of Indian warfare and was badly defeated by Miami war chief Little Turtle in a foray into Indian territory in 1790. (U.S. Department of State)

He was commissioned a captain in the 1st Pennsylvania Regiment on October 26, 1775, and served in Canada. He was promoted to major of the 3rd Pennsylvania Regiment on October 1, 1776, and to lieutenant colonel of the 6th Pennsylvania on June 6, 1777, in which unit he participated in the battles at Brandywine, Monmouth, and Stony Point.

Appointed lieutenant colonel and commander of the 7th Pennsylvania Regiment on August 9, 1780, Harmar transferred to the 3rd Pennsylvania upon the reorganization of the Pennsylvania Line on January 17, 1781. During the Yorktown Campaign he was second-in-command of Pennsylvania troops. On January 1, 1783, Harmar joined the 1st Pennsylvania Regiment and was brevetted colonel on September 30. When Congress approved the peace treaty in 1783, Harmar carried the news to France.

Because he had earned a reputation as a competent and reliable officer during the Revolution, Harmar was appointed by Congress as lieutenant colonel–commandant of the U.S. Infantry Regiment on August 12, 1784, and given the title of commander of the army. His unit of 700 men, stationed at Fort Pitt, was the only national army organization at the time. With this small regiment, he was expected to keep the Native Americans under control and evict squatters from Native American–held lands. He had neither the means nor the aptitude to succeed, and in the next few years he was engaged in almost perpetual warfare against various Native American tribes. On July 31, 1787, Harmar was brevetted brigadier general.

In 1790 Harmar was ordered to lead an expedition against the Native Americans in the Maumee Valley. He marched northward from Fort Washington (Cincinnati) at the end of September with 1,500 men, mostly Pennsylvania and Kentucky militia, and on October 15 he captured and pillaged Miami Town. His men then set about destroying the Native Americans' villages and burning their corn. One detachment, sent on October 19 to ravage a nearby village, was defeated by a Miami war party under Little Turtle, and Harmar decided to withdraw southward. However, he unwisely sent a party of 400 men under Major John P. Wyllys back to chastise the Native Americans at Miami Town. This force, ambushed on October 22 by a Pan-Indian party led by Little Turtle and Blue Jacket, barely managed to escape. Harmar's exhausted men stumbled into Fort Washington on November 3. Harmar immediately came under intense criticism from the government for his handling of the expedition.

Subjected to a court of inquiry in 1791, Harmar was exonerated but resigned from the army on January 1, 1792. Thereafter he lived quietly in retirement on the Schuylkill River near Philadelphia, although he did serve as adjutant general of Pennsylvania from 1793 to 1799. Harmar died at his home on August 20, 1813.

PAUL DAVID NELSON

See also

Blue Jacket; Little Turtle; Little Turtle's War; Miamis

References

Stewart, Richard W., ed. *American Military History*, Vol. 1, *The United States Army and the Forging of a Nation, 1775–1917*. Washington, DC: Center of Military History, 2005.

Sword, Wiley. *President Washington's Indian War: The Struggle for the Old Northwest, 1790–1795*. Norman: University of Oklahoma Press, 1985.

Harney, William Selby

Birth Date: August 27, 1800
Death Date: May 9, 1889

U.S. Army officer whose military career spanned nearly 50 years, from 1818 to 1862. William Selby Harney was born on August 27, 1800, in Haysboro, Tennessee, on the Cumberland River above Nashville. With a family heritage of frontier migration and military service and after attending a local academy, he was commissioned in 1818 by direct appointment to second lieutenant in the 1st Infantry Regiment. Physically impressive at more than 6 feet 3 inches in height and of military bearing, he was also ambitious, a disciplinarian, and argumentative, and he had a temper that brought him both personal and professional problems.

Harney's initial military service involved mostly regimental garrison duties, primarily at Baton Rouge, Louisiana, with breaks for recruiting duty and a short period as aide to Major General Andrew Jackson. In 1825 several 1st Infantry companies, including Harney's, were sent to St. Louis in response to a Native American attack on a group of fur trappers in the area of the current North Dakota–South Dakota border. The immediate problem was handled by a successful retaliatory operation, and the 1st Infantry companies remained in reserve.

Harney continued to serve almost exclusively in the upper Midwest until 1832. Accompanying an expedition aimed at resolving disputes regarding Native Americans and the fur trade on the upper Missouri River, he was exposed to the political-military problems of negotiating with Native Americans. His service included a minor role in the Black Hawk War (1832) as part of a force under Colonel Zachary Taylor.

After several years as a paymaster that included promotion to major, Harney gained appointment as regimental lieutenant colonel. In 1836 Congress had created a second regiment of dragoons. By December 300 men had been recruited, and five companies were sent dismounted to Florida to join the military effort to force the Seminoles to move to Oklahoma during the Second Seminole War (1835–1842). During the war, Harney emerged as one of the army's best-known and most skilled Indian fighters.

The start of the Mexican-American War (1846–1848) found the 2nd Dragoons mounted and serving in Texas. In June 1846 Harney was appointed commander of the regiment and promoted to colonel. During the operations of Major General Winfield Scott to capture Mexico City, Harney commanded all of Scott's mounted troops, providing effective service throughout the campaign.

Harney and his 2nd Dragoons were next ordered to Texas to guard frontier settlements. Harney was put in charge of a line of frontier posts. Commanding a force of 1,200 men with the brevet rank of brigadier general, he achieved a brutal victory over the Brulé Sioux at the Battle of Ash Hollow (September 2–3, 1855) on the south bank of the North Platte River and then conducted a winter operation designed to intimidate area tribes.

In early 1856, Seminole activities took Harney to Florida in command of the Department of Florida. There he demonstrated talent in unconventional warfare and amphibious tactics.

Passage of the 1854 Kansas-Nebraska Act soon brought violence to Kansas. In 1857 Harney was appointed to command federal forces there. He was then appointed to command the Utah Department and was soon promoted to regular army brigadier general. However, before he arrived in Utah, the Mormon problem was resolved, and he went instead to St. Louis to command the Department of the West.

In 1858 Harney was appointed commander of the new Department of Oregon, primarily to solve conflicts between Native Americans and whites. Harney's major problem, however, was related to a dispute between the British and the Americans as to who possessed the San Juan Islands near Vancouver Island. Harney's reaction to a series of relatively minor incidents almost resulted in an armed clash between the two countries, ultimately bringing about his relief from command.

In 1860 Harney returned to command at St. Louis. Although circumspect in his actions as the American Civil War (1861–1865) approached, his caution and southern background aroused suspicion, and in May 1861 he was relieved. He retired the following year.

With the Civil War over in 1865, there were renewed efforts to solve the situation with the Native Americans. No living army officer had more experience in Indian affairs than did Harney. Thus, during the period 1866–1870 he served the government both officially as a commissioner, active in the negotiations of both the Medicine Lodge and Fort Laramie treaties, and unofficially as an adviser. He was also much respected by the Native Americans themselves. Harney died on May 9, 1889, at his home in Orlando, Florida.

PHILIP L. BOLTÉ

See also

Ash Hollow, Battle of; Black Hawk War; Brulé Sioux; Jackson, Andrew; Military Divisions, Departments, and Districts; Seminole War, First; Seminole War, Second; Taylor, Zachary

References

Adams, George Rollie. *General William S. Harney: Prince of Dragoons.* Lincoln: University of Nebraska Press, 2001.

Downey, Fairfax. *Indian Wars of the U.S. Army, 1776–1865.* Garden City, NY: Doubleday, 1963.

Harper's Weekly

Popular nationally circulated illustrated newspaper begun in 1857 by Fletcher Harper, a principal in Harper and Brothers Publishing. *Harper's Weekly* is not to be confused with *Harper's Monthly*, which was also published by Harper and Brothers and was a general-interest monthly periodical. *Harper's Weekly* contained domestic and foreign news stories as well as poetry and fiction, including serializations of novels by well-recognized writers such as Wilkie Collins, Charles Dickens, and William Makepeace Thackeray. The newspaper sold for five cents per copy and was distributed each Saturday. During and after the American Civil War, the price per copy rose to six cents, which was then considered a major increase. The newspaper was an instant success, and by the eve of the Civil War in 1860, its circulation had topped 200,000.

For many years *Harper's Weekly* featured extensive illustrations made from woodcut engravings, many of which were produced by well-known artists. This was an era in which the technology for publishing photographs in print was not available. Many news items were accompanied by artists' renderings of events, which meant that like the accompanying copy, they were subject to the biases and interpretations of the person producing them. Artists such as Henry Mosler, Alfred R. Waud, Theodore Davis, Livingston Hopkins, and Winslow Homer helped cement the newspaper's

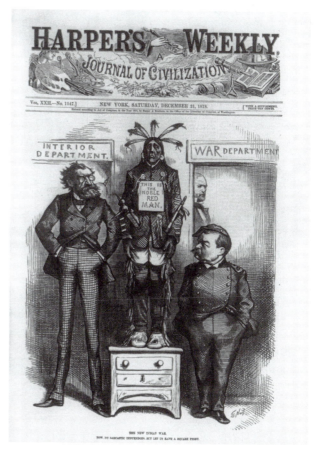

Cover by Thomas Nast of the December 21, 1878, issue of *Harper's Weekly*. The illustration depicts a Native American, labeled "This is the Noble Red Man," standing on a chest of drawers between Carl Schurz, representing the Department of the Interior, and General Philip Sheridan of the War Department. A peace pipe extends from his pocket toward Schurz and a tomahawk from another pocket toward Sheridan. U.S. Army commander General William Tecumseh Sherman stands in the shadow of the doorway behind Sheridan. (Library of Congress)

reputation as a serious news outlet with superlative illustrations. *Harper's Weekly* was also an outlet for humor, and soon it became known for politically oriented cartoons that often caricatured politicians and others in government service. Thomas Nast, who is considered the father of modern political cartoons, drew editorial and political cartoons for the newspaper for more than 25 years. His still-famous renderings of New York City mayor William Marcy "Boss" Tweed helped highlight the extent of graft and corruption in American politics.

In the years prior to the Civil War, *Harper's Weekly* took a decidedly neutral stance toward the issue of slavery, prompting some critics to label it "Harper's Weakly." However, when the war began in 1861, the newspaper became an avid supporter of the Union. Indeed, its news coverage and illustrations served as a powerful arm of the admittedly unorganized Union propaganda effort. Union soldiers were invariably pictured as heroic saviors, while Confederates were usually pictured as unkempt shady characters. Many of the wartime illustrations remain important pieces of interpretive art. In 1862 when the newspaper ran a story detailing Confederate defenses at Yorktown, Virginia, and the position and strength of nearby Union forces, Union secretary of war Edwin M. Stanton was furious, ordering a suspension of the paper's publication. Thanks to Fletcher Harper's intervention, however, that order was quickly rescinded.

Harper's Weekly remained popular after the Civil War and became a powerful arbiter in American politics. Some labeled it the "president maker," as its coverage and cartoons by Nast proved highly influential in presidential elections. Many credit Nast's support of Grover Cleveland for his electoral success when he ran for president the first time in 1884.

Harper's Weekly covered the Indian Wars in considerable depth and ran hundreds of illustrations of Native Americans and battles between whites and Native Americans. Often the coverage was one-sided, portraying the Native Americans as unnecessarily hostile and cruel. On occasion, however, reporters and illustrators attempted to portray the plight of the Native Americans in a more sympathetic light. The newspaper most certainly helped create the myths surrounding life in the western United States, usually making it appear more appealing and noble than it actually was. Not surprisingly, *Harper's Weekly* and similar publications often attributed attitudes and characteristics to Native Americans that were misleading and even inaccurate. The newspaper also tried to portray them in broad strokes, downplaying the fact that Native Americans varied greatly in terms of culture, attitudes, and outlook.

Harper's Weekly was absorbed by a newspaper called the *Independent* in 1916. Beginning in the 1880s when news photography became profitable and competition increased dramatically, the newspaper began losing readership. Changing public tastes also led to its demise.

PAUL G. PIERPAOLI JR.

See also
Literature and the American Indian Wars; Native American Warfare

References
Brown, Joshua. *Beyond the Lines: Pictorial Reporting and the Crisis of Gilded Age America.* Berkeley: University of California Press, 2002.
Coward, John M. *The Newspaper Indian: Native American Identity in the Press, 1820–90.* Urbana: University of Illinois Press, 1999.
Mott, Frank Luther. *American Journalism, a History: 1690–1960.* New York: Macmillan, 1962.

Harrison, William Henry
Birth Date: February 9, 1773
Death Date: April 4, 1841

U.S. Army officer, politician, and ninth president of the United States (March–April 1841). William Henry Harrison was born on February 9, 1773, on his family's plantation in Charles City County, Virginia. He studied classics at Hampden-Sydney College and medicine at the University of Pennsylvania.

Harrison joined the 1st U.S. Infantry Regiment as an ensign in August 1791. During the winter of 1791–1792 he led patrols into Native American territory and learned the rudiments of military life. In 1793 he served as an aide to Major General "Mad" Anthony Wayne, commander of the Legion of the United States. Harrison fought with distinction in the Battle of Fallen Timbers (August 20, 1794). The following year he was a signatory to the Treaty of Greenville.

Harrison remained in the army until June 1798, when he resigned his commission to become secretary of the Northwest Territory. Although he was appointed by Federalist president John Adams, Harrison's politics were more in line with Democratic-Republican Thomas Jefferson. In 1799 Harrison was elected the Northwest Territory's delegate to Congress.

In 1800 Congress divided the Northwest Territory into two parts. The first part eventually became the state of Ohio, and the rest was known as the Indiana Territory. Harrison became governor of the Indiana Territory and remained in that post until December 1812. During his tenure he negotiated 10 land treaties with the Native Americans, purchasing from them millions of acres of land.

Many Native Americans were unhappy with the treaties. Shawnee leader Tecumseh in particular refused to recognize their validity and worked to create a confederation of tribes to prevent further white incursions. Harrison and white settlers in the region also believed that the British were both provoking the Native Americans against the Americans and providing them with weapons.

These tensions and the murder of white settlers prompted Harrison, who was also a brigadier general in the militia, in late September 1811 to lead 970 men into Indian country. On November 6 Harrison's force arrived near Prophetstown, where Tenskwatawa (known as the Prophet), the half brother of Tecumseh, held sway. The two sides agreed to talks the next day. Tecumseh was away in the South recruiting for his confederation, and against Tecumseh's

As governor of the Indian Territory during 1800–1812, William Henry Harrison (1773–1841) negotiated numerous treaties with the Indians that resulted in the cession of millions of acres of land. He distinguished himself as a general in the War of 1812 and was elected president of the United Statres in 1840. (Chaiba Media)

orders Tenskwatawa goaded the warriors at Prophetstown into attacking the nearby American camp before the talks could occur.

Harrison had posted a strong guard and warned his men to be prepared for a night attack, but he neglected to throw up entrenchments or to consider the possibility that his men might be silhouetted against their own campfires. Nonetheless, when the warriors did strike early on November 7, Harrison's men rallied and won what became known as the Battle of Tippecanoe. Having suffered heavy casualties of up to a quarter of his force, Harrison burned Prophetstown and then withdrew. The battle made Harrison a nationally known figure and also caused many Native Americans to side with the British in the War of 1812.

At the beginning of the War of 1812, Harrison was appointed a major general of the Kentucky Militia. He led a rescue party to save the besieged Fort Wayne in September 1812 and secured a commission as a regular army major general. Replacing Brigadier General James Winchester, Harrison took command of the Army of the Northwest. He fought a siege and battle at Fort Meigs, near Perrysburg, Ohio, during May 1–9, 1813, and, in conjunction with Commodore Oliver H. Perry, following the latter's victory in the Battle of Lake Erie, recaptured Detroit that September, driving the British forces and Tecumseh down the Thames River to near Chatham, Ontario, Canada. There on October 5, 1813, Harrison and his troops defeated British and Native American forces led by Brigadier General Henry A. Procter and Tecumseh. Tecumseh was among those killed in the Battle of the Thames.

Harrison resigned his commission in May 1814 following ongoing disputes with Secretary of War John Armstrong. Nevertheless, Harrison's strong showing in the War of 1812 established his reputation as a bona fide military hero, which would stand him in good stead in his subsequent political career. Following the war, Harrison moved back to his Ohio home in North Bend, near Cincinnati. From 1816 to 1819 he served in the U.S. House of Representatives. He then served in the Ohio Senate but was defeated in a run for the U.S. Senate in 1821. In 1822 he lost his bid for a seat in the U.S. House of Representatives. Harrison won election to the U.S. Senate in 1825 and served until 1828. Throughout his congressional career, he was concerned with strengthening the military and with veterans' affairs. In 1828 President John Quincy Adams appointed Harrison minister to Colombia, a post he held until 1829.

Returning to North Bend, Harrison became clerk of the Court of Common Pleas for Hamilton County in 1834. Nominated by the Whig Party for president in 1836, he lost to Democratic nominee Martin Van Buren. Harrison was again nominated by the Whigs in 1840, his vice presidential running mate being John Tyler. Their campaign is often referred to as the first modern campaign and included the slogan "Tippecanoe and Tyler Too." Harrison handily won the election.

Harrison took office on March 4, 1841, and gave the longest inaugural address in U.S. history (100 minutes) amid a cold, driving rainstorm and soon fell ill. He died in Washington, D.C., on April 4, 1841, probably of pneumonia one month into his tenure. Harrison was the first American president to die in office.

WILLIAM TOTH

See also

Fallen Timbers, Battle of; Little Turtle's War; Native Americans and the War of 1812; Old Northwest Territory; Prophetstown; Tecumseh; Tenskwatawa; Thames, Battle of the; Tippecanoe, Battle of; Wayne, Anthony

References

Goebel, Dorothy Burne. *William Henry Harrison: A Political Biography.* Indianapolis: Historical Bureau of the Indiana Library and Historical Department, 1926.

Horsman, Reginald. "William Henry Harrison: Virginia Gentleman in the Old Northwest." *Indiana Magazine of History* 96 (June 2000): 125–149.

Millett, Allan R. "Caesar and the Conquest of the Northwest Territory: The Harrison Campaign, 1811." *Timeline* 14 (August 1997): 2–19.

Owens, Robert M. *Mr. Jefferson's Hammer: William Henry Harrison and the Origins of American Indian Policy.* Norman: University of Oklahoma Press, 2007.

Harrodsburg, Kentucky

Town located in central Kentucky (present-day Mercer County). Harrodsburg, or Harrodstown as it was initially known, became Kentucky's first permanent settlement. Harrodsburg was a crucial fortification and settlement during the American Revolutionary War (1775–1783) and served as a launching point for the campaigns led by George Rogers Clark into Ohio and the Northwest Territory.

James Harrod was a veteran of the French and Indian War (1754–1763) who had also fought in the relief of Fort Pitt during Pontiac's Rebellion (1763). Harrod and his brother Samuel began making hunting trips into central Kentucky as early as 1767. In 1773 the royal governor of Virginia, John Murray, Earl of Dunmore, ordered parties of surveyors to travel into present-day Kentucky and establish Virginia's claim to the region. The Harrods and several dozen others moved down the Ohio River to the mouth of the Kentucky River to what became known as Harrod's Landing. After a short march overland, the group selected a plot of ground and began laying out Harrodsburg and building a settlement.

Increasing clashes between whites and Native Americans led Dunmore to dispatch Daniel Boone to Harrodsburg to recall James Harrod and his men. They did not return to Harrodsburg until March 15, 1775, at which time they began building a fort and rebuilding the earlier structures.

In the late summer of 1775, Captain Clark became the leader of the growing colony. He and Gabriel Jones represented the region in the Virginia Assembly, where they requested and secured approval for Virginia's protection of the new Kentucky settlements.

The fort at Harrodsburg was of great strategic importance during the Revolutionary War. Not only was it one of the largest forts in Kentucky, but it also afforded better protection for pioneers from Native American attacks with its better-armed and better-experienced militia than did Boonesborough or Logan's Station.

At Harrodsburg, Clark planned his campaign through Ohio and the Northwest Territory. The Harrods were among the many settlers who fought with Clark through Chillicothe and Vincennes to end the threat from tribal attacks.

B. Keith Murphy

See also
Blue Licks, Kentucky, Action at; Boone, Daniel; Clark, George Rogers; Clark's Ohio Campaign, First; Lord Dunmore's War; Murray, John, Fourth Earl of Dunmore; Native Americans and the American Revolutionary War; Point Pleasant, Battle of

References
Aaron, Stephen. *How the West Was Lost: The Transformation of Kentucky from Daniel Boone to Henry Clay.* Baltimore: Johns Hopkins University Press, 1996.
Clark, Thomas D. *A History of Kentucky.* Ashland, KY: Jesse Stuart Foundation, 1992.
Harrison, Lowell H., and James C. Klotter. *A New History of Kentucky.* Lexington: University Press of Kentucky, 1997.

Hartford, Treaty of

Treaty signed on September 21, 1638, between English colonists in Massachusetts and the Pequot tribe, the terms of which were designed to eradicate the Pequot Nation after the Pequot War

(1636–1638). Angered by the Pequots' refusal to submit to English domination, leaders of the Massachusetts Bay Colony used the 1636 murders of several colonists as a pretext to declare war. By the end of July 1637 the colonists and their Narragansett and Wampanoag allies had soundly defeated the Pequots. In order to permanently eliminate the Pequot threat and send a warning to other tribes who might consider challenging the colonists, Massachusetts officials imposed a punitive treaty upon the Pequots.

The treaty, signed at Hartford, Connecticut, effectively dissolved the Pequot Nation. Of the estimated 2,500 Pequots who survived the war, at least 30 male captives were executed, and 180 other prisoners were given as slaves to the colonists' native allies. Colonial officials sold many other Pequots into slavery in the West Indies, and some women and children became household slaves in Massachusetts. The colonists divided most of the survivors among other Native American nations, with the majority, perhaps as many as 1,000, forced to integrate into the Mohegan tribe; a lesser number were allocated to the Narragansetts. One Pequot band was exiled to Long Island and made subject to the Metoac natives there.

In addition to enslaving or relocating the remaining Pequots, the Treaty of Hartford sought to eradicate their cultural identity. The terms prohibited the Pequots from returning to their lands, speaking their tribal language, or even referring to themselves as Pequots. When a few Pequots challenged the terms shortly afterward by settling on their former land at Pawcatuck, the colonists and their Mohegan allies quickly destroyed the encampment. Despite the prohibitions imposed by the treaty, the Pequots managed to retain their identity and gained federal recognition of their tribal status in 1983.

Jim Piecuch

See also
Mohegans; Narragansetts; Pequots; Pequot War; Wampanoags

References
Cave, Alfred A. *The Pequot War.* Amherst: University of Massachusetts Press, 1996.
Hauptman, Laurence M., and James D Wherry, eds. *The Pequots in Southern New England: The Rise and Fall of an American Indian Nation.* Norman: University of Oklahoma Press, 1990.

Hatch, Edward
Birth Date: December 22, 1832
Death Date: April 11, 1889

U.S. Army officer and well-regarded and long-serving colonel of the African American 9th Cavalry Regiment. Born in Bangor, Maine, on December 22, 1832, Edward Hatch studied at Norwich Military Academy (now Norwich University) in Vermont before moving to Iowa to engage in the lumber business. At the beginning of the American Civil War (1861–1865) he joined the 2nd Iowa Cavalry Regiment and was soon made a captain, rising through the ranks

Colonel Edward Hatch commanded both the African American 9th Cavalry Regiment and the Department of New Mexico. Through adroit diplomacy he quelled an uprising by the Utes but had less success in dealing with renegade Apache war chief Victorio. (Library of Congress)

In 1875 with Texas largely settled, the 9th Cavalry relocated to New Mexico, where Hatch served as district commander during a very tumultuous period. His first challenge was to quell an Apache uprising led by the skilled warrior Victorio. In 1877 Hatch was forced to intervene in a civil matter when violence erupted over access to salt mines east of El Paso, Texas (the so-called Salt War). Beginning in 1879, he faced major overlapping crises when a Ute uprising in Colorado threatened a much wider conflict and Victorio rose up again. Hatch proved an able diplomat by helping to broker a workable settlement with the Utes, but in dealing with Victorio he was less successful, despite persistent campaigning by his buffalo soldiers. The dreaded Apache leader was finally cornered and killed by Mexican troops in 1880.

In 1881 the regiment began four years of frustrating service, scattered about Indian Territory (Oklahoma) and its periphery in an effort to discourage encroachment of white settlers, known as Boomers. Regimental headquarters subsequently moved to Fort McKinney, Washington, but the companies were scattered as far away as Fort Robinson, Nebraska, where in March 1889 Hatch was injured in an accident. He died there on April 11, 1889. At the time of his death, he and Benjamin Grierson, commander of the all-black 10th Cavalry, were the most senior colonels in the army, both with almost 23 years with the same regiments.

DAVID COFFEY

See also

Apaches; Apache Wars; Buffalo Soldiers; Cavalry Regiment, 9th U.S.; Grierson, Benjamin Henry; Victorio

References

Leckie, William H., and Shirley A. Leckie. *The Buffalo Soldiers: A Narrative of the Black Cavalry in the West.* Norman: University of Oklahoma Press, 2003.

Starr, Stephen Z. *The Union Cavalry in the Civil War.* 3 vols. Baton Rouge: Louisiana State University Press, 1979–1985.

Utley, Robert M. *Frontier Regulars: The United States and the American Indian, 1866–1891.* New York: Macmillan, 1973.

to colonel in June 1862. He distinguished himself in a number of engagements in the western theater, including at Island No. 10, and commanded a brigade in the Battle of Corinth and the Battle of Iuka. He was also conspicuous in Colonel Benjamin Grierson's spectacular raid during the Vicksburg Campaign of 1863. After sustaining a wound during a raid in Tennessee, Hatch received an appointment as brigadier general of U.S. Volunteers in April 1864. He commanded a cavalry division for the balance of the war, most notably in opposition to Confederate general John B. Hood's invasion of Tennessee, for which Hatch earned a brevet to major general of volunteers. He mustered out of the service in January 1866.

In July 1866 Hatch was named colonel of the new 9th Cavalry Regiment, an all–African American unit. He received the command over several more senior and better-known officers, some of whom refused to serve with a black regiment. Hatch embraced the opportunity, however, beginning a remarkable tenure. After organizing the regiment—with substantial difficulty—in Louisiana, he moved the regiment to Texas, where it spent the next eight years in near-constant activity, especially along the U.S.-Mexican border. The black soldiers and white officers faced persistent suspicion and hatred from the people they sought to protect and engendered ridicule and discrimination within the army itself.

Hatteras Indians

See Croatans

Haudenosaunee

See Iroquois Confederacy

Havasupais

Native American tribe indigenous to northern Arizona. The name "Havasupai" means "People of the Blue-Green Water." Along with the Hualapais, from whom the Havasupais may be descended, they are also called the Pais (Pa'as, or "the People"). Hualapais are western Pais, and Havasupais are eastern Pais. Along with the Hualapais and the Yavapais, the Havasupais are also Upland Yumas, in contrast to River Yumas such as the Mojaves and Quechans. The Havasupais spoke Upland Yuman, a member of the Hokan-Siouan language family. Since approximately 1100, the Havasupais lived at Cataract Canyon in the Grand Canyon as well as on the nearby upland plateaus.

The Havasupais probably descended from the prehistoric Cohoninas, a branch of the Hakataya culture. Thirteen bands of Pais originally hunted, farmed, and gathered in northwestern Arizona along the Colorado River. The Havasupais were comfortable in an extreme range of elevations. They gathered desert plants from along the Colorado River at 1,800 feet and hunted on the upper slopes of the San Francisco peaks, at 12,000 feet.

Formal authority among the Havasupais was located in chiefs, hereditary in theory only, of 10 local groups. Their only real power was to advise and persuade. The Havasupais held few councils; most issues were dealt with informally by men in the sweat lodge.

In Cataract Canyon the Havasupai people grew corn, beans, squash, sunflowers, and tobacco. During the winter they lived on the surrounding plateau and hunted game such as mountain lions, deer, antelopes, mountain sheep, fowl, and rabbits. Wild foods included piñon nuts, cactus and yucca fruits, agave hearts, mesquite beans, and wild honey.

The Havasupais often traded with the Hopis and other allied tribes, exchanging deerskins, baskets, salt, lima beans, and red hematite paint for food, pottery, and cloth. They also traded with tribes as far away as the Pacific coast.

With the possible exception of Francisco Garces in 1776, few if any Spanish or other outsiders disturbed the Havasupais into the 1800s. Spanish influences did reach them, however, primarily in the form of horses, cloth, and fruit trees through trading partners such as the Hopis.

In the early 1800s a trail was forged from the Rio Grande to California that led directly through Pai country. By around 1850, with white encroachment and treaty violations increasing, the Pais occasionally reacted with violence. When mines opened in their territory in 1863, they perceived the threat and readied for war. From 1865 to 1869 they waged periodic warfare against U.S. Army forces. After the Pais were defeated by the United States, some served as army scouts against their old enemies, including the Yavapais.

Although the Hualapais were to suffer relocation, the United States paid little attention to those who returned to their isolated homes. At this point the two tribes became increasingly distinct. Despite the remote location of the Havasupais, American encroachment eventually affected even them, and an 1880 executive order established their reservation along Havasu Creek. The final designation in 1882 included just 518 acres in the canyon; the Havasupais also lost their traditional upland hunting and gathering grounds.

The Havasupais intensified farming on their little remaining land and began wide-scale cultivation of peaches. In 1912 they purchased cattle. Severe epidemics in the early 20th century reduced their population to slightly more than 100. At the same time, the Bureau of Indian Affairs, initially slow to move into the canyon, proceeded with a program of rapid acculturation. By the 1930s, Havasupai economic independence had given way to a reliance on limited wage labor. Traditional political power declined as well, despite the creation in 1939 of a tribal council.

Feeling confined in the canyon, the Havasupais stepped up their fight for permanent grazing rights on the plateau. The 1950s were a grim time for them, with little employment. Conflict over land led to familial divisions, which in turn resulted in serious cultural loss. In the 1960s, however, an infusion of federal funds provided employment in tribal programs as well as modern utilities. Still, croplands continued to shrink, as more and more land was devoted to the upkeep of pack animals for tourists, the tribe's limited but main source of income. In 1975 after an intensive lobbying effort, the government restored 185,000 acres of land to the Havasupais.

BARRY M. PRITZKER

See also

Bureau of Indian Affairs; Hualapais

References

Hirst, Stephen. *I Am the Grand Canyon: The Story of the Havasupai People.* Grand Canyon, AZ: Grand Canyon Association, 2007.

Lliff, Flora Gregg. *People of the Blue Water: A Record of Life among the Walapai and Havasupai Indians.* Tucson: University of Arizona Press, 1985.

Hayfield Fight
Event Date: August 1, 1867

Failed Indian attack on a hay-cutting party outside of Fort C. F. Smith. On July 23, 1867, Fort C. F. Smith, located in Montana Territory and established to protect travelers along the Bozeman Trail, acquired several mowing machines for cutting hay, allowing the fort's garrison to gather its own hay rather than have to purchase it from local farmers.

On July 29 garrison commander Lieutenant Colonel Luther P. Bradley ordered a mowing party of 6 civilians with the new machines to gather hay for the fort. He assigned newly arrived Lieutenant Sigismund Sternberg and a detail of 19 soldiers as an escort to a meadow approximately three miles from the fort, despite the fact that Crow Indian scouts had repeatedly warned of an impending attack from hostile Cheyenne and Sioux warriors in the area. However, there had been only two reported clashes in the last seven months.

Oglala Sioux chief Red Cloud meanwhile regrouped a coalition of nearly 1,000 Indian warriors to resume attacks along the Bozeman Trail. He learned from his scouts of the hay-cutting party and quickly convened a war council to formulate an attack plan for the morning of August 1.

Once at the mowing site, soldiers constructed a makeshift corral of brush and logs to serve as both a pen for draft animals and an improvised fortification. At 11:00 a.m. on August 1, a band of warriors attacked the civilian laborers working the mowing machines and chased them back into the corral. The Native Americans then deployed several decoys in an attempt to lure the soldiers out of their fortification. When this failed, the Native Americans shifted their tactics to assaulting the position en masse. The attackers expected to encounter slow-firing muzzle-loading muskets and anticipated long pauses between volleys of fire. The soldiers, however, had just been issued M-1866 Springfield-Allin breech-loading rifles that were capable of a considerably higher rate of fire. The initial Native American assault faltered, but the warriors regrouped and charged the corral two more times. Frustrated by these failures, the Indians charged desperately once more against the south wall of the corral on foot.

During the fighting, Lieutenant Sternberg refused to take cover and in consequence suffered a fatal gunshot wound to the head in the first minutes of the battle. When the detail's only noncommissioned officer, Sergeant James Norton, fell severely wounded shortly afterward, command passed to civilian Don Colvin, a veteran of the American Civil War (1861–1865).

Meanwhile, the garrison at the fort could not see the fighting only a short distance away because of the surrounding hills. When a messenger from the battlefield arrived at the fort, Bradley hesitated to send reinforcements, remembering the trap set during the Fetterman Massacre the previous December. He dispatched a mounted reconnaissance party at 3:30 p.m. that confirmed the severity of the fighting. Thirty minutes later Bradley mobilized a relief force of two infantry companies and a light howitzer to aid the beleaguered hay-cutting party. The arrival of the reinforcements forced the Indians to withdraw after nearly six hours of assaulting the corral. In the battle, U.S. forces suffered 3 killed and 3 wounded. No official count of Indian casualties exists, but estimates range from 18 to 23 killed and several dozen wounded.

BRADFORD A. WINEMAN

See also
Bozeman Trail; Fetterman Massacre; Red Cloud; Red Cloud's War

References
Hagan, Barry J. "Exactly in the Right Place": A History of Fort C. F. Smith, Montana Territory, 1866–1868. El Segundo, CA: Upton and Sons, 1999.

Herbert, Grace Raymond, and E. A. Brininstool. The Bozeman Trail: Historical Accounts of Blazing of the Overland Routes into the Northwest, and the Fights with Red Cloud's Warriors. 2 vols. Cleveland, OH: Arthur H. Clark, 1922.

Hazen, William Babcock
Birth Date: September 27, 1830
Death Date: January 16, 1887

U.S. Army officer. William Babcock Hazen was born on September 27, 1830, in West Hartford, Vermont, although his family moved to Ohio several years later. There, during childhood, he met future president James A. Garfield, who would become his lifelong friend as well as political patron. Hazen determined that the best way to escape drudgery on the family farm would be to receive an education at the U.S. Military Academy, West Point. After some difficulty, he received his appointment in August 1851 and graduated in 1855.

Like many other officers in the antebellum army, Hazen saw service along the western frontier. His first assignment in 1855 saw him posted to the Pacific Northwest until his reassignment to Texas in 1857. During his time in Texas, Hazen was wounded during a brief skirmish with the Comanches. Following a period of recuperation at home, he received a position teaching at West Point. Promoted to first lieutenant in April 1861, he was advanced to captain in the 8th Infantry a month later.

After the outbreak of the American Civil War, Hazen managed with the help of Garfield to be appointed colonel of the 41st Ohio Volunteer Infantry Regiment in September 1861. In January 1862 Hazen received command of a brigade in the newly organized Army of the Ohio. He first saw combat on April 6, 1862, on the second day of the Battle of Shiloh. Hazen also saw action at

Willam B. Hazen rendered distinguished service as a major general during the Civil War. He remained in the army after the war as a colonel and sought to scrupulously follow the terms of treaties with the Indians, despite the opposition of many of his superiors. (Library of Congress)

Stones River (December 31, 1862–January 2, 1863), after which his promotion to brigadier general of Volunteers was approved, to date from November 29, 1862. Hazen later fought in the Battle of Chickamauga (September 18, 1863) and the Battle of Missionary Ridge (November 25, 1863) and marched across Georgia with Major General William T. Sherman's army. Hazen was promoted to major general of Volunteers in December 1864.

After the Civil War, Hazen returned to the regular army as a colonel of the 38th Infantry, moving to the 6th Infantry in 1869. He resumed service in the West and negotiated with Native Americans along the Washita River in 1868 and 1869. Hazen sought to scrupulously follow the terms of the treaties that the United States had signed with the Native Americans, but he also spent his time arguing with superiors and rivals; several times he was court-martialed, although he was never convicted of serious offenses. He became embroiled in the controversy surrounding corruption in the War Department that hastened Secretary of War William Belknap's resignation. Hazen was also engaged in a running public feud with Lieutenant Colonel George A. Custer, whom he disliked intently, and Hazen even managed to alienate General Sherman, a former friend who had publicly defended Hazen. The writer Ambrose Bierce once referred to Hazen as the "best hated man I ever knew."

In 1880 Hazen began service with the Signal Corps with an appointment to chief signal officer and promotion to brigadier general, largely due to the influence of President-elect Garfield. After attending a party, Hazen caught a chill on January 14, 1887. He died in Washington, D.C., two days later.

PETER C. LUEBKE

See also

Belknap, William Worth; Comanches; Custer, George Armstrong; Sherman, William Tecumseh

References

Cooper, Edward S. *William Babcock Hazen: The Best Hated Man.* Madison, NJ: Fairleigh Dickinson University Press, 2005.

Hazen, William B. *A Narrative of Military Service.* Boston: Ticknor, 1885.

Reid, Whitelaw. *Ohio in the War: Her Statesmen, Her Generals, and Soldiers,* Vol. 1, *History of the State during the War, and the Lives of Her Generals.* Cincinnati: Moore, Wilstach and Baldwin, 1868.

Henderson, Archibald

Birth Date: January 21, 1783
Death Date: January 6, 1859

U.S. Marine Corps commandant, often referred to as the "Grand Old Man of the Marine Corps," having served for nearly 53 years. Archibald Henderson was born near the village of Dumfries, Virginia, on January 21, 1783. After working in his father's ironworks for a time, he secured a commission as a second lieutenant in the U.S. Marine Corps on June 4, 1806. He was promoted to first lieutenant on March 6, 1807, and to captain on April 1, 1811.

Henderson commanded the marine detachment in the frigate *President* during 1811–1812 and was assigned to the Charleston Navy Yard at the beginning of the War of 1812 during 1812–1813. In June 1814 he took command of the marine detachment in the frigate *Constitution,* and he took part in the engagement with and capture of the British frigate *Cyane* and sloop *Levant.* In 1816 he was brevetted major, to date from August 1814.

From September 16, 1818, to March 2, 1819, Henderson was acting U.S. Marine Corps commandant. On October 17, 1820, following the cashiering of Lieutenant Colonel Commandant Anthony Gale, Lieutenant Colonel Henderson was appointed the fifth commandant of the corps. He served in this position for almost 39 years, the longest tenure in that position in history. On July 1, 1834, he was promoted to colonel commandant.

As commandant, Henderson not only restored the reputation of the U.S. Marine Corps but is generally credited with preserving the corps, thwarting an attempt by President Andrew Jackson in 1829 to combine it with the army. Instead, in 1834 Congress passed the Act for the Better Organization of the Marine Corps, ensuring that the marines would remain part of the Navy Department. Henderson proved to be an able administrator who established the rigid, spartan training regimen for which the marines became famous, and he secured better facilities for the men. He also made standard the carrying of the Mameluke-pattern sword by marine officers. Henderson was able to expand the role of the U.S. Marine Corps beyond mere ship service and naval yard security. Taking advantage of the Indian Wars, he developed select marine battalions that could serve in the field in conjunction with the army.

Indeed, Henderson took to the field himself while commandant. Jackson ordered Henderson to send marines to assist in fighting during the Creek War of 1836. Henderson personally led two battalions of marines, more than half of the corps, in fighting in Alabama and Georgia. On the conclusion of the Creek War of 1836 that summer, the marines transferred to Florida, where they fought in the Second Seminole War (1835–1842). Henderson was brevetted brigadier general on January 27, 1837, for his role in the fighting.

Henderson lobbied unceasingly for an expansion in the size of the U.S. Marine Corps, but he achieved this as a consequence of the Mexican-American War (1846–1848), although the battalion he organized to take part in amphibious operations with the navy did not arrive in Mexico until three months after the fall of Veracruz. (Some 180 marines from the ships of the Home Squadron did take part in the landings, however.) Attached to Major General John A. Quitman's division, the marine battalion gained laurels in the assault of Chapultepec Castle on September 13, 1847.

Henderson was a strong advocate for the U.S. Marine Corps acquiring its own artillery units, and he secured authorization for artillery training in 1857. This helped ensure the future role of the corps in amphibious warfare. In June 1857 Henderson played an important role in suppressing rioters supporting the No-Nothing

Party in Washington, D.C. He died suddenly in Washington, D.C., on January 6, 1859.

Spencer C. Tucker

See also
Creek War; Jackson, Andrew; Seminole War, Second

References
Dawson, Joseph G. "With Fidelity and Effectiveness: Archibald Henderson's Lasting Legacy to the U.S. Marine Corps." *Journal of Military History* 62(4) (October 1998): 727–753.
Millett, Allan R. *Semper Fidelis: The History of the United States Marine Corps.* New York: Macmillan, 1980.

Hendrick, Chief
See Theyanoguin

Hichitis
See Creeks

Hillabee Massacre
Event Date: November 18, 1813

Massacre of Native Americans instigated by American forces under the command of Major General John Cocke on November 18, 1813. The action took place against the Creeks from the Hillabee towns along the Tallapoosa River in present-day Cherokee County, Alabama, 20 miles east of Talladega. The incident resulted from political jealousy between Cocke and Major General Andrew Jackson and from the complicated situation within the Creek Nation during the Creek War (1813–1814), then subsumed by the larger conflict known as the War of 1812.

The War of 1812 had further splintered an already divided Creek confederacy, and many militants from the Upper Creek towns, known as Red Sticks, supported Tecumseh's call for a Pan-Indian confederacy to oppose continued American expansionism. The Red Stick capture of Fort Mims and the subsequent massacre of its garrison on August 30, 1813, panicked whites in the Mississippi Territory and terrified people along the entire frontier. Consequently, Tennessee governor William Blount called out the state militia under Major General Jackson, then commanding the western Tennessee militia, and Major General Cocke, commanding the eastern militia, and sent them into the Mississippi Territory.

Jackson's subsequent campaign led to victories at Tallashatchee on November 3, 1813, and at Talladega on November 9, after which he called on Cocke, his nominal subordinate, to join him for an invasion of the Red Stick heartland along the Tallapoosa River. Disheartened by their recent defeats, the principal chiefs of the Hillabee towns sent Robert Grierson, a released prisoner, to

Jackson to request peace terms, which were then agreed upon. Jackson then sent word to Cocke at Fort Armstrong and informed him of the Hillabee capitulation.

It is debatable whether Cocke actually heard of the surrender before he took action, but he was nevertheless determined to match Jackson's military success and to punish the Hillabee towns for their previous militancy. On November 18 Cocke dispatched a mounted force under Brigadier General James White and a Cherokee auxiliary force under Colonel Gideon Morgan to attack the towns. Caught by surprise and believing that their terms had been accepted, the Hillabee Creeks offered little or no resistance as White's men destroyed three towns, killing 64 Creek warriors and forcing prisoners, which included more than 200 women and children, to return with them to Fort Armstrong. Creek warriors who managed to escape later became Jackson's implacable enemies and fought resolutely at the Battle of Horseshoe Bend (March 17, 1814), which finally crushed Creek resistance and helped end the Creek War.

Jackson was furious at Cocke's actions, and if Cocke had complied with Jackson's earlier request to join forces at Fort Strother, the massacre could have been avoided. Relations between the two Tennessee generals remained strained after their forces were united in December 1813, resulting finally in Cocke's arrest and court-martial for continually refusing to obey Jackson's orders. Acquitted, Cocke went on to serve four terms in the U.S. House of Representatives from 1819 to 1827.

Rory T. Cornish

See also
Creeks; Creek War; Fort Mims, Battle of; Horseshoe Bend, Battle of; Jackson, Andrew; Red Sticks; Tallushatchee, Battle of

References
Owsley, Frank L., Jr. *Struggle for the Gulf Borderlands. The Creek War and the Battle of New Orleans, 1812–1815.* Gainesville: University Presses of Florida, 1981.
Wright, J. Leitch, Jr. *Creeks and Seminoles: The Destruction and Regeneration of the Muscogulge People.* Lincoln: University of Nebraska Press, 1986.

Hin-mah-too-yah-lat-kekt
See Joseph, Chief

Ho-Chunks
See Winnebagos

Holata Micco
See Billy Bowlegs

Holy Ground, Battle of

See Econochaca, Battle of

Hook Nose

See Roman Nose

Hopewell, Treaty of

The Treaty of Hopewell was signed in 1785 and 1786 at Hopewell, Fort Prince George, on the Keowee River near Seneca Old Town, which is in present-day Pickens County, South Carolina. The treaty was an agreement between the United States and the Cherokees, Choctaws, and Chickasaws. The U.S. commissioners were Benjamin Hawkins, Andrew Pickens, Joseph Martin, and Lachlan McIntosh.

All previous treaties with the Native Americans had been made before and during the American Revolutionary War (1775–1783). The Treaty of Hopewell was the first treaty between Native Americans and the new U.S. government and also marked the first guarantee from the new government against further white settlement on Cherokee land. The treaty redefined the boundaries of Native American lands and put the Cherokees under the protection of the federal government. In addition, the treaty gave the responsibility for regulation of Cherokee trade to the United States.

The Treaty of Hopewell had three parts. The first and most important part was finalized on November 28, 1785, and addressed the Cherokees. The second part of the treaty, finalized on January 3, 1786, addressed the Choctaws. The third part, finalized on January 10, 1786, dealt with the Chickasaws. All three contained the same wording and promises and are together known as the Treaty of Hopewell.

The purpose of the treaty was to end fighting and bring peace between the Native American nations and the United States. Instead, the treaty created new problems. Indeed, the treaty demonstrated one of the shortfalls of the new confederated United States. Some of the new states had already ceded portions of their western land to the federal government to end disputes over conflicting territorial claims that had delayed ratification of the Articles of Confederation (Western Reserve), but Native American peoples were already living on much of the land that the federal government now controlled. Native Americans disagreed with the new boundary lines and largely disregarded the treaty, seeing the U.S. government as too weak and ineffective to enforce it.

White settlers were also already living in the contested areas, and the Treaty of Hopewell put them on the wrong side of the new boundaries. Suddenly finding themselves on Native American land, they nonetheless refused to move. These white settlers saw the government as uninterested and unwilling to protect them from Native Americans. The settlers also largely disregarded the treaty.

There were short periods of peace after the Treaty of Hopewell, but within three years sporadic fighting escalated into war. The Choctaws and Chickasaws remained at peace for years after the agreement, but such was not the case with the Cherokees. In 1788 peace chief Old Tassel was killed under a flag of truce. His murder united the Cherokees under Little Turkey, and the wars continued. Shortly after the death of Old Tassel, Congress issued a proclamation for the U.S. settlers that reemphasized the articles of the treaty. In 1790 President George Washington issued a similar proclamation. The Treaty of Holston of 1791 was an attempt to clarify and expand the Treaty of Hopewell, but the so-called Indian problem was never fully resolved by treaties, which served only to delay the relocation of most Native Americans.

BILLIE FORD

See also

Cherokees; Chickasaws; Choctaws; Washington, George; Western Reserve

References

Aron, Stephen. *How the West Was Lost: The Transformation of Kentucky from Daniel Boone to Henry Clay.* Baltimore: Johns Hopkins University Press, 1996.

Carter, Clarence Edwin, ed. *Territorial Papers of the United States,* Vol. 4. Washington, DC: U.S. Government Printing Office, 1934.

Kappler, Charles J., comp. and ed. *Indian Affairs: Laws and Treaties,* Vol. 2. Washington, DC: U.S. Government Printing Office, 1904.

Hopkins, Sarah Winnemucca

See Winnemucca, Sarah

Horses

Before horses diffused into Native American territory from Spanish settlements, the only beast of burden used by North American natives was the dog, which could pull small loads on a travois (a frame slung between trailing poles). Not surprisingly, horses were first greeted as a larger, stronger kind of dog. Native peoples who acquired horses usually affixed travois to them before learning to ride them. Ultimately horses, having both economic and military applications, radically transformed Native American culture.

Horses may have been introduced to some Native American peoples by Francisco de Vázquez de Coronado's expedition of the early 1540s, but the most likely genesis of Native American horse culture probably sprang from the herds that the Spanish kept at Santa Fe following the expedition of Juan de Oñate a half century later. Some horses escaped Spanish herds and bred wild in New Mexico and Texas. These were so-called Indian ponies averaging less than 1,000 pounds in weight, smaller than modern-day riding horses. These agile fast horses were interbred with larger animals acquired from Spanish (and later Anglo-American) herds. The Pawnees especially had access to these horses and to others traded to them by native

Shoshone buffalo-skin robe stretched and painted with figures that record tribal history and show the horse herds used for trade, warfare, and hunting. (Angel Wynn/Nativestock Pictures/Corbis)

merchants who tapped supplies in Mexico and became among the best and most prolific horse traders on the Plains.

By 1659 Spanish reports indicate that the Apaches were stealing horses from the Spaniards. At roughly the same time, the Apaches and Pueblos traded for horses; by 1700 the Utes and Comanches had also acquired mounts. After that, native peoples' use of horses spread throughout the continent. By 1750 the horse was widely recognized as a unit of barter and wealth. By roughly 1700 the horse frontier had reached a line stretching roughly from present-day eastern Texas northward through eastern Kansas and Nebraska and then northwest through Wyoming, Montana, Idaho, and Washington. Horses became such an essential part of many Native American cultures that the Apaches, for example, incorporated them into their oral history as gifts of the gods.

Having acquired horses, a number of native peoples migrated to the Plains because mounts made economic life there, especially the buffalo hunt, easier. Some of these natives were also being pressured westward by the European-American settlement frontier. The various Lakota-Nakota-Dakota bands moved westward before widespread white contact, as did the Omahas and many others. The horse extended the range of native peoples as well as control over their environment. A native group on foot was limited to a few miles' travel a day, while with horses a camp could

be moved 30 miles or more in the same period. A small party of warriors on horseback could cover 100 miles of rough country in a day or two.

Native Americans explored different ways of training horses. Unlike the Europeans, the Cheyennes, for example, did not usually break their horses. Instead they gentled them. Boys who tended horses stroked them, talked to them, and played with them. An owner of a horse might sing to it or smoke a pipe and blow smoke in its face. At age 18 months the horse would begin more intense training but was still gentled. Gradually the horse was habituated to carrying a human being and gear. Horses meant for war or hunting were trained specifically in those skills.

The horse shaped economic behavior in many ways. One was the productivity of raiding, which acquired considerable status. By the early 19th century raiding on horseback was the Apaches' major economic activity; the greatest fame that a Crow could earn came when he was able to snatch a tethered horse from under the nose of an enemy.

The horse turned a subsistence lifestyle on the harsh High Plains of North America into a festival of abundance for a few decades, until diseases also imported from Europe killed a large majority of the native peoples there. Many native nations on the Plains and near the adjacent Rocky Mountains, such as the various divisions of the Lakota, Nakota, and Dakota as well as the Crow and Nez Perce tribes, became rich in horses. The wealth in horses and the wealth produced by them affected ceremonialism as well, which among many Plains groups became more lavish than in pre-equine days.

Horses changed some peoples' housing styles from fixed lodges to mobile tepees. Horses also allowed the size of the average tepee to increase because a horse could haul a tepee as large as 18 to 20 feet in diameter, much larger than a dog or a human being could carry. Some tepees weighed as much as 500 pounds and required three horses to carry. The horse reduced economies of scale in hunting, especially of buffalo, making hunting parties smaller. The increased mobility brought by horses energized trade as well as intertribal conflict because ease of transport brought more contact between diverse peoples, friendly and not. When fighting whites, Native Americans found in the horse a reliable, sturdy mode of transportation that was every bit the equal of white transportation. This along with the introduction of firearms helped even the odds.

BRUCE E. JOHANSEN

See also

Buffalo; Spain

References

Calloway, Colin G. *New Worlds for All: Indians, Europeans, and the Remaking of Early America.* Baltimore: Johns Hopkins University Press, 1997.

Denhardt, Robert M. *The Horse of the Americas.* Norman: University of Oklahoma Press, 1975.

Wissler, Clark. "The Influence of the Horse in the Development of Plains Culture." *American Anthropologist* 16 (1914): 1–25.

Horseshoe Bend, Battle of

Event Date: March 27, 1814

Decisive American victory by Major General Andrew Jackson of the Tennessee Militia during the Creek War (July 1813–August 1814), considered to be a part of the War of 1812. A war party among the Creeks, who occupied most of present-day Alabama, had been resisting American encroachments upon their homeland. Led by Peter McQueen and William Weatherford, the Creeks enjoyed some initial military success, particularly in southern Alabama in the sacking of Fort Mims, commanded by Major Daniel Beasley, on August 30, 1813.

Soon the tables were reversed. In the autumn of 1813 militiamen from Georgia and the Mississippi Territory launched expeditions against the Creeks. Jackson successfully led 2,500 Tennessee militia against the Creek settlements of Tallushatchee on November 3 and Talladega six days later. Meanwhile, Brigadier General James White successfully led other Tennessee militia against Hillabee on November 18.

In January 1814 Jackson returned to the offensive with a force of 1,000 militiamen. He defeated the Creeks at Emuckfaw Creek

on January 22 and at Enitachopco Creek two days later, sustaining about 100 casualties while inflicting twice that number on the Native Americans.

By February 1814 Jackson's force had grown to some 4,000 men, mostly militia but including the 600-man 39th U.S. Infantry Regiment. The Creeks, some 1,200 strong, fortified their encampment on a peninsula of about 100 acres formed by the Tallapoosa River and called Horseshoe Bend. They constructed a log breastwork across the neck of the peninsula and collected canoes to flee across the river should that prove necessary. Jackson was determined to attack the encampment.

Jackson arrived at Horseshoe Bend on the morning of March 27, 1814. He had with him some 3,000 men, including allied Cherokee and Creek warriors. Sensing the weakness of the Creek defensive position, he sent Brigadier General John Coffee of the Tennessee Militia with mounted infantry and the allied Native Americans to take position behind the bend and block the hostile Creeks' escape. Some of the Cherokees swam across the river and seized the canoes.

At about 10:00 a.m. Jackson ordered his two small cannon to shell the hostile Creeks' fortifications. Coffee then used the captured canoes to get some of his men across the Tallapoosa and assault the Creeks from the rear. Flaming arrows fired by the Native American allies set much of the Creek settlement on fire.

At about 12:30 Jackson ordered the 39th Infantry to carry out a frontal assault with bayonets on the Creek breastworks. Although the Creeks fought desperately, they were quickly overwhelmed and driven from the works. Fighting in small bands, the survivors were soon pinned against the river.

The battle now turned into a massacre. Many of the Creeks refused to surrender, and others were shot while swimming across the river to escape. Jackson, a hardened soldier, described the carnage as "dreadful." Perhaps 800 hostile Native Americans were killed, and another 350, mostly women and children, were captured. Casualties among the militia and U.S. regulars were 26 killed and 106 wounded, while the allied Cherokees and Creeks suffered 23 killed and 47 wounded.

The Battle of Horseshoe Bend brought major combat in the Creek War to an end. Weatherford fled with a few survivors into Spanish territory but soon surrendered. On August 9, 1814, Jackson compelled the Creeks, both friend and foe, to sign the Treaty of Fort Jackson, ceding half of Alabama and part of Georgia to the United States.

PAUL DAVID NELSON

See also

Cherokees; Coffee, John; Creeks; Creek War; Emuckfaw Creek, Battle of; Enitachopco Creek, Battle of; Fort Mims, Battle of; Jackson, Andrew; McQueen, Peter; Native Americans and the War of 1812; Tallushatchee, Battle of; Weatherford, William

References

Burstein, Andrew. *The Passions of Andrew Jackson.* New York: Knopf, 2003.

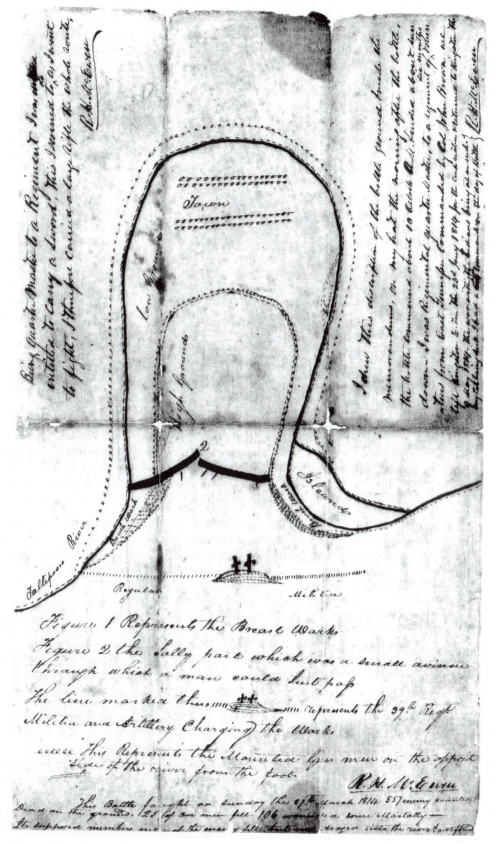

Diagram by a participant showing the location of American troops in the decisive Battle of Horseshoe Bend, fought along the Tallapoosa River, Alabama, on March 27, 1814, during the Creek War. (Hulton Getty/Archive Photos)

Heidler, David S., and Jeanne T. Heidler. *Old Hickory's War: Andrew Jackson and the Quest for Empire.* Mechanicsburg, PA: Stackpole, 1996.

Owsley, Frank L., Jr. *Struggle for the Gulf Borderlands. The Creek War and the Battle of New Orleans, 1812–1815.* Gainesville: University Presses of Florida, 1981.

Horseshoe Bend, Treaty of

See Fort Jackson, Treaty of

Hotoa-qa-ihoois

See Tall Bull

Houston, Samuel
Birth Date: March 2, 1793
Death Date: July 26, 1863

Soldier, frontiersman, and politician who led Texan forces during the struggle for independence from Mexico and subsequently became the president of the Texas Republic. Samuel (Sam) Houston was born on March 2, 1793, in Rockbridge County, Virginia, but moved to Tennessee as a boy. A rebellious youth, Houston left the family farm at age 16 and lived with the Cherokees, from whom he received his Native American name "Raven." He remained with the Cherokees for two years before he returned to Maryville and established a school for frontier children.

Following the outbreak of the War of 1812, in 1813 Houston enlisted in the army as a private, but his leadership skills were quickly recognized, and he was commissioned an ensign four months later. During the war he served with Major General Andrew Jackson in the campaign against the Creeks, including the Battle of Horseshoe Bend, where Houston was wounded three times. His heroism and leadership caught the attention of Jackson, who subsequently helped Houston at several points during his career.

Houston remained in the army after the war and was promoted to second lieutenant. In 1817, he was assigned to participate in the removal of the Cherokees from their lands to the Indian Territory (Oklahoma). In 1818 Houston resigned from the army after he was given an official reprimand by Secretary of War John C. Calhoun for appearing before the secretary in Cherokee garb.

Houston then studied law, passed the bar, and practiced law in Lebanon, Tennessee. On Jackson's recommendation, Houston was appointed a colonel and then was elected major general of the state militia. Houston also became active in politics and was elected attorney general for Nashville and then to the U.S. House of Representatives in 1823. In Congress, Houston worked to support Jackson's candidacy for the presidency following the election of 1824. In 1827 he left the House and became governor of Tennessee. Although he was reelected in 1829, Houston abruptly left politics and Tennessee after a brief failed marriage.

Once again Houston lived among the Cherokees, this time in Indian Territory. During this three-year period he met and married a woman of mixed Cherokee and European ancestry. The couple established a trading post on the Neosho River. In 1832 Jackson, now president, dispatched Houston to Texas, then part of the Mexican state of Coahuila y Texas, to negotiate with tribes in the region.

Houston soon became involved in regional politics in Texas and emerged as one of the foremost proponents of independence from Mexico. He attended the San Felipe Convention in 1833 that drew up a constitution for the territory and a petition to the Mexican government requesting that the area be made a separate state. In 1835 he was appointed commander of the Army of Texas with the rank of major general. The following year Houston was a delegate when the Texas Assembly declared independence. Although the Mexican forces initially enjoyed military success against the rebellious Texans, Houston was able to win a major victory at the Battle of San Jacinto on April 21, 1836. During the engagement he

Sam Houston, who later led Texan forces against Mexico and served as president of the Republic of Texas, first distinguished himself during the Creek War (1813–1814) and for a time lived among the Cherokees. (National Archives)

was wounded and had his horse shot from under him. After the battle the Mexican commander General Antonio López de Santa Anna was captured. The battle confirmed Texan independence, although Mexico officially refused to accept the loss of Texas until after the Mexican-American War (1846–1848).

Houston's great popularity led to his election as president of Texas in 1836. He worked hard to convince the United States to annex Texas as a new state and to improve relations between white settlers and Native Americans. After his first term as president ended in 1838, Houston served in the Texas House of Representatives but was reelected president in 1841. After Texas joined the Union in 1845, Houston served two terms in the U.S. Senate, where he supported the Mexican-American War.

In the Senate, Houston urged compromise on the issue of slavery and became well known as a staunch Unionist Democrat. His support for the Union and his efforts on behalf of Native Americans eroded his popularity in Texas, however. He ran unsuccessfully for governor of Texas in 1857 and left the Senate in 1859. He again ran for governor that same year and won. Once in office, Houston favored the use of force to establish a protectorate over Mexico and other areas of Central America as a way to divert attention from the growing sectional strife in the Union.

Following the election of Abraham Lincoln in 1860, Houston called a special session of the Texas legislature to debate secession. Although he opposed secession, the convention voted overwhelmingly to leave the Union. Houston oversaw the initial steps to sever ties with the Union but refused to take the oath of allegiance to the Confederacy. On March 16, 1861, the legislature removed him from office. Houston and his family moved to Huntsville, Texas, where he died on July 26, 1863.

JACK COVARRUBIAS AND TOM LANSFORD

See also

Cherokees; Creeks; Creek War; Horseshoe Bend, Battle of; Jackson, Andrew; Trail of Tears

References

Braider, Donald. *Solitary Star: A Biography of Sam Houston.* New York: Putnam, 1974.

Bruhl, Marshall de. *Sword of San Jacinto: A Life of Sam Houston.* New York: Random House, 1993.

Williams, John Holt. *Sam Houston: A Biography of the Father of Texas.* New York: Simon and Schuster, 1993.

Howard, Oliver Otis

Birth Date: November 8, 1830
Death Date: October 26, 1909

U.S. Army officer. Oliver Otis Howard was born in Leeds, Maine, on November 8, 1830. Graduating from Bowdoin College in 1850 and the U.S. Military Academy, West Point, in 1854, Howard was a first lieutenant teaching mathematics at West Point when the American Civil War (1861–1865) began. He resigned his regular

commission to become colonel of the 3rd Maine Regiment. He led a brigade during the First Battle of Bull Run (Manassas) on July 21, 1861, and helped cover the Union retreat. His performance won him promotion to brigadier general of volunteers. On May 31, 1862, Howard was conspicuous for his bravery at Seven Pines during the Peninsula Campaign, being wounded twice. His right arm was amputated close to the shoulder. For his actions at Seven Pines, he received the Medal of Honor in 1893.

During Howard's convalescence he became convinced that God had spared his life for the purpose of liberating the slaves. Back in command, Howard fought with distinction in the Second Battle of Bull Run (Manassas) (August 28–30, 1862) and the Battle of Antietam (September 17, 1862). Promoted to major general of volunteers, Howard led his division in the desperate frontal assault at Fredericksburg on December 13, 1862.

In April 1863 Howard took command of XI Corps, composed largely of German immigrants. Hit on May 2 by Confederate lieutenant general Thomas "Stonewall" Jackson's flank attack in the Battle of Chancellorsville, Howard's corps virtually disintegrated. Notwithstanding this defeat and the considerable controversy about his role in it, Howard retained his command. During Confederate general Robert E. Lee's second invasion of the North, on the morning of July 1, 1863, Howard selected Cemetery Ridge as the key defensive position at Gettysburg. Although the performance of his troops over the next two days of battle could best be called mediocre, Howard enjoyed the ultimate satisfaction of receiving the Thanks of Congress for his actions in the battle.

Howard then shifted to the western theater, commanding a corps at Chattanooga. During the subsequent Atlanta Campaign, Major General William T. Sherman chose Howard to command the Army of the Tennessee following the death of Major General James McPherson. At both Ezra Church and Jonesboro, Howard's army won easy victories.

When Sherman marched from Atlanta for Savannah in November 1864, he assigned Howard the honor of commanding the right wing of the army. In the Carolinas, Howard's army impressed all with the rapidity of its movement over flooded swamp country. Although Howard publicly justified the harsh treatment meted out to Southerners during the march, he attempted to check gratuitous violence. In North Carolina, Howard's army fought at Bentonville and Goldsboro. At the close of the war he was appointed brigadier general in the regular army.

Throughout the war, Howard won the admiration of his men for his great personal bravery. He also attracted attention for his churchgoing and for his puritanical ways: he opposed profanity, drinking, and gambling. Some admirers characterized Howard as "the Christian general." Skeptics called him "Old Prayer Book." Certainly Howard saw more than his share of battle and was, in Sherman's eyes, the consummate soldier.

Howard's straight-laced demeanor led President Andrew Johnson to appoint him head of the Bureau of Refugees, Freedmen, and Abandoned Lands in May 1865. While in this post Howard championed African Americans in various ways. In 1867 he became the key figure in the establishment of one of the earliest black institutions of higher education, which was named in his honor (now Howard University); he served as its first president until 1874.

Howard also played an active role in the settlement of the western frontier. In 1872 he had taken time off from his post to travel with an aide and three civilian guides (two of whom were Apaches) to the remote camp of the Chiricahua Apaches who had taken up arms against the whites. He entered the camp unarmed and, following 11 days of talks, negotiated a lasting peace settlement with Chiricahua leader Cochise.

In 1874 Howard assumed command of the Department of the Columbia, going west to Fort Vancouver. Here he was forced to deal with white settler demands that the Nez Perces under Chief Young Joseph be removed from the Wallowa Valley. Howard ordered his adjutant, Major Henry Clay Wood, a trained lawyer, to study the 1855 and 1863 treaties. Wood concluded that the Nez Perces had a legal claim to the land in question. Howard himself wrote in a report of 1876 that "I think it is a great mistake to take from Joseph and his band of Nez Perces Indians that valley . . . and possibly Congress can be induced to let these really peaceable Indians have this poor valley for their own." It was not to be.

First Wood in 1876 and Howard himself in 1877 met with the Nez Perces. In the course of the second meeting Howard reportedly lost his temper and, in the words of Yellow Wolf, "showed the rifle." (In Chief Joseph's famous speech in Washington, D.C., in 1879, he said that if Howard had given him sufficient time to gather his stock there would have been no war.)

When war broke out later in 1877, Howard sought a quick end to the hostilities, and in the Battle of the Clearwater River his men outnumbered the Nez Perces some six to one. However, the Nez Perces escaped through Lolo Pass and began their epic 1,500-mile flight in an attempt to find refuge in Canada. Howard's forces pursued Joseph's small band but never directly engaged the Nez Perces in battle again, and Howard was soon the target of public criticism. Four months later Joseph surrendered to Colonel Nelson A. Miles at Bear Paw, Montana.

Howard's last engagement in the Indian Wars took place in 1878 when his forces quickly and easily defeated the Bannock Indians, some of whom had served as scouts for the army in the Nez Perce War. Howard was superintendent of the U.S. Military Academy during 1881–1882 and was promoted to major general in 1886. After various other peacetime assignments, he retired from active duty in 1894. Howard died in Burlington, Vermont, on October 26, 1909.

MALCOLM MUIR JR.

See also
Bannock War; Clearwater River, Battle of; Cochise; Joseph, Chief; Miles, Nelson Appleton; Nez Perces; Nez Perce War

References
Greene, Jerome A. *Nez Perce Summer, 1877: The U. S. Army and the Nee-Me-Poo Crisis*. Helena: Montana Historical Society Press, 2000.
Howard, Oliver O. *Autobiography of Oliver Otis Howard*. New York: Baker and Taylor, 1908.
Howard, Oliver O. *My Life and Experiences among Our Hostile Indians: A Record of Personal Observations, Adventures, and Campaigns among the Indians of the Great West*. 1907; reprint, New York: Da Capo, 1972.
Howard, Oliver O. *Nez Perce Joseph: An Account of His Ancestors, His Lands, His Confederates, His Enemies, His Murders, His War, His Pursuit and Capture*. Whitefish, MT: Kessinger, 2007.
McCoy, Robert. *Chief Joseph, Yellow Wolf, and the Creation of Nez Perce History in the Northwest*. New York: Routledge, 2004.

Hualapais

Southwestern Native American group indigenous to northwestern Arizona. The Hualapais (Walapais), or "Pine Tree People," were named after the piñon pine nut. Along with the Havasupais, the Hualapais are called the Pais (Pa'as), or "the People"; the Hualapais are the western Pais, and the Havasupais are the eastern Pais. The Hualapais are also described, along with the Havasupais and the Yavapais, as Upland Yumas, in contrast to the River Yumas, such as the Mojaves and Quechans. The Hualapais spoke Upland Yuman, a member of the Hokan-Siouan language family.

The Pais, who traditionally considered themselves one people, probably descended from the prehistoric Patayans of the ancient Hakataya culture. Thirteen bands of Pais originally ranged in northwestern Arizona along the Colorado River. They engaged chiefly in hunting, farming, and gathering. By historic times, three subtribes had been organized: the Middle Mountain People, the Plateau People, and the Yavapai Fighters. Each subtribe was further divided into several bands, which in turn were divided into camps and families.

Traditional political authority was decentralized. The headmen of both a camp (roughly 20 people) and a band (roughly 85 to 200 people) led by fostering consensus. Headmen served as war chiefs and spokespeople when necessary. The position of headman was occasionally hereditary but more often was based on personality and ability. There was little or no tribal identity until the early 20th century, when the Hualapais created a fledgling tribal council. In the 1930s they adopted a constitution and elected their first tribal president.

Occasionally the Hualapais grew the standard American crops (corn, beans, and squash) near springs and ditches due to the arid climate in which they lived. Corn was made into mush, soup, and bread; pumpkins were dried in long strips. Mainly, however, they obtained their food by hunting and gathering, leaving their summer camps to follow the seasonal ripening of wild foods. The women gathered piñon nuts, cactus and yucca fruits, agave (mescal) hearts, mesquite beans, and other plants. The men hunted deer, antelope, mountain sheep, rabbits (in drives), and small game. The Hualapais also ate fish.

The Hualapais were part of an extensive system of trade and exchange that stretched from the Pacific Ocean to the Pueblo region. Shell decorations and horses came from the Mojaves and the Quechans. Rich red ocher pigment was a key trade item, as were baskets and dried mescal and dressed skins. Meat and skins were traded for crops, and lima beans were traded for Hopi peaches.

Although the Pais encountered Europeans in 1540 or perhaps as late as 1598, neither the Spanish nor the Mexicans settled in Hualapai country, which remained fairly isolated until the 1820s. Around that time a trail was blazed from the Rio Grande to California that led directly through Pai country. After the Mexican Cession in 1848, the Hualapais began working in white-owned mines. With American invasions and treaty violations increasing and the mines ever exploitative, in 1865 the Hualapais met violence with violence. A warrior named Cherum forced a key U.S. retreat but later scouted for his old enemy. Later, the United States selected Hualapai Charley and Leve Leve as principal chiefs because they were amenable to making peace. The conflict ended in 1869.

Because the eastern Pais played a minor role in the conflict, they were allowed to return home afterward; it was at this juncture that the Hualapais and Havasupais became increasingly separate. In 1874 the U.S. Army forced the Hualapais, who had failed to escape, to march to the Colorado River Reservation. There the low altitude combined with disease and poor rations brought the Hualapais much suffering and death. When they filtered back home several years later, they found their land in nonnative hands. Still, they applied for and received official permission to remain, and a reservation was established for them in 1883.

The reservation consisted of 1 million acres on the South Rim of the Grand Canyon, a fraction of their original land. Before long, overgrazing by whites' livestock had ruined the Native American food supply, and ranchers and cattlemen were directly threatening the Native Americans with physical violence. A series of epidemics struck the Hualapais as well. Most Hualapais lived off the reservation, scrambling for wage work and sending their children to American schools. As the Hualapais formed an underclass of cheap unskilled labor, their way of life began to vanish. The railroad depot at Peach Springs became the primary Hualapai village, but the railroad brought only dislocation, disease, and few jobs. The Hualapais' new condition strengthened their differences with the still-isolated Havasupais.

The Hualapais began herding cattle in 1914, although their herds were greatly outnumbered by those of nonnatives. Extensive prejudice against the Native Americans diminished somewhat after World War I (1914–1918) out of respect for Native American war heroes. Through the mid-20th century the Hualapais retained a strong sense of their own culture, although economic progress was extremely slow.

BARRY M. PRITZKER

See also
Havasupais

References
Dobyns, Henry F., and Robert C. Euler. *The Havasupai People.* Phoenix: Indian Tribal Council Series, 1976.

Lliff, Flora Gregg. *People of the Blue Water: A Record of Life among the Walapai and Havasupai Indians.* Tucson: University of Arizona Press, 1985.

Hudson River School

Term used to identify a group of U.S. landscape artists whose oil paintings portrayed the natural beauty of the Hudson River Valley and, later, the American West. The Hudson River School endured from 1825 to 1875. Some of its most famous artists were Thomas Cole, Asher Durand, and Albert Bierstadt. While the Hudson River Valley was the early focus of this movement, artists also depicted nearby areas such as the Catskill, Adirondack, and White mountains.

Following the War of 1812, young artists from the United States studying in Europe were swept up by the Romantic movement's interest in nature. A powerful upsurge in nationalism and a desire to quell European critics, who claimed that the United States had no culture of its own, led these artists, upon returning to their homeland, to concentrate on American themes. The beauty of the new nation's landscape became the focus of their attention. These painters envisioned landscapes as a more universal and democratic artistic expression of the endless possibilities for the future greatness of the young nation.

The school's first noted painter was Thomas Cole. The completion of the Erie Canal in 1825, along with the nation's post–War of 1812 optimism and prosperity, convinced Cole to focus on the purity of the natural ideal. As the pioneer painter of the American wilderness, Cole's paintings such as *Sunny Morning on the Hudson River* (ca. 1827) and *Schroon Mountain, Adirondacks* (1838), along with more ambitious worldly themes such as *Course of Empire* (1836) and *Voyages of Life* (1842), strengthened feelings of nationalism and cultural awareness. Many more young artists in the United States also began depicting the beauty of the frontier in majestic settings.

By the 1850s almost all of the Hudson River School painters conducted their work in large studios in their 15 West Tenth Street building in lower Manhattan. Upon Cole's death in 1847, Asher Durand became the leading figure. Durand painted directly from nature. His close-up oil sketches of woodland scenes remain as some of his most important contributions to American art. His *Kindred Spirits* (1849), depicting Cole and poet William Cullen Bryant on a cliff overlooking a stream in the mountains, symbolizes the work of the Hudson River School. Other important artists included Worthington Whittredge, Sanford Gifford, John Kensett, Frederick Church, and Jasper Cropsey. Cropsey's *Autumn on the Hudson* (1860) established his reputation as the foremost painter of detailed autumn landscapes.

As the pioneers pushed farther west especially after the acquisition of California as a consequence of the Mexican-American War (1846–1848), the school's artists took their brushes and easels with them beyond the Mississippi River. Albert Bierstadt's *Rocky*

Mountains–Landers Peak (1863) and *Yellowstone Falls* (1881) elevated him to first rank among American artists. By the mid-19th century the Hudson River School's painters were accepted on the same footing as their European counterparts. However, after the conclusion of the American Civil War (1861–1865), the Romantic movement and the school had reached their peak. Younger painters now began emulating the Barbizon style then popular in France. This new style captured the artists' subjective emotional responses to nature as opposed to the earlier emphasis on faithful detail. By 1880 the Hudson River School's style of painting had fallen completely out of favor.

The school's contribution to American history and culture lies in its romantic depiction of nature and its beauty. For 50 years the Hudson River School highlighted the potential greatness of the American landscape and its resources. In the process the school strengthened nationalistic feelings. Although early adherents of the Hudson River School eschewed depictions of Native Americans in favor of traditional landscapes, some late-school painters depicted Native Americans at work and in their relationship to nature.

CHARLES FRANCIS HOWLETT

See also

Bierstadt, Albert; Custer's Last Stand in Art; Literature and the American Indian Wars; Romanticism

References

Boas, George, ed. *Romanticism in America.* Baltimore: Johns Hopkins University Press, 1940.

Flexner, James T. *That Wilder Image: The Painting of America's Native School from Thomas Cole to Winslow Homer.* Boston: Little, Brown, 1962.

Minks, Louise. *The Hudson River School.* New York: Crescent Books, 1989.

Hudson's Bay Company

Privately held fur-trading company and the oldest commercial corporation in North America, established in 1670 by Britain's King Charles II. The company traded mainly with Native Americans living in central and northern Canada. The trade consisted of European goods in exchange for animal furs. The company's original territory embraced the area drained by the rivers and streams flowing into Hudson Bay, or some 1.5 million square miles, representing more than one-third of present-day Canada.

The company derived its name from Henry Hudson, the English explorer. In 1610 Hudson, who in the previous year had claimed the shores of the Hudson River for Holland, sailed to the New World in search of the Northwest Passage, a sea route across northern North America connecting the Atlantic and Pacific oceans. His ship, the *Discovery,* sailed around Iceland into the strait between Baffin Island and Labrador and into Hudson Bay in northern Canada. Trapped by ice, the *Discovery* wintered in the bay. As the spring of 1611 approached, the crew mutinied and set

Hudson, his son, and several sailors adrift in a small open boat, never to be seen again.

In the 1600s France had a monopoly on the Canadian fur trade. Two French traders, Pierre-Esprit Radisson and Médard des Groseilliers, wanted to establish a trading post on the bay to eliminate the cost of moving furs overland. Jean-Baptiste Colbert, appointed French controller-general of finances in 1665, hoped to promote farming in New France. He thus opposed further exploration and fur trapping and turned them down.

The two entrepreneurs then contacted some English businessmen in Boston, Massachusetts, and went to England to obtain financing. On June 5, 1668, two ships left England to explore Hudson Bay, but one, the *Eaglet,* turned back. The *Nonsuch,* with Radisson aboard, continued on to Hudson Bay. He established Fort Rupert at the mouth of the Rupert River, both named after Prince Rupert of Bavaria, the expedition's sponsor and a first cousin of Charles II. After a successful trading expedition over the winter of 1668–1669, the *Nonsuch* returned to England.

On May 2, 1670, Charles granted a Royal Charter that incorporated "The Governor and Company of Adventurers of England trading into Hudson's Bay," the company's original name, and granted it a monopoly over trade, especially the fur trade, with the Native Americans in the huge area along the shores of Hudson Bay.

The company established its first post at Fort Nelson at the mouth of the Nelson River in present-day northeastern Manitoba. Others around the edge of Hudson Bay in present-day Manitoba, Ontario, and Quebec soon followed. During the spring and summer, traders of the First Nations, the non-Inuit aboriginal peoples of Canada, traveled to the fort by canoe to exchange their pelts for metal tools and hunting gear.

After war broke out in Europe between France and England in the 1680s, expeditions from both countries regularly raided and captured each other's trading posts. In March 1686 a French raiding party captured the company's posts along James Bay. In 1697 a small French naval squadron defeated three British Royal Navy ships in the largest naval battle in the history of the North American Arctic. York Factory on Hudson Bay changed hands several times in the next decade, but Britain permanently received the post by the Treaty of Utrecht (1713).

Until the late 1800s, the Hudson's Bay Company controlled the fur trade throughout much of British North America from its headquarters at York Factory. The company's trappers explored much of the region. The company served as the de facto government and also later formed the nucleus of official authority in many areas of western Canada and the United States.

In 1821 the Hudson's Bay Company merged with the North West Company of Montreal, giving it a combined territory of 3 million square miles that reached north to the Arctic Ocean and west to the Pacific. In the 1820s and 1830s the company controlled nearly all trade in the Pacific Northwest from its headquarters at Fort Vancouver on the Columbia River. Although the Anglo-American Convention of 1818 granted the United States and

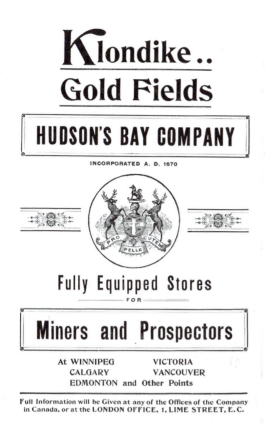

Advertisement for the Hudson's Bay Company, 1898. Originally chartered in 1670 by England's King Charles II, the Hudson's Bay Company is the oldest corporation in North America. (Library of Congress)

Britain joint authority over the Oregon Territory, the Hudson's Bay Company, through its effective monopoly on trade, actively discouraged Americans from settling in the region. However, after 1843 thousands of Americans poured into the Willamette Valley, and in 1846 the United States acquired full control of the Oregon Territory south of the 49th Parallel.

The Hudson's Bay Company also sent trapping brigades from Fort Vancouver into northern California as far south as the San Francisco Bay area. These trapping brigades were often the first to explore what were some of the last unexplored regions of North America.

The company's vast territory became the largest component in the Dominion of Canada, formed in 1867, and the company was the largest private landowner at the time. In 1868 the Hudson's Bay Company relinquished ownership of Rupert's Land to Canada, and two years later Britain abolished the company's monopoly on trade in the region. As the fur trade declined the company evolved into a mercantile business, selling goods to settlers in the Canadian West. These trading posts evolved into department stores, called The Bay Canada, and are the only part of the company operation still in existence. Until quite recently, these stores were often the only ones in many remote Canadian towns.

ROBERT B. KANE

See also
Fur Trade; Native American Trade

References
Creighton, Donald. *Dominion of the North: A History of Canada.* Boston: Houghton Mifflin, 1958.
MacKay, Douglas. *The Honourable Company: A History of the Hudson's Bay Company.* Indianapolis: Bobbs-Merrill, 1936.
Morton, W. L. *The Kingdom of Canada: A General History from Earliest Times.* Indianapolis: Bobbs-Merrill, 1963.

Hunkpapa Sioux

One of seven subbands of the Teton (western) Sioux. Referred to as the Lakota or Western Sioux, the Tetons inhabited parts of Nebraska, Wyoming, Montana, and the Dakotas during the late 1700s and early 1800s. They relocated there shortly after they acquired horses around 1740. By the 1830s almost all the Tetons, including the Hunkpapas, had adopted the Plains lifestyle, which relied heavily on buffalo and the buffalo hunt, required well-organized bands, and exalted raiding and combat. When the seven Lakota bands were camped together, the Hunkpapas were originally called *hukpapa,* which in Lakota refers to the band's location at the entrance to the camp, or those who camp at the entrance. Early students of the Sioux anglicized the name to Hunkpapa.

The Hunkpapas joined the larger Sioux migration from their original home in central Minnesota onto the Plains in the mid-1700s. After settling on the Plains, the Hunkpapas warred incessantly with neighboring nations, including the Crows, Assiniboines, Mandans, Arikaras, and Hidatsas, over access to hunting territory and trade. The Hunkpapas eventually expanded their territory at the expense of these tribes.

The Hunkpapa population increased during the first half of the 19th century, evidence of the successful adjustment by the Hunkpapas to buffalo hunting and a nomadic lifestyle. From an estimated 750 in 1833, their population increased to 2,920 members by 1850. The Native American wars at century's end, however, saw Hunkpapa numbers decline to 1,734 by 1890. A 1990 census showed a total of 6,083 people, mostly Hunkpapas and Blackfoot Sioux (Sihasapas), living on the South Dakota portion of the Standing Rock Reservation.

As a result of the Fort Laramie Treaty of 1868 and the creation of the Great Sioux Reservation, the Hunkpapas along with the Blackfoots, Lower Yanktonais, and Upper Yanktonais were placed in the new Grand River Agency at the confluence of the Grand and Missouri rivers in 1869. The agency was moved to Fort Yates in 1873 and given the name Standing Rock after a Lakota legend. The Hunkpapas lived between the Grand and Cannonball rivers in the late 19th century and remain along the Grand River today.

As the buffalo gradually disappeared in the last half of the 19th century, many Hunkpapas left the reservation to follow the remaining herds. In 1876 their departure led the U.S. government to send military expeditions to force their return to Standing Rock.

Hunkpapa leaders Sitting Bull and Gall defied the military, however, and Hunkpapa warriors played a major role in the Battle of the Little Bighorn (June 25–26, 1876).

By 1877 many Hunkpapas had fled into exile in Canada, where they settled near Wood Mountain in Saskatchewan. Most Hunkpapas returned to the United States in 1881 and were sent to Standing Rock. After Sitting Bull's death in 1890, the Hunkpapas were encouraged to adopt farming and ranching and adapt to American cultural practices. Today many Hunkpapas retain important parts of their traditional cultural beliefs.

STEVE POTTS

See also

Fort Laramie, Treaty of (1851); Fort Laramie, Treaty of (1868); Great Sioux Reservation; Great Sioux War; Little Bighorn, Battle of the; Sitting Bull; Standing Rock Reservation

References

DeMallie, Raymond J., ed. *Handbook of North American Indians: Plains,* Vol. 13, pt. 2. Washington, DC: Smithsonian Institution, 2001.

Gibbon, Guy. *The Sioux: The Dakota and Lakota Nations.* Malden, MA: Blackwell, 2003.

Hurons

See Wyandots

Hweeldi

See Fort Sumner

I

Illinois

Algonquian-speaking tribes living in the upper Mississippi River Valley in present-day Ohio, Illinois, Missouri, Iowa, and Wisconsin. The Illinois tribes comprised the Kaskaskias, the Cahokias, the Peorias, the Tamaroas, and the Michigameas.

During the 17th century the Illinois suffered heavy losses from the Beaver Wars (1641–1701) as the Iroquois drove tribes, including the Pottawatomis, Miamis, Kickapoos, Sauks, Foxes, and Osages,

out of the eastern Great Lakes region. Iroquois encroachment onto Illinois lands forced the Illinois to relocate in present-day southern Illinois along the Ohio River and its tributaries. The French first established contact with the Illinois in 1667 as Jesuit priest Claude Allouez was traveling to Chequamegon Bay on Lake Superior and encountered Illinois fur traders. In 1673 the Jesuit Jacques Marquette and the fur trader Louis Jolliet (Joliet) established contact with the Illinois while exploring the upper Mississippi River, and in

Contemporary depiction of Illinois Native Americans passing the peace pipe with settlers in the early 1700s. (Library of Congress)

1675 Marquette returned to establish a mission among the Illinois at Grand Kaskaskia near present-day Utica.

By the beginning of the 18th century the Illinois had lost most of their traditional lands and were reduced to territory along the Mississippi River and the Illinois River. The Illinois joined forces with the French in the Fox Wars (1712–1737), which would see the Illinois settle old scores with their Fox enemies. Illinois warriors from the Peoria band participated in the Detroit massacre of the Foxes, which in turn led to a cycle of revenge between the two tribes. Although the Illinois prevailed in battles with the Foxes (who were almost wiped out), they lost many of their warriors.

In the aftermath of the Fox Wars, the Illinois became even more dependent on the French and as a consequence would suffer heavy losses while fighting alongside the French in the Chickasaw Wars (1736–1740). As other tribes sought to take advantage of their increased weakness, the Illinois sought protection from the French. The Peoria band, for example, relocated to the French mission at Kaskaskia. Although the Illinois had fewer than 500 warriors left by the outbreak of the French and Indian War (1754–1763), they remained loyal to the French and participated in attacks against British settlements in Pennsylvania and Virginia. While participating in the campaign of Major General Louis-Joseph, Marquis de Montcalm, in northern New York in 1757, Illinois warriors contracted smallpox, which they brought back to their villages, further devastating the tribe.

Following the end of the French and Indian War, in May 1763 the Illinois supported Pontiac's Rebellion against the British. When Pontiac made peace with the British, the Illinois regarded this as a betrayal and murdered Pontiac when he visited Caholia in 1769. To avenge Pontiac's murder, the Ottawas, Ojibwas, Pottawatomis, Sauks, Foxes, Kickapoos, Mascoutens, and Winnebagos joined forces against the Illinois, nearly wiping out the tribe. Approximately 600 Illinois survived and fled to Kaskaskia, and their enemies divided up their lands. In 1803 the Illinois ceded all claims to their homeland and placed themselves under U.S. protection. In 1818 the Illinois agreed to removal west of the Mississippi, settling first in Missouri in 1818 and then in eastern Kansas in 1832. The Illinois merged with the Weas and the Piankashaws in 1854 and relocated with them in 1867 to northeastern Indian Territory (Oklahoma), where their descendants live today.

KATJA WUESTENBECKER

See also
Chickasaws; Fox Wars; French and Indian War; Iroquois; Kickapoos; Ogoula Tchetoka, Battle of; Ojibwas; Osages; Ottawas; Pontiac; Pontiac's Rebellion; Sauks and Foxes

References
Callender, Charles. "Illinois." In *Handbook of North American Indians*, Vol. 15, edited by B. G. Trigger, 673–680. Washington, DC: Smithsonian Institution Press, 1978.

Scott, James. *The Illinois Nation.* 2 vols. Streator, IL: Streator Historical Society, 1976.

Warren, Robert E., and John A. Walthall. "Illini Indians in the Illinois Country, 1673–1832." *Living Museum* 60(1) (1998): 4–8.

Indian Agents

Individuals assigned by either the British or U.S. governments to act as official liaisons with Native American tribes and nations. Since the late colonial period, Indian agents who lived among or near the various tribes of North America have served as on-the-scene representatives of their government. Agents answered directly to superintendents, who were powerful individuals controlling all Indian affairs in a given region.

In the colonial era, the British government appointed two superintendents of Indian affairs: Edmond Atkin in the South, who was succeeded by John Stuart, and Sir William Johnson in the North. The Ohio River served as the dividing line between the two districts. Johnson Hall, Sir William Johnson's home on the border between New York and Iroquoia, set an early precedent for the policy of stationing representatives in areas close to the Indian groups they sought to influence. Johnson tended to employ Indian traders, such as George Croghan, as agents because they were comfortable in both white and Native American societies.

Soon after the American Revolutionary War (1775–1783), U.S. secretary of war Henry Knox hoped to use Indian agents to ensure the pacification of unruly tribes, especially the Creeks. He thus appointed Benjamin Hawkins the first agent to the Creeks with the objective that he serve as the government's eyes among them and attempt to dissuade them from open resistance.

Yet the bureaucracy of the Indian service remained highly disorganized until 1834, when Andrew Jackson's administration finally codified many of its practices. Under the umbrella of the War Department, Indian agents were primarily civilian officials appointed by the president and approved by Congress. Each of these agents was dispatched to live among a specific Indian group for a period of four years and was given authority to employ a blacksmith, a farmer, a mechanic, a teacher, and an interpreter. The last of these jobs proved to be the most troublesome. A salary of $300 per year was insufficient to attract a qualified interpreter, and relations often suffered due to lack of good communications. Although Congress hoped that these subordinate roles would be filled by Native Americans, the agents usually employed whites.

Jackson reserved the right to appoint U.S. Army officers as agents, an economically advantageous policy because they could be paid less than civil servants. However, army officers usually resented being assigned to serve as Indian agents. Colonel Zachary Taylor, who had to act as an Indian agent in the mid-1830s, considered it a boring and tiresome position. The army high command also disliked the drain on their officer corps, which they complained resulted in poor efficiency among infantry and artillery units. In 1849 the Bureau of Indian Affairs was transferred from the War Department to the Department of the Interior, and military officials were forbidden from holding appointments as agents.

Corruption was a widespread problem among Indian agents. They had little supervision and nearly dictatorial powers in their region, and many abuses therefore resulted. Following the American Civil War (1861–1865), President Ulysses S. Grant attempted to

Judge

THE REASON OF THE INDIAN OUTBREAK.
General Miles declares that the Indians are starved into rebellion.

Cartoon showing an Indian agent profiting from unscrupulous practices in his dealings with Native Americans. From the December 20, 1890, issue of *Judge*. (Library of Congress)

solve this problem by reassigning army officers as agents, but Congress refused to accept this plan. As a compromise, church officials were given authority to nominate agents throughout the 1870s in an effort to ensure that only honest men were assigned to the posts. This plan also proved to be ineffectual. In the final analysis, Indian agents did little to stave off serious hostilities between Native Americans and white Americans and indeed may have inflamed the situation by the agents' corruption and biased approach to Indian affairs.

CAMERON B. STRANG

See also

Bureau of Indian Affairs; Croghan, George; Jackson, Andrew; Johnson, Sir William; Stuart, John

References

Priest, Loring Benson. *Uncle Sam's Stepchildren: The Reformation of United States Indian Policy, 1865–1887*. Lincoln: University of Nebraska Press, 1975.

Satz, Ronald N. *American Indian Policy in the Jacksonian Era*. Lincoln: University of Nebraska Press, 1975.

Washburn, Wilcomb E. *The Indian in America*. New York: Harper and Row, 1975.

Indian Creek Massacre
Event Date: May 20, 1832

A Native American raid on a white homestead located on Indian Creek in north-central Illinois (near present-day Ottawa) on May 20, 1832, during the Black Hawk War. Each year from 1829 to 1839 Chief Black Hawk and his Sauk and Fox followers returned to their summer encampment on the eastern shore of the Mississippi River in what is today northern Illinois, only to find the area inhabited by white settlers despite provisions of the 1825 Treaty of

Prairie du Chien. Black Hawk made various pleas for their removal and brought 1,000 men, women, and children from the western side of the river in the spring of 1832 in an effort to resettle the tribe's ancestral lands.

In the opening phases of the resulting Black Hawk War, the rout of almost 300 members of Major Isaiah Stillman's Illinois militia by a detachment of 40 warriors and the burning of homesteads by the Native Americans created panic among settlers in the territory. Warnings to evacuate extended throughout the region. William Davis, a white settler who refused to leave despite the warnings, had moved with his family from Kentucky to Indian Creek, some six miles north of present-day Ottawa, Illinois. Determined to stay, he also persuaded others, including the Hall and Pettigrew families, to do likewise.

Some months earlier Davis had alienated his Native American neighbors by building a dam on the creek that cut off an important supply of fish to a Pottawatomi village upstream. Keewasee, a member of that tribe, subsequently tried to dismantle the dam. Davis caught the man and severely beat him with a stick. Humiliated, Keewasee bore a grudge and used the violence associated with the Black Hawk War as cover by which to exact revenge.

Keewasee recruited some 40 Native Americans who had disagreed with their chief's decision not to support Black Hawk's incursion into the area. Three of Black Hawk's Sauk warriors also joined the group, which attacked the Davis homestead late in the afternoon on May 20, 1832. The Native Americans killed 15 people, including 7 children, in and around the cabins within 10 minutes. Several men who were working in the fields survived. The raiders withdrew quickly, taking teenage sisters Rachel and Sylvia Hall with them as captives. Although the Pottawatomis thought that Black Hawk would want the captives for bargaining purposes, he rejected the idea, and the girls were ransomed on June 1.

News of the killings and the kidnapping traveled quickly through the territory. Although the news adversely affected morale among some Illinois Militia units, the main effect was intensification of the fear and hatred of the local tribes. This prompted the raising of additional militia companies, spurred the construction of blockhouses, and motivated many settlers to seek refuge in army forts.

Following the Black Hawk War, three brothers were identified as the Sauk warriors among the attackers who perpetrated the massacre, but charges were dropped when witnesses failed to positively identify them. No evidence has suggested that Black Hawk himself sanctioned the attack or even knew about it in advance; rather, it appears to have been entirely a Pottawatomi-inspired operation.

MATTHEW J. KROGMAN

See also
Black Hawk War; Pottawatomis; Prairie du Chien, Treaty of; Sauks and Foxes

References
Jung, Patrick J. *The Black Hawk War of 1832*. Norman: University of Oklahoma Press, 2007.
Remini, Robert Vincenti. *Andrew Jackson and His Indian Wars*. New York: Penguin, 2001.
Trask, Kerry A. *Black Hawk: The Battle for the Heart of America*. New York: Holt, 2006.

Indian New Deal
See Indian Reorganization Act

Indian Presents

Term used to describe goods designated as gifts for use in diplomacy between Native American peoples and Europeans. Because such items were used by diplomats as well as traders who interacted with Native Americans, Indian presents are also referred to as Indian goods or trade goods. All European powers used presents in their diplomacy with native peoples during the colonial era. After that time presents continued to be used by traders, but the U.S. government usually favored lump-sum cash or annuity payments to secure Native American cooperation and land cessions.

Wampum (shell or other beads strung in the form of collars, girdles, belts, or strings) is commonly associated with diplomatic meetings. However, toys, fishing equipment, lead shot for firearms, knives, food, scalps, furs, tomahawks, rum, tobacco, clothing, and other textiles were also used in these rituals of exchange between colonists and natives. Metal objects were particularly sought after by American Indians. These included such items as silver medals, gorgets (half-moon–shaped or round metal plaques, often worn on a string like a necklace), earrings, and rings. Iron axes and knives and other small metal goods, such as thimbles, fishhooks, and bells, were likewise exchanged. Glass mirrors and glass beads were highly prized by native recipients, as were cloth goods such as wool coats and blankets (often made of imported fabrics called stroud, duffle, and ratteen) and decorative accessories such as ribbons and handkerchiefs. Every type of European-style clothing was exchanged except for wigs and breeches. Mind-altering products such as tobacco, rum, and other alcoholic beverages were also used as barter. Ivory objects and pigments for face painting are likewise often listed in inventories of trade goods and presents.

Although some of the objects presented by traders and diplomats were of utilitarian value, they were also often highly decorative. They sometimes served the aesthetic needs or desires of the native recipients. Objects used for trade were both manufactured in America (silver and iron) and imported from Europe (textiles and beads). Many colonial forts and military encampments or expeditions included craftsmen capable of creating trade goods.

Although Indian presents were goods designated for diplomatic exchange between agents of the colonial governments and native leaders, the same types of goods were also used in purely economic exchanges. Gifts were often presented as part of reciprocal giving for diplomacy or were given to natives as military awards. In contrast, the goods used for trade were exchanged for furs or other items. Documents reveal that the types of goods used for Indian presents were also purchased by Native Americans, and some were even manufactured by native craftsmen for use within their own communities or for trade.

Presents were an essential part of native diplomacy and played a major role in colonial warfare and diplomatic relations with native peoples. Gift giving and reciprocity had been a routine part of native life before European arrivals. Gifts were often given to commemorate events such as births, deaths, marriages, and ceremonies. They were also sometimes exchanged during council meetings and treaty negotiations. Gift exchanges acted as material signs of commitment to agreements made between groups. Often these agreements concerned access to land, trade rights, and other political matters.

Well versed in these gift-giving practices, many natives used presents to negotiate among European political groups and to maintain power in an ever-encroaching imperial world. From the earliest years of settlement, Europeans realized the importance of reciprocity with native peoples and quickly adopted the diplomatic practices of gift giving to achieve their goals for settlement and expansion in the New World.

Reciprocal exchanges of gifts continued throughout the colonial era. However, there was a significant rise in the number of gifts given between the late 1740s and the 1760s. This coincided with an increased level of contact and conflict between natives and colonists as encroachment onto native lands increased and colonial wars, particularly the French and Indian War (1754–1763), took place. In addition, there was a dramatic rise in the creation and use of certain types of goods, such as silver objects, after the mid-1700s.

After the 1760s the price of many of these goods began to fall, and the availability and variety of goods increased. When the United States gained independence in 1783, the U.S. government tended to eschew the use of presents in diplomacy with Native Americans, although the British continued the tradition into the 19th century.

A number of Indian presents exist today in museums and private collections. Inventories and accounts in private manuscript collections and governmental records also record the variety of goods used. Indeed, they underscore the importance of Indian gifts for understanding colonial diplomacy, native-white relations, and westward expansion throughout the colonial era.

CATHARINE DANN ROEBER

See also
French and Indian War; Native American Trade; Wampum

References
Jacobs, Wilbur R. *Diplomacy and Indian Gifts: Anglo-French Rivalry along the Ohio and Northwest Frontiers, 1748–1763.* Stanford, CA: Stanford University Press, 1950.

Richter, Daniel K. *The Ordeal of the Longhouse: The People of the Iroquois League in the Era of European Colonization.* Chapel Hill: University of North Carolina Press, 1992.

Richter, Daniel K., and James H. Merrell, eds. *Beyond the Covenant Chain: The Iroquois and Their Neighbors in Indian North America, 1600–1800.* Syracuse, NY: Syracuse University Press, 1987.

Indian Removal Act

Congressional legislation signed into law by President Andrew Jackson on May 26, 1830, that provided legal justification for the wholesale and forcible removal of Native Americans from the East to west of the Mississippi River, principally Indian Territory (present-day Oklahoma and parts of Kansas). The Indian Removal Act of 1830 was the culmination of a decades-long struggle between whites and Native Americans over who would control vast tracts of territory that had been Native American lands for many centuries. The Indian Removal Act rendered most prior agreements and treaties between the U.S. government and Native American nations null and void and set the stage for the government to negotiate new treaties with various tribes that would effect their removal to Indian Territory. Jackson believed that prior Indian treaties were an "absurdity" and that Native Americans were "subjects" of the United States who could not claim any rights to sovereignty, as a foreign nation could.

The Indian Removal Act was aimed immediately at the so-called Five Civilized Tribes (the Choctaws, Cherokees, Chickasaws, Creeks, and Seminoles), who had inhabited lands in the Southeast, including parts of Alabama, Mississippi, Tennessee, the Carolinas, Georgia, and Florida. Many southerners, principally wealthy planters, coveted the lands that these tribes inhabited because they were prime agricultural lands that could be planted with crops such as cotton, an extremely lucrative commodity in the early 19th century. Of course, the land would be worked with slave labor, making large-scale agricultural enterprises even more profitable.

During the election campaign of 1828, Jackson and the Democratic Party made Indian removal a major issue, and Jackson saw the Indian Removal Act, which proved quite controversial, as a campaign pledge fulfilled. While Jackson was intent on placing relations with Native Americans within the complete purview of the federal government, some states sought to control Native American tribes themselves. In 1830, for example, Georgia enacted a law that made it illegal for whites to live on Native American lands without explicit authorization and that placed tribal lands under state jurisdiction. This was aimed at white missionaries, who in some cases were helping Native Americans resist removal to the west. When this was challenged in the courts, in 1831 the U.S. Supreme Court under Chief Justice John Marshall (*Cherokee Nation v. Georgia*) ruled that Native American tribes were indeed sovereign nations, meaning that state laws (and by extension

INDIAN REMOVAL TO THE WEST

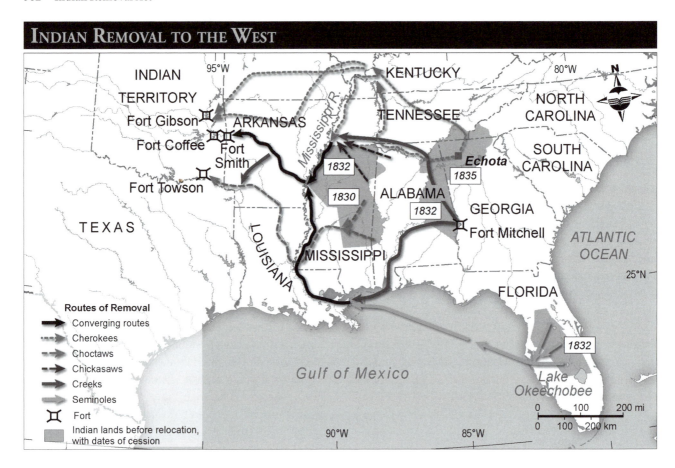

federal laws) could not apply to them. Jackson derisively spurned the court decision and essentially ignored it, as did his successors.

Within a decade or so of the 1830 Indian Removal Act, treaties had been signed with the five nations that allowed for their removal. While nothing in the act suggested forcible removal per se, that is in fact what occurred in many cases. While some tribes or factions of tribes resisted fiercely, most saw little choice but to acquiesce, with disastrous results in many instances. Many left their ancestral homelands under the watch of well-armed U.S. Army soldiers.

The first removal treaty was with the Choctaws (chiefly in Mississippi) and saw the movement of some 14,000 Choctaws to the Red River Valley. About 7,000, however, refused to leave and stayed behind. In the ensuing years they came under increasingly greater white encroachment. In 1838 and 1839 the U.S. Army used force to remove thousands of Cherokees to Indian Territory, precipitating the so-called Trail of Tears during which thousands died of exposure, starvation, and disease. Only a few hundred remained behind, having fled into mountainous areas. There were in fact numerous trails of tears, as most of the affected tribes suffered similar fates. The refusal of the Seminoles to accept forcible removal triggered the Second Seminole War (1835–1842). The Seminoles fought intrepidly and were not ultimately subdued until the end of the Third Seminole War (1855–1858). The Indian

Removal Act also affected tribes farther north and west, including the Shawnees, Pottawatomis, Sauks, and Foxes, who were eventually removed to Indian Territory. The Black Hawk War of 1832 was largely a result of attempts to relocate the Sauks and Foxes as well as the Kickapoos.

The Indian Removal Act was certainly not without controversy, and many Americans did not support it, for varying reasons. Numerous Christian missionaries, who had been living among the Native Americans for years, were opposed to the act, realizing that relocation would have to be de facto a forcible process, meaning that lives would likely be lost. Some northerners were against the legislation because they knew it would mean the empowerment of southern planters who would expand slavery-based agriculture into newly acquired lands. Still others abhorred the act because it seemed to subordinate states' rights to the federal government.

The Indian Removal Act was bitterly debated in Congress before its passage and was not universally supported. In most cases, individual removal treaties negotiated with the Native Americans involved the cession of Native American land in the East in exchange for land in Indian Territory. The exchange was almost never equal, however, meaning that tribes gave up far more land than they gained. Most treaties also continued earlier annuity payments by the federal government and had provisions for additional annuities after relocation was complete.

By 1883, 25 reservations had been established in Indian Territory, occupied by 37 Native American tribes. It is estimated that as many as 100,000 Native Americans were forced to move between 1830 and 1869. This mass relocation caused untold suffering. Perhaps as many as one-third of those forcibly removed died on the marches west or died shortly after because of disease, starvation, dehydration, or exposure in an environment and climate vastly different from their original homelands. The removal permanently altered tribes' cultures, social constructs, and familial institutions. Some, such as the Senecas, Navajos, Seminoles, and Cherokees, were partly or wholly successful in resisting removal. Some of these people remain today on part of their ancestral homelands. Other tribes that were removed to the west became the beneficiaries of new lands that had rich natural resources, such as minerals and oil. Those people and tribes who did relocate quickly established their own communities and began farming with considerable success. However, by the end of the 19th century many were once more under pressure to cede land to whites in Indian Territory, where oil attracted white speculators in droves.

PAUL G. PIERPAOLI JR.

See also

Black Hawk War; Cherokees; Choctaws; Chickasaws; Creeks; Indian Territory; Jackson, Andrew; Navajo Removal; Pottawatomis; Sauks and Foxes; Seminoles; Seminole War, Second; Seminole War, Third; Senecas; Shawnees; Trail of Tears

References

Cave, Alfred A. "Abuse of Power: Andrew Jackson and the Indian Removal Act of 1830." *Historian* 65 (Winter 2003): 1130–1153.

Jahoda, Gloria. *The Trail of Tears.* New York: Holt, Rinehart and Winston, 1975.

Johansen, Bruce E. *Shapers of the Great Debate on Native Americans: Land, Spirit, Power.* Westport, CT: Greenwood, 2000.

Satz, Ronald N. *American Indian Policy in the Jacksonian Era.* Lincoln: University of Nebraska Press, 1975.

Wallace, Anthony F. C. *The Long, Bitter Trail: Andrew Jackson and the Indians.* New York: Hill and Wang, 1993.

Indian Reorganization Act

Legislation passed by Congress on June 18, 1934, that substantially altered U.S. government policy toward Native American tribes and nations. With the Indian Reorganization Act of 1934, the U.S. government reversed its Indian policy of more than 130 years and finally focused on the needs of tribal governments to preserve their sovereignty, culture, and heritage. Prior to 1934, the United States had focused on acquiring native land for its citizens and eradicating native culture to the point that Native Americans would be assimilated into American society and lose their ethnic identities.

Specifically, the Indian Reorganization Act (also known as the Wheeler-Howard Act and the Indian New Deal) had several provisions. First, the act nullified the 1887 Dawes Severalty Act and ended the allotment of Native American land. Second, the Indian Reorganization Act made provisions for buying back land for Native American tribes and restoring to the tribes surplus land that had been previously assigned to be allotted. Third, the act allowed the formal organization of tribal governments but specified that they had to be ratified by a majority of their members. These governments were allowed to manage their own property and seek counsel to protect their rights. The tribal governments were also allowed to negotiate with federal, state, and local governments on behalf of their people but could not engage in land transactions without majority approval of their tribe. Fourth, the U.S. government set up a fund to lend money to tribes in an effort to promote economic development on tribal reservations. Fifth, in terms of making appointments to administrative and service positions serving the various tribes, the act gave preference to those Native Americans qualified to fill such positions and provided loans to Native American students for training in vocational and trade schools.

John Collier, the U.S. commissioner of Indian affairs in 1934, was the primary author of this landmark legislation. He intended to end exploitation of Native American resources, establish a solid economic foundation for reservations, and restore tribal self-government. Up until World War II (1939–1945), the Bureau of Indian Affairs vigorously pursued this policy, but the reduction of Department of Interior budgets because of the war effort ultimately limited the scope and impact of the Indian Reorganization Act and its ability to accomplish Collier's goals. Additionally, many tribes chose not to participate in the act to prevent further interference in their affairs by the federal government.

Changes in the American political climate in the aftermath of World War II led to another reversal in U.S. Indian policy. At this time the government sought to end its trust relationship with Native American tribes and encouraged Native Americans to move off reservations by promising to help them acquire jobs and housing. This government assistance was minimal at best and nonexistent in many cases. Unfortunately, this new postwar policy eradicated most of the benefits that Native Americans had gained from the Indian Reorganization Act.

DIXIE RAY HAGGARD

See also

Dawes Severalty Act

References

Taylor, Graham D. *The Indian New Deal and American Indian Tribalism: The Administration of the Indian Reorganization Act, 1934–45.* Lincoln: University of Nebraska Press, 1980.

Philp, Kenneth R. *John Collier's Crusade for Indian Reform, 1920–1954.* Tucson: University of Arizona Press, 1977.

Prucha, Francis Paul. *The Great Father: The United States Government and the American Indians.* 2 vols. Lincoln: University of Nebraska Press, 1984.

U.S. secretary of the interior Harold Ickes presents the Confederated Tribes of the Flathead Indian Reservation with the first constitution and bylaws to be issued under the Indian Reorganization Act (1934). The act advocated tribal organization on reservations as a formula for the improvement of Indian life. (Library of Congress)

Indian Ring Scandal
Start Date: 1869
End Date: 1876

One of several scandals during the presidency of Ulysses S. Grant. The Indian Ring Scandal involved corruption in the Bureau of Indian Affairs and the supply system for the U.S. Army in the West. Political favors and cronyism, also known as the spoils system, led to rampant corruption in many facets of American politics in the period following the American Civil War (1861–1865) and certainly tainted Grant's cabinet. There is no evidence to suggest that Grant himself was involved in these scandals, although he certainly was guilty of many poor or questionable appointments.

The federal government's failure to provide supplies to Native American tribes as promised by various treaties had strained relationships between Washington and Native American leaders. Substantial portions of the supplies and annuity payments owed to the tribes were routinely siphoned off by traders, in cooperation with corrupt federal Indian agents, in the form of compensation for debts allegedly incurred by the tribes. Many private individuals and government officials welcomed the resulting unrest, hoping that warfare with Native American tribes would result in further cessions of tribal lands that could be opened to mining, settlement, and other profitable economic activities.

In an effort to curb such abuses, Grant appointed Ely S. Parker, a Seneca and a member of Grant's Civil War staff, commissioner of the Bureau of Indian Affairs. Parker, however, became a victim of the Indian Ring in which Grant's secretary of war, William W. Belknap, accepted bribes from companies with licenses to trade on the reservations of many Native American tribes. Looking to embarrass Parker for reforms made within the bureau as well as for being the architect of Grant's peace policy toward Native Americans in the West, the Indian Ring delayed funding for urgently needed supplies. In response, Parker bypassed Congress and the War Department, purchased the supplies on credit, and shipped them to the reservations in need. Parker's action became fodder for the members of the Indian Ring, who accused him of corruption and launched a congressional investigation. Although

Parker was cleared of any wrongdoing, he resigned his position in August 1871.

Corruption also extended to the War Department, as the secretary of war held the power to appoint trading firms to supply the various reservations as well as the sutlers who supplied army posts. Army sutler contracts in the West were trading monopolies and could be highly profitable for the appointed trader. Knowing this, corrupt politicians along with groups such as the Indian Ring sought to benefit by collecting bribes from those seeking appointment.

In 1869 Grant appointed William Worth Belknap, a former brigadier general in the Union Army, as secretary of war. Belknap appointed Caleb Marsh to one of the coveted sutler positions at Fort Sill in Indian Territory (present-day Oklahoma) after Marsh and his wife had assisted Belknap's wife Carrie during childbirth in 1870. Unbeknownst to Belknap, Carrie promised the Marshes that she would lobby her husband to grant them that lucrative position in exchange for an annual payment of $1,250 to the Belknaps. Although Carrie Belknap died shortly after the arrangement took effect, William Belknap's second wife, Amanda Belknap, continued to collect payments from Caleb Marsh according to the original agreement.

Early in the presidential election year of 1876, probably at the behest of Democrats seeking to follow up on the previous Grant administration scandal known as the Whiskey Ring Scandal, the House Appropriations Committee began investigating U.S. Army expenditures. Belknap, who by then must have been aware of the agreement, quickly resigned, and the Indian Ring's activities were curtailed. The House of Representatives impeached Belknap, but the U.S. Senate, lacking jurisdiction following his resignation, acquitted him.

JIM PIECUCH AND JASON LUTZ

See also

Belknap, William Worth; Bureau of Indian Affairs; Grant, Ulysses Simpson; Grant's Peace Policy; Parker, Ely Samuel

References

Armstrong, William H. *Warrior in Two Camps: Ely S. Parker, Union General and Seneca Chief.* Syracuse, NY: Syracuse University Press, 1978.

Brown, Dee. *Bury My Heart at Wounded Knee.* New York: Holt, Rinehart and Winston, 1970.

Summers, Mark Wahlgren. *The Era of Good Stealings.* New York: Oxford University Press, 1993.

Utley, Robert M. *The Indian Frontier of the American West, 1846–1890.* Albuquerque: University of New Mexico Press, 1984.

Indians, Confederate

Native American tribes and bands that fought for the Confederacy during the American Civil War (1861–1865). The Civil War divided the loyalties of many Native American nations as the conflict spread into the Indian Territory (present-day Oklahoma). While many individual Native Americans fought for the Confederacy, the Cherokee, Creek, Choctaw, Chickasaw, Osage, and Seminole nations formed entire Native American units for home guard duties. Native American units fought on the side of the Confederacy in the Battle of Pea Ridge (March 7–8, 1862) in Arkansas, and Cherokee brigadier general Stand Watie was credited as being the last Confederate general to surrender his unit to Union authorities in 1865.

At the opening of the Civil War, the federal government withdrew most of its soldiers from Indian Territory for service in the East. The Confederate government then approached Cherokee chief John Ross, who attempted to remain neutral in the conflict, while Watie argued that the nation should support the Confederacy. Early Confederate victories and internal pressure forced Ross to transfer Cherokee treaty obligations to the Confederate government in October 1861. Watie received a Confederate commission as a colonel and began to raise an all-Cherokee unit.

During the autumn and winter of 1861, Brigadier General Albert Pike and Colonel Douglas Cooper formed three Confederate regiments with troops from the Cherokee, Creek, Choctaw, Chickasaw, and Seminole nations for service within Indian Territory. As with their Cherokee neighbors, the Creeks also were divided in their loyalties, with Chief Hopoeithelyohola (Opothleyahola) and most of the Creeks favoring the Union and former chief McIntosh offering his allegiance to the Confederacy. Colonel Cooper, with Creek, Choctaw, Chickasaw, Cherokee and non–Native American troops, engaged the Creek and Seminole forces loyal to Hopoeithelyohola in the Battle of Round Mountain (November 19, 1861), the Battle of Chusto-Talasah (December 9, 1861), and the Battle of Chustenhlah (December 26, 1861) before eventually forcing them and their families into Kansas.

Native American regiments under Pike, including Colonel Watie's unit, participated in the Battle of Pea Ridge (March 7–8, 1862). Federal forces captured Chief Ross in the summer of 1862, resulting in Colonel Watie emerging as the Cherokees' principal chief. As such, Watie drafted all able-bodied men of the Cherokee Nation between the ages of 18 and 50 for Confederate military service in Indian Territory. Native Americans fought on both the Confederate and Union sides across Indian Territory for the next two years. In May 1864 Watie became the only Native American Confederate general officer and assumed command of a cavalry brigade consisting of the 1st and 2nd Cherokee Cavalry regiments and battalion-sized units of Creek, Osage, and Seminole troops.

While many individual Native Americans served in Confederate units during the campaigns east of the Mississippi River, two nations stand out as groups. A number of Cherokees living in North Carolina fought under Colonel William Thomas in their own battalion, known initially as the Junaluska Zouaves. The Thomas legion performed home guard types of duties in eastern Tennessee, western North Carolina, and Virginia and remained in the field for more than a month following General Robert E. Lee's surrender of the Army of Northern Virginia at Appomattox on April 9, 1865.

Although the small Catawba Nation, whose reservation was located in South Carolina, numbered only 60 males, nearly one-third of them volunteered for duty in the Confederate Army. Most of the Catawbas joined one of three South Carolina regiments and were among the defenders in the Battle of the Crater (July 30, 1864) during the siege of Petersburg, Virginia. Brigadier General Watie surrendered his command to Union authorities two months after Appomattox, officially ending Native American participation on the Confederate side in the war.

Native Americans suffered greatly during the Civil War. In particular, civil conflict among factions of the Cherokees and Creeks resulted in many deaths due to combat, hunger, and disease, and many homes were burned as the combatants roamed across Indian Territory. The suffering of Native Americans from the conflict would continue for decades after the war.

TERRY M. MAYS

See also
Cherokees; Indian Territory; Watie, Stand

References
Abel, Annie Heloise. *The American Indian in the Civil War, 1862–1865.* Lincoln: University of Nebraska Press, 1992.
Crow, Vernon H. *Storm in the Mountains: Thomas' Confederate Legion of Cherokee Indians and Mountaineers.* Cherokee, NC: Press of the Museum of the Cherokee Indian, 1982.
Cunningham, Frank. *General Stand Watie's Confederate Indians.* Norman: University of Oklahoma Press, 1998.
Hauptman, Laurence M. *Between Two Fires: American Indians in the Civil War.* New York City: Free Press, 1995.

Indian Territory

Located in the south-central United States, largely present-day Oklahoma, Indian Territory was home to numerous Native Americans who had been relocated there, often forcibly, by the U.S. government. By the eve of the American Civil War (1861–1865), approximately 55,000 Native Americans lived in the territory. These inhabitants were not U.S. citizens, nor was the area a legal territory of the United States. It had no territorial governor or legislature; instead, the U.S. Bureau of Indian Affairs managed the region. A great many tribes were relocated there in the aftermath of the 1830 Indian Removal Act.

The U.S. government enforced its Indian policy through a string of fortifications in Indian Territory that originally included Fort Towson on the Red River and Fort Gibson on the Arkansas in the eastern part of the territory. The army later added Fort Washita, Fort Arbuckle, and Fort Cobb along the Washita River and in 1869 built Fort Sill in the western section of the territory. A number of temporary forts and camps also came into use. Posts in Texas and Kansas also played a role in controlling events in the territory. Most residents of Indian Territory belonged to the larger tribal affiliations of the so-called Five Civilized Tribes (Cherokees, Creeks, Choctaws, Chickasaws, and Seminoles), while the

remainder (Quapaws, Wichitas, Senecas, Shawnees, Delawares, Comanche, Osages, and others) were fewer in number. Eventually elements of some 50 tribes resided in the territory. As white populations moved across the Mississippi, western tribes faced removal into an increasingly crowded Indian Territory. Lands set aside for the eastern tribes now were subdivided to accommodate Plains tribes, which reduced hunting grounds and created new rivalries among Indian groups.

Conditions on the reservations in Indian Territory were far from ideal. Some of the areas were not well suited for agriculture, and tribes that had been accustomed to seasonal hunts were severely limited in their ability to range over a wide area. Educational facilities were marginal at best, and many Native Americans lived in poverty. Worse, many Indian agents were corrupt, making life in Indian Territory all the more bleak. Conflict between tribes was also an intermittent problem.

Some tribes established towns and settlements that later became cities, including Tulsa, Ardmore, and Muskogee. The Five Civilized Tribes also brought with them African American slaves, which swelled the African American population of what would later become Oklahoma. Members of these tribes sided largely with the Confederacy during the American Civil War (1861–1865), a conflict that greatly affected tribes living in Indian Territory.

Conditions in Indian Territory throughout the Civil War mirrored the larger conflict in terms of the factionalism and intensity of the political and military conflict. Native American tribes, particularly the Creeks and the Cherokees, fought their own internal battles to determine their affiliation with the Union or the Confederacy, which both vied for their support. By mid-1861 many tribal governments had signed treaties of alliance with the Confederate States. The tribes agreed to oppose Union forces in the territory and to contribute several regiments of Native American soldiers to the Confederate Army. In return the Confederate States recognized Indian land titles, assumed the financial and treaty responsibilities of the United States, and agreed to supply and pay Native American troops.

These relationships soon deteriorated, as long-term political divisions within the tribes affected Native American participation in the Civil War. When a band of Creeks under Opothleyahola attempted to flee to Kansas, tribal members loyal to the Confederates opposed their action. Some managed to escape, enlisted in the Union forces, and returned to Indian Territory determined to take revenge on their political opponents.

In 1862 Union forces responded to divisions within the Cherokee tribe by invading the Cherokee Nation. Union troops captured the principal Cherokee chief, John Ross, and escorted him to Washington, D.C., as their prisoner. There he later issued a proclamation of loyalty to the U.S. government on behalf of the Cherokee Nation. Other Cherokees under the military and political leadership of Stand Watie (a brigadier general in the Confederate Army), however, remained true to their alliance with the South. These internal divisions contributed to the intense conventional

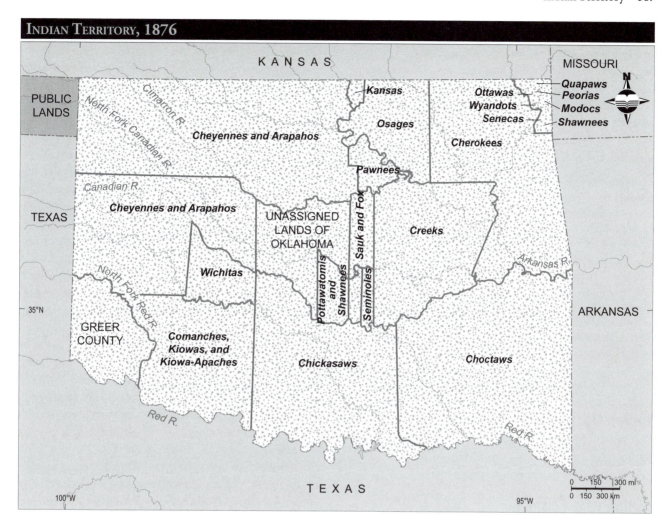

INDIAN TERRITORY, 1876

and guerrilla warfare that included indiscriminate murder, destruction of property, and continued political strife. The war left an unhappy legacy in Indian Territory.

By 1863 Union troops had largely defeated organized Confederate forces in Indian Territory, although continued military actions, guerrilla fighting, and enforcement of Indian policy required the use of significant Union and Confederate military resources in the region. Watie continued as a useful ally for the Confederacy. Indeed, under his command the Cherokee Rifles fought effectively at the Battle of Pea Ridge, harassed Union forces, and interdicted valuable supplies destined for Fort Scott and Fort Leavenworth. For the Native Americans themselves, the intense political divisions that the removal era inspired were exacerbated by the Civil War, making economic and political recovery after the conflict all the more difficult.

After the war, the alliances that the tribes entered into with the Confederacy contributed to unfavorable treaty provisions and shaped future Indian policies. These included detribalization and forced assimilation. With the South's defeat, Native American groups loyal to the Confederacy reestablished their relationship with the U.S. government. The exploding westward expansion of

the United States brought a flood of settlers into traditional Indian hunting grounds in Kansas, and soon railroads cut across the plains and eventually into Indian Territory itself. Cattle drives from Texas pushed through the territory en route to railheads in Kansas. In the decade following the Civil War, the Indians of the southern Plains who were still challenging white encroachment (the Comanches, Kiowas, Cheyennes, and Arapahos), unleashed their fury on white settlements, railroad crews, and westward-bound wagon trains. Treaties that sought to curtail these activities created a new reservation for the Cheyennes and Arapahos and one for the Kiowas and Comanches. But the Indians quickly learned how to use the reservations as refuge while raiding into Texas and Kansas. This brought the inevitable military response, and the territory saw many confrontations until the Red River War (1874–1875) substantially ended hostilities on the southern Plains.

Gradually many Native Americans were forced out of Indian Territory as the area designated for Indian use shrunk to make way for white settlement, aggressively promoted by so-called boomers. This process was hastened by the 1887 Dawes Severalty Act, which established the process for settling "unused" Indian lands. In 1889 the U.S. government organized the first of numerous runs in which white settlers grabbed up former Indian lands. Soon the non-Indian population swelled as new cities sprang from the prairie. In 1890 when the territory was organized as the Oklahoma Territory, the Native Americans' land area was further reduced. Native Americans tried to gain admission to the Union but were rebuffed. In 1907 Oklahoma became a state, with most of the remaining tribes confined to the eastern part of the state, where many still reside today.

DEBORAH KIDWELL

See also

Cherokees; Chickasaws; Choctaws; Creeks; Dawes Severalty Act; Indian Removal Act; Indians, Confederate; Native Americans; Native Americans and the Civil War; Seminoles; Watie, Stand

References

Fischer, Leroy Henry. *The Civil War Era in Indian Territory*. Los Angeles: L. L. Morrison, 1974.

Gibson, Arrell Morgan. *America's Exiles: Indian Colonization in Oklahoma*. Oklahoma City: Oklahoma Historical Society, 1982.

Spencer, John D. *The American Civil War in the Indian Territory*. New York: Osprey, 2006.

Indian Uprising of 1747

See Uprising of 1747

Indian War of 1864

See Sand Creek Massacre

Infantry Regiment, 7th U.S.

One of the oldest regular army units that has fought in every major conflict of the U.S. since the War of 1812. The 7th Infantry Regiment was officially established on January 11, 1812, as the 8th Infantry and in 1815 was consolidated with other units and designated the 7th Infantry Regiment. It has the most battle streamers of any army outfit and the second-highest number of Medal of Honor winners. The unit earned its nickname, the "Cottonbalers," during the Battle of New Orleans (January 8, 1815) when its men supposedly made their stand behind cotton bales.

The Indian Wars found the 7th Infantry patrolling the Montana Territory, but its only significant combat during this period was at the Battle of the Big Hole (August 9–10, 1877) against the Nez Perce tribe.

After distinguished service in the Mexican-American War (1846–1848) and with the Army of the Potomac during the American Civil War (1861–1865), the 7th Infantry was ordered to Jacksonville, Florida, to maintain peace during the tumultuous Reconstruction period. The regiment was transferred to the Montana Territory in 1869, where its ranks were bolstered by a consolidation with the disbanded 36th Infantry Regiment. With its headquarters at Fort Shaw, the 7th Regiment performed monotonous garrison duty until 1876.

In the summer of 1876 during the Great Sioux War (1876–1877) the 7th Infantry, now commanded by Colonel John Gibbon, was ordered to take part in a three-pronged punitive expedition against the Sioux. Lieutenant Colonel George Custer, commander of the 7th Cavalry, planned to attack a Sioux village along the Little Bighorn River and drive the fleeing warriors into the path of the 7th Infantry. These plans went awry when Custer met with disaster on the first day of the Battle of the Little Bighorn (June 25–26, 1876). Arriving at the battlefield two days later, the Cottonbalers relieved the last survivors of the onslaught and had the grim task of burying the mutilated soldiers. The regiment spent the remainder of that summer and autumn chasing the elusive Sioux before turning back to Fort Shaw on October 6, having trekked more than 1,700 miles.

In June 1877 certain bands of the Nez Perces refused to be moved to reservations in Idaho, and fighting broke out. After a series of skirmishes with Brigadier General Oliver O. Howard's command throughout July, the Nez Perces sought sanctuary in Montana, marching right into the path of two companies of the 7th Infantry posted at the newly built Fort Missoula. The Nez Perces headed toward a mountain pass known as the Lolo Trail (the soldiers referred to it as Lou Lou pass). There the two companies commanded by Captain Charles Rawn attempted to block their passage, but the Nez Perces managed to skirt around the soldiers' meager defenses.

On August 3, 1877, Gibbon arrived with the rest of the regiment at Fort Missoula and the next day set off with 15 officers, 149 enlisted men, and 35 civilian volunteers. On the night of August 8–9 Gibbon was able to place the 7th Infantry undetected around the Nez Perce bivouac at Big Hole Creek, a rare achievement for infantry during the Indian Wars. The troops charged across the creek at dawn, taking the village by complete surprise. A bloody 20-minute melee ensued, but the largely outnumbered soldiers were soon surrounded and were forced to fall back and dig in. The Native Americans fought with extra ferocity upon seeing many of their women and children killed. By nightfall the soldiers had expended more than 9,000 rounds of ammunition. The next day, Nez Perce warriors set the surrounding brush on fire in an attempt to force out the entrenched soldiers and kept up rifle fire while the rest of the tribe escaped. The Nez Perce evacuation was complete when Howard arrived with reinforcements on August 11. In this engagement the Cottonbalers suffered 28 killed and 39 wounded, with the Nez Perces suffering between 60 and 90 killed. The Nez Perces would not be subdued until October 1877.

The 7th Infantry retired from the campaign after the Battle of the Big Hole and continued its garrison duty at Fort Shaw until 1888, when it was transferred to Fort Snelling, Minnesota. The regiment participated briefly in a campaign against the Utes in 1889.

The 7th Infantry Regiment continued its distinguished service in the major wars of the 20th century and remains in existence today.

WILLIAM WHYTE

See also

Big Hole, Battle of the; Cavalry Regiment, 7th U.S.; Custer, George Armstrong; Gibbon, John; Great Sioux War; Howard, Oliver Otis; Little Bighorn, Battle of the; Nez Perces; Sioux; Utes

References

McManus, John C. *American Courage, American Carnage: 7th Infantry Chronicles.* New York: Tom Doherty, 2009.

Utley, Robert M. *Frontier Regulars: The United States and the American Indian, 1866–1891.* New York: Macmillan, 1973.

Infantry Regiment, 24th U.S.

U.S. Army infantry regiment established in 1869 during the general reorganization of the army and composed of African American soldiers commanded usually by white officers. The 24th and 25th Infantry regiments were created by the consolidation of four African American infantry regiments—the 38th, 39th, 40th, and 41st—established in 1866 following the American Civil War (1861–1865). Soldiers of the 24th and 25th Infantry regiments, along with the 9th and 10th Cavalry regiments, came to be collectively known as the buffalo soldiers as a consequence of their service in the various Indian Wars from 1869 to 1891. The regiment was commanded originally by Colonel R. S. Mackenzie and by Colonel J. H. Potter during its most active years, although Lieutenant Colonel W. R. Shafter frequently headed the unit in the field.

The Civil War infantry regiment provided the organizational model for the 24th Infantry Regiment, which consisted of 10 companies, each composed of up to 100 privates and 19 officers and noncommissioned officers (NCOs). Total strength was set at 1,046 men, although that figure was rarely met. Post–Civil War regiments seldom operated as regiments; instead, 1 or 2 companies were assigned to more than 50 widely scattered forts, and these units were often further dispersed for various duties. By 1891, the 24th Infantry had operated in the state of Texas as well as in the Arizona, Indian, and New Mexico territories. The 24th Infantry also served briefly in Mexico.

The 24th Infantry performed garrison duties such as constructing barracks, repairing buildings, maintaining and cleaning facilities, and garrisoning forts. This work was often routine and boring, but conditions were nevertheless extremely difficult particularly in far frontier posts, which were often isolated in rugged terrain and harsh climates. At the San Carlos Indian Reservation in southeastern Arizona, for example, conditions were so poor that some army officials believed it inhumane to station troops there. The 24th Infantry often had to build new post facilities and found existing buildings in poor shape upon arrival in a new locale. Funds were limited, and some units slept in tents and worked in buildings that could not be protected from wind, rain, blowing sand, and cold weather. Rations included flour, lard, bacon, hardtack (a tasteless hard biscuit), and a few other staples, all in short supply. Supplementing this were gardens tended by the soldiers and game that was shot near the forts or during expeditions. The army had no provisions for care of dependents, but some soldiers did have their wives and children close by, with wives often employed as laundresses, cooks, and maids. In spite of such hardships, the 24th Infantry had the lowest desertion rate of any U.S. Army regiment from 1880 to 1886.

Soldiers sought relief from the tedium of garrison life through off-post duties such as the construction of wagon roads and telegraph lines, escorting wagon trains, guarding key points, protecting payroll transports, shielding railroad crews from Native American attack, and responding to requests for army protection. These duties, however, exposed the soldiers to the constant threat of attack, and not just from hostile Native Americans. In 1889 two soldiers of the 24th Infantry earned the Medal of Honor for their actions against white bandits who had attacked a payroll wagon.

The 24th Infantry participated in numerous campaigns against hostile Native Americans. The Red River War (1874–1875) earned the regiment four Medals of Honor in actions against the Comanches and their Arapaho, Cheyenne, and Kiowa allies in Texas and New Mexico. Other campaigns included an 1874 raid into Mexico, which involved chasing a Kickapoo and Lipan raiding party, and the pursuit of the Apache leader Victorio (1877–1880) that resulted in his withdrawal to Mexico, where he was killed by Mexican militia.

After the Indian Wars, the 24th Infantry continued service as an all-black regiment, participating in the assault on San Juan Hill in Cuba during the Spanish-American War (1898), helping to suppress Filipino rebels during 1899–1911, joining Brigadier General John J. Pershing's pursuit of Pancho Villa in 1916, and service in World War II (1939–1945) and the Korean War (1950–1953). Racial integration of the army during the Korean War led to the deactivation of the 24th Infantry on October 1, 1951. In 1995 the U.S. Army revived the unit designation of the 24th Infantry as a parent unit under the Army Regimental System.

DANIEL E. SPECTOR

See also

Apaches; Arapahos; Buffalo Soldiers; Cavalry Regiment, 9th U.S.; Cavalry Regiment, 10th U.S.; Cheyennes; Comanches; Infantry Regiment, 25th U.S.; Kickapoos; Kiowas; Lipan Apaches; Red River War; Victorio

References

Fowler, Arlen L. *The Black Infantry in the West, 1869–1891.* Norman: University of Oklahoma Press, 1996.

Leckie, William H., and Shirley A. Leckie. *The Buffalo Soldiers: A Narrative of the Black Cavalry in the West.* Norman: University of Oklahoma Press, 2003.

Schubert, Frank N. *Black Valor: Buffalo Soldiers and the Medal of Honor, 1870–1898.* Wilmington, DE: Scholarly Resources, 1997.

Infantry Regiment, 25th U.S.

U.S. Army infantry regiment established during the general army reorganization in 1869 and composed exclusively of African American soldiers, usually with white officers. The regiment was commanded for most of the Indian Wars era by Colonel George Andrews. The 25th Infantry Regiment and the 24th Infantry Regiment were created by the consolidation of four African American infantry regiments—the 38th, 39th, 40th, and 41st—established in 1866 following the American Civil War (1861–1865). The men of the 25th Infantry and three other regiments—the 9th and 10th Cavalry and the 24th Infantry—are collectively known as the buffalo soldiers. They won renown fighting in the various Indian campaigns in the American West.

The Civil War infantry regiment provided the organizational model for the 25th Infantry: 10 companies, each with up to 100 privates and 19 officers and noncommissioned officers (NCOs). Total strength was 1,046, although this figure was rarely met. Post–Civil War regiments seldom operated as regiments. Usually, 1 or 2 companies were assigned to more than 50 widely scattered

An African American "Buffalo Soldier" of the 25th Infantry Regiment at Fort Custer, Montana, between 1884 and 1890. African Americans formed four regiments—two cavalry and two infantry—in the West after the Civil War. (Library of Congress)

forts, and often they were further dispersed for various duties. By 1891, the 25th Infantry had operated in Minnesota, Texas, and the Dakota, Indian, Montana, and New Mexico territories.

Dispersed among numerous isolated posts in usually harsh climates, the 25th Infantry set about repairing rundown buildings and constructing new ones. There was also tedious guard duty as well as details for cleaning, maintenance, cooking, and cutting firewood. Funding was seldom adequate, and rations, when available, included staples such as flour, bacon, lard, salt, and hardtack (a dry tasteless biscuit), sometimes supplemented by garden produce and game. There were no provisions for dependents, but some soldiers managed to have family travel with them. Despite the often trying conditions, morale remained high, with a much better reenlistment rate than in white infantry regiments.

Soldiers were relieved from the tedium of garrison life by such duties as constructing wagon roads and telegraph lines, escorting wagon trains, guarding key points, protecting payroll transports, shielding railroad crews from attack, and responding to requests for protection. Escort duties routinely required soldiers to travel 500 miles in a month, often on foot and always subject to attack from hostile Native Americans as well as American and Mexican bandits.

The 25th Infantry spent most of its first decade of service in Texas participating in numerous campaigns and expeditions against Indians, much of it in far western Texas and along the turbulent Mexican border. In 1873 a group of Comanches arrived at the Wichita Indian Agency for settlement, where they refused to surrender their weapons. The presence of numerous unarmed Native Americans nearby complicated the situation, but a two-day firefight resolved the issue with minimal casualties. In 1878 elements of the 25th Infantry participated in Colonel Ranald S. Mackenzie's brief punitive expedition into Mexico.

In the 1880s the 25th Infantry was posted to the Dakotas, Montana, and Minnesota. Its basic duties did not change. There was more woodcutting because of the cold and an emphasis on providing relief for white settlers beset by floods and other natural disasters. There was some prejudice toward the soldiers but less so than in Texas. The regimental band proved extremely popular and responded to numerous requests for performances. For the most part the Native Americans were not generally hostile, and the regiment enjoyed a satisfactory relationship with Sitting Bull. The unit participated in the suppression of the Ghost Dance movement in the Dakota Territory (November 1890–January 1891) but was not involved in the death of Sitting Bull on December 15, 1890, and was not present for the Battle of Wounded Knee (December 29, 1890). After the Indian Wars, the 25th Infantry served in the Spanish-American War (1898), the Philippine-American War (1899–1902), and World War II (1939–1945) and was finally deactivated in 1946.

Daniel E. Spector

See also

Buffalo Soldiers; Cavalry Regiment, 9th U.S.; Cavalry Regiment, 10th U.S.; Infantry Regiment, 24th U.S.; Wounded Knee, Battle of

References

Fowler, Arlen L. *The Black Infantry in the West, 1869–1891*. Norman: University of Oklahoma Press, 1996.

Leckie, William H., and Shirley A. Leckie. *The Buffalo Soldiers: A Narrative of the Black Cavalry in the West.* Norman: University of Oklahoma Press, 2003.

Schubert, Frank N. *Black Valor: Buffalo Soldiers and the Medal of Honor, 1870–1898.* Wilmington, DE: Scholarly Resources, 1997.

Inkpaduta

Birth Date: ca. 1815
Death Date: 1882

Wahpekute Dakota–Santee Sioux leader who arguably can be credited for having initiated the 30-year period of warfare between the Sioux and the U.S. government. Inkpaduta (Red Cap, Scarlet Point) was born in southern Minnesota around 1815. Little is known of his early life except that he probably suffered from small-pox as a youth or young man, a disease that left him permanently scarred. Inkpaduta and his people found themselves increasingly in the path of mounting white migration into the region. Left out of treaty negotiations at Traverse des Sioux in 1851, Inkpaduta's band relocated to Iowa.

The 1854 murder of Wahpekute leader Sintomniduta (Ink-paduta's older brother) and nine family members by Henry Lott, a white whiskey trader, led to Inkpaduta's assumption of leadership of the band. Unable to obtain justice for the murders, Inkpaduta sought vengeance. On March 8, 1857, near Lake Okoboji, Iowa, his band killed between 35 and 40 white settlers in what became known as the Spirit Lake Massacre.

Forced to flee into the Dakota Territory with his band and its white captives, Inkpaduta sought refuge among the Lakotas. Following the Dakota Uprising (1862) in Minnesota, the U.S. government and Minnesota authorities jointly launched military expeditions into the Dakota Territory to track down Inkpaduta and other Santee refugees.

Inkpaduta played a major role in the battles that ensued. In the Battle of Big Mound (July 24–25, 1863), Brigadier General Henry H. Sibley's troops drove the Sioux from the battlefield. In the Battle of Whitestone Hill (September 3, 1863), Brigadier General Alfred Sully's 300-man scouting party encountered a large Sioux camp. The engagement turned on Sully's sudden arrival as the battle began, ensuring a U.S. victory. In the Battle of Killdeer Mountain (July 28, 1864), Inkpaduta fought a delaying action to allow women and children to escape as the battle turned against him.

During the next decade Inkpaduta allied with western Lakota bands and joined fellow Santee exiles in Canada. On June 25, 1876, he joined the Hunkpapas and others in the Battle of the Little Big-horn in which he played a major role in the routing of Lieutenant Colonel George A. Custer's cavalry regiment. Fleeing with other Sioux into exile in Canada, Inkpaduta settled at Oak Lake Indian Reserve in Manitoba. He died there in 1882.

Steve Potts

See also

Custer, George Armstrong; Great Sioux War; Hunkpapa Sioux; Killdeer Mountain, Battle of; Little Bighorn, Battle of the; Minnesota Sioux Uprising; Sibley, Henry Hastings; Sioux; Spirit Lake Massacre; Sully, Alfred; Whitestone Hill, Battle of

References

Anderson, Gary Clayton. *Kinsmen of Another Kind: Dakota-White Relations in the Upper Mississippi Valley, 1650–1862.* St. Paul: Minnesota Historical Society Press, 1997.

Meyer, Roy W. *History of the Santee Sioux: United States Indian Policy on Trial.* Rev. ed. Lincoln: University of Nebraska Press, 1993.

Van Nuys, Maxwell. *Inkpaduta: The Scarlet Point.* Denver, CO: Self-published, 1998.

Interior, Department of the

See Bureau of Indian Affairs

Inuna-Ina

See Arapahos

Iroquois

At the time of European contact, the Iroquois Confederacy, which consisted of five tribes—the Mohawks, Oneidas, Onondagas, Cayugas, and Senecas—was located in what is now upstate and western New York. A sixth nation, the Tuscaroras, joined the confederacy in the 1720s. By virtue of their numbers, geographic location, and military reputation, the Iroquois served as a potent counterweight to the ambitions of both the English and the French in the American Northeast for most of the colonial period.

The five Iroquois tribes lived in large villages, usually on eas-ily defensible hilltops. Organized into clans that were headed by a matriarch, the Iroquois believed that in order to sustain spiritual and temporal power, captives had to be obtained to replace the dead. According to the founding myth of the Iroquois Confeder-acy, the five tribes warred against one another until a supernatu-ral being, Deganawida, and his human helper, Hiawatha, traveled among them, preaching a message of peace and unity. However, this message did not preclude the Iroquois from attacking other groups of native people, who were outside the longhouse, the traditional Iroquois dwelling that was used metaphorically to describe the confederacy. The founding of the confederacy created something of a paradox, however. While the Iroquois now lived in peace with one another, they increasingly engaged other native

Eighteenth-century depiction of an Iroquois warrior. (Library and Archives Canada/(R9266-3492) Peter Winkworth Collection of Canadiana)

peoples in warfare in an attempt to secure captives and strengthen their power.

Samuel de Champlain encountered the Iroquois on July 30, 1609, when his native allies encouraged him to join them in an expedition against the Mohawks, during which Champlain personally killed three warriors. Some historians have pointed to this small battle as the genesis of the century and a half of enmity between the Iroquois and the French.

For the rest of the 17th century the Iroquois remained embroiled in conflicts with the French and their native allies that were occasionally punctuated by brief truces. In order to maintain access to European trade partners to secure metal, cloth, firearms, and other items of European manufacture, the Iroquois fought other native people. The Mohawks forced the Mahicans to leave the vicinity of New Netherland's Fort Orange (now Albany, New York) after a bloody four-year conflict in the 1620s.

Unlike the Hurons, the Iroquois did not have direct access to the western Great Lakes and the regions south of Hudson Bay, where the best furs were to be found. Beginning in the 1630s and escalating in the 1640s, the Iroquois launched attacks on Huron fur-trading parties, taking both furs and captives. The rerouting of

furs to the Dutch traders at Fort Orange, and away from the French in Montreal, threatened New France's economic survival.

While the French and the Iroquois remained locked in a conflict that varied in intensity for much of the 17th century, this hostility between the two actually helped the other economically. The Iroquois served as a barrier that separated northern Native Americans from the Dutch at Fort Orange and their high-quality and reasonably priced trade goods. Northern natives, who had access to higher-quality pelts, were forced to trade with the French in order to obtain European goods. Thus, the Dutch could not obtain better-quality furs except for those that the Iroquois pillaged from other native peoples.

In the late 1640s the Iroquois, needing captives to replace the dead and wanting to gain the Hurons' middleman position in the fur trade, launched a series of attacks that destroyed two major Huron towns and prompted the Hurons to abandon their country, with the majority of them becoming refugees throughout the Ohio Country and the western Great Lakes region.

The assaults against the Hurons, however, were only partially successful. While the Iroquois did gain an impressive number of captives, French Jesuits claimed that there were more non-Iroquois adoptees than natives among the Iroquois, and they did not gain control of the fur trade. Instead, the focus of the trade shifted farther west, and peoples such as the Ottawas replaced the Hurons as middlemen. With the founding of the English Hudson's Bay Company in the 1660s, both the Iroquois and the French lost access to many of the high-quality furs of the north.

The Iroquois did not give up on their attempts to gain control over the fur trade, however. From the 1640s to the end of the 17th century, they routinely attacked other native peoples in the Ohio Country and the Great Lakes region. In the early 17th century the Iroquois could easily obtain firearms from the Dutch, the English, or the Swedes. After the 1660s other native peoples were at least equally well armed, and the Iroquois suffered horrible losses as a result. But this did not stop the warfare. The dead, according to Iroquois tradition, still had to be replaced.

Beginning in the 1660s a series of events forced the Iroquois to reevaluate their position. In 1664 the English seized New Netherland without firing a shot. The English promised that they, like the Dutch, would be faithful trade partners and allies. But when a French expedition devastated Seneca villages in the late 1680s, the English provided no help. Iroquois warriors continued to die in large numbers as the Beaver Wars (1641–1701) continued.

The Iroquois response to this was what has become known as the Grand Settlement of 1701. In two separate treaties, the Iroquois promised the French that they would remain neutral in any future conflict between France and England. However, in a separate agreement the Iroquois informed the governor of New York that they would consider lending the English military assistance provided that the English secure Iroquois hunting grounds in Ontario. The Iroquois, of course, realized that it was impossible for the English to fulfill this condition in 1701. Throughout the first half of the 18th century, the Iroquois played the English and the French against one another, threatening to join one side or the other and receiving gifts intended to keep them neutral or encourage them to join in a war (which they never did).

The 1701 treaties, however, did not diminish Iroquois influence, particularly among the English. For years the Iroquois, having dealt almost exclusively with the colony of New York, also formed an alliance with the colony of Pennsylvania, evicting the Delawares (Lenni Lenapes) on the colony's behalf after the fraudulent Walking Purchase of 1737. But the Iroquois did not always enjoy good relations with the English. Indeed, in the 1720s the Iroquois tried to persuade the Delawares and the Shawnees to join them in a war against the English. Both tribes refused to take part, and the scheme was never put into effect.

The Iroquois became more useful to the English as time went on. The Iroquois Confederacy claimed that it owned the lands comprising the Ohio Country, and the British government, arguing that the Iroquois were their subjects, used this claim to assert that it held legal title to the region. The French, however, also claimed the area. Iroquois diplomats oversaw some of the Delaware and Shawnee towns in the area, and their presence caused resentment among some of these peoples. Offered a chance to join the French and the possibility of regaining their lands, many of the peoples of the region went to war against the British.

For the most part the Iroquois sat on the sidelines and watched as British forces performed poorly in the early phases of the French and Indian War (1754–1763). Despite being given wagonloads of gifts at the 1754 Albany Congress, most Iroquois, with notable exceptions such as the Mohawk sachem Hendrick, chose to remain neutral.

In the later phases of the war as the British began to win some significant victories, the Iroquois entered the conflict on the side of the Crown. Realizing that a British victory could mean the eviction of the French from the continent, the diplomatic maneuvering that served the Iroquois so well for half a century would be useless. The next best thing was to be on the winning side and then to later remind the British of their usefulness as allies.

After the French and Indian War, Iroquois relations with the British remained unsettled. The Senecas sent a war belt to the western tribes in an attempt to raise a rebellion against the British, but none accepted. In the 1768 Treaty of Fort Stanwix, the Iroquois ceded most of present-day Kentucky and Tennessee to the British, which led to conflicts when colonists entered the region and came into conflict with Cherokees, Shawnees, and other peoples who lived there.

With the beginning of the American Revolutionary War (1775–1783), most of the Iroquois initially decided not to become involved in what they regarded as a family dispute. However, British partisans such as Joseph Brant (Thayendanega) of the Mohawks and Guy Johnson, Sir William Johnson's successor as British agent to

the northern tribes, were able to make a compelling case that an American victory would not be in the best interests of the Iroquois Confederacy. The Oneidas and some Onondagas, however, chose to side with the Americans, rupturing the Iroquois Confederacy.

After the war ended in 1783, Joseph Brant and a sizable group of Iroquois left New York to settle in Canada. To reward them for their loyalty, the Crown granted the Iroquois a large tract of land along the Grand River. Other bands stayed in the United States, but the cohesion of the original Iroquois Confederacy had been diluted by conflicting wartime allegiances.

The Iroquois had a highly sophisticated form of government, which among other things provided for a system of checks and balances to ensure that no individual or small group would come to dominate the political structure. Scholars have pointed out that the Iroquois' plan for political union informed the design of the U.S. Articles of Confederation. Today perhaps 40,000–45,000 people of Iroquois ancestry reside in Canada. Tribal registrations in the United States in the mid-1990s claimed about 32,000 Iroquois. However, many others have claimed Iroquois ancestry, and in the 2000 census 80,822 people claimed Iroquois ancestry.

ROGER M. CARPENTER

See also

Beaver Wars; Brant, Joseph; Cherokees; Delawares; French and Indian War; Iroquois Confederacy; Iroquois Treaties of 1700 and 1701; Mahicans; Mohawk-Mahican War; Mohawks; Mourning War; Native Americans and the American Revolutionary War; Native American Warfare; Oneidas; Onondagas; Ottawas; Senecas; Shawnees; Trois-Rivières, Treaty of; Tuscaroras; Walking Purchase; Wyandots

References

Jennings, Francis. *The Ambiguous Iroquois Empire: The Covenant Chain Confederation of Indian Tribes with English Colonies from Its Beginnings to the Lancaster Treaty of 1744.* New York: Norton, 1984.

Richter, Daniel K., and James H. Merrell, eds. *Beyond the Covenant Chain: The Iroquois and Their Neighbors in Indian North America, 1600–1800.* Syracuse, NY: Syracuse University Press, 1987.

Richter, Daniel K. *The Ordeal of the Longhouse: The People of the Iroquois League in the Era of European Colonization.* Chapel Hill: University of North Carolina Press, 1992.

Iroquois Confederacy

The Iroquois Confederacy was made up of different Native American nations that inhabited present-day upper and western New York state. Originally the league consisted of five tribes closely related by language: the Senecas, the Cayugas, the Onondagas, the Oneidas, and the Mohawks. In 1721 the Tuscaroras, who migrated from North Carolina, joined. Only the French called these people the Iroquois; the English referred to them as the Five Nations and then the Six Nations or simply used the individual nation's name. Within the confederation itself, however, the preferred self-descriptor was Haudenosaunee, meaning "People of the Longhouse," "the extended house," or "the whole house." Most

**Estimated Population
of the Iroquois Confederacy, 1763**

Tribe	Fighting Men	Total Population
Cayugas	200	1,000
Mohawks	160	800
Oneidas	250	1,250
Onondagas	150	750
Senecas	1,050	5,250
Tuscaroras	140	700
Total	1,950	9,750

scholars date the confederation from 1570, although some have it beginning much earlier. Iroquois oral tradition recounts the story of how two prophets, the Peacemaker and Hiawatha, brokered a peace to reduce conflict and bring the Haudenosaunee together.

Rarely did the members of the confederation act as a single unit. Rather than present a unified front to the French or the English, the confederation's primary purpose was to maintain peace among its component nations. Within the confederation, the village rather than the nation was the primary political unit.

From the mid-1600s the Iroquois were involved in a series of conflicts known as the Beaver Wars (1641–1701) that were essentially struggles for control of the fur trade. In the 1640s the Iroquois attacked Huron towns along the Saint Lawrence River and by the end of the decade had displaced the inhabitants. During the latter half of the 17th century and throughout the 18th century, however, the confederation suffered many setbacks. The Five Nations lost their Dutch trading partners as a result of the Second Anglo-Dutch War (1664–1667) and at the same time faced invading French troops, who burned a number of Mohawk villages. This was followed by French and Huron attacks against the Senecas in 1687, the Mohawks in 1693, and the Onondagas and the Oneidas in 1696. The confederation sued for peace in 1698 and signed the Grande Paix in Montreal in 1701, bringing to a temporary end a century of nearly continuous conflict. The confederation then remained largely neutral throughout the first half of the 18th century, although it maintained good relations with the British. Its component nations did, however, eventually side with Britain against the French during the latter years of the French and Indian War (1754–1763).

The final blow to the cohesion of the confederation came as a consequence of the American Revolutionary War (1775–1783). Initially neutral, the Six Nations eventually divided their loyalties between the Patriots and Britain. After the conflict, many Iroquois migrated to Canada; those who remained had to contend with the expansionary land policies of the United States. The Iroquois in the United States played only a very limited role in the wars of the Northwest Territory that followed.

JONATHAN A. CLAPPERTON

See also
Algonquins; Beaver Wars; Cayugas; Champlain, Samuel de; Dutch-Indian Wars; Dutch-Mohawk Treaty; Firearms Trade; French and Indian War; Iroquois; Iroquois Treaties of 1700 and 1701; Mohawk-Mahican War; Mohawks; Mourning War; Oneidas; Onondagas; Senecas; Senecas, French Attack on; Tuscaroras; Tuscarora War; Wyandots

References
Engelbrecht, William. *Iroquoia: The Development of a Native World.* Syracuse, NY: Syracuse University Press, 2003.
Richter, Daniel K. *The Ordeal of the Longhouse: The People of the Iroquois League in the Era of European Colonization.* Chapel Hill: University of North Carolina Press, 1992.
Snow, Dean R. *The Iroquois.* Malden, MA: Blackwell, 1994.

Iroquois Treaties of 1700 and 1701

Agreements between the Iroquois and the French (September 1700) and the Iroquois and New York colony (August 1701). By the end of the 17th century, the Iroquois Confederacy had been significantly weakened. Suffering from the losses sustained during the Beaver Wars (1641–1701) and King William's War (1689–1697), the Iroquois began to search for a way out of their predicament.

For much of the Beaver Wars, the Iroquois dominated their native enemies to the west. The Iroquois combined the economic motives for control of the fur trade with the traditional impetus of the Mourning War, which sought to replace their dead with captives. By the 1690s, however, Iroquois enemies were at least as well equipped with European weaponry as were the Europeans. With the disappearance of their previous technological advantage, the Iroquois began to sustain heavy losses.

The excessive number of casualties left the Iroquois vulnerable to attacks by their native enemies and the French. Indeed, in 1689 the French successfully invaded Seneca country, the westernmost portion of Iroquoia. There the French destroyed several Seneca towns and immense stores of maize.

The Iroquois also engaged in substantial fighting with the French during the 1690s on behalf of their English allies. However, the reaction (or rather inaction) of the colony of New York to the French invasion taught the Iroquois a valuable lesson. Although the English may have been desirable as trading partners, as military allies they were at best unreliable.

The Iroquois hoped to end the conflicts with the French and their native allies, yet their English allies restrained them from doing so. In 1698 English diplomats attempted to negotiate peace with the French on behalf of the Iroquois. However, both the French and the English had claimed the Iroquois as subjects. The French realized that they could not parley with English representatives acting on behalf of the Iroquois Confederacy. To do so would have implied that the Iroquois were subjects of the English Crown.

In September 1700 the Iroquois, over English objections, negotiated a treaty with the French. Under the terms of the accord, the Iroquois Confederacy promised to remain at peace with New France's native allies and to remain neutral in future conflicts between the French and the English. In this way the Iroquois actually helped the French, who were in something of a difficult economic and diplomatic position. The fur trade, the economic underpinning of French Canada, was if anything too successful. Warehouses in Montreal were glutted with furs, with the inevitable result that France's native trade partners would now be paid less for their pelts.

The treaty with the Iroquois allowed the French to keep the Five Nations in place as a barrier between the English colonies and other native peoples. This helped preserve France's trade and, more importantly, its alliances with the natives. If other native people had been able to trade with the English at Albany, they would have discovered that they offered cheaper and better-quality trade goods. The long-term result of that would have been disastrous for New France.

In August 1701 a year after the treaty with New France, the Iroquois parleyed with English representatives and signed a treaty with the colony of New York. Although the Iroquois did not pledge neutrality, they did deed to the Crown rights to lands in southern Ontario that they claimed were theirs "by right of conquest." However, to secure these lands the English would have to wrest control of them from the French, something that the Iroquois knew was impossible in 1701.

Taken together, the two treaties have come to be known as the Grand Settlement of 1701 and formed the basis of Iroquois diplomatic policy for half a century. The two treaties allowed the confederation to pursue a policy of aggressive neutrality by which it extracted concessions from both the French and the English. The English valued Iroquois trade, whereas the French had to have free access through lands controlled by the Iroquois in order to have communications between their colonies in Louisiana and in Canada. The Iroquois also took advantage of the long period of peace to foster peaceful relations with their native neighbors to the west and the north. In addition, the Iroquois forged closer ties with the English colony of Pennsylvania, as a counterweight to New York, and found that they were free to continue their wars against their smaller, weaker enemies to the south, with minimal English interference.

ROGER M. CARPENTER

See also

Beaver Wars; Covenant Chain; Decanisora; Iroquois; Iroquois Confederacy; King William's War; Mourning War

References

Aquila, Richard. *The Iroquois Restoration: Iroquois Diplomacy on the Colonial Frontier, 1701–1754.* Detroit: Wayne State University Press, 1983.

Jennings, Francis, et al., eds. *The History and Culture of Iroquois Diplomacy: An Interdisciplinary Guide to the Treaties of the Six Nations and Their League.* Syracuse, NY: Syracuse University Press, 1985.

Iroquois Wars

See Beaver Wars

Itazipcos

See Sans Arc Sioux

J

Jackson, Andrew
Birth Date: March 15, 1767
Death Date: June 8, 1845

U.S. general and president (1829–1837). Born the posthumous son of a poor Scotch Irish immigrant father in the Waxhaws Settlement on the South Carolina frontier on March 15, 1767, Andrew Jackson received little formal education. During the American Revolutionary War (1775–1783) he fought in guerrilla operations against the British in the Carolinas in 1780–1781 and was captured in 1781. A British officer slashed Jackson's face with a saber, allegedly because Jackson refused to polish the officer's boots. Jackson contracted smallpox while a prisoner, and his mother and both older brothers died during the war. These events no doubt influenced Jackson's subsequent hatred for the British.

Following the war Jackson first read and then practiced law, in North Carolina and then in Tennessee, where he was highly successful. He became state prosecuting attorney in 1788, and although his poor investments almost led to bankruptcy, he was a delegate in the state constitutional convention of 1796 and was Tennessee's first representative in the U.S. House of Representatives in 1796–1797. Appointed U.S. senator in 1797, Jackson resigned the next year because of financial problems. He then served as a superior court judge from 1798 to 1804 but again resigned because of financial difficulties.

Jackson found his calling when he was elected major general of the Tennessee Militia in 1802. He and his men entered federal service at the beginning of the war with Britain in June 1812. Jackson led his men to Natchez, Mississippi, in preparation for an invasion of Florida, which was canceled by Congress. He then marched his men back to Tennessee, earning the nickname "Old Hickory" for his toughness.

When a civil war between nativist and accommodationist factions split the Creek Confederacy in Alabama and Georgia during the War of 1812, Americans assumed that the nativist Red Stick Creeks had allied with the British. Although not technically true, British traders in Spanish Florida had provided the Red Sticks with arms and ammunition, and as the Red Sticks began attacking white settlers, Americans demanded that the government take action. Jackson was ordered to suppress the Red Sticks. A strict disciplinarian, he drilled his Tennessee militiamen thoroughly, believing that militia, if well trained and adequately supplied, could prove an effective fighting force. After carefully stockpiling supplies, he began a campaign against the Creeks that November when their own food supplies were low. Part of his force, under Brigadier General John Coffee, defeated the Creeks at Tallasahatchee, Alabama, on November 3, while Jackson himself won a lesser victory at Talladega on November 9. After reorganizing his forces, Jackson invaded the Creek heartland in March 1814, defeating the main Red Stick force in the Battle of Horseshoe Bend on March 27, 1814.

Appointed major general in the regular army in May 1814, Jackson assumed command of the Seventh Military District. He improved the defenses of Mobile, Alabama, and then defended it against a British naval attack on September 15, 1814. He then marched into Florida without official authorization. Taking Pensacola on November 7, he destroyed its fortifications and then hastened to New Orleans in December to defend the city against an expected British attack. Jackson hastily assembled a force of regulars, militia, and volunteers that repulsed British lieutenant

Among Native Americans, U.S. president Andrew Jackson is most closely identified with the Indian Removal Act of May 26, 1830, which led to the forcible removal of tens of thousands of Native Americans from their ancestral homelands to the West and the deaths of thousands of them in the process. (Library of Congress)

general Sir Edward Pakenham's assault on January 8, 1815, making Jackson a national hero.

Following the end of the war, Jackson assumed command of the Southern Division at New Orleans. Ordered to put an end to Native attacks during the First Seminole War (1817–1818), he invaded Florida. Taking advantage of the vagueness of his orders, he not only seized Pensacola on May 24, 1818, but also created an international incident that April by hanging two British subjects for allegedly supplying the Seminoles with arms. The James Monroe administration used Jackson's actions to induce Spain to sell Florida to the United States in 1819.

While Jackson began his military career as a rank amateur, he proved to be a military genius. A strict disciplinarian and a careful planner, he understood the need for thorough training before committing his men to battle, yet he could act quickly in an emergency, as he had done at New Orleans.

Resigning his commission in June 1821, Jackson served briefly as military governor of Florida during March–October 1821 before returning to his plantation home, the Hermitage, near Nashville. Elected to the U.S. Senate from Tennessee in 1823, he resigned after one session to run for president. In the election of November 1824 he won a plurality of the popular vote and electoral votes but

lost the election in the House of Representatives to John Quincy Adams. Jackson denounced Adams's deal with Henry Clay that secured the former's election as a "corrupt bargain," and Jackson's supporters responded by working to expand voting rights by eliminating property requirements. Their efforts led to his election to the presidency by wide margins in both 1828 and 1832.

As president, Jackson maintained U.S. neutrality but encouraged his friend Sam Houston in the Texas Revolution (1835–1836), also known as the Texas War of Independence. In 1830 he secured congressional approval for the Indian Removal Act that forced many Native Americans, especially the Cherokees, to move west of the Mississippi River. Jackson insisted that Indian removal was a humanitarian gesture to prevent the Native Americans from being engulfed and exterminated by the growing white population, but thousands of Native Americans died during the moves. Removal also led to both the Black Hawk War (1832) in Illinois and the Second Seminole War (1835–1842) in Florida. Among other events during his presidency were the Nullification Crisis in South Carolina and the elimination of the Second Bank of the United States.

On the completion of his second term in 1837, Jackson returned to Nashville. He died at the Hermitage on June 8, 1845.

Spencer C. Tucker

See also

Black Hawk War; Coffee, John; Creek War; Horseshoe Bend, Battle of; Indian Removal Act; Seminole War, First; Seminole War, Second

References

Remini, Robert Vincenti. *Andrew Jackson and the Course of American Empire, 1767–1821.* New York: Harper and Row, 1977.

Remini, Robert Vincenti. *Andrew Jackson and the Course of American Freedom, 1822–1832.* New York: Harper and Row, 1981.

Remini, Robert Vincenti. *Andrew Jackson and His Indian Wars.* New York: Penguin, 2001.

Jackson, Helen Hunt
Birth Date: October 15, 1830
Death Date: August 12, 1885

Noted poet, author, and champion of Native American rights. Helen Hunt Jackson was born Helen Maria Fiske on October 15, 1830, in Amherst, Massachusetts, the daughter of a professor of languages at Amherst College. Variously portrayed as brilliant and something of a pest, the young Helen Fiske learned to read and write earlier than most children, drawing largely from her collegiate surroundings. As a girl she became close friends with the poet Emily Dickinson. In her own time Fiske was a better-known poet than Dickinson, who spent much of her life in obscurity. At the age of 11, Fiske was sent to the first of several boarding schools. By age 19 she had been orphaned. Early in her life she was determined to support herself as an independent woman, not an easy role in a society in which women were defined as men's property. She decided to make her living as a writer.

First known as a romantic poet, Fiske later expanded her scope to include travel articles, short stories, novels, and books for children. Before becoming famous for her efforts to reform Indian policy, she led a widely varied life with her first husband Edward B. Hunt. Before the treatment of the Ponca tribe sparked her indignation, Helen Hunt Jackson had been a nearly apolitical person, having taken no published position on women's suffrage or slavery.

Within 15 years of marrying Hunt, the author had lost both her sons and husband. She assuaged her loneliness by writing poetry, becoming one of the most well-regarded poets of 19th-century America. Ralph Waldo Emerson often carried her poetry in his pocket to show to friends. In 1875 she married William S. Jackson, whose name she carried when her Indian reform work became well known. At the age of 49 Helen Hunt Jackson took up the cause of the Indians with a fervor that consumed her attention and energies for the few remaining years of her life.

Jackson's attention was turned toward the condition of Native Americans during October 1879 shortly after U.S. judge Elmer Dundy's ruling in *Standing Bear v. Crook.* While in Boston, Jackson heard a speech describing the travails of Standing Bear and the Poncas who, forced off their land in northern Nebraska, had escaped reservation life in Indian Territory (Oklahoma). Dundy ultimately ruled that Standing Bear must be regarded as a human being under the law of habeas corpus.

Portrait of author Helen Hunt Jackson. (Library of Congress)

After the trial Standing Bear and a group of Poncas visited several cities, including Chicago, New York City, Philadelphia, and Boston. It was in Boston, however, that support was greatest; $3,000 of the $4,000 that the Poncas thought they would need to pursue their land claim was raised there.

After hearing their story, Jackson collected funds for the Poncas and encouraged others to take an active part in their struggles. Jackson herself joined Standing Bear and others on a tour throughout New England. Her support was cited as being one of the major factors in the Poncas' ultimate victory.

Jackson's acquaintance with the Poncas also started her down a new literary road. Within two years of first hearing the Poncas' story, Jackson published *A Century of Dishonor,* a factual sketch of broken treaties and corruption in the Bureau of Indian Affairs. Three years later with a pledge to write a novel that would become the Native American version of *Uncle Tom's Cabin,* she published the best seller *Ramona,* a fictional account of the abuses suffered by the Mission Indians of California that was based on Jackson's travels in that area. Both books were among the best sellers of their time.

Jackson's books may have been so immensely popular during the 1880s because many people in the expanding United States, finding a need to reconcile the taking of a continent with notions of their own civility, sought to deal with the so-called Indian problem in what they believed to be a civilized and humane manner. Thus, cultural genocide (a late-20th-century phrase) was advanced in the modulated tones of civility, of doing what was believed to be best for Native Americans.

Jackson's books fueled a national debate over what would become of Native Americans who had survived subjugation by immigrant nonnatives. Most of her books combined condemnation of the government's earlier behavior with advocacy of popular solutions to the problems, such as religious instruction, boarding schools, and land allotment.

After *A Century of Dishonor* was published, Jackson sent a copy to each member of Congress at her own expense. She died before Congress passed the Dawes Severalty Act in 1887 that officially adopted allotment, which she had believed would save Native Americans from extinction. *Ramona,* which was reprinted 300 times after Jackson's death, was adapted for stage and screen several times.

After experiencing failing health, Jackson died on August 12, 1885, in San Francisco. Dickinson penned a eulogy in verse in honor of her friend.

BRUCE E. JOHANSEN

See also

Bureau of Indian Affairs; Dawes Severalty Act; Standing Bear; *Standing Bear v. Crook*

References

Banning, Evelyn L. *Helen Hunt Jackson.* New York: Vanguard, 1973.
Mathes, Valerie Sherer. *Helen Hunt Jackson and Her Indian Reform Legacy.* Austin: University of Texas Press, 1990.

Jamestown

The first permanent English settlement in North America. Jamestown was founded on an islandlike peninsula adjacent to the north bank of the James River in eastern Virginia. The settlement served as the epicenter of colonial Virginia during the 17th century and played an important role in conflicts between and among Europeans and Native Americans between 1607 and 1699. Jamestown (or James Town, as it was originally known) was a privately financed venture with a decidedly military flavor. The location was established on May 14, 1607, by 104 settlers of the Virginia Company of London and derived its name from King James I.

Investors hoped that the colonists, carried aboard the ships *Susan Constant, Godspeed,* and *Discovery,* would either trade with or quickly conquer local Native American tribes and possibly discover precious metals as a means of returning vast riches to England. Yet the investors feared that the colony would provoke an attack by Spain, which claimed all of North America as its own. The investors therefore included a number of former soldiers among the colonists and ordered Captain Christopher Newport to choose a site for Jamestown that was both hidden and easily defensible. Newport selected a peninsula that was virtually an island five miles upstream from the mouth of what settlers named the James River on terrain connected to the mainland by a very narrow, marshy neck of land. This site provided an obstacle to the landward approaches of Native Americans and made the new settlement accessible to seagoing ships while keeping it far enough from the open ocean to avoid arousing the suspicion of passing Spanish vessels.

Unfortunately, Jamestown had few other geographic advantages. The land was low and swampy, was infested with disease-carrying mosquitoes, and was so close to the ocean that the adjacent river was a brackish, swirling stew of saltwater and freshwater that stagnated close to shore. Because colonists dumped their waste into and drew their drinking water from the river in the same places, dysentery and other ailments ran rampant. Indeed, only 38 of the original 104 settlers survived the first nine months. Although new immigrants arrived to keep Jamestown going, colonists died so quickly that by 1610 only 60 out of 220 people who had arrived from England were still alive. Moreover, the early settlers were disproportionately gentlemen who hoped to get rich quickly and had no interest in working. They hunted and planted far too little to provide enough food for the winter, and thus those who endured the heat, insects, and disease of the summer months often froze or starved to death the following winter.

Predictably, these abysmal conditions led to enormous infighting and desperation, which combined with racism to drive many colonists to mistreat nearby Native Americans, whose gifts of food were the only reason some settlers survived. Captain John Smith famously brought order to the colony by imposing military discipline and forcing colonists to work six hours a day in 1608 and 1609. He also attempted to stay on good terms with the local Powhatan Confederacy.

All of this proved a brief respite, however, for his harsh measures provoked a revolt that, along with Smith's injury in an explosion, drove him from Jamestown and allowed the colony to descend into the so-called Starving Time of 1609–1610. So many settlers died that Jamestown was briefly abandoned in the spring of 1610. When they encountered a relief expedition in Chesapeake Bay, the colonists returned and submitted to martial law under governors Thomas Dale and Thomas Gates, but long-term success came only after the discovery of tobacco as a profitable export, the establishment of a head-right system that allowed private individuals to work their own farms, and a gradual inland movement of settlers that took them away from the disease-infested coast.

As a military position, Jamestown began without fortifications of any kind, but after a raid by Native Americans in May 1607, the settlers built palisades made of upright logs and a triangular fort with turretlike emplacements for artillery at the corners. This was the first of many English forts in North America, and it served as a base during the first (1610–1614) and second (1622–1632) wars against the Powhatans and as a haven from attacks by other tribes such as the Kecoughtans, Appomattocks, Rappahannocks, and Paspaheghs.

These Native American attacks were occasionally widespread, as evidenced by a colony-wide assault that left 347 settlers dead on March 22, 1622, and another in 1644 that killed more than 400 settlers. In each case the English exacted a terrible retribution, as in 1623 when they lured 250 natives to their deaths with the promise of peace talks. Over time the relentless influx of English settlers, their steady movement westward, catastrophic loss of habitat for wild game, and deliberate crop destruction by colonial forces destroyed Native American power in the region. The Algonquian-speaking tribes, for example, were reduced from an estimated population of 24,000 in 1607 to just 2,000 by 1669, and by the latter half of the 17th century tribes were forced to either accept English dominance or flee elsewhere.

As the center of economic power shifted farther inland, Jamestown gradually declined in importance. It was completely burned during Bacon's Rebellion in 1676 and then was destroyed yet again by accidental fire in 1699. At that time a new capital for Virginia was established at Williamsburg, and Jamestown was virtually abandoned thereafter.

LANCE JANDA

See also

Algonquins; Anglo-Powhatan War, First; Anglo-Powhatan War, Second; Anglo-Powhatan War, Third; Appomattocks; Bacon's Rebellion; Powhatan; Powhatan Confederacy

References

Rosen, Daniel. *Jamestown and the Virginia Colony.* Washington, DC: National Geographic Society, 2004.

Vaughan, Alden T. *American Genesis: Captain John Smith and the Founding of Virginia.* Boston: Little, Brown, 1975.

Jefferson, Thomas

Birth Date: April 13, 1743
Death Date: July 4, 1826

Planter, politician, writer, diplomat, and president of the United States (1801–1809). Thomas Jefferson was born on April 13, 1743, at Shadwell in Albemarle County, Virginia. He received a private classical education in preparation for the College of William and Mary, where he became interested in mathematics and science. From 1762 until 1767 he studied law at William and Mary. Admitted to the bar in 1767, Jefferson practiced law, but his principal activity was managing his large plantation.

Jefferson's political career began in 1768, when he was elected to the Virginia House of Burgesses. As a legislator he was efficient at committee work, but his poor oratorical skills limited his effectiveness. He soon gained a reputation, however, for his eloquent prose, and in the summer of 1774 he wrote *A Summary View of the Rights of British America,* which immediately became popular.

Jefferson was elected to the Second Continental Congress in 1775. In June 1776 Congress appointed a committee to draft a Declaration of Independence. Its members were John Adams, Benjamin Franklin, Robert Livingston, Roger Sherman, and Jefferson, the only southerner. The committee assigned Jefferson the task of drafting the document. The first draft of the declaration was only slightly amended by Adams and Franklin. In late June, however, Congress made extensive revisions to the text, and although Jefferson thought that Congress had "mutilated" his work, he accepted the changes. The Declaration of Independence was approved by Congress on July 2 and signed two days later.

Shortly after independence Jefferson returned to Virginia, where he participated in forming a new state government. He also served as governor from 1779 to 1781. This was a particularly difficult time for the state, and Jefferson's term was a disaster. In late December 1780 the traitor Benedict Arnold, now a British brigadier general, ravaged much of the eastern part of the state, while British major general William Phillips proceeded up the James River in March 1781. Then in May, Lieutenant General Charles Cornwallis marched in from North Carolina. Only weeks later, Jefferson himself narrowly escaped capture when British dragoons raided Charlottesville.

Soon thereafter, Jefferson's wife died. Utterly devastated, he served another term in Congress during 1783–1784. In 1784 Jefferson accepted appointment to a joint commission in Paris, with Franklin and Adams, to negotiate commercial treaties with European powers. In France, Jefferson renewed his close friendship with Adams. In 1785 Jefferson replaced the retiring Franklin as American minister to France.

Personal business led Jefferson to return to America in 1789. That same year he accepted President George Washington's offer to serve as secretary of state. Jefferson held this post until his resignation in 1793 because of an increasingly bitter conflict

Portrait of Thomas Jefferson, third president of the United States during 1801–1809. Jefferson arranged the Louisiana Purchase from France but pursued a harsh policy toward Native Americans, favoring their removal to the West. (BiographicalImages.com)

with Secretary of the Treasury Alexander Hamilton and Jefferson's perception that Washington favored Hamilton. By now, Americans who disagreed with Hamilton's Federalist policies began calling themselves Democratic Republicans. Although ostensibly in retirement, Jefferson came to lead this new political faction.

In 1796 in a close contest, the Federalist John Adams defeated Jefferson, his old but now estranged friend, to become the second president of the United States. Jefferson became the nation's second vice president but soon found this role so distasteful that he spent most of his time at his home of Monticello in Charlottesville, Virginia.

Elected president in December 1800, in March 1801 Jefferson assumed the presidency. His major achievement in office was to purchase the Louisiana Territory from Napoleon in 1803. Jefferson then sent Meriwether Lewis and William Clark on the 1804–1806 expedition to survey the lands that had doubled the size of the United States. But Jefferson's second term was plagued with difficult relations with Britain that tested his resiliency and ended in a fruitless economic embargo.

As early as the late 1770s, Jefferson had advocated the removal of Native Americans from lands in the East for resettlement farther west. He specifically had in mind the Shawnees and Cherokees. Soon after becoming president, Jefferson struck a deal with Georgia wherein the federal government would help drive the Cherokees from the state if Georgia gave up its western land claims. This would be in direct conflict with a prior treaty that had guaranteed the Cherokees their Georgia lands. Forcible removal of the Cherokees did not occur until the 1830s, but Jefferson's plan certainly informed the federal government's Native American policies for many decades. As a proponent of western expansion, Jefferson firmly believed that the United States could not allow Native Americans to impede that activity. He also believed that the best way to ensure Native American cooperation was to encourage them to abandon their cultures in favor of white American culture. This was to include proper education, conversion to Christianity, and the adoption of a sedentary agriculture-based lifestyle. If tribes resisted, Jefferson believed that forcible removal and forced assimilation were appropriate measures.

In 1809 Jefferson eagerly retired to Monticello, where he maintained a voluminous correspondence with a wide range of American and foreign leaders and luminaries. He also took great pride in founding the University of Virginia in Charlottesville in 1819. Jefferson died at Monticello on July 4, 1826, the 50th anniversary of the signing of the Declaration of Independence.

ANNETTE RICHARDSON

See also
Cherokees; Indian Removal Act; Reservations; Shawnees

References
Cunningham, Noble, Jr. *In Pursuit of Reason: The Life of Thomas Jefferson*. Baton Rouge: Louisiana State University Press, 1987.
Maier, Pauline. *American Scripture: Making the Declaration of Independence*. New York: Knopf, 1997.
Mapp, Alf J., Jr. *Thomas Jefferson, Passionate Pilgrim: The Presidency, the Founding of the University, and the Private Battle*. New York: Madison Books, 1991.

Jemison, Mary
Birth Date: ca. 1742
Death Date: September 1833

Pennsylvania frontier woman taken prisoner by Native Americans during the French and Indian War (1754–1763). Born about 1742 on a ship destined for Pennsylvania from Ireland, Mary Jemison worked on her family's farm in western Pennsylvania. On April 5, 1758, the Jemison family came under attack by Shawnee warriors and their French allies. Mary was the only family member to escape death. The Shawnees took her captive and subsequently turned the young woman over to the Senecas. Two

sisters cared for her and adopted her in place of their deceased brother. Jemison subsequently twice married Iroquois men and raised several children strictly according to native culture. She fully assimilated into the Seneca culture and became a noted leader among her adopted people.

Although Jemison remained with the Senecas for the rest of her life, becoming known as "the White Woman of the Genessee," she retained fluency in English and later told her experiences to Dr. James E. Seaver, who published them in 1824. The immensely popular story was subsequently reprinted in many editions and remains the most complete single source among Native American captivity narratives from colonial times, although scholars dispute to what degree Seaver edited or changed Jemison's story in order to provide the moral lessons that he believed it should impart. Jemison also indicated that she had withheld substantial portions of her life story from Seaver. These unanswered questions have given the text a life well beyond that of a true-life thriller or a morality play. Jemison died in September 1833 at a reservation near Buffalo, New York.

GRANT WELLER

See also
Captivity Narratives; Captivity of Europeans by Indians; French and Indian War; Senecas; Shawnees

References
Doyle, Robert. *Voices from Captivity: Interpreting the American POW Narrative*. Lawrence: University Press of Kansas, 1994.
Seaver, James. *A Narrative of the Life of Mrs. Mary Jemison*. Edited by June Namais. Norman: University of Oklahoma Press, 1992.
Walsh, Susan. "'With Them Was My Home': Native American Autobiography and *A Narrative of the Life of Mrs. Mary Jemison.*" *American Literature* 64(1) (March 1992): 49–70.

Jesup, Thomas Sidney
Birth Date: December 16, 1788
Death Date: June 10, 1860

U.S. Army officer and quartermaster general of the army from 1818 to 1860. Thomas Sidney Jessup was born in Berkeley County, Virginia (now West Virginia), on December 16, 1788, and was the son of a well-regarded American Revolutionary War officer. Jesup entered army service in 1808 as a second lieutenant in the 7th Infantry Regiment. He saw action during the War of 1812, earning promotion to major, 19th Infantry Regiment, in 1813. Jesup was taken prisoner at Detroit when Brigadier General William Hull surrendered that place in August 1812. Later exchanged, Jesup subsequently served most effectively, including during the Battle of Chippewa in July 1814 for which he was brevetted lieutenant colonel. That same month he was brevetted colonel for his performance in the Battle of Lundy's Lane during which he was badly wounded.

Jesup continued in the army after the war, earning promotion to lieutenant colonel in 1817. In 1818 President James Monroe appointed him quartermaster general at the rank of brigadier general, a post that Jesup would hold for 42 years until his death in 1860. Jesup is considered the father of the modern quartermaster corps. He immediately set about creating efficient, effective quartermaster procedures designed to provide adequate supplies of quality products, flexible and mobile delivery systems, and strict accountability on the part of suppliers and officers tasked with producing, requisitioning, and paying for military items. This marked the first time in which supplying the U.S. Army became a well-organized endeavor based on modern business techniques. Most of Jesup's improvements made their way into *Army Regulations,* and many of the procedures he pioneered remain in use today. In 1828 he was brevetted to major general for 10 years of meritorious service at the same grade.

Jesup also held field commands. In 1836 he served briefly against recalcitrant Creeks in Alabama and Georgia before moving to Florida, where during the Second Seminole War (1835–1842) he took over command from Brigadier General Winfield Scott, whom Jesup had severely criticized for his performance in Florida. Jesup proved to be an aggressive and imaginative field commander, breaking from Scott's conventional approach by sending smaller detachments into Seminole sanctuaries. Although these raids did not force a decisive engagement, they were disruptive and in some cases devastating, as soldiers destroyed villages and badly needed supplies. They also helped to erode the Seminoles' sense of security. But Jesup stirred up controversy when he violated a flag of truce, more than once, to capture hundreds of Seminoles and their leaders, including Chief Osceola, in 1837. Although widely condemned for this breach of the rules of conduct, Jesup argued that his approach was preferable to killing the Indians.

The largest battle of the Second Seminole War came during Jesup's 18-month tenure in command when Colonel Zachary Taylor defeated a Seminole force near Lake Okeechobee in December 1837. Taylor replaced Jesup as commander in Florida in May 1838, and Jesup resumed his quartermaster duties. During his time in Florida, however, Jesup fine-tuned his system of employing base supply camps and advance depots that greatly aided the U.S. Army in the prosecution of the war. He would use these same procedures, with considerable success, during the Mexican-American War (1846–1848).

When the Mexican-American War began, Jesup was first charged with setting up a supply center along the Rio Grande opposite Matamoros, Mexico, for Brigadier General Zachary Taylor's force. This assignment called forth Jesup's resourcefulness, and he proved equal to the challenge. In 1847 Jesup was tasked with supplying Major General Winfield Scott's army during its assault on Veracruz and the subsequent Mexico City Campaign. Planning for this operation, the largest amphibious landing undertaken by the U.S. Army to that point in time, began in late 1846. It was Jesup who arranged for and supervised the construction of landing craft. During the war numerous commanders, including Taylor and Scott, criticized Jesup for supply shortages, but overall he performed admirably well given the distinct limitations under which he labored. And compared to the Mexicans' logistics operation, Jesup's operation was a model of efficiency.

After the war ended Jesup retained his post, fighting to keep his systems functional during draconian budget cuts that occurred in the 1850s. Jesup died at his home in Washington, D.C., on June 10, 1860, still on active duty and the longest-serving quartermaster general in U.S. Army history.

PAUL G. PIERPAOLI JR. AND DAVID COFFEY

See also

Osceola; Scott, Winfield; Seminole War, Second; Taylor, Zachary

References

Kieffer, Chester L. *Maligned General: A Biography of Thomas S. Jesup.* Novato, CA: Presidio, 1979.

Winders, R. Bruce. *Mr. Polk's Army: The American Military Experience in the Mexican War.* College Station: Texas A&M University Press, 1997.

John O'Bail

See Cornplanter

Johnson, Sir William
Birth Date: 1715
Death Date: July 12, 1774

Noted British-born frontier trader, intermediary between North American colonists and Native Americans, and superintendent of Indian affairs for the region north of the Ohio River (1754–1774). William Johnson was born in 1715 in County Meath, Ireland, and arrived in North America in 1738 to manage his uncle's estates. Not long afterward, Johnson established his own trading house in the Hudson River Valley near Albany, New York.

Johnson soon developed a close association with the Mohawk tribe, the easternmost of the Iroquois Six Nations, and learned the Iroquois language, customs, and diplomatic protocol. The Iroquois named him Warraghiyagey, which roughly translates to "he who does great things." Indeed, Johnson's relationship with the Iroquois and his deep knowledge of native diplomacy were the primary reasons the Crown appointed him superintendent of Indian affairs in 1754, shortly after the beginning of the French and Indian War (1754–1763).

Adhering to the Grand Settlement of 1701, most of the Iroquois Six Nations remained neutral in the 18th-century imperial conflicts between France and England. However, this began to change when Johnson secured some influence with the Mohawks in the 1740s. During King George's War (1744–1748), the Crown appointed Johnson a colonel of the Six Nations. Working with the elderly Mohawk sachem Hendrick, Johnson was able to mount several military expeditions against French Canada.

William Johnson, British superintendent of Indian Affairs in the American colonies, 1754–1774. Johnson proved highly effective in working with the Iroquois to British benefit. (National Archives of Canada/C-083497)

Johnson further cemented his standing in the Mohawk community in the 1750s when he married into the prominent Brant family of the Mohawks, taking as his wife Molly Brant, one of Hendrick's female relatives. Johnson, however, referred to her as his housekeeper. As a clan matron, Brant wielded a great deal of authority in Mohawk governance. In fact, one of the primary reasons Johnson was appointed superintendent of Indian affairs was the intense Mohawk lobbying effort on his behalf.

The poor performance of British forces in the early phases of the French and Indian War convinced most of the Iroquois to remain neutral. However, Johnson worked with his friend Hendrick to raise a force of Mohawks and colonial militia that defeated a sizable French force at Lake George in August 1755. The battle had a mixed outcome for Johnson. His old adviser Hendrick was killed during the fighting, but the Crown rewarded Johnson by making him a baronet.

The Iroquois officially entered the war as allies of Great Britain in 1759, but for most of the remainder of the war the Iroquois, including the Mohawks, provided only token assistance to the British. In fact, much to Johnson's frustration, a good number of the Senecas, the westernmost of the Six Nations, sided with the French. But although he seldom led Iroquois warriors in battle, Johnson exercised his considerable diplomatic skills on the Crown's behalf, convincing many of the Delawares (Lenni Lenapes) and the Shawnees to abandon the French and remain neutral. Not until the closing phases of the war, when British victory seemed assured, would the Iroquois join the British in large numbers.

With the end of the conflict in 1763, the new commander in chief of British forces in North America, Major General Jeffrey Amherst, decided to stop the practice of gift giving with native peoples of the Great Lakes and the Ohio Country, arguing that they should not be bribed for good behavior. Johnson protested, arguing that gifts were a necessary part of native diplomacy. In 1763, partly as a result of Amherst's polices, Pontiac's Rebellion began, and Johnson was frustrated to learn that the Iroquois had little sway over the natives to the west. It was Johnson, however, who met with Pontiac at Oswego in 1766 and convinced him to make peace with the British.

For the last 10 years of his life Johnson continued to exercise a great deal of influence in Native American affairs. He also closely mentored one of his kinsmen, Mohawk leader Joseph Brant. Johnson died during a conference with representatives of the Six Nations at his home, Johnson Hall, in New York on July 12, 1774.

ROGER M. CARPENTER

See also
Brant, Joseph; French and Indian War; Great Britain; Iroquois Confederacy; King George's War; Mohawks; Native American Warfare; Pontiac's Rebellion

References
Flexner, James Thomas. *Mohawk Baronet: A Biography of Sir William Johnson.* Syracuse, NY: Syracuse University Press, 1989.

Hamilton, Milton W. *Sir William Johnson, Colonial American, 1715–1763.* Port Washington, NY: Kennikat, 1976.

O'Toole, Fintan. *White Savage: William Johnson and the Invention of America.* New York: Farrar, Straus and Giroux, 2005.

Johnson's 1780 Campaign

Two expeditions conducted by Sir John Johnson during the spring and autumn of 1780 in upstate New York designed to rescue Loyalists and their allies during the American Revolutionary War (1775–1783). Johnson was a prominent and wealthy Loyalist leader from New York's Mohawk Valley who, as superintendent of Indian affairs for the region north of the Ohio River, worked closely with the British throughout the Revolutionary War. He also recruited colonists and Native Americans to fight throughout the region. His father, Sir William Johnson, had immigrated to America from Ireland in 1739, built an estate along the Mohawk River, and preceded his son as superintendent of Indian affairs.

In May 1780 John Johnson set out from his base in southern Canada with a regiment of 300 whites and many Mohawks, whose land had been ravaged by Continental Army major general John Sullivan's expedition the previous summer. Johnson's mission was to rescue Loyalists in his old home town of Johnstown, New York, after information had been received that the revolutionaries intended to press them into military service.

On May 22 Johnson's force reached the vicinity of Johnstown and proceeded to ravage the countryside, while most of those loyal to the British cause flocked to his force. Wary of a counterattack from colonial militia in the area, Johnson then fell back toward Lake Champlain with his regiment, a number of prisoners, and the Loyalists and Native Americans.

The Oneidas were the only Iroquois to side with the colonists during the American Revolution. The governor of Quebec, General Frederick Haldimand, planned to cut off the Oneidas, but most of all he wanted to destroy their crops. Johnson was charged with executing this strategy. Johnson's plan was to cross the Saint Lawrence River to Oswego, New York. From this staging area he would march overland to the Schoharie Valley and destroy the Oneidas' autumn harvest. After that Johnson's forces would return via the Mohawk Valley to wreak more havoc there.

Johnson departed Montreal on September 11, 1780, and proceeded to Carleton Island in the Saint Lawrence, where he was reinforced. Johnson's force of 943 men, including 678 regulars of the King's Royal Regiment of New York and 265 Native Americans, departed Oswego on October 2, having waited for troops from Niagara who had been delayed. Fifteen days later Johnson's men plundered and burned the Schoharie Valley region, while locals sought refuge in the three forts in the area. The raiders then turned west toward the Mohawk River, with New York state militia under the command of General Stephen van Rensselaer in hot pursuit. Johnson then crossed the Mohawk on October 18 and defeated a small contingent of colonials, resulting in more than 40 colonists killed, while Johnson counted only 4 killed and 5 wounded.

Johnson's campaign was a success. He had destroyed an estimated 150,000 bushels of wheat along with more than 200 homes. But it was also the last foray Johnson led into New York. After a visit to England in 1781 to secure pay and recognition for his regiment, he returned to Canada as superintendent and inspector general of the Six Nations. Johnson then settled in Canada, receiving both land and money for his service to the Crown.

WILLIAM WHYTE

See also

Iroquois; Iroquois Confederacy; Johnson, Sir William; Mohawks; Native Americans and the American Revolutionary War; Oneidas; Sullivan-Clinton Expedition against the Iroquois

References

Calloway, Colin G. *The American Revolution in Indian Country: Crisis and Diversity in Native American Communities.* Cambridge: Cambridge University Press, 1995.

Tiedemann, Joseph S., and Eugene R. Fingerhut, eds. *The Other New York: The American Revolution beyond New York City, 1763–1787.* Albany: State University of New York Press, 2005.

Walker, Mabel G. "Sir John Johnson." *Mississippi Valley Historical Review* 3(3) (December 1916): 318–346.

Watt, Gavin K. *The Burning of the Valleys: Daring Raids from Canada against the New York Frontier in the Fall of 1780.* Toronto: Dundurn, 1997.

Joseph, Chief
Birth Date: 1840
Death Date: September 12, 1904

Nez Perce chief, Wallowa headman, and leader during the Nez Perce War (1877). Chief Joseph, also known as Young Joseph or Hin-mah-too-yah-lat-kekt, was born in Oregon's Wallowa Valley in 1840, the son of the Christianized Nez Perce chief Old Joseph. As a child the boy was baptized and renamed Young Joseph. He spent a short time at the Spalding Mission School. Young Joseph developed diplomatic and leadership skills by accompanying his father to councils and other negotiations. Old Joseph, however, refused to sign an 1863 treaty with the United States, renounced Christianity, and influenced his son to reject any white attempts to purchase Nez Perce land. When Old Joseph died in 1871, Young Joseph became chief of the Wallowa Band.

Growing friction between settlers and the Nez Perces prompted U.S. Army brigadier general Oliver Otis Howard to meet with headmen in July 1876. Chief Joseph and his brother Ollokot represented

Nez Perce chief Joseph, photographed by William H. Jackson circa 1875. Joseph led his people on an epic three-month trek through Oregon, Idaho, Wyoming, and Montana toward the Canadian border. Forced to surrender in October, Joseph proclaimed: "From where the sun now stands I will fight no more forever." (National Archives)

the nontreaty Nez Perces and presented testimony regarding settlers' crimes against their people. Chief Joseph was not satisfied with Howard's response, which virtually ignored the charges brought by Joseph. In January 1877 Howard gave Joseph an ultimatum: Joseph and the Wallowas were to leave for a reservation in Idaho by April 1, 1877, or face forcible removal. Joseph's refusal prompted Howard to send two companies of the 1st Cavalry from Fort Walla Walla (Washington) to the mouth of the Wallowa Valley.

Despite constant infringements on their lands, Joseph counseled his people to be patient and restrain their actions. Joseph and Howard again met, this time negotiating at Fort Lapwai in early May. Under threat of military reprisal, Joseph finally agreed to move his people to the reservation.

On June 14, 1877, three Nez Perce warriors killed four settlers, and the war that Chief Joseph had hoped to avoid erupted. Joseph decided that he would not take his people to the reservation, and he embarked with them on a trek that ultimately covered more than 1,500 miles in an effort to reach Canada.

On June 17 troops of the 1st Cavalry caught up with Joseph's small band in White Bird Canyon. Joseph, Ollokot, and about 60 warriors defeated the soldiers and began what turned out to be a three-month trek through Oregon, Idaho, Wyoming, and Montana toward the Canadian border. Leading about 800 people, Joseph evaded or engaged U.S. Army detachments throughout June and July. He earned a reputation as a civilized fighter, allowing noncombatants to escape and refusing to scalp or mutilate dead soldiers. On August 7, 1877, at Big Hole, Montana, Colonel John Gibbon, with the 7th Infantry and the 2nd Cavalry, fought another battle, attacking the Nez Perces when they were encamped. The tactical draw at Big Hole was followed by fierce fighting with Howard at Canyon Creek. Colonel Nelson Miles's command joined the pursuit, chasing Joseph to the Bear Paw Mountains in Montana, where he was forced to surrender with about 400 of his followers on October 5 less than 40 miles south of Canada. Some 300 Nez Perces managed to escape into Canada. Chief Joseph told Miles on his surrender that "From where the sun now stands I will fight no more forever."

The government dispersed the Nez Perces, and Joseph was eventually sent to the Colville Reservation in Washington. He remained a staunch advocate for his people for the rest of his life, always seeking to return to Wallowa, where his father was buried. Chief Joseph died on September 12, 1904, in Colville, Washington.

DAWN OTTEVAERE NICKESON

See also
Bear Paw Mountains, Battle of; Big Hole, Battle of the; Canyon Creek, Battle of; Howard, Oliver Otis; Miles, Nelson Appleton; Nez Perces; Nez Perce War

References
Gidley, M. *Kopet: A Documentary Narrative of Chief Joseph's Last Years.* Seattle: University of Washington Press, 1981.
Greene, Jerome A. *Nez Perce Summer, 1877: The U. S. Army and the Nee-Me-Poo Crisis.* Helena: Montana Historical Society Press, 2000.
McCoy, Robert. *Chief Joseph, Yellow Wolf, and the Creation of Nez Perce History in the Northwest.* New York: Routledge, 2004.

Moulton, Candy. *Chief Joseph: Guardian of the People.* New York: Tom Doherty, 2005.

Julesburg Raids
Event Dates: January 7, 1865 and February 2, 1865

Military engagement that pitted the Southern Cheyennes, Northern Arapahos, and Oglala and Brulé Sioux against U.S. forces in northern Colorado in the winter of 1865. The stage and telegraph station at Julesburg, Colorado, became the first target in a series of retaliatory raids by Native Americans for the Sand Creek Massacre of November 29, 1864. The slaughter of more than 200 Cheyennes, including many women and children, by Colorado militia under Colonel John Chivington had outraged the Native Americans, who promptly united and planned a series of reprisals.

The town of Julesburg was established in 1859. It is located in the northeast corner of Colorado, bordering southwest Nebraska. Situated along the confluence of the South Platte River and Lodge Pole Creek, the town was a major supply center. It possessed a large telegraph and stage office and a general store for travelers but was only lightly defended. Camp Rankin, located one mile west of the settlement and commanded by Captain Nicholas J. O'Brien, housed a small contingent of the 7th Iowa Cavalry.

The Native Americans, more than 1,000 strong, launched their attack on January 7, 1865. Native American scouts lured the troops away from Camp Rankin and then ambushed and killed 15 soldiers and 4 civilians. They then surrounded the hamlet's stockade and fired upon it to keep the inhabitants at bay while they ransacked the town. The Native Americans destroyed telegraph wires and scalped many of the inhabitants, just as Chivington's volunteers had scalped their victims at Sand Creek.

The raid then continued throughout the South Platte Valley. At nearby Harlow's Ranch, all the men living there were killed, and one woman was taken captive. Fifty miles upriver at Washington's Ranch, the Native Americans seized some 500 head of cattle and burned stores of government hay.

On February 2 a Native American war party again attacked Julesburg and Camp Rankin. This time, however, the soldiers remained within their defenses. The town was burned to the ground after being looted for a second time. The natives then proceeded north, continuing their depredations.

WILLIAM WHYTE

See also
Arapahos; Brulé Sioux; Cheyennes; Cheyennes, Northern; Chivington, John; Oglala Sioux; Platte Bridge, Battle of; Sand Creek Massacre; Sioux

References
Hatch, Thom. *Black Kettle: The Cheyenne Chief Who Sought Peace but Found War.* Hoboken, NJ: Wiley, 2004.
McChristian, Douglas C. *Fort Laramie: Military Bastion of the High Plains.* Norman: University of Oklahoma Press, 2008.
Ware, Eugene F. *The Indian War of 1864.* New York: St. Martin's, 1960.

K

Kaiiontwa'ko

See Cornplanter

Kamiakin

Birth Date: ca. 1800–1810
Death Date: 1877

Yakima political and military leader, influential among several tribes of the Columbia Plateau. Kamiakin was born in the Yakima Valley (present-day Washington state) sometime between 1800 and 1810 and emerged as a leader of the Yakima tribe by the 1840s. Initially peaceful toward white settlers, he grew increasingly alarmed as the extent of white settlement and the demands of white leaders increased.

Kamiakin opposed but eventually signed the 1855 Walla Walla Council Treaty that opened new lands east of the Cascades to white settlement while consigning the Native Americans to reservations not yet defined. The ensuing white encroachment, including those drawn by a new gold strike on the upper Columbia River, proved more than Kamiakin would tolerate. He led his Yakimas and their allies in an uprising known as the Yakima-Rogue War, which ended inconclusively when heavy troop deployments compelled Kamiakin's bands to disperse.

In 1858 in response to a near disaster that befell Lieutenant Colonel Edward Steptoe's command at the hands of agitated Spokanes and their confederates, the U.S. Army launched a major offensive that sought, among other things, to punish the perpetrators of Steptoe's debacle and to capture or drive away Kamiakin, whom the army held responsible for fomenting unrest. In the final engagement of the campaign, Colonel George Wright led a sizable column to a devastating victory against the Spokane alliance in the Battle of Four Lakes (Battle of Spokane Plain) on September 1, 1858, during which Kamiakin was badly wounded. He managed to elude capture by fleeing into the Rockies and then to Canada as the Washington Territory tribes endured the subjugation mandated in the 1855 treaty.

Kamiakin eventually returned to his homeland and died near Rock Lake, Washington, in 1877.

DAVID COFFEY

See also
Four Lakes, Battle of; Spokanes; Steptoe, Edward Jenner; Wool, John Ellis; Wright, George; Yakima-Rogue War

References
Scheuerman, Richard D., and Michael O. Finley. *Finding Chief Kamiakin: The Life and Legacy of a Northwest Patriot*. Pullman: Washington State University Press, 2008.
Splawn, A. J. *KA-MI-AKIN: Last Hero of the Yakimas*. Portland, OR: Metropolitan Press, 1944.
Utley, Robert M. *Frontiersmen in Blue: The United States and the Indian, 1848–1865*. Lincoln: University of Nebraska Press, 1967.

Kan-dazis-tlishishen

See Mangas Coloradas

Karankawas

Name for a number of Native American tribes—probably five or more loosely related bands—that lived on the Texas coast until they became extinct around 1850. The specific area that they inhabited was the coastline roughly between western Galveston Bay and just north of present-day Corpus Christi. At their most numerous, the Karankawas probably never exceeded 10,000 in number.

The Texas coast is a flat low-lying region protected by a string of barrier islands. Numerous rivers flow into its bays of Galveston, Matagorda, Aransas, and Corpus Christi. The natives who settled along these rivers from Galveston to Corpus Christi comprised the groups of the Karankawas. They were the Charrucos, the Hans, the Deguenes, the Carancaquacas (Karankawas), the Guaycones, the Quitoles, the Camolas, and possibly the so-called Fig People. The Karankawas spoke an unusual language that may have been originally related to Caribi.

The Karankawas were nonsedentary hunter-gatherers who also planted small gardens. Living in wigwamlike structures, they moved from place to place in large dugout canoes to search for food. They engaged in ritualistic ceremonies (*mitotes*) during which they drank an intoxicant brewed from the yaupon plant. Their worship was centered on the sun, to which they gave homage when it disappeared at sunset.

The Karankawas were not well organized politically. Leadership was not inherited but instead was earned by merit, often through battle. The Karankawas employed the longbow for both hunting and battle. They acquired a reputation for cannibalism, probably from the ritualistic or magical practice of eating the flesh of a dead enemy.

The first European encounter with the Karankawas came in 1532, when survivors of a Spanish expedition into the Florida Panhandle originally led by Pánfilo de Narváez were cast ashore. Álvar Núñez Cabeza de Vaca, a member of the expedition, lived among the Karankawas for six years as a captive. He eventually returned to Spanish territory, and his report provides the most extensive information available on the Karankawas.

After the Spaniards, the French were the next Europeans to encounter the Karankawas, specifically René-Robert Cavelier, Sieur de La Salle, who visited in 1685 and established Fort St. Louis along Garcitas Creek on the edge of Matagorda Bay. Relations between the French and the Karankawas quickly turned violent, and the natives killed the French settlers, ending this attempt at a permanent settlement.

In 1722 the Spanish established a presidio, Nuestra Señora de Loreto, and a mission on the ruins of the French fort. However, Spanish efforts to convert and pacify the Karankawas failed. In 1754 the mission of Nuestra Señora del Rosario was established at what soon became known as Goliad. Again the Karankawas resisted efforts to convert them. Undeterred, the Spanish erected the mission Nuestra Señora del Refugio in 1791 near the mouth of the Mission River. It too experienced little success.

In 1817 the privateer Jean Lafitte fought with the Karankawas, inflicting heavy losses on them. Stephen F. Austin, the Texas colonial leader, led a force against the Karankawas in 1825. By 1850 or so, disease, hostile actions by other tribes, and white encroachment resulted in the extermination of the Karankawas.

ANDREW J. WASKEY

See also

La Salle, René-Robert Cavelier, Sieur de; Narváez, Pánfilo de; Spain

References

Gatschet, Albert S. *The Karankawa Indians: The Coast People of Texas.* Millwood, NY: Kraus Reprints, 1974.

Ricklis, Robert A. *The Karankawa Indians of Texas: An Ecological Study of Culture Tradition and Change.* Austin: University of Texas Press, 1996.

Kearny, Stephen Watts
Birth Date: August 30, 1794
Death Date: October 31, 1848

Career U.S. Army officer and commander of the Army of the West during the Mexican-American War (1846–1848). Stephen Watts Kearny was born on August 30, 1794, in Newark, New Jersey, one of fifteen children. His father was a prosperous merchant, but much of his wealth was confiscated as a result of his support for the Loyalists during the American Revolutionary War (1775–1783). Kearny attended school in Newark and was admitted to Columbia College in 1811.

The War of 1812 cut his college career short, as Kearny joined the army in March 1812. He demonstrated great bravery in the Battle of Queenston Heights (October 13, 1812), during which he was captured; he was subsequently released in a prisoner exchange with the British. Beginning in 1819, he served almost exclusively on the western frontier and rose rapidly through the ranks. In 1820 Kearny made an exploratory march through the upper Midwest, during which he kept a detailed diary. He achieved literary fame posthumously when the diary was published in book form 88 years later.

During the late 1820s and early 1830s, Kearny was responsible for establishing numerous forts throughout the West, including Jefferson Barracks, Fort Des Moines, and what would later be called Fort Kearny in present-day Nebraska. In 1825 he made an expedition to the edge of Yellowstone, and in 1828 he assumed command of Fort Crawford in present-day Wisconsin. He was promoted to major in 1829, and in 1833 he was made lieutenant colonel of the 1st Dragoons. In 1836 he was transferred to Fort Leavenworth, Kansas, and promoted to colonel. Throughout his travels and expeditions, he made detailed notes of his dealings with Native Americans. By the early 1840s, Kearny had ordered small military units under his command to escort white settlers and travelers along the Oregon Trail. Kearny's decision became de facto government policy for many years.

At the beginning of the Mexican-American War, Kearny received command of the Army of the West. In June 1846 he and

U.S. Army career officer Stephen Watts Kearny established many forts throughout the West in the 1820s and 1830s. He commanded the Army of the West during the Mexican-American War and was in part responsible for the U.S. victory in California. He served for a time as California's military governor. (Library of Congress)

a force of 1,660 men departed Fort Leavenworth and headed west. Their goal was to assist in the conquest of California. Kearny's force took Santa Fe, New Mexico, on August 18, 1846, without resistance. President James K. Polk advanced Kearny to brigadier general and ordered him to proceed to California to augment U.S. forces there. Leaving most of his force behind to garrison New Mexico, Kearny set out on September 25 with some 300 men. On October 6 he encountered Lieutenant Christopher "Kit" Carson, who informed Kearny, incorrectly, that California had already been conquered. As a result of this misinformation, Kearny sent two-thirds of his men back to Santa Fe and continued on with only 121 men.

On December 6, 1846, shortly after his arrival in California, Kearny attacked a force of Californios (Spanish-speaking inhabitants of California) northeast of San Diego, but the Californios inflicted heavy losses on Kearny's forces in the ensuing Battle of San Pascual. Kearny himself was badly wounded in the fighting.

His escape route blocked, Kearny sent word to San Diego for help and a relief column was quickly dispatched, so that he and his men were able to continue on to San Diego. There he joined forces with new Pacific Squadron commander Commodore Robert F. Stockton, and they proceeded to Los Angeles, winning two victories on the way: the Battle of San Gabriel on January 8 and the Battle of La Mesa on January 9. On January 13, 1847, the Mexican governor surrendered California.

There now immediately arose the question of who was in charge of California: Kearny or U.S. Mounted Rifles lieutenant colonel John C. Frémont, who had accepted the surrender. Frémont claimed that Stockton had named him California's military governor. Kearny, who outranked Frémont, sent word to Washington, D.C., about the impasse. Washington backed Kearny, and Frémont was subsequently tried and convicted of insubordination. Kearny served as military governor for three months before turning over authority to Colonel Richard Barnes Mason.

In 1847 Kearny became civil governor of Veracruz, Mexico, and for a time governor of Mexico City. In September 1848 he received a brevet to major general. While in Veracruz, however, he caught a fever—most likely malaria—and, after returning to St. Louis, died there on October 31, 1848.

CRAIG CHOISSER

See also
Carson, Christopher Houston; Frémont, John Charles; Oregon Trail

References
Clarke, Dwight L. *Stephen Watts Kearny: Soldier of the West.* Norman: University of Oklahoma Press, 1961.
Von Sachsen Altenberg, Hans, and Laura Gabiger. *Winning the West: Stephen Watts Kearny's Letter Book, 1846–1847.* Boonville, MO: Pekitanoui Publications, 1998.

Keepers of the Eastern and Western Doors

Important largely symbolic metaphors involving the Iroquois Confederacy's political system and its relations with the outside world. According to Mohawk legend, the Iroquois Confederacy emerged after an extended period of struggle and warfare that engulfed the region encompassing present-day New York state and its peripheral areas. Tired of the senseless and destructive violence, Deganawida, the son of a Huron virgin, traversed the Great Lakes region from present-day Canada to New York preaching a message of peace and enlisting followers. As a result of his efforts and those of an Iroquois convert named Ayonhwathah (Hiawatha), the Mohawk, Oneida, Onondaga, Seneca, and Cayuga tribes formed the Great League of Peace, also known as the Iroquois Confederacy.

To maintain the Great League of Peace, the confederation members created a political system with several levels of government based on their social structures. Essentially, six levels of authority existed: fireside, longhouse, clan, settlement, tribe, and league. Additionally, two spheres of control existed: the outside (international) world and the inside (domestic) world. In both worlds, the concepts and reality of family, obligation, and peace stood at the heart of all levels of government.

The Iroquois viewed the Great League of Peace as a large metaphorical longhouse, with the Mohawks as the protectors of the Eastern Door, the Senecas the protectors of the Western Door, and the Onondagas the symbolic center and location of the sacred fire. Like the longhouse, the league operated on the premise of familial relationships, and the apparatus of government, the Council of Elders, existed as the forum by which to maintain the Great League of Peace.

The role of doorkeeper for both the Mohawks and the Senecas proved both symbolic and real and involved the political, military, and economic affairs of the Iroquois Confederacy. In a symbolic sense, the confederation charged the doorkeepers with the protection of the league from the outer world. In reality, however, although the principles of peace and consensus influenced the confederacy, each of the nations acted independently of one another. Occupying fairly specific geographic locations on the peripheries of the confederation, the Mohawks and the Senecas enjoyed access to the outer world. The other nations remained relatively distant from external happenings because of their positions within the metaphorical longhouse. As the doorkeepers, the Mohawks and Senecas essentially directed and influenced the international affairs of the confederacy. On more than one occasion, for instance, the Mohawks acted independently of the league and significantly altered the political world of New York, as was the case when they chose to go to war with the Mahicans over the lucrative Dutch trade along the Hudson River.

Because of their positions, the Mohawks and Senecas empowered themselves within the confederation by acting as middlemen in an elaborate trade network that stretched from the Atlantic seaboard to Lake Michigan and involved European colonists, Iroquois, and western Great Lakes tribes. Likewise, the two doorkeepers found themselves acting as the confederacy's liaison with many western and southern Native American nations who were at odds with the Hurons and the Iroquois themselves. Subsequently, in conjunction with the Onondagas, the Mohawks and the Senecas enjoyed much political influence both inside and outside the confederation, in large measure because of their positions as the Keepers of the Eastern and Western Doors.

JOSEPH P. ALESSI

See also

Iroquois Confederacy; Mohawks; Senecas

References

Morgan, Lewis H. *League of the Ho-de-no-sau-nee or Iroquois.* New York: Dodd, Mead, 1901.

Richter, Daniel K. *The Ordeal of the Longhouse: The People of the Iroquois League in the Era of European Colonization.* Chapel Hill: University of North Carolina Press, 1992.

Snow, Dean R. *The Iroquois.* Malden, MA: Blackwell, 1994.

Kelly, Luther Sage
Birth Date: July 27, 1849
Death Date: December 17, 1928

Soldier, frontiersman, scout, and Indian agent. Luther Sage Kelly, widely known as "Yellowstone Kelly," was born in Geneva, New York, on July 27, 1849. At the age of 16 he enlisted in the U.S. Army

as the American Civil War was about to end. Kelly was ordered to the West and, after his discharge, began hunting and trapping in the Yellowstone River Valley of Montana.

Kelly was soon taken with the natural beauty of the region and befriended a band of Lakotas (Sioux), in the process learning their language. He also began acting as an army scout and courier. In 1873 he scouted during an expedition to the geyser hot springs in Yellowstone Park, which is likely how he earned his nickname. Impressed with Kelly's knowledge of Native Americans and of the region, Colonel Nelson A. Miles tapped Kelly to be his lead scout. Serving in that capacity from 1876 to 1878, Kelly served Miles during his campaigns in the Great Sioux War (1876–1877) and the Nez Perce War (1877). He also saw action during the Battle of Wolf Mountains and the Battle of the Tongue River and participated in the Ute War in 1880 and in the pursuit of the Nez Perces.

Upon Miles's recommendation, Kelly next served as a clerk for the War Department, first in Chicago; next on Governor's Island, New York; and finally in Washington, D.C. Beginning in 1898 he scouted on two army expeditions to Alaska and also served as a captain of volunteers during the Philippine-American War (1899–1902). In 1904 Kelly became the Indian agent at the San Carlos Reservation (Arizona), a post he held until 1908. He returned to for a time to Montana, where he hunted and trapped. He later retired to California and wrote a popular book titled *Yellowstone Kelly: The Memoirs of Luther S. Kelly* (1926). Kelly died near Paradise, California, on December 17, 1928. He was buried near the summit of Kelly's Mountain near Billings, Montana, overlooking the land that he had explored, scouted, and loved.

PAUL G. PIERPAOLI JR.

See also

Crazy Horse; Joseph, Chief; Lakota Sioux; Miles, Nelson Appleton; Nez Perce War; San Carlos Reservation; Sitting Bull; Ute War; Wolf Mountains, Battle of

References

Keenan, Jerry. *The Life of Yellowstone Kelly.* Albuquerque: University of New Mexico Press, 2006.

Wooster, Robert. *Nelson A. Miles and the Twilight of the Frontier Army.* Lincoln: University of Nebraska Press, 1993.

Keokuk
Birth Date: ca. 1780
Death Date: 1848

Sauk chieftain. Keokuk was born probably in 1780 near present-day Rock Island, Illinois. He was known as Watchful Fox and led the faction that sought cooperation with the United States as the best way to protect the Sauk people against white expansion. Although he was not a hereditary civil chief, Keokuk rose in prominence because of his leadership in battle and his considerable oratorical skills. His main political rival among the Sauks was Black Hawk, who advocated traditional styles of Indian warfare to

Sauk chief Keokuk (ca. 1780–1848) led the faction of his people who sought accommodation with the whites as the best way to prevent further encroachment on Sauk tribal lands. (Smithsonian American Art Museum, Washington, DC/Art Resource, NY)

protect Sauk honor and land, a practice that would contribute to the outbreak of the Black Hawk War (1832).

In 1831 when U.S. forces under Major General Edmund P. Gaines were ordered to drive the Sauks out of their village of Saukenok and across the Mississippi River, Keokuk managed to convince most of his people to abandon their lands and flee to safety. He even sought—but was denied—a presidential audience in an attempt to ensure peace with the United States. Nevertheless war broke out, and Black Hawk blamed Keokuk for failing to resist removal in 1831 and for continuing to advocate cooperation with the United States during the war.

Following the defeat of Black Hawk's followers in 1832, Major General Winfield Scott proclaimed Keokuk to be the primary civil chief of the Sauks. Since Keokuk did not belong to the ruling clan, this decision was poorly received. In the ensuing 1832 Treaty of Fort Armstrong, Keokuk had little choice but to cede most of eastern Iowa to the United States. He remained the recognized chief of the Sauk Nation until his death near Franklin County, Kansas, in 1848.

CAMERON B. STRANG

See also

Black Hawk; Black Hawk War; Gaines, Edmund Pendleton; Sauks and Foxes; Scott, Winfield

References

Eby, Cecil. *"That Disgraceful Affair": The Black Hawk War.* New York: Norton, 1973.

Nichols, Roger L. *Black Hawk and the Warrior's Path.* Arlington Heights, IL: Harlan Davidson, 1992.

Kickapoos

Native American group first encountered by Europeans in the Green Bay region (present-day Wisconsin). The Kickapoo tribe belongs to the Algonquian linguistic group. The name "Kickapoo" means "he who moves about, standing now here, now there." This title is borne out by the movements of the Kickapoos, who changed geographic locations several times during the 17th and 18th centuries. Nevertheless, the Kickapoos exhibited a great deal of closely guarded cultural homogeneity. Although they were often forced into contacts with various Europeans, the Kickapoos consistently remained hostile and aloof. They were chiefly agriculturalists who also engaged in seasonal buffalo hunts.

The Kickapoos probably originated in the area of southeastern Michigan and northwestern Ohio. They were forced to relocate in present-day Wisconsin as a result of their involvement in the Beaver Wars (1641–1701). It was during their residence in Wisconsin that the Kickapoos first appeared in French records. In the first decades of the 18th century, they moved into what is now central Illinois, near present-day Peoria. Between 1729 and 1749 the Kickapoos split into two distinct groups. The tribe separated in an effort to make itself less vulnerable to a single large-scale enemy attack.

Culturally the Kickapoos were conservative, and they repeatedly shunned any efforts to assimilate into European culture. Such was the case even after trade with the French made assimilation almost imperative for their survival. Part of their conservatism stemmed from their small size, as the tribe never exceeded 3,000 in number. The Kickapoos' social organization was clan-centered and patrilineal, with descent traced through the father.

The Kickapoos vigorously resisted interactions with Europeans but often formed alliances with other Native American tribes. In 1685, for example, the Kickapoos formed a confederacy with the Foxes and several other tribes. The purpose of the alliance was to resist incursions by the Sioux. Indeed, the Kickapoos remained important allies of the Foxes during the Fox Wars (1712–1737).

Later the Kickapoos switched allegiance, becoming a French ally and turning against the Foxes. The Kickapoos continued in their alliance with the French, eventually fighting against the British in the French and Indian War (1754–1763). Members of the Vermillion Kickapoos took part in the siege of Fort William Henry in 1757. As a result of these activities, they were infected with smallpox, which they brought back to their villages that winter.

Almost immediately following the French defeat in the conflict, the Kickapoos took part in Pontiac's Rebellion (1763) and remained hostile toward the British longer than many other tribes in the Midwest. When Kickapoo resistance to British domination finally ended, it came not by way of military force but rather

An 1869 print showing a group of Kickapoo Indians that were presented in 1865 to Emperor Maximilian of Mexico. (Library of Congress)

because of the efforts of the frontier diplomat and trader George Croghan, whom the Kickapoos had captured in a raid.

The Kickapoos joined Little Turtle's War (1785–1795) against the United States, participated in Tecumseh's Pan-Indian rebellion in the early 1800s, and waged war against the United States during the War of 1812. In 1819 after being forced to cede their territory in Illinois to white settlers, the tribe moved to Missouri. Two bands, however, would not leave Illinois, and they waged a low-level conflict against white settlers from 1819 to 1831. These same bands joined the Sauks and Foxes in the Black Hawk War (1832). In 1832 the Missouri Kickapoos were driven out of Missouri and into northeastern Kansas. One Kickapoo band joined the Cherokees in Texas.

In 1839 the Texas Kickapoos were relocated to the Choctaw Reservation in Indian Territory (Oklahoma). In 1851 they left the reservation for Mexico. Another Kickapoo band that had gone to Texas joined the Creeks in Indian Territory, but that group also left for Mexico.

After several years of border skirmishes, the Kickapoos in Mexico were defeated in 1873 by Colonel Ranald Mackenzie and were forced to move to Indian Territory, where they were given a small reservation in 1883. Ten years later the reservation was closed, and individual Kickapoos received an allotment of 80 acres. Today there is still a small tribe in Texas as well as a tribe in Oklahoma.

JAMES R. McINTYRE

See also

Algonquins; Black Hawk War; Croghan, George; Fox Wars; French and Indian War; Mackenzie, Ranald Slidell; Mesquakies; Pontiac's Rebellion; Sauks and Foxes; Tecumseh

References

Anderson, Fred. *Crucible of War: The Seven Years' War and the Fate of the Empire in British North America, 1754–1766.* New York: Vintage Books, 2001.

Neilson, George R. *The Kickapoo People.* Phoenix, AZ: Indian Tribal Series, 1975.

Kieft, Willem
Birth Date: ca. 1600
Death Date: September 27, 1647

Director general (governor) of New Netherland (the Dutch West India Company) from 1638 to 1646. Willem Kieft was born around 1600 in the Netherlands. Little is known of his early years, although he had apparently suffered serious financial problems that led to bankruptcy before he left Europe for New Amsterdam. The Dutch West India Company had apparently learned little following the failures of the previous director general, Wouter von Twiller.

Kieft arrived in New Amsterdam in March 1638 and was not pleased with the settlement that he found there. Indeed, he complained of the crumbling fort and the shoddy houses that surrounded it. Kieft subsequently oversaw repairs to the fort and the construction in 1642 of the Stadt Huys (City Hall), which was a place where visitors could be entertained. He also ordered the construction of a church within the already-cramped Fort Amsterdam, against the wishes of the people.

Kieft encouraged English settlers who were being persecuted in New England for religious reasons to settle in New Netherland. English settlers became so numerous in New Amsterdam that an official translator had to be employed. Nevertheless, Kieft was wary of English encroachment on Dutch territory and watched with consternation as English settlements grew in Connecticut, just to the east. He also tried to dissuade former New Netherland governor Peter Minuit from establishing a settlement in 1638 for the Swedes on the Delaware River (near present-day Wilmington, Delaware).

Although Kieft had officially prohibited the sale of guns or gunpowder to Native Americans, the Dutch settlers could not resist the opportunity to make money by such ventures. They were indeed quite pleased to receive 20 beaver skins for a single firearm. Hoping for more money for his coffers, Kieft hatched a scheme to charge local natives a tax for protection by Dutch soldiers. When the natives balked at this, Kieft retaliated against the Raritan tribe for an incident involving a hog theft. As tensions ran high, the murder of a Dutchman by a Wickquasgeck warrior precipitated a full-scale war.

In February 1643 Kieft ordered the massacre of two groups of nonhostile Wickquasgecks who had camped near New Amsterdam seeking shelter from the Mohawks. The conflict that this action initiated became known as Kieft's War (1639–1645), which cost many lives and much destruction of property. Kieft's growing unpopularity was a direct result of the war and of his stubborn rejection of any compromise. In 1647 Kieft was ordered to return to Holland and account for his actions, including his policy toward the Native Americans. His ship sailed from New Amsterdam on August 17, 1647. Off the coast of England on September 27 a storm sent the vessel onto a rocky shoal, and most of the passengers, including Kieft, perished. Petrus (Peter) Stuyvesant replaced Kieft as director general.

RICHARD PANCHYK

See also
Dutch-Indian Wars; Kieft's War; Mohawks; Stuyvesant, Petrus

References
Ellis, Edward Robb. *The Epic of New York City.* New York: Kodansha America, 1997.
Lyman, Susan Elizabeth. *The Story of New York: An Informal History of the City.* New York: Crown, 1975.
Shorto, Russell. *The Island at the Center of the World: The Epic Story of Dutch Manhattan and the Forgotten Colony That Shaped America.* New York: Doubleday, 2004.

Kieft's War
Start Date: 1639
End Date: August 1645

Conflict largely conducted in the vicinity of New Amsterdam and precipitated by a massacre of Native Americans under orders of Dutch governor Willem Kieft. Kieft's War is also known as Governor Kieft's War and Willem Kieft's War. Since the founding of New Amsterdam in 1624, relations with local Native Americans had been mostly peaceful. This changed, however, when Kieft became director general (governor) of New Netherland in 1638. Kieft first provoked the Raritan tribe, allegedly in retaliation for their theft of pigs on Staten Island. In response, the Raritans burned a Dutch farmhouse and killed four Dutch settlers.

In the summer of 1641 a Wickquasgeck tribesman showed up at the door of a wheelwright named Claes Smit, who lived a few miles north of New Amsterdam. The tribesman pretended to be interested in buying cloth but then killed Smit in revenge for the murder of the tribesman's uncle in 1625. Kieft demanded that the Wickquasgecks produce the killer at once and hand him over to Dutch officials. They refused to comply.

In August 1641 Kieft assembled the citizens of the town to appoint an advisory council of 12 men to deal with the brewing Native American crisis. The questions facing the committee were fourfold. Should the Dutch seek revenge for the murderer of Smit; should the natives' whole village be destroyed in the process; how and when should retaliation be exacted; and who should conduct such an endeavor? Kieft's hope was that the council would simply draft plans for a war that he himself had already been plotting. To his dismay, however, the council was not so eager to engage in warfare.

The council's response to Kieft's questions was a diplomatic one. The council did agree that force should be used if necessary, but its petition recommended a careful course of action. The council also seemed to understand the position that Kieft was trying to put them in, so its members cleverly replied that since he was director general, he must lead the way in any plan of attack. The councilmen did favor continuing to advise Kieft, however. Angry at the council's response, Kieft issued a decree thanking its members for their help but forbidding the 12 councilmen from meeting again.

On February 25, 1643, Kieft ordered Dutch soldiers to attack two groups of unsuspecting Wickquasgecks at Corlaer's Hook (Manhattan) and Pavonia (New Jersey). The natives had encamped at those spots from points north seeking refuge from the Mohawks, their adversaries. That evening the former leader of the advisory council, David de Vries, tried in vain to convince Kieft of the folly of his plan, even as the soldiers prepared for attack. The raid went ahead, and more than 100 natives were massacred while they slept. Although Kieft's order specified that women and children be spared, such was not the case.

In his journal De Vries recorded the vicious brutality directed against the natives, reporting that he could hear the screams of

New Netherland governor Willem Kieft discusses the terms of a peace treaty with Native American tribal leaders at Fort Amsterdam in 1645. The treaty ended Kieft's War (1639–1645). (Library of Congress)

victims at Pavonia. He wrote that the Native Americans were "massacred in a manner to move the heart of a stone." The colonists were not happy that Kieft had gone against their wishes. Indeed, they knew that a state of war with the natives would seriously affect the fur trade, as they did not trap animals themselves but instead relied on Native Americans as their main source for furs.

Safety was also a major concern for the Dutch colonists. Despite orders to the contrary, Dutch settlers had continued to trade and sell guns and gunpowder to various native tribes. As the conflict expanded beyond the Wickquasgeck tribe that Kieft had ordered attacked, the colonists realized that their forces were badly outnumbered by Native American warriors by about 1,500 to 200. Native warriors killed colonists all over New Netherland, also destroying their homes, crops, and livestock. Safety could only be found within and around the walls of the crumbling Fort Amsterdam, whereas the farms in outlying areas to the north were constant targets of nighttime strikes by natives. An appeal for help to the English settlement at New Haven was rebuffed.

Natives murdered the recently arrived Anne Hutchinson (a refugee from Massachusetts) and six of her children on isolated land in the Bronx that Kieft had given her. The settlement at Mespat (in present-day Queens) was wiped out during Kieft's War, and

the village's founder, the Reverend Francis Doughty, fled to New Amsterdam. A settlement across the North (Hudson) River in present-day New Jersey was decimated. Gravesend in present-day Brooklyn came under native attack but was not destroyed.

The fighting continued into 1644. As the war became more expensive and destructive, it nearly bankrupted the colony. Kieft proposed levying taxes on beaver skins and beer, to the outrage of citizens.

The tide turned in 1644 when the Dutch hired English mercenaries led by Captain John Underhill. Combining his men with newly arrived Dutch forces, he raided a Native American settlement in Connecticut at night, killing hundreds. Hundreds more natives were slain soon after in another raid north of Manhattan Island. Beginning in April 1644, Underhill led skirmishes on Long Island, and his men killed more than 100 natives at Massapequa.

Finally, by the summer of 1645 both sides were ready to end the bloodshed, and a peace treaty was negotiated in August 1645. Kieft and the representatives of several native tribes held a ceremony in front of Fort Amsterdam to mark the end of hostilities. The terms of the peace treaty stated that the Dutch would stay away from Native American settlements and that armed natives were not allowed to approach Dutch settlements.

The fallout from the war was significant. Most of the farms in Manhattan had been damaged or destroyed during the war, leaving only a scant few unharmed. In the colonists' minds, the war erased any good that Kieft may have done while governor. Indeed, a petition of grievances against Kieft was smuggled to Holland in the autumn of 1644 that ultimately resulted in his ouster in 1647.

RICHARD PANCHYK

See also

Dutch-Indian Wars; Kieft, Willem; Underhill, John

References

Ellis, Edward Robb. *The Epic of New York City*. New York: Kodansha America, 1997.

Innes, J. H. *New Amsterdam and Its People: Studies, Social and Topographical, of the Town under Dutch and Early English Rule*. Princeton, NJ: Princeton University Press, 1902.

Lyman, Susan Elizabeth. *The Story of New York: An Informal History of the City*. New York: Crown, 1975.

Shorto, Russell. *The Island at the Center of the World: The Epic Story of Dutch Manhattan and the Forgotten Colony That Shaped America*. New York: Doubleday, 2004.

Trelease, Allen W. *Indian Affairs in Colonial New York: The Seventeenth Century*. Ithaca, NY: Cornell University Press, 1960.

Killdeer Mountain, Battle of
Event Date: July 28, 1864

A clash between 2,200 soldiers of the U.S. Volunteers commanded by Brigadier General Alfred Sully and 1,800 Sioux warriors (Dakota, Yanktonai, and Lakota) that occurred on July 28, 1864, near present-day Killdeer, North Dakota. The clash is also known as the Battle of Tahkahokuty Mountain. It was the culmination of two years of fighting that began when angry warriors attacked Minnesota settlements in response to treaty violations. The battle broke the back of Sioux resistance in the area.

When Brigadier General Henry Hastings Sibley, the former Minnesota governor, pushed the hostile Sioux west into Dakota Territory, residents there demanded protection. Major General John Pope, commander of the Department of the Northwest, responded with force. On September 3, 1863, Sully's forces routed the Sioux at the Battle of Whitestone Hill. Despite the victory, Native American frontier raids continued.

In 1864 Pope ordered Sully to establish a string of forts in Dakota Territory while simultaneously crushing the troublesome Sioux. Sully's 1st Brigade (also known as the Missouri River Brigade), marching northward along the Missouri from Sioux City, Iowa, included 4 companies of Minnesota cavalry led by Major Alfred B. Brackett, 11 companies of the 6th Iowa Cavalry under Lieutenant Colonel John Pattee, 3 companies of the 7th Iowa Cavalry, 2 companies of Dakota Cavalry led by Captain Nelson Miner, 1 company of Nebraska scouts (with Native American allies), and 1 Prairie Battery of four howitzers commanded by Captain Nathaniel Pope. The 2nd Brigade (also known as the Minnesota Brigade),

commanded by Colonel Minor Thomas, marched westward from Fort Ridgely in Minnesota with most of the 8th Minnesota Infantry (mounted), 6 companies of the 6th Minnesota Cavalry, 2 sections of the 3rd Minnesota Battery, and some 40 scouts. The two columns met on the Missouri in early July.

On July 7, 1864, Sully's men established Fort Rice at the mouth of the Cannonball River. On July 19 Sully's forces, accompanied by a caravan of 123 wagons destined for the Montana goldfields, left Fort Rice to engage hostile Native Americans who were massing between the Heart and Cannonball rivers. After detaching several hundred troops to guard the civilian trains and garrison Fort Rice, Sully marched with some 2,200 men in the two brigades. When scouts spotted the Sioux on July 28, Sully formed his soldiers in a phalanx, a hollow square that extended 1.25 miles on each side. In the middle of the formation Sully placed the artillery battery, wagons, and every fourth man holding four horses each.

A short time later Sully's force engaged the Sioux on the southern slopes of Killdeer Mountain. The Native Americans had selected the location for their camp based on the advice of the Santee leader Inkpaduta, who instructed his Lakota allies to retreat to the rugged Badlands for defensive purposes.

Spotting the advancing soldiers, Sioux warrior Long Dog led the attack. Despite the charges, Sully's phalanx held and pushed toward the Native American camp. Meanwhile, Captain Pope's artillery fire scattered the attackers. Major Brackett's Minnesota cavalry drove the Native Americans from the hills. Sergeant George W. Northrup, the "Kit Carson of the Northwest," and another soldier were killed during the battle. Sully estimated that 100–150 warriors died in the engagement, although the Indians claimed considerably fewer casualties.

The Native American survivors withdrew to the Badlands, a tangle of nearly impassable buttes and canyons. Believing that pursuit was too risky, Sully ordered the soldiers to destroy everything in the abandoned camp. By morning, only a few ponies and buffalo robes had been spared. Hostile activity in the area convinced Sully to return to Fort Rice. Tragically, the civilian wagon train pushed on without a military escort, only to be ambushed by Native Americans a short time later.

While the Battle of Killdeer Mountain scattered the hostile Dakota and Lakota bands and eliminated the imminent threat posed by the region's hostile tribes, the Sioux eventually regrouped and continued their efforts to drive encroaching settlers from the Dakota Territory.

JON L. BRUDVIG

See also

Dakota Sioux; Great Sioux War; Inkpaduta; Pope, John; Sully, Alfred; Sully-Sibley Campaigns; Whitestone Hill, Battle of

References

Sully, Langdon. *No Tears for the General: The Life of Alfred Sully, 1821–1879*. Palo Alto, CA: American West Publishing, 1974.

Utley, Robert M. *Frontiersmen in Blue: The United States and the Indian, 1848–1865*. Lincoln: University of Nebraska Press, 1967.

King George's War
Start Date: January 25, 1744
End Date: October 1748

One in the series of imperial wars of the 18th century involving Great Britain and France that spilled over from Europe to North America. In December 1740, taking advantage of the accession of young Austrian archduchess Maria Theresa to the Austrian throne, King Frederick II of Prussia initiated the First Silesian War, sending Prussian troops into Silesia and seizing that rich Austrian province. The major European powers took sides, and the conflict grew into what was later known as the War of the Austrian Succession (1740–1748). In the war France sided with Prussia, whereas Britain supported Austria. This situation was complicated by the Anglo-Spanish War (1739–1744), popularly known as the War of Jenkins' Ear. This war spread to North America and led to some clashes involving Spanish and British forces along the North Carolina, Georgia, and Florida coasts. As a consequence of the Second Family compact between France and Spain (October 23, 1743), France declared war on Britain on March 4, 1744, and King George II issued a counterdeclaration of war on March 29.

News of the declarations of war reached North America by the end of April. Perhaps wishing to steal a march on the British, the French began hostilities in North America, although neither side prosecuted the fighting there with great vigor. In May the French launched an attack from their great Cape Breton Island fortress of Louisbourg against Canso (Canseau), a small English fishing settlement in extreme northeastern Nova Scotia. The French took Canso without difficulty on May 13. The attack turned out to be a mistake in the sense that it fully alarmed New England.

A few weeks after the French took Canso, a French-allied Native American force appeared before Annapolis Royal (formerly Port Royal), Nova Scotia. The natives showed little inclination to attack a fortified position, even one defended by only about 100 men, and they soon withdrew on the arrival of 70 Massachusetts reinforcements. In August native warriors returned, this time with some French troops, but Massachusetts reinforcements again caused the attackers to depart.

Meanwhile, Governor William Shirley of Massachusetts prepared an expedition against the French fortress of Louisbourg on Cape Breton Island, an operation strongly supported by Massachusetts public opinion. Eliminating this important French base would, it was hoped, end French support for Native American attacks along the northern frontier. Also, Louisbourg was in times of peace the chief base for French fishing vessels, which were in direct competition with those of New England for the rich fishing grounds of the Grand Banks. In wartime, the harbor at Louisbourg served as the principal base for French privateers preying on New England merchant vessels as well as attacks on the British colonists' fishing boats. Exchanged British prisoners convinced Shirley that Louisbourg was undermanned and vulnerable to attack.

Other New England colonies sent men for the expeditionary force, although it was largely composed of citizens of Massachusetts. William Pepperell Jr. had command of the land force, which was supported by a British Royal Navy squadron. The force of some 100 ships of all sorts carrying 3,500 men arrived near Louisbourg at the end of April and captured the fortress on June 17. Although the Royal Navy had made possible the capture of Louisbourg through its effective blockade, Pepperell and the colonials justly received the credit for the victory, heralded as a remarkable achievement for a militia force and indeed certainly the greatest accomplishment of colonial arms before the American Revolutionary War (1775–1783). Many colonials falsely took this to mean that militia forces were superior to regular forces. A colonial force remained in garrison at Louisbourg, but dysentery, smallpox, and yellow fever claimed a high toll.

Governor Shirley meanwhile urged an immediate assault on Quebec in order to seize all of Canada. London approved the plan and even ordered the other colonial governors to cooperate. The British government also promised to pay for the troops raised and pledged to contribute a fleet and regular forces to meet the colonial force in Louisbourg. All the New England colonies plus New York, Maryland, and Virginia supplied troops. Mohawk warriors agreed to join as well. The colonial militia was in place by July 1746.

Unfortunately for the British colonists, the result was a repeat of 1709, as the British troops and ships were never sent. European considerations led to their diversion there. The assault on Canada was called off, and the colonial troops dispersed.

However, the French were not able to take advantage of London's quiescence. Recognizing the importance of Louisbourg to New France, the French mounted a considerable effort under Admiral Jean-Baptiste-Louis-Frédéric de la Rouchfoucauld de Roye, Duc d'Anville. The assembled force included 76 ships lifting 3,000 men with the goal of retaking Louisbourg and Annapolis Royal. The ships had a difficult three-month passage to America during which they were buffeted by hurricanes, and the men in the crowded ships fell prey to an outbreak of smallpox. On the fleet's arrival in American waters, d'Anville died of apoplexy. His successor attempted suicide and was in turn succeeded by the Marquis de la Jonquière, governor designate of New France. Before the fleet limped back to France, the infected troops inadvertently spread smallpox ashore among the Native Americans. The disease would exact a higher human toll on France's allies than the latter sustained in fighting during the entire war.

New Englanders had dared to believe that the capture of Louisbourg would bring an end to native attacks along the northern frontier, but this did not prove to be the case. Indeed, after the fall of Louisbourg, native attacks in Maine, New Hampshire, and Massachusetts actually increased. Early in 1744, the Massachusetts General Court ordered construction of four new posts along the Connecticut River. These became Fort Shirley, Fort Pelham, Fort Massachusetts, and Fort at Number Four. Massachusetts also sent 440 militiamen to guard the northwestern frontier. These efforts came none too soon, for in July 1745 natives attacked the Great Meadow Fort in present-day Putney, Vermont, and St. George's Fort in present-day Thomaston, Maine.

In this activity the Six Nations of the Iroquois Confederacy occupied an important position because of their geographical location and influence. Ever since King William's War (1689–1697), the Iroquois had generally pursued a policy of neutrality. Throughout the war, the Iroquois position shifted based on self-interest. Clearly they did not trust the British. Fearful that they would be left in the lurch, during the war the Iroquois tilted somewhat toward the French.

A number of the raids against the British originated from the French-built Fort St. Frédéric at Crown Point near the south end of Lake Champlain. The fort served as a major post for attacks against British settlements in upper New York and New England. In November 1745 Lieutenant Paul Marin led a sizable party from Fort St. Frédéric consisting of some 520 Frenchmen, Iroquois, Nipissings, Wyandots (Hurons), and Abenakis and even a priest.

Marin's objective was the English agricultural community of Saratoga, New York. Located on the west bank of the Hudson River some 30 miles above Albany, Saratoga boasted a fort, but the fort was both poorly maintained and lacked a regular garrison. The raiders struck at night and achieved total surprise, setting fire to the fort, homes, farms, and mills. The raiders then withdrew, taking with them 109 prisoners as well as significant stocks of supplies. They arrived back at Crown Point on November 22.

The Saratoga raid had a devastating effect on morale in the British settlements of the upper Hudson River Valley. Most settlers simply abandoned their homes and fled south. There were even fears that Albany might be attacked next.

During the spring of 1746 British settlements between the Kennebec and Penobscot rivers in Maine came under native attack. In April 1746 natives struck at Fort at Number Four on the Connecticut River, located at present-day Charlestown, New Hampshire, but were driven back. The natives struck there again, twice in May and again in June. Attacks occurred all along the New York frontier. In August a strong 700-man French and native raid occurred against Fort Massachusetts on the upper Hoosick River only 25 miles east of Albany. There were only 29 people at the post, of whom 21 were men, but they held out until their ammunition supply ran low. The attackers took them all prisoner and then burned the fort. The colonial governments found it impossible to protect the thinly spread frontier population against such attacks. Those settlers who chose to remain did so at a high degree of risk. They might be killed in the fields or taken prisoner, their possessions seized or destroyed.

The situation for the British in Nova Scotia seemed particularly precarious. French forces were located nearby at Beaubassin on Chignecto Bay, and the Acadian population of Nova Scotia sought to maintain a neutral stance. At the Acadian village of Grand Pré, English colonel Arthur Noble commanded a 500-man garrison.

In early January 1747 Antoine Coulon de Villiers led a force of 200 Canadians from Beaubassin. The ground was covered with snow, and the attackers had to resort to snowshoes and sledges. Gathering native and Acadian recruits as they proceeded, this French and native force arrived at Grand Pré at the end of the month. With a snowstorm arriving, Noble's men were caught unawares. Noble and several other officers were killed in the initial assault. After a fight lasting several hours and with 80 British dead and an equal number wounded, both sides agreed to terms by which the British soldiers were allowed to withdraw to Annapolis Royal. The French did not control northern Nova Scotia for long. Soon they too departed, and Grand Pré was reoccupied by a strong Massachusetts force.

In April 1747 Ensign Boucher de Niverville led a French force of perhaps 700 men against British forts along the Connecticut River. They attacked Fort at Number Four, but after a three-day siege they gave up and withdrew. At London's request, British colonial leaders gathered a large force of more than 3,000 militiamen and Iroquois at Albany in the spring of 1747. But with pay late in arriving from England and with unrest growing among various colonial factions, the troops were dismissed in July 1747.

The French attacked Saratoga again in late June 1747 with a mixed force of 500–600 men. In the attack the British suffered 15 casualties. Forty-nine men were also captured before English reinforcements arrived from Albany. However, the New Yorkers decided that the fort at Saratoga was too costly to maintain and too vulnerable to attack. They burned the fort and abandoned the site.

Fighting along the frontier continued into 1748, with attacks by the British near Crown Point and near Fort at Number Four. The French struck twice near Fort Dummer and another time near Schenectady, New York. British efforts to mollify their Native American allies continued as colonial leaders held a third Iroquois congress at Albany in July 1748. There the Iroquois declared themselves ready to fight but also expressed disappointment with the failure to attack Quebec in 1747. In the meantime, other Native American tribes' relations with the British colonists grew even more strained.

Both sides engaged in considerable privateering activity during the war. Mostly this consisted of seizures of merchant vessels, but occasionally there were hit-and-run attacks on coastal settlements. A Rhode Island privateer attacked and sacked a Spanish town in northern Cuba, and the Spanish raided coastal settlements in South Carolina and Georgia. In 1747 the Spanish even raided Beaufort, near Cape Lookout in North Carolina. The next year the Spanish attacked and held for a time the town of Brunswick, on the lower Cape Fear River. In 1747 French and Spanish privateers were active farther north, even penetrating some 60 miles up the Delaware River.

At the same time, however, the Royal Navy was actively reducing the French and Spanish fleets in European waters. The growing strength of the Royal Navy vis-à-vis its opponents boded ill for the French and Spanish in America, for this meant that reinforcements of men and supplies could not get through and that the British colonies' far larger population advantage would come into play. Indeed, shortages of goods forced the French into illicit trade with the enemy British colonists. This impacted relations with the Native Americans as well; they now often turned to the better-supplied British colonists to procure needed goods. Certainly the scarcity of trade goods contributed to the revolt of the Miami tribe in the Ohio Country in 1747 and helped strengthen the pro-British faction among the Choctaws.

The long war ended with the October 1748 Treaty of Aix-la-Chapelle. As far as America was concerned, the key provision was the restoration of colonial conquests. In December news reached New England, where the treaty was regarded as a great betrayal and a revelation of the disadvantage of being part of a worldwide empire. The colonists were incensed that Britain had returned Louisbourg, whereas the French had handed back Madras in India, which they had captured from the British. The colonists held as insufficient Parliament's reimbursement to New England of £235,000, most of which correctly went to Massachusetts, and a knighthood for Pepperell. The war claimed some 500 British colonists dead in the actual fighting. More than 1,100 others died from disease and exposure. About 350 Frenchmen died in the fighting, with at least 2,500 dead from disease. Native American casualties are unknown.

The war left both the French and British empires in North America intact. Some dared to hope that peace would last, but wiser heads predicted a return to fighting and a final showdown over which would dominate North America.

MARCIA SCHMIDT BLAINE AND SPENCER C. TUCKER

See also

Abenakis; France; Great Britain; Iroquois; Iroquois Confederacy; King William's War; Wyandots

References

Clark, Charles E. *The Eastern Frontier: The Settlement of Northern New England, 1610–1673.* New York: Knopf, 1970.

Leach, Douglas Edward. *Roots of Conflict: British Armed Forces and Colonial Americans, 1677–1763.* Chapel Hill: University of North Carolina Press, 1986.

Peckham, Howard Henry. *The Colonial Wars, 1689–1762.* Chicago: University of Chicago Press, 1964.

King of the Pamunkeys

See Opechancanough

King Philip's War

Start Date: June 20, 1675
End Date: October 1676

Last and deadliest general war between Native Americans and English colonists in southern New England. King Philip's War was named for the Wampanoag sachem Metacom, known to the colonists as King Philip. Tensions between natives and English colonists in southern New England had been building for years, driven by such incendiary subjects as land rights and the subjugation of natives to colonial law. While the colonies continued to grow in numbers and seize more and more land, the natives, devastated by European diseases, diminished in number with each passing year. By 1660 the colonists of Massachusetts Bay, Connecticut, Plymouth, and Rhode Island greatly outnumbered the native tribes remaining in the area.

In the midst of this native decline, Metacom, the son of the influential chief Massasoit, took control of the Wampanoag people on his brother Alexander's death in 1662. Metacom was not nearly as patient with the colonists as his father had been. Taken into court several times for breaking colonial law, Metacom had no great love for colonial authorities.

For several years it had been rumored that Metacom was secretly plotting with nearby tribes to attack the colonists. In January 1675 Metacom's former translator John Sassamon, who had become an informant for the colonial authorities in Plymouth, was found murdered shortly after warning Plymouth officials of Metacom's plan. In early June the Plymouth authorities accused, tried, and executed three Wampanoag warriors for the crime. In revenge, on June 20, 1675, Wampanoags attacked the town of Swansea in southwestern Plymouth Colony. The conflict spread rapidly thereafter, becoming known to history as King Philip's War.

A number of tribes—specifically the Pocasset, Sakonnet, and Nipmuck peoples—joined Metacom and the Wampanoags. Other tribes, such as the powerful Narragansetts, remained neutral, while still other tribes, especially many Christian groups, sided with the colonists. Traditional enmities between tribes trumped the natives' common complaints against the English.

In June 1675 militia forces of the United Colonies, hoping for a quick end to the fighting, tried to blockade Metacom and his followers on Rhode Island's Mount Hope peninsula. However, Metacom and his followers escaped via boats into nearby swamps. The colonial forces pursued him throughout July, but they were compelled to pull back when their ill-equipped and undertrained militiamen lost a number of skirmishes in the swamps. Although the natives were used to making their way across the swampy landscape of southern Rhode Island, the thick brush and marshy ground slowed the English and frustrated their efforts to bring the enemy into open battle. Instead the colonists found themselves the victims of frequent ambushes and traps. In late July, Metacom and his main force headed north to Nipmuck country, where on July 14 the Nipmucks had attacked Mendon, the first but not nearly the last Massachusetts Bay town struck.

In the autumn of 1675 the fighting shifted to the Connecticut River Valley. By then, Metacom's forces were attacking colonial towns across the length and width of the valley. The United Colonies sent troops west to protect the towns, deciding on a strategy that called for defending all the towns. Major John Pynchon, the

Colonists and Wampanoags battle during King Philip's War, 1675. (Library of Congress)

founder and majority landholder of Springfield, had charge of the western theater of operations.

The natives besieged Brookfield in August and quickly devastated Northfield and Deerfield. The militia companies did little better in the woods of western Massachusetts than they had in the swamps of Rhode Island. Natives ambushed Captain Richard Beers's 40-man company in September 1675. In one of the most infamous incidents of the war, Captain Thomas Lathrop and his company of 70 men from Essex County were ambushed while securing a wagon train of food from abandoned Deerfield. On September 19 Lathrop's men, many of whom had placed their muskets in carts in order to eat wild grapes along their route, were surprised by hundreds of warriors and ambushed alongside the banks of the Muddy Brook, since known as Bloody Brook. At least 60 colonists, including Lathrop, were slain.

The worst blow to the colonial cause came in October, when native forces attacked and destroyed much of the town of Springfield, the main settlement and military command center for the entire valley. Major Pynchon subsequently resigned his post as western commander to help in the rebuilding of Springfield, and Captain (later Major) Samuel Appleton took over. Appleton and his men soon shifted their attention away from the western theater.

In November 1675 the commissioners of the United Colonies, having evidence that the neutral Narragansett tribe was in fact aiding Metacom, decided on a preemptive strike against the Narragansett homeland. Massachusetts Bay, Plymouth, and Connecticut put an army of more than 1,000 men in the field against the Narragansetts, with Governor Josiah Winslow of Plymouth in overall command. Charged with making the Narragansetts live up to their treaty obligations, the army soon abandoned this goal and

decided to stage a preemptive attack on the strong Rhode Island tribe. The wintry conditions, although harsh, allowed the English to march over the now-frozen swamps, and the now-thin brush allowed them to see farther in the thick forests. In place by mid-December 1675, the army based itself at Wickford, Rhode Island, and fought a number of small skirmishes before attacking the Narragansetts' main fortified village in the middle of the Great Swamp.

With the help of a native traitor, the colonial army found and attacked the Narragansett fort on December 19, 1675. The fighting was at first indeterminate. However, Winslow's order to burn the village with hundreds of people still inside shelters turned the tide of the battle. Initial casualties were about 20 dead and 200 wounded on the colonial side. Estimates of native dead, largely from the fires, range from 600 to more than 1,000. Having destroyed the fort, the colonial force then limped back to its base in Wickford in the midst of a horrible winter storm in which many of the wounded died. The remainder of the colonial force, along with some fresh troops, tried to pursue the escaping Narragansetts in the infamous Hungry March during January and February 1676. Although many considered the Great Swamp Fight a decisive English victory, it did bring to Metacom a large number of committed Narragansett warriors bent on revenge.

Metacom had hoped to spend the winter months to the west, readying his men for the spring campaign. In order to do this he needed the cooperation of the mighty Mohawk tribe. However, instead of welcoming their fellow natives, the Mohawks took the opportunity to lash out at a weakened rival. In February, 300 Mohawk warriors attacked a winter camp of 500 of Metacom's men east of Albany and routed them. Other such attacks occurred. Metacom was now fighting a two-front war, which had more to do with his ultimate demise than did any other development. In the spring Metacom once again took to attacking colonial towns in the western Connecticut River Valley. The natives raided towns up and down the valley. Some, such as Sudbury in April 1676, were amazingly close to Boston (within 20 miles). Civilian inhabitants abandoned more than 12 towns as the frontier moved eastward. Yet the two-front fighting in which Metacom was now engaged as well as English superiority in numbers, changes in tactics and militia preparedness, and the increased use of native allies as scouts and guides all began to take their toll. The Fall's Fight of May 1676, when a large group of warriors was ambushed and many perished plunging to their deaths over a high waterfall, demonstrated this fact. In her famous captivity narrative, Mary Rowlandson of Lancaster noted that her captors were tiring of the fight, and their food and supplies were dwindling by the late spring of 1676.

By the summer of 1676 many Native Americans, with almost no food (most of the native fields and food caches had been destroyed by colonial troops), gave up the fight and surrendered. In July 1676 forces under Captain Benjamin Church captured Metacom's wife and son who, along with hundreds (if not thousands) of captured natives, were sold into slavery in the West Indies. Metacom slipped back to the vicinity of his Mount Hope, Rhode Island, home with his most faithful followers.

On August 12, 1676, a native warrior under the command of Captain Church shot and killed Metacom. His head was taken to Plymouth town, where it was placed on a pike and displayed for a number of years, a grim warning to other natives who might think of resisting English authority. By October 1676 the other native leaders and their men had been captured, and the war came to an end except in Maine (then part of Massachusetts), where intermittent violence continued for a number of years.

King Philip's War was the deadliest war in American history in terms of numbers of casualties for the people involved. Colonial losses were between 800 and 1,000, with at least 12 towns totally destroyed, hundreds of houses and barns burned, and thousands of cattle killed. Native American losses were even more severe. Perhaps 3,000 warriors were killed in battle, with hundreds more men, women, and children killed or sold into slavery after the war. The native converts to Christianity did not escape unscathed. Fearing that they might aid Metacom, colonial officials rounded up the native inhabitants of the so-called praying towns and confined them on an island in Boston Harbor, where many died of disease and exposure. The tribes of southern New England never recovered from King Philip's War. Indeed, their ability to resist the colonial onslaught had ended.

KYLE F. ZELNER

See also

Bloody Brook Massacre; Brookfield, Siege of; Falls Fight; Great Swamp Fight; Metacom; Narragansetts; Native American Warfare; New England Confederation; Nipmucks; Rowlandson, Mary White; Skulking Way of War; Wampanoags

References

Bodge, George Madison. *Soldiers in King Philip's War.* 3rd ed. Baltimore: Genealogical Publishing, 1967.

Hubbard, William. *The History of the Indian Wars in New England, from the First Settlement to the Termination of the War with King Philip in 1677.* Edited by Samuel Gardner Drake. 1864; Facsimile reprint, Bowie, MD: Heritage Books, 1990.

Leach, Douglas Edward. *Flintlock and Tomahawk: New England in King Philip's War.* East Orleans, MA: Parnassus Imprints, 1992.

Lepore, Jill. *The Name of War: King Philip's War and the Origins of American Identity.* New York: Knopf, 1998.

Mather, Increase, and Cotton Mather. *The History of King Philip's War by Rev. Increase Mather; Also, A History of the Same War by the Rev. Cotton Mather.* Edited by Samuel Gardner Drake. 1862; reprint, Bowie, MD: Heritage Books, 1990.

Schultz, Eric B., and Michael J. Tougias. *King Philip's War: The History and Legacy of America's Forgotten Conflict.* Woodstock, VT: Countryman, 1999.

King William's War

Start Date: 1689

End Date: 1697

The North American extension of what began in Europe as the War of the League of Augsburg. The European conflict grew out of Catholic-Protestant tensions, French king Louis XIV's expansionary policies in the Low Countries and the Rhineland, and the accession of the Protestant William of Orange (King William III) and his wife Mary to the English throne. This occurred after the overthrow of Catholic King James II in the 1688 Glorious Revolution. Nevertheless, James II still enjoyed powerful support among Catholics in England and Ireland as well as from the French king. Louis XIV's expansionist ambitions on the continent and his desire to restore a Catholic to the English throne fueled Anglo-French rivalry.

Full-scale war in Europe commenced in September 1688 when France invaded Flanders and the Palatinate. England and the Netherlands then united to support the League of Augsburg—an alliance of Protestant German principalities—along with Austria, Spain, and Sweden against France.

Political and religious tensions in the New World mirrored those in the Old World. Catholic New France and the Protestant English colonies in New England and New York had been moving steadily toward confrontation. Rivalries surrounding fishing rights, the fur trade, and Native American violence on the northern frontier inflamed feelings on both sides. The resulting war produced a string of failures by the colonial forces of English America. This combined with a series of horrific native raids on the northern frontier triggered a panic in Massachusetts that influenced the Salem Witch Trials of 1692 and caused a general crisis of confidence between the English colonists and the government in London.

The ensuing war stimulated domestic industry (particularly shipbuilding) in the colonies and led them to find their own methods of financing military operations. Particularly significant was the Massachusetts Bay Colony's decision to print paper money to defray the cost of the 1691 naval expedition against Quebec.

Because of English military failures, relations with their closest Native American allies of the Iroquois Confederacy suffered greatly. For the home country, King William's War revealed the dangers involved in relying on separate colonies to cooperate with each other. Nevertheless, the frustrating stalemate led many colonists to question London's commitment to their interests. In neither Europe nor North America did this nine-year conflict resolve any of the issues between England and France. Indeed, the 1697 Treaty of Ryswick proved only a temporary truce before the onset of Queen Anne's War (1702–1713).

In North America, news of the 1688 English Revolution gave impetus to long-nourished desires in the colonies, particularly in New England and New York, to strike against French Canada. New England Puritans had chafed under James II's prohibition of attacks on the French and raged against encroachments by the latter on the fur trade and offshore fisheries and incitement of Native American violence.

For their part, the French regarded the English colonies as threats to New France. They harbored their own ambitions in the Mississippi River and Ohio River valleys and in northern Maine to the Kennebec River. French agents cultivated local tribes along the northern New England and New York frontiers, especially the Abenakis. In fact, the French had established a fort along the Penobscot River in Maine (then part of Massachusetts) to funnel arms to potential native allies. The governor of New France, Count Louis de Buade de Frontenac, an abrasive but skilled career soldier, actively strengthened ties with the pro-French tribes and encouraged them to attack the Iroquois and frontier settlements in northern Maine.

Indeed, war between the French and the Iroquois had already broken out in August 1689. That month, a large Iroquois war party fell on the French village of Lachine near Montreal, slaying or capturing most of the population. News from Europe ignited this tinderbox into full-scale war.

In the ensuing conflict, the English colonists set goals that were vastly different from those of their home country. In Europe, King William III's objectives were limited to protecting his throne and preventing French expansion into the Low Countries and to the banks of the Rhine. Protestant New England and New York, however, sought nothing less than the destruction of New France and the expulsion of the French from North America.

In neither the ground nor the naval dimensions of King William's War did events develop as English America had hoped. The English colonies began the war with three major advantages. First, they possessed a lopsided advantage in manpower. The population of English North America's colonies in 1689 was nearly 250,000 people, more than 20 times that of New France. This large population provided governing authorities with a formidable base from which to recruit troops. Second, the colonists believed that they could count on military and naval support from the mother country. And third, the English colonies were allied with the largest and most powerful Native American tribal group in the Northeast, the Iroquois Confederacy.

None of these strengths proved decisive, however. Although much smaller numerically, the French could draw on a large number of males, many of whom had military experience. England, though fielding a large army, had to post most of its troops to Flanders and Ireland to parry French threats and internal unrest among the ousted James II's Catholic supporters. The ground and naval forces sent by the English government to the Western Hemisphere were deployed mostly to the West Indies to protect its possessions there. Also, English America was divided among a number of colonies, each with sovereignty over finances and military manpower, while New France was unified under the authority of one governor. Finally, the Iroquois tribes, although eager for plunder in Canada, were beset with internal divisions and relentless guerrilla attacks from their pro-French rivals.

While colonial authorities in New York and New England struggled to organize their forces, Frontenac sent mixed French and native war parties into northern New York and New England to raid remote and vulnerable English towns. On February 8, 1690, one such force raided the village of Schenectady, New York, killing 60 people and carrying off 27 and burning the settlement. The French and their American Indian compatriots struck again about a month later, hitting Salmon Falls, New Hampshire, not far from Portsmouth. The attackers killed 34 and took 54 hostages. In yet another attack in May 1690, 500 French and natives laid siege to Fort Loyal (Portland), Maine, forcing the small garrison into submission. When the English colonists surrendered, the French commanders stood by while their allies killed some 100 men, women, and children before burning the fort.

News of these attacks triggered a wave of terror among the English colonists and moved authorities in New York, Massachusetts, and Connecticut to raise militias. The northern English colonies then tried to launch a two-pronged invasion of French Canada via Lake Champlain and through the Saint Lawrence Valley against Montreal and Quebec, respectively. Their efforts foundered on internal divisions growing from the upheavals of the Glorious Revolution.

In April 1690 the first intercolonial conference assembled in New York City, with representatives from Massachusetts Bay, Plymouth, Connecticut, and New York attending (Maryland and Rhode Island promised financial support). There they agreed to furnish troops for an overland expedition against Canada. In addition, the Iroquois promised to send 800 warriors.

Efforts to raise and organize militias and launch the expedition suffered amid political bickering, supply shortages, and an outbreak of smallpox that devastated both the Iroquois and the colonists. The joint expedition against Canada ended in an embarrassing failure. While the main body under Major Fitz John Winthrop, a former British Army officer, halted, Captain John Schuyler proceeded north on Lake Champlain with 29 soldiers and 120 native warriors on a raiding expedition. On August 23, having paddled the length of the lake and entered the Richelieu River, they attacked the French settlement of La Prairie, across the Saint Lawrence from Montreal. The attackers killed 6 men, took 19 prisoners, shot a number of cattle, and burned several houses, barns, and haystacks. Fearing a reaction from the large Montreal garrison and with no sign of the rest of the expedition, Schuyler withdrew. The main body under Winthrop had already returned to Albany. The collapse of this Lake Champlain expedition fanned discontent, damaged intercolonial cooperation, and undermined the confidence of the Iroquois in their English American allies.

In the summer of 1691 New York's new royal governor, Henry Sloughter, sent another expedition against Montreal. After shoring up support among the Iroquois at a May conference in Albany, he ordered a mixed band of colonists and natives organized by Albany mayor Peter Schuyler on another raid against Montreal. Schuyler departed Albany on June 22. The force reached Montreal a month later in canoes, again via Lake Champlain. On August 1 the force struck the village of La Prairie for a second time, overrunning it. Schuyler and his men repulsed one counterattack but were obliged to withdraw on the appearance of reinforcements from Montreal. Fighting through a French ambush, Schuyler's detachment returned to Albany.

Although more successful than the 1690 attempt, Schuyler's raid did not significantly alter the political and strategic balance between French and English America. The French did not mount any major raids in 1691 or 1692. And hampered by the unexpected death of Sloughter in July and with only limited funds for raising troops, New York authorities were content to maintain a small garrison of 150 men at Albany and encourage the Iroquois to raid into Canada and blockade the fur trade on the Saint Lawrence.

The arrival of a new governor, Benjamin Fletcher, in August 1692 did not alter New York's quiescence. Unable to raise money from the already overtaxed colonists, Fletcher had to be content with encouraging the Iroquois and asking the other colonies for help. The precariousness of New York's position became clear in July 1696 when a large French and native force, commanded by Frontenac himself, invaded central New York. The attackers terrorized the Onondaga tribe and burned several English settlements. By the time Fletcher was able to borrow money from the other colonies, the attackers had departed. The raid made clear to the Iroquois that New York authorities could not protect them.

Over the ensuing six years, the pattern established in New York persisted. The ground fighting followed a cycle of fierce raids interspersed with periods of inactivity. The French, driven by Frontenac's ambitions, continued to encourage native raids, particularly by the Abenakis, against both the Iroquois and the Anglo-Americans.

The English colonists, in turn, sought to raise sufficient manpower to protect their outlying settlements and deter French attacks. Like their counterparts in New York in the Lake Champlain Valley, leaders in Plymouth and Massachusetts Bay made independent efforts to take the offensive in northern New England. For this they commissioned Major Benjamin Church, a veteran of King Philip's War (1675–1676), to organize troops and take the offensive in Maine. With a force of 300 men, Church sailed to Casco Bay in September 1691 and raided Abenaki villages near present-day Brunswick and Lewiston.

Although Church did not achieve decisive success, his expedition hurt the Abenakis sufficiently that they agreed to a peace treaty at Kennebec in November. This agreement lasted only until the following winter and early spring when, under French prodding, the Abenakis struck the Maine villages of York and Wells. In retaliation the new governor of Massachusetts, Sir William Phips, accompanied Church on another expedition against the Abenakis. The attackers established a new post, Fort William Henry, on the Maine coast near Saco Bay and raided into Abenaki territory. An attempt by the French to take the fort by sea failed when the commander of the naval expedition, Pierre Le Moyne d'Iberville, decided that his forces were insufficient and withdrew without firing a shot.

The New England frontier remained stable for approximately three years. Massachusetts, by now in the throes of the Salem witch hysteria, could provide only limited forces. French authorities, smarting from their failure at Fort William Henry, were struggling to keep their native allies from negotiating with the English. A militia force of 300 under Captain James Converse kept the peace and deterred any serious American Indian raids. In August 1693 Converse negotiated a peace with 13 Abenaki chiefs. This broke down later when 250 Abenakis, aroused by the new French commandant at Penobscot, Sieur de Villieu, overran Oyster Bay, New Hampshire, in July 1694. This force ravaged the New England frontier as far west as New York. Subsequent attempts to reestablish peace fizzled, and sporadic raiding continued throughout 1694 and 1695.

The last major clash on the New England frontier occurred in July 1696 when a mixed detachment of two French regular companies and 250 Native Americans supported by two French warships appeared off Fort William Henry and induced the commander, Captain Pasco Chubb, to surrender without resistance. The French restrained their allies from killing Chubb or any of his men but spent three days plundering the fort before withdrawing back to their fort at Penobscot.

In response, Massachusetts raised 500 men and once again called on Major Church to command an expedition into Canada. Supported by three English ships, Church landed at Penobscot but found that most of the French and natives had departed. He then moved his men up the coast to the Bay of Fundy, killing a few natives and burning the settlements in his path. There was no organized resistance.

Maine remained relatively secure until the war ended. News of the Treaty of Ryswick, which concluded the War of the League of Augsburg in 1697, effectively ended the fighting between the English colonists and New France but did not end warfare between the Iroquois and the pro-French tribes.

WALTER F. BELL

See also

Abenakis; Church, Benjamin; Falmouth, Battle of; France; Great Britain; Iroquois; Iroquois Confederacy

References

Leach, Douglas Edward. *The Northern Colonial Frontier, 1607–1763.* New York: Holt, Rinehart and Winston, 1966.

Leckie, Robert. *"A Few Acres of Snow": The Saga of the French and Indian Wars.* New York: Wiley, 1999.

Nester, William R. *The Great Frontier War: Britain, France, and the Imperial Struggle for North America, 1607–1755.* Westport, CT: Praeger, 2000.

Norton, Mary Beth. *In the Devil's Snare: The Salem Witchcraft Crisis of 1692.* New York: Knopf, 2002.

Peckham, Howard Henry. *The Colonial Wars, 1689–1762.* Chicago: University of Chicago Press, 1964.

Steele, Ian K. *Warpaths: Invasions of North America.* New York: Oxford University Press, 1994.

Taylor, Alan. *American Colonies: The Settling of North America.* New York: Viking/Penguin, 2001.

Kintpuash
Birth Date: ca. 1840
Death Date: October 3, 1873

Modoc leader who murdered Brigadier General E. R. S. Canby. Born near Lost River, California, close to the Oregon border, probably in 1840, Kintpuash was the son of the Modoc chief. Although Kintpuash's father was killed fighting white settlers who had begun encroaching on Modoc lands in the 1850s, Kintpuash pursued a policy of accommodation upon becoming chief. He encouraged the Modocs to trade with settlers and frequently visited the white communities, the inhabitants of which called him Captain Jack.

In 1864 Kintpuash agreed to the federal government's demand that the Modocs give up their lands and relocate to the Klamath Indian Reservation in Oregon. Once there, however, the Modocs did not receive the promised supplies and frequently came into conflict with the Klamaths, who considered the Modocs intruders. Kintpuash thus led the 300 Modocs back to their Lost River homeland in 1872.

Federal officials sent troops to force the Modocs to return to the reservation. A confrontation turned violent when the troops

Kintpuash (Captain Jack) was a key figure in the 1872–1873 Modoc War and the individual who shot and killed U.S. Army brigadier general Edward Canby during a meeting on April 11, 1873. (Library of Congress)

attempted to disarm the Modocs on November 28, 1872. The troops then withdrew, and the Modocs took refuge in rugged lava beds near Tule Lake.

Army forces surrounded the lava beds in mid-January 1873. Kintpuash initially proposed surrender, but militants led by Hooker Jim dissuaded him. The Modocs repulsed an attack on January 17. At the end of February, both sides attempted to negotiate a settlement. Angered by Brigadier General Edward R. S. Canby's refusal to grant amnesty to the Modocs and pressured by the militants, Kintpuash shot and killed Canby during a meeting on April 11. The troops then launched a series of assaults on the Modocs. Fighting lasted until June 1, when troops guided by Hooker Jim, who had agreed to betray Kintpuash in exchange for amnesty, captured the Modoc chief.

At Fort Klamath in July, Kintpuash was convicted of murder and was hanged there on October 3, 1873. His corpse was later stolen and exhibited at carnivals in the eastern United States.

JIM PIECUCH

See also

Canby, Edward Richard Sprigg; Modocs; Modoc War

References

Brown, Dee. *Bury My Heart at Wounded Knee.* New York: Holt, Rinehart and Winston, 1970.

Murray, Keith A. *The Modocs and Their War.* 1959; reprint, Norman: University of Oklahoma Press, 2001.

Kiowas

A southern Plains tribe and member of the Kiowa-Tanoan language family, one of the smaller Native American language groupings. The traditions of the Kiowas place their earliest territory in the Rocky Mountains, probably in Wyoming and southern Montana. The other members of the Kiowa-Tanoan family were located along the Rio Grande Valley in New Mexico, yet Kiowa traditions make no mention of them. The Kiowas have many memories of northern tribes; the Crows, for example, introduced the Kiowas to the horse and the nomadic life of Great Plains bison hunting. The Kiowas exhibited the full range of Plains Indian traits, including dependence on the horse for mobility, the tepee for shelter, the travois for transportation, and the bison for survival as well as warrior societies and the Sun Dance ritual.

The Kiowas were familiar with the Missouri River groups such as the Mandans and Hidatsas and also had contact with the Cheyenne and Pawnee peoples. The Lakota Sioux were remembered as the people who drove the Kiowas from the region of the Black Hills, eastern Wyoming, and western Nebraska. Eventually their territory was confined to western Texas, Oklahoma, and eastern New Mexico.

A subgroup within the Kiowa Nation, the Kiowa Apaches speak a dialect of the Athabascan language family. The Kiowa Apache group, though speaking a different language, was fully acculturated within the Kiowa Nation. The only significant difference between the two elements beyond the obvious linguistic difference was the higher proportion of mixed-blood families among the Kiowa Apache peoples. Full members of the tribal circle, they appear to have joined the Kiowas very early, as there is no traditional memory among either peoples of a time in which they lived apart.

The first Kiowa contact with Europeans appears to have been in the late 17th or early 18th centuries by French explorers when the Kiowas were still on the northern Great Plains. The Kiowas were then gradually pushed farther south, caught between the Lakota alliance pushing them south and the Comanche tribe, which occupied the southern Plains from the Arkansas River deep into Texas and from the Cross Timbers in central Texas and Oklahoma to the foothills of the Rocky Mountains in Colorado and New Mexico. This was the heart of the southern bison range. After 20–30 years of intermittent conflict between the Kiowas and the Comanches, a peace agreement was worked out around 1840.

From then until 1875, the Kiowas and Comanches were partners in war and in hunting. Sharing the northern part of the Comancheria, the Kiowas were the buffer to the north along the Arkansas River. The Kiowas began to accumulate massive horse herds through their long-distance raiding into Mexico and Texas alongside the Comanches. Some of these raids were as long as 1,000 miles. The objectives of the raids were horses, captives, luxury goods, and glory for the young warriors. At times women and children would accompany these raiding parties, as the duration could be many months.

Relations with Americans were initially friendly, with the Kiowas and the Comanches both making clear distinctions between differing groups of non-Indians. Even with the incursion of American settlers into Texas under the Mexican Republic, the Kiowas still made a distinction between Americans and whites living in Texas. The former were perceived as friends, while the latter were the targets of increasingly severe raids.

The Kiowas and Comanches would raid into Texas and steal livestock, driving it across the territory to the Staked Plains, where they would meet up with the Comancheros, traders from New Mexico. The Comanches had come to peace with the province of New Mexico in the 1780s and were thus free to come and go, bringing horses and cattle as well as captives for ransom. The Kiowas joined in this lucrative trade. Together the Kiowas and Comanches would delay the expansion of the Texas frontier until the mid-1870s.

In the north along the Arkansas River, the Kiowas were pressed by a very aggressive move south by the Cheyennes, supported by both their Arapaho and Lakota allies. This culminated in the Battle of Wolf Creek in 1838, when virtually the entire Cheyenne Nation and its Arapaho allies attacked a large camp of Kiowas along with some of their Comanche allies. Unlike most intertribal conflict, the Cheyennes pushed this toward a decisive engagement.

Willing to accept high casualties in return for victory, the Cheyennes shocked the Kiowas who, while fearless themselves, had never encountered this intensity in war from other Native Americans and were instead used to the small-scale raid as the means of war. The result was the settlement of their differences in 1840, which resulted in a new alliance between the Cheyennes and the Kiowas, a deal that the Kiowas sealed with the gift of hundreds of horses. From that time forward there was a solid wall of Native American warriors across the Plains who were opposed to further white encroachment.

Beginning in the 1840s, the raiding in Texas intensified as more and more settlers moved first into the Republic of Texas and later the state of Texas. Raiding also continued into Mexico, with the Comanches and Kiowas unable to understand why the Americans who had so recently been at war with the Mexicans were upset that they continued to raid the rich Mexican rancheros.

The U.S. Army established a series of forts west of the Texas settlements to try to protect the settlers; however, the forts were too far apart, and the Kiowas simply went around them. Prior to the American Civil War (1861–1865), army troops and Texas Rangers had begun to take the war to the Kiowas on their home grounds, and a Kiowa peace party began to take shape. Kiowa warriors, however, continued to raid deep into Texas. The Civil War aggravated the situation when Union troops withdrew and the Confederacy failed to replace the garrisons. In places the Texas frontier receded by up to 100 miles.

With the end of the Civil War in 1865, U.S. troops returned but initially were focused more on Reconstruction tasks. However, as they faced the Kiowas, they resumed the more aggressive stance of the prewar era. Many Kiowas moved to the reservation in Indian Territory (Oklahoma) during at least part of the year. Raiding continued, however, and on May 18, 1871, a group of young Kiowa warriors led by several chiefs—among them Owl Prophet and Satanta—allowed a small party including the commanding general of the U.S. Army, General William T. Sherman, to pass through an ambush site and later ambushed a wagon train carrying supplies. Most of the men in the wagon train were killed. An army patrol then followed the trail back to the reservation. Three chiefs—Satanta, Satank, and Big Tree—were subsequently arrested and tried in civilian court for the massacre in Texas.

Sherman then ordered Colonel Ranald S. MacKenzie, commanding the 4th Cavalry, and Colonel Benjamin Grierson, commanding the 10th Cavalry, to root out the hostile Kiowas. In a series of campaigns during the next three years, the troops penetrated into the Staked Plains, previously a Kiowa and Comanche sanctuary. The final outbreak of Kiowa resistance in 1874, punctuated by the Second Battle of Adobe Walls (June 27, 1874), was crushed during the Red River War (1874–1875), and the Kiowas were subdued and placed on a large reservation in Indian Territory.

JOHN THOMAS BROOM

See also
Adobe Walls, Second Battle of; Cheyennes; Comanches; Grierson, Benjamin Henry; Mackenzie, Ranald Slidell; Satanta; Sherman, William Tecumseh; Texas Rangers

References
Carlson, Paul H. *The Plains Indians.* College Station: Texas A&M University Press, 1998.
Ferhenbach, T. R. *Comanches: The History of a People.* New York, Anchor Books, 2003.
Hoig, Stan. *Tribal Wars of the Southern Plains.* Norman: University of Oklahoma Press, 1993.
LaVere, David. *Contrary Neighbors: Southern Plains and Removed Indians in Indian Territory.* Norman: University of Oklahoma Press, 2000.
Mayhall, Mildred P. *The Kiowas.* Civilization of the American Indian Series. 1971; reprint, Norman: University of Oklahoma Press, 1984.
Meadows, William C. *Kiowa, Apache, and Comanche Military Societies: Enduring Veterans, 1800 to the Present.* Austin: University of Texas Press, 1999.

Kituhwas
See Cherokees

Kotsoteka Comanches

A major band of Comanches. The Kotsoteka Comanches spoke a language related to the Uto-Aztecan linguistic family. The larger Comanche group migrated south and east from the Rocky Mountains. Around 1700 they split from the Shoshones and moved toward the North Platte River in present-day Nebraska, where they fought with every tribe they came into contact with before moving toward Texas and present-day Oklahoma. They also raided Spanish settlements in New Spain.

The Kotsotekas lived north of the Nakonis and south of the Yamparikas. They were known as Kuhtsoo-ehkuh, which means "Buffalo-Eaters." Their range was in the area of western Oklahoma, and they spent their winters along the Canadian River. As their name suggests, buffalo provided the bulk of their economic and living needs. They used the animals for meat, clothing, housing, and tools and other implements. The Kotsotekas were semi-nomadic, and like most Plains peoples they oriented their lifestyle around the buffalo hunt. They also engaged in trading with other Native Americans and Europeans; the buffalo was at the center of this commerce.

The Kotsotekas were sufficiently numerous to survive without needing other Comanche bands to replenish their numbers and generally numbered some 500 warriors. By 1750 the Kotsotekas and their fellow Comanches had so completely eliminated or driven out all of their foes that few of the surrounding peoples dared to enter the extensive Comanche lands. The Apaches and Tonkawas remained at the southwestern edge in the trans-Pecos region, while the Cheyennes and Pawnees stayed north of the Arkansas River. The Utes rarely ventured eastward past the Rocky Mountains. The Wichitas were the only tribe that dared to venture from the east, but they were not sufficiently powerful to challenge the Comanches.

From 1750 to about the 1830s the land called La Comancheria, in which the Kotsotekas and their fellow Comanches roamed, stretched from south of the Arkansas River to north of the Rio Grande in Texas, almost to the base of the Rockies in New Mexico and the eastern edge of the Plains in Oklahoma and Texas. The Kotsotekas, along with their fellow Comanches, enjoyed considerable freedom and gained much respect from tribes outside Comancheria.

In 1779 Don Juan Bautista de Anza, a Spanish officer appointed to govern New Mexico, destroyed a Kotsoteka camp in the eastern Colorado Plateau, killing women and children. Cuerno Verde, the Kotsoteka chief whose camp De Anza and his men had destroyed, rode into an ambush. The battle south of the Arkansas River, near Greenhorn Peak, cost the chief and most of his warriors their lives; few escaped.

Around 1830 the Kiowas and the Kotsotekas along with two of the other Comanche tribes, the Yamparikas and the Nakonis, battled the Cheyennes and Arapahos, who had begun to intrude on Kotsoteka territory. After 10 years of feints and skirmishes the five tribes agreed to a truce, called the Great Peace of 1840.

In October 1865 the U.S. government tried to pacify the West with the Treaty of Little Arkansas. Although they had signed the agreement, the Kotsotekas, like their fellow Comanches, continued their usual practices, which included raiding and the procuring of slaves. Two years later the U.S. government again tried to bring peace to the West with the Medicine Lodge Treaty, which established reservations for the Comanches and Kiowas in Indian

Territory (Oklahoma). Most of the Kotsotekas showed up for the talks, but there was little hope that anything was going to change, as neither the United States nor the Comanches understood each other. As a result, war soon broke out. By 1875 the Kotsotekas, defeated, demoralized, and starving, came to settle on the reservation near Fort Sill in Indian Territory, there to remain.

JOHN THOMAS BROOM

See also
Buffalo; Comanche Campaign; Comanches; Fort Sill; Medicine Lodge Treaty; Nakoni Comanches

References
Ferhenbach, T. R. *Comanches: The History of a People.* New York: Anchor Books, 2003.
Hoig, Stan. *Tribal Wars of the Southern Plains.* Norman: University of Oklahoma Press, 1993.
LaVere, David. *Contrary Neighbors: Southern Plains and Removed Indians in Indian Territory.* Norman: University of Oklahoma Press, 2000.
Powers, William K. *Indians of the Southern Plains.* New York: Capricorn Books, 1972.
Wallace, Ernest, and E. Adamson Hoebel. *The Comanches: Lords of the South Plains.* 1952; reprint, Norman: University of Oklahoma Press, 1986.

Kwahadi Comanches

A major band of the Comanches. Speaking a language related to the Uto-Aztecan linguistic family, the Comanches migrated south and east from the Rocky Mountains sometime prior to the 18th century. Around 1700 they split from the Shoshones and moved toward the North Platte River in present-day Nebraska. Acquiring horses probably in the late 16th century, they fought with every tribe they came in contact with as they moved toward Texas and present-day Oklahoma. They also frequently raided settlements in New Spain in search of booty and captives.

The Kwahadis, or Kwah-heeher kehnuh ("Sun Shades on Their Backs"), were also known as Kwerhar-rehnuh ("Antelopes"). The Kwahadis' name came from their custom of making parasols out of bison skins. Their range was the barren Staked Plains located of the Texas Panhandle. The Kwahadis were fierce fighters who were also aloof and usually remote from the other Comanche bands. As with other Plains tribes, buffalo provided the bulk of the Kwahadis' dietary, clothing, and housing needs.

The Kwahadis, like the other major Comanche bands, were large enough to survive without needing the other bands to replenish their numbers. By 1750 the Kwahadis and their fellow Comanches had so completely eliminated or expelled their foes that few of the surrounding peoples dared to enter the Comanche lands, which were massive in size. The Apaches and Tonkawas remained at the southwestern edge of their range in the trans-Pecos region. The Cheyennes and Pawnees stayed north of the Arkansas River. The Utes rarely ventured east of the Rocky Mountains. The

Wichitas were the only group that dared to venture from the east, but they were not powerful enough to challenge the Comanches.

With their territory free from enemies, the Kwahadis developed their own interests and had little contact with other Comanche bands, but they shared the Comanche hatred of the Apaches. In spite of slight differences in ceremonies, dances, and accents, the Kwahadis remained Comanche in culture.

Until the mid-1840s the Kwahadis freely roamed the Staked Plains, carrying out raids to replenish supplies they needed, but the annexation of Texas in 1845 by the United States and the gold rush of 1849 brought them in direct conflict with white settlers. By then a high mortality rate from disease had also begun to take its toll on the Kwahadis. Settlers had immunity to many diseases, but the Kwahadis did not. During this period, a long drought and the increasing pressure of Texas authorities and the U.S. military presence had brought the Kwahadis to the point of near starvation.

The Kwahadis had refused to participate in the October 1865 Treaty of Little Arkansas, and they believed that the ceded Native American lands did not include the Staked Plains. In the meantime, Comanchero-related business became so profitable that it attracted cattle barons and wealthy New Mexicans to the Staked Plains. These groups usually protected the Kwahadis and other Comanches from government intervention. This allowed the Kwahadis and other Comanche groups to receive merchandise and supplies, and they were an integral part of regional trade. Indeed, the Comanches paid well for dry goods, horses, mules, slaves, guns, and ammunition.

By the early 1870s Chief Quanah Parker, the son of a powerful chief and his white captive wife, had become the most prominent leader of the Kwahadis. He led them in conflict with white settlers and led the attack on buffalo hunters at Adobe Walls in 1874 and

Kwahadi Comanche leader White Wolf's camp in Indian Territory (Oklahoma), circa 1891–1898. (Library of Congress)

was a particularly notable challenge for the U.S. Army until the Battle of Palo Duro Canyon later that year, which largely destroyed the Indians' food supplies and pony herd. Compelled to surrender, the Comanches subsequently settled on the Fort Sill Reservation in Indian Territory (Oklahoma) in 1875.

JOHN THOMAS BROOM

See also

Adobe Walls, Second Battle of; Comanche Campaign; Comanches; Mackenzie, Ranald Slidell; Palo Duro Canyon, Battle of; Quanah Parker; Staked Plains

References

Ferhenbach, T. R. *Comanches: The History of a People.* New York: Anchor Books, 2003.

Hoig, Stan. *Tribal Wars of the Southern Plains.* Norman: University of Oklahoma Press, 1993.

LaVere, David. *Contrary Neighbors: Southern Plains and Removed Indians in Indian Territory.* Norman: University of Oklahoma Press, 2000.

Wallace, Ernest, and E. Adamson Hoebel. *The Comanches: Lords of the South Plains.* 1952; reprint, Norman: University of Oklahoma Press, 1986.

L

La Barre, Joseph Antoine Le Fèbvre de
Birth Date: 1622
Death Date: ca. 1690

Tenth governor of New France (1682–1685) who tried unsuccessfully to establish a permanent fur trade in western Canada (in and around present-day Kingston, Ontario). Joseph Antoine Le Fèbvre de La Barre was born in France in 1622. He served as a counselor of the Parlement of Paris (High Court) in 1646, master of requests in 1653, and intendant of Paris during the revolts known as La Fronde from 1648 to 1653.

La Barre held successive offices until he became intendant of Bourbonnais in 1663. In that year he formed a company called the Compagnie de la France équinoxiale to colonize Guiana on the Caribbean coast of South America. Appointed lieutenant general and governor of French Guiana, La Barre left France in 1662 with the Marquis de Tracy, newly appointed viceroy of the French possessions in America. La Barre returned to France later that year and wrote an account of his mission and his hopes for Guiana. Soon afterward he was appointed commander of Guiana and the French Antilles, and in 1671 he became the captain of a French man-of-war.

In 1682 French King Louis XIV appointed La Barre governor of New France, replacing the frustrated Louis de Buade, Comte de Frontenac et de Palluau. Along with several Canadian merchants, La Barre tried to secure trade with the Illinois tribe by confiscating the trading posts of Robert de La Salle, a protégé of the previous governor.

In the following year La Barre, with a few hundred soldiers, set out to establish the fur trade in western New France, the area of present-day Ontario. He made camp at the future site of Oswego, New York, waiting for an expected Iroquois attack. Soon more than 100 of La Barre's men had fallen ill, and supplies ran out. La Barre signed a peace treaty with the Iroquois and returned to Montreal in humiliation.

In 1685 the French king, having learned of La Barre's disastrous expedition, replaced him as governor with Jacques-René de Brisay, Marquis de Denonville. La Barre left New France in October 1685 and returned to Cayenne, Guiana, as governor in 1687. He died there sometime in 1690.

ROBERT B. KANE

See also
France; Fur Trade; Illinois; Iroquois

References
Eccles, W. J. *Frontenac: The Courtier Governor.* Lincoln: University of Nebraska Press, 2002.
Nute, Grace Lee. *Caesars of the Wilderness.* New York: D. Appleton-Century, 1943.
Parkman, Francis. *France and England in North America,* Vol. 2, *Count Frontenac and New France under Louis XIV.* New York: Library Classics of the United States, 1983.

Lake Okeechobee, Battle of
Event Date: December 25, 1837

The largest battle of the Second Seminole War (1835–1842) and a victory for U.S. forces. Under orders from overall campaign commander Brigadier General Thomas Sidney Jesup to destroy any Seminole force he met, Colonel Zachary Taylor landed at Tampa Bay with 1,000 men, mostly regulars of the 6th Infantry Regiment but also some Missouri volunteers and Native American allies. He immediately marched toward Lake Okeechobee on November 27, 1837. Taylor first established Fort Garner north of Lake Kissimmee and then proceeded down the west bank of the Kissimmee River on December 19. On December 22 he built Fort Basinger and then crossed the river en route to Lake Okeechobee to engage the Seminoles who occupied the area.

Upon Taylor's arrival near Lake Okeechobee on December 25 the Seminoles took up a defensive position in a swamp obscured by palmetto trees and saw grass. The Native American force numbered about 400 warriors, led by Wildcat, Sam Jones, and Alligator. The Seminoles under Alligator's leadership formed the center, and Sam Jones's and Wildcat's men took positions on the right and left flanks, respectively. The Seminoles placed lookouts in the trees to direct their fire.

The initial Seminole volley hit Taylor's command after the troops had entered the swamp, killing or wounding all but one of the commissioned officers. A majority of the noncommissioned officers suffered wounds, some mortal. The Missouri volunteers turned and ran after the first volley. Reserves saved the day for Taylor's command, however, with a bayonet charge on the Seminole line. The Seminoles only abandoned the field after Taylor's line closed in and could use its superior numbers to maximum effect.

After retreating, the Seminoles broke into groups of 10 to 15 men and disappeared into the swampy lowlands around Lake Okeechobee and the Kissimmee River. In the battle the Americans suffered 26 dead and 112 wounded. The Seminoles had at least 11 dead and 15 wounded. Taylor also captured 100 ponies and 600 head of cattle by taking control of the territory on the northeast side of Lake Okeechobee. Although Taylor held the field at the end of the day, the Battle of Lake Okeechobee was a failure for Taylor and his command because they had done little to end the Seminoles' ability to resist forced removal to Indian Territory (present-day Oklahoma). Nonetheless, the battle helped establish Taylor's military reputation, earned him promotion to brigadier general, and led to the nickname "Old Rough and Ready."

DIXIE RAY HAGGARD

See also

Seminoles; Seminole War, Second; Taylor, Zachary

References

Covington, James W. *The Seminoles of Florida.* Gainesville: University Press of Florida, 1993.
Mahon, John K. *History of the Second Seminole War, 1835–1842.* Rev. ed. Gainesville: University Press of Florida, 1991.

Lakota Sioux

Westernmost of the three main Sioux tribes (Oceti Sakowin), otherwise known as the Council of the Seven Fires. The word "Sioux" is derived from the old French word *nadouessioux,* meaning "enemies," a name endowed by French traders. The Lakotas are also known as the Teton Sioux. The Teton Sioux were split into seven groups: Sicangu (Brulé, Brunt Thighs), Hunkpapa (End of the Camp Circle), Miniconjou (Planters by the Water), Oglala (They Scatter Their Own), Oohenonpa (Two Kettles), Itazipco (Sans Arcs or Without Bows), and Sihasapa (Blackfeet).

The French considered the Sioux the most powerful and warlike of all the northwestern tribes. The Lakota Sioux territory included large parts of present-day North and South Dakota and parts of Montana and Wyoming. A seminomadic people, the Lakotas followed herds of buffalo on the Plains and hunted them from horseback. From the buffalo they derived much of their means of subsistence including meat and hides, which they used to shield themselves from the brutal Great Plains weather. They also used the hides for trade.

With the conclusion of the War of 1812 in 1815, numerous Native American tribes east of the Mississippi River signed peace treaties with the U.S. government. In 1825 an agreement was reached guaranteeing the Sioux Nation control of lands in what are today the states of Iowa, Missouri, Wyoming, Minnesota, Wisconsin, and North and South Dakota. A considerable portion of this land was in the Great Plains region of the West. The Indian Removal Act of 1830 accelerated the movement of Native Americans from east of the Mississippi to western lands acquired through the 1803 Louisiana Purchase. The act, signed by President Andrew Jackson, did not authorize the removal of any Native Americans. However, it did permit the president to negotiate treaties providing for the exchange of tribal land in the East for lands in the West.

In 1837 the Sioux sold their possessions east of the Mississippi, and in 1851 they sold additional lands as well. While most Native American tribes peacefully complied with the terms of the removal treaties, some groups resisted. The Black Hawk War of 1832, the Creek War of 1836, and the lengthy Second Seminole War (1835–1842) were evidence of Native American distrust of and anger at the young nation and its thirst for additional lands.

The continuous movement of pioneers into the Great Plains and mountainous West—chiefly miners, ranchers, and farmers—led to increased friction with the Native Americans. The Sioux of the northern Plains provided some of the most significant opposition to the government's laissez-faire attitude to these migrations. In 1854 near Fort Laramie (Wyoming), Lakota Sioux killed 30 U.S. soldiers in what became known as the Grattan Massacre. The following year some 700 soldiers, led by brevet Brigadier General William S. Harney, attacked a Lakota village without warning in retaliation. The soldiers killed more than 100 men, women, and children in their Nebraska camp. The tribe's chief was also taken prisoner.

The passage of the 1862 Homestead Act encouraged more white settlement and further Native American distrust. One Lakota chief, Red Cloud, known as Chief Makhpyialuta by his people, was outraged that miners had begun moving into the sacred lands of the Black Hills shortly after the Civil War. In 1866 fighting erupted. Known as Red Cloud's War (1866–1868), it was one of

A Lakota man on horseback and four Lakota women, three holding infants in cradleboards, in front of a tipi, probably on or near Pine Ridge Reservation. Photograph by John Grabill, circa 1891. (Library of Congress)

the most successful campaigns against the United States during the Indian Wars, as the Lakotas compelled the army to abandon its three Bozeman Trail forts. In the Treaty of Fort Laramie of 1868 the U.S. government granted a large reservation to the Lakotas. The treaty guaranteed the absence of a military presence or oversight, no further settlements, and no reserved building rights. The resultant Lakota Reservation included the entire Black Hills territory, and the treaty represented a major diplomatic victory for the Lakota Sioux.

Despite the treaty, the U.S. government and military did little to prevent prospectors and miners from entering Lakota territory. The discovery of gold in the Black Hills in 1874 led to even more prospectors moving into the region. Military commanders in the area failed to block the influx of new settlers, and the result was the Great Sioux War (Black Hills War) of 1876–1877.

The situation was compounded by the failure of the Indian Bureau to send regular supplies to Native American tribes and pay the yearly annuity as promised. During 1876 large numbers of Native Americans, including the Arapahos and Cheyennes, moved

north and joined forces with the Lakota Sioux in defiance of the reservation policy.

When the government ordered the Lakotas to yield their promised Black Hills lands and move onto a prescribed reservation, two of the tribe's most powerful leaders, Sitting Bull and Crazy Horse, refused. During the spring of 1876 thousands of Indians, having left their reservations, gathered in the valley of the Little Bighorn River and the surrounding area (southeastern Montana and northeastern Wyoming). In response the army mounted a massive three-pronged campaign to compel the Indians to return to the reservation. On June 17, 1876, Brigadier General George Crook's column, moving from the south in concert with Brigadier General Alfred Terry's command, marching westward from Fort Abraham Lincoln (North Dakota), and Colonel John Gibbon's force pressing southeastward from Fort Ellis (Montana), struck a large war party composed of Lakotas and Cheyennes, which checked Crook's advance in the Battle of the Rosebud (June 17, 1876).

Lieutenant Colonel George A. Custer's 7th Cavalry, leading Terry's column, pressed on in search of Indian camps. On June 25

Custer and his troops marched into the midst of a vast Sioux camp on the Little Bighorn River. In the resulting Battle of the Little Bighorn, 268 members of the 7th Cavalry, including Custer, died. "Custer's Last Stand" reverberated throughout the nation, and army reinforcements were rushed to the area. The Sioux quickly dispersed. Most were caught and placed on reservations. In 1877 the Lakotas were forced to sign a treaty ceding the Black Hills to the United States.

The last of the Lakota Sioux wars occurred in 1890 as a result of the Ghost Dance movement that spread among the Sioux. On December 15, 1890, fearing uprising, Brigadier General Nelson A. Miles ordered the capture of Sitting Bull, then living on the Standing Rock Reservation in South Dakota. When Sitting Bull refused capture, Native American policemen killed him. Sitting Bull's half brother, Big Foot, assumed leadership of the last band of Sioux resisters. Leaving the reservation, they were overtaken on December 29, 1890, by Colonel James W. Forsyth's 7th Cavalry at Wounded Knee Creek near Pine Ridge, South Dakota. As the soldiers attempted to disarm the Lakotas, gunfire erupted. In the ensuing fight, sometimes termed a massacre, 500 troops faced perhaps 300 Sioux, 100 of whom were warriors. At least 150 Sioux, including Big Foot, were killed, and another 50 were wounded. Army losses came to 25 killed and 40 wounded. The Wounded Knee fight marked the end of the Indian Wars. The frontier was now officially closed to the land's original inhabitants.

After Wounded Knee, the Lakotas went back to their reservations. By the early years of the 20th century, many Lakotas adapted themselves to farming and the raising of cattle, making them less dependent upon U.S. government subsidies. The 1934 Indian Reorganization Act allowed the Lakotas much autonomy through their own reservation and tribal governance. In the late 1940s, government-sponsored flood control projects along the Missouri River brought electricity to the Lakotas, but the tribe also lost nearly 166,000 acres to the projects. Much of this land had been prime agricultural and grazing territory. Today many Lakota Sioux live on five reservations in western South Dakota: Rosebud, Pine Ridge, Lower Brulé, Cheyenne River, and Standing Rock. In total there are fewer than 9,000 individuals on these reservations, where unemployment is chronically high, and perhaps two-thirds of the people live in poverty.

CHARLES FRANCIS HOWLETT

See also
Arapahos; Big Foot; Buffalo; Cheyennes; Crazy Horse; Crook, George; Custer, George Armstrong; Fort Laramie, Treaty of (1868); Grattan Massacre; Harney, William Selby; Indian Removal Act; Little Bighorn, Battle of the; Little Crow; Miles, Nelson Appleton; Red Cloud; Red Cloud's War; Reservations; Rosebud, Battle of the; Sioux; Sitting Bull; Wounded Knee, Battle of

References
Behrman, Carol. *The Indian Wars*. Minneapolis: Lerner Publishers, 2005.
Bonvillain, Nancy. *The Teton Sioux*. New York: Chelsea House, 2004.
Brown, Dee. *Bury My Heart at Wounded Knee*. New York: Holt, Rinehart and Winston, 1970.
Koestler-Grack, Rachel A. *The Sioux: Nomadic Buffalo Hunters*. Mankato, MN: Earth Books/Capstone, 2003.
Remini, Robert Vincenti. *Andrew Jackson and His Indian Wars*. New York: Penguin, 2001.
Thornton, Russell. *American Indian Holocaust and Survival: A Popular History since 1492*. Oklahoma City: University of Oklahoma Press, 1987.

Lance

Long polearm cavalry weapon. Before the advent of firearms, lances were, next to swords, the primary weapon for horsemen. Ranging from 9 to 14 feet in length, lances were made of hardwood, usually ash, and were 1.5 to 2 inches in diameter. The tip was metal, pointed so as to penetrate armor. Although known in ancient times, lances became much more important with the advent of the stirrup, which allowed the rider to brace himself in the saddle. During the charge the rider held the lance stationary under the arm with the tip forward, using the momentum of the horse for shock power.

Even with the advent of firearms, cavalrymen relied on the lance in part because reloading carbines and pistols while moving on horseback was difficult. Lances were very much a fixture of European warfare and continued in use even into World War II (1939–1945). They were, however, rarely employed in colonial North America because there was little open land for cavalry warfare. There were also few cavalry units, even late in the colonial period. Lances were adopted by the Native Americans of the Great Plains after the arrival of the horse.

CHARLES D. GREAR AND SPENCER C. TUCKER

See also
Cavalry, Native American; Cavalry, U.S. Army; Native American Warfare

References
Blackmore, D. *Arms and Armour of the English Civil War*. London: Royal Armouries, 1990.
Davenant, Charles. *An Essay upon Ways and Means of Supplying the War*. London: Printed for Jacob Tonson, 1695.
Starkey, Armstrong. *European and Native American Warfare, 1675–1815*. Norman: University of Oklahoma Press, 1998.

Land Cessions, Northwest Ordinance

Areas of the United States situated between the Appalachian Mountains and the Mississippi River that various states ceded to the federal government in the late 1700s and early 1800s. The formal organization and governance of this area were provided for in the Northwest Ordinance of July 13, 1787, passed by the Congress of the Confederation. Two years later the Congress under the Constitution of 1789 reaffirmed the ordinance with just slight modification. The ceded territory had a land area of about 370,040 square miles, or 10.4 percent of the present United States, and makes up all or part of 10 states. Some of the land was part of the Western Reserve, much of which was claimed by Virginia and Connecticut.

The 13 original British colonies were established along the Atlantic coast of North America between 1607 (Virginia) and 1733 (Georgia). At the time, knowledge of North American geography was incomplete. The royal proclamations or charters that established many of these colonies defined their boundaries as stretching "from sea to sea," with no idea of just how far to the west was the other sea. Other colonies did not establish any western boundaries at all. As a result, some colonies technically had land that extended to the Pacific Ocean, conflicting with the claims of other European powers, not to mention numerous Native American nations. Others claimed land that overlapped the claims of other colonies. Still others claimed no lands beyond their original boundaries.

The Proclamation of 1763, which prohibited white settlement beyond the Appalachians, sought to prevent the westward movement of the colonists. Meanwhile, the British government negotiated treaties with the Native American tribes and established a policy toward them in the trans-Appalachian region, which had been acquired from France as a result of the Treaty of Paris of 1763 that ended the French and Indian War (1754–1763). The treaty did not resolve the disputes among the colonies over the conflicting trans-Appalachian land claims, however. Eastern colonists generally ignored the proclamation, and various frontier settlement enterprises, owing allegiance to conflicting colonial governments, continued to sponsor settlers into the newly acquired lands.

By 1776 most colonies east of the Appalachian Mountains had surveyed the boundaries with their neighbors and agreed upon them with the exception of the dispute between New York and New Hampshire over the land that would eventually become Vermont. The claims of some colonies corresponded in varying degrees to the actual reality on the ground in the western region in 1776. For instance, Virginia organized Kentucky into a western county and considered it a part of Virginia right up until its admission to the Union in 1792. North Carolina had similarly organized its western counties but ceded them to the federal government, which organized them into the Southwest Territory. In 1796 the Southwest Territory became the state of Tennessee. By contrast, the claims of Massachusetts and Connecticut to land in what is now Ohio, Michigan, and Wisconsin amounted to little more than lines drawn on a map.

The 1783 Treaty of Paris that ended the American Revolutionary War (1775–1783) ceded what became known as the Old Northwest Territory to the United States, and the task of determining how to resolve the land claims of the states and how to govern that land became the first major tasks for the new nation. One obvious problem was the conflicting claims by several states to the same territory, as clearly only one would be ultimately recognized as the owner. Also, of the 13 new states, only 7 had western land claims; the other "landless" states feared that they would be overwhelmed by states that had vast stretches of the new frontier, which

Native American Lands Purchased by the U.S. Government, 1795–1838

Year	Lands Purchased (acres)	Purchase Price
1795	11,808,499	$210,000
1801	2,641,920	—*
1802	853,760	$2,201
1803	10,950,250	$16,000
1804	11,841,920	$26,295
1805	9,167,300	$155,600
1806	1,209,600	$44,000
1807	7,862,400	$100,400
1808	50,269,440	$60,000
1809	3,395,840	$20,700
1814	14,284,800	$120,000
1816	2,814,080	$77,000
1817	4,807,680	$561,830
1818	51,925,120	$482,600
1819	8,060,800	$67,000
1820	4,510,240	$5,000
1821	5,500,000	$150,000
1823	Unknown	$106,000
1824	11,000,000	$79,900
1825	85,699,680	$2,451,400
1826	4,132,480	$5,938,000
1827	1,337,780	$533,718
1828	1,285,120	$63,741
1829	990,720	$189,795
1830	6,695,760	$1,143,401
1831	24,092,000	$23,409,661
1832	8,326,397	$16,440,767
1833	19,122,280	$6,958,187
1834	4,128,610	$549,676
1835	5,113,920	$7,631,619
1836	22,652,720	$9,257,616
1837	6,698,240	$1,082,063
1838	18,250,000	$3,738,000
Total	421,429,356	$81,672,170

* Figure included in 1802 total

eventually would mean larger populations. Virginia, already the home of one in five inhabitants of the new nation, laid claim to present-day Kentucky, Indiana, and Illinois, and the smaller states feared that Virginia's land claims would come to completely dominate the new country.

By 1800 the individual states and the U.S. government had peacefully resolved the problems. Between 1781 and 1787 the states with trans-Appalachian land claims ceded them to the federal government—New York in 1780, Virginia in 1784, and Massachusetts and Connecticut in 1785—in some cases in exchange for federal assumption of their Revolutionary War debts. In 1787 the U.S. government formed the Northwest Territory, stretching from the Appalachians to the Mississippi River and from the Ohio River to the Great Lakes and the border with Canada. New York, New Hampshire, and the de facto Vermont government had resolved their quarrels by 1791.

These land cessions had prevented early, perhaps catastrophic, differences among the states of the young republic and sufficiently assuaged the fears of the "landless" states for them to ratify the new U.S. Constitution of 1789. The cessions also set the stage for the settlement of the Northwest Territory and the country's expansion farther westward to the center of the North American continent. At the same time, of course, these land cessions paved the way for continual conflict, some of it armed conflict, between whites and Native Americans that lasted well into the 19th century. The Land Ordinance of 1785 established an equitable method of surveying and dividing the land for sale that by and large prevented land speculation and boundary disputes. The Northwest Ordinance of 1787 prohibited slavery and discrimination based on religion, established the process by which the territory would be organized into new states, and began the federal government's support of free public education.

ROBERT B. KANE

See also

Northwest Ordinances of 1785 and 1787; Old Northwest Territory; Western Reserve

References

Buley, R. Carlyle. *The Old Northwest Pioneer Period, 1815–1840*, Vol. 2. Bloomington: Indiana University Press, 1951.

Cunliffe, Marcus. *The Nation Takes Shape, 1789–1837*. Chicago: University of Chicago Press, 1959.

Kluger, Richard. *Seizing Destiny: How America Grew from Sea to Shining Sea*. New York: Knopf, 2007.

Land Rights

Basic Native American land law and limited tribal sovereignty were established very early in American history through the U.S. Supreme Court decisions of Chief Justice John Marshall. The decisions of the Marshall Court during the 1830s affecting the Cherokees and other southeastern tribes laid the foundation for tribal sovereignty over land. In *Cherokee Nation v. Georgia* (1831), the court declared that the Cherokees constituted a "domestic dependent nation" whose members were to be considered wards of the United States and whose rights were to be protected by the federal government.

The next year in *Worcester v. Georgia,* the Marshall Court explained the idea of tribal sovereignty in greater detail, when it declared that "Indian nations had always been considered as distinct, independent political communities, retaining their original natural rights, as the undisputed possessors of the soil." Even though President Andrew Jackson ignored the Supreme Court's decision confirming Cherokee land rights and the Cherokees were later moved over the Trail of Tears to Indian Territory (Oklahoma), the Marshall Court's opinions in these cases have been cited throughout American judicial history in a multitude of other suits as setting the precedent for confirming tribal land rights.

Land tenure rights for Native Americans were severely tested later in the 19th century through various federal actions aimed at forcing the assimilation of Native American peoples. Federal policy, as set forth in the 1887 Dawes Severalty Act, attempted to do away with Native American peoples' land bases through the distribution of 80- or 160-acre parcels of reservation land to individual tribal members. Not only did this act break up tribal reservation land, challenging the widely held Native American idea of communal land ownership and making even more land available for white settlement, but it also made the Native Americans who received their allotments U.S. citizens, causing them to be subject to the laws and taxes of the individual states.

The Supreme Court confirmed this change in American Indian land policy in *Lone Wolf v. Hitchcock* (1903). In this decision, the Court informed Native American tribes and nations that the courts themselves were no longer the final recourse for Native American attempts to protect their land rights against intrusion by the federal government through claims to sovereignty. Congress alone was deemed responsible for American Indian policy, and its decisions in these matters were held not to be open to judicial review.

The situation for the Pueblo nations was even more desperate during the opening decades of the 20th century. Because their landholdings had been conferred by the Treaty of Guadalupe Hidalgo (1848) and not by an act of Congress, the Pueblos were excluded from the provisions that established federal relationships with Native Americans as outlined in the Trade and Intercourse Act of 1834. This status granted the Pueblos citizenship as landowners and thereby subjected them to taxation and to the laws of the State of New Mexico. Regarding land law, this made the Pueblo nations subject to the same statutes that governed all landholdings in the state. Any recourse taken against non–Native Americans who squatted on Native American lands would have to be taken up with the New Mexico state courts—which, like many other state court systems, had a well-earned reputation of hostility toward the claims of Native American tribes—and not with the federal government or the Bureau of Indian Affairs (BIA).

The breakup of lands, the diminution of sovereignty, and the assimilation of Native American peoples formed the basis of American Indian policy until the 1930s. This negative view of Native American land rights and tribal sovereignty in general would not be challenged in any meaningful way until the rise to prominence of Red Progressive reformer John Collier during the 1920s; the publication of the 1928 Meriam Report, which outlined the deficiencies of the American Indian policy centered around the General Allotment Act; and, with Collier's appointment as commissioner of Indian affairs after Franklin D. Roosevelt's election to the presidency in 1932, the passage of the Wheeler-Howard Act of 1934, popularly known as the Indian Reorganization Act (IRA). Upon his confirmation, Collier immediately began to dismantle the prior system of Native American management and create a new system that included more protection and self-determination for the tribes. Although he faced stiff opposition from assimilated Native Americans and local BIA officials who feared that they might lose their jobs, Collier had his IRA introduced in Congress in 1934.

John Collier, Indian Affairs commissioner during 1933–1945, with Blackfoot chiefs. Collier was a staunch advocate for Indian rights. (Library of Congress)

The IRA, the centerpiece of Collier's efforts to reform Indian policy, stated that "hereafter no land of any Indian reservation, created or set apart by treaty or agreement with the Indians, Act of Congress, Executive order, purchase, or otherwise, shall be allotted in severalty to any Indian." Collier's plan envisioned each Native American nation submitting a charter that included its territorial limits and membership but reflected its own traditional governmental forms. Collier's bill also established its own charters as superseding previous forms of government, a move that was sure to antagonize traditional elements and place tribal government in the hands of more assimilated elements. The commissioner was authorized to arrange and classify the functions and services that the BIA administered, allowing tribes to choose which services they would like to assume.

Most importantly, the IRA reversed the policy of land allotment, authorizing the secretary of the interior to withdraw the remaining "surplus" lands after allotment. No more Native American land was to be sold. The IRA specified powers that tribal councils could exercise without seeking the permission of the federal government, reversing the tendency of the federal government until that point to place more and more restrictions on Native Americans' self-determination. Debates regarding the efficacy of Collier's reforms and the extent of his commitment to Indian cultural forms have continued ever since he took office. Some Native Americans, especially those who had been educated in white institutions, who adopted Christianity, or who otherwise assimilated, did not support Collier's call for an end to individual land allotments. Moreover, many agents and other BIA officials disagreed wholeheartedly with his program of cultural preservation, tribal government, and land consolidation, and they refused to implement much of his program on the local level. However, there can be no doubt that the dim view of Indian tribal sovereignty and American Indian land rights that previously characterized federal Indian policy had changed radically.

However, not long after Collier's resignation in 1945, Congress asked for a list of tribes that would be "ready to succeed on their own," initiating the policy of termination. In 1953, Public Law 83-280 (PL280) placed Native Americans in five western states under state law enforcement jurisdiction and allowed states wishing to assume jurisdiction to amend their state constitutions to make this possible. Senator Arthur Watkins became the leading advocate of termination, using some of the same tactics (such as counting silence as assent and mischaracterizing the tone of meetings) that Collier had used to claim that he spoke for Native American desires and interests.

The Klamaths, Menominees, and Utes found themselves trading one trustee (the federal government) for another (private banks that had no knowledge of or sympathy for their needs). In 1954 the National Congress of American Indians (NCAI) met to discuss how to fight termination, exerting pressure on Congress to vote against it. During the 1960s the Democrats waffled on termination, not implementing it but not decrying it. The NCAI tried to keep its distance from the Civil Rights Movement in the late 1950s, but the poor conditions created by PL280 resulted in the need for the group to approach Congress for redress.

All of these acts, laws, and decisions have had varying degrees of influence on the self-determination over land that Indian tribes have been able to exercise. Although cuts in federal funding during the Ronald Reagan administration damaged the ability of the tribes to exercise their sovereignty, in sum the amount of sovereignty increased greatly over the course of the 20th century. These changes in federal views toward tribal sovereignty and land rights demonstrate that during the 1920s and 1930s a shift occurred in both government and public perception of Native American tribes. Those changes have only haltingly been implemented and have many times been reversed when the federal government found them inconvenient, but the early 20th century did signal a fundamental change in how the government addressed the problem of Indian land rights.

STEVEN L. DANVER

See also
Bureau of Indian Affairs; Dawes Severalty Act; Indian Reorganization Act

References
Deloria, Vine, Jr., and Clifford M. Lytle. *American Indians, American Justice.* Austin: University of Texas Press, 1983.
Deloria, Vine, Jr., and Clifford M. Lytle. *The Nations Within: The Past and Future of American Indian Sovereignty.* Austin: University of Texas Press, 1984.
Prucha, Francis Paul. *The Great Father: The United States Government and the American Indians.* 2 vols. Lincoln: University of Nebraska Press, 1984.
Prucha, Francis Paul, ed. *Documents of United States Indian Policy.* 2nd ed. Lincoln: University of Nebraska Press, 1984.

Langlade, Charles Michel de
Birth Date: May 1729
Death Date: ca. 1800–1802

Métis fur trader, officer, and Indian agent under the colonial administrations of France and Great Britain. Charles Michel de Langlade was born sometime in May 1729 at the French trading post of Michilimackinac (located on the northern tip of lower Michigan along the Straits of Mackinac) to a French fur trader and the sister of the Ottawa chief Nissowaquet (La Fourche). Langlade

gained his first military experience at the age of 10 when Nissowaquet took his nephew on a campaign against the Chickasaws. A skilled intercultural broker, Langlade assembled and accompanied large Native American contingents during several important episodes of the French and Indian War (1754–1763) and the American Revolutionary War (1775–1783).

In 1750 Langlade's father purchased his son a commission in the colonial service of King Louis XV. Although Langlade never rose above the rank of lieutenant, he became vital to France's western Native American alliance and took instructions directly from Canada's governor general. In June 1752 as the contest for the colonial dominion of North America neared a head in the Ohio River Valley, Langlade and 250 Ottawa and Ojibwa warriors sacked the pro-British Miami trading town of Pickawillany. Subsequently named Indian agent for the western tribes, Langlade led significant Native American contingents during Braddock's Campaign (1755), the massacre at Fort William Henry (1757), and the Battle of the Plains of Abraham (1759).

Following the French and Indian War, Langlade swore fealty to Great Britain, which retained him as agent for the western tribes. During the American Revolution, he mobilized western warriors on behalf of the British (notably in support of Lieutenant General John Burgoyne's 1777 invasion of New York) but encountered limited success following France's alliance with the United States. Langlade remained a British agent and fur trader at Green Bay (Wisconsin) until his death there sometime between 1800 and 1802.

JOHN W. HALL

See also
French and Indian War; Native Americans and the American Revolutionary War; Ottawas; Pickawillany Massacre; Scouts, Native American

References
Tasse, Joseph. "Memoir of Charles De Langlade." In *Report and Collections of the State Historical Society of Wisconsin,* Vol. 7, 123–187. Madison, WI: E. B. Bolens, 1876.
Zipperer, Sandra J. "Sieur Charles Michel De Langlade: Lost Cause, Lost Culture." *Voyageur: Northeast Wisconsin's Historical Review* 15(2) (Winter–Spring 1999): 24–33.

La Petite Guerre
See Petite Guerre, La

La Salle, René-Robert Cavelier, Sieur de
Birth Date: November 21, 1643
Death Date: March 1687

French military officer, explorer of North America, and diplomat. Born on November 21, 1643, in Rouen, Normandy, René-Robert Cavelier, Sieur de La Salle, was educated by the Jesuits. In 1662 he arrived in Montreal, New France, where he received a grant of land along the Saint Lawrence River.

La Salle's great passion was exploration. In 1669 and 1680 he explored areas south of Lake Ontario and Lake Erie. In 1674 he returned to France as the representative of the governor of New France, Louis de Buade, Comte de Frontenac, to explain why Frontenac had taken the initiative in constructing Fort Frontenac at the site of present-day Kingston, Ontario, and to petition for command of the fort, in which La Salle was successful. La Salle returned to France again in 1677 to seek permission to explore and expand the fur trade to the west, and King Louis XIV awarded him a monopoly on trade in the Mississippi Valley.

In 1679 members of La Salle's expedition sailed in the *Griffin*, the first commercial ship on Lake Erie, through Lake Huron to present-day Green Bay, Wisconsin, on Lake Michigan, where the *Griffin* was loaded with furs that La Salle hoped would help settle his sizable debts in Montreal. However, the *Griffin* succumbed to a storm in Lake Michigan in 1679. Unaware of this, La Salle continued down the western shore of Lake Michigan, building first Fort Miami on the St. Joseph River and then Fort Crèvecoeur near Lake Peoria in present-day Illinois in order to protect his men from the elements and hostile Native Americans. La Salle then returned with some of his party to Fort Frontenac to secure supplies for the trip down the Mississippi. He returned to discover that in March 1680, Fort Crèvecoeur had been abandoned.

Undeterred, La Salle again traveled to Fort Frontenac. Meanwhile a number of his men, who had been captured by Native Americans, found their way to Green Bay. The expedition resumed with additional men and supplies, and descending the Mississippi, La Salle finally reached the mouth of the river and the Gulf of Mexico on April 9, 1682. He claimed the Mississippi River and all territory watered by it and its tributaries for France, naming it Louisiana after King Louis XIV.

La Salle returned to the north to establish Fort St. Louis on the Illinois River in December 1682. He hoped to free himself from the control of French authorities in Canada and establish himself as governor of an independent French colony. La Salle's merchant rivals carried on a campaign against him, obliging him to return to France, where his appeals met with royal favor. The French government saw control of the mouth of the Mississippi as essential to its interests in the imperial rivalry with Spain, with which France was then at war, and La Salle received the governorship of all of Louisiana.

Ordered to establish a settlement near the mouth of the Mississippi, La Salle sailed for Louisiana in 1684 with four ships and about 400 men. The French naval commander, however, refused to follow La Salle's orders, resulting in the Spanish capture of the expedition's principal supply ship. In the West Indies, La Salle fell ill with a fever, with the result that the expedition fell into total disorder. Recovering his health, La Salle continued on with only about 180 men in the remaining three ships but sailed too far west in the Gulf of Mexico, landing near present-day Matagorda Bay, Texas. La Salle assumed that this was the westernmost outlet of the Mississippi, but explorations on land soon convinced him of his mistake. Meanwhile two of his remaining three ships had been wrecked, and the third returned to France.

Down to only 45 men, the expedition's situation was desperate, and La Salle set out in January 1687 with a small party to try to reach Canada and secure aid. Along the way his men mutinied, and La Salle was murdered in March 1687 near the Trinity River. Some of his party did reach Fort St. Louis on the Illinois River, but Native Americans killed most of the colonists who remained. While La Salle failed to realize his personal ambitions, his labors gave France a vast new colonial empire and altered the history of North America.

Theresa L. Storey

See also
France

References

Caruso, John Anthony. *The Mississippi Valley Frontier.* New York: Bobbs-Merrill, 1966.

Muhlstein, Anka. *La Salle: Explorer of the North American Frontier.* Translated by Willard Wood. New York: Arcade, 1994.

Parkman, Francis. *La Salle and the Discovery of the Great West.* Boston: Little, Brown, 1907.

Lawton, Henry Ware
Birth Date: March 17, 1843
Death Date: December 18, 1899

U.S. Army officer. Born in Maumee, Ohio, on March 17, 1843, Henry Ware Lawton moved with his family to Fort Wayne, Indiana, that same year. He was a student at the Methodist Episcopal College there when the American Civil War (1861–1865) began. Lawton joined the 9th Indiana Infantry Regiment in late April and saw service in the early fighting in western Virginia before mustering out with his unit that July.

Returning to Fort Wayne, Lawton reenlisted in the army in the 30th Indiana Infantry that August and was promoted to first lieutenant the same month. His unit joined the Army of the Ohio in Kentucky, and Lawton saw combat in the bloody Battle of Shiloh (April 6–7, 1862). He was promoted to captain in June during the Corinth Campaign. In all Lawton fought in 22 major engagements. He ended the war a brevet colonel and was subsequently awarded the Medal of Honor for his conduct during the 1864 Atlanta Campaign.

Following the Civil War, Lawton briefly studied law but returned to the army in 1867, although as a second lieutenant. He joined Colonel Ranald S. Mackenzie's 41st Infantry, a black regiment that later became the 24th Infantry. Lawton later moved with Mackenzie to the 4th Cavalry Regiment and served in most of the Indian campaigns in the Southwest, including the Battle of Palo Duro Canyon (September 20, 1874). Lawton had the reputation of being a brave and able officer who fought hard in battle and was also respected for his compassion and fairness toward the defeated, including Native Americans. Lawton was promoted to captain in March 1879, and in 1886 he was commanding B Troop of the 4th Cavalry when he was selected by Brigadier

Captain Henry W. Lawton distinguished himself in the Indian Wars in the West. He led the column that pursued Chiricahua Apache leader Geronimo, leading to his surrender in September 1886. (Library of Congress)

General Nelson A. Miles to lead the column that pursued Chiricahua Apache leader Geronimo, leading to his ultimate surrender that September.

Lawton was promoted to major in September 1888 and to lieutenant colonel in February 1889. Following the declaration of war against Spain, in May 1898 Lawton was advanced to brigadier general of volunteers and assumed command of the 2nd Division of Major General William R. Shafter's V Corps for the invasion of Cuba. Lawton supervised the initial V Corps landing at Daiquirí on June 22, 1898. He participated in the advance on Santiago de Cuba and led the attack at El Caney before joining the engagement at San Juan Heights.

Promoted to major general of volunteers on July 8, Lawton favored lenient terms for the Spanish, including allowing the Spanish soldiers to return home with their arms. Following the end of the fighting, Lawton served briefly as military governor of Santiago and then of the entire province. Relieved of his command because of "ill health" (i.e., heavy drinking that had led him to physically attack the Santiago police chief), Lawton returned to the United States to command IV Corps at Huntsville, Alabama. Receiving a stern lecture from President William McKinley and swearing off liquor, in March 1899 the popular Lawton was transferred to the Philippines, where he commanded the 1st Division and exhibited a lack of strategic sense combined with a reckless bravery in battle that on several occasions almost brought his death.

For whatever reason, Lawton chose to lead in person a small punitive action against Montalban and San Mateo near Manila. Walking the firing line in the open with complete disregard for his own safety during fighting near San Mateo on December 18, 1899, Lawton was struck by a bullet in the chest and died almost instantly, the only American fatality that day. Widely respected for his courage and leadership, Lawton was much mourned by the army and by the American public.

SPENCER C. TUCKER

See also

Adobe Walls, Second Battle of; Cavalry Regiment, 4th U.S.; Geronimo; Mackenzie, Ranald Slidell; Miles, Nelson Appleton; Palo Duro Canyon, Battle of

References

Cosmas, Graham. *An Army for Empire: The United States Army in the Spanish-American War.* College Station: Texas A&M University Press, 1998.

Linn, Brian McAllister. *The Philippine War, 1899–1902.* Lawrence: University Press of Kansas, 2000.

Rau, Rudy. *Lawton: Forgotten Warrior: A Commemorative Biography.* Washington, DC: Library of Congress, 1998.

Legion of the United States

Unique organization of the military land forces of the United States from 1792 to 1796 that was designed to counter the Indian threat on the northwestern frontier. Following the disastrous defeat of almost the entire U.S. Army in November 1791 by Native Americans in Ohio, Congress authorized raising a new army, and President George Washington selected Major General Anthony Wayne as commander. Wayne had proven to be a capable general during the American Revolutionary War (1775–1783) and had earned a reputation for hard fighting and strict discipline.

On December 27, 1792, President Washington formally designated this new U.S. Army the Legion of the United States. The legion concept was unique because it merged infantry, cavalry, and artillery into a single light and highly mobile combined arms force. Military theorists, including Maurice de Saxe, Henry Bouquet, Baron Friedrich von Steuben, and Henry Knox, were strong proponents of legion organization for independent operations in rugged terrain, since the legion would be trained to fight both conventional European-style armies and unconventional Native Americans of the frontier.

The total authorized strength of the Legion of the United States was 5,280 officers and enlisted men, although it never recruited more than 3,692 men, of whom 2,643 would participate during its single campaign. The legion had a headquarters staff and four equal sublegions of 1,348 officers and men, each commanded by a brigadier general and organized into eight infantry companies, four rifle companies, one light dragoon company, and one light artillery company. Each sublegion had its own distinct color. The sublegion was the primary maneuver unit capable of independent operations, with regular infantry used for firepower, riflemen used for skirmishing, light dragoons used for reconnaissance, and artillery used for heavy mobile fire support.

In 1792 Wayne established a training camp known as Legionville near Pittsburgh, Pennsylvania, where stern discipline and regulations were enforced. Offenses such as drunkenness were prevented by limiting passes and restricting men to camp. Disobedience was punished by reduction in rank, discharge, or whipping. Thieves were forced to walk a gauntlet of men and were drummed out of camp.

The legion's training was strenuous. Wayne applied Baron von Steuben's regulations during up to 10 hours of drill each day, including marksmanship and bayonet drill. The men skirmished, shot at targets, and attacked mock Indians. Effective marksmanship was rewarded with whiskey, and competitions were staged between sublegions. Practice battles were an essential part of training, and the riflemen served as the opposing force to stage mock attacks using blank ammunition on the remainder of the legion.

Wayne introduced several technical changes to improve efficiency, such as modifying muskets with new touch holes so that a soldier could prime them without looking. Fine gunpowder was issued so that it would easily fill the touch hole inside the barrel when the musket was tamped on the ground, thereby increasing the rate of fire and enabling soldiers to load on the run.

Wayne's legion trained through 1793 while fruitless peace talks with the Native Americans went forward. In October 1793 the legion took to the field and established a camp near Cincinnati, Ohio. The subsequent campaign of 1794 resulted in a resounding victory over the Native Americans in the Battle of Fallen Timbers (August 20, 1794). With Little Turtle's War (1790–1794), also known as the Northwest Indian War, won, the Legion of the United States was disbanded on November 1, 1796, and the sublegions were redesignated as the 1st, 2nd, 3rd, and 4th Infantry regiments. Wayne had proven that with proper organization and training, soldiers of the United States could successfully operate in wilderness and defeat the Indians on their own terms. The legion also showed that the fledgling U.S. government could raise and equip an army capable of providing for the common defense.

STEVEN J. RAUCH

See also
Fallen Timbers, Battle of; Washington, George; Wayne, Anthony

References
Birtle, Andrew J. "The Origins of the Legion of the United States." *Journal of Military History* 67 (October 2003): 1249–1262.

Gaff, Alan D. *Bayonets in the Wilderness: Anthony Wayne's Legion in the Old Northwest.* Norman: University of Oklahoma Press, 2004.

Lenni Lenapes
See Delawares

Lewis, Meriwether
Birth Date: August 18, 1774
Death Date: October 11, 1809

Soldier, personal secretary to President Thomas Jefferson, and leader, with William Clark, of the Corps of Discovery's expedition through the Louisiana Territory and the Oregon Territory (1803–1806). Meriwether Lewis was born on August 18, 1774, near Charlottesville, Virginia. Following his education by a private tutor, he inherited a plantation, which he managed from 1792 to 1794. In 1794 he volunteered as a private in the Virginia Militia and participated in putting down the Whiskey Rebellion. Later that same year he received a commission as an ensign in the regular U.S. Army. Serving in the army under Major General Anthony ("Mad Anthony") Wayne, Lewis first met William Clark in 1795.

After his election in 1800, President Thomas Jefferson—long a friend of Lewis's family—selected Lewis to serve as his private

Meriwether Lewis, along with William Clark, led the expedition bearing their names that explored the Louisiana Territory and the Oregon Country during 1804–1806. (Library of Congress)

secretary. In 1803 when Congress appropriated funding for an expedition to explore the new Louisiana Territory, Jefferson chose Lewis to lead the Corps of Discovery. Lewis invited Clark to share command as unofficial coleader.

Before departing for the West, Lewis undertook a crash course in the natural sciences, studying in Philadelphia with some of the nation's leading scientific minds. In the spring of 1804 Lewis joined Clark at their base camp near St. Louis. On May 22, 1804, Lewis and Clark with more than 40 soldiers, boatmen, and explorers launched their boats up the Missouri River.

Jefferson had instructed Lewis to follow the Missouri River to its source and find the best passage through the Rocky Mountains to the headwaters of the Columbia River and the Pacific Ocean. The president had also directed Lewis to make detailed maps of the terrain through which they passed, contact and establish relations with the Native American peoples and make ethnographic observations of them, investigate soils and the productive capacity of the land for agriculture, identify and collect specimens of plant and animal species, survey the territory's mineral resources and geological features, and record detailed observations of the region's weather.

Lewis and Clark constructed Fort Mandan on the Missouri River near present-day Bismarck, North Dakota, where they spent the winter of 1804–1805. There they were joined by Sacagewea, a Shoshone woman who helped navigate the Rocky Mountains and served as an interpreter and liaison with Native Americans. In April 1805 they resumed their trek west. They arrived in Oregon in November 1805 and erected Fort Clatsop near present-day Astoria, Oregon. In March 1806 they began the return trip eastward. At Traveler's Rest, located in the Bitterroot Valley of present-day Montana, Lewis and Clark divided the party. While Clark went south to explore the Yellowstone Valley, Lewis went north to explore the Marias River country. While separated, Lewis's party had a violent encounter with the Blackfoot Sioux on July 27. On August 11 Pierre Cruzatte, a member of the exploration party, accidentally shot Lewis in the thigh, but Lewis recovered from the injury. The next day Lewis and Clark reunited their expedition on the Missouri River and continued downstream, reaching St. Louis on September 23, 1806.

As a naturalist, Lewis had kept detailed scientific records and specimens for the expedition. He described approximately 100 new animal species and 70 new plant species. The expedition also established relations with several Native American tribes and recorded ethnographic information that remains valuable to researchers to this day. When Lewis reached Washington, D.C., in December 1806, he shared his discoveries with Jefferson.

The expedition was the high point of Lewis's short life. He never completed the task of preparing the expedition's journals, notes, and maps for publication. Jefferson appointed Lewis governor of the Louisiana Territory, but deepening depression, debt, and alcoholism consumed him. In 1809 while returning to Washington, D.C., Lewis twice tried to commit suicide. At a rural inn along the Natchez Trace in Tennessee (about 70 miles south of present-day Nashville), he finally succeeded. After shooting himself twice and cutting himself with a razor, Lewis died on October 11, 1809, at the age of 35.

PAUL G. PIERPAOLI JR.

See also

Clark, William; Jefferson, Thomas; Lewis and Clark Expedition; Louisiana Purchase; Sacagawea

References

Ambrose, Stephen E. *Undaunted Courage: Meriwether Lewis, Thomas Jefferson, and the Opening of the American West.* New York: Simon and Schuster, 2003.

Cutwright, Paul Russell. *Lewis and Clark: Pioneering Naturalists.* Lincoln: Bison/University of Nebraska Press, 2003.

Moulton, Gary, ed. *The Journals of the Lewis & Clark Expedition.* Lincoln, NE: Bison Books, 1983.

Lewis and Clark Expedition
Start Date: 1804
End Date: 1806

Expedition authorized by U.S. president Thomas Jefferson in 1803 to explore the newly acquired Louisiana Territory, which had been purchased from France. The expedition accomplished its primary goal of reaching the Pacific Ocean and also yielded a comprehensive map of the western terrain, descriptions of flora and fauna in the wilderness, and interaction with western Native Americans.

Jefferson had conceived the idea of westward expansion long before it came to fruition in 1803. Having inherited his father's skill at surveying and love of exploration, Jefferson had already considered a major westward expedition before he was elected president in 1800. When he became president he hired U.S. Army ensign Meriwether Lewis, a family acquaintance, as his personal secretary. In 1801 Jefferson sent Lewis to the University of Pennsylvania to learn scientific skills. Lewis was also trained in celestial navigation and wilderness survival techniques in preparation for the overland expedition to come.

Jefferson secretly sent a message to Congress in January 1803 asking for funds to explore the Louisiana Territory. His request was granted during the spring; coincidentally, Jefferson's opportunity to purchase the Louisiana Territory from the French government came about in May. Jefferson then named Lewis the commander of the Corps of Discovery expedition, and Lewis immediately set about preparing for the arduous journey. He tapped William Clark, with whom he had served in the army, to serve as unofficial cocaptain of the expedition. Once certain technicalities were resolved, Lewis, Clark, and their cadre of 29 men, plus an additional contingent of soldiers and boatmen who would return to St. Louis after the winter with reports and specimens for President Jefferson, set out from St. Louis, Missouri, on May 14, 1804.

Captain Meriwether Lewis shooting an Indian. Illustration from *A Journal of the Voyages and Travels of a Corps of Discovery: Under the command of Capt. Lewis and Capt. Clarke of the Army of the United States [. . .] during the years 1804, 1805 and 1806 [. . .]* by Patrick Gass, 1810. (Library of Congress)

The Corps of Discovery began the long journey up the Missouri River, suffering the only fatality of the entire expedition when Sergeant Charles Floyd died, apparently of appendicitis. By late October the men had traveled more than 1,000 miles and reached a settlement of 4,500 Hidatsa and Mandan people in what is now North Dakota. Lewis decided to camp there for the winter in a structure they named Fort Mandan, located across the river from the Native American settlement. There they hired the French fur trader Toussaint Charbonneau and his Shoshone wife, Sacagawea, to serve as guides and interpreters for their journey to the Pacific. Sacagawea's role became highly romanticized in the decades following the expedition, but she did help with navigation and in fostering cordial relations with Native Americans they met along the way.

Throughout the trip Lewis kept multiple copies of his maps and detailed notes of observations of the climate, vegetation, fauna, and people. Indeed, both Lewis and Clark kept diaries with complex scientific observations of the animal and plant life encountered by the expedition. In the spring of 1805 Lewis sent 12 of his men toward St. Louis with his various reports and a selection of artifacts—including a small selection of previously unknown live animals—for shipment to Washington, D.C.

Lewis and Clark meanwhile crossed the continental divide, and the party began the long trek to the Pacific Coast. For the rest of August and September 1805 the expedition struggled through the mountains of what are now Montana and Idaho. By September the expedition reached a tributary of the Columbia River that enabled the explorers to resume their travel by canoe. In late November 1805 the men reached the Pacific Ocean at the mouth of the Columbia near present-day Astoria, Oregon. After wintering on the coast, Lewis and Clark began the journey homeward up the Columbia River. In July Lewis and Clark split for a time, with Lewis and a small detachment cutting a new path to the Missouri but also exploring the Marias River, almost to the present-day Canadian border. It was during this separate adventure that the only deadly encounter with Indians occurred: a confrontation with Blackfoot warriors in which two Indians were killed. Clark meanwhile led the bulk of the expedition along the Yellowstone River before the two groups reunited on the Missouri in early August 1806. On September 23, 1806, they returned to St. Louis.

Lewis rested in St. Louis for several months but headed east again in November. In late December he arrived in Washington, D.C., and was received as a hero. Lewis and his men all received double pay and land grants from the government. Jefferson appointed Lewis governor of the Louisiana Territory and Clark official Indian agent for the West. Despite Lewis's success on the frontier, however, depression and financial problems beset him in the years following his famous expedition. On October 11, 1809, he committed suicide at a rural inn about 70 miles south of Nashville, Tennessee, while en route from St. Louis to Washington, D.C.

Paul G. Pierpaoli Jr.

See also
Clark, William; Jefferson, Thomas; Lewis, Meriwether; Louisiana Purchase; Sacagawea

References
Ambrose, Stephen E. *Undaunted Courage: Meriwether Lewis, Thomas Jefferson, and the Opening of the American West.* New York: Simon and Schuster, 2003.
Moulton, Gary, ed. *The Journals of the Lewis & Clark Expedition.* Lincoln, NE: Bison Books, 1983.
Ronda, James P. *Lewis and Clark among the Indians.* 2nd ed. Lincoln: University of Nebraska Press, 2002.

Lipan Apaches

One of the eastern Apache tribes. In seminomadic bands, the Lipans hunted buffalo and deer and planted seasonal crops across tribal lands that stretched from the Edwards Plateau (a fertile area of central Texas) across the arid southern Texas Plains to the Rio Grande, a region as large as the state of Oklahoma. Throughout the 18th century the Lipans, relying on their skills as horsemen and hunters, resisted and finally repelled Spanish invasion; however, between 1850 and 1880 the U.S. Army decimated and scattered the Lipans in relentless campaigns targeting Apache encampments.

Beginning in 1823, the newly independent nation of Mexico continued Spanish efforts to invite emigrants from the United States to

A Lipan Apache woman and child in partial native dress outside their tipi, 1900. (National Anthropological Archives, Smithsonian Institution, NAA INV 02029700)

settle in Texas. The Lipans befriended the Anglo-American settlers and supported them during the Texas Revolution against Mexico (1835–1836). After Texas won independence in 1836, the Lipans, signing treaties of friendship, were among the first allies of the new Republic of Texas, even joining in military actions against the Comanches. In 1842 Mexico's Army of the North invaded Texas, recapturing San Antonio and several nearby towns. While the Texans were raising a militia to oppose this invasion, Lipan warriors defended Austin, Houston, and other Texas cities from surprise attack by Mexican forces. And when Alexander Somervell led a daring punitive expedition into Mexico in November 1842, Lipan warriors rode alongside him, prompting Texas president Sam Houston to promise that Texas would always be "kind" to the Lipans.

The United States annexed Texas in 1845 and subjected the state's Native Americans to its national policies of Indian removal, but the Apaches refused to surrender. In response, the U.S. Army increased troop strength at forts on or near Lipan lands, and throughout the 1850s the U.S. Army mounted missions against Lipan encampments. When Brigadier General Albert J. Myer was an army surgeon in southern Texas from 1854 to 1857, he observed military action against the Lipans. "The war on this frontier is one of extermination," he wrote, adding that U.S. troops were ordered "to take no prisoners" and "to spare no one."

During the American Civil War (1861–1865), attacks against the Lipans stopped. After the war, however, the regular army reentered Texas in force. In 1872 the United States conducted a brutal campaign of annihilation against the Lipans. In raids on both sides of the Rio Grande, U.S. cavalry units attacked Apache encampments, killing Lipans on sight—sometimes women along with the men—and destroying their homes, crops, livestock, and ponies, thus rendering desperate any Lipan who might have escaped the raiders. By 1880 most of the surviving Lipans had scattered, giving up their land and traditional way of life to hide among the Tejano population (Hispanic Texans), especially around San Antonio, Corpus Christi, and the Rio Grande. Today the Lipan Apache tribe is petitioning the State of Texas for official recognition.

PATRICK RYAN

See also
Apaches; Houston, Samuel

References
Opler, Morris E. *American Indian Ethnohistory: Indians of the Southwest,* Vol. 10, *Lipan and Mescalero Apache in Texas.* Edited by David Agee Horr. New York: Garland, 1974.
Schilz, Thomas F. *Lipan Apaches in Texas.* El Paso: Texas Western Press, 1987.

Liquor

During the American Indian Wars, liquor was an important trading commodity. Usually available in the form of brandy, whiskey, or rum, it proved tremendously disruptive to Native American culture and did much to intensify violence between whites and Native Americans. Throughout the history of Native American wars with Europeans and later with American settlers, alcohol played a crucial role in devastating Native American society. Indians bore a considerable amount of complicity by participating willingly in a trade that proved so detrimental to their societies' well-being. Nevertheless, although it would be difficult to attribute the causes of any Native American war solely to liquor, the trade in spirits most certainly paved the way for white encroachment on Native American lands.

British and American officials, seeking to expand westward, frequently plied Native Americans with liquor to render them more agreeable to ceding extensive stretches of land in exchange for minimal compensation. Alcohol played an equally important role in intensifying frontier conflict. The reduced judgment and relaxation of inhibitions caused by liquor often incited violence between warriors and white settlers. Alcohol-induced killings reinforced hostile sentiments between whites and Native Americans on the frontier, magnifying the violence of the Indian Wars if not contributing to the causes of them.

The French also engaged in the trade in spirits. The French frequently recruited Native American allies with promises of brandy. Indeed, some French officers attributed their highly successful Native American recruiting efforts during the summer of 1756 to rumors spread by Ojibwas and Menominees that large quantities of alcohol accompanied French battlefield victories over the British.

Liquor itself did little to provoke war between Native Americans and European settlers. The trade in alcohol, however, remained a symbol of what each culture found lacking in the other. Settlers saw in the Indians' tendency to drink to excess an innate racial inferiority. Native Americans, contrary to popular stereotypes, remained well aware of their susceptibility to liquor. They in turn looked down on the morality of a European and American culture that would not prevent its traders from dealing in such a harmful substance. Indeed, Native American resistance to white encroachment, including the rejection of the European trade in alcohol, did much to stimulate perhaps the most successful Pan-Indian movement in North America, Pontiac's Rebellion (1763).

Following the French and Indian War (1754–1763), Pontiac, an Ottawa chief, organized a loose coalition of primarily Algonquian-speaking tribes to resist British expansion into the Ohio Valley. To recruit allies, Pontiac tapped into the nativist teachings of the Delaware prophet Neolin, who called for the rejection of European culture, including liquor, and a return to traditional Native American ways of life as they existed prior to contact with the whites. In this conflict, liquor was a symbol of each society's sense of superiority over the other. Recognizing the damage that European culture, and particularly alcohol, had done to their societies, Native Americans readily embraced rhetoric that called for the rejection of these influences.

Despite these motivations, however, warriors participating in the conflict could not evade the temptation of alcohol. The capture of two groups of Europeans—one a small party of traders and another of British soldiers—in early June 1763 by Mississaugi Ojibwas and Pottawatomis led to a night of drinking from the traders' supplies and ensuing violence. Natives not so tempted would have regretted the immorality of European traders who continued to deal in destructive spirits.

Alcohol remained a source of tension between settlers and Indians throughout the early history of the United States. Following American independence, as early as 1790 U.S. federal laws prohibited the trade of whiskey to Native Americans. The army was given the task of enforcing the laws. Even so, Americans continued to use alcohol to wrangle concessions from Native Americans. In 1809, for example, William Henry Harrison, governor of the Indiana Territory, wooed various chiefs with liquor while Tecumseh, a Shawnee chief preaching resistance to American encroachment, was away recruiting followers. Harrison succeeded in convincing the intoxicated Native American leaders to cede 3 million acres of land in exchange for payment of $7,000 and a modest annuity.

Some Indians protested the ban on alcoholic beverages. In one of the final episodes of U.S.–Native American conflict, Chiricahua Apaches on the San Carlos Reservation protested Brigadier General George Crook's policy against the consumption of an alcoholic beverage known as tiswin. In May 1885, 42 men, including Geronimo, and 92 women fled the reservation for the Mexican border. Although Geronimo would eventually surrender, another drunken episode led to a second escape and his subsequent legendary contest with Brigadier General Nelson A. Miles in 1886.

James K. Perrin Jr.

See also

Crook, George; Geronimo; Harrison, William Henry; Miles, Nelson Appleton; Neolin; Pontiac's Rebellion; Tecumseh; Tenskwatawa

References

Mancall, Peter C. *Deadly Medicine: Indians and Alcohol in Early America.* Ithaca, NY: Cornell University Press, 1995.

Utley, Robert M., and Wilcomb E. Washburn. *Indian Wars.* New York: American Heritage Press, 2002.

White, Richard. *The Middle Ground: Indians, Empires, and Republics in the Great Lakes Region, 1650–1815.* New York: Cambridge University Press, 1991.

Literature and the American Indian Wars

In 1699 New England Puritan minister Cotton Mather, writing in *Decennium Luctuosum: A History of Remarkable Occurrences in the Long [Indian] War,* told about "a body of terrible Indians" who had abducted a colonial mother, Hannah Duston. He concluded gloatingly that the captured woman and her companions escaped by striking dead their sleeping captors with hatchets, not forgetting moreover to slice off 10 scalps for the sake of a later bounty. An alternate voice sounded from Seneca chief Red Jacket more than a century later in 1812, when he claimed that white people, whom the natives had originally viewed as friends, "wanted our country. Our eyes were opened, and our minds became uneasy. Wars took place."

These two assessments mirror the polarities of literature arising from the most protracted American conflict, one that began with colonization in 1607 and continued into the 20th century. The controversial history of the Indian Wars has inspired a large body of fiction, history, biography, and memoirs. Many of these works can, however, only be viewed as creative rewritings of history based on fragmentary sources and the ethnocentric views of individual writers. In spite of their historical inaccuracy, many of the works mentioned below demonstrate how past and present wars became part of an ongoing cultural discourse that reflects shifting views of the indigenous population of North America and American territorial expansion.

With the outbreak of colonial hostilities such as the Anglo-Powhatan wars (1610–1614, 1622–1632, and 1644–1646), the Pequot War (1636–1638), and King Philip's War (1675–1676), all of which took place during the first 70 or so years of English colonization, the white settlers' initial view of the "friendly savage" who could be Christianized (see John Eliot's *A Late and Further Manifestion of the Progress of the Gospell amongst the Indians in New England,* 1655) shifted to one of fear and hatred. Captivity narratives, reflecting the experience of approximately 1,640 New Englanders taken hostage between 1675 and 1763, began to predominate as the western and northern frontiers became a vast battleground. Central to many of these narratives, of which Mary Rowlandson's *Sovereignty and Goodness of God* (1682) is the best known, is the idea that the captive, held hostage in the devilish clutches of savages, is redeemed through the grace of God. This view of Native Americans as vicious savages was further reinforced by an anonymous pamphlet titled *A Brief and True Narration of the Late Wars Risen in New-England, Occasioned by the Quarrelsome Disposition, and Perfidious Carriage of the Barbarous, Savage, and Heathenish Natives There* (1675).

While 18th-century Enlightenment writers, such as French philosopher Jean-Jacques Rousseau in his *Discourse on Inequality* (1754) and to some extent Benjamin Franklin in his *Remarks Concerning the Savages of North America* (1784), viewed Native Americans as "noble savages," hostility between Europeans and Native Americans peaked with the French and Indian War (1754–1763), during which tribes took different sides depending on where they thought their interests lay. Consequently, subsequent literature reflects a dichotomy wherein hostile tribes are demonized and friendly ones lionized. This either-or attitude prevails in the novels of 19th-century author James Fenimore Cooper. His *Last of the Mohicans* (1826), for instance, idealizes the "good Indians" Chingachook and Uncas but demonizes Magua and the other Hurons, who are allied with the French and are portrayed as cannibals and baby killers in this novel centering on the siege of Fort William Henry in 1757. Other novels by Cooper focusing on the Indian Wars include *The Pioneers* (1823), *The*

Prairie (1827), *The Pathfinder* (1840), and *The Deerslayer* (1841). Memoirs from the period include *The Journals of Major Robert Rogers* (1765), leader of the famous Rogers' Rangers attached to the British Army, and *George Washington Remembers,* based on Washington's 1786 account of his early military career, including British major general Edward Braddock's disastrous Fort Duquesne expedition in 1755.

In Cooper's wake, tales evoking Native American conflicts became a popular theme of 19th-century literature. Particularly interesting in the context of shifting views of the native is John Augustus Stone's drama *Metamora; or, The Last of the Wampanoags* (1829), which depicts Native American leader Metacom (King Philip) as a noble savage victimized by English colonists. Interestingly, this play, with the title role played by the celebrated actor Edwin Forrest, nearly provoked a riot on the first night of its run in Augusta, Georgia, in 1831, a sensitive time that coincided with the Cherokees' protest against the Indian Removal Act. Another potboiler of the 19th century, Ann Stephens's immensely popular dime novel *Malaeska: The Indian Wife of the White Hunter* (1860), takes a somewhat less controversial stand in highlighting the dangers of miscegenation. Malaeska's white lover is killed by Native Americans, and the son she bears him leaps from a cliff when he discovers his mixed-race background.

Popular short stories and novels further reflected the growing conflict over America's treatment of Native Americans, a tendency reinforced when abolitionist writing before the American Civil War (1861–1865) intersected with protests against Native American resettlement and the increasing expropriation of tribal territory. Here again a dichotomy is evident: while James Hall's "Indian Hater" (1829), for instance, indirectly justifies a settler's vendetta against the Native Americans who have killed his family and burned his home, other writers such as Julia Dumont in "Tecumseh" (1824) and Caroline Hentz in "The Indian Martyrs" (1832) condemn white atrocities and plead for peaceful coexistence. Helen Hunt Jackson's *Ramona* (1884), however, was the most significant development in popular literature dealing with Native American conflicts. In her earlier polemic *A Century of Dishonour* (1881), Jackson had already focused on the broken treaties and unfulfilled promises in a passionate indictment of American policies toward Native Americans. Her novel *Ramona,* set in southern California in the aftermath of the Mexican-American War (1846–1848), deals with a part–Native American woman who falls in love with a young full-blooded Native American sheepherder, Alessandro. After their elopement the two are chased from several of their homes by American greed. Alessandro's insanity precedes his murder by a white landholder. Sometimes called "The Uncle Tom's Cabin of Southern California," the novel enjoyed immense popularity when it was published.

Poetry provided a particularly fertile ground for 19th-century protests against what modern writers such as David Stannard (1992) have referred to as the "American Holocaust." Prominent American poets such as William Cullen Bryant mourned "a noble race" now gone in his "Disinterred Warrior" (1832), and John Greenleaf Whittier predicted in "Metacom, or Philip, the Chief of the Wampanoags" (1831) that the curse of the vanquished warrior would continue to haunt the fledgling nation. Concurrently, translators throughout the century familiarized English-speaking readers with Native American war songs, such as Frances Denmore's translation of Sitting Bull's last song after his surrender to U.S. authorities and Edwin T. Denig's "Prayer of a Warrior" (ca. 1854).

Much popular literature from the early 20th century to the present day focuses largely on intrigue and sensation. Popular novels include Kenneth Roberts's *Northwest Passage* (1937) about Rogers' Rangers, Hervey Allen's *Disinherited* trilogy (1943–1948) about the Texas Rangers, and Cormac McCarthy's *Blood Meridian, or the Evening Redness in the West* (1985) about a group of scalp hunters in the borderlands between Mexico and America. In a more serious vein, however, Native American and non–Native American voices, particularly since the civil rights era of the 1960s, have become increasingly prominent in challenging previous historiography. While much Native American fiction addresses contemporary problems, Forrest Carter's *Watch for Me on the Mountain* (1978) centers on Geronimo and the Apaches' struggle against the U.S. military. Juvenile fiction has been particularly prominent in its focus on American–Native American conflicts. Two books—Scott O'Dell's *Sing Down the Moon* (1970) and Beatrice Harrell's *Longwalker's Journey: A Novel of the Choctaw Trail of Tears* (1999)—focus on young people's harrowing experiences during Indian removal.

Contemporary writers have also explored the legacy of conflict in other genres. Poetry has been a fertile field, and examples include James Wright's "A Centenary Ode: Inscribed to Little Crow, Leader of the Sioux Rebellion in 1862" (1971) and Duane Niatum's "Tribute to Chief Joseph" (1980). A prominent biography to emerge in recent years has been John Sugden's *Tecumseh: A Life* (1997). Two recent dramas by native writers include Ray Louis's *Butterfly of Hope: A Warrior's Dream* (1974), which tells of a mid-19th-century band of Native Americans who fought against and hid from the U.S. cavalry to avoid displacement, and Wallace Tucker's *At the Sweet Gum Bridge* (1976), focusing on the Choctaw warrior Pushamataha and his alliance with U.S. forces during the War of 1812.

ANNA M. WITTMANN

See also

Captivity Narratives; Film and the American Indian Wars; Jackson, Helen Hunt

References

Berkhofer, Robert. *The White Man's Indian: Images of the American Indian from Columbus to the Present.* New York: Vintage, 1978.
Churchill, Ward. *Fantasies of the Master Race: Literature, Cinema, and the Colonization of American Indians.* San Francisco: Libri, 1998.
Geiogamah, Hanay, and Jaye T. Darby, eds. *Stories of Our Way: An Anthology of American Indian Plays.* Los Angeles: UCLA Indian Studies Center, 1999.
Goldensohn, Lorrie, ed. *American War Poetry: An Anthology.* New York: Columbia University Press, 2006.

Little Bighorn, Battle of the
Start Date: June 25, 1876
End Date: June 26, 1876

Battle that occurred during June 25–26, 1876, between units of the U.S. Army's 7th Cavalry Regiment, commanded by Lieutenant Colonel George Armstrong Custer, and Lakota Sioux, Arapaho, and Cheyenne warriors, led by Sitting Bull, Crazy Horse, Rain-in-the-Face, and Gall. The battle, also known as Custer's Last Stand and to Native Americans as the Battle of Greasy Grass Creek, took place along the Little Bighorn River in eastern Montana and was part of the wider Great Sioux War (Black Hills War) of 1876–1877. The Battle of the Little Bighorn is arguably the most famous battle of the American Indian Wars and the most important victory by the Plains Indians over the U.S. Army.

In the late 1860s gold was discovered in the Black Hills of South Dakota, sacred ground to the Lakota Sioux and off-limits to white settlement according to the 1868 Fort Laramie Treaty. In 1874 a U.S. Army expedition, led by Custer, confirmed the presence of gold in the region. As news of the discovery spread, white prospectors began pouring into the area. When the U.S. government tried to purchase the area with the gold in the Black Hills, the tribes refused to sell.

In late 1875 many Native Americans, outraged over the continued intrusions of whites onto their sacred lands, left their reservations and began raiding the miners' camps. The government then abrogated the Fort Laramie Treaty, and the commissioner of Indian affairs decreed that all Native Americans must return to their reservations by January 31, 1876. If they did not, they would be considered hostile. Defying the decree, several thousand Native Americans gathered in eastern Montana to fight for their lands.

The U.S. government and the army appeared to welcome the showdown with the Native Americans. The result was the Powder River–Bighorn–Yellowstone Campaign of 1876. To force the Native Americans back to the reservations, the army dispatched three large columns to the Black Hills region. Commander of the Department of Dakota Brigadier General Alfred Terry had overall command. Driving on the Sioux from the east, he had at his disposal some 1,000 men, including Custer's 7th Cavalry. Brigadier General George Crook moved north from Fort Fetterman in Wyoming with some 1,000 troops and 250 allied Native Americans. A third column of some 450 men under Colonel John Gibbon would march from Fort Ellis in western Montana. The plan was for the three columns to converge on the Native American camp

Estimated Casualties at the Battle of the Little Bighorn

	Killed	Wounded
U.S. Army Officers	16	1
U.S. Army Enlisted	242	51
Civilians	10	Unknown
Native Americans	36–300	About 160

Custer's Last Fight, depicting the defeat of members of the 7th Cavalry Regiment under Lieutenant Colonel George A. Custer in the Battle of the Little Bighorn, June 25–26, 1876. (Corel)

in eastern Montana on June 26 and force the Indians back to their reservations. With some 3,000 men involved, the army leaders were confident of victory.

The coordinated attack never occurred. Crook's column fought a much larger group of warriors in the Battle of the Rosebud on June 17 and was forced to retire in order to regroup. Unaware of Crook's situation, Gibbon and Terry proceeded forward and joined forces in late June near the mouth of Rosebud Creek. They decided that Terry's largest unit, the 7th Cavalry under Custer, would proceed up the Rosebud while Terry and Gibbon moved toward the Bighorn and Little Bighorn rivers, hoping to trap the Native Americans between them.

Custer had won some renown as a major general of cavalry in the Union Army during the American Civil War (1861–1865) and was resentful that he had still not recovered his wartime rank 10 years later. A veteran of the Plains wars, he was a glory seeker and was contemptuous of the ability of Indians to fight. Yet the camp toward which Custer was moving was probably the greatest concentration of Indian power ever: some 10,000–15,000 people, at least 4,000 of them warriors.

Terry's strategy was to place the Indians between Custer and Gibbon's mixed force of infantry and cavalry. The plan called for Gibbon's Montana column to move west along the Yellowstone River to its confluence with the Bighorn River. At that point

Gibbon, with Terry accompanying, was to turn south to be in position to cooperate with Custer's cavalry, which it was hoped would be driving the Indians from the east. Terry made it clear to Custer that he was to strike the Indians wherever they could be found but allowed him ample latitude in which to exercise tactical judgment.

Custer's force, which departed at noon on June 22, numbered 647 men: 32 officers, 566 enlisted men, and 35 Arikara, Crow, and Dakota scouts. Discovering a large Indian trail, Custer followed it to the west, reaching the valley of the Little Bighorn River in southeastern Montana very early on June 25. From the Crow's Nest, a high point on the divide separating the valleys of the Rosebud and the Little Bighorn, Custer's scouts detected the Sioux pony herd some 15 miles distant. Initially planning to rest his regiment through the day and then attack the Indian village at dawn on June 26, Custer was forced to revise his plan when it appeared that the Native Americans had discovered his presence. He decided to attack immediately.

Custer divided the regiment into three battalions. Breakup and dispersal of an Indian village before an attack could be launched was always of paramount concern to the officer in command of an attack, and Custer ordered three companies under Captain Frederick Benteen to scout to the left to ensure that the Indians did not escape in that direction. Custer directed that a second battalion of three companies together with the Indian scouts, under Major

Marcus Reno, cross the Little Bighorn River, charge down the valley, and attack the village. Meanwhile, the third and largest of the three battalions, five companies commanded by Custer himself, would approach the Indian village on a course roughly parallel to that of Reno's but above and to the right, hidden from Reno's view by the intervening bluffs above the river. No one really knows Custer's exact strategy that sultry Sunday afternoon, but most historians believe that Reno's attack was intended as a diversionary movement, which would have allowed Custer, with the largest battalion of the regiment, to strike the village from an unexpected quarter with the main body.

Encountering much stiffer resistance than he anticipated, Reno halted his charge down the valley. He then retreated into the timber along the river and finally abandoned that location. Panicking, he withdrew in disorderly flight across the Little Bighorn River to the safety of the bluffs above it. In the process he lost perhaps a fourth of his men. Here the survivors dug in.

Whether and to what extent Custer was aware of Reno's situation has been debated ever since. Also unclear is whether Custer actually attempted to cross the river and attack the village or was in fact himself attacked and driven back before he had an opportunity. Regardless, Custer's battalion was eventually forced to seek the higher ground north-northeast of the river. At some point Custer's five companies were forced to assume a defensive posture and were eventually overwhelmed. The final act of the drama saw Custer and a few others gathered atop what became known as Custer Hill in the famous last stand for which the battle is best known. In the fighting Custer himself sustained two wounds, but it is not clear whether he was hit early in the fight or later, during the last stand. Compounding the situation for Custer was the fact that his troops were armed with the single-shot Trapdoor Springfield carbine, while many of the Indians had the faster-firing Winchester repeating rifle.

Meanwhile, some five miles to the southeast at what is known as the Reno-Benteen defense site, Major Reno's three companies were joined by the pack train and Captain Benteen's battalion, returning from its earlier scout to the left. Here the Reno-Benteen command, although suffering substantial casualties, managed to hold out until relieved by Gibbon's column on June 27.

In the battle the 7th Cavalry lost 268 men killed, including about 210 on what has become known as Custer Field. This was nearly 40 percent of the regiment's prebattle strength. The Custer family lost four of its members in addition to George: two brothers, Captain Tom Custer and Boston Custer; a nephew, Armstrong Reed; and a brother-in-law, Lieutenant James Calhoun. No real consensus seems to exist on Indian losses, although these may have been as few as 50. The battle was at once the apex and the nadir for the Sioux and their allies.

When Terry and Gibbon reached the field on June 27, there were no Indians. They had moved off to the south immediately after the battle, and soon the separate clans went their own ways. The Indians lacked the ability to maintain a large force in the field for long. Had they stayed together for a few more days, the Indians might have defeated both Terry and Gibbon.

The Battle of the Little Bighorn shocked the entire nation. The government immediately sent reinforcements to the northern Plains, and by the spring of 1877 virtually all of the hostile Sioux, including Crazy Horse, had been hunted down and removed to reservations or had followed Sitting Bull to Canada.

ROBERT B. KANE, JERRY KEENAN, AND SPENCER C. TUCKER

See also
Cavalry, Native American; Cavalry, U.S. Army; Crazy Horse; Crook, George; Custer, George Armstrong; Great Sioux War; Mackenzie, Ranald Slidell; Merritt, Wesley; Miles, Nelson Appleton; Native American Warfare; Rosebud, Battle of the; Scouts, Native American; Sioux; Sitting Bull

References
Connell, Evan S. *Son of the Morning Star: Custer and the Little Bighorn.* New York: North Point Press, 1984.

Fox, Richard Allan, Jr. *Archaeology, History, and Custer's Last Battle.* Norman: University of Oklahoma Press, 1993.

Miller, David H. *Custer's Fall: The Native American Side of the Story.* Norman: University of Nebraska Press, 1985.

Nichols, Ronald H., ed. *Reno Court of Inquiry.* Hardin, MT: Custer Battlefield Historical and Museum Association, 1996.

Sarf, Wayne Michael. *The Little Bighorn Campaign, March–September 1876.* Conshohocken, PA: Combined Books, 1993.

Sklenar, Larry. *To Hell with Honor: Custer and the Little Big Horn.* Norman: University of Oklahoma Press, 2000.

Vestal, Stanley. *Warpath: The True Story of the Fighting Sioux Told in a Biography of Chief White Bull.* Lincoln: University of Nebraska Press, 1934.

Wert, Jeffrey D. *Custer: The Controversial Life of George Armstrong Custer.* New York: Simon and Schuster, 1996.

Little Carpenter
See Attakullakulla

Little Crow
Birth Date: ca. 1810
Death Date: June 10, 1863

Mdewakanton Sioux (Dakota) chief. Little Crow, or Taoyateduta, was born circa 1810 in a Mdewakanton Sioux village on the west bank of the Mississippi River south of present-day St. Paul, Minnesota. He inherited the chieftaincy of the Mdewakantons on the death of his father, Wakenyantaka. Little Crow signed the Treaty of Mendota on August 5, 1851, ceding a large amount of Sioux territory west of the Mississippi to the United States. Under the terms of the treaty, the Mdewakantons and Wahpetons relocated to their remaining lands near the Lower Sioux Agency on the Minnesota River near present-day Mankato, Minnesota. They were to receive annuity payments for the sale of their territory, although the Sioux

Mdewakanton Sioux chief Little Crow, who had previously been accommodating toward white settlers, led the bloody Minnesota Sioux Uprising of 1862. He was shot and killed by a settler in 1863. (Library of Congress)

had unknowingly signed a second document allocating most of those funds to cover their alleged debts to white traders.

Criticized by many Sioux for signing the treaty, Little Crow declared his opposition to further land cessions. However, he continued to pursue a policy of peace with the whites. He farmed in the settlers' manner and joined the Episcopal Church. In 1857 Little Crow organized a group of warriors to oppose fellow Sioux leader Inkpaduta after the latter's attack on white settlers at Spirit Lake, Minnesota. The following year Little Crow traveled to Washington, D.C., hoping to remedy injustices that had arisen from the 1851 treaty. Instead, federal officials persuaded him to sign another treaty ceding more Sioux land.

In August 1862 the annuity payment failed to arrive on time. Little Crow asked Agent Thomas Galbraith to issue provisions from the well-stocked storehouses to feed his people until the funds arrived, but Galbraith refused. Two days later angry young warriors killed five whites. At a council that night, Little Crow argued against war. Accused of cowardice by many Sioux, he reluctantly agreed to lead a campaign against the whites. The next day, August 18, Little Crow attacked the Lower Agency, killing 20 people. The Sioux then moved to strike Fort Ridgely, ambushing a company of soldiers and killing 21 on their way.

On August 19 Little Crow assembled 400 warriors to attack Fort Ridgely. The Sioux attacked the following day but were repulsed.

Joined that night by additional warriors who doubled the size of his force, Little Crow renewed the attack on August 22. Again the Sioux were driven off, and Little Crow was wounded. Learning that Colonel Henry Sibley was on the way with 1,400 soldiers, Little Crow decided to shift the attack to New Ulm. His injury prevented him from participating in the fight, in which the Sioux burned nearly 200 buildings and inflicted more than 100 casualties on the defenders but failed to take the town. Meanwhile, small parties of warriors raided isolated settlements.

Many Sioux became disheartened with their lack of success and dropped out of the fight. Little Crow and his remaining warriors attacked Sibley's force at Birch Coulee on September 23. Defeated, Little Crow withdrew to Devils Lake. He continued to launch sporadic raids and on one of these was shot and killed by a settler on June 10, 1863.

JIM PIECUCH

See also
Birch Coulee, Battle of; Dakota Sioux; Inkpaduta; Mendota, Treaty of; Minnesota Sioux Uprising; New Ulm, Battles of; Sibley, Henry Hastings

References
Anderson, Gary Clayton. *Little Crow: Spokesman for the Sioux.* St. Paul: Minnesota Historical Society Press, 1986.
Brown, Dee. *Bury My Heart at Wounded Knee.* New York: Holt, Rinehart and Winston, 1970.

Little Turtle
Birth Date: ca. 1747
Death Date: July 14, 1812

Last major war chief of the Miami tribe and primary Native American leader in Little Turtle's War (1785–1795), also known as the Northwest Indian War. Little Turtle (Mishikinakwa) was born around 1747 probably in the Miami village of Kekionga 20 miles northwest of present-day Fort Wayne, Indiana. His father, Mishikinakwa ("Turtle"), was a powerful Miami chief; tradition says Little Turtle's mother was a Mahican. The diminutive "Little" was applied to Little Turtle's name to distinguish him from his father.

Early on Little Turtle displayed both military and leadership skills. Chosen as the war chief of the Atchatchakangouen division of the Miamis, he became a brilliant war leader and strategist, widely acknowledged to have been one of the most successful Native American war chiefs. Determined and brave, Little Turtle was also noted for his oratorical skills. He was not the head chief of the Miamis, however; that position was hereditary.

On November 5, 1780, Little Turtle established his reputation as a war leader by defeating along the Eel River forces led by French adventurer Augustin Mottin de la Balme, who was attempting to capture Fort Detroit. After the American Revolutionary War (1775–1783), white settler inroads in the Northwest Territory led to the forming of a Native American confederation

Little Turtle's War 449

aimed at keeping the whites east of the Ohio River. Little Turtle was one of the leaders of the confederation, and the ensuing fighting became known as Little Turtle's War. When the U.S. government sent in 1,300 men (320 of them regulars and the remainder militia) under Brigadier General Josiah Harmar to end the unrest, in two battles in October 1790 Little Turtle and Shawnee leader Blue Jacket defeated Harmar's men, inflicting some 300 casualties. The next year Little Turtle and Blue Jacket again defeated U.S. forces numbering 600 regular troops and 1,500 militia, this time led by Major General Arthur St. Clair. This Battle of the Wabash (November 4, 1791) was the worst defeat ever suffered by U.S. forces at the hands of the Native Americans. St. Clair sustained some 800 casualties, while Native American losses were reported as 21 killed and 40 wounded.

A third U.S. expedition into the Northwest Territory, this one in 1794 by numerically superior well-trained forces led by Major General Anthony Wayne, caused Little Turtle concern. When Wayne sent a peace offer, Little Turtle urged its acceptance, pointing out the strength of the opposing force and expressing doubts about British support. Blue Jacket and British agents wanted war, which a majority of the chiefs then approved.

Reportedly Little Turtle then ceded leadership to Blue Jacket. Little Turtle's role in the resulting Native American defeat in the Battle of Fallen Timbers (August 20, 1794) is unclear; he may not have been present. Little Turtle and other Native American leaders were then obliged to sign the 1795 Treaty of Greenville. Little Turtle realized that the Native Americans could no longer expect to stop the advance of the American settlers. He therefore rejected the position taken by Shawnee leader Tecumseh and counseled Native Americans to keep the peace, including during the War of 1812.

Little Turtle met President George Washington as well as presidents John Adams and Thomas Jefferson. In 1809 Little Turtle broke with other Miami leaders on the occasion of a meeting at Fort Wayne with Governor William Henry Harrison, when Little Turtle supported Harrison. Little Turtle retired to a village near present-day Columbia City, Indiana. After the Siege of Fort Wayne in September 1812 during the War of 1812, Major General Harrison ordered retaliation against Miami villages in the vicinity, and the village of Little Turtle was among those destroyed. Little Turtle died from gout on July 14, 1812, not far from Kekionga, Indiana, and was honored with a military funeral at Fort Wayne.

BILLIE FORD AND SPENCER C. TUCKER

See also

Blue Jacket; Fallen Timbers, Battle of; Greenville, Treaty of; Harmar, Josiah; Harrison, William Henry; Little Turtle's War; Miamis; St. Clair, Arthur; Tecumseh; Wabash, Battle of the; Wayne, Anthony

References

Anson, Bert. *The Miami Indians*. Norman: University of Oklahoma Press, 1971.
Axelrod, Alan. *Chronicle of the Indian Wars: From Colonial Times to Wounded Knee*. New York: Prentice Hall, 1993.
Carter, Harvey Lewis. *The Life and Times of Little Turtle: First Sagamore of the Wabash*. Urbana: University of Illinois Press, 1987.
Sugden, John. *Blue Jacket: Warrior of the Shawnees*. Lincoln: University of Nebraska Press, 2000.

Little Turtle's War

Start Date: 1785
End Date: 1795

A series of battles and skirmishes fought in the Old Northwest Territory between a loose confederation of Native American tribes and the U.S. Army from 1785 to 1795. Little Turle's War, also known as the Northwest Indian War, is called the Miami Campaign by the U.S. Army. The conflict arose from competition over lands that are now part of Ohio and Indiana.

After the Northwest Ordinance of 1785 encouraged development of the lands newly acquired from Britain following the American Revolutionary War (1775–1783), American settlers began migrating farther west, across the Ohio River. The British provided the Native Americans in the region with arms and other supplies. As a result, Chief Little Turtle's Miamis and Blue Jacket's Shawnees, aided by other tribes, were strong enough to inflict more than 1,000 casualties on the white settlers and prevent them from moving out of the Ohio River Valley.

The security of the Northwest Territory was a major concern for the new U.S. government, and in the autumn of 1790 it sent a force of 300 regulars and more than 1,000 militia under Brigadier General Josiah Harmar to secure the region. The initial engagements in the war went badly for the Americans. Harmar divided his force, and two detachments were badly mauled in ambushes, forcing Harmar to fall back to Fort Washington (present-day Cincinnati, Ohio). In all Harmar lost some 130 men during the campaign.

In the spring and summer of 1791 the War Department orchestrated an enlargement of the army, and that summer Congress commissioned Northwest Territory governor Major General Arthur St. Clair to lead two 300-man regiments of regulars and 1,400 ill-trained levies and militiamen against the main Miami town, Kekionga. However, Little Turtle, Blue Jacket, and Tecumseh, leading a contingent of 2,000 warriors, surprised the force's poorly defended camp at present-day Fort Recovery, Ohio, near the headwaters of the Wabash River on November 4, 1791. More than half of the Americans were killed or wounded, and the survivors were forced into a haphazard retreat toward Fort Washington. In 1792 U.S. emissary Colonel John Hardin, on a peace mission to the Shawnees authorized by President George Washington, was killed by Shawnee warriors, which further intensified the ongoing war.

Convinced of the strategic necessity of securing the trans-Ohio region, Congress doubled the authorized size of the army, and

Depiction of Shawnee warriors defeating U.S. Army regulars and militia under Brigadier General Josiah Harmar in the Northwest Territory in 1790 during Little Turtle's War (1785–1795). (North Wind Picture Archives)

President Washington appointed a new military commander, Major General "Mad" Anthony Wayne. Wayne now took command of the new Legion of the United States in the late autumn of 1793; paid more attention to discipline, training, and provisioning than his predecessors; and moved methodically into the Native American lands in 1794, building defensive structures along the way. Seeking to avenge St. Clair's earlier defeat, Wayne ordered the construction of Fort Recovery, which Little Turtle and his warriors unsuccessfully attacked in June 1794.

The Native Americans, led by Blue Jacket, attacked Wayne's force of about 3,000 men near present-day Toledo. In the ensuing Battle of Fallen Timbers (so-named for the large number of trees felled there in an earlier tornado), the soldiers withstood the initial Native American onslaught and used a bayonet charge to push the warriors from their position onto open ground, where mounted soldiers quickly shattered the force. This stinging defeat for the Native Americans all but ended Little Turtle's War.

The defeat, coupled with the knowledge that Britain would soon finally abandon its frontier forts in accordance with Jay's Treaty (1794), effectively broke the Native Americans' resistance, and they ceded most of the disputed lands to the United States in the Treaty of Greenville, signed on August 3, 1795.

MATTHEW J. KROGMAN

See also

Blue Jacket; Fallen Timbers, Battle of; Greenville, Treaty of; Harmar, Josiah; Land Cessions, Northwest Ordinance; Legion of the United States; Little Turtle; Miamis; Old Northwest Territory; Shawnees; St. Clair, Arthur; Tecumseh; Wabash, Battle of the; Wayne, Anthony

References

Carter, Harvey Lewis. *The Life and Times of Little Turtle: First Sagamore of the Wabash.* Urbana: University of Illinois Press, 1987.

Dowd, Gregory Evans. *A Spirited Resistance: The North American Indian Struggle for Unity, 1745–1815.* Baltimore: Johns Hopkins University Press, 1992.

Stewart, Richard W., ed. *American Military History,* Vol. 1, *The United States Army and the Forging of a Nation, 1775–1917.* Washington, DC: Center of Military History, 2005.

Sugden, John. *Blue Jacket: Warrior of the Shawnees.* Lincoln: University of Nebraska Press, 2000.

Little Wolf
Birth Date: ca. 1820
Death Date: 1904

Northern Cheyenne chief whose warriors played a role in the defeat of U.S. forces under Lieutenant Colonel George A. Custer in the Battle of the Little Bighorn on June 25, 1876. Little Wolf was born circa 1820 in present-day Montana. A gifted warrior and military strategist, he soon became a war chief, having participated in Red Cloud's War (1866–1868) along the Bozeman Trail and having signed the Treaty of Fort Laramie in 1868. Little Wolf's bravery and military prowess further elevated him in Cheyenne society, and by the late 1860s he was among the most revered of all the Cheyenne chiefs.

In the mid-1870s Little Wolf, along with Dull Knife, another important Cheyenne chief, allied with the Lakota Sioux and other area tribes in an attempt to defeat U.S. military forces in the Montana Territory. Little Wolf did not participate in the Battle of the Little Bighorn, but Custer's discovery of his scouts there on June 25, 1876, led the cavalry commander to order an immediate attack on the distant Native American village rather than wait until the next day, as he had originally planned. This decision led directly to the near annihilation of Custer's command in the Battle of the Little Bighorn.

After the battle, Little Wolf and his allies fled into the Bighorn Mountains. Reinforced U.S. troops were soon in pursuit. By 1878 Little Wolf and his Cheyenne followers, along with other Native American groups, had been herded into Indian Territory (Oklahoma). With their people lacking adequate food and shelter, Little Wolf and Dull Knife defied U.S. government orders that they remain in Oklahoma and set out for their homeland in Montana in mid-August 1878. Their march of several hundred miles was grueling, and scores of people died en route. The day after the march began, U.S. cavalry caught up with the column of about 300 Native Americans, who refused to surrender. They continued on their march while repelling numerous attacks.

After reaching White Clay Creek in Nebraska, the column split. Dull Knife's contingent of about 150 people went to the Red Cloud Agency, where he finally surrendered. Little Wolf's contingent, with about as many people as that of Dull Knife, sought refuge in Nebraska's Sand Hills. Holding out until March 1879, Little Wolf was forced to surrender to U.S. forces and their Native American allies in Nebraska. Little Wolf's contingent was eventually allowed to remain in the area, and the chief became a scout for the U.S. Army for a short time. In December 1880 Little Wolf accidentally shot a warrior during an altercation. Little Wolf had been intoxicated at the time of the shooting and was mortified by what had transpired. He then went into virtual self-imposed exile, eventually taking up residency on the Northern Cheyenne Indian Reservation in Montana, where he died in 1904.

PAUL G. PIERPAOLI JR.

See also
Bozeman Trail; Cheyennes; Dull Knife; Little Bighorn, Battle of the; Red Cloud's War

Chief Little Wolf was revered among the Northern Cheyennes for his military prowess. In 1878, he helped lead his followers in a breakout from Indian Territory in order to return to their homeland in Montana. (Library of Congress)

References
Sandoz, Mari. *Cheyenne Autumn.* 1953; reprint, Lincoln: University of Nebraska Press, 1992.
Wiltsey, Norman B. *Brave Warriors.* Caldwell, ID: Caxton, 1963.

Llano Estacado
See Staked Plains

Logan, Benjamin
Birth Date: ca. 1742
Death Date: December 11, 1802

American frontiersman, soldier, and politician. Benjamin Logan was born in Augusta County, Virginia, around 1742. When Logan was 15 years old his father died, and Logan inherited his father's farm. Logan fought with Colonel Henry Bouquet against the Shawnees during the 1754–1763 French and Indian War. In 1774 as a lieutenant in a volunteer Virginia militia unit, Logan fought in Lord Dunmore's War against the Shawnees and Mingos.

The next year Logan moved to western Virginia (present-day Kentucky), founded the settlement of St. Asaph's near Stanford, and built Logan's Fort there. The following year he was appointed sheriff and justice of the peace. During the American Revolutionary War (1775–1783) he was a colonel in the Virginia Militia for Kentucky County and fought Native Americans in Kentucky and the Ohio Country, where he and Brigadier General George Rogers Clark, Logan's superior officer, frequently disagreed on strategy.

In the autumn of 1786 Logan led a force of U.S. soldiers and Kentucky militiamen in a campaign against Shawnee towns along the Mad River in the Ohio Country. Logan's men burned the towns, which had been inhabited primarily by noncombatants while the warriors were raiding forts in Kentucky. Logan destroyed food supplies and killed or captured a considerable number of Native Americans, including a chief. The Shawnees, in retaliation, escalated their attacks on white settlements. The campaign became part of Little Turtle's War (1785–1795), also known as the Northwest Indian War.

From 1781 to 1787 Logan sat in the Virginia House of Delegates, where he advocated for Kentucky statehood. He served as a delegate to the Danville Convention, which produced the first Kentucky Constitution in 1791–1792. After statehood Logan served in Kentucky's House of Representatives from 1792 to 1795. He ran unsuccessfully for governor in 1796 and 1800. On December 11, 1802, Logan died of a stroke at his home near Shelbyville, Kentucky.

ROBERT B. KANE

See also
Bouquet, Henry; Clark, George Rogers; Clark's Ohio Campaign, First; Clark's Ohio Campaign, Second; Little Turtle's War; Lord Dunmore's War; Mingos; Shawnees

References
Nester, William R. *The Frontier War for American Independence.* Mechanicsburg, PA: Stackpole, 2004.
Sword, Wiley. *President Washington's Indian War: The Struggle for the Old Northwest, 1790–1795.* Norman: University of Oklahoma Press, 1985.
Talbert, Charles G. *Benjamin Logan, Kentucky Frontiersman.* Lexington: University of Kentucky Press, 1962.

Logan, John
Birth Date: ca. 1725
Death Date: 1780

Mingo leader. Born around 1725 and also known as Chief Logan, the Mingo Chief, and Tachnedorus, John Logan resided in the western Virginia and Kentucky region during the American Revolutionary War (1775–1783) period. He was named after the secretary of the colony of Pennsylvania. Logan befriended many of the local white settlers in his role as tribal leader. He had a reputation for being a bridge builder between Native Americans and British colonists.

In 1774 the continuing sporadic violence between natives and settlers on the frontier led a group of settlers under Colonel Michael Cresap and Dan Grealborne to murder two of Logan's family members. This action helped trigger Lord Dunmore's War (1774). Logan responded by leading attacks against English settlements in the Monongahela River Valley, killing hundreds of settlers there. Colonial officials reacted by opening a campaign against the natives. Logan then decided to seal an alliance with Shawnee tribal leader Cornstalk.

In the Battle of Point Pleasant (October 10, 1774), the more numerous colonials defeated Cornstalk and Logan and their warriors. As a result, Cornstalk was forced to surrender all of his tribal land claims in Kentucky. Logan, however, refused to surrender. Over the next few months he raided settlements in both British and Native American territories. During the fighting, he gave a speech in which he declared that the authorities would never catch him. Continuing his attacks on local settlements, Logan died at an unknown location in 1780.

JAIME RAMÓN OLIVARES

See also
Cornstalk; Lord Dunmore's War; Mingos; Shawnees

References
Stuart, John. *Memoir of Indian Wars and Other Occurrences.* New York: New York Times, 1971.
White, Richard. *The Middle Ground: Indians, Empires, and Republics in the Great Lakes Region, 1650–1815.* New York: Cambridge University Press, 1991.

Logstown, Treaty of

Agreement among representatives of several Native American tribes, the Ohio Company, and officials from Pennsylvania and Virginia chiefly regarding land rights in the trans-Allegheny region. The treaty was signed on June 13, 1752, after negotiations had taken place at Logstown, a Native American settlement some 18 miles south of present-day Pittsburgh, Pennsylvania. Ultimately the Treaty of Logstown would aggravate the conflicting interests of the Iroquois Confederacy, New France, Virginia, and British land speculators in the Ohio River Valley. This helped contribute to the outbreak of the French and Indian War (1754–1763).

Immediately following the Iroquois cession of all land claims in western Maryland and Virginia in the Treaty of Lancaster (1744), the Virginia House of Burgesses moved to assert its claim over the entire Ohio Country. In 1745 the House of Burgesses granted nearly a third of a million acres of land to the Ohio Company of Virginia. The company sought to sell lands around the Forks of the Ohio River (present-day Pittsburgh, Pennsylvania) to promote trans-Allegheny settlement and trade. King George's War (1744–1748) delayed these plans. However, by the early 1750s the Ohio Company had established a fortified storehouse at the confluence of Wills Creek and the northern branch of the Potomac River (present-day Cumberland, Maryland). The company also planned to survey the Ohio Valley and sell land and manufactured goods to settlers there.

In June 1752 Christopher Gist, the leader of the survey, and George Croghan, a Pennsylvania trader who had established a large trading post at the Miami town of Pickawillany, convened a treaty conference at Logstown. Their goal was to convince the Iroquois, the Shawnees, and the Delawares to support the Ohio Company's goals. Also in attendance were commissioners from Virginia and Pennsylvania, whose interests generally intersected with those of the Ohio Company. Gist and Croghan sought Native American consent for the construction of a company-owned fortified storehouse at the confluence of the Allegheny River and the Monongahela River. They promised that the storehouse would offer Native Americans favorable trade rules. Actually, however, it would give the company control over a strategic point in the Ohio Valley that would promote trans-Allegheny settlement and trade. Influenced by abundant gifts, assurances of goodwill, and concern over recent French efforts to reassert former claims in the Ohio Valley (Céleron de Blainville's expedition), Tanaghrisson, the spokesman for the Iroquois Confederacy, accepted Gist and Croghan's proposal. In doing so, Tanaghrisson acknowledged Virginia's claim to all territory in the valley south of the Ohio River.

On learning of the treaty, the French destroyed the British trading post at Pickawillany on June 21, 1752, killing a number of people and forcing the Miamis back into alliance with France. The French also fortified their trading posts in the Ohio Valley and erected forts at Presque Isle, Le Boeuf, and Venango in northwestern Pennsylvania. Virginia's efforts to repel French encroachments in the region, including Lieutenant Colonel George Washington's 1754 expedition and Major General Edward Braddock's ill-fated 1755 campaign, marked the opening volleys of the French and Indian War.

Dean Fafoutis

See also

Croghan, George; French and Indian War; Iroquois Confederacy; King George's War; Ohio Company of Virginia; Pickawillany Massacre; Tanaghrisson

References

Anderson, Fred. *Crucible of War: The Seven Years' War and the Fate of the Empire in British North America, 1754–1766.* New York: Vintage Books, 2001.

Jennings, Francis. *Empire of Fortune: Crowns, Colonies, and Tribes in the Seven Years War in America.* New York: Norton, 1988.

White, Richard. *The Middle Ground: Indians, Empires, and Republics in the Great Lakes Region, 1650–1815.* New York: Cambridge University Press, 1991.

Lone Wolf
Birth Date: ca. 1820
Death Date: Mid-1879

Kiowa chief who led his followers in resistance to U.S. reservation policies. Lone Wolf (Guipago) was born probably around 1820 and became associated with the Tsetanmas, an elite warrior grouping among the Kiowas. He ultimately came to lead one of the chief militant factions of the Kiowas, who opposed accommodation with whites and the U.S. government. Lone Wolf did not trust whites and showed great animosity toward them.

In the summer of 1856 Lone Wolf's Kiowa band left its permanent settlement near Bent's Fort (Colorado), which was to be watched over by the trader William Bent. While the band was buffalo hunting, Bent offered the Kiowas' lodgings to the Cheyennes. Lone Wolf was furious and attempted to evict the Cheyennes by force, an effort that was unsuccessful. By 1860, however, the Kiowas had generally made peace with other Plains tribes.

Lone Wolf had not forgotten Bent's treachery and soon emerged as a principal militant, vowing not to submit to white demands. On October 18, 1865, Lone Wolf signed the Little

Kiowa chief Lone Wolf spent years battling the federal government's attempt to extinguish the Kiowa Reservation. The Supreme Court ruled against him in *Lone Wolf v. Hitchcock*, upholding the right of Congress to amend unilaterally the original treaty with the Kiowa people. (National Archives)

Arkansas Treaty, which included other Plains tribes and had been negotiated with the federal government. Lone Wolf soon abrogated the treaty, however, and began raids in Texas in the winter of 1866. In 1867 Lone Wolf refused to sign the Medicine Lodge Treaty because he believed that it did not offer his people sufficient concessions.

By 1868 Lone Wolf had become the coleader of the Kiowas along with Kicking Bird, who headed the peace faction. Try as he did, Lone Wolf was unable to unite the Kiowas under his authority. That same year when hostilities flared anew with white settlers and the U.S. Army, Lone Wolf and Satanta, another chief, agreed to engage in negotiations with Lieutenant Colonel George A. Custer, under a flag of truce, at Fort Cobb, located on the Kiowa-Comanche Reservation in Indian Territory.

Upon their arrival on December 17 Lone Wolf and Satanta were taken prisoner, and Custer threatened to kill the men unless they agreed to return their bands to the reservation. The threat worked, as most of the Kiowas relocated to the reservation by February 1866, at which point Lone Wolf and Satanta were released. Thereafter Lone Wolf maintained peace for a time, although he was unable to convince other militant Kiowas to follow suit.

Disgusted with the broken promises of the U.S. government and its Indian commissioners, the Kiowas resumed offensive operations, this time on the San Antonio–El Paso Road in April 1872. Lone Wolf personally led a raid against a government wagon train in which 17 Mexican teamsters were killed. That autumn Lone Wolf was chosen to attend a peace conference in Washington, D.C. The negotiations went well initially but were thwarted when Lone Wolf's son, Taukania, was killed in December 1873 by U.S. cavalrymen. Deeply angered, Lone Wolf now led a war party to Kickapoo Springs in May 1874 to recover his son's body and that of his cousin, also killed by U.S. soldiers.

Lone Wolf and his warriors participated in the Second Battle of Adobe Walls (June 27, 1874), which was part of the larger Red River War (1874–1875). After briefly returning to the reservation, Lone Wolf and his followers tried unsuccessfully to raid another wagon train. Lone Wolf's Kiowas then sought refuge in Palo Duro Canyon; in the meantime, on September 28 U.S. forces razed the Kiowas' village. Unable to fend off U.S. Army attacks and realizing that his band would starve, Lone Wolf surrendered to U.S. forces at Fort Sill, Indian Territory (Oklahoma), in February 1875. He was subsequently imprisoned at Fort Marion (Florida) in the early spring of 1875 and remained incarcerated until 1878. Suffering probably from malaria, Lone Wolf died near Fort Sill in the summer of 1879.

PAUL G. PIERPAOLI JR.

See also

Adobe Walls, Second Battle of; Bent's Fort; Cheyennes; Custer, George Armstrong; Fort Sill; Kiowas; Medicine Lodge Treaty; Palo Duro Canyon, Battle of; Red River War

References

Jones, L. Lee. *Red Raiders Retaliate: The Story of Lone Wolf.* Seagraves, TX: Pioneer Press, 1980.

Mayhall, Mildred P. *The Kiowas.* Civilization of the American Indian Series. 1971; reprint, Norman: University of Oklahoma Press, 1984.

Longhouse

Native American dwelling used chiefly by the Iroquois Confederacy, who lived in present-day New York state, southern Ontario, southern Quebec, and Wisconsin. The Iroquois Confederacy consisted of the Mohawks, Oneidas, Onondagas, Senecas, and Cayugas and, after 1722, the Tuscaroras.

The Iroquois built longhouses of varying design, construction, and size, but all were longer than they were wide. The typical longhouse, which could house as many as 20 families, was at least 80 feet long and 18 to 20 feet wide. The roof, which was covered with animal skins in the winter to keep warmth in, had numerous openings through which smoke from fires burning inside could be vented. There were few windows, so the average longhouse tended to be dark inside. At either end was an opening for a door. Some longhouses, constructed in later periods, were reportedly as large as 325–350 feet long and 15–20 feet wide. These large dwellings could house as many as 100 families. In very large longhouses, there were several doors cut into the sides as well.

Although construction design and material varied, most anthropologists believe that the side frames were made of sharp fire-hardened wooden poles. Between the poles, which were driven deeply into the ground, bark and other material was woven to form walls. In the warm months the roofs were thatched with grass or leaves. Animal skins were laid atop that material in the cold months for better insulation. There were usually at least four or five roof vents for fires used to prepare food and to keep warm. Rooflines also varied. Some were straight and pitched, while others were arched, achieved by painstakingly bending wooden poles into shape. Most longhouses were built within a village setting and were protected by high timber palisades to keep out animals and hostile enemies.

Other groups besides the Iroquois built longhouses; these included the Eries, Wyandots (Hurons), Leni Lenapes (Delawares), and Pamunkeys. Several tribes in the Pacific Northwest also constructed longhouses, some of enormous size (500–600 feet long and 50–60 feet wide). Many of these were built close to the shoreline, at the edge of the maritime forest.

PAUL G. PIERPAOLI JR.

See also

Iroquois Confederacy; Pamunkeys; Wyandots

References

Richter, Daniel K., and James H. Merrell, eds. *Beyond the Covenant Chain: The Iroquois and Their Neighbors in Indian North America, 1600–1800.* Syracuse, NY: Syracuse University Press, 1987.

Richter, Daniel K. *The Ordeal of the Longhouse: The People of the Iroquois League in the Era of European Colonization.* Chapel Hill: University of North Carolina Press, 1992.

An Iroquois family stands next to a longhouse covered with wooden mats, a typical Indian dwelling in the Northeast. (Native Stock Pictures)

Looking Glass
Birth Date: ca. 1823
Death Date: October 5, 1877

Nez Perce leader. Looking Glass (Allilimya Takanin) was born probably in 1823 near the Middle Fork of the Clearwater River in what is now Idaho. His father, Apash Wyakaikt, head of the Asotin band of the Nez Perces, was known as Looking Glass for the small mirror he wore around his neck. When his father died in January 1863, Allilimya Takanin inherited leadership of the band along with the mirror and the name "Looking Glass."

The elder Looking Glass and several other Nez Perce leaders had refused to sign the 1855 treaty that confined the tribe to a reservation in Idaho. After assuming leadership of the Asotins in 1863, the younger Looking Glass joined Old Joseph of the Wallowa and White Bird of the Salmon River Nez Perce bands in refusing to sign a second treaty that greatly reduced the size of the reservation. Although not bound by the treaty, Looking Glass and his band lived just inside the border of the reservation.

Tension between those Nez Perces who had not signed the treaty and whites increased in 1874 and 1875, as a growing number of settlers occupied Nez Perce land. Some Nez Perces favored war, but Looking Glass joined Wallowa leader Young Joseph in arguing for peace.

In May 1877 Looking Glass joined Joseph and White Bird in arguing against Brigadier General Oliver O. Howard's order that the Nez Perces relocate to the reservation. However, the leaders finally agreed to go, and Looking Glass returned to his village near the forks of the Clearwater, where he hoped to remain at peace. After a detachment of troops attacked Looking Glass's village on July 1, 1877, he and his people escaped and united with the bands of Joseph and White Bird.

Looking Glass fought in the Battle of Clearwater River (July 11–12, 1877). The Nez Perces were defeated but escaped the pursuing soldiers. Uncertain of their next move, the Nez Perce leaders conferred on the night of July 15. Looking Glass proposed that they cross the Bitterroot Mountains and join their Crow allies in Montana. If that plan failed, he advised going to Canada, where Sitting Bull and many Sioux had taken refuge.

Looking Glass knew the Bitterroots well and led the Nez Perces safely through the mountains. Upon reaching the Big Hole River in Montana, he recommended a pause to rest. This proved to be a serious mistake, as the army found and attacked the Nez Perces on August 9. Although the Nez Perces checked the attack and held off the troops while the noncombatants escaped, the tribe lost 90 people in the engagement.

In mid-September the Nez Perces learned that the Crows were scouting for the army and would not assist them. The Nez Perces

Nez Perce leader Looking Glass figured prominently in the Nez Perce War of 1877. He was killed in battle on October 5, 1877, shortly before the Nez Perce surrender. (National Archives)

then marched toward Canada and were about 40 miles from the border when Looking Glass again insisted that the people be allowed to rest. The delay allowed Colonel Nelson Miles to catch up with the Nez Perces on September 30. Looking Glass urged the surrounded Nez Perces to resist but was shot and killed on October 5 shortly before Joseph surrendered to Miles.

JIM PIECUCH

See also

Big Hole, Battle of the; Clearwater River, Battle of; Crows; Howard, Oliver Otis; Joseph, Chief; Miles, Nelson Appleton; Nez Perces; Nez Perce War; Sioux; Sitting Bull; White Bird Canyon, Battle of

References

Brown, Dee. *Bury My Heart at Wounded Knee.* New York: Holt, Rinehart and Winston, 1970.

Josephy, Alvin M. *The Nez Perce Indians and the Opening of the Northwest.* New Haven, CT: Yale University Press, 1965.

Utley, Robert M. *The Indian Frontier of the American West, 1846–1890.* Albuquerque: University of New Mexico Press, 1984.

Lord Dunmore's War
Event Date: April 1774

Conflict that erupted in April 1774 when bands of frontiersmen attacked Native American settlements in the Ohio River Valley. Subsequent retaliatory raids by the natives prompted John Murray,

Fourth Earl of Dunmore and Virginia's governor since 1771, to send 2,000 men into the district that he named West Augusta. By month's end, Dunmore announced that Fort Pitt (Pennsylvania) was in imminent danger. Pennsylvanians and Virginians, particularly land speculators associated with the Loyal Company, proceeded to manipulate the evolving frontier dispute as a means of subverting the hated boundary delineated by the Proclamation of 1763. The proclamation had been the British Crown's attempt to maintain peaceful relations with potentially rebellious western natives by prohibiting settlement west of the Appalachians.

Tensions between the Shawnees and the British colonists first surfaced when Sir William Johnson, British superintendent of Indian affairs for the northern colonies, and Iroquois emissaries fixed the northern boundary line, originally expressed in the Proclamation of 1763, with the Treaty of Fort Stanwix in 1768. Native American communities in the upper Ohio Valley—particularly the Miamis, Shawnees, Wyandots, Delawares, and Mingos—rejected the right of the Iroquois to cede all of their hunting grounds south of the Ohio as far as the mouth of the Tennessee River. The tributary nations argued that their dependency was based on a compact of mutual responsibilities that did not involve the unilateral surrender of their land rights.

When Daniel Boone and other American colonists claimed the ceded territory in Kentucky, angry Shawnees and Wyandots sought to turn back the encroachers. By 1771 Delaware, Mingo, Miami, Ottawa, and Illinois leaders helped fashion a confederacy to repulse the British invaders. Yet as throngs of pioneers crossed the Appalachians, one Shawnee leader, Cornstalk, advocated peaceful restraint. Lord Dunmore's War began with a series of atrocities committed against unsuspecting Native Americans. In 1774 Dunmore, on learning that hostile Shawnees were ravaging the frontier settlements in retaliation, rallied Virginia's militia. A short time later he sent 2,000 militiamen into Shawnee territory. Instead of chastising the rebellious tribes, the violent raids, especially the murderous exploits of Captain Michael Cresap, only created greater hostility. Enraged Shawnee warriors, accompanied by some Mingos, swarmed the exposed western settlements in revenge.

When frontier clashes first erupted in the spring of 1774, John Logan, a Mingo chief, admitted that the Ohio tribes had just grounds for complaint. Unlike other native leaders who favored a more militant course of action, Logan reminded Mingo warriors of their own transgressions during council deliberations. After the tribal council ended, however, messengers arrived in early May 1774 with tales of more atrocities, including the ambush and murder on April 30 of 11 Mingos, among them 2 of the chief's relatives. Mingo and Shawnee warriors responded to the reports by increasing their raids against British settlements along the west bank of the Monongahela River.

Eager to subdue the hostile Native Americans, Dunmore promptly dispatched two militia columns into the Ohio Valley. He also ordered the men to build a stronghold at Wheeling (Fort Wincastle) and to destroy neighboring Shawnee villages. Angus

LORD DUNMORE'S WAR, 1774

Lake Superior

Ottawa R.

45°N

Lake Huron

Lake Michigan

Lake Ontario

Hudson R.

Detroit

Muskingum R.

Lake Erie

Allegheny R.

Tioga

Onoquaga

Easton

New York

40°N

Wyandots

Fort Miami

Gnaddenhutten

Fort McIntosh

Forty Fort

Valley Forge

Philadelphia

Piqua

Fort Pitt

Delaware R.

Susquehanna R.

Delawares

Fort Henry

Potomac R.

Chillicothe

Shawnees

Fort Randolph

Washington

Ohio R.

Monongahela R.

Vincennes

Ruddle's Station

Martin's Station

Kanawha R.

Richmond

Yorktown

Bryant's Station

Boonesborough

Harrodsburg

Fort Massac

35°N

Fort Jefferson

Tennessee R.

ATLANTIC OCEAN

Savannah R.

Tombigbee R.

Wabash R.

30°N

■ Indian village
○ White settlement
✠ Fort

85°W

80°W

0   100   200 mi
0   100   200 km

75°W

McDonald's subsequent expedition destroyed five Shawnee villages. Although successful, the Wapatomica campaign failed to halt Shawnee and Mingo raids against isolated frontier communities.

On July 12, 1774, Dunmore instructed Colonel Andrew Lewis, commander of the southwestern militia, to proceed from Camp Union (present-day Lewisburg, West Virginia) directly to the mouth of the Kanawha River, where Dunmore's army would join him from Fort Pitt. Lewis and his 1,100 militiamen arrived on October 6, 1774, and camped at Point Pleasant, a triangle of land at the confluence of the Kanawha and Ohio rivers. Messengers later informed Lewis that Dunmore had altered his plans. Instead of joining Lewis at Point Pleasant, Dunmore now wanted Lewis to join him in attacks against Shawnee villages along the Scioto River. Shawnee scouts, however, spotted the invaders before they had time to depart, and the Native Americans rushed to prepare an assault. Although the warriors wanted to strike the first blow, Shawnee leader Cornstalk counseled peace. After rejecting Cornstalk's pleas for negotiation, the tribal council voted to strike Lewis's force at dawn.

Cornstalk demonstrated his acceptance of the council's decision by leading some 1,000 Shawnee, Mingo, Delaware, Wyandot, and Ottawa warriors against the unsuspecting Point Pleasant encampment. The Battle of Point Pleasant began on October 10, 1774. The natives fought hard, but the attackers were eventually scattered after a day of bloody combat.

Following their defeat at Point Pleasant, the Native Americans fled through the forest to their towns on Pickaway Plains. After warriors had reassembled in council, Cornstalk upbraided the other chiefs for their refusal to let him negotiate a settlement. No one moved to answer Cornstalk's questions about how to stop the advancing enemy. Thus, a furious Cornstalk rose and struck his tomahawk in a post in the council house and offered to make peace. The humbled warriors concurred, and Cornstalk assembled a Shawnee delegation to accompany him.

Cornstalk set out for Camp Charlotte, Dunmore's headquarters. Dunmore received Cornstalk's peace overture and agreed to hold a conference. During the ensuing treaty negotiations, Cornstalk described the innumerable wrongs that his people had suffered before the outbreak of hostilities. A chastised Native American delegation later dejectedly agreed to the peace terms offered at the Treaty of Camp Charlotte. According to the provisions of capitulation on October 19, 1774, members of the Shawnee delegation pledged to surrender all prisoners and valuables, to deliver hostages as a guarantee of friendship, to never again attack the frontier, and to surrender all claims to lands south and east of the Ohio River. The Mingos, however, refused to come to terms with the Virginians. The recalcitrant Iroquoian band accepted the capitulation only after Major William Crawford's frontiersmen destroyed several of their towns. Terms of the treaty were later confirmed at Fort Pitt in the autumn of 1775 when Mingo, Shawnee, Delaware, Wyandot, Iroquois, and Ottawa chiefs ratified and confirmed Dunmore's original peace terms.

After the war, resentful Native Americans realized that the westward-moving American colonists, called the "Long Knives," would continue to invade their cherished homelands. In June 1774 Parliament passed the Quebec Act. The new legislation temporarily restrained land-hungry settlers by extending Quebec's boundaries to the Ohio Valley, thereby nullifying land seizures made by Virginia during Lord Dunmore's War. American colonists, especially veterans of the French and Indian War (1754–1763) and those with designs on the western territories, derided the legislation. Not surprisingly, restless colonists and land speculators openly violated another of Britain's feeble attempts to restore order along the frontier.

Lord Dunmore's War and the subsequent flood of colonial encroachers into the western territories represented the failure of the British Crown to live up to the goals enunciated in the Proclamation of 1763 and the Quebec Act of 1774. Despite repeated orders to treat American Indians with justice, colonial governors and royal officials failed to enforce existing laws. As a result, angry warriors patiently waited for opportunities to secure the return of their ancestral lands.

JON L. BRUDVIG

See also

Cornstalk; Delawares; Illinois; Iroquois; Johnson, Sir William; Logan, John; Mingos; Murray, John, Fourth Earl of Dunmore; Ottawas; Proclamation of 1763; Shawnees

References

Brand, Irene. "Dunmore's War." *West Virginia History* 40 (Fall 1978): 28–46.

Dowd, Gregory Evans. *A Spirited Resistance: The North American Indian Struggle for Unity, 1745–1815.* Baltimore: Johns Hopkins University Press, 1992.

Downes, Randolph C. *Council Fires on the Upper Ohio: A Narrative of Indian Affairs in the Upper Ohio Valley until 1795.* Pittsburgh: University of Pittsburgh Press, 1940.

Holton, Woody. "The Ohio Indians and the Coming of the American Revolution in Virginia." *Journal of Southern History* 60 (August 1994): 453–478.

McConnell, Michael N. *A Country Between: The Upper Ohio and Its Peoples, 1724–1774.* Lincoln: University of Nebraska Press, 1992.

Sosin, Jack M. "The British Indian Department and Dunmore's War." *Virginia Magazine of History and Biography* 74 (1966): 34–50.

Thomas, William H. B., and Howard McKnight Wilson. "The Battle of Point Pleasant." *Virginia Calvacade* 24 (Winter 1975): 100–107.

White, Richard. *The Middle Ground: Indians, Empires, and Republics in the Great Lakes Region, 1650–1815.* New York: Cambridge University Press, 1991.

Wickwire, Franklin B. "Go On and Be Brave: The Battle of Point Pleasant." *Timeline* 4 (August–September 1987): 2–15.

Louisiana Purchase

Large land acquisition negotiated by President Thomas Jefferson's administration on May 2, 1803, that added approximately 828,800 square miles of territory to the United States, effectively

Treaty

Between the United States of America and the French Republic

The President of the United States of America and the First Consul of the French Republic in the name of the French People desiring to remove all Source of misunderstanding relative to objects of discussion mentioned in the Second and fifth articles of the Convention of the {8th Vendimiaire an 9/30 September 1800} relative to the rights claimed by the United States in virtue of the Treaty concluded at Madrid the 27 of October 1795, between His Catholic Majesty, & the Said United States, & willing to strengthen the union and friendship which at the time of the Said Convention was happily reestablished between the two nations have respectively named their Plenipotentiaries to wit The President of the United States, by and with the advice and consent of the Senate of the Said States; Robert R. Livingston Minister Plenipotentiary of the United State and James Monroe Minister Plenipotentiary and Envoy extraordinary of the Said States near the Government of the French Republic; And the First Consul in the name of the French people, Citizen Francis Barbé Marbois Minister of the public treasury who after having respectively exchanged their full powers have agreed to the following

articles

The first page of the Louisiana Purchase document of May 2, 1803. (National Archives) more than doubling it in size. The United States purchased the territory from Napoleonic France for a total cost of $15 million. The Louisiana Purchase encompassed portions of 14 future states and 2 Canadian provinces west of the Mississippi River and included the strategic port city of New Orleans. At the time some Americans questioned the constitutionality of Jefferson's action, but Jefferson sought to take advantage of the Napoleonic Wars, which had left France strapped for cash. He also asserted that the purchase was a strategic necessity for the United States. Almost immediately after the purchase, Jefferson authorized the Lewis and Clark expedition to survey the territory. A Lemhi Shoshone woman named Sacagawea provided invaluable guidance to the expedition over the treacherous Rocky Mountains west to Oregon. She also helped secure cordial relations with Native Americans along the way.

Indeed, the Louisiana Purchase offered the United States a golden opportunity to limit the influence of foreign powers in the West, to gain some control over the Native American populations of North America, and to secure western lands for future settlement. The purchase also offered some serious challenges. The territory was inhabited by numerous tribes, most of whom were unwilling to simply move out of the way for the growth of the United States. This led to innumerable conflicts over the years that would not come to an effective end until 1890.

Between 1763 and 1800, the possession of Louisiana and Florida by the Spanish had been a persistent problem for the United States. The Spanish could use their territory along the U.S. borders to encourage Native Americans in the western and southern United States to make life difficult for Americans settlers. The transfer of Spanish Louisiana back to France in 1800 did not lessen the problems but instead simply placed a more dangerous foreign power on the U.S. border.

Thus, the purchase of Louisiana was a logical move for the United States. The purchase allowed the United States to remove a powerful foreign power from its border and control the Mississippi River and also gave the U.S. government the ability to deal with the Native Americans in the region with limited interference from Britain and Spain.

In the end, the Louisiana Purchase set into motion a pattern of white expansion that would radically alter the demographics of North America and that would prove catastrophic for the Native Americans. With France gone from the scene in 1803, the tribes had only a partly interested Britain and a declining Spain to act as counterbalances to rising U.S. dominance. From 1790 to 1840 about 4.5 million nonnatives moved across the Appalachians, more than the entire population of the United States in 1790 (which was estimated at 3.9 million). In 1790 two-thirds of those 3.9 million lived within 50 miles of the Atlantic coast or the waterways leading to it. Steadily the population center moved farther and farther west, aided by the Louisiana Purchase, so that by 1850 the United States stretched all the way to the Pacific.

There can be no denying the deleterious impact that such huge demographic shifts had on the Native Americans living west of the Mississippi River.

Once the transfer to the United States was complete, the real question of what to do with this massive new territory became a subject of much discussion. The region had only a limited American and European population but a large number of Native Americans. Early on, some politicians recommended that the new territory become a large reservation, allowing the nation to simply move its Native Americans west of the Mississippi River. In the 1830s this was carried out for a number of tribes under the 1830 Indian Removal Act.

The coming of the American Civil War (1861–1865) may have overshadowed the conflicts between the United States and its Native American populations but did not stop them, as witnessed by the Minnesota Sioux Uprising of 1862 and the massacre of Native Americans by Colorado volunteer forces at Sand Creek in 1864. To deal with this unrest, several Union generals, who had been less than successful in the Civil War in the East, and a number of so-called Galvanized Confederates (prisoners of war who decided to fight for the U.S. government) were sent west, where their loyalty would be less of an issue because they would not be fighting the South but rather defending the settlers from Native Americans. Six regiments of galvanized soldiers would be raised in the last 18 months of the war.

With the end of the Civil War and renewed focus by Americans on moving west, numerous conflicts occurred within the old Louisiana Territory between 1865 and 1890. The U.S. Army counts the Indian Wars as consisting of more than 1,000 actions of various sizes over the 25 years during 1865–1890 in all parts of the West. The more famous battles in this period are often known as much for their tragic nature as for the success of one side or the other. They include the Battle of the Little Bighorn (1876) and the Wounded Knee tragedy (1890). The Native Americans had numerous successes large and small against U.S. forces, including the Fetterman Massacre (1866), the Battle of the Rosebud (1876), and the Battle of the Little Bighorn. However, their successes were not enough to defeat the Americans militarily or stop the westward expansion of white settlers.

Donald E. Heidenreich Jr. and Paul G. Pierpaoli Jr.

See also

Demographics, Historical; Jefferson, Thomas; Lewis and Clark Expedition; Sacagawea

References

Stewart, Richard W., ed. *American Military History,* Vol. 1, *The United States Army and the Forging of a Nation, 1775–1917.* Washington, DC: Center of Military History, 2005.

Trigger, Bruce, and Wilcomb Washburn, eds. *The Cambridge History of the Native Peoples of the Americas,* Vol. 1, *North America,* Part 2. Cambridge: Cambridge University Press, 1996.

Yonne, Bill. *Indian Wars: The Campaign for the American West.* Yardley, PA: Westholme, 2006.

Loups

See Mahicans

Lovewell, John
Birth Date: October 14, 1691
Death Date: May 8, 1725

British colonial soldier and captain of an independent military company during Dummer's War (1722–1727). John Lovewell was born on October 14, 1691, in Dunstable, Massachusetts. His family had settled in Dunstable in the 1680s and eventually came to own land and a mill along Salmon Creek. Lovewell and his own family would eventually own and work 200 acres of land.

From an early age, Lovewell had experienced war with New England's Native American population. Indeed, Dunstable, a frontier town, came under attack in 1691 during King William's War (1689–1697) and in 1703 and 1706 during Queen Anne's War (1702–1713). Along with the other remaining inhabitants of Dunstable, the Lovewells crowded into several garrison houses, living fear-filled and circumscribed lives.

During Dummer's War, Native Americans raided Dunstable in September 1724, capturing two inhabitants and killing most of the pursuing force. In response, Lovewell and other Dunstable inhabitants petitioned the Massachusetts General Court for assistance. To minimize costs to the colony yet improve frontier defenses, the court offered a £100 bounty for every male Native American scalp in hopes of encouraging private citizens to form armed companies to patrol the borderlands.

Lovewell was elected captain of one such company and proceeded to wage war against the local natives. In two expeditions in December 1724 and January 1725, Lovewell's men took several scalps and prisoners, collecting cash bounties and receiving accolades in Boston. On a third expedition into the White Mountains on May 8, 1725, however, Lovewell's company fell into an ambush. Lovewell and several of his men were killed, and the remnants of his company straggled back to Massachusetts frontier towns. What came to be called Lovewell's Fight ended in disaster.

DAVID M. CORLETT

See also

Dummer's Treaty; Dummer's War; King William's War; Lovewell's Fight; Native American Warfare; Queen Anne's War; Scalp Bounty; Scalping

References

Eames, Steven C. "Rustic Warriors: Warfare and the Provincial Soldier on the Northern Frontier, 1689–1748." Unpublished PhD dissertation, University of New Hampshire, 1989.

Leach, Douglas Edward. *Arms for Empire: A Military History of the British Colonies in North America, 1607–1763.* New York: Macmillan, 1973.

Penhallow, Samuel. *The History of the Wars of New-England with the Eastern Indians; or a Narrative of Their Continued Perfidy and Cruelty, from the 10th of August, 1703, to the Peace Renewed 13th of July, 1713. And from the 25th of July, 1722, to Their Submission 15th December, 1725, Which Was Ratified August 5th, 1726.* Reprint ed. Cincinnati: J. Harpel, 1859.

Lovewell's Fight
Event Date: May 8, 1725

Battle between an English scalp-hunting party led by John Lovewell and Abenaki Native Americans near present-day Fryeburg, Maine (then part of Massachusetts), on May 8, 1725. During Dummer's War (1722–1727), a conflict between the New England colonies and the Abenakis across the New England frontier, the Massachusetts government offered £100 bounties for native scalps. This profit potential encouraged private citizens to form independent military companies, unsupported by the provincial government, that ranged the New England frontier in search of scalps.

Lovewell, of Dunstable, Massachusetts, formed one such company. He had led successful outings against Native Americans in late 1724 and early 1725, taking more than 10 scalps. Encouraged by his success, Lovewell led his company of 46 men north toward the White Mountains of New Hampshire in April 1725. At Lake Ossipee, Lovewell constructed a crude stockade to serve as a refuge for a sick soldier as well as a rally point in case of disaster. Leaving the ill man, the company's doctor, and an 8-man guard, Lovewell and his remaining men marched toward Pigwacket on the upper Saco River. The Pigwacket Abenakis had already staged numerous raids on border settlements in New England.

While bivouacking along Saco Pond near present-day Fryeburg, Maine, on May 7, Lovewell's band heard Abenakis moving in their vicinity. The next morning the scalp hunters heard a gunshot. Leaving their packs unguarded, the men investigated the sound and found a lone native hunting ducks. Although the company managed to kill the man (the chaplain claimed the scalp), Lovewell and another man were wounded, and the men failed to find other natives. Unbeknownst to Lovewell, during this action Paugus, the party's intended target, and at least 40 native warriors had returned from a reconnaissance and discovered Lovewell's unguarded packs. There they set an ambush and awaited the return of the British scalp hunters.

When Lovewell's company returned to their camp to claim their packs, the warriors fired on and rushed the colonists. Lovewell fell in the first volley, but his outnumbered men returned fire, took cover where they could, and kept up the battle until sunset. Several men on both sides knew one another, and they exchanged taunts and insults throughout the daylong battle. Casualties on both sides were heavy. With Paugus and at least 9 other warriors dead, the Abenakis gathered their casualties and abandoned the field. Only

23 Englishmen remained alive, and of these survivors 14 were wounded, 1 mortally and 2 more unable to travel. The remaining men marched toward the company's fortification on Lake Ossipee. Instead of finding relief and medical help there, the survivors found the post abandoned. Apparently, a man in Lovewell's company had run away at the fight's onset and had carried exaggerated news of a massacre to the guard detail, quickly sending them homeward. The remnants of Lovewell's band straggled back into Dunstable, Berwick, and Biddeford on May 11, losing 4 more men along the way.

While Lovewell's defeat led to a decline in the popularity of scalp hunting, his expedition forced the Pigwacket Abenakis to abandon their village until a peace settlement was negotiated.

DAVID M. CORLETT

See also

Abenakis; Dummer's War; Lovewell, John; Scalp Bounty; Scalping

References

Clark, Charles E. *The Eastern Frontier: The Settlement of Northern New England, 1610–1673*. New York: Knopf, 1970.

Leach, Douglas Edward. *Arms for Empire: A Military History of the British Colonies in North America, 1607–1763*. New York: Macmillan, 1973.

Penhallow, Samuel. *The History of the Wars of New-England with the Eastern Indians; or a Narrative of Their Continued Perfidy and Cruelty, from the 10th of August, 1703, to the Peace Renewed 13th of July, 1713. And from the 25th of July, 1722, to Their Submission 15th December, 1725, Which Was Ratified August 5th, 1726*. Reprint ed. Cincinnati: J. Harpel, 1859.